Mesolithic on the Move

Papers presented at the Sixth International Conference on the Mesolithic in Europe, Stockholm 2000

Edited by Lars Larsson
Hans Kindgren, Kjel Knutsson, David Loeffler and Agneta Åkerlund

Oxbow Books 2003

Published by
Oxbow Books, Park End Place, Oxford OX1 1HN

© Oxbow Books and the individual authors, 2003

ISBN 1 84217 089 9

A CIP record for this book is available from the British Library

Cover image: Provided by Lars Larsson and David Loeffler

This book is available direct from
Oxbow Books, Park End Place, Oxford, OX1 1HN
(Phone: 01865-241249; Fax: 01865-794449)

and

The David Brown Book Company
PO Box 511, Oakville, CT 06779, USA
(Phone: 860-945-9329; Fax: 860-945-9468)

and

via our website
www.oxbowbooks.com

Printed in Great Britain by
The Short Run Press
Exeter

Contents

List of Contributors	vii
Preface	xv

Introduction

The Mesolithic: What do we know and what do we believe? *(Stefan Karol Kozłowski)*	xvii
The Mesolithic of Sweden in retrospective and progressive perspectives *(Lars Larsson)*	xxii
Peopling a Forgotten Landscape *(Agneta Åkerlund, Per Gustafsson, Dag Hammar, Christina Lindgren, Eva Olsson and Roger Wikell)*	xxxiii
Landscape history of the Södertörn peninsula, eastern Sweden *(Jan Risberg)*	xlv

Colonisation Processes

1.	Introduction *(Peter Woodman)*	1
2.	Early Settlement on Tyrrhenian islands (8th millennium cal. BC): Mesolithic adaption to local resources in Corsica and Northern Sardinia *(L. Costa, J.-D. Vigne, H. Bocherens, N. Desse-Berset, C. Heinz, F. de Lanfranchi, J. Magdeleine, M.-P. Ruas, S. Thiebault and C. Tozzi)*	3
3.	Palynological visibility and the Mesolithic colonisation of the Hebrides, Scotland *(Kevin J. Edwards and Heather Sugden)*	11
4.	Colonisation of the west Estonian archipelago *(Aivar Kriiska)*	20
5.	Storlyckan. Investigations of an Early Mesolithic Settlement Site in Östergötland, Eastern Middle Sweden *(Mats Larsson)*	29
6.	The Colonisation of Northernmost Finnish Lapland and the Inland Areas of Finnmark *(Tuija Rankama)*	37
7.	Mesolithic Colonisation of South-Eastern Subbalticum *(Zofia Sulgostowska)*	47
8.	Colonisation – Event or Process *(Christopher Tolan-Smith)*	52
9.	Colonising the edge of Europe: Ireland as a case study *(Peter Woodman)*	57

Enculturating the Landscape

10.	Enculturation of Mesolithic Landscapes *(Marek Zvelebil)*	65
11.	The origins of monumentality? Mesolithic world-views of the landscape in western Britain *(Vicki Cummings)*	74
12.	The Mesolithic of the Swiss and French Jura and its margins: 10,150–6000 BP *(Christophe Cupillard and Nicole Perrenoud-Cupillard)*	82
13.	Highland occupation in the southern Alps during the Early Holocene *(Federica Fontana and Antonio Guerreschi)*	96
14.	Enculturating the Landscape beyond Doggerland *(Ingrid Fuglestvedt)*	103
15.	Cultural convergences of northern Europe and North Africa during the Early Holocene? *(Elena A.A. Garcea)*	108
16.	The Enigma of the Far Northeast European Mesolithic: Reindeer Herd Followers or Semi-Sedentary Hunters? *(Bryan Gordon)*	115
17.	Forest and Mobility. A Case from the Fishing Camp Site Dudka, Masuria, north-eastern Poland *(Witold Gumiński and Maria Michniewicz)*	119
18.	Investigating Post-Glacial Hunter Gatherer Landscape enculturation: Ethnographic Analogy and Interpretative Methodologies *(Peter D. Jordan)*	128
19.	Enculturation through fire: beyond hazelnuts and into the forest *(Jenny Moore)*	139
20.	*Sorbus aucuparia* or extremely red Rowanberries? Some naïve reflections on archaeology, paleo-ecology and the non-scientific dimensions of a scientific landscape *(Björn Nilsson)*	145
21.	Harvesting pike at Tłokowo *(R. Schild, K. Tobolski, L. Kubiak-Martens, B. Bratlund, U. Eicher, G. Calderoni, D. Makowiecki, A. and M.M Pazdur†, F.H. Schweingruber, W. Van Neer, M. Winiarska-Kabacińska and S. Żurek)*	149

Social Relations and Group Formation

22. Introduction *(Ericka Engelstad)* — 159
23. Do dogs eat like humans? Marine stable isotope signals in dog teeth from inland Zvejnieki *(Gunilla Eriksson and Ilga Zagorska)* — 160
24. Microliths and Multiple Authorship *(Nyree Finlay)* — 169
25. My way or your way. On the social dimension of technology as seen in the lithic strategies in eastern middle Sweden during the mesolithic *(Christina Lindgren)* — 177
26. Inferences about Mesolithic life style on the basis of anthropological data. The case of the Portuguese shell middens *(Eugénia Cunha, Francisca Cardoso and Cláudia Umbelino)* — 184

Spatial Organisation of Sites

27. Introduction *(Ole Grøn)* — 191
28. Encircling the living space of Early Postglacial reindeer hunters in the interior of southern Norway *(Sveinung Bang-Andersen)* — 193
29. The site of Verrebroek "Dok" (Flanders, Belgium): spatial organisation of an extensive Early Mesolithic settlement *(Philippe Crombé, Yves Perdaen and Joris Sergant)* — 205
30. Ethno-archaeology among Evenkian forest hunters. Preliminary results and a different approach to reality! *(Ole Grøn and Oleg Kuznetsov)* — 216
31. A Mesolithic Winter-Site with a Sunken Dwelling from the Swedish West Coast *(Robert Hernek)* — 222
32. A Sunken Dwelling from the Ertebölle Site Nivå 10, Eastern Denmark *(Ole Lass Jensen)* — 230
33. Some observations concerning the relationship between distribution patterns, floor size and social organisation *(David Loeffler)* — 239
34. A Recently Discovered Mesolithic Wet Site at Riihimäki, South Finland *(Heikki Matiskainen and Mikhail G. Zhilin)* — 249
35. Liencres Revisited: the Significance of Spatial Pattrering Revealed by Unconstrained Clustering *(Christopher A. Papalas, Geoffrey A. Clark and Keith W. Kintigh)* — 253
36. The function of the Mesolithic sites in the Paris basin (France). New data *(Christian Verjux)* — 262
37. Mesolithic Settlement Structures in Reichwalde – Preliminary Observations on New Mesolithic Sites *(Jürgen Vollbrecht)* — 269

Territoriality – Regionalisation

38. Introduction *(Berit Valentin Eriksen)* — 281
39. The spatial and chronological development of the Late Mesolithic Nøstvet period in coastal southeastern Norway from a lithic raw material perspective *(Evy Berg)* — 283
40. Mesolithic Ethnicity – Too Hard to Handle? *(Knut Andreas Bergsvik)* — 290
41. Between Quartz and Flint. Material Culture and Social Interaction *(Tom Carlsson, Göran Gruber, Fredrik Molin and Roger Wikell)* — 302
42. Initial Evaluation of Grahame Clark's Model of Mesolithic Transhumance in Northern England: A Perspective from the Pennine Uplands *(Randolph E. Donahue and William A. Lovis)* — 310
43. Mesolithic Territorial Behaviour in Central Scandinavia and Adjacent Regions *(Per Falkenström)* — 316
44. Regionalism in the Mesolithic of Southern Germany *(Michael Jochim)* — 323
45. Mesolithic hunter-gatherers in the Isle of Man: adaptations to an island environment? *(Sinéad B. McCartan)* — 331
46. Indications of regionalisation in Mesolithic Scotland *(Alan Saville)* — 340
47. Early Mesolithic settlement patterns in Holmegårds Bog on South Zealand, Denmark. A social perspective *(Henrik Schilling)* — 351
48. The Mesolithic in the Cantabrian Interior: Fact or Fantasy? *(Lawrence Guy Straus and Manuel González Morales)* — 359
49. Scotland's First Settlers: an investigation into settlement, territoriality and mobility during the Mesolithic in the Inner Sound, Scotland, First Results *(Karen Hardy and Caroline R. Wickham-Jones)* — 369

Exchange and Communication

50. Exchange: artefacts, people and ideas on the move in Mesolithic Europe *(Anders Fischer)* — 385
51. Knowledge and Interaction in the Stone Age: Raw materials for adzes and axes, their sources and distributional patterns *(Lisbeth Bengtsson)* — 388
52. Traffic in Stone Adzes in Mesolithic Western Norway *(Knut Andreas Bergsvik and Asle Bruen Olsen)* — 395
53. Trapping up the rivers and trading across the sea – steps towards the neolithisation of Denmark *(Anders Fischer)* — 405
54. Appropriation of the Past. Neolithisation in the Northern Scandinavian Perspective *(Kjel Knutsson, Per Falkenström and Karl-Fredrik Lindberg)* — 414
55. The marrying kind: evidence for a patrilocal postmarital residence pattern in the Mesolithic of southern Brittany? *(Rick Schulting)* — 431
56. Mesolithic Economic and Social Changes in the Southern Netherlands *(Leo Verhart)* — 442
57. The Deposits of Raw Materials and the Quarry-sites during Mesolithic in the Trégor in Brittany *(Estelle Yven)* — 451

Ritual and Symbolic Behaviour

58. Introduction *(Lars Larsson)* — 463
59. Art: Context and Tradition in the Palaeolithic-Mesolithic Transition in Northern Europe *(Helena Ahlbäck)* — 467
60. Mesolithic Human Skeletal Remains from Tågerup, Scania, Sweden *(Torbjörn Ahlström)* — 478
61. Three Cremations and a Funeral: Aspects of Burial Practice in Mesolithic Vedbæk *(Erik Brinch Petersen and Christopher Meiklejohn)* — 485
62. Childhood in the Epi-Palaeolithic. What do personal ornaments associated with burials tell us? *(Marian Vanhaeren and Francesco d'Errico)* — 494
63. Mobility and Aesthetcs. On the Palaeo-Inuit style in the Nuuk Fjord area of Greenland *(Maria Hinnerson Berglund)* — 506
64. Late Mesolithic Rock Art and Expressions of Ideology *(Trond Klungseth Lødøen)* — 511
65. Pre-Boreal elk bones from Lundby Mose *(Keld Møller Hansen)* — 521
66. A Taphonomy of Ritual Practice, a "field"-anthropological study of late Mesolithic burials *(Liv Nilsson Stutz)* — 527
67. To Touch the Mind *(Bengt Nordqvist)* — 536
68. Rituals at the Meso 2000 Conference and the Mesolithic-Neolithic Terminological Breakdown *(Jimmy Strassburg)* — 542
69. Decorated objects of the older Mesolithic from the northern lowlands *(Thomas Terberger)* — 547
70. Burial traditions in the East Baltic Mesolithic *(Guntis Gerhards, Gunita Zariņa and Ilga Zagorska)* — 558

Hunter-Gatherers in Transition

71. Introduction *(Douglas T. Price)* — 565
72. Long term change in Portuguese early Holocene settlement and subsistence *(Ana Cristina Araújo)* — 569
73. Mesolithic-Neolithic population relationships in Portugal: the evidence from ancient mitochondrial DNA *(Fiona Bamforth, Mary Jackes and David Lubell)* — 581
74. Interactions between the late Mesolithic hunter-gatherers and farming communities in Northern Poland *(Lucyna Domańska)* — 588
75. My place or yours? *(Fredrik Hallgren)* — 592
76. The Transition from Mesolithic to Neolithic in eastern Sicily: A Microscopic Point of View *(Maria Rosa Iovino)* — 600
77. The Hardinxveld sites in the Rhine/Meuse Delta, the Netherlands, 5500 – 4500 cal BC *(Leendert P. Louwe Kooijmans)* — 608
78. Late Mesolithic to Early Neolithic communities in the Dnieper Rapids region of Ukraine: chronology and socio-economic continuity? *(Malcolm Lillie)* — 625
79. New Investigations on Submarine Stone Age Settlements in the Wismar Bay Area *(Harald Lübke)* — 633

Miscellany

80. A Short Note on the Mesolithic Fauna from Zamostje 2 (Russia) *(Louis Chaix)* — 645
81. The Contribution of the Technological Study of Bone and Antler Industry for the Definition of the Early Maglemose Culture *(Eva David)* — 649
82. The Renadières aux Pins, Charente, France. A Pre-boreal Cave in west central France *(Véronique Dujardin and Bruno Boulestin)* — 658
83. Mesolithic settlement during the Preboreal period in Finland *(Timo Jussila and Heikki Matiskainen)* — 664
84. Butchering of Wild Boar (*Sus scrofa*) in the Mesolithic *(Ola Magnell)* — 671
85. Another life of bones: the use of Pleistocene faunal remains in the Post-Pleistocene sites of arctic Siberia *(Vladimir V. Pitulko)* — 680
86. Recent excavations at the Pre-boreal site of Lahti, Ristola in southern Finland *(Hannu Takala)* — 684
87. Early Mesolithic communication networks in the East European forest zone *(Mickle Zhilin)* — 688
88. Deep in Russia, deep in the bog. Excavations at the Mesolithic Sites Stanovoje 4 and Sakhtysh 14, Upper Volga region *(Mickle G. Zhilin and Heikki Matiskainen)* — 694

List of Contributors

Helena Ahlbäck,
Göksholmsbacken 21,
SE-124 74 Bandhagen,
Sweden
Bukka7white@hotmail.com

Torbjörn Ahlström,
Department of Archaeology and Ancient History,
University of Lund,
Sandgatan 1,
SE-223 50 Lund,
Sweden
Torbjorn.Ahlstrom@ark.lu.se

Agneta Åkerlund,
Södermanland County Aministrative Board,
SE-611 86 Nyköping,
Sweden
Agneta.Akerlund@d.lst.se

Ana Cristina Araújo,
Instituto Português de Arqueologia,
Av. da Índia, 136,
P-1300-300 Lisboa,
Portugal
cristina@ipa.min-cultura.pt

Fiona Bamforth,
Department of Laboratory Medicine and Pathology,
University of Alberta,
Edmonton AB T6G 2R7,
Canada
fiona.bamforth@ualberta.ca

Sveinung Bang-Andersen,
Stavanger museum of Archaeology,
Box 478,
NO-4002 Stavanger,
Norway

Lisbet Bengtsson,
Göteborg University,
Museion,
Box 111,
SE-405 30 Göteborg,
Sweden
lisbet.bengtsson@museion.gu.se

Evy Berg,
Directorate for Cultural Heritage,
Box 8196 Dep.,
NO-0034 Oslo,
Norway
evb@ra.no

Knut Andreas Bergsvik,
Department of Archaeology,
University of Bergen,
H. Sheteligs plass 10,
NO-5007 Bergen,
Norway
knut.bergsvik@bm.uib.no

Hervé Bocherens,
CNRS (UMR 162).
Laboratoire de Biogéochimie isotopique,
Université P. et M. Curie, case 120,
4 place Jussieu,
F-75252 Paris cedex 05,
France

Bruno Boulestin,
16 rue Paul Bert,
F-94130 Nogent-sur-Marne,
France
b.boulestin@netcourrier.com

Bodil Bratlund,
Archeoosteological Research Laboratory,
Department of Archaeology,
Stockholm University,
Royal Palace Ulriksdal.
SE-170 79 Solna.
Sweden

Gilberto Calderoni,
Department of Earth Sciences,
University of Roma 'La Sapienza',
P. le A. Moro 5,
IT-00185 Roma,
Italy
gilberto.calderoni@uniroma1.it

Francisca Cardoso,
Departamento de Antropologia,
Faculdade de Ciências e Tecnologia,
Universidade de Coimbra,
P-3000-056 Coimbra,
Portugal
cunhae@ci.uc.pt

Tom Carlsson,
National Heritage Board UV Öst,
Järnvägsgatan 8,
SE-582 22 Linköping,
Sweden
tom.carlsson@raa.se

Louis Chaix,
Department of Archaeozoology,
Museum of Natural History,
C.P. 6434,
1 route de Malagnou,
CH-1211 Genéve 6,
Switzerland
louis.chaix@mhn.ville-ge.ch

Geoffrey A. Clark,
Department of Anthropology,
Arizona State Universtity,
Tempe,
AZ 85287-2402,
USA
geoffrey.clark@asu.edu

Laurent Costa,
Laboratoire de Préhistoire et de Technologie (UMR 7550),
MAE, 21 allée de l'Université,
F-92000 Nanterre,
France

Philippe Crombé,
Ghent University,
Department of Archaeology and Ancient History of Europe,
Research unit Pre- and Protohistory,
Blandijnberg 2,
B-9000 Gent,
Belgium

Vicki Cummings,
School of History and Archaeology,
PO BOX 909,
Cardiff University,
Cardiff,
CF10 3XU,
United Kingdom
CummingsVM@cardiff.ac.uk

Eugénia Cunha,
Departamento de Antropologia,
Faculdade de Ciências e Tecnologia,
Universidade de Coimbra,
P-3000-056 Coimbra,
Portugal
cunhae@ci.uc.pt

Christophe Cupillard,
Service Régional d'Archéologie de Franche-Comté,
7 rue Charles Nodier,
F-25043 Besançon-Cedex,
France
Christophe.cupillard@culture.fr

Eva David,
Laboratoire d'Ethnologie préhistorique,
U.M.R. ArScAn - U.R.A. 275,
Maison René Ginouvès - MAE,
21, Allée de l'Université,
F-92 023 Nanterre Cedex,
France
davide@mae.u-paris10.fr

Nathalie Desse-Berset,
NDB, CEPAM-CNRS,
250 av. Albert Einstein,
Sophia Antipolis,
F-06560 Valbonne,
Paris,
France

Lucyna Domańska,
Institute of Archaeology,
University of Łódź,
PL-91-402 Łódź,
Pomorska 96,
Poland
lucynad@krysia.uni.lodz.pl

Randolph E. Donahue,
Department of Archaeological Sciences,
University of Bradford,
Bradford,
BD7 1DP,
United Kingdom
r.e.donahue@bradford.ac.uk

Véronique Dujardin,
Conservatrice du Patrimoine,
Service Régional de l'Archéologie de Poitou-Charentes,
102 Grand-Rue,
F-86020 Poitiers Cedex,
France
veronique.dujardin@culture.fr

Ulrich Eicher,
Physics Institute,
University of Bern,
Sidlerstrasse 5,
CH-3012 Bern,
Switzerland

Kevin J. Edwards,
Department of Geography and Environment and Northern
    Studies Centre,
University of Aberdeen,
Aberdeen,
AB24 3UF,
United Kingdom
kevin.edwards@abdn.ac.uk

Ericka Engelstad,
Faculty of Social Science,
University of Tromsø,
NO-9037 Tromsø,
Norway
erickae@sv.nit.no

Francesco d'Errico,
Institut de Préhistoire et de Géologie du Quaternaire,
UMR 5808 of the CNRS,
Université Bordeaux I,
Avenue des Facultés,
F-33405 Talence,
France
f.derrico@iquat.u-bordeaux.fr

Berit Valentin Eriksen,
Department of Prehistoric Archaeology,
University of Aarhus,
Moesgård,
DK-8270 Højbjerg,
Denmark
farkbve@moes.hum.aau.dk

Gunilla Eriksson,
Archaeological Research Laboratory,
Stockholm University,
Greens villa,
SE-10691 Stockholm,
Sweden
gerik@arklab.su.se

List of Contributors

Per Falkenström,
Department of Archaeology and Ancient History,
Uppsala University,
St Eriks Torg 5,
SE-75310 Uppsala,
Sweden
falk.harbo@swipnet

Nyree Finlay,
Department of Archaeology,
University of Glasgow,
The Gregory Building,
Lilybank Gardens,
Glasgow
G12 8QQ,
Scotland
n.finlay@archaeology.gla.ac.uk

Anders Fischer,
The National Cultural Heritage Agency,
Slotsholmsgade 1,
DK-1216 Copenhagen K.,
Denmark
AFi@KUAS.DK

Federica Fontana,
Dipartimento delle Risorse Naturali e Culturali,
Corso Ercole I d'Este, 32,
IT-44100 Ferrara,
Italy
grr@unife.it

Ingrid Fuglestvedt,
Museum of Archaeology,
Box 478,
NO-4001 Stavanger,
Norway
Ifu@ark.museum.no

Elena A.A. Garcea,
Università di Cassino,
Dipartimento di Filologia e Storia,
Via Bari 8,
IT-03043 Cassino (FR),
Italy
egarcea@libero.it

Guntis Gerhards,
Institute of Latvian History,
Department of Archaeology,
Akademijas laukums 1,
Riga LV 1050,
Latvia

Bryan Gordon,
Canadian Museum of Civilisation,
PO Box 3100,
Station B,
Hull,
Quebec J8X 4H2,
Canada
Bryan.Gordon@civilisations.ca

Ole Grøn,
NIKU (Norwegian Institute for Cultural Heritage Research),
P.O.Boks 736 Sentrum,
NO-0105 Oslo,
Norway
ole.gron@nikuosl.ninaniku.no

Göran Gruber,
National Heritage Board UV Öst,
Järnvägsgatan 8,
SE-582 22 Linköping,
Sweden
goran.gruber@raa.se

Antonio Guerreschi,
Dipartimento di Scienze della Terra,
Università di Ferrara,
Italy

Witold Gumiński,
Institute of Archaeology and Ethnology Polish Academy of
    Sciences,
Solidarno ci 105,
PL-00-140 Warszawa,
Poland
gum@iaepan.edu.pl

Per Gustafsson,
National Heritage Board,
Department of Archaeological Excavations,
UV Mitt,
Box 5405,
SE-114 84 Stockholm,
Sweden
per.gustafsson@raa.se

Fredrik Hallgren,
Department of archaeology and ancient history,
St Eriks Torg 5,
SE-753 10 Uppsala,
Sweden
fredrik.hallgren@arkeologi.uu.se

Dag Hammar,
Department of Archaeological Excavations,
UV Mitt,
Box 5405,
SE-114 84 Stockholm,
Sweden
dag.hammar@raa.se

Keld Møller Hansen,
Sydsjællands museum,
Slotsruinen,
DK-4760 Vordingborg,
Denmark
Sydsjaellands@museum.dk

Karen Hardy,
Department of Archaeology,
University of Edinburgh,
Old High School,
12 Infirmary Street,
Edinburgh,
EH1 1LT,
Scotland
mikar@clara.net

Christine Heinz,
Laboratoire de Paléobotanique,
Environnement et Archéologie (URA 1477),
163 rue A. Brousonet,
F-34000 Montpellier,
France

Robert Hernek,
Bohusläns museum,
Box 403,
SE-451 19 Uddevala,
Sweden
Robert.Hernek@bohusmus.se

Maria Hinnerson Berglund,
The Greenland National Museum and Archives,
Box 145,
3900 Nuuk,
Greenland
mhbnatmus@greennet.gl

Maria Rosa Iovino,
Faculty of Archaeology,
Leiden University,
NL-2300 RA Leiden,
The Netherlands
miarosa@tin.it

Mary Jackes,
Department of Anthropology,
University of Alberta,
Edmonton AB T6G 2H4
Canada
mjackes@ualberta.ca

Ole Lass Jensen,
Hørsholm Egns Museum,
Sdr. Jagtvej 2,
DK-2970 Hørsholm,
Denmark
ole.lass@hoersholmmuseum.dk

Michael Jochim,
Department of Anthropology,
University of California,
Santa Barbara,
CA 93106,
USA
jochim@anth.ucsb.edu

Peter D. Jordan,
Institute of Archaeology,
University College London,
31–34 Gordon Square,
London
WC1H 0PY,
United Kingdom
P.Jordan@ucl.ac.uk

Timo Jussila,
Microlith Ltd,
Kotitontuntie 17 F,
FIN-00230 Espoo,
Finland
Mikroliitti@dlc.fi

Keith W. Kintigh.
Department of Anthropology,
Arizona State Universtity,
Tempe,
AZ 85287-2402,
USA
kintigh@asu.edu

Kjel Knutsson,
Institute of Archaeology and Ancient History,
Uppsala University,
St Eriks torg 5,
SE-75310 Uppsala,
Sweden,
Kjel.Knutsson@arkeologi.uu.se

Leendert P. Louwe Kooijmans,
Faculty of Archaeology,
Leiden university,
PO Box 9515,
NL-2300 RA Leiden,
The Netherlands
l.p.louwe.kooijmans@rulpre.leidenuniv.nl

Stefan Karol Kozłowski,
Institute of Archaeology,
Wasaw University,
Ul. Zwirki i Wigury 97/99,
PL-00-972 Wasaw,
Poland

Aivar Kriiska,
University of Tartu,
Lossi 3,
EE-50090 Tartu,
Estonia
aivark@ut.ee

Lucyna Kubiak-Martens,
BIAX Consult,
Research and Consultancy Services for Biological Archaeology
    and Environmental Reconstruction,
NL-1506 AL Zaandam,
The Netherlands
biax@biax.nl

Oleg Kuznetsov,
Chita Museum of Human and Natural History,
Babushkina str. 113,
RU-672000 Chita,
Russia
zabaikal@yahoo.com

Francois de Lanfranchi,
Centre de Recherches Archéologiques de l'Alta Rocca,
F-20170 Lévie,
France

Lars Larsson,
Department of Archaeology and Ancient History,
University of Lund,
Sandgatan 1,
SE-223 50 Lund,
Sweden
lars.larsson@ark.lu.se

List of Contributors

Mats Larsson,
University of Kalmar,
SE-391 82 Kalmar,
Sweden
mats.larsson@hik.se

Malcolm Lillie,
Wetland Archaeology and Environments Research Centre,
Department of Geography,
University of Hull,
Hull,
HU6 7RX,
United Kingdom
m.c.lillie@geo.hull.ac.uk

Karl-Fredrik Lindberg,
Institute of Archaeology and Ancient History,
Uppsala University,
St Eriks torg 5,
SE-75310 Uppsala,
Sweden

Christina Lindgren,
Department of Archaeology,
Stockholm University,
SE-106 91 Stockholm,
Sweden
christina.lindgren@ark.su.se

David Loeffler,
Department of Archaeology and Saami Studies,
University of Umeå,
SE-901 81 Umeå,
Sweden
david.loeffler@arke.umu.se

William A. Lovis,
MSU Museum and Department of Anthropology,
Michigan State University,
East Lansing,
MI 48824-1045,
USA
William.Lovis@ssc.msu.edu

David Lubell,
Department of Anthropology,
University of Alberta,
Edmonton AB T6G 2H4
Canada
dlubell@ualberta.ca

Harald Lübke,
Archäologisches Landesmuseum und Landesamt für
    Bodendenkmalpflege Mecklenburg-Vorpommern,
Schloss Wiligrad,
DE-19069 Lübstorf,
Germany
archaeomuseum.m-v@t-online.de

Trond Klungseth Lødøen,
Department of Archaeology,
University of Bergen,
Haakon Sheteligsplass 10,
NO-5007 Bergen,
Norway
trond.lodoen@bm.uib.no

Jacques Magdeleine,
Route sup. du Cardo,
F-20200 Bastia,
France

Ola Magnell,
Department of Historical Osteology,
Institute of Archaeology and Ancient History,
Sandgatan 1,
SE-223 50 Lund,
Sweden
Ola.Magnell@ark.lu.se

Daniel Makowiecki,
Poznań Branch
Institute of Archaeology and Ethnology,
Polish Academy of Sciences,
Zwierzyniecka 20,
PL-60-814 Poznań
Poland
makdan@man.poznan.pl

Heikki Matiskainen,
The Finnish Glass Museum,
Tehtaankatu 23,
FIN-11910 Riihimaki,
Finland
heikki.matiskainen@riihimaki.fi

Sinéad B. McCartan,
Department of Archaeology and Ethnography,
Ulster Museum,
Botanic Gardens,
Belfast,
BT9 5AB,
Northern Ireland
Sinead.McCartan.UM@nics.gov.uk

Christopher Mejklejohn,
Department of Anthropology,
University of Winnipeg,
Winnipeg,,
Manitoba,
Canada R3B 2E9
c.meiklejohn@uwinnipeg.ca

Maria Michniewicz,
Institute of Archaeology and Ethnology Polish Academy of
    Sciences,
Centralne Laboratorium,
Długa 24/26,
PL-00-950 Warszawa,
Poland

Fredrik Molin,
National Heritage Board UV Öst,
Järnvägsgatan 8,
SE-582 22 Linköping,
Sweden
fredrik.molin@raa.se

Jenny Moore,
19 Storrs Hall Road,
Walkley Bank,
Sheffield,
S6 5AW,
United Kingdom
Jenny.m@virgin.net

Manuel González Morales,
Departamento de Ciencias Históricas,
Universidad de Cantabria,
39005 Santander,
España
moralesm@unican.es

Björn Nilsson,
Institute of Archaeology and Ancient History,
Department of Archaeology,
Sandgatan 1,
SE-223 50 Lund,
Sweden
bjorn.nilsson@ark.lu.se

Liv Nilsson Stutz,
Institute of Archaeology and Ancient History,
Department of Archaeology,
Sandgatan 1,
SE-223 50 Lund,
Sweden
liv.nilsson@ark.lu.se

Bengt Nordqvist,
National Heritage Board,
Archaeological Excavations Department,
UV Väst,
Box 102 59,
SE-434 23 Kungsbacka,
Sweden
bengt.nordqvist@raa.se

Asle Bruen Olsen,
Department of Archaeology,
University of Bergen,
H. Sheteligs plass 10,
NO-5007 Bergen,
Norway
asle.bruenolsen@nm.uib.no

Eva Olsson,
National Heritage Board,
Department of Archaeological Excavations,
UV Mitt, Box 5405,
SE-114 84 Stockholm,
Sweden
eva.olsson@raa.se

Christopher A. Papalas,
Department of Anthropology,
Arizona State Universtity,
Tempe,
AZ 85287-2402,
USA
papalas@imap2.asu.edu

Anna Pazdur,
14 C Laboratory,
Institute of Physics,
Silesian Technical University,
Gliwice,
Poland

Yves Perdaen,
Ghent University,
Department of Archaeology and Ancient History of Europe,
Research unit Pre- and Protohistory,
Blandijnberg 2,
B-9000 Gent,
Belgium
yves.perdaen@rug.ac.be

Nicole Perrenoud-Cupillard,
Association pour les Fouilles Archéologiques Nationales,
Antenne Inter-Régionale Grand-Est,
Espace Linar 41/43 route de Jouy,
F-57160 Moulins lès Metz
France

Erik Brinch Petersen,
Institut for Arkeologi og Etnologi,
Vandkunsten 5,
DK-1467 København K,
Denmark
ebp@hum.ku.dk

Vladimir V. Pitulko,
Institute for the History of Material Culture,
RAS,
18 Dvortsovaya nab,
RU-191186 St. Petersburg,
Russia
archeo@archeo.ru

T. Douglas Price,
Department of Anthropology,
1180, Observatory Drive,
University of Wisconsin, Madison,
Madison
WI 53706
USA
tdprice@facstaff.wisc.edu

Tuija Rankama,
Isonpellonkuja 6,
FIN-02880 Veikkola,
Finland
Tuija.rankama@helsinki.fi

Jan Risberg,
Department of Physical Geography and Quaternary Geology,
Stockholm University,
SE-106 91 Stockholm,
Sweden
jan.risberg@geo.su.se

Marie-Pierre Ruas,
CNRS (UMR 5608),
Unité Toulousaine d'Archéologie et d'Histoire,
Maison de la Recherche,
Université Toulouse Le Mirail,
5 allées Antonio Machado,
F-31058 Toulouse cedex 1,
France

List of Contributors

Alan Saville,
Archaeology Department,
National Museums of Scotland,
Chambers Street,
Edinburgh
EH1 1JF,
Scotland
as@nms.ac.uk

Romuald Schild,
Institute of Archaeology and Ethnology,
Polish Academy of Sciences,
Al. Solidarnodci 105,
PL-00-140 Warsaw
Poland
RSCHILD@iaepan.edu.pl

Henrik Schilling,
Lolland-Falsters Stiftsmuseum,
Museumsgade 1,
DK-4930 Maribo,
Denmark
maribo@museum.dk

Rick J. Schulting,
School of Archaeology and Palaeoecology,
Queen's University Belfast,
Belfast UK BT7 1NN,
Northern Ireland
r.schulting@qub.ac.uk

Fritz H. Schweingruber,
Swiss Federal Institute for Forest and Landscape Research,
Birmensdorferstrasse 111,
CH-8903 Birmensdorf,
Switzerland

Joris Sergant,
Ghent University,
Department of Archaeology and Ancient History of Europe,
Research unit Pre- and Protohistory,
Blandijnberg 2,
B-9000 Gent,
Belgium
joris.sergant@rug.ac.be

Jimmy Strassburg,
The Central Board of National Antiquities,
Box 5405,
SE-114 84 Stockholm,
Sweden
Jimmy.Strassburg@raa.se

Lawrence Guy Straus,
Department of Anthropology,
University of New Mexico,
Albuquerque,
NM 87131,
USA
lstraus@unm.eu

Heather Sugden,
Department of Archaeology and Prehistory,
University of Sheffield,
Sheffield,
S1 4ET,
United Kingdom
H.Sugden@sheffield.ac.uk

Zofia Sulgostowska,
Institute of Archaeology and Ethnology,
Polish Academy of Sciences,
Al. Solidarności 105,
PL-00-140 Warszawa,
Poland
sulg@iaepan.edu.pl

Hannu Takala,
Museum of Lahti,
P.O. Box 113,
FIN-15111 Lahti,
Finland
Hannu.Takala@Lahti.fi

Thomas Terberger,
Lehstuhl für Ur- und Frühgeschichte,
Historisches Institut,
Universität Greifswald,
Hans-Fallada-Strasse,
DE-17489 Greifswald,
Germany
erberge@mail.uni-greifswald.de

Stéphanie Thiebault,
CNRS (UMR 7041), MAE,
21 allée de l'Université,
F-92000 Nanterre,
France

Kazimierz Tobolski,
Quaternary Research Institute,
Adam Mickiewicz University,
Poznań,
Poland

Christopher Tolan-Smith,
Department of Archaeology,
University of Newcastle,
Newcastle upon Tyne,
NE1 7RU,
United Kingdom
chris.tolan-smith@ncl.ac.uk

Carlo Tozzi,
Università di Pisa,
Dip. Di Scienze Archeologiche,
via S. Maria, 53,
IT-56100 Pisa,
Italy

Cláudia Umbelino,
Departamento de Antropologia,
Faculdade de Ciências e Tecnologia,
Universidade de Coimbra,
P-3000-056 Coimbra,
Portugal
cunhae@ci.uc.pt

Marian Vanhaeren,
Institut de Préhistoire et de Géologie du Quaternaire,
UMR 5808 of the CNRS,
Université Bordeaux I,
Avenue des Facultés,
F-33405 Talence,
France
m.vanhaeren@iquat.u-bordeaux.fr

Wim Van Neer,
IUAP,
Interdisciplinary Archaeology,
Royal Museum of Central Africa,
B-3080 Tervuren,
Belgium
vanneer@africamuseum.be

Leo Verhart,
National Museum of Antiquities,
PO Box 11114,
NL-2301 EC Leiden,
The Netherlands
l.verhart@rmo.nl

Christian Verjux,
Service régional de l'archéologie,
DRAC Centre,
6 rue de la manufacture,
F-45043 Orléans Cedex,
France
christian.verjux@culture.gouv.fr

Jean-Denis Vigne,
CNRS (ESA 8045),
Archéozoologie et Histoire des Sociétés,
Muséum national d'Histoire naturelle,
Laboratoire d'Anatomie comparée,
55 rue Buffon,
F-75005 Paris,
France

Jürgen Vollbrecht,
Landesamt für Archäologie Sachsen,
Arbeitsstelle Braunkohle,
Schadendorfer Straße 46,
DE-02943 Reichwalde,
Germany
vollbrechtj@t-online.de

Caroline R. Wickham-Jones,
Department of Archaeology,
University of Edinburgh,
Old High School,
12 Infirmary Street,
Edinburgh,
EH1 1LT,
Scotland
c.wickham-jones@dial.pipex.com

Roger Wikell,
National Heritage Board,
Department of Archaeological Excavations,
UV Mitt,
Box 5405,
SE-114 84 Stockholm,
Sweden
roger.wikell@raa.se

Małgorzata Winiarska-Kabacińska,
Poznań Archaeological Museum,
Wodna 27,
PL-61-781 Poznań,
Poland
muzarp@man.poznan.pl

Peter Woodman,
Department of Archaeology,
University College Cork,
Cork,
Ireland
PWoodman@arts.ucc.ie

Estelle Yven,
Centre de Recherche Bretonne et Celtique,
Faculté des Lettres et Sciences,
speciales 20,
rue Duquesne,
F-29285 Brest,
France
yven.e@club-internet.fr

Ilga Zagorska,
Institute of Latvian History,
Department of Archaeology,
Akademijas laukums 1,
Riga LV 1050,
Latvia

Gunita Zariņa,
Institute of Latvian History,
Department of Archaeology,
Akademijas laukums 1,
Riga LV 1050,
Latvia

Mikhail G. Zhilin,
Planernaya street, 3-2-235,
RU-123480 Moscow,
Russia
mizhilin@yandex.ru

Sławomir Żurek,
Institute of Geography,
Jan Kochanowski Academy,
M. Konopnickiej 15,
PL 25-406 Kielce,
Poland

Marek Zvelebil,
Department of Archaeology and Prehistory,
University of Sheffield,
Northgate House,
West Street,
Sheffield
S1 4ET,
Uinted Kingdom
M.Zvelebil@Sheffield.ac.uk

Preface

The 92 articles in this book (by 136 authors from 23 countries) include most of the oral and poster presentations presented at the 6th International Conference on *The Mesolithic in Europe* which took place at Nynäshamn, just south of Stockholm, in Eastern Central Sweden, between the 4–8 September 2000. The Conference was held under the auspices of the 12th Commission of the International Union of Pre- and Protohistoric Sciences.

At the preceding conference (Grenoble 1995) a group of participants from the universities in Sweden successfully campaigned to host the next meeting. This joint project, entitled *Meso 2000*, involving the universities of Lund, Gothenburg, Stockholm, Uppsala and Umeå. There are several reasons why we wished to host the conference in Sweden. Not least because Swedish archaeologists have been actively taking part in these meetings since they began in 1973. We also suspected that much of what others knew about the Mesolithic in this part of the world probably concerned southern Sweden, a situation that we felt uncomfortable with, especially in light of the new material that has been coming out of Middle and Northern Sweden, research which has developed and expanded considerably during the last decade. Thus, one of our aims was to promote knowledge about the Mesolithic in these poorly known areas situated along the northern fringe of Europe. We also decided to place the conference, not in the vicinity of the famous archaeological sites located the South, but in Eastern Central Sweden, where more than fifty new sites have been excavated during the last ten years. In order to illustrate the large variability that once existed during the Mesolithic in these different areas, pre- and post conference excursions were organised, as well as a small exhibition that was on display during the conference week.

Attendance has increased with each conference. The first was held at Warsaw, Poland and brought together some thirty-five scholars. Just over 200 participated in this latest gathering, of which almost half gave a presentation. Because of the limited time available, a program with parallel sessions was implemented. The number of papers presented orally had to be restricted and some applicants were advised to present their material as posters. The publication of all presentations, oral or otherwise, was encouraged.

Participants were invited to submit presentations that addressed one of eight topics or sessions: *Colonisation Processes, Enculturating the Landscape, Social Relations and Group Formation, Spatial Organisation of Sites, Territoriality – Regionalisation, Exchange and Communication, Ritual and Symbolic Behaviour* as well as *Hunter-Gatherers in Transition*.

These topics were chosen by the conference organisers in collaboration with two colleagues from abroad, Douglas Price and Clive Bonsall. This selection was based on our shared perceptions as to what was currently going on within the field of Mesolithic research. Although the topics chosen are somewhat limited in scope, there is still reason to believe that they do reflect current interests within the subject, and that the articles clearly show that Mesolithic studies are on the move.

The preliminary call for papers initially generated a particularly large response to the session on *Hunters and Gatherers in Transition* and *Enculturating the Landscape*, a circumstance that is not altogether evident from the number of papers that were finally published.

There seems to be a marked difference between the interests of female and male scholars. The later presented all the papers given on the *Spatial Organisation of Sites* while the former gave all the papers presented in *Social Relations and Group Formation*. Two of the sessions, *Hunters and Gatherers in Transition* and *Colonisation Processes*, were clearly dominated by male speakers. This illustrates the importance of actively encouraging a variety of directions within research, otherwise we will end up with a lopsided and/or limited view of the past.

The articles in this book are grouped in accordance with the thematic sessions in which they were first presented, with the addition of a ninth group that contains papers that could not be sorted according to one of the above eight topics. Each session was chaired by an archaeologist, invited to do so by the organising committee, chosen in light of their research in relationship to one of the above topics. These chair persons have each written a short introduction to the articles in their respective session.

This publication begins, however, with three introductory papers. The first takes a look at Mesolithic research in Europe, the second is a short review of what has been happening in Sweden, while the third presents recent work in Eastern Central Sweden.

Many people helped bring this conference about. Eva Hyenstrand and Dag Hammar designed the conference website while Elisabeth Green kept it up to date. Birgitta M. Johansson handled communications and correspondence prior to the conference. Helena Albäck, Helena Andersson, Kim von Hackwitz, Birgitta M. Johansson, Björn Karlsson and Cecilia Rodehn assisted in keeping the audio-visual equipment up and running during the presentations. The exhibition was arranged by Jackie Taffinder. We thank you one and all for your considerable efforts.

Two excursions were held prior to and after the conference. The former took place in southern most Sweden and along the West Coast under the direction of

Lars Larsson, Arne Sjöström and Hans Kindgren, while the latter travelled through Northern Sweden together with David Loeffler.

From Oxbow Books we would like to thank Julie Choppin for her work on the layout of this book and David Brown for his valuable support.

Finally, special recognition must be given to those institutions and foundations who generously provided the financial support for this endeavour: The Royal Academy of Letters, History and Antiquities, The Berit Wallenberg Foundation, The Bank of Sweden Tercentenary Foundation (RBJ), the Swedish Council for Research in the Humanities and Social Sciences (HSFR), The Åke Wiberg Foundation, The Wenner-Gren Centre Foundation, The Swedish Institute (SI), The Section for Planning, Budget and Quality at the University of Umeå and The Seth M. Kempe Memorial Foundation in Örnsköldsvik.

The Editorial Board

Introduction

The Mesolithic: What do we know and what do we believe?

Stefan Karol Kozłowski

The author reviews with skepticism some recently propounded hypotheses concerning the European Mesolithic, finding them to be in part too general, hence banal (see Figure 1). He emphasises numerous elements of the internal differentiation of this formation, demonstrating how they can be revealed in the course of a cartographic analysis.

Twenty-seven years have passed since our first meeting in Warsaw in May 1973. Later we met in Potsdam (1978), Edinburgh (1985), Leuven (1990) and Grenoble (1995). It is perhaps a good opportunity here, in Nynäshamn, to consider our accomplishments and our failures, to take a look at what we really know and what we only believe we know about the Mesolithic. The Meso-Comix (Figure 1) shows some of our recent achievements/discoveries. The picture is somewhat pessimistic (cf. below).

What is the Mesolithic?

There are those who would like to believe that the Mesolithic is characterised by some highly specific attributes, such as a uniform economic model based on individual hunting, gathering and fishing; which was adapted to specific interglacial (Early and Middle Holocene) forest conditions; also believed to be in opposition to the Late Glacial model (Palaeolithic/tundra viz. Mesolithic/forest); with a developed social and territorial organisation (ownership and borders of highly organised territories, settlement hierarchy and structuring, e.g. base viz. satellite camps, seasonal population movement, e.g. seasonal change of hunting niches and seasonal gatherings, cemeteries); raw material procurement systems (well organised mines/extraction points, specialised workshops, far reaching distribution); microlithisation and

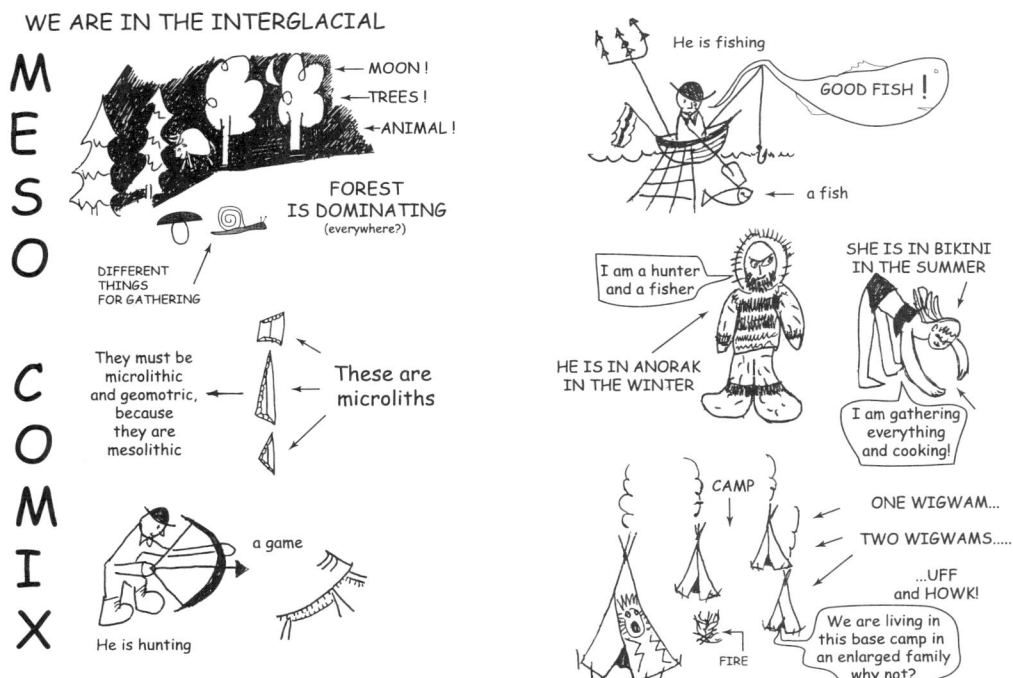

Figure 1 Meso Comix

geometrisation of backed and truncated points/bladelets serving as arrowheads (for hunting small game, of course?). Indeed, there is a man who fails to recognise the existence of the Mesolithic in Russia because of the lack of geometrics there.

According to this restricted definition, the European Mesolithic (not including the Scandinavian Peninsula and the Russian Plain) seems to be, in the eyes of some authors, surprisingly uniform or practically uniform with regard to technology and typology (=culture), something that does not fit well with our experience concerning the preceding (Palaeolithic) and following (Neolithic) periods. It is even believed (cf. below) that the evolution of the flint industry of this practically uniform Mesolithic is unidirectional and follows the sequence: broad triangles-narrow triangles-trapezes.

There is, even now, a tendency to abandon traditional cultural/taxonomic subdivisions and to replace them with more neutral names, like Early or Late Mesolithic. These chronological terms, when employed to describe contemporary phenomena from distant regions are totally misleading, if they do not take into consideration that they are describing completely different stylistic units/structures/worlds (e.g. Sauveterriano in Italy and Maglemose in Scandinavia).

Consequently, existing (often local) definitions and characteristics of the Mesolithic are based on criteria that are frequently contradictory. They are as follows (cf. Figure 1):

1   ecological (interglacial forest),
2   techno-stylistic (alleged uniformity featuring microlithism, geometrism, microburin technique and a common evolutionary rhythm),
3   economic (hunters-gatherers-fishers),
4   social (highly organised, developed and specialised hunting-gathering communities, featuring a social hierarchy, territorial systems, raw material procurement, seasonality),
5   chronological (Early and Middle Holocene).

Definitions of this kind consist of contradictions, while not covering phenomena that have been considered traditionally as Mesolithic (cf. below).

With regard to ecology, there were never any forests north of the Black and Caspian seas, for example, in the Holocene, nor were there any forests in the northern extremes of the continent. By contrast, the entire southern part of Europe was thickly wooded during the Late Glacial.

As for technology and typology, while there are no geometrics coming from Russia and the territories of the East Baltic states, such elements are well known from the Late Magdalenian, Epi-Gravettian and Ahrensburgian, as well as from the Late Glacial industries of the Middle East and Northern Africa. The same concerns microliths. In eastern areas of Europe and on the Scandinavian Peninsula the microliths/geometrics were replaced with tanged points.

The evoked socio-territorial organisation had in fact developed at least during the Middle Palaeolithic period, and some of these accomplishments are well known from the animal world! (social hierarchisation, territorial organisation, primitive dwellings).

The only remaining feature in common is the chronology, which places the Mesolithic in a period between ca. 8000 (or perhaps better 7800/7700?) years BC (uncalicrated) and the time of local/regional neolithisation.

The incoherent description presented above is indeed a simple summary of various regional experiences and definitions, and it demonstrates clearly enough how much we need to apply the extra-regional approach in studies of the Mesolithic, and also how little success we have had in this approach.

The approach we are still dependent on is the one applied by local priests/pastors or schoolteachers. Those first Mesolithic explorers and experts in many places and regions had only their local/parish experience/perspective, and were obviously incapable of achieving an extra-regional understanding of the problem.

Most of the evoked attributes are in fact either poorly documented or not exclusive/discriminant, some of them even banal. The former are mostly based on biological and ethnological/anthropological experience, and suggest nothing more than a banal and naive picture of the hunter-gatherer community on a developed, specialised level (Figure 1).

In turn, seasonality, raw material procurement, territory, settlement hierarchy, all appear real enough (documented), but are hardly exclusively Mesolithic in nature (cf. above). Indeed, even the geometrics, backed pieces, microliths and microburins on one hand, and the tanged points on the other, were invented and used before the Holocene (respectively by the Late Magdalenians, Epi-Gravettians and the Tanged Point Complex, all of whom were Palaeolithic populations).

The other question is; what do we actually know?

Instead of the above described picture of an allegedly uniform European Mesolithic, we are suggesting a more professional and thorough/subtle description of the phenomenon, based on a study of extra-regional differences. These differences concern a variety of environmental attributes, as well as cultural traditions, which can be determined on the grounds of styles and technology.

The Early and Middle Holocene European environment differed in many ways:

1   morphology of terrain (plain/plateau/mountain),
2   hydrography (sea/lakes/rivers/streams),
3   raw materials (outcrops for extraction/mining viz. surface sources; rocks diversity),
4   climate (subarctic/cool/temperate/Mediterranean; dry/wet; oceanic/continental),

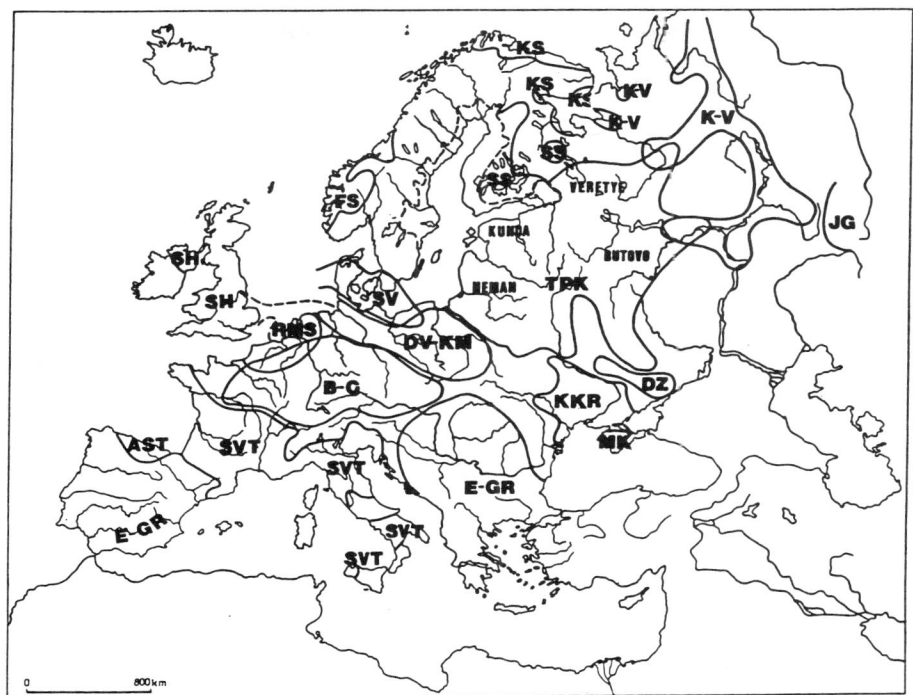

Figure 2 Mesolithic Europe in the second half of the 7th millenium b.c. KS – Komsa, FS – Fosna, SS – Suomusjärvi, KV – Kama-Vychegda, JG – Yangelka, TPK – Kunda Tanged Points, SV – Sværborg, DV-KM – Duvensee-Komornica, SH – Shippea Hill, RMS – Rhein-Meuse-Skhelde, BC – Beuron-Coincy, SVT – Sauveterrian, E-GR – Balkan Epi-Gravettian, KKR – Kukrek, DZ – Donetz, MK – Murzak-Koba.

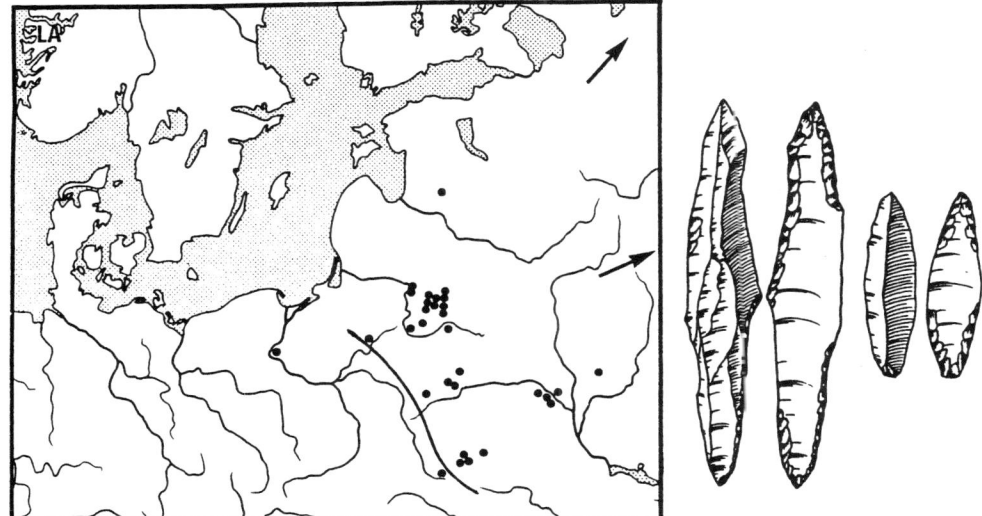

Figure 3 Western border of the North-Eastern Kunda Mesolithic Complex, as indicated by the Kunda tanged points.

5 flora (tundra/coniferous/mixed/deciduous forests/ steppes),
6 mammals (reindeer, elk, mixed forest fauna, aurochs, all occupying specific habitats),
7 goods for gathering (nuts, lentil, land and marine snails).
8 as for manufacturing technologies, the stylistic, typological and technological differentiation that can be observed in the tools concerns both technology (shape and mode of core pre-formation, e.g. conical, subconical, discoidal, single-, double-platform, etc.; modes of exploitation, e.g. pressure viz. punch technique; size, e.g. big Castelnovian items viz. smaller Sauveterrian; kinds of retouching, e.g. abrupt, semi-steep, flat; special techniques, e.g. microburin, pseudo-microburin, blade sectioning, etc.) and morphology (mostly shapes of alleged arrow- and spearheads, e.g. flint/stone tanged points, feuilles de

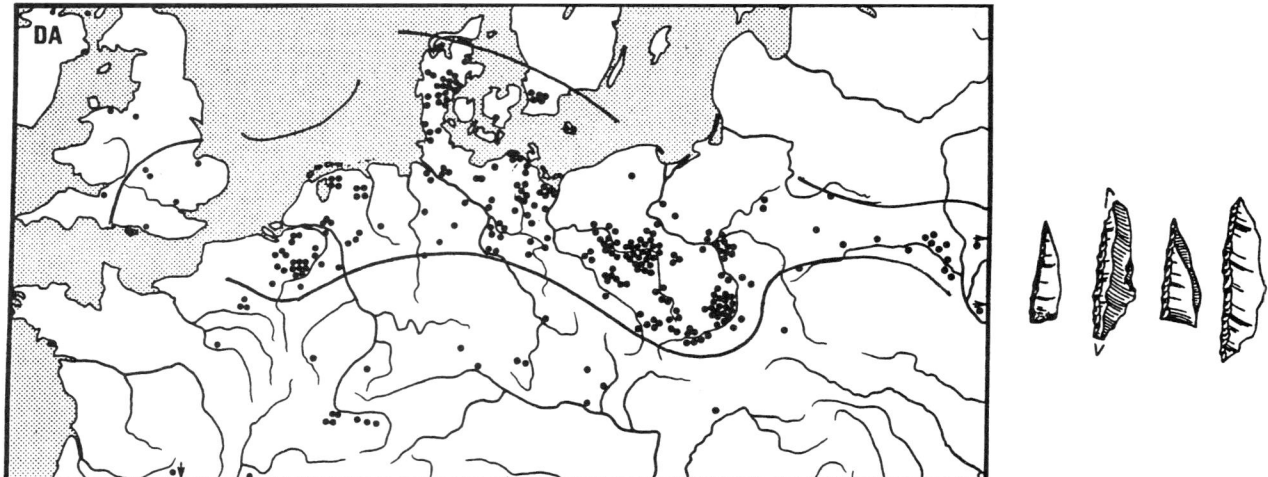

Figure 4 Territory of the Maglemosian/Northern Mesolithic complex (except for the most eastern region), as indicated by the Early/Middle Holocene backed points.

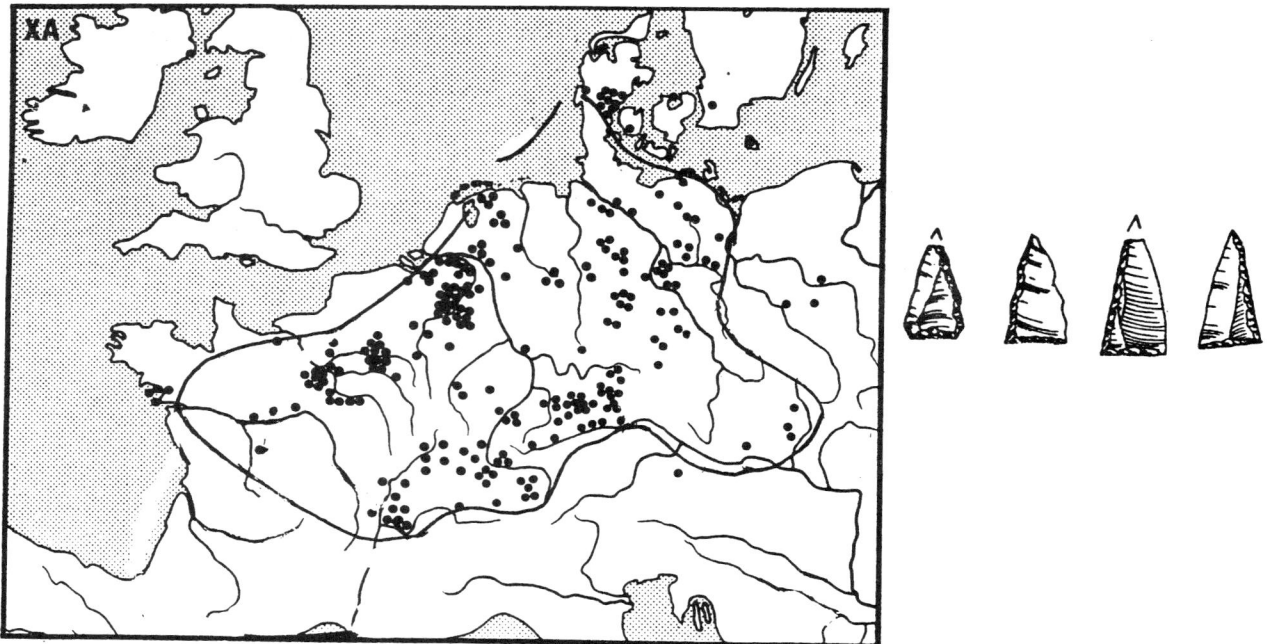

Figure 5 Northern part of the Western Mesolithic Complex territory, as indicated by the Tardenois points.

gui, backed points/bladelets, various triangles, microtruncations, microretouched bladelets, various trapezes, etc.; also bone/antler barbed, slotted, spindle-shaped or biconical points, unpolished and polished axes/adzes/chisels, denticulated Montbani bladelets, denticulated flakes, etc.).

To judge by our historical experience, environmental differentiation of the kind evoked above could strongly condition human culture, imposing differentiation/zonation/regionalisation/territorial separation. This is what we observe in the European Mesolithic (cf. below).

As for style/typology/technology, Mesolithic Europe demonstrates an extra-regional differentiation and zonation (Figure 2) that can be summarised in the following list of big, extra-regional taxonomic entities (techno-complexes): Scandinavian Tanged Points, Maglemosian or Northern, Western or Tardenoisian, North-Eastern or Kunda, Epi-Gravettian, Caucaso-Caspian, Castelnovian. The extent and borders of these entities (and their regional components-cultures, see Figure 2) can be traced cartographically, showing the territorial distribution of selected characteristic attributes. The maps (Figures 3–5), taken from the author's *Atlas of the Mesolithic in Europe* reveal the existence of borders between the North-Eastern and

Northern Mesolithic Complexes (Figures 3 and 4), as well as a transition zone between the Maglemosian and Western Mesolithic Complex (Figures 4 and 5).

These, as well as other maps, indicate the existence of extra-regional, regional and even local territories/zones, characterised by evident almost linear borders, each with their own distinct tradition. This is what we expected. It also means that the European Mesolithic was not as uniform as supposed.

Conclusion

To sum up what has been said here, what we do know is that:

The Mesolithic is a Postglacial/Interglacial continuation (in the south) and/or adaptation (in the north) of a culture of Late Glacial specialised hunters in a temperate climate and for the most part in a forested environment, which dominates almost the entire continent from the beginning of the eight millennium bc.

There is no shared attribute (except for the chronology) that could be safely used to define the entire Mesolithic formation.

The Mesolithic population was a highly specialised hunter-gatherer-fisher structure that was not invented in the Holocene, but was inherited from Late Glacial predecessors. This observation concerns not only material objects (flint tools, tanged points, geometrics, microliths, microburins, bone and antler industry), but also the more intangible and hence only selectively known elements of social culture, like territorial organisation, raw material procurement system, seasonality, settlement pattern and hierarchy of settlements, hunting strategies, etc.

Last but not least and contrary to what has often been suggested, the Mesolithic represents a highly differentiated phenomenon.

The Mesolithic of Sweden in retrospective and progressive perspectives

Lars Larsson

Because of its oblong shape, Sweden includes several different topographic as well as geological and climatic zones, and hence has obvious ecological differences. Contacts with surrounding areas were of importance for the formation of societies, with cultural influences from continental Europe in the south, links with the Atlantic coast in the west and with the Baltic region via the archipelago in eastern Sweden and the circumpolar network in northern Sweden. As a result, the Swedish territory includes several partly different prehistories.

Just as the lives of Mesolithic people were influenced by the specific environment – physical as well as social – research into the Mesolithic has been affected by the find conditions and the scholarly networks.

In the south, finds and sites in bogs as well as sites on the former coast were recognised early and attracted interest. The special conditions with transgressions and regressions served to inspire archaeological research on the west coast. Isostasy in eastern Sweden has provided an excellent perspective on life in archipelagos as well as the reaction of societies to marked changes of the coastline in northern Sweden. Inland settlement, not directly affected by the coastal dynamism, has been influenced by other circumstances.

In current archaeological research there are attempts to find new ways to analyse and structure results in order to discern which regulations and norms governed society and how these affected the position and action of individuals. One has to realise that world-views had a penetrating influence on everyday life.

Archaeology today provides good proof that we, as a product of the modern world, cannot act as independent observers of prehistory. Consciously or unconsciously, our attitude affects the prehistory we want to describe or interpret. In order to evaluate models concerning the value norms which existed in prehistory, we try to recognise patterns which suggest some kind of structure. Not ony those we can trace in the material culture but also those in connection with features and burials as well. To combine these indications into a contextual view of prehistoric society, to observe the shadows of their world-view, which leavened the life of the people, is therefore a most desirable but very difficult goal.

Introduction

Because of its oblong shape, Sweden includes several different topographic as well as geological and climatic zones, and hence has obvious ecological differences (Figure 1). This makes it very difficult to present an overview of the Swedish Mesolithic as well as other prehistoric periods. As a matter of fact, the Swedish territory includes several partly different prehistories. This is a very good example of the fact that it is almost impossible to describe the prehistory of a region with present-day political delimitations.

The southernmost part of Sweden is not only climatically but also geologically linked to the continental part of Northern Europe. The North Sea and the Baltic act as

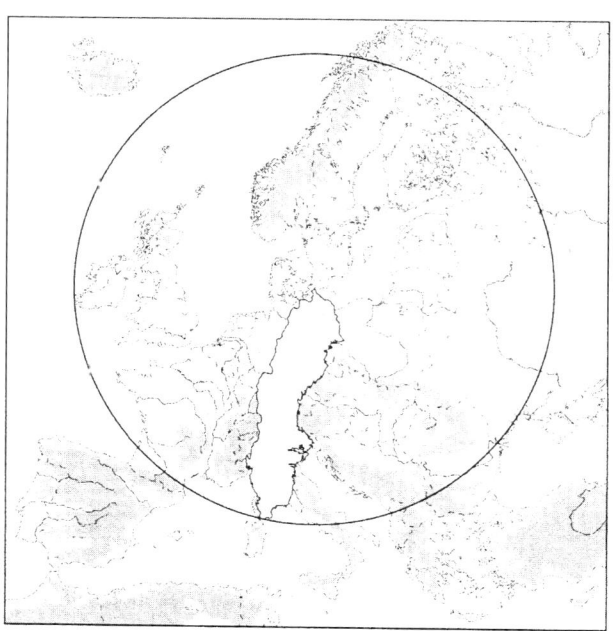

Figure 1 Sweden in Europe.

moderating factors for temperature changes during summer and winter, providing moderate winters and rather cool summers in western Sweden and in parts of the south-eastern coastal area of Sweden (Figure 2). A levelled area in the central part of southern Sweden provides climatic conditions parallel to areas further north. The Fenno-scandic mountains effectively hinder western winds from the North Atlantic from warming the interior of northern Sweden, except through some mountain passes in southern Norrland. Due to this situation, northern Sweden has a continental climate with cold winters and fairly warm summers. The topographic gradient is rather weak and drastic climatic zonation such as in Norway or parts of the Mediterranean does not exist in Sweden.

This means that the difference in July temperature between south and north is small, 16°C and 13°C respectively, with the exception of the high mountains, while the same difference during January is much higher, 0°C in the south and -15°C in the north.

Owing to considerable changes in the relation between land and water, marked alterations in climate must have taken place in Sweden, with a more continentally influenced climate during the early Mesolithic and a more maritime climate during the later part. The sea-ice situation during winters must have varied depending on the size and salinity of the Baltic. During the middle part of the Mesolithic, with the Ancylus Lake, the ice probably covered larger areas than, for example, the Littorina Sea during the late Mesolithic.

Environment and society

One does not need to be a natural determinist to claim that man's relations to his surroundings must have been influenced, both physically and mentally, by climatological conditions. However, climatological conditions in the Mesolithic have mostly been regarded in a teleological perspective, as a continuous rise in temperature.

The relations between society and environment are not viewed as an important agent for cultural changes. Interest has focused on aspects of general importance for hunter-gatherer societies, such as purely economic elements. Often the social-environmental situation is perceived as unproblematic. The question is whether this was the case. A couple of examples will show that this factor affected the social context.

In several palaeoecological studies of north-western Europe, a dramatic climatic decrease has been found at ca. 6200 BC cal. which in uncalibrated values is equal to 7400 BP (Bond *et al.* 1997). Interestingly enough, this date is contemporaneous with the transition from the Early to the Late Mesolithic. Elements such as large base camps and cemeteries indicate the increasing complexity of the social structure. A link between climatic change and social change cannot be proved, but the chronological relation is of such interest that further analysis should be conducted.

Attention should also be paid to the fact that late

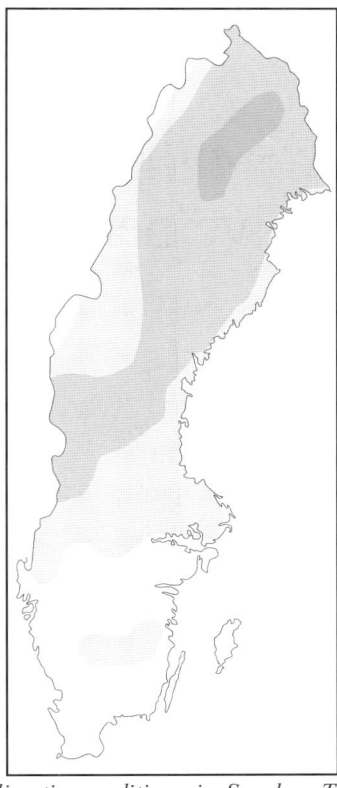

Figure 2 Climatic conditions in Sweden. The darker the area, the more affected it is by continental climate. From Vedin 1995.

Mesolithic sites are found in several lakes in southernmost Sweden at a level of one to two metres below the present water table (Karsten 1986). One has to consider that the present sea level is the result of intensive drainage since the 19th century, which caused a reduction of the water level by one and often two metres. Judging by the location of the late Mesolithic sites with an even lower water table, most lakes were missing or had a very reduced outlet. This situation must have made the coastal zone even more attractive for habitation in order to give rise to social changes. Climatic changes occurred during the Mesolithic, and their social implication should not be neglected.

Contact zones

Contacts with surrounding areas were of importance for the formation of the Mesolithic societies. Their form suggests that there are several feasible channels through which cultural influences could have reached present day Sweden (Figure 3). During the early part of the Mesolithic until about 7500 BP, southern Sweden was accessible almost dry-shod from present day eastern Denmark (Larsson 1999). The Danish island of Bornholm was linked to the continent during the early Mesolithic and the passage by sea was rather short. In contrast, the sea voyage from northern Jutland to western Sweden – of importance at least during the Neolithic – was somewhat

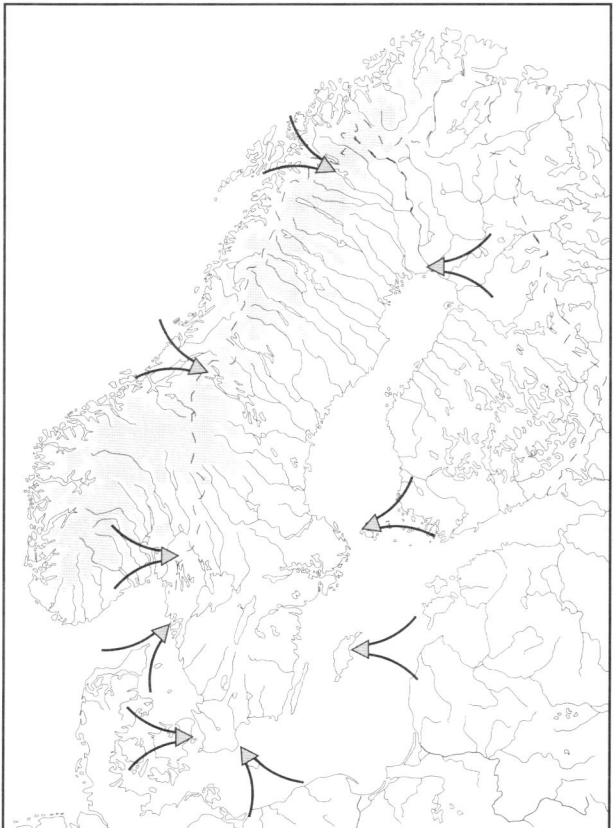

Figure 3 The most important routes of influence.

longer than today, as part of northern Jutland was still submerged. Links with the coastal societies along the North Sea and the North Atlantic could be established and maintained in at least three different regions: in the south along the coast, from the centre in present day Trøndelag, and from the north. The connection to present day northern Finland and perhaps from the arctic areas of Scandinavia was easy accessible mainly along the rivers. A circumpolar network connected northern Sweden.

The creation of an archipelago between south-western Finland and central Sweden might have become an important link with the Baltic region, at least during the latest part of the Mesolithic (Åkerlund 1996).

A voyage across the high sea was necessary in order to cross the Baltic to the island of Gotland. Gotland was settled from the Swedish side since at least the middle part of the Mesolithic. The distance between the Baltic region and Gotland is not that much further than to the Swedish coast.

These contact zones were of course not one-way. Societies within present day Sweden might have affected the surrounding world to a greater or lesser extent.

Retrospective view of research in the Mesolithic

The geographical variety has meant that Mesolithic research has been implemented on the basis of divergent intentions and preconditions. In southern Sweden the archaeological research in Denmark was a guiding star. The excavations of shell-middens in northern Jutland towards the end of the 19th century encouraged the excavation of a settlement in the Littorina ridge at Limhamn in south-western Scania, where remains similar to those at Ertebølle were found in 1903 (Kjellmark 1903). The bog excavation at Mullerup on Zealand encouraged Swedish archaeologists to look for the same type of settlement site and the first bog excavation was conducted in 1908 at Bare Mosse in western Scania (Welinder 1971).

Peat digging in the late 19th and early 20th centuries has revealed several bone and antler artefacts similar to those found in Danish bogs (Broholm 1924). However, the number of bog sites found in Denmark because of peat extraction during the two world wars did not have any counterpart in southern Sweden. The reason might be that the information links between antiquarian authorities and peat diggers were not as close in Sweden as in Denmark. However, no surveys were made with the aim of finding sites.

Intensive excavation was started after the Second World War because of finds made in the late 1930's (Althin 1954). Excavations of inland as well as coastal sites were conducted in the 1970's and 1980's (Welinder 1971; Larsson 1978, 1982). Not until very recently has the excavation of Mesolithic sites come under the attention of rescue archaeology.

Large areas of the present southern Baltic were land during the Early Mesolithic. From a low level during the Pre-boreal the water level rose – especially during the late Boreal – and reached the present situation in the early Atlantic. However, it is only rather recently that any research has been aimed at surveys and consequently the excavation of submerged sites (Larsson 1999).

In the western part of Sweden, Mesolithic research started in the 1910's (Sarauw and Alin 1923). At an early stage the location of sites in relation to the isostasy became an important aspect in the dating of the settlement. Somewhat later the eustatic phenomenon was recognised, as occupation layers covered with transgression layers were identified (Alin *et al.* 1934). Most Mesolithic sites during the last few decades have been found and excavated in rescue digs.

In general the very early and middle part of the Mesolithic are well known in western Sweden, with a large number of sites (Kindgren 1996), while several aspects of the latest Mesolithic are still not so well documented. The western part of Sweden is the only area where shell middens from the late Mesolithic, albeit small in numbers and size, are to be found (Alin 1935).

The Mesolithic settlement of south-eastern Sweden and central Sweden has not until very recently attracted any special interest. This area was looked upon something of a zone with influences from the south as well as from the north (Welinder 1977). It was not until the isostatic changes were geologically well understood that Meso-

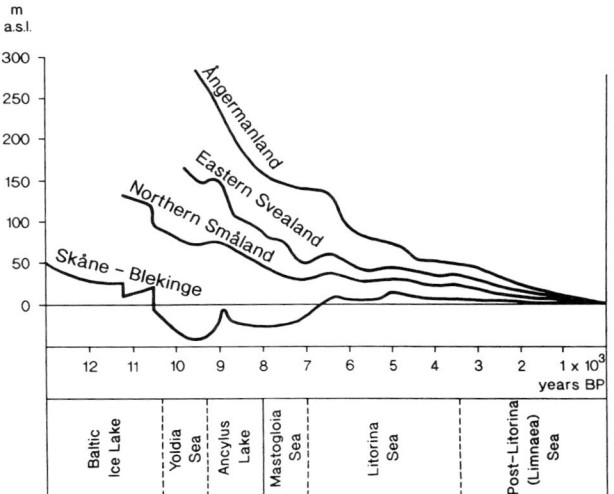

Figure 4 Isostatic and eustatic movements in different parts of Sweden. After Åkerlund 1996.

lithic sites with a very small number of formal tools could be reasonably well dated (Åkerlund 1996) (Figure 4). Settlement from the actual mainland all the way out to the outer archipelago can thus be traced.

Because of the damming of the large rivers in Norrland, large-scale surveys were undertaken after the Second World War and a large number of Stone Age sites were identified (Baudou 1992). It was not until the 1970's, however, that Mesolithic settlement was recognised (Broadbent 1979). The isostatic changes in Norrland, which in places might have been as much as 200 m during the Mesolithic, caused radical changes to the coastline, and in certain flat regions the coast might have receded about 200 km (Halén 1994). Its marked effects on the environment as well as on the cognitive aspect are not difficult to comprehend.

Several excavations have revealed an intensive settlement history which in its expressions has similarities to the settlement of southernmost Sweden, such as an intensification of exchange networks and the introduction of pottery and cemeteries (Halén 1995).

Cultural frameworks

For some time the Swedish Mesolithic has been divided into different regions, southernmost Sweden, the west coast and northern Sweden being the most characteristic divisions. With few exceptions (Welinder 1973, 1977), research has been kept within these regions, which has meant that new viewpoints about other and more complex network systems have had difficulty in finding acceptance. A couple of examples may demonstrate the problems with this division.

It may seem simplest to discern special cultural phenomena in the southernmost and westernmost parts of the country. Here the Maglemose and Hensbacka cultures have been distinguished in the early Mesolithic, the Kongemose and Sandarna cultures in the middle Mesolithic, and the Ertebølle and Lihult cultures in the later part of the Mesolithic. For the rest of Sweden there are no real culture designations. The main reason for this may be sought in the history of modern ideas, since scholars in recent years have avoided naming newly identified cultural phenomena. This is basically a correct approach, since one can easily become a prisoner within the frames that have already been set up. On the other hand, it becomes difficult to handle phenomena which have to be constantly redefined. For southern Sweden one clearly notices how divisions into cultural phases have attracted greater attention at the expense of cultural designations. Archaeologists speak of the Villingebæk phase, rarely of the Kongemose culture (Vang Petersen 1984). Depending on which variables are considered, individual scholars construct their own chronological frameworks, but in some cases this makes comparative studies difficult.

Chronological and chorological divisions of the Mesolithic can be done according to several variables. One division between north and south has often been based upon the use of different raw material, flint in the south and quartz in the north, with the dividing line somewhere in the northern part of southern Sweden (Welinder 1977) (Figure 5). New excavations in the northern part of the province of Scania and southern Småland (Figure 5) have shown that at some early Mesolithic sites quartz makes up 90% of the knapped material (Knarrström 2000a, 2000b). The same is also true for sites further to the east. These finds are excellent reminders of how fragile our information is about areas outside of traditional research regions.

It must also be openly admitted that there are also isolated finds of quartz and rock crystal at the flint bearing settlement sites in south-western most Scandinavia. It should be a task for the future to go through the finds to assess whether they are exotic items of symbolic or psychological importance from the north (Bang-Andersen 1998), comparable to the sporadic finds of slate objects in southern Sweden from the late Mesolithic (Taffinder 1998).

The influences and lack of influences may have changed considerably during different stages of the Mesolithic as well. There might be certain changes from an early stage with a larger element of flint to a later stage with raw material of local origin (Welinder 1977), but this is not always the real situation (Åkerlund 1996).

Another question is what should be designated as, say, Maglemose culture, and when does a hunter-gatherer society show Maglemose influences. The chronological division is based on a few tool forms, with arrowheads occupying a special position.

This considerable geographical and geological diversity is not only problematic, it also allows us to examine general and specific features.

All groups of material include more or less clearly identifiable functional categories, stone fragments that

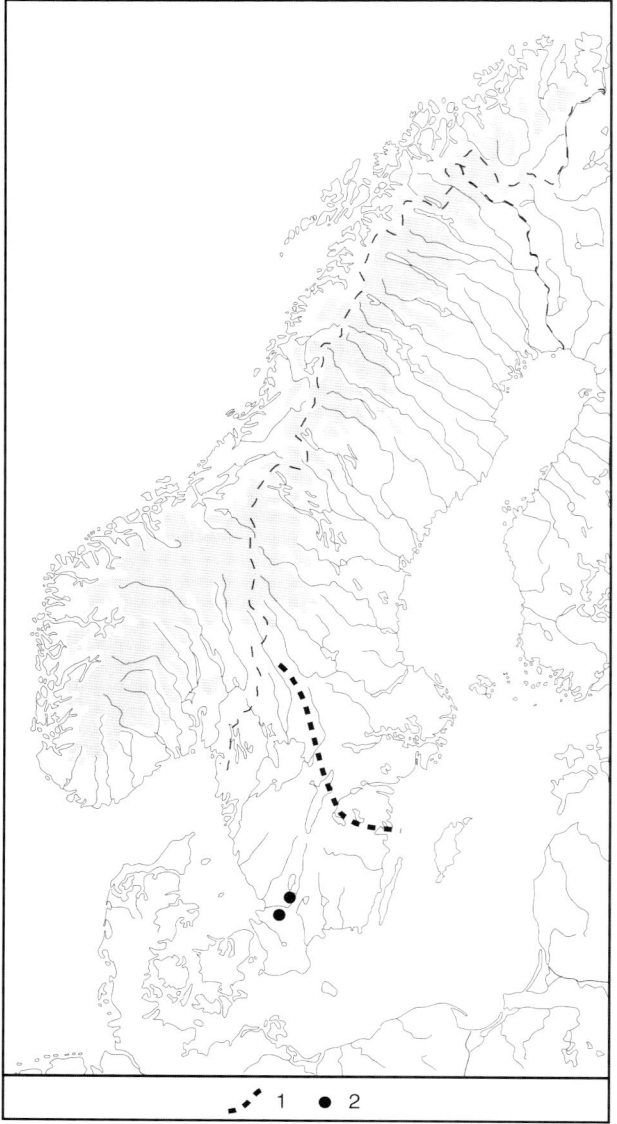

Figure 5 Divisions of the Mesolithic according to raw material. 1) divisions between settlement sites dominated by flint and those dominated by quartz and 2) southernmost sites with a majority of quartz.

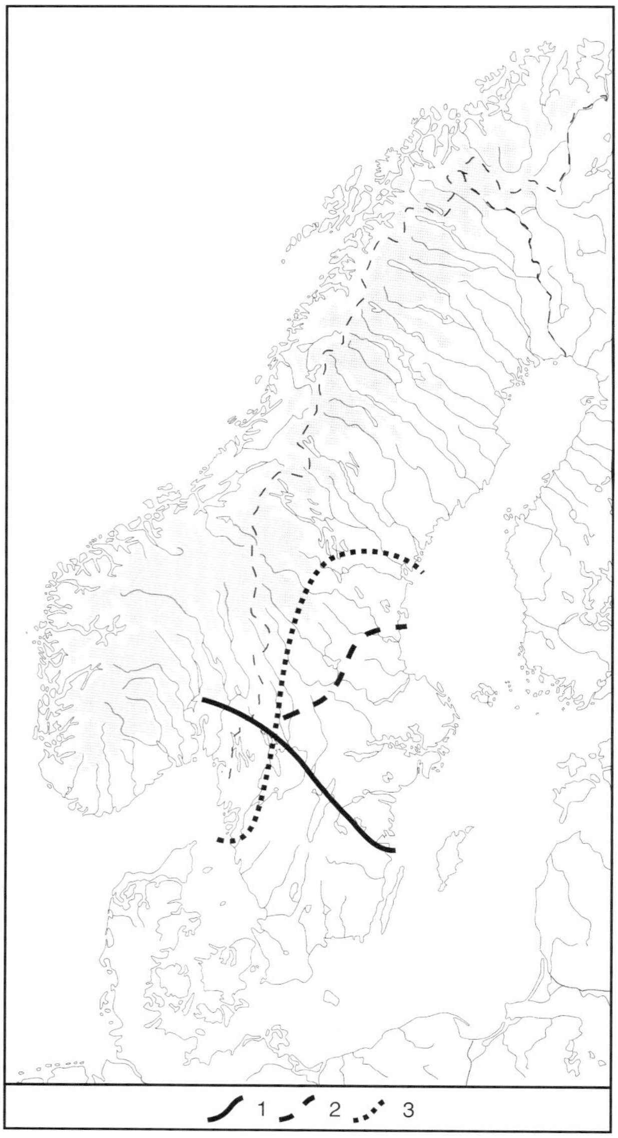

Figure 6 Divisions of the Mesolithic according to, certain tool types and expressions of art. 1) northern extent of microliths, 2) northern extent of stone axes and 3) southern extent of rock art.

were used for special activities, with or without reshaping. Of special interest, however, is the social categories, those which can have a practical function but which are in addition deliberately used as a marker in a social context.

I would say that the majority of all tools, especially those which we perceive as cultural and chronological markers, are totally unnecessary for maintaining basal activities in a society. It should also be borne in mind that there are remains of material culture which largely lack distinguishable formal tools, as we see, for example, at the Mörby settlement site in Östergötland (Kaliff et al. 1997) and at Garaselet in northern Västerbotten (Forsberg and Knutsson 1999). In both these examples the archaeological remains seem to be the initial settlement at each of these sites, dated to 9000–8500 BP and ca. 8000 BP respectively.

In many parts of the country the question of an arrowhead chronology is quite irrelevant, since there are no formal arrowheads. This clearly shows that specially shaped points are of no significance for hunting, fishing, or any other form of food acquisition for which the points were used. The points were primarily social markers. The same applies to axes. Hunting was evidently quite successful without any sharpened points or special axe forms. The cultural markers in the form of arrowheads, in both the early and the late Mesolithic (Figure 7), agree relatively well with the previously stated boundary between the use of flint and quartz (Figure 5). Microliths are

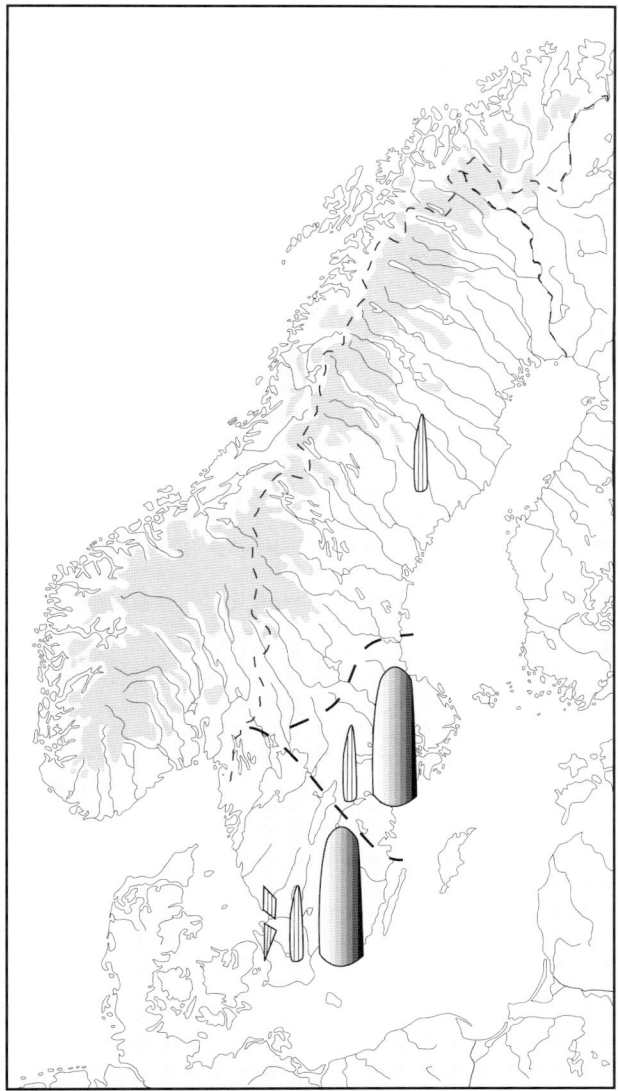

Figure 7 The division of Sweden according to artefacts of symbolic importance during the middle Mesolithic.

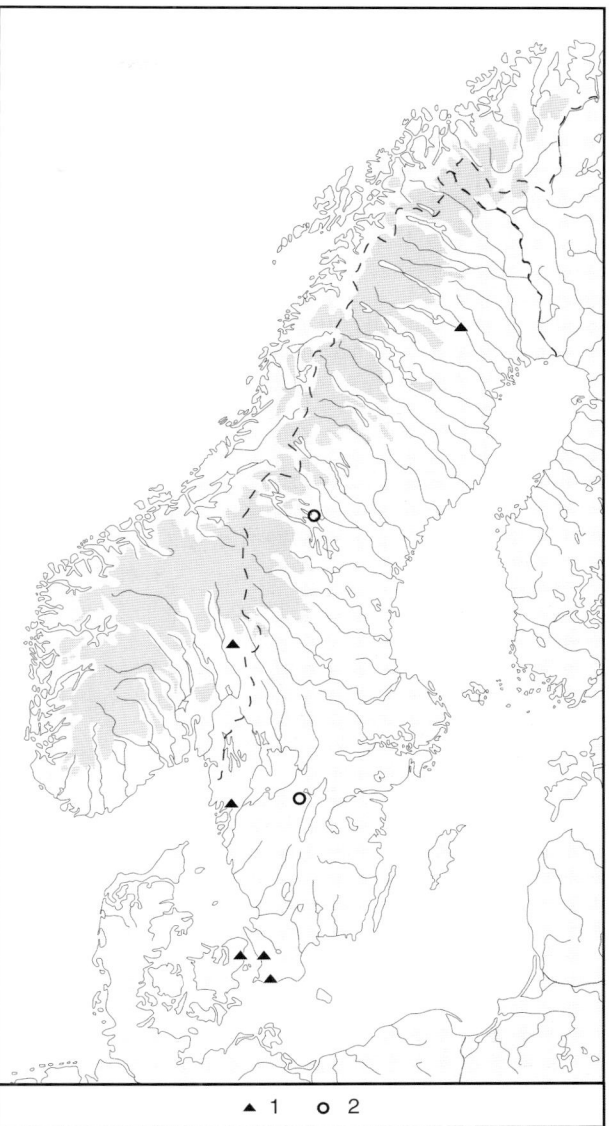

Figure 8 Some sites with Mesolithic houses with sunken floors (triangles) and the northernmost inland finds of slotted bone tools (rings).

restricted to a more southerly border zone (Rajala and Westergren 1990) and transverse arrowheads are spread somewhat further north (Knutsson *et al.* 1999:Fig. 7).

When one considers the expressions of material culture from the south towards the north, one sees that it is arrowhead forms, with their significant variations, that have the narrowest distribution (Figure 7). Stone axes of various shapes have a more northerly spread. After this, microblades, or more correctly, small blades, appear to cover virtually the whole country, with examples from south to north. Most of them were struck from handle cores which appear around 8000 BP in the south. A slower northward spread has been suggested, with examples around 7000 BP in western Sweden (Kindgren 1996), while recent excavations in the same region suggest that they were introduced almost at the same time as in the very south (Kindgren and Schaller Åhrberg 1999:231) and in eastern central Sweden (Knutsson *et al.* 1999). In

the interior of Norrland, handle cores appear later, around 6700 BP (Forsberg 1996:249).

The microblades, not infrequently of exotic material, which occur at a considerable number of Mesolithic settlement sites outside the southernmost and westernmost cultural spheres are scarcely essential for catering to the basic metabolism. However, as an example of contact networks of considerable dignity, they functioned as important social markers.

It has been suggested that microblades were brought to the find spot attached to composite tools such as slotted bone points or bone daggers (Lindgren 1998). In this connection it is interesting to note that in the second most northerly inland find of slotted bone point, a bog find from the Falköping district, has revealed that most of the flints in the edges are not microblades but small flint flakes, some of them retouched (Larsson 1977) (Figure 8). This might indicate that the edges for bone tools of this kind could very well have been made from unretouched or retouched flakes in other kinds of stone. However, a circumstance that suggests an extensive distribution of slotted bone tools is the find at Offerdal in Jämtland of a richly decorated bone point or dagger with grooves which are unfortunately empty (Montelius 1917: Fig. 62) (Figure 8). As regards both decoration and form, it fits in well with the finds from south-westernmost Scandinavia (Larsson 2000).

In this division of forms of material expression, the flint syndrome may very well be significant. The majority of the material has been classified on the basis of the nature of the flint. This source critical aspect has been pointed out by several archaeologists, but there is still, to my knowledge, no one who has developed a categorisation of, say, quartz, which clarifies tools as social markers, until much later in the Stone Age (Knutsson 1998; Lindgren 1998).

Places of central character

When one considers the remains of Mesolithic settlement sites in a broader geographical perspective, several aspects become obvious. One is the amount of the material remains. Settlement sites from the coasts of southern Sweden, with tons of debitage, contrast with, for example, sites in the interior, with only a few kilos of debitage. Naturally, this can be explained in part by the denser settlement, with large habitation sites and activities carried on over a long period of time and by the fact that certain cultural phenomena use a wasting technology while other societies have a saving technology. I think, however, that these are only partial explanations. Something more fundamental may be contained in these anomalies. As the refuse from most Mesolithic sites in northern Sweden shows, not much raw material is needed to maintain the basic functions of a society.

On the other hand, blade production in the middle Mesolithic of southern Sweden may be perceived as having been on an extremely large scale. It is hard to escape the impression that blades were primarily made as internal and external markers to highlight the skill of the flint knappers. In other parts of the Mesolithic it may be a question of both flint and stone axes or specific artefacts of bone and antler. A great deal of labour was expended and a huge amounts of refuse arose in order to maintain and demonstrate various forms of symbolism and control of the societies.

This discussion brings us into the problem concerning places of a central character; for example, that large settlement sites can be related to ceremonial expressions such as assemblages of graves and special representations which we usually call art.

To use the terminology of nuclear physics, I get the impression that a "critical mass" must occur if a need to express signs of social integration is to arise. Unlike nuclear physics, however, it is not a question of the accumulation of one component, but rather a mixture of several different components. One of the ingredients is the geographical conditions. Another ingredient is population density, which should not be confused with population growth, although there is often a certain association. A third ingredient is the scope of contact with other social groups. Further ingredients are the shaping of traditions as regards the social structure and hence the structure of the conceptual world and the composition of the economic base. The mental capacity, charisma or cunning of particular individuals, to consolidate or suppress control over other people, should not be underestimated.

This does not mean that exactly the same mixture was necessary on every occasion for the "critical mass" to arise. We must reckon with different combinations and varying significance for the above variables. Some general ideas may have existed, but we should not therefore ignore the conditions and conceptions that were specific to each region.

I thus believe that the reason why places of a central character appear is that increased contact between people and groups have resulted in a need to express oneself through different forms of socially connected markers. The reason why these places of central character appear in bays and river deltas on the coast is that people in large groups could support themselves in these environments and which were also easy to reach by water transports. Another likely factor is that the coast was constantly subject to reshaping, which must have repeatedly tested people's creativity. In these coastal environments, change was a normal state, whereas changes in the inland were much slower.

That central places arise at different times in different parts of Sweden is due to several factors. Immigration to southern Sweden took place earlier than in northern Sweden, which means that the population was in fact larger in the former area during the Mesolithic. Another important factor is that the extent of land in the south shrank as the sea level rose, thus leading to denser settlement. In the north the sea level fell and the area of land expanded, giving more room for the increasing population. This is therefore an explanation why central places arise earlier in the south than in the north. The oldest central places are considered by some scholars to have come into existence in south-west Scandinavia in the middle Mesolithic around 7500 BP. Here, however, one must also consider that this point in time also coincides with a coastline corresponding to today's. We have only very limited information about what the now submerged coastal settlement was like. Based on the finds from the inland, I would date the earliest central places to around 8000 BP. In northern Sweden corresponding central places arose during a very late part of the

Mesolithic at about 5400 BP or early in the Neolithic (Halén 1994).

There are differing opinions about the function of central places, with some scholars believing that they are an expression of ordinary settlement (Price and Gebauer 1992; Larsson 1995), while others think that they had a special function and were only occupied on special occasions when acts of a ceremonial nature were performed (Knutsson 1995; Strassburg 2000). In my view, there are elements that support both of these opinions, but the most reasonable ones are those which integrate the central places with the settlement system.

Matters of interest concerning the relationship between south and north are found at central places in both areas. An example of possible north-south relations concerns special forms of house structures. The excavation of the Skateholm sites revealed oval, partially sunken pits with stains left by posts; on the basis of earlier finds, these were interpreted as house remains with sunken floors (Larsson 1975, 1985). The interpretation was vigorously questioned, but the house form has been confirmed by similar structures uncovered by excavations at the late Mesolithic find spot of Tågerup in western Scania (Karsten and Knarrström 1999), and in Jutland and Zealand (Sørensen 1995, Lass Jensen 1997). Houses of similar form are represented in the interior of northern Sweden (Loeffler and Westfal 1985; Lundberg 1997) and in eastern Norway (Boaz 1998:142 pp), where the oldest are dated to the late Mesolithic. Could the similarity in design also reflect a common cultural expression, despite a distance of roughly 550 km between southern Sweden and eastern Norway? As it happens, the spatial distance between eastern Norway and northern Scandinavia is roughly as large.

New investigations show that this considerable distance in western Scandinavia can be bridged by finds of small house foundations with sunken floors at Husaby Klev and Timmerås on the west coast of Sweden (Hernek and Johansson 1999; Hernek, this volume).

Perishable and Non-Parishable markers

Archaeology today provides good proof that we, as a product of the modern world, cannot act as independent observers of prehistory. Consciously or unconsciously our attitude affects the prehistory we want to describe or interpret. In order to discern a model for the value norms which existed in prehistory, we try to sort out reoccuring patterns which suggest some kind of structure. Not only those we can trace in the material culture but also those in connection with features and burials as well. To combine these indications in a contextual view of the prehistoric society, to observe the shadows of the world view which leavened the life of the people, is a most desirable but very difficult goal.

In current archaeological research there are attempts to find new ways to analyse and structure the results in order to discern which regulations and norms governed society and how these affected the position and action of individuals. Bridging the intellectual distance between explaining and understanding might be almost insurmountable. However, it is when we try to take that step that the prehistoric world reveals something other than artefacts, constructions and features.

While rock carvings and paintings have been regarded as constituting an important part of the mental world of the hunter-gatherer people of northern Scandinavia, expressions of art in southern Scandinavia have rarely been ascribed the same importance.

An interesting aspect is the role of decoration in understanding the reaction of a society to external ideas. Sites with rock carvings dating to the Mesolithic were perceived as significant in manifesting the cosmology of a world view where shamans act as a transmitter between worlds (Helskog 1999). The importance of the sacral location is marked with additional activities for centuries, in some cases for millennia (Hallström 1960; Helskog 1988; Forsberg 1993). The obvious designs in rock make it easy to fulfil traditional ritual behaviour but could be an important mental as well as physical obstacle to changes, especially if they had a major influence on social interaction, including the sacral sites with carvings – resistible mentally as well as physically.

In southern Scandinavia there are no obvious centres such as those in northern Sweden. When dealing with decoration on organic material, the problem of representation is of major importance and complicates the elucidation. Most decorated artefacts have been found either in the refuse layer of large settlement sites or as single finds in wetlands. A direct relationship exists between the distribution of decorated objects and areas with a concentration of settlements and thus most probably a dense population (Andersen 1998:Fig. 7; Nash 1998:Fig. 3.1).

The question is whether sacral sites, such as the concentration of rock carvings in northern Scandinavia, existed in the south. Most of the decoration was done on perishable material in southern Scandinavia. The decorated paddles from the Danish Ertebølle culture hint at a habit of decorating large wooden objects (Andersen 1987). Decorated panels and poles might have been erected in special places. It might seem like a far fetched idea, but large poles, at locations similar to the Early Neolithic decorated menhirs of continental Europe, do appear in the Mesolithic. A huge post hole was documented in connection with a cremation grave at Skateholm I, southernmost Sweden, and large post holes excavated close to Stonehenge have been dated to the Mesolithic (Larsson in print). In both cases the poles were erected on sacral sites. Sacral sites could also be marked in many different ways. The deposition of humans in graves, common in the large sites of southern Scandinavia, is one way. To assemble decorated objects that are linked to the spirits to selected areas such as the "refuse" of settlements,

Figure 9 *A forest at Örup, south-eastern Scania, affected by elm decease.*

or wetland deposits without connection to sites might be another.

In a society where sacral places are kept in active use, as in northern Scandinavia, the introduction of new ideas – just like new techniques which might have implications for the society – must have been much more difficult than in areas where the marking of sacral places was not as non-parishable as rock carvings. The sacral sites in southern Scandinavia, if they were ever marked by perishable materials and designs, would have been much more difficult to maintain, which made it easier to successively confront the traditions with new ideas – with major consequences for the world view of the people.

Signs of the gods

Elm disease plays an important part in the discussion of the introduction of agriculture. Today, the elm decline is interpreted as a result of elm disease. This phenomenon can be detected all over northern Europe (Friman 1997).

At the present time southern Sweden is suffering from elm disease, thus it is possible to follow its effects, which in some places are very obvious. Within a few years a forest afflicted by elm disease will be transformed into an area of dead tree trunks with rapidly flourishing bushes and other undergrowth (Figure 9).

The Mid-Holocene elm disease arrived at a turbulent period. Ideas from the south about cattle breeding and agriculture and especially aspects of a new world view which was linked to the new economy had been partially accepted or were at least known to most people. Old traditions were confronted with new behaviour.

The ravages of elm disease may have seemed like the interference of supernatural forces, probably as a sign from the gods that the people should intensify the change to a new social order. This might be the most important aspect of the elm disease for the spread of the Neolithic in large parts of northern and north-western Europe. Who could withstand the signs of the gods?

References

Alin, J. 1935. En bohusländsk kökkenmödding på Rotekärrslid, Dragsmark. *Göteborgs och Bohusläns Fornminnesförenings Tidskrift* 1935, 1–38.

Alin, J., Niklasson, N. and Thomasson, H. 1934. *Stenåldersboplatsen på Sandarna vid Göteborg*. Göteborg.

Althin, C.-A. 1954. *The Chronology of the Stone Age Settlement of Scania, Sweden. I. The Mesolithic Settlement*. Acta Archaeologica Lundensia series 4°. No. 1. Lund.

Andersen, S.H. 1987. Mesolithic Dug-outs and Paddles from Tybrind Vig, Denmark. *Acta Archaeologica* 57 (1986), 87–106.

——— 1998. En mønstret pragtøkse fra ældre Ertebøllekultur. *Kuml* 1997–98, 9–26.

Bang-Andersen, S. 1998. Why All These White and Shiny Stones? On the Occurrance of Non-flint. Lithic Material on Mesolithic Inland Siters in South-western Norway. In: Holm, L. and Knutsson, K. (eds.) *Proceedings from the third flint alternative conference at Uppsala, October 18–20 1996*. Occasional Papers in Archaeology 16, 39–54. Uppsala.

Baudou, E. 1992. *Norrlands forhistoria – ett historiskt perspektiv*. Viken.

Boaz, J. 1998. Pioneers in the Mesolithic: The Initial Occupation of the Interior of Eastern Norway. In: Boaz, J. (ed.) *The Mesolithic of Central Scandinavia*. Universitetets Oldsaksamlings Skrifter. Ny rekke nr. 22, 125–152. Oslo.

Bond, G., Shovers, W., Cheseby, M., Lotti, R., Almasi, P., deMenocal, P., Priore, P., Cullen, H., Hajdas, I. and Bonani, G. 1997. A Pervasive Millennial-Scale Cycle in North Atlantic Holocene and Glacial Climates. *Science* 278, 1257–1265.

Broadbent, N. 1979. *Coastal Resources and Settlement Stability. A Critical Study of a Mesolithic Site Complex in Northern Sweden*. Aun 3. Uppsala.

Broholm, H.C. 1924. Nye Fund fra den Ældste Stenalder. Holmegaard- og Sværdborgfundene. *Aarbøger for Nordisk Oldkyndighed og Historie* 1924, 1–144.

Forsberg, L. 1993. En kronologisk analys av ristningarna vid Nämforsen. In: Forsberg, L. and Larsson, T.B. (eds.) *Ekonomi och näringsformer i nordisk bronsålder*. Studia archaeologica universitatis umensis 3, 196–246. Umeå.

——— 1996. The Earliest Settlement of Northern Sweden – Problems and Perspectives. In: Larssson, L. (ed.) *The Earliest Settlement of Scandinavia and its Relationship with Neighbouring Areas*. Acta Archaeologica Lundensia series 8°. No. 24, 241–250. Lund.

Forsberg, L. and Knutsson, K. 1999. Converging conclusions from different archaeological perspectives: the early settlement of Northern Sweden. In: Thévnin, A. (ed.) *L'Europe des derniers chasseurs. Épipaléolithique et Mésolithique*, 313–319. Paris.

Friman, B. 1997. Neolithization and "Classical" Elm Decline: A Synthesis of Two Debates. *Lund Archaeological Review* 2 (1996), 5–16.

Halén, O. 1994. *Sedentariness during the Stone Age of Northern Sweden. In the Light of the Alträsket site, c. 5000 B.C., and the Comb Ware site Lillberget, c. 3900 B.C. Source Critical Problems of Representativity in Archaeology*. Acta Archaeologica Lundensia series 4°. No. 20. Lund.

Hallström, G. 1960. *Monumental Art of Northern Sweden from the Stone Age. Nämforsen and Other Localities*. Stockholm.

Helskog, K. 1988. *Helleristningene i Alta. Spor etter ritualer og dagligliv i Finnmarks forhistorie*. Alta.

—— 1999. The Shore Connection. Cognitive Landscape and Communication with Rock Carvings in Northernmost Europe. *Norwegian Archaeological Review* 32, No. 2, 73–94.

Hernek, R. 2002. A Mesolithic Winter-Site with a Sunken Dwelling from the Swedish West Coast. (in this volume).

Hernek, R. and Johansson, G. 1999. Mesolitiska hyddor i Bohuslän. In: Burenhult, G. (ed.) *Arkeologi i Norden* 1, 206–209. Stockholm.

Kaliff, A., Carlsson, T., Molin, F. and Sundberg, K. 1997. *Mörby. Östergötlands äldsta boplats. Arkeologisk slutundersökning RAÄ 168, Hogstads socken, Mjölby Kommun, Östergötland*. Riksantikvarieämbetet, Avdelningen för arkeologiska undersökningar, Rapport UV-Linköping 1997:38.

Karsten, P. 1986. Jägarstenåldern kring Yddingen. *Limhamniana* 1986, 65–89.

Karsten, P. and Knarrström, B. 1999. Tågerup. Tvåtusen år av mesolitisk bosättning i sydvästra Skåne. In: Burenhult, G. (ed.) *Arkeologi i Norden* 1, 202–205. Stockholm.

Kindgren, H. 1996. Reindeer or seals? Some Late Palaeolithic sites in central Bohuslän. In: Larsson, L. (ed.) *The Earliest Settlement of Scandinavia and its Relationship with Neighbouring Areas*. Acta Archaeologica Lundensia series 8°. No. 24, 191–205. Lund.

Kindgren, H. and Schaller Åhrberg, E. 1999. From Sandarna to Lihult: Fredsjö's Enerklev phase revisted. In: Boaz, J. (ed.) *The Mesolithic of Central Scandinavia*. Universitetets Oldsaksamlings Skrifter. Ny rekke nr. 22, 217–233. Oslo.

Kjellmark, K. 1903. En stenåldersboplats i Järavallen vid Limhamn. Antikvarisk tidskrift.

Knarrström, B. 2000a. Materialstudier av Skånes äldsta stenålder – om tiden efter Bromme och tidigmesolitisk expansion i norra Skåne. In: Ersgård, L. (ed.) *Människors platser – tretton arkeologiska studier från UV*. Riksantikvarieämbetet, Avdelningen för arkeologiska undersökningar skrifter No. 31, 149–166. Stockholm.

—— 2000b. Tidigmesolitisk bosättning i sydvästra Småland. En komparativ studie över stenteknologi och regionala bosättningsmönster med utgångspunkt i en boplats vid Hamneda. In: Lagerås, P. (ed.) *Arkeologi och paleoekologi i sydvästra Småland – Tio artiklar från Hamnedaprojektet*. Riksantikvarieämbetet, Avdelningen för arkeologiska undersökningar skrifter no. 34, 15–33. Lund.

Knutsson, H. 1995. *Slutvandrat? Aspekter på övergången från rörlig till bofast tillvaro*. Aun 20. Uppsala.

Knutsson, K. 1998. Convention and lithic analysis. In: Holm, L. and Knutsson, K. (eds.) *Proceedings from the third flint alternative conference at Uppsala, October 18–20 1996*. Occasional Papers in Archaeology 16, 71–93. Uppsala.

Knutsson, K., Lindgren, C., Hallgren, F. and Björck, N. 1999. The Mesolithic in Eastern Central Sweden. In: Boaz, J. (ed.) *The Mesolithic of Central Scandinavia*. Universitetets Oldsaksamlings Skrifter. Ny rekke nr. 22, 87–123. Oslo.

Larsson, L. 1975. A Contribution to the Knowledge of the Mesolithic Huts in Southern Scandinavia. *Meddelanden från Lunds universitets historiska museum* 1973–1974, 5–28.

—— 1977. Ett fynd av en flinteggad benspets från äldre stenålder. *Falbygden* 31, 33–37.

—— 1978. *Ageröd I:B – I:D. A Study of Early Atlantic Settlement in Scania*. Acta Archaeologica Lundensia series in 4°. No. 12

—— 1982. *Segebro. En tidigatlantisk boplats vid Sege ås mynning*. Malmöfynd 4. Malmö.

—— 1985. Of House and Hearth. The Excavation, Interpretation and Reconstruction of a Late Mesolithic House. In: Backe, M., Bergman-Hennix, I., Forsberg, L., Holm, L., Liedgren, L., Lindqvist, A-K., Mulk, I-M., Nejati, M., Perstrand, P. and Ramqvist, P.H. (eds.) *In Honorem Evert Baudou*. Archaeology and Environment 4, 197–209. Umeå.

—— 1995. Man and Sea in Southern Scandinavia during the Late Mesolithic. The role of cemeteries in the view of society. In: Fischer, A. (ed.) *Man and Sea in the Mesolithic. Coastal settlement above and below present sea level*. Proceedings of the International Symposium, Kalundborg, Denmark 1993. Oxbow Monograph 53, 95–104. Oxford.

—— 1999. Submarine settlement remains on the bottom of the Öresund Strait, Southern Scandinavia. In: Thevénin, A. (ed.) *L'Europe des derniers chasseurs. Épipaléolithique et Mésolithique*. Peuplement et paléoenvironnement de l'Épipaléolithique et du Mésolithique, 327–334. Paris.

—— 2000. Expression of art in the Mesolithic societies of Scandinavia. In: Butrimas, A. (ed.) *Prehistoric art in the Baltic region*. Acta Academiae Artium Vilnensis 20, 31–61. Vilnius.

—— in print. The Mesolithic period in southern Scandinavia: with special reference to burials and cemeteries. In: Ashmore, F. (ed.) *Mesolithic Scotland. The Early Holocene Prehistory of Scotland and its European Context*. Edinburgh..

Lass Jensen, O. 1997. Nivå 10. *Arkæologiske udgravninger i Danmark 1996*, 125. København.

Lindgren, C. 1998. Shapes of quartz, shapes of minds. In: Holm, L. and Knutsson, K. (eds.) *Proceedings from the third flint alternative conference at Uppsala, October 18–20 1996*. Occasional Papers in Archaeology 16, 95–103. Uppsala.

Loeffler, D. and Westfal, U. 1985. A Well-preserved Stone Age Dwelling Site. Preliminary Presentation of the Investigations at Vuollerim, Lappland, Sweden. In: Backe, M., Bergman-Hennix, I., Forsberg, L., Holm, L., Liedgren, L., Lindqvist, A-K., Mulk, I-M., Nejati, M., Perstrand, P. and Ramqvist, P.H. (eds.) *In Honorem Evert Baudou*. Archaeology and Environment 4, 425–434. Umeå.

Lundberg, Å. 1997. *Vinterbyar ett bandsamhälles territorier i Norrlands inland 4500–2500 f.Kr*. Studia Archaeologica Unversitatis Umensis 8. Umeå.

Montelius, O. 1917. *Minnen från vår forntid*. Stockholm.

Nash, G. 1998. *Exchange, Status and Mobility. Mesolithic portable art of southern Scandinavia*. BAR International Series 710. Oxford.

Price, T.D. and Gebauer, M.A. 1992. The Final Frontier: Foragers to Farmers in Southern Scandinavia. In: Price, T.D. and Gebauer, M.A. (eds.) *Transitions to Agriculture in Prehistory*, 97–116. Madison.

Rajala, E. and Westergren, E. 1990. Tingby – a Mesolithic Site with the Remains of a House, to the West of Kalmar, in the Province of Småland. *Papers of the Archaeological Institute University of Lund*, New Series 8 (1989–1990), 5–30.

Sarauw, G.F.L. and Alin, J. 1923. *Götaälvsområdets fornminnen*. Göteborgs Jubileumspublikationer III. Göteborg.

Sørensen, S. 1995. Lollikhuse – a Dwelling Site under a Kitchen Midden. *Journal of Danish Archaeology* 11 (1992–93), 19–29.

Strassburg, J. 2000. *Shamanic Shadows. One Hundred Generations of Undead Subversion in Southern Scandinavia, 7,000–4,000 BC*. Stockholm Studies in Archaeology 20. Stockholm.

Taffinder, J. 1998. The *Allure of the Exotic. The social use of non-local raw materials during the Stone Age in Sweden.* Aun 25. Uppsala.

Vang Petersen, P. 1984. Chronological and Regional Variation in the Late Mesolithic of Eastern Denmark. *Journal of Danish Archaeology* 3, 7–18.

Vedin, H. 1995. Lufttemperatur. In: Raab, B. and Vedin, H. (eds.) Klimat, sjöar och vattendrag. *Sveriges Nationalatlas*, 44–57. Höganäs.

Welinder, S. 1971. *Tidigpostglacialt mesoliticum i Skåne.* Acta Archaeologica Lundensia, series tertia in 8° minore 1. Lund.

—— 1973. *The Chronology of the Mesolithic Stone Age on the Swedish West Coast.* Studies in North European Archaeology 9. Göteborg.

—— 1977. *The Mesolithic Stone Age of Eastern Middle Sweden.* Antikvariskt arkiv 65. Stockholm.

Åkerlund, A. 1996. *Human Responces to Shore Displacement. Living by the Sea in Eastern Middle Sweden during the Stone Age.* Riksantikvarieämbetet. Arkeologiska undersökningar Skrifter no. 16. Stockholm.

Introduction

Peopling a Forgotten Landscape

Agneta Åkerlund, Per Gustafsson, Dag Hammar, Christina Lindgren, Eva Olsson and Roger Wikell

The forested highlands of Hanveden at Södertörn have been regarded as inaccessible wasteland; it is a landscape with few place-names and no memories. In the beginning of the 1990s, exploitation of the area was proposed. At that time, no remains of any cultural historical interest were known in the area. Since then, hundreds of previously unknown prehistoric sites have been found at altitudes from c. 85 to c. 25 m a.s.l. It has been assumed that these sites were located close to the shore and moved progressively downwards across the landscape as the land rose. Shoreline dating suggests that the sites located at altitudes above c. 75 m a.s.l. must be older than c. 9000 ^{14}C years BP. The pioneer phase seems to have been rapidly succeeded by more permanent settlements. Quartz is the dominate material throughout the Stone Age. It seems that green-stone, flint and quartzite were not used by the pioneers, but they do appear later. One general reason for taking an interest in the peopling of the landscape in this region is that it allows us to study a complete course of colonisation from the Weichselian ice-withdrawal onwards. Because of shore displacement, all of the prehistoric landscapes can be found above the present shoreline, which is not the case in the southern Baltic region.

Introduction

It was long thought that eastern middle Sweden was entirely unpopulated during the Mesolithic, but once the first discoveries were made they were soon followed by more. The title of this paper implies that it will focus on the first occupation of the land, but it also alludes to a research process. During the last decade, the archaeologists behind this paper have cultivated a particular interest in the Stone Age of this region and they will interpret the material remains according to all the different themes presented at the 6th conference on The Mesolithic in Europe. There might be different opinions within the group, but we do not consider that to be a problem. Rather, the situation whereby we critically scrutinise each other's ideas has regularly given rise to new insights.

History of Research on the Mesolithic of the Region

Early archaeologists were primarily interested in collecting stone axes, and at the turn of the last century scholars such as De Geer and Hollender studied the relationship between sea levels and these stray finds. Only limited excavations, usually consisting of test pits, were carried out in the early part of the 20th century, particularly on Neolithic sites with rich assemblages of pottery. Knapped quartz was occasionally found, but it was assessed with great uncertainty. When quartz was encountered at Neolithic pottery-bearing sites, it was interpreted as temper to be used in the production of pottery. No pre-pottery sites were excavated in the region until the Florin's began their geological and archaeological investigations at the Dammstugan site in the 1930's. When they excavated the site of Hagtorp in the late 1930's, quartz was retrieved more systematically, the whole assemblage being collected. At the beginning of the 1950's there was still only a handful of excavated Mesolithic sites in the area. However, in the last decades things have changed dramatically and 45 sites have now been excavated, the majority as a result of real estate development. Large-scale investigations have provided a rapidly growing database of artefacts. Some of the biggest excavations have been carried out at Eklundshov, Kyrktorp, Smällan, Jordbro industriområde and Jordbromalm (Drotz and Ekman 1999; Lindgren and Lindholm 1999; Gustafsson and Lindgren ms; Olsson *et al.* ms-a, ms-b).

Eastern middle Sweden is an example of a region where Stone Age research has been conducted intermittently. Apart from a golden age in the 1930's, when Sten Florin, Ivar Schnell and Axel Bagge made valuable contributions both in the field and by publishing the results of their excavations, Stone Age studies in this area were undertaken discontinuously and only by one person at a time. At the beginning of the 1970's Mesolithic research projects in the region were initiated by Stig Welinder (1973, 1977). Previously *known* sites were chosen for excavation. Rescue excavations were also undertaken at previously known sites.

M A.S.L.	SITE SIZE	RAW MATERIAL	REDUCTION METHOD (valid for quartz, dominating method in extra bold type)
85–80	"small"	quartz	**platform**
80–70	"small" – "medium"	quartz	platform and **bipolar**
70–40	"small" – "large"	quartz, greenstone, flint, sandstone	platform and **bipolar**
40–35	"small" – "medium"	quartz, greenstone, flint, sandstone, slate	**platform** and bipolar

Figure 1 Approximate sizes of sites, frequently occurring raw materials and stone technology at different altitudes 85–35 m a.s.l. in Södertörn. (According to Risberg et al. 1991 the shoreline at 85 m a.s.l. corresponds to a situation older than 9000 BP or 8000 cal. BC, and 35 m a.s.l. to c. 5500 BP or 4500 cal. BC). The observations refer to excavated as well as surveyed sites.

A common pool of knowledge about the Mesolithic of the region, knowledge which could influence the course of further excavations, did not begin to accumulate until the end of the 1970's when it became clear that Mesolithic sites in the region were repeatedly found in specific topographic situations. Some field surveys have been carried out by private individuals (e.g. Hammar and Wikell 1994, 1996; Åkerlund *et al.* 1995, 2002), and changes in heritage management laws have resulted in investigations being undertaken, conducted in phases: survey – test excavation – final excavation. As a consequence of these two factors a large number of previously *unknown* sites, as well as different assemblages from those previously discovered, have been identified in the region. Due to the fact that a whole group of archaeologists have cultivated a particular interest in the Mesolithic of the region, the number of excavations has increased considerably in the last few years (e.g. Lindgren 1997; Gustafsson 1998; Knutsson *et al.* 1999; Lindgren and Lindholm 1999; Åkerlund *et al.* ms).

General Description of Sites

In Södertörn (see Figures 3 and 4) the remains of prehistoric human activities have been found through field surveys as well as excavations. The Swedish register of ancient monuments provides an unusually clear picture of the stock of archaeological remains of any particular country, but the large-scale field surveys performed in connection with the compilation of economic maps since the 1940's gave low priority to the recording of Stone Age sites. Special surveys directed at Stone Age sites have been carried out privately. The archaeological record from the Mesolithic consists of open-air sites composed of scatters of stone debitage.

Mesolithic sites have been found at altitudes between *c.*85 and *c.*35 meters above the present sea level (m a.s.l.). The sites vary in size, from ten to many thousands square meters, and the terms "small" and "large" have been used to express a rough relation between them. The Early Mesolithic sites at the highest altitudes, above 80 m a.s.l., are all small and located in sheltered positions, but at around 70 m a.s.l. sites are larger with a more pronounced connection to broader, sandier locations. There are also some interesting lithic differences between altitudes, quartz is the sole material found at the highest altitudes while greenstone (dolerite, diabase) appears from *c.*70 m a.s.l. downwards. Flint and quartzite, which are not uncommon in Late Mesolithic contexts, are completely absent at the highest altitudes. So far, very little quartz has been collected above *c.*80 m a.s.l., and the material is dominated by the platform method of reduction. Finds are more numerous below 80 m a.s.l., where both the platform and bipolar methods occur, the bipolar method being strongly represented (Figure 1). The limited variation in site size, use of raw materials and technology indicates that the early sites represent the remains of short visits by small groups. From the Middle Mesolithic, as well as the Late Mesolithic, there are sites of varying size and content, which indicates differentiated activities of varying length.

The large sites of the region can be internally subdivided into several smaller concentrations. For some of them a chronological disparity has been established between the subareas, and hence they have been regarded as re-occupied. At other sites no chronological disparity has been established among the concentrations of finds, and they can be regarded as seasonally used by a large number of people or inhabited on a yearly basis by a few (cf. below). Few hut remains and no graves have been recorded from the Mesolithic. Organic materials are poorly preserved in sandy soils, because of this few details are known about the mode of subsistence.

There are very few finds of bone, they are usually burnt and highly fragmented. The sites investigated represent different geographical locations, viz. the outer archipelago, the inner archipelago and the interior, but the bones from the Mesolithic periods reflect an economy dominated by sealing and coastal fishing while the remains of large land mammals and birds are few.

The carbonised plant macrofossils that were recovered (hazelnut shells, juniper berries, rose hips and bearberries) could have all originated from the natural vegetation within the areas near the sites. In other words, there are no clear indications that organic materials from far away have been brought into the area.

Dates

The apparent lack of formal types made out of quartz from eastern middle Sweden has presented difficulties in constructing a useful typology, thus we have had to rely on shoreline dating and radiocarbon dates to elucidate the regional Mesolithic chronology. Until the 1970's no sites were known in eastern middle Sweden that were older than c.6500 BP (cal. 5500 BC). There are now about 150 radiocarbon dates from Mesolithic contexts, the oldest was obtained from the Eklundshov site which dated 8030±210 BP (Ua-340, cal. 7200 BC). In this paper we will express dates in radiocarbon years BP (not cal.) as well as in cal. BC in order to facilitate a comparison between geological and archaeological dates. The geological dates have not been calibrated because the reservoir ages for the sampled basins are unknown (cf. Risberg in this volume).

A comparison has been made of the dating and location of excavated Mesolithic sites at Södertörn, 20 of them being radiocarbon dated (Åkerlund et al. ms). A comparison between the altitude of these sites and the current shore displacement model for Södertörn (cf. Risberg in this volume) shows that all sites were shore-bound. If the assumption that the sites were shore-bound is correct then the sites found at higher altitudes must be older than those at lower ones. Thus sites located at altitudes above c.75 m a.s.l. in the Stockholm region should be older than c.9000 BP (cal. 8000 BC).

Interpretations

One general reason for taking an interest in the peopling of this landscape is the possibilities in this region to study a complete course of colonisation from the withdrawal of the Weichselian ice sheet onwards. Because of the shore displacement (cf. Risberg in this volume) all of the prehistoric landscapes can be found above the present shoreline, which is not the case in the southern Baltic region. Below we will make some interpretations of the current find pattern in connection with the various themes presented at this conference.

First colonisation

The highest post-glacial coastline in eastern middle Sweden is at c.160 m a.s.l. which means that the region was completely submerged after the retreat of the Weichselian ice sheet. Soon afterwards the first skerries emerged as a result of the rapid crustal rebound (Figure 2). Ever since, new virgin land has been formed and the process is still continuing today, as can be seen in the Stockholm archipelago. One result of this process is that the fossil Mesolithic archipelago with sites, can now be found on dry ground in remote forested areas (Figure 3).

Figure 2 The first humans entered a rocky archipelago. They must have reached the islands by canoe or by crossing the ice during winter. This view from the outer archipelago of today shows the appearance of the Mesolithic archipelago. Photo Roger Wikell.

These areas, dominated by till, bedrock and bogs, are unsuitable for cultivation, and have remain virtually intact. This means that these areas are almost ideal for studies concerning the changing Mesolithic cultural landscape from the first pioneers and onwards.

Most studies, so far, have been carried out in the Hanveden forest on the Södertörn peninsula, some 20 km south of Stockholm (see also below). This forest is a wasteland, which is surprising since the area is very close to the most densely populated parts of Sweden. Its restricted use is reflected on the maps, where there are very few place-names. In comparison, even the smallest rocky islet in the nearby archipelago of today has been named on maps. This land is frequently used by fishermen as well as holiday-makers.

The first peopling probably took place during the Baltic freshwater stage, the Ancylus lake, c.9000 BP (cal. 8000 BC), when the sea level was approximately 80–85 m a.s.l. The sites from this first phase are very limited both in size and amount of finds. The small sites, some tens of square meters in size, indicate that they were visited by small groups of people. They are located in sheltered areas in the landscape, often in small bays with connections to wider straits. So far only worked quartz has been found. Both the platform and the bipolar method of reduction occur, with platform strongly dominating (cf. Fig.1). Somewhat later, at c.70 m a.s.l., the lithic assemblage has changed. The bipolar method dominates and worked greenstone is present for the first time. The sites have increased both in number and size, and are often located towards the open sea. A possible interpretation of this change is that people had become permanently settled in the outer archipelago. Both small tools (quartz) and axes (greenstone) were manufactured locally, and the more exposed locations of the sites could indicate the use of some type of permanent dwelling structure.

In this early phase of occupation, the Södertörn peninsula consisted of an extreme outer archipelago some

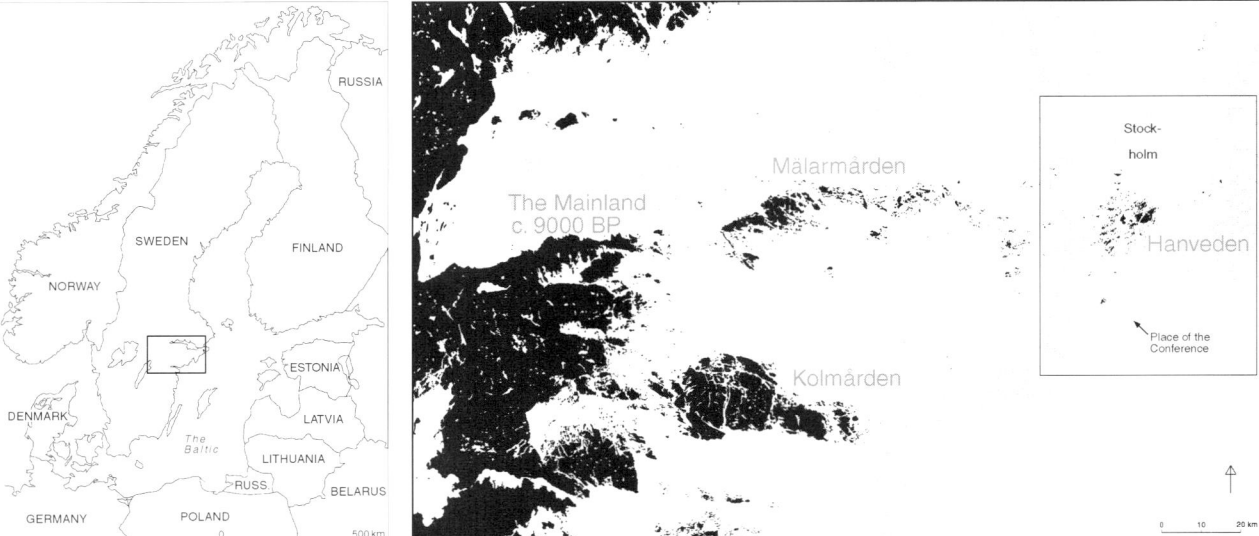

Figure 3 a. Map of northern Europe, where the area outlined is shown. b. Map of eastern middle Sweden, where land above 75 m a.s.l. is marked as well as the names of the forest highland areas mentioned in the text. The area outlined is shown in Figure 4. Based on Röda kartan, Lantmäteriverket. Drawing by Roger Wikell and Dag Hammar.

130 km from the mainland. Where did the first settlers come from? From the outermost islands, a narrow chain of skerries and islands stretches westwards to the mainland. This seems to be a probable route for the first inhabitants, where the islands served as stepping-stones. Some preliminary surveys along this chain of islands and on the neighbouring mainland have given promising results. In the Mälarmården forest, c.80 km west of Hanveden, sites have been found at altitudes up to 85 m a.s.l. One of the sites, found at the highest level, covers a large area and contains, apart from worked quartz, some greenstone. This picture contrasts with the outer archipelago and it could mean that a more permanent settlement, closer to the mainland, was established at an early phase. On the mainland, sites have been found up to c.90 m a.s.l. However, because of the differences in shore displacement they probably represent a later stage of occupation than sites at the same altitude further east. A larger archipelago was situated c.80 km SW of Hanveden, nowadays located in the higher parts of the Kolmården forest. Surveys carried out in this area have resulted in a number of new sites. The sites at the highest level, c.85–90 m a.s.l., are all very small, which is in accordance with the earliest sites at Hanveden (Åkerlund et al. 2002).

The preliminary dates suggest that the early sites at Hanveden, Mälarmården and Kolmården are contemporaneous with the Maglemose complex of southern Scandinavia, the Fosna/Hensbacka complex of western Norway and western Sweden, and the Kunda complex east of the Baltic, all of which are dominated by flint, and the Suomusjärvi complex in Finland, which is dominated by quartz. Accordingly, the peopling of eastern middle Sweden took place at a time when the regions to the east, south and west were already populated.

The Early Mesolithic sites hitherto found in eastern middle Sweden are completely dominated by worked quartz. This is in sharp contrast to the contemporaneous flint-dominated techno-complexes in southern and western Sweden. This means that there is an unknown transitional zone to be sought in the intervening areas towards the south and/or west, or that the first inhabitants came from elsewhere. The nearest parallel to the eastern middle Swedish quartz industry is found in Finland to the east of the Baltic. This long distance, across open water, seems rather hazardous to cross, but the voyage is not impossible.

The small sites dating to the pioneer phase can be regarded as the remains of short visits by small groups. A fact that contradicts the notion that these small sites represent a few lost souls who left an archaeological mark but failed to survive genetically, is the fact that these pioneer visits seem to have been succeeded by more permanent settlements, as indicated by the larger sites at lower altitudes. A model for settlement in the archipelago could proceed from the assumption that the islands were first used by people who made temporary visits to both the archipelago and some part of the nearby mainland, and later by islanders who settled there.

It can be assumed that the colonisers brought cultural traditions from outside, including choices of raw material with certain qualities, which may be regarded as normative for that society. Perhaps in this environment they did not have much of a choice, but if the colonisation was planned then people would possibly have tried to calculate the risks involved by first sending out some explorers. If the above mentioned finds are the remains of colonisers from the south, one would have expected some flint tools.

Not all individuals have the same opportunities for exploration. It has been suggested elsewhere that exploration in the context of calculated migration was carried out by adolescents, most probably males (Gamble 1995:110). The role of women in exploratory groups will have to be discussed some other time. Our reflections on the pioneer situation so far focus on what it means to be first and how to meet the risks associated with not having close neighbours to turn to if difficulties arise. In pioneer situations one is on one's own and must be able to estimate risks, make plans and work out risk reducing strategies.

Erret Callahan (1987:62 pp) has described the regional stone technology as simple and more flexible than that of southern Scandinavia. At the same time he questions whether simplicity must necessarily imply crudeness, and if it is right to interpret a simple system as less efficient. Like Callahan, one should have doubts about regarding these regional societies as being less complex than those of southern Sweden on account of their simpler technology. Should beautiful and carefully made objects necessarily be viewed as expressions of a more developed society with a greater complexity of ideas? We may well be taken in by our own ideas about what is complex and thus expressive of greater capabilities. Access to an easily available raw material that everyone can work with to satisfy their basic needs, permits great freedom.

Reflections on the choice of raw material and the changes in technology of the toolkit of explorers is well illustrated by the discussions of the remains characteristic of the Bromme complex from the late Palaeolithic of southern Scandinavia, that is, conditions preceding the ones discussed here. The blade technology of the Bromme complex has been regarded as simpler in terms of technical refinement than those of the preceding and following periods, and it has consequently been claimed that the pioneer societies of the deglaciated landscape of southern Scandinavia demonstrates a cultural degeneration as concerns stone technology. At the same time, the pioneer situation has been regarded as an advance in living conditions, as it provided more space, food and raw materials than in previous periods. In line with Anders Fischer's (1991) views, there was no incentive for the people to utilise a complex technology to conserve raw materials since life was easy.

We can consider the fact that a straightforward technology, with small flakes of simple form made from local raw materials, would allow real freedom to move around in the landscape, where raw materials of any size and quality might prove usable. This technology implies a contrast to that of corresponding groups with large, formal tools, who are restricted to fine raw materials. It would therefore seem logical for explorers of new environments to prefer a simple technology (Åkerlund 2002).

Enculturating the Landscape and Ritual and Symbolic Behaviour

Obvious traces of ritual activities such as graves or rock carvings/paintings have not been found from the Mesolithic of eastern middle Sweden. The remains are characterised by sites containing knapped quartz deposited in small concentrations, scattered depositions or as isolated finds. The analyses and interpretations of this regional archaeological record has often focused on the economical meaning of the remains. Utilisation of resources in the natural environment has also been of interest. In order to discuss ideology, ritual behaviour and enculturation of the landscape, we have to attach alternative meanings to the present record.

The topography of the study area in the Hanveden forest on the Södertörn peninsula is varied (Figure 4). It contains characteristically shaped topographical features made up of narrow fissure valleys flanked by ridges, outcrops of bedrock with both steep and gentle slopes and exposed quartz veins. Due to land upheaval, these features are preserved at high altitudes and have not, until recently, been disturbed by exploitation.

The excavation sites in the Gladö area could be divided into three main types:

1 Small concentrations of knapped quartz, deposited in an area measuring about 400 m^2. This type of site had clear spatial restrictions, a sandy slope surrounded on two or three sides by outcrops of bedrock and open or exposed towards the former shore (Figure 5).

2 Quartz debitage deposited in an area measuring more than 5000 m^2. This second type of site was unbounded in character and the spatial distribution of quartz did not always coincide with the best topographical localities. Quartz debitage was spread along the Mesolithic shore and in some cases (but not consistently) in larger or smaller concentrations. The site had no obvious outer limitations (in contrast to the situation on the small site).

3 The quartz quarry, in this case an exposed quartz vein, in an outcrop of bedrock surrounded by quartz debitage. The quartz vein was partially removed.

The spatial distribution of artefacts within the first and second types of sites shows both similarities and differences. The small and well-restricted sites contain distinct concentrations of quartz debitage, while the larger sites show both scattered remains and more closed concentrations of quartz (Gustafsson 1998). As a result of the perspectives prevailing at the time of excavation these differences were explained in economical terms. The small sites were interpreted as the remains of temporary camps or merely as isolated knapping floors, while the larger sites were seen as more intensively used for less specialised activities. One explanation for the relatively high frequencies of debitage that lacked the characteristics of ordinary knapping methods, noted at the larger sites, was the close position of these sites to the quartz veins. Since preservation conditions for features, bones and other ecofacts are unfavourable, the basis for

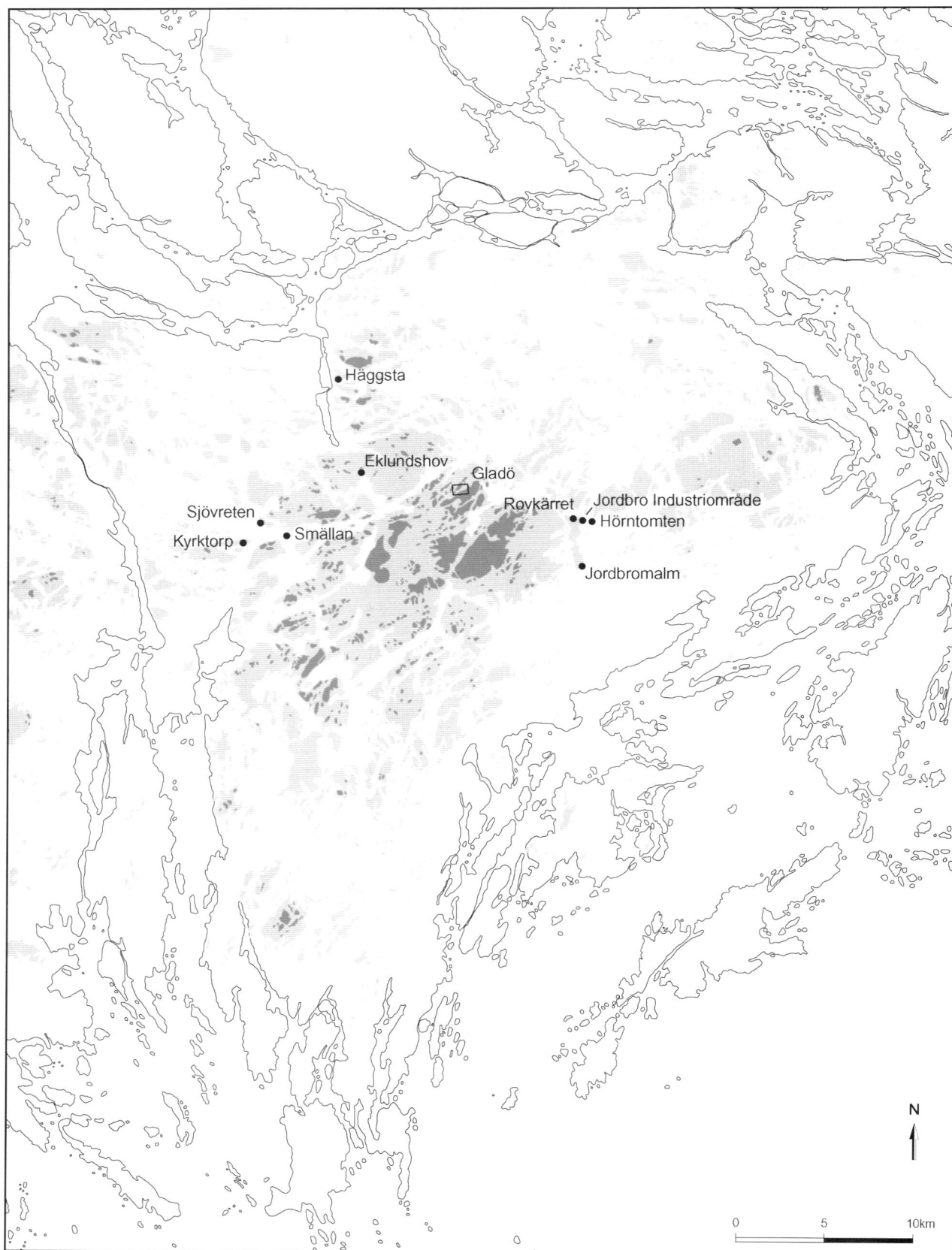

Figure 4 Map of the Södertörn peninsula with Mesolithic sites mentioned in the text. Land above 75 m a.s.l. is dark grey and land between 75 and 50 m a.s.l. light grey. These land areas correspond approximately to the Hanveden forest. Based on Röda kartan, Lantmäteriverket. Drawing by Dag Hammar.

Figure 5 A small site which will be excavated on a terrace in a sheltered position at Gladö in Hanveden south of Stockholm. See also site 305 in Figure 6. Photo Per Gustafsson.

further analyses of economical issues and resource utilisation is poor.

If we accept a pluralism of meaning in the archaeological record, then issues concerning ideology and ritual behaviour can be studied. Thus quartz depositions could be interpreted as culturally meaningful in a wider sense and not primarily as reflections of economical necessities. The primary intention of a human action may be to establish a camp or to prepare a tool. But the way an action is performed and the ideas underlying a choice of a specific place for a certain activity may be interpreted in terms of ideology or ritual behaviour.

It can also be assumed that natural features in the landscapes of Mesolithic hunter-gatherer's were classified according to mythical cosmologies and were given a symbolic meaning. If we manage to include the morphology of the natural environment in the analyses, it would provide us with a complement to the analysis of material culture. To enable this, the material culture has to be interpreted in terms of ideology. An interpretation that reaches beyond the economical and technological aspects requires a reclassification of the archaeological record. Since the remains seem to have an obvious connection with economical and technical functions, a new classification must aim at detecting underlying cognitive structures. One way of carrying this out may be the application of analytical principles inspired by structural-

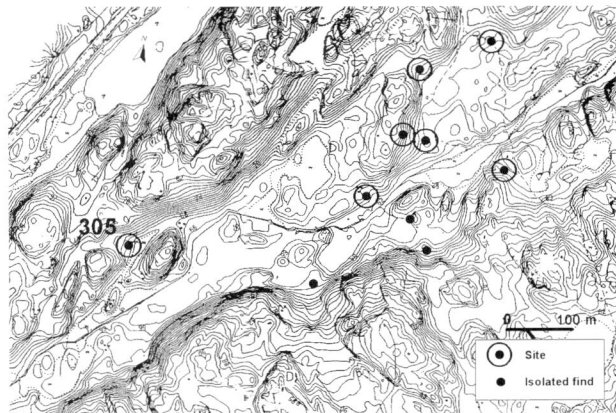

Figure 6 The well restricted site 305 at Gladö in Hanveden is separated from a cluster of open sites.

ism, preferably in the tradition of Claude Lévi-Strauss´. If the analyses comprise of binary oppositions, such as open-closed, concentrated-scattered, hidden-exposed, prepared-unprepared and light-dark, an alternative classification of the archaeological record can be made (Lévi-Strauss 1972). The structural principles characterising the intra-site conditions may be translated to features in the landscape. The set of binary oppositions relevant to the material culture should also be related to concepts that in our opinion seem to be general to the human world-view.

Examples of such concepts are nature-culture, female-male, sky-earth, land-water and life-death. If this re-classification turns out to be successful according to the archaeological record it may also have potential for application beyond the sites, such as the classification of features in the natural environment which are spatially related to the sites.

A point of departure taken from the archaeological record may be the comparison of various types of sites. Two site types, a smaller and a larger type, illustrate how the structuralistic approach may be attached to the archaeological record present in the Hanveden forest. The smaller site-type has a clear spatial restriction. It may be classified as restricted, closed or hidden. The larger site with its unlimited appearance may be termed unrestricted, open or exposed. The smaller site has an inside and an outside. The limitations of the inside are marked by culturally manufactured items, whereas natural features mark the boundary to the outside. The unlimited site has no inside/outside relations of the same kind, and there are less indications of a nature-culture contradiction. Material culture seems to flow without boundaries. The debitage left at the smaller site is well ordered. The cultural impact is more obvious at the smaller site, where most fragments can be determined to be the result of tool preparation. At the larger site there are relatively high frequencies of crushed pieces, which do not show the characteristic remains associated with tool production. This may also be viewed as a natural-cultural contradiction or as a dichotomy between the domesticated and the wild. A look at the site distribution pattern within the Gladö area at Hanveden reveals that the bounded sites are isolated from the rest of the sites in the area, while the open sites belong to a concentration of similar sites (Figure 6)(Gustafsson 1998).

Territoriality – Regionalisation

When and how did the people come to regard the archipelago as home? The question of territoriality and regionalisation depends on how we view the different topographic/geographic areas, in this case the archipelago in relation to the mainland of eastern middle Sweden. Eastern middle Sweden is a poorly defined region. One reason for this is the lack of research within the region as well as in the neighbouring areas (Åkerlund 2000:9, Fig.1). This makes it difficult to interpret signs of ethnicity based on observed variations in the material culture. There are, however, indications that can be used as a starting point when discussing the region of eastern middle Sweden and territoriality within that region.

During the Middle and Late Mesolithic the region was separated from the more well known areas in the southern and western parts of Scandinavia by the use of greenstone axe and bipolar knapped quartz. The greenstone axe is common on most Stone Age sites from this area, but it is not found on sites in southern Scandinavia. The shape of the axes also indicates affiliation with other areas such as

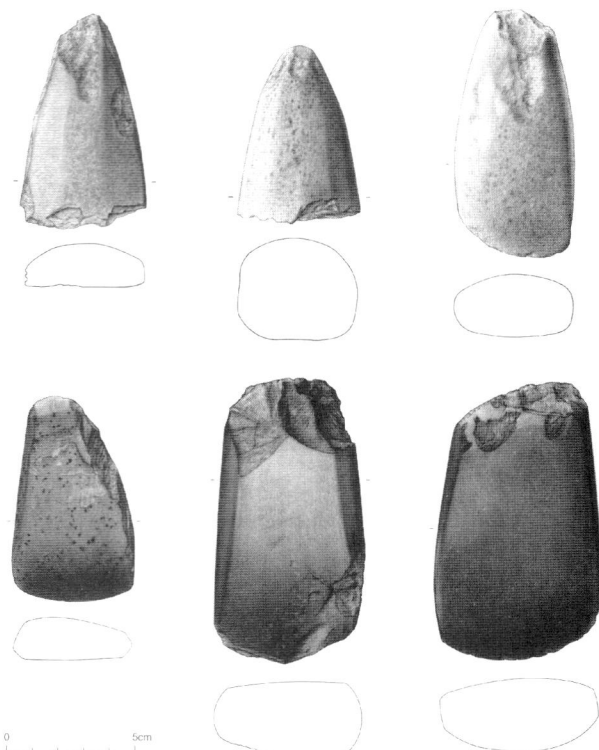

Figure 7 Examples of polished greenstone axes from eastern middle Sweden that are contemporaneous with the Lihult/Nöstvet phase. Drawing by Anders Eide.

the greenstone axes of the Lihult/Nöstvet complex (Figure 7) (Lindgren and Nordqvist 1997). The intensive use of the bipolar-on-anvil method of quartz reduction also serves as a marker of identification with other quartz using groups in the northern parts of Sweden, where this method is common during the later parts of the Stone Age (Forsberg 1989:59).

The physical landscape in eastern middle Sweden is characterised by the archipelago and the surrounding mainland. Although the landscape changes due to shore displacement, the archipelago – mainland relation continues during the Mesolithic. This seems to be reflected in the material remains. Differences in regional material patterns could be a manifestation of different social units, one of which is connected with the archipelago. So far, differences can be discerned concerning the type of economy, the choice of raw materials, external contacts and technology used during the Middle and Late Mesolithic (Åkerlund 1996, 2000; Lindgren 1997; Knutsson *et al.* 1999). On the mainland there are inland sites as well as coastal sites, where the economy was based on the hunting of both big and small game as well as marine resources. Several different local raw materials were utilised, flint was predominantly used for micro blade production. The inhabitants of the archipelago had an economy based on small game hunting and marine resources, and they occupied only coastal sites, with quartz as the dominant raw material and in which flint was not processed within the area, but only occurred in the form of ready-made objects. This unique combination of remains which tends to coincide with the archipelago and the mainland can be considered to have resulted from a social reproduction of traditions within and between equal social units. This means that we have changed our focus of the archipelago from viewing it as a resource area that complemented other areas situated on the mainland to an independent area with its own traditions. The archipelago is not only a resource area that was exploited and used during part of the year. Even though the Mesolithic people no doubt led an itinerant life compared to our own it is not obvious that their moving had to be based on efficiency concerning the exploitation of resources.

Within the archipelago the material remains show a remarkable variation in regard to site location, site size, economy, technology and raw materials. This variation supports an interpretation of the archipelago as being inhabited all year round. The variation among different sites also suggests that the sites were not used permanently. The people lived a life on the move but within the archipelago. This is, of course, something that changed over time. Initially the peopling of the archipelago was no doubt in the form of shorter visits. But for one or another reason those visits came to be longer and longer, and after some time the people started to think of the archipelago as home, rather than as islands in some far away place (cf. Engelstad 1990).

Spatial Organisation of Sites and Social Relations and Group Formation

One of the differences between the archipelago and the mainland is the large sites found on the former, that is, sites with artefacts covering an area of 5000 m^2 or more. The Middle and Late Mesolithic sites situated on Södertörn form a spatial pattern of large and small sites interpreted respectively as base camps or aggregation sites and sites for other activities (cf. Figure 1). These large sites are problematic as well as enigmatic. The problem is not only one of interpretation, but also concerns excavation. One result from the excavations is huge amounts of knapped quartz that has to be sorted and classified. In the days before computers, the registration of data was extremely time consuming. Instead the description of the site was based on observations in the field. Examples of large sites are the Eklundshov site excavated in 1986 and Jordbro Industriområde site excavated in 1993 (cf. Fig. 4, Lindgren 1997; Lindgren and Lindholm 1998; Gustafsson *et al.* ms;). Some of the earlier excavated sites have now also been reinterpreted as large sites, such as Hagtorp and Sjövreten (Florin 1959; Welinder 1977). These sites cover more than 5000 m^2 each. Examples of small sites, that is < 1000 m^2, are the Kyrktorp subarea 9B, Häggsta I, Hörntomten and Rovkärret (cf. Fig. 4, Olsson 1996; Drotz and Ekman 1998; Olsson *et al.* ms-a).

The interpretation of the large sites is an important part of understanding the Mesolithic society in the archipelago. Usually, sites of this kind are interpreted as either being the result of a large group living together for some time or the result of several visits from smaller groups. According to the first alternative, the sites have had a base camp function, while the second alternative correlates with aggregation sites (cf. Forsberg 1985:11; Åkerlund 1996:11). So far there is no conclusive evidence that supports the idea that these large sites are the result of intensive utilisation of specific resources.

Traces of a variety of activities, such as the making of axes, quartz knapping, hunting, fishing, possible storage and evidence of contacts with distant regions, are things that fall well into place with the interpretation of these large sites having been used as base camps. Even though the base camp model seems plausible, there are some discrepancies: the large sites contained hearths although not in large numbers, which makes it questionable whether these sites should be interpreted as base camps. The lack of hut remains at all sites also puts the base camp interpretation into question.

There are also differences among the sites. For example, the making of greenstone axes does not occur on all of the large sites, but only on some, and one may well ask why? Furthermore, the Eklundshov and Jordbro Industriområde sites also show interesting differences in the spatial distribution of knapped quartz. While the quartz at Eklundshov is distributed in several smaller agglomerations, the knapped quartz at Jordbro Industriområde shows a more distinct centre-periphery distribution (Lindgren 1997; Gustafsson *et al.* ms).

It seems as if the quartz is the key to understanding these large sites. The distribution of quartz is what makes these sites large, and it is also used in creating different rooms at the sites. The knapped quartz is not only the result of specific activities such as tool making, tool using and waste handling. It is also part of creating meaningful places on an intra-site level (Figure 8).

These large sites play an important part in the process of understanding social organisation. It is easy to accept a dichotomy between large and small sites. But the variation among the large sites complicates the picture. If the sites are examples of the gathering of large groups, then the social group formation/consolidation took different forms at different large sites. To achieve social stability, a variation among the large gathering sites might have been needed. Future research including GIS analyses may provide opportunity for new interpretations concerning the utilisation of the large sites. The quartz assemblages have the potential to yield more information about the large sites. A spatial analyses that takes the hitherto noted classes into consideration ought to be carried out on a broader level, something that has so far not been undertaken.

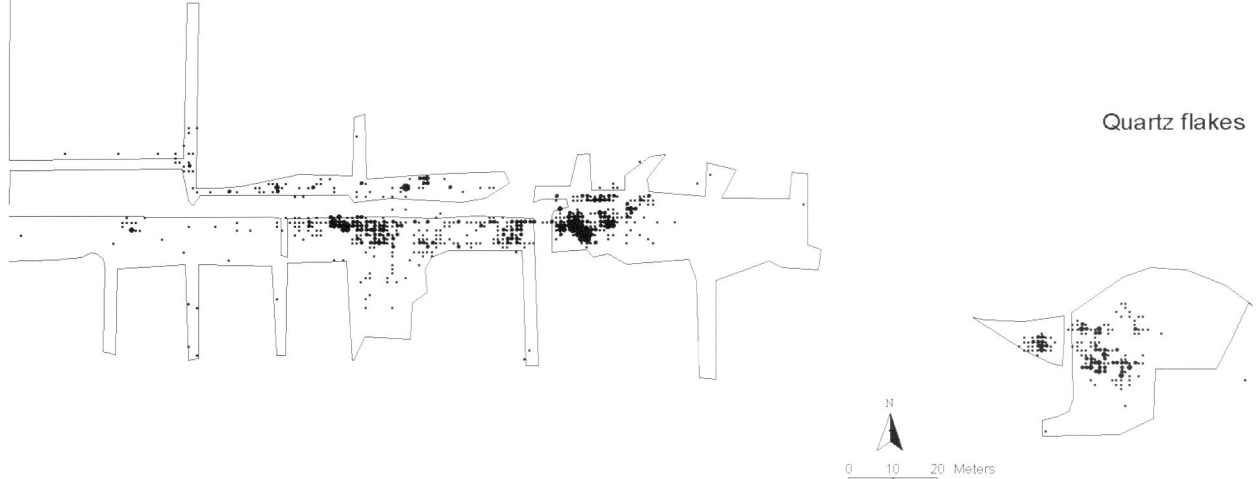

Figure 8 The spatial distribution of quartz flakes at the Eklundshov site creates different rooms within the site.

Exchange and Communication and Fisher-Hunter-Gatherers in Transition

In the archipelago direct signs of exchange and communication with people in other areas, for instance the mainland of eastern middle Sweden, are the artefacts made of raw materials that are not available locally. Indirect contact and indications of territoriality are implied in the shapes of axes, as discussed above. Finds of flint artefacts point to contacts with Scania or Västergötland, the latter of which is at least 250 kilometers away. Slate, on the other hand, was available on the mainland at a distance of 150–200 km (cf. Taffinder 1998:117) and so-called Gävle-sandstone at a distance of c.180 km. The earliest finds of these raw materials date to around 7500–6000 cal. BC, and they are thereafter found throughout the Mesolithic, although in different quantities (cf. Figure 1). The different sources of raw materials thus points to varying and possibly long-distance exchange.

The flint finds mainly consist of micro blades, which appear from around 7500 cal. BC to c.4500 cal. BC. Micro blades have been recovered from only a few sites and at these sites they are found in concentrations. This factor, as well as the lack of any traces of local production, indicate that they were brought to the archipelago as ready-made artefacts (Lindgren 1997:26; cf. Knutsson et al. 1999:Fig. 8; Åkerlund 2000:Fig. 6). The micro blades are mainly found on large sites, possible aggregation sites (see above), and might indicate a special distribution system between groups. The occasional finds of slate, which are mostly projectile points, which have been found on sites of different sizes, might indicate the existence of a parallel although different type of exchange system. This implies that, although contact with both the south and the north/west is manifested by the presence of projectiles, the artefacts were imbued with different meanings.

Traces of exchange and communication with other regions increases dramatically at the beginning of the Neolithic, with finds of polished flint axes, saddle-shaped grinding stones, Funnel Beaker pottery, long-houses and indications of farming (Hallgren et al. 1997; Kihlstedt 1997). Recent dates show that the introduction of the Neolithic c. 3900 cal. BC occurred quickly, spreading from southern Scandinavia to the whole of eastern middle Sweden. The dates show that Neolithic assemblages overlap those with Mesolithic finds. So far the Neolithic evidence differs between the archipelago and the mainland, as long-houses and traces of agriculture have only been recovered on the mainland. However, sites in the archipelago have traces of husbandry as well as hut-remains (Biwall and Kihlstedt 1997; cf. Åkerlund 2000: Fig. 8).

Earlier views interpreted the apparently simultaneous appearance of the Funnel Beaker Culture as an immigration from southern Scandinavia (Hulthén and Welinder 1981). At that time there was a clear lack of excavated sites dating from the last part of the Mesolithic (Hulthén and Welinder 1981:151, 173). During the last decade at least ten Late Mesolithic sites have been excavated in the archipelago, while excavated sites on the mainland remain relatively scarce.

The Late Mesolithic sites in the archipelago are found close to the Litorina shore, as were earlier sites, and show reliance on marine hunting and fishing. There are extremely few inland sites. Many Early Neolithic sites have been found on the exact same coastal locations, where they contain similar types of faunal remains, but at this time there were also inland sites with a different economy. During both periods there were sites of varying sizes. The settlement pattern for the Late Mesolithic is hard to ascertain, while the Early Neolithic sites, as well as later sites, appear in clusters.

A comparison between Late Mesolithic sites and Early Neolithic ones shows both similarities and dissimilarities, indicating not a quick and abrupt change but a slow and continuous process.

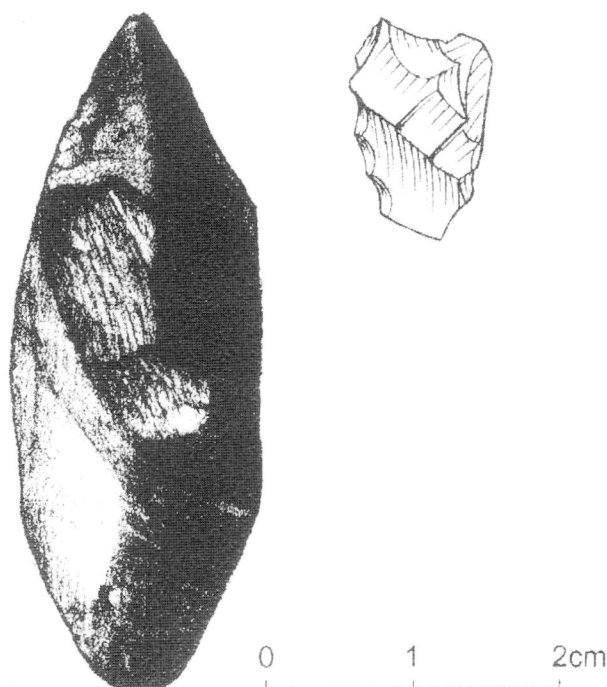

Figure 9 Contacts with different regions are exemplified in different types of projectile points, from the Late Mesolithic-Early Neolithic a transverse arrowhead of flint and a slate point. Drawing by Anders Eide.

There is continuity, but also change, in the lithic industry. The pecked axes of local greenstone with polished edges and a rounded cross-section still exist, but new shapes are also produced from around 5500 cal. BC. These axes are completely polished, with more angular cross-sections. The sites are dominated by knapped quartz (cf. Åkerlund 1996:Fig. 2:6). The amount of quartz at the Late Mesolithic sites does not differ from earlier sites, but it does differ significantly from the later ones, as the amount of quartz drops dramatically on Neolithic sites. During the latest part of the Mesolithic, from around 4500 BC, however, remains of the bipolar-on-anvil method decreases while traces of the freehand platform method show higher frequencies (Lindgren 1996:33, 1997:30). Thus, the lithic production in everyday use shows changes at different points of time. There are changes not only in how the quartz was worked but also where it was worked – at the quarries or on the pebble beaches?

During the same time, that is during the last part of the Mesolithic, the micro blades of flint are not found. Occasional finds of transverse arrowheads of flint and quartz start to occur, a find category that is common on Early Neolithic sites (Figure 9). From this period there is also an occasional find of a saddle-shaped grinding stone, in this case combined with a polishing stone (Hallgren et al. 1995), as well as a site with a large amount of slate artefacts, including northern forms (Blomqvist and Åhman 1999). During this time, however, there are no finds of pottery, long-houses, nor indications of farming, as they seem to come into use slightly later.

The examples of exchange from the earlier part of the Mesolithic may be regarded as different systems of exchange and value operating in the community at the same time. The contacts with southern Scandinavia during the Late Mesolithic might indicate a network based on a kinship (see Hallgren in this volume), while the more rare, and possibly therefore more exotic finds of northern/western slate could indicate ties on a non-egalitarian level. Thus, it would not seem odd if values changed at different times, presenting us with a heterogeneous picture of slow and continuous change within the local community.

Concluding Remarks

The forested highlands of eastern middle Sweden have long been regarded as an inaccessible wasteland; it is a landscape with few place-names and no memories. When the exploitation of the Hanveden forest south of Stockholm was proposed in the beginning of the 1990's, hardly any remains of any cultural-historical interest were known. Since then hundreds of Mesolithic sites have been found. The anonymity of prehistoric sites means that they are easily overlooked and thus face destruction. Knowledge of the Mesolithic in the region is increasing, and the authors maintain that this can be ascribed to the emergence of a research-conscious environment of a certain size, the results of which have inspired new perspectives on the Mesolithic landscape. We would like to conclude that archaeologists working with excavation missions must be given the opportunity to continuously formulate interpretations of their finds, since it is this knowledge, their questions and choices which determine the information that will be selected in future investigations.

References

Biwall, A. and Kihlstedt, B. 1997. Stenålderns hyddor och hus i Östra Mellansverige. In: Larsson, M. and Olsson, E. (eds) *Regionalt och interregionalt. Stenåldersundersökningar i Syd- och Mellansverige*. Riksantikvarieämbetet Arkeologiska undersökningar Skrifter nr 23, 282–293. Stockholm.

Blomqvist, M. and Åhman, S. 1999. *Skifferspetsar och kvartsavslag – senmesolitikum på östra Södertörn*. Arkeologisk förundersökning och delundersökning av Jordbroboplatsen, Raä 182a, Österhaninge sn, Södermanland. Riksantikvarieämbetet UV Mitt Rapport 1998:95. Stockholm.

Callahan, E. 1987. *An evaluation of the lithic technology in Middle Sweden during the Mesolithic and Neolithic*. Archaeological Studies, Uppsala University, North European Archaeology (Aun) 8.

Drotz, M. and Ekman, T. 1998. *Två senmesolitiska kustboplatser – Rovkärret och Hörntomten*. Arkeologiska förundersökningar och undersökningar av Raä 238 och 239, Österhaninge sn, Södermanland. Riksantikvarieämbetet UV Mitt Rapport 1998:35. Stockholm.

—— 1999. *Jordbromalm. Säl- och vildsvinsjägare i Haninge under senmesolitikum*. Arkeologisk förundersökning och undersökning av Raä 230, Österhaninge sn, Södermanland. Riksantikvarieämbetet UV Mitt Rapport 1998:48. Stockholm.

Engelstad, E. 1990. The meaning of sedentism and mobility in an archaeological and historic context. *Acta Borealia* 7/2, 21–35.

Fischer, A. 1991. Pioneers in deglaciated landscapes: the expansion and adaptation of Late Palaeolithic societies in southern Scandinavia. In: Barton, N., Roberts, A.J. and Roe, D.A. (eds) *The Late Glacial in North-West Europe: Human adaptation and environmental change at the end of the Pleistocene*, 100–121. Council for British Archaeology Research Report 77. Oxford.

Florin, S. 1959. En kvartsförande prekeramisk fångstboplats från Litorinatid. *Tor* V, 7–51.

Forsberg, L. 1985. *Site variability and settlement patterns.* Archaeology and environment 5. Umeå.

—— 1989. Economic and social change in the interior of northern Sweden 6000 bc – 1000 ad. In: Larsson, T. and Lundmark, H. (eds) *Approaches to Swedish prehistory.* BAR International Series Nr 500, 55–82. Oxford.

Gamble, C. 1995. *Timewalkers. The prehistory of global colonisation.* London.

Gustafsson, P. 1998. The earliest Stone Age occupation of Eastern Middle Sweden. *Current Swedish Archaeology* 6, 47–62.

Gustafsson, P., Lindgren, C. and Risberg, J. manuscript. The Eklundshov site. In: Åkerlund, A., Olsson, E., Miller, U. and Gustafsson, P. (eds) *Södertörn. Interdisciplinary investigations of Stone Age sites in Eastern Middle Sweden.* Riksantikvarieämbetet Arkeologiska Undersökningar Skrifter.

Hallgren, F., Bergström, Å. and Larsson, Å. 1995. *Pärlängsberget, en kustboplats från övergången mellan senmesolitikum och tidigneolitikum.* Arkeologisk undersökning av Raä 143, Överjärna sn, Södermanland. Tryckta rapporter från Arkeologikonsult AB 13. Upplands Väsby.

Hallgren, F., Djerw, U., af Geijerstam, M. and Steineke, M. 1997. Skogsmossen, an Early Neolithic settlement site and sacrificial fen in the northern borderland of the Funnel-beaker Culture. *Tor* 29, 49–111.

Hammar, D. and Wikell, R. 1994. Nyupptäckta stenåldersboplatser på Södertörn. *Arkeologi i Sverige* 3, 217–223. Riksantikvarieämbetet. Stockholm.

—— 1996. 250 nyupptäckta stenålderslokaler på Södertörn. In: Bratt, P. (ed.) *Stenålder i Stockholms län*, 15–21. Stockholms länsmuseum.

Hulthén, B. and Welinder, S. 1981. *A Stone Age economy.* Theses and papers in North-European Archaeology 11.

Kihlstedt, B. 1997. Neolitiseringen i Östra Mellansverige. In: Larsson, M. and Olsson, E. (eds) *Regionalt och interregionalt. Stenåldersundersökningar i Syd- och Mellansverige.* Riksantikvarieämbetet Arkeologiska undersökningar Skrifter nr 23, 110–127. Stockholm.

Knutsson, K., Lindgren, C., Hallgren, F. and Björck, N. 1999. The Mesolithic in Eastern Central Sweden. In: Boaz, J. (ed.) *The Mesolithic of Central Scandinavia.* Universitetets Oldsaksamlings Skrifter Ny rekke Nr 22, 87–123. Oslo.

Lévi-Strauss, C. 1972. *The Savage Mind. The Nature of Human Society.* London.

Lindgren, C. 1996. Kvarts som källmaterial: Exempel från den mesolitiska boplatsen Hagtorp. *Tor* 28, 29–52.

—— 1997. Mesolitikum i Östra Mellansverige – en presentation av undersökningar under åren 1986–1993. In: Larsson, M. and Olsson, E. (eds) *Regionalt och interregionalt. Stenåldersundersökningar i Syd- och Mellansverige.* Stockholm: Riksantikvarieämbetet Arkeologiska undersökningar Skrifter nr 23, 21–32. Stockholm.

Lindgren, C. and Lindholm, P. 1999. *En mesolitisk boplats vid Jordbro industriområde.* Riksantikvarieämbetet UV Mitt Rapport 1998:73. Stockholm.

Lindgren, C. and Nordqvist, B. 1997. Lihultyxor och Trindyxor. Om yxor av basiska bergarter i östra och västra Sverige under mesolitikum. In: Larsson, M. and Olsson, E. (eds) *Regionalt och interregionalt. Stenåldersundersökningar i Syd- och Mellansverige.* Riksantikvarieämbetet Arkeologiska undersökningar Skrifter nr 23, 57–72. Stockholm.

Olsson, E. 1996. *Stenåldersboplats vid Häggsta.* Riksantikvarieämbetet UV Mitt Rapport i ATA dnr 2987/84. Stockholm.

Olsson, E., Gustafsson, P., Karlsson, S., Kihlstedt, B., Lindgren, C., Miller, U., Risberg, J., Vinberg, A. and Åkerlund, A. manuscript-a. The Kyrktorp site. In: Åkerlund, A., Olsson, E., Miller, U. and Gustafsson, P. (eds) *Södertörn. Interdisciplinary investigations of Stone Age sites in Eastern Middle Sweden.* Riksantikvarieämbetet Arkeologiska Undersökningar Skrifter.

Olsson, E., Gustafsson, P., Lindgren, C., Miller, U. and Risberg, J. manuscript-b. The Smällan site. In: Åkerlund, A., Olsson, E., Miller, U. and Gustafsson, P. (eds) *Södertörn. Interdisciplinary investigations of Stone Age sites in Eastern Middle Sweden.* Riksantikvarieämbetet Arkeologiska Undersökningar Skrifter.

Risberg, J. 2002. Landscape History of the Södertörn peninsula, eastern Sweden. (in this volume).

Taffinder, J. 1998. *The allure of the Exotic. The social use of non-local raw materials during the Stone Age in Sweden.* Archaeological Studies, Uppsala University, North European Archaeology (Aun) 25.

Welinder, S. 1973. *The pre-pottery Stone Age of Eastern Middle Sweden.* Antikvariskt arkiv 48. Stockholm.

—— 1977. *The Mesolithic Stone Age of Eastern Middle Sweden.* Antikvariskt arkiv 65. Stockholm.

Åkerlund, A. 1996. *Human responses to shore displacement. Living by the sea in Eastern Middle Sweden during the Stone Age.* Riksantikvarieämbetet Arkeologiska Undersökningar Skrifter nr 16.

—— 2000. Separate Worlds? Interpretation of different material patterns in the archipelago and the surrounding mainland areas of east-central Sweden in the Stone Age. *European Journal of Archaeology* 3/1, 7–29.

—— 2002. Life without close neighbours. Some reflections on the first peopling of east central Sweden. In: Bratlund, B. and Eriksen, B.V. (eds) *Recent Studies in the Final Palaeolithic of the European Plain*, 43–47. Proceedings of the UISPP symposium in Stockholm October 1999.

Åkerlund, A., Hammar, D. and Wikell, R. 1995. Pioneers in the archipelago of Eastern Middle Sweden 9000 BP. In: Robertsson, A.-M., Hackens, T., Hicks, S., Risberg, J. and Åkerlund, A. (eds) *Landscapes and Life. Studies in honour of Urve Miller*, 109–120. PACT 50. Rixensart.

Åkerlund, A., Risberg, J., Hammar, D., Wikell, R., Luthander, A., Pettersson, M., Andersson, H. and Asplund, M. 2002. *Människan i det tidiga landskapet. Rapport från inventeringar i höglänta skogsområden i nordvästra Södermanland, sydöstra Närke och nordöstra Östergötland.* Stockholm Archaeological Reports. Field Studies 8.

Åkerlund, A., Olsson, E., Miller, U. and Gustafsson, P. (eds) manuscript. *Södertörn. Interdisciplinary investigations of Stone Age sites in Eastern Middle Sweden.* Riksantikvarieämbetet Arkeologiska Undersökningar Skrifter.

Landscape history of the Södertörn peninsula, eastern Sweden

Jan Risberg

The first land to rise out of water was the peak of Tornberget, now situated 112 m above the present day sea level. This event occurred when the Weichselian ice front was located approximately at what is today the center of Stockholm, c. 10,000 ^{14}C years BP. The water that surrounded this isolated island was fresh. At about the same time, the Baltic Ice Lake was drained at Billing Mountain and the water level dropped 26 m. Weak traces of the brackish water phase of the Yoldia Sea has been noted at 87 m a.s.l. During the first 1000 years after deglaciation land uplift was intense, resulting in the formation of large land masses. There are perhaps traces of a short transgression in the Ancylus Lake phase. It is not until the ingression of saline water through the Öresund and Store Belt straits 8500 ^{14}C years BP that the speed of the regressive shore displacement slowed down. This is recorded as a c. 1000 year long standstill, or even as a transgression. Since then the isostatic component has out-competed the eustatic one, but the land uplift was now slower. It is only during shorter periods that sea water re-covered land areas, as the result of either small scale neo-tectonic movements or higher eustatic rises of the ocean level. As the land areas grew and the climate improved, plants colonised these new areas. The first trees to immigrate were hazel and alder (c. 9500 and 9000 ^{14}C years BP, respectively). In the beginning of the warm Atlantic period, linden followed c. 7500 ^{14}C years BP. The elm decline is clearly detected at c. 4500 ^{14}C years BP. The latest tree to immigrate was spruce at about 2500 ^{14}C years BP.

Introduction

The following text deals with the late glacial and Holocene environmental changes as recorded from the Södertörn peninsula, south of Stockholm, as presented during the international conference MESO 2000 (Figure 1). When stated, calibrated ages follow Stuiver et al. (1998).

Bedrock

The bedrock of the Södertörn peninsula is formed from the roots of the Svecofennian mountain range, which was created around 2000–1800 million years ago (Möller and Stålhös 1969). Tectonically, the bedrock is made up from different antiforms and synforms, resulting in a pronounced fissure valley landscape (Stålhös 1976). Several of the faults and fractures have been considered to be of both glacial and Post-glacial age (Mörner et al. 1989), i.e. neo-tectonic movements are likely to have occurred.

Shore displacement

During the latest glaciation, the Weichselian, the bedrock was deeply pressed down. A subsequent re-appraisal puts the highest coast line at about 150 m above the present day sea level (Persson and Svantesson 1972). This means that the whole Södertörn peninsula was covered by water at the time of deglaciation. The first land to protrude above the water was the peak of Tornberget now situated at

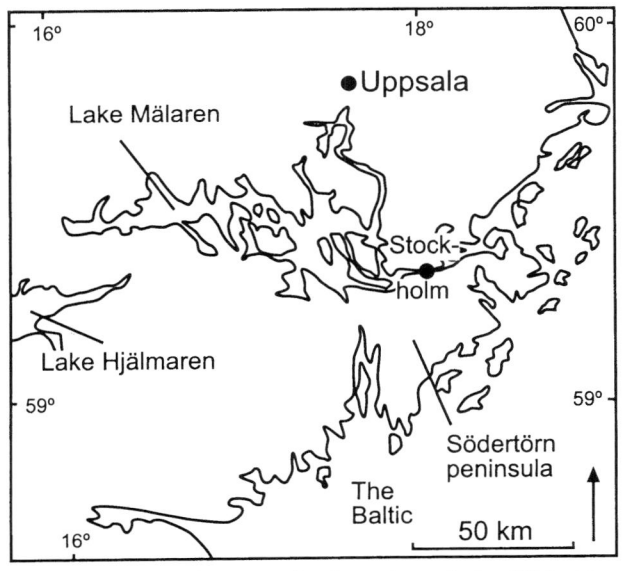

Figure 1 Map showing the location of the Södertörn peninsula, south of Stockholm.

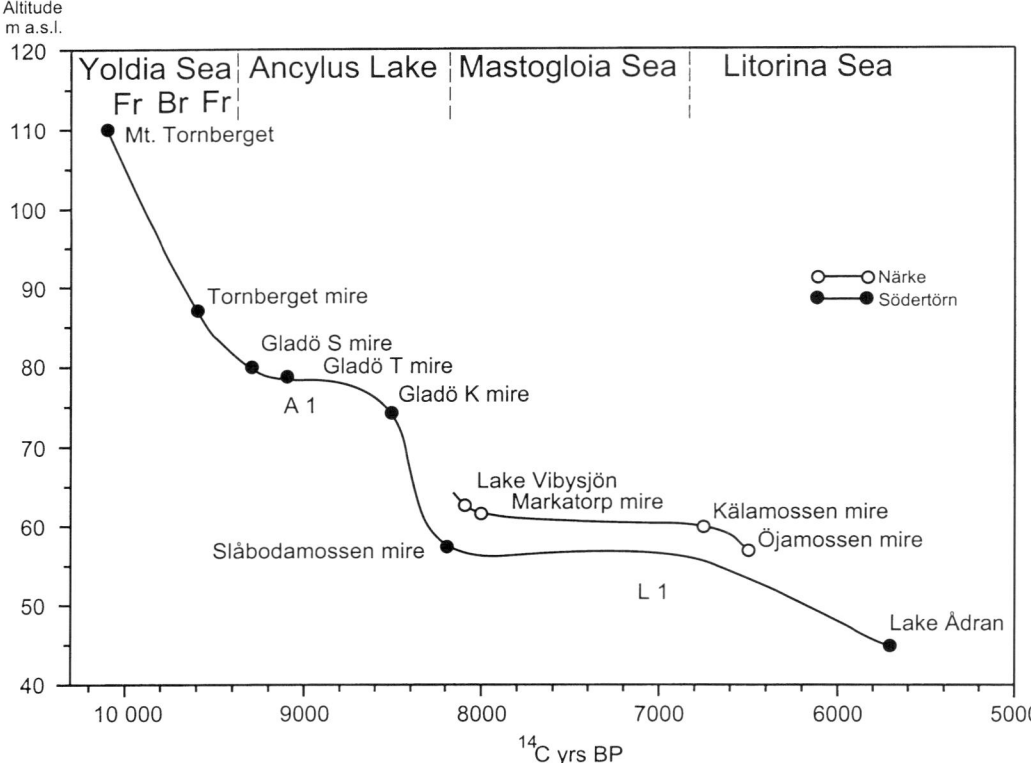

Figure 2. Shore displacement curve for the central part of the Södertörn peninsula and the province of Närke, west of Lake Mälaren (from Hedenström and Risberg 1999, fig. 11). A 1 represents a slight increase in water depth during the Ancylus Lake stage. L 1 represents the first rise in sea level during the Litorina Sea. Fr = fresh water stage of the Yoldia Sea. Br = brackish/marine stage of the Yoldia Sea.

112 m above the present day sea level (Figure 2). This event occurred when the Weichselian ice front was located approximately at what is today the center of Stockholm c. 9900 ^{14}C years BP (10,400 clay varve years BP or 11,300 cal. years BP; Sandgren *et al.* 1988; Strömberg 1989; Brunnberg 1995; Björck 1999). The water that surrounded this isolated island was fresh, originating from the receding glacier as melt water. This stage of the Baltic is referred to as the Baltic Ice Lake (cf. Donner and Raukas 1989). The rapid emergence of Mt. Tornberget was caused by the drainage of the Baltic Ice Lake c. 200 years earlier, c.11,500 cal. BP, at Mt Billingen, causing a drop in the water level of c. 26 m (Björck 1999). This event also marks the end of the Younger Dryas stadial. There after saline water penetrated into the Baltic basin via the Närke Strait, which resulted in the establishment of the Yoldia Sea (Wastegård *et al.* 1998). This event is divided into threes phases, where the oldest and youngest phase are characterised by fresh water. The middle phase is characterised by brackish water which, according to clay varve years, entered the Baltic basin during a period of 120 years. In time the water level in the Baltic basin was in balance with that of the ocean, from 9900 to 9500 ^{14}C years BP (11,300 to 10,600 cal. years BP; Björck 1999). On the Södertörn peninsula weak traces of the short brackish water phase has been noted at 87 m a.s.l.

(Hedenström and Risberg 1999). This altitude is believed to approximately correspond to the first human use of this archipelago for hunting and fishing (Åkerlund 1996; Åkerlund *et al.* 1995). In general, land uplift was intense during the first c.1000 years after the deglaciation resulting in the formation of large land masses. This process also led to the drying up of the Närke strait, again allowing the establishment of a fresh water lake in the Baltic basin, i.e. the Ancylus Lake (Hedenström and Risberg 1999). Due to the more intense isostatic uplift in the northern part of the Baltic basin, the southern part experienced a transgressive phase. Towards the north it is possible to trace the transgressive trend approximately to the Södertörn peninsula where the occurrence of planktonic diatoms indicate a minor rise in lake level around 9000 ^{14}C years BP (10,100 cal. years BP; Hedenström 1996; Hedenström and Risberg 1999).

At around 8500 ^{14}C years BP (9500 cal. years BP), the relatively rapid regression is replaced by a standstill, or even a slight transgressive shore line, traces of which can be seen on the Södertörn peninsula (Risberg 1991; Hedenström and Risberg 1999). This was caused by an ingression of saline water through the Öresund and Store Belt straits and represents the global postglacial climatic optimum. At this time the eustatic sea level rise had reached approximately the same position as present. This event also marks the onset of the Litorina Sea stage of the Baltic basin. Because of the initial low salinity, the first c. 1000 years is referred to as the Mastogloia Sea after the brackish water diatom genus. Since c. 7500 ^{14}C years BP (8400 cal. years BP), the isostatic component has outcompeted the eustatic one, resulting in a gradually slower rate of land uplift. It is only during shorter periods that sea water recovered land areas, either as a result of small scale neo-tectonic movements or short term eustatic rises of the ocean level (Miller 1973; Miller and Robertsson 1981; Miller and Hedin 1988; Olsson and Risberg 1996). These transgressive phases have not been detected along all of the Baltic basin shores and might therefore be of local character. One reasonable explanation might be small scale neo-tectonic movements along the pronounced fissure valleys. During the above described brackish water phases, salinity never reached the levels of the ocean (30–35 ‰). The maximum salinity is estimated to have occurred around c. 5000 ^{14}C years BP (5800 cal. years BP) reaching c. 15 ‰ or possibly 20 ‰ (Westman et al. 1999).

Quaternary deposits

The above described Holocene environmental changes have resulted in a specific range of soil stratigraphy. The Weichselian ice deposited till on top of the bedrock. In the deep water immediately after the deglaciation clay and silt accumulated. Within the Baltic Ice Lake and the Yoldia Sea, fine grained sediments formed annually varved sequences with grey or reddish colours. During the Ancylus Lake phase, water depth was still deep enough to allow for the sedimentation of clay. This stratigraphic unit, however, differs from the older clay by its bluish colour, higher organic carbon content and its low carbonate content. Today, these fine grained deposits can be found in valleys and depressions in the bedrock topography. Due to the combined effect from the formation of archipelagos and climate improvement, gyttja clay and clay gyttja was accumulated. Another phenomena caused by the regressive shore displacement was the isolation and formation of lake basins at progressively lower altitudes. In these basins gyttja accumulate, and after being filled in with sediment developed into various types of mires. These basins are excellent archives for the study of natural landscape changes and anthropogenic activities.

Vegetation changes

As the isostatic uplift continued and the climate improved plants were able to colonise the emerging land area. The first trees to immigrate were hazel and alder at c. 9500 and 9000 ^{14}C years BP (11,000 and 10,100 cal. years BP), respectively (Florin 1969, 1977; Robertsson 1995; Robertsson and Olsson 1995). In the beginning of the warm Atlantic period linden followed c. 7500 ^{14}C years BP (8400 cal. years BP). The debated elm decline is clearly detected at c. 4500 ^{14}C years BP (5100 cal. years BP; Miller and Hedin 1988). The latest tree to immigrate was spruce at about 2500 ^{14}C years BP (2600 cal. years BP). Note that pollen studies on sediments accumulated in Lake Ådran indicate that scattered stands of spruce were already growing in the area by 6000 ^{14}C years BP (6800 cal. years BP; Risberg and Karlsson 1989). All tree species, except spruce, followed the receding ice front northwards. Spruce immigrated from the east, via Finland and the Åland archipelago, thus reaching the northern parts of Södertörn first (cf. Miller and Robertsson 1981).

The earliest human impact on the vegetation, recorded as local clearances, is dated to about 5000 ^{14}C years BP (5800 cal. years BP; Karlsson et al. 1996). Extensive clearances are recorded from about 2000 ^{14}C years BP (2000 cal. years BP). The earliest cultivation is recorded from c. 4000 ^{14}C years BP (4500 cal. years BP). The major expansion started around 1000 ^{14}C years BP (900 cal. years BP).

References

Björck, J. 1999. Event stratigraphy for the last glacial-Holocene transition in eastern middle Sweden. Stockholm University, Department of Quaternary Research. *Quaternaria* A6.

Brunnberg, L. 1995. Clay-varve chronology and deglaciation during the Younger Dryas and Pre-boreal in the easternmost part of the Middle Swedish Ice Marginal Zone. Stockholm University, Department of Quaternary Research. *Quaternaria* A2.

Donner, J. and Raukas, A. 1989. On the geological history of the Baltic Ice Lake. *Proceedings of the Academy of Sciences of the Estonian SSR* 38, 128–137.

Florin, M.-B. 1969. Late-glacial and Pre-boreal vegetation in central Sweden. *Svensk Botanisk Tidskrift* 63, 143–187.

— 1977. Late-glacial and Pre-boreal vegetation in southern Sweden. II. Pollen, spore and diatom analyses. *Striae* 5.

Hedenström, A. 1996. Preboreal shore displacement on central Södertörn peninsula, eastern middle Sweden. Stockholm University, Department of Quaternary Research. *Quaternaria* B7.

Hedenström, A. and Risberg, J. 1999: Early Holocene shore-displacement in southern central Sweden as recorded in elevated isolated basins. *Boreas* 28, 490–504.

Karlsson, S., Risberg, J. and Miller, U. 1996. South-central Sweden. Type region S-h, fissure-valley landscape of Södermanland and Uppland. In: Berglund, B.E., Birks, H.J.B., Ralska-Jasiewiczowa, M. and Wright, H.E. (eds) *Palaeoecological events during the last 15 000 years*, 254–265. Chichester.

Miller, U. 1973. Belägg för en subboreal transgression i Stockholmstrakten. University of Lund. *Department of Quaternary Geology. Report 3*, 96–104.

Miller, U. and Hedin, K. 1988. The Holocene development of landscape and environment in the south-east Mälaren valley, with special refenerence to Helgö. *Excvations at Helgö* XI. Kungliga Vitterhets Historie och Antikvitets Akademien, Stockholm.

Miller, U. and Robertsson, A.-M. 1981. Current biostratigraphical studies connected with archaeological excavations in the Stockholm region. *Striae* 14, 167–173.

Möller, H. and Stålhös, G. 1969. *Description of the geological map Stockholm SO*. Sveriges Geologiska Undersökning Ae 3.

Mörner, N.-A., Somi, E. and Zuchiewicz, W. 1989. Neotectonics and paleoseismicity within the Stockholm intercratonal region in Sweden. In: Mörner, N.-A. and Adams, J. (eds) *Paleoseismicity and Neotectonics. Tectonophysics* 163, 289–303.

Olsson, E. and Risberg, J. 1996. Archaeological data and models of sea-level change c. 6000–3500 BP south of Stockholm, eastern Sweden. In: Robertsson, A.-M., Hackens, T., Hicks, S., Risberg, J. and Åkerlund, A. (eds) *Landscapes and life*. PACT 50, 219–230.

Persson, C. and Svantesson, S.-I. 1972. The highest shore-line on Jakobsdalsberget in Kolmården, Sweden. *Geologiska Föreningens i Stockholm Förhandlingar* 94, 353–356.

Risberg, J. and Karlsson, S. 1989. *The pollen stratigraphy in a sediment core from Lake Ådran, Södertörn, central eastern Svealand, Sweden.* University of Stockholm. Department of Quaternary Research. Report 14.

Risberg, J. 1991. *Palaeoenvironment and sea level changes during the early Holocene on the Södertörn peninsula, Södermanland, eastern Sweden. Stockholm University.* Department of Quaternary Research. Report 20.

Robertsson, A.-M. 1995. Palaeoenvironment during Preboreal-Boreal in Närke, south central Sweden. *Quaternary International* 27, 103–109.

Robertsson, A.-M. and Olsson, I.U. 1995. A Late Pleistocene/Early Holocene sequence at Kopperöd, SW Sweden. In: Hackens, T., Königsson, L.-K. and Possnert, G. (eds) *^{14}C methods and Applications*. PACT 49, 141–158.

Sandgren, P., Björck, S., Brunnberg, L. and Kristiansson, J. 1988. Palaeomagnetic records from two varved clay sequences in the Middle Swedish ice marginal zone. *Boreas* 17, 215–227.

Stålhös, G. 1976. Aspects of the regional tectonics of eastern central Sweden. *Geologiska Föreningens i Stockholm Förhandlingar* 98, 146–154.

Strömberg, B. 1989. Late Weichselian deglaciation and clay varve chronology in east-central Sweden. Sveriges Geologiska Undersökning Ca 73.

Stuiver, M., Reimer, P.J., Bard, E., Beck, J.W., Burr, G.S., Hughen, K.A., Kromer, B., McCormack, G., van der Plicht, J. and Spurk, M. 1998. Intcal98 radiocarbon age calibration, 24,000–0 cal BP. *Radiocarbon* 40, 1041–1083.

Wastegård, S., Björck, J. and Risberg, J. 1998. Deglaciation, shore displacement and early-Holocene vegetation history in eastern middle Sweden. *The Holocene* 8:4, 433–441.

Westman, P., Wastegård, S., Schoning, K., Gustafsson, B. and Omstedt, A. 1999. *Salinity change in the Baltic Sea during the last 8,500 years: evidence, causes and models.* SKB Technical Report TR-99-38.

Åkerlund, A. 1996. *Human responses to shore displacement.* Riksantikvarieämbetet. Arkeologiska Undersökningar Skrifter nr 16.

Åkerlund, A., Hammar, D. and Wikell, R. 1995. Pioneers in the archipelago of eastern middle Sweden 9000 BP. In: Robertsson, A.-M., Hackens, T., Hicks, S., Risberg, J. and Åkerlund, A. (eds) *Landscapes and life*. PACT 50, 109–120.

SESSION I

COLONISATION PROCESSES

Colonisation Processes

1. Introduction

Peter Woodman

Although only a few papers were delivered in the colonisation processes session a number of significant questions were raised and similarly a number of papers in other sessions could be considered to contribute to the discussion. Therefore where these other papers have made a relevant contribution to issues associated with colonisation processes they will be referred to in the introduction.

Several themes emerge at the conference. Perhaps the most noticeable aspect was that an explicit interest in the colonisation processes was strongest in regions where the first known settlement was either dated to the early Holocene or the end of the late glacial. Regions where settlement could be documented to an earlier date did not seem to have the same interest in questions associated with the initial human settlement at the end of the ice age. The main geographical spread of the papers in this session are therefore, not surprisingly, from the northern and western part of the British Isles and Fenno-Scandinavia with Zofia Sulgostowska's paper as an extension down the eastern edge of the Baltic. At first sight the paper by Costa and colleagues on the Tyrrhenian Islands of Sardinia and Corsica might appear to present a different series of issues as they are from a different geographical region but some of the problems discussed are similar in particularly when compared to questions raised about other island such as Ireland. The most obvious is the question of how human communities can survive on islands when they only had access to a significantly reduced range of resources. The question of continuity of settlement on islands can be seen to be an issue not only on the Tyrrhenian Island but is also of importance when considering the Mesolithic settlement of the Isle of Man (McCartan this volume).

It is evident that there has been a shift away from research based on the often common desire to "grab" at objects either from within an assemblage or stray finds as well as relying on individual ^{14}C dates. These forms of evidence were then used to stake a claim that human settlement could be pushed back to an earlier than expected point in time. While some of the papers from this session provide new evidence of earlier settlement, the recurrent themes of most are based on 1) a desire to consider the criteria by which early and initial phases of settlement can be identified, 2) what was meant by an initial phase of colonisation and 3) what are the factors which limit or encourage the expansion of human settlement into new areas.

It is very clear that, as early Holocene settlement can now be identified throughout much of the western and northern edges of Europe, the idea that significant time lags are to be expected is a truism which can no longer be simply and uncritically accepted. However the discovery of early settlement in many parts of Arctic Europe raises questions about the apparent initial delay in settlement in areas such as Ireland and Scotland or areas such as the Outer Hebrides where a Mesolithic occupation has yet to be discovered. In the latter case, given the difficulty in even finding the types of localities where Mesolithic settlement might occur i.e. due to the existence of extensive areas of quaternary deposits such as peat bogs and machair sand dunes. It has been necessary to consider the type of approaches used by Edwards and Sugden. In these cases even an indication that disturbances in the pollen record would be best explained as being anthropogenic would encourage further investigations focused on finding other evidence in the form of settlements and artefacts.

Rankama has identified the potential danger in working across national boundaries where very different paradigms could exist. She notes, in particular, that Norwegian Archaeology has always identified the potential of the coastal zone as vector for colonisation, while Finnish Archaeology, especially in the north of Finland, has always functioned within a terrestrial framework. It is therefore of interest that she suggests the quite early movements of human settlement from the south into the arctic region. However, aside from the continuing debate on the route of the initial colonisation of the Arctic, she has also proposed that the expansive inland Finnmarksvidda was first settled from the south rather than from the coast – a movement across present day national boundaries. Although it is not usually dealt with explicitly, issues of early colonisation are often fraught with problems created by implicit biases derived from national perspectives.

Two other sets of parameters are considered in these papers. It should not be surprising that, in a subject area such as the Mesolithic where ecological studies have played such an important role, attention is given to the potential for an area to receive and maintain human settlement – whether in areas such as Ireland or Scandinavia. It is clear from certain papers that potential for human settlement did not always pre-ordain a human presence at an early date. Both Tolan-Smith and Rankama have referred to the fact that there can be social limitations which may condition settlement and that these may be as important as the ecological potential for settlement.

Similarly, theories based on colonisation due to crises induced by changes in the resource base in the economy are no longer as prevalent as they were in the past. In fact it is probable that such forced colonisation would often lead to failure through maladaptation to the new environment. There is in these papers a clear recognition that three factors must be taken into consideration. These are:

- Do the potential resources to support human settlement exist?
- Have the colonising communities, where necessary, acquired or developed the required technology to exploit these resources?
- Have they networks and other social mechanisms to make the process work?

One point which kept recurring throughout the session itself but which is not fully reflected in the published papers is worth noting. It is necessary to identify the type of settlement whose traces are being recovered. Is it the initial short term pioneering settlement or is it the beginning of a more long-term consolidated phase of settlement.

In this context a number of other interesting issues were raised in papers presented in other sessions. Who were the first explorers of new territories? Instead of seeing whole communities involved in an initial move, could it have been small bands of adolescents as Akerlund and colleagues have noted that Gamble suggested in *Time Walkers*? Young adults were allowed latitude in marginal landscapes. In societies as far apart as the Inuit or in late Medieval Ireland, where in the summer the young looked after cattle in the hills, they were away from the controlled and prescribed world of their elders. This is surely an indication that exploration of new land need not be driven by the parallels of the commercial navigator/explorers of the 15th and 16th centuries. Perhaps we also need to consider the implications of the challenge and shock of something new as is explored by Fuglestvedt in her paper on the implications of societies from the low lying coastal regions exploring the spectacular mountain world of Southern Norway. Are these new territories immediately utilised or is the information on new landscapes, sources of food and raw materials banked for future use in the communal knowledge of Mesolithic societies? In other words do initial visits always have to be immediately followed by settlement.

Mats Larsson as well as Akerlund and colleagues have examined the early stages of settlement in Eastern Central Sweden and have slightly but not entirely different perspectives on the problems and potentially different strategies in exploiting stone raw material in a new environment. Larsson has suggested that there was an initial concentration on the continued use of the familiar flint with only a second stage adaptation to the use of more local material such as quartz. This is a theme that has echoes in a similar debate further north in the Arctic but the origins of the flint remains uncertain. Were the familiar raw materials imported or searched for in the new environment? In contrast Akerlund and colleagues emphasise the need for initial explorers to retain a simple but flexible technology that could have been adapted to serve a range of needs some of which would have been expected to be outside their previous experience. In this case it is highly probable that pioneering settlement phases would not necessarily be marked by a convenient range of artefacts which were identical to those used "Back Home"!

Numerous issues are raised for the first time in these papers. Hopefully it is the beginning of a long and fruitful discourse.

2. Early Settlement on Tyrrhenian islands (8th millennium cal. BC): Mesolithic adaption to local resources in Corsica and Northern Sardinia

L. Costa, J.-D. Vigne, H. Bocherens, N. Desse-Berset, C. Heinz, F. de Lanfranchi, J. Magdeleine, M.-P. Ruas, S. Thiebault and C. Tozzi

Mesolithic peoples are responsible for the earliest Holocene colonisation of the Tyrrhenian islands at around the 8th millennium cal. BC. Their presence in Corsica and Northern Sardinia is now documented by eight archaeological sites. New observations and reflections considerably improve our knowledge of subsistence practices during this period. In this paper, the exploitation of terrestrial and marine animals, wood, and lithic resources will be examined. Each of these categories indicates that the Mesolithic groups exploited resources that were directly available in proximity to the sites. Moreover, the chipped stone artefacts also suggest that their lithic production was adapted to the particular conditions of the Tyrrhenian islands. Along with the topographical distribution and spatial organisation of the sites, these observations allow us to propose an initial hypothesis concerning the way of life of these peoples in Corsica and Northern Sardinia.

The islands of Corsica and Sardinia have been isolated from the mainland since at least the Middle Pleistocene (Conchon 1976:241 pp; Van Andel 1989:733 pp). The question of the first human presence on these islands has not yet been resolved and it is possible that traces of human occupation during the Late Palaeolithic will be discovered (Vigne 1999a:308 p). For the moment, however, there is no real proof of human presence before the Holocene, 20,000 to 10,000 years ago.

The first evidence for the presence of "Preneolithic people" in Corsica was revealed in the sixties by Lanfranchi and Weiss (1973:7 pp). This was the first discovery of Pre-Neolithic groups in a truly isolated territory in the Mediterranean Basin. At the time, these groups were characterised by a total absence of ceramics, imported stone (flint and obsidian) and domestic animals, rare, crude lithic tools made exclusively from local stones (quartz and grainy rocks), and calibrated dates of approximately 9000 to 8000 BC. Lacking a more accurate characterisation, these groups were then called "Pre-neolithic". They were later renamed Mesolithic after their status as true Early Holocene hunters was confirmed (Lanfranchi 1998:537 pp).

Until 1990, the Mesolithic period was documented by only three small excavations (Figure 2.1), at Barbaggio-

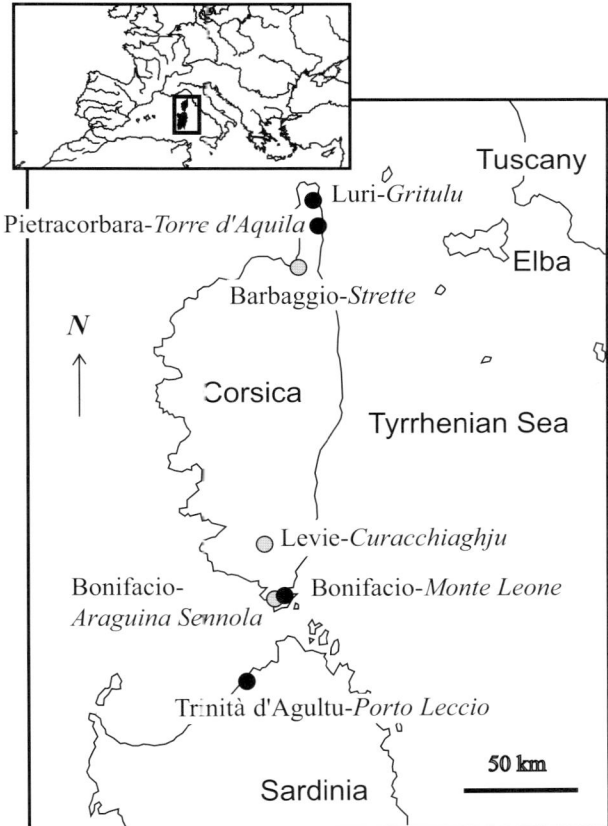

Figure 2.1 Location of Tyrrhenian islands in the Mediterranean area and of the Mesolithic sites in Corsica and northern Sardinia.

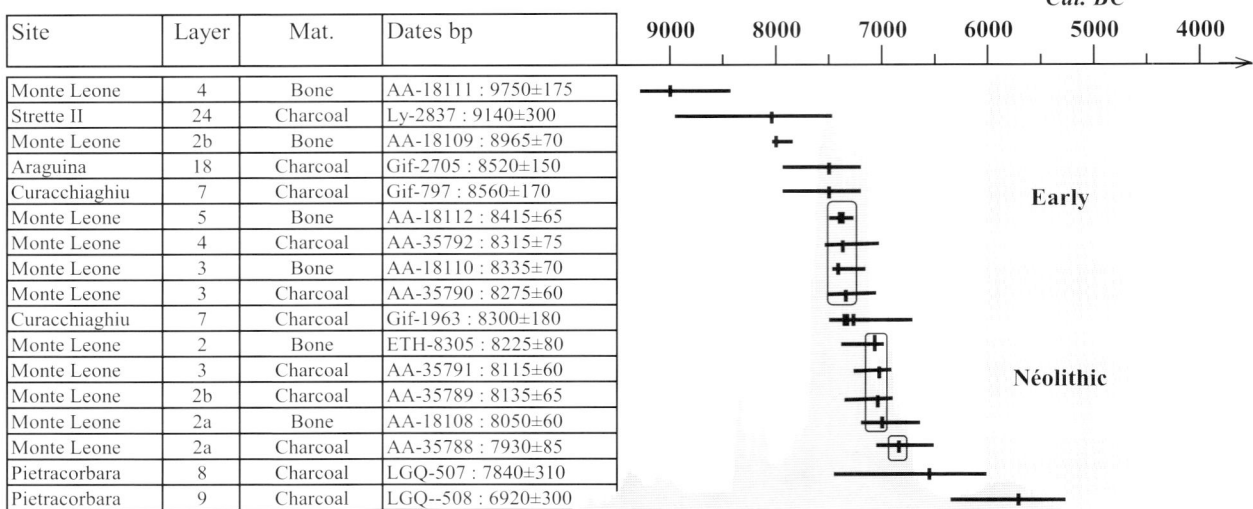

Figure 2.2 Calibrated radiocarbon dates from Corsican Mesolithic sites (modified from Vigne et al. 1998).

Strette (Magdeleine and Ottaviani 1986: 61 pp), Lévie-Curacchiaghju (Lanfranchi 1967:587 pp) and Bonifacio-Araguina-Sennola (Lanfranchi and Weiss 1973:7 pp). Since this time, four additional sites have been recorded and excavated, at Trinità d'Agulto-Porto Leccio in northern Sardinia (Tozzi 1996:9 pp), Luri-Gritulu (Magdeleine and Vigne 1994:53; 1997:51; Vigne 1999c:52 pp), Pietracorbara-Torre d'Acquila (Magdeleine 1991:80; Magdeleine 1995:362 pp) and Bonifacio-Monte Leone (Vigne and Desse-Berset 1995:309 pp; Vigne *et al.* 1998:251 pp; Vigne 1999b:645 pp). The latter is the largest site. These have provided many new data, especially concerning the nature of the settlements, the diet, the procurement of raw materials and lithic production. These new observations considerably improve our understanding of the occupations during this period, and allow us to propose an initial hypothesis concerning the way of life of these Mesolithic peoples in Corsica and northern Sardinia.

New radiocarbon dates and the origin of the Tyrrhenian Mesolithic people

Except for Porto Leccio, all of the Mesolithic sites have provided radiocarbon dates, especially the Monte Leone shelter, which has recently provided eleven dates. The total number of reliable dates is 17 (Figure 2.2), with calibration probabilities indicating that the Corsican Mesolithic spans essentially from the first half of the 8th millennium until the very beginning of the 7th millennium.

Gritulu cave is the only site where the Mesolithic layers are included in a long stratigraphy, spanning from the Middle Late Glacial to the Middle Neolithic (Vigne 1999c:53 p). This stratigraphy confirms that no human occupation occurred before the Mesolithic. In addition, *Megaloceros cazioti*, which is the only endemic large mammal of the island, became extinct before the Preboreal layer, and had no apparent relationship with the presence of Mesolithic people (Vigne *et al.* 1997:587 pp; Vigne 1999a:309, 2000:132 pp).

Both of these observations indicate that there was no significant human occupation in Corsica during the Late Glacial period. Consequently, Mesolithic groups probably first arrived from the mainland by sea during the Preboreal or Early Boreal period, suggesting they had some knowledge of sailing techniques.

Locations of the Mesolithic sites in Corsica and Northern Sardinia

The Mesolithic sites were located mainly on the present day coastline (Figure 2.1). Only Curacchiaghju shelter, a very small site probably corresponding to a small occupation, is located inland on the Corsican island, at 700 meters above sea level. Between the 8th millennium BC and modern times, the sea level has risen by 20 meters in the area surrounding these islands (Van Andel 1989:733 pp, 1990:151 p). This value does not take into account local tectonic phenomena or coastal sand accumulation. Today, part of the Mesolithic coastline is immersed. Since the continental shelves of Corsica are very abrupt, the present day coastlines do not differ significantly from the Mesolithic ones, except in the Bonifacio area where the sea bottom is not very deep. All Mesolithic sites of the Corsican-Sardinian region were located on the coast, never very far from the sea. Thus, not only did Mesolithic groups come from the continent by sea, they also settled the coastline.

Settlement characteristics

Except for Gritulu cave, all of the Corsican-Sardinian Mesolithic sites are located in rock shelters. No open-air sites are yet known. Except for the Monte Leone shelter, which seems to have covered 80 to 150 square meters, all of these settlements are characterised by a their small size, probably between 10 and 40 square meters. This suggests the presence of small human groups.

The dates yielded by the Monte Leone layers (Figure 2.2) suggest that this site was occupied for more than 500 years. This is consistent with other data, such as the large quantity of bones attributed to a small endemic lagomorph (*Prolagus sardus*), which is estimated to represent 75,000 to 150,000 individuals consumed at the site (Vigne *et al.* 1998:257 pp). Others sites such as Torre d'Acquila and Strette, have yielded abundant faunal remains (Vigne 1995:381 pp; Vigne and Desse-Berset 1995:309 pp), indicating that the occupations lasted at least several weeks.

In contrast, Strette could not have been occupied year round since it is located in a narrow area between the river and a cliff and was probably flooded at each river swelling. At this site, two distinct Mesolithic layers are separated by a thick sterile deposit (Magdeleine and Ottaviani 1986:61 pp). The Curacchiaghju shelter is situated in the mountainous area. Due to cold winters, continuous occupation of this site is also unlikely. At Monte Leone shelter, 18 to 38% of the rodent teeth display digestion marks. This provides evidence of interstratified owl pellet deposits, most of which were probably accumulated by the endemic small eagle owl (*Bubo insularis*). This suggests periods of human absence, which probably lasted longer than a season. At this same site, the Mesolithic sedimentation is clearly separated into several phases, also suggesting discontinuous occupation.

All of these observations together suggest long-term but discontinuous occupations. Corsican Mesolithic sites thus appear to correspond to a succession of occupations, which were interrupted by periods of abandonment sometimes lasting several decades or centuries. It is therefore probable that the small human groups that occupied these sites were nomadic.

Raw material origins

The faunal assemblages of Corsican-Sardinian Mesolithic sites are constituted primarily of shells and small vertebrate bones (Vigne and Desse-Berset 1995:309 pp). The reconstruction of subsistence practices thus requires exhaustive collection of these materials by fine mesh water sieving. Unfortunately, this method has been applied only at the Monte Leone shelter, whose results are thus the most reliable.

These results show that subsistence during this period was based mainly on small game. According to the osteological remains, *Prolagus* represented 70 to 80 % of the diet (Vigne and Desse-Berset 1995:309 pp). The presence of burn marks demonstrate that this species was actually cooked and eaten (Vigne *et al.* 1981:222 pp; Vigne and Marinval-Vigne 1983:239 pp). At Monte Leone, such marks have also been observed on 12 to 18% of the bones of endemic small rodents, the large field mouse *Rhagamys orthodon*, and also the large vole *Tyrrhenicola henseli*. Birds were very scarce in the diet, but consumption of great bustards is attested at Monte Leone (Cuisin and Vigne 1998:831 pp). Shellfish are also scarce, though more abundant at Torre d'Acquila than at Monte Leone (Vigne 1995:381 pp). At Monte Leone, fishes account for about 20 % of the diet. Most of these are small species, such as eels (*Anguilla anguilla*) or sardines (*Sardinia* sp.), the heads of which were systematically removed for storage (Vigne and Desse-Berset 1995: 309 pp).

Fish storage at Monte Leone suggests that the bones and shells found in the sites may represent only a small portion of the animals that were actually consumed, and that percentages based on bone remains may give a biased estimation of the diet. For this reason, analyses of Carbon (δ^{13}C) and Nitrogen (δ^{15}N) isotopes from different fish species, *Prolagus*, monk seal and great bustard, as well as from two human individuals from Araguina-Sennola and Monte Leone, have been processed. While not yet completed, and based on only two human individuals from the same Bonifacio area, these analyses seem to confirm that the diet was primarily composed of terrestrial game, and secondarily of marine resources.

All of the dietary components observed at Monte Leone come from the immediate surroundings of the site. Both the littoral fish and shellfish, and *Prolagus* from the coastal plains, originate from less than 5 km away. We can thus conclude that all food resources were local.

Charcoal and seed analyses at Monte Leone (Heinz, Ruas and Thiébault, in Vigne *et al.* 1998:251 pp) show that firewood was procured almost exclusively from the surrounding thermomediterranean mattoral (*Juniperus*, *Phillyrea*, *Pistacia lentiscus*, *Erica* sp...) (an unusually high percentage of cf. *Celtis* charcoal is probably not related to fire activities, see below). Mesomediterranean bush is poorly represented (wood of *Arbutus unedo*, seeds of *Sambucus nigra*), while Pine wood (*Pinus laricio*) from mountain forests is represented by only one charcoal piece found in layer C.3. In addition, seed analyses show the presence of reed bed herbaceous plants, probably obtained from wet areas in the bottom of the Bonifacio ria, which were immersed at the time. It thus appears that wood resources and herbaceous plants were also exclusively local.

Flint and obsidian are totally absent in Corsica. Mesolithic people used only local materials, especially quartz and coarse-grained rocks, such as rhyolite and granite (Figure 2.3). These materials, which come from lodes, are very difficult to shape or knap. However, they are very easy to find everywhere on the littoral. Flint, which is present only in Northern Sardinia, was used at Porto Leccio, but in small quantities (27%) compared to quartz and 'rhyolite'. Analysis of the lithic supply at each site indicates that most of the raw materials were obtained from pebbles, which were collected locally in the rivers or on the beaches close to the sites.

sites\materials	CORSICA						SARDINIA
	Gritulu	Strette	Torre d'Aquila	Curacchiaghju	Araguina-Sennola	Monte Leone	Porto Leccio
quartz	4	468	295	152	131	704	148
grainy rocks	5	508	234	116	9	490	29
flint	0	0	0	0	0	0	58
TOTAL	**9**	**976**	**529**	**268**	**140**	**1194**	**215**

Figure 2.3 Lithic materials used at Corsican and northern Sardinian Mesolithic sites. The counts include tools, flakes and fragments. Splinters are small flakes or debris less than 1 cm long. We have considered these separately because Monte Leone is the only site where these small remains have been systematically collected.

This exclusively local raw material procurement pattern for animal, plant and lithic resources, indicates that these human groups rarely obtained resources from the inland portions of the island. We can thus suppose that their activities were mainly concentrated within a small area in proximity to their camps, thus suggesting a strong association with the seashore. In our opinion, all these data suggest that these groups moved often and did not remain in the same place for long periods of time. In other words, their raw material procurement practices were particularly well adapted to the conditions of a nomadic lifestyle.

Adaptations to local exploitation

Animal exploitation

It must be emphasised that large terrestrial game was not a factor in this island situation. The only local ungulate, *Megaloceros cazioti*, is completely absent from Mesolithic assemblages, and apparently became extinct at around the 10th millennium BC in Corsica (Vigne 1999a:295 pp) and Sardinia (Klein Hofmeijer 1997; Tozzi and Vigne 2000:177 pp). The available evidence shows that Mesolithic people did not exploit large coastal game either. Monk seal (*Monachus monachus*) is represented by only two bones, one at Araguina-Sennola and another at Monte Leone. Dolphins (*Delphinus delphis*, cf. *Tursiops*) are attested by only 15 isolated teeth and bone fragments at Monte Leone (Vigne et al 1998:251 pp). Preliminary isotopic analyses also indicate that these meat resources were not extensively exploited.

There is evidence for the consumption of large birds, such as the European shag (*Phalacrocorax aristotelis*), geese and ducks (*Anser* sp., *Anas platyrhynchos*), raptors and Corvidae, and especially the great bustard, but always in small quantities (Cuisin and Vigne 1998:831 pp). Therefore, the animal resources exploited consisted almost exclusively of small species, such as fish, shellfish, rodents and *Prolagus*, the latter being highly abundant. In other regions of the world (e.g. Prummel 1994:316 pp; Shaffer and Gardner 1997:263 pp), all of these species were collected with nets or traps. A portion of the resources was kept and stored for later consumption. This is attested by the systematic absence of the bones of the heads of small fish, and several small pits at Monte Leone that may have been used for storage (Vigne and Desse-Berset 1995:309 pp; Vigne et al. 1998:251 pp; Vigne 1999b:645 pp).

Finally, since there was no large game in the environment, these human groups were not hunters. Rather, they relied exclusively on trapping and fishing.

The lithic industry

A technological analysis of 3320 remains from seven Corsican and Sardinian sites (Figure 2.4) has revealed the use simple debitage techniques and methods. The objective of this production was to obtain very simple flakes. While a very small number of these flakes have an elongated form, none can be considered as true blades or bladelets, as would be produced by intentional blade debitage methods.

The first step of the operational sequence consisted of breaking pebbles into two halves, probably by bipolar, anvil percussion. Flakes were then removed by direct, hard-hammer percussion, using a unidirectional method. Depending on their morphology, the fracture surface of the pebbles could be used either as a striking platform, or as a flaking surface. Since the pebbles were between 5 and 10 cm in diameter, the debitage products were rather small, more than 80 % being less than 3 cm long.

The tools (Figure 2.5, Figure 2.6) consist primarily of scrapers, notched flakes and denticulate flakes. Although they are characteristic of Mesolithic periods in the western Mediterranean, microliths are absent.

The number of tools in each assemblage is very small. We have identified only 21 notched flakes, 19 denticulate flakes, 10 scrapers and 16 other retouched flakes, for a total 66 tools among the 3320 objects studied (2%). All of the tools were made either from large flakes or directly shaped from pebbles. It follows that the dimensions of the majority of the tools do not correspond to the debitage products. The latter are too small, as is demonstrated by the core removals (Figure 2.6). Therefore, significant proportion of the pebble debitage was undoubtedly aimed at the production of small cutting flakes, which were probably used unretouched. Close examination of these small flakes reveals cutting edges with visible wear traces (blunted and scarred edges). Moreover, some of them

GRITULU							
raw materials	debris	cores	flakes	Tools	TOTAL	splinters	total
quartz	1	0	3	0	**4**	0	4
grainy rocks	1	2	2	0	**5**	0	5
TOTAL	**2**	**2**	**5**	**0**	**9**	**0**	**9**
TORRE d'AQUILA							
raw materials	debris	cores	flakes	tools	TOTAL	splinters	total
quartz	72	17	195	5	**291**	4	295
grainy rocks	196	8	25	4	**234**	0	234
TOTAL	**268**	**25**	**220**	**9**	**525**	**4**	**529**
STRETTE							
raw materials	debris	cores	flakes	tools	TOTAL	splinters	total
quartz	65	8	150	5	**229**	239	468
grainy rocks	230	4	157	8	**402**	106	408
TOTAL	**295**	**12**	**310**	**13**	**631**	**345**	**976**
CURACCHIAGHJU							
raw materials	debris	cores	flakes	tools	TOTAL	splinters	total
quartz	34	9	106	2	**151**	1	152
grainy rocks	36	8	66	4	**114**	2	116
TOTAL	**70**	**17**	**172**	**6**	**265**	**3**	**268**
ARAGUINA-SENNOLA							
raw materials	debris	cores	flakes	tools	TOTAL	splinters	total
quartz	16	2	79	2	**99**	32	131
grainy rocks	0	0	7	0	**7**	2	9
TOTAL	**16**	**2**	**86**	**2**	**106**	**34**	**140**
MONTE LEONE							
raw materials	debris	cores	flakes	tools	TOTAL	splinters	total
quartz	114	22	131	4	**273**	431	704
grainy rocks	144	24	208	24	**390**	100	490
TOTAL	**258**	**46**	**339**	**28**	**663**	**531**	**1194**
PORTO LECCIO							
raw materials	debris	cores	flakes	tools	TOTAL	splinters	total
quartz	11	7	92	5	**115**	13	128
grainy rocks	2	1	19	1	**26**	3	29
flint	12	2	37	6	**53**	5	58
TOTAL	**25**	**10**	**146**	**8**	**194**	**21**	**215**

Figure 2.4 Lithic remains from Mesolithic sites in Corsica and northern Sardinia.

materials \ tools	scrapers	notched flakes	denticulate flakes	others
quartz	0	9	6	7
grainy rocks	10	10	13	9
flint	0	2	0	0
TOTAL	**10**	**21**	**19**	**16**

Figure 2.5 Tool types and frequencies from seven Mesolithic sites in Corsica and northern Sardinia.

also possess one or several abrupt edges, which could not result from the pebble debitage. Therefore, we assume that they were obtained by intentional breakage, probably to be fit into a handle. We have identified approximately 125 small calibrated flakes with this type of "backing". Some of may have played the role of more typical Mesolithic microliths. If this is the case, they can be considered as technical adaptation to the poor quality of the local quartz and coarse-grained stones.

The distribution of different categories of lithic artefacts shows little relation to the different types of raw materials, such as quartz or coarse-grained stones (Figure 2.7). It thus appears that the lithic production took equal advantage of the different available stones and was not based on a true economy of raw materials ("économie de matières premières", Perlès 1980:37 pp, 1991:35 pp).

We also observe that lithic tools are very scarce and not very diversified, suggesting they were used for a restricted range of activities. Consequently, we can suppose that many tools were made from other, non-lithic, materials. Meanwhile, no bone or tooth tools have been recovered from these Mesolithic sites. Wood and vegetal

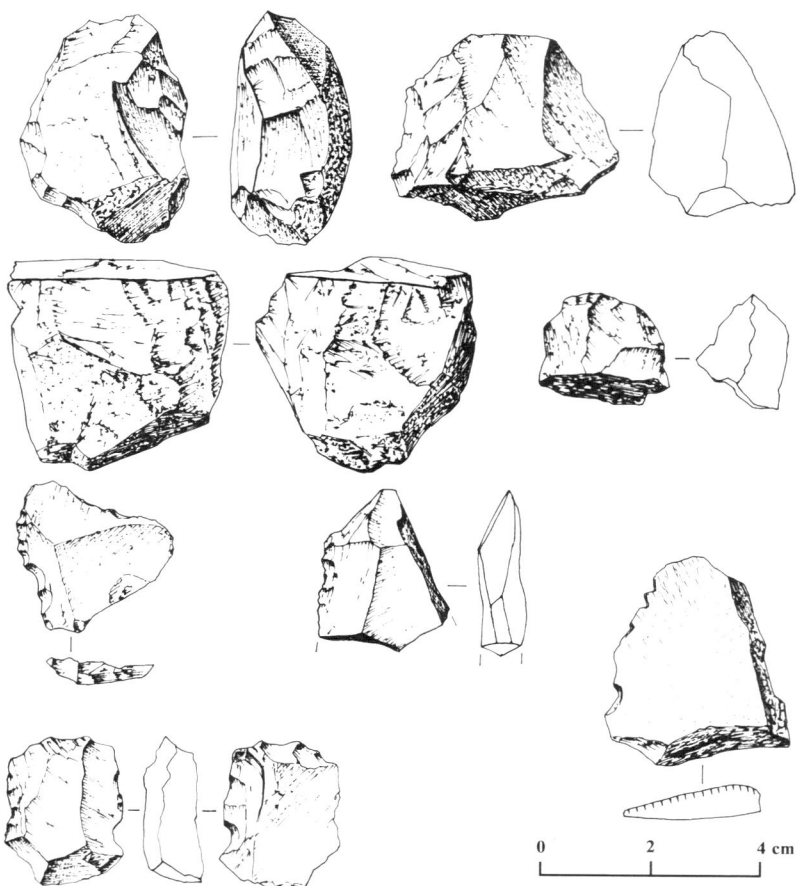

Figure 2.6 Cores and tools (drawings by F. Negrino).

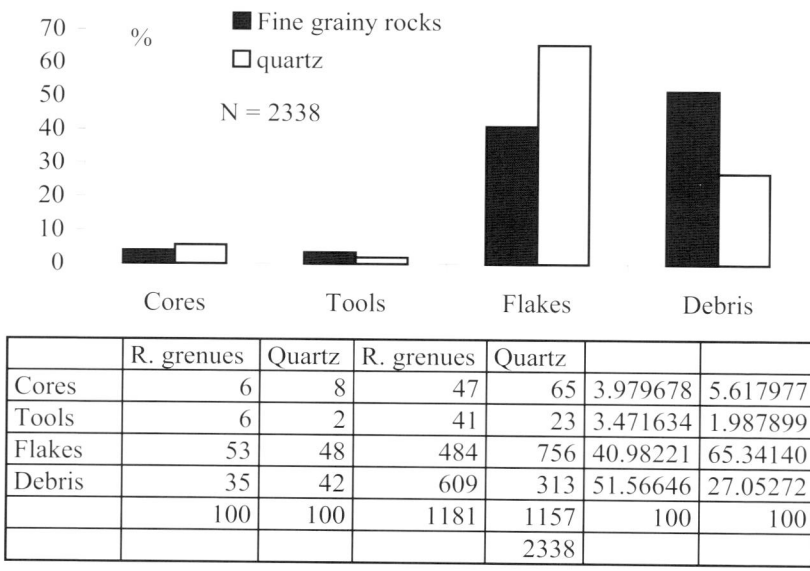

	R. grenues	Quartz	R. grenues	Quartz		
Cores	6	8	47	65	3.979678	5.617977
Tools	6	2	41	23	3.471634	1.987899
Flakes	53	48	484	756	40.98221	65.34140
Debris	35	42	609	313	51.56646	27.05272
	100	100	1181	1157	100	100
				2338		

Figure 2.7 Distribution of the lithic artefacts according to raw materials.

fibres, on the other hand, probably played an important role. This is suggested by the abundance of nettle tree (cf. *Celtis*) in the charcoal samples of the three main layers at Monte Leone (46.3%, 23% and 28.3% in C4, C3 and C2, respectively). This is a rather rare species in the context of meso-mediterranean vegetation, but it is known to provide a good quality wood for shaping. The use of plants from the nearby wet areas of the Bonifacio ria, which might have been used for basketry (traps, nets, etc.) is also suggested at Monte Leone by the presence of Cyperaceae and Juncaeae seeds (respectively *Scripus lacustris*, *Cladium mariscus* and *Luzula* sp. account for 55% of the 40 recorded seeds).

Conclusion

In conclusion, we can first remark that analyses of a great number of new data, most from the Monte Leone shelter, have extensively improved our understanding of the first Mediterranean Mesolithic islanders. Some important aspects of their way of life are now becoming clear. These can be summarised by five main points:

- these Mesolithic groups had sailing capabilities;
- their settlements were mainly coastal;
- the sites were very small and probably resulted from occupations by small human groups;
- these sites were occupied discontinuously, probably with long phases of abandon. Raw materials (food, wood, herbaceous plants, lithics) all originate from local sources and were most often collected in proximity to the sites. These different features suggest a coastal, nomadic lifestyle.
- the technical characteristics of these groups consist of the local exploitation of coastal resources. Their diet was based mainly on small, littoral game, small fish and shellfish, which were easy to catch and store. These groups did not practice hunting, but were trapper-fishers. They used few lithic tools, which were probably complimented by wood tools, nets and basketry. One of the aims of the lithic debitage might have been the production of small cutting flakes, which would have been used unretouched.

Despite the crude nature of the lithic production, these technical characteristics can be seen as efficient adaptations to the local environmental resources and a coastal, nomadic, trapper-fisher lifestyle. Consequently, they must be considered as genuine cultural characteristics, based on their choice of a particular lifestyle.

Generally speaking, these groups were not significantly different from the Mesolithic groups of the continental region of the Tyrrhenian Sea, as described by Tozzi or Martini (Tozzi 1996:7 pp). Therefore, it is still unclear whether they were exclusively, or only partly, islanders. However, Corsican and Sardinian sites have thus far provided no evidence for a link with the continent. Meanwhile, it is possible that if Mesolithic people crossed the sea once, they could have returned at some point. In this case, they might have lived on either side of the Tyrrhenian Sea, depending on the period. However, we have no material evidence for this hypothesis.

We are dealing here with small groups of "trapper-fisher-coastal-nomads" who were very well adapted to the exploitation of local resources in proximity to their sites, and who frequented the Corsican and Sardinian coasts on several occasions during the 8th millennium BC. In our opinion, the fragile balance of the littoral ecosystem must have played an important role in determining the way of life of these Mesolithic peoples. In order to assure their subsistence, they were probably required to move on a regular basis. These frequent displacements could explain the local character of their raw material supply: these Mesolithic peoples perhaps based all of their technical production on materials that could be found anywhere on the coast in order to retain a their freedom of movement.

Acknowledgements

This paper is the result of the work of several members of the international research project, PREFACTH (Paysages, Renouvellements de Faune et Anthropisation de la Corse au Tardiglaciaire et au début de l'Holocène), which benefits from grants by the Services Régionaux de l'Archéologie de la Région Corse (PCR), the Centre National de la Recherche Scientifique (Programme PeH), and the Projet de Parc International des Bouches de Bonifacio. We are grateful to J. Cuisin who allowed us to present his results in this paper, as well as to A. Tresset and M. O'Farrell, who made helpful comments on earlier drafts.

References

Conchon, O. 1976. The human settlement of Corsica: palaeogeographic and tectonic considerations. *Journal of Human Evolution* 5, 241–248.

Cuisin, J. and Vigne, J.-D. 1998. Présence de la grande outarde (*Ottis tarda*) au Boréal, dans la région de Bonifacio (Corse-du-Sud, France, 8ème millénaire av. J.-C.). *Geobios* 31, 6, 831–837.

Klein Hofmeijer, G. 1997. *Late Pleistocene deer fossils from Corbeddu cave: implications for human colonization of the island Sardinia*. British Archaeological Reports, International Series 663. Oxford.

Lanfranchi, F. (de) 1967. La grotte sépulcrale de Curacchiaghju (Levie, Corse). *Bulletin de la Société préhistorique française* 64, 2, 587–612.

—— 1998. Prénéolithique ou Mésolithique insulaire? *Bulletin de la Société préhistorique française* 95, 4, 537–545.

Lanfranchi, F. (de) and Weiss, M.C. 1973. La sépulture prénéolithique de la couche XVIII de l'abri d'Araguina-Sennola (Bonifacio, Corse). *Bulletin de la Société des sciences historiques et naturelles de la Corse* 606, 7–17.

Magdeleine, J. 1991. Une deuxième sépulture prénéolithique de Corse. *Bulletin de la Société préhistorique française* 88, 3, 80.

—— 1995. Préhistoire du cap Corse: les abris de Torre d'Aquila, Pietracorbara (Haute-Corse). *Bulletin de la Société préhistorique française* 92, 3, 363–377.

Magdeleine, J. and Ottaviani, J.C. 1986. L'abri préhistorique de Strette. *Bulletin de la Société des sciences historiques et naturelles de la Corse* 650, 61–90.

Magdeleine, J. and Vigne, J.-D. 1994. Luri, grotte de Gritulu, Tufo. *Bilan scientifique 1993 du Service Régional de l'Archéologie, Corse*, Ministère de la Culture et de la Francophonie, Ajaccio, 53.

—— 1997. Luri, Grotte de Gritulu. *Bilan scientifique 1996 du Service Régional de l'Archéologie, Corse*, Ministère de la Culture, Ajaccio, 51.

Martini, F. 1993. Grotta della Serratura a Marina di Camerota. In: Martini, F. (ed.) *Culture e ambienti dei complessi olocenici*. Florence: Garlatti e Razzai.

Perlès, C. 1980. Economie de la matière première et économie du débitage : deux exemples grecs. *Préhistoire et technologie lithique*. CNRS Paris, 37–41.

—— 1991. Economie des matières premières et économie du débitage: deux conceptions opposées? *25 ans d'études technologiques en préhistoire: bilan et perspectives*. Actes des rencontres de Juan-les-Pins (octobre 1990), Editions APDCA, 35–45.

Prummel, W. 1994. Birds and mammals as indicators for fishing methods. *Offa* (Neumünster, Netherland), 51, 316–318.

Shaffer, B.S. and Gardner, K.M. 1997. Reconstructing animal exploitation by Puebloan peoples of the Southwestern United States using Mimbres pottery, AD 1000–1150. *Anthropozoologica* 25–26, 263–268.

Tozzi, C. 1996. L'abri prénéolithique de Porto Leccio (Sardaigne septentrionale). *Actes des 3ème journées universitaires corses de Nice* (19–20 mai 1995). Université de Nice, 11–16.

Tozzi, C. and Vigne, J.-D. 2000. Il contributo dell'Archeozoologia alla conoscenza del Mesolitico sardo-corso. *Atti 2° Convegno di Archeozoologia* (Asti, nov. 1997). Forlì: ABACO, 177–181.

Van Andel, T.H. 1989. Late Quaternary sea-level changes and archaeology. *Antiquity* 63, 733–745.

—— 1990. Addentum to "Late Quaternary sea-level changes and archaeology". *Antiquity* 64, 151–152.

Vigne, J.-D. 1995. Préhistoire du cap Corse : les abris de Torre d'Aquila, Pietracorbara (Haute-Corse): La faune. *Bulletin de la Société préhistorique française* 92, 3, 381–389.

—— 1999a. The large "true" Mediterranean islands as a model for the Holocene human impact on the European vertebrate fauna ? Recent data and new reflections. In: Benecke, N. (ed.) *The Holocene history of the European vertebrate fauna. Modern aspects of research* (Workshop, 6th–9th April 1998, Berlin). Deutsches Archäologisches Institut, Eurasien-Abteilung, (*Archäologie in Eurasien*, 6), Berlin, 295–322.

—— 1999b. L'abri du Monte Leone (Bonifacio, Corse du Sud): vaste site pré-néolithique en contexte insulaire. In: Thévenin, A. (ed.) and Bintz, P. (dir.), *L'Europe des derniers chasseurs. Peuplement et paléoenvironnement de l'Epipaléolithique et du Mésolithique* (5ème Colloque International UISPP, septembre 1995). CTHS, Paris, 645–650.

—— 1999c. Luri, grotte de Grítulu. *Bilan scientifique 1998 du Service Régional de l'Archéologie, Corse*, Ministère de la Culture, Ajaccio, 52–53.

—— 2000. Les chasseurs préhistoriques dans les îles méditerranéennes. *Pour la Science*, Dossier Hors série "La valse des espèces", Juillet 2000, 132–137.

Vigne, J.-D., Bailon, S. and Cuisin, J. 1997. Biostratigraphy of Amphibians, Reptiles, Birds and Mammals in Corsica and the role of man in the Holocene turnover. *Anthropozoologica* 25–26, 587–604.

Vigne, J.-D. and Desse-Berset, N. 1995. The exploitation of animal resources in Mediterranean islands during the Pre-Neolithic: the example of Corsica. In: Fisher A. (ed.) *Man and Sea in the Mesolithic*. Oxbow Monograph 53, 309–318, Oxford.

Vigne, J.-D. and Marinval-Vigne, M.-C. 1983. Méthode pour la mise en évidence de la consommation du petit gibier. In: Clutton-Brock, J. and Grigson, C. (eds) *Animals and Archaeology, 1 – Hunters and their Prey* (4th Int. Council for Archaeozoology, Londres, 1982), B.A.R. Int. Series 163, 239–242.

Vigne, J.-D., Marinval-Vigne, M.-C., Lanfranchi, F. de and Weiss, M.-C. 1981. Consommation du "Lapin-rat" (*Prolagus sardus* Wagner) au Néolithique ancien méditerranéen. Abri d'Araguina-Sennola (Bonifacio, Corse). *Bulletin de la Société préhistorique française* 78, 7, 222–224.

Vigne, J.-D., Bourdillat, V., André, J., Brochier, J.-E., Bui Thi Mai, Cuisin, J., David, H., Desse-Berset, N., Heinz, C., Lanfranchi, F. de, Ruas, M.-P., Thiébault, S. and Tozzi, C. 1998. Nouvelles données sur le Prénéolithique corse: premiers résultats de la fouille de l'abri du Monte Leone (Bonifacio, Corse-du-Sud). In: Anna, A. (d') and Binder, D. (eds) *Production et identité culturelle. Actualité de la recherche*. Rencontres méridionales de préhistoire récente, actes de la deuxième session, Arles (8–9 novembre 1996), Antibes, 251–260.

Colonisation Processes

3. Palynological visibility and the Mesolithic colonisation of the Hebrides, Scotland

Kevin J. Edwards and Heather Sugden

The Inner and Outer Hebridean island chains off Scotland's west coast are producing increasing numbers of high resolution palynological records. Those from the Inner Hebrides are interpretable in terms of anthropogenic impacts upon vegetation which are consistent with archaeological evidence of a Mesolithic. New evidence for climate change may, however, confuse the issue. Pollen and charcoal data from the Outer Hebrides reveal similar patterns, but the archipelago has produced no Mesolithic archaeological evidence. The significance of the palynological data for hunter-gatherer colonisation is considered alongside discussion of the distribution of sites which appear to show no convincing signs of human activity. These 'mute' sites may be mapping areas seldom visited or which functioned as throughways for mobile populations. In island situations they may tell us that the whole island environment was not used or manipulated, or perhaps that human and/or animal populations were small. Such arguments must be tempered by an awareness of changes in land area as a result of sea-level rise, as well as limitations in available data.

Introduction

The contribution of pollen analysis (palynology) to archaeological research in both on- and off-site contexts is undoubted (Dimbleby 1985; Whittington and Edwards 1994). The method can furnish a reconstruction of environment, it can demonstrate land use, and, where continuously accumulating deposits are present, and where appropriate high resolution approaches are deployed, it has the capability of showing near-continuous environmental and land use change over long time periods (a perspective generally unavailable to archaeology).

The applicability of palynology to the island chains of the Inner and Outer Hebrides off Scotland's west coast (Figure 3.1) is especially pertinent. The Inner Hebrides have a proven Mesolithic archaeological presence (e.g. Wickham-Jones 1990; Mithen and Lake 1996), whereas no material archaeological finds of the period have been recovered from the Outer Hebrides (Edwards 1996). This apparent difference between the two archipelagos may reflect a real situation, it may be a function of the intensity of Mesolithic-orientated survey and excavation in the two areas (the Inner Hebrides have benefited from extensive archaeological research over the last 15 years or so), or it may show the problematic survival of evidence in the Outer Hebrides where a rise in sea-level, landward movement of sand deposits, and the spread of blanket peat may hide signs of an early Holocene hunter-gatherer presence. Pollen analysis has the ability to provide evidence enabling an evaluation to take place of the status of the environment as a resource base, and to assess the impact of hunter-gatherers upon vegetation and the wider landscape.

This contribution cannot address in detail questions of, for example, fire and vegetation history, woodland management, faunal impacts or the transition to the adoption of agriculture. It is concerned with the pollen records covering the putative Mesolithic period in the Hebrides (10,000–5000 BP) and it is able to take advantage of the increasing number of high resolution palynological records available for the area. Three key questions are addressed:

1. How comparable were the resource bases of the two island groups?
2. Are there signs of vegetational disturbance which could be ascribed convincingly to human activity?
3. Conversely, do sites with no signs of obvious disturbance convey a message?

How comparable were the resource bases of the two island groups?

The islands of the Inner Hebrides are currently more wooded, have a more diverse flora and possess richer agricultural land than those of the Outer Hebrides. The Outer Hebrides are more windswept and have a more extensive peat cover. The relative lushness of the Inner Hebrides is partly caused by less exposure, although levels of precipitation are often greater than in the outer isles.

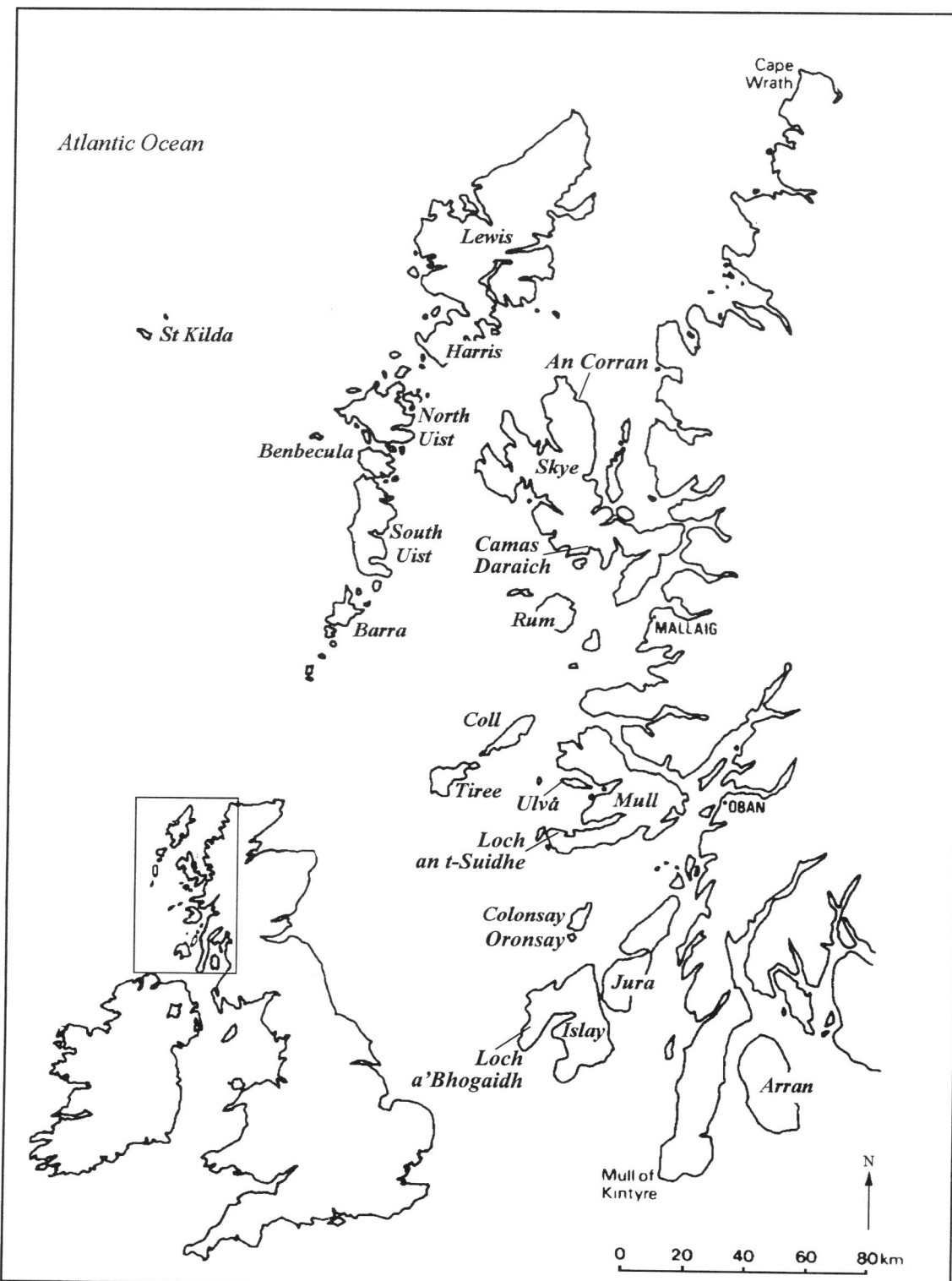

Figure 3.1 Location of the Inner and Outer Hebrides.

Each island group has mixtures of good and poor soils. It could be misleading to assume that the aforementioned provides an indication of conditions during Mesolithic times. While the postglacial climate may have been relatively harsher to the Outer Hebrides, the vegetational cover would not have been unfavourable to settlement. It is quite clear from the evidence of present and past vegetation that the Inner Hebrides possessed a good tree and shrub cover including dominant birch (*Betula*), hazel (*Corylus avellana*) and oak (*Quercus*) together with elm

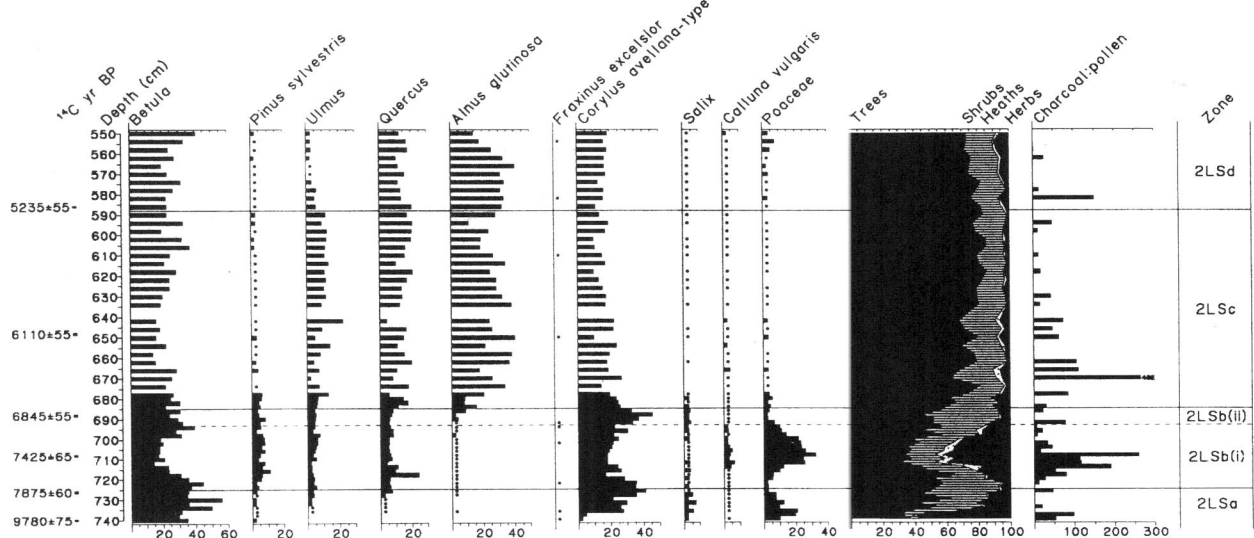

Figure 3.2 Selected pollen and spore taxa and charcoal to pollen ratios from Loch an t-Suidhe, Mull, Inner Hebrides (Sugden 1999). Taxa are expressed as percentages of total land pollen.

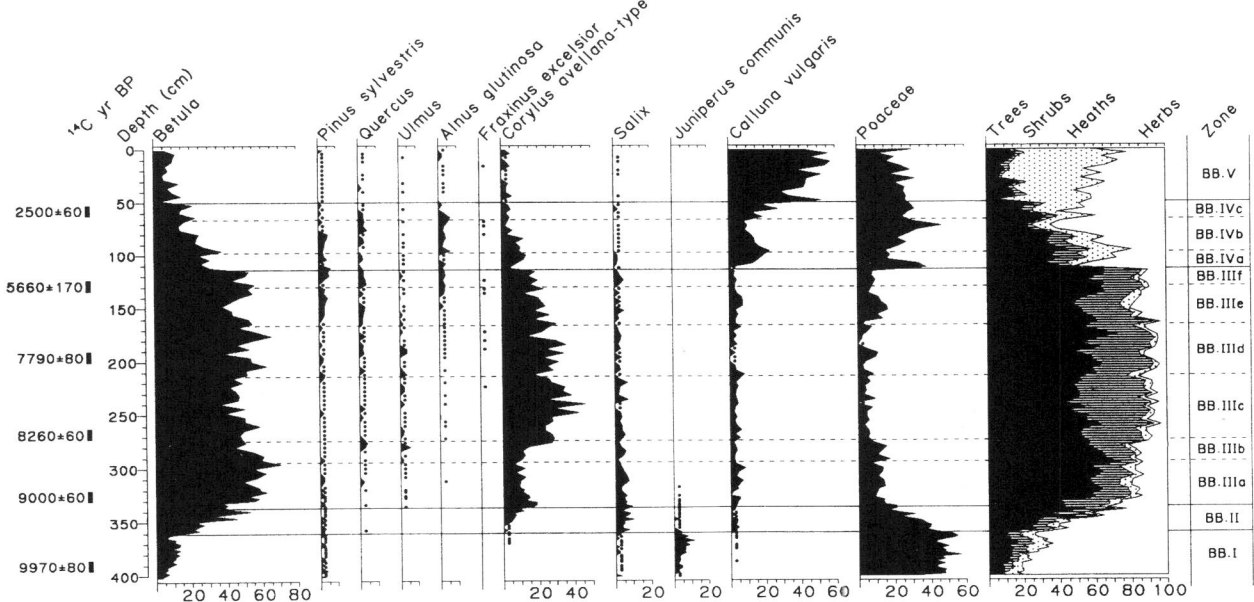

Figure 3.3 Selected pollen and spore taxa from Loch na Beinne Bige, Lewis, Outer Hebrides (Lomax 1997; Edwards et al. 2000). Taxa are expressed as percentages of total land pollen.

(*Ulmus*), Scots pine (*Pinus sylvestris*), alder (*Alnus glutinosa*), ash (*Fraxinus excelsior*), willow (*Salix*) and juniper (*Juniperus communis*) (cf. Figure 3.2). The time of appearance and representation of these taxa varied of course, and in some areas, especially close to coasts, at altitude, and in valley bottoms, peat formation was already occurring (Andrews *et al.* 1987; Edwards in press). Arboreal taxa in the Outer Hebrides certainly included birch and hazel dominants with alder and willow in damper areas (cf. Figure 3.3). Pine cover was good in at least the Isle of Lewis and while elm, oak and ash may well have been present, their pollen abundances are less than were found in Inner Hebridean fossil profiles (Edwards *et al.* 2000). A thing to note is that exposure and proximity to salt-laden winds may have led to a reduced woodland density in the Outer Hebrides compared with areas closer to the mainland (Edwards in press).

If the general aspect of the vegetational landscape was fairly similar between the Hebridean archipelagos, albeit with a lower woodland density in the Outer isles and a more extensive development of peat, what of the resource value of the flora? This may be summarised in relation to those plants listed by Price (1989) as being of economic importance during the Mesolithic in northwest Europe,

Scientific name	Common name	Product(s)
Corylus avellana	hazel	nuts
Crataegus spp.	hawthorn	leaves/fruit
Malus spp.	crab apple	fruit
*Prunus avium	wild cherry	fruit
*Quercus spp.	oak	acorns
Fragaria vesca	wild strawberry	leaves/fruit
Rosa spp.	wild rose	fruit
Rubus spp.	bramble/raspberry	fruit
Sambucus nigra	elder	fruit
Empetrum nigrum	crowberry	fruit
Vaccinium spp.	bilberry	fruit
Atriplex spp.	orache	seeds
Chenopodium spp.	goosefoot	seeds
Galeopsis tetrahit	common hemp-nettle	leaves
Persicaria bistorta	common bistort	leaves
Poaceae	grasses	seeds
Polygonum spp.	knotweed	seeds
Potentilla anserina	silverweed	roots
Rumex crispus	curled dock	leaves
Stachys palustris	woundwort	roots
Stellaria media	chickweed	leaves
Taraxacum officinale	dandelion	leaves
Urtica dioica	common nettle	leaves
Vicia spp.	vetch	seeds
**Alisma plantago-aquatica	water plantain	rhizomes
Menyanthes trifoliata	bog bean	rhizomes
Nuphar lutea	yellow water-lilly	seeds
Nymphaea alba	white water-lily	tubers/seeds
Phragmites australis	common reed	rhizomes
Typha latifolia	bulrush	rhizomes

* status uncertain in Outer Hebrides
** absent from Outer Hebrides

Figure 3.4 Plants of potential economic importance in the Mesolithic of the Hebrides

but with appropriate modification to exclude those taxa which would not have been present in western Scotland during this period (Figure 3.4). It can be seen that virtually all of the relevant plants found in the Inner isles (and in much of northwest Europe) were also to be found in the Outer Hebrides. The area was clearly not lacking in useful plants.

Good examples of exploitation of the Mesolithic landscape of the Inner Hebrides include the shell middens of Oronsay with their shell fish, fish bone and remains of red deer (Mellars 1987), the rock shelter and cave sites at An Corran, Skye (Saville and Miket 1994) and Livingstone's Cave, Ulva (Bonsall *et al.* 1991), and the pit at Staosnaig on Colonsay which contained an estimated 160,000–320,000 charred hazelnut shells (Mithen and Lake 1996; Mithen 2001). In addition there are the numerous lithic and occupation sites from Skye down to Islay (e.g. Mercer 1979; Wickham-Jones 1990; Finlayson and Edwards 1997; Mithen 2001). The possible antiquity of sites may be shown by the tanged points from a range of Inner Hebridean locations (Edwards and Mithen 1995), including most recently the two recovered from Camas Daraich, Skye (Wickham-Jones and Hardy 2000).

The resource base of the islands is also contingent upon their land area. Relative sea-level changes consequent upon eustatic (world-wide effects following global ice-sheet decay) and isostatic (rebound of crustal areas local following ice sheet decay) processes determine that the Inner Hebrides are areas of Holocene emergence and those in the Outer Hebrides are characterised by submergence (Ballantyne and Dawson 1997). Whereas the Mesolithic land area of the Inner Hebrides was smaller than today, though not greatly, that of the Outer Hebrides was larger. This would have been most apparent along the western littoral where the shallow Atlantic rock platform would have been dry land, perhaps to a distance of around 2 km. Furthermore, a rise in sea level, some 9.0 m since deglaciation (Ritchie 1985), would have drowned the low-lying landscapes between the Uists and Benbecula, as well as the shallow areas of sand on Harris and Barra, creating a series of smaller islands. The area of the Outer Hebrides may even have formed one large island that was later fragmented by rising seas during late Mesolithic times (Sissons 1967; Ritchie *et al.* in press), perhaps around 6000 BP. The currently submerged, but presumably emergent Mesolithic areas of the Outer Hebrides would have consisted largely of peat, bare rock, sand dunes, sand bars, beach ridges and lagoons (Ritchie 1979), although birch and hazel scrub at least would also have been prominent. Indeed, given that coastal exploitation was particularly favoured by Mesolithic communities in northwestern Europe (Fischer 1995; Coles 1998), the now-hidden 'coastal plain' would have constituted a fine resource for hunter-gatherer-fishermen. The sand which was a major part of the changing coastal geomorphology is not evident in submarine Admiralty charts, and is now doubtless to be found on land as part of the machair – the calcareous and silicic sand plain which fringes the western coasts of the Outer Hebrides and which in its present guise dates to around 5200 BP (Whittington and Edwards 1997; Ritchie *et al.* 2001).

It seems possible that the coastal environments of the Outer Hebrides would have represented a desirable habitat for the Mesolithic biota, including *Homo sapiens*. Whether it was sufficient to overcome the friction of distance from the mainland (about 40 km at closest, though the isle of Skye is a stepping stone only 25 km distant) is another matter. In other respects, there may have been little to choose between the two archipelagos.

Are there signs of vegetational disturbance which could be ascribed convincingly to human activity?

Given the proven existence of Mesolithic peoples in the Inner Hebrides, the existence of inferred palynological evidence for their vegetational impacts becomes pertinent as models for what may have been taking place in the Outer isles. The first Inner Hebridean site claimed to produce appropriate evidence was that of Kinloch, Rum (Hirons and Edwards 1990), close to the site of one of Scotland's earliest known occupation areas (Wickham-Jones 1990). Pollen, charcoal and sedimentological data revealed a record which spans the period *c.* 7800 BP to the present, which only partly overlaps the more restricted and upper limits of the Mesolithic archaeological record (*c.* 8590–7570 BP). The sharp changes in alder, willow and grass, and to a lesser extent in hazel are difficult to understand in simple autecological terms. While alder and willow may be seen as responding to hydrological changes at and around the raised beach site, this is less obvious for hazel and grass (unless the latter derives from *Phragmites australis* [common reed]). Pronounced and sustained changes in the charcoal curve, corresponding to changes in pollen representation, demand an explanation and this may be provided by an anthropogenic cause. The use of fire may not be instrumental in burning standing vegetation (which would be difficult in normal circumstances in hydroseral situations in the Hebrides – though cf. Mellars and Dark [1998]), but domestic burning of firewood cleared by axe might produce the patterns seen at Kinloch.

Subsequent research has produced patterns of floristic change which are compelling. Thus at the site of Loch a'Bhogaidh I, Islay, marked early Holocene fluctuations in the pollen curves for hazel, birch and grasses may result from human impact, with removal of hazel and an expansion of birch and grasses into a resultant clearing (Edwards and Berridge 1994; Edwards and Mithen 1995). Later evidence for possible woodland disturbance (*c.* 7550–7310 BP) occurs chronologically close to dates for organic materials from the Bolsay Farm and Gleann Mor excavations, beside Loch a'Bhogaidh. At Loch an t-Suidhe, Ross of Mull (Sugden 1999), there are also striking reductions in birch and hazel with expansions in grasses (Poaceae), heather (*Calluna vulgaris*) and charcoal between *c.* 7700 and 7200 BP, suggesting that reduction of woodland taxa was accompanied by an increased herbaceous cover and burning. There are no known Mesolithic artefacts from around the site, but lithics are known from the island. The small island of Ulva lies off the west coast of Mull, and a pollen diagram (Sugden 1999) from close to the Mesolithic site of Livingstone's Cave (Bonsall *et al.* 1991) portrays a similar pattern, but dating to a more prolonged 7500–5740 BP.

A complicating factor could be that climatic fluctuations (cf. Whittington *et al.* 1996; Edwards and Whittington 1997; Ammann *et al.* 2000) may have a part to play in this. Early Holocene temperature oscillations may be influencing the earliest patterns seen at Loch a'Bhogaidh, while the marked changes seen in the eighth millennium BP portions of the diagrams may correspond with the so-called '8.2 ka event' of Alley *et al.* (1997), the coldest climatic event since the Younger Dryas and lasting from 8400–8000 cal BP (ice core dates; *c.* 7650–7200 BP) and a response to probable changes in North Atlantic ocean circulation following the drainage of glacial lakes associated with the Laurentide ice sheet (Barber *et al.* 1999). This is still under investigation, but it is also possible that vegetational changes caused initially by a climatic revertence were sustained by human activities (hence the longevity of the episode reported above from the Ulva pollen site). There is no reason to believe that humans abandoned such areas and the enhanced charcoal records during these phases, if not a response to greater aridity and lightning frequency, may denote the need to burn fires to keep warm or to maintain heathland browse to attract game. The human angle may be reinforced by the finds from Staosnaig, Colonsay (Mithen and Lake 1996). Here, an estimated 160,000–320,000 charred hazel nut shells were recovered from within a large (4.8 m diameter) circular feature and produced a radiocarbon date of *c.* 7720 BP from burnt hazel nut fragments in the basal fill. This clearly argues for more than a casual gathering of nuts. In the pollen diagram from a valley mire beside Loch Cholla, almost 2 km south of Staosnaig, and for the time of collection of the hazel nuts, the profile (Andrews *et al.* 1987) displays a massive fall in cf. hazel pollen (zone Lcs, *c.* 7800–6200 BP) and expansions in the pollen of grass, sedge and heath communities. The reduction in *Corylus avellana*-type is certainly of interest, but may be a function of *in situ* peat growth or, indeed, it could embrace (though not in its entirety), the 8.2 ka event. This example serves to highlight the multiplicity of causes which could be involved in palynological investigation. It is hoped that new pollen and charcoal data from the Loch Cholla site (Edwards, Borejsza and Solomon unpublished) will provide more secure inferences.

If the Inner Hebridean sites are accepted as providing evidence which points to possible human impacts, what is the status of such studies in the 'unpeopled' Outer Hebrides (Figure 3.5)? At a coastal site close to Callanish, Lewis, Bohncke (1988) produced palynological evidence for a sustained, major decrease in birch pollen (from 72 down to 17 %), and increases in charcoal, heather, grasses, tormentil/cinquefoil (*Potentilla*-type) and bracken (*Pteridium aquilinum*) between *c.* 8400 and 4860 BP. This he inferred to be a response to burning by hunter-gatherer communities in order to assist in the clearance of woodland and the creation of browse.

A number of sites in South Uist have produced interesting records. Thus the near-coastal site of Loch an t-Sil may be displaying evidence of two woodland clearance phases, lasting around a century each at about 8040 and 7870 BP (Edwards 1996), in which birch and hazel are reduced and grasses, heather and charcoal increase. A multiple hypothesis approach to interpreting the site can be adopted including woodland removal, the intentional or incidental spread of heathland as a management tool, and either domestic burning or muirburn. The estuarine site of North Locheynort has a sustained charcoal peak from 7280–4460 BP associated with reductions in trees and shrubs (Edwards 1990). The nearby site of Loch Lang also has decreases in arboreal taxa and a rise in the charcoal curve from *c.* 9000 BP for which a Mesolithic camp-fire explanation has been advance (Bennett *et al.* 1990). High charcoal values accompanied by reductions in tree and shrub taxa are also evident at the upland site of Reineval, especially around 6500–6000 BP (Edwards *et al.* 1995). The east coast South Uist site of Loch Hellisdale has a fall in hazel with concomitant rises in birch and grasses, but not in charcoal (Brayshay and Edwards 1996). Could this be indicating human impact without burning, an autogenic change, or a climatic effect?

Two inter-tidal peat sites from the Outer Hebrides are especially interesting. At Peninerine, South Uist, the high *Calluna* pollen values are associated with high charcoal representation (Edwards *et al.* 1995). If *in situ* burning was involved, it may not have been responsible for the rise in heather, but it could have assisted in the maintenance of heathland from *c.* 7700 BP onwards. At Borve, an inter-tidal peat site on the west coast of Benbecula, there are rises in charcoal between (7680 and 7100 cal BP 1-sigma) decreases in hazel and birch woodland and a rise in the sand content of the deposits (Whittington and Edwards 1997). It is possible that human activity may have accelerated the spread of sand at this site as well as elsewhere (e.g. Kallin, Grimsay).

Whatever the proximal causes of the changes seen in the pollen records, it is clear that the patterns evident in the Inner Hebrides and ascribable *inter alia* to anthropogenic impact, are also replicated in the Outer isles. Nine of the 21 sites under consideration from the Outer Hebrides have produced possible records of impact (Figure 3.5). Six of the sites are in South Uist, with single instances being found in the islands of Benbecula, Grimsay and Lewis. Five sites are in current coastal or near-coastal situations, one is estuarine with another close by, and two are in easily accessible inland locations. In the absence of a denser network of sites, it is almost certainly too soon to make more of this distribution, but the possible coastal emphasis is no great surprise.

Do sites with no obvious signs of disturbance convey a message?

Superficially, it would seem that pollen sites which do not display patterns of potential human disturbance are telling us that the relevant pollen catchment areas did not witness vegetational interference. This would have clear implications regarding settlement (*vide infra*), but to what extent should this negative evidence be taken at face value? The pollen data can only reflect the pollen received from the pollen catchment area at the time when the pollen was being deposited – this will typically be from a wider area in the case of lakes (which will often be in receipt of palynomorphs from incoming streams) than in peat deposits (Birks and Birks 1980). While the microfossil record in peat may contain a more local and sensitive signal, the deposit may be dominated by vegetation growing on the bog surface whose pollen and spores may numerically obscure records of interference taking place within the catchment area. Pollen counts which are low (e.g. less than 300–500 grains) may not reveal minor vegetational disturbances. Perhaps most important of all, the pollen sample resolution exerts a powerful limitation on inference. A single sample may typically represent anything from say 10–100 years of pollen deposition, enough to hide short-term hunter-gatherer activity, and a sample taken say every 5–10 cm up a core could thus represent an interval of between 50 and 1000 years. The solution is to adopt a high resolution strategy by closing-up on sampling intervals and preferably to sample contiguous levels, excluding unsampled sections of core (cf. Turner and Peglar 1988; Edwards and McIntosh 1988; Edwards 1996) and to employ multiple-coring approaches in order to optimise the detection of human impacts (Edwards 1982, 1983; Sugden and Edwards 2001).

With the above provisos in mind, what does the pattern of 'mute' sites tell us? They may not disclose episodes of

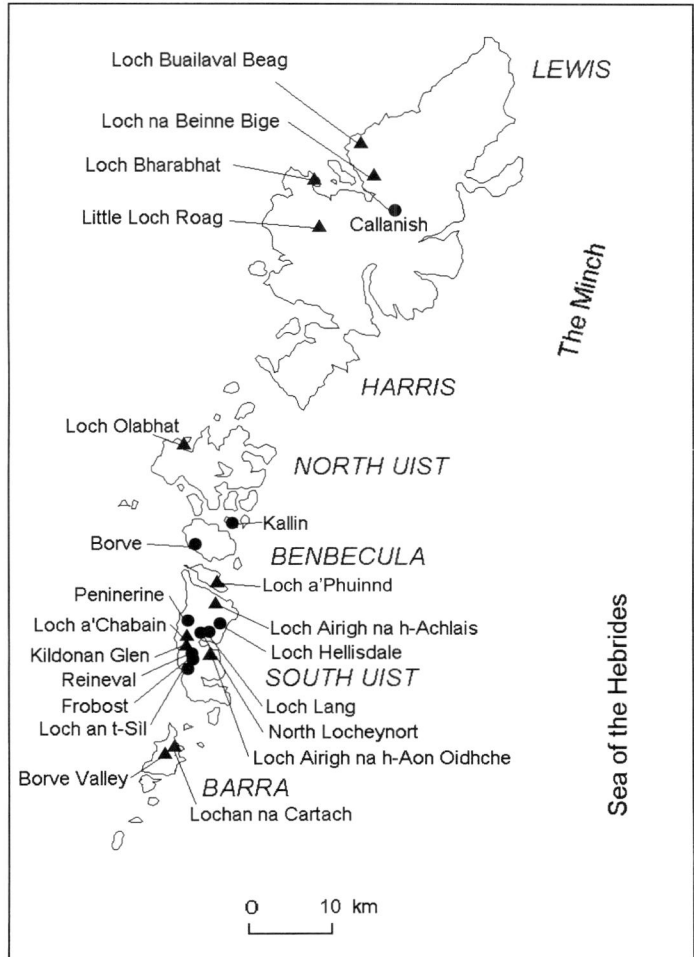

Figure 3.5 Pollen sites from the Outer Hebrides containing possible signs of human impact (circles) or no evidence of human impact (triangles).

impact, but they provide information on the potential resource base of an area (Edwards 2000). An area with diverse woodland provides varied woodland resources in terms of timber and foodstuffs; grassland and heathland may attract browsing animals; low density shrubland may provide cover for hunters as may coastal reedswamp. If the testimony of absence of impact is accepted, then the distribution of sites which appear to show no convincing signs of activity could be very informative in indicating areas seldom visited or which functioned as throughways for mobile populations of people and animals. For the Hebrides, they may be showing that the whole-island environment was not used or manipulated, or perhaps that human or animal populations were small. As we have seen, rising sea levels will have reduced the land area to the west of the Outer Hebrides especially, and it would be necessary to be aware of this before estimating resource availability and population sizes.

Many sites in the Outer Hebrides do not display inferred human impact and many of these are not high resolution sites. There are sufficient, however, to indicate whether inferred phases of longstanding impact had been occurring (Figure 3.5). Amongst these, nothing is claimed for the Mesolithic age levels at sites such as Little Loch Roag (Birks and Madsen 1979), Loch Buailaval Beag (Fossitt 1996), Loch na Beinne Bige and Loch Bharabhat (Lomax 1997; Edwards et al. 2000) in Lewis, Loch Olabhat (Mulder 1999; Edwards et al. 2000) in North Uist, Loch a'Phuinnd, South Uist (Fossitt 1996), Loch a'Chabhain, Frobost, Loch Airigh na h-Achlais and Loch Airigh na h-Aon Oidhche (Mulder 1999; Edwards et al. 2000) also South Uist, and the Barra sites of Borve Valley (Ashmore et al. 2000) and Lochan na Cartach (Brayshay and Edwards 1996).

Twelve of the 21 sites under consideration here have produced no convincing 'impact' (Figure 3.5). These sites are frequently in locations which are well inland and/or would be considered less accessible today. Given the relative small size of the southern islands, however, it cannot be said that any sites are difficult to reach. Some of the sites might still be thought to be in less convenient locations although they are not distant from current coastlines. Loch Bharabhat, for example, is at the head of a narrow, steep ravine; Little Loch Roag is currently 6 km from the open sea and above a steep valley side; Loch Airigh na h-Aon Oidhche occupies an isolated basin surrounded by steep sided rocky slopes; while Borve (Barra) is at the head of a valley. This does not preclude the possibility that the vicinities of such sites provided tree or shrub cover or food resources for passing populations of people and animals.

The situation in the Inner Hebrides is arguably less propitious for an initial appraisal given the fewer high resolution diagrams (though see Sugden 1999) and such an exercise has not therefore been attempted.

Conclusions

If we are to be confident about detecting palynological signs of Mesolithic colonisation in the Hebrides, then we obviously require a greater density of sites and these must be high resolution in nature. Until a material archaeological presence of the Outer Hebridean Mesolithic is available, the significance of the palynological data is clear. Confidence in such records is high, even if we can't always be precise in our interpretations. The major perturbations in past vegetational communities clearly mean something. The recent evidence for climate oscillations – especially the 8.2 ka event, based on ice core and geomorphological findings – are urgently in need of independent testing at pollen sites and insect data derived from Coleoptera (beetles) or Chironomidae (non-biting midges) could achieve this.

There is a dearth of high resolution studies from the Inner Hebrides, an area with a proven Mesolithic and one which is capable of furnishing model patterns in the behaviour of pollen spectra which could be compared with those from the Outer Hebrides. In these respects, the islands of Skye, Mull and Jura would repay further study. The recent discoveries of tanged points at Camas Daraich, Skye (Wickham-Jones and Hardy 2000) reinforce this need.

The submergence of the Atlantic coastal shelf of the Outer Hebrides has inundated possible intact areas of peat (cf. Ritchie 1979; Ritchie 1985). Given the apparent palynological sensitivity of the coastal sites, these may hold the greatest potential for recovering a palaeoecological record of Mesolithic impacts. The currently available sites provide hints of what the submarine records may have to offer.

The Hebrides are of special interest in that they act currently as a 'frontier' between the known and the unproven Mesolithic. A similar situation once applied to the mainland and Orkney – yet Orkney now has a proven Mesolithic (cf. Saville 1996) which is complemented by the Mesolithic inferred from its palynological record (Edwards 1996). The comparable palynological record for Shetland has yet to receive an archaeological counterpart. The reality of a cultural fault-line between the Inner and the Outer Hebrides, as for the Northern Isles, is surely more apparent than real?

Acknowledgements

Financial support for fieldwork came from the Natural Environment Research Council (NERC) and the Leverhulme Trust. Radiocarbon dates for Loch na Beinne Bige and Loch an t-Suidhe were obtained, respectively, from the University of Glasgow laboratory at East Kilbride under the supervision of Gordon Cook with finance from Historic Scotland and at the NERC laboratory at East Kilbride under the supervision of Charlotte Bryant with finance from NERC. All are gratefully acknowledged.

References

Alley, R.B., Mayewski, P.A., Sowers, T., Stuiver, M., Taylor, K.C. and Clark, P.U. 1997. Holocene climatic instability: a prominent, widespread event 8200 yr ago. *Geology* 25, 483–486.

Ammann, B., Birks, H.J.B., Brooks, S., Eicher, U., von Grafenstein, U., Hofmann, W., Lemdahl, G., Schwander, J., Tobolski, K. and Wick, L. 2000. Quantification of biotic responses to rapid climatic changes around the Younger Dryas – a synthesis. *Palaeogeography, Palaeoclimatology, Palaeoecology* 159, 313–349.

Andrews, M.V., Beck, R.B., Birks, H.J.B., Gilbertson, D.D. and Switsur, V.R. 1987. The past and present vegetation of Oronsay and Colonsay. In: Mellars, P. (ed.) *Excavations on Oronsay, prehistoric human ecology on a small island*, 52–77. Edinburgh.

Ashmore, P., Brayshay, B.A., Edwards, K.J., Gilbertson, D.D., Grattan, J.P., Kent, M., Pratt, K.E. and Weaver, R.E. 2000. Allochthonous and autochthonous mire deposits, slope instability and palaeoenvironmental investigations in the Borve Valley, Barra, Outer Hebrides, Scotland. *The Holocene* 10, 97–108.

Ballantyne, C.K. and Dawson, A.G. 1997. Geomorphology and landscape change. In: Edwards, K.J. and Ralston, I.B.M (eds) *Scotland: environment and archaeology, 8000 BC–AD 1000*. 23–44. Chichester.

Barber, D.C., Dyke, A., Hillaire-Marcel, C., Jennings, A.E., Andrews, J.T., Kerwin, M.W., Bilodeau, G., McNeely, R., Southon, J., Morehead, M.D. and Gagnon, J.-M. 1999. Forcing of the cold event of 8,200 years ago by catastrophic drainage of Laurentide lakes. *Nature* 400, 344–348.

Bennett, K.D., Fossitt, J.A., Sharp, M.J. and Switsur, V.R. 1990. Holocene vegetational and environmental history at Loch Lang, South Uist, Scotland. *New Phytologist* 114, 281–298.

Birks, H.J.B. and Birks, H.H. 1980. *Quaternary palaeoecology*. London.

Birks, H.J.B. and Madsen, B.J. 1979. Flandrian vegetational history of Little Loch Roag, Isle of Lewis, Scotland. *Journal of Ecology* 67, 825–842.

Bohncke, S.J.P. 1988. Vegetation and habitation history of the Callanish area. In: Birks, H.H., Birks, H.J.B., Kaland, P.E. and Moe, D. (eds) *The cultural landscape – past, present and future*, 445–461. Cambridge.

Bonsall, C., Sutherland, D.G., Lawson, T.J., Russell, N. and Coles, G. 1991. *Ulva Cave excavation report No. 3*. Department of Archaeology, University of Edinburgh.

Brayshay, B.A. and Edwards, K.J. 1996. Lateglacial and Holocene vegetational history of South Uist and Barra. In: Gilbertson, D.D., Kent, M. and Grattan, J.P. (eds) *The Outer Hebrides: the last 14,000 years*, 13–26. Sheffield.

Coles, B.J. 1998. Doggerland: a speculative survey. *Proceedings of the Prehistoric Society* 64, 45–81.

Dimbleby, G.W. 1985. *The palynology of archaeological sites.* London.

Edwards, K.J. 1982. Man, space and the woodland edge: speculations on the detection and interpretation of human impact in pollen profiles. In: Bell, M. and Limbrey, S. (eds) *Archaeological aspects of woodland ecology*, 5–22. British Archaeological Reports, International Series 146, Oxford.

—— 1983. Quaternary palynology: multiple profile studies and pollen variability. *Progress in Physical Geography* 7, 587–609.

—— 1990. Fire and the Scottish Mesolithic: evidence from microscopic charcoal. In: Vermeersch, P.M. and Van Peer, P. (eds) *Contributions to the Mesolithic in Europe*, 71–79. Leuven.

—— 1996. A Mesolithic of the Western and Northern Isles of Scotland? Evidence from pollen and charcoal. In: Pollard, T. and Morrison, A. (eds) *The early prehistory of Scotland*, 23–38. Edinburgh.

—— 2000. Pollen, archaeology, and burdens of proof. In: Young, R. (ed.) *Mesolithic lifeways: current research from Britain and Ireland*, 67–74. Leicester Archaeology Monographs 7, University of Leicester.

—— in press. Palaeoenvironments of Late Upper Palaeolithic and Mesolithic Scotland and the North Sea area: new work, new thoughts. In: Saville, A. (ed.) *Mesolithic Scotland: the early Holocene prehistory of Scotland and its European context.* Society of Antiquaries of Scotland Monograph Series, Edinburgh.

Edwards, K.J. and Berridge, J.M.A. 1994. The Late-Quaternary vegetational history of Loch a'Bhogaidh, Rinns of Islay S.S.S.I., Scotland. *New Phytologist* 128, 749–769.

Edwards, K.J. and McIntosh, C.J. 1988. Improving the detection rate of cereal-type pollen grains from *Ulmus* decline and earlier deposits from Scotland. *Pollen et Spores* 30, 179–188.

Edwards, K.J. and Mithen, S. 1995. The colonisation of the Hebridean islands of western Scotland: evidence from the palynological and archaeological records. *World Archaeology* 26, 348–365.

Edwards, K.J. and Whittington, G. 1997. A 12 000-year record of environmental change in the Lomond Hills, Fife, Scotland: vegetational and climatic variability. *Vegetation History and Archaeobotany* 6, 133–152.

Edwards, K.J., Whittington, G. and Hirons, K.R. 1995. The relationship between fire and long-term wet heath development in South Uist, Outer Hebrides, Scotland. In: Thompson, D.B.A., Hestor, A.J. and Usher, M.B. (eds) *Heaths and moorland: cultural landscapes*, 240–248. H.M.S.O., Edinburgh.

Edwards, K.J., Mulder, Y., Lomax, T.A., Whittington, G. and Hirons, K.R. 2000. Human-environment interactions in prehistoric landscapes: the example of the Outer Hebrides. In: Hooke, D. (ed.) *Landscape, the richest historical record*, 13–32. Society for Landscape Studies Supplementary Series 1.

Finlayson, B. and Edwards, K.J. 1997. The Mesolithic. In: Edwards, K.J. and Ralston, I.B.M. (eds) *Scotland: environment and archaeology, 8000 BC–AD 1000*, 109–125. Chichester.

Fischer, A. (ed.) 1995. *Man and sea in the Mesolithic: coastal settlement above and below present sea level.* Oxford.

Fossitt, J.A. 1996. Late Quaternary vegetation history of the Western Isles of Scotland. *New Phytologist* 132, 171–196.

Hirons, K.R. and Edwards, K.J. 1990. Pollen and related studies at Kinloch, Isle of Rhum, Scotland, with particular reference to possible early human impacts on vegetation. *New Phytologist* 116, 715–727.

Lomax, T.M. 1997. *Holocene vegetation history and human impact in western Lewis, Scotland.* Unpublished PhD thesis, University of Birmingham.

Mellars, P.A. 1987. *Excavations on Oronsay: prehistoric human ecology on a small island.* Edinburgh.

Mellars, P. and Dark, P. 1998. *Star Carr in context: new archaeological and palaeoecological investigations at the early mesolithic site of Star Carr, North Yorkshire.* McDonald Institute Monographs Cambridge.

Mercer, J. 1979. The Palaeolithic and Mesolithic occupation of the Isle of Jura, Argyll, Scotland. *Almogaren* 9–10, 347–367.

Mithen, S.J. (ed.) 2001. *Hunter-gatherer landscape archaeology: the Southern Hebrides Mesolithic Project, 1988–1998.* Volumes 1 and 2. McDonald Institute Monographs, Cambridge.

Mithen, S. and Lake, M. 1996. The Southern Hebrides Mesolithic Project: reconstructing Mesolithic settlement in western Scotland. In: Pollard, T. and Morrison, A. (eds) *The early prehistory of Scotland*, 123–151. Edinburgh.

Mulder, Y. 1999. *Aspects of vegetation and settlement history in the Outer Hebrides, Scotland.* Unpublished PhD thesis, University of Sheffield.

Price, T.D. 1989. The reconstruction of Mesolithic diets. In: Bonsall, C. (ed.) *The Mesolithic in Europe*, 48–59. Edinburgh.

Ritchie, W. 1979. Machair chronology and development in the Uists. *Proceedings of the Royal Society of Edinburgh* 77B, 107–122.

—— 1985. Inter-tidal and sub-tidal organic deposits and sea level changes in the Uists, Outer Hebrides. *Scottish Journal of Geology* 21, 161–176.

Ritchie, W., Whittington, G. and Edwards, K.J. 2001. Holocene changes in the physiography and vegetation of the Atlantic littoral of the Uists, Outer Hebrides, Scotland. *Transactions of the Royal Society of Edinburgh: Earth Sciences* 92, 121–136.

Saville, A. 1996. Lacaille, microliths and the Mesolithic of Orkney. In: Pollard, T. and Morrison, A. (eds) *The early prehistory of Scotland*. 213–224. Edinburgh.

Saville, A. and Miket, R. 1994. An Corran, Staffin, Skye. *Discovery and Excavation in Scotland*, 40–41.

Sissons, J.B. 1967. *The evolution of Scotland's scenery.* Edinburgh.

Sugden, H. 1999. *High resolution palynological, multiple profile and radiocarbon dating studies of early human impacts and environmental change in the Inner Hebrides, Scotland.* Unpublished PhD thesis, University of Sheffield.

Sugden, H. and Edwards, K.J. 2001. The early Holocene vegetational history of Loch a'Bhogaidh, southern Rinns, Islay, with special reference to hazel (*Corylus avellana* L.). In: Mithen, S. (ed.) *Hunter-gatherer landscape archaeology: the Southern Hebrides Mesolithic Project, 1988–1998.* Volume 1, 129–135. McDonald Institute Monographs, Cambridge.

Turner, J. and Peglar, S.M. 1988. Temporally-precise studies of vegetation history. In: Huntley, B. and Webb, T., III. (eds) *Vegetation history*, 753–777. Dordrecht.

Whittington, G. and Edwards, K.J. 1994. Palynology as a predictive tool in archaeology. *Proceedings of the Society of Antiquaries of Scotland* 124, 55–65.

—— 1997. Evolution of a machair landscape: pollen and related studies from Benbecula, Outer Hebrides, Scotland. *Transactions of the Royal Society of Edinburgh: Earth Sciences* 87, 515–531.

Whittington, G., Fallick, A.F. and Edwards, K.J. 1996. Stable isotope and pollen records from eastern Scotland and a consideration of Late-glacial and early Holocene climate change for Europe. *Journal of Quaternary Science* 11, 327–340.

Wickham-Jones, C.R. 1990. *Rhum: Mesolithic and later sites at Kinloch, excavations 1984–1986.* Society of Antiquaries of Scotland Monograph Series No. 7, Edinburgh.

Wickham-Jones, C.R. and Hardy, K. 2000. *Camas Daraich 2000. Data structure report.* Centre for Field Archaeology, University of Edinburgh, Edinburgh.

4. Colonisation of the west Estonian archipelago

Aivar Kriiska

The inhabitation of the Baltic islands is closely connected to changes in the Baltic Sea itself. The higher points of the Estonian islands emerged from the water in about 9600 cal BC when the Baltic Ice Lake joined the ocean and the level of the lake subsided nearly 25 m in the Baltic basin. In spite of the unstable water level that has at times caused massive floods, the general trend has been towards an increase in island acreage. Another influence on the rise of early island settlement was seal hunting as a rapidly developing subsistence strategy. The exploitation of marine products was a matter of course for island livelihood. In the Late Mesolithic, about 6500 to 5000 cal BC, the transition to specialised seal hunting took place. From that time on seal meat became an important part of the local diet. It was probably on these sealing trips that the hunting groups discovered the west Estonian islands that were dozens of miles from the Estonian mainland. Radiocarbon dates provide evidence for the earliest habitation of Saaremaa in about 5800 cal BC, on Hiiumaa in 5700 cal BC, and in Ruhnu in 5300 cal BC. Archaeological finds and the geographical situation indicate that the initial home for the colonisers of the islands was the coastal region of west Estonia. The bone assemblages from the oldest campsites of Saaremaa and Hiiumaa contain mostly seal bones. The hunters presumably stayed in these camps in early spring, which is the best seal-hunting season, but it is possible that permanent island settlements date from the end of the Mesolithic period, and the earliest of these were probably located in the middle and northern parts of Saaremaa.

Introduction

The investigation of the early settlement of the west Estonian islands began in the second half of the 19th century with the collection and identification of stray finds (e.g. Grewingk 1871). This has, however, been sporadic and limited activity until recent years. The course of the investigations has been determined by chance rather than by scientific interest. The first archaeological excavations of a Stone Age site only took place in 1943 when Richard Indreko excavated the Late Neolithic settlement site at Undva, north-western Saaremaa (Ösel) (The border between the Mesolithic and the Neolithic in Estonia begins with the introduction of pottery) (Indreko 1964:127 pp). Since then separate fieldwork has continually been carried out at brief intervals, but until the beginning of the 1980's these were confined to Saaremaa. Five monuments were excavated: the Neolithic sites of Loona in 1956–1957, Naakamäe in 1961–1962 (Jaanits 1965:28 pp), Kuninguste in 1971 (V. Lõugas 1974), Paju in 1975–1976 (Tamla and Jaanits 1977:69 p) and Kõnnu from 1976–1986 (Jaanits 1979). A few Stone Age finds were discovered while excavating in 1987–1988 and in 1996 the iron-smelting centre in Tuiu that dates from the end of the Iron Age and Middle Ages was discovered (Peets 1988:386). A Neolithic settlement phase was also identified in the 1938 find material from the fortified settlement of Asva (V. Lõugas 1970:343). The first Mesolithic site on the island, the Võhma I settlement on north-western Saaremaa, was discovered in 1986 (Pesti and Rikas 1991).

Since 1994 the author of the present article has been engaged in systematic research aimed at determining the time of the colonisation of the islands, the origin of the settlers and the correspondence of Stone Age development on the islands to corresponding processes on the mainland. The main region of investigation has been Hiiumaa, where in the course of the research 14 new Stone Age settlement sites have been discovered on Kõpu peninsula, representing all known phases and cultures of the Estonian Stone Age. Archaeological excavations have been carried out on five of the sites (partly published in Kriiska 1995; 1996b; Kriiska and Lõugas 1999). Several new Stone Age sites have also been discovered on Saaremaa (Kriiska 1998) and on Ruhnu (Runö) (Kriiska and Saluäär 2000). Though the excavations there have been carried out on one and two sites respectively, the presumably oldest settlement traces on either island have been investigated. These works, together with earlier information mainly concerning the Late Neolithic, enable us to begin dating the settlement processes of the islands and reconstruct their development and background.

Site	¹⁴C-year (BP)	Calibrated date 2 sigma (cal BC)	Calibrated date 1 sigma (cal BC)	Lab.-no.	Sample material	Archaeological culture
Võhma I	6950±100	6010–5640	5970–5720	Ta-2659	charcoal	Kunda
Võhma I	6750±50	5730–5560	5715–5620	Ta-2646	charcoal	Kunda
Võhma I	6330±100	5480–5040	5470–5140	Ta-2649	charcoal	Kunda
Võhma I	6245±200	5650–4700	5500–4900	Ta-2652	charcoal	Kunda
Kõpu IV	6757±50	5730–5560	5715–5625	Tln-2016	charcoal	Kunda
Kõpu IV	6640±60	5670–5470	5620–5490	Ta-2533	charcoal	Kunda
Ruhnu II	6400±170	5700–4850	5530–5080	Le-5629	charcoal	Kunda
Ruhnu II	6150±60	5290–4850	5230–4990	Le-5627	charcoal	Kunda
Pahapilli I	6370±180	5650–4850	5510–5070	Le-5452	charcoal	Kunda
Kõpu VIII	6172±51	5290–4950	5260–5040	Tln-2024	hazelnut shells	Kunda
Kõpu I	5698±70	4710–4360	4670–4450	Tln-1901	charcoal	Narva
Kõpu I	5604±52	4540–4340	4490–4360	Tln-1873	charcoal	Narva
Kõpu I	5575±50	4520–4330	4455–4355	Le-5452	charcoal	Narva
Kõpu I	5464±96	4500–4040	4450–4160	Tln-1898	charcoal	Narva
Kõpu I	5460±100	4500–4040	4450–4110	Ta-2686	charcoal	Narva
Kõpu I	5370±68	4340–4040	4330–4050	Tln-1871	charcoal	Narva
Kõpu I	5330±90	4340–3980	4320–4040	Ta-493	charcoal	Narva
Ruhnu II	5400±150	4550–3800	4360–4040	Le-5628	charcoal	Narva
Ruhnu II	5400±100	4450–3980	4340–4050	Ta-2716	charcoal	Narva
Loona	4270±75	3100–2600	3020–2700	Ua-4824	bone	Late Combed Ware
Loona	4050±80	2900–2350	2860–2460	Ua-4825	bone	Late Combed Ware
Naakamäe	4125±85	2890–2470	2870–2580	Ua-4822	bone	Late Combed Ware

Figure 4.1 Table of radiocarbon dates from Stone Age sites on the islands.

Early settlements on the west Estonian islands

Presently, 35 Stone Age settlement sites are known on the west Estonian islands. Twentyfive of these belong to the Late Mesolithic or Early Neolithic. Since both Late Mesolithic and Early Neolithic materials are important from the point of view of the origin of the habitation of the islands (and are also very similar, the only difference being the occurrence or absence of pottery), I will briefly below discuss the sites and finds from both periods. Nineteen reliable ¹⁴C analyses have been performed on charcoal excavated from the fire-pits of various early settlements on the islands, dating the Late Mesolithic sites to an average age of 5800–5000 cal. BC (the basis for the calibration is CAL40.DTA OxCal v2. 18 cub r:4 sd:12 prob[chron]), and the Early Neolithic settlements to 4500–4200 cal. BC (Figure 4.1). In the light of the earliest date of the Narva Culture on the mainland (Kriiska 1996a:416), traces of settlement from the very beginning of the Early Neolithic have not yet been discovered on the islands.

A common feature on the islands is the location of early settlements along the coastal zone or its immediate vicinity. On Saaremaa, the largest island of the region under discussion, monuments have unfortunately only been sought systematically in the north-western part of the island. The Late Mesolithic settlements known there are located on the shores of larger or smaller ancient bays or coves, and often on the promontories that extended into them (Figure 4.2). The peninsula of Kõpu on the islet of Hiiumaa, which is only about 5 km across, emerged from the sea at the beginning of the Litorina Sea. In the southern part of the island there was a lagoon with a diameter of about 1 km. All the early settlements are located on the open shore of the south-east part of the ancient island, but a couple of these are also found near the lagoon (Figure 4.3). At that time Ruhnu was smaller, rising above water as a horseshoe shaped island of about 3–4 km². A narrow strip of land 50–500 m wide surrounded the 2.5 km wide lagoon which itself was divided in two by a narrow 1 km long spit. The settlement sites are located on the shore of the ancient lagoon (Figure 4.4). The most extensive cultural layer lies at the end of the fossil spit.

The size and thickness of the cultural layers of the settlement sites on the islands varies, containing different activity areas from different periods. In one of the most extensive of these, the Kõpu I settlement, the period of exploitation has been 300 years, according to the average of the ¹⁴C dates. Relying upon the fact that the difference in the altitudes of the upper and lower ends of the settlement is 3 m, and only the upper part has been investigated, the period of exploitation must have been longer still, but interrupted. The Ruhnu II settlement, where the land rose at a considerably slower rate, contains both Late Mesolithic and Early Neolithic strata, the difference in the ¹⁴C dates is as much as 1100 years. The density of finds also varies, from 18–797 finds per m² in

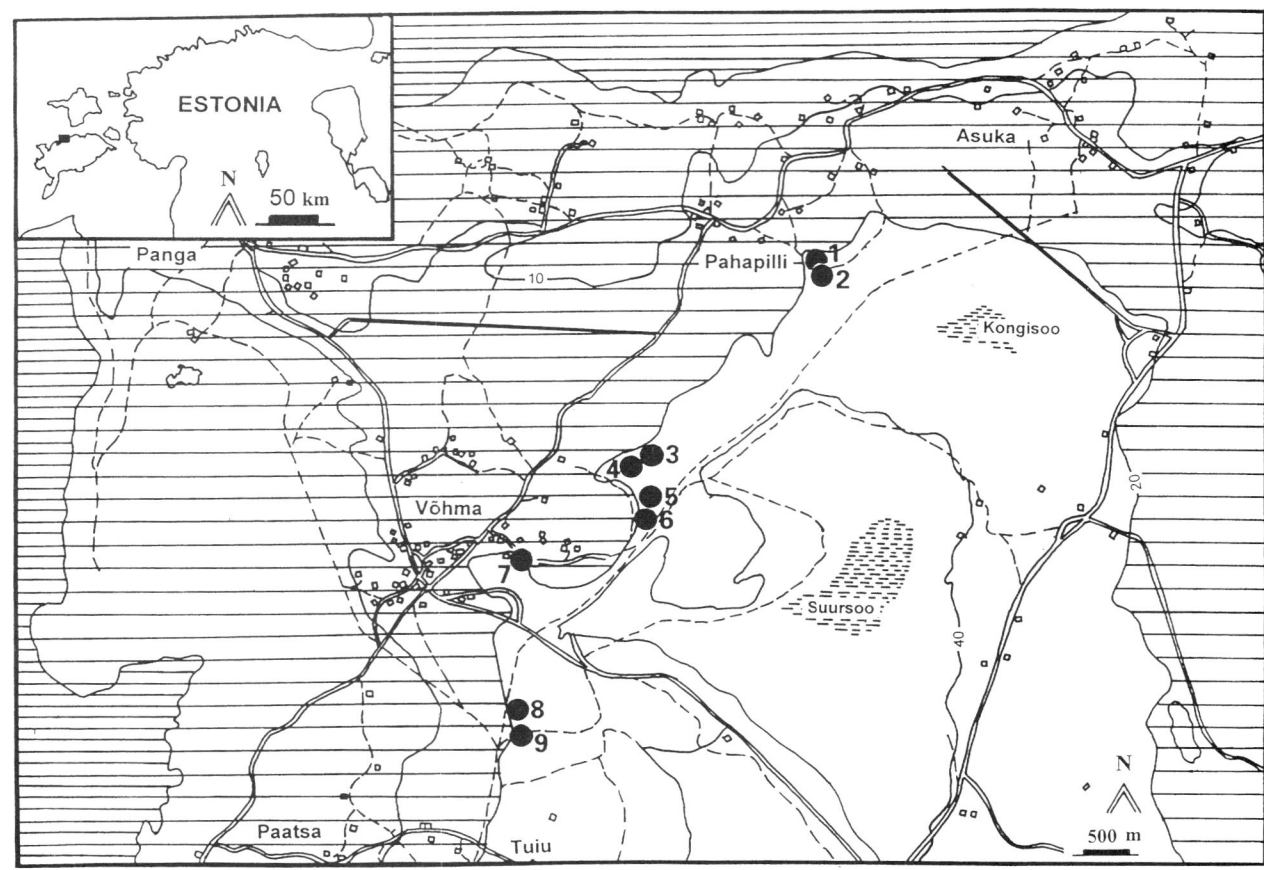

Figure 4.2 Mesolithic sites in north-western Saaremaa: 1 – Pahapilli II, 2 – Pahapilli I, 3 – Võhma VI, 4 – Võhma VII, 5 – Võhma IV, 6 – Võhma V, 7 – Võhma I, 8 – Võhma II, 9 – Võhma III. The heavily shaded area marks the presumable coastline of the Late Mesolithic and the lightly shaded area the present sea.

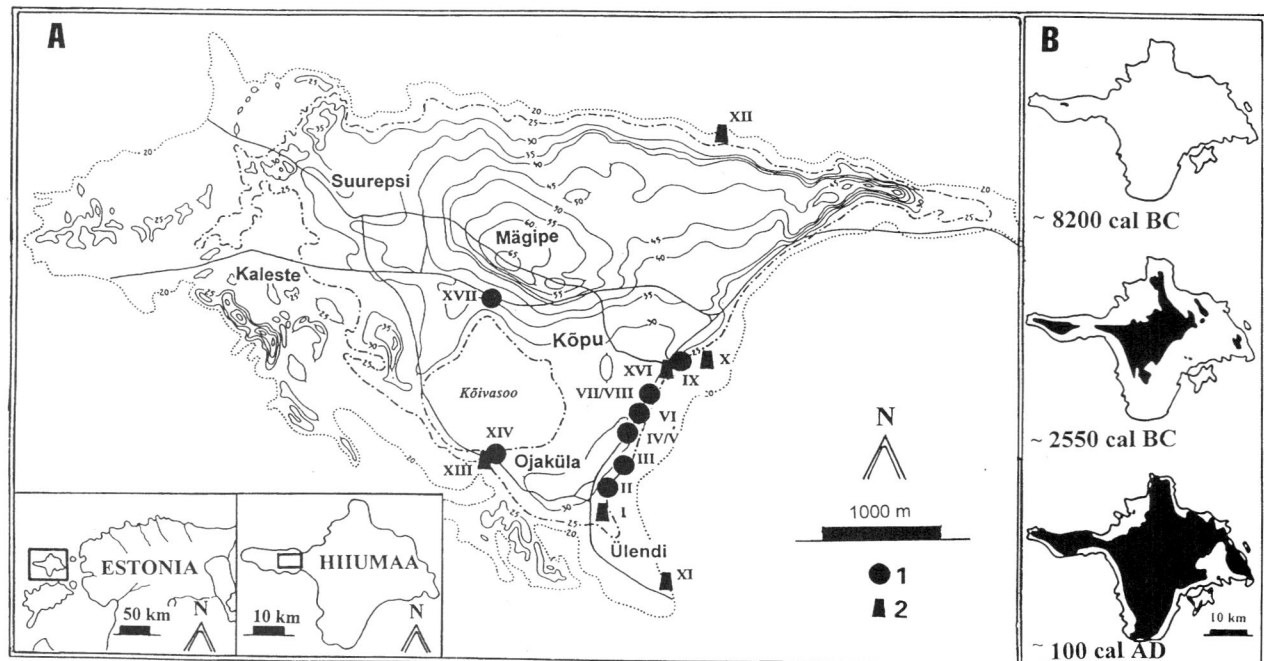

Figure 4.3 The ancient island of Kõpu, as reflected in the contour lines at present altitudes of 25–20 m and the known Mesolithic (1) and Neolithic (2) sites. B. Evolution of the island Hiiumaa during the Holocene (by Raukas and Ratas 1996).

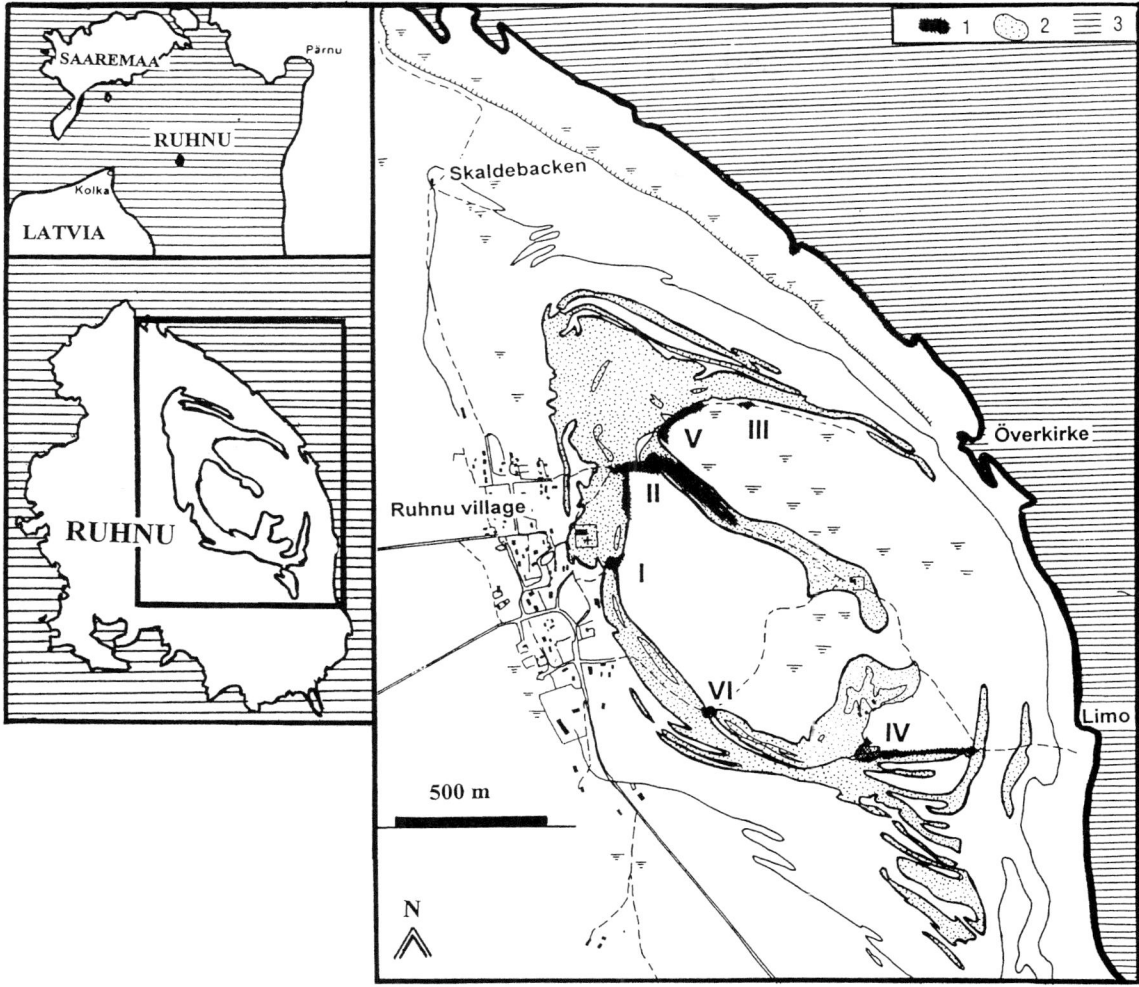

Figure 4.4 Stone Age sites on Ruhnu island. 1 – Stone Age sites, 2 – island (12,5 m a.s.l.) at the beginning of the Litorina Sea.

the settlements investigated by the author, using the same excavation methods.

The only distinguishable features are fire-pits. As a rule these are round or oval, lined with tightly packed stones. The average diameter is 1±0.5m. An exceptionally large fire-pit with a diameter of 5 m was excavated in the Kõpu IV/V settlement. While the smaller hearths could have been located in dwellings, it could hardly be so with the large one. Presumably it served some special purpose, perhaps it was used to melt seal grease.

Organic matter is not preserved in sandy soil. Only a small number of animal bones, mostly calcined in fire, and some nutshells, have been found. The quantity of nutshells in the Kõpu VII/VIII settlement site was exceptional – more than 2000 fragments of nutshells were found in 10 m^2.

Finds

On the islands tools made from quartz dominates over flint together with a small number of other rocks. The amount of quartz in the assemblages consisting of both quartz and flint (with some quartzite) is 41–98 % in the settlements investigated by the author (Figure 4.5). The local flint used is of poor quality, greyish or beige, most likely from the Silur limestone. It occurs in Holocene sediments on all three islands. A unique feature on the islands was the use of Baltic red quartz-porphyry when making small tools. Apart from the islands, the distribution area of this rock covers only a strip of mainland in west Estonia. In the early phase the distribution of Baltic red quartz-porphyry is quite limited, but it occurs in the finds from Saaremaa and Hiiumaa and also in those from Ruhnu.

Both blade and flake techniques have been used, the latter clearly prevailing. The number of blades is small, only 0.8–6.9 % of the stone finds from the investigated settlement sites. Apparently hard percussion was used for primary processing. As can be seen from structure faults at the ends of cores and blades and the specific thinning

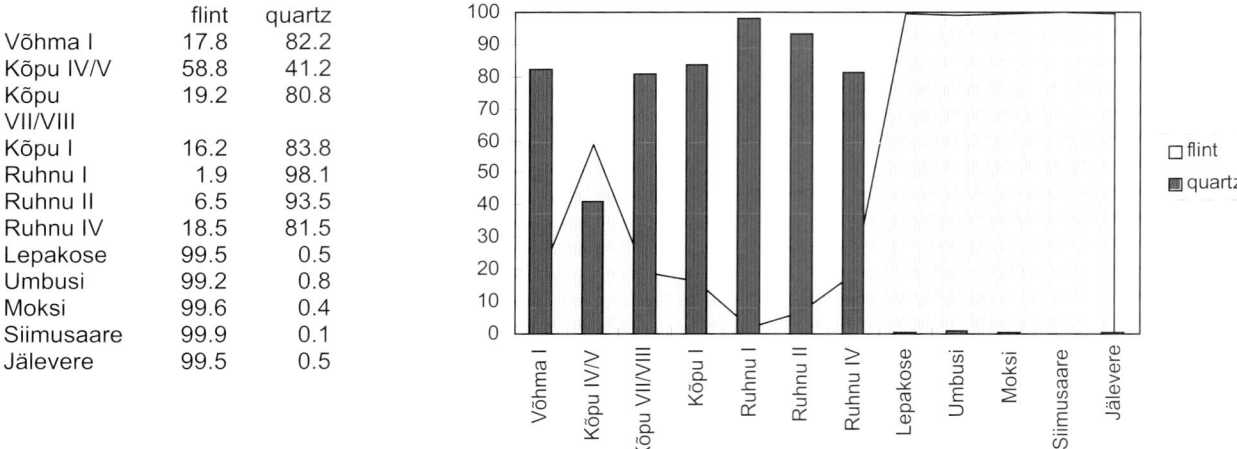

	flint	quartz
Võhma I	17.8	82.2
Kõpu IV/V	58.8	41.2
Kõpu VII/VIII	19.2	80.8
Kõpu I	16.2	83.8
Ruhnu I	1.9	98.1
Ruhnu II	6.5	93.5
Ruhnu IV	18.5	81.5
Lepakose	99.5	0.5
Umbusi	99.2	0.8
Moksi	99.6	0.4
Siimusaare	99.9	0.1
Jälevere	99.5	0.5

Figure 4.5 Utilisation of the two most common lithic materials from the Late Mesolithic and Early Neolithic on the islands and from central Estonian Mesolithic sites (Lepakose, Umbusi, Moksi, Siimusaare and Jälevere by K. Jaanits 1989).

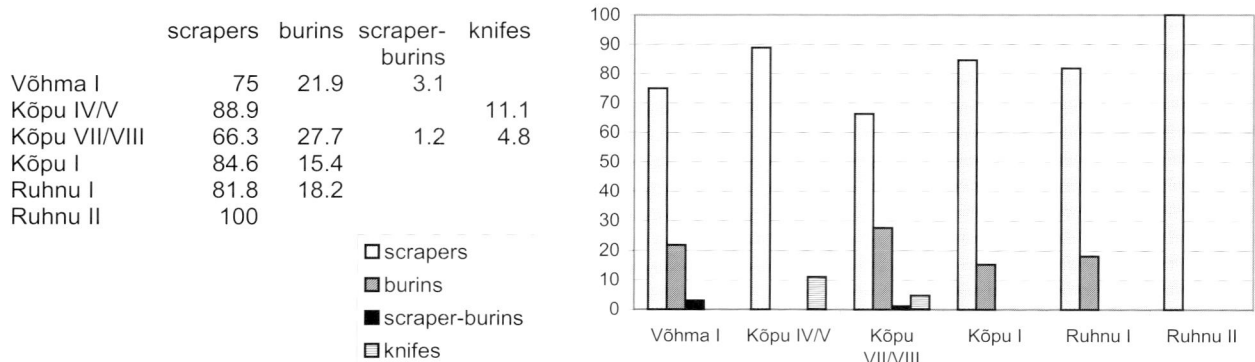

	scrapers	burins	scraper-burins	knifes
Võhma I	75	21.9	3.1	
Kõpu IV/V	88.9			11.1
Kõpu VII/VIII	66.3	27.7	1.2	4.8
Kõpu I	84.6	15.4		
Ruhnu I	81.8	18.2		
Ruhnu II	100			

Figure 4.6 The proportions of the four most common tools from the Late Mesolithic and Early Neolithic on the islands sites.

of the latter, the primary knapping was mainly bipolar. Secondary processing can be observed only on the blades of tools and is the result of direct knapping. Since the investigations necessary for more accurate identification haven't yet been carried out, the use of both percussion and pressure flaking can be assumed. Flaking complicates the recognition of cores in the find material. Quartz cores also outnumber flint ones in the overall material. The cores are usually small, with a height of 2.3–8.0 cm, rectangular parallelepipeds by shape (over 30%), less often conical-pyramidal, oval, or of some other shape, but mostly bipolar as mentioned above.

The percentage of tools that have undergone secondary processing is quite small, 0.4–3.3% in the early settlements on the islands. Scrapers (66.3–100%) clearly prevail over burins (up to 27.7%) together with a few scraper burins and knives (Figures 4.6 and 4.7). The majority of these (54.2–100%) are made of quartz, the use of flint is less common. With the exception of a few blade scrapers, they are all made from flakes. On most of the settlement sites, side scrapers are slightly more numerous than end scrapers, and the proportion of side-and-end scrapers is small. The majority of burins (75.6%) are also made of quartz. They are made, with the exception of one blade burin, from triangular (62%), trapezoidal, oval, circular or irregularly shaped flakes. Angle burins and side burins occur with roughly equal frequencies. Side burins were usually produced by striking at right angles, and sometimes the point protrudes like a beak.

Polished stone artefacts are rare in the find material from early settlements on the islands: one or two chisels or fragments of, per settlement site, and in some cases also blanks for stone axes. Chopping tools from the early settlement phase were not found on Ruhnu. The only exceptional site is Kõnnu in southern Saaremaa, where nearly 500 stone axes and chisels were found. Still, irregularly shaped polishing stones and fragments made from sandstone or quartzite have been found at all settlement sites. They make up 0.1–1.3% of the stone artefacts. Although bone and perhaps even wooden artefacts were polished in the Stone Age, the severe wear of the polishing stones, especially the very hard quartzite ones, can only be explained as resulting from stone processing.

To the present day, Early Neolithic pottery has been found at only four settlement sites on the islands. The

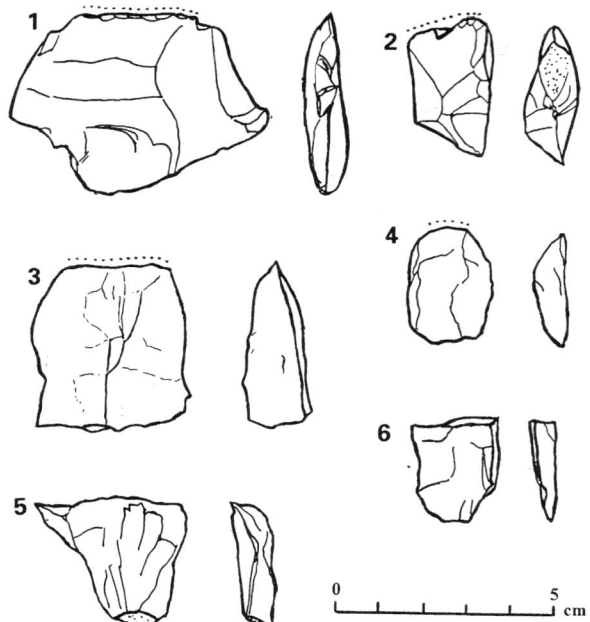

Figure 4.7 Scrapers (1–4) and burins (5–6) from Kõpu I (1, 4), Kõpu IV/V (2) and Võhma I (3) sites. 1, 2, 5 flint and 3, 4, 6 quartz (AI 6007:48, AI 6021:141, TÜ 600:214, AI 6007:68, AI 6007:59, AI 6007:189)

early potsherds from Saaremaa, Hiiumaa and Ruhnu can be determined as belonging to the Narva type on the basis of their conical shape, narrow clay coil with convex-concave connection, and the decoration of comb impressions, notches and pits. Unlike the Narva pottery of the mainland, stone rubble has been used for temper instead of ground shells and plant remains. The earthenware from the islands is less decorated than the pottery from the mainland, especially southeast Estonia, quite often decoration is completely absent. A specific feature occurring only on the islands is a decoration consisting of rows of small pits on the rim of the vessels. There are also differences in surface finish, striated surfaces occur less frequently than on the mainland.

Discussion and interpretation

The interpretation of archaeological material is always to some extent precocious, since the shortage of material always sets boundaries for archaeologists. Another group of problems arises in connection with the existing material – different method of fieldwork, different principles of collecting stray finds, etc. The west Estonian islands are no exception. Yet I think that the discussion of the general processes of the colonisation of the islands is already possible and the collected material represents the main line of colonisation and not a marginal one.

The post-glacial development of the islands of the Baltic Sea depended on the development of the water bodies in the Baltic basin and the compensational land rise. The higher areas of Saaremaa, Hiiumaa and Ruhnu rose above the water about 9600 cal. BC, when an opening appeared at Billingen between the Baltic Ice Lake and the ocean, and the water level fell about 25 m (Andrén et al. 1999:369). Large areas were also flooded later, in the transgression of the Ancylus Lake and the Litorina Sea, but the main trend was towards an increase in the amount of land.

The cause of the colonisation of the west Estonian islands was the formation of coastal settlements – communities living by the sea and engaged in a maritime economy. On the coast of the Estonian mainland this was formed by the end of the Mesolithic. The beginning of the formation might be principally dated to the period of the Ancylus Lake. From Antrea, Karelia, a net fragment and other artefacts probably lost due to a boat wreck were discovered. They were dated to 8500 cal. BC (Carpelan 1999:160 p). On the basis of artefact typology it was possible to connect this complex to the Kunda Culture. The oldest settlement sites in southeast Finland are also located on the shores of the Yoldia Sea or the straits of the maximum extent of Ancylus Lake (Jussila 2000:24).

At the present stage of investigation, coastal settlement in Estonia is mainly connected with the beginning of the Litorina Sea. Presently only one settlement site, Sõitme I in north Estonia, has been discovered, and this may have been located on the shore of the Ancylus Lake (Vedru 1998:19). At the same time we must keep in mind that this is an area of relatively modest land rise compared to that of Fennoscandia, the shores of the final minimum extent of Ancylus Lake were later flooded by the Litorina Sea. The discovery of buried sites is more complicated than finding sites where the cultural layer lies on the surface.

In any case, clear traces of coastal settlements date from the beginning of the Litorina Sea. The Narva Joaoru settlement in NE Estonia was established in about 6500 cal. BC (^{14}C dates published by Ilves et al. 1974:173 pp). It was not located on the seashore but on the river, a few kilometres upstream from the mouth of the river. In Siivertsi, only a few kilometres from Joaoru, artefacts (bone arrowheads, bone points, and a processed elk antler) and the remains of nets (net-sinkers, a float of pine bark and pine bark fragments) have been found (Indreko 1932). According to the results of pollen analysis (Jaanits et al. 1982:48) these were drowned in the one-time lagoon during the transitional phase between the Boreal and the Atlantic climatic period, i.e. somewhere at the turn of the 8th–7th millennium cal. BC. The settlement sites of Vihasoo I and maybe also Vihasoo II, north Estonia, and Valge-Risti, west Estonia, where people lived in the delta of the river and on the shore of a spit extending into the sea, respectively, belong to the end of the Mesolithic period.

The traces of both economic and settlement displacement at the end of Ancylus Lake and the beginning of the Litorina Sea can also be observed elsewhere around the

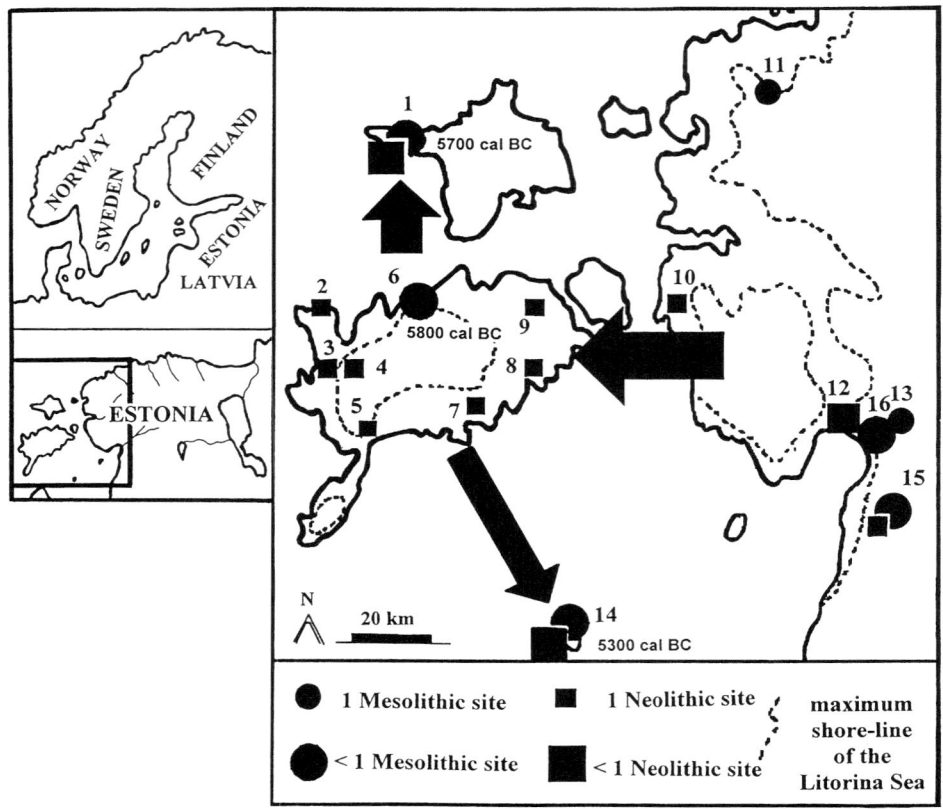

Figure 4.8 Stone Age settlement sites in west Estonia and the presumed pattern of the settlement of the islands. Sites: 1 – Kõpu I–XVII, 2 – Undva, 3 – Loona, 4 – Paju, 5 – Naakamäe, 6 – Võhma I–VII and Pahapilli I–II, 7 – Kõnnu, 8 – Asva, 9 – Kuninguste, 10 – Kaseküla, 11 – Valge-Risti, 12, Lemmetsa I- II and Malda, 13 – Pulli, 14 – Ruhnu I-VI, 15 Metsaääre I–III, 16 – Sindi Lodja I–II.

Baltic. The first traces of settlement on several Finnish islands, e.g. Kemiö (Asplund 1997:218), Åland (Nuñez and Gustavsson 1995:233) and Vantaa Kilteri and Jönsas (Purhonen and Ruonavaara 1994:91) date from that period.

The reason for the formation of the maritime hunter economy is not clear. Among other hypotheses, it has been explained by ecological pressure that had its background in the presumed decrease of the elk population (Siiriäinen 1982:18). The Estonian material does not permit one to draw such a conclusion, and the hypothesis that the sea became more productive (Nuñez 1996:24) seems more plausible here. The Litorina Sea, which was saltier, evidently offered excellent conditions for the general increase of biomass, and thus also for seals at the end of the food chain, remarkably increasing their populations.

The typical artefact complex and rock materials from the settlements indicate that the colonisation of the west Estonian islands began from the Estonian mainland (Figure 4.8). Thus the use of quartz precludes Latvia as an area of origin, and the use of flint precludes Finland. A more accurate identification of the area of origin is not yet possible, since the Stone Age of west Estonia, the nearest and most likely origin for the colonisation, has hitherto been rather poorly investigated. Chronologically, only the settlement sites of Metsaääre I, II and Sindi Lodja I, II (southwest Estonia), and some of the bone artefacts found from the bottom of Pärnu River fall between the Early Mesolithic Pulli (9000 cal. BC) and Valge-Risti (which is presumably contemporaneous with the early settlement of the islands).

Many features connect the early material from the islands with a coastal variant of the Kunda Culture. Firstly, the rock use in both areas is similar: the proportion of flint and quartz used is the same in coastal Estonia and on the islands. In three Early Neolithic settlements excavated by the author the amount of quartz (together with a small amount of quartzite) is 45.0–96.6%. Thus both areas differ from the complexes of central Estonia where flint prevails (over 99%; Figure 4.5). The stone processing technique is also analogous, flakes prevail and the bipolar technique has often been used for knapping both quartz and flint. The minimal number of small tools with secondary processing is typical of both the islands and the coastal area. The amount of morphological artefacts in the archaeological material naturally depends on several factors, some of them distorting reality, which complicates interpretation. Firstly, the excavated areas are small, encompass different types of activities and were excavated using different methods (screening, etc.). The finds from

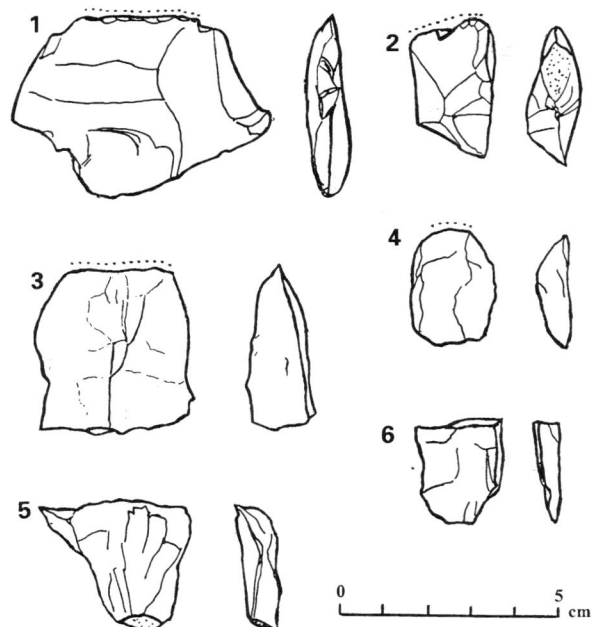

Figure 4.7 Scrapers (1–4) and burins (5–6) from Kõpu I (1, 4), Kõpu IV/V (2) and Võhma I (3) sites. 1, 2, 5 flint and 3, 4, 6 quartz (AI 6007:48, AI 6021:141, TÜ 600:214, AI 6007:68, AI 6007:59, AI 6007:189)

early potsherds from Saaremaa, Hiiumaa and Ruhnu can be determined as belonging to the Narva type on the basis of their conical shape, narrow clay coil with convex-concave connection, and the decoration of comb impressions, notches and pits. Unlike the Narva pottery of the mainland, stone rubble has been used for temper instead of ground shells and plant remains. The earthenware from the islands is less decorated than the pottery from the mainland, especially southeast Estonia, quite often decoration is completely absent. A specific feature occurring only on the islands is a decoration consisting of rows of small pits on the rim of the vessels. There are also differences in surface finish, striated surfaces occur less frequently than on the mainland.

Discussion and interpretation

The interpretation of archaeological material is always to some extent precocious, since the shortage of material always sets boundaries for archaeologists. Another group of problems arises in connection with the existing material – different method of fieldwork, different principles of collecting stray finds, etc. The west Estonian islands are no exception. Yet I think that the discussion of the general processes of the colonisation of the islands is already possible and the collected material represents the main line of colonisation and not a marginal one.

The post-glacial development of the islands of the Baltic Sea depended on the development of the water bodies in the Baltic basin and the compensational land rise. The higher areas of Saaremaa, Hiiumaa and Ruhnu rose above the water about 9600 cal. BC, when an opening appeared at Billingen between the Baltic Ice Lake and the ocean, and the water level fell about 25 m (Andrén et al. 1999:369). Large areas were also flooded later, in the transgression of the Ancylus Lake and the Litorina Sea, but the main trend was towards an increase in the amount of land.

The cause of the colonisation of the west Estonian islands was the formation of coastal settlements – communities living by the sea and engaged in a maritime economy. On the coast of the Estonian mainland this was formed by the end of the Mesolithic. The beginning of the formation might be principally dated to the period of the Ancylus Lake. From Antrea, Karelia, a net fragment and other artefacts probably lost due to a boat wreck were discovered. They were dated to 8500 cal. BC (Carpelan 1999:160 p). On the basis of artefact typology it was possible to connect this complex to the Kunda Culture. The oldest settlement sites in southeast Finland are also located on the shores of the Yoldia Sea or the straits of the maximum extent of Ancylus Lake (Jussila 2000:24).

At the present stage of investigation, coastal settlement in Estonia is mainly connected with the beginning of the Litorina Sea. Presently only one settlement site, Sõitme I in north Estonia, has been discovered, and this may have been located on the shore of the Ancylus Lake (Vedru 1998:19). At the same time we must keep in mind that this is an area of relatively modest land rise compared to that of Fennoscandia, the shores of the final minimum extent of Ancylus Lake were later flooded by the Litorina Sea. The discovery of buried sites is more complicated than finding sites where the cultural layer lies on the surface.

In any case, clear traces of coastal settlements date from the beginning of the Litorina Sea. The Narva Joaoru settlement in NE Estonia was established in about 6500 cal. BC (^{14}C dates published by Ilves et al. 1974:173 pp). It was not located on the seashore but on the river, a few kilometres upstream from the mouth of the river. In Siivertsi, only a few kilometres from Joaoru, artefacts (bone arrowheads, bone points, and a processed elk antler) and the remains of nets (net-sinkers, a float of pine bark and pine bark fragments) have been found (Indreko 1932). According to the results of pollen analysis (Jaanits et al. 1982:48) these were drowned in the one-time lagoon during the transitional phase between the Boreal and the Atlantic climatic period, i.e. somewhere at the turn of the 8th–7th millennium cal. BC. The settlement sites of Vihasoo I and maybe also Vihasoo II, north Estonia, and Valge-Risti, west Estonia, where people lived in the delta of the river and on the shore of a spit extending into the sea, respectively, belong to the end of the Mesolithic period.

The traces of both economic and settlement displacement at the end of Ancylus Lake and the beginning of the Litorina Sea can also be observed elsewhere around the

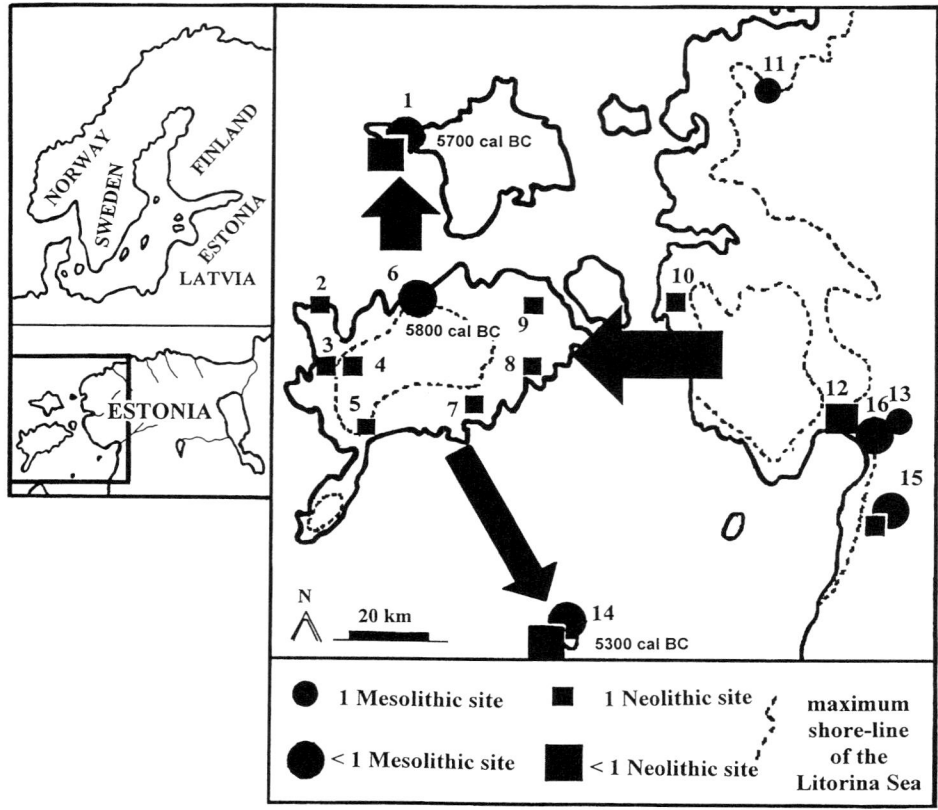

Figure 4.8 Stone Age settlement sites in west Estonia and the presumed pattern of the settlement of the islands. Sites: 1 – Kõpu I–XVII, 2 – Undva, 3 – Loona, 4 – Paju, 5 – Naakamäe, 6 – Võhma I–VII and Pahapilli I–II, 7 – Kõnnu, 8 – Asva, 9 – Kuninguste, 10 – Kaseküla, 11 – Valge-Risti, 12, Lemmetsa I- II and Malda, 13 – Pulli, 14 – Ruhnu I–VI, 15 Metsaääre I–III, 16 – Sindi Lodja I–II.

Baltic. The first traces of settlement on several Finnish islands, e.g. Kemiö (Asplund 1997:218), Åland (Nuñez and Gustavsson 1995:233) and Vantaa Kilteri and Jönsas (Purhonen and Ruonavaara 1994:91) date from that period.

The reason for the formation of the maritime hunter economy is not clear. Among other hypotheses, it has been explained by ecological pressure that had its background in the presumed decrease of the elk population (Siiriäinen 1982:18). The Estonian material does not permit one to draw such a conclusion, and the hypothesis that the sea became more productive (Nuñez 1996:24) seems more plausible here. The Litorina Sea, which was saltier, evidently offered excellent conditions for the general increase of biomass, and thus also for seals at the end of the food chain, remarkably increasing their populations.

The typical artefact complex and rock materials from the settlements indicate that the colonisation of the west Estonian islands began from the Estonian mainland (Figure 4.8). Thus the use of quartz precludes Latvia as an area of origin, and the use of flint precludes Finland. A more accurate identification of the area of origin is not yet possible, since the Stone Age of west Estonia, the nearest and most likely origin for the colonisation, has hitherto been rather poorly investigated. Chronologically, only the settlement sites of Metsaääre I, II and Sindi Lodja I, II (southwest Estonia), and some of the bone artefacts found from the bottom of Pärnu River fall between the Early Mesolithic Pulli (9000 cal. BC) and Valge-Risti (which is presumably contemporaneous with the early settlement of the islands).

Many features connect the early material from the islands with a coastal variant of the Kunda Culture. Firstly, the rock use in both areas is similar: the proportion of flint and quartz used is the same in coastal Estonia and on the islands. In three Early Neolithic settlements excavated by the author the amount of quartz (together with a small amount of quartzite) is 45.0–96.6%. Thus both areas differ from the complexes of central Estonia where flint prevails (over 99%; Figure 4.5). The stone processing technique is also analogous, flakes prevail and the bipolar technique has often been used for knapping both quartz and flint. The minimal number of small tools with secondary processing is typical of both the islands and the coastal area. The amount of morphological artefacts in the archaeological material naturally depends on several factors, some of them distorting reality, which complicates interpretation. Firstly, the excavated areas are small, encompass different types of activities and were excavated using different methods (screening, etc.). The finds from sporadic surveys must be considered to be somewhat selective (unintentional). Nevertheless the material is reliable enough to reflect general tendencies.

The small scraping and cutting tools of both areas possess several common features. In the case of scrapers this is the correlation of end, side and side-and-end scrapers, but also their general shapes. In burins the similarities lie in production techniques, shapes and the position of the blades. Thereby, the burin complex of the Early Neolithic site of Kroodi in north Estonia corresponds in every feature to those in the islands, including among others a specimen with a beak-like protrusion on the blade (Kriiska 1997:10, Fig. 2–3).

Naturally we cannot exclude that single sporadic trips to the (offshore) islands took place even in earlier times, but the colonisation that led to permanent settlement became possible only with the formation of a maritime economy and settlement mode. It is possible that the more distant islands were discovered only in the course of long seal-hunting trips. Initially the islands were used for temporary camps. Firewood could be obtained locally on the islands, it was not necessary to carry it along on long trips from the mainland. Raw material for tools could be found and some supplies could be left behind.

At present the direct evidence of the formation of a permanent settlement on the islands is poor. In all hitherto investigated settlements we encounter features indicating seasonality, e.g. the small variety of artefacts and animal bones, etc. The amount of seal bones is large in the osteological material received from the early settlements, while on the Mesolithic settlements all mammal bones could be determined according to species as belonging to seals. These sites were most likely used in late winter/early spring, which is the best time for hunting ringed seal and grey seal, when they are giving birth to their young (Aul et al. 1957:268 p) and are easiest to catch. Although both species can to some extent be hunted year round, early spring has evidently been the best and most productive season for hunting these seals throughout the period (Kalits 1963:136; Art 1988:13). The direct evidence of hunting during this time is provided by a bone belonging to a ringed seal about a week old found from the Kõpu I settlement site (Moora and Lõugas 1995:479).

The Early Neolithic settlement of Kõnnu in south Saaremaa gives a somewhat different picture. There (as mentioned above), unlike other early settlements on the islands, many chopping tools have been found. Their amount is large even if we consider that the excavated area is considerably larger than that of other sites. The abundance of chopping tools evidently reflects prolonged and miscellaneous activities on the site. The osteological material is of a wider selection, containing, besides seal bones, some elk, beaver and wild boar bones. The carnivores are represented by pine marten and fox bones (L. Lõugas 1997: appendix II.A).

Despite the absence of direct evidence we may presume that a permanent settlement formed on the islands at the end of the Mesolithic. Thus the existence of a distinctive group of the Narva Culture on the west Estonian islands at the beginning of the Neolithic could be interpreted as a result of local and to some extent isolated development. The basis of this hypothesis is, of course, the presumption that the new kind of artefact, i.e. pottery, which was introduced at that time reflects the regional peculiarities that had already developed there at an earlier time (Kriiska 1997:17), and not differences in the development and spread of pottery from different areas of innovation (e.g. Jaanits 1954:356; Girininkas 1985: 121). The earliest permanent settlement must evidently have been the largest island of the region, in the western and northern part of present-day Saaremaa. The similarity of material culture with the finds from Hiiumaa supports the idea that the people who settled on Saaremaa also used the other surrounding islands and islets. Ancient Kõpu Island, as well as Ruhnu were then, however, too small for the formation of year-round settlement.

A very clear shift in life styles can be observed in the materials from Saaremaa and Hiiumaa during the Late Neolithic. Artefact assemblages show greater variety and, most important of all, now include animal bones of species which indicate that hunting was or could be carried out during a greater number of seasons. This would in turn seem to indicate that year round villages had now been established. Along side the grey and ringed seal, which are easiest to hunt during the early spring, we now find the harp seal, which no longer can be found in the Baltic but which is easiest to hunt during the autumn and early winter. As concerns fishing, the favourite species was cod. The only *Cetacea* of the Baltic was porpoise, which was also caught, the main hunting season being summer and autumn. Kõpu Island in the western part of Hiiumaa was, by the latest, permanently inhabited during the Late Neolithic. In comparison with the Estonian mainland, tillage on the islands was introduced quite early. The pollen analysis of a sample taken at Kõivasoo on Kõpu peninsula shows that barley might have been cultivated there as early as 3900 cal. BC. This is one of two pollen diagrams from Estonia (Kriiska 2000:tab. 1), which shows that the people of the Combed Ware Culture possibly engaged in tillage if only marginally. However, tillage as a phenomenon affecting settlement strategies is connected with the Late Neolithic Corded Ware Culture, sites which have been discovered on Saaremaa, Muhu and Hiiumaa. At least on Saaremaa the Corded Ware Culture existed along side that of the Combed Ware Culture, the latter which subsisted on an economy based mainly on hunting and fishing.

References

Andrén, T., Björck, J. and Johnsen, S. 1999. Correlation of Swedish glacial varves with the Greenland (GRIP) oxygen isotope record. *Journal of Quaternary Science* 14 (4), 361–371.

Art, E. 1988. Hülged ja hülgepüük. *Hülgepüüük. Hülgepüügi meenutusi möödunud aegadest*, 5–15. Stockholm.

Asplund, H. 1997. Kemiön suurpitäjän esihistoria. *Kemiön suurpitäjän historia* I. Tammisaari, 213–286.

Aul, J., Ling, H. and Paaver, K. 1957. *Eesti NSV imetajad.* Tallinn.

Carpelan, C. 1999. On the Postglacial Colonisation of Eastern Fennoscandia. In: Carpelan, C., Hakinen, P., Kirkinen, T., Laulumaa, V., Lavento, M. and Lönnqvist, M. (eds) *Dig it all. Papers dedicated to Ari Siiriäinen*, 151–171. Helsinki.

Girininkas, A. 1985. Narvos kultkros raida. *Akmens amžiaus gyvenviets ir kapinynai.* Lietuvos archeologija 4. 119–134. Vilnius.

Grewingk, C. 1871. Zur Kenntniss der in Liv-, Est-, Kurland und einigen Nachbargegenden aufgefundenen Steinwerkzeuge heidnischer Vorzeit. *Verhhandlungen der Gelehrten Estnischen Gesellschaft zu Dorpat* VII:1, 1–56. Dorpat.

Ilves et al. 1974 = Ильвес Э., Лийва А., Пуннинг Я.-М. *Радиоуглеродный метод и его применение в четвертичной геологии и археологии Эстонии.* Таллин.

Indreko, R. 1932. Kiviaja võrgujäänuste leid Narvas. *Eesti Rahva Muuseumi Aastaraamat* VII, 1931, 48–67. Tartu.

—— 1964. *Mesolithische und frühneolithische Kulturen in Osteuropa und Westsibirien. Kungl. Vitterhets Historie och Antikvitets Akademiens Handlingar. Antikvariska Serien 13.* Stockholm.

Jaanits, K. 1989. Янитс К. Л. Кремневый инвентарь стоянок кундаской культуры. Диссертация на соискание ученой степени кандидата исторических наук. Таллинн. (Manuscript in the archives of Institute of History)

Jaanits, L. 1954. Neoliitilised ja varase metalliaja asulad Emajõe suudmealal. *Eesti NSV Teaduste Akadeemia Toimetised. Ühiskonnateadused* 3:3, 350–356.

—— 1965. Über die Ergebnisse der Steinzeitforschung in Sowjetestland. *Finskt Museum* LXXII, 5–46.

—— 1979. Die neolithische Siedlung Kõnnu auf der Insel Saaremaa. *Eesti NSV Teaduste Akadeemia Toimetised. Ühiskonnateadused* 28:4, 363–367.

Jaanits, L., Laul, S., Lõugas, V. and Tõnisson, E. 1982. *Eesti esiajalugu.* Tallinn.

Jussila, T. 2000. Pioneerit Keski-Suomessa ja Savossa. Rannansiirtymisajoitusmenetelmien perusteita ja vertailua. *Muinaistutkija* 2, 13–38.

Kalits, V. 1963. Kihnlaste elatusalad XIX sajandi keskpaigast tänapäevani. Tartu. (Manuscript in the Library of University of Tartu)

Kriiska, A. 1995. Archäologische Ausgrabungen auf dem Standort der ehemaligen Steinzeitsiedlung Kõpu I (Ristipõllu). *Proceedings of the Estonian Academy of Science. Humanities and social sciences* 44:4, 410–416.

—— 1996a. Archaeological excavations on the neolithic site of Riigiküla IV. *Proceedings of the Estonian Academy of Science. Humanities and social sciences* 45:4, 410–419.

—— 1996b. Archaeological studies on the Kõpu Peninsula. *Proceedings of the Estonian Academy of Science. Humanities and social sciences* 45:4, 398–409.

—— 1997. Kroodi ja Vihasoo III asula Eesti varaneoliitiliste kultuurirühmade kontekstis. *Journal of Estonian Archaeology* 1, 7–25.

—— 1998. Mesoliitilised asustusjäljed Loode-Saaremaal. *Ajalooline Ajakiri* 1 (100), 13–22.

—— 2000. Corded Ware Culture Sites in north-eastern Estonia. In Lang, V. and Kriiska, A. (eds) *De temporibus antiquissimis ad honorem Lembit Jaanits.* Muinasaja teadus 8, 59–79. Tallinn.

Kriiska, A. and Lõugas, L. 1999. Late Mesolithic and Early Neolithic Seasonal Settlement at Kõpu, Hiiumaa Island, Estonia. In: Miller, U., Hackens T., Lang, V., Raukas, A. and Hicks, S. (eds). *Environmental and Cultural History of the Eastern Baltic Region.* PACT 57, 157–172. Rixensart.

Kriiska, A. and Saluäär U. 2000. Archaeological fieldwork on the island of Ruhnu. In: Tamla, Ü. (ed.) *Arheoloogilised välitööd Eestis 1999*,18–28. Tallinn.

Lõugas, L.1997. Post-Glacial development of vertebrate fauna in Estonian water bodies. *A palaeozoological study.* Dissertationes Biologicae Universitatis Tartuensis 32. Tartu.

Lõugas, V. 1970. *Eesti varane metalliaeg (II a.-tuh. keskpaigast e.m.a. – 1. sajandini). Dissertatsioon ajalooteaduste kandidaadi kraadi taotlemiseks.* Tallinn. (Manuscript in the Institute of History, Tallinn).

—— 1974. Die Bodendenkmäler in der Umgebung von Kuninguste und Tagavere auf der Insel Saaremaa. *Eesti NSV Teaduste Akadeemia Toimetised. Ühiskonnateadused* 23:1, 79–84.

Moora, H. and Lõugas, L. 1995. Natural conditions at the time of primary habitation of Hiiumaa Island. *Proceedings of the Estonian Academy of Science. Humanities and social sciences* 44:4, 472–481.

Nuñez, M. 1996. When the water turned salty. *Muinaistutkija* 4, 23–33.

Nuñez, M. and Gustavsson, K. 1995. Prehistoric Man and Ice Conditions in the Åland Archipelago 7000–1500 Years ago. In: Robertsson, A.-M., Hackens, T., Hicks, S., Risberg, J. and Åkerlund, A. (eds) *Landscape and Life. Studies in honour of Urve Miller.* PACT 50, 233–244. Rixensart.

Peets, J. 1988. Vorzeitliches und frühmittelalterliches Eisenverhüttungzentrum in Tuiu auf der Insel Saaremaa. *Eesti NSV Teaduste Akadeemia Toimetised. Ühiskonnateadused* 37:4, 385–390.

Pesti, O. and Rikas, K. 1991. *Saaremaa ajaloo- ja kultuurimälestised. Kaitstavad mälestised. 2., parandatud ja täiendatud trükk.* Tallinn.

Purhonen, P. and Ruonavaara, 1994. On subsistence economy at the prehistoric dwelling-site area of Jönsas in Vantaa, southern Finland. In: Purhonen, P. (ed.) *Feno-ugri et slavi 1992. Prehistoric economy and means of livelihood. Papers presented by the participants in the Finnish-Russian archaeological Symposium "Pre-historic economy and means of livelihood", 11–15 May 1992 in the National Museum of Finland.* Museoviraston arkeologian osasto julkaisu, 5, 88–97.

Raukas, A. and Ratas, U. 1996. Holocene Evolution and Palaeoenvironmental Conditions of Hiiumaa Island, northwestern Estonia. In: Robertson, A.-M., Hicks, S., Åkerlund, A., Risberg, J. and Hackes, T. (eds) *Landscapes and Life. Studies in Honour of Urve Miller.* PACT 50, 167–174. Rixensart.

Siiriäinen, A. 1982. Recent Studies on the Stone Age Economy in Finland. *Fennoscandia antiqua* I, 17–26.

Tamla, T. and Jaanits, K. 1977. Das Gräberfeld und der spätneolithiche Siedlungsplatz von Paju. *Eesti NSV Teaduste Akadeemia Toimetised. Ühiskonnateadused* 26:1, 64–71.

Vedru, G. 1998. *Kahala ümbruse asustuspiirkond muinasajal. Magistritöö.* Tartu. (Manuscript in the Institute of History, Tallinn).

5. Storlyckan. Investigations of an Early Mesolithic Settlement Site in Östergötland, Eastern Middle Sweden

Mats Larsson

The article discusses the internal structure of an early Mesolithic site in the district of Östergötland, Eastern Middle Sweden that was excavated in 1997. One of the interesting finds from the site is a hut structure. Close to the hut there was also a small area used for working quartz containing waste from tool manufacture. Quartz and flint show completely different patterns of distribution, which indicates that these different types of material are related in different ways to the hut. This leads to a discussion of pioneers in a new landscape and their relationship to both the "new" world and the "old" one. Using terms such as "micro-space" and "macro-space", paths of contact and the structuring of the landscape are discussed.

Introduction

In the last fifteen years our picture of the Mesolithic period in Östergötland, eastern central Sweden, has changed (Larsson *et al.* 1997). Field surveys around Tåkern have yielded many new and valuable discoveries, in the form of both stray finds and settlement sites (Browall 1981, 1999). New settlement sites excavated during later years include Högby, Mörby, Lilla Åby and Motala (Appelgren 1995; Carlsson *et al.* 1999; Kaliff *et al.* 1997; Larsson 1996; Molin and Larsson 1999). At the first two of these sites, remains of post-built huts have been found, along with occupation layers and hearths. At the Lilla Åby site a possible hut construction has also been reconstructed (Carlsson *et al.* 1999). The oldest dated remains of a house hitherto found in Sweden were excavated at the Mörby site (Kaliff *et al.* 1997:22 pp).

In much of today's archaeological research there is often a focus on how people shaped and reshaped the landscape. Based in many cases on ethnographical analogies the landscape is viewed as an active part of people's lives. The structuring of landscapes reflects both practical and ritual activity and a range of long term similarities can be identified in both habitual use of the landscape and in the use of certain areas for ritual activity (Zvelebil and Jordan 1994:121). It has been pointed out that people distinguish themselves from natural objects by being equipped with a memory, a "living past" (Nordin 1996:95). This notion can in many ways be compared to Braudels the *Long Duree* as landscapes are structured in time and space.

A fruitful way to discuss Mesolithic society could be to study how the settlement sites were organised. The historian Dick Harrison (1998:50 p), in his research into medieval man's spatial perception, has used the terms "micro-space" and "macro-space", the former referring to the empirically known world, that is, the world known to the individual, while the latter represents a cosmological category which can include everything from religion to cultural contacts between people in a geographical context (Harrison 1998:51). Zvelebil and Jordan (1994:121 p) have argued that locales existed in the landscape, where different aspects of ideology and cosmology found their expression. In Harrison's words this can be seen as the "macro-space". All contacts with other groups of people may have changed not only their perception of ritual practice, but also aspects in the material culture. In the following article a newly excavated site, Storlyckan, will be discussed.

The Storlyckan site

The settlement site at Storlyckan was situated in a sheltered spot on a natural terrace below the highest coastline, about 135 m above sea level. The terrace is naturally demarcated to the west, east, and south in the form of the swash zone of the highest coastline and by a steep slope down towards a fen.

During the excavation four distinct features were documented in the bottom layer, a hearth pit and three stone-lined post-holes. The hearth pit was oval, measuring 1.05 by 0.70 m, with a rounded bottom profile, 0.20 m deep. A large quantity of fire-cracked stone was found in the hearth-pit. The post-holes had a rounded form, between 0.25 and 0.30 m across and 0.20–0.30 m deep, with rounded bottom profiles. The features coincided with an area that had obviously been cleared of stones, which was

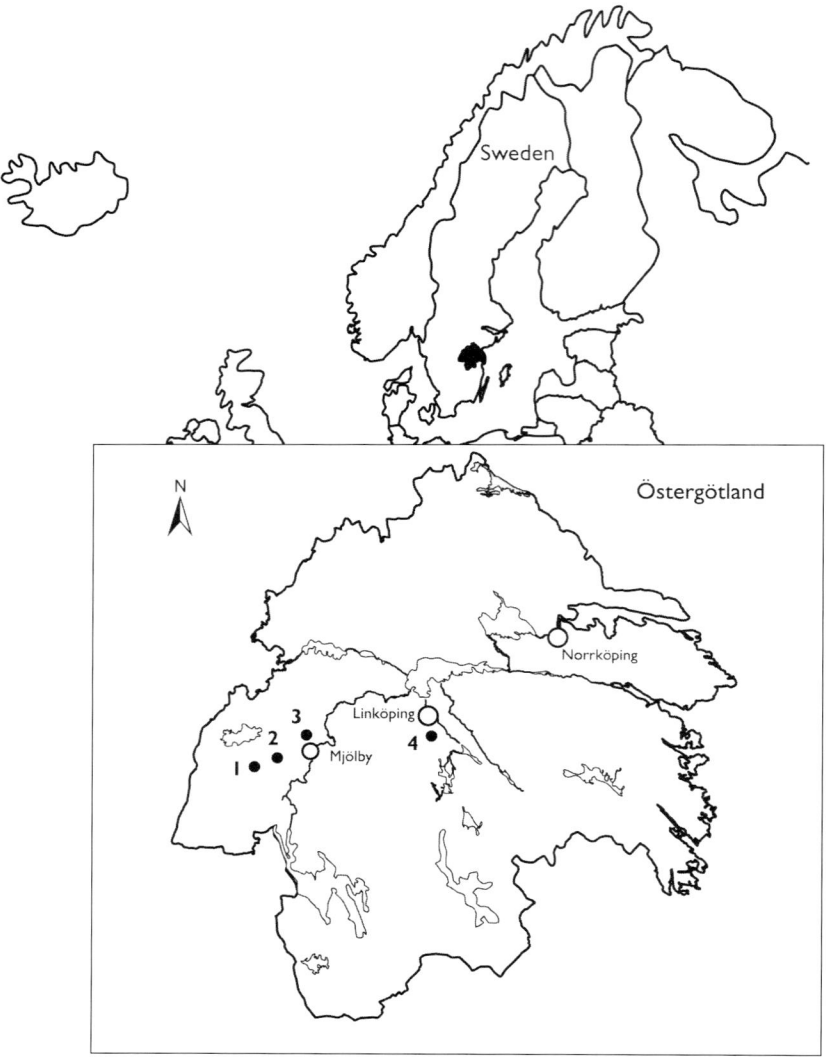

Figure 5.1 Map of Östergötland showing the settlement sites discussed in the text 1 Storlyckan, 2 Mörby, 3 Högby, 4 Lilla Åby. Graphics Lars Östlin.

mostly lined by a number of large moraine boulders lying in a semicircle. This area was at an early stage interpreted as the site of a dwelling structure. It appeared as if stone had been thrown up against a wall which had been supported by the kerb of boulders. The hut opened to the east, and here too the area seemed to have been cleared of stones. When viewed in this way, the three post-holes would be the remains of the roof-supporting structure. The hut measures about 4.70 by 3.75 m, thus giving an living area of about 15 m².

About ten metres down the slope, an oval hearth pit was found, measuring 2.00 by 1.50 m, 0.30 m deep, with a rounded bottom profile. The filling contained a large quantity of fire-cracked stone and a concentration of soot and charcoal. Close to the hearth pit was a grindstone of granite, almost rectangular, deliberately cut to shape and with a roughly ground surface.

Two Mesolithic features from Storlyckan have been ^{14}C-dated. The samples (Ua-8945 and Ua-8946) were from charcoal found in hearth pits both in the hut and in the activity area with the grindstone. The charcoal comes from pine. The dates agree, placing the settlement site between 7905 and 7865 BP, or 7000–6550 cal BC 1 sigma.

The finds

The analysed stone-material consists of flint, rhyolite (hälleflinta in Swedish), and quartz, comprising a total weight of 4,665 kg and 241 items. Flint and quartz items are most numerous. The distribution of the artefacts is as follows 43% are of quartz, 47% of flint, and 10% of rhyolite. In terms of weight, quartz shows an overwhelming dominance, 80% as against 15% flint and 5% rhyolite. Rhyolite is a local stone type. This in some ways looks and appears like the Baltic flint. The proportion of definable artefacts is moderate. Apart from a large quantity of micro blades there were in all thirteen scrapers, eight of flint, three of quartz, the other two of rhyolite.

The analysed finds are summed up in table 5.1. It is interesting that the proportion of flint (including rhyolite) is so high. This means that Storlyckan differs significantly from the majority of excavated sites in eastern central Sweden. However, the distribution is similar to that at the nearby settlement site of Högby (Åkerlund 1996:37 p). The vast majority of the flint material consists of blades and blade fragments (approx. 41%). The scrapers made from flakes are small, 16–20 mm in size and semicircular in shape, while the blade scrapers have a rectangular shape and are generally smaller. The micro blades show traces of having been pressed, seen in the form of small platforms and bulbs of percussion. All in all, this indicates that at least some of the blades originated from conical micro blade cores.

If we then turn to the quartz, we see that the material comes from both veined quartz and collected stray nodules. The reduction methods for quartz working represented on the site can be studied mainly from the cores and flakes. Both bipolar knapping and reduction by means of the platform method are represented. They probably represent different stages in the working of the quartz. It has previously been claimed that a bipolar reduction method occurs frequently at Mesolithic sites in eastern central Sweden (Lindgren 1994; 1996).

Table 5.1 Classification of the artefacts from Storlyckan.

Category	Material	Number	Weight, g
Drills	Flint	1	0.5
Scrapers	Flint	8	8.5
Blades/fragments	Flint	69	38.5
Cores/fragments	Flint	10	16.0
Flakes/fragments	Flint	13	9.0
Debris	Flint	25	11.5
Scrapers	Rhyolite	2	7.5
Blades/fragments	Rhyolite	5	2.5
Cores/fragments	Rhyolite	3	7.5
Flakes	Rhyolite	1	2.5
Debris	Rhyolite	14	4.0
Scrapers	Quartz	3	10.5
Blades	Quartz	1	0.5
Cores/fragments	Quartz	12	89.5
Flakes/fragments	Quartz	56	143.0
Debris	Quartz	75	20.0

The spatial distribution of the finds

The flint material is almost totally confined to the hut, and an area to the north, beside the entrance. The distribution of flint cores and scrapers also agrees with

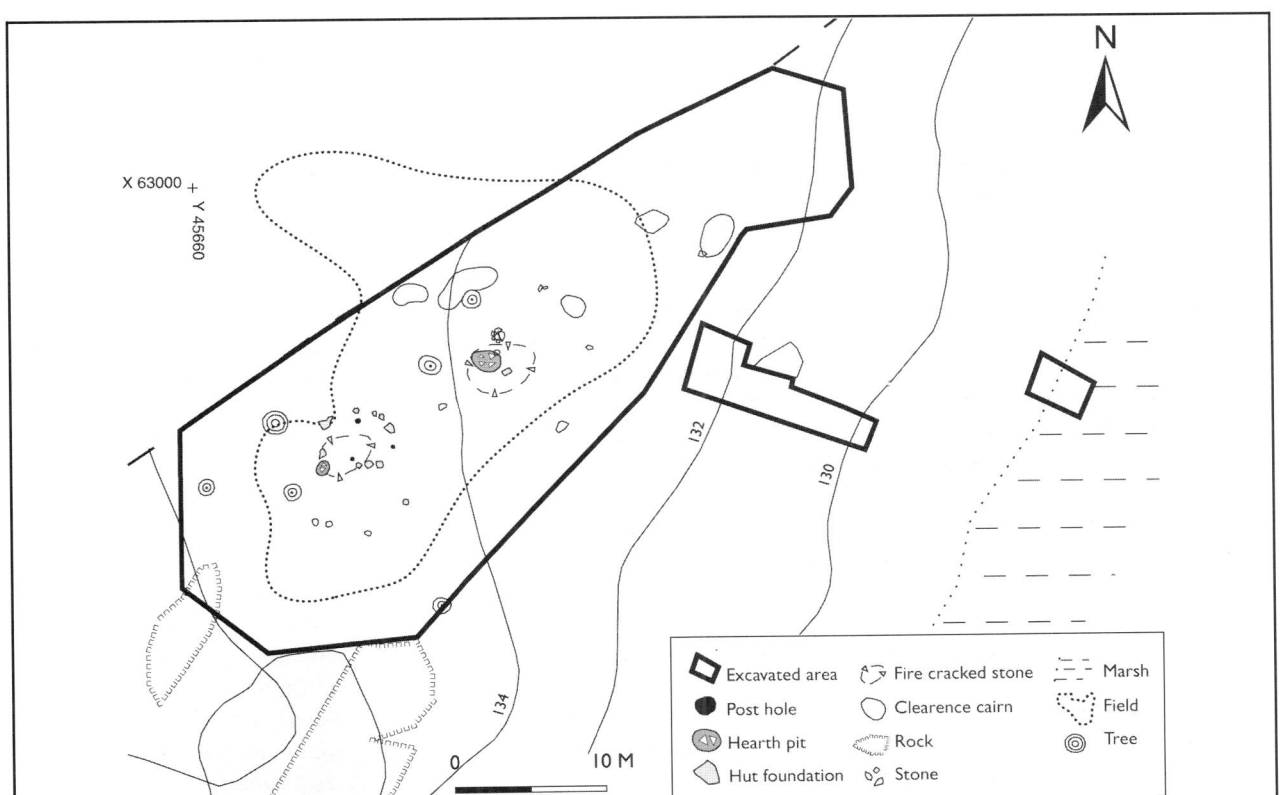

Figure 5.2 Survey plan of the settlement area with the hut. Graphics Lars Östlin.

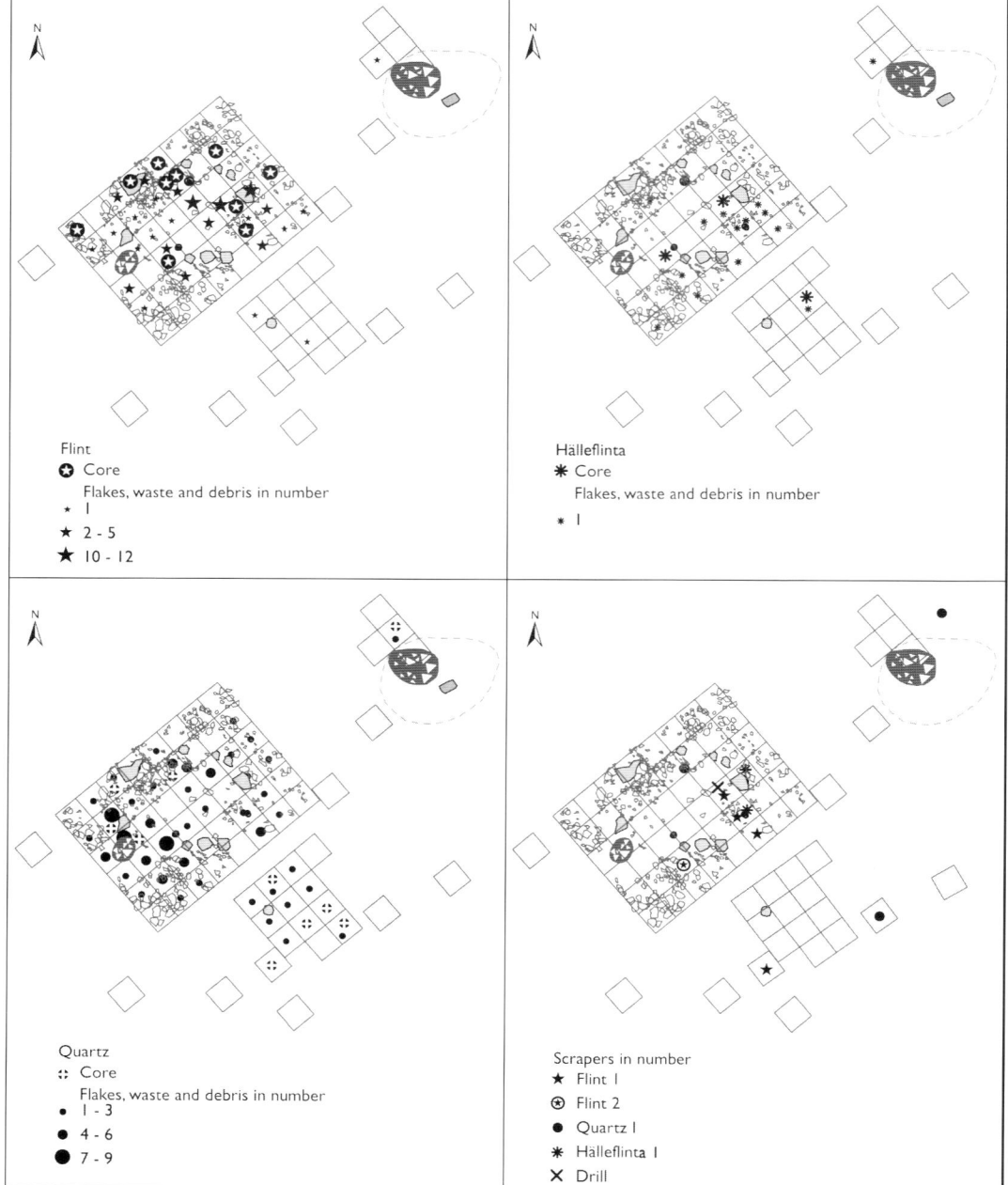

Figure 5.3 Distribution of the finds: flint, rhyolite (hälleflinta in Swedish), quartz, and tools. Graphics Lars Östlin.

this picture. The analysis of micro debitage also showed the occurrence of flint debitage in this area, and also outside the hut. This might support a view that waste was cleared out of the hut (Geijerstam 1999). If we view this distribution pattern in a wholly functionalistic way one probable explanation of the concentration of waste might be that this area was a knapping place where the primary working of the flint was carried out. As will be discussed later on there are other ways to interpret this pattern. The flint micro blades, on the other hand, show a completely different picture, almost all of them being inside the hut, with a large concentration in the middle. Here it is obvious that the material was deposited in connection with a specific activity inside the hut. Interestingly enough, the distribution of the few whole micro blades does not agree with this picture. These were instead found around the hearth pit in the hut, probably along the wall, and outside the hut. Three whole micro blades were found close together in what was obviously a closed deposit beside the hearth pit. This may be interpreted as a votive offering. As Zvelebil and Jordan (1994:122) note there are obviously ritual depositions in a "domestic context" as well. The three blades are of the same type of flint and were in all probability pressed from the same flint core.

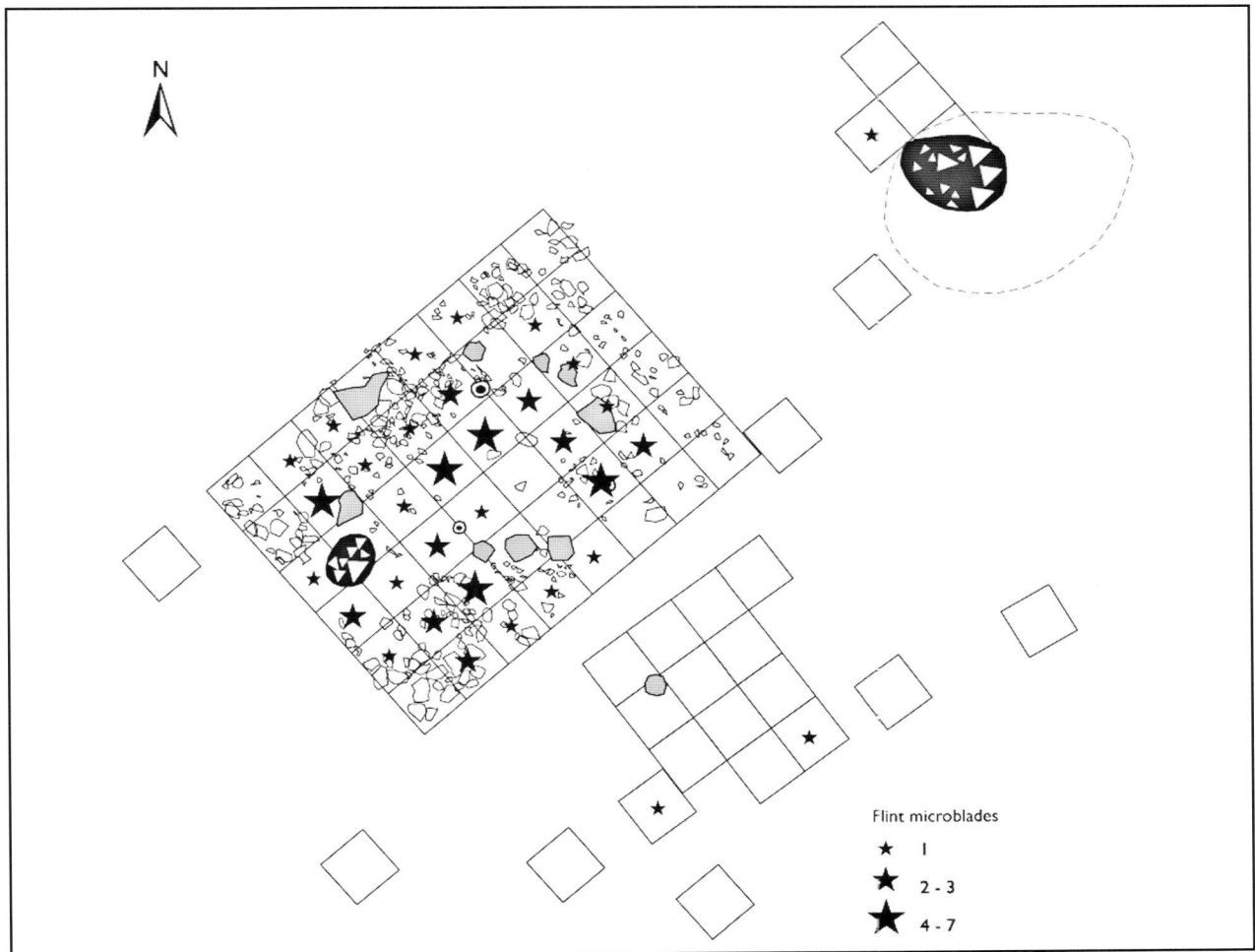

Figure 5.4 Distribution of microblades at the hut. Graphics Lars Östlin.

The quartz objects were also found beside the hut and within an area just south of it where a probable anvil stone was located. The anvil stood upright. The top of it consisted of a worked circular area. Five bipolar cores of quartz and one core of rhyolite were scattered around the anvil stone. In addition, there was an even distribution of mainly flakes, flake fragments, and debris. A large proportion of quartz micro debitage likewise corroborates the hypothesis that the anvil stone and the area around it was a knapping place.

The distribution of the quartz shows both similarities and differences with respect to the distribution of flint. The similarity is seen in the fact that the hut appears to have been cleared of waste, which, like the flint waste, was accumulated around the wall of the hut. On the other hand, there was no noticeable concentration in the front of the hut, around the entrance; instead the material was found more towards the back of the hut, particularly outside the assumed line of the wall. This coincides with the distribution of the quartz cores which also lay at the back of the hut.

Judging by the finds, the area just inside the entrance, especially the northern half, seems to have been a knapping place, mostly for working flint, combined with a more general activity area. The back of the hut is above all associated with quartz debris. The distribution of flint micro blades reflects an activity associated with the blades, concentrated in the centre of the hut. Perhaps also a votive offering. Another interesting observation on the basis of the distribution and proportions of quartz and flint was that it was possible to see in the hut itself how the majority of the flint was found in a limited part of the hut, whereas the vast majority of the quartz was found outside or in the peripheral parts of the hut. We can thus see a marked division of the "micro-space" of the hut. A possible interpretation for this will be further elaborated below.

Living areas and the organisation of space

It is now time to discuss the obvious similarities between the Mesolithic huts excavated in Östergötland in recent years. They all share the round-oval shape, for instance. There are admittedly minor differences as regards the size and constructional details, but the shared features predominate. The structures do show differences, however, in the spatial organisation of activity areas. When different regions are discussed, on the other hand, the comparative perspective reveals differences in how people perceived and shaped their "micro-space". The variations in the function of the huts in relation to other activities indicate that space was arranged differently depending on where one was (Carlsson and Hennius 1998). It is obvious that it is very difficult, even dangerous, to make to general remarks concerning the organisation of Mesolithic living floors because the material remains found during archaeological excavations were originally created and organised by people who were steered and influenced by social and gendered norms. The localisation of settlements affects the utilisation of the surrounding landscape and the form taken by the flow of material and artefacts between settlements and between regions. The density and location of settlement sites influenced all aspects of life.

If we return to the "micro-space", that is, the spatial organisation of the huts, we can, as we have seen, distinguish a characteristic round-oval shape. This shape would then be culturally conditioned and, like the micro blades, be seen as one of the elements binding the material culture together. The striking differences between the Maglemose huts of southern Scandinavia and the huts from Högby and Mörby in Östergötland have previously been discussed. The differences are supposed to lie in the lack of a clear link between the artefacts and the hut (Carlsson et al. 1999; Kaliff et al. 1997:49 p). The analysis of the Storlyckan site shows that there might be no such correlation. Unlike the other sites, Storlyckan shows a clear agreement between the hut and the artefacts. Due to the spatial analysis of the find material on the site an interesting difference in the use of flint and quartz was revealed, which is of great interest for the following interpretation. The majority of the flint was found in the actual hut whereas the quartz was outside and in a more peripheral part of the hut. How shall we then interpret this? As has sometimes been pointed out all material culture possesses a ritual and ideological aspect (Zvelebil and Jordan 1994:102). The micro blades may for example be seen as an important part of the exchange system between different regions. They may have acted as a link between the old word left behind and the new unknown world. The accumulation of micro blades, and the supposed votive offering of micro blades, may be seen as a link between the familiar, that is, the flint, the living area and the people. They acted in this way as both social and even ritual markers. It is most likely that many of the blades at one time were part of slotted bone points and it is obvious that very few of these actually reached Eastern Middle Sweden judging from the small number of micro blades on most sites (Larsson et al. 1997:45 pp). The elaboration of material culture in hunter-gatherer cultures is an elaboration of social relations, ties between people can be objectified through things (Zvelebil 1996). In this way it is quite likely that we ought to see the slotted bone points as social markers.

Christopher Gosden (1994:35) has pointed out that standardised material forms were a support for people in their dealing with a new world and the rapid changes that take place with colonisation. It is interesting to note that the so familiar microliths of southern Scandinavia are completely missing in eastern Sweden. These points, and the variation in form, have often been interpreted as a part of a group's social identity (Larsson et al. 1997:47 pp). The colonisation of new areas with which we are dealing here gradually created new constellations in which elements from the old area survived while certain other elements were reshaped to suit the new situation better. By partly changing their material culture, the newcomers created their own identity but also forged associations with what they had left behind. In other words, there is a link between the new area and the old one (Boaz 1999). In this way we may interpret the existence of micro blades but not microliths. It was more important for people during the early Boreal to confront the new hitherto unknown landscape than to make different types of points. Some aspects of the material culture "needed" replacement and so they chose to exclude the points. In the words of Marek Zvelebil (1996:58 p) this can be seen as part of a negotiation for power, control, or the attainment of goals between different segments of society, which is played out at different scales of organisation, starting with individuals, and then moving on to households and larger units. The use and meaning of symbols will change as a part of this negotiation. This is an interesting and challenging view in which gender relations are also an important part, if we accept gender as socially constructed. As discussed above we should look at the micro blades as social markers. The form of the huts could of course also be seen as a link between the old and the new and perhaps also as a form of social marker showing group identity.

During investigations in northern Scania and southern Småland interesting observations regarding the use of flint and quartz have been made (Knarrström 2000a:15 pp, 2000b:159 pp). At lake Hjälmsjön in northern Scania the first quartz dominated settlement site in Scania has been found (Knarrström 2000b:159 p). Knarrström (2000b: 161) discusses a model where during the early Mesolithic the material culture is in a broad sense comparable to the Maglemose culture. In this area it is possible to see how people during the course of the Early Mesolithic increasingly replaced flint with local raw material like for example quartz.. It is quite possible that this pattern is the result of a more permanently settled population in the interior of northern Scania and southern Småland. A more settled population probably also developed its own material culture. This pattern is comparable to the picture discussed above. In southern and western Östergötland it is obvious that we can distinguish a group of settlement sites where quartz dominate but with a rather large proportion of flint. The use of material culture in the creation of a new identity in a "new world" is quite probable.

The first settlers in an area were confronted with a

new problem: the landscape had no history or identity (Boaz 1999:139). Existing ideological and mythological frameworks could be used to some extent, but mostly new frames of reference were needed. These first colonists in Östergötland mainly used flint which they brought with them. As time passed by quartz and other local rocks were gradually incorporated in the material culture. This pattern can be studied at both Högby, Storlyckan and Mörby. The quartz, representing a new material, may have been regarded as an alien element and therefore potentially dangerous. As time passed, the alien element, the quartz, was gradually accepted, and it also became predominant in the future centuries. By changing parts of their material culture, Mesolithic man could create his or her own social identity. This enabled both differentiation and contacts between different social groups. As we have seen the proportion of flint declined, but micro blades existed all the time. We may look upon these as the links with the past; in other words, they are part of the social relations in the form of the exchange of material culture, for example the slotted bone points, that survived and which we can see throughout the Mesolithic. The supposed votive offering in the back of the hut at the Storlyckan site is clearly part of how material culture during the Mesolitihic had both ritual and ideological implications.

This is how the mental space – "macro-space" – was created. Myths, events, and experiences acted together in the shaping and creation of a meaningful world, and for these people also a new world. Places such as topographical markers and special locations became part of mans experience, heritage and future. In this way it is perhaps possible to explain why sites as Högby and Mörby were visited several times over a long time span. They had in a way become mythical, ancestral places and not only favourable hunting stands or good settlement sites. Stories and myths were created about certain places in the landscape, which later became a part of the group's shared history, while others did not acquire this significance. People met at specific places or they met by pure chance. Information and perhaps goods would also have been exchanged at these meetings (Edmonds 1999: 23 pp).

There are no doubt gaps in the above argument. We do not know today how specific or general the Storlyckan site was. This settlement gives the impression of having been used for a relatively short time, and there is no evidence of later visits during the Mesolithic. This is quite different from the sites discussed above. Due to archaeological work in the surrounding area during the late 1990´s we have some further clues to how the landscape was used and influenced by people (e.g. Ericsson and Österström 1999). These small sites mostly consist of only one or two hearths and hardly any finds to speak of. These scattered hearths may be seen as evidence of a mobile settlement pattern. The landscape was gradually influenced by humans, small clearances were made, and stone waste from tool manufacture was deposited in some places and slowly these places became part of Mesolithic mans "macro-space".

Acknowledgements

I would like to thank my friend and colleague Fredrik Molin, Linköping, for all help. English revised by John Airey (Kalmar).

References

Appelgren, K. 1995. *Lilla Åby*. Arkeologisk undersökning. Riksantikvarieämbetet UV Linköping Rapport 1995:19.

Boaz, J. 1999. Pioneers in the Mesolithic. The Initial Occupation of the Interior of Eastern Norway. In: Boaz, J. (ed.) *The Mesolithic of Central Scandinavia*. Universitetets Oldsaksamlings Skrifter. Ny Rekke 22, 125–153.

Browall, H. 1981. Mesolitisk stenålder vid Tåkern. *Östergötland* 1980, 47–59.

—— 1999. Mesolitiska mellanhavanden i västra Östergötland. In: Gustafsson, A. and Karlsson, H. (eds) *Glyfer och arkeologiska rum – en vänbok till Jarl Nordbladh*. Gotarc Serie A vol 3, 289–305. Göteborg.

Carlsson, T. and Hennius, A. 1998. Invisible Activities. Early Neolithic House Remains in Western Östergötland. *Lund Archaeological Review* 1998, 29–37.

Carlsson, T., Kaliff, A. and Larsson, M. 1999. Man and the Landscape in the Mesolithic. Aspects of Mental and physical Settlement Organisation. In: Boaz, J. (ed.) *The Mesolithic of Central Scandinavic*. Universitetets Oldsaksamlings Skrifter. Ny Rekke 22, 47–73.

Edmonds, M. 1999. *Ancestral Geographies of the Neolithic. Landscapes, Monuments and Memory*. London.

Ericsson, A. and Österström, K. 1999. *Lugnet. Boplatslämningar från äldre järnålder och mesolitikum*. Riksantikvarieämbetet Rapport UV Linköping 1999:13.

Geijerstam, M. 1999. Mikrodebitage på boplatsen Storlyckan. Analysrapport. RAÄ 275, Väderstads socken, Östergötland. In: Molin, F. and Larsson, M. (eds) *Mesolitikum vid Storlyckan – hyddlämning och fyndmaterial*. Riksantikvarieämbetet Rapport UV Linköping 1999:1, appendix 1.

Gosden, C. 1994. *Social Being and Time*. London.

Harrison, D. 1998. *Skapelsens geografi föreställningar om rymd och rum i medeltidens Europa*. Svenska humanistiska förbundet 110. Stockholm.

Kaliff, A., Carlsson, T. Molin, F. and Sundberg, K. 1997. *Mörby. Östergötlands äldsta boplats*. Riksantikvarieämbetet Rapport UV Linköping 1997:38.

Knarrström, B. 2000a. Materialstudier av Skånes äldsta stenålder om tiden efter Bromme och tidigmesolitisk expansion i norra Skåne. In: Ersgård, L. (ed.) *Människors platser – tretton arkeologiska studier från UV*. Riksantikvarieämbetet Arkeologiska Undersökningar Skrifter Nr 31, 149–167.

—— 2000b. Tidigmesolitisk bosättning i Sydvästra Småland. In: Lagerås, P. (ed.) *Arkeologi och paleoekologi i sydvästra Småland*. Riksantikvarieämbetet Arkeologiska Undersökningar Skrifter Nr 34, 15–35.

Larsson, M. 1996. *Mesolitiska och Senneolitiska boplatser vid Högby i Östergötland. Bosättningsmönster och materiell kultur*. Riksantikvarieämbetet Rapport UV Linköping.

Larsson, M., Lindgren, C. and Nordqvist, B. 1997. Regionalitet under mesolitikum. Från senglacial tid till senatlantisk tid i Syd- och Mellansverige. In: Larsson, M. and Olsson, E. (eds) *Regionalt och interregionalt. Stenåldersundersökningar i Syd- och Mellansverige*. Riksantikvarieämbetet. Arkeologiska undersökningar Skrifter 23, 13–51.

Lindgren, C. 1994. Ett bipolärt problem – om kvartsteknologi under mesolitikum. *Aktuell Arkeologi* IV. Stockholm Archaeological Reports 29, 77–86.

—— 1996. Kvarts som källmaterial – exempel från den mesolitiska boplatsen Hagtorp. *Tor* 28, 29–52.

Molin, F. and Larsson, M. 1999. *Mesolitikum vid Storlyckan – hyddlämning och fyndmaterial.* Riksantikvarieämbetet Rapport UV Linköping 1999:1.

Nordin, S. 1996. *Det pessimistiska förnuftet. Filosofiska essäer och porträtt.* Nora.

Zvelebil, M. 1996. Ideology, society and economy of the Mesolithic communities in temperate and Northern Europe. *Origini. Prehistoria e protohistoria delle civilta antiche* XX, 51–70.

Zvelebil, M. and Jordan P. 1994. Hunter fisher gatherer ritual landscapes-questions of time, space and representation. In: Goldhahn, J. (ed.) *Rock Art as Social Representation.* BAR International Series 794, 101–127, Oxford.

Åkerlund, A. 1996. *Human Responses to Shore Displacement. Living by the Sea in Eastern Middle Sweden during the Stone Age.* Riksantikvarieämbetet Arkeologiska Undersökningar Skrifter nr 16. Stockholm.

6. The Colonisation of Northernmost Finnish Lapland and the Inland Areas of Finnmark

Tuija Rankama

The paper discusses the earliest Mesolithic colonisation of the inland areas of northernmost Finnish Lapland and Norway. It argues that for a model of immigration to work, it needs to take into account a wide array of variables ranging from archaeological chronology to environmental development, resource availability, adaptation, technology, and so-called cultural factors. On the basis of a discussion of these factors, the paper attempts to pinpoint the direction of the immigration, focussing specifically on the coast–inland dichotomy that is evident in this area. The environmental development of the area during the time of the first inland occupation, including the development of the fauna, is reconstructed using palaeobotanical and ecological data. The economic adaptations and resource utilisation strategies of the populations of the surrounding areas are discussed, including lithic resource availability and use. It is suggested that lithic resources and lithic technology were a vital factor for the populations of the area, and that the geological boundary that bisects the study area may have been, for cultural reasons, as significant as the boundary between a maritime and an inland hunting adaptation. Consequently, a southern inland origin for the immigrants is considered more likely than a northern coastal one.

Introduction

In the course of the last century, a variety of views has been expressed both in Finland and in Norway concerning the early Postglacial colonisation of the Norwegian coast and the inland areas of Finnmark and northern Lapland (Figure 6.1) (see e.g. Bjerck 1994 for a brief history of ideas in Norway; also Olsen 1994; Thommessen 1996a; Woodman 1999; for Finland, e.g. Luho 1956; Siiriäinen 1981; Huurre 1983; Meinander 1984; Nuñez 1996, 1997; Carpelan 1996; Rankama 1995, 1996, 1997b; Halinen

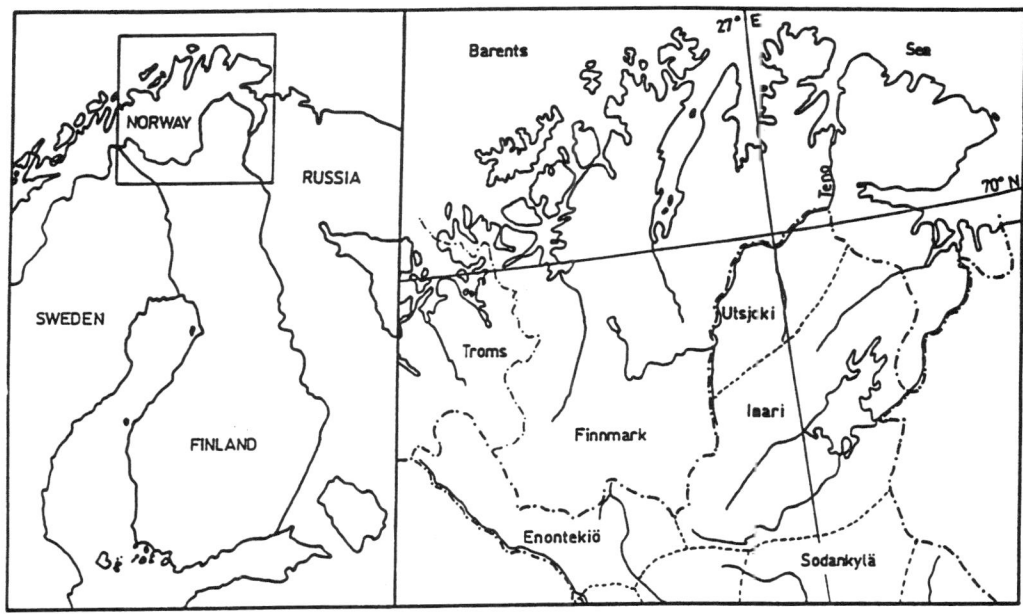

Figure 6.1 The location of the research area in northern Fennoscandia.

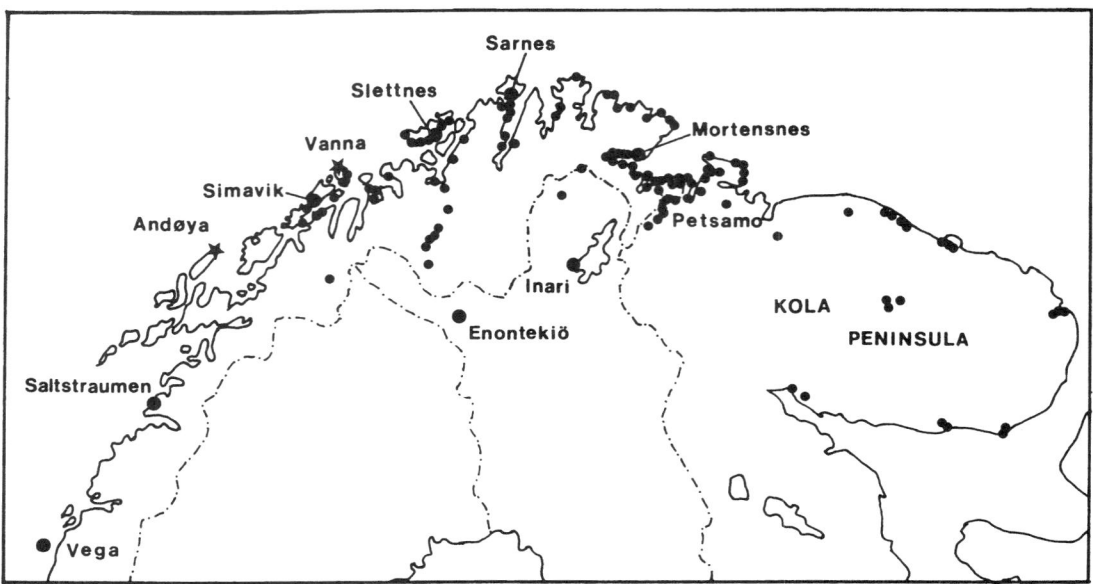

Figure 6.2 Mesolithic sites in northernmost Fennoscandia. In Finland, only the most significant settlement areas are indicated without displaying each individual site. The earliest dates are the following:

Radiocarbon dates:
Sarnes, Magerøya[1]	10,280±80 BP
	9,800±60 BP
Slettnes, Sørøya[2]	9,610±80 BP
Saltstraumen[3]	9,580±90 BP
Vega[4]	9,350±270 BP
Simavik, Ringvassøy[5]	9,200±200 BP
Saamenmuseo, Inari[6]	8,760±75 BP
	8,380±90 BP
	8,290±110 BP
Myllyjärämä, Enontekiö[7]	8,320±110 BP

Shoreline dates:
Mortensnes, Varanger[8]	10,000 BP
Petsamo (Kola Peninsula)[9]	10,000–9,000 BP

Indirect evidence:
Andøya[10]	11,500–11,000 BP
Vanna[10]	11,500–11,000 BP

References: [1]Thommessen 1996a, 1996b; [2]Hesjedal et al. 1996; [3]Hauglid 1993; [4]Pettersen 1982, Bjerck 1994; [5]Sandmo 1986, 1996; [6]Arponen & Hintikainen 1993, Carpelan 1999, Schulz 1996; [7]Carpelan 1999, Schulz 1996; [8]Schanche 1996; [9]Šumkin 1990; [10]Møller 1996.

1996; Havas 1999). The discussion has been mostly concerned with the origin and direction of the immigration, but questions pertaining to adaptation have also been addressed (Bjerck 1994; Rankama 1995, 1996, 1997b; Halinen 1996; Woodman 1999).

The subject offers the makings of a lively debate, not least because of the equivocal character of the available archaeological data. One source of controversy are the available radiocarbon and other dates (Figure 6.2), which tend to place the earliest Holocene settlement of both countries in the north. In Norway, the earliest occupation sites are in Sarnes and Mortensnes on the northern coast, with dates reaching 10,000 BP (uncalibrated) and beyond (Thommessen 1996a, 1996b; Schanche 1996). The earliest date of a settlement site in Finland derives from Vanha Kirkkosaari Island in Suomussalmi, northeastern Finland (Hel-2313, 8950±120 BP; Carpelan 1999:162; Schulz 1996:42), but the first Lapland date, from the Saamenmuseo site in Inari, is only two hundred years later (Ua-4296, 8760±75 BP; Arponen and Hintikainen 1995:14; Carpelan 1999: 165; Schulz 1996:43), and a date from the Myllyjärämä site in Enontekiö follows closely at 8320±110 BP (Hel-2710; Carpelan 1999:159; Schulz 1996:43). All dates cited in this paper are in uncalibrated radiocarbon years BP.

Another feature, which concerns particularly the origin of the inland settlement, is the fairly undiagnostic character of the archaeological assemblages, especially the fact that most of the artifacts are made of quartz, a ubiquitous raw material that does not easily lend itself to the manufacture of characteristic formal tool types. The early coastal assemblages are problematic, too, because few detailed studies of the archaeological material have been carried out (but see Woodman 1993; 1999) and clear counterparts for the tool forms have been missing in the possible source areas for the occupation.

This situation makes it possible to suggest on the one hand both a western and an eastern immigration route for the coastal population, and on the other both a northern and a southern origin for the inland population. The expressed views have, naturally, been affected by the research situation at the time of each publication, and the increased research activity during the 1980's and the 1990's has made it easier to solve some of the problems. Nevertheless, opposing views concerning the matter still exist.

The proponents of a western origin and immigration route for the early coastal population have included, for example, Nummedal (1924), Odner (1966), Siiriäinen (1981), Bjerck (1994), Carpelan (1996), Nuñez (1996, 1997), and Woodman (1999), while an eastern or southeastern origin has been favoured by Luho (1956) and Meinander (1984) and, lately, Anundsen (1996). Olsen (1994) and Thommessen (1996a) consider a western origin more likely in the present research situation. However, due to recent information that suggests an early date for the deglaciation of the Kola Peninsula (e.g. Møller 1996), they leave the possibility of an eastern immigration route open.

The currently available archaeological material from the Kola Peninsula shows that the earliest settlement of the region occurred on the northern coast and was contemporaneous with and related to the earliest north Norwegian settlement, i.e. the Komsa complex. The inland areas and the south coast were not settled before the late Mesolithic, i.e. by *c.* 7000–6000 BP. Influence from Karelia in the south can be seen only in the relatively late occupation of the southern part of the peninsula, and no actual eastern antecedents for the Komsa type material can be identified. It seems thus obvious, at least at this stage of research, that the initial colonisation of the peninsula, or the north Norwegian coast, did not originate in the east (Gurina 1987; Šumkin 1990; Woodman 1999).

As regards the inland region of Finnmark (i.e. the Finnmarksvidda), its settlement began considerably later than on the coast, and although few thorough studies of the subject have been carried out, it has been more or less taken for granted among Norwegian and Norwegian-trained or -influenced scholars that the origin of the settlers was in the coastal area (e.g. Helskog 1974; Hood 1992; Olsen 1994; Havas 1999; Woodman 1999). Olsen (1994) acknowledges the possibility that some immigration from the south might have occurred, but bases all his subsequent discussion on the assumption of a northern coastal origin. In the most recent extensive treatise of the subject, Havas (1999) also reaches the conclusion that the likeliest source for the occupation was on the coast.

In Finland, studies concentrating on the archaeology of northern Lapland are very few indeed (but see Halinen 1996; Rankama 1996, 1997a), and the source of the earliest inland population has seldom been discussed. Carpelan (1996) prefers the coast, because to him an origin in the coastal area and, ultimately, among the Late Palaeolithic population of Western Europe, would help explain the genetic uniqueness of the Sámi people. Apart from Carpelan and, to a degree, Nuñez (1997), researchers, however, tend to favour the idea that the origin lies in the south or southeast, that is, within the sphere of the Finnish Mesolithic and its more eastern predecessors,

and that this population, and not the coastal Norwegian Mesolithic people, also settled the Finnmarksvidda (Huurre 1983:121 pp; Halinen 1996; Nuñez 1996; Rankama 1996:524 pp, 1997b).

These views reflect the cultural idiosyncrasies of both countries. Norwegians tend to see the coast as the primary settlement area and the inland as a periphery to be taken into use by the coastal population only when need arises. Finns, on the other hand, are more used to inland settlement and inland adaptations, and view the hinterland not as a periphery but as a part of the normal sphere of subsistence pursuits into which settlement can be easily extended.

This paper attempts to use the widest possible array of information to look at the colonisation of the inland areas of Finnmark and northern Finnish Lapland, and to reach a conclusion based not only on archaeological finds but on variables as far apart as rock type distributions and the self-image of potential settlers.

The Environmental Background

A model of colonisation, of necessity, must take as its starting point the available archaeological information. In some cases, where the evidence is unequivocal, this may be sufficient, but in others, such as in my opinion the case discussed here, other factors must be taken into account. These include local geography, geology, environmental development, resource availability, subsistence systems, and technology. In addition, a number of cultural factors are important. Probably the most significant of these is adaptation with all of its cultural "by-products", such as self image, mindsets concerning attitudes towards available resources, approaches to technology and raw materials, and the ideas and aims of tool production, traditional ritual behaviour, territoriality, etc.

Together, these variables form a system in which no element can be ignored, not even if all the rest fits. The environment and its changes through time determine the resources present; the resources are reflected in subsistence and adaptation, as well as in technology; adaptation and its cultural consequences, in turn, are reflected in resource use. The term "available resources" is very much culturally defined: not everything present is necessarily used, and the order of preference depends on a variety of cultural factors (see e.g. Fitzhugh 1972:183; Jones 1978; Meehan 1977; Nelson 1983).

The environmental development of the area under scrutiny begins with deglaciation. The maps in Figure 6.3 (Eronen *et al.* 2001) show the size of the Scandinavian Ice Sheet at 10,300, 10,000, 9300–9200 and 7500–7000 BP. At 10,300 BP (and, indeed, already at 11,000 BP; see Hyvärinen 1997, Fig. 3) a narrow strip of coastal Norway was already free of ice. In theory, immigration along the coast from the south was already possible for a population with a marine adaptation and the necessary technology, that is, first and foremost, boats. The eastern

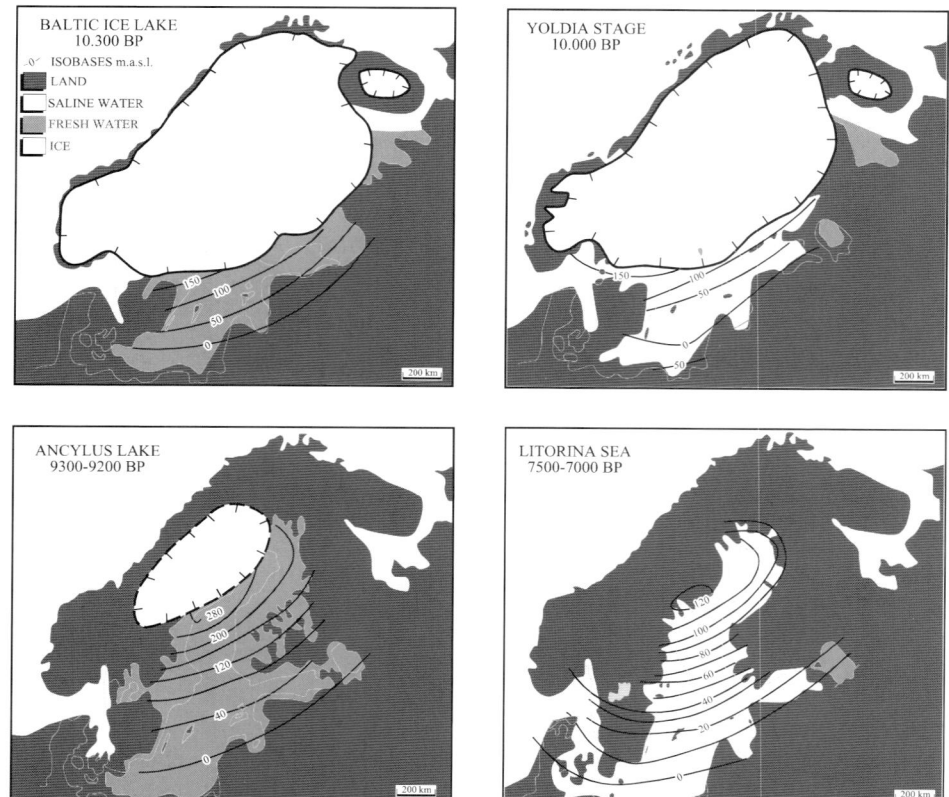

Figure 6.3 The deglaciation of Fennoscandia from 10,300 BP to 7000 BP. From Eronen et al. 2001.

route through Kola Peninsula is problematic, since its deglaciation history is still debated (Hyvärinen 1997:21 p). A route along the north coast and directly across the northern part of the White Sea would probably have been possible, but as pointed out above, no antecedents for the population have been detected in the projected area of origin in the east.

After the stagnation of the ice edge between c. 10,500 and 10,200 BP, it began to retreat again after 10,000 BP. The melting of the ice was now very rapid especially along the eastern edge of the glacier, and all of Finnish Lapland was freed from ice in a thousand years (Hyvärinen 1997:22). Since most of Lapland was supra-aquatic after the Ice Age (Figure 6.3; see also Donner 1995, Fig. 11.7), human immigration was possible very soon after the retreat of the ice.

The development of the vegetation was characterised by fairly rapid changes. During the stagnation of the ice edge the coastal area was covered by periglacial tundra characterised by low herbs and wormwood (Hyvärinen 1975, 1976). When deglaciation recommenced, the mean annual temperature rose rapidly and reached the present level by 9000 BP (Eronen 1997). Since the climate was already favourable for trees, the early postglacial pioneer vegetation stage characterised by low herbs and shrubs only lasted a couple of centuries (Hyvärinen 1975, 1976, 1997; Hicks and Hyvärinen 1997), and by 9000 BP all of the lower-lying areas in northern Lapland were already covered by birch forest (Figure 6.4).

The spread of pine forest began in the Varangerfjord area (Figure 6.5) in the northeast, where pine was dominant already at 8000 BP. At this time the mean annual temperature was already higher than today, and continued its upward trend until c. 5000 BP (Eronen 1997). This meant a rapid increase in pine, and by 7500/7000 BP (Figure 6.6) pine forest covered most of northern Finnish Lapland and the Finnmarksvidda, as well as large stretches of the shoreline of the northern fiords. Compared to the present situation, it means that most of the areas now carrying birch forest were covered by pine – a situation that lasted until c. 5000 BP, when the retreat of pine from the northernmost areas began (Hyvärinen 1975, 1976; Hicks and Hyvärinen 1997; Rankama 1996).

The vegetation was, thus, undergoing change through most of the Mesolithic in northernmost Lapland and Norway (see Rankama 1996 for a review of the development). This was, naturally, reflected also in the fauna. The terrestrial fauna can be divided in three ecological groups. The tundra or arctic fauna includes the tundra reindeer (*Rangifer tarandus tarandus* L.), the arctic fox (*Alopex lagopus* L.), the Norwegian lemming (*Lemmus lemmus* L.), and the rock ptarmigan (*Lagopus mutus* Montin). In this area the salmon (*Salmo salar* L.) and the arctic char (*Salvelinus alpinus* L.), which originate in the

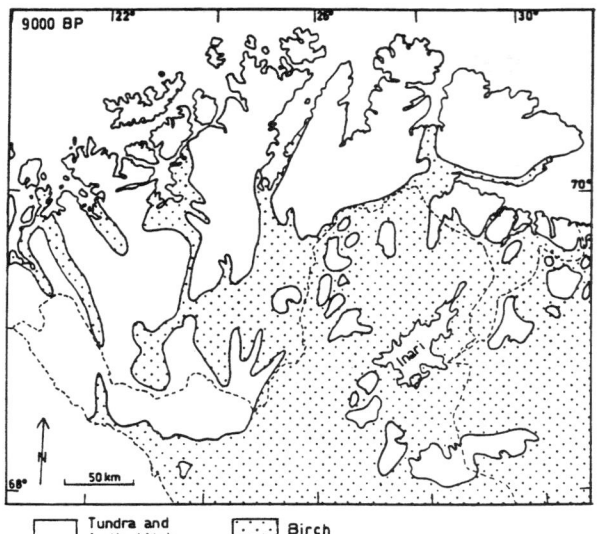

Figure 6.4 Main vegetation zones in northern Lapland and Finnmark at 9000 BP. Modified from Hicks and Hyvärinen 1997:Fig. 2.

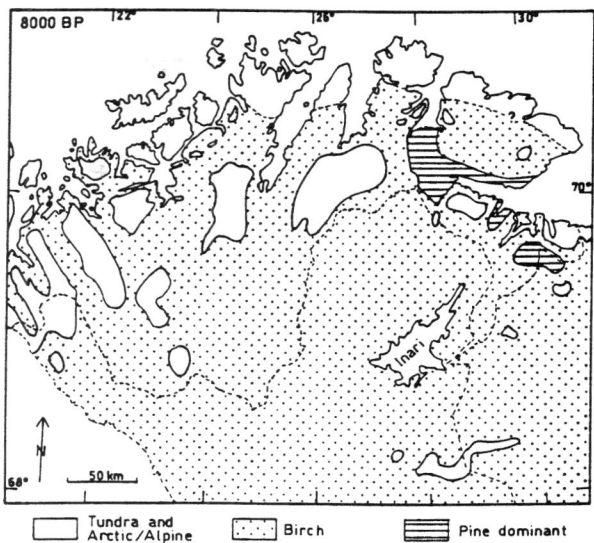

Figure 6.5 Main vegetation zones in northern Lapland and Finnmark at 8000 BP. Modified from Hicks and Hyvärinen 1997:Fig. 3.

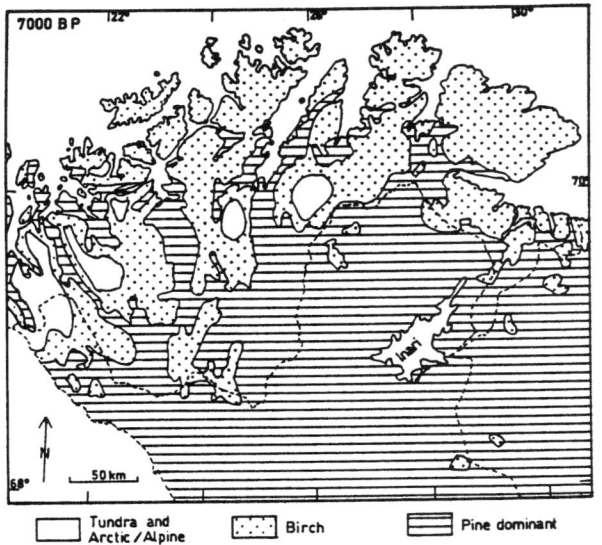

Figure 6.6 Main vegetation zones in northern Lapland and Finnmark at 7000 BP. Modified from Hicks and Hyvärinen 1997:Fig. 4.

Arctic Ocean, can also be grouped with the tundra fauna. The boreal forest fauna includes the forest reindeer (*Rangifer tarandus fennicus* Lönnb.), the elk (*Alces alces* L.), the beaver (*Castor fiber* L.), the squirrel (*Sciurus vulgaris* L.), the pine marten (*Martes martes* L.), the capercaillie (*Tetrao urogallus* L.) and the black grouse (*Tetrao tetrix/ Lyrurus tetrix* L.). In addition, there is a group of generalists or "cosmopolitans" that are as much at home in the forest as in the tundra. These include the brown bear (*Ursus arctos* L.), the wolf (*Canis lupus* L.), the wolverine (*Gulo gulo* L.), the lynx (*Lynx lynx/ Felis lynx* L.), the fox (*Vulpes vulpes* L.), the otter (*Lutra lutra* L.), the arctic hare (*Lepus timidus* L.), the willow ptarmigan (*Lagopus lagopus* L.), and the several species of freshwater fish (Rankama 1996:431 pp; see also Pruitt 1978:41 pp).

The marine fauna includes a number of seals, for example the common seal (*Phoca vitulina* L.), the grey seal (*Halichoerus grypus* Fabr.), the ringed seal (*Pusa hispida* Schreb.), the harp seal (*Phoca groenlandica* Erxl.), and the bearded seal (*Erignathus barbatus* Erxl.), as well as the walrus (*Odobenus rosmarus* L.), the polar bear (*Thalarctos maritimus* Phipps), and various large and small whales. Marine fish species are, of course, numerous, and include, among many others, the salmon, the cod (*Gadus morhua* L.), the polar cod (*Boreogadus saida* Leperchin), and various kinds of flatfish, such as the halibut (*Hippoglossus hippoglossus* L.), the plaice (*Pleuronectes platessa* L.), and the dab (*Limanda limanda* L.).

No archaeological refuse faunas exist from the north Norwegian Mesolithic, and the reconstruction of the earliest fauna must consequently be based on ecological factors, the availability of immigration routes, and other kinds of finds from Finnmark and from further south. These suggest that tundra reindeer immigrated to northern Norway along the Norwegian coast by 12,000–11,500 BP at the latest (Hakala 1991, 1997). An eastern migration route is also possible, but at present difficult to assess. A later migration from the southeast following the retreating ice is less likely, since the rapid spread of forest in the east (Jelina 1985) and south made the environment unsuitable for tundra reindeer soon after deglaciation (Rankama and Ukkonen 2001).

The presence of the other tundra species was also likely already during the periglacial stage of the coast. Likewise,

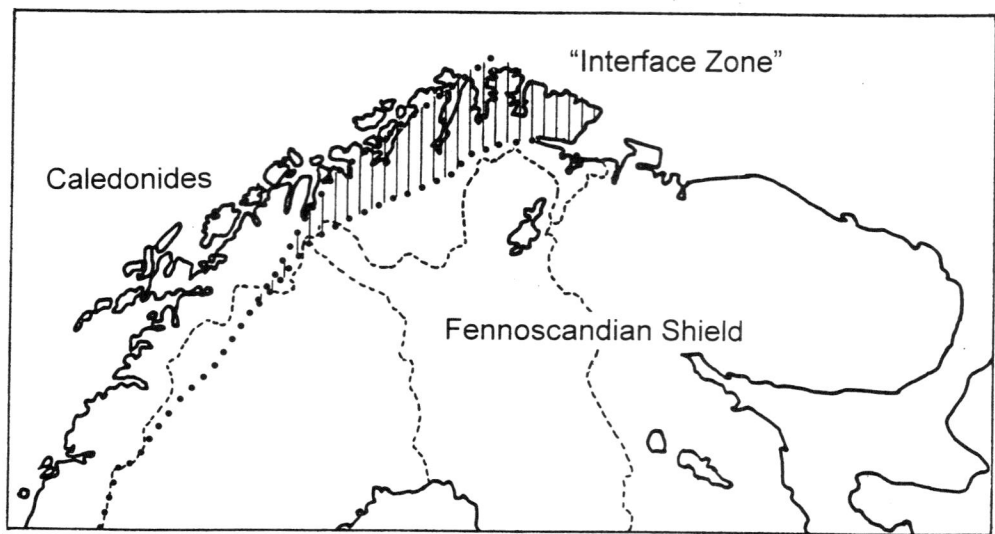

Figure 6.7 Main units of bedrock in northernmost Fennoscandia. Based on Silvennoinen et al. 1997.

the presence of a full range of marine fauna was probable. As the ice retreated from the inland, these areas became available for colonisation by fauna. The tundra species migrated south from the coast, but some of the generalists could also make their appearance from the southeast at this stage. Fish also invaded the lakes and rivers, both from the ocean and along other routes from the south and east. The earliest archaeological bone assemblages from northern Finnish Lapland are dated to *c.* 7700 BP in Enontekiö and 7600 BP in Inari and consist exclusively of reindeer bones. They predate the spread of pine forest and can thus be considered evidence of the presence of tundra reindeer (Rankama 1996; Ukkonen 1997; Rankama and Ukkonen 2001).

With the spread of pine forest between 7500 and 7000 BP the immigration of boreal forest species became possible. The elk appeared in refuse faunas slightly before 7000 BP, the beaver somewhat later. During the Climatic Optimum the distribution of the forest species covered the same area as the pine forest, that is, it was far wider than today. At this time, also, the tundra reindeer in the inland areas were replaced by forest reindeer that had migrated into Finland from the east (Rankama 1996; Ukkonen 1997; Rankama and Ukkonen 2001).

This pattern of faunal development means that the resource base available for exploitation in the inland grew more varied with time. The situation on the coast may have been different. The area available for tundra species shrank, and this may have caused a decline in their numbers. In pace with the warming of the climate, ocean temperatures also rose (Koç Karpuz and Jansen 1992:508 pp, Fig. 9.). What the effect of this might have been on the marine fauna has yet to be studied.

A discussion of resources also needs to take into account other things than food. The area under scrutiny is bisected by a significant geological boundary (Figure 6.7), that between the Fennoscandian Shield and the Caledonian mountain chain (Silvennoinen *et al.* 1987; Donner 1995:Fig. 2.1), which denotes a major difference in the available lithic resources. In the area of the Fennoscandian Shield, practically the only usable raw material for flaked stone implements is quartz. The Caledonian mountain chain and the "interface zone", on the other hand, provide a variety of good quality cherts and quartzites for exploitation (see Hood 1992; Rankama 1996). Given the character of quartz as a raw material that lends itself poorly to the manufacture of formal tool types, which, on the other hand, are easy to achieve in the so-called better raw materials, this difference has the makings of a major distinction.

In addition to the geological boundary, the Caledonian mountains mark a major topographical change as well, from the low undulating contours of the ancient Fennoscandian Shield to the much younger and, consequently, higher and sharper silhouette of the coast. This difference is significant from the point of view of travel, although there are river valleys and passes that cross the higher mountains.

The Archaeological Data

The Mesolithic in Finnmark has been divided in three phases on the basis of the archaeological material (Olsen 1994:23 pp; Woodman 1993, 1999). The settlement began at 10,000 BP at the latest. At this time, the inland was still covered by ice and the conditions were periglacial. The significant features of Phases I and II of the Finnmark Mesolithic are the exclusive use of the coastal zone, the prevalence of cherts and quartzites as lithic raw materials, and similarities in the assemblages with material from western Norway. Phase I is characterised by a macrolithic industry with such artifact forms as large tanged points, flake axes, macro blades and globular cores. Microblades and single platform microblade cores made their appearance in Phase II, by which time the ice had retreated from the inland and birch forest had spread into the area. Phase III, the beginning of which coincided with the spread of pine forest all the way to the northern coast, marked a significant change: settlement appeared in the inland (the Finnmarksvidda), the use of quartz increased and was followed by changes in lithic technology, including the disappearance of microblades and microblade cores. Oblique quartz arrowheads and ground slate implements appeared at the same time as similarities with western Norway disappeared. The oldest coastal rock carvings also derive from Phase III of the Finnmark Mesolithic. In addition to marine elements, they depict inland fauna such as the elk, the bear, and the reindeer (Olsen 1994:23 pp).

According to present evidence, the Mesolithic settlement of northern Finnish Lapland began some centuries after 9000 BP, that is, during the birch forest chronozone and Phase II of the Finnmark Mesolithic, and continued until 6000 BP. No phase division has been attempted. The lithic assemblages are characterised by the practically exclusive use of quartz, with the oblique arrowhead as the only really chronologically diagnostic tool form. Microblades and microblade cores are absent (but see Siiriäinen 1982), but ground slate implements, such as leaf shaped arrowheads and so-called primitive axes, occur (Huurre 1983:81 pp; Halinen 1996; Havas 1999). The assemblage, thus, differs dramatically from the Finnmark Phase II assemblage on the coast, during which the Finnish inland settlement began, but is very similar to the assemblage of the Finnmark Phase III.

The exact character of the adaptation of the early coastal inhabitants cannot be studied because of the absence of faunal remains. It has to be deduced from the location of the occupation sites on the islands and the outer shores of the fiords (Bøe and Nummedal 1936; Odner 1966; Sandmo 1986, 1996; Hauglid 1993; Bjerck 1994; Olsen 1994; Hesjedal et al. 1996; Schanche 1988; Thommessen 1996b), and from the route the colonisers used to reach the area. Both of these indicate a developed maritime adaptation, that is, the use of fish and marine mammals as the core of the diet (cf. Woodman 1999:306 pp). Reindeer may also have been hunted near the coast, at the very least because their skins would have been needed for good-quality clothing, bedding, and tent covers. The lithic assemblages suggest the use of local raw materials and specialised techniques, such as the production of macro- and microblades in Phases I and II, respectively (Bøe and Nummedal 1936; Woodman 1992, 1999; Olsen 1994).

Judged by the refuse faunas, the inland adaptation in northern Finnish Lapland was originally very much geared towards exploiting the tundra reindeer. With the spread of the pine forest, it became more generalised and utilised a variety of boreal forest species, together with freshwater fish (Ukkonen 1997; Rankama and Ukkonen 2001). The latter had, in fact, probably been part of the diet from the beginning, although no evidence of this survives in the refuse faunas. The lithic assemblage indicates a generalised quartz technology with few diagnostic tool types.

Discussion

What, then, was the origin of the inland population in the north? Given the data summarised above, it seems obvious that the coastal maritime population and the inland population had very little in common. Likewise, it seems obvious that the first inland population of the Finnmarksvidda had more in common with the inland population of northern Finnish Lapland than with the coast. The colonisation of northern Finnish Lapland occurred earlier than that of the Finnmarksvidda, and if it is argued that the settlers came from the coast, an explanation is required for why the extensive Finnmarksvidda plateau was skipped in the process, only to be taken into use somewhat later.

I would argue, instead, that we are dealing with two separate populations, and that the origin of the inland population was in the Finnish Mesolithic and its eastern predecessors, who had a well-established boreal inland adaptation and were also accustomed to the use of quartz as their primary lithic raw material. The expansion of the boreal forest northward made the colonisation easier. For the coastal population to have colonised the inland, it would have been required to change its subsistence system and adaptation. It would also have needed to settle for the use of quartz – and the fact that traditional tool types were not executable in quartz – instead of continuing to use the better coastal raw materials, or else it should have started an extensive import of cherts and quartzites into the inland, of which there is no archaeological evidence.

As stated before, Norwegian scholars, nevertheless, prefer to think of the inland as an extension of the coast, waiting to be taken into use whenever the coastal inhabitants felt the inclination. The eventual inclination itself is taken for granted and not questioned; the potential reasons for the inclination are barely discussed, or are waved aside with vague references to social pressures and conflicts within the coastal communities – the reasons for which are, again, not discussed in detail (Hood 1992; Olsen 1994; Havas 1999). The scholars criticise studies geared towards environmental factors and subsistence for "ecofunctionalism" (Hood 1992) or for an excessive focus on resources (Havas 1999).

To me, however, the key issue is not the environment or the resources *per se*, but human adaptation to different resources, whether faunal or lithic. Adaptation is much more than learning to use the available resources in a newly settled area. Adaptation, defined as the way an individual or a society reacts to environmental stimuli, is a process that both defines culture and is subsequently culturally defined. Consequently, it is in the adaptation that we can begin to see cultural idiosyncrasies, social mechanisms, and cognitive responses to the environment. In other words, adaptation, not simply resources or territoriality, is what potentially differentiates between coastal and inland populations – and since adaptation is a cognitive process, it will have consequences on a cognitive level. That is, we can assume that adaptation is very much about people's perceptions about themselves and each other, and this is what we are dealing with when we talk about coast-inland dichotomies.

If resources were the key issue, we could easily imagine hunter-fisher-gatherers moving between the coast and the inland with little difficulty, simply shifting their economic focus from one group of animals to another, for example on a seasonal basis – and examples of this type of subsistence pattern abound in the ethnographic literature. In my view the situation in Mesolithic coastal north Norway and northern Finnish Lapland is different, however. Here we are dealing with two separate well established populations and types of adaptation, one maritime and one geared towards inland resources, and we have to decide which was the more likely to have colonised a new inland area that had become available.

When the concept of adaptation is introduced into the equation, it is followed by cognitive ideas of self-definition, by institutionalised ritual behaviour in relation to game and other resources, by set practices of distributing specific economic goods, and by established ways of gaining prestige within the community. Fitzhugh (1972:193) quotes an example of the inland-adapted Naskapi Indians of Labrador, who had to move to the coast in the early 20th century because of a crash in the local caribou population. Despite the absence of traditional resources, the Naskapi were not able to change into fishermen or marine hunters, since their whole culture was centred on the caribou and other inland game. The butchering and sharing of all inland game species, as well as the disposal of the bones, had been ritualised. Leadership and prestige was derived from the ritual complex centred on inland foods, and the traditional behaviour in relation to the inland resources strengthened social integration. It was not possible to integrate the coastal prey species or the new, individual methods of catching them into the traditional culture, and the result was starvation.

In addition to food resources, the lithic resources and the technologies and traditions associated with them, *i.e.*, the adaptation pertaining to tool manufacture, is also important. It is easy to think of lithic technology from a purely pragmatic point of view, and to assume that there are no particular cultural values associated with it – and, consequently, that a shift from one raw material to another means simply applying previously learned skills to something slightly different. However, different groups of people have always had their own particular ways of using stone, as well as their traditional tool forms, as shown already by the fact that archaeologists have been able to use these traditional "types" as cultural and chronological indicators. The social and cultural ties to tool types and manufacturing processes may be quite as strong as the ties to food resources. In other words, there is no reason to assume that the cognitive aspects of adaptation to raw materials and technology should be any less powerful than the cognitive aspects of adaptation to game.

What, then, will happen, when a lithic user faces a type of raw material that does not behave in the accustomed way, and the production of traditional tool forms becomes difficult or impossible – for example when somebody used to using easily workable raw materials, such as flints, cherts, and quartzites, has to start using exclusively quartz? The first consequence is frustration, since the raw material does not obey the knapper. In the long run, if alternatives do not exist, the second consequence is re-adaptation.

Re-adaptation to quartz is not simple, however, because it requires a completely different way of thinking about lithic production. Since quartz does not lend itself easily to the production of strictly defined formal tool types, quartz users, at least in Finland, seem to have had a different approach to lithic technology. Their expectations concerning the products have been pragmatic: the important thing is for the piece to work in the projected task, not its precise shape. Quartz tools, therefore, often display little elaborate modification. Expedient tools seem to be the rule: any edge will do, as long as it does the cutting. In addition, since quartz is ubiquitous in the terrain, there is usually no shortage of raw material, and since the reduction process produces a large quantity of flakes, a dulled blade can easily be discarded and replaced with a sharp one.

The consequence of this pragmatic attitude to lithic production and the incidental shapes of the tools is that lithic small tools do not easily absorb cultural meaning: there is no *our* scraper or knife type as distinct from *their* scraper or knife type. The need to produce "meaningful" implement types may instead be satisfied through other raw materials, for example organic ones that are rarely preserved for the archaeologist to observe.

The users of other lithic raw materials than quartz, on the other hand, may have attached a wide array of cultural connotations to lithic tool types and technologies. As a corollary to this, it can be stated that

> adaptation to a new raw material is not only a technical problem, but may entail extensive cultural consequences that make adjustment difficult,

and that

> the wider the range of cultural meanings that are attached to raw material usage, the more difficult it will be to adjust to using a new raw material type that is poorly suited for expressing those cultural meanings.

Consequently, cultural problems pertaining to both lithic and food resources may have been severe obstacles for the colonisation of the inland. These problems would have been felt especially by the coastal population that had a maritime adaptation and was accustomed to using easily workable lithic raw materials. Although it is impossible to make definite claims about what the situation actually was, the above discussion should suffice to show that there are several aspects to adaptation and that we have to at least take into account the possibility that shifting the resource base is not necessarily an altogether effortless process.

We also need to take into account the time perspective, that is, the length of time a particular adaptation has prevailed. It seems reasonable to think that the longer the time, the stronger the cognitive ties of the people to their type of adaptation. In consequence, if a coastal or inland adaptation has prevailed for a few thousand years, changing it will be more difficult than if it is only a few centuries or decades old. In any situation it is easier to colonise areas that offer the opportunity to continue the same kind of adaptation as the colonising group has had of old than to move into an area that requires a change in adaptation. At the very least, the impetus for colonising regions that differ strongly from the home area needs to be very strong – in other words, if such a process seems to have taken place, as archaeologists we have to start looking for drastic changes in the environment or the society that have necessitated such population movement.

A corollary of this is also that moving into unknown areas may be easier in the initial stages of the colonisation process, when the population has not yet become rooted into an area or into an adaptation – if such a situation has existed. At the time of the colonisation of the inland areas of northern Lapland, however, this was not the situation. The present colonisation theories that prefer an immigration from the north propose the migration of people who had already been living on the coast for at least 1500 years, and totally ignore the cognitive problems such a change might have involved.

Conclusion

In the light of the above discussion I, again, suggest that the colonisation of the inland areas of Finnmark and northern Lapland took place from the south and not from the north. This is by far the more parsimonious explanation. It does not, of course, rule out the possibility of some individual north to south, coast to inland movement – it just makes it unlikely that the coast was the primary source of the inland population.

The fact that the changes in the lithic assemblage at the beginning of Phase III of the Finnmark Mesolithic occurred also on the coast leads to the further suggestion that even that area might have been taken over by the inland populations. If the coastal resources declined with the warming of the ocean water, it might have led to the demise of the maritime-adapted population. The resulting void could have been easily filled by the inland people, especially since the spread of the pine forest and the boreal fauna down to the coastal zone would have meant that their traditional adaptation did not require significant adjustment in the process.

References

Anundsen, K. 1996. The Physical Conditions for Earliest Settlement during the Last Deglaciation in Norway. In: Larsson L. (ed.) *The Earliest Settlement of Scandinavia and its relationship with neighbouring areas*. Acta Archaeologica Lundensia Series in 8°, No. 24, 207–217.

Arponen, A. and Hintikainen, E. 1995. Strandförskjutningen i Enare Träsk mot bakgrunden av de arkeologiska fynden. *Finskt Museum* 1993, 5–25.

Bjerck, H.B. 1990. Mesolithic Site Types and Settlement Patterns at Vega, Northern Norway. *Acta Archaeologica* 60, 1–32.

—— 1994. Nordsjøfastlandet og pionerbosetningen i Norge. *Viking* LVII, 25–58.

Bøe, J. and Nummedal, A. 1936. *Le Finnmarkien. Les origines de la civilisation dans l'extrême-nord de l'Europe*. Instituttet for Sammenlignende Kulturforskning B XXXII. Oslo.

Carpelan, C. 1996. Mikä on alkuperämme? *Hiidenkivi* 4/96, 10–14.

—— 1999. On the Postglacial Colonisation of Eastern Fennoscandia. In: Huurre, M. (ed.) *Dig it All. Papers Dedicated to Ari Siiriäinen*, 151–171. The Finnish Antiquarian Society and The Archaeological Society of Finland. Helsinki.

Donner, J. 1995. *The Quaternary History of Scandinavia*. World and Regional Geology 7. Cambridge.

Eronen, M. 1997. Ilmaston kehitys Pohjois-Euroopassa viime jääkauden loppuvaiheista nykyaikaan (Abstract: Climatic variations in northern Europe since the last glacial time). *Helsinki Papers in Archaeology* 10, 7–18.

Eronen, M., Glückert, G., Hatakka, L., van de Plasche, O., van der Plicht, J. and Rantala, P. 2001. Rates of Holocene isostatic uplift and relative sea-level lowering of the Baltic in SW Finland based on studies of isolation contacts. *Boreas* 30, 17–30.

Fitzhugh, W.W. 1972. *Environmental Archeology and Cultural Systems in Hamilton Inlet, Labrador. A Survey of the Central Labrador Coast from 3000 BC to the Present*. Smithsonian Contributions to Anthropology 16.

Gurina, N.N. 1987. Main stages in the cultural development of the ancient population of the Kola Peninsula. *Fennoscandia Archaeologica* IV, 35–48.

Hakala, A. 1991. Aspects of the origin of the Scandinavian mountain reindeer and the early man in Fennoscandia with some comments on the history of small mammals. *Aquilo Series Zoologica* 28, 11–21.

—— 1997. Origin and prehistory of the Fennoscandian reindeer with reference to the taxonomy and background in glacial Europe. *Helsinki Papers in Archaeology* 10, 59–80.

Halinen, P. 1996. *Ounasjärven alueen esihistoriallisten peuranpyytäjien asutusmallit*. Unpublished Lic.Phil. thesis in archaeology, University of Helsinki.

Hauglid, M.A. 1993. *Mellom Fosna og Komsa. En preboreal "avslagsredskapskultur" i Salten, Nordland*. MA thesis in archaeology, University of Tromsø.

Havas, H. 1999. *Innlana uten landegrenser. Bosetningsmodeller i det nordligste Finland og Norge i perioden 9000–6000 BP*. MA thesis in archaeology, University of Tromsø.

Helskog, K. 1974. Stone Age Settlement Patterns in Interior North Norway. *Arctic Anthropology* XI-Suppl., 266–271.

Hesjedal, A., Damm, C., Olsen, B. and Storli, I. 1996. *Arkeologi på Slettnes. Dokumertasjon av 11.000 års bosetning*. Tromsø museums skrifter XXVI.

Hicks, S. and Hyvärinen, H. 1997. The vegetation history of Northern Finland. *Helsinki Papers in Archaeology* 10, 25–34.

Hood, B.C. 1992. *Prehistoric Foragers of the North Atlantic: Perspectives on Lithic Procurement and Social Complexity in the North Norwegian Stone Age and the Labrador Maritime Archaic*. Ph.D. dissertation, University of Massachusetts. University Microfilms International. Ann Arbor.

Huurre, M. 1983. *Pohjois-Pohjanmaan ja Lapin esihistoria*. Pohjois-Pohjanmaan ja Lapin Historia I. Kuusamo.

Hyvärinen, H. 1975. Absolute and relative pollen diagrams from northernmost Fennoscandia. *Fennia* 142.

—— 1976. Flandrian pollen deposition rates and tree-line history in northern Fennoscandia. *Boreas* 5, 163–175.

—— 1997. The Fennoscandian ice sheet and the deglaciation history of Lapland. *Helsinki Papers in Archaeology* 10, 19–24.

Jelina, G.A. 1985. The history of vegetation in Eastern Karelia (USSR) during the Holocene. *Aquilo Series Botanica* 22, 1–36.

Jones, R. 1978. Why did the Tasmanians stop eating fish? In: Gould, R.A. (ed.) *Explorations in Ethnoarchaeology*, 11–48. Santa Fe.

Koç Karpuz, N. and Jansen, E. 1992. A High-Resolution Diatom Record of the Last Deglaciation from the SE Norwegian Sea: Documentation of Rapid Climatic Changes. *Paleoceanography* 7, 499–520.

Luho, V. 1956. Die Komsa-Kultur. *Suomen Muinaismuistoyhdistyksen Aikakauskirja* 57.

Meehan, B. 1977. Man does not live by calories alone: the role of shellfish in a coastal cuisine. In: Allen, J., Golson, J. and Jones, R. (eds) *Sunda and Sahul*, 493–531. London.

Meinander, C.F. 1984. Kivikautemme väestöhistoria. Suomen väestön esihistorialliset juuret. *Bidrag till kännedom av Finlands natur och folk* 131, 21–48.

Møller, J.J. 1996. Issmelting og strandforskyving. Modell for utforsking av strandnær bosetning. *Ottar* 4/96, 4–13.

Nelson, R.K. 1983. *Make Prayers to the Raven. A Koyukon View of the Northern Forest*. Chicago.

Nummedal, A. 1924. Om flintpladserne. *Norsk geologisk tidsskrift* 7, 89–141.

Nuñez, M. 1996. Pohjoisen Fennoskandian varhainen asuttaminen. *Sukutieto* 4/1996, 4–7.

—— 1997. Finland's settling model revisited. *Helsinki Papers in Archaeology* 10, 93–102.

Odner, K. 1966. *Komsakulturen i Nesseby og Sør-Varanger*. Tromsø Museums Skrifter XII.

Olsen, B. 1994. *Bosetning og samfunn i Finnmarks forhistorie*. Oslo.

Pettersen, K. 1982. Steinalder på Vega. En introduksjon og et analyseforsøk. *Rapport Arkeologisk Serie* 1982/9. UNIT, Vitenskapsmuseet.

Pruitt, W.O. 1978. *Boreal Ecology*. London.

Rankama, T. 1995. Review of Bjørnar Olsen: *Bosetning og samfunn i Finnmarks forhistorie (Settlement and Society in Finnmark's Prehistory)*. Oslo, 1994. *Norwegian Archaeological Review* 28, 137–142.

—— 1996. *Prehistoric Riverine Adaptations in Subarctic Finnish Lapland: the Teno River Drainage*. Ph. D. dissertation, Brown University. University Microfilms International. Ann Arbor.

—— 1997a. Ala-Jalve. Spatial, technological, and behavioral analyses of the lithic assemblage from a Stone Age-Early Metal Age site in Utsjoki, Finnish Lapland. *British Archaeological Reports International Series* 681.

—— 1997b. Lapin ensimmäiset asukkaat – idästä vai lännestä? *Hiidenkivi* 1/97, 42–43.

Rankama, T. and Ukkonen, P. 2001. On the early history of the wild reindeer (*Rangifer tarandus* L.) in Finland. *Boreas* 30, 131–147.

Sandmo, A.-K. 1986. *Råstoff og redskap – mer enn teknisk hjelpemiddel*. MA thesis in archaeology, University of Tromsø.

—— 1996. En gang for lenge, lenge siden i Simavik. *Ottar* 4/96, 14–17.

Schanche, K. 1988. *Mortensnes, en boplass i Varanger. En studie av samfunn og materiell kultur gjennom 10 000 år*. MA thesis in archaeology, University of Tromsø.

—— 1996. Boplasser og strandlinjeforskyving i Ceavccageadge/Mortensnes i Varanger. *Ottar* 4/96, 34–37.

Schulz, H.-P. 1996. Pioneerit pohjoisessa. (Zusammenfassung: Die frühmesolithische Besiedlung Finnlands im Lichte neuerer archäologischer Daten.) *Suomen Museo* 1996, 5–45.

Siiriäinen, A. 1981. Problems of the East Fennoscandian Mesolithic. *Finskt Museum* 1977, 5–31.

—— 1982. A Communication relating to a Stone Age find from the village of Inari (Lapland). *Fennoscandia Antiqua* I, 5–12.

Silvennoinen, A., Gustavsson, M., Perttunen, V., Siedlecka, A., Sjöstrand, T., Stephens, M.B. and Zachrisson, E. 1987. *Geological Map, Prequaternary Rocks, Northern Fennoscandia, 1:1 mill.* Compiled at the Geological Surveys of Finland, Norway, and Sweden. Printed in Finland by the Publications Division of the National Board of Survey, Helsinki.

Šumkin, V.Y. 1990. On the Ethnogenesis of the Sami: An Archaeological View. *Acta Borealia* 2/1990, 3–20.

Thommessen, T. 1996a. The Early Settlement of Northern Norway. In: Larsson, L. (ed.) *The Earliest Settlement of Scandinavia and its relationship with neighbouring areas*. Acta Archaeologica Lundensia Series in 8°, No. 24, 235–240.

—— 1996b. Steinalderfunnene på Sarnes, Magerøya. *Ottar* 4/96, 25–29.

Ukkonen, P. 1997. Pohjois-Suomen eläimistön historiaa. *Helsinki Papers in Archaeology* 10, 49–57.

Woodman, P. 1993. The Komsa Culture. A Re-examination of its Position in the Stone Age of Finnmark. *Acta Archaeologica* 63, 57–76.

—— 1999. The Early Postglacial Settlement of Arctic Europe. In: Cziesla, E., Kersting, T. and Pratsch, S. (eds) *Den Bogen spannen. Festschrift für B. Gramsch zum 65. Geburtstag*. Beiträge zur Ur- und Frühgeschichte Mitteleuropas 20, 297–312.

7. Mesolithic Colonisation of South-Eastern Subbalticum

Zofia Sulgostowska

The discussed territory has revealed new data concerning the vegetation, fauna and economy at the end of the Pleistocene and beginning of the Holocene. The reconstruction of the environment contradicts the theory regarding the retardation of the Holocene conditions and Mesolithic colonisation of the area. Chronology based on tens of C14 measurements shows that during the Preboreal territory constituted the terminal outskirts for two North European Early Mesolithic units: Maglemose to the west, Kunda and Veretie to the east differing not only in their lithic technology but also in their forest animal hunting strategies. The destination of the Final Pleistocene reindeer hunters connected with the Tanged Point Technocomplex typical for Poland, Lithuania and Latvia is considered.

The first Mesolithic societies exhibit a hunting, fishing and plant gathering economy. Flint mining and processing in specialised workshops – typical for the Final Palaeolithic groups – are not continued. Cemeteries from Poland, Latvia, Russia show the complex burial rites of these first Mesolithic societies.

Introduction

Owing to numerous new data from the area of southeast Subbalticum, Mesolithic colonisation can be discussed as being a result of field activity in the territory, including Finland, Russia, Estonia, Latvia, Lithuania and Poland. The map (Figure 7.1) shows the location of Pre-boreal and Boreal sites with ^{14}C-measurements, faunal remains and palynological analysis in the region earlier considered not available for settlement as early as the Pre-boreal time.

The existing myth about hostile environmental conditions preventing Mesolithic colonisation of the region is changing due to systematic research into the peat sites, which were started in the sixties and developed fifteen years ago. This changes opinion about the regionalisation of the Mesolithic colonisation, and the long survival of Pleistocene conditions in the region of northeast Poland. This territory was regarded as a refuge for reindeer and final Palaeolithic groups hunting it till the Boreal period.

Territory of Lithuania, Latvia, Estonia and northern Russia were considered even more hostile for settlement. But recent environmental analysis shows a picture, different from that published earlier and still being published.

Recent results

I shall discuss only sites dated with ^{14}C measurements (Figure 7.3). This situation is special, because not only settlements but also numerous burial grounds are present in this territory. This is due to the fact that they are located on mineral grounds and are easier to find than sites covered by peat. Only such sites however provide source informations.

Vegetation

Palynological analysis is not yet complete for all the sites but we have data from Całowanie (Dąbrowski 1981); Chwalim (Wasylikowa 1993); Dudka (Nalepka 1995); Tłokowo (Schild *et al*. this volume); Pulli, Antrea, Heinola, Veretye I (Spiridonova 1997). They reveal the presence of pine and birch forest in the Pre-boreal. Especially important, considering the geographical position of the site – the most north-eastern – is the palynology of Veretye I site (Spiridonova 1997). Relics of peryglacial flora (Efedra) are present in Layer I, dated to the Pre-boreal period. But in Layer II, saturated with Mesolithic cultural remains, no peryglacial relics were found.

Fauna

Figure 7.2 shows mammals present among faunal remains. When the sample was sufficient to count percent, the dominant species are marked. All sites present species considered as typical for a Holocene forest. Some preferences can be observed: red deer is dominant in the west, elk and beaver in the east. There are transitional sites where both species are present (Dudka, where red deer is dominant and Kabeliu). Elk is present in the oldest assemblages from Oleni Ostrov, Pestschanitsa and Popovo.

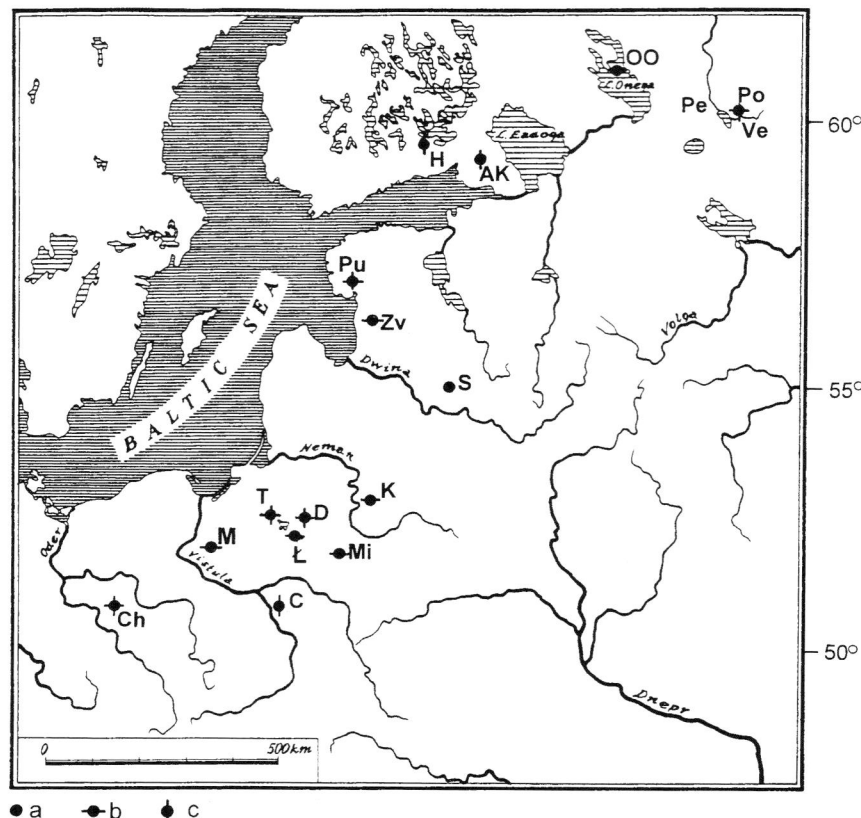

Figure 7.1 Location of the discussed Preboreal and Boreal sites: Antrea Korpilati /AK/ – Matiskainen 1996; Całowanie /C/ – Schild 1996a; Chwalim /Ch/ – Kobusiewicz and Kabaciński 1993; Dudka /D/ – Gumiński and Fiedorczuk 1990; Heinola /H/ – Matiskainen 1996; Kabeliu /K/ – Ostrauskas 1999; Łajty /Ł/ – Sulgostowska 1996; Miłuki /Mi/ – Brzozowski and Siemaszko 1996; Mszano /M/ – Marciniak 1993; Oleni Ostrov /OO/ – Gurina 1956; Oshibkina 1989; Pestchanitsa /P/ – Oshibkina 1994; Popovo /PO/ – Oshibkina 1994; Pulli /Pu/ – Jaanits and Jaanits 1975; Sulgalis /S/ – Loze 1988; Tłokowo /T/ – Schild 2002; Veretie I /V/ – Oshibkina 1997; Zvejnieki /Zv/ – Zagorska 1981.
Key: a – C14 measurements; b – faunal remains; c – palynology.

	Red deer	Roe deer	Wild boar	Aurochs	Horse	Elk	Beaver	Dog	Bear	Reindeer	Arctix fox	Blue hare
OLENI OSTROV						○	○		○			
PESTCHANITSA						○						○
POPOVO						●	○	○	○	○		
PULLI						○	●					
CHWALIM	○			○		○						
DUDKA	●	○	○	○		○						
ŁAJTY	●	○	○		○							
KABELIU 2	○					○	○					
ZVEJNIEKI						●	○					
VERETIE I						○	●	○	○	○	○	

● dominant species

Figure 7.2 Mammal remains (Pre-boreal and Boreal sites).

The early appearance of the dog is significant in Popovo, and a high percentage in Veretye (the same as beaver – 25.4%).

The Pleistocene relics – reindeer, arctic fox and blue hare are present in the Sukhona river basin faunal assemblages. But their ratio is low (reindeer in Popovo – 7.8%) or very low in the Boreal site Veretye I (reindeer – 0.6%, arctic fox – 0.3%) compared with the dominant elk – 59.6%. Rich, representative faunal Pre-boreal assemblages from Poland – Dudka and Łajty did not provide remains of reindeer.

No longer was it possible to hunt reindeer herds as the

SITE	AGE 14C BP	FAUNA	ARCHAEOLOGY
Oleni Ostrov **grave 100**	9910± 80 GIN-4836	Mammals	*Cemetery* Gurina 1956 Oshibkina 1989:403 Veretie culture
Pestchanitsa	9890±120 GIN-4858	Mammals Birds Fish	*Burial complex*: grave, pits, animal bones Oshibkina 1994 52-55 Veretie culture

Popovo
   Grave IX
   Grave III
   Grave I
	
	 9730±110 GIN-4856
	 9520±130 GIN-4442
	 9430±150 GIN-4447
		Mammals	*Cemetery*
			 (9730-7150 BP)
			 Oshibkina 1994:49-52
			 Veretie culture

Pulli	9600±120 TA-245 9575±115 TA-176 9300±75 TA-175 9285±120 TA-284	Mammals	*Settlement* Jaanits & Jaanits 1975 Kunda culture
Dudka	9710±150 Gd-4305 9620±60 Ki-5730 9610±70 Gd-3310 8740±70 Gd-3309	Mammals Birds Fish	*Settlement, cemetery* Gumiński&Fiedorczuk 1990; Gumiński 1995, 1999; Fiedorczuk 1995 Narvian
Chwalim	9565±90 Gd-1164 9500±75 Bln-1766 9385±90 Gd-1164	Mammals	*Settlement* Kobusiewicz & Kabaciński 1993:77 Gautier 1993, Wasylikowa 1993
Sulgalis	9570±80 TA-1317		*Settlement* Loze 1988
Łajty	9420±110 Gd-8027 9240±320 Gd-4584 9150±200 Gd-4588 8870±110 Gd-6982	Mammals	*Settlement* Sulgostowska 1996 Narvian
Całowanie	9410±110 Gd-2734 9380±80 Gd-1721 9370±80 Gd-1719 9350±100 Gd-2198 9350±100 GrN-5251 9200±75 GrN-5442		*Settlement* Schild 1996 a Narvian
Miłuki	9280±50 Gd-7595 9160±50 Gd-7594	Mammals	*Settlement* Brzozowski& Siemaszko 1996, Narvian+Kunda
Kabeliu 2	9100±180 Ta-2600 8680±90 Ta-2604	Mammals	*Settlement* Ostrauskas 1999 Narvian + Kunda
Antrea Korpilati	9310±140 Hel-1303 9230±210 Hel 296		*Net, bark floats* Matiskainen 1996:258
Suomussalmi- **Kirkkosaari**	8950±120 Hel-2313		*Settlement* Matiskainen 1996:255
Mszano	8890±180 Gd-6432 8840±170 Lod-491 8680±130 Gd-6436	Mammals	*Cemetery, pits dwelling* Marciniak 1993:9 Narvian
Heinola	8840±90 Su-1710		*Sledge - pine wood* Matiskainen 1996:259
Veretye I	9370±80 GIN-4833 9050±80 GIN-4031 8790±100 GIN-4869 8750±70 LE-1472 8560±120 GIN-2452 8520±80 GIN-4030 8520±130 GIN-2452 8340±120 GIN-4832 8240±140 GIN-4869 8200±80 GIN-4869	Mammals Birds Fish	*Settlement* Oshibkina 1997 Spiridonova 1997 Veretye Culture

Figure 7.3 Pre-boreal and Boreal sites.

main prey animal and new forest species demanded new hunting strategies.

When we accept that more favourable, Holocene, conditions existed in south-eastern Sub-balticum making possible Mesolithic colonisation as early as in the Preboreal the next important questions are:

1 Was Mesolithic settlement the first one?
2 Was there continuity with the Palaeolithic tradition?
3 What about reasons for settling these new territories and directions of new arrivals?

The proposed answers are:

1 Tens of Palaeolithic sites connected with Tanged Point technocomplex are recorded in the territories of NE Poland, Lithuania and Latvia, mainly Mazovian=Sviderian, but sites with Lyngby and Ahrensburgian points are also present. In the current state of research it is clear that Mesolithic colonisation was the first only for Estonia, Finland and NW Russia.
2 Relations with the Palaeolithic Tanged Points Mazovian=Sviderian tradition and new cultures – Narvian connected with Maglemose tradition sensu largo, Kunda and Veretie connected with North-Eastern complex, are diverse. Discontinuity between Mazovian and Narvian is proved by 14 C measurements, the abandonment of raw material exploitation, distribution and a new tool-kit: the use of geometric insets (Schild 1996 b). Because of the persistent opinion that Kunda and Veretye cultures were continuation of the Masovian "exodus" towards the north-east to continue a reindeer hunting subsistence it is evident that new environment forced these societies to change their style of life. Not only in their hunting strategy – from reindeer herds to forest fauna – but also in their lithic provision and processing.

The Kunda and Veretye cultures used a very efficient lithic processing technique "by pressure", extremely useful in a situation of deficiency of high quality raw materials – which is a situation typical in Karelia, Latvia and Estonia. The one platform cores were processed to produce regular, slim blades, specially broken to obtain insets. The origin of this technology can be traced in Sybiria to the Late Palaeolithic (Vasilev 1992). Grave No. 100 from Oleni Ostrov contains a bunch of 15 "Sviderian like" points with a flat, ventral retouch on the tang but the flint processing is completely different. The same situation occurs in the Ristola inventory from Finland, considered to be Sviderian (Matiskainen 1996).

The anthropological data indicated among the Mesolithic population of Latvia, Karelia and the Sukhona basin, two components of Europoids: the western and the archaic eastern regarded earlier as mongoloid (Denisova 1975; Potekhina 1999).

3 The colonisation of new territories was a continuing process following changes in the environmental conditions. The tradition of Palaeolithic contacts with territories possible to settle is reflected in the raw material distribution (Sulgostowska 1997). Prospection for raw materials can also be considered.

When we consider Narvian – Kunda-Veretie relations it is important that Narvian and Kunda were contemporaneous but in the early phases they had occurred in different territories. The NE region of Poland is the area where both units met. The Veretie sites are located to the east of the Kunda territory. The temporal and spatial relations of mentioned units will be solved when more homogenous sites are recorded.

The mentioned taxons shared numerous general traits:

– The subsistence strategy consisted mainly hunting for megafauna, but fishing and plant gathering were also important;
– The presence of dwelling structure suggesting semi-permanent settlement;
– The presence of cemeteries revealing complex burial customs;
– The mobile art performance using the same decorative motives;
– Very effective processing of lithics, bone, antler and wood.

Differences reflect environmental diversity or different traditions: preference to hunt red deer as the main pray in the Narvian, or elk and beaver in the Kunda and the Veretie; diverse technology and morphology of lithics with the same functionality of their tool-kit.

Conclusion

The Early Mesolithic colonisation of the south-eastern Sub-balticum is supported by records from less than twenty sites. It is not much when we consider that the area covers approximately million square kilometres. There are also some doubts concerning 14C measurements from bone and antler, which are considered not as exact as from wood or charcoal. Other doubts concern the directions of colonisation: archaeological and anthropological records suggest the possibility of colonisation from West and East. More data is also needed to explain the chrono-spatial relation of sites, regions and taxons.

I believe that the first steps have been taken and each new site will enrich our approach. The situation is especially promising because of the presence of numerous burial grounds, in Oleni Ostrov, Popovo, Zvejnieki, Dudka and Mszano or single graves, which are the best archaeological source to investigate past societies.

References

Brzozowski, J. and Siemaszko, J. 1996. Dolnomezolityczne obozowisko kultury kundajskiej w Miłukach, stanowisko 4, w świetle datowań dendrochronologicznych I radioweglowych. *Zeszyty Naukowe Politechniki śląkiej. Matematyka-Fizyka* z. 80. Geochronometria 14, 229–238.

Dąbrowski, M. 1981. Analiza pyłkowa torfowiska Całowanie (woj. warszawskie). *Archeologia Polski* 26 (2), 269–294.

Denisova, R.J. 1975. *Antropologia drevnikh Baltov.* Riga.

Fiedorczuk, J. 1995. Mesolithic Finds at Dudka 1, Great Masurian Lakeland, and their Chronological-Taxonomic Relations. *Przegląd Archeologiczny* 43, 47–59.

Gautier, A. 1993. The faunal remains. In: Kobusiewicz, M.and Kabaciński, J. (eds) *Chwalim. Subboreal Hunter-Gatheres of the Polish Plain*, 77–89. Institute of Archaeology and Ethnology Polish Academy of Sciences. Poznań.

Gumiński, W. 1995. Environment, Economy and Habitation during the Mesolithic at Dudka, Great Masurian Lakeland, NE Poland. *Przegląd Archeologiczny* 43, 6–46.

—— 1999. Środowisko przyrodnicze a tryb gospodarki i osadnictwa w mezolicie i paraneolicie na stanowisku Dudka w Krainie Wielkich Jezior Mazurskich. *Archeologia Polski* 44 (1–2), 33–74.

Gumiński, W. and Fiedorczuk, J. 1990. Dudka 1. A Stone Age Peat-Bog Site in North-eastern Poland. *Acta Archaeologica* 60, 52–70.

Gurina, N.N. 1956. Oleneostrovskij mogilnik. *Materialy i issledovania po arkheologii SSRR* 47. Moskva-Leningrad. Akademia Nauk SSRR.

Jaanits, L.and Jaanits, K. 1975. Frühmesolitische Siedlung in Pulli. *Eesti Teaduste Akademia Toimetisted* 24/1, 64–78.

Kobusiewicz, M. and Kabaciński, J. 1993. *Chwalim. Subboreal Hunter-Gatheres of the Polish Plain.* Institute of Archaeology and Ethnology Polish Academy of Sciences. Poznań.

Loze, I. 1988. *Poselenia kamennogo veka Lubanskoi Niziny: Mezolit i Srednij Neolit.* Zinatne. Riga.

Marciniak, M. 1993. Mesolihic burials and dwelling structure from the Boreal period excavated at Mszano site 14, Toruń District, Poland. Preliminary report. *Mesolithic Miscellany* 14, 1–2, 7–11.

Matiskainen, H. 1996. Discrepances in Deglaciation Chronology and the Appearance of Man in Finland. In: Larsson, L. (ed.) *The Earliest Settlement of Scandinavia and its relationships with neihbouring area.* Acta Archaeologica Lundensia. Series in. 8, no. 24, 251–262. Stockholm.

Nalepka, D. 1995. Palynological investigation of an archaeological site at Dudka (profile D1–26). *Przegląd Archeologiczny* 43, 61–64.

Oshibkina, S. V. 1989. The Material Culture of the Veretye type Site in the Region to the east of the lake Onega. In: Bonsall, C. (ed.) *The Mesolitic in Europe*, 402–412. Edinburgh.

—— 1994. Mezoliticheskie pogrebenia vostochnogo Prionezhia. *Arkheologiceskije Vesti* 3, 48–57.

—— 1997. *Veretye I. Poselenie epokhi mezolita na Severe Vostocnoi Evropy.* Rossijskaia Akademia Nauk, Institut Arkheologii. Moskva. Nauka.

Ostrauskas, T. 1999. Kabelių 2-oji akmens amziaus gyvenviete. *Lietuvos archeologija* 16, 31–66.

Potekhina, I.D. 1999. Postswiderian population of of North-Eastern Europe as seen from the anthropological data. In: Kozłowski, S. K., Gurba, J. and Zaliznyak, L. (eds) *Tanged Points Cultures in Europe*, 333–336. Lublin.

Schild, R. 1996a. Raciochronology of the early Mesolithic in Poland. In: Larsson, L. (ed.) *The earliest Settlement of Scandinavia and its relationships with neihbouring area.* Acta Archaeologica Lundensia. Series in. 8, no. 24. 285–295. Stockholm.

——1996b. The North European Plain and Eastern Subbalticum between 12,700 and 8000 BP. In: Strauss, L.G., Eriksen, B.V., Erlandson, J.E. and Yesner, D.R. (eds) *Humans at the End of the Ice Age. The Archaeology of the Pleistocene-HoloceneTransition*, 129–157. New York and London.

—— 2002. Harvesting the pike at Tłokowo (in this volume).

Spirydonova, E.A. 1997. Zaklucenie po rezultatam sporovopylcevovo analiza stoianki Veretye I v Arkhangelskoi oblasti. In: Oshibkina, S.V. (ed.) *Veretye I. Poselenie epokhi mezolita na Severe Vostocnoi Evropy*, 189–191 Rossijskaia Akademia Nauk, Institut Arkheologii. Moskva. Nauka.

Sulgostowska, Z. 1996. The Earliest Mesolithic Settlement of North-Eastern Poland. In: Larsson, L. (ed.) *Earliest Settlement of Scandinavia and its relationships with neihbouring areas.* Acta Archaeologica Lundensia. Series in 8. no. 24, 297–304. Stockholm.

—— 1997. The Phenomenon of Chocolate Flint Distribution on the North European Plain during the Final Palaeolithic. In: Schild, R. and Sulgostowska, Z. (eds) *Man and Flint. Proceedings of VIIth International Flint symposium*, 313–318. Institute of Archaeology and Ethnology Polish Academy of Sciences. Warszawa

Vasiliev, S.A. 1992. The Late Palaeolithic of the Yenisei. A New Outline. *Journal of World Prehistory* 6, 337–383.

Wasylikowa, K. 1993. History of vegetation. In: Kobusiewicz, M. and Kabaciński, J. (eds) *Chwalim. Subboreal Hunter-Gatherers of the Polish Plain*, 91–101. Institute of Archaeology and Ethnology Polish Academy of Sciences. Poznań.

Zagorska, I. 1981. Das Frühmesolithicum in Lettland. *Veroffentlichungen des Museums fur Ur-und Fruhgeschichte Potsdam* 14/15, 183–190.

8. Colonisation – Event or Process

Christopher Tolan-Smith

Several processes are implicated in the Late glacial and early Post glacial settlement of NW Europe. First, there is the natural tendency of species to expand to fill their ecological niche. Second, human communities adapted to life in the boreal/tundra transitional zone may have moved north with that zone as a policy designed to maintain a successful adaptation. Third, population growth and displacement by rising sea levels provided a stimulus to expansion into unoccupied areas. Considerations of these processes have paid little attention to the role of social relations and social practice in the everyday experience of the groups involved. Viewed as a simple process proceeding at a constant rate, the spread of human settlement from 50N to 70N over five millennia need have involved a barely perceptible adjustment of annual hunting ranges of 13km per generation. However, when account is taken of the wider environmental circumstances in which this expansion occurred, the movement into new areas may well have constituted a significant event to the communities involved. This paper looks at the social context within which the expansion of settlement into NW Europe took place and suggest that it was a concomitant of significant social developments.

Colonisation; an 'event' and a 'process'

Hitherto the settlement of northern Europe has been considered mainly in terms of chronology, and as such, has been viewed as an archaeological event. The date and rate at which the formerly glaciated and periglacial areas of Europe north of latitude 50N were settled during the late Pleistocene and early Holocene has been well established by several hundred radiocarbon dates (Smith and Openshaw 1990; Gob 1991; Charles 1996; Smith 1997; Housley *et al.* 1997; Tolan-Smith 1998; Tolan-Smith and Bonsall 1999; Blockley *et al.* 2000; Housley *et al.* 2000). The details of this process need not been gone into here, though it should be noted that the data do not document an even rate of demic expansion across the areas studied; for example, a major standstill occurred in the colonisation of the British Isles between 11,000 BP and 9000 BP (Tolan-Smith 1998). It should be noted that uncalibrated dates are used throughout this paper.

From the perspectives of archaeology and palaeogeography a number of processes are implicated in the colonisation of formerly uninhabited regions. First, there is the natural tendency of species to expand to fill their ecological niche. Secondly, human communities adapted to life in the boreal-tundra transitional zone are likely to have moved north with that zone as a policy designed to maintain a successful adaptation. Thirdly, population growth will have provided a stimulus to expansion into unoccupied areas. In an important recent paper drawing on data from an ethnographic study of recent hunter-gatherer communities dependent upon terrestrial animals, Binford (1999:8) has suggested that a critical threshold is reached at 1.57 persons per 100 km (0.0016/km) at which point structural changes take place that may involve a diversification of subsistence or the budding-off of the surplus component in the population to found new communities. Population displacement caused by rising sea levels will have had the same effect by creating population increases in areas not subject to inundation. However, simply enumerating these processes pays little attention to the role of social relations and social practice in the everyday experience of the groups involved, although such issues must have been a feature of each of these scenarios. Although it may be a principle of ecology that species expand to fill their niche, in the case of humans this is not a random process but the result of decisions taken by individuals to venture into new, and at times unfamiliar, areas. Any deviation from the normal annual cycle is likely to have been a significant social event. The ability to find new hunting grounds or sources of raw materials may have been an additional social *chacet* to that of being a successful hunter, while the skill to help the group maintain a traditional way of life in the face of often rapid environmental change probably brought similar benefits to the individual concerned, as would the ability to successfully negotiate social relations within the context of a rising population. The benefits to the individuals concerned are likely to have been a stimulus

State 1	State 2	
Residential foragers	Logistic collectors	(Binford 1980)
Immediate return systems	Delayed return systems	(Woodburn 1980)
Local group alliance systems	Local group growth systems	(Ives 1990)

Figure 8.1 Models of socio-economic relations among hunter-gatherers, past and present

to expansion and the possibility of an 'ethos' of expansion and colonisation is worth considering, particularly at a time when significant environmental changes were occurring within the span of a single generation. One of the most significant, perhaps the most significant, feature in any group's environment is other groups and similar considerations apply at the level of the co-residential, or local, group. Those groups best fitted to coping with the pressures presented by a dynamic environmental and social arena are likely to be those with strongly cohesive but flexible social relations.

A model of socio-economic relations

Drawing on ethnographic data, several models have been proposed as a means of making generalisations about the ways in which hunter-gatherers organise their lives, each with implications for the social practices of the groups involved.

This first example is the well known Binford 'residential forager/logistic collector' model, the prime focus of which is the way in which communities map their economic strategies onto the pattern of resource availability. However, the ability to recruit and logistically deploy specialist task groups implies a level of social organisation unnecessary in the case of a community of residential foragers.

My second example is James Woodburn's 'immediate and delayed return' model. Unlike the Binford model the social content of Woodburn's model is more explicit in that communities, or 'societies' to use Woodburn's term, pursuing an immediate return economic strategy are usually found to be more egalitarian than the complex hierarchical societies who have adopted delayed return systems.

The third example is Jack Ives explicitly social 'local group alliance formation/local group growth' model. In a study of northern Athapaskan societies in prehistoric and historic times Ives focused on the principles which underlie group formation and found two broad patterns. In the first kinship structures promoting exogamy regulated the size of local groups and led to the formation of extensive alliance networks with the higher levels of social organisation functioning at the level of the regional group. In the alternative case, endogamy was promoted leading to growth of the local group and the emergence of social complexity within the group.

I find striking similarities between these three models and suggest that they can be combined to produce a model of socio-economic relations. Immediate return societies are usually residential foragers and have kinship systems which limit local group size and promote the formation of alliance networks while delayed return societies are usually logistic collectors and have kinship rules which promote local group growth and, axiomatically, social complexity. I refer to these contrasting patterns of socio-economic relations as States 1 and 2 respectively.

The Late Upper Palaeolithic and Mesolithic colonisation of the British Isles

In a series of publications (Smith and Openshaw 1990; Smith 1997; Tolan-Smith 1998; Tolan-Smith and Bonsall 1999) I have proposed that the spatial and temporal distribution of the radiocarbon dated records of an initial human presence in the British Isles allows three broad phases of settlement to be identified. The first I regard as the phase of initial colonisation. This began around 12,500 BP, towards the end of the Late glacial Interstadial (Dryas Ib, Ic and II), and was marked by the rapid and widespread dispersal of human groups into the lowlands of central, southern and eastern England. The second phase, corresponding to the Loch Lomond Stadial (Dryas III) and the Pre-boreal (Godwin Zone IV), and dating from c. 11,000–9000 BP, was an episode of consolidation with little further spread of settlement. The third phase, from c. 9000–7000 BP, witnessed a rapid expansion of settlement that involved most of the rest of the British Isles, including Ireland. The mechanisms behind each phase of this process are likely to have been different.

During the initial phase of colonisation people moved into Britain overland from adjoining areas of the north European plain. The world they encountered in southeast and central Britain differed little from the one they were familiar with and is unlikely to have presented many challenges. One area in which unfamiliarity may have exerted a premium is in the availability of raw materials. As groups move into unfamiliar territory it may take some time before a full appreciation of raw material availability can be established leading to a tendency during the initial stages of occupation for raw materials to be transported over long distances (Kelly and Todd 1988:237–8). In a recent analysis of Late Upper Palaeolithic material from southern Britain, Barton and Dumont (2000:155) have noted that their initial phase of settlement, dated to the mid part of the Late glacial Interstadial and termed by them the 'Creswellian', is characterised by the use of non-local (>160 km distant) sources or raw material.

This phase can be viewed ecologically as a case of a population expanding to fill its niche. The radiocarbon dates for a human presence across the north European plain, from the shores of the Baltic to the English Midlands, a spread of 12 degrees of longitude, are barely distinguishable and the spread of communities throughout this area need have involved no more than a barely perceptible adjustment of annual hunting ranges of 20 km per generation. Simulation studies by Surovell (2000) of the North American case have shown that regions can be populated very rapidly as a result of the accumulation of numerous small scale moves by 'residential foragers'. This situation, in which a small population rapidly expands into a new area, is likely to be an example of my State 1. The groups involved can be expected to have pursued a policy of 'local group alliance formation' while practicing a 'residential foraging' economic strategy designed to produce more-or-less 'immediate returns'. Some support for this interpretation is provided by the archaeological record for the Late Upper Palaeolithic in southern Britain, which is characterised by the generalised nature of the assemblages recovered, whereas a more complex State 2 level of socio-economic relations would be expected to have led to a range of clearly defined site categories.

The second, or consolidation, phase is one during which little further expansion occurred and population growth was accommodated by the infilling of areas already occupied. Archaeologically this is reflected regionally by an increase in the evidence for a human presence in southern Britain (Tolan-Smith 1998:23–25 and figs 2(b) and 3(a)) and on a site-by-site basis by a greater interest in the use of locally available raw materials (Barton and Dumont 2000:157), precisely what would be expected as communities became familiar with the resources of a newly occupied region. But why did the process of colonisation stop in Britain at the end of the Late glacial Interstadial, around 11,000 BP? I do not think we can avoid an explanation that is, at least in part, environmental or ecological, though in practice it was limitations of the social structures and practices of the groups involved that actually called a halt to expansion. They were confronted with two adverse sets of circumstances. First, by the beginning of the twelfth millennium BP the climate in northern Europe had begun to deteriorate with the onset of the Dryas III cold stage; in Britain represented by the return to glacial conditions in much of the north. At just the time when groups were beginning to extend their ranges west and north, conditions in those areas began to deteriorate. Second, even without the problems presented by a deteriorating climate, the way of life that had developed during the Late glacial on the north European plain had reached its geographical limit in the west and north. The people that had so successfully extended that way of life became confronted with very different and unfamiliar landscapes in the mountains of western and northern Britain and on the shores of the Atlantic ocean. The west and north were *terra incognita* in the most literal sense, and knowledge could only be acquired by trial and error.

When expansion did resume after 9000 BP it was rapid with communities being established in the north of Ireland and throughout the length of western Scotland and most of the Hebridean archipelago by the mid eighth millennium BP. While the acquisition of knowledge and an understanding of the opportunities presented by the new situation was an essential prerequisite, I have suggested two major factors that may account for this spectacular extension of human settlement (Tolan-Smith 1998). The first is ecological and acknowledges the role played in the development of the climate, and indirectly the biomass, by the migrations of the Polar Front. During the tenth millennium BP the Polar Front migrated from the latitude of Galicia to that of Iceland. This brought the warm and biologically productive waters of the North Atlantic Drift to the shores of northern and western Britain. It is unlikely to have been a coincidence that the colonisation of northern and western Britain began at this time. These new opportunities are nevertheless likely to have presented difficulties to groups whose way of life had formerly been adjusted to the exploitation of terrestrial resources. Recently acquired data on the *delta* ^{13}C and *delta* ^{15}N stable isotope ratios of late Pleistocene and early Holocene humans from the British Isles have shown that even those living within a relatively short distance (<20 km) of the contemporary coastline nevertheless had diets dominated by terrestrial resources (Richards *et al.* 2000, Richards and Schulting in press). Acquiring knowledge about the potential of the new circumstances would not have occurred overnight, but neither is it likely to have taken millennia and other factors must be invoked. The second major factor that I suggest should be taken into account can be seen as a social response to the challenges presented by those new ecological circumstances. The exploitation of marine resources (other than the collection of shellfish) and the occupation of offshore islands is an activity involving high levels of investment in equipment such as fish traps, nets and, most expensive of all, boats. The high status of boat owning and handling is well documented ethnographically and coastal hunter-gatherers provide some of the best examples of 'delayed return' systems, characterised by levels of social organisation of greater complexity than normally found among terrestrially oriented groups. It is also the case that 'delayed return' systems are characteristically those of 'logistic collectors' while the levels of social organisation required for the development of such systems are usually found to arise from a policy of 'local group growth'. Accordingly, the expansion phase in the settlement of the British Isles can be seen as an example of State 2 in the model of socio-economic relations. The preceding consolidation phase can be regarded as a transitional period during which groups at first tried to maintain familiar lifeways, but eventually succumbed to the demands and opportunities of a new and unfamiliar world. Differentiation in site type of the kind associated with the logistic deployment of specialist task groups is a feature of the later Mesolithic with shell middens, upland hunting camps, and lithic procurement localities being familiar examples.

The establishment of appropriate levels of social organisation were a prerequisite to the development of a way of life capable of fully responding to the opportunities presented by the Atlantic shores of north-west Europe. Put simply, the colonisation of the Atlantic coastal zone required a quantum leap in social organisation, but once this had occurred its consequences were rapid and far-reaching. The Mesolithic settlement of north-west Britain seems to have been mainly a maritime venture and the stable isotope data document a virtually exclusively maritime diet for the groups involved (Richards and Mellars 1998, Richards and Hedges 1999(a), 1999(b), Richards and Schulting in press). The fact that most of the earliest radiocarbon dates for the presence of humans in the area come from the Inner Hebridean islands of Islay, Jura, Ulva, Rum and Skye suggests that settlement may have been accomplished by movement along the island chain with occupation of the nearby mainland occurring as a secondary process. Such an 'island-hopping' scenario would certainly explain the rapidity with which the region was occupied and can be paralleled elsewhere in the world during many different periods.

Conclusion

In conclusion, I should like to make two propositions:

- First, that the colonisation of new territories should be seen not only as part of an ecological process but also as a social event taking place within a social arena, and

- second, that the challenges and opportunities presented by unfamiliar environments also challenged prevailing patterns of socio-economic relations and in extreme cases led to a renegotiation of relationships within, and probably between, groups.

I have suggested, in what is almost certainly an over-simplification, that the patterns of socio-economic relations found amongst hunter-gatherers can be classified as belonging to one of two alternative states. State 1, in which exogamous local groups with far reaching alliance networks pursue patterns of residential foraging designed to produce a more-or-less immediate returns, appears to have been the prevailing mode during the Late Upper Palaeolithic when communities continued their expansion across the North European Plain into the lowlands of southern Britain. However, the ability to continue that expansion on to and along the shores of the Atlantic Facade required fundamental developments in socio-economic relations of the kind that I have described as State 2. In this situation endogamous local groups with a tendency towards growth and increasing social complexity logistically deploy specialist task groups in a variety of delayed return strategies. These developments enabled human settlement to spread at an exponential rate. The establishment of State 2 patterns of socio-economic relations is one of the defining characteristics of the Mesolithic in Europe.

Acknowledgments

I should like to acknowledge the contribution to my thinking on this matter of Jack Ives, of the Provincial Museum of Alberta, Edmonton who first suggested to me the notion of an 'ethos' of expansion or colonisation. I am also grateful to Mike Richards for discussion of the stable isotope work and for allowing me to quote work in advance of publication.

References

Barton, N. and Dumont, S. 2000. Recolonisation and settlement of Britain at the end of the Last Glaciation. In: *L'Europe Centrale et Septentionale au Tardiglaciare* Table-ronde de Nemours, 13–16 mai 1997, Memoires du Musee de Prehistoire d'Ile de France 7, 151–162.

Binford, L.R. 1980. Willow smoke and dogs' tails: hunter-gatherer settlement systems and archaeological site formation. *American Antiquity* 45, 4–20.

—— 1999. Time as a Clue to Cause? *Proceedings of the British Academy* 101, 1–35.

Blockley, S.P.E., Donahue, R.E. and Pollard, A.M. 2000. Radiocarbon calibration and Late Glacial occupation in northwest Europe. *Antiquity* 74, 112–119.

Charles, R. 1996. Back into the North: the Radiocarbon Evidence for the Human Recolonisation of the North Western Ardennes after the Last Glacial Maximum. *Proceedings of the Prehistoric Society* 62, 1–18.

Gob, A. 1991. The early Postglacial occupation of the southern part of the North Sea Basin. In: Barton, N., Roberts, A. and Roe, D.A. (eds) *The Lateglacial in north-west Europe*, 227–233. Council for British Archaeology. London.

Housley, R.A., Gamble C.S., Street, M. and Pettitt, P. 1997. Radiocarbon evidence for the Lateglacial Human Recolonisation of Northern Europe. *Proceedings of the Prehistoric Society* 63, 25–54.

Housley, R.A., Gamble, C.S. and Pettitt, P. 2000. Reply to Blockley, Donahue and Pollard. *Antiquity* 74, 119–121.

Ives, J.W. 1990. *A Theory of Northern Athapaskan Prehistory*. Calgary.

Kelly, R.L. and Todd, L.C. 1988. Coming Into the Country: Early Paleoindian Hunting and Mobility. *American Antiquity* 53, 231–244.

Richards, M. and Mellars, P.A. 1998. Stable isotopes and seasonality of the Oronsay middens. *Antiquity* 72, 178–183.

Richards, M.P. and Hedges, R.E.M. 1999(a). Stable Isotope Evidence for Similarities in the Types of Marine Foods Used by Late Mesolithic Humans at Sites Along the Atlantic Coast of Europe. *Journal of Archaeological Science* 26, 717–722.

—— 1999(b). A Neolithic revolution? New evidence of diet in the British Neolithic. *Antiquity* 73, 891–897.

Richards, M.P., Hedges, R.E.M., Jacobi, R., Current, A. and Stringer, C. 2000. FOCUS: Gough's Cave and Sun Hole Cave Human Stable Isotope Values Indicate a High Animal Protein Diet in the British Upper Palaeolithic. *Journal of Archaeological Science* 27, 1–3.

Richards, M.P. and Schulting, R.J. in press. Characterising subsistence in Mesolithic Britain: New information from stable isotope analysis. *Les nouvelles de l'Archeologie*.

Smith, C. 1997. *Late Stone Age Hunters of the British Isles*. London.

Smith, C. and Openshaw, S. 1990. Mapping the Mesolithic. In: Vermeersch, P.M. and van Peer, P. (eds) *Contributions to the Mesolithic in Europe*, 17–22. Leuven.

Surovell, T.A. 2000. Early Paleoindian Women, Children, Mobility and Fertility. *American Antiquity* 65, 493–508.

Tolan-Smith, C. 1998. Radiocarbon chronology and the Lateglacial and early Postglacial resettlement of the British Isles. In: Eriksen, B.V. and Straus, L.G. (eds) *As the world warmed; human adaptations across the Pleistocene/Holocene boundary. QUATERNARY INTERNATIONAL The Journal of the International Union for Quaternary Research* Vols 49/50, 21–27.

Tolan-Smith, C. and Bonsall, C. 1999. Stone Age studies in the British Isles: the impact of accelerator dating. In: Jacques, E. *et al.* (eds) *14C and Archaeology Acts of the 3rd International Symposium (Lyon 6–10April* 1998) Memoires de la Société Prehistorique Francaise Tome XXVI, 1999 et Supplement 1999 de la Revue d'Archeometrie Rennes: Universite de Rennes, 249–257.

Woodburn, J. 1980. Hunters and gatherers today and reconstruction of the past. In: Gellner, E. (ed.) *Soviet and Western Anthropology*, 95–117, London.

9. Colonising the edge of Europe: Ireland as a case study

Peter Woodman

This paper examines the reasons for the apparent absence of human settlement in Ireland during the Late Glacial and Early Holocene. Ireland as an island is not unusual in having an apparent delayed human settlement and a narrower range of faunas in comparison to equivalent areas on adjacent continental landmasses. The paper emphasis the fact that factors other than the sea barrier itself could have been the major inhibitors to extensive early settlement.

Introduction

It has virtually become a mantra for the author and others to refer to the fact that, in the case of Ireland, known human settlement begins well after the commencement of the Holocene and while this has been noted as anomalous (Woodman 1986; 2000) and the possibility of earlier settlement has been alluded to, no objective assessment of the potential for Late Glacial/Early Holocene settlement has been made. To some extent, the possibility of earlier settlement before the Last Glacial maximum has been discussed (Woodman 1998) and in that case, a time span of at least 20,000 years, alongside known, if intermittent human settlement in Britain, provided a tantalising prospect for a human presence in Ireland.

In the case of Late Glacial/Early Holocene Ireland, there is a much shorter interval of time when a series of quite obvious environmental changes take place. A realistic reassessment of the earlier known Mesolithic human settlements in Ireland (Woodman forthcoming) suggests, that the notional 9000 bp date for the earlier human settlement in Ireland, based primarily on dates provided from Mount Sandel, could be slightly too old. In fact, the initial phase of Mount Sandel (Woodman 1985) could date to 8800 bp or slightly later! While this could provide a better chronological framework for relating the British and Irish Mesolithic, it also lengthens the period during which human settlement is known elsewhere in North West Europe, but not known in Ireland. Therefore, human settlement would appear to be absent from Ireland for a period of approximately 4000 years, or in other words, not only are the Late Glacial lithic technologies absent, but the earliest Holocene assemblages of the Star Carr and Thatcham types (Reynier 1997) are also absent. In one instance, (Housley *et al.* 1997) a case can be made for a human presence by 13,000 bp, the Late Glacial in Southern Britain, while it would appear that human settlement was taking place north of the Scandinavian ice sheet well before 9000 bp, if not 10,000 bp (Woodman 1999).

Perhaps we do not examine closely enough our own perspectives towards the processes of island colonisation. Irrespective of even the issue of islands, for many living on the so-called edge of Europe, it has been a long and difficult struggle to escape from concepts of these 'marginal regions' as part of a Mesolithic *ultima Thule* (Woodman 1996). These have often been seen as regions, which were only first colonised by communities forced out from their original environment due to change. While many of the more extreme and contradictory elements have fortunately vanished, i.e. Palaeolithic survivals, the underlying the assumption of late arrivals of human settlement has remained. For this reason, the apparent early human presence in Norway and on the Kola Peninsula clearly indicates, that delayed colonisation on the periphery need not necessarily happen. In fact, it would appear that a good case can be made for an extremely rapid movement of settlement into the European Arctic (the author's preferred choice would be along the coast, see Rankama this volume for further discussion of this problem) It would also seem probable that, while certain technologies are not transferred to new environments, e.g. the handle core technology has a limited occurrence further north than the West Norwegian coast, other forms such as the micro blade technology can be found as early in Finnmark as in Southern Scandinavia, i.e. by 8000 bp (Woodman 1993). Bjerck (1995) has suggested that rather than regard distance, inhospitality etc. as a barrier to movement, it may be more a case of developing the appropriate technology, which would allow a particular rich environment to be fully utilised. Perhaps one of the classic instances of this type of expansion takes place across the islands of Arctic Canada with the development of the Bladder float technology. In that case, there would appear to have been an initial several thousand years delay, before, with the advantage of the new technology, a rapid expansion took place. In summary, we should perhaps assume, that successful colonisation of the beginning of the Holocene is not a product of pushing into the margins, groups who failed to adapt to changing environments elsewhere.

The ecology and settlement of other islands

Islands, of course, need to be considered differently. Ireland is not unique in that many islands of similar size would appear to have been colonised at quite a late date. Therefore, islands as diverse as the Caribbean islands, e.g. Barbados (Drewett 1991) or even some of the larger Mediterranean islands (see Vigne 1999 for a recent overview), either lack early settlement or else only have very intermittent, ephemeral or even controversial indications of early, or in the case of the Mediterranean islands, pre-Holocene settlement.

This frequent late colonisation can be matched to a great extent by the fact, that many islands have a very narrow faunal range. Even islands such as those in the Mediterranean, which escaped the ravages of glaciations, have narrow faunal ranges (see Vigne 1999 for Corsica and Sardinia, where sea distance has obviously created a barrier). Similarly, it would appear, that the deep channel between Honshu and Hokkaido on the Japanese archipelago created a significant barrier to the mammalian colonisation of Hokkaido as well as Sakhalin (Dobson 1994). Therefore, it would appear that distance to an island, as well as the length of time available, can combine to limit a range of colonisation processes of both plants and animals. Thus Britain, which was not isolated until well into the Holocene, enjoyed a range of Late Glacial and Early Holocene mammalian faunas similar to that of adjacent areas of mainland Europe. In contrast, during the comparatively long OI stage 3 which preceded the Late Glacial Maximum, Ireland had its richest mammalian fauna at a time, when many aspects of the environment were not particularly accommodating (Woodman *et al.* 1997), but on the other hand, had at any one point in the Late Glacial/Early Holocene a narrow range of fauna. Ireland, can therefore, be seen as quite typical in having a late human presence and a reduced range of animals present. In fact, even within the known indigenous fauna of the Holocene (Figure 9.1), there is as yet no unequivocal evidence that several species, including red deer *Cervus elaphus*, badger *Meles meles*, and pine marten *Martes martes*, were present during the Mesolithic.

Placing Ireland in context

In many of the discussions on either early human settlement or the origins of Ireland's flora and fauna, attention has often focused on the issue of the land bridge. Even early monks speculated on the role of the land bridge, while in the last few decades there have been various suggestions: a morainic land bridge across the middle of the Irish sea (Mitchell 1976), a low-lying land bridge, which allowed the nesting pygmy shrew *Sorex minutus*, but not the burrowing common shrew *Sorex araneus* into Ireland (Yalden 1981), the (Sleeman *et al.* 1984; Devoy 1985) suggestion of a northern low discontinuous land bridge and, more recently, (Wingfield 1995) a series of sand ridges across the Irish sea.

Late Glacial
    Megaloceros giganteus — Giant Deer
    Rangifer tarandus — Reindeer

Holocene
Species, which extend to subarctic regions of Europe
    Sorex minutus — Pygmy Shrew
    Canis lupus — Wolf
    Vulpes vulpes — Fox
    Ursus arctos — Brown Bear
    Martes Martes — Pine Marten
    Mustela erminea — Stoat
    Lutra lutra — Otter
    Lepus timius — Mountain Hare

The temperate woodland element of Irish mammal fauna
    Meles meles — Badger
    Fekus silvestris — Wild Cat
    Sus scrofa — Wild Boar
    Cervus elaphus — Red Deer
    Sciurus vulgaris — Red Squirrel
    Apodemus sylvaticus — Woodmouse

Figure 9.1 Late Glacial and Holocene faunas (after Stuart and Van Wijngaarden-Bakker, 1985)

It would, however, appear that any island successful colonisation must contend with three factors:

Is it possible to reach the island? In the case of Ireland, this factor and the significance of land bridges has tended to dominate discussions.

On arrival, is it possible to sustain an initial population? Are there sufficient resources, notably food, which would allow any initial settlers to survive?

Is it possible to sustain a long-term population on an island?

While the 'land bridge' debate was really more about the origins of elements other than human settlement, the fixation on land bridges is an indication as to how much attention was, and is, being paid to the first of the three factors, i.e. an implicit assumptions that the Irish sea represented a major and frequently impassable barrier. As noted earlier, islands can have delayed settlement, obviously in part due to the sea, though its significance as an obstacle itself may be exaggerated. The very fact that Mesolithic artefact types, of albeit as yet uncertain ages, are now being recognised in Orkney, further emphasises the fact that hostile stretches of water, such as the Pentland Firth, were not barriers for stone-age hunter-gatherers (Wickham Jones and Firth 2000). This would also be evident in the early settlement of islands such as Vega, which are located well off the Norwegian coast (Bjerck 1995). The question, therefore, surely must be, whether there were Late Glacial or Early Holocene societies, which exploited the sea as part of their normal range of economic activities. The loss of the early coastline on either side of the Irish Sea presents an obvious problem. While the effects of Glacial Isostatic adjustments were marked in Northern Britain, the rise of over 50 metres in eustatic sea level (Roberts 1998) has resulted in the loss of much of the early coastline of Southern Britain and Ireland; therefore many of the British cave sites would have been quite removed from the contemporaneous coastlines. As has been shown by the δ^{13}C levels of the 'Red Lady' of Paviland at 26,000bp (Aldhouse Green and Pettitt 1998), the use of marine resources was established even before the Last Glacial Maximum, therefore, it is possible, as indicated by Richards *et al.* (2000), that much of the known British Late Glacial and earlier Holocene archaeology is representative of only an inland focus of the economy. We can, therefore, presume that populations living on the Atlantic coast of England had access to boats and would not have seen the Irish Sea as a barrier. After all, there are numerous points in Britain from which Ireland is clearly visible. The one exception in Britain associated with a Late Glacial date is at Kendrick's Cave, on the north coast of Wales, where some of the human remains are associated with a δ^{13}C suggestive of a marine component in the economy, even as far back as 12,000 bp or earlier (Richards pers. comm.). Elsewhere, the evidence from La Riera in Cantabria (Strauss and Clarke 1986) would also indicate that the sea was used prior to the later parts of the Mesolithic, as is indicated by many Mesolithic sites in Western Sweden such as Bua and Balltorp (Wigforss 1995), where the economy contained a significant marine element but was probably not as specialised towards the use of the sea as in the final stages of the Mesolithic (Richards pers. comm.).

In terms of Ireland being available for and sustaining human settlement, the documentation of the presence of differing ranges of animals in Ireland during the Late Glacial and the Early Holocene has two important implications for the examination of human colonisation. On the positive side, the fact that there is evidence for different faunas during different phases suggests that, while certain species may not have been able to survive climatic change, classically the giant deer *Megaloceros giganteus*, there would appear to be a continued replenishment of new species arriving in Ireland (see Figure 9.2).

It is assumed that the various woodland temperate species were added throughout the Holocene, but at what

13,000 bp	
	Reindeer, hare
12,000 bp	
	Giant Deer, wolf, bear, Red Deer, stoat? hare?
11,000 bp	
	Arctic lemming, reindeer, stoat, hare
10,000 bp	
	Stoat, hare, boar, lynx, wildcat, wolf, brown bear
9000 bp	

Figure 9.2 Range of mammals thought to have been present in Ireland at various stages of the Late Glacial and Early Holocene.

date is uncertain (see McCormick 1999). What is most noticeable about Figure 9.2 is the significant absence of species, which would traditionally have been hunted in Britain, particularly before the Younger Dryas. These include wild horse *Equus caballus* in particular, which was of much significance before 12,000 bp, but also aurochs *Bos primegenius* and elk *Alces alces* and to a lesser extent red deer *Cervus elaphus*, which would appear to have a very limited presence in Late Glacial Ireland.

This raises the points, brought out by Housley *et al.* (1997), that on the basis of ^{14}C dates, the initial colonisation of many parts of North-western Europe can be divided into two phases, i.e. a colonising phase and a residential phase. In the case of Ireland, it is possible, that there could be an initial colonising phase, as the range of other species surviving in Ireland in the Late Glacial demonstrates the feasibility of getting there; however, there is a question, as to whether at any phase in particular the sustaining of the initial population was possible. At any one point in time, it would appear that there was an extremely limited range of species to be found in Ireland and it is difficult to imagine, there being enough diversity in fauna to support a long term Late Glacial settlement in Ireland. In fact, the only viable lifestyle might have been one based on the exploitation of marine resources or species such as salmon. It is easy to dismiss this alternative lifestyle, on the grounds that the sites are buried below present day sea level, however it is a realistic possibility. In contrast, so far, there is no evidence of a substantial land based mammal hunting economy.

It is instructive to examine the potential of a Late Glacial occupation of Ireland from the perspective of the known, intermittent occupation of Britain. It is interesting therefore, that the initial intensive phase of human settlement in Britain, i.e. the Cresswellian, occurs at a time when, other than reindeer and hare, there is no apparent mammalian presence in Ireland (David 1991; Jacobi 1991). Housley *et al.* (1997) have demonstrated that even the Cresswellian residential presence existed before 12,000 bp, while there is a lesser presence of human settlement in the west of Britain in the Windermere interstadial. In the equivalent Irish Woodgrange interstadial, in spite of the presence of a profusion of giant deer, there is no evidence of their exploitation. It is

Figure 9.3 The extant of human settlement in Late Glacial Britain (shaded areas marks the known extant of Late Younger Dryas settlement).

possible to argue that their spongy antlers were not particularly suited to the use of tool manufacture, and that much of their discovery was based on trophy hunting for the antlers and so other portions of the skeleton were not examined. There was, during the 19th century case in particular, a very informal debate on the potential contemporanity between giant deer and humans and the issue of the marks were debated (see Carte 1865). The only documented presence of a giant deer antler artefact would appear to be a re-used portion of an antler from the Bronze Age (Liversage 1957). Therefore, no trace of the human use of giant deer remains has been found. In contrast, in the Irish Nahanagan stage/British Loch Lommond Re-advance, it is questionable as to whether there was a significant human presence on the western shores of Britain (see Figure 9.3). As can be seen from Barton (1991) and Barton and Dumont (2000), the final phase is not only restricted spatially, but may be confined to a very short period from 10,200 to 10,000 bp. There would, therefore, be less possibility of a human presence in Ireland, particularly as it is suggested that cold conditions in Ireland at this period were very severe. The one exemption to this limited eastern human settlement in Britain in the Loch Lommand Re-advance is a 10,000 bp date from Kendrick's Cave on the North coast of Wales (Green and Walker 1991).

It is, of course, tempting to go looking for artefacts, which resemble those which characterise Late Glacial assemblages, e.g. pieces, which resemble Ahrensburgian tanged points (see Wickham Jones and Woodman 1998), but are probably later. There can also be forms, which resemble penknife or cresswellian points, but taken on an individual basis it would be dangerous to infer a Late Glacial presence on one or two- stray artefacts. Woodman (2000) suggests, that the unusual occurrence of scrapers and what appeared to be burins incorporated in the lower gravels at Cushendun (Movius 1940) could be an indication of a Late Glacial presence as these implements are quite rare in the Irish Mesolithic (Woodman 2000), but Finlay (pers. comm.) has pointed out that several small scrapers occur in the Mesolithic assemblage at Lough Boora (Ryan 1980).

Summary

In summary, we must at some point search for Late Glacial *assemblages* in Ireland, but this will not be helped by claiming that individual pieces are an indication of a Late Glacial presence. This type of approach will only lead to sterile debates, to which there can be no solution. The reasons for the lack of settlement in Late Glacial Ireland may be less to do with the opportunity to get to Ireland, irrespective of the extent of development of the Irish Sea, and have more to do with the capacity of a population to sustain itself in Ireland. Certainly if this was a land based economy, the narrow range of mammalian fauna associated with Late Glacial Ireland would have been unlikely to have supported a long term human presence in Ireland. Perhaps, as an afterthought, we should consider why in the Early Holocene the apparent Mesolithic settlement in Ireland should be delayed for a period of up to 2000 years. There are now a significant number of sites and assemblages, which can be dated, either typologically or by ^{14}C dating, to the Irish Early Mesolithic, which begins at or after 9000 bp, but yet, as in Scotland (Wickham-Jones and Woodman 1998), there is no convincing evidence of material older than the Mesolithic.

References

Aldhouse-Green, S. and Pettitt, P. 1998. Paviland Cave: conceptualising the Red Lady. *Antiquity* 72, 756–772.

Barton, N. 1991. Technological Innovation and continuity at the end of the Pleistocene in Britain. In: Barton, N., Roberts, A.J. and Roe, D.A. (eds) *The Late Glacial in North-west Europe*. CBA Research Report No. 77, 234–245. London.

Barton, N. and Dumont, S. 2000. *Recolonisation and Settlement of Britain at the end of the Last Glaciation*. Memoires du Musee de Prehistoire d'ile de France 7, 151–162.

Bjerck, H.B. 1995. The North Sea Continent and the pioneer settlement of Norway. In: Fischer A. (ed.) *Man and the sea in the Mesolithic*. Oxbow monograph 53, 131–144. Oxford.

Carte, A. 1865. On some indented bones of the *cervus megaloceros* found near Lough Gur Co. Limerick. *Journal of the Royal Geological Society of Ireland* 11, 151–153.

David, A. 1991. Late Glacial archaeological residues from Wales: a selection. In: Barton, N., Roberts, A.J. and Roe, D.A. (eds) *The Late Glacial in Northwest Europe*. CBA Research Report No. 77, 141–160. London.

Devoy, R.J.N. 1985. The problems of a Late Quaternary land bridge between Britain and Ireland. *Quaternary Science Reviews* 4, 43–58.

Dobson, M. 1994. Patterns of distribution in Japanese land mammals. *Mammal Review* 24, 91–111.

Drewett, P.L. 1991. *Prehistoric Barbados*. Institute of Archaeology. London.

Green, S. and Walker, E. 1991. *Ice Age Hunters*. National Museum of Wales. Cardiff.

Housley, R.A., Gamble, C.S., Street, M. and Pettitt, P. 1997. Radiocarbon evidence for the Lateglacial Human Recolonisation of Northern Europe. *Proceedings of the Prehistoric Society* 63, 25–54.

Jacobi, R. 1991. The Cresswellian, Cresswell and Cheddar. In: Barton, N., Roberts, A.J. and. Roe, D.A. (eds) *The Late Glacial in North-west Europe*. CBA Research Report No. 77, 128–140. London.

Liversage, D. 1957. An object of giant deer antler. *Journal of the Royal Society of Antiquities of Ireland* 55, 159.

McCormick, F. 1999. Early evidence for wild animals in Ireland. In: Benecke N. (ed.) *The Holocene History of the European vertebrate fauna*, 355–371. Rahden/Westf.

Mitchell, G.F. 1955. The Mesolithic site at Toome Bay Co. Derry. *Ulster Journal of Archaeology* 18, 1–16.

—— 1976. *The Irish Landscape*. London.

Movius, M.L. 1940. An early Post-Glacial archaeological site at Cushendun Co. Antrim. *Proceedings of the Royal Irish Academy* 46C, 1–48.

Rankama, T. 2002. The Colonisation of Northernmost Finnish Lapland and the Inland Areas of Finnmark (in this volume).

Reynier, M. 1997. Radiocarbon dating of Early Mesolithic stone technologies from Great Britain. In: Fagnart J.P. and Thevenin A. (eds) *Le Tardiglaciaire en Europe du Nord-Ouest*. Editions du CTMS, 529 – 542. Paris.

Richards, M.P., Hedges, R.M., Jacobi, R., Cuwene, A. and Seringer, C. 2000. Focus: Goughs Cave, Sunhole Cave. Human stable Isotopes indicate a high animal protein diet in the British Upper Palaeolithic. *Journal of Archaeological Science* 27, 1–3.

Roberts, N. 1998. *The Holocene*. Oxford.

Ryan, M. 1980. An early Mesolithic site in the Irish midlands. *Antiquity* 54, 46–47.

Sleeman, D.P., Devoy, R.J. and Woodman, P.C. 1984. *Proceedings of the Postglacial colonisation conference*. Occasional Publications of the Irish Biogeographical Society. No.1. Cork.

Straus, L.G. and Clark, G. 1986. La Riera Cave. *Stone Age Hunter-gatherer adaptations in Northern Spain*. Arizona State University Anthropological Research Papers No. 36. Tempe.

Stuart, A.J. and Van Wijngaarden Bakker, L. 1985. Quaternary vertebrates. In: Edwards, K.J. and Warren, W.P. (eds) *The Quaternary History of Ireland*, 221–250. London.

Vigne, D. 1999. The large 'true' Mediterranean islands as a model for the Holocene Human impact on the European vertebrate fauna? Recent data and new reflections. In: Benecke, N. (ed.) *The Holocene History of the European vertebrate fauna: Modern Aspects of Research*, 295–322. Rahden/Westf.

Wickham-Jones, C.A. and Firth, C.R. 2000. Mesolithic Settlement of Northern Scotland: first results of fieldwork in Caithness and Orkney. In: Young, R.M. (ed.) *Mesolithic Lifeways: Current Research from Britain and Ireland*. Leicester Archaeology Monographs No. 7, 119–132. Leicester.

Wickham-Jones, C.A. and Woodman, P.C. 1998. Studies on the Early Settlement of Scotland and Ireland. *Quaternary International* 49/50, 13–20.

Wigforss, J. 1995. West Swedish Mesolithic settlements containing faunal remains – aspects of the topography and economy. In: Fischer, A. (ed.) *Man and the sea in the Mesolithic*, Oxbow monograph 53, 197–206. Oxford.

Wingfield, R.T.R. 1995. A model of sea levels in the Irish and Celtic seas during the end of the Pleistocene to the Holocene transition. In: Precce, R.C. (ed.) *Island Britain: a Quaternary Perspective*, Geological Society Special Publications No. 96, 209–242. London.

Woodman, P.C. 1985. *Excavations at Mount Sandel Co. Derry 1973–77*. Her Majesty's Stationary Office (Northern Ireland) Belfast.

—— 1986. Why not an Irish Upper Palaeolithic? In: Roe, D.A. (ed.) *Studies in the Upper Palaeolithic of Britain and North-west Europe*. BAR International 296, 43–54. Oxford.

—— 1993. The Komsa culture: a re-examination of its position in the Stone Age of Finnmark. *Acta Archaeologica* 63, 57–76.

—— 1996. Archaeology on the edge: Learning to fend for ourselves. In: Pollard, T. and Morrison, A. (eds) *The early Prehistory of Scotland*, 152–161. Edinburgh.

—— 1998. Pushing out the boat for an Irish Palaeolithic. In: Ashton, N., Healy, F. and. Pettitt, P. (eds) *Stone age Archaeology*. Oxbow Monographs 102, 146–157. Oxford.

—— 1999. The Early Postglacial settlement of Arctic Europe. In: Cziesla, E., Kersting, T. and Pratsch, S. (eds) *Den Bogen Spannen*, 297–312. Weissbach.

—— 2000. Hammers and shoeboxes: New agenda for prehistory. In: Desmond, A., Johnson, G., McCarthy, M., Sheehan, J. and Shee Twohig, E. (eds) *New Agendas in Irish Prehistry*, 1–14. Bray.

—— forthcoming. Retrospect and Prospect. In: Saville, A. (ed.) *Mesolithic Scotland; the early Holocene prehistory of Scotland and its European context*. Society of Antiquaries of Scotland. Edinburgh.

Woodman, P.C., McCarthy M. and Monaghan, N. 1997. The Irish Quaternary Faunas Project. *Quaternary Science Review* 16(2), 129–159.

Yalden, D. 1981. The occurrence of the pigmy shrew *Sorex minutus*, on moorland and the implications for its presence in Ireland. *Journal of Zoology* 195, 147–156.

Session II

Enculturating the Landscape

10. Enculturation of Mesolithic Landscapes

Marek Zvelebil

In this contribution, I discuss the ways in which hunter-gatherers enculturate their landscape, and how we can identify such practices in the archaeological record. I discuss what is a cultural landscape, what do we mean by landscape enculturation among hunter-gatherers, and what is the social and political significance of this concept. In so doing, I draw a methodological distinction between practical and ritual landscapes, using examples from two ethnographic case studies. I go on to discuss different traditions of research in landscape-oriented archaeology, and show, how this results in different forms of understanding of the archaeological record. Finally, I address the social and political significance of recognising hunter-gatherer landscape enculturation for contemporary hunter-gatherers.

Hunter-gatherer landscapes and their enculturation

Until quite recently, people – professionals and the broader public – believed that hunter-gatherer intervention in the landscape has been minimal. It was generally agreed that post glacial hunter-gatherers left few, if any, enduring traces of permanent landscape changes in the archaeological and palaeoenvironmental records. It has now become clear that hunter-gatherers intervene in and enculturate their landscape using a number of practical and symbolic strategies, the signatures of which have often passed unnoticed by researchers far too influenced by minimalist, social evolutionary and typological perceptions of hunter-gatherer communities. While a major shift from mainly functionalist to more inclusive social and symbolic approaches to the understanding of past landscapes has become evident in studies of the Neolithic and later prehistoric landscapes (i.e. Fleming 1987, 1999; Cooney 1994, 1999; Barker 1991; Bender 1993; Bradley 1993, 1997, 1998, 2000; Barrett 1994; Tilley 1994; Edmonds 1999; Ucko and Layton 1999), the reappraisal of the symbolic perception and social use of landscape by hunter-gatherers in the Mesolithic is only beginning (i.e. Tilley 1994; Zvelebil 1997; Zvelebil and Jordan 1999; Bradley 2000; Young 2000; Jennbert 2000).

For the first time, the enculturation of landscapes by post glacial hunter-gatherers formed a theme of a separate session at an international UISPP congress on the Mesolithic in Stockholm, yet as papers in this volume show, there is great variation in approaches, revealing the early stages in our quest for the understanding of this issue. This raises a number of fundamental questions. What is a cultural landscape? What do we mean by landscape enculturation among hunter-gatherers, and what is its significance? How can we identify it in the archaeological record?

Landscape can be comprehended as natural and cultural features, which give character and diversity to the earth's surface. Landscapes reflect the use of geographical space by individuals and communities over extended periods of time, which include the organisation of settlement in terms of seasonality, hierarchy and function, the prosecution of resource use strategies and the enactment of ritual activities. They are structured by their users in time and space to reflect practical and ritual activities. In turn, landscapes are modified and enculturated through such activities.

Enculturation, then, is an imposition of practical and/or symbolic properties to land and water through practical use and symbolic activity. It is an act of 'inhabitation' (Barrett 1994) that involves symbolic and practical appropriation and includes a cognitive shift in perception from an alien and incomprehensible landscape to a familiar and structured one. For example, Åkerlund's account (this volume) of naming places in a Swedish landscape, emphasising the maritime focus of the (pre)historic communities is an act of inhabitation and enculturation, encoding a past cultural landscape in a region which, through isostatic uplift, is removed from the sea today.

Because of the recursive relationship between people and the landscape, landscapes can play an active role in generating constraints and opportunities for the communities involved, in terms of landscape antecedents and landscape successors. Landscape antecedents impose constraints and opportunities for human users, landscape successors are landscapes shaped by the human use of landscape and can act as antecedents for the succeeding groups of people. It follows, then, that landscapes are not passive recipients of human activities but dynamic and interactive elements in the evolution of past societies.

Practical and ritual landscapes: some examples

Landscapes are structured in time and space. Both of these entities are real, and at the same time perceptual, entities, social constructs modified by the conceptual frameworks of the users. Both dimensions, in their modified, historically and socially situated form, influence in a fundamental way the structuring of landscapes.

At the practical level, hunter-fisher-gatherer land use is guided by the ecological structure of resources, seasonality, the balance between population and resources, technology, and by the motivation guiding resource use strategies, such as social competition, long-term risk minimisation, adequate food provision, procurement for market and exchange or a combination of all such concerns. Together, these considerations impose a certain structure on hunter-gatherer activities in space (Binford 1983; Mithen 1990; Rowley-Conwy and Zvelebil 1989; Tolan-Smith 1992; Zvelebil 1997, etc.).

At the same time, practical landscapes are also the ritual landscapes. Practical activities are embedded in a broader framework of ideology and ritual; profane time is linked to ritual time. Cosmology and ritual impose a web of meaning on the landscape, and in its turn, landscape enculturated through symbolism and ritual plays a role in the processes of social production and reproduction. The relationship between the practical, or routine use of the landscape and the ritual use of the landscape is a complex one, and in a sense it would be wrong to separate the two when trying to comprehend societies unstructured by our own western world-view. Yet, paradoxically, the use of this categorical distinction as a heuristic device does help in promoting our understanding of hunter-gatherer patterns of land use, and in the translation of the meaning and significance of their activities into our own frame of reference. Philosophically, this is the only course of action we can pursue with any clarity within the framework of the established discourse based on western rational thought, and in so doing, we can identify and illuminate people-land relationships within hunter-gatherer societies which have been dismissed or ignored until very recently.

To illustrate this point, I would like to use two from a number of ethnographic studies now available (i.e. Chase 1984, 1989; Chatwin 1989; Myers 1991; Morphy 1995; Ucko and Layton 1999; Zvelebil and Jordan 1999; Brody 2000; and Jordan, this volume): one from western Siberia, the other from South America. The Kets of western Siberia (Zvelebil 1997) are one of the traditional hunting and gathering groups settled along the Yenisei and Ob rivers in western Siberia (others are Selkups, Nentsy, Mantsy and Khantsy). Among the Kets, those settled along the river Pokamennaya Tunguzka (ca.160 people in the first census ca. 1600) are said to have remained hunting-fishing and gathering people without reindeer herding or reindeer transport until the end of the 19th century (Resketov 1972; Aleksenko 1967).

Based on the information from ethnographic sources (Resketov 1972; Aleksenko 1967; Zvelebil 1997 with lit.), it is possible to comprehend how the Kets as hunting-gathering people enculturated their landscape even though this process of 'inhabitation' escaped the notice of earlier ethnographers and archaeologists. In practical terms, the Kets appropriated their landscape following patterns of seasonality, residence and mobility, which provided an underlying structure to their territorial organisation. The calendar year of P.T. Kets – their secular time – was divided into 12 months and reflected the subsistence activities and mobility patterns of the group. The autumn was spent in tents along Yenisei, Tunguzka and tributaries fishing, fowling and gathering berries. With first frosts people moved to their winter settlement upriver. The early part of the winter was spent hunting bear and fur game in a logistical pattern of resource use: hunting parties of three to four men would leave the settlement for four to five days in search of prey, following a system of paths known as 'small roads' (or journeys). This was followed by a festive season, the month of 'short days', marked by aggregation, mid-winter festivals and social activities. From mid-January, the entire group broke into smaller units and set out on the 'great road' or 'great journey' in the major residential move of the year. The entire move lasted about three months and involved movement from one temporary camp to another. Elk, reindeer and fur animals were the main game. At the end of this period people returned to the main settlement, where they remained during the snow-melt and the break-up of ice. The month of the pike (May) was marked by a dispersal to the traditional fishing grounds, owned by each household. There people built fish and waterfowl dams, fish weirs, fish traps, as well as fishing by hook and net. The main summer activities were fishing, fowling and gathering of plant food. The midsummer also marked the second social season, marked by the organisation of fairs along the main river Yenisei. Fairs served as a focus for the exchange of goods, long-distance trade, for interaction with other groups, the making of marriages and for ceremonial activities marking the rites of passage. So in summary, we have four organisational structures: residential aggregation at the main settlement (early winter, early spring), logistical mobility (early winter hunting parties), group residential mobility on the 'great road', and household-based dispersal in the summer. Each group had at its disposal several hunting districts marked out by the small and great roads, so different journeys were taken in different years.

How does the practical use of space among the Kets relate to the generation of socially constructed landscapes? The cosmology of the Kets is a part of a broader belief system, prevalent among the hunter-gatherers of northern Eurasia, which, in summary, seems to focus on two things (Aleskenko 1967; Balzer 1980; Ingold 1986):

1. the division of the universe into three horizontal layers: sky, earth, and the underworld, which corresponds to air, land and water respectively. These layers are linked by a 'cosmic pilar', or 'cosmic river', symbolised in shaman's Turu, or a tree often placed in the centre of shaman's tent

2. the division of humans and animals into the physical self, the body-soul and the free-soul. Human beings and those animals who are masters of their animal charges, such as the bear, possess all three substances. Wild animals normally possess physical self and the body soul (their collective 'free soul' residing in the animal master), while among domestic animals 'the spirit of the domestic animal is the soul of man, controlling the animal from without' (Ingold 1986: 255): domestic animals have no soul (see also Zvelebil and Jordan 1999; Jordan, this volume)

Within this cognitive framework, elk, bear and waterbirds play clearly defined roles as guardians of other animals and as channels of communication with other, non-terrestrial worlds. The 'heavenly elk' for example, is an inhabitant of the heavens, and a central actor in the myths of revival and regeneration, as well as in the mediation between the world of the spirits and of the humans. The bear plays an analogous but somewhat different role as the chief guardian of wild animals and a mediator between animal beings and human beings. Waterbirds are perceived as the messengers between the other-world and the earth, guarding the entrance to the lower world, and acting as guides to the 'sea of the deceased' in some myths, to the 'burial beyond the water' in others (Aleksenko 1967; Balzer 1980; Ingold 1986).

With this background information in mind, we can identify aspects of landscape as a social and ritual construct among the Kets. These serve as points of reference linking the landscape to their cosmology and ritual, through which the landscape becomes symbolically enculturated and appropriated. The Ket 'small roads' and 'great roads' were more than just migration routes. They imposed a network of paths representing a pattern of activity in time and space, journeys at once practical and ritual, during which routine tasks and ritual activities were performed; they encapsulated seasonal strategies by which a particular time of the year was defined (see also Tilley 1994:29pp.; Zvelebil and Jordan 1999).

Physical marks of enculturation were present along these paths. They included site locations themselves with temporary structures such as tents and more permanent ones, such as the earth-houses of the main settlement and fixed facilities, such as fish weirs, traps and dams, pits and traps for fur animals. They also included marks made on trees, or ski and sledge remains placed to communicate specific claims of ownership or exclusive rights of use (Aleksenko 1967; Resketov 1972). So such features symbolised collective ownership of the landscape by the PTK as a group, and the ownership of locations in the landscape by individual households. They symbolised social order in the landscape and encoded visually the relations between households, lineage groups and broader political units.

Such symbols of enculturation were legitimised by reference to ancestors and linked to the overarching cosmology of the Kets. For example, at the first camp of the 'great road', at the beginning of the journey, ceremonies were performed to communicate with female ancestral being (the 'old woman of the road', Resketov 1972). Similar ceremonies were performed on return. Other ancestral rituals, linked to death and regeneration, were also performed at summer fairs and other major gatherings.

Rituals linking cosmology and landscape were also embedded into the course of regular subsistence activities. For example, after the first killing of animals serving as guardians or messengers in Ket cosmology, the soup remaining after cooking such animals: bear, elk, reindeer, waterfowl or fish, was returned to the river at specific holy places in an act of symbolic regeneration (i.e. the essence of messenger animals returned to the 'cosmic river'). Ceremonies associated with the bear hunt defined sacred, ritual places in the landscape by reference to bear as the guardian of other animals and a creature responsible for ensuring hunting success: this was for instance symbolised by specific bear bones (jaws, scapulas) being hung from trees (Resketov 1972; Aleksenko 1967). Collectively, all these activities served to enculturate the landscape, to appropriate it for Kets as a group and specify patterns of use and ownership, and to impose a conceptual structure and order over it.

The Nukak are a hunter-gatherer group in the Amazonian rainforest. A study by Politis (2000) showed that the Nukak were not only collecting, but also manipulating and cultivating plants to varying degrees within the broader framework of the hunter-gatherer mode of production (sensu Ingold et al. 1988; i.e. Politis 105–108). Politis' excellent study also shows that such plant manipulation and the associated practical and ritual inhabitation of the broader forest landscape constitutes enculturation in both the practical and conceptual sense as defined in this paper.

Politis (2000) correctly argues that social and ideological factors are crucial to understanding how the Nukak utilise, manipulate and regenerate rainforest resources. According to him, Amazonian cosmology and its ideological framework can be summarised in a basic concept 'Animals, plants and inanimate objects are integrated in several hierarchical levels; their use and exploitation is mediated by a complex mythical system in which spirits/ancestors played a significant role being the 'owners' of places and the 'managers' of situations'

(Politis 2000:100). Within this ideological framework, which resembles in some key aspects the Siberian belief system, humans are not in any superior position in the natural order.

The Nukak organise their landscape in five spatially-referenced territorial dimesions, ranging from a territory of a co-resident group or a domain (sensu Chase 1989:45; Politis 2000:104) to the mythical dimension, which includes the land surface, the underworld and the overworld – all three inhabited by spirits/ancestors. Patterns of landscape appropriation, land use conventions and resource use strategies are specified for each domain along household, kinship and gender lines, and are validated by reference to ancestral and cosmological myths.

The Nukak practical use of the landscape includes patterned woodland clearance during residential camp movements, promotional planting and tending of certain plants such as palm and guana trees, clearance, burning and sowing, and similar forms of management and use of forest resources. These strategies of inhabitation alter the composition of the forest and lead to the development of anthropogenic woodlands, where the forest layers are structured as a result of human intervention, and often result in 'wild orchards' with concentrations of useful plants. As Politis notes:

> 'The Nukak construct a residential camp, which, after being abandoned, becomes transformed into a type of wild orchard, which augments the resource potential of the area.... Due to the fact that abandoned camps are not reoccupied, edible wild species are not destroyed by subsequent human activity. During the summer the dry roof leaves which still remain are sometimes burned, as well as the garbage piles, creating a fine layer of ash which increases the fertility of compacted soil... This sophisticated settlement and mobility system is also connected to the rainforest layers, as the Nukak displace the lowest stratum of the rainforest ecosystem, and leave the forest canopy intact' (idem 2000:115).

In so doing, the Nukak are creating 'domuses' (Chase 1989), anthropogenic landscapes, to which they can return during periods of high productivity of the 'wild orchards'. Such routine practices are also acts of enculturation, creating ordered, familiar and productive landscapes within tropical forest, qualities which invite the reuse of the locality. In this way, *landscape antecedents* are generated for subsequent settlement and use. But the 'domuses' are a consequence of both, ecological and ideological factors. As Politis notes, 'the conceptualisation of environment is framed in the Nukak cosmology, resulting in a 'map' of the territory where places are favoured or forbidden and where spirits/ancestors/owners integrate the perception and determine the access to them' (idem 2000:199). Practical enculturation is embedded within symbolic enculturation – and both are used to mark and symbolise the possession of the territory. Similar horticultural practices have been observed among other hunter-gatherer groups in South America, Africa and Australia (Politis 2000:116 with references; Harris and Hillman 1989; Gosden and Hather 2000).

Traditions of research, forms of understanding: archaeological applications

Against this background, it is useful to consider next the different traditions of research and different forms of understanding now current in Mesolithic archaeology which relate to landscape. We are dealing here with a plurality of approaches, evident for example in the present volume (comp. Moore, Cummings, Cupillard, Schild, this volume). These differences reflect the disparate theoretical underpinnings and historical origins of various approaches to reconstructing ancient landscapes.

First, there is spatially focussed reconstruction of a dwelling place and its broader catchment, the community or settlement area, designed to understand patterns of land use, subsistence and transhumance. This approach has come into prominence with the palaeoeconomy school of Eric Higgs, where site catchment analyses were used to reconstruct land use patterns within site territories, extended (group or community) territories, and annual territories (Higgs 1972; Higgs and Jarman 1975; Clarke 1972; for application to hunter-gatherer land use, see Jochim 1976; Dolukhanov 1979; Bailey *et al.* 1983; Clark 1983; Rowley-Conwy 1983; Zvelebil 1981, 1986, etc.). The inspiration for the development of this approach was drawn initially from geography (Vita-Finzi and Higgs 1970; Higgs and Vita-Finzi 1972); it was later enhanced and elaborated by ethnographic and archaeological studies carried out by Binford (i.e. 1983) and others (i.e. Flannery 1976; Yellen 1977; Jochim 1983; Moore 1983; Keene 1983). Although set aside for a while as overly normative and insensitive to cultural variation in decision making by hunter-gatherers (see Jochim 1983, 1998; Keene 1983; Bettinger 1991), this and similar approaches have been redeveloped in Central Europe recently using site-oriented concepts of settlement area and community area, ultimately inspired by the same geographical sources (Neustupný 1991, 1998; Kuna 1991; Jochim 1998). These approaches, focussed as they are on the probable utilisation of landscapes around settlements, address principally functional questions of land use patterns, economic exploitation, and resource viability in relation to the human population and the size of the resident group. There is reticence to explore conceptual or symbolic aspects of hunter-gatherer landscapes, either on their own, or in relation to the practical, routine use of the landscape. As a consequence, such studies, while acknowledging hunter-gatherers as skilful and adept at utilising their landscape, reinforce the notion of them leaving few if any permanent traces within it, and claiming no practical or symbolic possession of it.

The second approach to landscape reconstruction takes

its inspiration from palaeoenvironmental, and especially palynological investigations. This approach has a long and distinguished tradition in Scandinavian archaeology, and needs not to be detailed here. It was imported into British archaeology through the early work of Grahame Clark (1936, 1949, 1952) and has entered mainstream archaeological research traditions throughout Europe since then. Of importance here are the implications of this approach to our understanding of hunter-gatherer landscapes in prehistory. Partly because of the stratigraphic and chronologically-controlled nature of the evidence, palaeoenvironmental landscape investigations tend to focus on landscape reconstruction and on long-term changes in the landscape, allowing for the reconstruction of economic landscape histories. For example, Stålfelt's wonderful book *Plant Ecology* includes, in reality, a culture history of the Swedish landscape (Stålfelt 1960); more explicitly, Frank Mitchell's *Reading the Irish Landscape* (1986) was inspired by geomorphological investigations, and the landscape history of Scania, published as edited volumes by Berglund (1990) and Larsson (1992), relies first and foremost on palaeoenvironmental studies for its landscape reconstructions. Within this approach, a greater emphasis is placed on landscape reconstruction and history rather than economic utilisation alone. The focus becomes the landscape itself rather than human settlement, and human – including hunter-gatherer – intervention in the landscape is addressed explicitly (i.e. Simmons 1996), acknowledging the capacity of prehistoric hunter-gatherers to generate long-lasting, sometimes permanent changes in the character of the landscape. At the same time, this approach is ill-equipped to address the issues landscape perception, enculturation and appropriation by prehistoric hunter-gatherers.

The shift in focus from an archaeological site (usually treated as a dwelling site by default) to a landscape covered with archaeological residues and signatures of human occupation has been further developed in a distributional approach, also known as off-site, or non-site archaeology. Field surface collection survey, test-pitting, coring, and other field techniques are the hallmark of this approach, the origin of which can be traced to developments in processual archaeology, and to questions it posed about the formation of archaeological residues, the meaning of an archaeological site as a concept and its spatial and cultural integrity, the meaning of archaeological cultures and their relationship to human behaviour (i.e. Clarke 1968; Hodder 1978; Binford 1983; Shennan 1985; Schofield 1991; Rossignol and Wandsneider 1992; Needham and Macklin 1992 etc.). For our understanding of the past hunter-gatherer landscapes, the important outcome of this approach was the demonstration that past landscapes were comprehensively inhabited and utilised beyond the settlement (with 'background scatters' often as archaeological signatures) and the clear recognition of structure to such patterns of use (i.e. Shennan 1985;

Zvelebil *et al.* 1987; Zvelebil 1992). This structuring in the archaeological record and zonation of landscape by the hunter-gatherer communities implicit in it suggested a range of new questions, including the existence of ritual zones, areas of exclusion, of territorial appropriation, and other uses of the landscape hitherto recognised only among more 'complex', later farming societies.

We can now move into the area of 'landscape archaeology', a concept usually applied to prehistoric societies later than Mesolithic hunter-gatherers. Investigating the origins of landscape archaeology would take a paper of its own. Philosophically, this approach has a peculiarly British focus rooted in a sentimental perception of English traditional landscapes, encapsulated in *The Making of the English Landscape* (Hoskins 1985). A related phenomenon on the Continent is the sentimental view of traditional farming landscapes, celebrated as ancestral to the creation of national and ethnic identity, where farmers are seen as harbingers of true and original national values (Zvelebil 1996). As such, landscape archaeology would seem an unpromising approach to apply in an effort to understand hunter-gatherer landscapes. And yet Mesolithic archaeology has a lot to learn from this approach.

Landscape archaeology came into existence, arguably, as a result of conceptual fusion between traditional landscape historical approaches, practised within historical geography and history (see Roberts 1987 for summary), and post-processual, or post-modernist critique of archaeological theory and practice. Equipped with this conceptual heritage, landscape archaeology, operationalised by methodologies appropriate to archaeological data (such as field surveys, aerial photography, remote sensing), was often applied to bridge the gap between the parsimony of archaeological evidence and socially aware, broadly post-processual agendas (i.e. Fleming 1987, 1999; Cooney 1994, 1999; Hodges 1991; Bender 1993; Tilley 1994; Barrett 1994; Edmonds 1999; Gojda 2000; Jennbert 2000). This is an approach where interpretation becomes explicit, and which is based on full awareness of the recursive relationship between the landscape and its users – a relationship which I have tried to characterise in terms of landscape antecedents and successors. It is an approach, too, that emphasises social and symbolic conditions of routine and practical human activities, and tries to apprehend their meaning. Ethnographic examples noted earlier illustrate the recursive nature of the practical-ritual use of among hunter-gatherers quite clearly. Using this approach, we may come to realise the meaning and social symbolism of material culture signatures, which we may have identified in the material culture of the Mesolithic, but which appeared symbolically unintelligible to us, until we combine the concepts used in current social theory with ethnographic analogies such as those discussed earlier.

Finally, we can also use another perspective, where interpretation, rather than reconstruction, in emphasised. In here, landscapes are regarded, in the main, as socially constructed phenomena, perceived and manipulated through a hermeneutic process of recognition and representation: at first by the people in the past, then by ourselves. It is clear that such hermeneutic cycles can be repeated many times over by each succeeding generation of users. The emphasis is on comprehension, on phenomenology and 'reading the past' (Tilley 1994), on 'promenoren' (Jennbert 2000). This approach recognises the key symbolic value of the landscape and its role in the formation of past and present societies. As Simon Schama, writing about the constitution of German identity, put it:

> 'German woods were more than simply an economic resource: they were in some mysteriously indeterminate way an essential element in the national character, they were ... what made Germany German.' (Schama 1995:116)

The general point is that we perceive the past landscape through our own imperfect eyes, not dispassionately, but as we experience it, informed by our knowledge, and as a social, political and psychological resource. This can make us blind to the significance of some features in the landscape at the expense of others. Such conditions of understanding, possession and consequent transformation of landscapes existed in the past, within every community of users. A number of contributors in the present volume address these issues (Jordan, Cummings, Moore, Fuglestvedt, all this volume).

In practice, each of these approaches to prehistoric landscapes addresses a portion of the entire reality of prehistoric human existence, of the hunter-gatherer inhabitation of the landscape; and so it follows that archaeological investigations should adopt a multiple approach strategy. Students of the Mesolithic have been traditionally reticent to move beyond the descriptive, and use more interpretational approaches associated with landscape archaeology. However, in so doing, they may have inadvertently reinforced the notion of hunter-gatherer societies as nomadic, unsocialised, non-territorial, and unable to manage their resources or landscapes they inhabited. Such reconstructions by default have, of course, political implications, as the cases below show.

Conclusion: The politics of hunter-gatherer landscape enculturation

Hugh Brody spent much of his life mapping hunter-gatherer territories, researching Land Claims and representing aboriginal interests in disputes with national governments in North America, South Africa and elsewhere. As he notes in his recent book, *The Other side of Eden*, the Canadian government requires that in land claim disputes, the litigants from hunter-gatherer societies have to prove that

> 'they use and occupy a definite territory to the exclusion of all other peoples; they have used and occupied the territory 'since time immemorial'; they are 'an organised society'.

The problems inherent in proving the first two requirements – exclusive use and occupancy – are severe. In many hunter-gatherer systems, there are imprecisions and overlaps of territory that unsettle the demand for boundaries and boundary maintenance that the colonial model requires. For oral cultures to prove continuity of land use beyond the present generation is also a daunting undertaking. The imposition of legal process and rules on the peoples that colonists have sought to dispossess makes it hard for hunter-gatherers to give evidence of their own kind in their own way. But the difficulties that arise with questions about use and occupation of land do not challenge the hunter-gatherers' humanity. It is in the 'organised society' test that the deepest prejudices reveal themselves' (Brody 2000:283).

Brody goes on to make a key link between 'organised society', political rights, and land ownership:

> 'Both British and American courts have at times made the existence of organised society a test of aboriginal claims to ownership of their lands. Hunter-gatherers have duly been failed, on the grounds that they lack the minimally necessary social institutions. The accusation of nomadism has been a repeated, if rather general, way in which colonists express this failure of others to achieve their self-styled levels of society. The proposition that nomadism is evidence of lack of rights to land is a great and terrible paradox of the agriculturists' judgement upon others. Great because it speaks to the entire range of frontiers that displace peoples whose territories are wanted for new farms; terrible because this process gives rise to, and then relies upon, a racism that is relentless and purposeful.' (Brody 2000:160).

How consonant are Brody's conclusions with the views of 19th century anthropologists, inspired by social evolutionism and employed in the service of colonial expansion! For example:

> 'the dispossession by a newcomer of a race already in occupation of the soil has marked an upward step in the intellectual progress of mankind. *It is not priority of occupation, but the power to utilise, which establishes a claim to the land.* Hence it is a duty which every race owes to itself, and to the human family as well, to cultivate by every possible means its own strength...' (Sollas 1911:383, ital. mine).

These views articulate fundamentally the difference in the perception of land ownership attributed to farmers and hunter-gatherers. The question arises how far is this difference real. Is it a product of social and economic conditions of hunter-gatherer and farmer existence, and of their different cosmologies and ideologies, or have such categorical distinctions been created, at least in part, by our own (mis)representations (Ingold 1980, 1986, 1993; Zvelebil 1998; Pluciennik 1998; Mulk and Bayliss-Smith 1999; Rudebeck 2000)?

Despite the implicit generalisation, it is clear for example, that what was regarded as aimless nomadism among modern hunter-gatherers consists, in fact, of complex patterns of mobility and sedentism within territories conceptually 'owned', managed, and claimed in ways radically different from more fixed and sedentary land use and ownership patterns conventional among farming communities (Chase 1984, 1989; Chatwin 1989; Morphy 1995; Binford 1978, 1983; Zvelebil 1997; Zvelebil and Jordan 1999; Brody 2000, etc.). The two are not as different in practice as pure nomadism and tethered sedentism, yet different enough symbolically to generate misunderstanding and incomprehension. As Brody shows, this apparent gulf between 'nomadic' hunter-gatherers and 'sedentary' farmers survived despite the recent re-appraisal of hunter-gatherers (Brody 2000: 122pp., and in passim) and found its political use as a major criterion in settling land claims to ownership. Earlier, this perceived difference was used routinely to justify the dispossession and genocide against hunter-gatherers throughout the world (i.e. Sollas op. cit.; see Gamble 1993). The key point is that the possession of the land and land 'ownership' is contingent on symbolic appropriation as well as on practical use; on symbols of social organisation marked upon the land, on landscape enculturation. Herein lies the fundamental importance of recognising the antiquity of such practices among hunter-gatherers, arguably extending back to the Mesolithic.

In their discussion of the representation of Saami cultural identity through landscape enculturation, Mulk and Bayliss-Smith (1999) elaborate on the relationship between the symbolic appropriation of the landscape and its practical use, and on the significance this has had on the competing claims to land and resources between the Swedish farming and Saami hunting and reindeer herding inhabitants of Norrland. They note how the prevailing notion of a cultural landscape in Sweden today still remains the one defined by the presence of agriculture. In their view 'The entire prehistory of the Saami is rendered invisible by this negative definition of their landscape' (1999:363).

Mulk and Bayliss-Smith (1999) go on to illustrate how the Saami enculturate their landscape, and how such forms of enculturation would go unrecognised, or not acknowledged, by settled agricultural communities. They show how this leads to conflicting interpretations of the Saami prehistory: to conflicts in understanding the development of cultural landscape, and to the consequent general failure to recognise the antiquity and the extent of inhabitation of the landscapes of northern Sweden by hunting and reindeer herding communities who now form a part of the Saami identity. Zachrisson (1994) covers similar ground. Both studies show how the enculturation of the landscape has become a major criterion in settling land claims, and as such is a major tool in a political struggle for land and resources, yet the material and symbolic evidence of landscape enculturation eludes recognition because it continues to be evaluated by the standards and expectations set essentially for farming communities.

References

Aleksenko, E.A. 1967. *Kety*. Moskva.
Bailey, G. 1983. *Hunter-gatherer economy in prehistory. A European perspective*. Cambridge.
Balzer, M.M. 1980. The route to eternity: cultural persistence and change in Siberian Khantsy burial ritual. *Arctic Anthropology* 27 (1), 77–89.
Barker, G. 1991. Two Italys, one valley: an Annaliste perspective. In: Bintliff, J. (ed.) *The Annales School and Archaeology*. Leicester.
Barrett, J. 1994. *Fragments from Antiquity*. Oxford.
Berglund, B.E. 1990. The Cultural Landscape during 6000 years in southern Sweden – the Ystad project. *Ecological bulletin* No. 41. Copenhagen.
Bender, B. 1993. *Landscape: Politics and Perspectives*. Oxford.
Bettinger, R. 1991. *Hunter-gatherers: Archaeological and evolutionary theory* New York.
Binford, L.R. 1978. *Nunamiut Ethnoarchaeology*. New York.
—— 1983. *In Pursuit of the Past*. London.
Bradley, R. 1993. *Altering the Earth. The Origins of Monuments in Britain and Continental Europe*. Society of Antiquaries of Scotland, Edinburgh.
—— 1997. *Rock Art and the Prehistory of Atlantic Europe*. London.
—— 1998. *The Significance of Monuments. On the Shaping of Human Experience in Neolithic and Bronze Age Europe*. London.
—— 2000. *An Archaeology of Natural Places*. London.
Brody, H. 2000. *The other side of Eden. Hunter-gatherers, farmers and the shaping of the world*. London.
Chase, A. 1984. Belonging to country: territory, identity and environment in Cape York peninsula, Northern Australia. *Oceania* 27, 104–122.
—— 1989. Domestication and domiculture in northern Australia: a social perspective, In: Harris, D.R. and Hillman, G.C. (eds) *Foraging and Farming: The Evolution of Plant Exploitation*, 42–53. London.
Chatwin, B. 1989. *The Songlines*. London.
Clark, J.G.D. 1936. *The Mesolithic Settlement of Northern Europe*. Cambridge.
—— 1949 (with Godwin, H., Fraser, F.C. and King, J.E.). A Preliminary Report on the Excavations at Star Carr, Seamer, Scarborough, Yorkshire, 1949. *Proceedings of the Prehistoric Society*, 1949, 52–69.
—— 1952. *Prehistoric Europe. The Economic Basis*. London.
Clark, G.A. 1983. The Asturian of Cantabria. *Anthropological Papers of the University of Arizona*. Tucson.
Clarke, D.L. 1968. *Analytical Archaeology*. London.
—— (ed.) 1972. *Models in Archaeology*. London.
Cooney, G. 1994. Sacred and secular Neolithic landscapes in Ireland. In: Carmichael, D.L., Hubert, J., Reeves, B. and Schanche, A. (eds) *Sacred Sites, Sacred Places*, 32–43. London.
—— 1999. *Landscapes of Neolithic Ireland*. London.
Cummings, V. 2002. The origins of monumentality? Mesolithic world-views of the landscape in western Britain (in this volume).
Cupillard, C. 2002. The Mesolithic of the Swiss and French Jura and its margins: 10,150–6000 BP (9550–4700 BC) (in this volume).

Dolukhanov, P.M. 1979. *Ecology and Economy in Neolithic Eastern Europe.* London.

Edmonds, M.E. 1999. *Ancestral Geographies.* London.

Flannery, K.V. (ed.) 1976. *The Early Mesoamerican Village.* New York.

Fleming, A. 1987. Coaxial field systems: some questions of time and space. *Antiquity* 61, 232, 182–202.

—— 1999. Small-scale communities and the landscape of Swaledale (North Yorkshire, UK). In: Ucko, P.J. and Layton, R. (eds) *The Archaeology and Anthropology of Landscape.* One World Archaeology, 65–72. London.

Fuglestvedt, I. 2002. Enculturating the Landscape beyond Doggerland (in this volume).

Gamble, C. S. 1993. *Timewalkers: the prehistory of global colonisation.* Stroud.

Gojda, M. 2000. *Archeologie Krajiny.* Czech.

Gosden, C. and Hather, J. 2000. *The Prehistory of Food.* One World Archaeology. London.

Harris, D.R. and Hillman, G.C. (eds) 1989. *Foraging and Farming.* London.

Higgs, E. (ed.) 1972. *Papers in Economic Prehistory.* Cambridge.

Higgs, E.S. and Jarman, M.R. 1975. *Palaeoeconomy.* Cambridge.

Higgs, E.S. and Vita-Finzi, C. 1972. Prehistoric Economies: A Territorial Approach. In: Higgs, E.S. (ed.) *Papers in Economic Prehistory.* Cambridge.

Hodder, I. (ed.) 1978. *The Spatial Organisation of Culture.* London.

Hodges, R. 1991. *Wall-to-Wall History. The story of Roystone Grange.* London.

Hoskins, W.G. 1955 (1985). *The Making of the English Landscape.* Harmondsworth

Ingold, T. 1980. *Hunters, Pastoralists and Ranchers.* Cambridge.

—— 1986. *The appropriation of nature. Essay on human ecology and social relations.* Manchester.

—— 1993. The temporality of landscape. *World Archaeology* 25 (2), 152–174.

Ingold, T., Riches, R. and Woodburn, J. (eds) 1988. *Hunters and Gatherers.* Oxford.

Jennbert, K. 2000. Peopling the Landscape. The Landscape – Variable, Invisible, and Visible. In: Olausson, D. and Vandkilde, H. (eds) *Form, Function and Context. Material Culture Studies in Scandinavian Archaeology.* Acta Archaeologica Lundensia 8:31, Lund.

Jochim, M.A. 1976. *Hunter-Gatherer Subsistence and Settlement: A Predictive Model.* New York.

—— 1983. Optimization Models in Context. In: Moore, J. and Keene, A. (eds) *Archaeological Hammers and Theories.* New York.

—— 1998. *A Hunter-Gatherer Landscape. Southwest Germany in the Late Paleolithic and Mesolithic.* New York.

Jordan, P. 2002. Investigating Post-glacial hunter gatherer landscape enculturation: ethnographic analogy and interpretative methodologies (in this volume).

Keene, A.S. 1983. Biology, Behaviour and Borrowing: A Critical Examination of Optimal Foraging Theory in Archaeology. In: Moore, J.A. and Keene, A.S. (eds) ~*Archaeological Hammers and Theories*, 137–156. New York.

Kuna, M. 1991. The structuring of prehistoric landscape. *Antiquity* 65, 247, 332–347.

Larsson, L. 1992. Neolithic settlement in the Skateholm area, southern Sweden. *Papers of the Archaeological Institute University of Lund* 1991–1992, 5–44.

Mitchell, F. 1986. *Reading the Irish Landscape.* Dublin.

Mithen, S.J. 1990. *Thoughtful Foragers: A Study of Prehistoric Decision Making.* Cambridge.

Moore, J.A. 1983. The Trouble with Know-It-Alls: Information as a Social and Economic Resource. In: Moore, J.A. and Keene, A.S. (eds) *Archaeological Hammers and Theories*, 173–220. New York.

—— 2002. Enculturation through fire: beyond hazelnuts and into the forest (in this volume).

Morphy, H. 1995. Landscape and the reproduction of the ancestral past. In: Hirsch, E. and Layton, R. (eds) *The anthropology of landscape.*

Mulk, I-M. and Bayliss-Smith, T. 1999. The representation of Sámi cultural identity in the cultural landscapes of northern Sweden: the use and misuse of archaeological knowledge. In: P.J. Ucko and Layton R. (eds) *The Archaeology and Anthropology of Landscape*, 358–396. One World Archaeology. London.

Myers, F.R. 1991. *Pintupi Country, Pintupi Self.* California.

Needham, S. and Macklin, M.G. 1992. Introduction to the volume. In: Needham, S. and Macklin, M.G. (eds) *Alluvial archaeology in Britain.* Oxbow Monograph 27, 1–8. Oxford.

Neustupný, E. 1991. Community areas of prehistoric farmers in Bohemia. *Antiquity* 65, 247, 326–331.

—— 1998. *Space in prehistoric Bohemia.* Czech Republic.

Plucciennik, M. 1998. Deconstructing 'the Neolithic' in the Mesolithic-Neolithic transition. In: Edmonds, M. and Richards, C. (eds) *Understanding the Neolithic of North-Western Europe*, 61–83. Glasgow.

Politis, G.G. 2000. Plant exploitation among the Nukak hunter-gatherers of Amazonia: between ecology and ideology. In: Gosden, C. and Hather, J. (eds) *The Prehistory of Food*, 99–126. One World Archaeology. London.

Resketov, A. 1972. *Okhotniki, Sobirateli, Rybolovy.* Moskva.

Roberts, B.K. 1987. Landscape archaeology. In: Wagstaff, J.M. (ed.) *Landscape and culture*, 77–95. Oxford.

Rossignol, J. and Wandsneider, L. 1992. *Space, Time and Archaeological Landscapes.* New York.

Rowley-Conwy, P. 1983. Sedentary hunters, the Ertebølle example. In: Bailey, G.N. (ed.) *Hunter-Gatherer Economy in Prehistory.* Cambridge.

Rowley-Conwy, P.A. and Zvelebil, M. 1989. Saving it for later: storage by prehistoric hunter-gatherers in Europe. In: Halstead, P. and O'Shea, J. (eds) *Bad Year Economics*, 40–56. Cambridge.

Rowley-Conwy, P., Zvelebil, M. and Blankholm, H.P. (eds) 1987. *Mesolithic Northwest Europe: Recent Trends.* Sheffield.

Rudebeck, E. 2000. *Tilling Nature Harvesting Culture. Exploring Images of the Human Being in the Transition to Agriculture.*

Schama, S. 1995. *Landscape and Memory.* London.

Schild, R. *et al.* 2002. Harvesting pike at Tłokowo (in this volume).

Schofield, A.J. 1991. *Interpreting Artefact Scatters.* Oxford.

Shennan, S. 1985. *Experiments in the Collection and Analysis of Archaeological Survey Data: The East Hampshire Survey.* Sheffield.

Simmons, I.G. 1996. *The Environmental Impact of Later Mesolithic Cultures.* Edinburgh.

Sollas, W.J. 1911. *Ancient hunters and their modern representatives.* London.

Stålfelt, M.G. 1960. *Stålfelt's Plant Ecology.* (Trans M.S. Jarvis and P.G. Jarvis). London.

Tilley, C.Y. 1994. *A Phenomenology of Landscape: Places, Paths and Monuments.* London.

Tolan-Smith, C. 1992. *Late Stone Age Hunters of the British Isles.* London.

Ucko, P.G. and Layton, R. (eds) 1999. *The Archaeology and Anthropology of Landscape.* London.

Vita-Finzi, C. and Higgs, E.S. 1970. Prehistoric economy in the Mount Carmel area of Palestine: site catchment analysis. *Proceedings of the Prehistoric Society* 36, 1–37.

Yellen, J. 1977. *Archaeological Approaches to the Present.* New York.

Young, R. (ed.) 2000. *Mesolithic Life ways. Current Research from Britain and Ireland.* Leicester.

Zachrisson, I. 1994. Archaeology and Politics: Saami Prehistory and History in Central Scandinavia. *Journal of European Archaeology* 2:2, 361–368.

Zvelebil, M. 1981. *From Forager to Farmer in the Boreal Zone.* British Archaeological Reports, International Series, 115, Oxford.

—— (ed.) 1986. *Hunters in Transition. Mesolithic Societies of Temperate Eurasia and their Transition to Farming.* Cambridge.

—— 1989. Economic intensification and postglacial hunter-gatherers in north temperate Europe. In: Bonsall, C. (ed.) *The Mesolithic in Europe*, 80–88. Edinburgh.

—— 1992. Hunting in farming societies; the prehistoric perspective, *Anthropozoologica* 16, 7–17.

—— 1996. The agricultural frontier and the transition to farming in the circum-Baltic region. In: Harris, D. (ed.) *The Origins and Spread of Agriculture and Pastoralism in Eurasia*, 323–345. London.

—— 1997. Hunter-gatherer ritual landscapes: spatial organisation, social structure and ideology among hunter-gatherers of Northern Europe and Western Siberia. *Analecta Praehistorica Leidensia* 29, 33–50.

Zvelebil, M., Moore, J.A., Green, S.W. and Henson, D. 1987. Regional Survey and Analysis of Lithic Scatters: a Case Study from Southeast Ireland. In: Rowley-Conwy, P., Zvelebil, M. and Blankholm, H.P. (eds) *Mesolithic Northwest Europe: Recent Trends*, 9–32. Sheffield.

Zvelebil, M. and Jordan, P. 1999. Hunter fisher gatherer ritual landscapes. In: Goldhahn, J. (ed.) *Rock Art as Social Representation*, 101–127. BAR International Series 794. Oxford.

Åkerlund, A., Gustafsson, P., Hammar, D., Lindgren, C., Olsson, E. and Wikell, R. 2002. Peopling a forgotten landscape (in this volume).

11. The origins of monumentality? Mesolithic world-views of the landscape in western Britain

Vicki Cummings

According to many readings of the archaeological record, people in the Neolithic seem to have inhabited a world filled with mythologies and symbolic places, while Mesolithic populations centred their lives around technological and economic considerations. This dichotomy may result from the evidence itself, as the Neolithic is dominated by monuments which are understood as venues for rituals. In contrast, Mesolithic sites tend to be interpreted as places devoid of ideological meaning. However, this dichotomy may be as much a result of opposing interpretations of the evidence as it is representative of social behaviour in prehistory. Using case-studies from south-west Wales and south-west Scotland, I will demonstrate how hunter-gatherers moved and positioned themselves in relation to a landscape imbued with meaning and myths. In particular, I will highlight the significance of water (the sea, lakes and rivers), rock outcrops, plants and animals in these regions. This does not deny that people during this period were unconcerned with subsistence, but that the places which they repeatedly visited, even as part of economic regimes, would have become intimately bound within a mythological understanding of the world. It was this landscape, and mindset, which would ultimately set the scene for the construction of monuments in the Neolithic.

Introduction

Our understanding of later British prehistory is still characterised by two rather different approaches to the evidence (Mithen 1991; Thomas 1991). On the one hand, it has been suggested that people in the Neolithic inhabited a world filled with mythical features and symbolic places (e.g. Tilley 1994; Bradley 1998b, 2000). However, technological, environmental and economic explanations have tended to dominate our understanding of the Mesolithic (see papers in Bonsall 1990; Mellars and Dark 1998). It seems likely that this is due in part to the nature of the British evidence, which, unlike other parts of Europe, has virtually no evidence of Mesolithic cemeteries and formalised rituals. In contrast, the archaeological record of the British Neolithic is dominated by sizeable ritual monuments which have encouraged a broad range of interpretative approaches. In recent years, one interpretative approach to the evidence has focused on the location of Neolithic monuments in relation to natural topographic features (Tilley 1994, 1996b; Bradley 1998a; Tilley et al. 2000; Cummings 2001). As a consequence, the importance of the meanings and metaphors inherent in the landscape have been considered in depth with respect to the Neolithic, but have remained largely neglected in Mesolithic studies.

Problems with the Mesolithic/Neolithic dichotomy: Mesolithic monumentality

It has been acknowledged for many years that the division of prehistory into defined epochs is not always reflected in the archaeological record (Armit and Finlayson 1992, 1996; Pluciennik 1998). Nevertheless, the Mesolithic and Neolithic continue to be treated as separate entities and are usually understood in quite different ways. Many scholars studying the origins of monumentality suggest that the construction of these buildings required a significant ideological change (e.g. Thomas 1988; Sherratt 1996; Bradley 1998b). I would like to suggest, however, that ideological changes which are frequently associated with the introduction of the Neolithic might have taken place over a far longer period of time, and may not even have become fully realised until the later Neolithic or even the Bronze Age.

However, it is possible to suggest that people in the Mesolithic were already building large and enduring places in the landscape and this may indicate that people had an understanding of the world that was not inconsistent with notions of Neolithic monumentality. Caistel nan Gillean I shell midden on the small island of Oronsay in western Scotland is one of several large middens on the island which has been interpreted as the remains of domestic refuse (Figure 11.1). Shell middens are usually interpreted as the remains of either food for humans or bait for fishing (Deith 1990:75). However, it

The origins of monumentality? Mesolithic world-views of the landscape in western Britain

Figure 11.1 The shell midden of Caistel nan Gillean, Oronsay (after a photograph by W. Galloway, published in Mellars 1987).

Figure 11.2 Distribution map of sites mentioned in the text.

has also been suggested that the meat within the shells may have been incidental to their collection (Classen 1991) and that they were collected to create middens. Whether or not the shellfish were collected for food, their remains did create large, permanent places in the landscape (Pollard 2000:130). These middens were locales which were repeatedly returned to, and there is clear evidence for successive episodes of deposition over many years (Mellars 1987). This is not unlike the way in which many Neolithic monuments are created and used. Materials were collected and special places marked out by the construction of a large and permanent structure. Monuments also enabled people to return to a specific point in the landscape over many years, and just as shell middens had received successive deposits, monuments also saw repeated, structured deposition.

There are other parallels between Neolithic monuments and shell middens. Monuments not only create permanent places but they also help people to remember. The Cnoc Coig shell midden was built over a site of earlier activity, which became sealed under the mound. This is reminiscent of the placing of Neolithic monuments over Mesolithic flint scatters such as at Gwernvale (Britnell and Savory 1984) and Hazleton (Saville 1990). In addition, human bones were found within the shell middens. The remains of at least seven individuals were represented including both children and adults. However, in contrast to midden burials abroad (e.g. Schulting 1996) articulated skeletons were not found. Rather the bones were primarily from the hands, feet and crania (Mellars 1987:290) leading the excavator to suggest that parts of corpses had been intentionally moved from other places to be incorporated into the midden (Mellars 1987:299). In continental Europe, there is evidence for the circulation of human bones within living populations (Bradley 1998b:27; Whittle 1996:202), perhaps as mementoes of named or unnamed ancestors. This practice also has parallels in the earlier Neolithic, where it has been suggested that the placing of remains within monuments was only part of a process which saw fragments of bodies being moved around the landscape (Bradley 1984:22 pp). There is also the possibility that whole bodies were placed on shell middens, perhaps as part of an excarnation ritual (Pollard 1996, 2000). There are ethnographic parallels for this; the Kajemby of Madagascar bury their dead on the beach, so that the burials were taken away by the sea (Radimilahy 1994:98). On Oronsay, bodies may have been left on the shell middens to be taken away at high tide or perhaps during storms. Excarnation would certainly provide the conditions under which hand and foot bones could easily have been lost and bones taken from the corpse. Excavations of Obanian shell middens elsewhere have found human bones, suggesting this phenomenon was not restricted to Oronsay (Schulting 1998:264). Is it possible that these monumental middens were highly symbolic and special places in the landscape, not unlike early Neolithic monuments? Even if this was not the original initiative behind their construction, they may have become meaningful places over time.

However, the practices which created the Oronsay shell middens are perhaps not representative of Britain as a whole. Oronsay was occupied in the latest Mesolithic (Mithen 2000), and it was only a few hundred years until there is clear evidence of Neolithic activity nearby at Carding Mill Bay (Connock et al. 1992). It is possible to argue that the Oronsay shell middens represent an 'intermediate' stage, when people knew about the Neolithic but did not adopt any Neolithic material culture (a shortened Ertebølle). However, the Oronsay shell middens were not the only permanent places in the Mesolithic landscapes of Britain. Other sites were clearly repeatedly visited, and many of these may have been places for rituals, feasting, exchange, or sites for dealing with the dead. One of the only known Mesolithic cemeteries from Britain, Aveline's Hole in the Mendips, contained at least 20 individuals, and at least 50 poorly contextualised bodies were found here prior to 1805 (Jacobi 1987:165). This represents a special location chosen for the disposal of the dead which was used over a considerable period of time (Pollard 2000:132). There is additional evidence for the use of natural places like caves such as those on Caldey Island in Wales, which has produced human remains (Lacaille and Grimes 1955) and Ulva Cave in Scotland (Bonsall et al. 1994). Other probable ritual sites have been found. Near the future site of Stonehenge in southern England, a series of enormous timbers were set upright into the ground (Cleal et al. 1995). Specialised ritual deposits were found in a pit under a stone surface at Culverwell, Portland (Palmer 1990). However, these kinds of sites are not commonplace in the British Mesolithic with activity more usually represented by lithic scatters. How can we begin to understand the importance of the settings where no structural evidence remains?

Landscape: a background

Ethnography and anthropology have demonstrated that the landscape is a highly evocative and symbolic medium through which people can understand their world. Landscapes are frequently imbued with meaning (Basso 1996), and places within a hunter-gatherer world are often viewed as populated by spirits, mythical powers or ancestors. In Australia, there is a strong bond between Aborigines and the landscape, people and places (Morphy 1993; Tilley 1994:37 pp). Mythology and ancestral knowledge are entwined in the landscape which acts as a central reference system for anchoring social identity as well as accessing resource areas (Morphy 1995:186). The landscape is not a passive recipient of meaning, however, as it also 'offers up' information on the invisible forces that created it and are embodied in it (Ritchie 1994). Indeed, in Western Arnhem Land, Australia, many stone sources are considered to be the remains of ancestral beings (Taçon 1991:197). A close relationship between people and places is found elsewhere. To the Nenet of the Arctic, the landscape is filled with holy places. These may be locales where an event occurred, or may be an unusual stone, tree, or simply a feature which captured their imagination (Ovsyannikov and Terebikhin 1994:58). The Saami landscape is also literally filled with sacred places and landscape features, from lakes and waterfalls to entire mountains (Bradley 2000; Mulk 1994). Although not hunter-gatherers, to the Wamira of Papua New Guinea, each stone has a history, name and life of its own. Some stones represent where elders sat in the past while others are considered to be the ancestors themselves (Kahn 1990). To the Ninaiskákis of America, entire mountains are sacred (Reeves 1994:265). Indeed, the whole landscape may have been used as a metaphor for an ancestral past or cosmological understanding of the world.

Thus, even people who do not build large monuments often conceive the landscape as embodying broader cosmologies, with natural places rooted in legend and origin myths. Places within a landscape can also become important because of events that happened there. Such sites often become the focus of ritual activities, but everyday places are also considered important in the overall mythos of the landscape. In '*A phenomenology of landscape*' Tilley (1994) suggested that Mesolithic sites were carefully positioned in relation to a meaningful and symbolic landscape. However the majority of projects which examine the importance of the landscape have focussed on the Neolithic. One exception is work in the Inner Hebrides, which has used GIS to show that Mesolithic sites were not positioned to have wide-ranging views of the landscape (Lake *et al.* 1998). Could this suggest that people were positioning sites in relation to a cosmological understanding of the landscape? I will now consider a series of Mesolithic locales as places which were immersed in an embodied and experienced landscape.

Case studies: south-west Wales and south-west Scotland

Water

As part of a broader project examining the significance of the landscape from the Mesolithic through to the late Neolithic I have examined a series of Mesolithic locales in south-west Wales and south-west Scotland (Cummings 2001). In both areas, many Mesolithic sites are located along the coastline and almost all have wide and expansive views of the sea. In south-west Scotland, a number of sites are also positioned along rivers and next to lochs, and dense lithic scatters have been found around Loch Doon and Clatteringshaw Loch (Edwards *et al.* 1983). In addition, many sites in south-west Wales are found next to springs or streams. Fresh water was undoubtedly an important resource, but I would like to suggest that water was also a highly potent symbol in the Mesolithic. It may

have been crucial in the creation of cosmologies, as it played such an essential role in the everyday lives of people. Within most societies water is a highly symbolic natural feature. Rivers and the sea can represent a boundary between the living and the dead and water is frequently associated with rituals. Water has cleansing properties (Douglas 1966) and may have been associated with renewal or rebirth. The sea has a rhythmical cycle which can appear to be timeless. The sea is also a liminal place, with the inter-tidal zone an interface between the land and the sea (Scarre 2000). The sea then, could have been seen as a creator, a transformer and recycler of life (Kahn 1990:59). It could also have been viewed as a metaphor for movement and journeys (Richards 1996). Indeed, there is evidence that people were moving around by water in the Mesolithic. A paddle was found at Star Carr (Clark 1954) and people were clearly visiting islands like Oronsay by boat.

The sea and water may also have been considered important because of the animals that live there. Water provided many key resources, and there is evidence that marine foods were heavily utilised in the Mesolithic (Price 1990; Schulting 1998; Mithen 2000). There is also considerable evidence to suggest that animals were a crucial source of symbolism in the lives of Mesolithic people and individual species of animals may have been invested with a whole series of meanings and significances (Whittle 2000). Furthermore, there is ethnographic evidence to suggest that animals may also have been treated as social beings with motives, values and morals (Tapper 1994:51). Amongst the Inuit the realms of humanity and nature are not separated (Ingold 1994) and in the past, myths tell that humans and animals were interchangeable (D'Anglure 1990:179; Guenther 1988). Indeed, many modern hunter-gatherer groups see animals and humans as intelligent in an otherwise non-intellectual world (Kent 1992). Creatures like seals are common on the coastline of south-west Wales and the presence of these animals may have embodied places in the landscape as particularly significant. Likewise, whales may also have been regarded as mythical creatures (Whittle 2000) which may have been stranded on the shoreline from time to time. Indeed, between 1913 and 1926, 407 whales were stranded on British shores (Clark 1952:63).

Given the virtual absence of formal burials in the British Mesolithic, is it also possible that people were disposed of in important natural places such as rivers, lakes, or the sea? The transformative properties of water may have been considered appropriate for the transformation of the living body to the dead spirit or ancestor. In Denmark there is evidence from the Mesolithic of bodies being placed in boats and put on the water (Grøn and Skaarup 1991). Perhaps we could envisage a similar situation in the British Mesolithic? Water, then, may have been one of the most potent elements in the Mesolithic, and sites may have been carefully positioned in the landscape in order to reference water and all its associations.

Rocky outcrops

Many of the Mesolithic sites in south-west Wales are located on low hills and crags which would have been encountered when moving inland from the coastal plain. This relationship has already been noted by Tilley (1994:80) who suggests that sites were positioned on these outcrops due to the wealth of resources the coast provided as well as their inherent cosmological significance. I have already outlined how rock and stone is frequently considered to embody the essence of the ancestral beings who formed the world, for example among the Aborigines in Australia (Morphy 1995; Tilley 1994). Rocks are seen as highly symbolic and their colour, hardness and durability are also important in assigning significance (Taçon 1991). It is thus of interest that many of the sites that were repeatedly used throughout the Mesolithic in south-west Wales were positioned in relation to distinctive rocky outcrops (Cummings 2000:91). It is difficult to be certain of the precise appearance of the south Welsh landscape in the Mesolithic, as there have been considerable rises in sea level (Heyworth and Kidson 1982). While these features would not have been coastal cliffs, it is feasible that people would have been aware of the rocks beneath their feet. Native American groups frequently consider subsurface features such as the soil and bedrock to be significant (Owoc forthcoming).

One of the largest sites known from south-west Wales is Nab Head. This place seems to have been repeatedly visited throughout the Mesolithic and excavations have uncovered many thousands of worked flints (David 1990). This locale was used for bead manufacture in the early Mesolithic and remains of drills, bead blanks and broken beads have been found, along with 690 finished beads (David 1990:245). The site has some more rather special finds, including two possible figurines (Jacobi 1980) which are likely to be early Mesolithic (Andrew David pers. comm.) and several later Mesolithic ground stone axes and a perforated stone disk (David 1990). Why was this particular location repeatedly used throughout the Mesolithic? We should certainly consider the idea that particular locations were significant places in a social landscape (Pollard 2000:124), perhaps tied to a broader mythological understanding of the world. In addition, this location may have been chosen and considered important because of the striking red colour of the underlying rock. Nab Head is now a coastal peninsular, and erosion has revealed the distinctive Old Red Sandstone bedrock. In the Mesolithic, people may have been able to see the rock outcropping nearby or were aware of the underlying geology. Even if they were not, the soil would have been a distinctive red colour. Perhaps the site was repeatedly visited because of the red of the soil and rock? There is certainly plenty of evidence to suggest that red was a highly potent colour in the Mesolithic, found, for example, in burials on the continent (Tilley 1996a) and on sites such as Star Carr (Clark 1954) and Morton (Coles 1971).

A little further along the coast from Nab Head, Freshwater East also stands on part of the coastline where the sea has revealed distinctive coloured banding in the geological strata. Is it possible that Mesolithic sites were deliberately positioned in relation to distinctive coloured outcrops? In south-west Scotland, the shores of Loch Doon were visited throughout the Mesolithic, and thousands of lithics have been found (Edwards *et al.* 1983). One of the major concentrations is located in the vicinity of distinctive rocky outcrops lined with bands of quartz. Although the loch has been dammed and the water levels raised, it seems likely that at least some of these outcrops would have been visible in the Mesolithic. Mesolithic lithic scatters have been found close to distinctive outcrops at Clatteringshaw Loch to the south of Loch Doon, and in each case it seems unlikely that vegetation would have concealed these outcrops. Of course, it could be argued that sites were fortuitously positioned next to these features, and it does remain to empirically test these relationships. Nevertheless, the distinctive and unusual qualities of these places would have demanded an explanation and people may have generated stories or mythologies to account for them. The technological value of rocks has been emphasised in the past, but studies in Australia have shown that locations where raw material was procured became invested with the most potent ancestral mythologies (Taçon 1991).

Vegetation

While certain landscape features might have had symbolic qualities, rather more ephemeral elements of the environment may also have been important. For instance, there is ethnographic evidence to suggest that trees are highly potent symbols and are frequently used as metaphors for broader conceptions of the world. To the Mdembu of Zaire the tree is a rich symbol and stands as a sign of strength and permanence (Davies 1988:34). Several cultures believe that a tree stands at the centre of the world where the roots represent the underworld, the branches represent heaven and the trunk stands for this realm (Davies 1988; Ovsyannikov and Terebikhin 1994). This world tree is thus a conceptual ordering of the universe. Amongst the Zafimaniry, wood is a crucial metaphor for the body and life cycles (Bloch 1995). Likewise, the Yolngu connect tree-trunks with bone and leaves with flesh (Keen 1990). Wood also seems to have been important in Mesolithic burials in Scandinavia (Bradley 1998b:24). At Skateholm it appears that wooden structures were built over the graves (Tilley 1996a:36). Trees may not just have been potent symbols but may also represent important places in the landscape. In the Arctic, sacred places are frequently marked by trees. Groves are also important, and the birch is a particularly potent tree (Ovsyannikov and Terebikhin 1994). Specific trees may have been named and were part of an inscribed landscape. In particular, distinctive trees may have been tied to local myths and legends (Basso 1996). Could sites in the Mesolithic have been located in relation to such ephemeral features? Plants would have been a valuable resource and may have been associated with their own myths and symbolism. As such, places where berries, fruit or fungi grew might have been bestowed with meaning. Likewise, the proximity of wild animals to an area may also might have been considered important (Cummings 2000:91). I have already suggested that people may have considered animals to be intelligent, sentient beings attributed with spiritual powers. Thus, the presence of wild animals may represent not only a possible source of food, but also a spiritual link to a specific place.

'Persistent places'

Many sites may have been important and symbolic simply because they had a history of use. Sites which were repeatedly used throughout the Mesolithic may have been termed 'persistent places' (Barton *et al.* 1995) and it has been suggested that these places would have engendered a sense of time and belonging (Pollard 2000:124). People may have become attached to certain places in the landscape which through use became important and symbolic places. At Nab Head, for example, the range of unusual finds suggests that this was a particularly special site, and it may have been considered important *because* it had a long history of occupation. This significance may have been further exemplified by the wide-ranging views over the landscape and the presence of the distinctive red rocks in the area. These persistent places may have been visible in a number of different ways. First, people could have encountered evidence of previous occupations, whether as worked stones or the regenerating vegetation of forest clearings. The sites may equally have survived as memories or myths, passed down through the generations perhaps as stories. Many sites in the British Mesolithic show clear evidence of being visited repeatedly, including Oronsay (Mellars 1987), Waun Fignen Felen (Barton *et al.* 1995) and even Star Carr (Clark 1954; Pollard 2000:125pp). These sites were not monuments, but they were permanent locales in the landscape that could be remembered, visited and referenced time and again. These are qualities of places which we would ordinarily attribute to Neolithic monuments.

Conclusion

The main obstacle to interpretation in the British Mesolithic seems to relate to the nature of the evidence, which lacks the mortuary data more commonly found on the continent. However, I have suggested that a Mesolithic understanding of the world may not have been entirely different to that of the first monument builders. While ethnography should not be uncritically applied to the archaeological record, there is evidence to suggest that people in the Mesolithic would have considered the landscape to be filled with symbolism and mythology.

Places such as mountains, outcrops, streams, springs and forests, and the plants and animals which inhabited these places, are likely to have been regarded as meaningful. In the Mesolithic, permanent locales and venerated natural places existed which may not have been conceptually too dissimilar to the monuments which appeared in the early Neolithic. Therefore, the fundamental change in ideology that we normally associate with the beginning of the Neolithic may instead have had its origins in the Mesolithic. Thus, it might have been the development of symbolic places in the Mesolithic which laid the foundations for the origins of monumentality.

Acknowledgements

I would like to thank Alasdair Whittle for comments on an earlier draft of this paper. Thanks also to Marek Zvelebil for accepting the paper for presentation at the Mesolithic 2000 conference in Stockholm, and to the other contributors in the landscape session for useful discussion.

References

Armit, I. and Finlayson, B. 1992. Hunter-gatherers transformed: the transition to agriculture in northern and western Europe. *Antiquity* 67, 664–676.
—— 1996. The transition to agriculture 1: Introduction. In: Pollard, T. and Morrison, A. (eds) *The early prehistory of Scotland*, 269–271. Edinburgh.
Barton, R., Berridge, P., Walker, M. and Bevins, R. 1995. Persistent places in the Mesolithic landscape: an example from the Black Mountain uplands of south Wales. *Proceedings of the Prehistoric Society* 61, 81–116.
Basso, K. 1996. Wisdom sits in places: notes on a Western Apache landscape. In: Feld, S. and Basso, K. (eds) *Senses of places*, 53–90. Santa Fe.
Bloch, M. 1995. The resurrection of the house amongst the Zafirmaniry of Madagascar. In: Carsten, J. and Hugh-Jones, S. (eds) *About the house; Levi-Strauss and beyond*, 52–71. Cambridge.
Bonsall, C. (ed.) 1990. *The Mesolithic in Europe*. Edinburgh.
Bonsall, C., Sutherland, D., Russell, N., Coles, G., Paul, C., Huntley, J. and Lawson, T. 1994. Excavations in Ulva Cave, western Scotland 1990–91: a preliminary report. *Mesolithic Miscellany* 15, 8–21.
Bradley, R. 1984. *The social foundations of prehistoric Britain: themes and variations in the archaeology of power*. London.
—— 1998a. Ruined buildings, ruined stones: enclosures, tombs and natural places in the Neolithic of south-west England. *World Archaeology* 30, 13–22.
—— 1998b. *The significance of monuments: on the shaping of human experience in Neolithic and Bronze Age Europe*. London.
—— 2000. *The archaeology of natural places*. London.
Britnell, W. and Savory H. 1984. *Gwernvale and Penywyrlod: two Neolithic long cairns in the Black Mountains of Brecknock*. Cardiff: The Cambrian Archaeological Association.
Clark, J.G.D. 1952. *Prehistoric Europe: the economic basis*. London.
—— 1954. *Excavations at Star Carr*. Cambridge.
Classen, C. 1991. Gender, shellfishing and the shell mound archaic. In: Gero, J. and Conkey, M. (eds) *Engendering archaeology*, 276–300. Oxford.

Cleal, R., Walker, K. and Montague, R. 1995. *Stonehenge in its landscape: twentieth century excavations*. English Heritage. London.

Coles, J. 1971. The early settlement of Scotland: excavations at Morton, Fife. *Proceedings of the Prehistoric Society* 37, 284–366.

Connock, K., Finlayson, B. and Mills, C. 1992. Shell-midden with burials at Carding Mill Bay, near Oban, Scotland. *Glasgow Archaeological Journal* 17, 25–38.

Cummings, V. 2000. Myth, memory and metaphor: the significance of place, space and the landscape in Mesolithic Pembrokeshire. In: Young, R. (ed.) *Mesolithic lifeways: current research from Britain and Ireland*, 87–95. Leicester: University of Leicester.

—— 2001. *Landscapes in transition? Exploring the origins of monumentality in south-west Wales and south-west Scotland.* Ph.D. thesis, Cardiff University. Cardiff.

D'Anglure, B. 1990. Nanook, super-male: the polar bear in the imaginary space and social time of the Inuit of the Canadian Arctic. In: Willis, R. (ed.) *Signifying animals: human meaning in the natural world*, 178–195. London.

David, A. 1990. Some aspects of the human presence in west Wales during the Mesolithic. In: Bonsall, C. (ed.) *The Mesolithic in Europe*, 241–253. Edinburgh.

Davies, D. 1988. The evocative symbolism of trees. In: Cosgrove, D. and Daniels, S. (eds) *The iconography of landscape*, 32–42. Cambridge.

Deith, M. 1990. Clams and salmonberries: interpreting seasonality data from shells. In: Bonsall, C. (ed.) *The Mesolithic in Europe*, 73–79. Edinburgh.

Douglas, M. 1966. *Purity and danger*. London.

Edwards, K., Ansell, M. and Carter, B. 1983. New Mesolithic sites in south-west Scotland and their importance as indicators of inland penetration. *Transactions of the Dumfries and Galloway Natural History and Antiquarian Society* 58, 9–15.

Grøn, O. and Skaarup, J. 1991. Møllegabet II – a submerged Mesolithic site and a "boat burial" from Ærø. *Journal of Danish Archaeology* 10, 38–50.

Guenther, M. 1988. Animals in Bushmen thought, myth and art. In: Ingold, T., Riches, D. and Woodburn, J. (eds) *Hunters and gatherers: property, power and ideology*, 192–202. Oxford.

Heyworth, A. and Kidson, C. 1982. Sea-level changes in southwest England and Wales. *Proceedings of the Geological Association* 93, 91–111.

Ingold, T. 1994. From trust to domination: an alternative history of human-animal relations. In: Manning, A. and Serpell, J. (eds) *Animals and human society: changing perspectives*, 1–22. London.

Jacobi, R. 1980. The early Holocene settlements of Wales. In: Taylor, J. (ed.) *Culture and environment in prehistoric Wales*, 131–206. British Archaeological Reports, British Series 76. Oxford.

—— 1987. Misanthropic miscellany: musing on British early Flandrian archaeology and other flights of fancy. In: Rowley-Conwy, P., Zvelebil, M. and Blankholm, H. (eds) *Mesolithic northwest Europe: recent trends*, 163–168. Department of Prehistory and Archaeology, University of Sheffield. Sheffield.

Kahn, M. 1990. Stone-faced ancestors: the spatial anchoring of myth in Wamira, Papua New Guinea. *Ethnology* 29, 51–66.

Keen, T. 1990. Ecological community and species attributes in Yolngu religious symbolism. In: Willis, R. (ed.) *Signifying animals: human meaning in the natural world*, 85–102. London.

Kent, S. 1992. The current forager controversy: real versus ideal views of hunter-gatherers. *Man* 27, 45–70.

Lacaille, A. and Grimes, W. 1955. The prehistory of Caldey. *Archaeologia Cambrensis* 104, 85–165.

Lake, M., Woodman, P. and Mithen, S. 1998. Tailoring GIS software for archaeological applications: an example concerning viewshed analysis. *Journal of Archaeological Science* 25, 27–38.

Mellars, P. 1987. *Excavations on Oronsay*. Edinburgh.

Mellars, P. and Dark, P. 1998. *Star Carr in context*. Cambridge: MacDonald Institute for Archaeological Research.

Mithen, S. 1991. A cybernetic wasteland? Rationality, emotion and Mesolithic foraging. *Proceedings of the Prehistoric Society* 57, 9–14.

—— 2000. Mesolithic sedentism on Oronsay: chronological evidence from adjacent islands in the southern Hebrides. *Antiquity* 74, 298–304.

Morphy, H. 1993. Colonialism, history and the construction of place: the politics of landscape in northern Australia. In: Bender, B. (ed.) *Landscape: politics and perspectives*, 205–243. Oxford.

—— 1995. Landscape and the reproduction of the ancestral past. In: Hirsch, E. and O'Hanlon, M. (eds) *The anthropology of landscape: perspectives on place and space*, 184–209. Oxford.

Mulk, I. 1994. Sacrificial places and their meaning in Saami society. In: Carmichael, D. Hubert, J. Reeves, B. and Schanche, A. (eds) *Sacred sites, sacred places*, 121–131. London.

Ovsyannikov, O. and Terebikhin, N. 1994. Sacred space in the culture of the Arctic regions. In: Carmichael, D., Hubert, J., Reeves, B. and Schanche, A. (eds) *Sacred sites, sacred places*, 44–81. London.

Owoc, M.A. forthcoming. Munselling the mound: the use of soil colour in British Bronze Age funerary ritual. In: Jones, A. and MacGregor, G. (eds) *Colouring the past: the significance of archaeological research*. Oxford.

Palmer, S. 1990. Mesolithic sites of Portland and their significance. In: Bonsall, C. (ed.) *The Mesolithic in Europe*, 254–258. Edinburgh.

Pluciennik, M. 1998. Deconstructing 'the Neolithic' in the Mesolithic-Neolithic transition. In: Edmonds, M. and Richards, C. (eds) *Understanding the Neolithic of north-western Europe*, 61–83. Glasgow.

Pollard, J. 2000. Ancestral places in the Mesolithic landscape. *Archaeological Review from Cambridge* 17, 123–138.

Pollard, T. 1996. Time and tide: coastal environments, cosmology and ritual practice in early prehistoric Scotland. In: Pollard, T. and Morrison, A. (eds) *The early prehistory of Scotland*, 198–210. Edinburgh.

Price, T.D. 1990. The reconstruction of Mesolithic diets. In: Bonsall, C. (ed.) *The Mesolithic in Europe*, 48–59. Edinburgh.

Radimilahy, C. 1994. Sacred sites in Madagascar. In: Carmichael, D., Hubert, J., Reeves, B. and Schanche, A. (eds) *Sacred sites, sacred places*, 82–88. London.

Reeves, B. 1994. Ninaustákis – the Nitsitapii's sacred mountain: traditional native religious activities and land use/tourism conflicts In: Carmichael, D., Hubert, J., Reeves, B. and Schanche, A. (eds) *Sacred sites, sacred places*, 265–295. London.

Richards, C. 1996. Henges and water: towards an elemental understanding of monumentality and landscape in late Neolithic Britain. *Journal of Material Culture* 2, 313–336.

Ritchie, D. 1994. Principles and practice of site protection laws in Australia. In: Carmichael, D., Hubert, J., Reeves, B. and Schanche, A. (eds) *Sacred sites, sacred places*, 227–244. London.

Saville, A. 1990. A Mesolithic flint assemblage from Hazleton, Gloucestershire and its implications. In: Bonsall, C. (ed.) *The Mesolithic in Europe*, 258–263. Edinburgh.

Scarre, C. 2000. *The perception of space and geometry: megalithic monuments of west-central France in their relationship to the landscape.* Paper given at EAA 2000, Lisbon.

Schulting, R. 1996. Antlers, bone pins and flint blades: the Mesolithic cemeteries of Teviec and Hoedic, Brittany. *Antiquity* 70, 335–350.

—— 1998. Slighting the sea: stable isotope evidence for the transition to farming in northwestern Europe. *Documenta Praehistorica* 25, 203–218.

Sherratt, A. 1996. Instruments of conversion? The role of megaliths in the Mesolithic/Neolithic transition in north-west Europe. *Oxford Journal of Archaeology* 14, 245–260.

Taçon, P. 1991. The power of stone: symbolic aspects of stone use and tool development in Western Arnhem Land, Australia. *Antiquity* 65, 192–207.

Tapper, R. 1994. Animality, humanity, morality, society. In: Ingold, T. (ed.) *What is an animal?*, 47–62. London.

Thomas, J. 1988. Neolithic explanations revisited: the Mesolithic-Neolithic transition in Britain and south Scandinavia. *Proceedings of the Prehistoric Society* 54, 59–66.

—— 1991. The hollow men? a reply to Steve Mithen. *Proceedings of the Prehistoric Society* 57, 15–21.

Tilley, C. 1994. *A phenomenology of landscape.* Oxford.

—— 1996a. *An ethnography of the Neolithic.* Cambridge.

—— 1996b. The powers of rocks: topography and monument construction on Bodmin Moor. *World Archaeology* 28, 161–176.

Tilley, C., Hamilton, S., Harrison, S. and Anderson, E. 2000. Nature, culture, clitter. *Journal of Material Culture* 5, 197–224.

Whittle, A. 1996. *Europe in the Neolithic: the creation of new worlds.* Cambridge.

—— 2000. 'Very like a whale': menhirs, motifs and myths in the Mesolithic-Neolithic transition of north-west Europe. *Cambridge Archaeological Journal.*

12. The Mesolithic of the Swiss and French Jura and its margins: 10,150–6000 BP

Christophe Cupillard and Nicole Perrenoud-Cupillard

The mountains of the Swiss and French Jura stretch from the valley of the Rhine to the valley of the Rhône, over 300 km. This region forms an area of cultural crossroads where continental and Mediterranean influences meet. The Jura is a calcareous range of moderate altitude, culminating at 1718 m, where karstic caves and rock shelters have been actively studied by prehistorian researchers from the end of the 19th century, and yielded the data which has been used to establish the chronologic and typologic frame of the Epipaleolithic and of the Mesolithic. The recent discoveries and the archaeological investigations of important Mesolithic open-air settlements have yielded new data, thus making it possible to discuss the organisation of the dwellings, the economic strategies and the funeral practices. Our paper is based on the synthesis of the environmental and the archaeological evidences dated between 10,000 and 6000 BP. We shall focus on the development of the Mesolithic hunter-gatherers communities and their gradual disappearance at the Neolithic transition.

The frame of the study

The relief and the hydrography

Geographically, the massif of Jura constitutes the border between Switzerland and France (Figures 12.1 and 12.2). The Jura covers an area of 14,000 km² forming a crescent 300 kilometre long situated between the Rhine and the Rhône valleys. This region forms an area of cultural crossroads where continental and Mediterranean influences meet. To the west, it is surrounded by plains and plateaux, to the northwest, we find the mountains of the Vosges, to the east we have the hills of the Swiss plateau and south the Prealps of Savoie. The relief is typically of an alpine foreland with altitudes ranging from 400 to 1700 m. It presents a dissymmetric structure:

- to the west, the outer Jura presents a monotonous sequence of plateaux and hills. The altitudes here range from 400 to 900 m

- to the east, the inner Jura is the centre of the massif with a sequence of parallely incurved secondary ranges, where altitude is between 900 and 1700 m. Altitude is gradually increasing in this hilly zone from the north to the south where the Jura forms a real barrier culminating at 1718 metres over the Swiss plateau.

Hydrography reflects the geological structure. Most of the water flows towards the Mediterranean except for a few rivers flowing to the Rhine and the North Sea from the north of Jura. The rivers are few. The Doubs and the Ain are draining most part of the Jura. The rivers are more or less hemmed in valleys constituting major roads of penetration. The plateaux exterior to the glacial area have subterranean rivers mostly infiltrated in the karstic system, whereas the plateaux interior to the glacial area are covered with many lakes, swamps and peat bogs.

The geology

The geology of the Jura presents limestone and marl covered by superficial quaternary formations of glacial, lacustrine or fluvioglacial origin. It is characterised by the presence of many caves and rock shelters which could yield an important archaeological potential as most of the stratified Mesolithic settlements recognised in the Franco-Swiss Jura were karstic sites (Figure 12.2).

We can note that many siliceous rocks can be found within the different layers of the Jurassian geologic stratigraphy. They are suitable for knapping and easily available to prehistoric man. These abundant and well distributed resources, were the subject of a systematic inventory and petrographic analysis since 1980 in order to study the economy and circulation of raw material during the Mesolithic (Cupillard 1998e).

The lacustrine and paludal formations have been investigated in the last 20 years by the laboratory of chrono-ecology in Besançon (UMR 6565 du CNRS). The significant results of this study define:

- the reconstruction of the vegetation and its evolution from 15,000 BP (Richard 1983; Ruffaldi 1993; Schoellammer 1997; Bégeot 2000; Richard et al. 2000),
- the recognition of evidences related to human influence on the vegetation (Richard 1994, 1995, 1997a, 1997b; Richard and Ruffaldi 1996; Richard et al. 2000),
- lake fluctuations probably linked to climatic variations: the phases of regression corresponding to climatic amelioration while the transgression phases reflect the deterioration of the climate (Magny 1992, 1995; Magny and Ruffaldi 1995; Magny et al. 1998; 2000).

The archaeological research

In Switzerland and in France, scientific research started around 1950 (Vilain 1966; Crotti 1993; Pignat and Winiger 1998; Thévenin 1998a; Frelin-Khatib and Thévenin 2000; Cupillard in press). Between 1950 and 1990, caves and rock shelters were mostly investigated. In the nineties, open-air sites have been investigated during rescue excavations. In Franche-Comté, for example, investigations were carried out on the site of the A 39 motorway (Séara and Ganard 1996; Rotillon 2000; Séara 2000a, 2000b, 2000c; Séara et al. in press). At the same time, a project of landscape archaeology developed together with extensive prospection allowing for the discovery of many more open air sites (Cupillard and Richard 1998).

Presently thirty stratigraphic settlements have been excavated and most are published (Figure 12.1). They provide a precise chronological frame and allow us to investigate different themes such as the structure of the dwelling, the strategies of acquisition, the funeral practices, and so on. Moreover complementary data were recorded at dozens surface sites.

Throughout this paper, C14 dates used are uncalibrated values BP.

The climatic and botanic context from the Pre-boreal to the end of the Early Atlantic between 10,150 and 6000 BP

The Pre-boreal between 10,150 and 9150 BP

The Holocene starts with the Pre-boreal and the sudden increase in the temperature is similar to what occurred at the start of the Bölling. The vegetation cover evolves rapidly, following the rise of the temperature. The heliophile herbaceous cover disappears as pine forests develop, but birch remains present in higher altitudes.

The Pre-boreal can be divided into three periods alternating two mild stages with a damper one around 9700 BP. The latter provoked the lacustrine transgression known as the "phase of Remoray", also characterised by the decrease of pine and the increase of birch and a specific herbaceous vegetation.

At the end of the Pre-boreal, pine forests were overrun by thermophile species such as hazel, oak and elm.

During the Pre-boreal, the vegetation cover did not reflect any human activity.

The Boreal between 9150 and 8000 BP

This period is often considered as the time of hazel. It corresponds to the general damper climatic conditions causing a series of lake transgressions. This "phase of Joux" culminates around 8300 BP and corresponds to the climax of hazel. Thereafter, the vegetation environment changes towards the end of the Boreal, as milder conditions precede the Atlantic. Hazel is then receding, dense forests develop with oak and elm combined with lime and maple.

The analysis of the peat-bog of Mouthe – in the high chain – shows abnormal variations in the hazel ratio at an altitude of 960 metres at the end of the Boreal (Figure 12.3). These fluctuations could have a natural cause such as, for instance, spontaneous fires followed by regeneration of the vegetation, but it might also result from human activity (Cupillard et al. 1994). This needs to be confirmed by further studies of Jurassian sites.

The Early Atlantic between 8000 and 6000 BP

The Early Atlantic can be divided into two climatic phases.

First, it is characterised by a general warming leading to the Post-glacial Optimum around 7500 BP. Oak is then at its climax.

The second phase is marked by a climatic deterioration with a diminution of oak forest and the rise of fir and beech.

Both phases were not constant and included short term variations of temperature. The warmer stages during the second phase influenced the neolithisation in progress during the 7th millennium BP in the Jura.

As a matter of fact, the most ancient pollen of cereals found in this region were dated to the later half of the Atlantic about 6900 BP. They were collected on a site of the upper Doubs valley, at 750 metres of altitude (Richard 1997a, 1997b; Richard et al. 2000). This very early evidence must yet be questioned, even though similar evidence were observed by the lake of Zurich on the Swiss plateaux (Haas 1996) and in the upper Rhône valley by the lake of "Mont d'Orge" (Welten 1982) (Figure 12.4).

Around 6500/6400 BP, human impact on the vegetation cover is recognised at the lake of Chalain, on the lower plateau and in the Doubs upper valley at Remoray (Cupillard et al.1994; Richard 1997a, 1997b) (Figure 12.5).

Around 6300/6000 BP, several sites indicate that by that time, neolithisation is almost accomplished throughout the Jura (Richard et al. 2000).

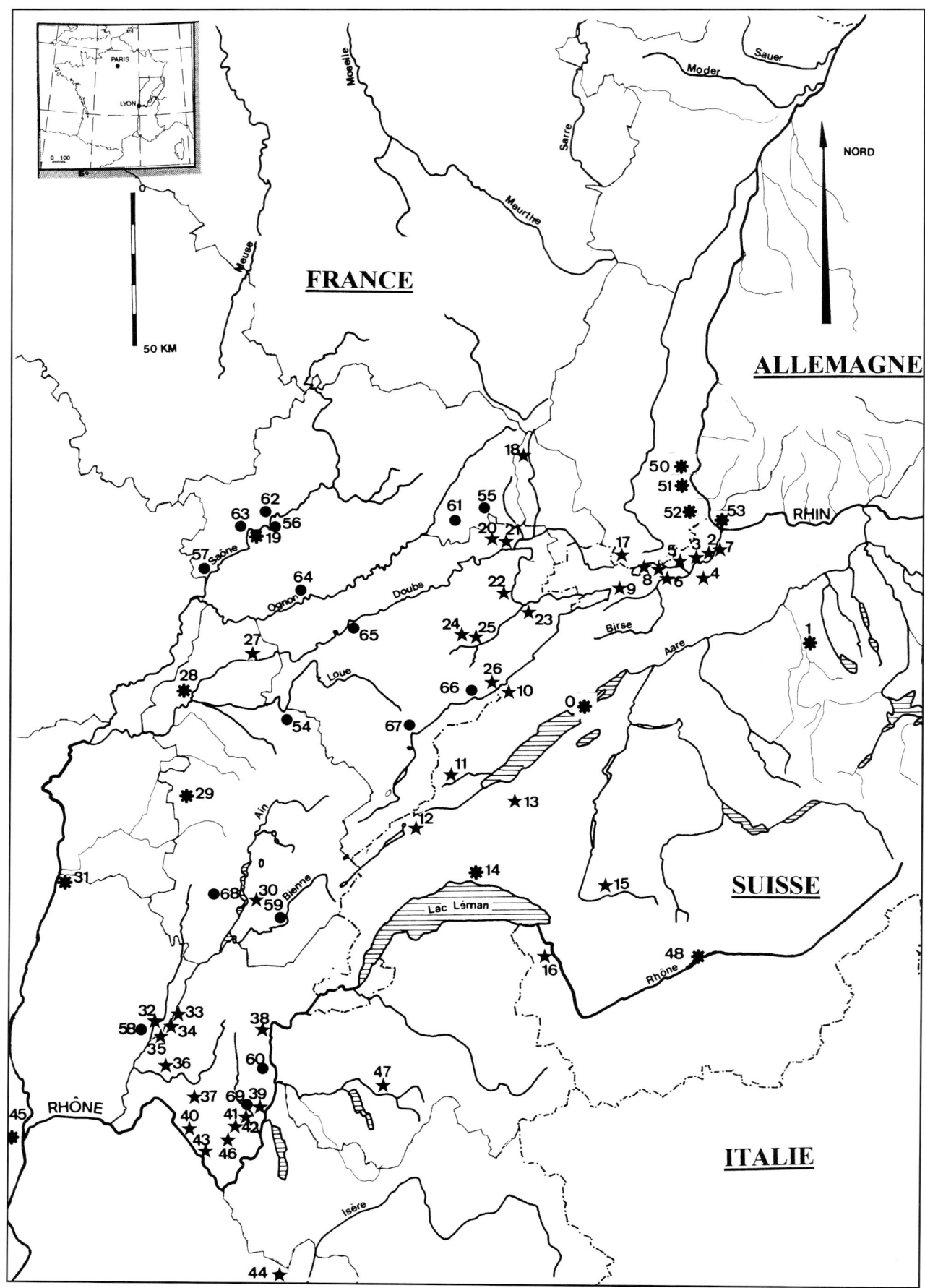

Figure 12.1 The main sites of the Mesolithic and Early Neolithic of the Eastern France and the Western Switzerland.

The main excavated karstic and open air sites from 0 to 53.

0. Open air site of "Jänet III", Gampelen, BE, Switzerland (Nielsen 1991)
1. Open air site of Schötz 7, Schötz, LU, Switzerland (Wyss and Stampfli 1979)
2. Rockshelter of Wachtfels, Grellingen, BE, Switzerland (Crotti 1993)
3. Cave of Birsmatten, Nenzlingen, BE, Switzerland (Bandi et al. 1963).
4. Rockshelter of Chesselgraben, Erschwil, SO, Switzerland (Spycher and Seldmeier 1985)
5. Rockshelter of Tschäpperfels, Röschenz, BE, Switzerland (Seldmeier 1967/1968)
6. Rockshelter of Liersbergmühle VI, Liesberg, BE, Switzerland (Hofmann-Wyss 1978)
7. Rockshelter of Zwingen, Zwingen, BE, Switzerland (Nielsen 1986)
8. Rockshelter of Ritzigrund, Roggenburg, BE, Switzerland (Jägher 1989)
9. Rockshelter of "Les Gripons", Saint-Ursanne, JU, Switzerland (Pousaz 1991)
10. Rockshelter of "Le Col-des-Roches", Le Locle, NE, Switzerland (Cupillard 1998c)
11. Rockshelter of "La Cure", Baulmes, VD, Switzerland (Egloff 1966–1967; Leroi-Gourhan and Girard 1971)
12. Rockshelter of "Le Mollendruz", Mont-la-Ville, VD, Switzerland (Pignat and Winiger 1998)
13. Cave of "La Baume d'Ogens", Ogens, VD, Switzerland (Egloff 1966–1967)
14. Open air site of "Vidy", Lausanne, VD, Switzerland (Crotti 1993)
15. Blockshelter of Château d'Oex, Château d'Oex, VD, Switzerland (Crotti 1993)
16. Rockshelter of Vionnaz, Collombey-Muraz, VS, Switzerland (Crotti 1993)
17. Rockshelter of "Mannlefelsen 1", Oberlag, 68, France (Sainty and Thévenin 1976, 1998)
18. Blockshelter of Giromagny, Giromagny, 90, France
19. Open air site of "Sur la Noue la Lande", Beaujeu, 70, France (Cupillard and Richard 1998)
20. Rockshelter of "Châtaillon", Bart, 25, France (Cupillard and Richard 1998)
21. Rockshelters of "Bavans", Bavans, 25, France (Aimé 1993)
22. Rockshelter of "Rochedane", Villars-sous-Dampjoux, 25, France (Thévenin 1982)
23. Rockshelter of "La Baume de Montandon", Saint-Hippolyte, 25, France (Cupillard et al. 2000)
24. Rockshelter of "Roche-Chèvre", Bretonvillers, 25, France (Baudais et al. 1993)
25. Rockshelter of "Gigot 1", Bretonvillers, 25, France (Vuaillat et al. 1984)
26. Rockshelter of "La Roche-aux-Pêcheurs", Villers-le-Lac, France (Cupillard 1998a)
27. Rockshelter of "Les Cabônes", Ranchot, 39, France (Cupillard 1998b)
28. Open air site of "Aux Champins", Choisey, 39, France (Séara 2000a, 2000b, 2000c)
29. Open air site of "A Daupharde", Ruffey-sur-Seille, France (Séara 2000a, 2000b, 2000c)
30. Cave of "Les Pestiférés", Moirans-en-Montagne, 39, France (Pétrequin and Vuaillat 1971)
31. Open air site of "Les Charmes", Sermoyer, 01, France (Frelin-Khatib and Thévenin 2000)
32. Rockshelter of "Le Roseau", Neuville-sur-Ain, 01, France (Wittig and Guillet 2000)
33. Rockshelter of "Les Layes 2", Serrière-sur-Ain, 01, France (Frelin-Khatib and Thévenin 2000)
34. Rockshelter of "Trosset", Serrière-sur-Ain, 01, France (Frelin-Khatib and Thévenin 2000)
35. Rockshelter "Gay", Poncin, 01, France (Frelin-Khatib and Thévenin 2000)
36. Cave of "Le Gardon", Ambérieu-en-Bugey, 01, France, Early Rhodanian Neolithic (NAR)(Voruz 1996)
37. Cave of "Chênelaz", Hostias, 01, France (Cartonnet 1995)
38. Rockshelter of "Sous Sac", Craz-en-Michaille, 01, France (Vilain and Dufournet 1970)
39. Rockshelter of "Sous Balme", Culoz, 01, France (Vilain 1966)
40. Cave of "Souhait", Montagnieu, 01, France (Desbrosse et al. 1961)
41. Cave of "La Touvière", Arbignieu, 01, France (Morelon 1973)
42. Cave of "L'Abbaye 1", Chazey-Bons, 01, France (Frelin-Khatib and Thévenin 2000))
43. Cave of "Glandieu 2", Saint-Benoit, 01, France (Frelin-Khatib and Thévenin 2000)
44. Rockshelter of "La Fru", Saint-Christophe, 73, France (Pion et al. 1990)
45. Open air site of "Vaise", Lyon, 69, France (Frelin-Khatib and Thévenin 2000)
46. Rockshelter of "Sous Vargonne", Andert-Condon, 01, France (Frelin-Khatib and Thévenin 2000))
47. Rockshelter of "La Vielle Eglise", La Balme de Thuy, 74, France (Ginestet et al. 1984)
48. Open air settlement of "Sous le Scex", Early Valaisan Neolithic (NAV), Sion, VS, Switzerland (Voruz et al. 1995)
49. Open air settlement of "Ricoh", Wettolsheim, 67, France, LBK (Jeunesse 1993)
50. Open air settlement of "Les Octrois", Ensisheim, 67, LBK (Jeunesse 1993)
51. Open air settlement "In den Nesseln", Bruebach, 67, France, LBK (Jeunesse 1993)
52. Open air settlement of "Ruetschyberg", Stetten, 67, France, LBK (Jeunesse 1993)
53. Open air settlement of "Pfaffenrainstrasse", Bottmingen, BL, Switzerland, LBK (Voruz et al. 1995)

The main scatter areas from 54 to 69.

54. Site of "Mornô", Pretin, 39, France (Roncin 2000)
55. Site of "Le Cimetière", Champey, 70, France (Thévenin 1990)
56. Site of "Le Châtelard", Beaujeu, 70, France (Cupillard and Richard 1998)
57. Site of "Les Mézières", Mantoche, 70, France (Roué 2000)
58. Site of "Sous le grand Molard", Druillat, 01, France (Cartonnet 1988)
59. Site of "Chaumont", Saint-Claude, 39, France (Pétrequin and Vuaillat 1971)
60. Site of "La Combe Merlin", Corbonod, 01, France (Cartonnet 1992)
61. Site of "Fonteneille", Aillevans, 70, France (Jaccottey et al. 2000)
62. Site of "La Planche", Fédry, 70, France (Cupillard and Richard 1998)
63. Site of "Mont-de-Saint", Ovanches, 70, France (Cupillard and Richard 1998)
64. Site of "La Corre 3", Motey-Bésuche, 70, France (Cupillard en préparation)
65. Site of "Sur la Vigne", Vaire-Arcier, 25, France (Cupillard and Richard 1998)
66. Site of "Courbebief", La Longeville, 25, France (Cupillard and Richard 1998)
67. Site of "Mont-Malinguin", Goux-les-Usiers, 25, France (Cupillard en préparation)
68. Site of "Les Massettes", Chavéria, 39, France (Cupillard en préparation)
69. Site of "Landaize", Culoz, 01, France (Khatib-Frelin and Thévenin 2000)

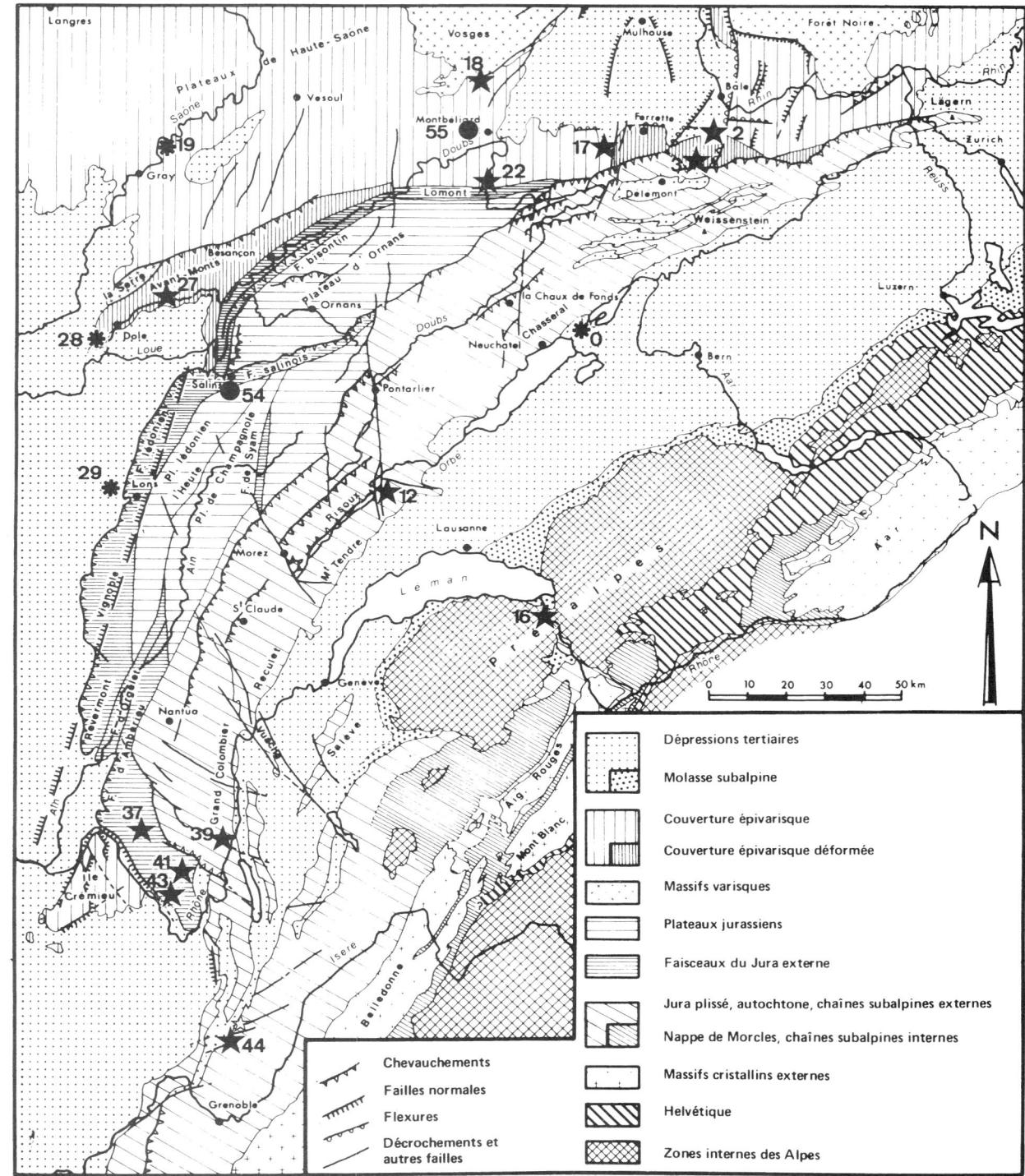

Figure 12.2 10,000–9000 BP (9550–8050 cal BC): The main sites of the Early Mesolithic of the Jurassian area and its margins during the Preboreal.

By the end of the Atlantic and at the start of Sub-boreal, evidence shows that the agricultural practice is clearly dependent on the climatic conditions. Therefore, the agricultural evidence prior to 6000 BP must be considered as originating as determined to certain extent by climatic changes (Richard and Ruffaldi 1996).

The cultural evolution between 10,000 and 6000 BP

The Early Mesolithic

The earliest Mesolithic industries of the Jura emerge towards 9700 BP in the middle of the Pre-boreal (Figure

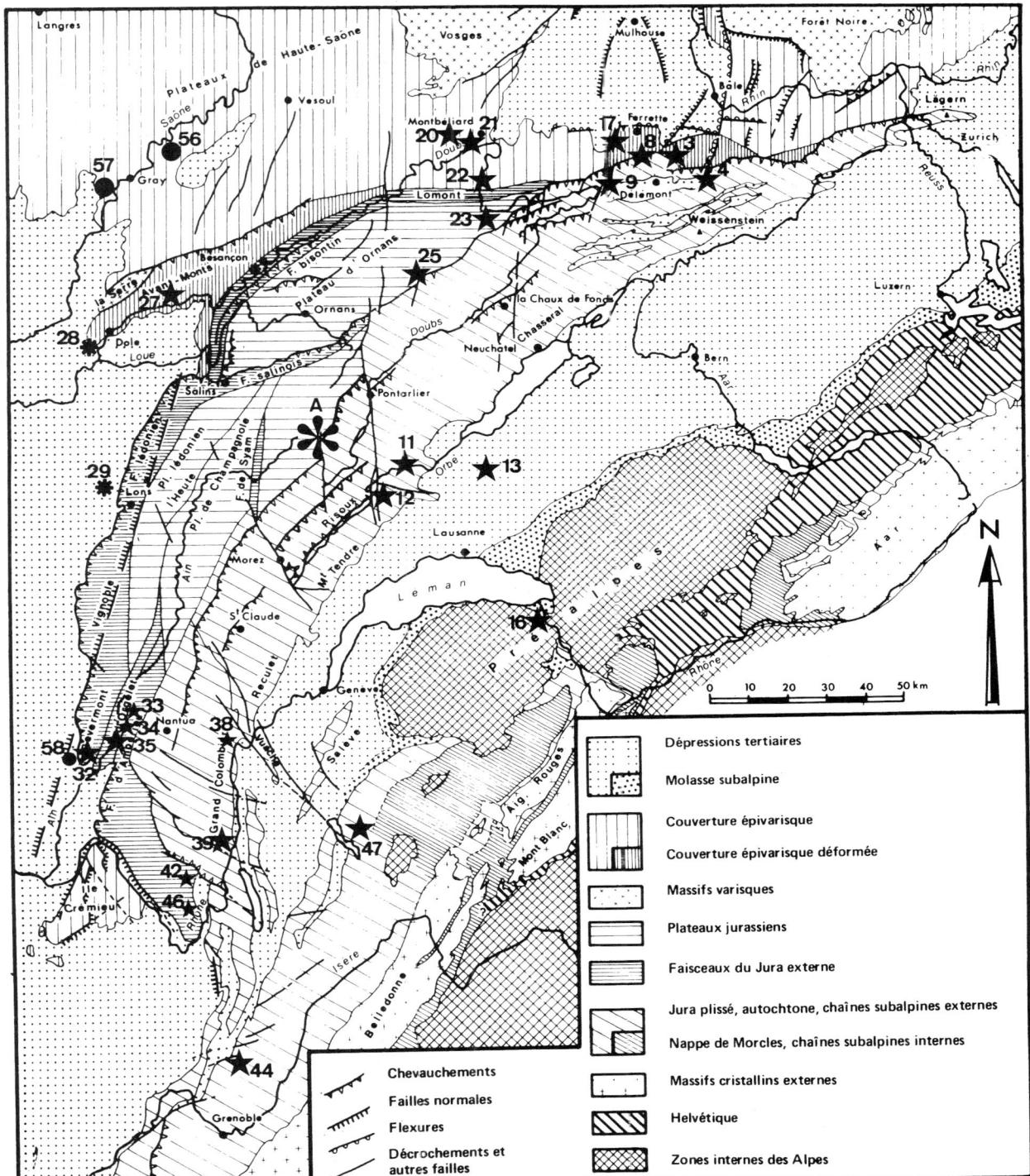

Figure 12.3 9000–8000 BP (8050–6900 cal BC): The main sites of the Middle Mesolithic of the Jurassian area and its margins during the Boreal. Pollen indications of human presence?: A: Peat-bog of "Les Seignes", Mouthe, 25, France (Cupillard et al.1994).

12.2). The settlement of Choisey "Aux Champins" is the only known site dated to this period, at the western margin of the massif. This open air site has yielded industries from the early Mesolithic of Ahrensburgian influence characterised by a microlithic arrowhead sequence where truncated points and isoscele triangles are prevailing (Séara and Ganard 1996; Thévenin 1998b, 1998c; Séara 2000b).

For the second part of the Pre-boreal between 9500 and 9000 BP, the number of early Mesolithic sites increases and can be divided into three technocomplexes, according to A. Thévenin (1998b, 1998c):

88 Christophe Cupillard and Nicole Perrenoud-Cupillard

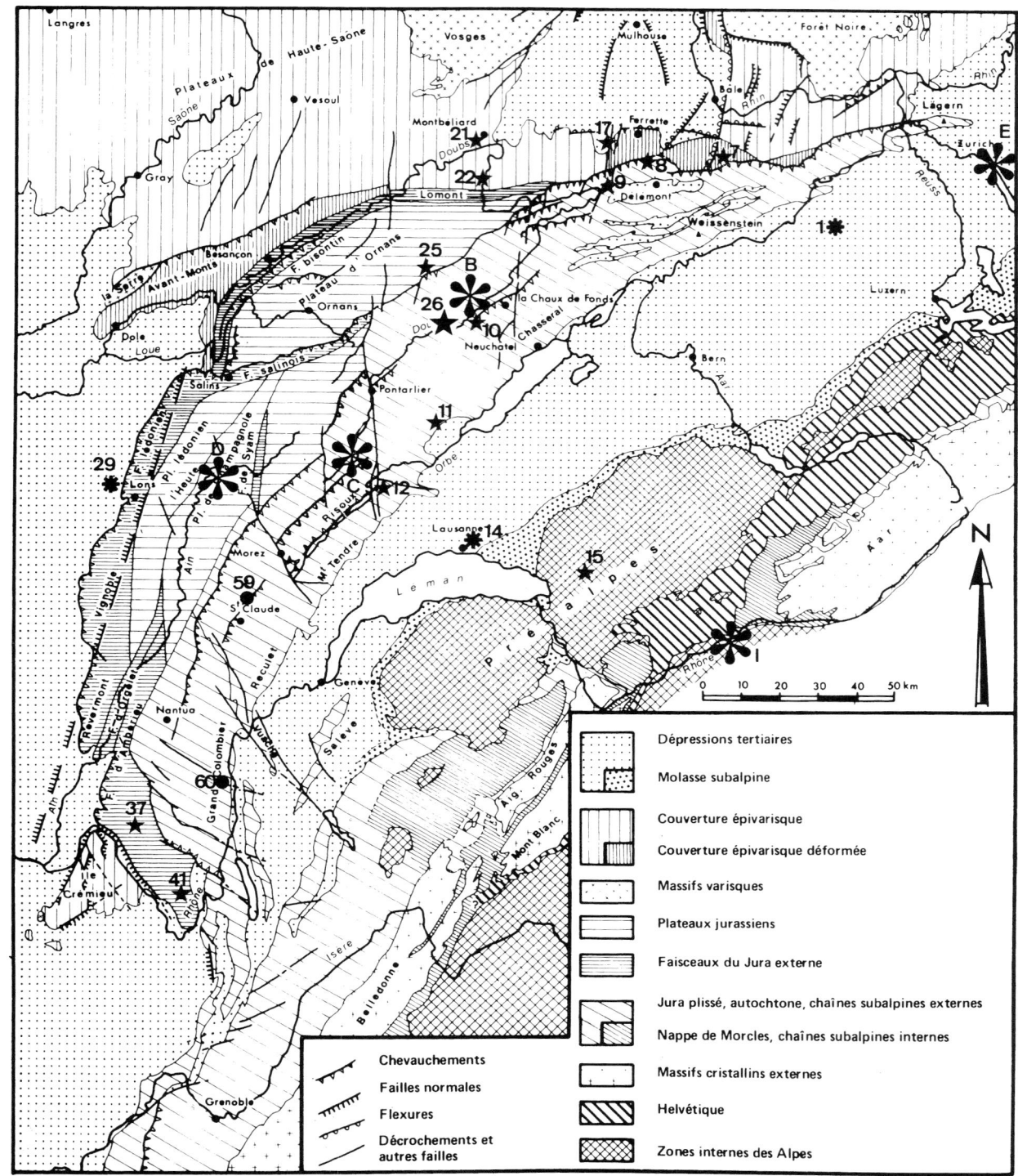

Figure 12.4 8000–6500 BP (6900–5300 cal BC): The main sites of the Late Mesolithic of the Jurassian area and its margins during the Early Atlantic. Pollen indications of human presence: B: Paleolake of Chaillexon, "Les Prés Mourey", Villers-le-Lac, 25, France (Richard et al.2000) C: Lake of Remoray, Remoray, 25, France (Richard et al. 2000) D: Lake of Chalain, Doucier, 39, France (Richard 1997; Richard et al. 2000) E: Wallisellen-Langachermoos, ZH, Switzerland (Haas 1996). I: Lake of "Mont d'Orge", VS, Switzerland (Welten 1982).

– first, the early Mesolithic with segments evolved from the epipaleolithic backed point industry. It is present on the western slopes of the Jura from the north (Thévenin and Sainty 1980; Thévenin 1982, 1991, 1998b, 1998c; Sainty and Thévenin 1998) to the south (Vilain 1966; Frelin-Khatib and.Thévenin 2000)

- second, the Beuronian defined by W. Taute and S. Kozlowski (Taute 1971, 1972; Kozlowski 1975), it presents a sequence of microlithic armature where basally retouched points and isoscele triangles prevail. It has been recognised to the northwest of Switzerland (Bandi et al.1963; Crotti 1993), and on the western slope of the central Jura, at Ruffey-sur-Seille "A Daupharde" (Séara and Ganard 1996; Thévenin 1998b, 1998c; Séara 2000b).
- third, the early Sauveterrian, where the scalene triangles prevail. It can be found in the southern part of the Jura, on the western and eastern slopes (Crotti 1993; Séara and Ganard 1996; Thévenin 1998b, 1998c; Frelin-Khatib and.Thévenin 2000; Séara 2000b).

The Middle Mesolithic

The Middle Mesolithic, between 9150 and 8000 BP, develops during the Boreal (Figure 12.3). The reference settlements are many and belong to two technocomplexes (Thévenin 1998b, 1998c): the Beuronian complex to the north characterised by the use of basally retouched points (Bandi et al.1963; Jägher 1989; Crotti 1993) and the mid-Sauvetterian complex to the centre and the south of the range (Frelin-Khatib and.Thévenin 2000; Cupillard in press) on the eastern (Pousaz 1991; Crotti 1993; Pignat and Winiger 1998) and western slopes (Séara and Ganard 1996; Roué 2000; Séara 2000b).

The Late Mesolithic

The Late Mesolithic between 8000 and 6500 BP corresponds to the longer part of the early Atlantic (Figure 12.4). It is characterised by the rise of the trapeze ratio and the absence of armatures. Between 8000 and 7000 BP, lithic series are not well known (Cupillard in press). While the number of sites increases between 7000 and 6500 BP and the trapezes technology prevail clearly (Thévenin 1991; Crotti 1993; Thévenin 1998b, 1998c). We can also note the appearance of antler harpoons (Hoffmann-Wyss 1978; Wyss 1968; Wyss and Stampfli 1979; Vuaillat et al. 1984; Cupillard et al. 1991, 2000; Vuaillat and Demars 1998).

The Final Mesolithic

The Final Mesolithic dated to 6500–6000 BP is a time of transition (Figure 12.5). The lithic industries of clearly Mesolithic provenience included trapezes with inverse retouch and new triangular arrowheads: Bavans and Montclus arrowheads and asymmetric triangular arrowheads with bifacial invasive retouch (Vilain 1966; Aimé 1993; Jaccottey and Daval 1997; Thévenin 1998c; Jaccottey 1999; Cupillard et al. 2000; Jaccottey et al. 2000).

They are rather frequent from the north to the south of the Jura. Some are associated with a few ceramics types, such as LBK or la Hoguette, also with elements of domestic fauna and some evidence of pollen of cereal and antler harpoons (Bandi et al. 1963; Vilain 1966; Leroi-Gourhan and Girard 1971; Hoffmann-Wyss 1978; Vuaillat et al.1984; Jeunesse 1987, 1993; Cupillard et al.1991, 2000; Jeunesse et al.1991; Nicod et al. 1996; Thévenin 1998c; Wittig and Guillet 2000).

Chronologically this final Mesolithic is contemporaneous with the late LBK of Alsace and with the Cardial from the north of the Rhône valley together with the Rhodanian Neolithic recognised in the cave of the Gardon to the south of the Jura (Nicod et al. 1996; Voruz 1996; Cupillard et al. 2000; Wittig and Guillet 2000).

We consider that these industries either belong to Mesolithic communities in the process of being acculturated, or to Neolithic group of a particular type (Cupillard et al. 2000). We probably find here a case of local Mesolithic communities integrated into a process of neolithisation by contact between two Neolithic frontier zones, that is the LBK and the Cardial, as M. Zvelebil describes it (Zvelebil and Dolukhanov 1991; Zvelebil 2000).

Human dispersal and settlement

The Early Mesolithic

The occupation of the Jura during the earliest phase of the Mesolithic around 9700 BP remains quite unknown: it has been recorded only in the plain and in the level C 1 of the open site of Choisey "Aux Champins" (Figure 12.2). This is an important settlement as it stretches over 5000 m^2 from which 1800 m^2 were excavated. The precise study of the spatial repartition within the central area has allowed us to recognise the existence of two dwellings whose structure can be compared with the Upper Magdalenian sites of the Parisian region (Séara and Ganard 1996; Séara 2000a, 2000c).

The site of Choisey is contemporaneous with the climatic deterioration phase in the mid-Preboreal. It is the only settlement recorded for this period or during the first part of the Pre-boreal yet climatically very favourable. But this fact may only reflect the present state of the research.

The peopling of the Jura really increases during the second part of the Pre-boreal: a very favourable climatic phase between 9500 and 9000 BP. Settlements are recorded in the open as well as under rock shelters, their number rises at every altitude from 175 m to 1088 m (Cupillard in press).

The most important sites are likely to be in the open, at a low altitude near a river as at Ruffey-sur-Seille "A Daupharde" (Séara and Ganard 1996; Séara 1999, 2000) or near a lake as at Gampelen "Jänet III" in the Swiss Mittelland (Nielsen 1991). The extension of the occupation is important, it varies from 400 m^2 to 2400 m^2 at Ruffey-sur-Seille. The dwelling structures are light and the spatial organisation is totally different from the earlier

90 Christophe Cupillard and Nicole Perrenoud-Cupillard

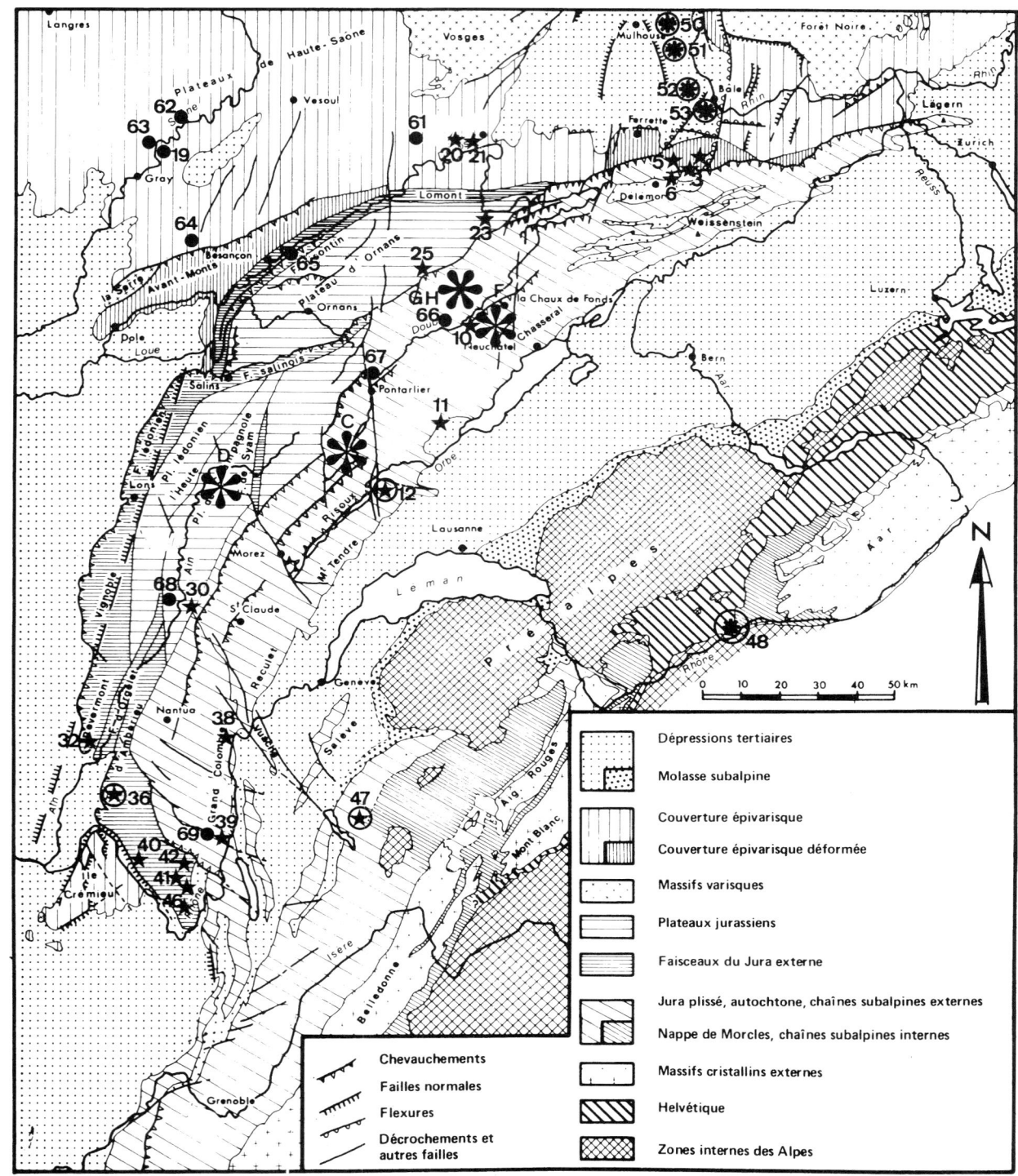

Figure 12.5 6500–6000 BP (5300–4700 cal BC): The main sites of the Final Mesolithic and Early Neolithic of the Jurasssian area and its margins at the end of the Early Atlantic. Pollen indications of human presence: C: Lake of Remoray, Remoray, 25, France (Richard et al. 2000). D: Lake of Chalain, Doucier, 39, France (Richard 1997; Richard et al. 2000). F: Peatbog of "Le Col-des-Roches", Le Locle, NE, Switzerland (Schoellammer 1997). G: Paleolake of Chaillexon, "Moulin Bournez", Montlebon, 25, France (Inédit). H: Paleolake of Chaillexon, "Morteau Stade", Morteau, 25, France (Inedit).

Mesolithic at the start of the Pre-boreal. This pattern of organisation persists during the Middle Mesolithic (Séara and Ganard 1996; Séara 2000a, 2000c).

Other surface sites were found on the edge of the lower jurassian plateau (Roncin 2000; Cupillard in press) and some isolated evidence reveal that the upper Doubs valley was also occupied between 780 to 900 m (Cupillard and Richard 1998, 1999).

Caves and rock shelters continue to be then more or less occupied. The significant data of this period is the exploitation of all the altitudinal stages and more particularly the mountain zone. At high altitude, like in the Mollendruz rock shelter at 1088 m, the occupations remain seasonal, short term and specialised in hunting tasks (Crotti and Pignat 1986; Pignat and Winiger 1998). The important lowland settlements of Choisey "Aux Champins" (Level C2) and Ruffey-sur-Seille "A Daupharde" (levels R 4 and R 3) correspond to long term installations which could be characterised as base camps (Séara and Ganard 1996; Séara 2000a, 2000c; Cupillard in press).

The Middle Mesolithic

The Boreal Middle Mesolithic between 9000 and 8000 BP corresponds to a period of climatic deterioration and, paradoxically, to a reinforcement of human presence, revealed by the increase in the number of sites in the whole massif and on the margins (Cupillard 1998d; Thévenin 1998b, 1998c; Cupillard in press) (Fig 3). This process of expansion goes together with the increase in the surface of the settlements of all kinds. For instance, at the site of Ruffey-sur-Seille "A Daupharde", the layer R 2 covers 10,500 m^2 (Séara and Ganard,1996; Séara 2000a, 2000c). In the mountain foreland and the lowland, the occupations become denser. Some of the lowland sites like the rock shelter of Ranchot or the open air site of Ruffey-sur-Seille "A Daupharde" are base camps and regularly re-occupied (Séara and Ganard 1996; Cupillard and David 1995; Roué 2000; Séara 2000a, 2000b; Séara et al. in press). The tasks performed there, are varied and more complex than during the early Mesolithic. Both sites yielded indications of domestic tasks and funeral practices such as human remains scattered at Ranchot (Valentin 1998; Valentin and Le Goff 1998) or the partial cremation found at Ruffey-sur-Seille (Séara and Ganard 1996; Le Goff 1998; Valentin and Le Goff 1998).

The increasing complexity of the occupations can be observed at other settlements situated in the lowland and in the middle mountain zone. The land exploitation differs here from the early Mesolithic in what seems to be longer term seasonal occupation at the Mollendruz rock shelter (1088 m), a probable base camp located at high altitude (Pignat and Winiger 1998).

We think that a model of human colonisation including base camps and peripheral sites can now be applied to every one of the Jurassian topographic zones regardless of altitude. This process could be directly a result of an increase in population during the Boreal. The consequent pressure on the environment, therefore, could explain the variation in hazel ratios noted palynologically in the upper Doubs valley (Cupillard et al.1994).

The late and the final Mesolithic

The early phase of the late Mesolithic from 8000 to 7000 BP is little known (Figures 12.4 and 12.5). This phenomenon is not restricted just to the massif of the Jura. This situation is disconcerting as this period is climatically very favourable (Magny et al. 2000; Cupillard in press). The scarceness of the data questions our research. Does this reflect a decrease in occupation or is it simply a problem of taphonomy? The latter might be the solution as many deposits of this period show traces of erosion between the end of the Boreal and the second part of the early Atlantic (Jägher 1989; Nielsen 1986; Crotti 1993; Pignat and Winiger 1998; Cupillard in press).

The period corresponding to the late and final Mesolithic, between 7000 and 6000 BP, is known through rather a better data and the sites are well documented. The second part of the early Atlantic is a time of climatic deterioration, still the number of settlements becomes paradoxically greater. The Mesolithic communities obviously appreciate the vicinity of rivers and lakes or streams and springs. This is particularly striking at the surface sites the location of which increases greatly in altitude (Cupillard and Perrenoud-Cupillard 1995; Cupillard 1998d, in press; Cupillard and Richard 1999).

The excavation of the level R 1 at Ruffey-sur-Seille "A Daupharde", a lowland site, reveals the extensive pattern of occupation exceeding 1000 m^2 (Séara and Ganard1996; Séara 2000a, 2000c; Séara et al. in press) and as do occupations of Schötz 7 by the Wauvilersee paleolake in the Swiss Mittelland (Wyss and Stampfli 1979).

Investigated rock shelters have yielded a great amount of data even in high altitudes (Cupillard 1998d). Some of the mountain sites, as at the "Baume de Montandon" at Saint-Hippolyte, were occupied even in winter (Cupillard et al. 2000).

Between 7000 and 6500 BP, settlements are occupied by hunter-gatherers strictly speaking as we can infer from the artefacts and from the fauna, dog being the only domestic species (Séara and Ganard 1996; Cupillard et al. 2000; Séara et al. in press). However, certain palynological evidence recorded in high altitude questions about the possible presence of an early agriculture. But this needs to be confirmed (Richard 1997a, 1997b; Richard et al. 2000).

Between 6500 and 6000 BP, positive indications reveal the presence of man on the upper Jurassian plateau and in the high mountain chain. During this period, contemporaneous with the late LBK and the end of the Cardial culture, we may suppose an acculturation of the Jurassian Mesolithic communities which practised seasonal agriculture (Cupillard et al.1994, 2000). Anyway, we can consider these communities as culturally belonging to the final Mesolithic or to the early Neolithic but the point remains that they shift then from a forager life style to one of agriculture.

Conclusion

From the Pre-boreal to the end of the early Atlantic and from the start of the Mesolithic to the Mesolithic-Neolithic transition, it is possible to reconstruct the progress of the human colonisation of the Jurassian massif. The process we are able to observe throughout this period is marked by greater and greater occupation of land regardless of the climatic conditions, except for the very end of the period. From our point of view, the increasing human occupation of the area can be explained by demographic and social change. We would now suggest a working hypothesis which outlines the possible pattern of the development of land use and of settlement structure.

In the middle of the Pre-boreal, the organisation of the site of Choisey is very similar to the upper Palaeolithic sites of the Parisian region. This is confirmed by the origin of lithic raw material (Cupillard 1998e). During this period residential mobility is the probable lifestyle of people in question.

For the second part of the Pre-boreal, the land exploitation requires logistic mobility on a large scale as the base camps lie in the plain or at the edge of the lower jurassian plateau while areas in higher altitudes are exploited seasonally, with short-term occupations.

During the Boreal, the communities of the Middle Mesolithic still practice logistic mobility but on another scale. The number of base camps is greater and lie at every altitudinal level in the same region as peripheral sites. The change observed between the Pre-boreal and the Boreal might be explained by an increasing demography, causing an intensification of land use. The pressure brought by man on the environment could be the cause of the variations in the hazel ratio observed in the upper Doubs valley.

Despite the scarcity of sites during the first part of the Early Atlantic caused by taphonomy, the shift towards a greater exploitation of the territory carries on between 7000 and 6500 BP. It brings the local communities into contact with the Neolithic groups of the periphery and leads to the adoption of agropastoralism between 6500 and 6000 BP. These scenarios are to be made more precise by further detailed research (Cupillard en préparation).

References

Aimé, G. (dir.) 1993. *Les abris- sous- roche de Bavans (Doubs)*. Vesoul: Mémoire de la Société d'Agriculture, Lettres, Sciences et Art de la Haute-Saône, Archéologie 3.

Bandi, H.G., Bay, R., Gfeller, C., Graffenried, C.V., Lüdin, C., Müller, E., Müller-Beck, H., Oakley, K.P. and Schmid, E., 1963. *Birsmatten-Basisgrotte, eine mittelsteinzeitliche fundstelle im Unteren Birstal*. Acta Bernensia I. Bern.

Baudais, D., Chaix, L., Pétrequin, P., Pétrequin, A.M., Piningre, J.F., Richard, H. and Urlacher, J.P. 1993. L'abri de Roche-Chèvre à Bretonvillers (Doubs), campements de chasse du Néolithique Moyen et de l'Age du Bronze. *Revue Archéologique de l'Est et du Centre -Est* 44, 261–292.

Bégeot, C. 2000. *Histoire de la végétation et du climat au cours du Tardiglaciaire et du début de l'Holocène sur le massif jurassien central à partir de l'analyse pollinique et des macrorestes végétaux*.Thèse Université de Franche-Comté, UFR des Sciences et des Techniques.

Cartonnet, M. 1988. Un site mésolithique et néolithique final à Druillat (Ain). *Revue Archéologique de l'Est et du Centre-Est* 39, 41–51.

—— 1992. Activités archéologiques 1992. *Les Cahiers de Dreffia* No 1, 21–24.

—— 1995. La grotte de Chênelaz à Hostias (Ain, France). *Livret-guide de l'excursion Préhistoire et Quaternaire en Chartreuse et Savoie. Epipaléolithique et mésolithique en Europe*, 104–117. Ve Congrès International U.I.S.P.P., XIIe commission, Grenoble 1995.

Crotti, P. 1993. L'Epipaléolithique et le Mésolithique en Suisse: les derniers chasseurs. In: *La Suisse du Paléolithique au Moyen-Age, Paléolithique et Mésolithique*, 203–243. Bâle: Société Suisse de Préhistoire, S.P.M.1.

—— (ed.) 2000. *Epipaléolithique et Mésolithique*. Actes de la table-ronde de Lausanne, 21–23 novembre 1997. Lausanne: Cahiers d'Archéologie Romande 81.

Crotti, P. and Pignat, G. 1986c. La séquence chronologique de l'abri Freymond près du Col du Mollendruz (Jura vaudois). *Archéologie Suisse* 9– 4, 138–148.

Cupillard, C. 1998a . L'abri de la Roche-aux-Pêcheurs à Villers-le-Lac (Doubs). In: Cupillard, C. and Richard, A.(dir.) *Les derniers chasseurs cueilleurs (13000–5500 av.JC) dans le massif du Jura et ses marges*, 106–107. Lons-le-Saunier.

—— 1998b. L'abri des Cabônes à Ranchot (Jura). In: Cupillard, C. and Richard, A.(dir.) *Les derniers chasseurs cueilleurs (13000–5500 av.JC) dans le massif du Jura et ses marges*, 112–113. Lons-le-Saunier.

—— 1998c. L'abri du Col-des-Roches au Locle (NE, Suisse). In: Cupillard, C. and Richard, A.(dir.) *Les derniers chasseurs cueilleurs (13000–5500 av.JC) dans le massif du Jura et ses marges*, 126–127. Lons-le-Saunier.

—— 1998d. Géographie et évolution du peuplement. In: Cupillard, C. and Richard, A.(dir.) *Les derniers chasseurs cueilleurs (13000–5500 av.JC) dans le massif du Jura et ses marges*, 131–132. Lons-le-Saunier.

—— 1998e. Matières premières siliceuses et territoires d'approvisionnement. In: Cupillard, C. and Richard, A.(dir.) *Les derniers chasseurs cueilleurs (13000–5500 av.JC) dans le massif du Jura et ses marges*, 153–156. Lons-le-Saunier.

—— in press. The last hunters-gatherers in Eastern France: the example of the Franche-Comté region between 10000–6000 BP. In: *Peopling the Mesolithic in a Northern Environment*. Papers from the Theorical Archeology Group Conference, Cardiff, 14–16 december 1999, Council for British Archaeology Research Report.

—— en préparation. *Le Mésolithique et la Néolithisation du Jura Franco-suisse*. Thèse, Université de Franche-Comté, UFR des Sciences de l'Homme, du Langage et de la Société.

Cupillard, C. and David, S. 1995. La prédation au Magdalénien final et au Mésolithique: les chasseurs-cueilleurs de l'abri des Cabônes à Ranchot (Jura). In: Richard, A. and Munier, C. (dir.) *Eclats d'histoire, 25000 ans d'héritages, 10 ans d'archéologie en Franche-Comté*, 104–109. Besançon.

Cupillard, C. and Perrenoud-Cupillard, N. 1995. Derniers chasseurs et premiers agriculteurs dans la Haute vallée du Doubs. In: Richard, A. and Munier, C. (dir.) *Eclats d'histoire, 25000 ans d'héritages, 10 ans d'archéologie en Franche-Comté*, 110–115. Besançon.

Cupillard, C. and Richard, A. (eds) 1998. *Les derniers chasseurs cueilleurs (13000–5500 av.JC) dans le massif du Jura et ses marges*. Lons-le-Saunier.

Cupillard, C. and Richard, H. 1999. Epipaléolithique et Mésolithique en zone de moyenne montagne jurassienne: l'exemple de la haute vallée du Doubs (France). In: Bintz, P. and Thévenin,

A. (ed. et dir.) *L'Europe des derniers chasseurs: Epipaléolithique et Mésolithique*. Actes du 5e colloque international de l UISPP, commission XII, Grenoble, 18–23 septembre 1995. Paris: édition du CTHS (Documents préhistoriques 12), 509–519.

Cupillard, C., Pétrequin, P., Piningre, J.F. and Richard, H. 1991. La néolithisation du Jura. In: *Mésolithique et néolithisation*, 269–280. Actes du 113e Congrès National des Sociétés Savantes, Strasbourg 1988. Paris.

Cupillard, C., Magny, M., Richard, H., Ruffaldi, P. and Marguier, S. 1994. *Mésolithisation et néolithisation a'une zone de moyenne montagne: évolution du peuplement et du paysage de haute vallée du Doubs*. Rapport ATP-CNRS Besançon: Laboratoire de Chronologie.UPR 7557 CNRS.

Cupillard, C., Chaix, L., Piningre, J.F. and Bourgeois, D. 2000. L'abri de la Baume de Montandon à Saint-Hippolyte (Doubs, France). In: Richard, A., Cupillard, C., Richard, H. and Thévenin, A. (eds) *Epipaléolithique et Mésolithique: les derniers chasseurs-cueilleurs d'Europe occidentale (13000–5500 av.J.C.)*. Actes du Colloque International de Besançon (Doubs, France). Paris: Les Belles Lettres, Presses Universitaires de Franche-Comté, Collection Annales Littéraires de l'Université de Franche-Comté, série "Environnement, sociétés et Archéologie", No1, 219–251.

Desbrosse, R., Parriat, H. and Perraud, R. 1961. La grotte du Souhait à Montagnieu (Ain). *Le Physiophile* 54, 3–68. Montceau-les-Mines: Société d'Archéologie de Briord et de ses environs.

Egloff, M. 1966–67. Le gisement préhistorique de Baulmes (Vaud). *Annuaire de la Société Suisse de Préhistoire et d'Archéologie* 53, 7–13.

Frelin-Khatib, C. and Thévenin, A. 2000. Le Mésolithique du département de l'Ain. In: Crotti, P. (ed.) *Epipaléolithique et Mésolithique*. Actes de la table-ronde de Lausanne, 21–23 novembre 1997. Lausanne Cahiers d'Archéologie Romande, No 81, 155–164.

Ginestet, J.P., Bintz, P., Chaix, L., Evin, J. and Olive, C. 1984. L'abri sous roche de "La Vieille Eglise". La Balme-de-Thuy (Haute-Savoie): premiers résultats. *Bulletin de la Société Préhistorique Française* 81, 320–342.

Haas, J.N. 1996. *Pollen and plant macrofossil evidence of vegetation change at Wallisellen-Langachermoos (Switzerland) during the Mesolithic-Neolithic transition 8500 to 6500 years ago*. Berlin and Stuttgart.

Hofman-Wyss, A.B. 1978. *Liesbergmühle VI.Eine mittelsteinzeitliche Abristation im Birstal*. Schriften des Seminars für Urgeschichte der Universität Bern, Heft 2. Bern.

Jaccottey, L. 1999. Le Mésolithique récent et final franc-comtois. In: Bintz, P. and Thévenin, A.(ed. and dir.) *L'Europe des derniers chasseurs-Epipaléolithique et Mésolithique: Peuplement et paléoenvironnement de l'Epipaléolithique et du Mésolithique*. Actes du 5e Colloque International de l'UISPP, commission XII, Grenoble,18–23 septembre 1995. Documents préhistoriques 12, 521–528. Paris.

Jaccottey, L. and Daval, D. 1997. La couche 5 de Bavans (Doubs) et la fin du Mésolithique en Franche-Comté. In: Jeunesse, C. (ed.) *Le Néolithique danubien et ses marges entre Rhin et Seine*. Actes du XXIIe colloque interrégional sur le Néolithique, Strasbourg 27–29 octobre 1995. Cahiers de l'Association pour la Promotion de la Recherche Archéologique en Alsace, Supplément No 3, 313–325.

Jaccottey, L., Petit, C., Huet, F., Krzyzanowski, J. and Thévenin, A. 2000. Les armatures évoluées (Pointes de Bavans et fléchettes asymétriques à base concave) de l'Est de la France: définition, répartition et chronologie. In: Thévenin, A. (dir.) *Actes de la table-ronde de Metz*. Bulletin de la Société préhistorique Luxembourgeoise 19, 195–215.

Jägher, R. 1989. Le gisement mésolithique de Roggenburg-Ritzigrund, Commune de Roggenburg.Canton de Berne (Suisse). In: Aimé, G. and Thévenin, A. (Dir.) *Epipaléolithique entre Ardennes et Massif Alpin*. Mémoire de la Société d'Agriculture, Lettres, Sciences et Arts de Haute-Saône, Archéologie 2, 105–123. Vesoul.

Jeunesse, C. 1987. La céramique de la Hoguette. Un nouvel "élément non rubané" du Néolithique ancien de L'Europe du Nord-ouest. *Cahiers Alsaciens d'Archéologie d'Art et d'Histoire* 30, 5–33.

—— 1993. *Recherches sur le Néolithique ancien du Sud de la plaine du Rhin supérieur et du Nord de la Franche-Comté*. Thèse de Doctorat. Université des Sciences Humaines, Strasbourg II, Institut des Antiquités Nationales.

Jeunesse, C., Nicod, P.Y., Vanberg, P.L. and Voruz, J.L. 1991. Nouveaux témoins d'âge néolithique ancien entre Rhône et Rhin. *Annuaire. de la Société Suisse de Préhistoire et d'Archéologie* 74, 43–78.

Kozlowski, S.K. 1975. The western technocomplex. In: Kozlowski, S.K. (ed.) *Cultural differentiation of Europe from 10th to 5th millenium BC*, 51–203. Warsow.

Le Goff. I. 1998. L'usage du feu dans la pratique funéraire observée à Ruffey-sur-Seille(Jura). In: Cupillard, C. and Richard, A. (dir.) *Les derniers chasseurs cueilleurs (13000–5500 av.JC) dans le massif du Jura et ses marges*, 187–189 Lons-le-Saunier.

Leroi Gourhan, A. and Girard, M. 1971. L'abri de la Cure à Baulmes (Suisse). Analyse Pollinique. *Annuaire. de la Société Suisse de Préhistoire et d'Archéologie* 56, 7–15.

Magny, M. 1992. Holocene lake-level fluctuations in Jura and subalpine ranges, France: regional pattern and climatic implcations. *Boreas* 21, 319–334.

—— 1995. *Une histoire du climat: Des derniers mammouths au siècle de l'automobile*. Paris: éditions Errance. Collection des Hespérides.

Magny, M. and Ruffaldi, P. 1995. Younger Dryas and early holocene lake-level fluctuations in the Jura mountains, France. *Boreas* 24, 155–172.

Magny, M., Schoellammer, P., Richard, H. and Bossuet, G. 1998. A high-resolution record of Late Younger Dryas to Mid-Holocene palaeohydrological changes from the palaeolake Le Locle, Swiss Jura. *Compte-Rendus de l'Académie des Sciences de Paris* 326, 787–793.

Magny, M., Marguet, A., Richoz, I. and Schoellammer, P. 2000. Variations du niveau des lacs et oscillations du climat dans le Jura et sur le plateau suisse de 14500 à 6500 BP. In: Richard, A., Cupillard, C., Richard, H. and Thévenin, A. (eds) *Epipaléolithique et Mésolithique: les derniers chasseurs-cueilleurs d'Europe occidentale (13000–5500 av.J.C.)*. Actes du Colloque international de Besançon (Doubs, France), 23–25 octobre 1998. Paris: Les Belles-Lettres, Presses Universitaires de Franche-Comté, Collection Annales Littéraires de l'Université de Franche-Comté, série "Environnement, sociétés et Archéologie", No 1, 19–28.

Morelon, N.S. 1973. *Le gisement préhistorique de la Touvière, commune d'Arbignieu (Ain)*. Documents du Laboratoire de Géologie de la Faculté des Sciences de Lyon, No 56. Lyon.

Nicod, P.Y., Voruz, J.L., Jeunesse, C. and Van Berg, P.L. 1996. Entre Rhône et Rhin au Néolithique Ancien. In: Duhamel, P. (dir.) *La Bourgogne entre les bassins Rhénan,Rhodanien et Parisien: carrefour et frontière*. Actes du XVIIIe Colloque Inter-régional sur le Néolithique, Dijon, 25–27/10/1991. Dijon: Revue Archéologique de l'Est et du Centre Est.,14e supplt, 85–94.

Nielsen, E.H. 1986. Zwingen: eine mesolithische Fundstelle im Birstal. *Annuaire de la Société Suisse de Préhistoire et d'Archéologie* 69, 7–34.

—— (dir.) 1991. *Gampelen-Jänet 3: eine mesolithische Siedlungstelle im westlichen Seeland*. Schriftenreihe der Erziehungsdirektion des Kantons Bern. Bern.

Pétrequin, P. and Vuaillat, D. 1971. Matériaux pour une carte archéologique de la région de Saint-Claude (Jura). *Revue Archéologique de l'Est et du Centre-Est* 22, 3–4, 277–294.

Pignat, G. and Winiger, A. (dir.) 1998. *Les occupations mésolithiques de l'abri du Mollendruz. Abri Freymond, commune de Mont-la-Ville (VD, Suisse)*. Cahiers d'Archéologie Romande 72. Lausanne.

Pion, G., Billard, M., Bintz. P., Caillat, B., Cataliotti-Valdida, J., Durand, J.M., Girard, M. and Montjuvent, G. 1990. L'abri de la Fru à Saint-Christophe (Savoie). *Gallia Préhistoire* 32, 65–123.

Pousaz, N. (dir.) 1991. *L'abri- sous- roche mésolithique des Gripons à Saint-Ursanne (JU, Suisse)*. Cahier d'Archéologie Jurassienne 2. Porrentruy.

Richard, H. 1983. *Nouvelles contributions à l'histoire de la végétation comtoise tardiglaciaire et holocène à partir des données de la palynologie*. Thèse de 3ème cycle.Université de Franche-Comté. Faculté des Lettres de Besançon.

—— 1994. Indices polliniques d'une néolithisation précoce sur le premier plateau du Jura (France). *Compte-Rendus de l'Académie des Sciences de Paris* 318-série II, 993–999.

—— 1995. Indices d'anthropisation dans les diagrammes polliniques du massif jurassien. *Palynosciences* 3, 37–49.

—— 1997a. Indices polliniques de néolithisation du massif jurassien aux VIème et Vème millénaires. *Quaternaire* 8–(1), 55–62.

—— 1997b. Analyse pollinique d'un sondage de 7,50m. In: Pétrequin, P. (dir.) *Les sites littoraux néolithiques de Clairvaux-les-Lacs et de Chalain (Jura), III: Chalain, station 3, 3200–2900 av JC*, 101–112. Paris.

Richard, H. and Ruffaldi, P. 1996. L'hypothèse du déterminisme climatique des premières traces polliniques de néolithisation sur le massif jurassien (France). *Compte-Rendus de l'Académie des Sciences de Paris*, 322-série II, 77–83.

Richard, H., Bégeot, C., Gauthier, E. and Ruffaldi, P. 2000. Evolution du couvert végétal du Tardiglaciaire et du début de l'Holocène sur la chaîne jurassienne: nouveaux résultats. In: Richard, A., Cupillard, C., Richard, H. and Thévenin, A. (eds) *Les derniers chasseurs-cueilleurs d'Europe occidentale (13000–5500 av. J.C.)*. Actes du Colloque international de Besançon (Doubs, France), 23–25 octobre 1998. Paris: Les Belles-Lettres, Presses Universitaires de Franche-Comté, Collection Annales Littéraires de l'Université de Franche-Comté, série "Environnement, sociétés et Archéologie", No 1, 29–36.

Roncin, O. 2000. *Etude de l'industrie lithique mésolithique du site d' "En Mornoz" à Pretin (Jura, France)*. Mémoire de Maîtrise. Université de Franche-Comté, UFR des Sciences du Langage, de l'Homme et de la Société, section d'Histoire de l'Art et Archéologie.

Rotillon, S. 2000. L'ajustement des systèmes fluviaux de la fin du Tardiglaciaire au début de l'Holocène en tant qu'indicateur des changements environnementaux: la Seille à l'aval d'Arlay (Jura, France). In: Richard, A., Cupillard, C., Richard, H. and Thévenin, A. (eds) *Les derniers chasseurs-cueilleurs d'Europe occidentale (13000–5500 av.JC)*. Actes du Colloque international de Besançon (Doubs, France), 23–25 0ctobre 1998. Paris: Les Belles-Lettres, Presses Universitaires de Franche-Comté, série "Environnement, sociétés et Archéologie", No1, 83–92.

Roué, S. 2000. Les armatures mésolithiques de l'abri des Cabônes à Ranchot (Jura). In: Richard, A., Cupillard, C., Richard, H. and.Thévenin, A. (eds) *Les derniers chasseurs-cueilleurs d'Europe occidentale (13000–5500 av.J.C.)*. Actes du Colloque international de Besançon (Doubs, France), 23–25 octobre 1998. Paris: Les Belles Lettres, Presses Universitaires de Franche-Comté, Collection Annales Littéraires de l'Université de Franche-Comté, série "Environnement, sociétés et Archéologie", No1, 133–141.

Ruffaldi, P. 1993. *Histoire de la végétation du Jura méridional depuis le retrait du glacier würmien à partir des analyses palynologiques du lac de Cerin (Ain,France)*. Thèse de Doctorat des Sciences de la Vie. Université de Franche-Comté. UFR des Sciences et Techniques.Laboratoire de Chrono-écologie, UPR 7557 du CNRS.

Sainty, J. and Thevenin, A. 1976. Les structures d'habitat mésolithiques du gisement d'Oberlag (Haut-Rhin). *Congrès Préhistorique de France*, XXème session Provence 1974, 560–566.

—— 1998. L'abri du Mannlefelsen I à Oberlag (Haut-Rhin). In: Cupillard, C. and Richard, A. (dir.) *Les derniers chasseurs cueilleurs (13000–5500 av.JC) dans le massif du Jura et ses marges*, 122–123. Lons-le-Saunier.

Schoellammer, P. 1997. Le marais du Col-des-Roches (NE, Suisse): Le site de référence pour l'histoire de la végétation pour le Jura Neuchâtelois. *Quaternaire* 8–(4), 365–375.

Séara, F. 2000a. Approche de l'organisation spatiale de campements de chasseurs-cueilleurs mésolithiques: le cas de Ruffey-sur-Seille dans le Jura (France). In: Crotti, P. (ed.) *Epipaléolithique et Mésolithique*, 139–150. Actes de la table-ronde de Lausanne, 21–23 novembre 1997. Cahiers d'Archéologie Romande 81. Lausanne.

—— 2000b. Les cadres chronologiques et culturel des occupations mésolithiques de Ruffey-sur-Seille "A Daupharde" et de Choisey "Aux Champins" (Jura). In: Richard, A., Cupillard, C., Richard, H. and Thévenin, A. (eds) *Les derniers chasseurs-cueilleurs d'Europe occidentale (13000–5500 av.JC)*. Actes du Colloque international de Besançon (Doubs, France), 23–25 0ctobre 1998. Paris: Les Belles Lettres, Presses Universitaires Franc-Comtoises, Collection Annales Littéraires de l'Université de Franche-Comté Série "Environnement, sociétés et archéologie No1, 125–132.

—— 2000c. Deux types d'organisation spatiale de campements mésolithiques: les cas de Choisey "Aux Champins" et de Ruffey-sur-Seille "A Daupharde" dans le Jura. In: Richard, A., Cupillard, C., Richard, H. and Thévenin, A. (eds) *Les derniers chasseurs-cueilleurs d'Europe occidentale (13000–5500 av.JC)*. Actes du Colloque international de Besançon (Doubs, France), 23–25 0ctobre 1998. Paris: Les Belles Lettres, Presses Universitaires Franc-Comtoises, Collection Annales Littéraires de l'Université de Franche-Comté Série "Environnement, sociétés et archéologie No1, 209–218.

Séara, F. and Ganard, V. (dir.) 1996. *Les gisements de Choisey "aux Champins" et de Ruffey-sur-Seille "A Daupharde": étude des occupations mésolithiques, néolithiques et protohistoriques de dux sites de plaine alluviale*. Document Final de Synthèse. Autoroute A 39 Dole-Bourg-en-Bresse. AFAN Coordination A 39/ SAPRR/ Services Régionaux d'Archéologie de Franche-Comté, Bourgogne et Rhône-Alpes.

Séara, F., Rotillon, S. and Cupillard, C. (dir.) in press. *Campements mésolithiques en Bresse jurassienne: Choisey et Ruffey-sur-Seille*. Document d'Archéologie Française. Paris.

Seldmeier, J. 1967/1968. Der Abri Tschäpperfels. Eine mesolithische Fundstelle im Lützeltal. *Jahrbuch des Bernischen Historischen Museums* 47/48, 117–145.

Spycher, H. and Seldmeier, J. 1985. Steinzeitfunde bei Erschwil im Schwarzbubenland. *Helvetia Archaeologica* 63/64, 78–80.

Taute, W. 1971. *Untersuchungen zum Mesolithikum und Spätpaläolithikum im südlichen Mitteleuropa*. Band I: Chronologie Süddeutschlands. Habilitationsschrift.Tübingen.

—— 1972. Funde aus der Steinzeit in der Jägerhaus-Höhle bei Bronnen. In: Thorbecke, J. (ed.) *Fridingen -Stadt an der oberen Donau*, 21–26. Sigmaringen.

Thévenin, A. 1982. *Rochedane. L'Azilien, l'Epipaléolithique de l'Est de la France et les civilisations épipaléolithiques de l'Europe occidentale*. Mémoire de la Faculté des Sciences Sociales. Ethnologie. Université des Sciences humaines. Strasbourg.

—— 1990. Du Dryas III au début de l'Atlantique pour une approche méthodologique des industries et des territoires dans l'Est de la France.1ere partie. *Revue Archéologique de l'Est et du Centre-Est* 41–2,177–212.

—— 1991. Du Dryas III au début de l'Atlantique pour une approche méthodologique des industries et des territoires dans l'Est de la France. 2ème partie. *Revue Archéologique de l'Est et du Centre-Est* 42–1, 3–62.

—— 1998a. Les recherches sur l'Epipaléolithique et le Mésolithique en Franche-Comté. In: Cupillard, C. and Richard, A.(dir.) *Les derniers chasseurs cueilleurs (13000–5500 av.JC) dans le massif du Jura et ses marges*, 22–23. Lons-le-Saunier.

—— 1998b. L'Epipaléolithique et le Mésolithique de l'Est de la France dans le contexte national: cadre d'étude et état des recherches. In: Cupillard, C. and Richard, A. (dir.) *Les derniers chasseurs cueilleurs (13000–5500 av.JC) dans le massif du Jura et ses marges*, 24–35. Lons-le-Saunier.

—— 1998c. L'abri de Rochedane à Villars-sous-Dampjoux. In: Cupillard, C. and Richard, A. (dir.) *Les derniers chasseurs cueilleurs (13000–5500 av.JC) dans le massif du Jura et ses marges*, 104–105. Lons-le-Saunier.

—— (dir.) 2000. *Actes de la table ronde de Metz*, 23 and 24 novembre 1996. Bulletin de la Société Préhistorique Luxembourgeoise 19.1997.

Thévenin, A. and Sainty, J. 1980. Un gisement préhistorique exceptionnel du Jura alsacien: l'abri du Mannlefelsen I à Oberlag (Haut-Rhin). *Annuaire de la Société d'Histoire Sundgauvienne*, 21–39.

Valentin, F. 1998. Les restes humains de l'abri des Cabônes à Ranchot. In: Cupillard, C. and Richard, A. (dir.) *Les derniers chasseurs cueilleurs (13000–5500 av.JC) dans le massif du Jura et ses marges*, 185–186. Lons-le-Saunier.

Valentin, F. and Le Goff, I. 1998. Sépultures et pratiques funéraires mésolithiques. In: Cupillard, C. and Richard, A. (dir.) *Les derniers chasseurs cueilleurs (13000–5500 av.JC) dans le massif du Jura et ses marges*, 182–184. Lons-le-Saunier.

Vilain, R. 1966. *Le gisement de Sous Balme à Culoz (Ain) et ses industries microlithiques*. Documents du.Laboratoire de Géologie de la Faculté des Sciences de Lyon, No. 13. Lyon.

Vilain, R. and Dufournet, P. 1970. l'abri de Sous-Sac à Craz-en-Michaille. Analyse des fouilles de Gabriel Salanville. *Le Bugey* 57, 24–58.

Voruz, J.L. (dir.) 1996. *La grotte du Gardon à Ambérieu-en-Bugey (Ain). Rapport de Fouilles. 1994–1996*. Ambérieu-en-Bugey: Société Préhistorique Rhodanienne.

Voruz, J.L., Nicod, P.Y. and de Ceuninck, G. 1995. Les chronologies néolithiques dans le bassin rhodanien: un bilan. In: Voruz, J.L. (dir.) *Chronologies néolithiques. De 6000 à 2000 avant notre ère dans le bassin rhodanien* 38. Actes du colloque d'Ambérieu- en- Bugey,19 et 20/09/1992 (XIe Rencontre sur le Néolithique de la région Rhône-Alpes). Documents du Département d'Anthropologie et d'Ecologie de l'Université de Genève 20 et Société Préhistorique Rhodanienne, Ambérieu-en-Bugey, 381–404.

Vuaillat, D. and Demars, P.Y. 1998. L'abri de Gigot à Bretonvillers. In: Cupillard, C. and Richard, A. (dir.) 1998. *Les derniers chasseurs cueilleurs (13000–5500 av.JC) dans le massif du Jura et ses marges*, 99–101. Lons-le-Saunier.

Vuaillat, D., Thévenin, A. and Heim, J. 1984. Un nouveau gisement épipaléolithique et mésolithique en Franche-Comté: l'abri de Gigot à Bretonvillers (Doubs): note préliminaire. In: Bocquet, A. *et al.* (dir.) *Eléments de pré et protohistoire européenne, Hommages au professeur J.P. Millotte*, Annales littéraires de l'Université de Franche-Comté, série archéologie No 32, 115–124. Paris.

Welten, M. 1982. *Vegetationgeschichtliche Untersuchungen in den westlichen Schweizer Alpen: Bern-Wallis*. Mémoire de la Société Helvétique des Sciences Naturelles 9. Basel.

Wittig, M. and Guillet, J.P. 2000. Le Mésolithique de l'abri du roseau (Ain, France). In: Crotti, P. (ed.) *Epipaléolithique et Mésolithique*. Actes de la table-ronde de Lausanne, 21–23 novembre 1997. Cahiers d'Archéologie Romande 81, 165–170. Lausanne.

Wyss, R. 1968. Das Mesolithikum. In: Drack, W. (dir.) *Ur- und Frügeschichtliche Archäologie der Schweiz. Band I. Die Altere und Mittlere Steinzeit*, 123–144. Schweizerische Gesellschaft für Ur-und Frügeschichte. Bâle.

Wyss, R. and Stampfli, H.R. 1979. *Das Mittelsteinzeitliche Hirschjägerlager von Schötz 7 im Wauvilermoos*. Archäölogische Forschungen. Schweizerischen Landesmuseums. Zürich.

Zvelebil, M. 2000. The last hunter-gatherers of temperate Europe. In: Richard, A., Cupillard, C., Richard, H. and Thévenin, A. (eds) *Les derniers chasseurs-cueilleurs d'Europe occidentale (13000–5500 av. J.C.)*. Actes du Colloque International de Besançon (Doubs, France), 23–25 octobre 1998. Les Belles Lettres, Presses Universitaires de Franche-Comté, Collection Annales Littéraires de l'Université de Franche-Comté No 699, série "Environnement, sociétés et Archéologie" No1, 379–406. Paris.

Zvelebil, M. and Dolukhanov, P. 1991. The transition to farming in Eastern and northern Europe. *Journal of World Prehistory* 5, 233–278.

13. Highland occupation in the southern Alps during the Early Holocene

Federica Fontana and Antonio Guerreschi

Highland occupation by post-glacial hunter-gatherers represents a widespread cultural phenomenon all over Europe. Research begun in the 70s on the southern slope of the Alps has revealed the presence of hundreds of sites and find-spots particularly on its central and eastern sides. These sites, which appear to be concentrated in proximity to the timber-line, can be considered as a seasonal aspect of a more complex settlement system based on the exploitation of the main Alpine valleys from their bottoms to highland territories. In this paper we have addressed the problem of highland occupation from a spatially focussed perspective: our aim is to understand the specific use of the sites and of their broader catchment territories and thus analyse the capacity of hunter-gatherers to intervene in the landscape. For this purpose we have considered the data emerging from the analysis of two pilot sites situated at the opposite sides of the southern Alps: Mondeval de Sora, in the eastern Dolomites (Belluno) and Alpe Veglia, in the Lepontine Alps (Verbania).

Introduction

In his introductory paper to the session *Enculturating the landscape*, Zvelebil (this volume) has pointed out the presence of different traditions of research in connection to the topic of landscape in Mesolithic archaeology. In this paper we would like to discuss the problem of highland occupation in the southern Alps during the early Holocene from a spatial perspective taking as a basis the preliminary data emerging from the analysis of two pilot sites situated on the two opposite sides of the Italian Alps, Mondeval de Sora (Dolomites, Belluno) and Alpe Veglia (Lepontine Alps, Verbania).

We stress that this perspective has not been developed in northern Italy so far, with some significant exceptions (Bagolini and Dalmeri 1987; Biagi *et al.* 1994; Fedele and Wick 1996). This is due both to the ephemeral nature of most of the sites identified (predominantly open-air) and to the lack of a solid tradition in this sense. On the contrary, the approach adopted by Italian researchers has mainly been addressed to a chrono-stratigraphical and environmental reconstruction, as well as to an assessment of settlement patterns form a deliberately long-term perspective (Broglio 1980, 1992; Dalmeri and Pedrotti 1994; Lanzinger 1996). In the first part of this paper we will summarise the data emerging from the above approach as a background to the information resulting from our analysis of the two pilot sites, which will be the object of the second part. All dates in the text are expressed in uncalibrated years.

Environmental context and human settlement

The occupation of mountain areas by groups of hunter-gatherers represents one of the most significant phenomena of cultural adaptation to the changing environmental conditions in Europe starting from the Late Glacial. Research carried out on the southern slope of the Alps by different institutions from the 70s onwards has revealed the presence of several sites and find-spots, particularly on its central and eastern sides. As a result the topic of highland occupation is today one of the most discussed among scholars specialised in Mesolithic studies in northern Italy.

Geomorphological and palaeobotanical data indicate that glaciers, on the central and eastern sides of the southern Alps, began to reduce about 15,000 years BP (Orombelli and Ravazzi 1996). As a consequence, vegetation and fauna progressively started to colonise highland territories; at the same time the main prealpine valleys which had been hollowed out by glacial erosion were occupied by lake basins, some of which still exist today. The subsequent phases of glacial expansion (Younger Dryas) did not have great impact on the environment except at very high altitudes, so that glacier reduction continued almost undisturbed until about 5000 BP (Orombelli and Ravazzi 1996) reaching higher positions than today at the end of the Boreal and the beginning of the Atlantic period.

The colonisation of these territories by vegetation was particularly intense during the temperate phases of the

Figure 13.1 Location of the sites of Mondeval de Sora (Belluno, Italy) and Alpe Veglia (Verbania, Italy).

Late Glacial (Bölling and Alleröd), when there was an important diffusion of arboreal species (particularly *Pinus*) together with a reduction of non arboreal plants. This situation underwent a marked regression between the end of the Alleröd and the beginning of the Younger Dryas but increased again considerably from the Preboreal onwards, with a diffusion of *Pinus* and *Larix* in the Pre-boreal phase and of *Picea* in the Boreal. From the end of the Pre-boreal the timberline was thus situated at a higher position than today (Oeggl and Wahlmüller 1992).

As deglaciation processes proceeded, human groups who had previously settled at the edges of the Prealpine plateaus started to occupy the main Alpine valleys. Settlement patterns during the Late Palaeolithic and early Mesolithic were thus characterised by a greater complexity which resulted in the occupation of different topographic positions: not only valley-bottoms and mountain areas but also high plateaus, as highlighted by the most recent research (Angelucci and Peresani 1995; Peresani *et al.* 2000).

Seasonal occupation of highland territories by human groups began during the temperate phases of the Late Glacial as a progressive phenomenon, reaching altitudes as high as 2300 meters in the early Mesolithic. The main watercourses and their tributaries were followed to gain access to the highland areas (Lanzinger 1996).

As far as the Mesolithic is concerned settlement patterns in the Alpine area has been reconstructed after analysing different aspects such as the topographic location of the sites, composition of lithic assemblages and raw material provenience. In a detailed study Lanzinger (1985) established an apparent correlation between the morphological locations of the sites and the composition of the lithic assemblages thus making a distinction between residential sites – which were characterised by a high variable assemblage and located either under large rock boulders or in the open-air, next to small lakes – and specialised hunting stations, to be identified by the presence of a high percentage of entire and broken microlithic armatures and situated near passes or in dominant positions. Furthermore, as far as the sites of the eastern Alps are concerned, the origin of most of the lithic raw materials used for manufacturing tools from the Jurassic and Cretaceous formations of the Prealpine belt suggests that mountain and valley-bottom sites were part of the same settlement system (Broglio 1992; Broglio and Lanzinger 1996).

Although some hundreds of sites have been brought to light, these are mostly represented by surface collections; the number of excavated sites is thus much smaller, and only a few have revealed the presence of visible or latent structures. Two of these, Mondeval de Sora and Alpe Veglia (Figure 13.1), have been the object of our research in the recent years, providing an opportunity to approach this subject from a different perspective which takes into account aspects such as the nature, function and organisation of dwelling space within sites.

Mondeval de Sora

Mondeval de Sora is a small basin situated at the top of the Fiorentina Valley, in the centre of the Dolomite region, at about 2165 metres a.s.l. Several secondary watercourses cross the valley which is delimited both to the north and east by imposing reliefs composed by Dolomitic and tufaceous sandstones as well as by important passes connecting with contiguous valleys. The presence of a lake basin which may have existed in the early Holocene was inferred after geomorphological and sedimentary research (Alciati *et al.* 1994). Pollen analysis on the sedimentary series deposited by the lake proved not to be possible due to the presence of high quantities of charcoals, indicating the existence of large fires, the origin of which has not been possible to determine so far.

Figure 13.2 Site VF1, sectors I and III at Mondeval de Sora

Several sites have been discovered in the area following non-systematic surveys carried out by local amateurs. Four of these are located under large dolomite boulders, while the others are open air find-spots mainly situated along ideal path-ways connecting different passes, where some tens or hundreds of lithic artefacts were collected.

In site VF1, which is protected by a large erratic boulder, two different sectors representing two separate sites have been explored (Figure 13.2). Interdisciplinary analyses have focused so far on site VF1-sector 1, located beneath the S-W facing side of the boulder; here an area of approximately 60 sqm has been excavated, revealing a complex stratigraphic series. It is the most exceptionally well preserved Mesolithic site on the southern slope of the Alps, where an important Late Mesolithic (Castelnovian) burial has also been identified.

The early Mesolithic (Sauveterrian) layers contain a paved area made of tufa slabs (Layer 14) and, outside it, an arrangement of blocks of dolomite stone (Layer 33). Layer 32 forms the bottom of a sub-circular structure interpretable as a hearth (Figure 13.3). These features were covered by two anthropogenic layers: Layer 8 – dated with ^{14}C to 9185 ± 240 years BP uncal. (GX-21788) – was very rich in charcoal and ecofacts and contained about 20,000 lithic artefacts, while Layer 31 was a light brown silty-sandy soil, characterised by the presence of abundant faunal remains and extending mostly into the area beyond Layer 8.

The two Mesolithic layers, which were cut and partially removed by subsequent occupation of the site in the north-western side of the excavated area, have provided the first information about the economy of mountain settlements in the southern slope of the Alps. Preliminary analyses indicate that red deer was the most hunted species, followed by ibex. Furthermore, some new-born specimens confirm that the site was occupied during the summer season (Alciati *et al.* 1994).

Techno-typological and spatial analyses with GIS have been performed on the lithic assemblage from Layer 8 with the aim of detecting behavioural aspects such as the organisation and function of the area. These will be completed with data on the faunal remains as soon as their study will be achieved. Data processing on Layer 31 is also in progress.

Analysis of the lithic assemblage from Layer 8 has highlighted that 87% of it is represented by *débitage*,

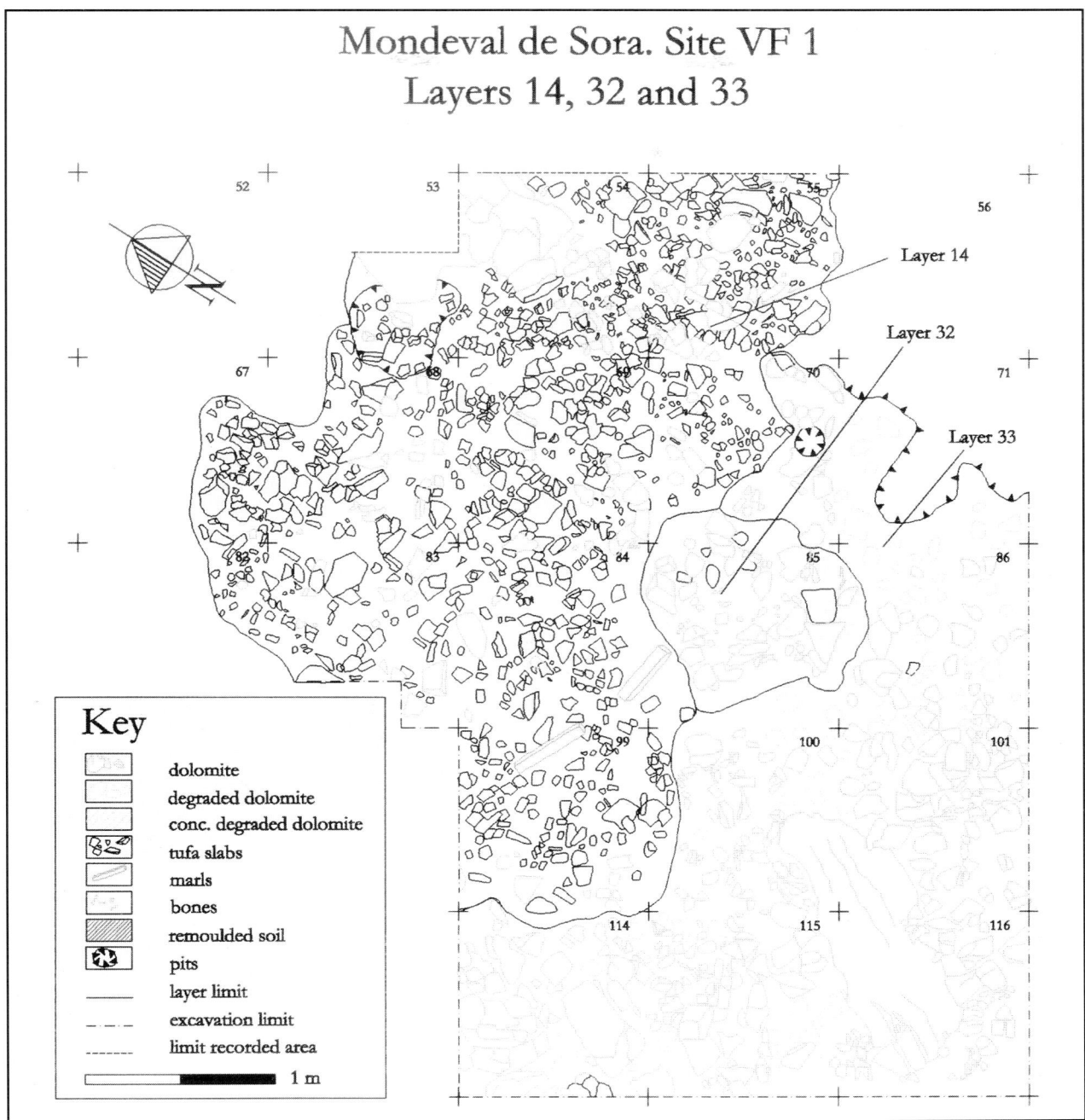

Figure 13.3 Map of the dwelling structures built with local stones at Mondeval de Sora, site VF1, sector I.

50% of which are burned. Among retouched artefacts, microliths are the best represented (88%), particularly crescents, triangles of the scalene type and double backed points which, in spite of their standardised shape, were mostly obtained from irregular flakes by the microburin technique. The raw material for lithic manufacture was mainly imported from the valley-bottom within an embedded procurement system, though local Alpine flint was also used (Fontana 1997).

The processing of distribution maps of the different main techno-typological classes (*débitage*, cores, microlithic tools, microburins and tools) – assuming that they have a functional value which can reflect the activities carried out in the site – has allowed relatively stable patterns to be identified. On the basis of the maps so far obtained, we can suggest that Layer 8 was occupied several times during the early Mesolithic following the same occupational behaviour. It was therefore used as a "complex polyfunctional area" where activities such as flintknapping and microlith manufacturing mostly took place, along with butchering and leather scraping (Vullo *et al.* 1999; Fontana and Vullo 2000).

Figure 13.4 Panoramic view of Alpe Veglia site.

Alpe Veglia

Alpe Veglia is the only Mesolithic site excavated to date in the western Italian Alps (Gambari *et al.* 1991). It lies in the upper Val d'Ossola (Alpi Lepontine) on an alluvial fan in the middle of a glacial valley at an altitude of 1750 m, and is surrounded by reliefs as high as 3000 m (Figure 13.4). An area of about 200 sqm has been uncovered so far. The approximately 25 cm thick archaeological layer is located immediately underneath the meadow and overlies a sterile surface of crio-nival origin, characterised by the presence of stones (Fontana *et al.* 2000). Because of soil acidity organic remains are not preserved, and the archaeological record consists exclusively of lithic artefacts. These are almost entirely made of local rock crystal, while only a few artefacts are manufactured from imported flint (0.01%).

Débris and fragmented artefacts represent almost 85% of the industry, due to structural features of the rock itself. Technological analysis indicates that knapping was mostly oriented towards the production of flakes rather that blades. Among retouched tools, microliths dominate (particularly scalene triangles and truncated bladelets) thus suggesting an attribution of this assemblage to the middle phase of the Sauveterrian. The microburin technique is underrepresented in comparison with the sites situated in the eastern Alps.

An understanding of the intra-site organisation and function of this deposit would not have been possible without the application of GIS to the spatial analysis of archaeological data. Two main concentrations of archaeological material have been detected which could be related to the presence of two areas of activity or dwelling units: these appear slightly different in composition due to the presence of all categories of objects in one of the areas and to a lack of cores in the other one. Moreover, these two units seem to correspond to zones where the density of stones on the soil decreases, an aspect which could suggest an intentional clearing of the area by the groups who settled in the site.

Conclusions

As emerges from the study of the sites of Mondeval de Sora and Alpe Veglia, the occupation of highland

	Mondeval de Sora, site VF1, III	Alpe Veglia
Location of the site	open air	rockshelter
Raw material exploitation system	mostly local	mostly imported
Presence of dwelling structures	not identified	yes
Identification of strongly structured spaces	*yes*	yes
Modes of occupation	Residential, polyfunctional area	Residential, identification of different concentrations of materials

Figure 13.5 Comparison of occupation strategies at the sites of Mondeval and Alpe Veglia.

territories by post-glacial hunter-gatherers in the southern slope of the Alps implied the adoption of practical strategies which could allow them to live at high altitudes for long periods during the summer season. The adoption of these strategies results in a more or less visible impact on the palaeoenvironmental and archaeological record, as testified by data relating to the organisation of space within the sites and, more in general, to land use.

Firstly the presence of dwelling structures built with local rocks on site VF1-I at Mondeval de Sora constitutes a visible sign of man's intervention on the landscape. Moreover, for the first time in the context of highland sites in the southern Alps, the exceptional preservation of organic remains has made it possible to appreciate the capacity of post-glacial hunter-gatherers to take advantage of both local faunal and vegetal resources.

Secondly, the presence of markedly structured spaces has been detected both at Mondeval and Alpe Veglia, thanks to specific intra-site spatial analysis performed with GIS. As a matter of fact these *structures latentes*, using Leroi-Gourhan's expression (Leroi-Gourhan and Brézillon 1972), which would not be visible to the naked eye, represent a further sign of early Holocene hunter-gatherers cultural interaction with the surrounding environment. We can therefore affirm that, although the composition of lithic assemblages shows a trend in the specialisation towards hunting activities, the two sites were used as seasonal residential camps. More specifically, the existence of an occupational palimpsest seems obvious at Mondeval, where the layer so far analysed (Layer 8) results from the repeated use of the area as a polyfunctional zone. On the contrary, at Alpe Veglia it is still not clear whether the two units identified – to be interpreted as different activity areas or dwellings – were formed contemporaneously or not.

Finally, from the point of view of their location, the two sites are situated in ideal and usual positions for high altitude residential sites (presence of flat surfaces, proximity to small lake basins, watercourses and passes). Nevertheless, different specialised behaviours have been detected which seem to be strictly connected to the morphology and environmental features of the territories where they are located. This aspect is reflected by site typology – which is represented at Mondeval by a rockshelter and at Alpe Veglia by an open air area – as well as by raw material exploitation systems. The use of local lithic materials (rock crystal) is almost exclusively documented at Alpe Veglia while flint, mainly imported from the southern Alps, dominates at Mondeval. Moreover, the presence of some artefacts made with rock crystal coming from the area north of Mondeval suggests either the presence on this site of groups coming from different areas, or exchanges between different groups.

In conclusion the two sites – which on the basis of different parameters can be considered as two seasonal residential camps – are characterised (see Figure 13.5) by different strategies in terms of the organisation of space, choice of settlement, resource exploitation and so on. All these aspects reflect the capacity of the last European hunter-gatherers to adapt to the territories where they settled according to the opportunities offered by the landscape.

References

Alciati, G., Cattani, L., Fontana, F., Gerhardinger, E., Guerreschi, A., Milliken, S., Mozzi, P. and Rowley-Conwy, P. 1994. Mondeval de Sora: a high altitude Mesolithic camp-site in the Italian Dolomites. *Preistoria Alpina* 28/1 (1992), 351–366.

Angelucci, D. and Peresani, M. 1995. I siti all'aperto di Val Lastari e Cima Dodici: nuovi contributi per lo studio del popolamento preistorico dell'Altopiano dei Sette Comuni. *Studi Trentini di Scienze Naturali – Acta Geologica* 70, 109–123.

Bagolini, B. and Dalmeri, G. 1987. I siti mesolitici del Colbricon – Analisi spaziale e fruizione del territorio. *Preistoria Alpina* 23, 7–188.

Biagi, P., Nisbet, R. and Scaife, R. 1994. Man and the vegetation in the Southern Alps: the Valcamonica-Valtrompia-Valsabbia watershed (Northern Italy). In: Biagi, P. and Nandris, J. (eds) *Highland zone exploitaion in Southern Europe*. Monografie di Natura Bresciana 20, 133–142.

Broglio, A. 1980. Culture e ambienti alla fine del Paleolitico e Mesolitico nell'Italia nord-orientale. *Preistoria Alpina* 16, 7–29.

—— 1992. Mountain sites in the context of North-East Italian Upper Palaeolithic and Mesolithic. *Preistoria Alpina* 28/1, 293–310.

Broglio, A. and Lanzinger, M. 1996. The Human population of the Southern slope of the Eastern Alps and the Würm Late Glacial and Early Postglacial. In: Evans, S.P., Frisia, S., Borsato, A., Cita, M.B., Lanzinger, M., Ravazzi, C. and Sala, B. (eds) Proceedings of the AIQUA Conference *Modificazioni climatiche ed ambientali tra il Tardiglaciale e l'Olocene antico in Italia*, Il Quaternario 9, 2, 499–508.

Dalmeri, G. and Pedrotti, A. 1994. Distribuzione topografica dei siti del Paleolitico superiore finale e Mesolitico in Trentino Alto-Adige e nelle Dolomiti venete (Italia). *Preistoria Alpina* 28/2 (1992), 247–267.

Fedele, F. and Wick, L. 1996. Glacial/postglacial transition South of Splügen Pass: environment and human activity. In: Evans, S.P., Frisia, S., Borsato, A., Cita, M.B., Lanzinger, M., Ravazzi, C. and Sala, B. (eds) Proceedings of the AIQUA Conference *Modificazioni climatiche ed ambientali tra il Tardiglaciale e l'Olocene antico in Italia*, Il Quaternario 9, 2, 541–550.

Fontana, F. 1997. *Il popolamento delle aree montane nell'Olocene antico. Analisi delle strutture e delle industrie litiche dei livelli sauveterriani del sito di Mondeval de Sora (Dolomiti Bellunesi)*. PhD Thesis, University of Ferrara.

Fontana, F. and Vullo, N. 2000. Organisation et fonction d'un camp de base saisonnier au coeur des Dolomites: le gisement mésolithique de Mondeval de Sora (Belluno, Italie). In: Richard, A., Cupillard, C., Richard, H. and Thévenin, A. (eds) *Les derniers chasseurs-cueilleurs d'Europe occidentale (13000–5500 av.J.C.)*. Actes du Colloque International de Besançon (Doubs, France) 23–25 octobre 1998. Paris: Les Belles Lettres, Collection Annales Littéraires de l'Université de Franche-Comté No 699, Série "Environnement, sociétés et archéologie" No 1, 197–208.

Fontana, F., Guerreschi, A. and Vullo, N. 2000. Le site méso-lithique de l'Alpe Veglia (Alpes Lepontines, Italie): analyse techno-typologique et spatiale. Résultats préliminaires. In: Crotti, P. (ed.) *"Meso '99*. Actes de la Table Ronde Epipaléo-lithique et Mésolithique, 21–23 Novembre 1997, Lausanne, Cahiers d'Archéologie Normande, 259–265.

Gambari, F., Ghiretti, A. and Guerreschi, A. 1991. Il sito mesolitico di Cianciàvero nel Parco Naturale di Alpe Veglia (Alpi Lepontine, Val d'Ossola, Novara). *Preistoria Alpina* 25, 47–52.

Lanzinger, M., 1985. Ricerche nei siti mesolitici della cresta di Siusi (auf der Schneide, siti XV e XVI dell'Alpe di Siusi) nelle Dolomiti. Considerazioni sul significato funzionale espresso dalle industrie mesolitiche della Regione. *Preistoria Alpina* 21, 33–48.

—— 1996. Sistemi di insediamento mesolitici come adattamento agli ambienti montani alpini. *XIII International Congress of Prehistoric and Protohistoric Sciences*, Colloquium 7, The Mesolithic, 125–140.

Leroi-Gourhan and Brézillon 1972. Fouilles de Pincevent: essai d'analyse ethnographique d'un habitat magdalénien, *Gallia Préhistoire* 2, 7.

Oeggl, K. and Wahlmüller, N. 1992. Vegetation and climate history of high Alpine Mesolithic camp-site in the Eastern Alps. *Preistoria Alpina* 28/1 (1994), 71–82.

Orombelli, G. and Ravazzi, C. 1996. The Late Glacial and early Holocene: chronology and palaeoclimate. In: Evans, S.P., Frisia, S., Borsato, A., Cita, M.B., Lanzinger, M., Ravazzi, C. and Sala, B. (eds) Proceedings of the AIQUA Conference *Modificazioni climatiche ed ambientali tra il Tardiglaciale Tardiglaciale e l'Olocene antico in Italia*, Il Quaternario 9, 2, 439–444.

Peresani, M., Di Anastasio, G. and Bertola, S. 2000. Epigravettien récent et Mesolithique ancien en contexte Préalpin: les odnnées du haut plateau du Cansiglio (Italie du Nord). In: Crotti, P. (ed.) *Meso '99*. Actes de la Table Ronde Epipaléolithique et Mésolithique, 21–23 Novembre 1997, Lausanne, Cahiers d'Archéologie Normande 81, 267–276.

Vullo, N., Fontana, F. and Guerreschi, A. 1999. The application of GIS to intra-site spatial analysis: preliminary results from Alpe Veglia (VB) and Mondeval de Sora (BL), two Mesolithic sites in the Italian Alps. In: Barceló, J.A., Briz, I. and Vila, A. (eds) *New Techniques for Old Times*. Proceedings of the 26th Conference of Computer Applications and Quantitative Methods in Archaeology, Barcelona, March 1998, BAR International Series 757, 111–115. Oxford.

Zvelebil, M. 2002. Enculturation of Mesolithic Landscapes (in this volume).

14. Enculturating the Landscape beyond Doggerland

Ingrid Fuglestvedt

The pioneer settlement of Southwest-Norway, 10,200/ 10,000 – 9800/9500 BP has traditionally been described solely in terms of subsistence and economy. The paper outlines alternative approaches, using concepts of 'centre and periphery', the 'sacred' and the 'profane', 'origin myths' and 'totemism'.

Introduction

This short paper is based on my doctoral thesis "Phenomenology of the pioneer settlement: Southwest-Norway and North-Europe in the period 10,200/10,000 – 9500 BP" (Fuglestvedt 2001). The focus of my work has been to understand the pioneer settlement in Southwest-Norway within a North-European context. My work includes a study of material from Late Upper Palaeolithic/Early Mesolithic sites in Southwest-Norway (i.e. Rogaland county). Comparisons with material from contemporary sites in West-Norway, East-Norway, Denmark and North-Germany have also been conducted (Fuglestvedt 1999a; Kutschera and Warås in prep.). However, the main goal of this thesis is to understand the pioneer settlement from the perspective of phenomenological thinking (Fuglestvedt 1999b), i.e. a thorough study of human experience, both in general as well as a historic specific event. The thesis examines issues related to the pioneer situation as a bodily experience – and as a situation in which the Late Upper Palaeolithic human beings had to change their world view and create new origin myths. Further, the pioneer settlement is understood in concepts of 'centre and perihery' and includes topics related to totemism.

The setting

The earliest settlement in West-Norway dates to the period 10,200 – 9800 BP. The sites represents a society of mobile hunters visiting a landscape only partly understood and experienced by Late Palaeolithic man. In other words, it involves a situation in where the new landscape is not wholly enculturated. Before I try to answer the question about what an enculturating process may be like, I will have to summon up the setting and the last results concerning the archaeological material of this period.

I have studied the flint collections from the coastal site Galta 3 in Rogaland ((Høgestøl 1995; Høgestøl et al. 1995; Prøsch-Danielsen and Høgestøl 1995; Fuglestvedt in prep. a) and Moldvika 1 (Gjerland 1990; Fuglestvedt in prep. b) in Rogaland. This has been done as a part of an informal collaboration in West-Norway comparing the material and site distribution patterns of contemporary sites. Along with this, I have studied the Early Mesolithic site of Stunner in East Norway (Fuglestvedt 1999a). Further, I have compared the Norwegian material with Danish and North-German sites, by way of studying the collections from Sølvbjerg, Bonderup, Stellmoor and the Teltwisch sites. Last year (1999) an internordic group of archaeologists working specifically with Late Upper Palaeolithic and Early Mesolithic flint artefacts gathered in Stavanger. The objective was to discuss the Scandinavian material of this period and provide access to the West-Norwegian material (Kutschera and Warås in prep.). This work of cooperation and comparisons has led to one main conclusion: The Earliest Fosna, that is, from about 10,200/10,000 until 9800/9500 BP must be called by its 'real' name – *Ahrensburg*. The correspondence with Norwegian material concerns both tools and technology (see also Fischer 1996; Kutschera 1999; Kutschera and Warås 2000), however there may be a difference in the use of flake axes. The only clear difference between Norwegian and continental assemblages, is the former's frequent use of poor quality flint.

The contents of the Ahrensburg-label must be modified to include new regions of Northwest-Europe, and a time period covering the first centuries of the Mesolithic period. This is fairly unproblematic as the activities at the classic Ahrensburgian site Stellmoor is C14-dated to the period 10,200 to 9800 BP (Fischer and Tauber 1986:9). This dating corresponds exactly to the geological dates of the Galta 3 site (Prøsch-Danielsen and Høgestøl 1995:129) and the shore displacement curve dating of Moldvika 1 (Gjerland 1990:21) in Rogaland, Southwest Norway. The group visiting the sites in what is now North-

Germany and Southwest-Norway, may very well have been the same people, or at least related socially and biologically.

In the Late Palaeolithic a similar site structure was common on the North-European plain. For instance the site Borneck (Rust 1958:Abb. 26) in Ahrensburger tunneltal has a very similar outline to what is found in the mountain areas of Rogaland, at lake Store Myrvatn, and at Store Fløyrlivatn (Bang Andersen 1990, 2000, this volume; Tørhaug and Åstveit 2000:38). As with the stated similarities in technology, we thus experience an often repeated site structure in North-Europe, the Norwegian sites included (see also Nærøy 1995, 2000). The site structure indicate a high degree of mobility and a group of three to five persons as the smallest social segment.

To return to the main scope of this paper – the process of enculturating a new landscape – we will have to look at the palaeographic situation. The dry North Sea area of the period has in a paper by Bryony Coles (1998) been given the name *Doggerland*. In line with Coles, Doggerland should be seen as an area of settlement in the Late Palaeolithic and Early Mesolithic periods. In other words, this drowned area is to be seen as an extension of the settlement area on the North-European plain. We do not have the details concerning the topography of Doggerland. However, from the data we have, the landscape was not too different from other parts of the plain – that is: Fairly small topographic differences and flood plains. The Thames and the Rhine of today are relics of an old river system as tributaries of a common main river, the Channel river.

The Norwegian trench, or an extended version of this ocean area, must have been regarded as a meaningful threshold between the old world 'here', and the new world on the far side. The landscape in West-Norway stands in a formidable contrast to the lowland area of Doggerland. This new landscape appeared as a large archipelago with an indefinite amount of islands and sounds – and a rocky coastline. In the near and far background there were fjords and chains of mountain plateaus. On clear days the glacial ice could be seen. Late Upper Palaeolithic man – and woman – had never experienced anything like this before. As a basis for an understanding of what a pioneer condition in this setting may involve, I will shortly refer generally to general conclusions after studying the ethnographic record concerning man-landscape relationships among mobile hunter-gatherers. When referring to general patterns in human life I need to make clear that I am talking about pre-modern societies, even if some of the models can be applied to modern societies as well.

The world perceived

The world is being perceived from the living centre of the human body. One of my basic assumptions is prehistoric man as a religious human being. Pre-modern conceptions of the inhabited landscape are thus closely connected to religious experience. I will base my interpretations on a body of thought which can be presented by the following key words:

- Centre and periphery
- The sacred and the profane – and hierophanies
- Origin myths
- Totemism

I will shortly present the issues

Centre and periphery

Most pre-modern societies regard their own territory as the centre of the world. It is usual to exaggerate its dimensions, and thereby its importance (see examples in Tuan 1990: Figs 2 and 7). The territory, or *life world* of a social group is normally conceived as the world's centre. This world is in most cases imagined as having a circular shape. This is the place for cosmic order and for proper existence – that means – for *real* human beings (Tuan 1990:32 pp). In the world's periphery, or outside it, there is no cosmic order, rather it is chaos and eventually a place for monsters or non-classifiable beings. The world is the place of sense, outside the world there is non-sense, disorder and anti-structure.

However, what is conceived as 'outside' the world may also be used constructively, as the anti-structure of the chaotic world outside is commonly conceived as the precondition of cosmos. The human being is by its very nature inclined to transcend the given. The transcending forces are to be found in chaos, and therefore, an opening towards chaos is important (Eliade 1994 [1957]:23).

The world's periphery or the threshold between chaos and cosmos may serve, in Arnold van Gennep's (1999 [1909]) terms, as a *liminal space* for rites of passage from child to adult. As known also from Victor Turner's studies of rites of passage, the liminal phase is where the novise leaves structure, and receives the non-identity lying 'betwixt and between' (Turner 1967:93 pp) the fixed identities associated with child- and adulthood.

The sacred and the profane – and hierophanies

Close to the centre and periphery approach is the concept of 'the sacred and the profane' (Eliade 1994; 1958: chapter 1). Space is not homogenic, but divided into profane and sacred places. Sacred places may correspond with notions of the world's centre, however, we will see that *within* a group's territory the concept of the world's centre is *not* always a fixed point in space – an *axis mundi* may be dynamic. In the case of mobile hunters and gatherers the construction of the world's centre represents an existential act of creating the world in a new place (Eliade 1994:37).

Pre-modern religious experience of space, is of a non-homogenic space. This division is a basic religious experience, prior to any reflection upon the world (Eliade 1994:15). It is only when this division is established that the world can be created – and the human being can create itself. A *hierophany* is a place were 'the sacred' is revealed. And it is only by the revelation of the sacred, that the world can get ontologically constituted. At the hierophany a centre, or a fixed point in space is disclosed, from which orientation in the world is possible. Thus the hierophany – the sacred point in the world – has existential value to the prehistoric human being. A fixed point is a precondition for any orientation in the world. This is why – metaphorically spoken – the pre-modern human being always tries to settle down in the world's centre, this centre being the ordered cosmos, opposite to chaos.

As stated above, the centre of the world may be constituted several places within a group's territory. The world's centre should therefore be understood metaphorically as well as substantially. Among Australian, as well as North American, Fennoscandian and Siberian hunters and gatherers we find the same pattern of certain points in the landscape as sacred places. It may be mountain peaks or plateaus, caves, sources, or bogs, islands and rivers (e.g. Hubert 1994; Mulk 1994; Theodoratus and LaPena 1994; Wandibba 1994).

The world's centre can be a very dynamic one. As in the example of the mobile Mescalero Apaches of Texas and New Mexico. Their house construction, the tipi, is in itself a symbol of the Apachian cosmology. The tipi has a conical shape and is constructed by a wooden frame and covered with hides. The wooden poles point upwards and keep the sky elements in place, simultaneously the hut encloses the earth elements. Sky and earth are associated with male and female deities, respectively (Carmichael 1994). Similarly, the house construction, or the choom, of the mobile Nenets at the Siberian tundra marks the world's centre. It constitutes a dynamic centre, independent of place within the territory. Any work operation connected with rising of the choom is of a religious value. When the choom is erected the world is created anew. In Nenets mythology the first human being is a female, therefore rising the choom is the women's duty (Ovsyannikov and Terebikhin1994).

Origin myths

To be able to live in a certain landscape, a social group must have origin myths connected to this landscape – otherwise living in this space has no sense.

In the example provided by the Australian Pitjantjatjaras sacred places (hierophanies) are connected to ancestral beings (see also Morphy 1995). The landforms may be seen as having been created in mythical time by heroes digging valleys, rising mountains or petrified other beings. The landforms serves as a reminder of the mythical heros' actions, and as such the landscape as a whole is made up of stories and memorials about the actions of mythical beings. These actions are regarded as moral actions that maintain the world, and well-being of both ancestors and living people. This case is an example of a common concept, that is: The landscape as a chart of the world view. This phenomenon of reproducing the ancestral past serves as an example of the extent to which human action finds its place in a context of landscape. We may say that landscape serves like a moral chart that gives meaning to certain actions in certain landscapes (Silberbauer 1994:123 pp).

A group's mental landscape may thus be described as a *total philosophical fact*. The chart is a corpus of traditional theories including myths about the origin of the world and the human race, the theories underlying various rites as well as moral notions.

Totemism

Much can be said about totemism (e.g. Levi-Strauss 1963). In these contexts, it is important to focus on what was recently said regarding actions in the context of a certain landscape. All actions are social actions. To be able to act in a landscape, ego has to stand in a social relation to it. Among hunters and gatherers this is interconnected with standing in a certain relationship – or rather 'a totemic kinship' – to a certain species in nature, either it be a hierophany, a plant or an animal. The late glacial fauna situation have provided conditions for various big game species as totemic animals for different segments of The Late Upper Palaeolithic society in North-Europe.

Most hunters and gatherers regard themselves as a being integrated in nature's order in the same way as other beings, as such nature being conceived as living. Hunting is commonly understood as a sacred act in which the animal 'gives itself' to the human being. A totemic animal may be a wanted prey in terms of subsistence. However, totemic animals also have a mental value far beyond the food resource aspect.

Conclusions

By going back to the prehistoric setting, I will finally refer to possible discussions based on the theories presented:
Based on what has been discussed regarding the great contrast between the Northwest-European plain and Southwest-Norway, the assumption is made that the Ahrensburgian social group conceived the Norwegian trench as a border zone, or threshold between the known and the unknown world. *Their* life world, their centre – and their concepts regarding landforms, the creation of the world and human beings, had a connection to life at the plain, Doggerland included. The land on the other side of the trench was only just becoming a part of their experience. They knew it was there, but it was outside the real world of real beings, and as such, chaotic and beyond any sense. There was no explanation neither to its origin,

nor to the human connection to it. To begin with, it had no personality. However, the anti-structure related to being in this new landscape may have provided a liminal space for rites of passage or places for shamanistic activities.

But how was it possible to really establish a life, meaning an *everyday life* i.e. a life world, in the landscapes of today's Southwest- and West-Norway?

Traditional or pre-modern societies do change, but unlike modern societies they change according to what is orally defined as being within the frames of tradition. Change happens, because man, as stated above, by his very nature is inclined to transcend what is already given. The human being will always try to make the world less indefinite and thereby more expectable. The pioneer settlement may be understood as an expression of man's *search* for meaning by experiencing the unknown, as well as a quest to *give* meaning to this same world.

Mobile hunters and gatherers, just by being mobile, are dynamic – also in their creation of the centre of the world. The archaeological record reveals how Late Upper Palaeolithic/Early Mesolithic human beings created themselves anew in the foreign landscape by conducting the same technological practice, often on the mediocre quality Norwegian flint. Further, they recreated their world by way of putting up their 'micro-cosmos', i.e. their circularly founded tents (e.g. Eliade 1994:34; Tanner 1979; Tuan 1990:16). This is what we as archaeologists recognise as a Late Upper Palaeolithic and Early Mesolithic site structure. Ahrensburgian groups created their world in the unknown, and by doing this, they created themselves *anew*, transcending the given.

The enculturating of a landscape corresponds to the process of creating origin myths connected to the earlier unknown landscape. It is also to personify, and thereby socialise it. However, as stated above, to be able to act in a landscape, one needs a social relation to it. A social relation is interconnected to a totemic relation, and perhaps transcending the threshold over the Norwegian trench was possible because of this special relationship.

The archaeological record contains material indicating a totemic way of thinking in Late Palaeolithic and Early Mesolithic North-Europe, like the 'totempole' of a reindeer from Stellmoor (Rust 1943: Fig. 28), or the shamanistic skull of deer from Star Carr (Clark 1971; Smith 1992: Fig. 7.4) and finally, the many rock carvings of reindeer, elk, probably wild horse, bear, whale and seal in North-Norway (Gjessing 1932) from this time period (Hesjedal 1994).

By being related to totemic animals, the Ahrensburgian perhaps saw themselves as in some way related to this new landscape after all. On this background, the pioneer settlement can be understood on the basis of certain relationships between man, animal and landscape.

In conclusion my research may not be very original: Late Upper Palaeolithic people followed their preferred big game, primarily the reindeer herds, into new and unknown areas. However, the traditional understanding (e.g. Hagen 1963; Indrelid 1975) of the pioneer settlement is based on the assumption that reindeers were good to eat. My interpretations involve reindeers and other big game species as part of a deeper value system. Of course the animals were good to eat – however – they were also good to *think* about.

Acknowledgement

I would like to thank Joel Boaz for correcting my English in an earlier version of this manuscript.

References

Bang-Andersen, S. 1990. The Myrvatn Group, A Preboreal Find-Complex in Southwest-Norway. In: Vermeersch, P.M. and Van Peer, P. (eds) *Contributions to the Mesolithic in Europe*, 215–226. Leuven.

—— 2000. Fortidens svarte gull. Nærmere om datering og miljøtolkning av Fløyrliboplassene. *Fra haug ok heidni* 4/2000, 27–32. Stavanger.

—— 2002. Encircling the living space of Early Post-glacial reindeer hunters in the interior of southern Norway. (in this volume).

Carmichael, D.L. 1994. Places of power: Mescalero Apache sacred sites and sensitive areas. In: Carmichael, D.L., Hubert, J., Reeves, B. and Schanche, A. (eds) *Sacred Sites, Sacred Places*. One World Archaeology 23, 89–98. London/New York.

Clark, J.G.D. 1971. *Excavations at Star Carr* (2nd ed.). Cambridge.

Coles, B.J. 1998. Doggerland: a Speculative Survey. *Proceedings of the Prehistoric Society* 64, 45–81.

Eliade, M. 1994 [1957]. *Det hellige og det profane*. Oslo.

—— 1958. *Patterns in Comparative Religion*. London.

Fischer, A. 1996. At the Border of Human Habitat. The Late Palaeolithic and Early Mesolithic in Scandinavia. In: Larsson, L. (ed.) *The Earliest Settlement of Scandinavia and its relationship with neighbouring areas*. Acta Archaeologica Lundensia. Series in 88, No. 24, 157–176.

Fischer, A. and Tauber, H. 1986. New C14 Datings of Late Palaeoltihic Cultures from Northwestern Europe. *Journal of Danish Archaeology* 5, 7–13.

Fuglestvedt, I. 1999a. The Early Mesolithic Site at Stunner, Southeast Norway: A Discussion of Late Upper Palaeolithic/Early Mesolithic Chronology and Cultural Relations in Scandinavia. In: Boaz, J. (ed.) *The Mesolithic of Central Scandinavia*. Universitetets Oldsaksamlings Skrifter. Ny rekke. Nr. 22, 189–202. Oslo.

—— 1999b. Phenomenology of the pioneer-settlement of SW-Norway. In: Selsing, L. and Lillehammer, G. (eds) *Museumslandskap. Artikkelsamling til Kerstin Griffin på 60-årsdagen*. AmS-Rapport 12B, 515–520. Arkeologisk museum i Stavanger.

—— 2001. *Pionerbosetningens fenomenologi: Sørvest-Norge og Nordvest-Europa 10 200/10 000 – 9 800/9 500 BP*. Unpublished doctoral thesis. Arkeologisk Institutt, Universitetet i Bergen.

—— in prep. a. The Ahrensburgian site Galta 3, Rennesøy, Southwest-Norway. Dating, technology and cultural affinity of a Late Upper Palaeolithic/Early Mesolithic Assemblage. Manuscript.

—— in prep. b. The Late Upper Palaeolithic/Early Mesolithic site Moldvika 1, Rogaland, SW-Norway: Spatial organisation at an Ahrensburgian Site. Manuscript.

Gjerland, B. 1990. *Arkeologiske undersøkingar på Haugsneset og Ognøy i Tysvær og Bokn kommunar, Rogaland*. AmS-Rapport 5. Stavanger.

Gjessing, G. 1932. *Arktiske helleristninger i Nord-Norge*. Instituttet for sammenlignende kulturforskning, Oslo.

Hagen, A. 1963. Mesolittiske jegergrupper i norske høyfjell. SynsmÂter om Fosnakulturens innvandring til Vest-Norge. *Universitetets Oldsaksamlings Årbok* 1960–1961, 109–142. Oslo.

Hesjedal, A. 1994. The Hunter's Rock Art in Northern Norway. Problems of Chronology and Interpretation. *Norwegian Archaeological Review* 27, No. 1, 1–28.

Hubert, J. 1994. Sacred beliefs and beliefs of sacredness. In: Carmichael, D.L., Hubert, J., Reeves, B. and Schanche, A. (eds) *Sacred Sites, Sacred Places*. One World Archaeology 23, 9–19. London/New York.

Høgestøl, M. 1995. *Arkeologiske undersøkelser i Rennesøy kommune, Rogaland, Sørvest-Norge*. AmS-Varia 23. Arkeologisk museum i Stavanger.

Høgestøl, M., Berg, G. and Prøsch-Danielsen, L. 1995. Strandbundne Ahrensburg- og Fosnalokaliteter pÂ Galta-halvøya, Rennesøy kommune, Sørvest-Norge. Arkeologiske Skrifter Nr. 8 – 1995, 44–64. Arkeologisk institutt, Universitetet i Bergen.

Indrelid, S. 1975. Problems relating to the Early Mesolithic Settlement of Southern Norway. *Norwegian Archaeological Review* 8, No. 1, 1–18.

Kutschera, M. 1999. Vestnorsk tidligmesolitikum i et nordvesteuropeisk perspektiv. In: Fuglestvedt, I., Gansum, T. and Opedal, A. (eds) *Vennebok til Bjørn Myhre på 60-årsdagen*. AmS-Rapport 11a, 43–52. Arkeologisk museum i Stavanger.

Kutschera, M. and Warås, T.A. 2000. Steinalderlokaliteten på 'Breiviksklubben' på Bratt-Helgaland i Karmøy kommune. In: Løken, T. (ed.) *Åsgard – Natur- og kulturhistoriske undersøkelser langs en gassrør-trasé i Karmøy og Tysvær, Rogaland*. Ams-Rapport 14, 61–96. Arkeologisk museum i Stavanger.

—— in prep. Technological diversity and similarities in southern and western Scandinavia during the Late Glacial – Boreal transition. Manuscript.

Levi-Strauss, C. 1963. *Totemism*. Boston.

Morphy, H. 1995. Landscape and Ancestral past. In: Hirsch, E. and O'Hanlon, M. (eds) *The Anthropology of Landscape. Perspectives on Place and Space*, 184–209. Oxford.

Mulk, I-M. 1994: Sacrificial places and their meaning in Saami society. In: Carmichael, D.L., Hubert, J., Reeves, B. and Schanche, A. (eds) *Sacred Sites, Sacred Places*. One World Archaeology 23, 121–131. London/New York.

Nærøy, A.J. 1995. *Early Mesolithic Site Structure in western Norway – a case study*. Universitetets Oldsaksamling. Årbok 1993/1994, 59–77. Oslo.

—— 2000. *Stone Age Living Spaces in Western Norway*. BAR International Series 857. Oxford.

Ovsyannikov, O.V. and Terebikhin, N.M. 1994. Sacred space in the culture of the Arctic regions. In: Carmichael, D.L., Hubert, J., Reeves, B. and Schanche, A. (eds) *Sacred Sites, Sacred Places*. One World Archaeology 23, 44–81. London/New York.

Prøsch-Danielsen, L. and Høgestøl, M. 1995. A coastal Ahrensburgian site found at Galta, Rennesøy, Southwest Norway. In: Fischer, A. (ed.) *Man and Sea in the Mesolithic. Coastal settlement above and below present sea level*. Oxbow Monograph 54, 123–130. Oxford.

Rust, A. 1943. *Die alt- und mittelsteinzeitlichen Funde von Stellmoor*. Neumünster.

—— 1958. *Die jungpaläolitischen Zeltanlagen von Ahrensburg*. Neumünster.

Silberbauer, G.B. 1994. A Sense of Place. In: Burch, E.S. and Ellanna, L. (ed.) *Key Issues in Hunter-Gatherer Research*, 119–143. Oxford.

Smith, C. 1992. *Late Stone Age Hunters on the British Isles*. London.

Tanner, A. 1979. *Bringing home animals. Religious Ideology and Mode of Production of the Mistassini Cree Hunters*. New York.

Theodoratus, D.J. and LaPena, F. 1994. Wintu sacred geography of northern California. In: Carmichael, D.L., Hubert, J., Reeves, B. and Schanche, A. (eds) *Sacred Sites, Sacred Places*. One World Archaeology 23, 20–31. London/New York.

Tuan, Y.-F. 1990. *Topophilia. A Study of Environmental Perception, Attitudes and Values*. New York.

Turner, V. 1967. *The Forest of Symbols. Aspects of Ndembu Ritual*. Ithaca/London.

Tørhaug, V. and Åstveit, L.I. 2000. Steinalderboplassene ved Store Fløyrlivatn. *Fra haug ok heidni* 1/2000, 35–39. Stavanger.

Van Gennep, A. 1999 [1909]. *Rites de passage. Overgangsriter*. Oslo.

Wandibba, S. 1994. Bukusu sacred sites. In: Carmichael, D.L., Hubert, J., Reeves, B. and Schanche, A. (eds) *Sacred Sites, Sacred Places*. One World Archaeology 23, 115–120. London/New York.

15. Cultural convergences of northern Europe and North Africa during the Early Holocene?

Elena A.A. Garcea

The Early Holocene spread of humans into North Africa extended from the Mediterranean coasts to the mountain ranges of the Central Sahara. Two distinct cultural and chronological horizons were identified which existed before the emergence of subsistence strategies based on food production. The earlier horizon had been named "Epipalaeolithic", the later one "Mesolithic". These terms were derived from Mediterranean-based terms, which are inappropriate for the North African context. Research in North Africa was long biased by Mediterranean cultural frameworks, which viewed the production of pottery and polished stone tools as evidence of "Neolithic" cultures. As a consequence, the "Epipalaeolithic", which already yielded the first ceramic and polished stone artefacts, was assimilated into the "Mesolithic", and these two with the "Pastoral Neolithic". In order to avoid confusion and to point out the main features of these horizons, new terms have been suggested, namely "Early Acacus" for the earlier horizon, and "Late Acacus" for the later horizon, based on their identification in the Tadrart Acacus mountain range in the Libyan Sahara. The Late Acacus, in particular, featured a number of innovations leading to a stronger enculturation of the landscape concerning technology, economy, site organisations and settlement patterns.

Preface

The Mesolithic has been correctly considered the "Cinderella of the Three Age system" (Zvelebil 1986:5). Various Mesolithic cultures existed in Europe with different and independent forms of adaptation. Among them, the Mesolithic of the Baltic, for example, was an autonomous development, and certainly not a periphery of the Near East (Zvelebil 1998).

To the contrary, southern European prehistory, and prehistorians as well, were greatly influenced by the Near Eastern and the Mediterranean cultures. As a consequence, it has long been assumed that similar cultural developments were also to be expected beyond the Mediterranean coasts, into the Sahara (cf. Balout 1955; Hugot 1963; Maitre 1972). This led to the creation of the term "Saharo-Sudanese Neolithic" (Camps 1974), based on the identification of pottery as "guide fossil" for any "Neolithic" culture. The result was a long, undifferentiated "Saharan Neolithic" period of about 6000 years, spanning from the earliest hunting/gathering occupations (c. 9000 BP) in the Holocene to the late pastoral evidence (c. 3000 BP). It took a long time before archaeologists realised that pottery and many other artefacts could be produced by hunter-gatherers as well. Furthermore, other variables concerning the economic organisation and the settlement system were long neglected (for further discussion, see Garcea 1993).

From technological to economic variables

Pottery and any other technological indicator appeared too generic for distinguishing the various cultural units that developed in the Sahara and North Africa between the Early and the Middle Holocene. On the other hand, economic bases could provide more reliable indicators in the long and widespread cultural development of those areas. Therefore, the distinction between "pre-pastoral" and "pastoral" cultures was the necessary priority as animal herding brought major cultural changes in the area. These broad contexts could be further differentiated into more specific local cultural units with regards to the Libyan Sahara. Within the pre-pastoral horizon, two different units could be separated. They were originally called "Epipalaeolithic" and "Mesolithic" (di Lernia 1996). Later, in order to avoid Mediterranean-biased correlations, they were re-named: *Early Acacus* and *Late Acacus* (di Lernia and Garcea 1997).

The study area

In the Tadrart Acacus mountain range in the Libyan Sahara, several excavated sites provided the archaeological evidence for distinguishing an early and a late horizon within the prepastoral period (Figure 15.1). They were: Ti-n-Torha East and Two Caves to the north (Barich

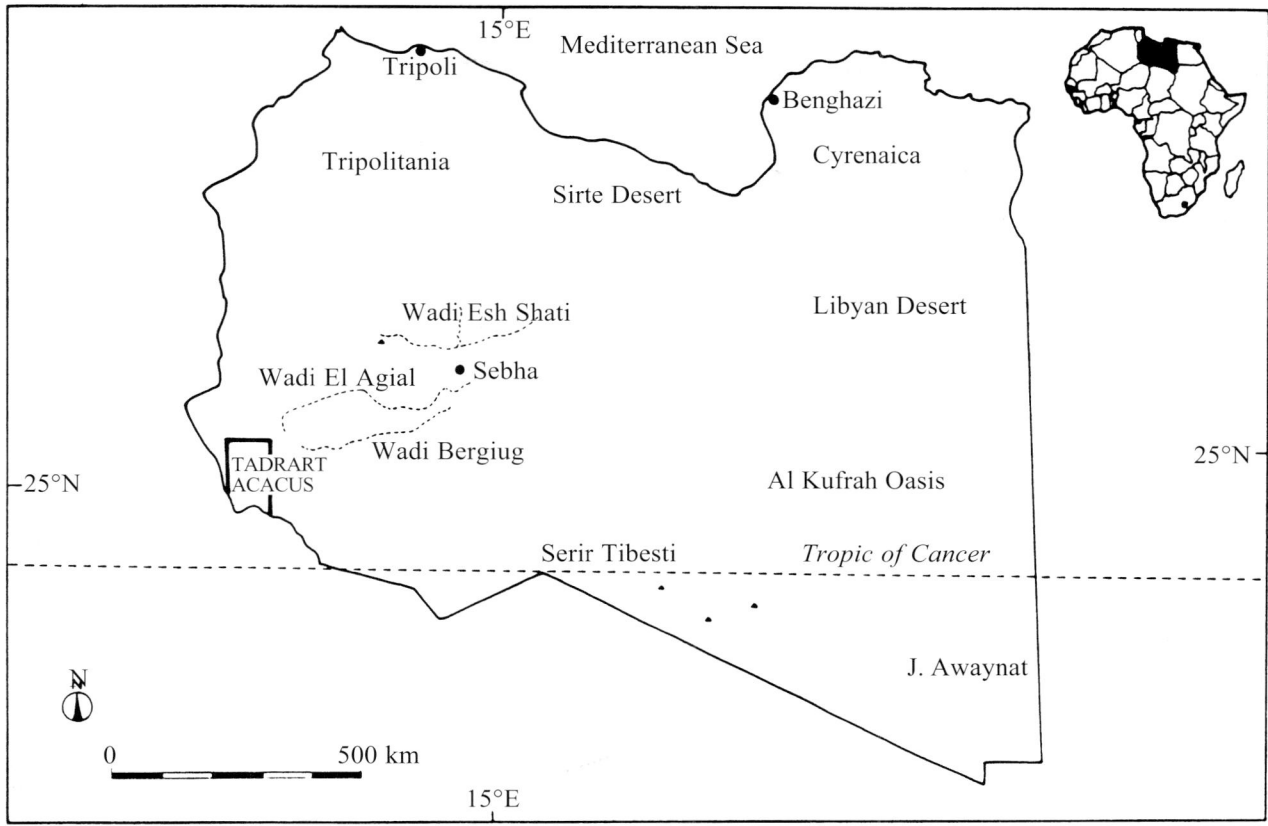

Figure 15.1 Map of Libya with the study area.

1974; 1987), Uan Tabu (Garcea 1998; 2001d), Uan Afuda (di Lernia 1998b; 1999a) and Uan Muhuggiag Wadi (di Lernia and Manzi 1998) in the centre, and Fozzigiaren to the south of the mountain range (di Lernia and Manzi 1998). Many other sites were surveyed in the area (Cremaschi and di Lernia 1998), within the research programme of the Joint Italo-Libyan Mission for Prehistoric Research in the Sahara of the Centro Interuniversitario per Ricerche sulle civiltà del Sahara Antico e delle zone aride (CIRSA), University of Rome "La Sapienza", both directed by Mario Liverani.

This paper presents some of the results of the excavations conducted at Uan Tabu, a rock shelter located in the Wadi Teshuinat, a seasonal water course. At this site, a 255-cm stratigraphic sequence included four main units, the upper three dating to the Early Holocene. Units I and II could be attributed to the Late Acacus and Unit III to the Early Acacus (Figure 15.2). Unit IV formed in the late Pleistocene and comprised late Middle Stone Age artefacts. Therefore, the present paper highlights the main features of the Late Acacus horizon represented at Uan Tabu in Units I and II, while Units III and IV are beyond the "Mesolithic" focus (for further information, see Garcea 2001c). With regards to the settlement and mobility patterns, these data are integrated in the general framework of the area.

Chronology

Thirteen radiocarbon measurements on wooden charcoal date the Late Acacus at Uan Tabu. Non-calibrated, conventional datings spanned from 8870 ± 100 (Rome-295) to 8580 ± 80 years BP (BO-344) and calibrated ages (at 68.2%) were between 8030–7880 and 7640–7500 cal years BC (Bartolomei and Rizzo 2001; Garcea 2001a). There was no evidence of a chronological gap between the Early and the Late Acacus.

The latest dates for the Late Acacus horizon came from Uan Muhuggiag Wadi and were 7823 ± 95 (Gx-17815 AMS) and 7550 ± 120 (Gx-17816 AMS) years BP (di Lernia and Manzi 1998).

Changes in climatic and environmental conditions

The climate in the Late Acacus was slightly drier than in the Early Acacus. Lakes existed until around 8500 BP, but were dried by the end of the 9th millennium BP (Cremaschi 1998; Cremaschi and di Lernia 1999). The environmental conditions were substantially similar during the shift from the Early to the Late Acacus (Castelletti et al. 1999). A more significant change occurred during the Late Acacus, as was sedimentologically and stratigraphically attested to at the site in

	EARLY ACACUS	*LATE ACACUS*
CHRONOLOGY BP (uncal.)	9810±75 / 8880±100	8870±100 – 8580±80
CHRONOLOGY BC (cal. at 68.2%)	9140–8940 8030–7880	8030–7880 7640–7500
STRATIGRAPHY	Unit III	Units II and I
CLIMATE	Relatively humid	Drier in Unit I
ANIMAL EXPLOITATION	90–100% Barbary sheep	45–60% Barbary sheep + smaller taxa Taming
PLANT EXPLOITATION	Low diversity: Food No Cerealia	Large spectrum: Accumulation Manufacturing Storing Roasting Empirical cultivation of wild cereals
SPATIAL ORGANISATION	Rare evidence	Hut Combustion structures
SETTLEMENT PATTERN	Numerous small sites	Fewer larger sites
MOBILITY	High (mountains and ergs)	Reduced (mountains) Long-distance trade
POTTERY	Extremely rare	Common, but imported
WOODEN/PLANT TOOLS	No	Perforators, baskets, cords
BONE TOOLS	No	Perforators, polishers, bevels, denticulates
CHIPPED LITHICS	Microliths Endscrapers, perforators, burins	Macroliths Notches, denticulates, sidescrapers
POLISHED STONE TOOLS	Not important	Large production
ROCK ART	No	Round Head paintings

Figure 15.2 Synthesis of the Early Acacus ("Epipalaeolithic") and Early Acacus ("Mesolithic") features at Uan Tabu.

the shift from Unit II to Unit I, which were both part of the Late Acacus horizon. Pollen spectra indicated a reduction of the savannah-like vegetation and an increase of shrubs, favouring a diversification of the habitats (Mercuri and Trevisan Grandi 2001).

Changes in the exploitation of resources

Wild Barbary sheep predominated in the Early Acacus faunal assemblages. They were reduced down to about 45–60% in the Late Acacus and was replaced by smaller taxa. Larger game hunting, such as Barbary sheep and gazelle, decreased due to intensive predation. A longer-term system of exploitation based on delayed and planned consumption was developed to compensate shortages (Gautier 1987; di Lernia 1999b).

Animal taming and penning became a common practise. Barbary sheep were kept in enclosures in the human settlements where large accumulations of straw, fodder and dung can be found (di Lernia 1996; 1998a; 1999c).

The wadi valleys could provide good seasonal grazing, establishing favourable prerequisites for animal domestication or adoption of domesticated herds. It is also possible that the exploitation of a broader faunal spectrum was a reaction to an enduring subsistence crisis, which may have brought to animal domestication (Holl 1998).

Plant exploitation also increased in the Late Acacus. Wild grasses were intensively collected and used for different purposes. Unit II, dated to 8900–8800 BP, indicated that a large spectrum of plant resources was exploited and that the accumulation of plants at the site doubled, in comparison to the previous phase. Unit I showed a higher specialisation over a slightly reduced spectrum of plant resources, with an intensive exploitation of cattails (Mercuri and Trevisan Grandi 2001).

Cattails must have been simultaneously used for food, bedding, weaving, and/or building. Gramineae, particularly Paniceae (*Panicum, Setaria, Echinochloa*), were abundant. Burned caryopses of Gramineae were only found in the Late Acacus, suggesting that they were stored and roasted for later consumption (Mercuri 2001).

Charcoal of *Tamarix* predominated in the earlier fuel resources and was complemented by Chenopodiaceae, namely *Calotropis procera* in Unit II, and the first scattered tropical elements, such as *Salvadora persica* and *Leptadenia pyrotechnica* in Unit I (Neumann and Uebel 2001).

The accumulation of charred plants was interpreted as a shift from short seasonal stays to longer occupations of sites. This also suggested an increase in human pressure (Mercuri 2001).

Some kind of empirical cultivation seems to have been attempted, which allowed the preservation and survival of the wild cereals and plants under human care, even when their habitat was reduced (Mercuri 2001). It has also been inferred that the first stages of the domestication process of *Sorghum* and *Pennisetum*, which later spread to the south, may have taken place in the Sahara (Neumann 1999).

Changes in the use of the landscape

A marked intra-site spatial organisation appeared as a peculiar feature of the Late Acacus sites. At Uan Tabu, a wooden hut was found in this horizon. A spatial analysis within the site indicated that some activities were carried out in the hut area, and others outside of it. Lithic equipments of good quality rocks and some specific tools, such as endscrapers, sidescrapers, backed and geometric tools, and microburins, were concentrated in the hut area. At the same time, tools related to activities that had to be performed in the open-air, such as perforators, notches and denticulates, and arrowheads, as well as cores and polished stone tools, were farther from the hut. Pottery, wooden and bone tools, ostrich eggshell beads, and colouring materials were all concentrated in the hut area. It has been suggested that fragile and delicate artefacts were intentionally kept, if not also used, in the hut in order to save them for repeated uses and to protect them from damage or loss (Garcea 2001b).

Combustion structures became another distinctive feature of the Late Acacus (Garcea 2001a). They were the most complex and the largest in all times of occupation of the site, reaching over 1 m in diameter and 20–30 cm in thickness. Some of them indicated polyphase organisations (according to Taborin 1989), which imply the repetition of the same activity or a series of activities over time; others suggested polycycle organisations, involving a sequence of several cycles of use.

In general, Late Acacus sites were less numerous, but larger than the Early Acacus ones. They were concentrated in the mountain areas, where resources were more abundant (Cremaschi and di Lernia 1998). It has been suggested that more concentrated and more permanent occupations caused a depletion of the landscape (Gautier 1984; Mercuri 2001). A population growth seems to have also been likely (di Lernia 1996; 1999b; Mercuri 1999). Mobility decreased, although interregional relations and long-distance trade and/or exchange developed.

Changes in the manufacturing of resources

Pottery became common in the Late Acacus. It was decorated with impression techniques. Petrographic analyses indicated that pastes included granite, which is not present in the Tadrart Acacus mountain range. Its closest source is located near the Algerian border, about 70 km south-west of the site (Livingstone Smith 2001). This indicated that all pottery was imported and may have not been an ordinary product for domestic use. It has been suggested that the earliest pottery could be linked to prestige, ownership of stored goods, and social interactions (Hayden 1995; Hoopes and Barnett 1995).

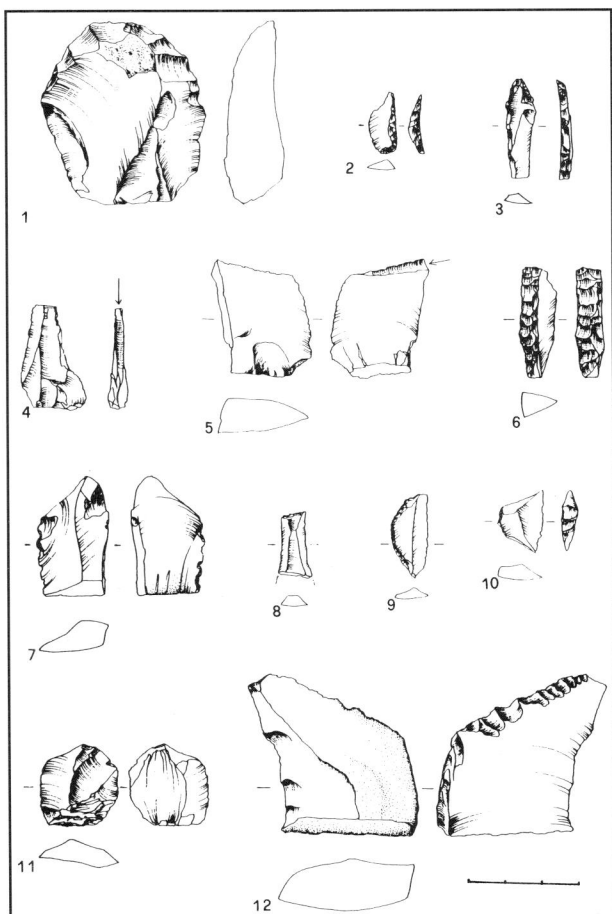

Figure 15.3 Late Acacus lithic tools. 1: endscraper on a retouched flake; 2: perforator on a backed bladelet; 3: double backed perforator; 4: angle burin on a fracture; 5: dihedral angle burin; 6: arch-backed bladelet; 7: denticulated flake; 8: truncation; 9: segment; 10: trapeze with a concave side; 11: scaled piece; 12: convergent sidescraper.

The lithic technocomplex mainly consisted of generic formal tools on a macroflake, comprising notches, denticulates and sidescrapers (Figure 15.3). This suggested activities that probably required longer time of processing, preparing and manufacturing food and secondary products (Garcea 2001b).

Wooden tools and plant artefacts, like perforators, baskets and cords, were also found. Baskets were likely used for either grain winnowing or storage even in other Mesolithic contexts (Zvelebil 1994). Polished bone tools were of different types (Figure 15.4). Ostrich eggshell beads, fragments, some of them decorated, were typical features of the Late Acacus (Garcea 2001b).

Polished stone tools were widely produced. Wild cereal grinding must have been a usual practise. Furthermore, grindstones were used for pounding ochre and other colouring materials probably used for the rock paintings present at the site (Garcea 2001d).

Rock paintings belonging to the so-called Round Head

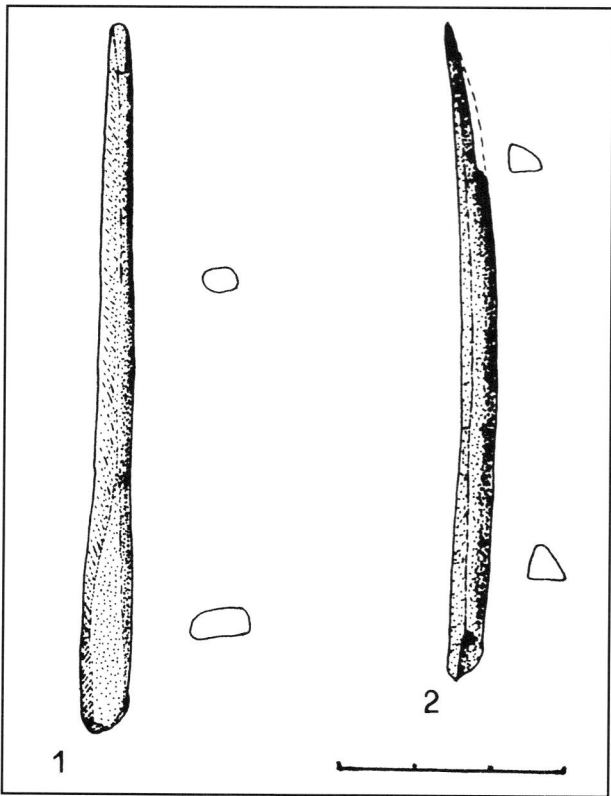

Figure 15.4 Late Acacus bone perforators.

phase could be related to the Late Acacus (Garcea 1998; di Lernia 1999d). They were the earliest paintings in the Saharan rock art and Round Head figures were the earliest anthropomorphic representations (Mori 1965; 1998). They were covered by later Pastoral paintings and, therefore, provided an important relative chronology for the Saharan rock art.

The presence of rock art suggested that the rock shelter had some ritual functions, even during the use of the place as a household. There are reasons to believe that ritual functions increased in later, pastoral times in conjunction with a reduced use of the site as a secular area. The Uan Tabu rock shelter must have been part of a "practical landscape" (*sensu* Zvelebil and Jordan 1999) during the Late Acacus, even though some rituals, in the sense that ideology was consciously expressed, did take place in the domestic environment. The need of marking the territory by means of permanent signs, such as rock paintings, was certainly an important cultural change of the Late Acacus. No burials were found at Uan Tabu. However, one burial was unearthed at Uan Muhuggiag Wadi, which is located in the same wadi, the Wadi Teshuinat, as Uan Tabu. The tomb exhibited two sub-circular stone structures. The head laid on a stone and two slabs covered the body (di Lernia and Manzi 1998). No evidence for funerary practices were attested to in the Early Acacus.

Final remarks

To conclude, the original question whether there were cultural convergences between the forms of landscape enculturation in northern Europe and in North Africa during the Early Holocene can only be answered in generic, although positive, terms. Analogical reasoning can support a broad application of approaches to interpret archaeologically similar phenomena. Obviously, comparisons should only be attempted at a general level. It may be legitimate to suggest convergences as long as they are accepted as apparently similar cultural adaptations. Any deeper interpretation would be misleading. Other relevant factors in culture, such as environmental conditions, are completely different in the two areas and their cultural horizons can only be thoroughly viewed within their local contexts and environments. Such an attempt is not meant to diminish the importance of the environment in the development of human cultures (see, for example, Åkerlund 1996, for an appreciation of the relationships between human cultures and landscapes in northern Europe). It only brings the discussion at a higher level of analysis. However, such a level can only be taken into account if specific and contextual investigations have already been carried out locally. The final interpretation of the archaeological evidence certainly needs a thorough understanding of the specific local context and can only be referred to that context (Zvelebil and Jordan 1999).

Within this perspective, the Mesolithic of northern Europe has been able to provide North African archaeologists with helpful hints for understanding their local archaeological indicators. As a matter of fact, some cultural adaptations are more comparable than others that may even be located in closer areas. The archaeological evidence on the Mediterranean cultures, for example, often misled the interpretations of the North African prehistory. On the other hand, farther regions such as northern Europe were able to suggest analogical hints on apparently similar adaptive dynamics.

To summarise, tentative analogies between North Africa and northern Europe can be suggested between several cultural outputs, such as reduced mobility with long-distance exchange of exotic items, production of pottery, bone tools, and polished stone tools, and animal management of wild species that were never domesticated (cf. among others, Rowley-Conwy 1983; 1993; Price 1985; Larsson and Lundmark 1989; Gebauer 1995; Zvelebil 1996).

The availability of resources and the reduction in mobility may be the common denominators that encouraged storage, animal and plant management and the production of prestige goods. It has also been suggested that reduced mobility favoured population growth (Hassan 1981; Fisher 1995). Larger human groups may have required a more complex social organisation and a more efficient economic system (see also Garcea 1996). Such a system may have been able to satisfy the subsistence needs of its components without requiring full domestication even over a long period of time, as long as the availability of resources was maintained.

Acknowledgments

I would like to express my sincere gratitude to Agneta Åkerlund for all the discussions and talks we shared since long before the Meso2000 Conference. She also read and commented on the preliminary manuscript of the present paper. I wish to thank her for her fruitful insights and suggestions.

References

Balout, L. 1955. *Préhistoire de l'Afrique du Nord. Essai de chronologie*. Paris.

Barich, B.E. 1974. La serie stratigrafica dell'Uadi Ti-n-Torha (Acacus, Libia). *Origini* 8, 7–184.

—— (ed.) 1987. *Archaeology and Environment in the Libyan Sahara. The excavations in the Tadrart Acacus, 1978–1983*. BAR International Series 368, Oxford.

Bartolomei, P. and Rizzo, A. 2001. Radiocarbon dates of charcoal samples from the Holocene sequence. In: Garcea, E.A.A. (ed.) *Uan Tabu in the Settlement History of the Libyan Sahara*. Firenze.

Camps, G. 1974. *Les civilisations préhistoriques de l'Afrique du Nord et du Sahara*. Paris.

Castelletti, L., Castiglioni, E., Cottini, M. and Rottoli, M. 1999. Archaeobotanical analysis of charcoal, wood and seeds. In: di Lernia, S. (ed.) *The Uan Afuda Cave: Hunter-Gatherer Societies of Central Sahara*, 131–148. Firenze.

Cremaschi, M. 1998. Late Quaternary geological evidence for environmental changes in south-western Fezzan (Libyan Sahara). In: Cremaschi, M. and di Lernia, S. (eds) *Wadi Teshuinat. Palaeoenvironment and Prehistory in south-western Fezzan (Libyan Sahara)*, 13–48. Firenze.

Cremaschi, M. and di Lernia, S. 1998. The geoarchaeological survey in central Acacus and surroundings (Libyan Sahara). Environment and cultures. In: Cremaschi, M. and S. di Lernia (eds) *Wadi Teshuinat. Palaeoenvironment and Prehistory in south-western Fezzan (Libyan Sahara)*, 243–296. Firenze.

—— 1999. Holocene Climatic Changes and Cultural Dynamics in the Libyan Sahara. *African Archaeological Review* 16(4), 211–238.

di Lernia, S. 1996. Changing adaptive strategies: a long-term process in the Central Saharan Massifs from Late Pleistocene to Early Holocene. The Tadrart Acacus perspective (Libyan Sahara). In: Aumassip, G., Clark, J.D. and Mori, F. (eds) *The Colloquia of the XIII International Congress of Prehistoric and Protohistoric Sciences. Vol. 15: The Prehistory of Africa*, 195–208. Forlì.

—— 1998a. Cultural control over wild animals during the early Holocene: the case of Barbary sheep in central Sahara. In: di Lernia, S. and Manzi, G. (eds) *Before food production in North Africa. Questions and tools dealing with resource exploitation and population dynamics at 12,000–7000 bp. XIII U.I.S.P.P. Congress*, 113–126. Forlì.

—— 1998b. Early Holocene pre-Pastoral cultures in the Uan Afuda cave, wadi Kessan, Tadrart Acacus (Libyan Sahara). In: Cremaschi, M. and di Lernia, S. (eds) *Wadi Teshuinat. Palaeoenvironment and Prehistory in south-western Fezzan (Libyan Sahara)*, 123–154. Firenze.

—— (ed.) 1999a. *The Uan Afuda Cave: Hunter-Gatherer Societies of Central Sahara*. Firenze.

—— 1999b. Assembling the evidence: cultural trajectories at Uan Afuda Cave. In: di Lernia, S. (ed.) *The Uan Afuda Cave: Hunter-Gatherer Societies of Central Sahara*, 223–237. Firenze.

—— 1999c. Delayed use of resources: significance of Early Holocene Barbary sheep dung. In: di Lernia, S. (ed.) *The Uan Afuda Cave: Hunter-Gatherer Societies of Central Sahara*, 209–222. Firenze.

—— 1999d. Rock art paintings of the "Round Heads" phase. In: di Lernia, S. (ed.) *The Uan Afuda Cave: Hunter-Gatherer Societies of Central Sahara*, 39–48. Firenze.

di Lernia, S. and Garcea, E.A.A. 1997. Some remarks on Saharan terminology. Pre-pastoral archaeology from the Libyan Sahara and the Middle Nile Valley. *Libya Antiqua* new series 3, 11–23.

di Lernia, S. and Manzi, G. 1998. Funerary practices and anthropological features at 8000–5000 BP. Some evidence from central-southern Acacus (Libyan Sahara). In: Cremaschi, M. and di Lernia, S. (eds) *Wadi Teshuinat. Palaeoenvironment and Prehistory in south-western Fezzan (Libyan Sahara)*, 217–242. Firenze.

Fischer, A. (ed.) 1995. *Man and sea in the Mesolithic. Coastal settlement above and below present sea level. Proceedings of the international symposium, Kalundborg, Denmark 1993*. Oxbow Monograph 53. Exeter.

Garcea, E.A.A. 1993. *Cultural Dynamics in the Saharo-Sudanese Prehistory*. Roma.

—— 1996. La culture des pucheurs d'*Early Khartoum*: un exemple dans la vallée du Nil. *Préhistoire Anthropologie Méditerranéennes* 5, 207–214.

—— 1998. Aterian and "Early" and "Late Acacus" from the Uan Tabu rockshelter, Tadrart Acacus (Libyan Sahara). In: Cremaschi, M. and di Lernia, S. (eds) *Wadi Teshuinat. Palaeoenvironment and Prehistory in south-western Fezzan (Libyan Sahara)*, 155–181. Firenze.

—— 2001a. Combustion structures as a Late Acacus feature. In: Garcea, E.A.A. (ed.) *Uan Tabu in the Settlement History of the Libyan Sahara*, 151–158. Firenze.

—— 2001b. The Early and the Late Acacus material cultures after the 1960–63 and the 1990–93 excavations. In: Garcea, E.A.A. (ed.) *Uan Tabu in the Settlement History of the Libyan Sahara*, 95–110. Firenze.

—— 2001c. The Pleistocene and Holocene archaeological sequences. In: Garcea, E.A.A. (ed.) *Uan Tabu in the Settlement History of the Libyan Sahara*, 1–14. Firenze.

—— (ed.) 2001d. *Uan Tabu in the Settlement History of the Libyan Sahara*. Firenze.

Gautier, A. 1984. New data concerning the prehistoric fauna and domestic cattle from Ti-n-Torha (Acacus, Libya). *Palaeoecology of Africa* 16, 305–309.

—— 1987. The Archaeozoological Sequence of the Acacus. In: Barich, B.E. (ed.) *Archaeology and Environment in the Libyan Sahara. The excavations in the Tadrart Acacus, 1978–1983*. BAR International Series 368, 283–308. Oxford.

Gebauer, A.B. 1995. Pottery Production and the Introduction of Agriculture in Southern Scandinavia. In: Barkett, W.K. and Hoopes, J.W. (eds) *The Emergence of Pottery: Technology and Innovation in Ancient Societies*, 99–112. Washington.

Hassan, F. 1981. *Demographic Archaeology*. New York.

Hayden, B. 1995. The Emergence of Prestige Technologies and Pottery. In: Barnett, W.K. and Hoopes, J.W. (eds) *The Emergence of Pottery: Technology and Innovation in Ancient Societies*, 257–265. Washington.

Holl, A.F.C. 1998. The Dawn of African Pastoralisms: An Introductory Note. *Journal of Anthropological Archaeology* 17, 81–96.

Hoopes, J.W. and Barnett, W.K. 1995. The Shape of Early Pottery Studies. In: Barnett, W.K. and Hoopes, J.W. (eds) *The

Emergence of Pottery: Technology and Innovation in Ancient Societies, 1–7. Washington.

Hugot, H.J. 1963. *Recherches préhistoriques dans l'Ahaggar nord-occidental*. Mémoires du C.R.A.P.E. 1. Paris.

Larsson, L. and Lundmark, H. (eds) 1989. *Approaches to Swedish Prehistory*. British Archaeological Reports, International Series 500. Oxford.

Livingstone Smith, A. 2001. Pottery manufacturing processes: reconstruction and interpretation. In: Garcea, E.A.A. (ed.) *Uan Tabu in the Settlement History of the Libyan Sahara*, 111–150. Firenze.

Maitre, J.P. 1972. Notes sur deux conceptions traditionelles du Néolithique saharien. *Libyca* 20, 125–136.

Mercuri, A.M. 1999. Palynological analysis of the Early Holocene sequence. In: di Lernia, S. (ed.) *The Uan Afuda Cave: Hunter-Gatherer Societies of Central Sahara*, 149–181. Firenze.

—— 2001. Preliminary analyses of fruits and seeds from the Early Holocene sequence. In: Garcea, E.A.A. (ed.) *Uan Tabu in the Settlement History of the Libyan Sahara*, 187–208. Firenze.

Mercuri, A.M. and Trevisan Grandi, G. 2001. Palynological analyses of the late Pleistocene, early Holocene and middle Holocene layers. In: Garcea, E.A.A. (ed.) *Uan Tabu in the Settlement History of the Libyan Sahara*, 159–186. Firenze.

Mori, F. 1965. *Tadrart Acacus. Arte rupestre e culture del Sahara preistorico*. Torino.

—— 1998. *The great civilizations of the ancient Sahara*. Roma.

Neumann, K. 1999. Early Plant Food Production in the West African Sahel: New Evidence. In: van der Veen, M. (ed.) *The Exploitation of Plant Resources in Ancient Africa*, 73–80. New York.

Neumann, K. and Uebel, D. 2001. The cold Early Holocene in the Acacus: evidence from charred wood. In: Garcea, E.A.A. (ed.) *Uan Tabu in the Settlement History of the Libyan Sahara*, 209–211. Firenze.

Price, T.D. 1985. Affluent Foragers of Mesolithic Southern Scandinavia. In: Price, T.D. and Brown, J.A. (eds) *Prehistoric Hunter-Gatherers: The Emergence of Cultural Complexity*, 341–363. Orlando.

Rowley-Conwy, P. 1983. Sedentary hunters: The Ertebølle example. In: Bailey, G.N. (ed.) *Hunter-Gatherer Economy in Prehistory*, 111–126. Cambridge.

—— 1993. Season and Reason. The Case for a Regional Interpretation of Mesolithic Settlement Patterns. In: Peterkin, G.L., Bricker, H.M. and Mellars, P. (eds) *Hunting and Animal Exploitation in the Later Palaeolithic and Mesolithic of Eurasia*. Archaeological Papers of the American Anthropological Association 4, 179–188. Washington.

Taborin, Y. 1989. Le foyer: document et concept. In: Olive, M. and Taborin, Y. (eds) *Nature et fonction de foyers préhistoriques. Actes du Colloque International de Nemours*. Mémoires du Musée de Préhistoire d'Ile de France 2, 77–80.

Zvelebil, M. 1986. Mesolithic prelude and Neolithic revolution. In: Zvelebil, M. (ed.) *Hunters in Transition. Mesolithic societies of temperate Eurasia and their transition to farming*, 5–15. Cambridge.

—— 1994. Plant use in the Mesolithic and its role in the transition to farming. *Proceedings of the Prehistoric Society* 60, 35–74.

—— 1996. Subsistence and social organisation of the Mesolithic communities in Temperate and Northern Europe. In: Kozlowski, K. and Tozzi, C. (eds) *The Mesolithic. The Colloquia of the XIII International Congress of Prehistoric and Protohistoric Sciences*, 163–174. Forlì.

—— 1998. Agricultural Frontiers, Neolithic Origins, and the Transition to Farming in the Baltic Basin. In: Zvelebil, M., Domanska, L. and Dennell, R. (eds) *Harvesting the Sea, Farming the Forest: The Emergence of Neolithic Societies in the Baltic Region*, 9–27. Sheffield.

Zvelebil, M. and Jordan, P. 1999. Hunter fisher gatherer ritual landscapes – questions of time, space and representation. In: Goldhahn, J. (ed.) *Rock Art as Social Representation*. BAR International Series 794, 101–127.

Åkerlund, A. 1996. *Human Responses to Shore Displacement: Living by the Sea in Eastern Middle Sweden during the Stone Age*. Arkeologiska undersökningar Skrifter No. 16. Stockholm.

16. The Enigma of the Far Northeast European Mesolithic: Reindeer Herd Followers or Semi-Sedentary Hunters?

Bryan Gordon

Just as migration ensures survival of migratory herds, following and intercepting these animals ensured the survival of prehistoric human groups. Season of site occupation and hence, human migration patterns can be ascertained from examination of long-term habits of prey and observation of hunting tools in different parts of reindeer range. In Canada, Alaska and the Taimyr Peninsula of Siberia, herds have been documented migrating north in early summer to calve on tundra and south by a parallel route to rut in autumn at the edge of the forest. They winter in forest. Such was probably the case in far NE European Russia. Fifty years of research in far NE European Russia has resulted in the discovery of 100 Mesolithic sites. Mesolithic origins relate to a south-west flint source on Timan Ridge and a south-east one in the Urals. Each flint type is distinct and traceable north and south through the main valley of each reindeer range. Blades (4,674) cores (118), core tablets (70), scrapers (191), points (17), knives (5), pushplanes (6), hammerstones (11), burins (32), adzes (2) and domiciles (7) in 74 sites were grouped and compared according to whether they were in forest or on tundra. Artifacts were examined in terms of material, plan, section, colour and traits diagnostic to each tool type. Less variety in type and colour of stone and smaller size is noted farther from the flint sources, as it was in similar Canadian studies. But in far NE Russia, some hunters summered in the forest, hunting forest animals, fishing and stockpiling flint for their own use and for the use of their herd-following kin who would return from the tundra each autumn.

Mesolithic people varied from semi-sedentary fisher-gatherers to nomadic hunters in temperate regions. In the sub-arctic or arctic they may have been fully migratory if tundra or sea resources were only seasonally available (Gordon 1992). I compare sub-arctic peoples of far north-east Europe and the Canadian Barrenlands. Both had a mixed forest-tundra environment and hunt the same animal (*Rangifer* caribou/reindeer).

Acid soil in both areas has dissolved bone. Consequently, we cannot identify fauna, nor date bone with radiocarbon. The oldest Canadian Barrenland sites are contemporaneous with European sites (Gordon 1996). In far north-east Europe, the Vis site (Figure 16.1, bottom left) dates 8080±90 (Le-776), 7820±80 (RUL-616), 7150±60 (Le-684), 7090±80 (Le685) and 7090±70 (Le-7134; Burov 1989; uncal.). I reconstructed ancient Barrenland *Rangifer* ranges using modern ranges and archaeological sites confined to them (Gordon 1975). Doing the same for north-east European tundra, I deduce both peoples hunted *Rangifer*, as other food was unavailable on the tundra. Survival depended upon moving in synchrony with herds (Gordon 1990). Differing major tool traits in adjacent ranges imply restricted band contact, especially so on tundra where hunter and herd follow migration paths (Gordon 1981). This restricted contact between ranges also lead to slightly different tool styles. Most tool size difference throughout the length of each range is due to distance from forest quarry sources and from seasonal use (Gordon 1996).

In comparing Barrenland and north-east European peoples, I focussed on known reindeer ranges of the Russian Komi Republic and Bolshe'zemle tundra farther north to the Arctic Ocean (Figure 16.1). Finland is west, Moscow southwest and the Urals and Siberia east. The tree-line follows the north border of the Komi Republic. The northeast and northwest European Mesolithics are not concurrent because warm Gulf Stream Atlantic air blocked by Scandinavian glaciation delayed and shortened the colder east European Mesolithic. While Danish Mesolithic people lived in small shoreline campsites, some Komi Mesolithic people migrated over tundra.

Reindeer ranges in the study area are from the Atlas of the Komi Republic. Calving grounds near the Arctic Ocean lead south to migration routes that join as they approach the forest in the south half of Figure 16.1, while a wide grey line separates Western and Eastern reindeer ranges. After wintering in Vychegda forests at bottom left, the Western herd followed the Ijhma River north, splitting into five minor migration routes following valleys and leading north to their calving grounds. The Eastern

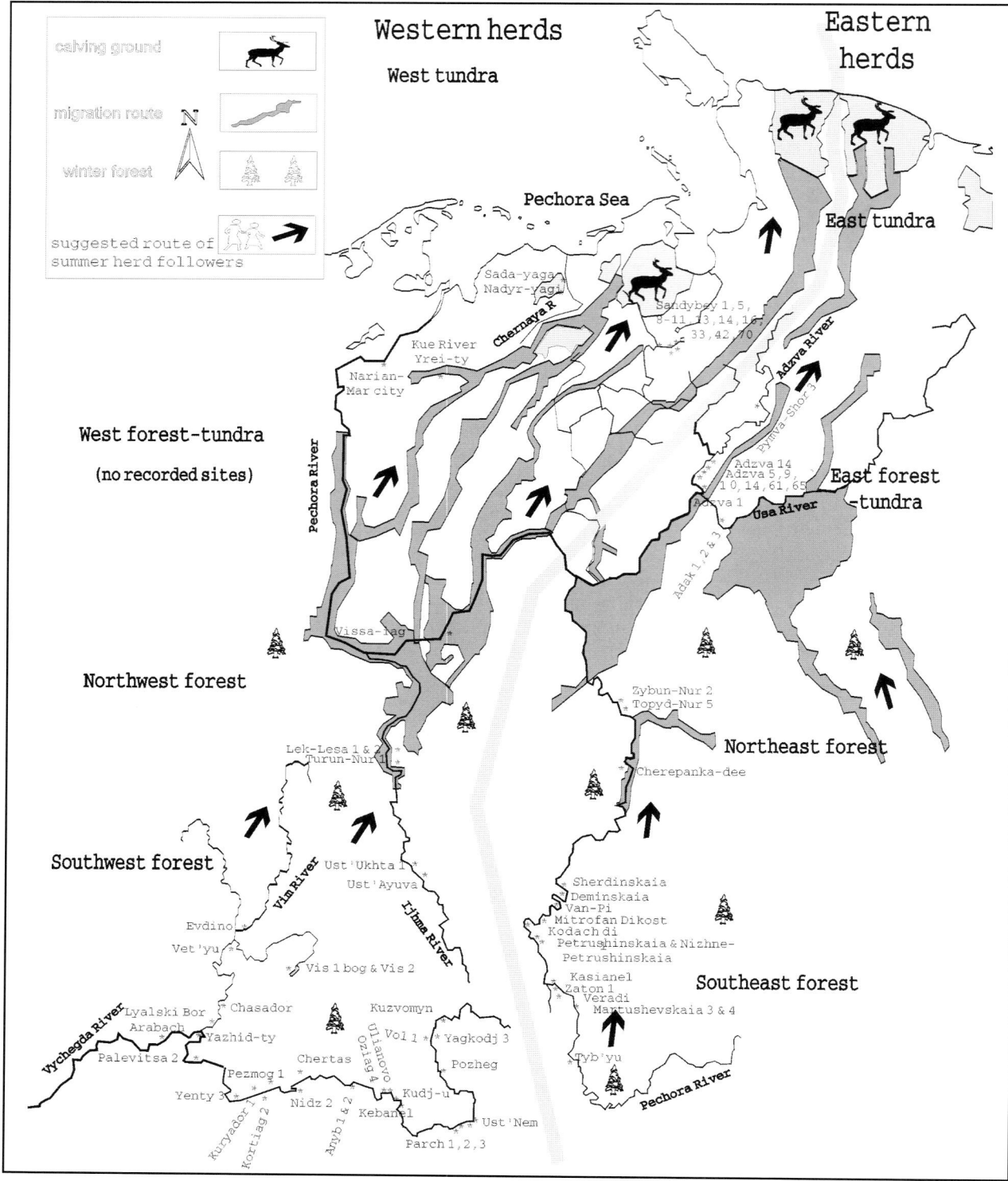

Figure 16.1 Mesolithic sites in reindeer ranges in far northeast European Russia

herd followed the Pechora River (bottom right) north to the Usa, before crossing the coastal plain on one major migration route to its calving ground. Equally divided among both ranges are 76 Mesolithic hunting camps.

Western range forest surrounds sites on the Vychegda River, where conifers mix with deciduous trees. Calcined faunal remains in the Parch sites in this area (bottom center) suggest some inhabitants lived on forest food but also reindeer. Reindeer bone occurs in the nearby radiocarbon-dated Vis 1 site. The Vychegda Basin is rolling meadow and forest with heavy moss, ideal reindeer winter range. The Usa in the Eastern range resembles

Artifact	R	South Forest	North Forest	Forest-Tundra	Tundra
Blades	W	large. 5 colours. Fewer bladescars	very large. 4 colours. Average bladescars	none	medium. 3 colours
	E	very large. 3 colours. Fewer bladescars	large. 2 colours. Average bladescars	med.2 colours. Many bladescars	very small. Grey. Most bladescars
Cores	W	medium. Many colours. Conical /blocky	None	none	medium. 2 colours. Conical
	E	large. Grey. Conical & blocky	small. 4 colours. More conical	smaller. 4 colours. Conical	none
Core tablet	W	large. Many colours. 9 bladescars	small. 3 colours. 7 bladescars	none	very small. Grey. 9 bladescars
	E	large. Many colours. 7 bladescars	moderate. 2 colours. 8 bladescars	huge (2). 2 colours.10 bladescars	none
Scrapers	W	medium. Most plans. Serrated. Ground ventral retouch 4 colours. Most cortex	medium. Many plans some serrated Grnd vent. ret. Worn base. Most grey. Some cortx	none	medium.Unserrated.Grnd. vent.ret. 3 colours. No cortex/worn base. 2 plans
	E	large. Serrated. Bif. ret. Most plans. 4 colours. Much cortex. Most worn bases	large. Some serrated. Worn bases. Some cortex. Few plans	smallest.Unserrated. Grey. No cortex. Few plans.	none
Points	W	4 sided & planoconvex. Many colours	None	none	none
	E	lanceolate/biconvex. Many colours, bases	None	none	none
Knives	W	Broken; unknown plans. 2 colours	None	none	none
	E	ovoid. Biconvex. Ungrnd. taper.1 colour	None	none	none
Pushplane	W	mixed plans, sections, colours & retouch	None	none	none
	E	lanceolate. Keeled. Thinned dorsal haft	None	lanc. Planoconvx. Bashed side	none
Ham'stone	W	mixed plan, section, colour, stone, pocking	(1) ovoid. Unipolar & equatorial pocking	none	none
	E	(1) ovoid. Bipolar end & angle pocking	None	none	none
Burins	W	mix plan, colour 11x27mm microblades	double burin. Bilateral retouch	none	none
	E	mixed retouch. 35–40mm long	None	none	none
Adzes	W	mix plans, sections, colour, material, bits	None	none	none
	E	none	None	none	none
Pithouse	W	mixed plans, hearths, postholes, NW-SE	ovoid, E-W orientation, central hearth	none	tentrings
	E	none	ovoid, mixed orientation, central hearth	tentrings	tentrings
Sum		larger. More plans, colour, stone, cortex	Decreasing size, plan, colour, cortex	Less size, plan, colour, cortex	Tiny grey flint. Few plans, cortex

Figure 16.2 Comparison of Western and Eastern range artifacts by subrange. R=range; W=west; E=east. From south forest to tundra subrange, artifact size, colour and attributes change, indicating multi-coloured flint source at Timan Ridge for West range, and primarily grey flint source in Central Urals for East range. Cores and core tablets have more bladescars to north. Domiciles and scrapers especially change.

Barrenland Rivers where herds cross and are intercepted. At clearings near rivers, camps are easily seen in surface artifacts or butchered bone. Farther north, herds crossed open tundra, sand blowouts, muskeg and bog to forest ambushes at tree-line. Here, hidden hunters erected brush drive-lanes and fences. Bolshe'zemle and Barrenland tundras are a mass of small esker-controlled lakes surrounded by gravel, glacial erratics, shrubs and flowers. Tents in both areas were erected with poles, with circles of stone to anchor skin covers.

Assigning hunting bands to West and East ranges derives from my Barrenland studies and interpretation of Upper Paleolithic tool evolution by Burov (1989), Vereshchagina (1973, 1989), Volokitin (1986, 1989, 1990, 1991, 1992a and b, 1995, 1997) and Zalyznyak (1989). Magdalenian hunters merged into Swiderian and Ahrensbourgian groups as they pursued reindeer herds north with glacial retreat. East European Swiderians formed the Kunda and Butova people, one south-west of my study area, the other south-east. (Note. Mikhail Zhilin at the Meso 2000 conference offered a different opinion, but until origin theories are resolved, I use my data; see Zhilin 1995:85 for other details). Reaching the Komi winter forest, each Mesolithic band continued to follow herds seasonally, leaving Western and Eastern range toolkits in their migrations. Evidence of their separation exists in Western range multicoloured flint and other stone traceable to the Timan Ridge to the south-west, while simple white and grey flint in the Eastern range comes from the Urals to the southeast. In addition, minor sources exist throughout both ranges.

Tools are made mainly from flint blades, including knives with retouched edges for cutting meat. Blades are struck from conical cores, their ridges indicating the number of blades removed. Tundra blades are smaller with more blade ridges from depletion. Scrapers are also made from blades and flakes, and like Barrenland winter scrapers, are serrated in the forest for use on frozen hides. Blades are also made into burins and Swiderian and Ahrensbourgian arrowheads.

Material, size, special traits, platform, retouch, colour, etc., are compared on 4674 blades, 118 cores and 70 tablets, 191 scrapers, 17 points, 5 knives, 6 pushplanes, 11 hammerstones, 32 burins, 2 adzes and 7 pit-houses from 76 forest and tundra sites of both ranges (Figure 16.2). Like Barrenland stone artifacts, tundra tools are smaller because their quarry sources are hundreds of km south and tools had to be used longer or cores had to be further reduced to make more blades. Tools also differ seasonally.

Despite some Komi forest dwellers being non-migratory, Barrenland and north European artifacts are comparable seasonally and according to range. Some Komi reindeer hunters left tools along the migration route in spring and autumn. While points and other tools are too few to compare, tundra blades, cores and tablets and scrapers are smaller, plus seasonal differences exist in their form. All of this indicates some Mesolithic peoples migrated long distances, only to return in autumn to their more sedentary forest kin when winter arrived on the tundra.

In conclusion, north-east European Mesolithic people were not so enigmatic after all. Some followed the reindeer for hundreds of km, a tradition that continued historically. Others remained in the forest, hunting boreal animals, fishing, gathering and stockpiling flint for themselves and their migratory kin.

References

Burov, G. M. 1989. Some Mesolithic wooden artifacts from the site of Vis I in the European northeast of the U.S.S.R. In: Bonsall, C. (ed.) *The Mesolithic in Europe*, 391–401. Edinburgh.

Gordon, B.C. 1975. Of men and herds in Barrenland prehistory. *Mercury Series no. 28, Archaeological Survey of Canada, National Museum of Man*, Ottawa.

—— 1981. Man-environment relationships in Barrenland prehistory. *The Musk-Ox* 29, 1–19.

—— 1990. More on the Herd-Following Hypothesis. *Current Anthropology* 31 (4), 399–400.

—— 1992. Were the Nganasan like Barrenland Herd Followers? In: Pusztay, J. and Savel'eva, E. (eds) Book 5, *The Arctic. Papers of An International Conference*, Syktyvkar, Russia, May 16–19. *Specimina Sibirica*, 95–115.

—— 1996. People of Sunlight; People of Starlight: Barrenland. Archaeology in the Northwest Territories of Canada. *Mercury Series no. 154, Archaeological Survey of Canada, Canadian Museum of Civilization*. Hull. Quebec.

Vereshchagina, I.B. 1973. Sites with Microlithic inventory in the Bolshoi tundra (Pamyathiki s mikroliticheskim inventarem Bolshezemelskoy tundry). *Materialy poarkheologii Evropeyskogo Severo-Vostoka* 5, 3–21. Syktyvkar (in Russian).

—— 1989. *Mesolithic and Neolithic of northeast Europe* (Candidate thesis in historical research). Leningrad (in Russian).

Volokitin, A. 1986. New data on the Northeast European Mesolithic. *Materials on the Archaeology of the European Northeast* 10, 19–82. Syktyvkar (in Russian).

—— 1989. On dating methods of some Stone Age sites in the Vychegda Basin. *Urgent problems of West Siberian Archaeology*. Novosibirsk (in Russian).

—— 1990. The Mesolithic in northeast Europe. *Kratkiya Soobsheniya* 200, 48–52 (in Russian).

—— 1991. *First Peopling of the Arctic*. International Symposium of Problems of the Historic and Cultural Environment of the Arctic. Syktyvkar.

—— 1992a. On the Mesolithic of the European Northeast. *Problems of Finno-Ugric Archaeology of the Urals and Volga*, 72–77. Syktyvkar (in Russian).

—— 1992b. On the peopling of Bolshezemelskaya Tundra in the Mesolithic Age. In: Pusztay, J. and Savel'eva, E. (eds) Book 5, *The Arctic. Papers of An International Conference*. Syktyvkar, Russia, May 16–19. *Specimina Sibirica*, 293–298.

—— 1995. On the problem of ethnogenesis of the Mesolithic of the European Northeast. Ethnocultural contacts in the Stone, Bronze and Early Iron Ages and Medieval Period in the northern Sub-Urals. *Materials on the Archaeology of the European Northeast* 13. Syktyvkar (in Russian).

—— 1997. The Mesolithic Age in the Territory of the Komi Republic. Chapter 2. In: Savel'eva, E. (ed.) *Komi Archaeology*, 91–145. Syktyvkar (in Russian).

Zalyznyak, L.L. 1989. Chap. 3. Economic-cultural Type of Reindeer Hunters. *Final Palaeolithic Reindeer Hunters in the Ukrainian Forest*, 98–129. Ukrainian Academy of Sciences. Kiev (in Russian).

Zhilin, M. 1995. The western part of Russia in the Late Palaeolithic-Early Mesolithic. In: Larsson, L. (ed.) *The Earliest Settlement of Scandinavia and its relationship with the neighbouring areas*, 273–284. Acta Archaeologica Lundensia 8:24. Lund.

17. Forest and Mobility. A Case from the Fishing Camp Site Dudka, Masuria, north-eastern Poland

Witold Gumiński and Maria Michniewicz

The paper presents a history of the natural environment, particularly concerning the forest and game mammals starting from the Allerød up to the beginning of the Early Sub-boreal on the Dudka island and mainland around one of the (former) Great Masurian Lakes. Accordingly, the human mobility, territoriality and the forest management are discussed for each period. From the Late Boreal some semi-farming exertions – hazel cultivation and game attracting are suggested.

Introduction

Dudka is a prehistoric site in the north-eastern Poland in the Masurian Lake District (Figure 17.1). The site is a big, flat island (c.12 hectares) of the former extensive lake (c. 25 km^2), nowadays a peat-bog. It resembles an elongated triangle in outline, in which the widest angle (promontory) is oriented to the south (Figure 17.2). The shortest distance between the mainland and the island is 0.5 km. The island was settled as a seasonal fishing campsite from the Allerød to the beginning of the Middle Sub-boreal, i.e. from the Late Palaeolithic to the end of the Neolithic. This was confirmed by complete stratification sequence dated by forty radiocarbon tests. Well preserved organic materials, such as wood and bone are excellent scientific sources to investigate the changes in environment and human activity in this particular region over the period of more then seven thousand radiocarbon years (Gumiński 1999:38 pp). The history of a local vegetation was reconstructed above all by analysing several hundred dendro fossil samples from which c. twenty-eight thousand of wood and charcoal pieces were determined (Figure 17.3) (Michniewicz 1998–2000). Palynological analysis were used as well (Gumiński 1995:17 pp; Nalepka 1995). The species composition of animal bones in the individual layers was determined and taken into consideration (Gumiński 1995:Tables 7 and 9, 1998:Tables 4 and 5, 1999:Table 4). The human mobility is suggested from the distribution and density of finds in particular periods and from the presence of certain rare

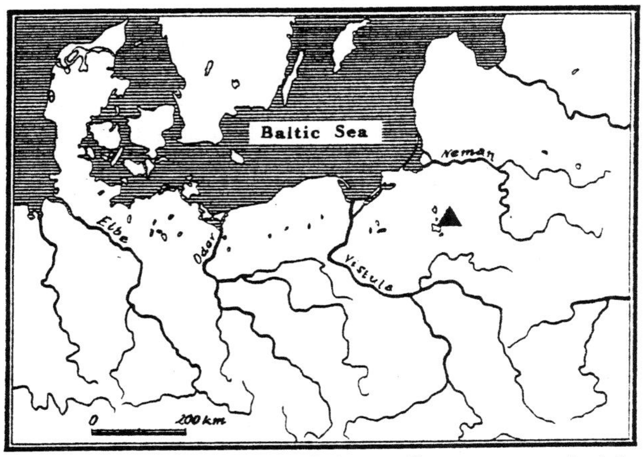

Figure 17.1 Localisation of the Dudka site – marked by "△".

Figure 17.2 Aerial photography of the Dudka island. "SP" – the southern promontory; "EB" – the eastern bay.

Type/species Taxon (wood and charcoal)	Forest community	Chronozones – Periods										
		Palaeolithic				Mesolithic					Para-Neolithic	
		AL	DR III	FR e.PB	DR IV	l. PB	e. BO	l. BO	e/m AT	m/l AT	l. AT	AT/ SB
Pine –*Pinus*	Open forest	8%	19%	73%	48%	76%	30%	14%	13%	3%	6%	8%
Birch –*Betula*		73%	27%	5%	14%	6%	9%	7%	15%	4%	13%	25%
Aspen /Poplar –*Populus*		1%	11%	x		x	2%	4%	x	3%	7%	4%
Willow –*Salix*	Bushes	18%	40%	17%	19%	5%	1%	x	1%	x	x	x
Juniper –*Juniperus*		(+)	1%	x	19%	3%	2%		x			
Hazel –*Corylus*						1%	7%	2%	x	3%	2%	1%
Alder –*Alnus*	Wet leafy			2%		6%	29%	34%	38%	26%	47%	22%
Elm –*Ulmus*						2%	14%	28%	8%	9%	4%	5%
Ash –*Fraxinus*						(+)	x	1%	10%	8%	10%	4%
Oak –*Quercus*	Broad-leaved					x	1%	2%	4%	6%	2%	5%
Lime –*Tilia*							1%	4%	10%	31%	2%	23%
Hornbeam –*Carpinus*						x	x	1%	x	1%	2%	1%
Maple –*Acer*							x	1%	1%	2%	1%	2%
Beech –*Fagus*								x	x		x	x
Larch –*Larix*	Conifer					x						
Spruce –*Picea*						1%	1%					x
Rowan –*Sorbus*	Undergrowth		3%	1%		x		x	x		x	
Sea buckthorn –*Hippophae*				1%		x		x				
Heathberry –*Ericaceae*				x		x	x					
Spindle-tree –*Euonymus*						x	2%	x	x	1%	1%	
Bird cherry –*Prunus padus*						x	x		x	x		
Cranberry-tree –*Viburnum*							x	x		x	1%	x
Alder buckthorn –*Frangula*							x	x	x	x	2%	x
Dogwood –*Cornus*							x	x	x		x	
Elder –*Sambucus*							x			x		
Clematis –*Clematis*							x			x		
Wild cherry –*Cerasus avium*								x	x			x
Buckthorn –*Rhamnus*								x				
Blackthorn –*Prunus spinosa*								x				
Barberry –*Berberis*								x				
Mistletoe –*Viscum*								x				
Ivy –*Hedera*									x			
Rosaceous –*Rosaceae*										x		
Honeysuckle –*Lonicera*										x		
Privet –*Ligustrum*											x	
No of dendro remains		62	113	248	103	2530	6236	7993	5446	2705	908	1610
Average share of charcoal		100%	–	4%	–	21%	70%	74%	56%	78%	45%	54%

Figure 17.3 Average percentages of determined taxa in dendro samples in each distinguished period at the Dudka site. "x" – present in less then 0.5% of a given period; "(+)" – present exclusively as an artefact.

species or raw materials which probably not occurred in surroundings of Dudka and which thus could be accessible far from this site (Gumiński 1999:72 pp). Some possibilities of semi-farming activities in the forest during the Mesolithic are discussed below.

Forest and human adaptation

The thin birch forest with pine admixture and willow-bush covered the island and mainland in the *Allerød* period (the Late Palaeolithic) (Figure 17.4). A bone of horse and that of elk found on the Dudka island well reflect the

Forest and Mobility. A Case from the Fishing Camp Site Dudka, Masuria, north-eastern Poland

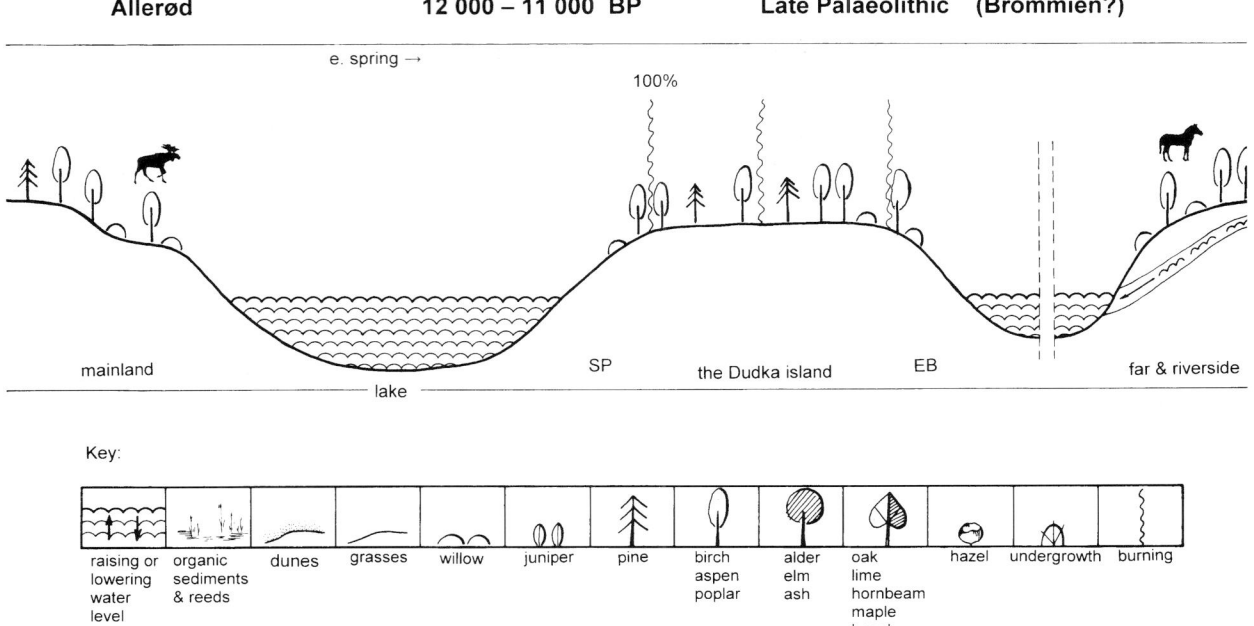

Figure 17.4 Dudka during the Allerød. Schematic view of the island, the lake and surrounding area showing the main kind of forest, game mammals and lake conditions.

Explanations to figures 5–10: *Percentage over an icon of the smoke indicates the share of a charcoal in dendro samples. Season above the lake→ occasionally visited the island, → recurrently.*

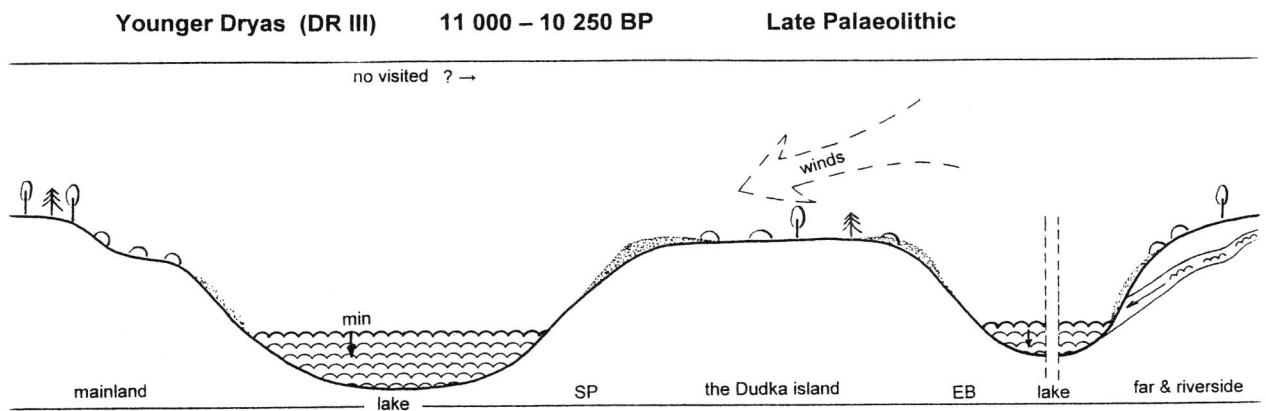

Figure 17.5 Dudka during the Younger Dryas (Dryas III). See explanations figure 17.4.

landscape mosaics. The horse bone suggests hunting rather in open grassy areas, while the bone of elk – in wooded and marshy ones. Occasional camps were pitched at different places on the island, which not fully forested ground enabled for. However, the southern promontory of the island was the most intensively used in this period (and later on) (Figure 17.2). Among small amount of dendro samples found in the Allerød layer only charcoal was present. Not even one piece of ordinary wood has been found. However, a wooden artefact, the hook made of juniper root, was preserved. Already at that time the main purposes for camping on the island were probably fishing and fowling. The wooden fishhook and the skull of cormorant confirm that hypothesis.

In the *Younger Dryas* period (Dryas III) (Figure 17.5) cold and windy weather heavily reduced most of the woods and dunes were formed on the island shore. The bushy landscape with dwarf, shrubby forms of willow, birch, aspen and rowan prevailed over forests containing mostly undersized pine and birch. There is still no evidence for human existence on the island during the period in question.

In the very beginning of the Holocene, i.e. oscillation of the Early Pre-boreal called *Friesland* (Figure 17.6) thin pine forest, still rather low, covered most of the area. Willows formed separate bushes as before. Similarly, as it was in the Allerød period, occasional visits to the southern promontory of the island took place during

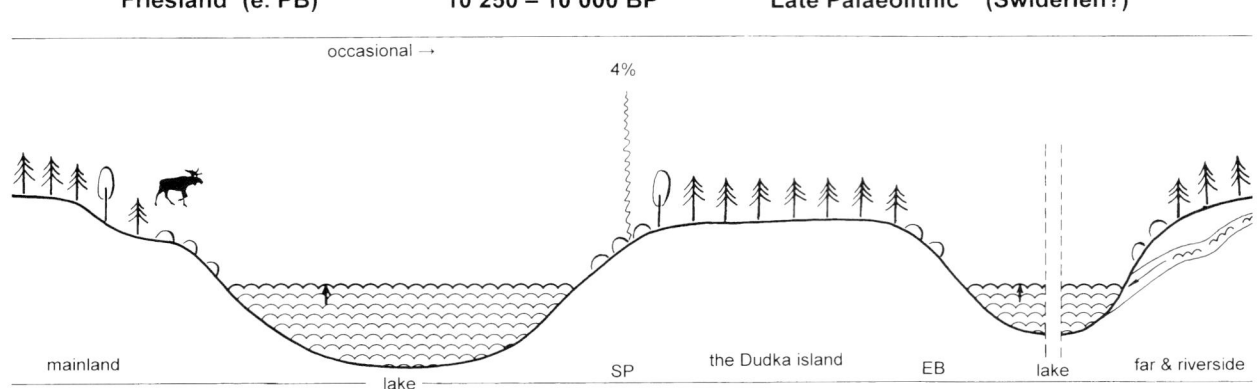

Figure 17.6 Dudka during the Friesland of the Early Pre-boreal. See explanations figure 17.4.

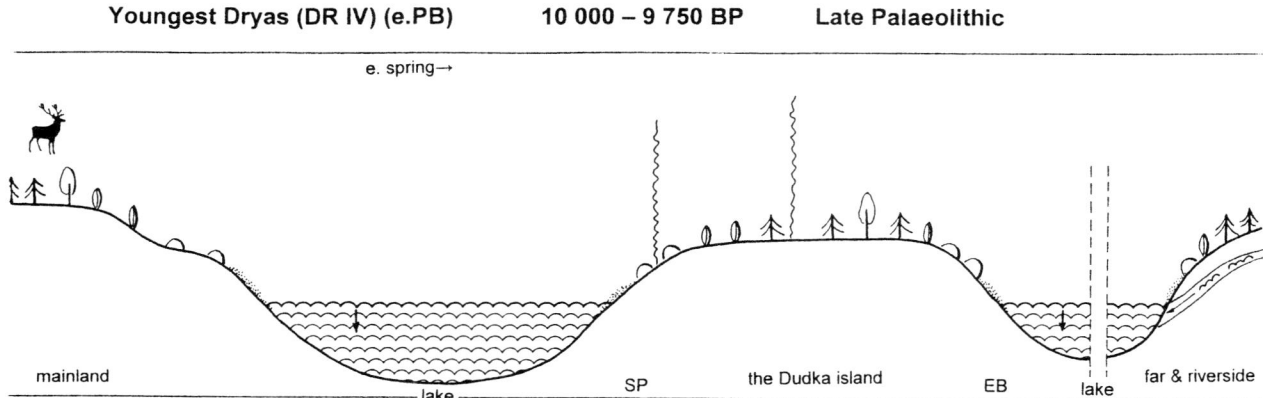

Figure 17.7 Dudka during the Youngest Dryas (Dryas IV) of the Early Pre-boreal. See explanations figure 17.4.

Friesland (Figure 17.2). A weak human activity can be confirmed by a low contribution (4%) of charcoal in dendro samples. A singular bones of elk, and maybe of red deer, roe deer and aurochs/bison suggests hunting in the wooded landscape rather then in opens.

The last, comparatively short period of the Late Palaeolithic, i.e. the *Youngest Dryas* (Dryas IV) of the Early Pre-boreal (Figure 17.7) was quite cold with the eolian activity again. The landscape backed to more bushy with willow and juniper communities. Park forests or coppices almost exclusively consisted of dwarfs pine and birch. Short time camps were pitched mainly along the south-eastern shore, as before (Figure 17.2). Fish and bird's bones confirmed fishing and fowling done at the end of the Late Palaeolithic. A rib of red deer was found, which may suggest hunting in a rather forested area. Such a game, however, is not likely to be frequent at that time.

At the beginning of the *Late Pre-boreal* (Figure 17.8) and thereby from the Early Mesolithic the landscape changed dramatically. The dense pine forest with some birch and the small admixture of other than pine coniferous species covered most of the area. The rest of undersized pine-trees disappeared during this period. Willow bushes and shrubs of the juniper gradually diminished, therefore partly open areas shrank. At the end of the period, bushes of the hazel appeared as well as the waterside wet leafy forest community with the alder and the elm began to grow.

Due to environmental changes (increase in the forested area) the main hunting weapon of Early Mesolithic hunters became a bow. This is indicated by the findings in the Late Pre-boreal layer of a flattened wooden arrow and a piece of a wooden artefact, possibly a fragment of a bow. According to the landscape structure, Early Mesolithic hunters first of all penetrated the prevailing habitats of grown, dense forests to hunt various ungulate games, such as red deer and wild boar. Comparatively the high share of elk bones among remnants from the Late Pre-boreal layers indicates hunting in marshlands as well. Besides, coppices and wood-edges where the roe deer occur abundantly and even open grasslands, suitable for the horse, could also be penetrated as bones of these species suggest. An artefact (the slotted point) made of a wood of the ash, a tree still very rare at that time (according to dendro samples it appeared at Dudka not earlier than in the middle of the Early Boreal), may suggest that distant expeditions were undertaken to find special raw materials.

The only habitation place used in the Late Pre-boreal

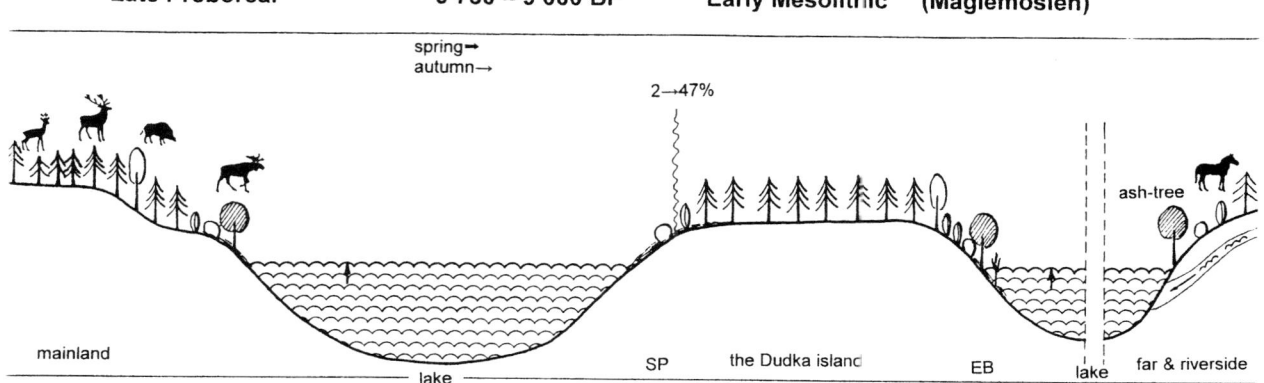

Figure 17.8 Dudka during the Late Pre-boreal. See explanations figure 17.4.

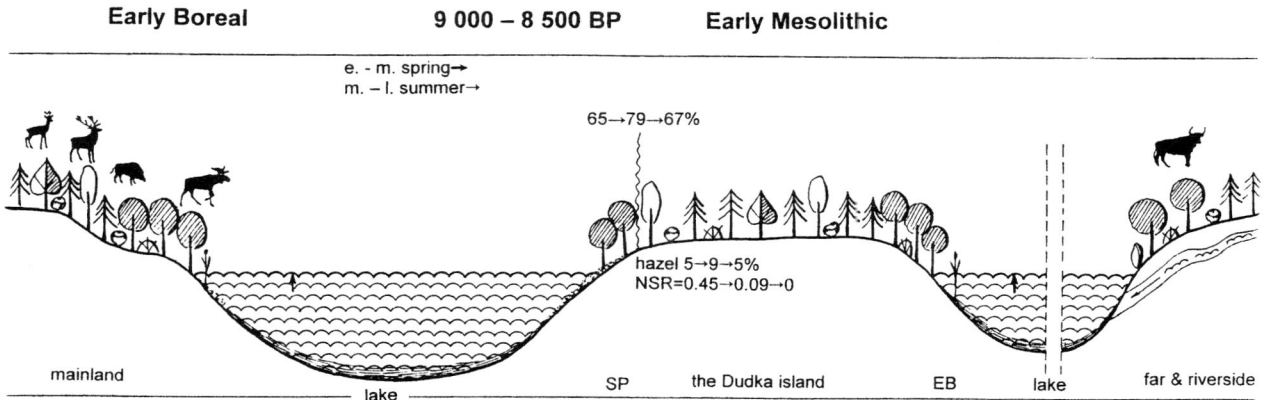

Figure 17.9 Dudka during the Early Boreal. See explanations figure 17.4. NSR= number of nuts and nutshells divided by number of hazel's wood and charcoal.

was again the southern promontory (Figure 17.2). From that period recurrent seasonal encampments were established on the island in the springtime and also in the late summer. The charcoal produced in those encampments constituted 2% of dendro samples at the beginning of the Late Pre-boreal, but as much as 47% at its end.

During the *Early Boreal* (Figure 17.9) the forest finally became mature and covered the whole ground surface. Pine lost its former absolute majority among trees, but grew up higher, reaching the sizes similar to that observed today. Typical pine forest began to change into mixed coniferous one, in which birch prevailed over other deciduous trees. The deciduous were not numerous, but their species richness was high. Relic willow and juniper bushes were on the decline. Instead of them, the wet leafy forest community consisting of alder and elm occupied lower situated grounds along shores. Entirely forested area caused the horse to disappear completely. Instead, aurochs appeared somewhere within Dudka hunters' reach.

In the Early Boreal hazel reached its Holocene maximum. Its share in the pollen profile increased by 19% at the beginning of the Early Boreal and by almost 9% in dendro remains in the middle of that period. Surprisingly, only some nutshells could be found in habitation vicinity mostly at the beginning of the Early Boreal and then they gradually disappeared towards the end of the period. The low share of hazelnuts and nutshells in relation to pieces of hazel-wood and hazel-charcoal can be well expressed by the NSR ratio (the nuts and nutshells ratio – NSR = number of nuts and nutshells divided by number of hazel's wood and charcoal), which never exceeded the value of 0.5. Recurrent, mainly early and mid springs but also mid and late summers, seasonal camps were still pitched at the same south-eastern place of the southern promontory (Figure 17.2). The charcoal produced in those camps comprised from 65 up to 79% of pieces in dendro samples.

In the *Late Boreal and the very beginning of the Early Atlantic* (Figure 17.10) the earlier tendency to replace pine forest with deciduous one was far-gone. Apart from the birch and the poplar, other admixtures of broad-leaved species, particularly the lime and the oak began noticeable. Shores and marshes were entirely occupied by alder-elm woods with well developed, various, thick undergrowth of high species diversity. This wet-ground leafy forest community reached its Holocene maximum at that time. Climate became changeable. Frequent storms occurred, water level considerably fluctuated but was generally higher than in the previous periods. An abrasion of lakes'

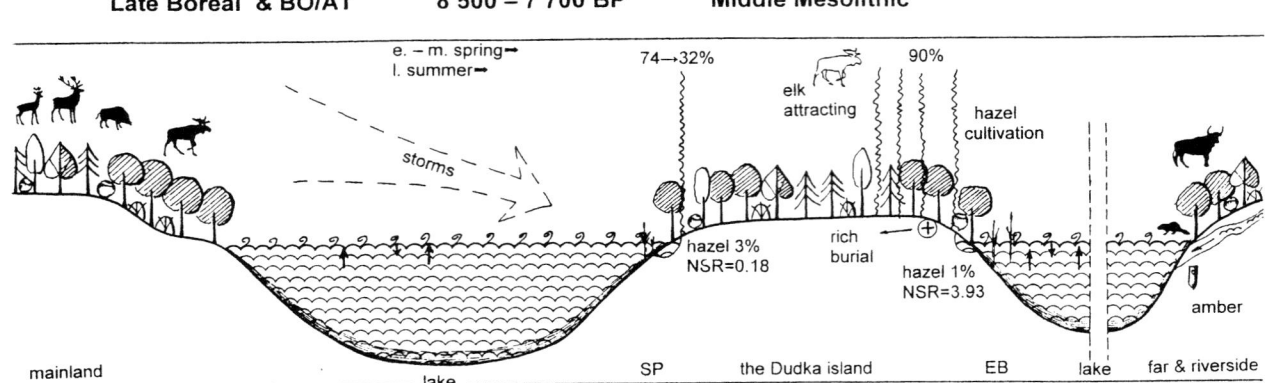

Figure 17.10 Dudka during the Late Boreal and turn to the Early Atlantic. See explanations figures 17.4 and 17.9.

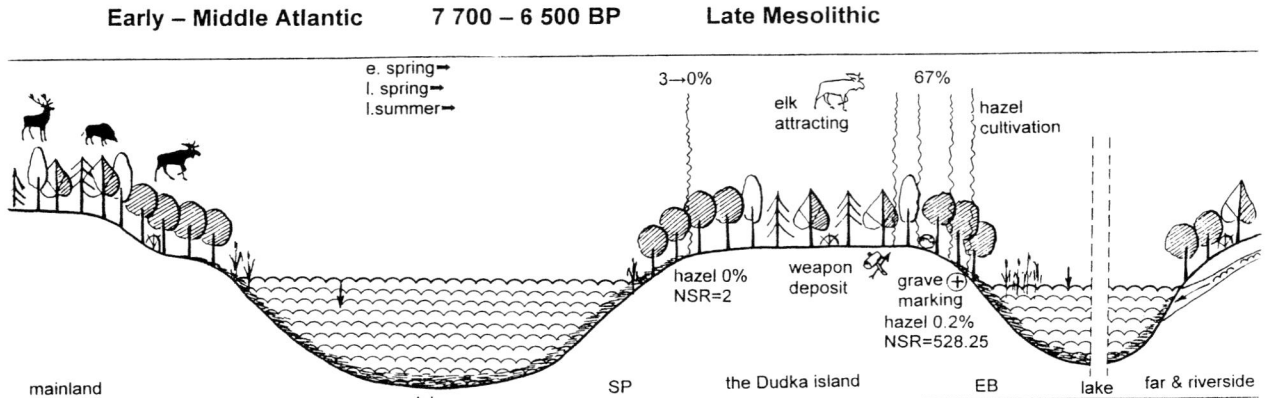

Figure 17.11 Dudka during the Early and the first half of the Middle Atlantic. See explanations figures 17.4 and 17.9.

shorelines and rivers' banks enabled people to successful seeking after the amber, ornaments of which have been found only from this period of Mesolithic. When the opportunity occurred, beaver was hunted along the riverside. Traditional habitation place was moved to the region over the eastern bay, more protected from winds by the local wood growing on the island and from waves by the belt of reeds (Figure 17.2).

At the new campsite charcoal consisted of up to 90% of dendro remains, while at the former one its share decreased to 32%. Such a high share of charcoal at the new place suggests that this originated not only from fireplaces, but mostly from intentional forest burning. Regular forest burning can additionally be confirmed by appearance of *Pteridium aquilinum* in the pollen-diagram. This fern is known to grow particularly just after forest clearance (Gumiński 1995:18 p; Nalepka 1995:64). The composition of charcoal is interesting, because indicates selected burning directed to: (1) alder and elm, which 99.9% of dendro remains were charred wood, (2) young twigs of deciduous trees, (3) shrubs, particularly prickly species. Bush burning off was obviously done to get clearings for encampment. Why did foragers burn alder or young deciduous twigs, although they are a very poor fuel? The more so as a smoke from alder produces pungent smell, whereas most of deciduous species that sprouts were damaged by fire shoot out proliferated. One can presume, that hunters of Dudka purposely "produced" young shoots for attracting elk, which specially prefers such a food. It should be mentioned that bones of elk reached their Holocene maximum in that period.

Alder and elm burning might be connected with hazel cultivation. Dendro samples contain only 1% of hazel wood and charcoal, while nutshells or nuts (which are not counted as dendro remains) are almost four times more numerous (NSR= 3.93). It is interesting that at old camping site on the southern promontory hazel was three times more frequent (3% of dendro remains), but NSR more then twenty times lower! (NSR= 0.18). As a photophilous plant, hazel can only fructify abundantly while growing in the open area. Therefore alder-elm forest, growing just on the SE island shore and thus shading hazel, should first of all be burned off if foragers would like to obtain plenty of hazelnuts. Since 60% of nutshells and nuts found at the new campsite over the eastern bay were charred, the site can be regarded as a place for hazel cultivation, nuts roasting and storage.

Dense deciduous forest with well-developed under-

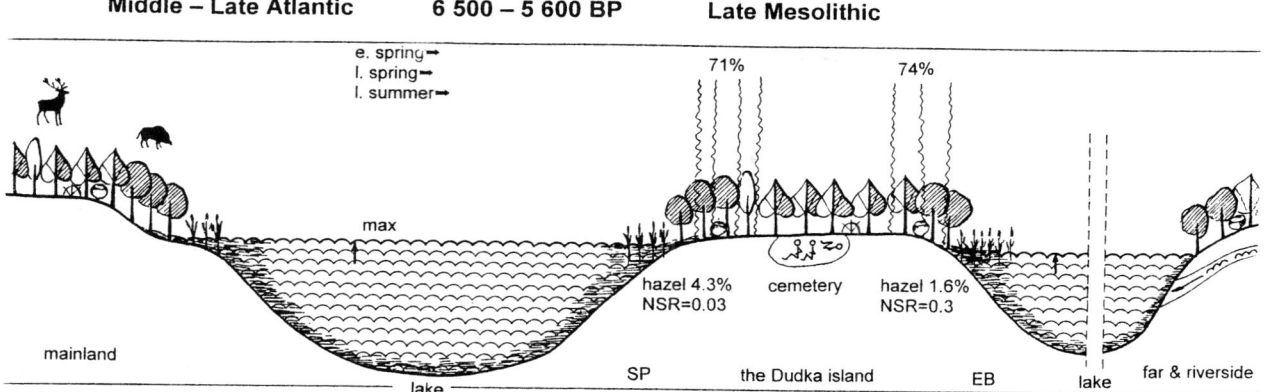

Figure 17.12 Dudka during the second half of the Middle and the first half the Late Atlantic. See explanations figures 17.4 and 17.9.

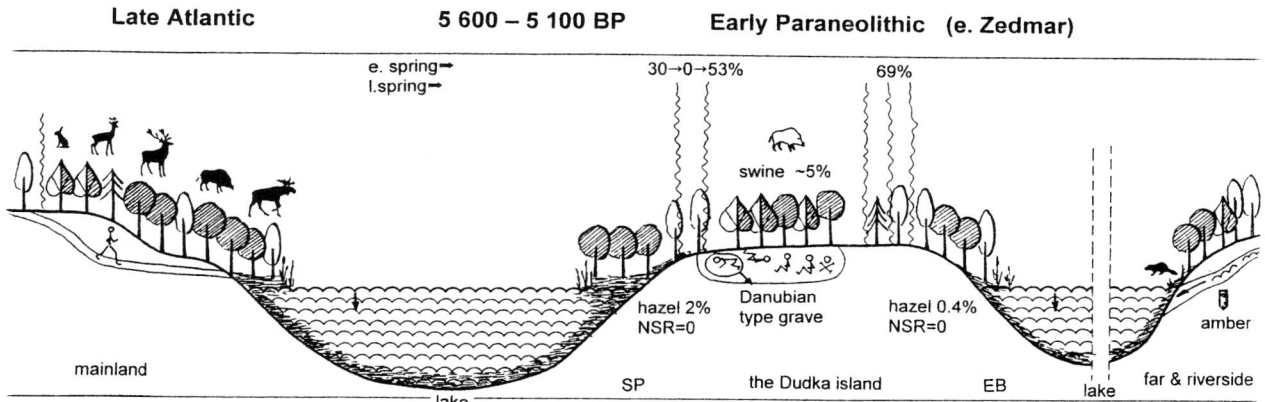

Figure 17.13 Dudka during the second half of the Late Atlantic. See explanations figures 17.4 and 17.9.

growth limited a view, was less passable and restrained foragers from the mobility. Living in such circumstances stimulated native society to display increasing territoriality. The social status of the dog, which became indispensable hunting companion as the best pursuer, probably also, increased. These processes are exemplified by remnants of the rich human burial furnished by the distinguishing amber ornament and with accompanying dog (Gumiński 1995:35 p).

In the *first half of the Atlantic* (Figure 17.11) warm temperate climate set in. Mixed deciduous forest with pine addition changed modestly. Elm declined distinctly in the wet-ground forest along the shores and was replaced by the ash. In the forest growing on drier, more elevated ground hazel decreased, while oak and particularly lime increased. It is noteworthy that also some undergrowth species, including all prickly shrubs and trees disappeared (at least on the island). Perhaps their extinction at Dudka could be attributed to the human activity. Twice higher share of birch comparing with the previous period could have anthropogenic reasons as well. Being a pioneer tree, birch could occur abundantly as a result of re-colonisation of cleared areas.

Passing the forest became more and more arduous; therefore hunting district and long distance raw material expeditions were restricted. Amber, bones of aurochs and even beaver disappeared from the Dudka island. Since human movement had been more and more limited within a given area, farther territorial manifestations were induced. One of them was a deposit of weapon buried in a small pit within the "new" encampment zone over the eastern bay. It contained an antler hatchet and an arrow from which quasi tanged point microlith remained (Gumiński 1995:35, Fig. 9). Other significant sign of territoriality was a big stone, which had been put just over the rich ancestor's grave (this with dog and amber pendant). This can be interpreted as marking the territory out and declaring right to the island.

In that time camping at the "traditional" site on the southern promontory was given up. Charcoal disappeared there, while at the "new" site selective forest burning was continued, although in a smaller degree (67% of dendro remains are charred). Some other noticeable changes have also been recorded. First of all, elm, lime and alder were burnt, but not the shrubs. Charcoal and wood of hazel are very scarce in contrast to lots of hazelnuts and nutshells (exceptionally high NSR= 528.25), from which only 5% have visible traces of roasting. Recurrent habitation, forest

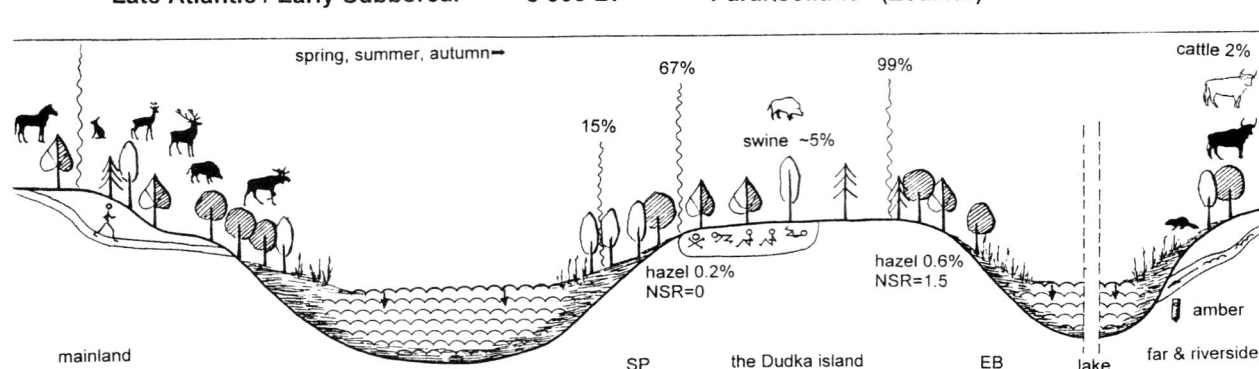

Figure 17.14 Dudka during the Late Atlantic/Early Sub-boreal transition. See explanations figures 17.4 and 17.9.

clearings, hazel cultivation and perhaps elk and red deer attraction stimulated the growth of synanthropic plants. According to pollen diagram they are ribwort (*Plantago lanceolata, P. media, P. major*), sorrel (*Rumex acetosa, R. acetosella* type) and heather (*Calluna vulgaris*) (Gumiński 1995:19, Table 3; Nalepka 1995:64). In this period the foragers visited the island for a shorter time, but more frequently – three times a year (Gumiński 1995:29 p; 1999:61, 73, Tables 3 and 4). Frequent campsite changes in the area covered by hard to pass forests interrupted by lakes' waters only, perhaps induced the necessity of using alternative means of movement and transportation. Dugout boats (a transom of such a boat have been found) might be commonly used at that time.

In the *second half of the Atlantic* period (Figure 17.12) pine and birch decreased to the Holocene minimum, while lime reached its Holocene maximum and became the most common tree, even outnumbering alder. Other species of broad-leaved forest community, such as oak, maple and hornbeam increased as well. The lowest share of NAP (6%) in the pollen diagram well indicates a shady, dense deciduous forest with thick undergrowth. Such conditions, with the highest Holocene water level and swampy shores caused that the exploitation district was highly restricted. Red deer and wild boar became almost the only prey. No Neolithic novelties were found at Dudka site, in spite of quite dense the Early Neolithic Danubian colonisation established less then 200 km away (towards the SW). The high level of isolation induced a new territorial manifestation – establishment of the cemetery located just between the "traditional" campsite and the "new" one. In this period the southern promontory was again inhabited, so both places were occupied and cleared out by fire. Hazel-bush grew up again, being more then twice more often at the southern promontory than over the eastern bay. However the low NSR (= 0.03 and 0.3 for the southern promontory and the eastern bay, respectively) indicates poor hazel harvesting. It is difficult to find a reasonable explanation of this.

In the *very Late Atlantic* period (Figure 17.13) the rate of lake shallowing increased distinctly. Lush vegetation overgrew the littoral zone and the shores. In contrast, the forest became less compact. In previously trackless forest vegetation the paths and glades were created. Thinning the forest out is suggested by: rising NAP in pollen diagram, increased share of birch and poplar/aspen in dendro samples, more bones of roe deer and the appearance of the bones of hare and beaver, as well as the occurrence of amber pendants.

The most spectacular, however are some Neolithic novelties, which were adopted from the middle and late Danubian communities (mainly from Brześć-Kujawski culture). Those are flat-bottomed pottery, small polished stone adzes, T-shaped antler axes and remnants of manufacturing them. Moreover, one of the graves from the Dudka cemetery was exactly in the Neolithic Danubian style, i.e. the contracted skeleton, laid on the right side, with head turned to the south and face to the east. The burial was furnished with small polished stone adze – typical for Danubian Neolithic (Gumiński 2001b:146, Fig.10d, 13).

Aborigines made also some attempt in swine domestication, however bones of semi-domesticated swine accounted for only 5% of all mammal bones. Surprisingly, hazel cultivation was given up (NSR= 0), although hazel-bush still grew on the island. Perhaps hazelnuts, the product that can easily be stored for a long time, lost their importance due to introducing some new methods of food preservation and storage. More kinds of food could be prepared and stored thanks to the usage of the pottery. Also semi-domesticated pigs could serve as a good food reserve since they could be killed and used at any moment.

On the *Late Atlantic/Early Sub-boreal transition* (Figure 17.14) surface of open areas increased considerably, as pollen diagram indicates (from 10 to 18% of NAP). The spectrum of game species from Dudka was changed accordingly. Horse and aurochs returned, hare, roe deer and badger became more common, and in the end a few cattle bones appeared. The more open landscape made exchange expeditions easier, which, beside the easily accessible food, was the main reason for an abrupt demographic growth (Gumiński 2001a: Tab.1). The recurrent forest burning, as well as keeping a herd of semi-domesticated swine on the island through the entire warm season caused forest degradation. Fireplaces were located even on the freshly formed, overgrown land of the former littoral zone, where fold down branches from the nearest vicinity (mainly birch) were taken to the fire. Maybe hazel was cultivated again at the same place (i.e. over the eastern bay – NSR= 1.5), however in a much lesser scale.

Conclusion

Generally, as the forest became less passable, foragers restricted the district of their activity, which led to the increase in the territoriality. Hunter-gatherers actively limited the forest growing and thickening by burning and treading. Apart from gaining living space, forest burning was directed to additional profits, such as multiplying hazelnuts or game. Such semi-farming exertions began at Dudka already in the Late Boreal. It is interesting, that the beginnings of the Neolithic caused disappearance of the hazel cultivation.

Acknowledgements

We would like to express our grateful to Ewa Gumińska for drawings. The participation of one of the authors (W.G.) at the Conference was possible thanks to The Institute of Archaeology University of Warsaw, as well as The Royal Academy of Letters, History and Antiquities in Stockholm.

References

Gumiński, W. 1995. Environment, economy and habitation during the Mesolithic at Dudka, Great Masurian Lakeland, NE-Poland. *Przegląd Archeologiczny* 43, 5–46.

—— 1998. The peat-bog site Dudka, Masurian Lakeland: An example of conservative economy. In: Zvelebil, M., Dennell, R. and Domańska, L. (eds) *Harvesting the Sea, Farming the Forest. The Emergence of Neolithic Societies in the Baltic Region*, 103–109. Sheffield.

—— 1999. Środowisko przyrodnicze a tryb gospodarki i osadnictwa w mezolicie i paraneolicie na stanowisku Dudka w Krainie Wielkich Jezior Mazurskich (English summary: Natural environment – and the mode of economy and settlement in the Mesolithic and Paraneolithic at the Dudka site in the Masurian Lakeland). *Archeologia Polski* 44, 31–74.

—— 2001a. Scattered human bones on prehistoric camp site Dudka, NE-Poland, as indication of peculiar burial rite. In: Vermeersh, P.M., Otte, M. and Derwich, E. (eds) *Préhistoire – Pratiques Mortuaires – Mort (Paléolithique, Mésolithique, Néolithique)*, Leuven (in press).

—— 2001b. Kultura Zedmar. Na rubieży neolitu "zachodniego". (English summary: The Zedmar Culture. On the Border of the "Western" Neolithic.) In: Czebreszuk, J., Kryvalcevič, M. and Makarowicz, P. (eds) *Od neolityzacji do początków epoki brązu. Przemiany kulturowe w międzyrzeczu Odry i Dniepru między VI i II tys. BC*, 133–152. Poznań.

Michniewicz, M. 1998–2000. Dendroflora ze stanowiska Dudka. (Manuscript in Polish).

Nalepka, D. 1995. Palynological investigations of an archaeological site at Dudka (profile D1-26). *Przegląd Archeologiczny* 43, 61–64.

18. Investigating Post-Glacial Hunter Gatherer Landscape enculturation: ethnographic analogy and interpretative methodologies

Peter D. Jordan

The analytical concept of landscape represents an important interpretive forum in which divergent "ecological" and "culturological" approaches to the study of hunter fisher gatherers may be combined. In the anthropological literature hunter gatherers tend to be portrayed as fluid social bands whose roaming lives constitute an eternal quest for ecological resources. Where processes of landscape enculturation have seen attention, this has been limited to investigating how mental constructs are draped over the unaltered physical terrain. Research is scarce into the ways in which natural features of the landscape are singled out for special veneration and physically transformed through the creation or deposition of material artefacts.

The ecological bias in anthropological hunter gatherer research has been imported into archaeological interpretations via an inevitable reliance on ethnographic analogy for exploring the material remains of the past, strengthening existing disciplinary trends of period specific theorisation. In this paper, I argue that solutions to these problems can be sought via the development of more appropriate sources of ethnographic analogy, that is, through actualistic studies of the production, use and deposition of material culture in a landscape context. Adopting a more resolutely social and symbolic interpretive framework brings a combined consideration of subsistence, cosmology and ritual to the fore.

The Eastern Khanty are mobile hunter fisher gatherers of the boreal forest zone of western Siberia. Recent ethnographic fieldwork is drawn upon to investigate how landscapes are structured by their users to incorporate routine and ritual activities, including the maintenance of a complex hierarchical network of sacred sites. People, artifacts and activity at these holy places are linked to

Figure 18.1 Khanty men relax back at the river-side base yurt by drinking brashka and eating fish, late Winter 1999.

concepts of tenure, kinship and gender pollution. Ritualised exchanges between human and spirit domains demand the use and deposition of artefacts as media of communication. Crucially, patternings in the material correlates to these practices have the potential to be archaeologically intelligible.

Introduction: the challenge of investigating landscape enculturation

There exists a growing acknowledgement in Mesolithic archaeology that post-glacial hunter gatherers in northern Europe did appropriate the landscape both practically and symbolically. In other words, while the changing Holocene environment may have created ecological opportunities and constraints, members of these prehistoric communities acted within and made sense of this material and social world through their own set of understandings rich in subjective meaning and symbolism. But how do we gain an understanding of that world? The challenge currently facing Mesolithic archaeologists is the need to develop appropriate research methodologies, which have the potential to adequately investigate questions of social and symbolic adaptation as well as the more familiar ecological ones.

Recent attempts to breathe fresh inspiration into the entrenched traditions of Mesolithic archaeology have their roots in broader intellectual currents, whereby methodologies of Enlightenment *explanation* (*erklären*) can be broadly contrasted with a quest for interpretative *understanding* (*verstehen*). For Layton (1997:184 pp.) causal explanation involves undertaking empirical investigation and the recording of statistical regularities in human behaviour in order to develop general laws. These laws are argued to be valid in all historical and cultural contexts and capture the overarching and objective (*etic*) "truth" of how the world works in a manner analogous to those of the natural sciences, rather than the humanities. In contrast, many engaged in the human sciences have argued that their subject matter must be differentiated from the natural sciences on qualitative grounds. This project of (*emic*) understanding demands the observation of "meaningful interaction, in order to discover meanings specific to that time and place and which actors attributed to their own and others' behaviour" (ibid. 1997:184). Writing in this interpretative vein, Geertz argues that:

> "the concept of culture I espouse....is essentially a semiotic one. Believing, with Max Weber, that man is an animal suspended in webs of significance he himself has spun, I take culture to be those webs, and the analysis of it to be therefore not an experimental science in search of law but an interpetive one in search of meaning" (Geertz 1973:5).

Geertz develops a sense of cultural relativism by layering up these contextual meanings:

> "what defines it [ethnography] is the kind of intellectual effort it is: an elaborate venture in, to borrow a notion from Gilbert Ryle, "thick description" (Geertz 1973:6).

The challenge of understanding another culture becomes a problem of interpretation:

> "Doing ethnography is like trying to read (in the sense of "construct a reading of") a manuscript – foreign, faded, full of elipses, incoherencies, suspicious emendations, and tendentious commentaries, but written not in conventionalised graphs of sound but in transient examples of shaped behavior" (Geertz 1973:10).

This promotes the anthropologists' notion of others cultures as a kind of alien text, in which local details have contextual significance and meanings, and which must then be "read" by the fieldworker through an exercise in hermeneutics (i.e the practice of interpretation) (Silverman 1990).

In the parallel discipline of archaeology the call to employ similar interpretative methodologies reached a crescendo in the later 1980's and recent years have witnessed the development of a suite of post processual (interpretative) approaches, which have been applied to the evidence from later prehistory. In this way, the apparently innovative shift towards a "thick description" of the Mesolithic period, complete with theories of meaning, action and individual intent mirrors – and is substantially pre-dated by – broader intellectual developments in the wider discipline. Yet it remains crucial to note that this disparity is an academic phenomenon, which reveals more about what van Gijn and Zvelebil have termed period specific theorisation in archaeology (ibid 1997:3) than any fundamental difference marking out human experiences in the different periods of the prehistoric past. How did this situation develop?

Firstly, and from a theoretical angle, the Mesolithic has been equated, either explicitly or implicitly, with historically documented hunter gatherers who, "thanks to a residual commitment to the comparative method of classical social evolutionism", have traditionally been portrayed as existing at the "absolute zero of cultural development" (Ingold 1986:130 pp.). Secondly, the physical evidence of the Mesolithic is scarce and impoverished in contrast to later prehistory lending itself to the investigation of broader ecological adaptations and tool typologies. These disparate currents have combined in the production of the widely accepted images of the Mesolithic as being a simple or primitive precursor to the Neolithic, its foraging populations ecologically adapted to a resource environment. Only in later periods does the archaeological story become more interesting, with agriculturalists enjoying rich social and symbolic relations while dwelling in an enculturated landscape bursting with impressive monumental architecture and populated by the ancestors. Indeed, the impressive physicality and obvious symbolism of this later evidence demands nothing less than a fully humanistic account of what it actually felt like – and meant – to move through the complex architecture of ritual spaces and boundaries. In turn, this directs attention to how these actions were central to process of social and symbolic reproduction in communities bound by webs of symbolism and riddled with unequal relations of power, resistance and authority (Thomas 1993; Barrett 1994; Tilley 1994 etc.)

While these latter issues are of equal importance in the Mesolithic the fragmentary evidence for this period – including a distinct lack of monumental architecture – requires a suitable interpretative forum. One obvious way forward is the employment of the analytical concept of landscape (Gosden and Head 1994). Here, an interpretive methodology has obvious attractions for the development of a Mesolithic landscape archaeology whereby the material remnants of processes of enculturation can be investigated and translated in terms of the social practices and belief systems which produced those remains. I would argue that pursuing these questions in a specifically Mesolithic context must also require a much more fundamental shift in our perception of both hunter gatherers and the way these groups bring meanings to the landscape through the creation, use and deposition of material culture. In particular, this demands a more subtle "translation" of the relationship between deposited Mesolithic artefacts and the "natural" places they occupy in the wider landscape (cf. Bradley 2000):

> "The places where collections [of artefacts] occur deserves a more searching analysis...deposits of bones are treated, quite misleadingly, as evidence of the subsistence economy...or feasts. In neither case is it asked why they should be found at distinctive places in the landscape, and that is where a new study might begin" (ibid. 2000:38).

In this way, we are seeking to grasp an understanding of procurement behavior, seasonal movements and tool technology within a more holistic – and landscape based – understanding of what these knowledgeable actions *meant* through a reference to the belief systems and cosmologies of the groups who enacted them.

Yet herein lies a crucial obstacle. Archaeologists cannot observe past societies directly, nor, in the case of the Mesolithic, move through the architecture of prehistoric spaces, but must build up this sense of "thick description" or "landscape reading" from the surviving material remains. Our only route into the meanings of this Mesolithic world begins with the selective use of ethnographic analogy, which forms a starting point in a hermeneutic circle linking a dialectic knowledge of the present and the past (cf. Tilley 1991). To date, however, this endeavour to "inhabit" the Mesolithic landscapes with knowledgeable actors through an inevitable reliance on ethnographic analogy (Wylie 1985) has been characterised by two fundamental problems:

Firstly, some of the most common sources of hunter gatherer ethnographic analogy (African, Australian) have few, if any, conceivable links with the north European prehistory other than in the context of externally imposed economic and socio-evolutionary frameworks. The resultant bridging arguments operate at the lowest level of certainty, that is, as weak general analogies. In addition, archaeologists have appeared keen to engage in an eclectic pick-and-mix of use of analogies without sufficient scrutiny of their specific content and of the theoretical climate within which they were created. All ethnographies are but subjective interpretations (Clifford and Marcus 1986) and few accounts have given explicit attention to the material and artefactual dimensions to social practices. Indeed, material culture – the basic "raw materials" upon which all archaeologists must build their interpretations – has seen only the most cursory attention from anglophone anthropologists (Lemonnier 1993:7).

Secondly, the more general Post Processual desire to seek emancipation from the constraints of explicit methodologies – and the dubious validity of "testable" hypotheses (cf. Hodder 1982:23) – has generated a significant gap between creative interpretations and the prehistoric material evidence. Consequently, Mesolithic lives come to be explored through reference to a series of – at times, rather banal – phenomenological truisms. It is, of course, almost certainly true that people of the past had myths and ancestors, that artefacts or places meant one thing in terms of another (metaphor) as part of a wider mind-set intimately linked to the inhabitation of a landscape rich in meaning and symbolism. The methodological problem is that these concepts grant abundant poetic license but fail to demand a rigorous engagement with the *specificty* of particular archaeological data sets. While this initial interpretative stage has raised questions and succeeded in pegging out a series of much broader prehistoric possibilities, we now need to re-engage with the evidence if we are to start to say something more specific – and therefore of *real* interest – about the Mesolithic of northern Europe.

How then to close this gap and forge stronger bridging arguments? Most of the work has approached the problem from an archaeological angle but there is another area in which more work might be done. Some of the most exciting and innovative work on Mesolithic landscape enculturation has drawn inspiration from the rich ethnographic record of adjacent Siberia. In contrast to more exotic sources of analogy, northern Europe and Siberia can be linked on a number of conceptual levels. Geographical proximity produces close parallels in seasonality, flora, and fauna. In addition, the prehistory, ethnohistory and ethnographic present of the two regions suggest that different communities have, at different times and in different ways, reproduced and transformed key elements in a broader circumpolar cosmology (Ingold 1986; Zvelebil 1997). In short, Fennoscandia is one of the few regions in Europe where the use of direct historical analogy may be justified.

Both Tilley (1991) and Zvelebil (1997) have investigated the symbolism of the rock carving site located at Nämforsen rapids, which was created and visited by hunter fisher gatherers between 3000 and 1500 BC in a social climate of growing contact and exchange with adjacent farming. Tilley employs Evenk – and Zvelebil Ket – analogies although neither worker explains why these particular Siberian groups are selected. More problematic is that neither of the ethnographies focus directly on the role of material culture in social practice. In particular, Tilley, appears content to gather normative ethnographic anecdotes and "lay" them onto Nämforsen so that the "link with Sel'kup Evenk Mythology is almost exact" Tilley (1991:136). The problem is that we are left with no sense of how these meanings and folklore ideas about rapids, elks and islands are created and sustained by routine or ritual practices grounded in the materiality of the Evenk world. These images do not help us to understand the physical alteration of sacred places through acts of special veneration. In effect we are doing nothing but blanketing the prehistoric past with a quilt of images gathered from the ethnographic present.

These observations provide the final element in to set of problems facing archaeologists in their quest to explore landscape enculturation in the Mesolithic: the lack of suitable ethnographies, which explore processes of landscape enculturation through a specific focus on both social practices and material culture. Improving our contemporary understandings of both the complexity and diversity of this *human:landscape* relationship is absolutely pivotal if our project to explore landscape enculturation is to advance anywhere beyond a superficial (rich in the poetics of discourse, poor in substance) acknowledgement that there were webs of meaning attached to places and spaces.

My aim in this paper is to explore landscape enculturation in a contemporary ethnographic context and to identify some of the implications raised by the study for the practice of Mesolithic archaeology. In an investigation of the Eastern Khanty – mobile hunter fisher gatherers of the west Siberia boreal forest – I will explore how landscapes are structured by their users to incorporate routine and ritual activities, which include the maintenance of a complex hierarchical network of sacred sites.[1] People, artefacts and activities at these holy places are linked to concepts of tenure, kinship and gender pollution. Ritualised exchanges between human and spirit domains demand the use and deposition of artefacts as media of communication. Crucially, it is the landscape patternings in the material correlates to these practices that have the potential to be archaeologically intelligible.

The Khanty of western Siberia

The Khanty have a long and complex history and while they are, along with Mansi, Ket and Sel'kup groups, the oldest indigenous inhabitants in western Siberia, they have never lived in isolation but have traded extensively with groups to the south and west. For the Khanty communities who reside on the middle sections of the Ob' River three historical developments have had particularly profound influences:

Firstly, the incorporation of northern Asia (i.e. Siberia) into the Russian Empire after the 16th C brought the imposition of colonial administrative policies whose primary focus was the extraction of *yasak* fur tax from the local taiga-forest hunting, fishing and gathering communities (Forsyth 1992; Konev 1998). At the same time, and despite a shift to a more dispersed settlement pattern, administrative territories appear to have been based, to a large extent, on pre-existing social groupings, with these, in turn, related closely to the drainage basins of the rivers tributary to the mighty Ob' (Martynova 1995). In order to pay the obligatory fur tax at annual *Jahrmarkt* trade fairs indigenous communities were obliged to spend most of the yearly procurement round away from main Russian settlement centres, thereby sparing them massive face to face exposure to outside contacts. The basic structures of this extractive colonial relationship amounted to *de facto apartheid*, and in much of western Siberia continued largely unaltered, right through the Communist period (Shimkin 1990).

Secondly, indigenous belief systems were attacked by successive waves of missionaries leading to a partial blending of native and Russian Orthodox religion. Shamans were singled out for special persecution in the Stalinist purges of the 1930's (Pentikäinen 1998) leading many to assume by that shamanism had died out entirely by the middle of the 20th C (Hoppál 1996). However, in the remoter areas seldom visited by state officials traditional beliefs and religious practices were maintained in secret and continue to be respected and observed to the present day. The imposition of Russian-language boarding school education on indigenous communities after the 1930's had major cultural impacts as did partially "successful" collectivisation programmes conducted during the 1950's Krushchev era.

Thirdly, and most recently, the large-scale industrial exploitation of Siberia's mineral wealth has wrought massive ecological destruction in areas occupied by indigenous communities still practising traditional hunting and fishing lifestyles (Massey-Stewart 1995; Wiget and Balalaeva 1997a, 1997b). In addition, the urban centres tied to mineral extraction have boomed in recent years bringing into the remote taiga landscapes large influxes of migrant workers who have shown little respect for either the local ecology or the traditional lifeways of the Khanty.

Malyi Iugan Khanty material culture

Amongst the widespread environmental destruction around Surgut, where, "from the window of a helicopter one can see 300 flames shooting up from oil rigs" (Pentikäinen 1998:103), pockets of traditional living continue to survive, albeit under the lengthening shadow

Figure 18.2 Riverside yurt with huts facing out to the river. The newest house is on the right and the river is flowing to the left.

cast by advancing mineral extraction industries (Massey-Stewart 1995; Wiget and Balalaeva 1997a, 1997b). This case-study explores the broader social, symbolic and material dimensions to practices of Khanty communities who maintain semi-nomadic lifestyles and reside on the upper stretches of the Malyi Iugan River, part of the larger Iugan River basin.[2]

The local taiga ecosystem is comprised of stands of woodland interspersed with lakes and extensive areas of bog. The climate is strongly continental, with warm summers and bitterly cold winters and deep snow cover. The summer thaw brings extensive flooding in this region of low-lying topography. The forests are home to numerous fur-bearing animal species including fox, wild deer, elk, sable, bear and squirrel. The rivers and lakes are rich in fish, especially in the summer and early autumn when migratory species return after the stagnant winter water has been flushed out during break up. This strong seasonality leads to an uneven distribution of resources over the landscape at different times of the year. Traditional semi-nomadic Khanty lifestyles, based around hunting, fishing and gathering, alternate between the winter dispersal of household groups for forest hunting and their summer aggregation at riverside fishing sites.

The term *yurt* is used in the ethnohistorical literature to describe a small community of indigenous people who occupy different seasonal settlements in order to exploit general hunting, fishing and gathering territories (Martynova 1995). On the Malyi Iugan River *yurt* communities comprise two-six households and are usually based around exogamous patrilocal lineages or *patronimia*. While successive generations of male hunters, bearing the same family name, tend to occupy the same territories, their wives are married into the *yurt* community from other *yurt*s in the wider river basin (comprising the Bolshoi and Malyi Iugan branches of the Iugan River). At a broader level these lineages group to form non-localised clans or *sir*, comprising bear, elk and beaver clans (*pupi sir*, *nekh sir* and *makh sir*).

While "Russians" (i.e. non-Khanty) are present in the local administrative centre located on the lower reaches of the main Iugan River the population of the Malyi Iugan River remains exclusively Khanty in ethnic composition. This colonial settlement pattern developed after the imposition of the *yasak* fur tax system, part of which involved the establishment of forts and later church-administrative settlements at strategic points on arterial rivers. The pattern continued through the historical *longue durée* with the Russian population of the taiga zone of western Siberia residing predominantly in urban settlements on the main Ob' River and having little, if any, contact with forest "Ostiaks" (Khanty)(Lukina 1985:16). Middle and upper reaches of tributaries like the Agan, Iugan and Vakh tended to remain indigenous "hinterlands" providing fish and fur to the state economy, although more recently the inexorable advance of mineral extraction activities has radically transformed this ethnic mosaic much to the detriment of indigenous communities.

For Malyi Iugan households the seasonal round comprises movement between isolated huts located in winter hunting grounds (a period described as being *v urmane*, literally "in the forest") and riverside base-settlement, also termed *yurt*. The hunting season is punctuated by a mid-winter break spent back at this base *yurt* when it becomes too dark and cold to hunt. Spring and autumn are also spent in the base *yurt* or at local fishing cabins. In the Communist era the whole community were obliged to take part in summer "expeditionary fishing", which involved travelling, often en masse, to rich fishing sites on the lower Iugan and main Ob' Rivers. Thus, a distinctive feature of this procurement activity is cyclical patterns of community aggregation and dispersal.

Places: Material culture of the riverside Yurt

Bones

If more ritualised forms of communication take place at the hierarchical network of sacred sites, linking the human collective with a range of spirit protectors, then these same relationships of respect are maintained through more routine practices. In Khanty views the outcome of hunting is as much about relationships with supernatural beings than about an individual's technical ability. The forest spirit, local holy site spirits and household spirits are all able to exert influence and, for elk in particular, the animal spirit master *Vojwort Iki* is thought to have "given" the animal to the successful hunter. After killing and consumption the appropriate treatment and deposition of animal bones is important if this respectful relationship is to be nurtured (Jordan in press a). Feeding the "clean" heart and head of elk to the dogs is thought particularly offensive and elk heads are often consumed at holy site, forming one of the best sorts of *pory* or fare for the spirits. Relationships with the bear are more complex but also involve appropriate treatment of bones and their deposition in deep pools, whereas elk bones are returned to the forest to a "clean place". At the elk kill site a piece of fur is cut out from the animal's throat and hung from a tree so that "*Vojwort Iki* will know his elk has been killed". For the bear special carvings are made in cedar trees beside the path leading back into the *yurt*. These represent the head and paws of the bear, parts of the anatomy where the soul is thought to reside, and are cut so that *Torum*, the master of the bear will not "waste time looking for him". The appropriate routine treatment of animals is also vital for the maintenance of the community's continued welfare.

Houses

There are certain traditions associated with the founding of new yurts or the building of new houses, both of which revolve around the perception of auspicious directions in the river flow. These are also linked to the location of the cemetery, which should never be located directly upstream from the yurt for fear that the illnesses of the dead will flow into the domain of the living. It is also thought very unlucky, for example, to found a new settlement downstream. One informant emphasised this point by relating a recent story of how one household had left an older established yurt on the upper river in order to found a new and separate residence site some kilometers downstream. All went well for a few years but then the family died tragically in a boating accident and the widow was left alone to bring up the children. Moving a yurt across the river to the opposite bank is also considered to be an inherently risky manouvre and therefore a reindeer must be slaughtered and the blood trailed across the river so that the ground upon which the new yurt will stand will be lucky.

Similar ideas about river flow also guide the construction of new houses and all informants emphatically agreed that a new house built by "locals" (i.e. from that yurt) should never be built downstream. Where houses were rebuilt in situ, the new house was constructed a few "symbolic" meters upstream, and sometimes, slightly inland. Through time, broad patterns emerge so that several yurts on the river are effectively growing upstream as new houses are built at the upstream end of the settlement while the older houses, of e.g. dead parents, are used for storage at the downstream end of the yurt. Also, if newcomers arrive in the yurt community it is considered unlucky if they locate at the top end of the yurt and they generally slot in behind other established households at the lower end of the settlement. Where lakes and old river bends block this pattern of upstream expansion the yurt tends to advance inland instead. Thus, through time, and as the community reproduces itself socially and biologically, so the settlement is reproduced through space and through the creation of durable material culture. In many cases, the social history of the yurt maps out as a series of floor plans that move gradually upstream.

Most houses face outwards to the river, which serves as the main route of summer access. Each household has a set of store-houses, clay ovens and summer kitchens, which are grouped around the hut. This central area of the yurt settlement is a well-trodden grassy area clear of trees but also devoid of refuse. While this inner core can be viewed as a busy workshop into which game, nuts and other raw materials are brought, consumed and transformed then most of the material remains are either passed on again as trade "exports" or are dumped away from the living areas. The river bank with moored up boats remains clean and so most discarded material culture is found in a broad arc of forest around the back of the yurt. Here, in this "clean area" – and away from the paths that radiate out into winter hunting grounds – are discarded animal bones and middens. Old clothes must also be disposed of carefully as they are closely bound up with the welfare of one of a person's many souls. Casual discard on the forest floor tempts the arrival of illness and death and so clothes are hung from trees of the benign upper world species – birch, pine and cedar (Jordan in press c).

When viewed from above, patterns of land-use and material culture deposition at Khanty riverside base-yurts can be comprehended in terms of a series of concentric circles around the settlement's inner living core, which itself is slowly being reproduced and shifted upstream through time. In the first – and forest-edge – circle are latrines, drums of fuel, dog kennels and firewood stacks. Beyond lies the "clean area" of bone and clothing deposition. Further away, and lying somewhere between the deep forest of winter hunting (where one is *"v urmane"*) and the busy places of riverside inhabitation is a broad tract of land, which is still talked of in terms of being "doma", that is, "at home". Here are located the cemetery abodes of dead clan members and the local

Figure 18.3 Sacred ambarchik *housing local protector spirit idols.*

sacred sites of communal veneration. Neither are located directly within the spheres of routine human movement or procurement but lie slightly outside, exerting an aloof presence, rather than being entirely distant. In this sense, the material culture of the immediate yurt area blends into wider processes of practical and symbolic landscape enculturation.

Wider landscape enculturation: holy sites and burial grounds

In order to secure success for the forthcoming hunting season the household must do *pory* gifts or fare (*ugoshenie* in Russian) for the forest spirit, *Wuhnt Lung* (*lesnoi shaitan* in Russian), who despatches game to the hunter. Although *Wuhnt Lung* is present in every part of the forest he is through to reside in a series of *kot mykh* "earth-houses", which, in the flat and boggy terrain, tend to be isolated island groves surrounded by open bog. At the sunny side of these islands white cloths are hung from trees, vodka drunk and elk heads cooked, consumed and the bones/bottles deposited. Each tract of the landscape has its own local *earth-house* and offerings must be left there when entering the area to hunt. Formerly, domestic reindeer were sacrificed at some of the more important earth-houses. As *yurt* communities tend to use the same hunting areas year after year knowledge of particular sites, and the stories associated with them, tend to be passed down within the group:

"Petka's parents were poor and hungry but his father dreamt that they should do *pory* at *byrishkin kot mykh* (grandfathers grandmothers earth house) so then went ahead and did that. Next morning, when they checked, they found a sable in every trap".

The members of the household are also protected throughout the course of the mobile seasonal round by the household idol who "sees and hears all and does not let the illness spirits come close". This anthropomorphic wooden idol is honoured monthly, often at times corresponding to the provisioning of the household with goods. The dolls themselves are fashioned from cedar wood and cut from trees growing on special *earth-house* island groves. Newly married couples travel to the girl's local grove where the male keeper (*khoziain*) of the site cuts the doll from a live tree. The couple make occasional return visits to leave offerings but after the death of the woman the doll is left "*bez khoziana*" (with no keeper) and is returned to foot of the same tree from which it was cut and left there to rot back into the ground.

In addition, each of the *yurt* communities strung out along the river has a local holy site spirit protector. These wooden images are housed in stilted *ambarchiks* or low open-fronted huts in dense areas of forest some distance away from the *yurt*. These places are known as settlements (*yurts*) but are described as being *bozhestvennyi* (i.e. sacred). Here live divine beings, the original residents of land who were powerful warriors, heroes and elders and who lived in the distant past by hunting, fishing and gathering in the same way that the modern Khanty inhabitants do. Around these sites are areas of forest closed to all procurement activity and while the game in these areas is thought to belong to the spirits these zones of exclusion serve as unique sacred nature reserves (Novikov and Mekrushina 1998). In order to request community health, welfare and hunting success these sites are visited at times in the seasonal cycle when the community has aggregated again or is about to disperse. Lengths of white cloth and coins are left at the site along with remains of ritual meals consumed at the site consisting of tea, vodka, elk heads and other fare. Reindeer and other domesticates are occasionally sacrificed and while the sacred sites remain fixed in place the wooden huts and dolls are replaced at intervals (Jordan in press a).

The chief of these local *yurt* protector spirits also resides in a stilted *ambarchik* and is the powerful patron protector of the wider river basin community. This hierarchical cultic tradition is found on other Khanty rivers (Martynova 1995:90) with the main river deity a son or daughter of *Torum* the sky god. For example, on the Bolshoi Iugan River this figure is *Iugan Iki*, the *Iugan Elder* while on the Kazym River it is *Kazym Imi*, the *Kazym Woman* of that Kazym River. On the Malyi Iugan this deity is *Lon Lor Iki*. As one informant explained, "*Lon Lor Iki* is the general and the other local spirits are his officers". Other important deities of this rank include the animal spirit master *Vojwort Iki*, who "lives between the earth and the sky", the fish master *As Iki*, who despatches fish up the rivers and *Kon Iki*. This latter figure rides on a horse and circles the world in an instant checking that all is well by acting as an intermediary between the high god and humans living on the middle earth (see also: Kulemzin 1984). Another first generation descendant of *Torum* is *Pugos Anki*, the "mother of all". Her daughters were sent to live on the Malyi Iugan where they reside on the middle reaches of the river. They are tended by the local *yurt* community and are a focus of worship for Khanty from the local and adjacent river basins. Domestic animal sacrifices take place more frequently at the sacred sites inhabited by these more important deities.

Other important deities reside in key topographic features in the landscape. High ground is rare in this flat and boggy landscape although a series of low hills forms the river-bank on the middle reaches of the river. At the "fourth mountain" resides *Lulgut Iki* who also provides health, welfare and hunting success. No specific social groups have any prescribed relationship with this holy place and there is no designated "keeper". Veneration of this deity formed an important stage in the journey to summer collective fishing lower on the river, when the upper river population would migrate south. Three shots were fired when passing and those with specific requests would consume vodka and leave offerings of white cloths or money on the forested summit of the hill, which affords a rare vantage over the seemingly endless taiga forests stretching in all directions.

In addition to these *settlements of the sacred* Khanty believe that the souls of the dead live on after death in the cemetery – the *settlement of the dead* (Kulemzin 1984: 146). The cemeteries are visited at special times in order to hold special remembrance feasts, a time for communion with dead relatives. If the human dead are made to feel comfortable in the cemetery there is less chance that their unsettled souls will wander back into the community at night. After communal visits the path is closed symbolically with felled saplings and at other times the cemetery is strictly avoided, especially in the course of procurement activity. Each *yurt* community has its own cemetery, often located inland or down stream but never upstream from the base *yurt* for fear that "the diseases of the dead will contaminate the living" (Jordan in press b).

"Animate" material culture in an enculturated landscape

Throughout the landscape the conceptual treatment of material culture is linked to ideas about animate and inanimate objects. The Khanty belive that humans and animals possess two essential life forces located within a material body (Kulemzin 1984; Kulemzin and Lukina 1977, 1992):

The first of these is the *free soul*, – an internal life force or *lil'* – which leaves the human body during dreaming, when it travels to the places seen in the dream. Involuntary departure is also caused by fainting but if the *lil'* soul does not, or cannot return then illness and death result. This ability to depart from the body for short periods means that the *free soul* is particularly susceptible to being kidnapped or stolen. Evil illness causing spirits (either *Kyn Lung* or the spirits he controls) may take the soul to the lower world, or it may be dragged away by souls of dead relatives who feel lonely in the world of the death and cannot settle. Thirdly the *lil'* soul may be displaced by the intrusion of illness causing spirits in the middle world. In contrast to other human persons, the shaman's *free soul* may leave the body and wander into different realms although this remains an inherently risky practice.

The second soul is the *body soul*, which remains with the body, yet can be destroyed when the physical integrity of the body is destroyed. This soul or "life force" is closely linked not only to the physical form of the body but also to the shadow, reflection or impression that the body casts or makes. For this reason, sharp objects should never be stuck into shadows or into foot-prints in the snow for fear that they will cause the owner harm. Old clothes must be discarded with care for they maintain the body's impression, and are hence associated with its life forces.

While the two life forces are to some extent independent they are both inextricably linked to the fate of an individual. Thus, illness and death can result from the loss of *lil'* but also from the destruction of the physical body, which in turn impacts upon or destroys the *body soul*. While the Khanty term *lilenky* describes living or animate beings (humans, animals) having the presence of

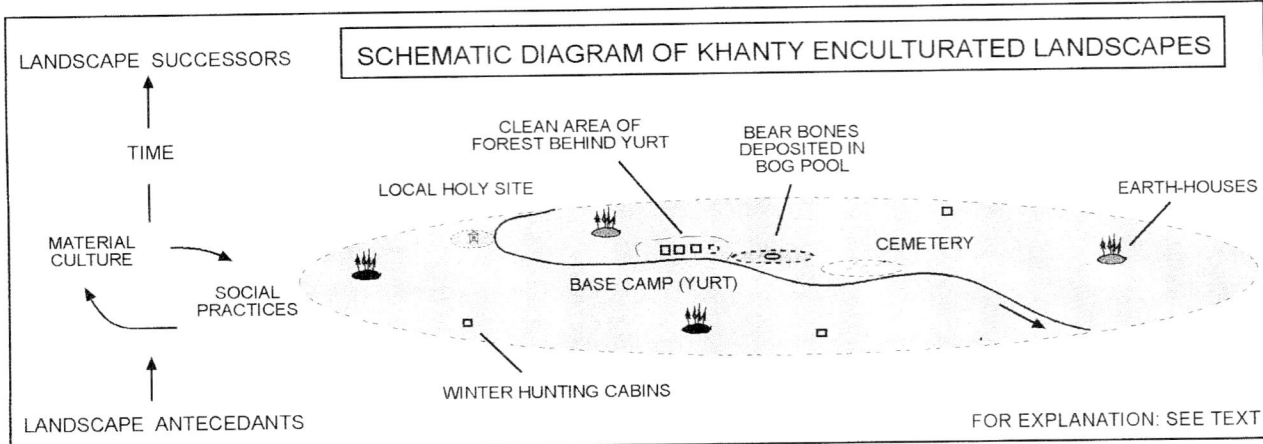

Figure 18.4 Schematic diagram of Khanty enculturated landscapes.

a (*lil'*) soul, the human dead are described as *suram*, that is not fully "dead" but possessing some life forces. In contrast truly inanimate objects are described as being *entelilenky* (Kulemzin 1984; Kulemzin and Lukina 1977, 1992).

Of crucial importance to the investigation of the role of material culture in social practices is the concept that not only humans may be termed *lilenky*. The presence of *lil'* is revealed by the act of breathing, transformation and the ability to move so that trees, animals, flowing water and falling snow are also conceived to be animate or *lilenky*. Where these indicators are absent a tree stump or stone may also become animate if a supernatural being (*lung*) settles within it, for while human souls look like humans, and animal souls like animals, supernatural beings can assume any form. However, material objects may also come to be regarded as being animate if, through their physical form, they resemble other animate beings like humans or animals. Hence, sacred anthropomorphic spirit dolls and other items of material culture are thought animate as are natural feaures of the landscape, which may resemble human or animal features (Kulemzin 1984; Kulemzin and Lukina 1977:154 p.). For example, at a holy site on the Malyi Iugan there is a boulder singled out for special veneration due to its close resemblance to the form of a bear's head.

These concepts are also expressed during the enactment of blood sacrifice of imported domesticates (reindeer, sheep, goats) and the hanging of their skulls and skins from trees. In this way, not only is the animal's *lil'* or free soul released to the appropriate deity but also their body soul, relating to their physical form. In this sense the "whole" animal is offered up, even though meat is consumed by humans at the meal (see e.g. Kulemzin and Lukina 1977:153). In return, it is hoped that the deity will supply game, health or welfare to the hunter or community as part of a wider "economy of souls" (see: e.g. Ingold 1986 for an interesting wider discussion). Skulls and skins (and clothing and cloths) may only be hung from pine, birch or cedar, all of which are upper world tree species.

Discussion

In this paper I have explored how Khanty understandings of the world are expressed through complex social practices and represent as much a "symbolic" as an ecological adaptation to this Siberian taiga landscape. Through a multi-scalar analysis of the relationship between human activity, land-use and material culture I have argued that landscape enculturation is constituted by:

a   cyclical patterns of physical movement between different places and zones of the landscape, and:
b   the creation, use and deposition of material artefacts in relation to – and in turn reproducing – a web of cosmological understandings of the world.

At an abstract conceptual level patterns of landscape enculturation can be argued to have *antecedants* (see Zvelebil, this volume). Individuals are born into the community and are socialised into particular ways of understanding, moving around and engaging with the places and spaces of an inhabited and enculturated landscape. These existing patterns of material and social interaction provide subsequent constraints and opportunities, which are then reproduced, transformed or overthrown with the re-enactment – through time – of subsequent routines of practice. Social interaction occurs in a broader material and spatial context so that the landscape represents an interactive forum within which material culture can perform a central role in these processes of social and cultural reproduction, in turn producing an unfolding sequence of *landscape successors*. This fundamental relationship between social practices, material culture and the temporality of landscape enculturation is explored in relation to a schematic diagram of Khanty land-use (Figure 18.4).

Conclusion

This paper is a contribution to the debate about how we can "people the Mesolithic" and explore complex processes of prehistoric landscape enculturation. I have argued that work towards these goals must proceed from both an archaeological and an ethnographic angle. The key goal is achieve a fundamental re-assessment of the potential richness and complexity of (a) the transformative bond of landscape enculturation and (b) the role of material culture within this process.

At a general level, the suitability of the current ethnographic case-study for this quest is enhanced through its potential use as a source of *direct historical analogy* for adjacent areas of prehistoric Fennoscandia. In basic terms this argument rests on each regions' geographical contiguity, similar landscapes and ecology, but may also extend to strong parallels in routine and ritual strategies, material culture and long-term cultural links (Zvelebil 1997). Studies of this kind enable us to start engaging more fully with the specificity of the past rather than blanketing prehistoric landscapes with universal phenomenological truisms (Zvelebil and Jordan 1999). However, the temptation to "cut and paste" images from the present to the past should be resisted and the archaeological material interpreted on its own terms by using the ethnography as a "point of departure". Moreover, the divergent historical trajectories of hunter fisher gatherer east and west of the Ural Mountains should not be downplayed to facilitate a deceptively simplistic route into lifeways of the north European Mesolithic.

At a more specific level the following heuristic framework can be outlined as a useful summary:
Hunter gatherers *do* enculturate the landscapes they inhabit: sacred sites, residential camps and interlocking routine and ritual zones are the practical expression of these beliefs and practices.

These processes of enculturation are not only mental – they are not merely the pegging of "invisible" mental constructs from natural features – but also involve the veneration and physical transformation of particular locations through the creation, use and deposition of material culture. Many "ritual" signatures of this kind may be intelligible in archaeological landscape contexts, so long as the *potential* for their existence is acknowledged.

The broader or "routine" set of material signatures produced by hunter fisher gatherer practices are not *devoid* of symbolism, that is, somehow guided by functional subsistence concerns alone. Cosmologies are not only reflected in the material culture of sacred sites but in the material expression and reproduction of wider culturally constructed understandings of the world.

Finally then, the conceptual treatment of material culture may be linked to ideas that objects, as a result of their physical form (occurring naturally or as a result of human action), may come to be perceived as being animate, that is, charged with life forces, and consequently demanding special attention. In addition, these *animate* artefacts or features of the landscape (e.g. rock outcrops (see Manker 1963) may have particular symbolic value in the relationships of communication and exchange, which often take place at key sacred sites and link *human:spirit* domains.

Notes

1. Data collection and fieldwork was carried out over 10 months in Siberia between 1996 and 1999. I would also like to thank all the people who made me welcome in their homes on the Iugan River. Fieldwork funding was provided by a Hossein Farmy Scholarship, (University of Sheffield), Emslie Horniman Scholarship Fund (Royal Anthropological Institute) and an Ethnographic Fieldwork Award (Finno – Ugrian Society). I am grateful to Mark Edmonds, Tim Ingold, Bob Layton, Mike Parker Pearson and Marek Zvelebil for references and assistance with these applications. Many thanks to Arkady Michaelev and Valery Shubin for allowing me access to the ethnographic film archives of VIZAN Studios, Tomsk, Russia.

2. The Iugan Khanty are struggling to establish legally protected status for their clan lands in order to protect them from the threat of encroaching mineral extraction. For more information please contact Dr. Andrew Wiget <awiget@NMSU.Edu>, who is an instrumental figure in these campaigns and Sophie Grig (Campaigns Officer) of *Survial International*, London.

References

Barrett, J.C. 1994. *Fragments from Antiquity: An Archaeology of Social Life in Britain c. 2900 – 1200 B.C.* Oxford.
Bradley, R. 2000. *An Archaeology of Natural Places*. London.
Clifford, J. and Marcus, G. (eds) 1986. *Writing Culture: the Poetics and Politics of Culture*. Berkeley.
Forsyth, J. 1992. *A History of the Peoples of Siberia: Russia's North Asian Colony 1581–1990*. Cambridge.
Geertz, C. 1973. *The Interpretation of Culture*. London.
Gosden, C. and Head, L. 1994. Landscape – a usefully ambiguous concept. *Archaeol. Oceania* 29, 113–116.
Hodder, I. 1982. *Symbols in Action: Ethnoarchaeological Studies of Material Culture*. Cambridge.
Hoppál, M. 1996. Introduction. In: Diószegi, V. and Hoppál, M. (eds) *Shamanism in Siberia*, vi–xv. Budapest.
Ingold, T. 1986. *The Appropriation of Nature*. Manchester.
Jordan, P.D. in press a. Ideology, material culture and Khanty ritual landscapes in western Siberia. In: Fewster, K.J. and Zvelebil, M. (eds) *Hunter Gatherer Ethnoarchaeology*. BAR International Series. Oxford.
—— in press b. Cultural landscapes in Colonial Siberia: Khanty Settlements of the Sacred, the Living and the Dead. *Landscapes Journal*. Autumn 2001.
—— in press c. The Materiality of Shamanism as a "World-View": Praxis, Artefacts and Landscape. In: Price, N. (ed.) *The Archaeology of Shamanism,* chapter 10. London.
Konev, A.I. 1998. The state and the peoples of north of western Siberia in XVII-beginning of XX centuries: experience of legal regulation and land relations. In: *Proceedings of the International Conference "Indigenous Peoples. The Oil. The Law"*, 127–128. Khanty-Mansijsk, Russia, March 23–5, 1998.
Kulemzin, V.M. 1984. *Chelovek i priroda v verovaniiakh Khantov*. Tomsk: Izdatel'stvo Tomskogo Universiteta.
Kulemzin, V.M. and Lukina, N.V. 1977. *Vasiugansko-Vakhovskie*

Khanty v kontse XIX - nachale XX vv. Izdatel'stvo Tomskogo Universiteta. Tomsk.

—— 1992. *Znakom'tec': Khanty.* Nauka. Novosibirsk.

Layton, R. 1997. *An Introduction to Theory in Anthropology.* Cambridge.

Lemonnier, P. (ed.) 1993. *Technological Choices: Transformation in Material Culture Since the Neolithic.* London.

Lukina, N.V. 1985. *Formirovanie material'noi kultury Khantov.* Izdatel'stvo Tomskogo Universiteta. Tomsk.

Manker, E. 1963. Seite-Kult und Trommelmagie der lappen. In: (s.n.) Glaubenswelt und Folklore der Sibirischen Völker, 29–45. Budapast.

Martynova, E.P. 1995. Obshchectvennoe ustroistvo v XVII–XIX vv. Chapter 4 in: Lukina, N.V. (ed), *Istoriia i kul'tura Khantov,* 77–121. Tomsk.

Massey-Stewart, J. 1995. The Khanty: Oil, Gas and the Environment. *Siberica* 1 (2), 25–34.

Novikov, V.P. and Merkushina, T.P. 1998. Ecological and economic significance of the "Sacral Rivers" for Khanty and Mansi. In: *Proceedings of the International Conference "Indigenous Peoples. The Oil. The Law",* 114–115. Khanty-Mansijsk, Russia, March 23–5, 1998.

Pentikäinen, J. 1998. *Shamanism and Culture.* (3rd, revised edition). Helsinki.

Shimkin, D.B. 1990. Siberian ethnography: historical sketch and evaluation. *Arctic Anthropology* 27 (1), 36–51.

Silverman, E.K. 1990. Geertz: towards a more "thick" understanding. In: Tilley, C. (ed.) *Reading Material Culture: Structuralism, Hermeneutics and Post-Structuralism,* 121–162. Oxford.

Sokolova, Z.P. 1989. A survey of the Ob-Ugrian shamanism. In: Hoppál, M. and von Sadovszky, O.J. (eds), *Shamanism: Past and Presen.* ISTOR Books 1–2, 155–164. Budapest/Los Angeles.

Thomas, J. 1993. Discourse, Totalization and "The Neolithic". In: Tilley, C. (ed.) *Interpretative Archaeology,* 357–394. Oxford.

Tilley, C. 1991. *Material Culture and Text. The Art of Ambiguity.* London and New York.

—— 1994. *A Phenomenology of Landscape.* London.

Wiget, A. and Balalaeva, O. 1997a. Saving Siberia's Khanty from Oil Development. *Surviving Together* 46 (SPR), 22–25.

—— 1997b. Black snow, oil and the Khanty of West Siberia. *Cultural Survival Quarterly* 20, 13–15.

Wylie, A. 1985. The reaction against analogy. In: Schiffer, M.B. (ed.) *Advances in Archaeological Method and Theory* 8, 63–112.

Zvelebil, M. 1997. Hunter-gatherer ritual landscapes: spatial organisation, social structure and ideology among hunter gatherers of northern Europe and western Siberia. In: van Gijn, A. and Zvelebil, M. (eds) *Ideology and Social Structure of Stone Age Communities in Europe.* Analecta Praehistorica Leidensia 29 (monograph), 33–50. Leiden.

—— 2002. Enculturation of Mesolithic Landscapes (in this volume).

Zvelebil, M. and Jordan, P. 1999. Hunter Fisher gatherer Ritual Landscapes: Questions of Time, Space and Representation. In: Goldhahn, M. (ed.) *Rock Art as Social Representation.* BAR International Series 794. Oxford.

19. Enculturation through fire: beyond hazelnuts and into the forest

Jenny Moore

Exploring social relationships in the Mesolithic is complex archaeologically and human modification of the landscape presents evidence of a more ephemeral nature than other aspects. In Britain, the search for modification of the landscape in the Mesolithic continues. A key aspect of this is the use of fire in removing woodland. The contradictions in this are the so-called 'silent' Mesolithic in Scotland and the unquestionable removal of woodlands in the uplands, to apparent lack of human modification of woodlands in the lowlands. Why is this so difficult to clarify? Leaving aside methodological problems such as pollen preservation in the lowlands and perceived lack of flammability of deciduous forests, this paper starts from first principles – how woodlands and individual trees may have been regarded by people in the Mesolithic. Interaction with the environment, specifically woodlands, may have been a significant societal dynamic, imbued with ritual and symbolism, rather than purely economic. By integrating ecological principles and ethnographic analogy, the additional application of social theory to palaeoecological data enhances cognition of prehistoric anthropogenic manipulation of the forested environment through the use of fire. By taking the Mesolithic back into forest, the symbolism of trees and their removal may say more about changing social structure than, for example, pots and domesticated crops say about Neolithic society.

Introduction

In 1984 (11) Richard Bradley wrote that '... successful farmers have social relations with one another, while hunter-gatherers have ecological relations with hazelnuts'. This statement neatly encapsulates the view that social relationships and societal construction were perceived as not commencing until the Neolithic, a view which is clearly unrepresentative of the Mesolithic as we understand it now, although the persistence of this idea continues to permeate literature on the subject. There is still the underlying idea that hunter-gatherers, untrammeled by the rigours of farming and a need to control land, wandered through the landscape primarily gathering, but occasionally killing a large mammal and having a feast. Beyond that, certainly in Britain, there is little said about social complexity or lives imbued with symbolism.

Spikins (1999:53) points out that studies of the Mesolithic have been dominated by an ecological approach, compared with more sociological or ideological orientation of studies of later periods. The definition of subsistence resources, although fraught with difficulty, has overshadowed more theoretical interpretations, and has largely been accepted uncritically. Notwithstanding, ecological relationships may have been a key factor in the development of social relationships and societal construction in the Mesolithic. Richard Bradley's quote should perhaps be modified: hunter-gatherers may not have had ecological relations with hazelnuts, but spiritual relationships with trees. Clearly, finding hard archaeological evidence of this is problematic. But then archaeologists have produced hypotheses of social behaviour and gender relationships, the evidence for which is often intangible, so why not trees, having meaning beyond the economic, in the Mesolithic?

The environment

How people related to their environment in the past is problematic and no more than in endeavouring to understand the symbolism of an otherwise natural feature (cf. Bradley 2000). We need to know what the wooded environment in the British Mesolithic was like and whether there was anything in the nature of these woodlands for them to have a symbolic and ideological significance. Making this argument even more tenuous is the fact that this natural feature no longer exists in a form that would have been recognisable in the Mesolithic. There are, however, other approaches.

There is a persisting myth relating to post glacial woodlands in Britain that by around 6500 BP Britain and Ireland had a solid cover of woodland, except for extreme environments (Rackham 1986). It is a common misconception despite the work of numerous palaeoecologists who have been saying for years that this is not how it was. Woodlands did not form a solid cover across the country. There were edges, patches and openings created through natural and anthropogenic action which opened up the forest to regeneration. It is often overlooked that if there were such a forest, it would be singularly unhealthy. Hypotheses as to the extent of tree cover are based on pollen diagrams and many palynologists are reluctant to admit that pollen can merely tell us that there were trees somewhere. Pollen can be transported great distances from source, it cannot tell us how dense, how tall, how mature or how healthy a forest was and it certainly cannot tell us if a forest was subject to human manipulation. In addition, there are no modern ecosystem parallels with which to compare, making exact interpretations as to species communities and interactions unattainable.

Moving away from the assumption that Britain and Ireland were covered by almost continuous woodland until the Neolithic, once climatic conditions permitted, post glaciation, tree species spread across Britain with the rapidity of shopping malls in the late twentieth century. Between 10,000 and 8000 yr BP, tree species chaotically colonised suitable vacant land forming localised associations of convenience between species which now have no contemporary analog (Roberts 1989). After the pioneer woods of willow, birch and pine, the first deciduous trees were hazel and elm, both of which spread in less than 500 years. Later arrivals were oak, lime, alder, ash, beech, hornbeam and poplar (Brown, pers.com.). Within this there is much variability both in relation to environments and species. There is not the inexorable successive progression so often implied. The picture is of a rapidly expanding wooded environment, but which was far more open and park-like than has been recognised previously. There are several ecological reasons to back up this argument, but perhaps the most cogent is simply that few native trees can grow in the shade of other trees.

So that was the post glacial forest, or rather it was more a series of woodland stands, varying in levels of closed and openness. This was an exciting time for trees, they were colonising like mad, dynamically utilising every scrap of land they could, they were vital, powerful and self-sustaining. Spikins (1999:83) comments that although the spread of trees in Britain took millennia, within a human lifetime changes in the woodland landscape would have been very noticeable. Perhaps trees and woodlands appeared to have magical properties in their ability to spring up and survive, apparently from nowhere.

Human/forest interaction in the Mesolithic

Human occupation of forests in the Mesolithic is assumed rather than proven (Simmons 1993), but using ethnographic analogy, the North American forests were occupied prior to pre-European contact and manipulated for economic purposes (Cronon 1983). Simmons (1975), Mellars (1976), Zvelebil (1994) and myself (Moore 1996) have proposed how fire may have been used in manipulating forest faunal and floral resources in the Mesolithic. From an environmental point of view there are contrasting evaluations of Mesolithic environmental manipulation through the use of fire, although the clearest examples come from uplands. Smith (1970) thought that peaks in hazel pollen or a rise in alder, associated with flints and charcoal suggested human activity had brought about vegetation change. Conversely, Bennett *et al.* (1990) and Edwards (1990) found that hazel type pollen peaks did not correspond to charcoal peaks, and could find no evidence for human activity associated with vegetation change.

My argument (Moore 1996, 1997, 2001) has always been that it was not a case of humans firing vast tracts of forest, but the expansion of naturally created openings such as the edges of streams and similar kinds of patchy environments that were being manipulated by the use of fire. The acknowledged end result of this activity is an increase in floral and faunal resources perhaps remaining productive for 10–15 years (Bell and Walker 1991). For example, hazel responds to firing by producing foliage at browse level which is higher in protein, as well as nutritious nuts (Simmons 1993). Additional but equally important factors may be the opening up of the landscape to improve access, and indeed the marking of the landscape (Brown 2000). Subsequently, the composition of plant communities may have been determined by the large herbivores that inhabited the landscape (Whelan 1995).

The environmental evidence, however, is not clear on human manipulation of the forested environment in the Mesolithic, either through the use of fire or other means. However, evidence of woodland management in the Mesolithic has been inferred from wooden fishing structures along the coasts of Denmark (Pedersen 1995). Notwithstanding this, there is enough evidence now to build a presumption of human manipulation of the forest through the use of fire – unless you are of the school of thought that rejects all such evidence unless it is of the nature of the struck flint at the base of a burnt tree. Taking these difficulties into account, how may we build a picture of the relationship that people had with trees, beyond the economic, and how did this relationship influence the lives and beliefs of those people?

Myths and symbolism

Frazer (1994:109) in *The Golden Bough* remarks that nothing could be more natural than the worship of trees. In many cultures, trees are regarded as sacred and by some even feared. It is acknowledged, however, that there has been relatively little research into the spiritual significance of trees (Rival 1998) and tree lore has a more substantive history in Ireland and northern Europe than in mainland Britain. Even so, there has been little consideration of the symbolism of trees in archaeology, and certainly none in relation to the Mesolithic.

Anthropologists have concerned themselves with the ways in which natural processes are conceptualised, the ways the natural world is classified and how human societies interact with their natural environments and use natural resources, but very little anthropological writing *per se* concerns trees (Rival 1998). Anthropologically and archaeologically, trees are seen as representing little more than a background to activity. Yet, is it so unrealistic to suggest that certain places could have acquired their symbolic value through the trees associated with them? Bradley (2000:22) reviews just such a proposition through the texts of Pausanias. Spiritual significance was attached to mountains, caves and trees many of the latter being found in groves. Bradley notes (2000:22) that woods, groves and trees are components of the landscape which cannot be identified today. It is clear, however, that Pausanias does not give trees a single meaning or regards them similarly wherever he finds them. He distinguishes a tree or stands of trees as being sacred or non-sacred depending on the social environment in which they grow, rather than on physical attributes such as species or number (Birge 1994:245). Symbolic trees and groves have a history and identity of their own, of greater import than the purely practical in terms of their place as signifiers in the landscape.

In many cultures, the world is animate and trees and plants are no exception. Sacrifices and specific ceremonies had to be undertaken before trees could be cut down and often fallen timber would be used in preference to cutting a tree down, a selection process that was more than simply economy of effort. In some cultures, damaging a tree has ferocious penalties, often equating with a life for a life (Frazer 1994). As well as trees being animate, they can be male or female, and they can be ancestral. They can have spirits that have to be tempted out of the tree into an alternative residence when, for example, an area of forest is to be cleared. There can, however, be a change in ideology where the tree is no longer the embodiment of the tree spirit, but simply its home which it is able to leave whenever it wishes. Instead of each tree being a living and conscious being, each is now merely an inert lifeless mass that the tree spirit inhabits, probably in a set of defined circumstances. As the spirit can now move freely from tree to tree it ceases to be a tree soul and becomes a forest god. As soon as the tree spirit is disengaged from the individual tree, its abstract spiritual form begins to assume the shape of a human being (Frazer 1994).

Frazer's exhaustive collection of customs relating to trees should not be dismissed as merely anecdotal. Strathern (1990) noted that such recurrences of customs and beliefs must be accounted for if we are to understand the social determination of myths and symbols and the comparability of beliefs. Trees often provide some of the most visible and potent symbols of social process and collective identity (Rival 1998). There is a recurrence in the symbolic correspondence between trees and human bodies, down to the level of tree parts and body parts, that is often quite explicit. Anthropomorphic representation of the tree spirit is often made simultaneously with the vegetable form, the human representation being a doll or puppet. The situation is such that there can be no doubt that the spirit of the tree is being represented in human form (Frazer 1994). Some Native Americans see themselves as natural extensions of the forest and the modifications to the forest made by their forebears are seen as naturalised. There are many examples of trees and wood linked to life crisis rituals and as Rival (1998) points out, these continue through to the present day with cemeteries and graves replaced with 'peace forests'. Trees are the true symbols of life and eternity.

Symbolism of trees
Human body
Living and eternal – symbolic of life
Regenerative
Ancestral

We seem to have lost sight of how the naturalised world is intricately combined with human culture and activity. This is particularly so in the case of trees and woodlands that are invariably seen as a background to human activity, their value being interpreted as purely economic. Trees and woodlands should not be viewed as merely part of the landscape, but may well have been a defining factor in ritualising the landscape. Human interaction with trees was imbued with ritual and symbolism.

Trees, woodlands and the Mesolithic

It would seem appropriate here to sum up the current position with a metaphor – am I barking up the wrong tree? I don't think so. In considering human interaction with the environment, we are swayed by the ideology of the pristine forest, despite environmentalists recording human manipulation of ecosystems from time immemorial. To quote Cronon (1995:37) 'The myth of Eden describes a perfect landscape, a place so benign and beautiful and good that the imperative to preserve or restore it could be questioned only by those who ally themselves with evil.' A powerful statement, and in this context implies that humans have always interacted with the wooded environment. We have been swayed by our own ideal of a symbolic pristine environment, untarnished by human interference. This, to my mind, is a factor in our inability to clearly identify a human relationship and interaction with the forested environment in the Mesolithic.

It is equally important not to separate the economic from the cultural, especially in relation to an understanding of human interaction with woodlands in the Mesolithic, but it is clear that this has occurred. For example, discussions regarding the firing of forests have concentrated on the perceived non flammability of mature deciduous woodlands in Britain, rather than on the symbolism of such firing, whether natural or anthropogenic. Mellars (1976) and Zvelebil (1994) explored the economic rationale and we now have a clearer picture of how human firing may have taken place (Moore 1996; 1997, 2001) in environments not perceived as flammable, but the crucial question is – what may this have meant?

For hardened empiricists, the evidence is tentative to say the least. Fortunately, a highly-respected archaeologist, Richard Bradley, recently published *An Archaeology of Natural Places* (2000) in which he argues for natural places to have an archaeology, because they acquired significance in the minds of people in the past. One way of recognising the importance of these locations is through the evidence of human activity remaining there (Bradley 2000:35). Bradley (2000:6) refers to the work of Manker (1957) who explored Saami ideology. In addition to stone images, there were a number of carved wooden idols but often the carving respected the original form of the wood. It was difficult to assess how common these were, as so few survived, but interpretation was further complicated by the fact that living trees also seem to have been worshipped and some may have been carved. Here we have the heart of the problem. In relation to the symbolism of trees, the evidence will not survive in the archaeological record, but that does not mean it should be disregarded.

Tilley (1994) proposed that during the Mesolithic the significance of place was understood in terms of its setting in the landscape. In the Neolithic this was reversed – the landscape was now understood in terms of its relationship to the setting of the monuments. There was a need to represent in physical form a permanency, a representation of ancestral connections with the landscape. Almost in a throwaway line, he says that in areas where there are no monuments, there is little or no evidence of Mesolithic activity either. Edmonds (1999:448) expands on this, suggesting lightning fires may have been seen as 'the hand of the ancestors' and areas cleared in this way were marked for settlement. Bradley (2000) considers that these monuments created their own significant natural places and were politically as much as ideationally situated in the landscape.

What is this telling us? The environmental evidence for woodlands associated with monuments is equivocal. It is often of the standard of 'there were some trees here somewhere', or even the more specific 'shady setting within localised clearance' (Evans *et al.* 1999:247). Brown (2000) argues that clearings had symbolic significance and on Dartmoor early Neolithic tombs and later monuments were constructed in clearings surrounded by a predominantly wooded landscape. Generally, the interpretation of the data is that the monument was constructed in an open landscape with some patches of woodland. My hypothesis is that some monuments were constructed in, or closely associated with, sacred groves of woodland, the trees of the ancestors and that that 'sacredness' had come about from the beliefs of Mesolithic people. In fact, Brown's (2000) arguments are not contradictory to this theory, far from it. Such early Neolithic monuments were situated where there *had* been sacred trees or woodlands.

Not every monument would have this association, but some may well have 'monumental' status for this reason. The ritual landscape in which Stonehenge is situated has underlying it the three massive pine timber posts which are dated to the eight millennium BC and predate the construction of Stonehenge by several thousand years (Richards 1991; Cleal *et al.* 1995). Darvill (1996) commented that the tree that stood beside these posts, evidenced by a treehole, was of more interest than the posts themselves, but had been largely ignored by the archaeologists. Other monuments where Mesolithic activity is evident below a later monument are Gwernvale, Powys (Britnell 1984), Hazleton North (Saville 1990), Kilham, Yorkshire (Manby 1976), West Cotton (Windell *et al.* 1990). Darvill (forthcoming) makes the point that it is not simply the case of a Mesolithic site followed by a Neolithic site but continuity in addressing the landscape in a particular way.

With monuments constructed of wood (e.g. Woodhenge in Wiltshire) the monument is seen as having a ritual focus, but the trees used to construct that monument are not. They are not really given any ritual credence in themselves and are viewed in terms of accessibility in that particular landscape. For this reason, the focus on the trees is economic and practical, rather than that the trees themselves were the ritual focus. Again referring to the work of Pausanias, Bradley (2000: 35) notes that it is perhaps just as important to appreciate the special character of the place from where the wood was obtained. The trees used to construct the monument may therefore be a signifying factor in the ritualisation of the monument.

What if it could now be suggested that humans, far from being overwhelmed by the progression of trees, post glaciation, were material in creating and managing the forest, not just for economic purposes but for symbolic and ideological reasons? Is it possible to plot the change in a belief system in understanding how woodlands were used?

Frazer (1994) outlines the development of a belief system where the tree is no longer the embodiment of a tree spirit, but merely an inert lifeless mass which the tree spirit inhabits. Once disengaged in this way the tree spirit, being able to move from tree to tree and becomes a forest god. It is no longer necessary to see the tree as the embodiment of a spiritual entity and as long as there is some forest for the forest god to reside in, tracts of woodland can be removed, say for agricultural purposes, with impunity. A convenient ideological change, or sanction for early farmers. Spikins (1999) refers to marked changes in lithic industries at the Early to Late Mesolithic transition, and that the establishment of oak is associated with the appearance of Late Mesolithic industries in northern Britain. She notes (1999:118) '...the spread of different technologies with environmental changes may be explained by other mechanisms, such as common adaptations to similar environments or through the spread of ideas...'. Indeed, and possibly those ideas were belief systems relating to trees and the forest.

I would argue that what we actually see is something far more significant than the simplistic removal of forests, the clearing of land for agriculture. It was a shift from interaction with nature to domination of nature, implicit in which is a shift in cultural and ideological tenets, paving the way for Neolithic belief systems represented by domination of the landscape through monumental construction. Human interaction with the environment and evidence of subtle shifts in such interaction may well mean far more than the search for an economic outcome, it has the potential to be interpreted as representative of ideological and social change as much as pots and monument construction.

Conclusion

One wonders why Bradley's statement is so heavily (mis)quoted when the context of the sentence is far more significant in relation to how we consider people in the Mesolithic. He points out that the Mesolithic is treated only as an economic phenomenon. The Mesolithic population loses its only role when its subsistence pattern is changed and thereafter it exists only as an 'influence' on Neolithic technology. The character of native populations is underestimated perhaps because burials and monuments are so often the only measures of social complexity.

At the heart of this may lie observations made by Spikins (1999) and Brown (2000). In relation to Mesolithic studies the dominance of an ecological economy approach, over the sociological or ideological is commented on by Spikins (1999) and Brown (2000) notes that palaeoenvironmentalists tend to interpret their data in subsistence terms – any 'ritual' or 'symbolic' interpretation of data is suspect. Pollen data which does not support a subsistence function is dismissed. On the other hand, landscape theoreticians have a tendency to ignore environmental data altogether, when hypothesising on 'visibility' and 'lines of site'. The polarity of the two camps has been commented on recently (Chapman and Gearey 2000) despite earlier analyses showing the benefits of marrying of hard ecological data with a theoretical framework (McGlade 1995; Brown 1997, 2000). For a full understanding of human interaction with the environment, there needs to be a firm integration of the two methodologies to interpret data and until there is such integration, potentially we miss the full picture.

We are influenced by the mindset 'Mesolithic people did not build monuments'. We create our own boundaries in examining archaeological remains and we need to become more aware of how those boundaries affect our interpretations. Neolithic ritual monuments with earlier Mesolithic associations should be interpreted as having obtained their ritual significance from a Mesolithic belief system. Can we plot a change in ideology from environmental data – where the tree spirit becomes the forest god and trees can be removed with impunity? Finally, in firing areas of woodland in the Mesolithic can this simply have been for economic reasons, or can we now imply a more symbolic context?

Trees are too often thought of as simply a 'backdrop' to the landscape, yet colonisation of trees post glaciation was remarkable – changes would have been observable within a generation (Spikins 2000). Surely this indicates that we should be thinking of trees as having more significance to Mesolithic people, beyond being an economic source. Their symbolic relationship with these vigorous life forms may have been material in social and ritual construction of society in the Mesolithic.

Acknowledgements

This paper has benefitted from refinements suggested by Tony Brown and Alex Gibson.

References

Bennett, K.D., Fossitt, J.A., Sharp, M.J. and Switsur, V.R. 1990. Holocene vegetation and environmental history at Loch Lang, South Uist, Western Isles, Scotland. *New Phytologist* 114, 281–298.

Bevan, L. and Moore, J. (eds) in press. *Peopling the Mesolithic in a northern environment.* BAR. Oxford.

Bradley, R. 1984. *The social foundations of prehistoric Britain.* Essex.

—— 2000. *An archaeology of Natural Places.* London.

Britnell, W.J. 1984. The Gwernvale long cairn, Crickhowell, Brecknock. In: Britnell, W.J. and Savory, H.N. (eds) *Gwernvale and Penywyrlod: two Neolithic long cairns in the Black Mountains of Brecknock.* Cambrian Archaeological Monograph 2, 43–154. Cardiff.

Brown, A.G. 1997. Clearances and clearings: deforestation in Mesolithic/Neolithic Britain. *Oxford Journal of Archaeology* 16, 133–146.

—— 2000. Floodplain vegetation history: clearings as potential ritual spaces? In: Fairburn, A.S. (ed.) *Neolithic plants in Britain and beyond,* 49–62. Neolithic Studies Group Seminar papers 5. Oxford.

Chapman, H.P. and Gearey, B.R. 2000. Palaeoecology and the perception of the prehistoric landscapes: some comments on visual approaches to phenomenology. *Antiquity* 74, 316–19.

Cleal, R., Walker, K.E. and Montague, R. 1995. *Stonehenge and its landscape. Twentieth-century excavations.* English Heritage Archaeological Report 10. London.

Cronon, W. 1983. *Changes in the Land. Indians, colonists, and the ecology of New England.* New York.

Darvill, T. 1996. *Billown Neolithic Landscape Project, Isle of Man, 1995.* Bournemouth University School of Conservation Sciences Research Report 1, Bournemouth and Douglas.

—— in press. Analytical scale, populations, and the Mesolithic-Neolithic transition in the far north west of Europe. In: Bevan, L. and Moore, J. (eds) *Peopling the Mesolithic in a northern environment.* BAR. Oxford.

Edmonds, M. 1999. Inhabiting Neolithic landscapes. In: Edwards,

K.J. and Sadler, J.P. (eds) Holocene environments of prehistoric Britain. *Journal of Quaternary Science* 7, 485–492.

Edwards, K.J. 1990. Fire and the Scottish Mesolithic: evidence from microscopic charcoal. In: Vermeersch, P.M. and van Peer, P. (eds) *Contributions to the Mesolithic in Europe*, 71–79. Leuven.

Evans, C., Pollard, J. and Knight, M. 1999. Life in woods: tree-throws, 'settlement' and forest cognition. *Oxford Journal of Archaeology* 18, 241–254.

Fairburn, A.S. 2000. *Neolithic plants in Britain and beyond*. Neolithic Studies Group Seminar papers 5. Oxford.

Frazer, J. 1994. *The Golden Bough*, abridged version. London.

Manby, T.G. 1976. Excavation of the Kilham long barrow, East Riding of Yorkshire. *Proceedings of the Prehistoric Society* 42, 111–159.

Mellars, P. 1976. Fire ecology, animal populations and man: a study of some ecological relationships in prehistory. *Proceedings of the Prehistoric Society* 42, 15–45.

Moore, J.M. 1996. Damp squib: how to fire a major deciduous forest in an inclement climate. In: Pollard, T. and Morrison, A. (eds) *The Early Prehistory of Scotland*, 62–73. Edinburgh.

—— 1997. The infernal cycle of fire ecology. In: Topping, P. (ed.) *Neolithic landscapes*, 33–40. Oxford.

—— 2001. Can't see the wood for the trees. Interpreting woodland fire history from microscopic charcoal. In: Albarella, U. (ed.) *Environmental archaeology: theory and purpose*, 211–228. The Netherlands.

Pedersen, L. 1995. 7000 years of fishing: stationary fishing structures in the Mesolithic and afterwards. In: Fischer, A. (ed.) *Man and sea in the Mesolithic. Preceedings of the International Symposium, Kalundborg, Denmark 1993*, 75–83. Oxbow Monograph 53.

Rackham, O. 1986. *The History of the Countryside*. London.

Richards, J. 1991. *Stonehenge*. Batsford/English Heritage. London.

Rival, L. (ed.) 1998. *The social life of trees*. Oxford.

Saville, A. 1990. *Hazleton North. The excavation of a Neolithic long cairn of the Cotswold-Severn group* (Historic Buildings and Monuments Commission for England Archaeological Report 13), English Heritage. London.

Simmons, I.G. 1975. Towards an ecology of Mesolithic man in the uplands of Great Britain. *Journal of Archaeological Science* 2, 1–15.

Smith, A.G. 1970. The influence of Mesolithic and Neolithic man on British vegetation. In: Walker, D. and West, R.G. (eds) *Studies in the vegetation history of the British Isles*, 81–96. London.

Spikins, P. 1999. *Mesolithic Northern England. Environment, population and settlement*. BAR British Series 283, Oxford.

Strathern, M. 1990. Out of context: the persuasive fictions of anthropology. In: Mangarano, M. (ed.) *Modernist anthropology. From fieldwork to text*, 78–89. Princeton, NJ.

Tilley, C. 1994. *A phenomenology of landscape*. Oxford.

Whelan, R.J. 1995. *The ecology of fire*. Cambridge.

Zvelebil, M. 1994. Plant use in the Mesolithic and its role in the transition to farming. *Proceedings of the Prehistoric Society* 60, 35–74.

20. *Sorbus aucuparia* or extremely red Rowan-berries? Some naïve reflections on archaeology, paleo-ecology and the non-scientific dimensions of a scientific landscape

Björn Nilsson

The following paper discusses some personal epistemological reflections on the interface between a non-functionalistic archaeology and paleo-ecology. With examples from a recently started project some theoretical and methodological wishes are expressed – from an archaeologist's point of view. As a conclusion, and in order to gain a specific and strictly human-related knowledge of the archaeological places and landscapes, a naïve approach is proposed.

Some days before the MESO 2000 conference I took a walk in the windswept Oak forest on a small island off the coast of Blekinge, south-eastern Sweden. I had a retired fisherman by my side. The fisherman, who has lived his entire life on this small island, and on the seas around it, where looking at the extremely red rowanberries on a small tree:

> "That colour makes me happy, and it makes me respect the ending of summer. If there was Rowanberries during the Stone Age, I bet they liked them as much as I do... What do you say, expert"

He was laughing, knowing the impossibilies of answering that question. Silence. And again I was reminded of the limited scope of archaeology, and how hard it is to grasp the real essential of culture.

The study of the non-agrarian cultural landscape

The enculturated hunter-gatherer landscape truly is a field of research that is in an interesting phase. Having left most of the functionalist approaches behind, hopefully – a new scope emerges. The non-functionalist archaeology tries to elucidate a specific human-related landscape, in contrast to a generalised and pure scientific landscape. The process of peopling the hunter-gather landscape is in a phase of finding its own data and words. Here we encounter an epistemological problem. Rhetorically we could call it the *non-Neolithic syndrome*. The effect of this is that the Mesolithic period per definition is concerned a *non-Neolithic* period. Some examples:

In Europe the traditional functionalist concept of a cultural landscape is the "opened" landscape. Even though traditional environmental archaeologists acknowledge prehistoric hunter-gatherers as responsible for such an impact, it's often understood as a mere function of economy and adaptation, as a natural change of conditions (Evans 1978:11 p). The "real" opened cultural landscape is still a pure Neolithic process. The indicators of the human influence are based on the agrarian anthropocores and apofyths, besides the proxy-data of agrarian economy itself. Thus the hunter-gatherer prehistory does not possess any own cultural landscape. This is one side of the problem. Another is connected to the landscape archaeology of the 90s, which have had great impact on non-functionalistic archaeology. The perspective is quite focused on the Neolithic stone monuments – especially those of Britain (cf. Bradley 1993, 1998; Tilley 1994, 1996). This has resulted in a wish and search for Neolithic substitutes. Prominent features of the landscape, e.g. rock-outcrops, large mountains, springs, plays the role of the megaliths (Bradley 2000).

It is obvious that the "epistemological transition" from Neolithic to Mesolithic thinking has been disadvantageous when it comes to the study of human landscapes. In this paper I would like to discuss the possibilities of constructing a non-monumental landscape archaeology of the Mesolithic. A landscape study can't rely only on remarkable, eternal landscape features, visible even today. We can presume that the totality of vegetation (and fauna) *itself* might be one of the most important parts of the culturally interpreted landscape.

The flora is an annually pulsing setting of human-natural interaction. It is an always present – and totally essential – cover of the world. In times of change, which undoubtedly the Holocene Stone Age can be understood as, it is a fast responding and changing entity. In landscape archaeology – and as a complement to manifest landscape features – I wish that the non-eternal scenery of nature could be permitted to play its real prominent role, especially the vegetation. The question is how archaeologists and paleo-ecologists – both theoretically and methodologically – should deal with this. The question arises: how can we discern early, and presumably more subtle, encultured nature when it, so to speak, hides in the woods?

I am aware of that this is a somewhat utopian wish. Nevertheless, in the following I will try to outline the outline of an archaeological and paleo-ecological research strategy beyond such a non-monumental landscape archaeology. The discussion, even though it primarily will stay rough and theoretical, is based on the examination of Mesolithic and Neolithic hunter-gatherer economies in the upland of Småland, an area in south-eastern Sweden. The sites are located in an area rich in mixed spruce and deciduous forests, lakes and fens. Since the agriculture has been of lesser importance – at least during the period of a motorised farming – a fossil prehistoric landscape is well preserved. The landscape topography and hydrology is suitable for different kinds of paleo-ecological analyses.

The study I will come back to is the result of a personal collaboration between Lund University (archaeology) and Växjö University (forest ecology and vegetational history), Sweden. The project is explicitly small-scale and is based upon collegial interests rather than funding and administrative connection. In much it is a spin off effect of different research projects that involves the same geographical region. The main concern is to study the very-near surroundings of prehistoric sites, spanning from the Mesolithic to the Bronze Age. Since the paleo-ecological and archaeological fieldwork gradually is conducted by master-students in forest biology – paleo-botany and paleo-entomology – the project will continue over a long time, and will hopefully grow over time. The students are supervised by Prof. Marie-José Gaillard Lemdahl and Dr Geoffrey Lemdahl, inst. of Bio-Sciences, Växjö University. Their knowledge and rather dynamic and non-linear ecological approach, relies upon a temporarily and spatially high-resoluted study of forest-structures. Here the general landscape history plays a sub-ordinate role. The main unit is the place, the mosaics of landscape, and the *specific* spatial histories. Hopefully, this project can give us an opportunity to once again align archaeological theoretical questions with paleo-ecological methodology, now with a non-functionalistic understanding rather than functionalistic.

The following text is based on some personal thoughts emanating from several discussions with my paleo-ecological and archaeological colleagues at the universities of Växjö and Lund, especially during excursions. I want to stress that possible errors and misconceptions are my own. I would like to continue with three different sets:

– Theory
– Methods
– Naïveté

Theory

With the risk of being either too obvious or pseudo-philosophical – which is easy – I would like to declare my standpoint when it comes to human ecology. Human ecology is culture rather than nature. Cultural systems are based upon value-dependant, symbolic structures. The human ecosystems are symbolic rather than energetic. Human Ecology is based upon societal and personal communication and is thus recursive. How we use the world, is a matter of how we look upon the world. How we look upon the world, is a matter of how we use the world.

Long-term historical human ecology can be studied as recursive and ever-changing mediation between the natural and the social. As a scientific discipline, human ecology includes the study of the societal, personal, natural and super-natural worlds. Thus, human ecology is a study of how people connect to, and how they communicate and use the totality of their surroundings. In this broad sense human ecology turns into an over-all perspective rather than a clear defined discipline. And that is how I want to see it. It is a point of departure and a monistic perspective on culture and nature which puts the Cartesian dialectics in question.

So, it is evident that human ecology is a matter of world-views and world-use. To understand and describe this we have to understand the setting in which people interact. We have to discover the surroundings of human day-to-day, week-to-week and year-to-year activities. Here Anthony Giddens' discussion on spatial conception and especially his notion *locale* might be of use (Giddens 1986:115 p.). The *locale* refers to the setting of human-environmental action, wherein not only physical geographical aspects are considered, but also social and mental meanings. A *locale* describes a person's, or a group's, relation to a certain spatial-temporal domain, and as an analytic instrument the concept could be coupled to a spatial human-ecological project. This is an important perspective. And it requires methods of tracing and describing the landscape properly, and on a specific often small-scale human level. And this is important: all too often we use a far too general level of description which in fact only exists in the landscape of science. We focus on spatial properties and temporal changes that in some cases might have been beyond reach for personal, social or cultural sensation. Without evoking the trauma of post-modern relativism, one could conclude: the paleo-ecological world of the past is far more archaeological than prehistorical.

However, the synergetic effects of new perspectives in both paleo-ecology (a non-linear, dynamic and structural approach) and archaeology (a non-functional and cultural understanding of the human ecosystem) might let us re-approach the prehistoric, enculturated landscape (cf. Lagerås 2000a; 2000b).

Methods

Followingly, I will present an utopian example of how I would like to work. This is an archaeologist's highly generalised view of the paleo-ecological research situation.

There is an interesting phenomenon that has to be reflected upon. It seems like non-agrarian cultural landscapes are extremely large, they are covering vast areas. In praxis this means that the hunter-gatherer does a lot of things in a lot of places. Though, the archaeological landscape is built upon places rather than areas. We are good to trace places of activities, but not the "passive" spaces in between. It is not much we can do for changing this. But what we can do is to examine different places – even the presumably not used – and compare their paleo-ecological and archaeological record. In the long-term archaeology we could use a place-biographical approach, which expects that not one single archaeological place will reveal the same paleo-ecological history. All due to the recursive character of ecology itself, which creates unique and unpredictable, irreversible environmental patterns. As times goes by every place gets a history and properties of their own.

Our point of departure is the archaeological place. We concentrate on three different kinds of places, which according to the archaeological situation have had quite different life histories.

The archaeological place of recurrent use
The archaeological place of occasional use
The archaeological place of no-use

The sites are located within the same natural and geographical area, which is rich in Mesolithic and Neolithic settlements. There are no general traces of an agrarian economy until the end of the Neolithic, even though archaeology proofs early Neolithic settlement. Sedimentological fieldwork hasn't been carried out on location I and II. Location III is thoroughly investigated by the department of quaternary geology, Lund University (Sjögren 1999).

In order to capture a high-resoluted picture of the structure and the dynamics of the very-near prehistoric environment, some conditions has to be fulfilled. We have selected (Place I, II) archaeological places that lie in the direct vicinity of the paleo-ecological sample sites. The cores are to be taken in extremely small lakes, fens or creek-beds. The data will primarily consist of sub-fossils (such as twigs, bark and seeds), insects and pollen, which are supposed to reflect the microenvironment. In order to understand the formation of the historic data, the present-day landscape is examined. Contemporary flora, fauna and pollen-rain are evaluated (personal message of Prof. Gaillard-Lemdahl).

The next methodological step is to compare the different life histories and the vegetation history of the different examined sites. The intention is to concentrate on both the differences and the similarities. Hopefully and after sequential research we might be able to sort out a *cultural* floristic *taxa* of the archaeological places. This could be a starting point for a vegetational cultural landscape archaeology. Successively, we might get a glimpse of how the structure of different prehistorically settings has been created over time, and how man and nature recursively shapes places in a landscape. And hopefully, we might get an ethnobotanical perspective on the human ecology of landscapes and places.

Naïveté

There is a tendency not to ask the "real" questions of archaeology – especially when we work together with natural historians. It is an urgent issue since the questioning itself will reproduce certain methodology, which in inference will cause epistemological effects. I would like to propose a *naïve* approach. Seriously, I would like to be more childish (i.e. basic thoughtful) in my scientific work, and I would like to see more child-to-motherish questions in archaeology.

When did spring arrive? Were the ices thick or thin in the winter, and what colour did the autumn have? How did it smell by the lake, which trees surrounded the dwelling?

I might be childish. I am aware of the gigantic problems that encompass such a farfetched goal, described above. It might be impossible to reconstruct the subtle cultural landscape of hunter-gatherers who died thousands of years ago. But I am also aware of that we – especially in Mesolithic archaeology – need a renewed discussion when it comes to landscape issues. We need these "optimistic" projects to cope with both post-modern ultra-relativism, and functionalistic general theory. There is an obvious danger in choosing either the " archaeology of subjective words " or the " archaeology of objective data". There must be a combination.

To let culture encompass nature and in addition call objectivity into question does not fit all. In his book *The Edge of Objectivity*, the historian C.C. Gillispie expresses his attitude towards this "pathetic theme" and declares that this is "the science of those who make botany of blossoms and meteorology of sunsets" (Gillispie 1960:199 p). I would say that it is only through the blossoms and the sunsets that we can learn to see the world as we once really saw it. So, from pollen record to sensation:

Were the Rowanberries as extremely red as they are today?

References

Bradley, R. 1993. *Altering the Earth, The Origins of Monuments in Britain and Continental Europe.* Society of Antiquaries of Scotland Monograph Series 8. Edinburgh.

—— 1998. *The Significance of Monuments*. London.
—— 2000. *An Archaeology of Natural Places*. London.
Evans, J.G. 1978. *An Introduction to Environmental Archaeology*. New York.
Giddens, A. 1986. *The Constitution of Society*. Cambridge.
Gillispie, C.C. 1960. *The Edge of Objectivity*. Princeton.
Lagerås, P. 2000a. Gravgåvor från växtriket. Pollenanalytiska belägg från en senneolitisk hällkista i Hamneda. In: Lagerås, P. (ed.) *Arkeologi och paleoekologi i sydvästra Småland. Tio artiklar från Hamnedaprojektet*. Riksantikvarieämbetet. Avdelningen för arkeologiska undersökningar. Skrifter No. 34, 65–85.
—— 2000b. Järnålderns odlingssystem och landskapets långsiktiga förändring. Hamnedas röjningsröseområden i ett paleoekologiskt perspektiv. In: Lagerås, P. (ed.) *Arkeologi och paleoekologi i sydvästra Småland. Tio artiklar från Hamnedaprojektet*. Riksantikvarieämbetet. Avdelningen för arkeologiska undersökningar. Skrifter No. 34, 167–231.
Sjögren, P. 1999. *Utmarkens vegetationsutveckling vid Ire i Blekinge, från forntid till nutid. En pollenanalytisk studie*. Examensarbete i geologi vid Lunds universitet. Lund.
Tilley, C. 1994. *A Phenomenology of Landscape: places, paths and monuments*. Oxford.
—— 1996. *An Ethnography of the Neolithic. Early Prehistoric Societies in Southern Scandinavia*. Cambridge.

21. Harvesting pike at Tłokowo

*R. Schild, K. Tobolski, L. Kubiak-Martens, B. Bratlund,
U. Eicher, G. Calderoni, D. Makowiecki, A. and M.M Pazdur†,
F.H. Schweingruber, W. Van Neer, M. Winiarska-Kabacińska and
S. Żurek*

Six seasons of excavations (1992, 1993, 1995–1998) in a Lateglacial/early Holocene palaeo-lake at Tłokowo, in north-eastern Poland, disclosed five horizons of finds. The two lower ones yielded many mysterious wooden objects, a result of the activity of beavers. The middle horizon included birch logs seemingly arranged in a platform or a gangway. The upper horizon contained a thin, charcoal rich cultural layer with numerous fish bones, rare mammal remains and isolated artifacts made of bone, antler, wood and flint as well as macro remains of plant food. Both, the radiocarbon measurements and the biogenic indicators place this horizon in the late Boreal, around 8300 BP (all radiocarbon ages reported in this article are uncalibrated). The recovered artifacts, on the other hand, point to an association with the Kunda complex. The assemblage of fish bones is mainly composed of cranial elements and vertebrae of adult pikes. The size classes of the recovered sample are characteristic for a population of spawning pike. The pike spawns in Poland in late March and April. The presence of the remains of a young female wild boar, probably killed between late winter and early summer, agrees with the timing of the use of the site. Charred fragments of several eatable plants occurring in the cultural layer suggest their utilisation by man. The organic materials recovered at Tłokowo imply seasonal exploitation of the lake as a locality used for harvesting the spawning pike as well as for gathering eatable water plants.

Introduction

In 1990, Mr. Wiesław Górnicki, the owner of a small meadow with a cattle pond in the middle, found a decorated bone point (harpoon) with two rows of microlithic flint insets, while deepening the pond. The following detailed survey failed to disclose traces of a settlement along the shores of the pond. Subsequently, the point was studied in detail and culturally associated with the Kunda complex of south-eastern Subbalticum (Sulgostowska and Hoffman 1993). Similar points, classified as Clark's Type 21, occur in the late Maglemose and Kongemose sites in south-western Scandinavia and in the sub-Baltic Mesolithic, where they are known as the Menturren type (Galiński 1990:18, Fig. 1.7). At Menturren, Kaliningrad Enclave, Russia, the cultural level containing two of these points has been dated to early Boreal and the beginning of rapidly rising *Corylus* curve (Gross 1938:90). The find at Tłokowo triggered a long-term field and laboratory project. At the beginning, the goal was to try to reconstruct a particular event in prehistory, above all the history of use and loss of a single, but complex Mesolithic tool. Soon, it appeared that the bone point was just one element of a much more intricate story.

Geomorphic Setting

The find place lies in north-eastern Poland in the region of the Mazurian Lakes, slightly to the north-east of the town of Olsztyn (Figure 21.1). It is a rolling country, a typical landscape of Lateglacial moraines of the Pomeranian phase. Numerous fossil and extant lakes of various sizes dot the landscape. The small lake or pond in which the point occurred had once been a part of a bigger lake system, a small sub-basin in the middle of a narrow channel linking two much larger basins (compare Figure 21.1). It was a typical dead ice lake formed by melting ice core, showing downthrown lakebeds of Lateglacial and early Holocene age.

General Stratigraphy, Bio and Radiochronology

Twenty cuts and trenches as well as numerous bore-holes provide a sound basis for detailed stratigraphy (Figure 21.2). Deep trenches near the center of the small lake as well as along the shores enable the microstratigraphic analyses of the finds and reconstruction of the dynamics

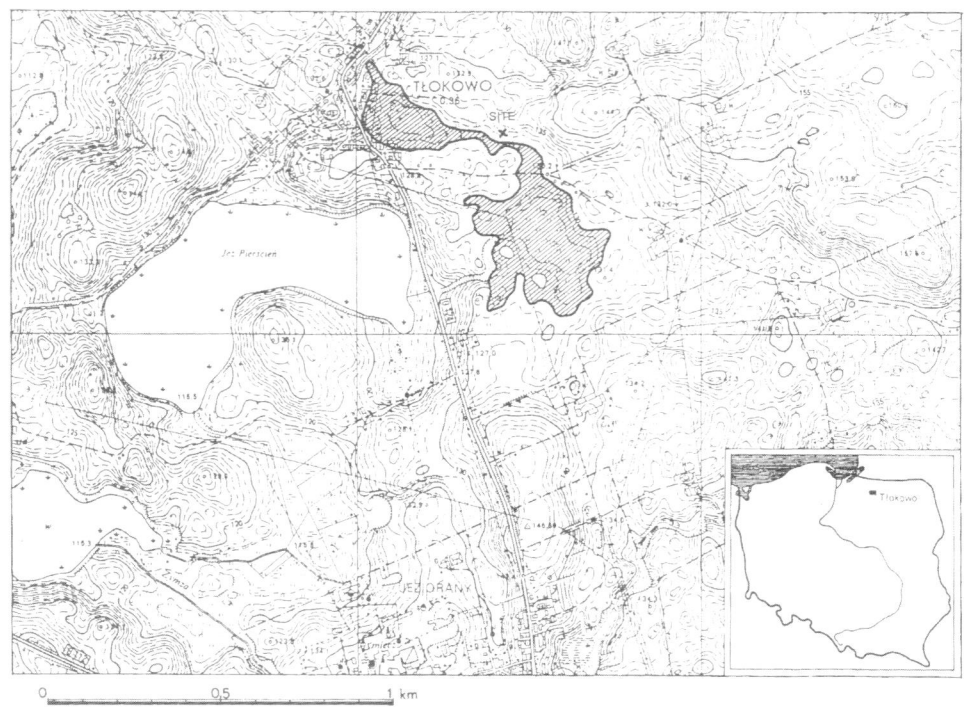

Figure 21.1 Location of Tłokowo Site and preliminary reconstruction of lake system at the high water stage in the early spring (late Boreal).

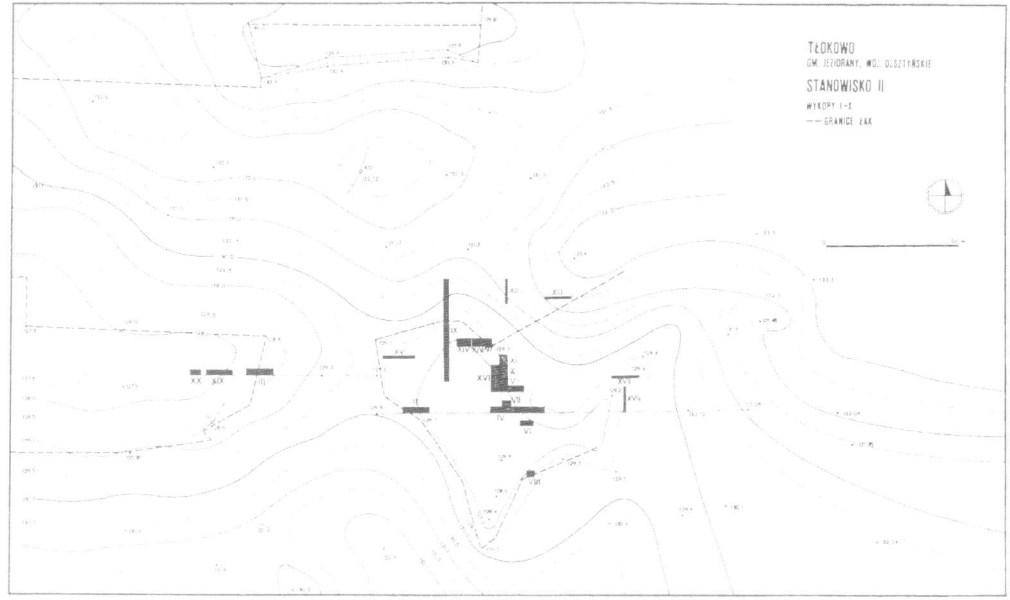

Figure 21.2 Tłokowo. Contour map and location of trenches.

of the formation of mineral and biogenic strata. In the present paper, however, only a synopsis of the stratigraphy shall be discussed (Figure 21.3).

The lake basin is inset into the Lateglacial till (Figure 21.3), dated by two TL assays at 16.2 ± 2.4 k (UG-2894) and 15.6 ± 2.3 k (UG-2893), i.e., of Pomeranian Phase chronology. The deposition in the basin begins with a bed of sandy silt, laid down in a shallow, littoral environment with macro-spores of *Selaginella* s*elaginoides,* oospores of *Charales* and rare fruits of *Betula 'alba'*, indicating a cold open landscape around the lake (Figure 21.4). The silt is conformably overlain by a bed of brown, coarse detritus gyttja (Figure 21.3), rich in wood, floral macro-remains and pollen, indicating a densely wooded landscape of interstadial (Bölling/Alleröd) character (Figure 21.4). Along the eastern shore, the detritus gyttja

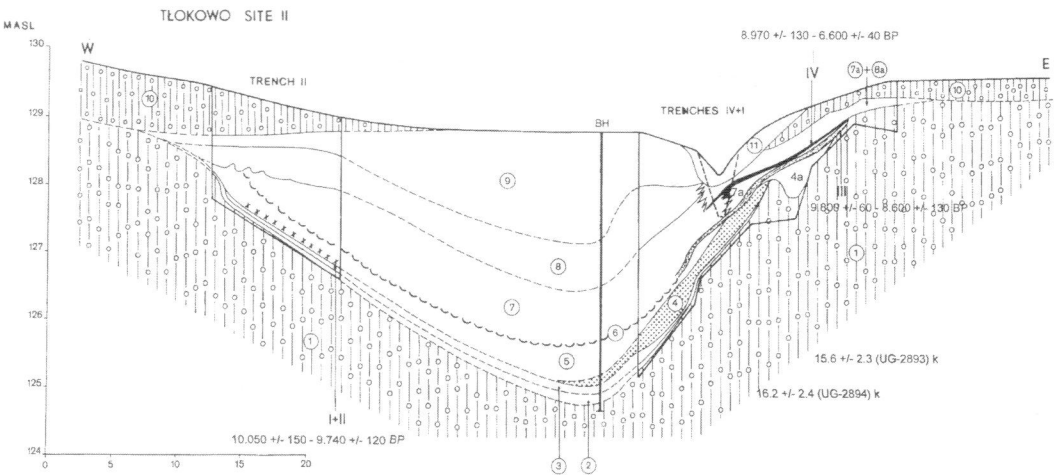

Figure 21.3 General cross-section through lake along northern faces of Trenches I, II and IV. See text for details.

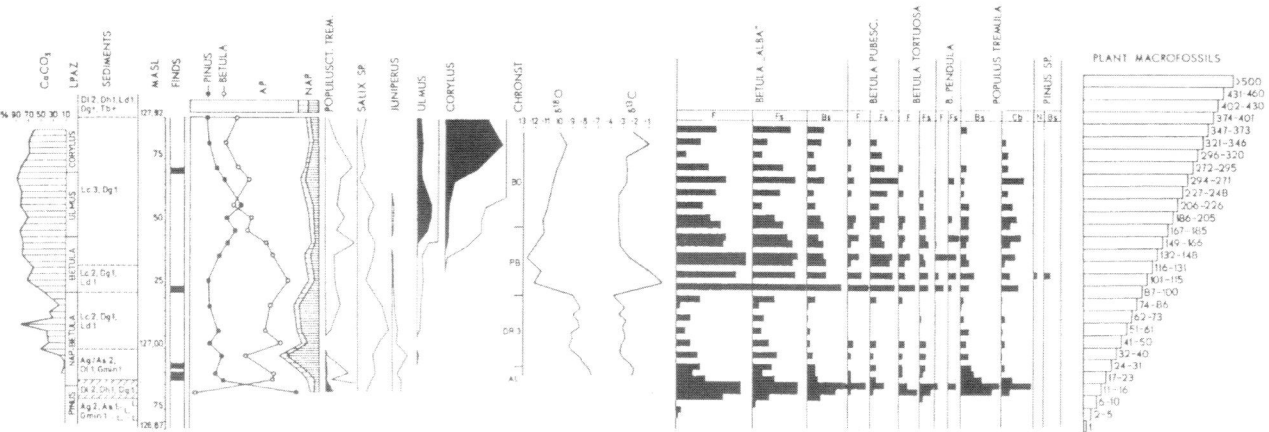

Figure 21.4 Compiled paleoecological signals from Trench II by U. Eicher (isotopes), L. Kubiak-Martens (plant macrofossils), and K. Tobolski (pollen). See text for details.

is, in turn, unconformably overlain by alluvial, gravelly sands (Figure 21.3) with pebbles and cobbles of a seasonal high-energy stream, radiocarbon dated at 9990 ± 110 ^{14}C years BP (Gd-10115). Channels of this rivulet are seen along the shore in shallow trenches (Figure 21.3:4a).

A bed of sandy, gray lacustrine silts with gastropods conformably overlies the brown detritus gyttja and the alluvial sands (Figure 21.3:5, base). Three major suits of rhythmically laminated calcareous gyttjas follow. At the base is a brownish gray, silty gyttja showing conspicuous bedding and variable carbonate content (Figure 21.3:5), topped by a thin bed of gray gyttja rich in *Unio* shells (Figure 21.3:6). A, brownish olive, calcareous, marly gyttja rich in tree leaves overlies the *Unio* bed (Figure 21.3:7, lower). In the littoral, it grades into a dark gray, fine detritus gyttja rich in reeds (Figure 21.3:7a). In the deep water section the brownish olive gyttja grades upward into a gray yellowish marly one, becoming light brown, heavily coquinoid near the top (Figure 21.3:7, upper).

The calcareous gyttjas near the shore are, in turn, uconformably overlain by a rather fine, brown detritus gyttja that interfingers with the top part of the gray, yellowish calcareous one in the central part of the basin. The former, on the other hand, grades upward into a coarse, brown detritus gyttja in the littoral (Figure 21.3:8a). The fine and coarse detritus gyttja eventually covers all the calcareous ones (Figure 21.3:8). It is topped by a brown, heavily decomposed peat (Figure 21.3:9).

Along the shores, the biogenic sediments are overlain by a relatively thick bed of clayey colluvium, thinning toward the center of the basin (Figure 21.3:10). The colluvium is made up of the redeposited till washed down the slopes after the tillage of the hills began, most probably in Medieval times. On the eastern shore, the cattle pond in which the bone point was found cuts the colluvium and the biogenic deposits. A bed of intersecting refill deposits indicates that the hole has been rejuvenated several times (Figure 21.3:11).

All the calcareous lacustrine deposits are rich in plant macrofossils, pollen and gastropods. Both, the macrofossils and pollen suggest the presence of five local pollen

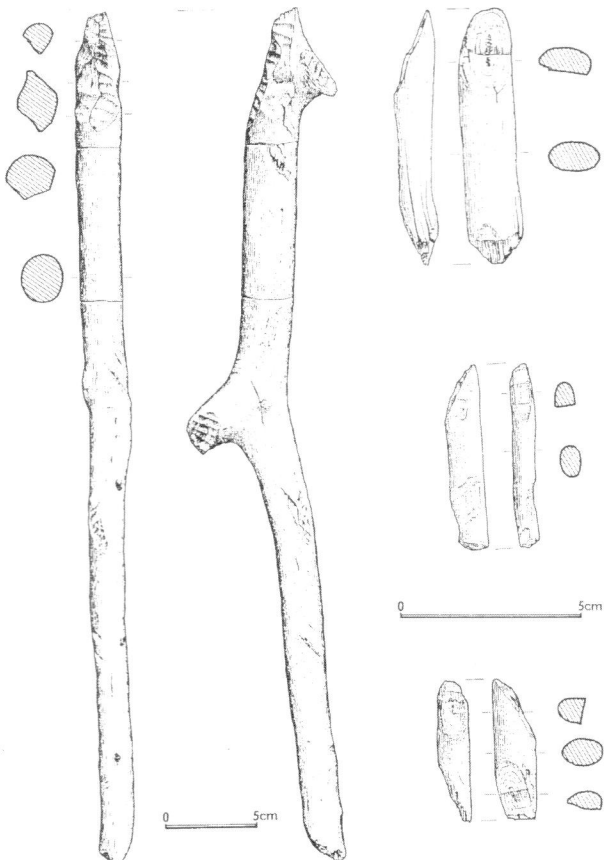

Figure 21.5 Horizons I and II. Selected beaver offcuts. (Drawn by Marek Puszkarski).

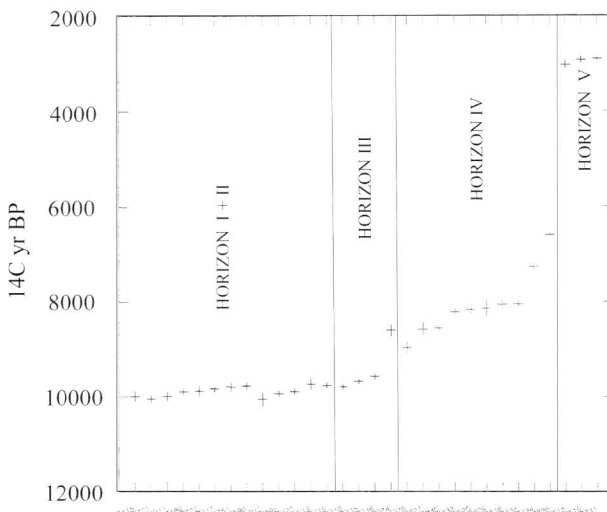

Figure 21.6 Radiocarbon ages BP from Tłokowo.

assemblage zones (L PAZ) and a general partition of the diagram into four chronozones: Alleröd, Younger Dryas, Pre-boreal and Boreal. The base of the diagram is of undetermined, cold Lateglacial character (Figure 21.4).

The behavior of isotopic curves in the early Holocene section is most absorbing (Figure 21.4). The oxygen curve registers fluctuations reaching more than 3 degrees, coeval with the reaction of the ^{13}C isotope. Usually such a set of events announces a rapid drop in temperatures at the beginning of Younger Dryas (see Schwander *et al.* 2000). At Tłokowo this phenomenon appears near the beginning of Holocene, together with an increase of the macro-remains of birch trees and the decrease of the macrofossils of juniper and willow, almost certainly indicating a cold pulsation called elsewhere the *Pre-boreal oscillation* (Ammann *et al.* 2000:342; Schwander *et al.* 2000).

The Finds

There are five levels of finds recognised. The lower two, in the gray silt (Horizons I and II), originally thought to be of anthropogenic character, are in fact results of the activity of beavers, which dammed the late Younger Dryas rivulet and created the first lake. The finds consist of hundreds of pieces of wood, mainly branches and twigs, many with characteristic facets left by the incisors (Figure 21.5). Largely similar biofacts were reported from the Somerset Levels (Coles and Orme 1982). These *offcuts* are the rejected stubs, stored foodstuff, and building material of one or two lodges. Thirteen radiocarbon ages were measured on pieces of *cut* wood, ranging from 10,050 ± 150 (Gd-4912) to 9740 ± 120 (Gd-4913) ^{14}C years BP (Figure 21.6). Most of these, however, cluster around the late Younger Dryas ^{14}C plateau of 10,000 BP.

One of the most intriguing problems associated with the discovery of the wooden *offcuts* is the specific composition of the wood (F. Schweingruber). Until now, 55 specimens have been defined to specific level. Of these 41 belong to *Salix* sp., nine to *Betula cf. nana*, four to *Salix cf. retusa*, and one to *Prunus cf. spinosa*. Six of the willow twigs are classified as to the season of cutting. All were removed from the trees at the peak moment of vegetation. The plum, (most probably blackthorn), on the other hand, was cut off the tree in the winter.

Finds associated with Horizon III, stratigraphically placed in the Pre-boreal oscillation, are represented in all the trenches dug along the eastern shore of the lake. The horizon contains numerous birch tree trunks and branches, mostly debarked, fallen toward the lake, most probably a result of rising lake level. The trees are embedded in the detritus gyttja with reed remains grading toward the deep-water section into the lower calcareous gyttja. Many complete skeletons of fish, as well as their fragments have been recovered from this horizon. Among these are 18 skeletons of roach (*Rutilus rutilus*), five skeletons of perch and one of a large pike, as well as several isolated bones of the same taxa. It is believed that the fish remains represent catastrophic death, probably resulting from a seasonal sudden drop of water level and the entrapment of the fish in the dense mat of branches of the fallen trees.

Three radiocarbon age estimates have been obtained from the logs: 9800 ± 60 years BP (Gd-7219), 9680 ± 60

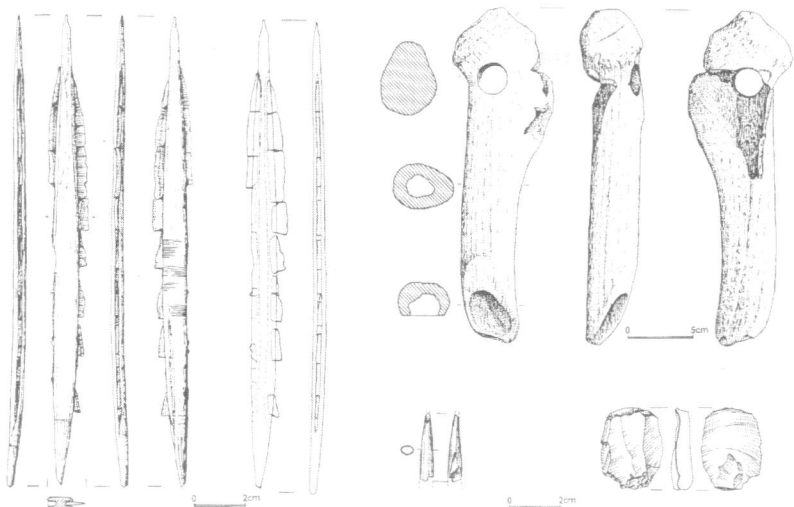

Figure 21.7 Horizon IV. Selected artifacts. Bone point with insets after Sulgostowska and Hoffman (1993). (Drawn by Ewa Gumińska and Marek Puszkarski).

years BP (Gd-7215), 9580 ± 60 years BP (Gd-7216). The fourth estimate of 8600 ± 130 years BP (Gd-6974), on seemingly burned bark, comes from the top of the detritus gyttja, certainly postdating the deposition of the trees (Figure 21.6).

Horizon IV occurs at the very base of the upper brown detritus gyttja in the littoral zone. It dips into the upper, gray yellowish marly gyttja in the deep-water section of the lake. In the pollen diagram (Figure 21.4), Horizon IV is near the base of the rapid rise of the hazel curve, a similar placement as at Menturren (Gross 1938:90). It is a very thin bed, 0.5 to 2 cm in thickness, of detritus, almost black gyttja extremely rich in charcoal and charcoal powder, containing burned pieces of wood, fish remains, rare mammal bones and occasional artifacts. The bone point with flint insets almost certainly came from this level. Toward the eastern shore, the blackish cultural layer pinches out. Redeposited, isolated flint artifacts occur in the topmost deposit, the clayey colluvium, a result of the slope wash phenomena that displaced the artifacts originally left on the dry shore.

Ten radiocarbon assays on charcoal and single pieces of burned branches recovered from Horizon IV range from 8970 ± 130 (Gd-6978) to 6600 ± 40 (Gd-7836) ^{14}C years BP. Most of the ages, however, cluster around 8300–8200 radiocarbon years BP (Figure 21.6).

Another thin horizon of charcoal powder containing few bone fragments occurs in the peat overlaying the brown detritus gyttja (Horizon V). Three radiocarbon ages of 3040 ± 90 (Gd-10515), 2940 ± 90 (Gd-10519) and 2910 ± 40 (Gd-7831) years BP pertain to this level.

Cultural, Archaeozoological and Archaeobotanical Elements of Horizon IV

The entire volume of the blackish cultural horizon was wet-sieved on the spot. As a result over one thousand fish bones, some fifty bird remains, nearly forty micro mammal fragments, a dozen large mammal bones, some amphibian remains, a dozen flint artifacts, a bone point polisher of stone, an axe/adze socket (*mattock*) of red deer antler, and a tip of a bone point, broken on impact, have been recovered (Figure 21.7). Some of the fragments of wood occurring in the cultural layer show traces of working. Among these is a flat, relatively large piece of soft wood with a regular burned ring suggesting a mark left by the initial use of a fire drill (identification by M. Michniewicz).

Nine species of fish have been identified (D. Makowiecki and W. Van Neer), of which large pikes comprise almost 80 per cent of the total. The breakdown of the fish bone assemblage is the following:

Species Present

Fishes	N	%
Pike	453	78,8
Carps	46	8,0
Roach	1	0,2
Chub	1	0,2
Tench	51	8,9
Crucian carp	2	0,3
Perches	4	0,7
Perch	16	2,8
Pikeperch	1	0,2
Identified	575	100
Not identified	508	
Total	1083	

Basic Anatomical Distribution

Parts of fish	Esox lucius L.		Other	
	n	%	n	%
Head	274	60,4	92	75,4
Vertebral column	165	36,4	10	8,2
Caudal skeleton	5	1,1	0	0
Rib	4	0,9	6	4,9
Fin	5	1,1	13	10,7
Others	0	0	1	0,8
Total	453	100	122	100

Size Distribution

TL limes	Esox lucius L.	Tinca tinca (L.)	Rutilus rutilus L.	Stizostedion lucioperca (L.)	Perca fluviatilis L.	Percidae	Carassius carassius (L.)	Leuciscus cephalus (L.)
10-15	0	1						1
15-20	0	0			9		1	
20-25	0	0	1		4			
20-30	2	0						
30-35	0	1					1	
30-40	18	0						
35-40	0	2						
40-45	0	17						
40-50	37	0						
45-50	0	13						
50-60	49			1				
60-70	36							
70-80	36							
80-90	3							
90-100	2							
100-110	4							

The following large mammal, bird and microfauna species have been recorded (B. Bratlund):

	NISP	MNI
Cervus elaphus	1	1
Capreolus capreolus	1	1
Sus srofa fer.	3	1+1
Sus sp.	1	1
Lutra lutra	6	1
Large ungulate indet.	2	1
Anas platyrhynchus	31	2
Anatinae	2	
Birds indet.	22	

Among the microfauna the following elements, seemingly of background character, are recorded:

	NISP	MNI
Neomys foetidens	1	1
Soricidae	1	1
Arvicola terrestris	18	1+3+?
Microtus arvalis/agrestis	2	1
Microstus sp.	6	

Sorting for plant macrofossils of several bulk samples of the cultural horizon (L. Kubiak-Martens) yielded a number of charred rhizomes, fruits, seeds, achenes and stem fragments of six eatable plant species as follows: *Typha latifolia* (cattail), rhizomes; *Phragmites australis* (reed); stem fragments; *Utrica dioica*, fruits; *Scroplaria/Verb.*, seeds; *Carex* sp., stem fragments; *Chenopodium album*, achenes.

The flint assemblage is very poor. Only two retouched tools have been recovered. One is an endscraper on a shortened blade and another is a bladelet with lateral retouch of Borki type. The latter, as well as the pressure method of bladelet production, used as blanks for the bone point insets, indicate association with the Kunda technocomplex of the Mesolithic (Sulgostowska and Hoffman 1993).

Dynamics of Formation, Taphonomy and Functional Character of Horizon IV

The archaeological bed of Horizon IV formed at the beginning of a considerable shallowing of the lake soon after the final collapse of lacustrine beds following the ultimate melting of the ice core. This is seen in the expansion of the littoral section of the basin, change of the deposition from calcareous gyttjas to detritus one in the former deep water zone, and in the composition of gastropod assemblages (Alexandrowicz 1999), in the deepest part of the sub-basin where the precipitation of calcium carbonate was still taking place (yellowish, coquinoid gyttja).

The archaeological materials concentrate almost exclusively in the north-eastern section of the basin. Because of the subsequent, sub-recent erosion of the shore, the remains of human activity are almost exclusively preserved in the biogenic, water-laid sediments. Except for the obvious biological background (e.g., microfauna), the bed contains artifacts that were disposed of and thrown into the lake (axe socket), lost during use (bone points), or washed in from the higher, dry ground (bones, charcoal), where most of the activity took place. Also, in the littoral zone of the lake at least one fragment of a wooden pole made of a plank of a large tree was found. The pole had been vertically thrust into the underlying calcareous gyttja and burned down to the level of the cultural bed. On the other hand, most of the cultural deposits that had been left on the dry ground, the then surface of a soil developed in the top part of the clayey till, were destroyed by chemical (acidic soil) or biological phenomena, and finally by the erosion that removed the topmost section of the surrounding mineral shores.

Composition of the finds suggests a multi purpose use of the locality, however, harvesting of the pike seems to be dominant. Most of the faunal remains are fish bones, by and large cranial elements and vertebrae. Nearly 80% of the bones come from the adult pikes in the size categories between 30 cm to 80 cm. These classes are characteristic for the composition of the population of spawning pike (Rolik and Rembiszewski 1987:145). The pike spawns in Poland in late March and April. During spawning, the pike comes to the very shallow water, often flooded meadows, where hands and baskets can gather it. In fact, very numerous, dense, and narrow depressions resembling footprints were found in Trench XVI, sunk into the calcareous gyttja from the base of the cultural layer. Furthermore, the common presence of the burned stems of reed in the cultural layer suggests the purposeful burning of the dense reed stands, in order to facilitate the access to the spawning grounds. On the other hand, a very rich presence of charcoal in the archaeological bed as well as the anatomical distribution of fish bones may indicate processing and smoking of the catch on the adjacent dry ground.

Single specimens represent mammal remains. Of these, of particular interest is a centrotarsal of a roe deer showing cut marks and a few bones of a boar, a young female most probably killed sometime between late winter and early summer. The scarcity of large mammal bones may suggest that they were brought to the place as parts of food supply used during harvesting and processing the fish.

Charred rhizomes, achenes, fruits, seeds, and stem fragments of several waterlogged plants may indicate that they were also uprooted or dug out for consumption. Perhaps, this may explain the presence of the adze socket in the cultural layer.

In this context, the two probably lost while spearing bone points are not necessarily associated with the catching of the fish. One cannot exclude their use in hunting large water mammals like the otter present in the bone assemblage from Tłokowo. The insets of the bone point show wear traces (M. Winiarska-Kabacińska) resulting from penetration of a soft tissue (Sulgostowska and Hoffman 1993).

Conclusions

The site at Tłokowo yielded intriguing; very unusual palaeoenvironmetal and biological materials that are often either disregarded or can misleadingly be mistaken for anthropogenic artifacts and constructions. Careful excavations and employment of a number of biological analyses permit better understanding of the archaeology and the environment of this very little known area of Europe. The archaeology of the small sub-basin of Tłokowo shows how complex even relatively poor localities can be and how differently Mesolithic populations could have used the same place during a year. It is very likely that the same may be said about many of the known waterlogged Mesolithic loci of Europe.

Acknowledgments

The work on Tłokowo was financed by the State Committee for Scientific Research grant (1 1663 91 02) awarded to R. Schild and K. Tobolski as well as by the Institute of Archaeology and Ethnology, Polish Academy of Sciences. We are grateful to Mr. Paul Barford for several stylistic suggestions concerning this article.

References

Ammann, B., Birks, H.J.B., Brooks, S.J., Eicher, U., von Grafenstein, U., Hofmann, W., Lemdahl, G., Schwander, J., Tobolski, K. and Wick, L. 2000. Quantification of biotic responses to rapid climatic changes around the Younger Dryas – a synthesis. *Palaeogeography, Palaeoclimatology, Palaeoecology* 159, 313–347.

Alexandrowicz, W.P. 1999. Evolution of the malacological assemblages in North Poland during the Late Glacial and Early Holocene. *Folia Quaternaria* 70, 39–70.

Coles, J.M. and Orme, B.J. 1982. Beaver in the Somerset Levels: some new evidence. *Somerset Levels Papers* 8, 66–75.

Galiński, T. 1990. Późoplejstoceńskie i wczesnoholoceńskie harpuny i ostrza kościane i rogowe na południowych wybrzeżach Bałtyku między ujściem Niemna i Odry. *Materiały Zachodniopomorskie* 32 (1986), 7–62.

Gross, H. 1938. Auf den ältesten Spuren des Menschen in Altpreussen. *Prussia* 32, 84–132.

Rolik, H. and Rembiszewski, M.J. 1987. *Ryby i krągłouste (Pisces et Cyclomasta)*. Warszawa.

Schwander, J., Eicher, U. and Ammann, B. 2000. Oxygen isotopes of lake marl at Gerzensee and Leysin (Switzerland), covering the Younger Dryas and two minor oscillations, and their correlation to the GRIP ice core. *Palaeogeography, Palaeoclimatology, Palaeoecology* 159:203–214.

Sulgostowska, Z. and Hoffman, M. 1993. Kościane ostrze mezolityczne z wkładkami krzemiennymi z Tłokowa, woj. olsztyńskie – aspekt technologiczny. *Archeologia Polski* 38(1), 75–88.

Session III

Social Relations and Group Formation

22. Introduction

Ericka Engelstad

Social relations and group formation is a theme that is essential for understanding the societies and the lives of individuals in the Mesolithic. This is not a theme that has been central to previous Mesolithic in Europe conferences. We can, however, thank the Swedish organisers of the 7th conference for especially including a session on "the social". Traditionally research on the Mesolithic has emphasised ecology, economics, typology, change and transition, and regional (cultural historical) studies. Although these themes are still in the forefront, one can see from an examination of papers in the other sessions of the conference that there is consistently a social aspect to these traditional themes. However, during the conference I was consistently reminded of Christopher Hawkes (1954) ladder of inference where the social and ritual were considered to be not only difficult to analyse, but also at the limits of archaeological inference and understanding. The climb from the concrete to the archaeological esoteric was simply too difficult and is still in many ways a (not insurmountable) barrier. The papers in this session have taken up this ever-present challenge and use a variety of methods and evidence to understand the everyday lives of people in the Mesolithic.

Gunilla Eriksson and Ilga Zvejnieki answer their question "do dogs eat like humans?" with a definite no. But one must not be fooled by their seemingly simple question, for central to their analysis are not only the different roles dogs fill in past societies and the symbiotic relationship between dogs and humans, but also the relations between inland and coastal populations, trade and intergroup exchange.

Studies of lithic technology are used by Christina Lindgren to study differences between and within different societies/groups. Different technological strategies and different raw material preferences not only reflect differences between societies and genders within a society, but are also used as symbolic capital to constitute and mark these differences. Thus technology is closely tied to identity, both gender identity and group identity. Gender identity has been an important subject in recent social theory and gender archaeology. Gender relations are not only an aspect of individual identity but also reflect the social structure of societies, a duality grasped by Lindgren's third case study from the middle Swedish archipelago.

The quality of people's lives is, in particular, reflected in Eugénia Cunha, Francisca Cardoso, and Cláudia Umbelino's analysis of the human skeletal material from shell middens in Portugal. On the basis of different analytical techniques they find that these Mesolithic populations suffered from no chronic illnesses, that childhood was characterised by good nutrition, and that although individuals suffered from accidents, there were no sign of violence. Incidences of traumatic events and infectious diseases were few. One gets the definite impression that these Mesolithic hunter-gatherers enjoyed "the good life".

Gender attribution is no longer an entirely adequate way of analysing gender relations in the past. Using the text metaphor to understand the meaning and significance of materiale culture Nyree Finlay challenges traditional functional interpretations as well as an assumed single maker of composite tools. The metaphor of multiple authorship enables Finlay to transform the study of lithic technology by developing a dynamic social relations perspective within the methodology of chaine operatoire. She also shows how conventional analytic techniques can effect what we are able to recognise – in terms of form, function, and meaning – in any microlithic assemblage and in particular notes the constraints of the "microlithic gaze".

There are several major themes that unite the papers in this session: daily life, identity, social group relations, gender processes and relations, and technological processes. It is clear that the papers emphasise the dynamic rather than the static. The authors are moving toward grasping the complexity and ambiguity of social relations between individuals, genders, social groups, and societies in the Mesolithic.

23. Do dogs eat like humans? Marine stable isotope signals in dog teeth from inland Zvejnieki

Gunilla Eriksson and Ilga Zagorska

The close association between dogs and people since early times has led some scholars to infer that dogs generally had the same diet as humans. In palaeodietary research where bone chemistry is employed, dogs have therefore sometimes been used as approximates for humans when human bone was not available. In this study, stable carbon and nitrogen isotope analysis is applied to pendants made from dog's teeth from Stone Age graves at Zvejnieki in northern Latvia to investigate the validity of using dogs to infer human diet. In addition, human and faunal remains are analysed. Analyses produced evidence for three different groups of dogs at Zvejnieki: scavenging dogs, dogs feeding on exclusively freshwater fish, and dogs with a completely marine diet. Humans consumed large amounts of freshwater fish, but none of them had any marine input to their diet. The marine dogs are therefore interpreted as evidence for contact with coastal people. The Zvejnieki inhabitants are likely to have acquired the dogs from coastal people either as living animals, or in the form of tooth pendants. The general conclusion is that dogs exhibit too great a variability in diet to be useful as approximations for human diet.

Introduction

The earliest known dog in the world, dated at c. 14,000 BP, was a mandible found in a human double grave at Oberkassel in Germany (Benecke 1987; Clutton-Brock 1995:10). In Scandinavia and the East Baltic countries, dog remains have been found at numerous Mesolithic sites, from the Preboreal onwards (Paaver 1965; Lepiksaar 1984; Benecke 1987; Larsson 1990; Lõugas et al. 1996). Dogs occur in various archaeological contexts, from occasional bones recovered in cultural layers, to dogs (complete or in parts) deposited in human graves, or even the whole animal interred in a grave of its own, with or without grave goods. Although some of these instances are obviously ritual, this is not to say that all Mesolithic dog remains were ritually deposited. Neither would it be correct to assume that, for example, all scatters of dog bones in cultural layers are simply traces of non-ritual waste disposal. There are no general criteria that apply cross-culturally to distinguish between ritual and non-ritual deposits of dog (Olsen 2000:72). Moreover, taphonomic processes do in some cases produce deposition patterns that are similar to those that result from intentional human disposal of dog remains. Olsen (2000: 90) has emphasised the importance of recording contextual information about dog deposits in detail, to enhance interpretation about sacred or secular use of dogs.

At the famous Mesolithic complex at Skateholm in southern Sweden all various manners of dog deposition mentioned above occur (Jonsson 1988:67 p; Larsson 1990). This clearly illustrates the multitude of different roles that dogs filled in past human societies. Dogs in prehistory presumably had a number of different functions, both ritual and practical, often simultaneously (Serpell 1995; Olsen 2000). Practical use of their skills included roles as hunting partners, draft animals, guard dogs, herding animals, and scavengers. Company, affection, and status, were other important features (Crockford 1995:302 p). Use of wool (Schulting 1994), fur (Noe-Nygaard 1995), meat (Serpell 1995), and teeth (the present study) of dog is also recorded. As for ritual purposes, dogs are often viewed as messengers between this world and the next, for example serving as underworld guides or for the invocation of spirits.

The various roles which dogs fill in human society are of course not mutually exclusive. Serpell (1995:247 p) reviews the ambivalence exhibited towards dogs, as exemplified by the Yurok Indians in California, where dogs were highly esteemed for their hunting capability, and treated with great affection by their owners, but at the same time regarded as taboo, not allowed into human habitations, not named, etc. Despite this, they could be buried with full ceremony. That is, the roles that the dog played in life may not be connected to its role in death, and hence the treatment displayed in burial rites could be much different from the daily treatment.

The close association between dogs and people has led some scholars to infer that dogs generally had the same diet as humans. In palaeodietary research where bone chemistry is employed, dogs have therefore sometimes been used as approximates for humans when human bone was not available for dietary analysis (e.g. Noe-Nygaard 1988; Clutton-Brock and Noe-Nygaard 1990). In the present paper, the feasibility of this approach is investigated by means of stable isotope analysis (carbon and nitrogen) of a particular type of dog deposition, dog-tooth pendants in human graves at Zvejnieki in northern Latvia. Furthermore, original stable isotope data of humans from Zvejnieki are presented, as well as faunal data from the same site.

Zvejnieki

The Stone Age complex at Zvejnieki in northern Latvia is situated some 50 km off the Baltic coast (the distance differing only marginally during the Stone Age), at Lake Burtnieki. The Zvejnieki cemetery comprises 315 burials, with adjacent Mesolithic and Neolithic settlement remains. The graves were excavated in the 1960s under the conduction of the late Francis Zagorskis, and a monograph in Latvian was subsequently published (Zagorskis 1987; for an outline of the research history of Zvejnieki, see Zagorska and Lõugas 2000).

Skeletal remains at the cemetery were generally very well preserved, and so far human bone from 24 graves has been radiocarbon dated, indicating continuous use during several thousand years (8150–4190 BP). Only some of the graves were furnished with grave goods, most frequently tooth pendants. Archaeological dating of graves with no, or only limited, grave goods is therefore mainly based on burial customs (position, orientation, presence of ochre, or structures), and location in the cemetery. Radiocarbon datings have mainly confirmed the presence of chronologically separate clusters at the cemetery, but location alone cannot be used for reliable dating.

During the excavation, the remains of two dogs were uncovered among the Neolithic graves. Since Stone Age dog graves were largely unknown at that time, they were interpreted as modern intrusions, and were consequently discarded after being recorded. However, it is not unlikely that they were in fact Stone Age burials of dogs. Dog bones were also numerous in the cultural layers of the Mesolithic settlement at Zvejnieki (Zagorska 1992:114).

Stable isotope studies of dogs

Skeletal bone or teeth can be used to produce information on the diet of individuals with the use of bone chemistry. In studies where stable carbon and nitrogen isotope analysis is employed, it has been shown that measurements on bone and tooth collagen mainly reflect protein intake (Ambrose and Norr 1993). Due to the constant turnover in skeletal tissue, stable isotope values from bone collagen represent an average diet of several years prior to death.

In the dentine of teeth, by contrast, no collagen turnover takes place, and stable isotope signatures therefore reflect the specific period in life when the teeth were formed, that is, in childhood. The stable carbon and nitrogen isotope values are denoted as $\delta^{13}C$ and $\delta^{15}N$ respectively, and expressed in per mil (‰).

A basic difference used in $\delta^{13}C$ analyses is that between terrestrial and marine protein sources, chiefly related to salinity. In the Baltic region, this could result in seemingly terrestrial $\delta^{13}C$ signatures for people living of protein from the sea during periods when the Baltic-Sea Basin contained freshwater, for example the Ancylus stage (cf. Lõugas et al. 1996). Another important difference is that between C_3 and C_4 plants, where C_3 plants have lower, i.e. more negative, $\delta^{13}C$ signatures than C_4 plants. Species such as maize, millet, and sorghum, which grow in warm and arid environments, are C_4 plants, which have different photosynthetic pathways than most terrestrial plant species, i.e. C_3 plants. In the Baltic region, all edible plants during the Stone Age were C_3 plants, and therefore have $\delta^{13}C$ values corresponding to those of terrestrial animals.

The $\delta^{15}N$ value increases c. 3‰ per trophic level (Minagawa and Wada 1984). This enrichment can be used to establish position in the food web, that is, to distinguish between plants, herbivores, and carnivores. Since marine food chains are generally longer than terrestrial chains, marine top predators have higher $\delta^{15}N$ values than terrestrial ones.

The first study applying stable isotope analysis to dog remains was made on hair (Burleigh and Brothwell 1978), but since hair is only rarely present in prehistoric contexts, most studies have focused on bone. One of the earliest analyses of dog bone in Europe was performed on Mesolithic/Neolithic Danish material by Noe-Nygaard (1988). Here, $\delta^{13}C$ analysis was employed on dogs and humans from 16 Mesolithic and Early Neolithic sites, both coastal and inland. An alleged great similarity in $\delta^{13}C$ values between humans and dogs from the same site is only based on two coastal sites, one Late Mesolithic, and one Neolithic. Although no bone collagen quality indicators were reported, the dog value from a third site, –30.9‰, is clearly out of range. Furthermore, the average for dog/humans from inland Mesolithic, –21.5‰, is cited in support of a mainly terrestrial diet, but this is based on only two humans and four dogs, with a range of 9.5‰. Altogether, the assumption that dogs and humans have similar diets is neither verified nor refuted by the stable isotope data.

A subsequent study by Clutton-Brock and Noe-Nygaard (1990) investigated dog bone from the Preboreal site of Seamer Carr, adjacent to the famous Star Carr site. Stable carbon isotope analysis indicated mainly marine protein input in the diet of dog at this inland site. In a recent review of their Seamer Carr study, Day (1996) suggested that the $\delta^{13}C$ values of dog were in fact not marine, but the result of freshwater food intake. However, her argument regarding $\delta^{13}C$ values of fish and waterfowl is purely hypothetical, and is contradicted by actual bone collagen isotope data (Schoeninger and DeNiro 1984; Katzenberg 1989; Little and Schoeninger 1995; the present study). A forthcoming paper by Schulting and Richards (in prep.), where new stable isotope measurements of both the Seamer and Star Carr dogs are presented, also contradict Day's view. In fact, the most important conclusion one should draw from Day's paper, is that in order to interpret data correctly, it is important to establish reference values by making background faunal measurements.

Katzenberg (1989) applied $\delta^{13}C$ and $\delta^{15}N$ analysis to human and faunal remains, including dog, from an Amerindian inland site in Canada. All dogs had high $\delta^{13}C$ values, around –11‰, which is interpreted as being caused by a high consumption of maize. Humans had similar $\delta^{13}C$ values, but about 3‰ higher $\delta^{15}N$ values, around 13‰. Katzenberg suggested that the humans consumed dog meat along with freshwater fish, since dogs were the only fauna to have such high $\delta^{13}C$ values, and maize consumption would not have produced such high $\delta^{15}N$ values. Moreover, dog-meat consumption was recorded in ethnohistoric literature among a neighbouring people with many cultural similarities.

In a study of prehistoric Asiatic Eskimos at Ekwen, Chu (1998) performed stable isotope analysis on humans as well as dogs and other available fauna, namely seal, walrus, and reindeer. Earlier archaeological research had indicated that the Ekwen people consumed mainly marine mammals, which was confirmed by stable isotope analysis. However, the contribution of walrus meat was considerably smaller than expected, judging by the extremely high trophic-level $\delta^{15}N$ signatures, around 20‰. Dogs, were roughly 1‰ more negative in $\delta^{13}C$ than humans, and on average were 2‰ lower in $\delta^{15}N$, but with considerable variation. According to Chu, the variation indicated that dogs were fed scrap food.

The assumption that dog bone can be used as a surrogate for human bone was allegedly tested by Cannon *et al.* (1999) on a Canadian Northwest Coast site, where frequencies of faunal remains indicated varying dependence on salmon during five subsequent periods (6060–1405 BP). Whereas human bone was mainly available from the salmon-peak periods, dog bone was preserved from all five periods. Dog diet did seem to co-vary chronologically to some extent with the faunal indications, but contrary to the authors' claim, the assumed similarity between dog and human was simply not proven. Even though the total average $\delta^{13}C$ for both humans and dogs matched, humans were from a narrower time span, and since the chronological change was investigated, the overall average is insignificant. Moreover, $\delta^{15}N$ values were roughly 3‰ lower for dogs than for humans, which is explained by Cannon *et al.* in terms of consumption of clams and human faeces by dogs. Despite a valuable contribution to the discussion of indications of seasonal differences in dogs, their arguments regarding dogs and humans remain circular.

In summary, for the dog–human approximation to be correct, one would expect the $\delta^{13}C$ and $\delta^{15}N$ values of dogs to largely coincide with those of humans from the same site. However, previous studies have frequently presupposed, rather than verified, this claim, and have instead demonstrated a great variability and inconsistency in the diet of dog as compared to human. In the present study, $\delta^{13}C$ and $\delta^{15}N$ analysis is employed on the remains of both humans and dogs from the same site to further test the claim.

Material and methods

Eight Zvejnieki graves with nine individuals, furnished with tooth pendants of dog, were studied more closely. The graves, which range from the Late Mesolithic to the Middle Neolithic, are presented in a table (Figure 23.1). One should bear in mind that the definition of the Neolithic in the Eastern Baltic differs somewhat from that generally used in Western Europe, resulting in for example 'Late Mesolithic' graves (in Western terminology) here being termed Early Neolithic. The buried individuals are four adult males, one female adult, and four adolescent/child (all morphologically identified). The sex and age distribution is not representative of the cemetery as a whole (Zagorskis 1987). All individuals were buried in extended supine position, accompanied by 9 to 88 tooth pendants in single burials, and as much as 340 tooth pendants in the only double burial (grave 122/123). Many of the graves were strewn with ochre, but only one, the double grave 122/123, had a stone structure over the upper part of the grave.

Collagen of ten dog-tooth pendants from these graves was extracted and subject to $\delta^{13}C$ and $\delta^{15}N$ analysis. Additional human and faunal material from these and other burials at Zvejnieki were also analysed in the same manner, forming reference values for the dog-tooth measurements.

The 15 human specimens originate from 12 graves with both Mesolithic and Neolithic dates. Samples were taken from bone as well as teeth, and in three cases human-tooth pendants. Since the collagen in teeth is formed during childhood, whereas bone collagen is continually remodelled throughout life, the Zvejnieki human stable isotope signatures represent a population consisting of both adults and children.

The faunal material included 39 specimens from 21 graves of the following species: elk (moose), red deer, aurochs, wild horse, wild boar, brown bear, badger, beaver, otter, pike, grey seal, and ringed/harp seal. The majority of samples were taken from tooth pendants, but a few (red deer, beaver, pike) were also represented by other bone elements (phalanges, astragalus, vertebrae).

A dentist's drill was used to obtain bone- and tooth powder. Collagen was extracted according to Brown *et al.* (1988), where high molecular-weight remnants (>30 kDa) were selected for. The stable isotope ratios were

Grave no.	Sex, age	Tooth pendants	Other grave goods	Filling, ochre, orientation	Archaeological dating	Radiocarbon dating
165	male adult	24 in neck region	bird bones	light gravel, ochre all over, SW	Late Mesolithic (?)	–
122/123	adolescent + male adult	340 all over	–	grey gravel, intense ochre, stone setting on upper part, S	Transition Late Mesolithic/Early Neolithic	6395±75 BP (OxA-5967)
121	adolescent	88	1 pebble, 1 figural stone in hip region, 1 piece of worked flint, bird bones in foot region, beaver bones	dark earth, intense ochre all over, S	Transition Late Mesolithic/Early Neolithic	–
158	male adult	22 in chest region	1 bone spearhead on the chest	black earth (grave severely damaged), E	Early Neolithic (?)	–
164	male adult (25–30 years)	9 by the head	17 bone spearheads by the legs, bird bones	black earth, ochre in head region, E	Transition Early/Middle Neolithic	5230±95 BP (Ua-15544)
233	female adult	9 by the hands	slate chisel (Neolithic form)	black earth, no ochre, SE	(Middle?) Neolithic	–
226	child	80 on the chest	–	grey earth, ochre all over, SE	Difficult to date; in the region of Neolithic graves, but old traditions	–
290	adolescent	37 by hands and legs	–	black earth, ochre in patches (grave damaged), SE	Difficult to date; in the region of Neolithic graves, but old traditions	–

Figure 23.1 The graves in this study, sorted according to archaeological dating. Sex and age based on morphological measurements only. Radiocarbon datings made on human bone.

determined using an Optima Fison mass spectrometer with a precision of <0.1‰. The $\delta^{13}C$ and $\delta^{15}N$ values are calculated as $\delta=(R_{sample}/R_{standard}-1)\times 1000‰$, where R is the $^{13}C/^{12}C$ and $^{15}N/^{14}N$ ratio respectively, expressed relative to the standards PDB limestone for carbon and AIR atmospheric N_2 for nitrogen.

Results

Results of the stable isotope analysis are presented in three tables (Figures 23.2–23.4) and a plot (Figure 23.5). The extracted collagen from bone and teeth of Zvejnieki was generally well preserved. Only 7 out of 64 samples failed to meet the quality requirements, which is a low number for Stone Age material. The atomic C/N ratio was out of the accepted range 2.9–3.6 (DeNiro 1985) in three cases (AZV08, ZVE04, and ZVE05). Four samples (AZV21, AZV31, AZV47, and ZVE01) yielded insufficient absolute quantities of collagen to produce reliable (or any) stable isotope measurements, although other samples might have lower percentage yields due to larger initial quantities. The samples with insufficient quality are excluded from further discussion (for a review on bone collagen quality indicators, see e.g. van Klinken 1999:689 pp).

For the fauna (excluding dogs) the $\delta^{13}C$ range was −25.3‰ to −15.4‰, and the $\delta^{15}N$ range was 4.3–14.5‰. Not surprisingly, seals had the most positive $\delta^{13}C$ values, as well as the highest $\delta^{15}N$ values, which is what can be expected for marine top-predators. Bearing in mind that this was an inland site, they could not have belonged to the immediate Zvejnieki ecosystem, although they are valuable indications of the marine end-value for this period, i.e. where in the diagram an individual with a 100% marine protein intake would be plotted. Apart from the seals, the highest trophic levels, as indicated by $\delta^{15}N$ values around 12‰, are represented by other carnivores, such as badger, otter, and pike. Whereas otters are known to feed mainly on freshwater fish (as do pikes), badgers consume for example worms, eggs, small rodents, and insects. This is compliant with a $\delta^{13}C$ signature considerably more positive for badger than for other species.

Omnivores such as the brown bear and the wild boar have a major input of plant food to the diet in addition to meat, which results in wide $\delta^{13}C$ ranges, from −19.8 to −24.7‰. Naturally they show a generally lower trophic level than carnivores, $\delta^{15}N$ values ranging from 4.8 to 8.7‰. The $\delta^{15}N$ range for herbivores, which feed exclusively on plants, is only slightly lower, 4.3–7.3‰, and $\delta^{13}C$ varies between −25.3 and −22.0‰. The ranges are by no means anomalous, taking into account the considerable natural stable isotope variation in plants, the

Lab code	Grave	Species	Common name	$\delta^{13}C$	$\delta^{15}N$	C/N	% collagen	%C	%N
AZV 27	37	*Alces alces*	elk (moose)	−22.0	4.3	3.3	3.7	42.7	15.0
AZV 28	153	*Alces alces*	elk (moose)	−22.9	6.4	3.2	4.2	38.5	13.8
AZV 29	170	*Alces alces*	elk (moose)	−22.3	6.1	3.3	3.6	37.0	13.0
AZV 02	62	*Cervus elaphus*	red deer	−22.4	4.5	3.5	0.6	40.7	13.6
AZV 01	62	*Cervus elaphus*	red deer	−22.0	6.0	3.4	0.4	38.9	13.2
AZV 18	164	*Bos primigenius*	aurochs	−22.2	6.4	3.5	3.8	43.8	14.6
AZV 20	62	*Castor fiber*	beaver	−23.1	5.3	3.3	3.4	40.2	14.2
~~AZV 21~~	~~62~~	~~*Castor fiber*~~	~~beaver~~	~~−23.8~~	~~4.7~~	~~3.3~~	~~0.8~~	~~31.5~~	~~11.0~~
AZV 07	206	*Castor fiber*	beaver	−23.7	4.4	3.6	1.4	30.3	9.8
~~AZV 08~~	~~252~~	~~*Castor fiber*~~	~~beaver~~	~~−24.0~~	~~4.5~~	~~4.0~~	~~2.1~~	~~40.4~~	~~11.7~~
AZV 22	27	*Cervus elaphus*	red deer	−24.4	5.1	3.6	0.7	37.4	12.1
AZV 23	124	*Cervus elaphus*	red deer	−23.2	7.1	3.4	4.4	39.3	13.3
AZV 24	170	*Cervus elaphus*	red deer	−23.7	7.3	3.5	5.6	42.5	14.2
AZV 09	12	*Equus ferus*	wild horse	−24.4	6.1	3.4	2.3	36.5	12.5
AZV 10	42	*Equus ferus*	wild horse	−24.5	6.3	3.5	5.5	42.0	14.1
AZV 11	42	*Equus ferus*	wild horse	−24.9	5.8	3.3	2.5	38.2	13.5
AZV 12	86	*Equus ferus*	wild horse	−23.4	5.6	3.4	2.9	40.7	14.2
AZV 13	100	*Equus ferus*	wild horse	−25.3	5.4	3.2	3.6	36.6	13.3
AZV 14	122/123	*Equus ferus*	wild horse	−24.3	5.6	3.3	6.9	43.6	15.5
AZV 16	226	*Halichoerus grypus*	grey seal	−15.4	14.5	3.1	5.7	38.4	14.5
AZV 25	164	*Lutra lutra*	otter	−23.3	11.9	3.4	4.1	37.9	12.9
AZV 48	122/123	*Meles meles*	badger	−18.6	12.1	3.4	2.4	36.1	12.5
AZV 17	290	*Phocidae indet.*	seal	−16.6	12.6	3.1	2.4	37.9	14.3
~~AZV 47~~	~~60~~	~~*Esox lucius*~~	~~pike~~	−	−	−	1.2	−	−
AZV 46	60	*Esox lucius*	pike	−23.6	11.7	3.5	0.6	21.1	7.0
~~AZV 31~~	~~31~~	~~*Sus scrofa*~~	~~wild boar~~	~~−25.2~~	~~5.3~~	~~3.5~~	~~3.7~~	~~37.5~~	~~12.5~~
AZV 32	31	*Sus scrofa*	wild boar	−23.1	6.8	3.5	4.2	41.4	13.7
AZV 40	76	*Sus scrofa*	wild boar	−23.6	8.1	3.2	2.0	54.6	19.9
AZV 33	124	*Sus scrofa*	wild boar	−24.0	7.0	3.5	5.1	42.1	14.0
AZV 34	153	*Sus scrofa*	wild boar	−23.4	4.8	3.3	7.9	40.4	14.4
AZV 35	168	*Sus scrofa*	wild boar	−22.6	7.9	3.3	7.5	41.9	14.6
AZV 36	170	*Sus scrofa*	wild boar	−24.7	6.3	3.5	3.4	41.4	13.7
AZV 37	206	*Sus scrofa*	wild boar	−22.9	4.9	3.3	5.8	41.7	14.5
AZV 26	146	*Sus scrofa*	wild boar	−22.7	6.1	3.3	5.5	40.5	14.5
AZV 50	122/123	*Ursus arctos*	brown bear	−19.8	8.7	3.5	3.8	36.9	12.3
AZV 51	122/123	*Ursus arctos*	brown bear	−20.2	8.0	3.5	4.0	40.5	13.3
AZV 49	122/123	*Ursus arctos*	brown bear	−20.0	7.8	3.5	4.7	41.3	13.8
AZV 38	122/123	*Ursus arctos*	brown bear	−22.7	6.5	3.3	4.6	39.4	13.8
AZV 39	153	*Ursus arctos*	brown bear	−22.2	6.1	3.2	6.3	39.5	14.5

Figure 23.2 Stable isotope data of faunal material (excluding dog), sorted according to species. ~~Marked~~ samples fall outside quality ranges.

diversity in choice of food plants among herbivores of different species, and also the differing physiology (Schoeninger and DeNiro 1984).

Stable carbon isotope values for the human samples vary between −24.3‰ and −20.7‰, the most positive value coming from a tooth pendant. These values are considerably more negative than what is generally recorded for western European material, where −21‰ is usually considered a terrestrial end-value. However, the values are compliant with evidence for regional variation due to climatic factors (van Klinken et al. 1994). Moreover, they are consistent with previously recorded values for Mesolithic and Neolithic humans of this region (Lõugas et al. 1996; Lillie and Richards 2000), and supported by the range for herbivores in Zvejnieki. In fact, considering the $\delta^{13}C$ values of freshwater fish and otter from Zvejnieki, it can be concluded that freshwater fish made up a considerable part of the human diet. The range of stable nitrogen isotope values, 10.6–14.0‰, supports this interpretation.

Lab code	Grave	Tooth/bone element	δ¹³C	δ¹⁵N	C/N	% collagen	%C	%N	Age of individual when collagen was formed
ZVE 03	5	second deciduous molar	−23.9	12.5	3.5	2.9	37.7	12.5	infant
ZVE 04	5	second deciduous molar	−24.4	11.9	3.9	1.3	31.0	9.3	infant
ZVE 05	5	deciduous incisor	−31.5	13.7	5.4	4.8	37.1	8.0	infant
ZVE 01	62	premolar (tooth pendant)	−25.0	12.1	3.6	1.1	39.3	12.9	child
ZVE 16	76	femur	−21.3	12.3	3.4	2.2	38.3	13.2	adult
ZVE 12	89	first molar	−21.8	11.8	3.4	1.9	35.1	12.1	child
ZVE 13	89	second premolar	−22.4	11.6	3.5	2.2	37.2	12.4	child
ZVE 02	114	first molar (tooth pendant)	−21.7	10.6	3.3	5.1	40.4	14.2	child
ZVE 14	121	canine (tooth pendant)	−20.7	11.7	3.5	5.8	41.3	13.9	child
ZVE 15	158	incisor	−24.3	14.0	3.3	5.0	37.7	13.2	child
ZVE 11	164	scapula	−21.9	13.0	3.2	3.4	35.1	12.6	adult
ZVE 17	179	pelvis	−22.4	11.7	3.4	1.7	39.2	13.5	adult
ZVE 10	186	ulna	−21.7	10.9	3.3	3.0	40.2	14.1	child
ZVE 06	189	femur	−23.4	12.5	3.4	2.3	40.1	13.9	infant
ZVE 07	199	fibula	−23.1	12.0	3.4	5.8	43.9	15.1	adult

Figure 23.3 Stable isotope data of human bone and teeth, sorted according to grave. Marked samples fall outside quality ranges.

Lab code	Grave	Tooth	δ¹³C	δ¹⁵N	C/N	% collagen	%C	%N	samples from same grave
AZV 41	121	incisor	−21.9	10.4	3.2	1.1	32.0	11.5	Homo
AZV 42	122/123	third incisor	−20.8	10.4	3.2	2.0	36.7	13.3	Equus, Ursus, Meles
AZV 43	158	third incisor	−16.8	14.7	3.2	3.0	39.3	14.3	Homo
AZV 19	164	incisor	−21.5	7.3	3.2	3.6	37.4	13.8	Homo, Lutra, Bos
AZV 44	165	third incisor	−16.7	14.8	3.3	3.1	40.7	14.3	-
AZV 04	226	premolar	−25.6	12.2	3.4	5.5	35.6	12.1	Halichoerus
AZV 03	226	incisor	−25.5	12.7	3.5	4.6	38.7	13.1	Halichoerus
AZV 45	233	third incisor	−25.6	13.5	3.3	2.7	37.9	13.6	-
AZV 05	290	canine	−15.9	16.0	3.5	4.4	38.6	12.9	Phoca/Pusa
AZV 06	290	first molar	−16.6	14.1	3.9	n.d.	42.8	12.6	Phoca/Pusa

Figure 23.4 Stable isotope data of dog-tooth pendants, sorted according to grave. Marked samples fall outside quality ranges.

Stable isotope analysis of the dog-tooth pendants gave an extremely wide range, 9.7‰ in δ¹³C, and 8.7‰ in δ¹⁵N, but the values can be grouped into three clusters, each with three samples. In the first cluster, the dogs seem to have consumed mainly seal meat or other marine mammals. Whereas the δ¹³C signatures are roughly the same as for seals, −16.8 to −15.9‰, δ¹⁵N values are approximately 3‰ higher, that is, one trophic level above the seals.

The second group is more terrestrial, comparable to human values in δ¹³C, but lower in δ¹⁵N, from 7.3 to 10.4‰, as compared to 10.6–14.0‰ in humans. The contribution of freshwater fish to the diet of these dogs is probably smaller than that for humans, and the considerable variation suggests scavenging.

The third group consists of three samples with extremely negative δ¹³C values, one is tempted to call them 'extra-terrestrial', and with very high δ¹⁵N values, indicative of high trophic-level protein consumption. Two of the specimens are from the same grave, and are likely to be from the same dog. Supposedly these dogs fed almost exclusively on freshwater fish.

Discussion

The human stable isotope values are derived from graves of both Mesolithic and Neolithic dates, but the small sample size in relation to the great chronological span does not allow any conclusions concerning temporal trends, or the effects of sex and age in the human diet at Zvejnieki. Seen in relation to faunal values, there is overwhelming evidence that people consumed large amounts of freshwater fish, supplemented by terrestrial animals and plant resources. The variability in δ¹³C and δ¹⁵N points to somewhat differing proportions of these dietary constituents among individuals, but the overall impression is that the people buried at the Zvejnieki cemetery belonged to a fishing/hunting/gathering com-

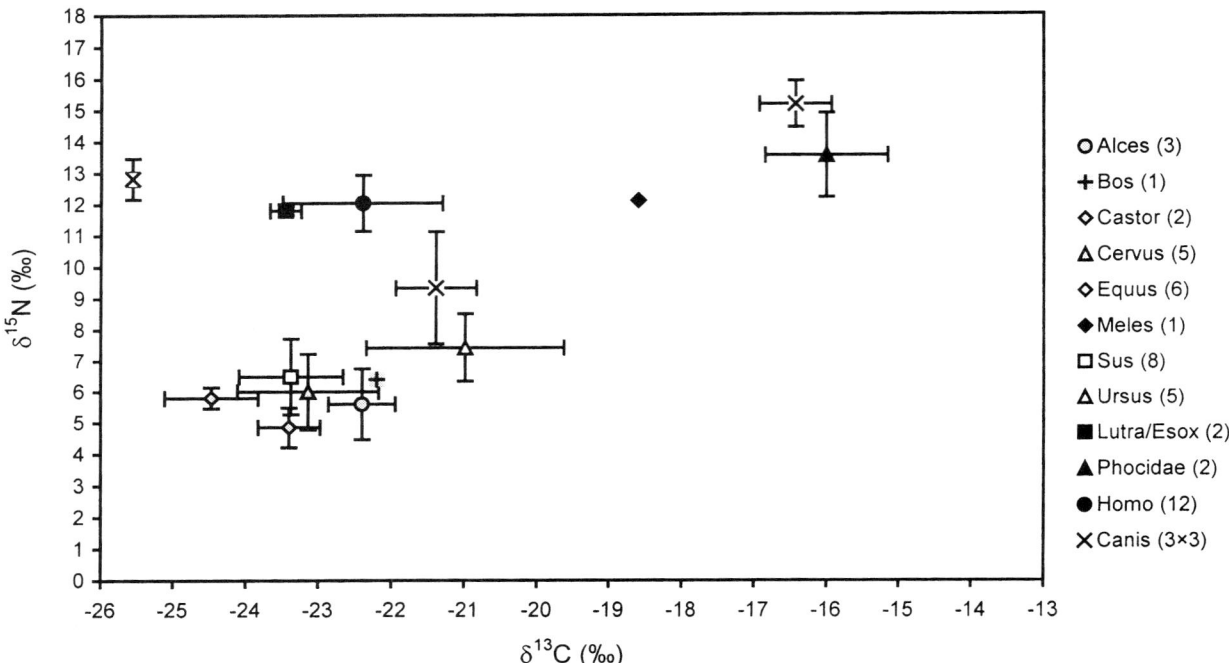

Figure 23.5 Collagen $\delta^{13}C$ and $\delta^{15}N$ values (average and one standard deviation) of all species at Zvejnieki. Number of samples indicated in brackets.

munity regardless of whether they were Mesolithic or Neolithic.

A possible explanation for the variability in human values is seasonality. Values representing children (including infants) have a higher standard deviation in both $\delta^{13}C$ and $\delta^{15}N$ than do adult values. Children's values derive from either adult teeth, which are formed during a limited period during childhood, or, in two cases, from children's bone which is likely to have a faster collagen turnover rate than adult bone, and thus represent a shorter period (cf. Lidén and Angerbjörn 1999 and references cited therein). Consequently, the isotopic signal in adult bone is levelled out during several years, whereas the signal recorded during childhood represents a much shorter time span, making it more likely to be affected by fluctuations caused by seasonal shifts in the diet.

The dog-tooth pendants in this study were mostly made out of permanent incisors, but also included one canine and one premolar (Figure 23.4). The sample was taken from the part of the tooth which is formed early in the pup's life, so what is recorded is actually what the dog was eating during its first five months (Hillson 1986:217). Suckling is likely to only leave traces in deciduous teeth, or the very earliest formed portion of the permanent teeth, and consequently it will not have affected stable isotope values in this study (cf. Katzenberg *et al.* 1996; Balasse *et al.* 1997; Schurr 1998; Wright and Schwarcz 1998; Lidén *et al.* in prep.).

The dogs fall into one of three groups which are very different from each other with regard to diet. There is no obvious correlation between these groups and the types of graves they were placed in, as regards dating, number of tooth beads, additional grave goods, orientation, ochre, or filling. Still, the number of graves analysed would have to be expanded considerably in order to draw any general conclusions.

The 'extra-terrestrial' dogs have the lowest $\delta^{13}C$ values so far measured at Zvejnieki, –25.6‰; only one specimen of wild horse comes close to them. However, horse meat is not likely to have made up any considerable part of the diet for these dogs, taking into account the very high $\delta^{15}N$ values in the dogs. The pike and the otter, on the other hand are closer in $\delta^{15}N$, but do not quite match the $\delta^{13}C$ values. Since these freshwater species are represented by only one specimen each, future studies will also include other freshwater species from Zvejnieki in order to investigate the potential variation of this freshwater ecosystem. From the present data it is reasonable to assume that the bulk of the dog diet consisted of freshwater fish. This suggests that the dogs were fed only fish, and did not have access to the scavenging of other food sources during their first months of life.

The group of dogs with intermediate $\delta^{13}C$ values may well have been scavengers at Zvejnieki. This includes the consumption of scrap food, that is, not only leftovers from human meals, but for example also pieces that were not considered edible by humans. An important element in scavenging is that humans are not in control of the dog's consumption, particularly the proportions of different components in the diet. This could explain the great variability among the scavenging dogs at Zvejnieki. White *et al.* (2001) have in a very recent study recorded even greater variability among what they interpret as scavenging Maya dogs, demonstrating the inconsistency in dog diet.

The idiosyncratic 'marine dogs' are intriguing. The first thought that comes to mind is the possibility that some of the Zvejnieki people were making expeditions to the coast to hunt seals. However, in grave 158, where one of the 'marine dogs' was found, a human specimen exhibits a completely non-marine stable isotope signature. One could of course argue that this sample, from this adult individual, is misleading because it was taken from an incisor, which is actually formed in early childhood. Nevertheless, there is no marine influence, as indicated by $\delta^{13}C$ measurements, in any of the 31 individual humans measured so far, that is, neither in the human bones or teeth included in this study, nor in the human bones that were radiocarbon dated (some specimens included in the present study were also radiocarbon dated).

Furthermore, there are no artefacts or faunal remains to support the idea of regular seal hunting among the Zvejnieki inhabitants. Tooth pendants of seal do occur at Zvejnieki, but only in a few graves. Three of those are included in this study, graves 121, 226, and 290 (Figure 23.4). These graves contain dog-tooth pendants which span all three dietary groups, $\delta^{13}C$ ranging from –15.9 to –25.6. In grave 121 there is also a human specimen, which is unfortunately a tooth pendant, resulting in only a weak connection to the interred individual. Still, the $\delta^{13}C$ value is terrestrial.

A factor that has to be taken into account when dealing with this part of Europe is the various stages that the Baltic Sea has passed through. Since $\delta^{13}C$ is to a great extent dependent on salinity, marine organisms will produce what appears to be 'terrestrial' stable carbon isotope signatures during freshwater stages of the Baltic Sea, such as the Ancylus stage. This has been shown in an earlier study by Lõugas, Lidén and Nelson (1996), where ringed seal bone from the Lammasmägi (Kunda) site in Estonia exhibited a $\delta^{13}C$ value of –23.3‰. The site is considerably older, c. 8500 BP, than the graves in this study, and the majority of the people buried at Zvejnieki seem to have lived after the Anclys stage of the Balitc Sea, so therefore the probability of a 'hidden' marine influence in the diet is negligible.

One could argue that the background faunal stable isotope data derive to a great extent from artefacts in graves. These artefacts could originate from distant regions, being deposited in the graves as 'exotics' (cf. Larsson 1978; Taffinder 1998). The faunal data would thus represent ecological conditions at places other than Zvejnieki. Tooth pendants of seal and of 'marine dogs' are obvious examples of such potential exotics, but other species at Zvejnieki do not readily qualify as rare or exotic. It is likely that some kind of local production of tooth pendants existed, and that to a great extent they do therefore represent local conditions. Nevertheless, future studies will include animal bone from cultural layers, as well as faunal remains from the graves, excluding artefacts, to rule out the possibility that the measured fauna was 'foreign'.

To sum up then, hunting seal at the coast does not seem to have been a habit among the Zvejnieki inhabitants. Another possible scenario to account for the presence of the 'marine dogs' could be that the people of Zvejnieki received dog-tooth pendants from people living by the coast in much the same way as they got the tooth pendants of seal. In contrast to seals, however, dogs are not only terrestrial animals, they are above all domesticated, and as such may be moved about in ways that seals cannot. A third possibility must therefore be considered, namely that the inland people at Zvejnieki acquired living dogs from coastal inhabitants. From the present data it is not possible to tell if the animals came to Zvejnieki in the form of tooth pendants or as living animals. The dogs were probably valued in both forms, and the evidence for contact with coastal people is clear.

Conclusions

The present study demonstrates that dogs do not necessarily eat like humans, and therefore cannot be used as approximations for human diet; that is, the stable isotope analysis of dog does not automatically tell what people ate. It does, on the other hand, tell us what dogs ate, which in this study has produced important evidence on contacts between inland and coastal inhabitants during the Stone Age in Latvia. Furthermore it has added to our knowledge of the Zvejnieki subsistence, and presented clues as to the relationship between dogs and people in Mesolithic society. Due to the number of roles that dogs may have in human society, it is not likely that they had homogenous diets within a particular community. The Zvejnieki case is a conspicuous example of this variability.

Acknowledgements

We wish to thank Janne Storå, Lembi Lõugas, Kerstin Lidén and Valdis Berzins for their invaluable help and support to this study. Furthermore, we thank Bo Edlén for running the mass spectrometer, and finally The Swedish Council for Research in the Humanities and Social Sciences (HSFR), The Royal Swedish Academy of Sciences, The Latvian Academy of Sciences, and Greta Arwidssons fond for funding.

References

Ambrose, S.H. and Norr, L. 1993. Experimental evidence for the relationship of carbon isotope ratios of whole diet and dietary protein to those of bone collagen and carbonate. In: Lambert, J.B. and Grupe, G. (eds.) *Prehistoric Human Bone: Archaeology at the Molecular Level*, 1–37. Berlin.

Balasse, M., Bocherens, H., Tresset, A., Mariotti, A. and Vigne, J.-D. 1997. Émergence de la production laitiére au Néolithique? Contribution de l'analyse isotopique d'ossements de bovins archéologiques. *Comptes rendus de l'Acadámie des sciences* 325, 1005–1010.

Benecke, N. 1987. Studies of early dog remains from northern Europe. *Journal of Archaeological Science* 14, 31–49.

Brown, T.A., Nelson, D.E., Vogel, J.S. and Southon, J.R. 1988. Improved collagen extraction by modified Longin method. *Radiocarbon* 30, 171–177.

Burleigh, R. and Brothwell, D. 1978. Studies on Amerindian dogs, 1: Carbon isotopes in relation to maize in the diet of domestic dogs from Early Peru and Ecuador. *Journal of Archaeological Science* 5, 355–362.

Cannon, A., Schwarcz, H.P. and Knyf, M. 1999. Marine-based subsistence trends and the stable isotope analysis of dog bones from Namu, British Columbia. *Journal of Archaeological Science* 26, 399–407.

Chu, P.P. 1998. Dietary variation among the prehistoric Asiatic Eskimo. Master thesis: Simon Fraser University. Vancouver.

Clutton-Brock, J. 1995. Origins of the dog: Domestication and early history. In: Serpell, J. (ed.) *The Domestic Dog: Its evolution, behaviour, and interactions with people*, 7–20. Cambridge.

Clutton-Brock, J. and Noe-Nygaard, N. 1990. New osteological and C-isotope evidence on Mesolithic dogs: Companions to hunters and fishers at Star Carr, Seamer Carr and Kongemose. *Journal of Archaeological Science* 17, 643–653.

Day, S.P. 1996. Dogs, deer and diet at Star Carr: A reconstruction of C-isotope evidence from early Mesolithic dog remains from the Vale of Pickering, Yorkshire, England. *Journal of Archaeological Science* 23, 783–787.

DeNiro, M.J. 1985. Postmortem preservation and alteration of *in vivo* bone collagen isotope ratios in relation to palaeodietary reconstruction. *Nature* 317, 806–809.

Hillson, S. 1986. *Teeth*. Cambridge Manuals in Archaeology. Cambridge.

Jonsson, L. 1988. The vertebrate faunal remains from the Late Atlantic settlement Skateholm in Scania, South Sweden. In: Larsson, L. (ed.) *The Skateholm Project: I. Man and Environment*. Acta Regiae Societatis humaniorum litterarum Lundensis, 56–88. Lund.

Katzenberg, M.A. 1989. Stable isotope analysis of archaeological faunal remains from Southern Ontario. *Journal of Archaeological Science* 16, 319–329.

Katzenberg, M.A., Herring, D.A. and Saunders, S.R. 1996. Weaning and infant mortality: Evalutating the skeletal evidence. *Yearbook of Physical Anthropology* 39, 177–199.

Larsson, L. 1978. Mesolithic antler and bone artefacts from Central Scania. *Meddelanden från Lunds universitets historiska museum* 1977–1978, 28–67.

—— 1990. Dogs in fraction – symbols in action. In: Vermeersch, P.M. and Peer, P.V. (eds.) *Contributions to the Mesolithic in Europe: Papers presented at the Fourth International Symposium 'The Mesolithic in Europe', Leuven 1990*, 153–160. Leuven.

Lepiksaar, J. 1984. Die frühesten Haustiere der skandinavischen Halbinsel, insbesondere in Schweden. In: Nobis, G. (ed.) *Der Beginn der Haustierhaltung in der 'Alten Welt'. Die Anfänge des Neolithikums vom Orient bis Nordeuropa*, 221–266. Köln.

Lidén, K. and Angerbjörn, A. 1999. Dietary change and stable isotopes: A model of growth and dormancy in cave bears. *Proceedings of the Royal Society of London: Series B* 266, 1779–1783.

Lidén, K., Olsson, A., Eriksson, G. and Angerbjörn, A. (in prep.) Nitrogen isotope analysis of teeth: A tool to trace individual dietary change. Manuscript.

Lillie, M.C. and Richards, M. 2000. Stable isotope analysis and dental evidence of diet at the Mesolithic–Neolithic transition in Ukraine. *Journal of Archaeological Science* 27, 965–972.

Little, E.A. and Schoeninger, M.J. 1995. The Late Woodland diet on Nantucket Island and the problem of maize in coastal New England. *American Antiquity* 60, 351–368.

Lõugas, L., Lidén, K. and Nelson, D.E. 1996. Resource utilization along the Estonian coast during the Stone Age. In: Hackens, T., Hicks, S., Lang, V., Miller, U. and Saarse, L. (eds.) *Coastal Estonia: Recent Advances in environmental and Cultural History*. PACT 51, 399–420. Rixensart.

Minagawa, M. and Wada, E. 1984. Stepwise enrichment of ^{15}N along food chains: Further evidence and the relation between $\delta^{15}N$ and animal age. *Geochimica et Cosmochimica Acta* 48, 1135–1140.

Noe-Nygaard, N. 1988. $\delta^{13}C$-values of dog bones reveal the nature of changes in Man's food resources at the Mesolithic–Neolithic transition, Denmark. *Chemical Geology (Isotope Geoscience Section)* 73, 87–96.

Noe-Nygaard, N. 1995. *Ecological, sedimentary, and geochemical evolution of the late-glacial to postglacial Åmose lacustrine basin, Denmark* (Fossils and Strata 37). Oslo.

Olsen, S.L. 2000. The secular and sacred roles of dogs at Botai, North Kazakhstan. In: Crockford, S.J. (ed.) *Dogs Through Time: An Archaeological Perspective*. BAR International Series, 71–92. Oxford.

Paaver, K. 1965. *Formirovanie teriofauny i izmencivost mlekopitajuscich Pribaltiki v golocene*. Tartu.

Schoeninger, M.J. and DeNiro, M.J. 1984. Nitrogen and carbon isotopic composition of bone collagen from marine and terrestrial animals. *Geochimica et Cosmochimica Acta* 48, 625–639.

Schulting, R.J. 1994. The hair of the dog: The identification of a Salish dog-hair blanket from Yale, British Columbia. *Canadian Journal of Archaeology* 18, 57–76.

Schulting, R.J. and Richards, M.P. (in prep.). Dogs, ducks, deer and diet: A reappraisal of the stable isotope evidence on Early Mesolithic dogs from the Vale of Pickering, North-East England. Submitted to *Journal of Archaeological Science*.

Schurr, M.R. 1998. Using stable nitrogen-isotopes to study weaning behavior in past populations. *World Archaeology* 30, 327–342.

Serpell, J. 1995. From paragon to pariah: Some reflections on human attitudes to dogs. In: Serpell, J. (ed.) *The Domestic Dog: Its evolution, behaviour, and interactions with people*, 245–256. Cambridge.

Taffinder, J. 1998. *The Allure of the Exotic: The social use of non-local raw materials during the Stone Age in Sweden*. Aun 25. Uppsala.

van Klinken, G.J. 1999. Bone collagen quality indicators for palaeodietary and radiocarbon measurements. *Journal of Archaeological Science* 26, 687–695.

van Klinken, G.J., van der Plicht, H. and Hedges, R.E.M. 1994. Bone $^{13}C/^{12}C$ ratios reflect (palaeo-)climatic variations. *Geophysical Research Letters* 21, 445–448.

White, C.D., Pohl, M.E.D., Schwarcz, H.P. and Longstaffe, F.J. 2001. Isotopic evidence for Maya patterns of deer and dog use at Preclassic Colha. *Journal of Archaeological Science* 28, 89–107.

Wright, L.E. and Schwarcz, H.P. 1998. Stable carbon and oxygen isotopes in human tooth enamel: Identifying breastfeeding and weaning in prehistory. *American Journal of Physical Anthropology* 106, 1–18.

Zagorska, I. 1992. The Mesolithic in Latvia. *Acta Archaeologica* 63, 97–117.

Zagorska, I. and Lõugas, L. 2000. The tooth pendant head-dresses of Zvejnieki cemetery. In: Lang, V. (ed.) *De temporibus antiquissimis ad honorem Lembit Jaanits*. Muinasaja Teadus, 223–244. Tallinn.

Zagorskis, F. 1987. *Zvejnieki akmens laikmeta kapulauks*. Riga.

24. Microliths and Multiple Authorship

Nyree Finlay

This paper develops the notion of multiple authorship in relation to Mesolithic microliths. Originating in Melanesian ethnography, multiple authorship is a construct that acknowledges the partible nature of people, events and things. Here it is used as a device to reconfigure the social dimensions of lithic technologies. A couple of ethnographic case studies are presented including David Clarke's alternative microlithic tool: the grater board. Making microliths involves a number of different skills and separate tasks. These have traditionally been perceived as the action of one, usually male, individual. Yet multiplicity is implicit in microlith manufacture and explicit in terms of the hafted component. Here it is beneficial to reconsider the dynamics of microlith manufacture and use as embodying collective effort: technology as a forum for group participation and expression rather than individual action. It is argued the concept of multiple authorship in conjunction with the chaîne opératoire offers a means to enrich our understanding of microlith biographies by allowing for the elaboration of age, gender and social relations in the realm of mesolithic tool production and use.

Introduction

This paper is concerned with the archetypal signifier of the Mesolithic: the microlith. As both an artefact and a metaphor the microlith can be identified with various stages in the development of mesolithic studies. Its small size appeared to encapsulate debates about cultural hiatus and the insignificance of the period in relation to those on either side. Here the moniker pygmy flint, used by the antiquarians, seemed more than apposite. Due to its identification as a projectile component the microlith has also become a metonym for male action: as such it is indelibly bound with other dominant narratives about the period that have centred on red deer hunters and their actions. As a mesolithic motif, the microlith has many meanings. As an artefact, attention is given to function at the expense of production. It is unfortunate that due to their perceived simplicity microliths have rarely been the subject of experimental replication. This has clearly been detrimental to our appreciation of production as performance and knowledgeable action. Moreover, functional studies have tended to conform to the dominant narratives with little consideration of alternative or multiple uses and interpretations. Another characteristic of our diminutive type fossil lies with its composite nature and the multiplicity inherent in the arrangement of lithic components. Here the practical benefits of such technologies are given precedence over any social significance or meaning. Yet, at one level, technological strategies can be seen as a metaphor for society at large and it is with these and other readings of the microlith that I concern myself in this paper.

Divided into four main sections the aim is to develop the notion of multiple authorship for the mesolithic and argue that such constructs offer a means to reconsider the character and meaning of composite technologies. The first part outlines multiple authorship as a construct and a gives a brief examination of its ethnographic background. The second section takes a closer look at grater board production and use as an example that revisits David Clarke's alternative vision of the mesolithic. While the following two sections seek to demonstrate the methodological strategies that can be used to elaborate elements of the microlith chaîne opératoire and their theoretical implications.

Multiple Authorship: appropriation of a construct

Some of the most potent approaches that we as archaeologists can draw from anthropology centre on reading material culture and in particular integrating the life cycles of people with things. Here an explicit focus on biography is rewarding at a number of levels, from developing notions of personhood to the complexities of reading past meaning in the present. Recent anthropological studies have demonstrated the potential of such biographical approaches, acknowledging the critical role of objects in the creation of personal and social identities (e.g. Appadurai 1986; Battaglia 1983; Hoskins 1998).

Marilyn Strathern developed multiple authorship as a construct in relation to gender dynamics in Papua New Guinea. Such ideas developed out of the tensions between Melanesian and western perspectives on social action. Tensions paralleled in our own negotiation between present and past. Multiple authorship combines a conceptualisation of legitimate ownership with a critique of the conscious individual agent who is the singular source of their actions (Strathern 1988:158). As such it engages with the notion of partible persons which directly challenge the western ideal of the individual. Partibility recognises the fragmented nature of the person where identity is not fixed but composed of a number of different properties. Personhood is, therefore, also defined by the exchange, circulation and meaning of things.

In *The Gender of the Gift* Strathern (1988) fragments the sociological categorisation of gender to encompass objects, events and transactions as well as people themselves. In doing so she challenges discourses of domination with a focus on the transformation of gendered action and power. Hence the production and exchange of pigs in Hagen society is the outcome of the nurturing power of female action that is transformed in the male exchange transaction. The former is not negated but reworked by the latter. The details of Strathern's argument are complex and context specific, most need not directly concern us here (see Gell 1999a for a diagrammatic translation of these ideas). Despite its ethnographic specifics, multiple authorship can be adopted as a general principle. A way to refocus attention on the complex of meaning surrounding identity and action. As Jolly (1992:143) has argued it need not imply equivalence: rather the emphasis is on mutuality and the underlying meanings of action. Here it is as important to consider symbolic as well as physical action. One is reminded of a different ethnographic situation described by Bodenhorn (1993) concerning the Inupiat of Alaska where the success of the male whale hunter is dependant upon the role of the whaling captains-wife in ritually facilitating the hunt. In this example where 'survival rather than biology' defines action, it is knowledge and skills that take precedence.

It is within the realm of material culture that multiple authorship offers a more tangible contribution to archaeological concerns. In her excellent examination of the manufacture and use of string bags or *bilums* in Papua New Guinea, Maureen MacKenzie (1991) explores the multiple authorship involved in the production of one of these items. Bilums serve a number of important functions for carrying produce back from the gardens, transporting infants, as well as ritual paraphernalia. While these items are made and used by women, they are not sex-exclusive, rather they are quintessentially androgynous objects: an amalgamation of the creativity of both men and women. Men often commission bags providing raw materials and paying in kind for labour, because bilums are time consuming to produce and it can take up to 15 hours to make one of the larger bags. Their size and shape varies as does the cordage techniques of their manufacture, and such variations are associated with different sexes, age sets and kin groups. As such bilums are the product of more than one individual involved in a network of social obligations. They serve many different functions and have different meanings and associations depending on the context, the individual and both their respective places in the life-course.

While multiple authorship originates in Melanesian ethnography the term can clearly be adopted for wider application particularly in the manner exemplified by MacKenzie (1991) and Hoskins (1998). It provides a link between different types of action and its material expression. It also enables the elaboration of narratives of transformation but retains sufficient ambiguity to prevent these from becoming proscriptive and bounded entities. One of the most significant advantages of borrowing notions like multiple authorship is that it provides us with the means of subverting established notions of the gendered attribution of artefacts. Multiple authorship acknowledges both male and female action in a manner that does not privilege one over the other but recognises that action and its meanings are fluid. Doing so releases us from over simplistic readings of objects and action to the dynamic interplay of constellations of knowledge and experience. It is not only gender distinctions that benefit, age and other social constructions of difference can be incorporated. Moreover, these need not remain fixed for either the author or the artefact. This makes it an ideal adjunct to biographical approaches that emphasis the metaphorical meaning of material culture. Although to date these remain relatively under-explored in archaeology, see Tilley (1999) for a notable exception.

Revisiting Clarke's Grater Board

David Clarke first proposed the grater board as the alternative composite artefact of the Mesolithic in *Mesolithic Europe: the economic basis* (Clarke 1976: Fig. 2). This paper marks an important benchmark in mesolithic studies, as a tribute to Graham Clark it is also a potent critique of traditional approaches to the Mesolithic and the stereotypical associations of the period. Unfortunately it tends to be cited for its over-estimates of plant productivity and inappropriate use of antipodean parallels (e.g. Bonsall 1981; Rowley-Conwy 1986), rather than its more subversive content. This is regrettable for Clarke encapsulates many of the problems and issues that continue to set the Mesolithic agenda. While his figure of composite artefacts has been reproduced on a number of occasions few have taken to heart the fervour of his critique against the faunal, artefactual and north European bias.

In this section I wish to revisit the grater board, not to argue for it as the missing artefact form of the Mesolithic, but rather to consider it from the perspective of multiple

Figure 24.1 Cassava Grater in action in Mawikà. © The National Museum of Denmark, Department of Ethnography. Photographer: Jens Yde.

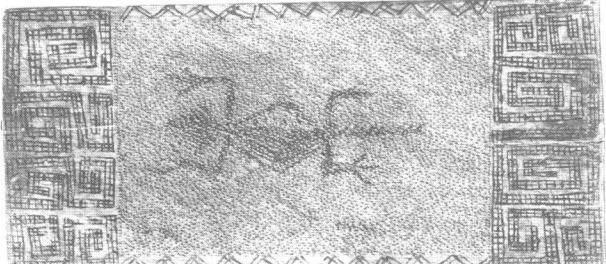

Figure 24.2 Waiwai Cassava Grater, length 75.5 cm. © The National Museum of Denmark, Department of Ethnography. Photographer: Lennart Larsen.

```
Task                                           ♀♂
Collection of raw materials                    ♂
  wood (Aspidospermum excelsa)
  stone (2 days distance); resin; pigments

Manufacture
  carving the board                            ♂
  red pigment outline on board                 ♀♂
  knapping of stone chips                      ♀♂
  insertion of stone chips                     ♀♂
  surface sealed with red pigment              ♀♂
  decoration with black pigment                ♂

Use
  use of board for grating cassava             ♀
```

Figure 24.3 Grater board chaîne opératoire showing tasks undertaken by husband and wife team (after Yde 1965)

23.1–23.2), necessitated by the need to remove toxins to render these tropical species edible. The tubers are grated on a wooden board embedded with several hundred if not thousands of small knapped stone chips (Mowat 1989). The stone chips are c. 8 mm in length and project several millimetres above the board (Sievert 1992). Ethnographic studies of grater board production and use emphasis collective production. Among the Waiwái of Guiana and Brazil, the manufacture of a cassava grater board is a shared undertaking; the woman knapping and inserting the lithics into the wood board fashioned by her husband. Following the coating of the inserted stone chips with resinous red pigment, she hands it to her husband who completes the board by decorating it with totemic animals and designs in black pigment (Yde 1965). Stages in the grater board chaîne opératoire are outlined in Figure 24.3. Janet Chernela (1992) who has explored the specialised production and exchange of boards in the northwest Amazon also stresses the shared and indebted nature of production. Among the Eastern Turkanoan, each language group exclusively specialises in the production of a matrimonial exchange item. These include grater boards, baskets, strainers as well as benches used in shamanic rituals. For the Baniwa groups who produce grater boards their value is further enhanced by the need to acquire non-local quartzite for the stone inserts.

The grater board is a composite artefact that encapsulates multiple authorship. It demonstrates the layers of meaning, social obligations and collective engagement embedded in the routines of technology. These obligations continue throughout the life-cycle of the grater board: relationships made explicit through the repetitive rubbing of the tuber on the grater, marking the transformation of the cassava from inedible crop to dietary staple. The significance of the grater board is matched by its symbolic role reflected in the relationship that produced it, the designs painted upon it, and the exchange value of such items. As a biographical object it embodies the combined efforts of the husband and wife team.

The grater board is not the only example that demonstrates the collective and indebted nature of artefact production. Others can be found among the wider ethnographic literature that show the social obligations and relationships central to tool production and use, for example Osgood (1940) identifies the makers, users and owners of tools among the Ingalik Inuit. Indeed one could argue that all aspects of technology are inherently social, even when a single individual controls all stages for this is clearly a statement to others about the ownership and possession of goods. Recent developments in theorising the social dimensions of technology are significant and provide a means to refocus on the broader meanings of action (in particular see Dobres 2000). Adopting constructs like multiple authorship and considering them along with the notion of the biographical object allows us to acknowledge these inherently social strategies in the artefact lifecycle.

authorship. It is unfortunate that Clarke directed his attention to the functional bias in artefactual studies rather than consider the broader implications in terms of production for it may be in this arena that the grater board analogy is more apposite.

The grater board is an implement type associated with the processing of manioc and cassava tubers (Figures.

In lithic analysis, we can identify a number of elements that have prevented the development of more explicit theoretical engagement with these issues. The first lies in lithic replication as contemporary practice with a focus on the knapping abilities of a number of prominent and proficient male individuals: the legacy of Bordes and Crabtree (see Gero 1991 for a detailed critique). Creating a gender bias it also reifies knapping as a specialist activity, giving undue emphasis to individual action. Secondly, our focus on reduction sequences and the chaîne opératoire tend to reinforce the notion of the singular artisan. While not inherent *per se* in the formation of these constructs, it is more often than not the by-product of methodological strategies used such as refitting. It also reflects a more general failure to consider tool production as a collective engagement rather than individual endeavour. Paradoxically it is these same methodological tools that offer potential for addressing these biases but for this to happen the theoretical context has to be made more explicit.

For the Mesolithic, the identification of microliths as masculine objects has characterised narratives of their production and use. In Britain such constructs originate in the post-war period during the 1950s when such discourses become dominant (Finlay 2000a). Such gendered identifications continue to the present and a more recent scandinavian example is the work by Ole Grøn on the Maglemosian sexual division of labour where microliths are seen as explicitly male signifiers (Grøn 1995). Yet the case studies cited above reveal that an object can have many authors and encompass several distinct meanings at any given time. These meanings can even be independent of the identity of the person making or using the item yet are of critical importance to its perceived value. The subject of who makes and uses microliths raises a whole range of issues. Traditional assumptions of microliths as relatively simple artefacts without complex manufacturing procedures have conditioned our approaches and treatment of them, while debates about style condition perceptions of these pieces as emblematic rather than seeing form as the outcome of a set of dynamic processes. In the next section, attention is focused on the microlith biography to explore whether multiple authorship has any currency and how we can identify it.

Methodologies for the Microlith Biography

To date discussion of microlithic technologies have focused on the functional benefits of their design principles rather than the social strategies embodied in their form. It is with the latter in mind that we turn our attention to consider the microlith biography: from blank production to archaeological artifice. The observations made here are informed from two main sources experimental replication and assemblage analysis. The former sought to address issues of skill and consistency in blade production and the constraints on microlith form (Finlay

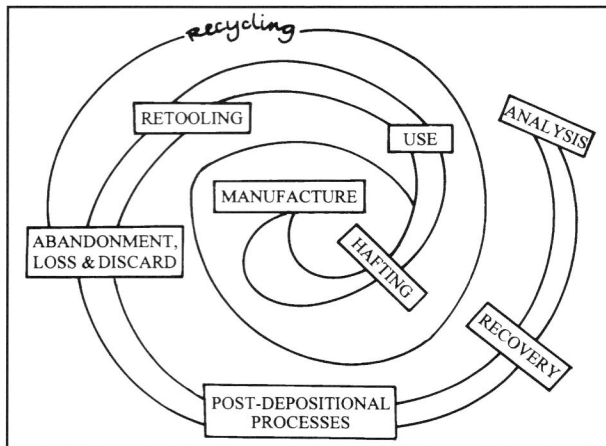

Figure 24.4 The Microlith Biography.

1997, 2000a) while the latter comprised archaeological material excavated under the aegis of the *Southern Hebrides Mesolithic Project* (Mithen 2000). Lithic assemblages were recovered from a series of later mesolithic sites on the islands of Islay and Colonsay, off the west coast of Scotland. Most activity dates to the mid 8th millennium BC (with a date range from 8110±60BP (AA-21627) at Staosnaig, Colonsay to 6800±40BP (Beta-37624) at Rockside, Islay. Therefore the specific examples given may only be relevant to these particular assemblages although what I am saying hopefully has broader application.

This section reviews various stages of the microlith biography (see Figure 24.4) as a means to develop approaches to consider the presence of multiple authorship and refocus on the social dimensions of lithic technology. This coverage cannot be exhaustive, rather the intention is to highlight a number of key aspects. The continuum of the microlith biography can be considered under four basic headings: manufacture, use-life, discard and finally, as archaeological entity. The latter conditions all approaches to our understanding of the other three stages and the strategies adopted to examine them and it is here that we begin.

The microlith as archaeological entity

The dominant motif of the Mesolithic is an archaeological creation. The microlith has served a number of different roles in the formation of Mesolithic narratives. These have conditioned the treatment of this component of lithic assemblages and how we have objectified the microlith as a signifier. As such, it is privileged from other debitage components in an assemblage by virtue of the presence of backing retouch. Moreover, we are conditioned by a two-dimensional appreciation of the microlith as a product of the conventional orientation of microliths in archaeological analysis. If we take any illustration of microliths, we can see the dorsal surface uppermost, vertical arrangement on the page arranged by the form in plan and typological treatment that typifies approaches to these implements. The microlith as conventionally illustrated determines our understanding of these pieces producing a *microlithic gaze* that establishes the microlith in the consciousness of the analyst. This constrains our reading of them in terms of plane symmetry leading to a tendency to recognise particular forms at the expense of others. Yet this is an artifice in relation to the reality of the microlith as a manufactured form. For a start, the dominant orientation is ventral, for this is the surface that is altered by backing retouch. This means that the creation of a simple scalene triangle form is a mirror image of the shape created during analysis. The conflicts between these etic/emic concepts of the microlith are important, but seldom do we consider the broader implications for our treatment of assemblages. This focus on the shape of the microlith in plan and the two-dimensional view perpetuated by the microlithic gaze also places undue emphasis on the microlith as a fixed form. Instead the three-dimensional manipulation and play on this can also occur during hafting and the configuration of complementary forms to create a continuous cutting edge instead of a biserial symmetric arrangement. Here envisaged scenarios of use have conditioned reconstruction of microlithic arrangements. At each stage of the microlith biography we need to question the microlith as a product of archaeological enquiry and refocus the microlithic gaze.

Manufacture

Discussions of microlith manufacture have tended to focus on technical details such as the microburin technique at the expense of the dynamic of the chaîne opératoire. Due to their perceived simplicity microliths have not been the subject of experimental replication. Where this has been undertaken it has tended to be relatively informal (e.g. Tixier 1963) and often conducted in the context of use related studies (e.g. Barton and Bergman 1982). This is unfortunate for a more explicit focus on microlith manufacture can reveal subtle differences in the realisation of microlith form. Their apparent simplicity masks a number of different routines of production from issues such as the type of retoucher utilised to whether the blank is rested on an anvil to be retouched or handheld and scraped against a stone. Blank thickness and the location of arris scars also determine the frequency and character of retouch, limiting both the formation of *enclume* retouch to determining the overall form (Finlay 1997, 2000a).

Detailed assemblage analysis does reveal subtle differences in the realisation of microlith shape. In assemblages excavated under the aegis of the *Southern Hebrides Mesolithic Project* on the islands of Islay and Colonsay (Mithen 2000), the dominant microlith is the scalene triangle, it accounts for 50–65% of the microliths at four sites. In many instances this is created by the backing of two sides only, leaving the base untrimmed; a

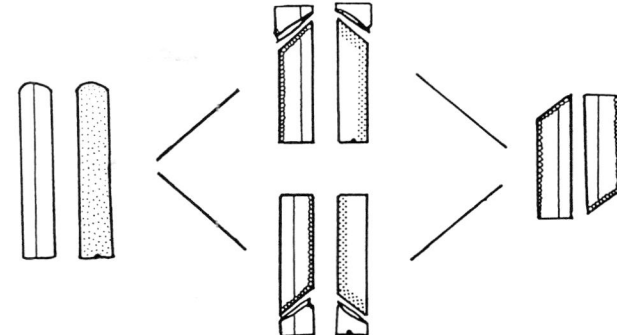

Figure 24.5 Schematic diagram of the two routines of scalene triangle production.

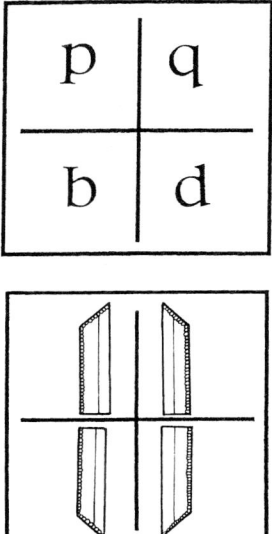

Figure 24.6 Issues of symmetry in scalene triangles.

common feature of microliths in the region, giving a final piece 10–15 mm in length. Scalene triangles can be realised by two different routines of backing, backed across the dorsal left side and distal end or the right side and proximal end (Figure 24.5). The issues are determined by how the piece is orientated during production, as there is a dominant ventral surface orientation to the execution of retouch. The issues are the same as those encountered with the letters b, d, p and q (Figure 24.6). Each are formed by a straight line and a loop, yet the perception and meaning of these letters is determined by their direction and orientation. Turn the page upside down and the d becomes p and vice versa. The left/distal forms of scalene triangles predominant at Bolsay Farm, Islay, whereas the right/proximal forms are prevalent at other sites (Staosnaig, Colonsay and Aoradh and Coulererach, Islay; full details of these assemblages and broader discussion can be found in Mithen 2000). This reveals differences in the orientation of pieces during manufacture and possibly preferences in terms of the internal geometry of forms. These observations also have implications regarding handedness but we do not know whether the blank was held vertical or horizontal during backing. The presence of *lamelle à cran* does, however, suggest that the lateral edge was backed first.

Unfortunately several of the sites are large palimpsests and the factors responsible for the variations identified may simply be the conflation of a number of different elements. Indeed one of these may be conditioned by our preference as analysts for recognising these forms (left/distal, right/proximal) over the left/proximal, right/distal variety. Psychological pattern recognition tests have demonstrated the problem of recognising the same form if it appears as a left/right reversal rather than a mirror image (Rock 1973). Analysis of other assemblages is revealing other symmetry preferences (Finlay in prep.). At the end of the day, these may simply reflect the product of different routines for holding and backing forms rather than indicating conscious choices of one form over the other, given that the internal geometry is the same and the difference is essentially one of orientation. However, it is interesting to note that there are only two microliths from different SHMP sites out of 1500 examined that have the same internal geometry as a scalene triangle but are backed along the longest lateral side instead of the shortest. This does suggest that there was a strong cultural preference for the classic scalene form in the region. The identification of these subtle differences reveals the benefits of detailed assemblage analysis and the value of attribute based typologies. Issues of surface and plane orientation have considerable potential for transforming our understanding of microliths both during manufacture and as hafted components.

Another manufacturing myths about microliths that needs to be challenged is the importance of the microburin technique. At least 20% of experimentally produced microliths using the microburin technique resulted in breakage and no identifiable microburin (Finlay 1997). Even when successful this method is often associated with unidentifiable small debitage fragments. The importance given to this technique needs to be revised in terms of making broader inferences on the basis of microburin ratios and frequencies. The identification of different routines for truncating blanks can enhance our appreciation of differences in the microlith chaîne opératoire (Finlay 2000c).

One of the dominant motifs of microlith manufacture is the sense of concealment. The transformation of the blank is essentially a hidden process, during backing the hand obscures the piece from both the maker and any observers. Microlith manufacture is in the sleight of the hand and this metaphor of concealment continues in the hafting where the haft or mastic conceals the piece. This concealment also serves to emphasise the transformation in form. Established notions of microlith manufacture credit production as the action of one person who makes the blank, retouches it and then secures it in the haft. This need not have been the case at all. Indeed one could argue that the contribution of materials or individual components would actively engender co-operation. Perhaps resulting in the claim to resources procured by the person using this tool or via other meanings of the relationship embedded in the hafted form. Clearly we should not assume that all microliths in a hafted composite were the product of one person for the metaphor of concealment also reveals potential multiplicity in production. Not simply in terms of the various components in the creation of a haft but the choices made in their selection.

Use Life

Discussions of microlith function are dominated by the mythology as a projectile component. While this was the element that Clarke (1976) attacked using the grater board as an alternative, projectile functions continue to dominate discussion of microlith use. This is despite microwear analysis that has revealed a range of alternative functions for the microlith in Britain and Ireland (Dumont 1988; Finlayson and Mithen 1997; Grace 1992). It is evident that we need to disconnect function from the meta-narratives that such inferred uses have created in order to develop multiple authorship as a viable challenge.

The use of macroscopic use wear indicators such as edge damage and impact fractures also needs to be questioned (cf Grøn 1992). During experimental microlith replication an impact fracture was fortuitously produced during backing (Finlay 1997). Located at the retouched proximal end, this piece has the macroscopic criteria that would be attributed to impact fractures. Given that one can be produced accidentally we should be cautious of using such features to imply projectile function without qualifying microwear or other supporting evidence.

Around forty microlithic arrangements and clusters are known from Britain (Rozoy 1978:Fig. 265; Myers 1986; David 1998). While no preserved hafts have yet been recovered, these clusters demonstrate the complexity of the original forms. At Readycon Dene, West Yorkshire a cluster comprised 35 microliths evenly spaced over a 2m length and is clearly suggestive of a more complex form than a simple arrow shaft. More extensive use-wear programmes are needed to examine the currency of microlith use lives and the frequency of replacement rates. As noted above these have tended to be dominated by projectile uses but other studies (such as Sievert 1992 for grater boards) are required. A focus on breakage patterns is another rewarding, but currently unexplored avenue (McBryde 1986; Finlay in prep.).

Discard

Another means of elaborating the multiple authorship of microliths lies with the identification of differential spatial patterning and attitudes to discard. Multiple authorship is already evidenced in the spatial distribution of knapping products. Rozoy (this volume) has identified notable differences between the Magdalenian and mesolithic in northern France in relation to the movement of different knapping products within open air sites. Different stages in the microlith biography can also be identified in the archaeological record, revealing whether microliths are recovered in forms representative of their original form (Finlay 2000b). Thus, different trajectories of use, retooling and repair have varying archaeological signatures.

It is also clear that not all microliths were used. At Gleann Mor, Islay microwear analysis revealed that microliths with clearly defined angles on both surfaces were more likely to retain use traces (Finlayson and Mithen 1997). Here we need to consider potential selection criteria and the manner by which microliths were chosen given the multiplicity of uses for these pieces.

Reconfiguring Microlithic Technologies

One of the striking aspects of microlithic technologies in addition to the size and the shape of the component pieces is its composite character. Technological rationales to account for the values inherent in this form of design have centred on elements like versatility; portability; ease of replacement and maintenance. There has been considerable attention given to the concept of risk avoidance and reduction in models such as those presented by Myers (1986) in relation to the shift from the broad to narrow blade forms in English mesolithic. Theoretical explanations for microlithic technologies have focused on the benefits of a plug-in, pull-out system in terms of advantages for the hunter (Zvelebil 1986). But microliths are multi-functional components, and the technology extends beyond that of the projectile.

While I acknowledge that component parts are an element in most tool forms, especially those that are hafted, there is something quite explicit about the reliance on small microlithic elements in the mesolithic. Multiplicity is implicit in microlith manufacture and explicit in terms of the hafted component. Because of its reliance and emphasis on multiple components, microlithic technology can be seen as a forum for group participation and expression rather than individual action. As Moss states 'backed bladelets do not require great skill or much time to manufacture, but including the haft, the final implement was labour intensive' (Moss 1983:143). Are the technological rationales of mobility and raw material constraints sufficient to explain the labour intensity of composite technologies or are there other aspects to these industries that demand further discussion and explanation. The basic question to be asked is what does this composite character engender in terms of social relations?

The patterns identified in the previous section reveal different strategies for the production of microliths. These different routines of production and use may have been the preserve of different members of the microlith using community. Such differences may have been specific to the social position of an individual and their realms of knowledge but equally may have been located in the biography of the component and its function. We must consider at what point in the production process were microliths embued with meaning. Was this specific and present at the start of artefact production, from blade through to finished implement? Alternatively, was microlith manufacture more generalised than this with the microlith only taking on cultural meaning through its use in certain contexts? These issues can be addressed by the adoption of a more explicit biographical focus and via the development and application of methodological and theoretical strategies to identify processes of multiple authorship in the Mesolithic.

The motifs of concealment and transformation are an example of the enchantment of technology (Gell 1999b) and one that serves to reinforce the need to focus on these routine actions in more detail. What was hidden yet known may have been more important that what was seen. This re-focusing on interpersonal action also has implications for the debates about the stylistic significance of microliths (e.g. Gendel 1988). There is evidence to suggest that this composite motif so readily acknowledged in relation to microliths may well apply to other mesolithic artefact types. Although at present these are more ambiguous. Roger Grace (op cit) has identified several unretouched flakes at Thatcham with identical patterns of use-wear which he suggests were hafted together as a single artefact. Here broader parallels can be made with the Danish unretouched microblades, not to mention the potential in organic media for such elaboration. This characteristic of microlith technology may have served to reinforce relationships and social obligations in food procurement and artefact production. A metaphorical reading of the microlith enables us to re-evaluate the social dimensions of microlithic technology and the emphasis on collective components. The importance of these lithic insets extended beyond the projectile function so readily ascribed to them, rather there are other dimensions of their multiple authorship that we need to consider.

Conclusion

This paper has explored the notion of multiple authorship and its application to the making of microliths during the Mesolithic. It has been argued that multiple authorship offers a solution to enable the development of more theoretically aware approaches to the social dimensions of lithic technology. Part of the appeal of borrowing these ideas lies with their ambiguity, for multiple authorship acknowledges the fluidity and partability of objects and actions within the life-course of both people and things.

As archaeologists we have tended to subsume the potential complexities represented by lithic industries for there has been little explicit theorising about the social significance of artefact production and, with a few notable exceptions, lithic technology as a forum for group action. An explicit focus on the microlith biography demonstrates the benefits of experimental replication and focused assemblage analysis for exploring the microlith chaîne opératoire in more detail. Such studies not only enrich perspectives on the routines of manufacture and use but also simultaneously challenge our treatment and objectification of such artefacts. Ultimately these strategies have a number of broader implications for our constructions of the mesolithic. Acknowledging multiple authorship allows for the elaboration of age, gender and social relations into our research. In doing so we begin to multiply the meanings and enrich the narratives of future Mesolithic pasts.

Acknowledgements

The content of this paper has had a long gestation and stem from doctoral research undertaken at the University of Reading. I take the opportunity to thank colleagues on the *Southern Hebrides Mesolithic Project* for many discussions of the ideas expressed here. I also wish to thank Peter Woodman for this support and I gratefully acknowledge the Archaeology Department Research Fund and the Arts Faculty Fund, University College Cork for funding my attendance at Meso2000. As always all faults and oversights remain my own.

References

Appadurai, A. (ed.). 1986. *The social life of things: commodities in cultural perspective*. Cambridge.
Barton, R.N.E. and Bergman, C.A. 1982. Hunters at Hengistbury: some evidence from experimental archaeology. *World Archaeology* 14, 237–48.
Battaglia, D. 1983. Projecting personhood in Melanesia: the dialectics of artefact symbolism on Sabarl Island. *Man* 18, 289–304.
Bodenhorn, B. 1993. Gendered spaces, Public places: public and private revisited on the North slope of Alaska. In: Bender, B. (ed.) *Landscape: Politics and perspectives*, 169–203. Oxford.
Bonsall, C. 1981. The coastal factor in the Mesolithic settlement of north-west England. In: Gramsch, B. (ed.) *The Mesolithic in Europe*. Veröffentlichungen des museums für Ur-und Fruhgeschicte 14/15, 451–72. Potsdam.
Clarke, D.L. 1976. Mesolithic Europe: the economic basis. In: G.de.G. Sieveking, Longworth, I.H. and Wilson, K.E. (eds) *Problems in Economic and Social Archaeology*, 449–481. London.
Chernela, J. 1992. Social Meaning and Material Transaction: the Wanano-Turkano of Brazil and Colombia. *Journal of Anthropological Archaeology* 11, 111–124.
David, A. 1998. Two assemblages of later mesolithic microliths from Seamer carr, north Yorkshire: fact and fancy. In: Aston, N., Healy, F. and Pettitt, P. (eds.) *Stone Age Archaeology*, 196–204. Oxbow Monograph 102. Oxford.
Dobres, M-A. 2000. *Technology and Social Agency*. Oxford.
Dumont, J.V. 1988. *A microwear analysis of selected artefact types from the mesolithic sites of Star Carr and Mount Sandel*. British Archaeological Reports, British Series 187. Oxford.
Finlay, N. 1997. *Exploring the social dimensions of microlithic technology: experimental and analytical approaches with a case study from Western Scotland*. Unpublished PhD thesis, University of Reading. Reading.
—— 2000a. Microliths in the making. In: Young, R. (ed.) *Mesolithic Lifeways: current research from Britain and Ireland*, 23–31. Leicester Archaeology Monograph 7. Leicester.

—— 2000b. Deer Prudence. *Archaeological Review Cambridge* 17(2), 1–8.
—— 2000c. Defining the Microlith chaîne opératoire. In: Mithen, S. (ed.) *Hunter-gatherer landscape archaeology. The Southern Hebrides Mesolithic Project 1988–98. Vol 2*, 581–3. Cambridge.
Finlayson, B. and Mithen, S. 1997. The microwear and morphology of microliths from Gleann Mor. In: Knecht, H. (ed.) *Projectile Technology*, 107–129. New York.
Gendel, P.A. 1984. *Mesolithic Social Territories in Northwestern Europe*. British Archaeological Reports S218.
Gell, A. 1999a. Strathernograms, or, the semotics of mixed metaphors. In: Hirsch, E. (ed.) *The Art of Anthropology: essays and diagrams*, 29–75. London.
—— 1999b (1992). The technology of enchantment and the enchantment of technology. In: Hirsch, E. (ed.) *The Art of Anthropology: essays and diagrams*, 159–186. London.
Gero, J.M. 1991a. Genderlithics: Women's Roles in Stone Tool Production. In: Gero, J. and Conkey, M. (eds), *Engendering Archaeology*, 163–193.
Grace, R. 1992. Microwear Analysis. In: Healy, F., Heaton, M. and Lobb, S.J. Excavations at a mesolithic site at Thatcham, Berkshire. *Proceeding of the Prehististoc Society* 58, 41–76.
Grøn, O. 1992. Maglemosian Microliths and their mounting. *Mesolithic Miscellany* 13, 9–11.
—— 1995. *The Maglemose Culture: A reconstruction of the social organisation of a mesolithic culture in Northern Europe*. British Archaeological Reports S616. Oxford.
Jolly, M. 1992. Partible Persons and Multiple Authors. *Pacific Studies* 15 (1), 137–149.
Hoskins, J. 1998. *Biographical objects: how things tell the stories of people's lives*. London.
MacKenzie, M. 1991. *Androgynous Objects: string bags and gender in Central New Guinea*. Amsterdam.
McBryde, I. 1986. The broken artefact and functional studies. In: Ward, G.K. (ed.) *Archaeology at ANZAAS*, 203–209. Canberra.
Mithen, S. (ed.) 2000. *Hunter-gatherer landscape archaeology: the Southern Hebrides Mesolithic Project 1988–1998*. Cambridge.
Moss, E. 1983. *The Functional Analysis of Flint Implements – Pincevent and Pont d'Ambon: two case studies from the French Final Palaeolithic*. British Archaeological Reports, International Series 177. Oxford.
Mowat, L. 1989. *Cassava and Chicha: bread and beer of the Amazonian Indians*. Princes Risborough.
Myers, A. 1989. Reliable and maintainable technological strategies in the Mesolithic of mainland Britain. In: Torrence, R. (ed.) *Time, Energy and Stone Tools*, 78–91. Cambridge.
Osgood, C. 1940. *Ingalik Material Culture*. New Haven.
Rock, I. 1973. *Orientation and Form*. London.
Rowley-Conwy, P. 1986. Between cave painters and crop planters: aspects of the temperate European Mesolithic. In: Zvelebil. M. (ed.) *Hunters in Transition.* 17–32. Cambridge.
Rozoy, J-G. 1978. *Les derniers chasseurs. L'Epialéolithique en France et en Belgique*. Société archéologique champenoise numéro spécial. Charleville.
Sievert, A.K. 1992. Root and tuber resources: experimental plant processing and resulting microwear on chipped stone tools. In: Anderson. P.C. (ed.) *Préhistorie de l'Agriculture: nouvelles approches expérimentales et ethnographiques*, 55–66. Paris.
Strathern, M. 1988. *The Gender of the Gift*. Berkeley.
Tilley, C. 1999. *Metaphor and Material Culture*. Oxford.
Tixier, J. 1963. *Typologie de l'epipaléolithique du Maghreb*. Memoire C.R.A.P. Paris.
Yde, J. 1965. *Material culture of the Waiwài*. National Museum of Copenhagen. Copenhagen.
Zvelebil, M. 1986. Postglacial Foraging in the forests of Europe. *Scientific American* 254(3), 86–93.

25. My way or your way. On the social dimension of technology as seen in the lithic strategies in eastern middle Sweden during the Mesolithic

Christina Lindgren

Technology as a part of society and as used by the people of that society has a strong social dimension. The technology reflects and affects the social organisation and social communication between people. Based on three case studies I will show different examples of how social communication was practiced on different levels through the medium of technology. The first case study is based on the differences in making tools in sandstone, greenstone and quartz. Structuring the production of tools in different raw materials becomes a way of supporting group identity on different levels. The second case study is based on the missing micro blade industry in the archipelago, which is an example of how cultural identity is formed toward groups living in neighboring areas. The third example is based on two different technological strategies of making quartz tools. Technologically the bipolar-on-anvil method of reduction is dominating the lithic scene for over 3000 years. There are however indications of two different technological strategies. The strategies are visible through different access to raw material, different method of reduction and different end products. These two lithic strategies are intimately linked to the social structure of the mesolithic society and more specifically to the division of labor.

For a long time and for many different reasons the mesolithic in Eastern Middle Sweden has been a white spot on the map (Åkerlund 2000:8 p). This is about to change following an increasing number of excavated sites during the last 20 years which has given us huge amounts of new data. At the same time as the amount of new data are increasing, the mesolithic research are beginning to change from an ecological, functional deterministic archaeology to a more social and symbolic archaeology (Conkey 1984:257). This means that we must seek elsewhere for theories and ideas that we can use in our interpretations of the past. By seeking inspiration not only from social anthropology but also sociology the mesolithic can be interpreted as a period not only of adaptive hunters and gatherers but also by active people with a social dimension.

Communicating through technology

One aspect of the social dimension is communication between people. Communication is really about expressing your self in comparison with other people as well as things. This kind of social communication is practised daily with your family, friends and neighbours but also with strangers and enemies. By doing things your way you express and communicate intangible things such as prestige, power, worldviews, and social relations.

The way we do things, the way we make and shape our material culture can be named technology. It can be defined as " artefacts, behaviour and knowledge to make and use products and that can be communicated between generations" (Schiffer 1987:595). It consist of both raw material and gestures, it also combines them with energy, knowledge and objects (Lemonnier 1992:5 p). Technology is an intriguing word with many associations, both in the present times and in prehistory. It can give associations of progress and development but it can also be associated with alienation and despair. Technology has often been interpreted in strictly functional and economic terms. It has also been regarded as something outside society, an external factor that affects society, a link between man and nature.

There is however during the last years a growing consensus among archaeologists as well as anthropologists that technology is as much a social act as anything else, both in present times as well as in prehistory (Lechtman and Merrill 1977; Ingold 1990; Lemmonier 1992, 1993; Pfaffenberg 1992; Dobres 2000). Since it is as social as anything else we humans do it cannot be separated from the rest of our social lives. If we challenge the separation between society and nature, technology no longer holds its mediating place between the two. Instead it becomes a way of dealing with the world around us. We need to combine knowledge about the hard things of technology – in our case the artefacts – with social theory that helps us understand human action.

Based on my observations from the excavations in the last ten years I will present three case studies. These case studies are examples of how patterns in the material world can be used to make interpretations how social communication was practised on different levels through the medium of technology during the mesolithic in Eastern Middle Sweden.

Hidden and open production – different ways of making axes, whetstones and quartz tools

My first example deals with the relations between technology and group formation as seen in the use of different raw materials. The three main raw materials used for tool production in the mesolithic archipelago were yellow or red sandstone for whetstones and grinding stones, dark greenstone for axes, adzes and chisels and white quartz for a variety of tools such as scrapers and knives. Artefacts of these three materials are found on almost every site in the region (Figure 25.1). During a period from approximately 7000 BC (cal) to 4500 BC the sites fall into two groups, based on size and number of artefacts (Lindgren 1997:25 p). The combinations of these three raw materials occur on sites of both types. They are often found in the cultural layer without signs of special depositions. There is reason to believe that the use of these three raw materials was no doubt part of everyday activities. This does not however make them non-ritual or non-symbolic. Instead they can make an excellent starting point for discussing the symbolic dimension of technology. These three materials: sandstone, greenstone and quartz have different colours, texture and are found in different geographic location. It is easy to read different symbolic meaning in these materials, based on their physical appearance. The colour and texture and origin were probably also involved in different metaphorical meanings. But the raw materials have one thing in common; they had to be transformed into tools. So let us focus on the technology.

If using tools from different raw materials was part of everyday activities the production was certainly not. There are several differences between the three raw materials in terms of access to raw material, distribution of raw material and tool production.

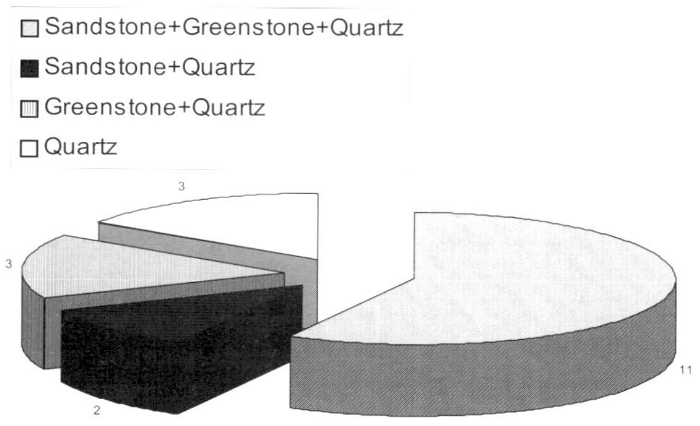

Figure 25.1 The combination of sandstone, greenstone and quartz are most common on mesolithic sites.

The sandstone used is mainly of two types, red or yellow. Red sandstone is coarse, occurs in slabs often with distinct wavemarks on them. Yellow sandstone is fine grained and does not occur as slabs. Geologically they probably represent at least two different raw materials sources. So far no quarry or manufacturing site has been found where sandstone of any kind has been processed. We have therefore no knowledge of how or where these tools were made. This can be interpreted as a strictly controlled process with limited access to raw material and a wide net of distribution of ready-made tools not unlike what is known from Australia (McBryde 1987). It also shows that the production of whetstones and grinding stones were part of a common mental concept, an idea within a common framework (Lidström Holmberg 1998: 132).

The axes are often made of diabase/dolerite or what is commonly known as greenstone. A thin section study has shown that the raw material is from different kinds of dolerites and amphibolites (Kars *et al.* 1991:218). These raw materials are obtained locally in dykes in the bedrock. No greenstone quarry has so far been found but there are some of the larger sites with axe manufacturing indicated by a number of axe preforms and large amounts of waste (Lindgren and Nordqvist 1997). This is rather an example of limited access to the source of the raw material but with a widespread distribution of raw material to be processed on certain sites.

The quartz is something completely different. Quartz can be obtained in two ways, as nodules in the moraine and glacifluvial deposits and from veins in the bedrock. Both these sources seem to have been used and several quartz quarries are known (Lindgren 1994; Lindholm 1998) Tool production occur more or less on every site. This seems to be your typical household production with easy access to raw material and a widespread production.

So there are differences both in the access to and the control of the raw material sources and in the production processes. Not everybody could acquire sandstone or greenstone, the origin of these raw materials were hidden from a lot of people. Making a whetstone or a grinding stone were also a secret to most people while some people at certain sites could witness the making of an axe. At the same time "everybody" could get their hands on some good quartz and make tools for them selves. The principles behind this differentiated structuring of tool making seem to be rooted in ideas of control, in hiding and displaying actions. By secluding the production of certain tools you give not only the finished objects but also the production of them a magic dimension (Gell 1992). On the other hand the quartz was easy accessible to a lot of people, maybe giving a sense of community, of equality. By using the concept of hidden and displaying as structuring the lithic technology you create a social tension within the group, between different subgroups of people and also between different types of sites within the archipelago. Technological strategies seems in this case support group identity on different levels as in the example of the quartz, but also serve as a marker of exclusivity as in the case with the greenstone and the sandstone.

Knowing but not doing – the case of the missing microblade production

The second example concerns the missing microblade industry. The microblade tradition in Scandinavia around 6500 BC is well known (Knutsson 1993). The production of microblades using handle cores is widely distributed all through Sweden (Figure 25.2) and occurs in several different raw materials. The mesolithic inhabitants of the archipelago were no doubt familiar with the microblade tradition as is shown by the findings of a number of microblades both in flint and in quartz on several of the sites in the archipelago. A few microblades in flint is found on almost every large site. Microblades in quartz are more common but still few compared to the number of flakes. But there is one thing missing – the handle cores themselves. Handle cores (or any type of cores) in flint or waste products from the production of microblades occurs only as single finds (Knutsson *et al.* 1997:103) handle cores in quartz are so far not known from the archipelago (Lindgren 1997:30, Fig 8). Occasionally you can observe singe microblade shaped flaking scars on especially bipolar cores in quartz. But there are very few observations that speak for an intentionally production of microblades by the use of handle cores, or from other types of cores.

In the surrounding mainland areas there are microblade production documented on several sites (Figure 25.3). Here microblades are made in flint, quartz, quartzite and hälleflinta. Microblade cores in these materials are also known from several sites (Welinder 1977; Larsson 1996; Apel *et al.* 1998; Kihlstedt 1998).

For one reason or another they have chosen not to produce microblades within the archipelago. There is no obvious functional explanation to this choice, such as unsuitable raw material or lack of knowledge. The rawmaterials are often the same in the archipelago as in the surrounding mainland and the occurrence of single microblades show that they had contact with microblade producing groups. The choice not to make microblades seems to depend on other, non-functional, factors. Technology is formed by things like tradition, contacts, raw material availability and of course the desired function. There is a strong momentum of choice in the use of a certain technology. These choices are not only based on rational, economic and physical factors, they are also based on social factors such as tradition and relation to social identity. The question is not whether a technological phenomenon has certain advantages, that decides if it shall be accepted or not. Instead it depends on the context, in each specific situation (Lemonnier 1992). In a given situation the decision not to accept a technological innovation or change is not primarily based on economical or functional factors. If the innovation is not compatible with the prevailing social standards there is only a small chance of acceptance. In this case the

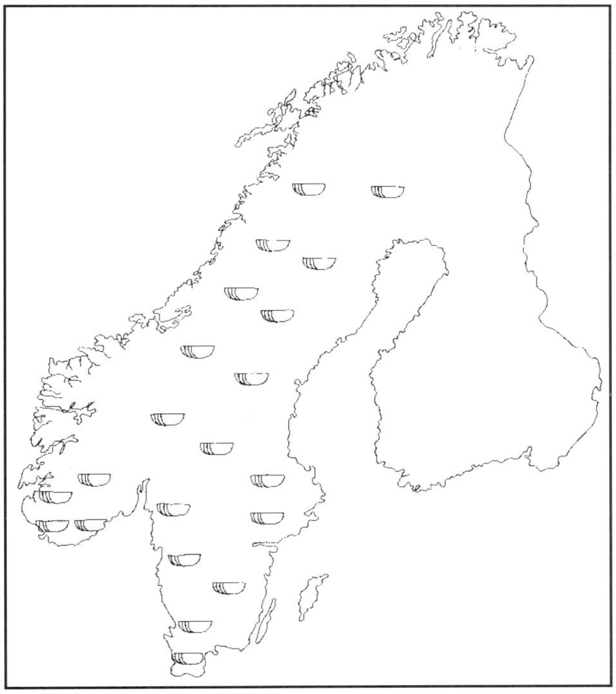

Figure 25.2 Map over Scandinavia and the distribution of handle cores around 8000 – 6000 BP (From Knutsson 1996, Fig.17)

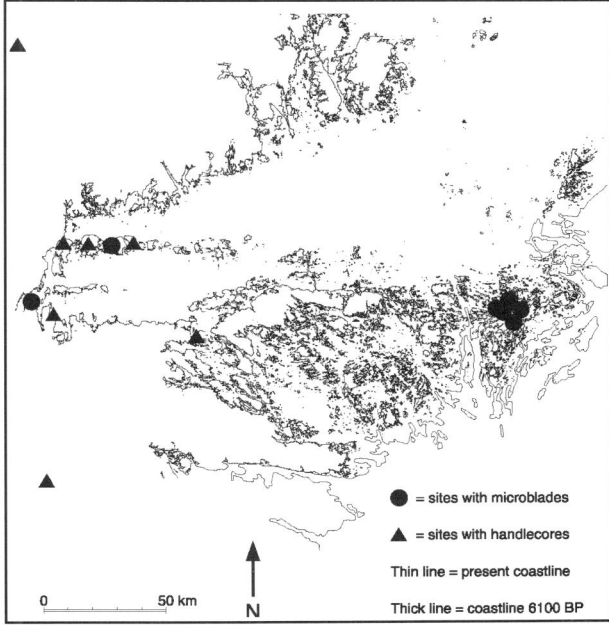

Figure 25.3 Map showing the Eastern Middle Sweden with a sea level corresponding to 5000 BC, showing sites with only micro blades in the archipelago and handle cores in the surrounding mainland. (Background map made by Leif Andersson SGU.)

choice not to make microblades works as a marker of identity towards other neighbouring areas with a lot of things in common regarding economy and material culture. Not making microblades was no doubt part of their way to do things, clearly related to creating social identity. In this case the technological differences between neighbouring areas create a sense of dualism between the archipelago and the surrounding mainland.

So these are two short examples of how technology can be used for studying social matters. It is important to stress that it is not my point to replace functional or physical explanations to technological variation with social ones. The point is that they are all intimately related. There is no such thing as one single reason for expressing material culture in one or the other way. It is always culturally and historically founded.

Two lithic strategies – two identities?

My third example deals with technological strategies in every day life. The use of quartz as I mentioned is interpreted as a typical household production, easy accessible raw material sources and the presence of tool production on almost every site. The process from raw material to the end product seems to be short, both in time and in space. There is a variation of reduction methods used, the two most common are freehand – platform and bipolar-on-anvil, the latter one being dominant during most of the mesolithic (Figure 25.4). The formal tools are few and most of the produced flakes where probably intended to be used without further modification. But for some reason, some flakes were modified secondary. There seems to be a dominance for platform flakes being retouched whereas bipolar flakes are not (Figure 25.5). Figure 25.5 shows the retouched objects from six sites and there is a clear tendency that it was the platform flakes that was secondly modified, not the bipolar flakes. This could be interpreted as representing two technological strategies.

This is a rather rough division and it should not be to easily interpreted as representing two different activities. The retouched platform flakes show considerable formal variation and were no doubt intended for several different purposes. Neither should we assume that the unmodified

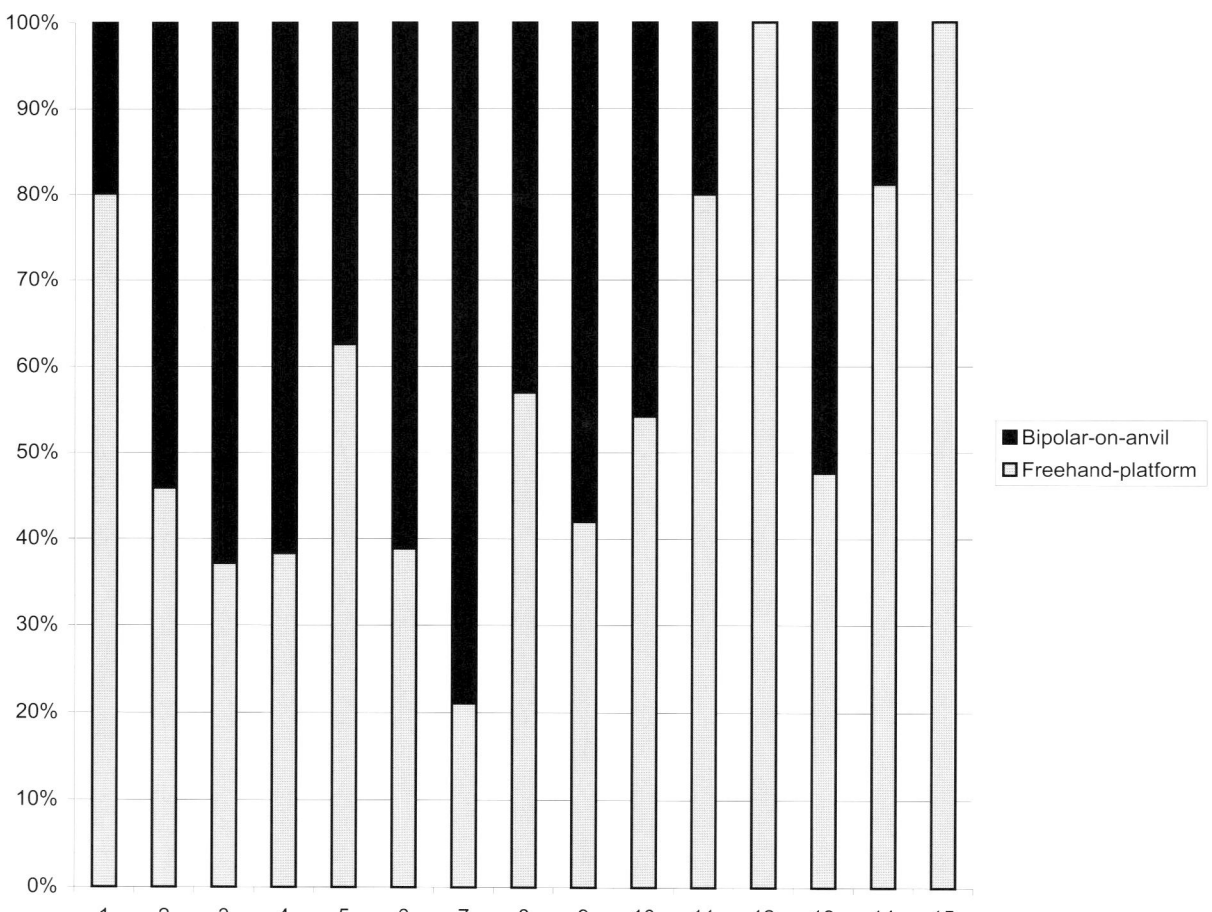

Figure 25.4 Bar chart showing the variation between freehand platform method of reduction and bipolar-on-anvil reduction method at 15 mesolithic sites. Note that sites are sorted chronologically with sites nr 11–15 belonging to the period after 4500 BC.

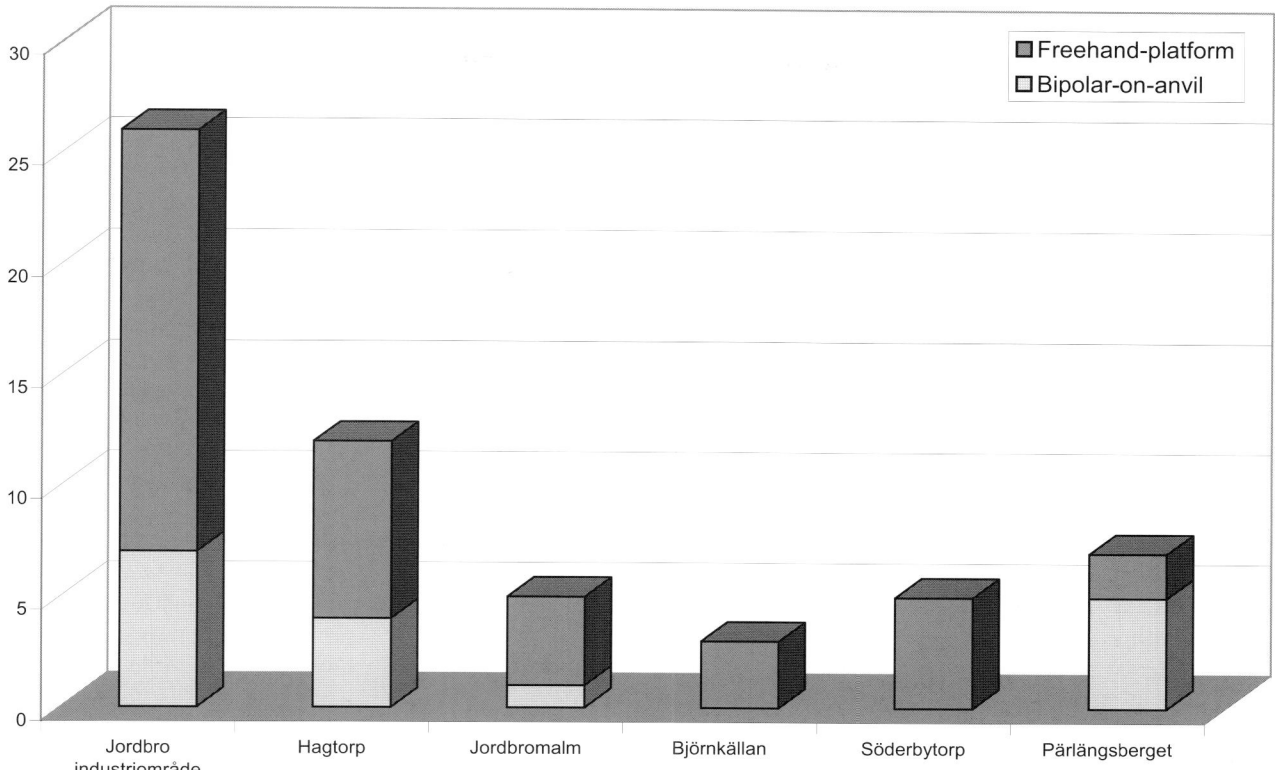

Figure 25.5 Bar chart showing the relation between retouched tools and technology.

bipolar flakes were used in one single activity. But technologically the production of quartz tools where structured according to two different strategies. One freehand – platform intended for second modification and one bipolar – on – anvil intended for immediate use.

The question we should ask ourselves are what does these two strategies tell us about the people using them. The key issue is whether they are indication of a structure of labour division in the mesolithic society. Division of labour, or rather work since the term labour may not be an adequate term for the tool production in the mesolithic, exists in every society.

By working, and in this case producing lithic tools, you are inevitable also dealing with such things as social relations, power, and prestige. Seeing technology as a social act makes it possible to discuss for example division of labour as a gendered practice. The issue is not to identify activity areas and infer labels of sex or age to them. Instead I would like to see technology here as a way to study how different groups, for example based on gender, act within a site.

Mesolithic sites in the archipelago around 6500 BC forms a pattern of large and small sites. Larger sites are sites extending over several thousands square meters and thick cultural layers often containing exotic raw material, lots of greenstone axes, the smaller sites are only 100–200 square meters of lithic scatter around one or two hearths. Neither the lithic technology nor the faunal remains at the smaller sites gives us any indication of the sites being specialised in any way. This settlement pattern could be an example of a large group of people, several households, living together for most of the year but during parts of the year the group scatters into smaller units of maybe one family. Social life on these two types of sites was probably very different. Regardless of why such a pattern was created it can be used as a starting point for interpretations of the social composition in the society. Since there are very few indications of specialisation of either the larger or the smaller sites I would like to suggest that both these types of sites where used by one or several groups resembling a household. And if there were households there were likely to be found groups defined by gender. The two above mentioned quartz reduction strategies are represented at both the larger and the smaller sites that are indicating that they were part of common every day life transcending size differences between sites.

By introducing gender in a discussion of technological variation you could end up with a discussion who did what in the mesolithic home. In this case, with two different technological strategies it is easy to see it as an example of how both men and women are active in the process of tool making, something that has not always been the case in archaeological research (Gero 1991). But I am at this point very unwilling to label the two strategies with being a male strategy and a female strategy. They are instead a good example of the dangerous pit falls in generalising male or female labels to different types of tools or technologies. Traditionally the scraper has often been used as an example of a tool used by women. This is an object that we find represented in one of the strategies. On the other hand the bipolar technology has often been considered simple, crude and expedient, terms that are also often associated with descriptions of what is considered "female" in lithic technology. No doubt have women used the bipolar-on-anvil technology as several ethnographic examples suggests (Willemark 1997:56). So we can actually suggest that women could be responsible for both strategies. This could imply women in general being in charge of most of the manufacturing of stone tools in the mesolithic in Eastern Middle Sweden. Even though the idea might be appealing I have several objections to this interpretation. It is based on ideas of women as non-capable of using more sophisticated techniques, as archaeological visible only in the domestic sphere, scraping hides as always. It could very well be the result of another scenario. If the bipolar strategy was connected to hunting, something that is not visible in the platform strategy it could just as easily be interpreted as a representation of a competing situation between older and younger men. Young hunters create and maintain their identity as hunters by, among other things, making their hunting tools in a certain way.

So there are no simple interpretations of who did what. But the two technological strategies in their context give us the possibility of introducing gender in a discussion of technological variation. Obviously the technological organisation involved several groups within the society. This also gives room for daily negotiating social roles and identities within the structure of labour division. Manufacturing stone tools were everybody's business. In order to further understand the relationship between social identity and lithic technology I will combine data on technological variation with spatial analysis from excavated sites. In this way I hope to be able to study how these two technological strategies were, not only visible, but formed an active part in creating social space.

This lithic scene described above seems to be stable for almost 2000 years, and this stability is interesting. Part of technology is concerned with passing on knowledge and learning how to do things. For a technology to be unchanging for a long time there had to be a powerful structure in the society that made it possible to uphold and reproduce the technology. If the technology were linked specially to labour division based on gender through these two strategies and thus accordingly this could very well be a structure that provided stability.

But around 4500 something changes. The system of larger and smaller sites seems to collapse, and the sites tend to be most of medium size, the use of the bipolar on anvil method drops dramatically and retouched tools were being produced with both methods (Figure 25.4). This is an example of a technological change that seems to represent so much more than just a different way of doing things. There are no indications of any technological innovation, or any signs of change in the economic structure, but the two technological strategies disappear. If it was a link between technology and the division of labour there were surely radical changes in both areas. The disappearance of the bipolar-on anvil strategy is no doubt an indication of a shift in the power relations between different groups of individual, perhaps based on gender. You did not do it your way any more.

Final remarks

The tree examples I have used have all been examples of how technology in some way has been actively used in communicating within a group or between groups. Hiding or displaying tool production, technological choices and communicating group identity are all different ways of creating and maintaining your social identity. To reach the daily social life of the mesolithic in the Eastern Middle mesolithic quartz technology can be a good starting point. No doubt was a lot of tool making made outdoors and visible to others. This means that it also played an important role in the daily negotiating between people. You did not only make tools, you also made yourself.

References

Bergold, H. and Holm, J. 1998. *Lämningar från mesolitikum till efterreformatorisk tid vid Skävi, E 20*. Arkeologisk undersökning, Riksantikvarieämbetet UV, Stockholm Rapport 1998:72. Stockholm.

Conkey, M. 1984. To find ourselves: Art and Social Geography of Prehistoric Hunter-Gatherers. In: Schrire, C. (ed.) *Past and Present in Hunter-Gatherer Studies*, 253–276. Orlando.

Dobres, M-A. 2000. *Technology and Social Agency. Outlining a Practice Framework for Archaeology*. Oxford.

Gell, A. 1992. The technology of enchantment. In: Coote, J. and Shelton, A. (eds.) *Anthropology, Art and Aestethics*, 40–63 Oxford.

Gero, J. 1991. Genderlithics: Womens Roles in Stone Tool Production. In: Gero, J. and Conkey, M. (eds.) *Engendering Archaeology*, 163–193. Oxford.

Ingold, T. 1990. Society, Nature and the Concept of Technology. *Archaeological Review from Cambridge* 9 (1), 5–17.

Kars, E.A.K., Kars, H. and McDonnell, R.D. 1991. Greenstone axes from eastern central Sweden. A technological-petrological approach. *Archaeometry* 34:2, 213–222.

Kihlstedt, B. 1998. *Arkeologisk undersökning: boplats och järnframställningsplats vid Sågebol, E 20, Närke, Viby sn, RAÄ 214*. Riksantikvarieämbetet UV Mitt Rapport 1998:50. Stockholm.

Knutsson, K. 1993. Garaselet – Lappviken – Rastklippan. Introduktion till en diskussion om Norrlands Äldsta Bebyggelse. *TOR* 25, 5–51.

Knutsson, K., Lindgren, C., Hallgren F. and Björck, N. 1999. The Mesolithic in Eastern Middle Sweden. In: Boaz, J. (ed.) *The Mesolithic of Central Scandinavia*. Universitets Oldsakssamlings Skrifter Ny rekke Nr 22, 87–123. Oslo.

Larsson, M. 1996. Högby. *Mesolitiska och senneolitiska boplatser vid Högby i Östergötland. Bosättningsmönster och Materiell kultur. Del 1* Arkeologisk slutundersökning Riksantikvarieämbetet UV Linköping 1996:35. Stockholm.

Lechtman, H. and Merrill, R.S. 1977. *Material Culture. Styles, Organisation and Dynamics of Technology*. St. Paul.

Lemonnier, P. 1992. *Elements for an Anthropology of Technology*.

Anthropological Papers No. 88. Museum of Anthropology University of Michigan. Ann Arbor.
—— 1993. *Technological choices*. Transformations in Material Culture since the Neolithic. London.
Lidström Holmberg, C. 1998. Prehistoric Grinding Tools as Metaphorical Traces of the Past. *Current Swedish Archaeology* 6, 123–142.
Lindgren, C. 1994. Prehistoric Quartz Quarryies in Eastern Middle Sweden. *Archaeologia Polonia* 33, 89–97.
—— 1997. Regionalitet under mesolitikum. Från senglacial tid till senatlantisk tid i Syd- och Mellansverige. In: Larsson, M. and Olsson, E. (eds.) *Regionalt och interregionalt*. Stenåldersundersökningar i Syd- och Mellansverige. Riksantikvarieämbetet Arkeologiska Undersökningar Skrifter nr 23, 21–32. Stockholm.
Lindgren, C. and Nordqvist, B. 1997. Lihultsyxor och Trindyxor. Om yxor av basiska bergarter i östra och västra Sverige under mesolitikum. In: Larsson, M. and Olsson, E. (eds.) *Regionalt och interregionalt*. Stenåldersundersökningar i Syd- och Mellansverige. Riksantikvarieämbetet Arkeologiska Undersökningar Skrifter nr 23, 57–72. Stockholm.
Lindholm, P. 1998. *Kvartsbrott vid Norrskogen, Arlanda Flygplats, tredje landningsbanan. Arkeologisk Förundersökning RAÄ 79 Skånela socken, Uppland*. Riksantikvarieämbetet UV Mitt rapport 1998:7. Stockholm.
McBryde, I. 1987. Goods from another country: exchange, networks and the people of Lake Eyre basin. P 253–274. In: Mulvaney, D.J. and White, J.P. *Australians to 1788*, 253–274. Broadway NSW.
Pfaffenberg, B. 1992. Social Anthropology of technology. *Annual rewiew of Anthropology* 21, 491–516.
Schiffer, M. and Skibo, J. 1987. Theory and experiment in the study of technological change. *Current Anthropology* 28:5, 595–622.
Welinder, S. 1977. *The Mesolithic of Eastern Middle Sweden*. Antikvariskt arkiv 65. Stockholm.
Willemark, K. 1997. Kvinnor, män och stenhantverk. In: Johnsen, B. and Welinder, S. (eds) *Gender och Arkeologi.*, 50–62. Östersund.
Åkerlund, A. 2000. Separate Worlds? Interpretation of the different material patterns in the archipelago and the surrounding mainland areas of east-central Sweden in the stone age. *European Journal of Archaeology* 3 (1), 7–29.

Unprinted references

Apel, J. *Skumparberget 1 och 2. En mesolitisk aktivitetsyta och tidigneolitiska trattbägarlokaler vid Skumparberget i Glanshammar sn, Örebro län, Närke*. För- och slutundersökningsrapport från Arkeologikonsult AB ATA Dnr 421-4806-1996.
Artursson, M. *Lysinge. Två mesolitiska boplatser i östra Mellansverige. Lillkyrka sn, Närke*. För- och slutundersökningsrapport från Arkeologiskonsult AB. ATA Dnr 421-4205-1995.

Social Relations and Group Formation

26. Inferences about Mesolithic life style on the basis of anthropological data. The case of the Portuguese shell middens

Eugénia Cunha, Francisca Cardosa and Cláudia Umbelino

The number of Mesolithic skeletons recovered in Portugal stands out within the European context. More than four hundred individuals have been found from both the classic shell middens of Muge as well as from the Sado River shell middens. These important osteological finds have been the subject of an exhaustive paleobiological analysis by our team. In the present paper, on the basis of paleodemographic, morphological and paleopathological results we try to infer some aspects concerning the life style of the last hunter gathers communities in Portuguese territory. The proportion of adults versus sub-adults is presented. Caries rates as well as general patterns of dental wear are given and discussed. Other pathological conditions are also described.

Introduction

Portugal is indeed particularly rich in human skeletons from the Mesolithic. Besides the famous Muge shell middens, there are also the less known shell middens from Sado. Yet, not withstanding its popularity, the osteological material of Muge was never the subject of a systematic and exhaustive analysis. This was done in the context of a research project about the Mesolithic-Neolithic transition in the Portuguese territory. In the present paper we will refer the main inferences taken from the paleobiological analysis of the Portuguese Mesolithic osteological material, with respect to daily life.

Before that, a brief description of each site will be presented.

Geographical setting and short history of their research

Sado shell middens

Discovered during the thirties, the Sado shell middens are located along the ancient estuary of the Sado River, at a distance of approximately 100 km from the well-known Muge shell middens.

These shell middens comprises eleven sites, divided into three main areas, the majority of them on the edge of a very steep slope some 40 to 50 m above the river bed. Várzea da Mó, is the exception, located just a few meters above the valley on a small tributary of the Sado and Poças de S.Bento which is located 3 km south of the valley, at c.80 m above sea level (Arnaud 1987:53 p; Arnaud 1989:616 p).

The settlement system was organised, according to the archaeologists (Arnaud 1989:629; Araújo 1995/7:149), around two main base-camps, Cabeço do Pez and Poças de S.Bento which are the larger shell middens, while the remaining sites, of lesser dimensions, were used as seasonal settlements.

In November 1997 our team undertook a paleobiological project having as main basis the anthropological material from the Sado shell middens, housed at the National Museum of Archaeology, in Lisbon, which includes 6 sites. No human bones were retrieved from the other sites.

All the burials were excavated in layers and contained occupation debris. There is however some heterogeneity among the shell middens, namely in the amount of shell and other detritus (from fishing and hunting) found, which could be related with some dietary differences.

Chronometrical framework

There are twelve radiocarbon dates from this Mesolithic site. Eight were provided by Arnaud (1989:618 p) and four were performed within our project (Cunha *et al.* n.d.). All of them proved both the antiquity of these shell middens as well as their contemporaneity with their Muge counterparts. While the ones obtained by Arnaud (1989: 619) were mainly done on shells, our dates are from samples taken from human bones. These later ones were performed at Beta Analytic Inc (AMS dates), and Instituto Tecnológico e Nuclear in Lisbon (conventional radiocarbon dates).

Taking into account all the available dates, it becomes clear that Arapouco seems to be the oldest site (Figure 26.1), immediately followed by Cabeço das Amoreiras. On the other hand, the dates obtained for Cabeço do Pez,

Site	C¹⁴ age BP	Lab ref.	C¹³/C¹²
Cabeço do Pez	6760±40	Beta-125109	-22.6 ‰
Cabeço das Amoreiras	7230±40	Beta-125110	-20.8‰
Arapouco	7200±130	Sac- 1560	-16.92‰
Cabeço do Pez	6740±110	Sac-1558	-19.28‰

Figure 26.1 Radiocarbon dates on human bones from the Sado shell middens.

Site	C¹⁴ age BP	Lab ref.	C¹³/C¹²
Cabeço da Arruda	7550±100	Beta-127451	-19.0 ‰
Cabeço da Amoreira	6850±40	Beta-127450	-16.5‰
Moita do Sebastião	7120±40	Beta-127449	-16.8‰
Cova da Onça	7140±40	Beta-127448	-17.2‰

Figure 26.2 Radiocarbon dates on human bones from the Muge shell middens.

suggest a slightly later occupation. On the basis of these dates, this Mesolithic site was occupied for at least around 1000 years.

Muge shell middens

The Muge shell middens are located on the shores of the Muge tributary of the Tagus river, a few kilometers from its junction, in central Portugal. Moita do Sebastião and Cabeço da Amoreira are situated on the left side of Muge river at 15–22 m above the sea level, and approximately 15 m above the river bed, while Cabeço da Arruda is on the right side, only 3 meters above the river bed. Furthermore there is the Cova da Onça shell midden, near the Magos riverside (Cunha and Cardoso 2002).

The Muge material is deposited in three different Portuguese museums, namely in Lisbon, Oporto and Coimbra. Subsequently, it was a difficult task to identify the exact provenance of some of the bones and to achieve an accurate minimum number of individuals. We can now identify three hundred individuals exhumed from the four Mesolithic sites.

Chronometrical framework

Several radiocarbon dates were performed in order to corroborate the authenticity of some of the human bones (Figure 26.2), besides strengthening previous dates obtained by other researchers (Lubell and Jackes 1994: 203; Jackes *et al.* 1997:642). Like the Sado shell middens, the ones from the Tagus River were as also inhabited for around 1000 years.

Inferences about life style

Funerary rituals

With respect to funerary rituals, it has been confirmed that the space used by the living (acropolis) was the same space used for the dead (necropolis). The proximity between necropolis and acropolis was constant throughout the period that the shell middens were in use.

The way the bodies were deposited varied not only between Muge and Sado, but even within the Muge site. That is, we cannot single out any type of burial as being typical for the complex.

At Muge, both fetal positions as well as *decubitus dorsalis* ones with the legs semi-contracted/fully con-

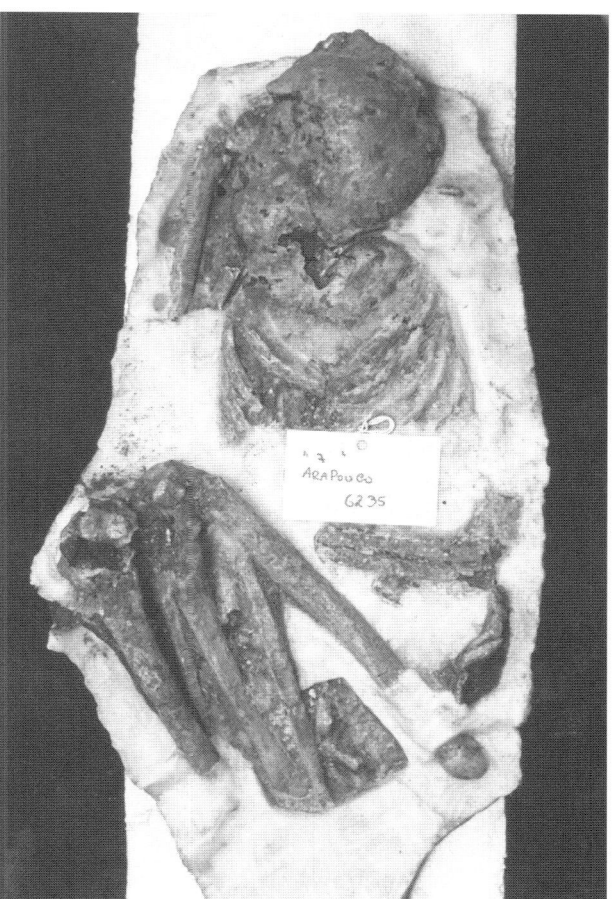

Figure 26.3 An illustration of one of the most frequent inhumation positions from Sado.

tracted and upright were found. In recent excavations performed in 2000, an individual was found with his legs stretched and crossed. The fetal position, or a semi-contracted posture was easily observed in some cases, namely in Sado, because of the way the skeletons were preserved (Figure 26.3).

In effect, during their excavation in the fifties and sixties, they were paraffined, preserving therefore, the original position of the bodies. Moreover they are involved in calcite.

Further, for both Muge and Sado, there are some excellent drawings illustrating the way the bodies were laid out on the ground. Both adults and sub-adults were submitted to this type of treatment at the time of their death.

Some paleodemographic parameters

Moving now to the world of the living, and starting with paleodemography, the incompleteness and fragmentation of vast quantities of the material precluded many age and sex estimations. Regarding the state of preservation of the human remains at Muge, while there are some remarkably well preserved and complete skeletons (at least around 30), there are also skeletons represented by a single bone (correctly labelled). This is an important data to take into account when performing a paleodemographic analysis.

All 112 individuals exhumed at Sado (Cunha and Umbelino 1995/7:165 p) were analysed, together with approximately 200 individuals from Muge.

The proportion of adults versus non-adults was more or less the same from all the sites at the Sado shell-middens: around 20% non-adults and 80% adults.

At Muge, our analysis shows that at Amoreira non-adults made up 22% of the material (4/18), while at Moita do Sebastião, using figures presented by Ferembach (1974:33) sub-adults made up 30% of the material (40/136). (The sub-sample from Moita, studied by us, consisted of 50 individuals, of which only four were sub-adults). For Arruda, the 78 individuals analysed by us, point to an equal percentage of adults and sub-adults (38/78). Finally, the Cova da Onça site yeilded the lowest proportions of sub-adults: only 16% (5/32).

The sub-adult Muge sample, studied by the authors, consists of 59 skeletons (including 8 skeletons with unknown specific provenance), ranging in age at death from new-born to 20 years old. In Sado, 23 sub-adults were retrieved.

However, it is impossible to accurately quantify child mortality from these remains. On the one hand and in some cases the state of preservation of the osteological material precludes a precise age at death estimation, and on the other hand, we have to wait for the final results from the Muge material (combining the results from Jackes' work with ours). But we are certain about the presence of very young children, there is a 8–9 month old fetus at Poças de S.Bento (Sado) and a 18 month old child from Cabeço da Arruda, although there is a clear under representation of children under 5 years of age.

Regarding the sex distribution of the adults, it seems that there are not any strong asymmetries among Muge and Sado sites, with the exception of Cabeço das Amoreiras (from Sado), where of the 5 adults retrieved 4 were males. At Poças de S. Bento, also a Sado shell midden, preservation conditions only allowed the recognition of adult remains, but it is not possible specify either their age at death or sex. At Muge the majority of the material did not allow for the recognition of sex to be established, while for the remaining cases, male individuals make up 44% of the total (Amoreira, Arruda and Moita).

With respect to adult longevity we can only hypothesize. There are some skeletons that clearly seem to have belonged to adults who had lived beyond fifty years of age. This inference was made on the basis of skeletal signs, namely a conjunction of indicators, such as differential molars dental wear, alveolar resorption, suture closure, pubic symphisis and degenerative pathology such as osteoarthrithis.

Although we do not know whether the affect of the senescence process was then as it is today (probably not), it is still clear that some individuals were older than 50 years of age. Some examples can be seen among the adult skeletons from Arruda, housed at the Oporto Museum, namely skeleton 3, where besides severe dental wear affecting all the posterior dentition, suture closure was very advanced.

Brief summary to paleopathological data

The oral pathological data which are most informative about daily life is that on caries and dental wear. Whereas caries incidence from the total number of observable teeth is around 4.1% (67/1624) at Muge, at Sado the figure is 3.9% (41/1049). These values imply the existence of some cariogenic foods such as fruits. It should be noted however that an analysis of caries could not be conducted on 13.9% (263/1887) of the teeth from Muge and on 10.95% (129/1178) of the teeth from Sado.

Dental wear was evaluated according to Smith's scale (1984:46). The severe pattern detected on the anterior teeth led us to suppose that the mouth was used for other functions besides mastication. This would suggest that some cutting functions were performed using the teeth. It is possible that both severe and angulated patterns of dental wear on the anterior dentition was caused by the way the bivalve were ingested. Bivalves, once mixed with some sand, could also be responsible for the degree of dental wear found on the posterior dentition. Furthermore, the strong dental wear might have obliterated some dental caries. Finally, concerning the oral cavity, there is no evidence of dental care.

Regarding degenerative, infectious, traumatic and metabolic events that were detected, and the reasons behind them are as follows.

With the exception of a severe lesion on a temporo-mandibular joint (Figure 26.4), all other osteoarthritic lesions are not only infrequent but are not severe, a fact that might be related with the general demographic profile of the series.

Enthesopathies, lesions on the muscular and tendon insertion sites, are also not common, indicating a lack of any need to perform repetitive or strenuous physical tasks. Once again, exceptions exist, such as the case of skeleton

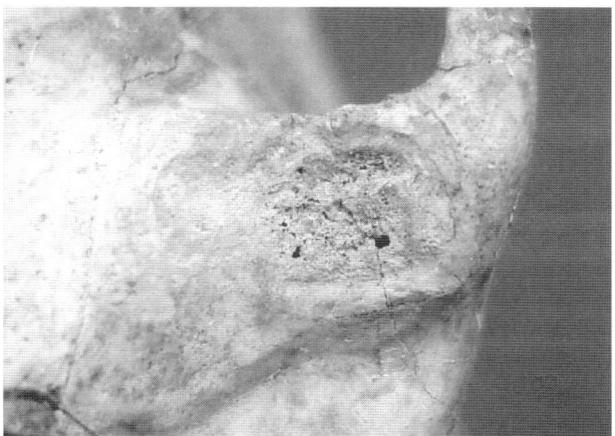

Figure 26.4 Severe temporomandibular osteoarthritis in a male individual from Muge.

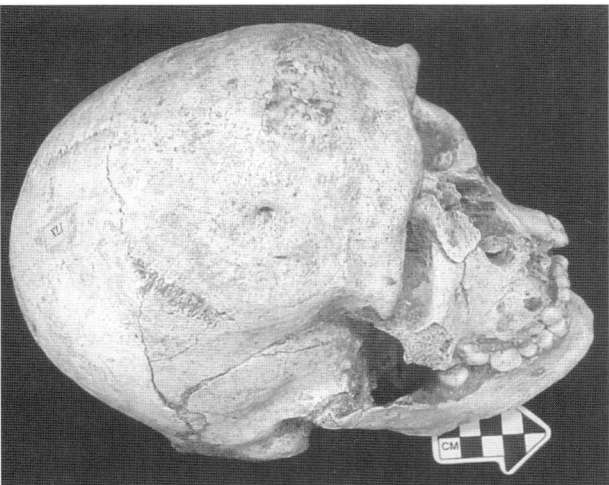

Figure 26.5 Eventual trepanation located on the right antero-lateral portion of the frontal bone, from an individual from Moita do Sebastião.

3 from Moita do Sebastião (Oporto), who does seem to have a series of enthesopathies in the lower limbs.

Regarding traumatic events, there are only a few cases and they show that fractures were not correctly set, suggesting that treatment for this kind of trauma was unknown. The most relevant cases are the following: A radius and ulna fracture on a non-adult individual from Cabeço da Arruda, Muge. A fracture on the distal portion of a 3rd metatarsian belonging to a female from Arapouco, with at the age of death was over 40 y.o. This kind of trauma seems to have occurred as a consequence of daily accidents, precluding any kind of inter personal violence.

The most striking case found refers to an eventual trepanation from Moita do Sebastião (Crubézy et al. 2001). It is a hole located on the right antero-lateral portion of the frontal bone of a male individual over 40 years old (Figure 26.5). Contrary to the previous examples, this traumatic injury reflects, in a way, some kind of concern and treatment.

Specific infectious diseases are almost absent. Regarding periostitis, although verified, it has not reached significant levels. Nevertheless, in many cases periosteum could not be fully evaluated.

Metabolic diseases such as scurvy and rickets were not found. The only pathology found in this group of diseases might have been caused by a case of Paget's disease. A skull fragment, from Cabeço do Pez, shows a massive thickening of the skull vault which was also very perceptible on the X-ray where, one could see that, both the inner and outer tables had thickened to such a point that it was difficult to recognise radiologically.

Skeletal stress indicators

Linear enamel hypoplasias, one of the most accurate non-specific stress indicators, was looked for in all the dentitions. While this nutritional stress indicator was almost absent in the deciduous dentition, meaning that part of growing period (prenatal) was free of major disturbances, the frequency of enamel hypoplasias in permanent dentitions was moderate. In Muge 13.2% (177/1339) of the observed teeth were affected. Regarding Sado, 2.07% (21/1010) of the analysed teeth showed dental enamel hypoplasias. However, 29% (548/1887) of the teeth from Muge and 14.26% (168/1178) of the teeth from Sado could not be analysied (Cardoso, 2001). In any case, the frequency noted does not indicate that there were periods of severe disturbances of growth among the Mesolithic children. It seems that, in general, growing was a process that was in equilibrium with the environment.

Final comments

In all, it seems that the average adult and sub-adult individual was not frequently affected by chronic diseases. Furthermore, a comparison of the incidence of the above mentioned pathologies among the Mesolithic and Neolithic Portuguese communities does not confirm a higher incidence of traumatic events among the hunter-gather communities of the Mesolithic or, for that matter, a higher prevalence of infectious diseases among the first farmers. This seems to indicate that a certain degree of sedentharisation had already been achieved by the last Mesolithic communities in the Portuguese territory.

Acknowledgements

This paper is funded by a Praxis grant, from Fundação da Ciência e Tecnologia, namely PCNA /BIA/ 114/96.

Dr. J. Brandão (from Serviços Geológicos de Portugal) facilitated this research in many ways. Dr. H. Bacelar (Museu de História Natural da Universidade do Porto) has also help us a lot. We are also indebted to Dr. Luís Raposo and Dra. Ana Cristina Araújo from the Museu Nacional de Arqueologia.

Participation to the Mesolithic meeting was partially supported by Fundação Calouste Gulbenkian.

References

Araújo, A.C. 1995/7. A indústria lítica do concheiro de Poças de S.Bento (vale do Sado) no seu contexto regional. *O Arqueólogo Português*, série IV, 13/15, 87–159.

Arnaud, J.M. 1987. Os concheiros mesolítico dos vales do Tejo e Sado: semelhanças e diferenças. *Arqueologia 15*, 53–64.

—— 1989. The Mesolithic communities of the Sado valley, Portugal, in their ecological setting. In: Bonsall, C. (ed.) *The Mesolithic in Europe: Papers Presented at the Third International Symposium, Edinburgh 1985*, 614–631. Edinburgh.

Cardoso, F.A. 2001. *Problemas de Crescimento no Mesolítico Português. Contribuição de Alguns Indicadores de Stress.* Tese de Mestrado em Evolução Humana. Departamento de Antropologia. Universidade de Coimbra. Coimbra.

Crubézy, E., Bruzek, J., Guilaine, J., Cunha, E., Rougé, D. and Jelinek, J. 2001. The antiquity of cranial surgery in Europe and in the Mediterranean basin. Ancienneté de la chirurgie crânienne en Europe et dans le Bassin Méditerranéen. *Comptes Rendus de l'Academie de Sciences de Paris*. Accepted for publication.

Cunha, E. and Umbelino, C. 1995/7. Abordagem antropológica das comunidades mesolíticas dos Concheiros do Sado. *O Arqueólogo Português*, Série IV, vol.13/15, 161–179.

Cunha, E. and Cardoso, F. 2002. New data on Muge shell middens: a contribution to more accurate numbers and dates. *Proceedings of O Mesolítico no território Português*. Universidade Autónoma and Câmara Muncipal de Salvaterra de Magos edition. In press.

Cunha, E., Umbelino, C. and Cardoso, F. n.d. New anthropological data on the Mesolithic communities from Portugal: the shell middens from Sado. *Human Evolution*. In press.

Ferembach, D. 1974. *Le gisement Mésolithique de Moita do Sebastião. Muge. Portugal*. II Anthropologie. Direcção Geral dos Assuntos Culturais. Lisboa.

Lubell, D. and Jackes, M. 1994. The Mesolithic-Neolithic transition in Portugal: Isotopic and dental evidence of diet. *Journal of Archaeological Sciences* 21, 201–216.

Jackes, M., Lubell, D. and Meiklejohn, C. 1997. Healthy but mortal: human biology and the first farmers of western Europe. *Antiquity* 71, 639–58.

Smith, B.H. 1984. Patterns of Molar Wear in Hunter-Gathers and Agriculturalists. *American Journal of Physical Anthropology* 63, 39–56.

Session IV

Spatial Organisation of Sites

27. Introduction

Ole Grøn

In biology it is an established fact that the organisation of each living organism is encoded in the genes found in each of its cells. For archaeologists engaged in the study of the scanty material remains of what were once living cultural systems with behavioural codes and spiritual concepts, it may appear optimistic or even presumptuous to adopt a similar attitude: to search for a reflection of cultural systems in the organisation of their settlements and dwellings. It might be an easier task to get the proverbial camel through the eye of the needle.

Meanwhile, it is also an established fact that one of the few 'very general' statements about indigenous cultures is that their dwellings play a central role in their world concepts and cosmologies. The dwelling is very often conceived as a micro version of the real cosmos and organised spatially to reflect this symbolically. But its spatial organisation also reflects the social organisation of the group living in it. The literature on this subject is about as comprehensive as the lack of interest it has so far received from most archaeologists (e.g. Ränk 1951: 141; Bourdieu 1970:739 pp; Ohnuki-Tierny 1972:427 pp; Eliade 1976:3, 41 pp; Tanner 1979:73, 88, 1991; Bernot 1982; Fock 1986:61 pp; Gracheva 1989; Doxtater 1991:156 pp.; Parvia 1991:150 pp).

Were the prehistoric cultures so primitive that they were deprived of the use of symbolic and ritual behaviour? This possibility is ruled out by, among other things, the few archaeological cases where it has been possible to directly observe the repetitive organisation of dwelling units in well preserved settings – for instance Skara Brae and Çatal Hüyük (Childe 1946:28 pp; Melaart 1967:56 pp; Clarke and Sharples 1985:70). The importance of such sites, meanwhile, has not gained sufficient attention.

The basic problem, as I see it, has been that archaeology employs many concepts which in fact are very different from and incompatible with those used in sciences that study living humans. Becker states for instance that 'on none of the Maglemosian settlements on Zealand lived more than one small-family at a time' (Becker 1953). But did they never meet other families? Did they never camp together and have a party? Hunt together? The 'size' of the settlements is sometimes used as a diagnostic factor in the study of cultural change. But who really believes that humans lived in settlements that only measured 5, 10, or 20 metres in diameter. How did they manage that, did they tie up their kids and dogs to prevent them from enlarging the 'settlement area?'. What kind of features are we talking about when we use the term 'settlement'?

An obvious starting point has been to try to demonstrate that Mesolithic settlements were in fact well organised areas, as one should expect, and that there existed a behavioural code that sometimes can be distinguished in the material remains (Grøn 1995:9 p, 1999). Repetition of patterns is important. When they can be observed, when they have not been disturbed or blurred by overlapping settlement phases, geological processes, human activities etc., they allow for a more 'anatomically' and even culturally correct approach to the sites.

The papers in this session demonstrate an increasing interest and focus on settlement organisation in Mesolithic research. That is a very positive and promising development. Recent excavations have revealed repetitive patterns occurring on north European Mesolithic sites. More importantly, archaeologists have now begun to disentangle some of the more complex site palimpsests that initially did not yield immediate results with regard to spatial organisation. In both cases is it important that new excavations are carried through with a more systematic registration of the material, something that was often lacking in some of the earlier investigations.

An improvement of, together with a more realistic attitude towards, analysis that employ more sophisticated statistical methods of distribution patterns is welcome. Some of the earlier methods assumed fundamentalistic behavioural principles that must have made life difficult for the prehistoric people. Such techniques can of course never fully reveal all of the behavioural aspects of the archaeological material in detail, but they can be helpful in visualising significant spatial tendencies that are difficult to distinguish through visual inspection alone.

In this and other sessions the subject ritual has popped

up. To me it is obvious that ritual is a factor we cannot reject in archaeology. It has most likely played an active role in the deposition of material on sites – like it or not. At times it represents an irritating factor that is somewhat difficult to control archaeologically. But that it is difficult does not allow us to ignore it – if our aim is to conduct serious research. Ethnoarchaeology may be one way of overcoming some of the shortcomings inherent in the excavated materials with regard to this aspect – even though traditional archaeologists should be very much aware that ethnoarchaeology is not a magic box which contains answers to everything an archaeologist could possibly hope for.

In general I feel that the papers presented in this session clearly indicate that Mesolithic archaeology has reached a new stage and that we have accumulated so much material that it is now possible to formulate more refined generalisations than previously. One can now only hope for that the disturbing lack of resources for the excavation of new and informative Mesolithic sites, a situation that has been experienced in some countries, shall not stop this positive development.

References.

Becker, C.J. 1953. Die Maglemosekultur in Dänemark: Neue Funde und Ergebnisse. *Congrés International des Sciences Préhistoriques 1950, Actes de la IIIe Session*, 180–183.

Bernot, L. 1982. The two-door house. In: Izikowitz, K.G. and Søensen, P. (eds.) *The Intha example from Burma. East and Southeast Asia. Anthropological and architectural Aspect*, 41–48. London.

Bourdieu, P. 1970. La maison Kabyle ou le monde renversé. In: Pouillon, J. and Maranda, P. (eds.) *Échanges et communications. Mélanges offerts à Claude Lèvi-Strauss à l'occassion de son 60ème anniversaire*, 739–758.

Childe, G.V. 1946. *Scotland before the Scots*. London.

Clarke, D.V. and Sharples, N. 1985. Settlements and subsistence in the third millennium B.C. In: Renfrew, C. (ed.) *The prehistory of Orkney*, 54–82. Edinburgh.

Doxtater, D. 1991. Reflections on the Anasazi cosmos. In: Grøn, O., Engelstad, E. and Lindblom, I. (eds.) *Social Space. Human Spatial Behaviour in Dwellings and Settlements*, 155–184. Odense.

Eliade, M. 1976. *A History of Religious Ideas* I. Chicago.

Fock, N. 1986. Et sted i skoven – en verden – et univers. *Jordens folk* vol 21(2), 61–69.

Grøn, O. 1995. *The Maglemose Culture. The reconstruction of the social organisation of a mesolithic culture in Northern Europe*. BAR International Series 616. Oxford.

Gracheva, G. 1989. Nganasan shamans' ways and worldview. In: Hoppal, M. and Pentikänen, J. (eds.) *Uralic Mythology and Folklore*, 233–238. Budapest – Helsinki.

Mellaart, J. 1967. *Çatal Hüyük. A Neolithic Town in Anatolia*. London.

Ohnuki-Tierney, E. 1972. Spatial concepts of the Ainu of the Northwest Coast of Southern Sakhalin. *American Anthropologist* vol.74(3), 426–457.

Parvia, R. 1991. The Finnish concept of space. A mythical spiritual view. In: Grøn, O., Engelstad, E. and Lindblom, I. (eds.) *Social Space. Human Spatial Behaviour in Dwellings and Settlements*, 149–154. Odense,

Ränk, G. 1951. *Das System der Raumeinteilung in den Behausungen der nordeuroasischen Völker* vol.2. Stockholm.

Tanner, A. 1979. *Bringing Home Animals. Religious Ideology and Mode of Production of the Mistassini Cree Hunters*. London.

Tanner, A. 1991. Spatial organization in social formation and symbolic action: Fijian and Canadian examples. In: Grøn, O., Engelstad, E. and Lindblom, I. (eds.) *Social Space. Human Spatial Behaviour in Dwellings and Settlements*. Odense, 21–39.

28. Encircling the living space of Early Postglacial reindeer hunters in the interior of southern Norway

Sveinung Bang-Andersen

Seven tent rings, six evident and one analytically segregated, found on sites at Store Myrvatnet and Store Fløyrlivatnet in the mountains of SW Norway, are presented. C14-dated between c. 9600 and 9000 uncal. BP these range as the oldest dwelling structures so far known in Norway. The size, form, function and cultural-historical background of the tents used by the "Myrvatn-Fløyrlivatn group" of logistic-mobile reindeer hunters is tentatively interpreted in the light of ethnographical and archaeological data. Further studies will be needed to separate more precisely the different dwelling constructions and activity patterns expressed in the tent rings.

Introduction

In southern Scandinavia, as in other parts of Northern Europe, faint remains of hutfloors often appear on sites from Pre-boreal and Boreal hunter-gatherer groups adapted to densely vegetated environments. These sites provide important – still highly fragmentary – evidence about seasonality, camp organisation and indoor/outdoor work activities (Fredsjö 1953:46 pp; Larsson 1974:5 pp; Blankholm 1987:109 pp; Johansson 1990:15 pp). Some sites have even been interpreted to reflect social factors determining the spatial use of the hutfloors (Grøn 1989:99 pp, 1995:59 p).

As a contrast, dwelling remains from preceding pioneer populations inhabiting open tundra or park tundra landscapes, are of even more slender character, despite the careful excavation of a large number of well-preserved sites in Denmark and on the North European plain. Interpretations of Late Glacial dwellings have mainly been of indirect nature, based on the spatial localisation of hearths, special activity areas, postulated door dumps or potential walls reflected by the artefact dispersal (Andersen 1973:16 pp). Alleged "tent" or "hut" structures do, with some very few exceptions (e.g. Terberger 1997:25 pp), not appear convincing.

The aim of this paper is to bring into discussion tent rings found in Pre-boreal inland sites bordering the mountain lakes *Store Myrvatnet* and *Store Fløyrlivatnet* in Southwest-Norway. Focus will be on the tent rings and their cultural-historical setting within a North-European and Circumpolar context. Other important archaeological aspects opened by these sites will be subject for later analyses, and are not considered in any detail here.

The two lakes are situated 20 km apart in the mountain areas on the southern side of the Lysefjord, 40 and 45 km E and ESE of the city of Stavanger (Figure 28.1).

Both the topographical setting and the character of the sites exhibit important common traits. The lakes are surrounded by open low-alpine landscapes, now only

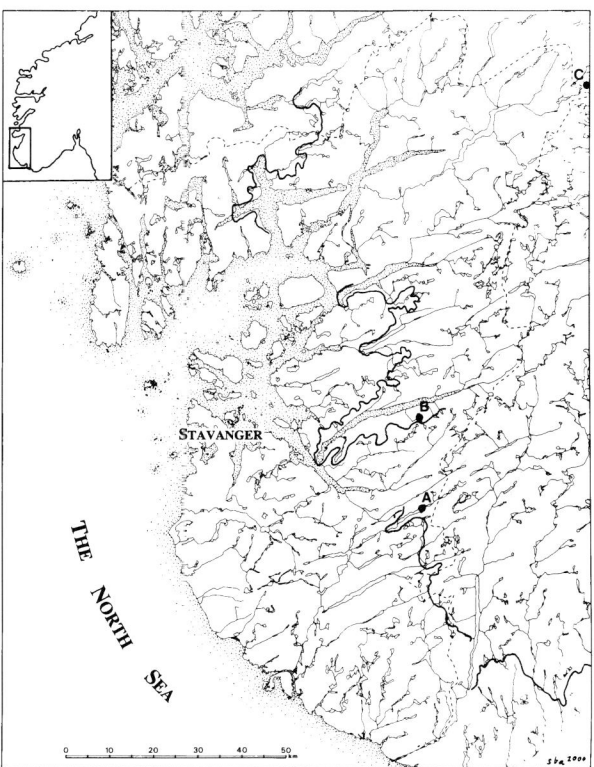

Figure 28.1 Map of SW Norway with solid lines indicating the Younger Dryas ice front position, A: Store Myrvatnet, B: Store Fløyrlivatnet, and C: Holmavatnet.

sporadically used by wild reindeer. As both lakes have been utilised for hydro-electrical purposes since the early 1920s, large beach zones emerge strongly eroded due to water-level alterations. With regard to ice recession chronology, the sites are situated within or immediately behind the Younger Dryas main frontal moraine, the Lysefjord stage, dated between c. 10,900 and 10,700 BP (Andersen 1979:86). Accordingly, any settlement remains found here in unprotected position should be younger than about 10,500 radiocarbon years.

Until now 17 Early Mesolithic sites have been localised: 7 alongside Myrvatn, 10 at Fløyrlivatn. All are open air sites dominated by lithic inventories devoid of organical remains other than charcoal. In both areas the physical preservation of the sites varies due to differential exposure to the main erosional processes: inundation, wave abrasion and ice pack action. The Myrvatn sites, due to superimposition of thick bog formations, generally contain the physically best preserved cultural layers. In spite of this, the most complete dwelling structures have, paradoxally, come to light at Fløyrlivatn.

A total of 10 Pre-boreal sites have been excavated: 3 at Myrvatn between 1985 and 1998 (Bang-Andersen 1990:215 pp), 7 at Fløyrlivatn in 1999 (Tørhaug and Åstveit 2000:35 pp). The investigated sites contain findbearing activity areas between c. 10 and 45 sq.m. with lithic inventories ranging from about 100 to 3900 artefacts. According to a total of 26 radiocarbon analyses of charcoal, the Myrvatn sites date between 9600 and 9000 BP (Bang-Andersen 1990:218 pp) and the Fløyrlivatn sites between 9750 and 9350 BP (Bang-Andersen 2000:28 p). The radiological time setting is supported by the artefact material in the sites: rich projectile inventories based on tanged points and microliths, a flint manufacture technology dominated by unifacial blade cores with opposed tilted platforms, and rock crystals reduced bipolary.

All sites were excavated in an optimally uniform manner by hand-troweling units of 1/4 sq.m followed by water screening to ensure approximately total find recovery. Accordingly, a sound basis should exist both for inter- and intrasite comparisons.

The Myrvatn sites

The discovery of a group of Pre-boreal settlement sites at Lake Store Myrvatnet (610 m a.s.l.) in 1984 was sensational by the favourable preservational conditions in some sites with plentiful survival of charcoal for radiocarbon datings and palaeo-ecological reconstructions (Bang-Andersen 1988a:124 pp, 1988b:45 pp, 1990:215 pp, 1995:65 pp, 1996b:229 p). Indications of dwelling structures were, however, of slender nature and confined to three sites (Figure 28.2).

Site I, containing an inventory of 1350 stone artefacts within the investigated area of 32.5 sq.m, has been interpreted as the result of one short encampment episode (Bang-Andersen 1990:216).

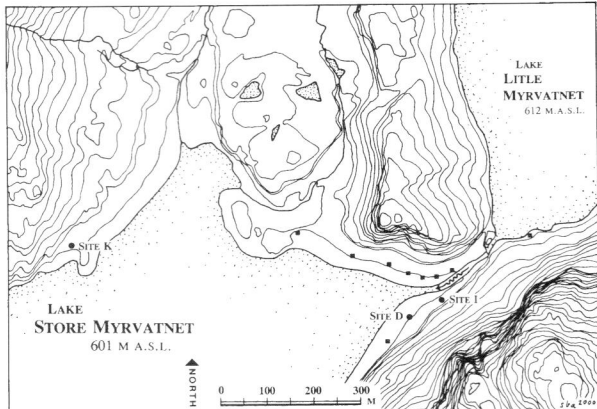

Figure 28.2 Reconstructed shore-line of NE part of Store Myrvatnet with Mesolithic sites (squares) and sites containing tent rings (dots) specified. Contour intervals: 5 m.

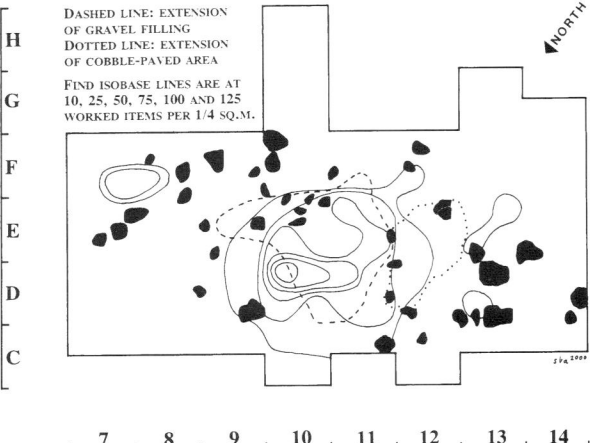

Figure 28.3 Simplified plan of Myrvatn Site I with stones (in black) interpreted as tent weights out of context. Plan size units: 1 m.

Tent rings or other evident dwelling structures were not recognised during excavation. In spite of this, 40 to 45 rounded stones measuring between 20 and 45 cm, spread widely on a homogenous level, may well be taken as structural stones deriving from some kind of tent- or windbreak construction. Charcoal and flint artefacts, directly under the bases, indicate a number of the stones to have been relocated from former positions.

The horizontal distribution of the lithics, with about 75% of the total find amount concentrated within a oval/circular stone-cleared area 2.8–3.2 m across, probably outlines a c. 7 sq.m large tent floor. A 2.8 m wide filling of charcoal-mixed gravel coincided with the artefact concentration (Figure 28.3).

The distribution of burnt flints on Site I, located inside the postulated tent floor, indicates use of interior fire, despite a lack of distinct hearts. Two radiocarbon analyses of charcoal independently date the site to c. 9000 BP (see Appendix for lab. references). Possible tent openings marked by "find tongues" or "door dumps" are not

Figure 28.4 Gravel filling (close to camera) and stone paving at Myrvatn Site I. Photo: S. Bang-Andersen.

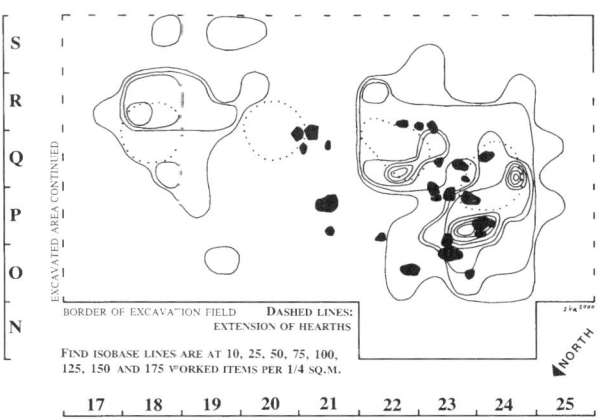

Figure 28.5 Simplified plan of the central parts of Myrvatn Site D with stones interpreted as belonging to a tent ring (in black). Plan size units: 1 m.

apparent from these horizontal distribution of finds. A 1.2 x 1.9 m wide stone paving may, however, have served as drainage outside a highly hypothetical SW facing entrance (Figure 28.4).

Site D, located just 50 m WSW of Site I, contained three find scatters 2–3 meters apart, each interpreted to reflect separate visits. About 3850 stone artefacts were recovered from the 92 sq.m large excavated area (Bang-Andersen 1990:219 pp).

An alignment of stones, evidently a tent ring, soon appeared on the best preserved SW part of the living floor. The structure consisted of about 25 rounded stones, 15–40 cm large, arranged as an irregular oval or rhomb with inner diameter between 1.8 and 2.8 m and net floor area c. 5.0 sq.m. A majority of the stones measured between 20–25 cm. Some stones, superimposing flint artefacts or charcoal appear to have been removed some short distance. No indications of tent openings were found.

Three circular hearths, between 1.0 and 1.4 m in diameter, located to the southern and eastern periphery of the tent ring, stratigraphically reflect one or several settlement episodes *antedating* the construction of the tent ring. This may also apply to most of the stone artefacts, as the highest frequencies of finds were underneath the western tent weight stones (Figure 28.5). As there were only minor amounts of charcoal and burnt flint inside the stone alignment, the tent has probably been without internal hearth. Also by a low number of artefacts inside the tent ring the Site D tent is indicated to have served a more passive function than the analytically segregated Site I tent.

Three radiocarbon analyses of charcoal from super-imposed hearths, all dating around 9400 BP (Bang-Andersen 1990:221), determine a maximum age of the tent ring.

Site K was found in 1991 denuded by wave erosion on the opposite northern beach of the lake and first noticed by a partly intact tent ring and a concentration of about 100 flint artefacts including a Zonhoven point. The

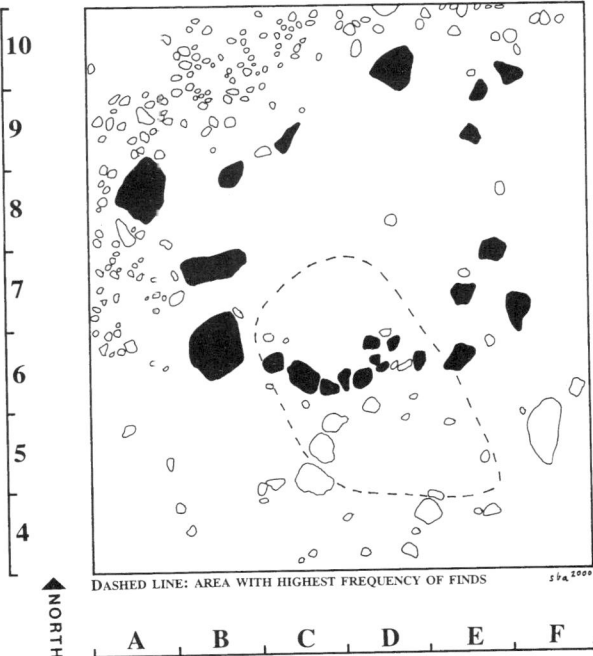

Figure 28.6 Simplified plan of Myrvatn Site K with stones interpreted as belonging to a tent ring (in black). Plan size units: 1 m.

archaeological treatment has so far been restricted to documentation, investigation of intact contexts underneath the tent weight stones and collection of surface finds of lithics and charcoal.

The tent ring consists of 23 rounded stones and blocks, 15–85 cm wide; a majority head-sized. The inner diameter measures 3,8 m, producing a circular or slightly oval tent floor covering 11.4 sq.m (Figure 28.6). A lack of stones in the NW sector facing the land side may indicate a tent opening, or could be the result of ice push or wave abrasion. However, the distribution of surface finds, concentrated within a 5–6 sq.m large area covering the southern sector of the ring and the adjacent area outside, more convincingly reflects a tent door and a restricted outdoor activity area facing the lake. Charcoal in the southern part of this area, evidently the remains of an exterior hearth, has been radiocarbon dated to about 9500 BP.

Considering the uneven state of preservation and a still awaiting total excavation, the potentiality also of an interior use of fire should not be excluded.

In sum, the Myrvatn sites have left evidence of three tents in Pre-boreal contexts: one *latent* tent floor (Site I) segregated mainly by the distribution of artefacts and a charcoal-mixed floor filling, and two *evident* tent rings (Site D and K) appearing as partly disturbed open oval stone alignments. More "textbook like" tent rings formed as regular, closed stone circles have not been verified.

The net tent floor areas are estimated from 5.0 to 11.4 sq.m, and an interior hearth is only apparent from Site I. The amount of stones interpreted as structural weights used to secure the tent covers to the ground, between 21 and 25, should be taken as absolute minimum numbers. C-14 datings of the Myrvatn dwelling structures range from c. 9500 to 9000 BP.

The Fløyrlivatn sites

The totally distorted or partly blurred tent remains at Myrvatn may be better understood by the results of investigations carried out at lake Store Fløyrlivatn (760 m a.s.l.) as late as 1999.

Four tent rings in all were recorded from three sites (Figure 28.7). A fifth structure, a 3 m long curved stone alignment on Site 15, dated to 9700–9600 BP (Bang-Andersen 2000:28) and interpreted during excavation as a tent ring (Tørhaug and Åstveit 2000:35), more probably represents the foundation of a windbreak and will not be taken into further consideration.

At *Site 9,* atypically located in a boulder terrain bordering the south-western part of the lake, about 120 lithics were recovered within the 27 sq.m large excavated area. The site emerged as strongly eroded, devoid of humic sediments and plant cover. As a number of flint artefacts appeared surficial, an unknown amount of lithics is likely to have been washed into the lake.

The structural feature at Site 9 is an almost closed alignment of 21 rounded stones adjacent to a large erratic with level upper part. Both a 0.5 x 0.7 m wide stone in the central part of the tent ring, and about 10 stones found in the immediate surroundings, may be weight stones in secondary positions. The structural stones interpreted to lie *in situ* were between 15 and 55 cm in diameter, forming an oval, NE-SW oriented, 2.0 x 2.4 m wide enclosure covering 4.5 sq.m. The SE sector appeared as intact by five weight stones, 22–36 cm in diameter, evenly placed with internal spacing between 12 and 22 cm (Figure 28.8).

Distinct hearths were not found. A slight occurrence of charcoal less than 1 m outside the tent ring, dated by two radiocarbon analyses between c. 9700 and 9500 BP (see Appendix), probably represents an exterior hearth. The horizontal distribution of the sparse remaining stone

Figure 28.7 Reconstructed shore-line of S parts of Store Fløyrlivatnet with Mesolithic sites (squares) and sites containing tent rings (dots) specified. Contour intervals: 5 m.

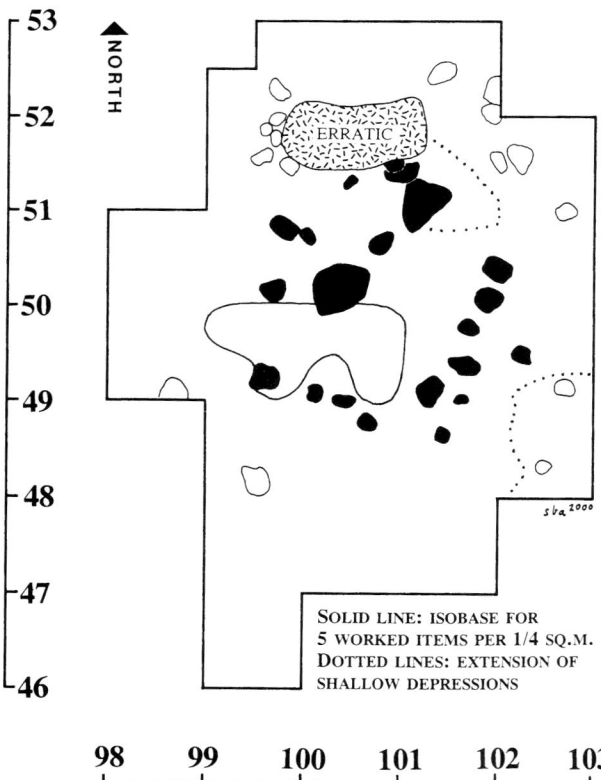

Figure 28.8 Simplified plan of Fløyrlivatn site 9 with stones interpreted as belonging to a tent ring (in black). Plan size units: 1 m.

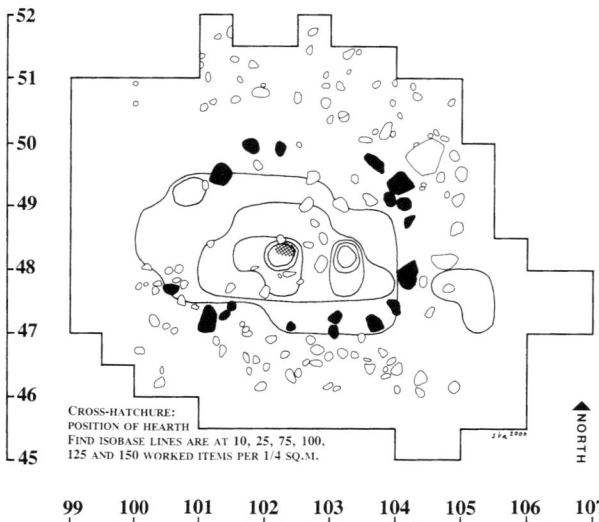

Figure 28.9 Simplified plan of Fløyrlivatn Site 7 with stones interpreted as belonging to a tent ring (in black). Plan size units: 1 m.

Figure 28.10 The NW part of Fløyrlivatn Site 6 with two tent rings. Line of boulders in the background represent the former shore line. Photo: V. Tørhaug.

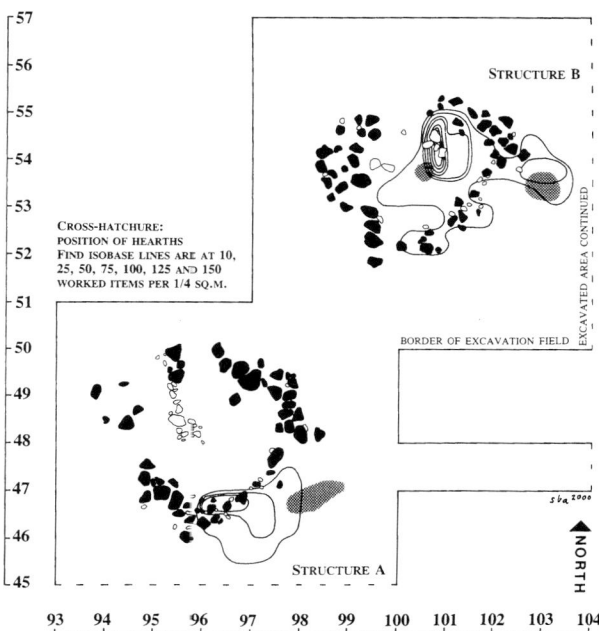

Figure 28.11 Simplified plan of NW part of Fløyrlivatn Site 6 with stones interpreted as belonging to two tent rings (in black). Plan size units: 1 m.

artefact material, concentrated to the SW sector of the tent ring, may further indicate a tent opening facing the hearth and the waterfront.

Site 7, on a wide outwash delta on the south-eastern lakeshore, 900 m E of Site 9, contributes with even more detailed dwelling data. The excavation covered a 38.5 sq.m large area, producing about 1700 lithics. 19 stones, arranged as a ESE-WNW oriented open circle, between 2.7 and 3.3 m in inner diameter and covering 8.0 sq.m, formed an almost "ideal" tent ring (Figure 28.9).

The weights, 10–60 cm in diameter, were spaced at irregular intervals with a certain number of stones out of place. Some of these may have been removed to the NW interior part of the structure, where artefacts occurred under the bases of head-sized stones. A stone-free area facing West, reducing the tent ring to a 4/5 of a complete circle, may be due to recent erosion or reflect a former door opening facing the lake. Provided a regular spacing, the tent ring has probably consisted of minimum 25 stones.

A 20 x 30 cm wide scatter of charcoal in the centre of the tent floor, C14- dated to c. 9400 BP, represents a partly washed out interior hearth. Indications of outside hearths are not recorded. The find distribution is clear-cut, with no less than 83 % of the total lithic assemblage concentrated inside the tent ring, most pronounced to the central and southern part.

Site 6 was found on the sloping eastern lakeside 600 m N of Site 7. By its discovery in 1997 the site, like Myrvatn K, emerged as partly surface eroded with flint and rock crystal artefacts and a stone circle (Structure A) clearly visible. The excavation of 168 sq.m produced about 2300 lithics. This states a minimum of artefacts originally deposited, as an unknown amount has been removed by erosion.

Two tent rings were uncovered on the NW part of the site (Figure 28.10).

Structure A appeared as an approximately circular or rhombic alignment of 55 well-rounded stones, all more or less *in situ*. The tent ring was about 3.2 m by inner diameter, encircling a 7.2 sq.m large floor area. The weight stones varied between 10 and 50 cm in diameter. Three 0.6–0.8 m wide disjunction's in the NW quadrant of the stone circle may be interpreted as one (or several) tent openings facing the lake. Most pronounced of these is a 0.6–0.7 m long north-oriented "corridor" (Figure 28.11).

Interior hearths, or other indications of fire as scatters

of charcoal or burnt artefacts, were not recorded. Containing a highly restricted number of artefacts, the tent floor may seem to have served passive site functions e.g. as area for sleep or rest. A concentration of flint artefacts deposited outside the SSE margin of the tent ring and superimposed by structural stones may be interpreted to result from site activities *antedating* the tent ring, determined by C14-datings to c. 9600–9400 BP. A 1.2 m long aggregation of charcoal 0.8 m outside the SE sector of the tent ring, apparently an external hearth, has been dated within the same time range.

Structure B, 3–4 m NE of Structure A, had the shape of an irregular oval or rhombic stone circle with inner diameter between 3.0 and 3.2 m covering a net area of about 6.7 sq.m. The tent ring was made up by 51 rounded stones measuring between 10 and 40 cm, mainly 20–25 cm. A 1.0 m wide disjunction may represent a tent opening facing NNW, or could be the result of erosion. More likely the entrance has been by a 0.4–1.2 m long southwards oriented "corridor" similar to the feature in the northern part of Structure A (Figure 28.11).

The lithic material was clearly concentrated to the central and NE part of the tent floor with no indications of door dumping. A circular 0.4 wide hearth in the geometrical centre of the tent ring has been dated between to about 9400 BP, and a circular 0.7 m wide stonelined hearth 0.6 m outside the ESE part of the dwelling to 9750 BP. Based on the age of an interior hearth, which seems functionally related to the tent ring, Structure B *may* – but need not necessarily – be contemporaneous with Structure A. The only possible method to prove this, is by future identification of lithic refit patterns.

In sum the Fløyrlivatn investigations have brought into light four evident tent rings in the shape of oval or circular alignments of c. 20–55 structural stones. Three of the rings are closed, except for short intercepts indicating the possible position of tent openings. The inner diameter varies between 2.2 and 3.3 m, and the net floor space between 4.5 and 8.0 sq.m.

Two structures (Site 6B and 7) contain centrally positioned interior hearths, while one (Site 9) seems functionally related to an exterior hearth. In addition two structures (Site 6A and 6B) are surrounded by hearths appearing not to be contemporary with the tent structures. C-14 datings of the Fløyrlivatn tent rings cluster between c. 9600 and 9400 BP.

The Myrvatn-Fløyrlivatn group

The campsites: situation, size, and artefact inventory

Based on the presentations above, the Early Mesolithic sites at Myrvatn and Fløyrlivatn exhibit a number of common traits:

- All are closely lakeside oriented, normally positioned between 2 and 10 m away from the former waterfront and overlooking wide landscape areas.
- The sites are, with just one exception (Fløyrlivatn 9), situated on well-drained fine-sorted late glacial outwash.
- In spite of surface erosion, all find areas still contain remains of undisturbed cultural levels potent to define roughly the former extension and character of the sites.
- The horizontal scattering of artefacts is extremely restricted, ranging from about 8 to c. 50 sq.m. As the two largest sites (Myrvatn D and Fløyrlivatn 6) have been subject to re-use, the spaces occupied per encampment episode hardly exceed 10–15 sq.m.
- The artefact assemblages consist mainly of medium to high quality flint with minor supplements of rock crystal or quartz (except Myrvatn F). The inventory of formal tools is normally restricted to projectile points and lower amounts of scrapers. Other types as burins and borers occur as a clear element only in Myrvatn D.
- Of particular importance is the good preservation of charcoal, providing high-resolution datings of the Myrvatn sites to c. 9600–9000 BP and the Fløyrlivatn sites to c. 9750–9350 BP, and occurrence of tent ring structures.

The tent rings: basic elements, main function, dating

All tent rings found at Myrvatn and Fløyrlivatn are localised to horizontal, stone-cleared areas on the sites.

The archaeological visibility varies from a *latent* tent floor segregated mainly from the distribution of lithic artefacts (Myrvatn I) to *evident* "text-book like" stone-lined circles (Fløyrlivatn 6 and 7). As the most disturbed tent structures were found in the by all other respects best preserved sites (Myrvatn I and D), human behaviour appears to have been more decisive for the preservation of the tent rings than the cumulative effect of all natural and man-triggered erosion during the subsequent millennia. In one extreme case the tent weight stones appear to have been deliberately tossed away before breaking up from the site. Normally the stones lie slightly dislocated from their original positions due to removal of the tent sheet.

The shape of the *tent floors* is circular, or slightly elongated as an irregular oval or rhombe. Two of the tent rings (Myrvatn K and Fløyrlivatn 7) are partly open alignments of placed stones, while the remaining four appear as basically closed. The inner dimension varies between 1.8 and 3.8 m and the net floor area from 4.5 to 11.4 sq.m. with 7.1 as a mean value (Figure 28.12).

Possible *tent openings*, indicated by stone-free disjunction's or find-tongues exceeding the border of the tent ring, seem to have existed in most cases; facing the water (Myrvatnet K, Fløyrlivatn 7) or the adjacent beach

Site name	Tent ring type	Ground plan lay-out	Inner dimension in metres	Floor area in sq.m	Indoor fire	C14 age BP
Site I, Store Myrvatnet	I	oval/circular(?)	2.8 x 3.2	7.0	+	9000
Site D, Store Myrvatnet	IIIa	oval/rhombic	1.8 x 2.8	5.0	−	9400
Site K, Store Myrvatnet	IIa	circular/oval	3.8 x 3.8	11.4	−	9500
Site 9, Store Fløyrlivatnet	IIIa	oval/circular	2.0 x 2.4	4.5	−	9600
Site 7, Store Fløyrlivatnet	IIa	circular	2.7 x 3.3	8.0	+	9400
Site 6A, St. Fløyrlivatnet	IIIb	circular/rhombe	3.2 x 3.2	7.2	−	9600
Site 6B, St. Fløyrlivatnet	IIIa	oval/rhombic	3.0 x 3.2	6.7	+	9400

Figure 28.12 Collocation of tent ring data from the investigated areas. The codes, partly based on Newell (1981), distinguish: I. Structural stones lacking a discernible pattern. II. Open alignments of structural stones (IIa. partly distorted, IIb. intact). III. Enclosed alignments of structural stones (IIIa. partly distorted, IIIb. intact). Radiocarbon ages are expressed as approximate mean values.

line (Fløyrlivatn 6A and 6B). The evidence of tent openings is however generally of a hypothetical character and needs to be tested by later analyses.

The tent rings consist of between 20 and 70 *weight stones*, mostly c. 20–30 cm by largest dimension and well-rounded to prevent tearing up the tent cover. As some weights appear to be missing from most tent rings, removed by the campsite inhabitants or dislocated by later natural agents, this states absolute minimum numbers. The amount of structural stones actually necessary for fixing the tent sheets firmly to the ground depended on factors as wind exposure, tent height and size, and local availability of stones. Indications of other supporting elements as stakeholes, outside drainage ditches or guystones have not been documented from any site, but may well have existed.

Interior hearths were used in at least two of six tent rings (Fløyrlivatn 6B and 7) centrally positioned on the tent floor. Contemporary *exterior hearths* appear to have existed in at least two cases (Myrvatn K and Fløyrlivatn 9) adjacent to postulated door openings. Alternatively these outside hearths may represent ashes dumped out from former interior campfires.

Considering the distribution of finds, one half of the tents had most or all artefacts concentrated *in*side, and the other half the main artefact distributed *out*side. In both tent rings with internal hearths most or all artefacts were found indoor. Presupposing the total amount of lithic artefacts to be valid as a coarse indicator of function, and precluding the possibilities of interior clean-ups with door dumping, this may indicate some differentiation in the use of the tents. Beyond a basal function as shelter against wind, rain and snow, some tents were also areas for cooking, heating and tool manufacture, or more passive seclusions for rest and reflection.

The radiological datings of the tent rings need some further consideration.

Expressed in *uncalibrated* radiocarbon years, the oldest and youngest dates of the Myrvatn tent rings, or hearths functionally related to these, range between 9570 (9495±75 /Tua -1692) and 8910 (9040±130 /T-7994) BP, indicating a maximum time span of 660 years. The corresponding values from Fløyrlivatn are 9830 (9750±80/ Beta-141301) and 9280 (9360±80 /Beta-141293) BP, or a maximum period of use covering 550 years. Two tent rings from Fløyrlivatn Site 6B and 9, predating all Myrvatn dates (see Appendix), suggest Early Mesolithic hunter groups to have pitched tents in this area some few hundred years earlier than at Myrvatn. On the other hand, as the tent floor in Myrvatn I postdates all Fløyrlivatn tent rings, the use of tents probably lasted some few hundred years longer at Myrvatn.

Conclusions as these may easily be turned over by sources of error inherent in the C14-method. As known for a long time (e.g. Gulliksen 1980:101 pp; Gowlett 1986:98 pp) clear deviations exist between conventional dates and tree-ring calibrated calendar year dates, in particular during the Pre-boreal. Radiological research has proved plateaux of constant radiocarbon ages to existed at 9950 and 9550 uncalibrated years BP, the last covering as many as 400 calendar years (Becker and Kromer 1991:22 pp).

Calibrations of the Myrvatn and Fløyrlivatn dating series according to the latest available data using two sigma confidence intervals (Stuiver *et al.* 1998:1041 pp), determine the Myrvatn tent rings between 9200 and 7750 cal BC, or a period of maximum 1450 solar years. The values for the Fløyrlivatn tent rings range between 9350 and 8250 cal BC, or a maximum period of use covering 1100 years. Based on the lowest standard deviations, the tents in each area need not have been used longer than about 850 and 660 solar years respectively (see Appendix).

Without involving further details, calibrations confirm:

- the oldest tent rings to be at Fløyrlivatn (Sites 6 and 9),
- the youngest evidence of tent use to Myrvatn (Site I),
- some of the Myrvatn and Fløyrlivatn tent rings (e.g. Myrvatn D and Fløyrlivatn 7) as potentially contemporaneous; and
- tents in both areas to have been used over a longer

period of time than indicated by the uncalibrated radiocarbon datings.

The background: ecological setting, subsistence system

The dating of most of the Myrvatn and Fløyrlivatn tent rings to 9600–9400 BP, or the middle part of the Preboreal, determines human enterprise to have occurred within or soon after the Trollgaren ice-advance stage about 9700–9500 BP (Anundsen 1985:220). Tents also seem to have been used at Fløyrlivatn during a minor ice advance around 9300 BP.

With the inland ice sheet still covering mountain areas just some few kilometres further East, the environmental setting of the sites in both areas is likely to have been that of a periglacial tree-less landscape, climatically influenced by the continued presence of inland ice.

This is supported by wood-anatomical analyses of the charcoal from the Myrvatn sites, reflecting a low-alpine pioneer vegetation of willow scrubs and dwarf birch established on fresh mineral soils (Bang-Andersen 1990:224). The charcoal from Fløyrlivatn is more problematic palaeobotanically as some samples have turned out to contain oak and pine wood, most likely brought in from lowland areas (Bang-Andersen 2000:27 pp). Pollen analyses able to reconstruct the middle Preboreal non arboreal vegetation in the mountain areas South of Lysefjord, or high-resolutive quaternary deglaciation studies, have so far not been completed.

Concerning potential food resources available in recently deglaciated mountain landscapes as these, one is confined to use indirect evidence or qualified guesswork due to the complete lack of faunal remains in the sites.

Compared with groups known to have lived under similar natural conditions, wild reindeer *(Rangifer tarandus)* emerge as the only likely big game of importance. The reindeer herds need however not necessarily have been predated primarily for their meat. Skins, sinews and antler for tool production may have been even more demanded. The interpretation of the Myrvatn and Fløyrlivatn sites as special purpose hunting camps seems to be supported by the expedient flint tool inventories in the sites, almost exclusively projectile points and scrapers.

In logistic terms the sites appear to be the products of short-lasting early autumn hunting activities performed by mobile groups with home bases on the coast of SW Norway (Bang-Andersen 1990:224 pp, 1996b:435 pp). C14-datings in both study areas point to discontinuous series of stays of sporadic character, not separated by extremely long intervals.

The tents of reindeer hunters

Evident tent rings dating to the Late Pleistocene or Early Holocene are not known in other parts of southern Scandinavia, in spite of a the discovery and investigation

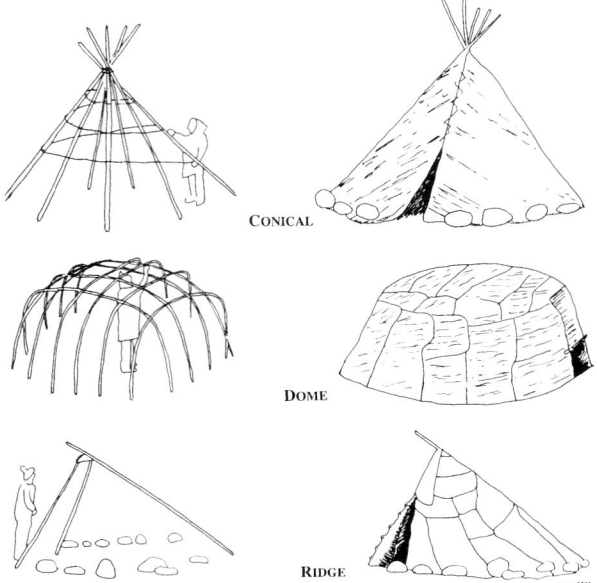

Figure 28.13 The three main types of tents within the circumpolar zone, based mainly on Faegre (1979).

of a increasing number of short-term camps or kill sites attributed to reindeer hunting (Holm and Rieck 1992:9 pp, Vang Petersen and Johansen 1993:20 pp; Larsson 1994:159 pp).

Tent ring like structures do occur in Late Glacial sites on the continental lowland plains. Within the Stellmoor valley in NW Germany a number of circular or semi-circular stone alignments interpreted as tent rings have been recorded from different chronological contexts (Rust 1958:29 pp). The main part of these, as an alleged 3.5–4 m wide tent ring in the Ahrensburgian levels of the site *Borneck-Ost*, turn out as problematic due to insufficient documentation, or possible sources of error as surface deformation by later trefalls. Some few structures like "Konzentration IV", a partly disturbed tent ring with central hearth in the late Magdalénien site *Gönnersdorf* in the upper Rhine valley (Terberger 1997:25 pp), may however prove to be of relevance for the interpretation of the Myrvatn-Fløyrlivatn tent rings, despite a wide gap in time and space and obvious differences in palaeo-ecolgcial setting.

The most relevant basis for comparison and interpretation of tent foundations and framings seems to exist within the circumpolar tundra zone. Fundamentally the tents of recent Inuit reindeer or combined reindeer/seal hunting groups are of three types: conical, domed or ridged tents (Faegre 1979:99 pp) (Figure 28.13).

The *conicals* of caribou Eskimos, resembling the "larvos" of the Fennoscandian Saami population and the "tipis" of the North American plain Indians, have a circular frame of 7 or 8 poles tied together on the top, eventually strengthened by horizontal lines around the poles. The tent cover is usually 10 to 20 reindeer skins

Figure 28.14 Inuit ridge tent at Angmagssalik, SE Greenland around 1900. Photo: J. Petersen (reproduced with kind permission from Nationalmuseet, Etnografisk samling, Copenhagen).

sewn together in a half circle or as two separate sheets, drawn over the back of the tent and latched over the door opening. Stones are placed on the outside edge of the cover hold it in place, forming a circular alignment.

The *domes* are more typical winter tents framed by 20–30 bent willow poles planted to the ground. As the edges of the tent cover were not fixed with weight stones, this type seems of minor importance for the interpretation of tent rings.

The *ridge* tents form the most characteristic Inuit tent, existing in a great variety of forms and formats. One main feature common to all types is the ridge pole supported by one or more, usually about ten upright poles. The tent covering, sewn together by 10 to 15 seal- or reindeer skins, is wrapped around the frame, laced together over the door and rolled over on the edges by stones. Most ridge tent variants will leave oval or ovate semi-open stone alignments after dismounting. Greenlanders use of these tents less than one century ago has been described by Kaj Birket-Smith (1924:154 pp) and Therkel Mathiassen (1928:131 pp) (Figure 28.14).

Both conical and ridged tents are designed for simple use and easy transportation; weight depending of tent size, the number of poles and the skin type used as cover. An advantage of the conical is a generous interior height with facilities for a centrally positioned hearth. The lower and tilted ridge tents are, on the other hand, more stable to prevailing strong winds. They may also be framed by far fewer poles, a scarce resource in most circumpolar and periglacial areas.

Palaeo-Eskimo research covering large parts of East and West Greenland, High-arctic Canada and North Alaska (e.g. Binford 1978:268; Grønnow et al. 1983:50 pp; Sandell and Sandell 1996:161 pp; Appel and Pind 1996:131 pp; Helmer 1996:97 pp) have demonstrated a wide time-span for the use of tents during seasonal reindeer or seal hunting. Like the tent rings from recent Inuit camps, the tent structures on the Palaeo-Eskimo sites

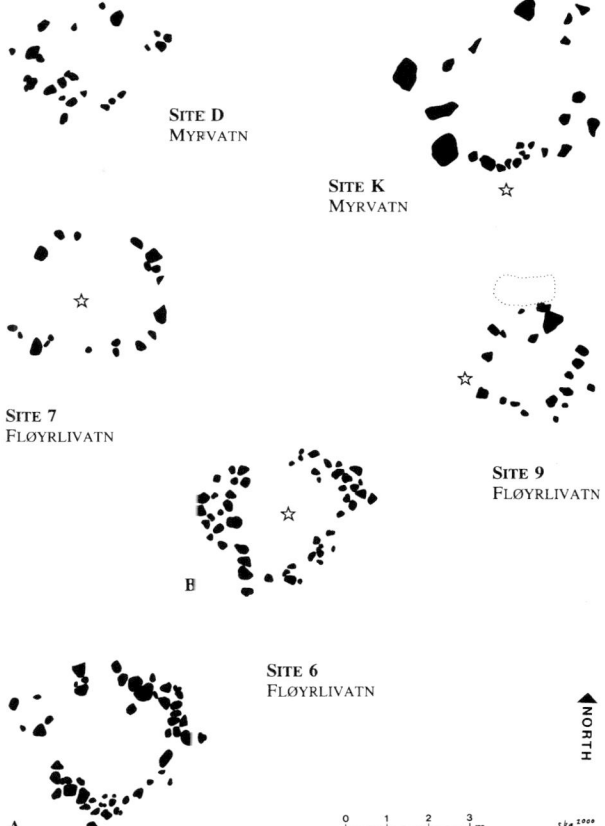

Figure 28.15 Comparison of tent rings at Myrvatn and Fløyrlivatn with contemporary hearths indicated by asterisks. All plans are to the same scale and compass point.

vary more by extension than by shape. In SW Greenland and High-Arctic Canada rings as wide as 5 or 6 m by inner dimension are reported (Appelt and Pind 1996:131 pp; Helmer 1996:98). Normally the tents appear to have been smaller, 3 or 4 m in diameter, producing floor areas of 7 to 12 sq.m.

A feature common to many circular Palaeo-Eskimo tent rings is a rectangular axial passage of partly upright stone slabs set 0.7–1,0 m apart. "Mid-passage structures" as these, often filled up with fire-cracked stones, are interpreted as places for heating and cooking (Appelt and Appelt 1996:131).

In the light of the ethnographical and archaeological data from wide circumpolar areas, some leads should exist for a further interpretation of the Myrvatn/Fløyrlivatn tent rings regarding the size, shape and handling of the *tents* once pitched inside the stone alignments (Figure 28.15).

As the weight stones have been rolled onto the edges of the tent covering, the inner diameter of the tent rings states a maximum tent floor area. Normally the actual floor-space must have been smaller due to a radically relocation of weight stones some short distance by the removal of the tent sheets. The sloping of the walls further limited the utilsable space.

Presupposing that the *net living floor* on the average was restricted to 80 % of the tent ring area, the efficient floor space of the Myrvatn and Fløyrlivatn tents has varied from 3.6 to 9.1 sq.m, with 5.7 sq.m as mean value. Compared to the interior space of present-day mountain tents, normally allotting about 1.2 sq.m per person, the tents used at Myrvatn and Fløyrlivatn group could hardly manage to accommodate more than 3 to 7 persons each. Interior use of fire may have further reduced the bed area in some of the tents.

Concise information about the height and shape of the Myrvatn-Fløyrlivatn tents appears difficult to arrive at due to the displacement of weight stones from their original positions. Generally oval or rhombic floor plans (as in Myrvatn D) should be supposed to reflect ridge constructions, and circular plans (Fløyrlivatn 7) conical tents. A conical shape is probably also indicated by centrally positioned hearths (as in Fløyrlivatn 6B), or by a circular artefact distribution (Myrvatn I). Accordingly, conical tents appear to have been dominating at Fløyrlivatn while both main types were probably used at Myrvatn.

The preference of conical tents may seem surprising. High efforts connected to the transportation of tent sheets and poles into these elevated areas and the harsh environment prevailing 9500 radiocarbon years ago taken into account, ridge tents should logically emerge as the most applicable type. However, at least at Fløyrlivatn, a basic requirements for tent warmth appears to have dominated more practical considerations as pack weight reduction and wind resistibility.

Despite extensive archaeological investigations in wide parts of the south Norwegian mountains, bringing to light a high number of well-preserved sites e.g. in the inner Sognefjord mountains, at the Hardangervidda plateau and in the Setesdal mountains (Johansen 1969:38 pp; Bang-Andersen 1989:338 pp; Indrelid 1994:11 pp), similar Mesolithic tent rings have only been recorded in one restricted area.

At lake *Holmavatnet* (1030 m a.s.l.), about 100 kms NNE of the Myrvatn-Fløyrlivatn area (Figure 28.1), tent rings were found in three sites excavated in 1963–1965. No radiocarbon datings are available. According to the artefact inventories two sites appear to be of Late Mesolithic or Early Neolithic age (Mikkelsen 1989:86 pp). A third site, *Bamsebubukta*, dated between 8000 and 6000 BP by occurrence of microblades and microblade cores, and containing the best preserved tent rings at Holmavatn (Rognes 1964:130 pp), attracts particular interest.

Two oval or hearthshaped tent rings, about 2.4 x 3.8 m and 2.4 x 3.3 m by inner dimension, were situated just two meters apart from each other. The main amount of artefacts and the only diagnostic hearth was located to the south-western tent ring. Irrespective of a time gap covering several thousand years, the Bamsebubukta site seems to exhibit close parallels to Fløyrlivatn 6 with its remains of two equally sized, possibly contemporary and activity-specific tents placed almost side by side.

However, a vast majority of the Middle/Late Mesolithic and Early/Middle Neolithic sites in the southern Norwegian mountains are virtually without any discernible traces of dwelling structures as tent rings or foundations for wind shields. Small rectangular huts, circular sunk pit houses and rock shelters seem, with some few exceptions, first to have been taken into use during the Late Neolithic, c. 3800–3500 BP (Indrelid 1994:229).

As apparently contradictory, the widespread occurrence of open, unprotected Mesolithic sites in the high mountains is a matter deserving far more intensive study. One explanation among several possible is that tents may perfectly well have been used *without* weight stones during climatic periods of milder and less windy conditions. This may for instance be relevant for the southern parts of the Hardangervidda which were covered by pine forests during parts of the Mesolithic (Moe *et al.* 1978:76 pp). The total lack of tent rings in the Late Glacial southern Scandinavian reindeer hunting sites is, however, far more difficult to comprehend in the light of the ethnographical evidence from sub-polar environments evincing tents as a prerequisite for subsistence and survival.

Appendix

C14 datings of tent ring structures in the two study areas

T-6489 *Site I*, Myrvatn (conv.)***: 9040 ±120 BP, calibrated age: BC 8600–7800

T-7994 *Site I*, Myrvatn (conv.)***: 9040 ±130 BP, calibrated age: BC 8600–7750

T-8293 *Site D*, Myrvatn (conv.)**: 9440 ±50 BP, calibrated age: BC 9150–8950 and BC 8900–8550.

T-8294 *Site D*, Myrvatn (conv.)**: 9460 ±80 BP, calibrated age: BC 9150–8450

T-8296 *Site D*, Myrvatn (conv.)**: 9420 ±80 BP, calibrated age: BC 9150–8450

TUa-1691 *Site K*, Myrvatn (AMS)*: 9485 ±65 BP, calibrated age: BC 9150–8600

TUa-1692 *Site K*, Myrvatn (AMS)**: 9495 ±75 BP, calibrated age: BC 9200–8600

Beta-141295 *Site 9*, Fløyrlivatn (AMS)*: 9720 ±80 BP, calibrated age: BC 9350–8800

Beta-141296 *Site 9*, Fløyrlivatn (AMS)*: 9490 ±70 BP, calibrated age: BC 9150–8600

Beta-141293 *Site 7*, Fløyrlivatn (AMS)****: 9360 ±80 BP, calibrated to: BC 9150–9000 and BC 8850–8250

Beta-141294 *Site 7*, Fløyrlivatn (AMS)****: 9400 ±70 BP, calibrated to: BC 9150–8950 and BC 8900–8450

Beta-141304 *Site 6A*, Fløyrlivatn (AMS)**: 9450 ±70 BP, calibrated age: BC 9150–8450

Beta-141305 *Site 6A*, Fløyrlivatn (AMS)**: 9630 ±80 BP, calibrated to: BC 9240–8780 and BC 8770–8740

Beta-141302 *Site 6A*, Fløyrlivatn (AMS)*: 9560 ± 80 BP, calibrated age: BC 9220–8640

Beta-141303 *Site 6A*, Fløyrlivatn (AMS)*: 9430 ± 70 BP, calibrated to: BC 9110–9005 and BC 8830–8545

Beta-141289 *Site 6B*, Fløyrlivatn (AMS)****: 9360 ±80 BP, calibrated to: BC 9150–9000 and BC 8850–8250

Beta-141300 *Site 6B*, Fløyrlivatn (AMS)****: 9460 ±70 BP, calibrated age: BC 9200–8600

Beta-141301 *Site 6B*, Fløyrlivatn (AMS)*: 9750 ± 80 BP, calibrated to: BC 9305–9125 and BC 8990–8910.

* Indirect datings deriving from external hearths
** Maximum datings by charcoal superimposed by tent weight stones
*** Datings of structural charcoal occurrences within tent floors
**** Datings of internal centrally positioned hearths

Uncalibrated ages are stated with the standard 1 sigma (68.2 %) confidence interval. All calibrated ages are with 2 sigma (95.4 %) confidence intervals according to atmospheric data from Stuiver *et al.*(1998) using database OxCal v.3.3. (Bronk Ramsey 1999).

References

Andersen, B.G. 1979. The deglaciation of Norway 15,000 – 10,000 B.P. *Boreas* 8, 79–87.

Andersen, S.H. 1973. Bro, en senglacial boplads på Fyn. *KUML* 1972, 7–60.

Anundsen, K. 1985. Changes in shore-line and ice-front position in Late Weichsel and Holocene, Southern Norway. *Norsk Geografisk Tidsskrift* 39, 205–225.

Appelt, M. and Pind, J. 1996. Nunnguaq – A Saqquaq Site from Godthåbsfjorden. In: Grønnow, B. and Pind, J. (eds.) *The Paleo-Eskimo Cultures of Greenland*, 129–142. Copenhagen.

Bang-Andersen, S. 1988a. Oppsiktsvekkende funn ved Myrvatnet. *Frå haug ok heidni*, 1998 No. 4, 124–134.

—— 1988b. New Findings spotlighting the Earliest Postglacial Settlement in Southwest-Norway. *AmS-Skrifter*, Vol. 12, 39–51.

—— 1989. Mesolithic Adaptations in the Southern Norwegian Highlands. In: Bonsall, C. (ed.) *The Mesolithic in Europe*, 338–350. Edinburgh.

—— 1990. The Myrvatn Group, a Preboreal Find-Complex in Southwest- Norway. In: Vermeersch, P.M. and Van Peer, P. (eds.) *Contributions to the Mesolithic in Europe*. Studia Praehistorica Belgica, Vol.5, 215–226.

—— 1995. Den tidligste bosetning i Sørvest- Norge i nytt lys. In: *Steinalderkonferansen i Bergen 1993*. Arkeologiske Skrifter, No. 8, 65–80.

—— 1996a. The Colonization of Southwest Norway. An Ecological Approach. In: Larsson, L. (ed.) *The Earliest Settlement of Scandinavia and its relationship with neighbouring areas*. Acta Archaeologica Lundensia. Series in 8°, No.24, 219–234. Lund.

—— 1996b. Coast/inland relations in the Mesolithic of Southern Norway. In: Rowley-Conwy, P. (ed.): *Hunter-Gaterer Land Use*. World Archaeology 27, No.3, 427– 443.

—— 2000. Fortidens svarte gull. Nærmere om datering og miljøtolkning av Fløyrliboplassene. *Frå haug ok heidi 2000*, No. 4, 27–32.

Becker, B. and Kromer, B. 1991. Dendrochronology and radiocarbon calibration of the early Holocene. In: Barton, N., Roberts, A.J. and Roe, D.A. (eds.) *The Late Glacial in Northwest Europe*. CBA research report 17, 22–24. Oxford.

Binford, L.R. 1978. *Nunamiut Ethnoarchaeology*. New York.

Birket-Smith, K. 1924. Ethnography of the Egedesminde District. *Meddelelser om Grønland* LXVI. Copenhagen.

Blankholm, H.P. 1987. Maglemosian Hutfloors: an Analysis of the Dwelling Unit, Social Unit and Intra-site Behavioural Patterns in Early Mesolithic Southern Scandinavia. In: Rowley-Conwy, P., Zvelebil, M. and Blankholm, H.P. (eds.) *Mesolithic Northwest Europe: Recent Trends*, 155–162. Sheffield.

Bronk Ramsey, C. 1999. *OxCal. v.3.3*. Internet address: www.rlaha.ox.ac.uk/oxcal/oxcal

Faegre, T. 1979. *Tents. Architecture of the nomads*. London.

Fredsjö, Å. 1953. *Studier i Västsveriges Äldre Stenålder*. Göteborg.

Grøn, O. 1989. General Spatial Behaviour in Small Dwellings: a Preliminary Study in Ethnoarchaeology and Social Psychology. In: Bonsall, C. (ed.) *The Mesolithic in Europe*, 99–10. Edinburgh.

—— 1995. *The Maglemose Culture: The reconstruction of the social organisation of a mesolithic culture in Northern Europe*. BAR International Series 616. Oxford.

Grønnow, B., Meldgaard, M. and Nielsen, J.B. 1983: *Aasivissuit – The Great Summer Camp. Archaeological, ethnographical and zoo-archaeological studies of a caribou-hunting site in West Greenland*. Meddelelser om Grønland. Man and Society 5. København.

Gulliksen, S. 1980. Calibration of Radiocarbon Dates: A Review. *Norwegian Archæological Review* 13, No.2, 101–109.

Gowlett, J.A. 1986. Radiocarbon accelerator dating of the Upper Palaeolithic in Northwest Europe: a provisional view. In: Collcutt, S.N. (ed) *The Palaeolithic of Britain and its Nearest Neighbours: Recent Trends*, 98–102.

Helmer, J.W. 1996. Archaeology of the Middle Pre-Dorset Twin Ponds Site, Northern Devon Island N.W.T., High Arctic Canada. *Tübinger Monographien Zur Urgeschichte* 11, 97–109.

Holm, J. and Rieck, F. 1992. *Istidsjægere ved Jelssøerne. Hamburgkultur i Danmark*. Skrifter fra museumsrådet for Sønderjyllands amt, 5. Haderslev.

Indrelid, S. 1994. *Fangstfolk og bønder i fjellet. Bidrag til Hardangerviddas førhistorie 8500 – 2500 år før nåtid*. Universitetes Oldsaksamlings Skrifter. Ny rekke, No.17. Oslo.

Johansen, A.B. 1969. Høyfjellsfunn ved Lærdalsvassdraget. I. Årbok for Universitetet i Bergen. Hum. ser. 1969, No. 4. Bergen.

Johansson, A.D. 1990. *Barmosegruppen. Præboreale bopladsfund i Sydsjælland*. Aarhus.

Larsson, L. 1974. A Contribution to the Knowledge of Mesolithic Huts in Southern Scandinavia. *Meddelanden från Lunds Universitets Historiska Museum* 1973–1974, 5–28.

—— 1994. The Earliest Settlement in Southern Sweden. Late Paleolithic Settlement Remains at Finjasjön, in the North of Scania. *Current Swedish Archaeology* 2, 159–177.

Mathiassen, T. 1928. Material Culture of the Iglulik Eskimos. *Report of the Fifth Thule Expedition 1921–24*, VI. No.1. Copenhagen.

Moe, D., Indrelid, S. and Kjos-Hanssen, O. 1978. A Study of Environment and Early Man in the Southern Norwegian Highlands. *Norwegian Archaeological Review* 11, No.2, 73–83.

Mikkelsen, E. 1989. fra jeger til bonde. Utviklingen av jordbrukssamfunn i Telemark i steinalder og bronsealder. *Universitetets Oldsaksamlings Skrifter. Ny rekke* No.11. Oslo.

Newell, R.H. 1981. Mesolithic Dwelling Structures: Facts and Fantasy. *Veröffentlichungen des Museums für Ur- und Frühgeschichte Potsdam*. Band 14/15/1980, 235–284.

Rognes, K. 1964. Innberetning om utgravning av steinaldertuft i Bamsebubukta ved Holmevann på Haukelifjell sommeren 1964. In: *Arkeologiske undersøkelser i Røldal-Suldal 1964 (File Report)*, 130–137.

Rust, A. 1958. *Die jungpaläolitische Zeltanlagen von Ahrensburg*. Offa-Bücher 15. Neumunster.

Sandell, H. and Sandell, B. 1996. Paleo-Eskimo Sites and Finds in the Scoresby Sound Area. In: Grønnow, B. and Pind, J. (eds.) *The Paleo-Eskimo Cultures of Greenland*, 161–173. Copenhagen.

Stapert, D. 1990. Within the tent or outside? Spatial patterns in late Palaeolithic sites. *Helinium* XXIX/1, 14–35.

Stuiver, M., Reimer, P.J., Bard, E., Beck, J.W., Burr, G.S., Hughen, K.A., Kromer, B., McCormac, G., van der Plicht, J. and Spurk, M. 1998. INTCAL98 Radiocarbon Age Calibration, 24000–0 cal BP *Radiocarbon* 40(3), 1041–1083.

Terberger, T. 1997. *Die Siedlungsbefunde des Magdalénien-Fundplatzes Gönnersdorf. Konzentrationen III und IV*. Stuttgart.

Tørhaug, V. and Åstveit, L.I. 2000. Steinalderboplassene ved Store Fløyrlivatnet. *Frå haug ok heidni 2000*, No.1, 35–39.

Vang Petersen, P. and Johansen, L. 1993. Sölbjerg – An Ahrensburgian Site on a Reindeer Migration Route through Eastern Denmark. *Journal of Danish Archaeology* 10 (1991), 20–37.

29. The site of Verrebroek "Dok" (Flanders, Belgium): spatial organisation of an extensive Early Mesolithic settlement

Philippe Crombé, Yves Perdaen and Joris Sergant

In this paper the formation process of one of the largest Mesolithic settlements currently known in Belgium is discussed. Based on the results of a preliminary spatial analysis and extensive radiocarbon dating this complex is interpreted as an agglomeration of relatively small artefacts units, resulting from recurrent occupations during the second half of the Pre-boreal and the first half of the Boreal.

Introduction

Since 1992 the Department of Archaeology of the Ghent University has been doing large-scale salvage excavations on an extensive Early Mesolithic settlement situated in the municipality of Verrebroek in north-western Belgium. The site (Figure 29.1), which covers a surface of at least 3 hectares is under constant threat by harbour expansion and will be entirely destroyed in the near future by the construction of a new dock, the so-called Verrebroek dock. The investigation, financed by the Research Fund of the Ghent University, is organised in a multi-disciplinary way, including spatial analysis, refitting, microwear analysis, radiocarbon dating, petrographical analysis and various kinds of palaeo-environmental analyses (soil-, botanical and faunal analysis). As most of these investigations are still in progress final results are not yet available. Hence, the results discussed in the present paper must be regarded as preliminary and subject to later modifications.

Excavation

Field-research at Verrebroek "Dok" started in 1992 (Crombé 1993) with a pilot excavation to test the potential of the site for further research. It was followed in 1993–1994 and 1997–2000 by 6 additional excavation campaigns (Crombé 1994; Crombé and Van Strydonck 1994; Crombé *et al.* 1997, 1998, 1999a) resulting in the investigation of ca. 6000 sq.m or 20% of the total site-surface. In 1996 (Crombé and Meganck 1996) the site and its surroundings were submitted to an extensive and detailed augering survey, in order to get a better insight in its preservation, extension and palaeo-topographical setting.

From the very start of the project, excavations have been executed by water-screening of the soil (mesh width 2 mm) according to a fixed grid of 1/4 sq.m squares and artificial layers of 10 cm thickness. Features of presumed anthropogenic origin, such as surface-hearths, hearth-pits and pits, have been intensively sampled for various palaeo-environmental analyses.

General situation and stratigraphy

The site of Verrebroek "Dok 1" is situated in the so-called "Scheldepolders", which constitutes a low-lying coastal-landscape (ca 3 m above sea-level) close to the estuary of the Schelde river into the Westerschelde. This specific position is responsible for the fact that the site was covered first by peat and later by alluvial (peri-marine) deposits (Figure 29.2). According to the first palynological analyses (Louwagie *et al.* in press) peat

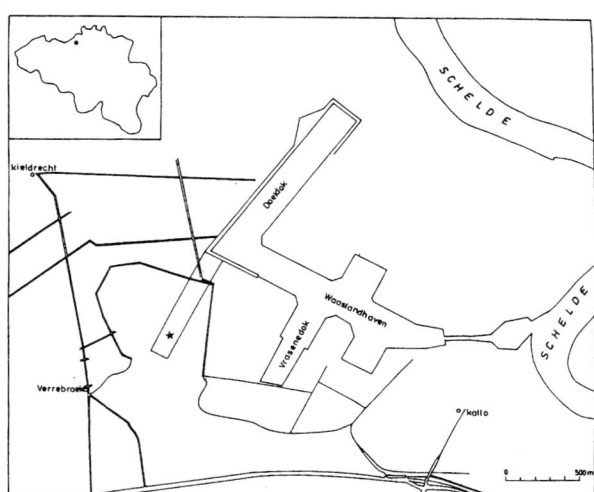

Figure 29.1 Location of the site of Verrebroek "Dok" within Belgium and the harbour of Antwerp.

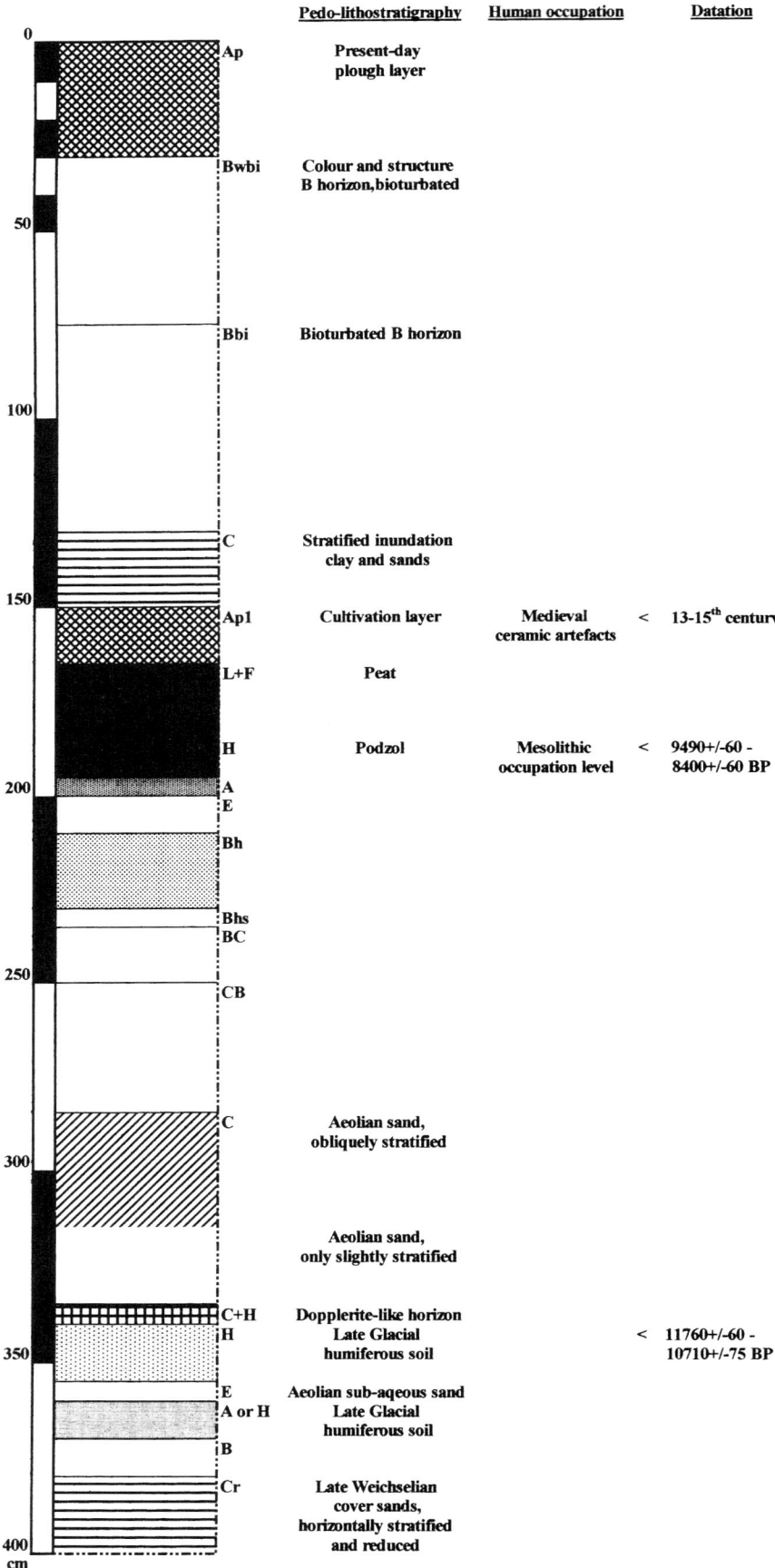

Figure 29.2 Schematic profile of the pedo-lithostratigraphical units at Verrebroek "Dok".

growth started on the site around 4000 BP and ended roughly between 2000 and 1500 BP. The clay deposits, which are related to natural and strategic inundations of the Schelde, mainly date back to the late 15th and 16th century AD. Intercalated between these peat and clay sediments is situated a strongly organic sand layer which is stratigraphically connected with some large drainage ditches and numerous spade-ditches. These are the remains of a late medieval cultivation of the peat bog (13th–15th century AD).

Underneath this 0.70 to 2.0 m thick cover the original Late-glacial/Early Post-glacial topography is well-preserved in the coversand deposits. It seems that the Mesolithic settlement was installed on the eastern flank of a large, east-west oriented sand ridge, facing the Pleistocene valley of the Schelde to the east. The Late-glacial origin of this sand ridge has recently been confirmed by the discovery of two sub-aquatic humiferous to peaty soils of Allerød age (base 11,760±60 BP; top 10,710±75 BP) at about 1.2 to 1.5 m below the top of the coversands. The Mesolithic remains are situated in the upper 30–40 cm of these coversand deposits, indicating that aeolian sedimentation had stopped at last at the mid of the Pre-boreal.

The surface of the coversand ridge presents a typical micro-relief of alternating shallow depressions and small elongated sand dunes with an average height difference of less than 0.5 m. Mesolithic finds have been collected both in depressions and on dunes, yet under different preservation conditions. In general the preservation is at its best in the depressions, whereas the higher grounds of the former landscape are generally truncated to a certain degree as a result of medieval activities and transgressions.

General dating

The site of Verrebroek is currently dated by a series of 81 AMS-radiocarbon dates, carried out by the laboratory of the Royal Institute for Cultural Heritage of Brussels (M. Van Strydonck) in collaboration with the Van de Graaff laboratory of Utrecht (The Netherlands) and the Rafter Radiocarbon Laboratory of Lower Hutt (New Zealand). The dating strategy (Crombé et al. 1999b) which has been applied consists of single entity dating of charred hazelnut shells from 45 surface-hearths and charcoal from 8 hearth-pits (Figure 29.3). Referring to a recent paper (Van Strydonck et al. 2001), in which the dating results are discussed in detail, the main conclusions can be summarised as follows.

Based on the hazelnut dates the main occupation of the site is situated between ca. 9490 BP and 8650/8400 BP (floruit: 8410–7930 cal BC 1-sigma; 8710–7570 cal BC 2-sigma), corresponding to the second half of the Pre-boreal and first half of the Boreal. This seems to agree fairly well with the relative dating based on tool typology. Three younger hazelnut dates (7720±60 BP, 7020±60 BP

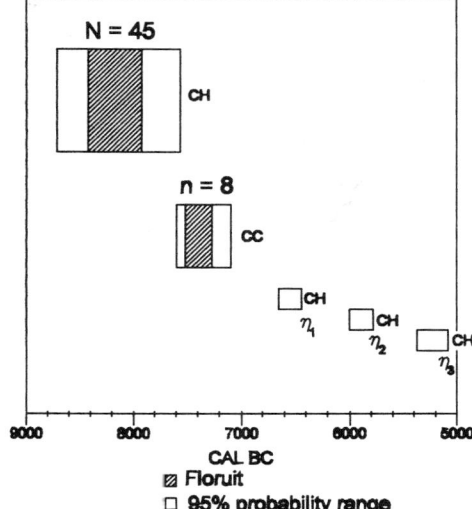

Figure 29.3 Floruit and 95% probability range of the dates from 45 surface-hearths dated on charred hazelnut shells (CH), 8 hearth-pits dated on charcoal (CC) and 3 individual charred hazelnut shells.

and 6260±50 BP) however indicate presumably incidental re-use of the site during the Late Mesolithic. This was recently confirmed by the discovery of some trapezes and regular Montbani-like blades on the site.

The interpretation of the charcoal dates from 8 hearth-pits on the other hand is much more difficult as they are apparently not compatible with the hazelnut dates. So far the charcoal dates are situated between 8500/8450 BP and 8250/8230 BP (floruit: 7520–7280 cal BC 1-sigma; 7600–7110 cal BC 2-sigma); hence there is hardly any overlap with the hazelnut dates. It would appear that the dated hearth-pits were in use at the end and/or after the main occupation of the site. Yet there is currently no material evidence in the lithic inventory which supports an occupation during the second half of the Boreal.

Site structure

Features

Due to various post-depositional soil processes structural features dating back to the Mesolithic occupation are extremely scarce. The formation of a heather podzol, for example, has led to a total blurring of shallow features within the upper 30/40 cm of the coversand deposits. Hence, only the deepest features are generally preserved as soil marks. Besides various old, pre-podzolic tree-fall features, a number of small pits with a charcoal-rich filling occur on the site. Amongst these are 12 circular to elliptical shaft-like pits with a homogeneous charcoal filling which can be determined as hearth-pits (Groenendijk 1987). Their size (Figure 29.4) is generally limited to 0.50/0.70 m in diameter and 0.35/0.50 m in depth.

Figure 29.4 Section of hearth-pit S.100.

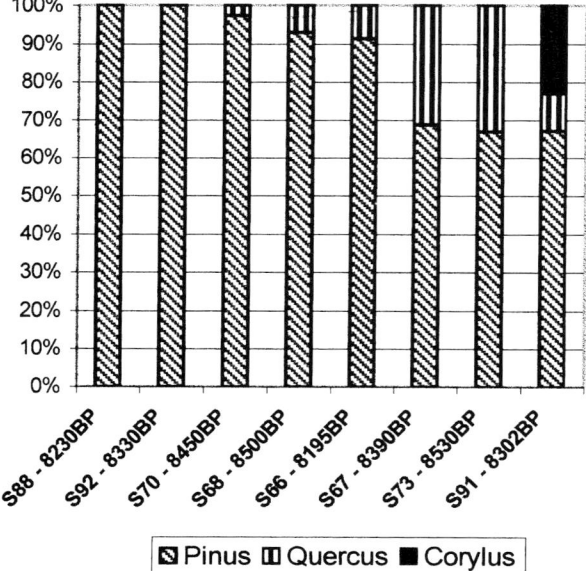

Figure 29.5 Results of anthracological analysis on charcoal from hearth-pits.

Anthracological analysis of 8 hearth-pits (Louwagie *et al.* in press) reveals that *Pinus* is the most important and in some hearth-pits even the only wood species (Figure 29.5). In six pits an amount of *Quercus* wood is found next to *Pinus*. One of them also contains some fragments of *Corylus* wood. Mixed with these charcoal fragments small proportions of flint artefacts (mainly small chips) and carbonised hazelnut shells are generally found. According to the results of ^{14}C-dating, both lithics and shells presumably have to be regarded as residual material, which slipped into the hearth-pits at the time of filling. Double dating of hearth-pit S.88 for example resulted in incompatible charcoal and nutshell dates. On a spatial level (Figure 29.6) the excavated hearth-pits display a remarkably limited distribution. Within the excavated area they have been found clustered in the south-western corner, which formerly corresponded with one of the highest grounds of the coversand landscape. According to the radiocarbon evidence from 8 hearth-pits there is little chance that these features are contemporaneous.

Besides these hearth-pits numerous other charcoal features were registered on the site. Compared to the above hearth-pits, these features are much more diffuse in outline and less uniform in size. Furthermore their filling usually contains smaller amounts of charcoal, the latter mainly consisting of small fragments of *Pinus*. Another difference with respect to the hearth-pits is the apparent absence of a significant spatial patterning. These diffuse charcoal features occur randomly spread over the excavated site-surface both within and outside the boundaries of artefact units. Although some small pits to a certain degree resemble post- or stake-holes, it is more likely that they represent natural features.

At three locations vague traces of shallow pits filled with numerous carbonised hazelnut shells, in some cases mixed with charcoal fragments, were found. They were situated in the periphery of artefact units C.22 and C.14. At present it is not yet clear how these features should be interpreted, but one cannot exclude that they are remains of shallow roasting-places or small storage-pits.

Artefact loci

In absence of other structural features the reconstruction of the internal organisation of the site of Verrebroek can only be achieved by analysing the spatial distribution of the recovered artefacts and ecofacts. Due to the large amount of findings (more than 0.5 million of lithic artefacts) unfortunately only part of the excavated area could be analysed so far. Hence, the following will be mainly based on the results of spatial analysis of the finds gathered in 1992–1994 (Crombé 1998) and part of those recovered in 1997–1998. Information related to the remaining finds is solely based on field-observations and not on detailed spatial studies.

In the present state of analysis at least 55 spatially independent artefact units could be located (Figure 29.6). Though they were found scattered over the entire excavated area, the density is clearly higher in the western sector towards the top of the sand ridge. There is reason to believe that the excavations have more or less reached the eastern limit of the Mesolithic site. All excavated units mainly consist of stone artefacts, mostly made of local flint of inferior quality that could be collected in a radius of about 5 km around the site. In some units small amounts of exotic raw material were also found. It includes quartzite of Wommersom and Tienen both imported from approximately 75 km away and various kinds of sandstones from southern Belgium (distance >100 km). Due to unfavourable preservation conditions (Ph-value and oxidation degree) organic material is extremely badly conserved on the site. Only carbonised organic residue, such as charcoal, hazelnut shells and bones, appears to have been preserved.

Among the recorded artefact units there seems to exist

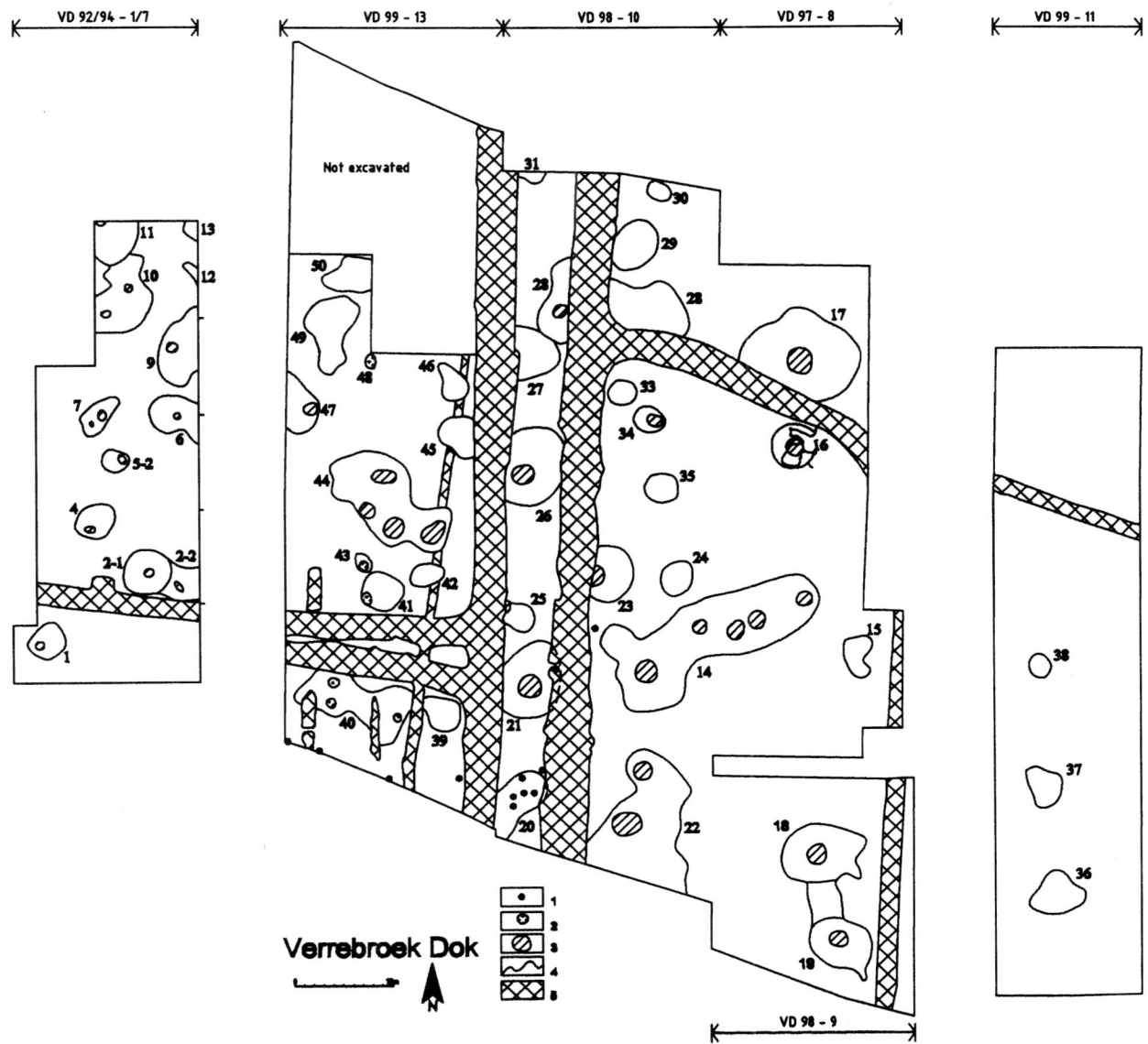

Figure 29.6 Schematic and preliminary draft of the artefact loci excavated at Verrebroek "Dok" between 1992 and 2000. Key: 1. Hearth-pit 2. Bone cluster 3. Surface-hearth 4. Artefact locus 5. Medieval ditch.

an almost infinite variation in size, artefact-density, amount of artefacts, spatial arrangement and tool-typology. A simple classification, as proposed earlier on the basis of observation gathered between 1992 and 1994 (Crombé 1998:51 p), seems no longer possible. In order to allow a reliable inter-unit comparison all artefact loci should be defined in the same way. Due to the presence of numerous "stray-finds" in between the dense artefact units, however, the latter cannot be defined simply on the basis of the one artefact per grid-unit (Newell and Dekin 1978). In high-density areas, e.g. nearby the top of the sand ridge, the 10 artefacts per 0.25 sq.m-line must be used to delimit the individual loci. In the less dense eastern sector on the other hand the limit of the artefact units already appears at the 5 artefacts per 0.25 sq.m-line. In view of a comparative analysis in this article, the limit of all units has been set to 10 artefacts per 0.25 sq.m.

From figure 29.7 it can be deduced that the size of the excavated units varies from very small (<5 sq.m), over small (5–10 sq.m), to medium (10–15 sq.m) and (very) large (>15 sq.m). The smallest units cover a surface of 1.5 to 3 sq.m (e.g. C.2.3, C.5.1, C.5.2, C.5.3, C.15.2), the largest ones (C.14, C.17, C.22, C.28, C.44) are usually more than 50 sq.m large. The majority however is obviously smaller than 10–15 sq.m.

On the level of the find-density (Figure 29.8) a clear distinction between high-density and low-density units can be made. Within the latter the density is generally below 40 artefacts per 0.25 sq.m. The density within the high-density loci amounts to 80 to 155 artefacts per 0.25

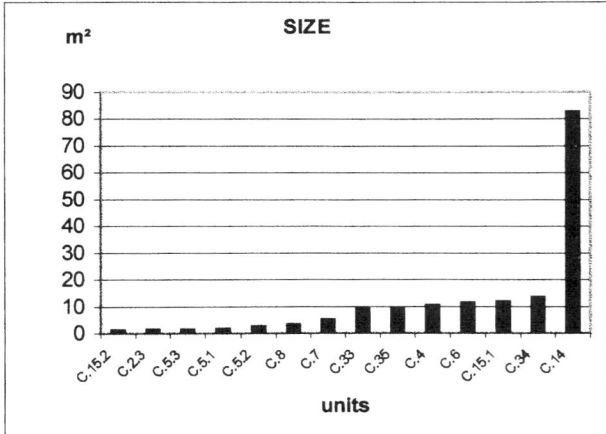

Figure 29.7 Diagram representing the intra-site variation in the size of the artefact loci.

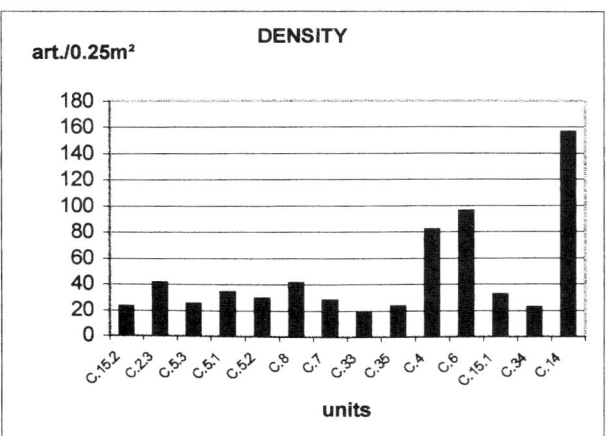

Figure 29.8 Diagram representing the intra-site variation in find-density.

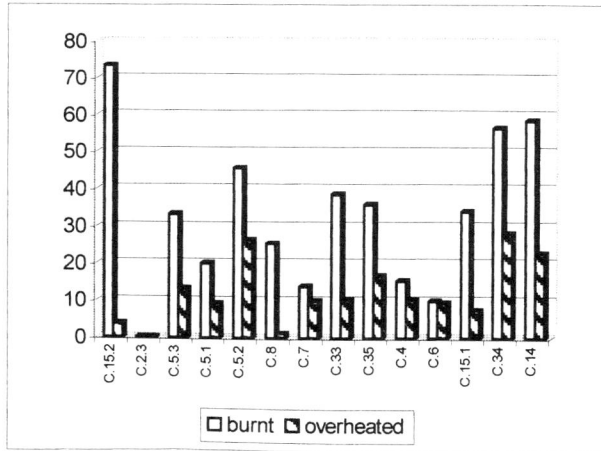

Figure 29.9 Diagram representing the intra-site variation of the burnt artefacts.

sq.m. Although there is apparently no clear correlation between the find-density and the size of the units, it appears that high-density only occurs within the medium and large units.

A common characteristic of all units (except C.2.3) is the occurrence of numerous burnt artefacts, most likely indicating the presence of former fire-places. From figure 29.9 it appears that there is quite a considerable inter-unit variation in the frequency of burnt items, with minimum values of 9.73% (C.6) and maximum values of 73.33% (C.15.2). Looking at the overheated artefacts only, a clear grouping appears. In most units overheated artefacts represent 7% to 16% of the total industry. Extremely low frequencies are noted in two very small units, C.15.2 (3.7%) and C.8 (1.14%), extremely high frequencies in units C.5.2 (26.07%), C.14 (22.56%) and C.34 (27.87%). The true meaning of these variations so far remains unclear, yet it is not impossible that they point to differences in intensity and duration of use of the fire-places. The exact outline of these fire-places is unfortunately not known, due to later soil-processes (cf. supra), which led to a complete blurring of all shallow features. The only way to locate the former position of hearths is by plotting the burnt artefacts, assuming that the squares with the highest density coincide with the centre of former hearths. This is confirmed to a certain degree by the perfect spatial coincidence between the burnt artefacts and burnt ecofact, e.g. charred hazelnut shells and bone fragments, which are found in numerous units. Knowing from better preserved sites in northern Germany and south Scandinavia that Mesolithic surface-hearths are often centred around (Grøn 1995:38), the burnt artefacts found outside the centre can be considered to belong to the so-called "expanded hearth area". Applying these principles to the various units, it turns out that all units smaller than 10–15 sq.m (small- to medium-sized units) generally posses one single surface-hearth (Figure 29.6). Larger artefact clusters on the other hand have more surface-hearths, usually two but occasionally up to 4 or even 5 specimens. A good example is unit C.14, which revealed at least 5 different surface-hearths more or less aligned according to a SW-NE axis. Along the western limit a small hearth-pit filled with *Pinus* charcoal was also found.

The artefact-typology clearly indicates that in most units, except the smallest ones, a broad spectrum of activities took place around these fire-places. Flint knapping was apparently one of the major activities, resulting in sometimes huge accumulations of knapping debris, including cores, rejuvenation products, un-retouched flakes and blades as well as numerous chips. The latter generally constitute 75% to 90% of the total industry. Flint knapping probably directed the manufacturing of different kinds of tools, some of which may have been used and discarded within the structure. Although extensive refittings and detailed microwear results are still lacking, the latter assumption is already partly corroborated by the presence in numerous units of tool fabrication waste such as microburins and burin spalls.

Within most artefact loci tools tend to be distributed asymmetrically around the hearth (Figure 29.10). The majority of tools are usually situated along one half of the hearth, possibly indicating that most activities took place on this side. Apparently the orientation of this tool-rich half is not constant but varies among the different units and even among different hearths within one unit. In the eastern half of unit C.14 (Figure 29.11), for example, the orientation of the tool-rich half changes from south (hearth 1), to east (hearth 2) to north (hearth 3).

A detailed look at the tool distribution reveals traces of a possible functional arrangement of the living-floor within various artefact loci. In units with abundant microliths, microburins and scrapers and/or burins (e.g. C.15, C.2.1., C.6, C.14, etc.) a clear spatial patterning could be observed (Figure 29.12; 13). Microliths and microburins are always found spatially separated from scrapers and burins. Large waste items, such as cores and large preparation flakes, can be found distributed either randomly or clustered in a small area within the artefact unit. The latter probably points to cleaning activities of the living-floor, as documented in the ethnoarchaeological record (Binford 1983b:299 pp). Judging by the peripheral position within the artefact loci these small waste areas most likely have to be interpreted as dumps of aggregated waste.

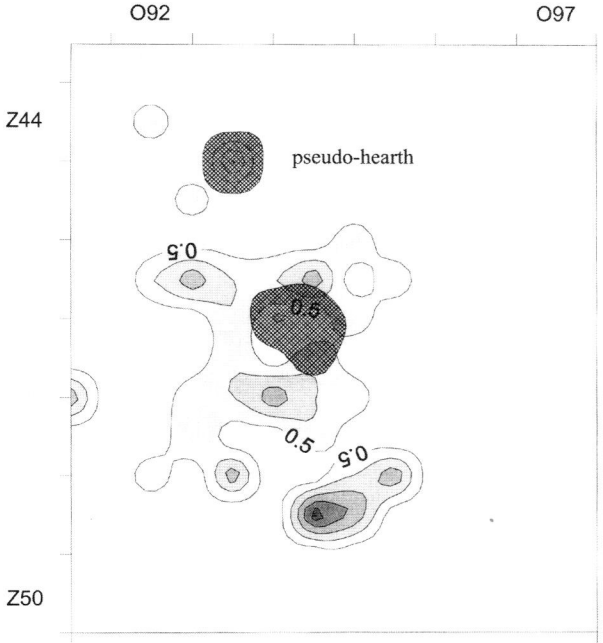

Figure 29.10 Contour map of all tools within artefact locus C.15 in relation to a presumed surface-hearth (black).

Discussion

Without the results of extensive refitting and microwear analysis a reliable interpretation of the intra-site variability and spatial patterning, as just described, remains particularly difficult. However it is beyond any doubt that different factors, such as the range of activities performed,

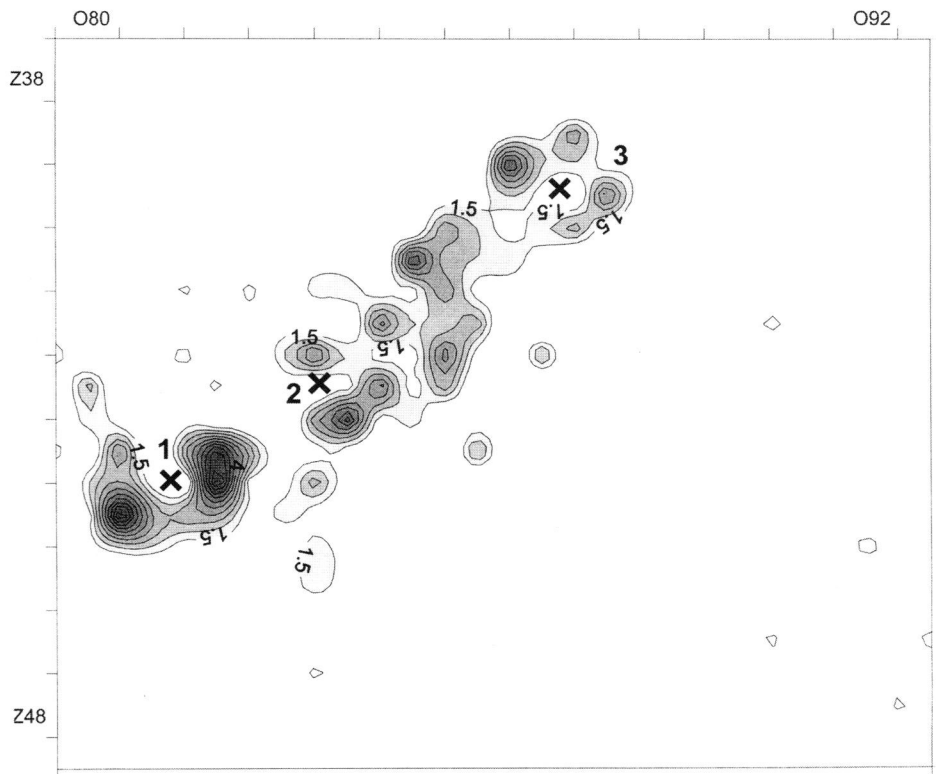

Figure 29.11 Contour map of all tools within artefact locus C.14 in relation to three presumed surface-hearths (cross). Since the western half of this unit in not yet submitted to a detailed spatial analysis, only the eastern part is plotted here.

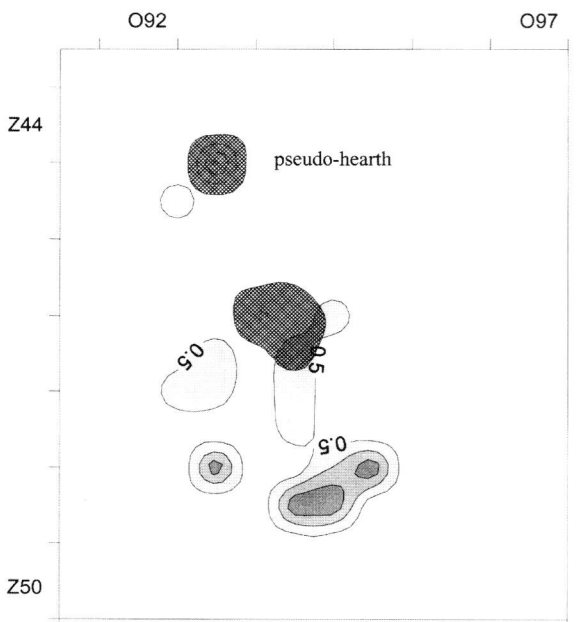

Figure 29.12 Contour map of all microliths found within artefact locus C.15.

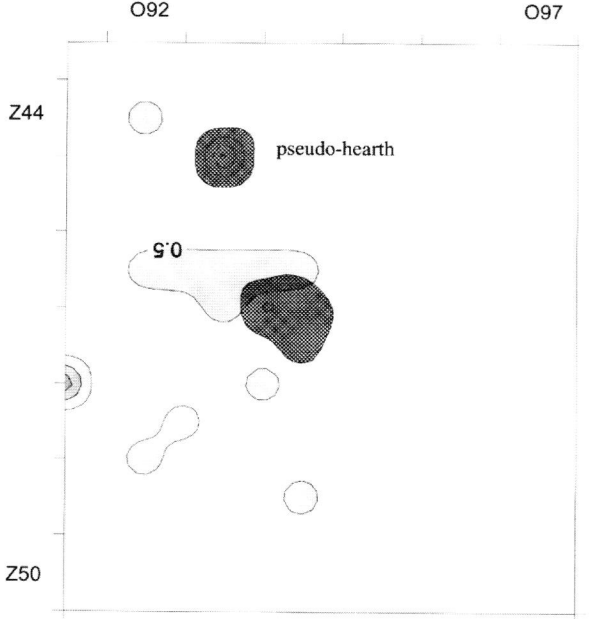

Figure 29.13 Contour map of all scrapers found within artefact locus C.15.

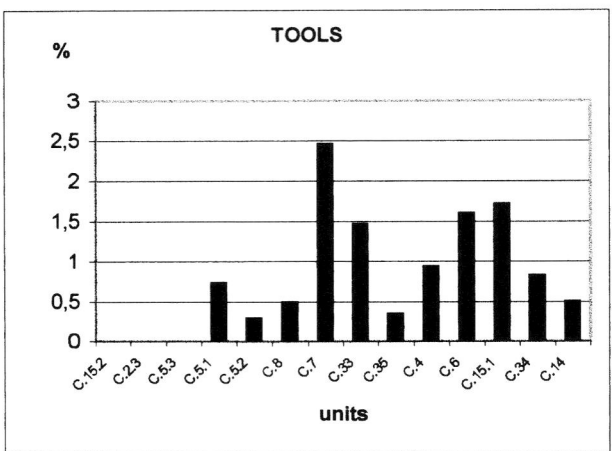

Figure 29.14 Diagram representing the intra-site variation in the tool frequency.

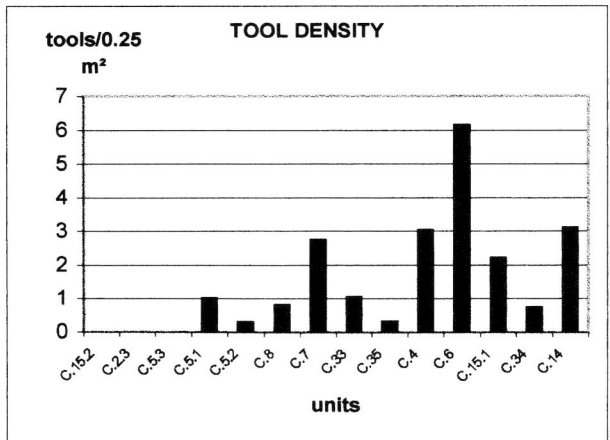

Figure 29.15 Diagram representing the intra-site variation in the tool-density.

group size, duration of occupation and frequency of re-use of the individual artefact loci, will have played a role in the formation of the site.

Based on major inter-unit variations in tool typology and tool frequency a certain functional variability can be assumed. In most units tools represent less than 1% of the total industry (Figure 29.14). Higher frequencies up to 1.5–2.5% however do occur, e.g. in units C.6, C.7, C.15.1 and C.33. Expressed in mean tool-density per 0.25 sq.m (Figure 29.15) a somewhat different picture is obtained. Obviously the highest densities (3 to 6 tools/0.25 sq.m) exclusively occur within the medium- and large-sized high-density units (e.g. C.4, C.6, C.14). The tool-density is at its lowest (< 1 tool/0.25 sq.m) in the smallest artefact loci (e.g. C.5–1, C.5–2). Three such units (C.2.3, C.5.3 and C.15.2) even yielded no tools at all. Although the exact function of these small units so far remains unclear, it may be assumed that some of them are hearth dumps or knapping dumps while others the vague remains of small (satellite?) hearths.

On a typological level too, inter-unit variations are very common. A hierarchical cluster analysis on a sample of 13 units points to the existence of at least four different tool groups within the site:

- group 1: dominance of microliths (45%–59%), completed with mainly simply retouched artefacts (units C.14(1), C.14(2), C.4, C.10, C.6, C.9)
- group 2: predominance of microliths (70%–83%) (units C.16, C.18, C.7 and C.1)

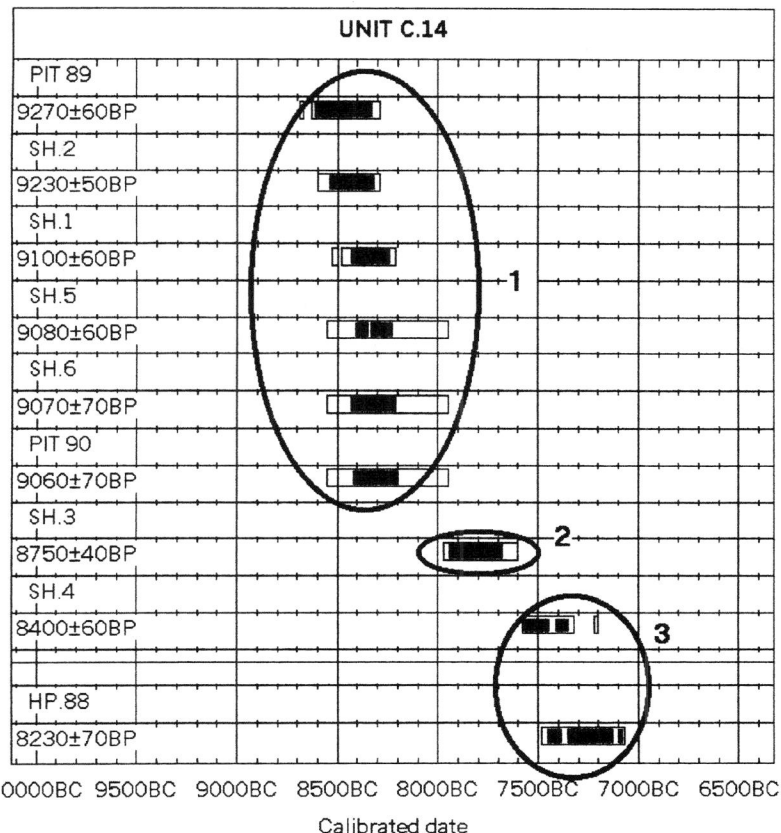

Figure 29.16 Probability distribution of the calibrated dates obtained on samples from artefact locus C.14.

- group 3: predominance of scrapers and microliths (75%–86%) (C.15, C.2.1, C.14(3))
- group 4: all tool types (microliths, scrapers, borers and simply retouched artefacts) more or less evenly represented (unit C.2.2)

It may be assumed that these statistical-typological differences to some degree reflect functional differences between the artefact loci of the site. Yet, this must be further verified by means of microwear analyses, which are currently in progress.

Group size and duration of occupation are other variables which have to be taken into account when discussing the intra-site variability. It is beyond any doubt that both variables have a certain effect on the size and the artefact-density of the units. It can be presupposed that artefact-density and size will increase as the number of inhabitants and/or the length of time a unit is occupied increases. If we follow this reasoning, this would imply that the largest units of the site were inhabited by larger groups than the smaller units.

This however is contradicted to a certain degree by either the lithic industry or the radiocarbon datings. Major intra-unit differences in the composition of the tool kit, the tool typology and the raw material distribution between different hearth-areas indirectly point to a repeated rather than to a single occupation of the large artefact units of the site. In unit C.14 for example the lithic industry collected around the three easternmost hearths presents considerable variations. The tool kit around hearths 1 and 2 is dominated by microlithic armatures (± 60%), whereas scrapers (± 11%) and simply retouched tools (± 15%) occur in low frequencies. Among the microliths crescents are predominant with ± 47%. Besides a few artefacts in Wommersom quartzite, the entire lithic industry is made of flint. The assemblage around the easternmost hearth 3 on the other hand is characterised by numerous microliths (± 44%), especially scalene triangles (± 29%) and points with retouched base (± 36%), and scrapers (± 35%) as well as by a high frequency of artefacts in Tienen quartzite (± 35%).

The above assumptions are further corroborated by the available radiocarbon datings, which clearly indicate that the largest units are chronologically not uniform, but rather represent palimpsests of different diachronic occupations. Unit C.14 for example (Figure 29.16) is currently dated by 9 different samples, amongst which 8 samples of charred hazelnut shells and one of charcoal. The latter was selected from the filling of a small hearth-pit lying at the western limit of the unit. The hazelnut samples originate from 5 surface-hearths, a possible sixth surface-hearth and two shallow roasting or storage pits (cf. supra). From the available dates it can be deduced that unit C.14 was inhabited in at least three different intervals. One centred around 9270 BP and 9070 BP (hearths 1, 2, 5 and 6; pits 98 and 90), a second one around 8750 BP (hearth 3) and a last one around 8400–8230 BP (hearth 4 and hearth-pit 88). This means that the above assumed diachrony between hearths 1/2 and hearth 3 is confirmed by the radiocarbon evidence. Radiocarbon evidence from other large units leads to similar conclusions. Units 17 and 22 represent accumulations of at least 3 different occupation phases, whereas ^{14}C-dates point to two different visits within units 28 and 44. It thus seems that the larger units of the site are the results of overlaps and intersections of different smaller units, which were inhabited diachronically. Theoretically it is even possible that each individual hearth reflects one visit, but this of course is difficult to prove by means of radiocarbon dating. It is hoped that refittings, which will be organised in the near future, will provide additional chronological information.

Although the chronological integrity of the small- and medium-sized units of the site has not yet been tested by means of radiocarbon datings, it may be assumed that these represent single occupation loci, occupied by relatively small groups, e.g. a nuclear family or a task group. Arguments in favour of this hypothesis are the small dimensions, the presence of generally one single surface-hearth, the technological and typological homogeneity of the lithic industry, the relatively small number of tools and the preservation of a spatial arrangement of the living-floor. In this respect the small- and medium-sized units of Verrebroek show great similarity with better preserved dwelling structures excavated at various Early Mesolithic sites in northern Europe, such as the Duvensee sites 8 and 13 (Bokelmann 1981, 1985), Mount Sandel (Woodman 1985), Ulkestrup II (Andersen et al. 1982), Klosterlund (Brinch Petersen 1966) and Bare Mosse II (Grøn 1995:66 p). According to recent studies by Blankholm (1987) and Grøn (1995) these Early Mesolithic dwellings were built according to a fixed behavioural pattern, which has also partly been recognised at the site of Verrebroek. Grøn even states that most of these structures represent one-family dwellings inhabited during the summer. The recently excavated peat-bog site of Duvensee 19 (Bokelmann 1995) however proves that Early Mesolithic living areas expanded beyond the limits of these dwelling structures. Excavations at this location, situated close to the "large" dwelling structure Duvensee 13, revealed a scatter of spaced or overlapping no-flint or faint-flint activities, associated with bark floors and small hearths. Similar activity-areas can also be expected within the excavated area of Verrebroek, though they are much more difficult to define as non-carbonised organic material is lacking. It looks as if the smallest artefacts units, small scatters of charred hazelnut shells and/or bone fragments as well as the scattered lithics recovered in between the different artefact loci at Verrebroek must be interpreted as the faint remains of peripheral activities, the nature of which remains to be determined.

Conclusion

In the present state of analysis the extensive settlement of Verrebroek can best be regarded as a location with a very high locational redundancy (Binford 1983a), intensively visited during the second half of the Pre-boreal and the first half of the Boreal presumably by small groups of recurring hunter-gatherers. Unfortunately, due to the bad organic preservation it is impossible to determine whether the site was occupied within the same season throughout the whole Early Mesolithic, nor can we decide whether it always had the same function within the settlement system. Indeed, it is perfectly possible, given the important intra-site variability of the tool kit, that the site was used in different seasons and within different structural poses. It could for example have been used at a given moment as a hunting camp (e.g. microlith dominating units), while at another moment it functioned as a base camp.

Another problem to resolve is related to the question why Mesolithic hunters kept returning to this spot. From the ethnographic record (Houtsma et al. 1996:98 p) it appears that areas with high concentrations of food resource, such as river eddies, creek mouths and shallow lakes, generally show a significant higher incidence of annual re-occupation than adjacent areas within the same territory. Similar observations have been done in parts of Sandy Flanders, where the density of Final Palaeolithic and Early Mesolithic sites is considerably higher around the banks of former lakes and rivers (Crombé and Verbruggen in press). Hence, the existence of an important open water system in close vicinity of the Verrebroek site can be expected. In our opinion the river Schelde, which runs approximately 2.3 km east of the site, was too far removed from the site to play any significant role. It seems more likely that open water (river or lake) was present immediately to the south of the site, more precisely along the eastern edge of the sand ridge. In order to verify this hypothesis the area to the south of the site is currently drilled systematically in view of a detailed palaeo-environmental reconstruction.

References

Andersen, K., Jörgensen, S. and Richter, J. 1982. *Maglemose hytterne ved Ulkestrup Lyng.* Nordiske Fortidsminder Serie B, 7. Kopenhagen.

Binford, L. 1983a. *In Pursuit of the Past. Decoding the Archaeological Record.* New York.

—— 1983b. *Working at Archaeology.* New York.

Blankholm, H.P. 1987. Maglemosian Hutfloors: an Analysis of the Dwelling Unit, Social Unit and Intra-Site Behavioural Patterns in Early Mesolithic Southern Scandinavia. In: Rowley-Conwey, P., Zvelebil, M. and Blankholm, H.P. (eds.) *Mesolithic Northwest Europe: Recent Trends,* 109–120. Sheffield.

Bokelmann, K. 1981. Duvensee, Wohnplatz 8; neue Aspekte zur Sammelwirtschaft im frühen Mesolithikum. *Offa* 38, 21–31.

—— 1985. Duvensee, Wohnplatz 13. *Offa* 42, 13–27.

—— 1995. "Faint flint fall-out": Duvensee, Wohnplatz 19. *Offa* 52, 45–56.

Brinch Petersen, E. 1966. Klosterlund-Sönder Hadsund-Böllund;

les trois sites principaux du Maglemosien ancien en Jutland. Essai de typologie et de chronologie. *Acta Archaeologica* 37, 77–185.

Crombé, P. 1993. Epipaleolithische en mesolithische bewoning in zandig Vlaanderen; resultaten van de opgravingscampagne 1992 op vier Oostvlaamse sites. *Notae Praehistoricae* 12, 83–94.

—— 1994. Recherche poursuivie sur le Mésolithique en Flandre orientale. *Notae Praehistoricae* 13, 71–78.

—— 1998. *The Mesolithic in Northwestern Belgium, Recent Excavations and Surveys*. British Archaeological Reports, International Series 716. Oxford.

Crombé, P. and Van Strydonck, M. 1994. Recherche poursuivie sur le site Mésolithique ancien de Verrebroek (Flandre orientale): résultats de la campagne 1994. *Notae Praehistoricae* 14, 95–102.

Crombé, P. and Meganck, M., 1996. Results of an auger survey research at the Early Mesolithic site of Verrebroek "Dok" (East-Flanders, Belgium). *Notae Praehistoricae*,16, 101–115.

Crombé, P., Perdaen, Y. and Sergant, J. 1997. Le gisement mésolithique ancien de Verrebroek: campagne 1997. *Notae Praehistoricae* 17, 85–92.

—— 1998. The Early Mesolithic site of Verrebroek "Dok": preliminary results of the 1998 excavation campaign. *Notae Praehistoricae* 18, 101–105.

—— 1999a. The Early Mesolithic site of Verrebroek "Dok 1": preliminary results of the 1999 excavation campaign. *Notae Praehistoricae* 19, 71–74.

Crombé, P., Groenendijk, H. and Van Strydonck, M. 1999b. Dating the Mesolithic of the Low Countries: some methodological considerations. In: *Actes du 3ème Congrès International "14C et Archéologie", 6–10 Avril 1998, Lyon, Mémoires de la Société Préhistorique Française, XXVI and Supplément 1999 de la Revue d'Archéométrie*, 57–63.

Crombé, P., Deforce, K., Langohr, R., Louwagie, G., Perdaen, Y., Sergant, J. and Verbruggen, C. 1999c. A small Final Palaeolithic knapping site at Verrebroek "Dok 2" (Flanders, Belgium). *Notae Praehistoricae* 19, 63–68.

Crombé, P. and Verbruggen, C. in press. Late Glacial and Early Post Glacial occupation of northern Belgium: the evidence from Sandy Flanders. In: *Acts of the international U.I.S.P.P. symposium "Behavior and Landscape Use in the Final Palaeolithic", Stockholm 14–17/10/1999.*

Groenendijk, H. 1987. Mesolithic hearth-pits in the Veenkoloniën (province Groningen, The Netherlands); defining specific use of fire in the Mesolithic. *Palaeohistoria* 29, 85–102.

Grøn, O. 1995. *The Maglemose Culture. The Reconstruction of the Social Organization of a Mesolithic Culture in Northern Europe*. British Archaeological Reports, International Series 616. Oxford.

Houtsma, P., Kramer, E., Newell, R.R. and Smit, J.L. 1996. *The Late Palaeolithic Habitation of Haule V: From Excavation Report to the Reconstruction of Federmesser Patterns and Land-Use*. Assen.

Louwagie, G., Langohr, R., Deforce, K., Verbruggen, C. and Klinck, B., in press. Perception of landscape change through the soilscape study at the archaeological excavation of Verrebroek "Dok" (Province of eastern Flanders, Belgium). In: *Acts of the Geoarchaeology Workshop "Landscape Changes over Archaeological Timescales", University of Reading, UK, 15th–17th December 1999.*

Newell, R.R. and Dekin, A.A. 1978. An integrative strategy for the definition of behaviorally meaningful archaeological units. *Palaeohistoria* XX, 7–38.

Van Strydonck, M., Crombé, P. and Maes, A. 2001. The site of Verrebroek « Dok » and its contribution to the absolute dating of the Mesolithic in the Low Countries. In: Carmi, I. and Boaretto, E. (eds.) *Proceedings of the 17th International Radiocarbon Conference, Judean Hills, Israël, Radiocarbon*, 43 (2B), 997–1005.

Woodman, P. 1985. *Excavations at Mount Sandel 1973–77*. Northern Ireland Archaeological Monographs 2. Belfast.

30. Ethno-archaeology among Evenkian forest hunters. Preliminary results and a different approach to reality!

Ole Grøn and Oleg Kuznetsov

The paper is based on ethno-archaeological data collected by the authors among the Evenki reindeer hunters in northern Transbaikal, Siberia. It focuses on the background for and the spatial effect of ritual manipulation of the material during site formation that may have a greatly underestimated impact on where objects are located on sites.

Introduction

A general problem for archaeology is that 'irrational' cultural elements such as cult and ritual undoubtedly have played an important role in most of the prehistoric societies whereas our ability to deal with spiritual phenomena that control the material culture is restricted in our interpretations. The central point we wish to stress in this paper is that ritual behaviour must also be considered an important agent in site formation. This seems to have been overseen in a many archaeological and ethno-archaeological settlement studies.

Extensive social anthropological data show that human cultures follow certain rules when they organise themselves in space. These rules are often related to religious and cosmological ideas. In some cases it is possible in prehistoric settlements to distinguish repeated spatial patterns in specific object categories that seem to reflect such spatially patterned behaviour (Ränk 1951; Tanner 1979; Grøn 1989, 1991, 1995, 1998; Yates 1989). To better understand the nature of such rules, their relation to religion and cosmology, and how they work in practice, ethnoarchaeological studies were started in 1997 among the Evenkian reindeer hunters in Northern Transbaikal, Siberia. The field work is carried out as a collaboration between NINA•NIKU, Norway, the Centre for Cultural Anthropology and Ecology of the Transbaikal Natives, the Chita State Technical University, The Chita Regional Museum of Human and Natural History, and The Evenks community in Chapo Ologo.

Our results demonstrate that ritual manipulation of the material in settlements may have a greatly underestimated impact on where many types of objects are deposited and indicate that such conscious differentiation in the handling of different categories of waste, for instance, may have been an important factor in the formation of archaeological sites. In spite of this 'blurring' of the activity patterns, it is interesting that some object types still seem directly to reflect the repeated spatial patterns controlling behaviour in the dwellings.

It should be noted that our study area is only a fraction of the enormous area where the Evenkian Culture is found. Whereas most Evenks today subsist as farmers or herders, nomadic hunter-gatherers are still found in some areas. Because of the variance in the Evenkian Culture, observations from one restricted area cannot all be regarded as general for this culture and should accordingly not be used directly as a model for all hunter-gatherers. Meanwhile, we are convinced that they in combination with other social anthropological and ethno-archaeological data can be used to point out some themes of general value.

Some of the behavioural elements we have observed are barely mentioned in the literature on the Evenkian Culture and have never been described in detail. It is surprising that there still is such basic information to gather. Unfortunately, if present development continues, it would also be surprising if the same phenomena can be observed in 10–20 years.

The urgency of the collection of ethnoarchaeological data from hunting cultures living in forested environments closely resembling those of Mesolithic Europe appears from the fact that the majority of the examples we use as a basis for interpretation of European Mesolithic Cultures derive from extreme environments such as polar areas or deserts. Our results from the Evenks indicate that forest cultures with access to firewood in large amounts may behave differently.

The Evenks – and the Northern Transbaikal

Apart from *Orochen* and *Tungus* a large number of other names have been applied to groups with a closer or more distant relation to the Evenkian Culture (Shirokogoroff 1979). In spite of the fact that many sources give the impression that no Evenks follow a traditional way of life any more (e.g. Vasilevich and Smolyak 1964), we found that some – in spite of the influence from modern civilisation – still live as nomadic reindeer hunters and have large parts of their old beliefs and behaviour preserved. Bark tents were used by some till the early '80s, and the traditional religion seems little influenced by the restricted activities of missionaries in the area. Hunting families often use 15–30 domesticated reindeer for transportation – riding them or using them to pull the sledges – but they are hunters not herders. The domesticated reindeer of the Evenks can be compared to the dogs of the Greenland Inuit. The hunting groups subsist on the meat of wild reindeer, elk, red deer, musk deer and mountain sheep, as well as birds and fish from the lakes and rivers (Shirokogoroff 1979; Anderson 1991).

The Transbaikal region is part of the mountain zone that separates the Central Asiatic Steppe in the south from the Siberian Plateau in the north. The steepest and highest mountains with heights up to 3.073 metres are found in the Northern Transbaikal. Above the open grass areas in the broader valleys is an open forest of pine, larch, fir, a little Siberian cedar and some birch in the moister places and with reindeer mosses strongly represented in its floor. This 'taiga' continues up to the tree line at an altitude of about 2.000 metres. The average temperatures vary from -36 °C in winters to 18 °C in summer with extremes around -55 °C and 35 °C. This, combined with the restricted snow cover due to the low average precipitation in the area, maintains permafrost conditions even though the centre of the Northern Transbaikal is as far south as 57°30' N, 150 km north and 550 km east of the northernmost point of the Lake Baikal (Baulin et al. 1984; Wright and Barnovsky 1984; Ivanenkov and Fraicheva 1997).

We never move – it's the world that moves – the organisation of space

The world concept of the Evenks is surprising to us and gives insight into their ideas about the space within which their settlements exist. When travelling from A to B their idea is that they 'don't move it's the world that moves'. According to this concept they always stay in the same place and therefore their different settlements are in the same place – they are 'the same place'. Therefore their dwellings and settlements are organised 'in the same way'.

Such an idea is not unique. Tanner has recorded a similar idea from the Mistassini Cree in the James Bay Area and comparable 'egocentric' ideas have been observed in other nomadic hunter-gatherer cultures (Holmberg 1922; Schmidt 1935, 1941; Tanner 1979:73; Eliade 1983:212 p). From a psychological point of view, it seems quite plausible that nomadic people create stability in their ever changing world by locating themselves in a place that is always the same.

With the Evenks of Northern Transbaikal the most sacred part of the dwelling is the 'malu' at the back of the dwelling. Here was a sacred passage for bringing sable (Siberian marten) into the tent when it was killed. It could not be brought in through the normal entrance. Behind the dwelling was also the tree with the 'Barrilak-dolls'. Barrilak is a god in the shape of a little old man clad in a hunter's clothes. He is the god of the land and lives in the hearth. The 'Barrilak'-dolls hung in the tree in small leather bags. They brought the hunters luck in their hunt. The dolls were cut out of wood and dressed in clothes of reindeer skin. In the Northern Transbaikal the dolls were not taken into the tent as described by Shirokogoroff (Shirokogoroff 1979:255).

In a one-family dwelling, one side of the entrance area is regarded as the women's side and the other as the men's side. Kitchen utensils, containers and food are stored against the wall just inside the entrance on the women's side in the area called 'tjungal' (with a box for plates, etc.). Male equipment such as hunting gear, male clothes, etc., is stored against the wall further back in the tent on the men's side. The guns are placed horizontally resting on two Y-shaped sticks adjacent to the tent wall just beside the men's sleeping places, so that there is quick access to them.

The firewood is piled up between the entrance and the hearth/oven and to some degree around the latter for drying. This also functions as a visual marking of the border between the 'male side' and the 'female side'. If the door – seen from the outside – opens on the left side (this means it must be moved outwards and to the right to open), the women's side is to the left inside the entrance and the men's to the right. If the door opens on the right, this scheme is reversed. The first pattern is definitely the most used one. We have not yet been able to find out what controls which way the door opens. The Evenks reject that it is the right or left-handedness of the man, as it is with the Sami in the Swedish Lule district (Ränk 1951:88).

For the night the wife moves to the men's side, and the couple normally sleeps parallel to the wall with their feet to the door in the area called 'be'. The wife lies along the wall and the man beside the oven. It was explained to us that he has to hold the warmest position, but also that it is his duty to tend the fire during the night. If the tent is full, some or all of the occupants may lie radially with their feet to the fire. In this case the man will lie nearest to the entrance. The place of the children is at the back of the tent, 'because that is the warmest place', as one informant stated. Normally they are arranged so that the smallest child has its place closest to the 'man's side' where the couple sleep. During the night, the children sleep along the wall or with their feet to the fire.

Single elder members of the family (parents of the married couple, uncles, aunts, etc.) will during the day, seen from the entrance, have their place in the tent beside and behind the woman if they are female and beside and behind the man if they are male. Their sleeping place is along the wall opposite the place where the host couple sleeps – also called 'be'. Thus they sleep in the women's side of the dwelling. Guests will during the day follow the same pattern as described here. At night they will sleep in the most sacred part of the tent, the malu, between the children.

The organisational pattern described here resembles closely that described in the creation myth describing the Evenk's descent from the bear recorded from the Sym and Bayakit Evenks by Vasilevich (Vasilevich 1963):

> "A girl, Kheladan, was walking on and on until at last she came to the bear. The bear said: 'Kill me and cut me up. Place my heart to sleep beside you, put my kidneys in the place of honour (the malu) behind the hearth, my duodenum and rectum place opposite you, spread out my fur in a dry ditch, hang my small intestines on a dry, bent-over tree, and put my head to sleep near malu (the place of honour).' Kheladan killed the bear and did all as he had ordered. In the morning she awoke and looked. At the place of honour there were two children (the kidneys) playing, an old man (the head) was sleeping near them, while opposite him were sleeping an old man and an old woman (the intestines). She glanced outside – there were some reindeer (the fur) walking about and the little valley was full of reindeer. She ran out of the yurt, and there were some halters (the small intestines) hanging on the slanting tree."

This shows how the organisation of space inside the dwelling can be controlled and 'legitimated' by mythology. Our studies also show that the settlements are organised in accordance with a set of spatial rules. The spatial relation between the dwellings, the activity areas, the waste platforms, and the banks the settlements are located on, etc., also seems to be regulated by a set of spatial rules.

The archaeological point is that the dwellings and settlements are organised spatially in accordance with a set of rules that are formally 'explained' by cosmology and mythology. From an anthropological point of view, it may also be relevant to be aware of the social-psychological effects of such spatial patterns (Grøn 1991).

Reuse of dwellings – an old dwelling

Especially in the summer base camps, dwellings are often re-used year after year. Earlier, the Larch bark *duytchars* (pointed tents of the 'tipi'-type) used on such sites were left as they were and then repaired next time the site was inhabited. With the modern canvas tents, a frame of stakes is left in position so that the cover can easily be put over it again.

In 1998 we excavated an old summer dyutchar that, according to the oral information we could obtain as well as the datable finds, was constructed around 1930 and destroyed around 1970. From the stakes that were still preserved below ground level it could be seen that it had

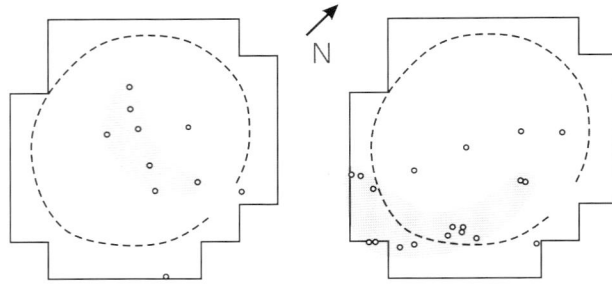

Figure 30.1 The distributions of two object types found during excavation of the site St.Martin nr.1, Lake Chikalovski, Chara River, used from approximately 1930–1970 by three different families.

been round with a diameter of approximately 6 metres. Three different families had used it in this period. Dimitri Danilov and his wife had used it for approximately 15 years, in the late '40s and '50s. Another family had used it before them and a third after them.

The distribution of caps, bullets and whole cartridges shows a clear concentration centrally in the dwelling, whereas none of these were found in its southwestern half (Figure 30.1). The different types that were found show that they were not deposited during one season. Probably, the spatially discrete concentration has accumulated through the 40 years the tent was in use.

The distribution of net floats differs clearly from that of cartridge parts. It is concentrated in the southwestern part of the excavated area (Figure 30.1). The net floats are mainly of the traditional type made as rolls of birch bark, while a few are carved out of wood and a couple cut out of Styrofoam. Also here it is most likely that the floats excavated have been deposited through several seasons.

The fact that some types through time seem to have been deposited in the same zones, even though they were maybe not even deposited by the same group of inhabitants, can most reasonably be explained by assuming that the objects found were handled by persons seated in accordance with a general set of spatial rules as discussed above.

At the Maglemose site Ulkestrup II, where the bark floor was well preserved, it has been suggested that the presence of two partly overlapping hearths inside the dwelling, repair of one of the walls (two rows of wall stakes), and the appearance of left-retouched triangles only in the bottom of the culture layer and right-retouched ones only in its top most likely reflects that the dwelling was inhabited – at least twice. The distributions of the left- and the right-retouched triangles conjoin inside the dwelling and form one small concentration (Andersen 1982; Grøn 1995:27 pp).

The Evenks – parallel to the Maglemose Culture – use floors of twigs and sometimes thin trunks in their dwellings. New twigs are added when the old ones are worn flat (approximately every third day). When a settlement is abandoned, the old floor twigs are removed. When the dwelling is re-occupied a new floor is laid. If small objects such as microliths or parts of cartridges fall through this type of flooring, the danger that they be removed from their position is minimised. Outside the dwelling, the Evenks keep the settlement surface orderly and clean. Here the chances of removal of even small items is considerably larger.

If a dwelling is cleared out between the occupations, the material found in it may well reflect its spatial organisation, but only from the last phase of occupation, as Møbjerg concludes on the basis of the data from her ethnoarchaeological investigation of an Inuit winter house in Greenland (Møbjerg 1991).

The re-use of the same settlements year after year seems to be facilitated in locations where sufficient amounts of fuel are accessible (firewood or fat from sea mammals). Hunting cultures in areas with less fuel often avoid old settlement sites for longer periods (e.g. Rogers 1967:9 p; Silberbauer 1981:222, 245 p). In general, our possibilities for finding preserved patterns in the archaeological material that reflect the social organisation of a society may depend on the amounts of fuel available.

The size of the settlements

One must be aware that a settlement is more than a central area with one or more dwellings. Around the dwellings will be different types of platforms, storage pits, storage areas, shades for humans and animals, activity areas, outdoor hearths, etc. Around the structures belonging to the central living area will normally be a zone with a heavy impact on the vegetation from traffic, toilet activities, collection of firewood, bark for roofing, etc. This can also be regarded as a part of the settlement as far as it is a zone where daily and regular activities are carried out. Such zones can probably be observable in the vegetation for hundreds and in some cases thousands of years (Grøn et al. 1999; Holm-Olsen et al. 1999).

As archaeologists we tend to think of Stone Age 'settlements' as features with a size closely related to the concentrations of material we excavate. Newell even states:

> "the maximum distribution of the retouched tools is a more reliable indicator of the settlement area (total activity area) than is the maximum distribution of the waste material (possible midden, etc.)"

(Newell 1973). I have earlier argued that a single archaeological settlement may consist of several contemporaneous dwellings reflected as several concentrations of material (Grøn 1987). Meanwhile this point of view still seems too restricted.

At an Evenkian settlement we visited in 1999 and 2000, the area with structures related to the settlement is about 600x500 metres. If one includes an old storage platform still in use, even though it originally belonged to another camp, the area increases to nearly 1.000x500 metres. The surrounding zone with a visible impact from cutting firewood, taking bark from the larch trees, etc., has a radius of several kilometres. The site was inhabited by 5 persons in 1999 and 4 in 2000. This is a large area for a site according to Evenkian standards, but even the structures of 'small' sites will seldom take up an area smaller than 20x20 to 30x30 metres. In addition to this comes the 'impact-zone'.

If a settlement is used for longer stays, it is normal to place the platforms and other external structures at a greater distance from the dwellings than if it is used only for shorter stays. Thus, there is a direct relation between the area a settlement takes up and the length of the periods of occupation.

The areas the Evenkian settlements take up are considerably larger than the areas we normally excavate during investigations of Old Stone Age settlements. This fits data from other hunter-gatherers (Turnbull 1962:10; Boas 1966:24; Yellen 1977; Johnson et al. 1999:66). That the older Evenkian sites in the area look smaller than the more recent ones is most likely because many structures disintegrate with time and become 'invisible'. This most likely also explains the 'restricted size' of many Stone Age sites: we investigate only the areas where the well-preserved lithic materials appear in significant concentrations.

Where to put the waste/re-circulation of souls

An understanding of how the prehistoric cultures handled and manipulated their waste is essential for our possibilities of interpreting their sites. The way the Evenks dispose of their waste is complex and thought-provoking and a good example of the impact spiritual culture can have on the concrete handling of material objects.

The settlement surfaces are kept clean. For many waste categories there are special procedures of disposal that must be followed. These procedures seem generally to serve purposes related to the souls or remains of souls thought to be present in the waste. Therefore it is obvious that mythology and cosmology not only play an important role for the spatial organisation of daily life on the settlements, but also to a high degree control the disposal of the waste from it.

Old clothes are regarded as sacred because they contain 'remains' of the soul of the person who wore them. Therefore they must not be placed so that they touch the ground when they are discarded. We observed old clothes hanging on trees and on branches stuck into the ground in the old settlements. In some cases old platforms are used for dumping old clothes. When people die it is normal to hang their clothes on a tree besides their grave or in the forest.

For humans, the idea of reincarnation is well described. Their souls can after a stay with the dead souls in the lower world 'return' to the clans 'storehouse' of souls in the upper world waiting for re-birth into the middle world – our real physical world (Anisimov 1963a; Vasilevich 1963). With regard to the bear, who is regarded as human and even more intelligent than humans, it is not strange to find documentation of a similar idea expressed in the spectacular bear cult. Meanwhile, the published Siberian data on re-circulation of the souls of the other consumed animals that make up the absolute majority of the diet is surprisingly thin. This rather overlooked aspect is important because it has consequences for where and how the main part of the bones are deposited (Anisimov 1963b; Paproth 1976).

The bear ritual exists in a number of different versions in the Evenkian culture (Paproth 1976). In the northern part of our area, the following version is still in use. The dead bear is addressed grandfather/grandmother and other names, and the hunters tell it that they didn't kill it. The bones and the skull are 'buried' on a platform (a '*dalken*' or '*talken*' with sides) similar to a traditional human burial structure in this area. This structure can be placed on the kill site or close to the settlement. There can be several bears on such a platform, but they cannot be deposited together with other animals. In the southern part of the Northern Transbaikal (the area around Kalar Village) they have never used platforms but formerly buried the skull of the bear under a heap of stones with the face against the ground – so that it could not see who killed it.

The bones of wild hoof-animals are put on a platform or in a 'halbo' (a log-built box standing on the ground), normally on the periphery of the settlements. As with the bear, the idea is that the souls of the dead animals must feel good, so that their reincarnations will return to the same area. In this way it is thought that their population in the area can be maintained. Moose and musk deer are not regarded as hoof-animals. Their bones must not be placed on the platforms for these. The skull and pelvis of musk deer are put on young trees, often close to the settlements. One can imagine that this reflects the fact that the musk deer sometimes grazes on the lower branches of the trees (Prikhodko and Ovsyanikov 1998), although the Evenks deny ever having observed such a thing. The moose bones may be deposited in the water. This also seems logical, since this is where the moose grazes during summer. Sable (Siberian marten) was traditionally brought into the dwelling through a sacred opening at the rear. After the fur has been removed, what remains of the body is deposited in a hole in a tree to 'bring him home' or placed on a small specialised platform near the settlement.

The depositional behaviour outlined here explains the problem we met from the start: there was almost no waste left in the central parts of the settlements, even though we knew they had been inhabited year after year. Generally, the platforms and halbos for deposition of bones are located at some distance from each other 20 to some hundred metres behind the dwellings 'just at the edge of the forest'. It seems that the locations where musk deer bones are put on trees follow the same pattern.

Archaeologically, we may end up with a situation where the central settlement area apart from the dwelling areas will appear as a dark 'culture layer' (due to the reindeer dung) with very few finds in it. Bear bones, bones of hoof-animals apart from musk deer and bones of sable will form separate concentrations behind the site if they are preserved.

When old platforms collapse, the bones tend to spread on the forest floor due to animal activity. If the settlement is occupied, the inhabitants may decide to collect the bones and throw them into the river because the domesticated reindeer may eat them to get calcium and become ill. Such waterlogged 'waste layers' will mostly be dispersed by the current in the rivers, whereas they should be preserved in situ in most lacustrine situations.

Archaeological implications – conclusion

The results presented here from the Northern Transbaikal are in themselves only valid as inspiring examples of how the relation between inhabited settlements and their archaeological remains can be. No general model for solving the problem of archaeological interpretation is postulated. We can conclude that:

a   With the Evenks studied, the dwellings and settlements are organised spatially in accordance with a set of rules that are formally 'explained' by cosmology and mythology.
b   The dwelling floors of branches may serve as traps for small objects that can yield statements about the organisation of the dwelling space – even though the dwellings have been inhabited several times.
c   The settlement sizes we operate with for hunter-gatherer settlements in archaeology seem unrealistically small.
d   The manipulation of the major find category in this case – the bones – is enormous, and different spatial procedures are used for the bones of different animal species.

The implication of these observations is that one must take the possibility of manipulation of the archaeological material in accordance with spiritually based rules and customs very seriously when interpreting prehistoric settlements. Especially the study of material from outside dwellings appears problematic, whereas the study of material from inside the dwellings can provide a basis for some optimism.

The use of strict spatial rules by different cultures for their organisation of the dwelling spaces seems from an archaeological point of view to be one of the most useful general features observed in social anthropology. Because it provides an interface between spiritual and material culture, we have a chance of extracting information about the social organisation of prehistoric hunting societies in cases where the cultural and natural conditions have preserved traces of it.

Whereas graves as well as the dwelling areas of the settlements may reflect aspects of the social organisation of prehistoric societies, the former do not represent ordinary daily-life situations as those found in dwellings. Because the relatives of the deceased in a burial situation will react to an extreme situation, their actions are unlikely to reflect daily life. They may, in such a situation, accentuate and maybe even overemphasise aspects of the social organisation that are not visible in daily life. The studies of social organisation based on the material from settlements and from graves will therefore most likely supplement each other.

The preliminary results we have obtained from our expeditions to Transbaikal stress the importance of a continuation of the careful registration and documentation of the Evenk tradition. Especially the possibilities of gaining an understanding of the relation between settlement behaviour, use of and handling of natural resources, and cosmology appear important.

References

Andersen, K. 1982. *Maglemose hytterne ved Ulkestrup Lyng*. Copenhagen.

Anderson, D.G. 1991. Turning hunters into herders: A critical examination of Soviet development policy among the Evenki of Southeastern Siberia. *Arctic* 44, No.1, 12–22.

Anisimov, A.F. 1963a. The shaman's tent of the Evenks and the origin of the shamanistic rite. In: Henry, N.M. (ed.) *Studies in Siberian Shamanism*, 84–123. Toronto.

—— 1963b. Cosmological concepts of the peoples of the north. In: Henry, N.M. (ed.) *Studies in Siberian Shamanism*, 84–123 Toronto.

Baulin, V.V., Belopukhova, Y.B. and Danilova, N.S. 1984. Holocene permafrost in the USSR. In: Velichko, A.A., Wright Jr., H.E. and Barnosky, C.W. (eds.) *Late Quaternary Environments of the Soviet Union*, 87–91. Minneapolis.

Boas, F. 1966. *Kwaikiutl Ethnography*. Chicago.

Eliade, M. 1983. *Le Chamanisme et les techniques archaïques de l'extase*. Paris.

Grøn, O. 1987. Seasonal variation in Maglemosian group size and structure. *Current Anthropology* 28, nr.3, 303–327.

—— 1989. General spatial behaviour in small dwellings: a preliminary study in ethnoarchaeology and social psychology. In: Bonsall, C. (ed.) *The Mesolithic in Europe. Papers presented at the third International Symposiu*, 99–105. Edinburgh.

—— 1991. A method for reconstruction of social organization in prehistoric societies and examples of practical application. In: Grøn, O., Engelstad, E. and Lindblom, I. (eds.) *Social Space. Human spatial behaviour in dwellings and settlements. Proceedings of an interdisciplinary conference*, 100–117. Odense.

—— 1995. *The Maglemose Culture. The reconstruction of the social organisation of a mesolithic culture in Northern Europe*. Oxford.

—— 1998. Neolithisation in southern Scandinavia – A mesolithic perspective. In: Zvelebil, M., Dennell, R. and Domanska, L. (eds.) *Harvesting the Sea, Farming the Forest: The Emergence of Neolithic Societies in the Baltic Region*, 181–191. Sheffield.

Grøn, O., Holm-Olsen, I.M., Tømmervik, H., and Kuznetsov, O. 1999. Reindeer hunters and herders: settlement and environmental impact. In: *NIKU 1995–1999. Kulturminneforskningens mangfold*, 20–26. Oslo.

Holm-Olsen, I.M., Grydeland, S.E. and Tømmervik, H. 1999. *Samiske kulturminner og kulturlandskap i Mauken Blåtind øvings- og skytefelt. Utvikling av en GIS- og fjernmålingsbasert metode*. NIKU-Oppdragsmelding 082. Oslo.

Holmberg, U. 1922. *Der Baum des Lebens*. Helsinki.

Ivanenkov, P.M. and Fraicheva, L.B. (eds.) 1997. *Atlas Chitinskoi oblasti i Aginskogo Buriatskogo avtonomiogo okruga*. Federalnayar Cluhva Geodesii i kartografii Rossii. Moscow.

Johnson, P., Bannister, A. and Wannenburgh, A. 1999. *The Bushmen*. Cape Town.

Møbjerg, T. 1991. The spatial organization of an inuit winterhouse in Greenland. An ethnoarchaeological study. In: Grøn, O., Engelstad, E. and Lindblom, I. (eds.) *Social Space. Human spatial behaviour in dwellings and settlements. Proceedings of an interdisciplinary conferenc*, 40–48. Odense.

Newell, R.R. 1973. The Post-glacial adaptions of the indigenous population of the Northwest European Plain. In: Kozlowski, S.K. (ed.) *The Mesolithic in Europe*, 399–440. Warszaw.

Paproth, H.-J. 1976. *Studien über das Bärenzeremoniell. I. Bärenjagdriten und Bärenfeste bei den tungusischen Völkern*. Uppsala.

Prikhodko, V. and Ovsyanikov, N.G. 1998. Does the Musk Deer Have a Future in Russia? *Russian Conservation News* No.16, Summer 1998, 17–21.

Ränk, G. 1951. *Das System der Raumeinteilung in den Behausungen der noreuroasischen Völker. Ein Beitrag zur nordeuroasischen Ethnologie vol. II*. Stockholm.

Rogers, E. 1967. *The Material Culture of the Mistassini*. Ottawa.

Schmidt, W. 1935. *Der Ursprung der Gottesidee vol. VI. Eine historisch-kritische und positive Studie. 2. Abteilung: Die Religionen der Urvölker V. Endsyntese der Religionen der Urvölker Amerikas, Asiens, Australiens, Afrikas*. Münster.

—— 1941. Analecta et Additamenta. *Anthropos* 35–36 (1940–1941), 966–969.

Silberbauer, G.B. 1981. *Hunter and Habitat in the Central Kalahari Desert*. Cambridge.

Shirokogoroff, S.M. 1979. *Social Organization of the Northern Tungus*. New York. Reprint of 1929 version, Shanghai.

Tanner, A. 1979 *Bringing Home Animals. Religious Ideology and Mode of Production of the Mistassini Cree Hunters*. London.

Turnbull, C.M. 1962. *The Forest People*. New York.

Vasilevich, G.M. 1963. Early Concepts about the Universe among the Evenks (Materials). In: Henry, M.M. (ed.) *Studies in Siberian Shamanism*, 46–83. Toronto.

Vasilevich, G.M. and Smolyak, A.V. 1964. The Evenks. In: Levin, M.G. and Potapov, L.P. (eds.) *The Peoples of Siberia*, 620–654. Chicago and London.

Wright, H.E. and Barnosky, C.W. 1984. Introduction to the English Edition. In: Velichko, A.A., Wright Jr., H.E. and Barnosky, C.W. (eds.) *Late Quaternary Environments of the Soviet Union*, xiii–xxii. Minneapolis.

Yates, T. 1989. Habitus and social space: some suggestions about meaning in the Saami (Lapp) tent ca. 1700–1900. In: Hodder, I. (ed.) *The Meanings of Things. Material Culture and Symbolic Expression*, 249–262. Cambridge.

Yellen, J.E. 1977. *Archaeological Approaches to the Present. Models for Reconstructing the Past*. New York.

31. A Mesolithic Winter-Site with a Sunken Dwelling from the Swedish West Coast

Robert Hernek

This article deals with the excavation of a Middle Mesolithic site at Timmerås in the province of Bohuslän on the Swedish West Coast. The site was situated on a 50x20 m large terrace at the foot of a mountain and was, in the Mesolithic, surrounded by water on three sides. In the central part of the site were the remains of a dwelling with a sunken floor. This was situated on slightly sloping ground and the dwelling-pit had been dug in order to achieve a flat living surface, which was oval in shape and measured 5x4 m. The culture layer within the dwelling-pit was homogeneous and almost totally black in colour. It is likely that four posts arranged in a square supported the roof. At the centre of the dwelling there were two fireplaces and those were at different levels within the fill. There was a distinct layer of charcoal and burnt hazelnut shells in connection with the upper hearth, which shows that this one had been used for roasting hazelnuts. In the area around the dwelling there were a large number of features such as hearth-pits, hearths lying directly on the ground and other types of pits whose functions are difficult to estimate. All together the C14-dates from Timmerås, originating both from the dwelling-pit and hearth-pits, lie within the interval 8385–8060 uncalibrated BP. It is likely that the dwelling was inhabited on seasonal basis for a number of years and there are good reasons to believe that this was a winter camp for a small unit, probably an extended family.

Introduction

The sites from the Middle Mesolithic in Western Sweden, i.e. the Sandarna culture, are known for the transgressed sites such as Sandarna, Bua Västergård, Balltorp and Huseby klev. On these sites sand, gravel and/or clay covered the find layer. Due to disturbances and erosion caused by wave movements during process of transgression there is normally nothing that is left of the actual living surfaces. This means that the finds were in secondary context and that cultural layers and features had been washed away. In that sense the well-known site at Sandarna, excavated in 1930, was an exception. Surprisingly, not only hearths but also even cultural layers are preserved. Due to geological circumstances transgressed sites is only seen in the Gothenburg area and the southern part of the province of Bohuslän. Further north there is only "open sites" from the Mesolithic and the majority of these sites lack culture layers with soot and charcoal. The artefacts are normally found in humus-free layers of gravel and sand. This circumstance in combination with previous excavation technique had revealed very few Mesolithic features from western Sweden. In those cases where hearths and cooking-pits are found on the sites, the C14-dates have, with just a few exceptions, showed that they were constructed during Bronze- or Iron Age. The excavation in 1997 of a small settlement site at Timmerås in the middle of Bohuslän was therefore of particular interest. This was an "open site" with dark culture layers, the remains of a sunken dwelling and a number of other Mesolithic features. The excavation took place under the management of The Central Board of National Antiquities (Riksantikvarieämbetet UV Väst) and was caused by a road project. Unfortunately the site

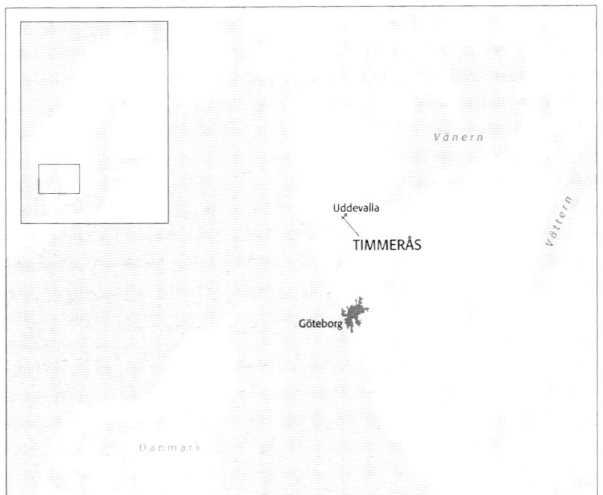

Figure 31.1 Map over the province of Bohuslän with the location of Timmerås.

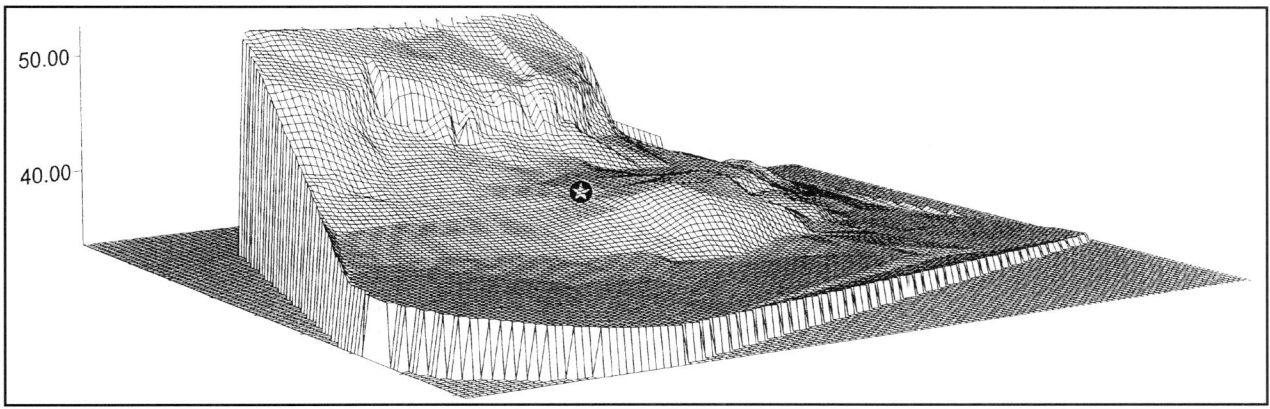

Figure 31.2 Topographic view of Timmerås. According to the upheaval of land the site lay 40 metre above sea level. The symbol shows the location of the dwelling.

was first discovered during a small excavation of a nearby site with remains from the Late Bronze Age. In spite of some extra resources for the excavation some less favourable priorities had to be done regarding the excavation methods. The analysis of the site is not completed but a publication can be expected in 2002.

The dwelling at Timmerås

The site at Timmerås was situated on a 50x20 m large terrace at the foot of a rather steep mountain. To judge from the topography it is almost certain that it had been shore-bound during the settlement, which means that the site was surrounded by water in three directions (Figure 31.2). In the Mesolithic the area can be described as an inner archipelago and the site itself was situated on a rather big island but yet close to the mainland.

The very small terrace, where even a great part was rocky without covered earth, had been cultivated, probably at the end of the 19th century. However, before the excavation took place the site was covered with high trees of fir. Under the thin ploughing-layer there were dark, up to 35 cm thick, occupation layers which covered an area of about 200 m². At the centre of this dark layer it was possible to detect an even darker area where the earth was totally black in colour (Figure 31.7). What was seen was the upper part of a sunken dwelling. The dwelling was situated on a slightly sloping ground and the actual dwelling-pit had been dug in order to achieve a flat living-surface. This means that the northern part of the dwelling was deeper cut into the ground than the southern side (Figure 31.3). At first, when the surface was cleared, the dark layer, that is the filling of the pit, had a more or less rectangular shape with rounded corners. After the removal of the upper decimetre of the cultural-layer the dwelling became more oval in shape and measured about 5x4 m and that extension remained all the way down to the bottom of the pit (Figure 31.4). This difference in extension is one indication that the walls of the super-structure at some parts did not coincide with the walls of

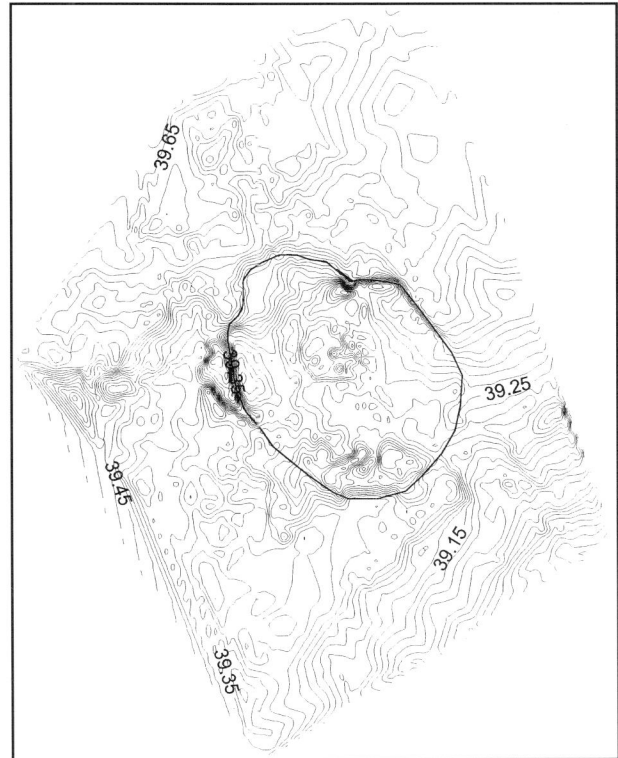

Figure 31.3 A terrain model showing the sunken dwelling.

the dwelling-pit. The distance between the pit and the outer wall was probably less than one metre and the space in between could have been used for storage of clothes, tools etc. The thickness of the culture-layer within the pit varied from 10 to 30 cm. The layer was thinnest in the southern part and this could, probably to some extent, be explained by damage caused by the cultivation. The entrance was probably in the north where it was possible to see a sloping down to the actual dwelling-floor. This means that there could have been a hearth-pit just outside the entrance (Figure 31.4).

The black layer within the dwelling-pit stood out

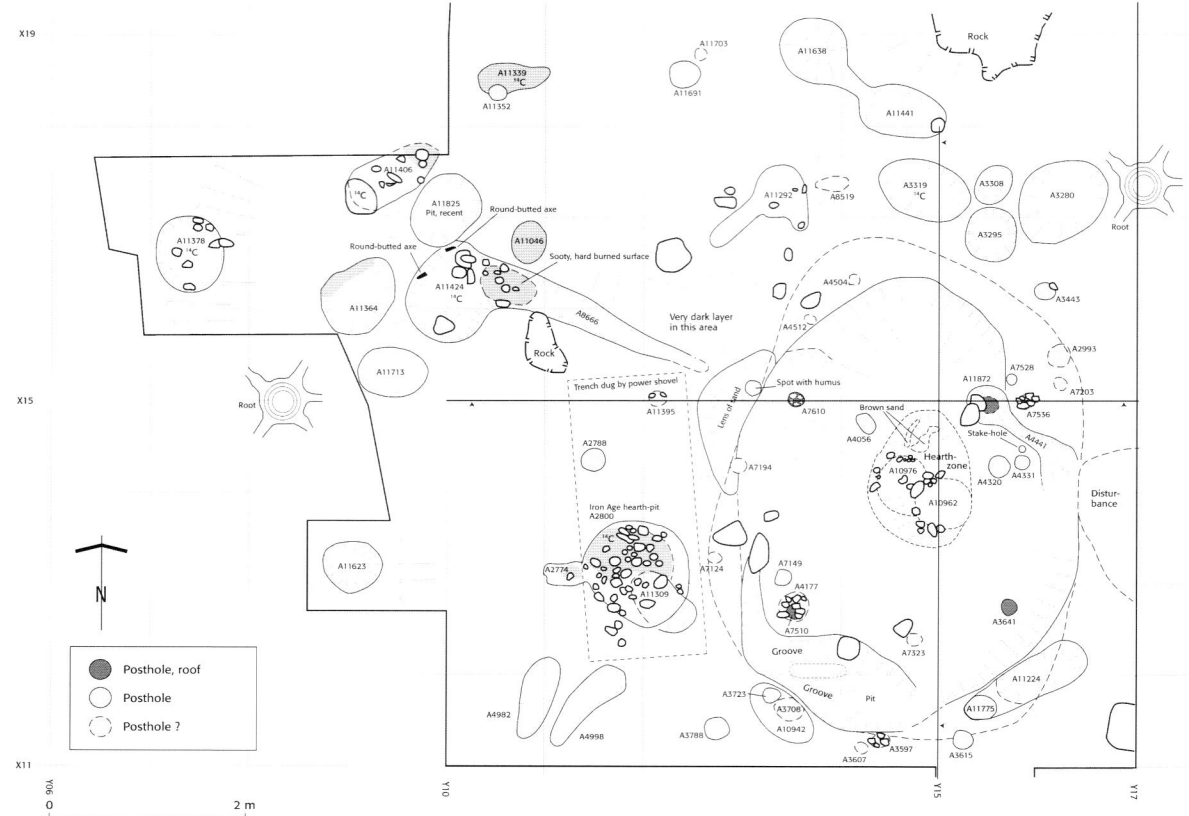

Figure 31.4 The central area of the site as it appeared after removal of the culture layer.

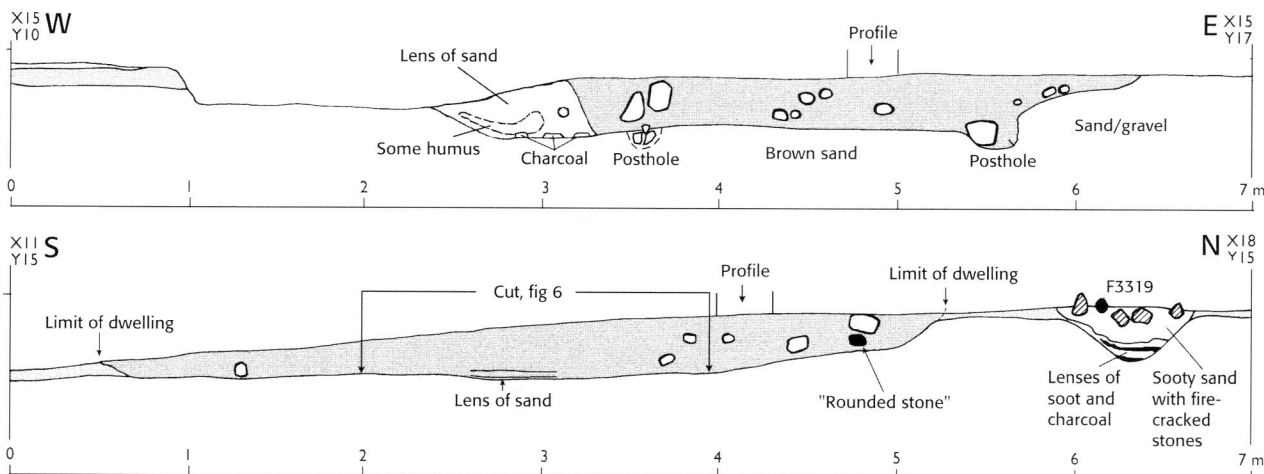

Figure 31.5 Profiles through the dwelling-pit. The hearth-pit, feature 3319, on the N–S profile has been dated to 8060±95 BP (Ua-9590). An enlarged cut of the S–N profile is seen in figure 31.6.

clearly against the surrounding soil (Figure 31.5). The limit was most clear in the north-eastern part where the boarder between the black coloured culture layer and the sterile gravely sand was very distinct. The situation was similar in the north-western part but here the culture layer met against an almost vertical edge of light-brown sand. Contrary to the other side this sand was not totally sterile and the reason for this was that the sand did not coincide with the wall of the dug pit (Figure 31.5). Instead the sand lay like a two metre long and about thirty centimetre broad lens between the pit and the culture layer within the dwelling. One could easily imagine that the sand, probably in the form of turf, was spread as an extra isolation on the lower part of the wall. For different reasons it is instead more likely the sand was built up to form the dwelling-pit before the superstructure was raised.

Since the limits between the culture layer and the surrounding material was almost vertical one can assume that the walls of the pit must have been covered in order to prevent the earth-walls to erode onto the floor. It is likely that they solved this problem by covering the pit-walls with birch-bark, just as they have suggested for dwellings with sunken floors in the northern part of Sweden (Lundberg 1997:124).

The construction of the dwelling

When it comes to the construction of the dwelling nothing can be said with certainty, but there are strong indications of its basic framework. Around the border of the dwelling there were some small colourings but the gravely sand made it almost impossible to decide if those really were the remains of small posts or stakes or simply from roots or burrowing animals. Yet, their position indicates that at least some of them really were traces of thin stakes. At the bottom of the dwelling there were also larger colourings and some of them could almost certainly be described as post-holes. It is very likely that four posts supported the roof and those posts were arranged in a square. In the middle of this square was the position of the fireplace (Figure 31.4). It is reasonable to believe that the four posts were connected at the top with horizontally stakes. As will be discussed further in the publication it is likely that this main construction created a support for a skeleton made of thinner stakes which created a foundation for one or more layers of bark, probably from birch. In order to prevent the bark from drying and as an extra isolation, the construction was probably covered with turfs of grass or seaweed or a combination of these materials. Another observation worth mentioning is that there were grooves along some parts at the edge of the pit. Since these grooves were at the very bottom it is likely that they were the remains of tree-trunks which in part had been dug into the ground. Such tree-trunks could have served as an extra support for the earth-walls and to secure the birch-bark mentioned before. The dwelling was consequently a solid construction that was built with intention to be used for several years. It can be mentioned that the so called "birch-bark kotes" that were used by the Lapps in northern Scandinavia could be in use for 50–60 years without repairing the main construction (Liedegren 1992:146). However, the dwelling at Timmerås was probably in use for a much shorter period, maybe not more than 5–10 seasons.

The culture layer within the dwelling-pit

There can be no doubt that the culture layer within the dwelling-pit was built up during the settlement. This means that no material came into the pit after it was abandoned. Although the dwelling probably has been in use for several years, the fill within the pit was homogenous and it was not possible to see any stratigraphy in the black layer. The same pattern is seen in other dwellings of the same type such as Saxtorp and Skateholm I in Scania (Larsson 1975, 1985), Svanemose 28 in Jutland (Grøn 1995:75) and Huseby Klev in Bohuslän (Hernek and Nordqvist 1995:71, Nordqvist 2000:213). The culture layer was rich in finds and the majority was found in the upper part of the fill whilst the number of finds successively decreased towards the bottom. Three squares were excavated in mechanical layers with 4-cm thickness. Taken those squares together the total numbers of flints were, from the top: 267, 185, 128, 110, 110, 55 and 48. To some extent this could be the result of vertical movements caused by freezing but again the same pattern was obviously seen in the dwellings just mentioned.

As proposed by Grøn (1995:36) and Sørensen (1995: 25) it is likely that the flooring-material within the sunken dwellings from Southern Scandinavia were of the same type as on the bog-sites, that is, branches, barks and twigs. Such a floor could explain the creation of the homogeneous layers inside the dwellings and how it was possible to live among the many sharp flint-pieces – the loose structure would simply absorb the flint (Grøn 1995:36, 2000:197 p). One indication that this kind of materials were used in dwellings in the archipelago of western Sweden, was seen from the oldest Mesolithic settlement phase at Huseby Klev. This site, dated to 9100–8600 BP, was transgressed and the finds were covered with more than one metre of clay (Hernek and Nordqvist 1995; Nordqvist 2000:210). The condition of preservation for organic material was extremely good and among the flints, unburned bones, resin-pieces and chopped wood there were also a great number of burned and unburned hazelnut shells, bark-pieces and branches. There were also thinner stakes and some of them were burnt in one tip. It is likely that much of this material originate from dwelling-floors that eroded into the sea during the process of transgression.

Fireplaces inside the dwelling

At the centre of the dwelling there were two fireplaces and those were at different levels within the fill. There were also indications that there had been yet another fireplace in the level between those two. One of the fireplaces was at the very top of the culture layer and this one was first observed when the 30-cm thick profile bench was excavated (Figure 31.7). The other fireplace was situated at the bottom of the dwelling-pit but it was slightly raised above the sterile sand. Both hearths contained fire-cracked stones and had a hard burnt layer of charcoal. Another thing in common was that they appeared as two different hearths lying next to each other (Figures 31.4 and 31.6). Although it was not possible to detect a border between the two hearths the first interpretation was that there had been two central hearths in the dwelling which had been in use simultaneously.

This was probably wrong and the imagination of a

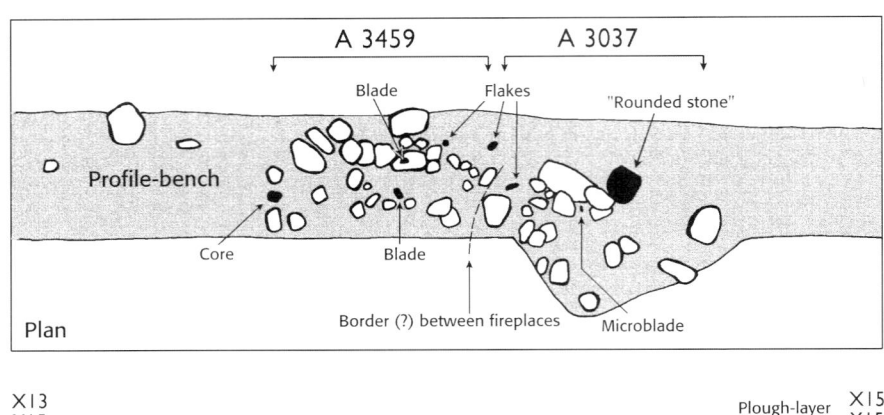

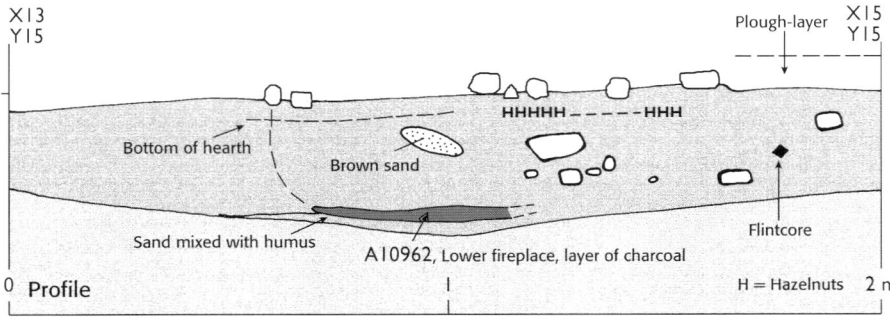

Figure 31.6 The figure at the top is a plan over a part of the profile-bench through the dwelling (see figure 31.5) and what are seen is the remains of the "upper" fireplace. The figure at the bottom is the actual profile.

divided hearth could be explained in another way. It is not unusual that hearths from the Maglemose culture are divided horizontally and thus appear as two individual hearths (Grøn 1987:70 pp). As proposed by Grøn, the reason for this is that the fireplaces have been used for roasting hazelnuts. This means that the hearth-zone is separated into a regular fireplace and adjacent sand depot. The hazelnuts were mixed together with red-hot charcoal taken from the actual fireplace and during the roasting process the hazelnuts were covered with sand (Grøn 1987:73). It is obvious that, at least the upper fireplace at Timmerås had been used for roasting hazelnuts. This fireplace was oblong in shape and about two meters long and less than one metre broad. The southern part had a thicker and more pronounced layer of charcoal and also contained more fire-cracked stones. The northern part of the fireplace also contained a layer of dark brown sand and underneath there were almost a compact layer of charcoal mixed with burnt hazelnut-shells (the H:s at figure 31.6). A makrofossil-analysis showed that one litre of earth from this layer contained about 100 burnt shells. Since there were blotches of sand and burnt hazelnut shells also in connection with the other fireplace, i.e. the one at the bottom, it is likely that even this one had been used for roasting hazelnuts.

Several habitations?

The fact that there were two fireplaces on different levels indicates at least two settlement phases within the dwelling

Figure 31.7 Photo over the profile-bench (N–S). The lens of sand that delimited the north-western part of the pit is seen in the right upper corner. The small stones at the top belong to the fireplace that was situated at the top of the culture layer.

and, as mentioned, there were signs of yet another fireplace in the level between those two. Apart from this it was not possible to see any stratigraphy in the dwelling-pit but it is reasonable to believe that the culture layer were the remains of several floors. It is also likely that the upper part of the culture layer, which contained most flints and most tools, reflects the very last occupation-phase within the dwelling. However it is less probable that the culture layer underneath were the remains of intact floors. My interpretation is that the old floor was cleaned up

Figure 31.8 Part of the excavation area with the dwelling and the surrounding features. All stones within the dwelling, which were at least 5 cm in size, are shown. Outside the dwelling were a number of such stones but these were not documented.

before every new seasonal habitation, which anticipate the building of the new floor. It seems though, that they for some reason did not clear out all of the material but saved the lowest part of the old floor. One can only speculate why, but it may well have been irrational reasons governed by certain rules in the society. Apart from this seasonal cleaning it is also likely that the floor, to some extent and especially the hearth zone, was cleaned repeatedly during every seasonal occupation. The interpretations made mean that no habitation has taken place on the actual bottom of the dwelling-pit and this seems to be in agreement with other dwellings of the same type, for example at Nivå 10 in Zealand (Lass Jensen in this volume). Although the "lower" fireplace was slightly raised above the sterile sand its vertical position raises the question if this, almost intact, fireplace actually reflects a habitation phase. Instead, it is possible that this fireplace was of ceremonial character and was used only on one particular occasion, namely just after the dwelling was built. The fireplace could thus have been used on an initiation feast and should for that reason not be cleared. It is well known that the fireplaces often attend a special symbolic value. This can be exemplified from a Mesolithic dwelling at Sunde on the Norwegian West Coast. Under the fireplace within the dwelling was a small "offering-pit" with an intact greenstone axe (Braathen 1985:74 p).

When it comes to the horizontal distribution of finds, this analysis is not yet completed but, as expected, it seems that the pattern is rather blurred. However, there is a discernible pattern in the distribution of stones. All stones within the dwelling that were at least 5 cm in size were documented and as seen in figure 31.8, the southern and eastern parts was free from stones. It is likely that this stone-free area in the inner part of the dwelling were the sleeping-places. This is, for example, in accordance with dwelling-pits from the northern part of Sweden where the sleeping places seemed to have been situated as far from the entrance as possible (Rydström 1986:103). It is also possible, but more of a speculation, that there had been some kind of a sleeping-platform within this area. In the stone-free area the cultural layer was slightly lighter in colour and there were also fewer finds. A big shallow pit in the southern side may have served as a storage-pit under a sleeping platform (Figure 31.4).

Finds and dating

There were no organic materials apart from charcoal, burnt hazelnut shells and some pieces of resin. The flint material consists of blades and micro-blades. Some are stuck from conical cores but they mainly derive from one-sided cores with one platform. It is worth to emphasise that there are no microliths. The most common tool is small burins made of flakes. There is also a great deal of non-flint material such as flakes from diabases, which is surprising since this is a characteristic trait for the Late Mesolithic. One unusual artefact found in the dwelling was a made of soapstone. It is shaped like an "ice-hockey puck" and has probably been used for some kind of grinding. There were also a lot of round or round-oval stones with smooth surfaces within the dwelling. The stones had no traces of pounding or other kind of use.

From the filling of the dwelling-pit there are four C14-dates and the samples originate from burnt hazelnut shells and one piece of resin. These four dates lie within the interval 8300–8200 uncalibrated BP. In all there are eight C14-dates from the actual settlement and these span from 8385±145 BP (T-14057) to 8060±60 BP (Ua-9590). In chronological terms this means the latest phase of the Sandarna culture. The lack of microliths and the fact that there were a great deal of non-flint material indicates that Timmerås can be considered as transitory-site between Middle- and Late Mesolithic. According to the flint material from a site in Bro parish in the middle of Bohuslän, Fredsjö called this phase "The Enerklev phase" (1953:89 pp). Another site with a find material similar to Timmerås is Dammen, which is situated not far from the Enerklev site. Some C14-dates from Dammen is somewhat younger, 7600–7900 BP (Kindgren and Schaller Åhrberg 1999:221), but the results from some new analysis are in degree with the dates from Timmerås (Eva Schaller Åhrberg, pers.com.).

Features outside the dwelling

In the area around the dwelling there were a large number of features of different types (Figure 31.8). Many were simple hearths lying directly on the ground while others were hearth-pits. The latter category contained various amounts of fire cracked stones. There were also other types of pits, whose functions were difficult to estimate.

It is likely the features were contemporary with the dwelling and one argument for this is that not a single feature disturbed the centrally located dwelling. Charcoal from four hearth-pits has been dated and the results are in agreement with the dates from the dwelling. It should be mentioned though that one hearth-pit was dated to the Late Mesolithic and in addition there was one big hearth-pit that differs from the others and this one has, as expected, been dated to the Early Iron age. One of the Mesolithic features can be mentioned. It was a hearth-pit (F11424) where two round-butted axes were found. Both were intact and about the same size and these were the only greenstone axes found at the site. From this particular hearth-pit, which was dated to 8280±60 BP (GrA-16548), a groove followed towards the dwelling (Figures 31.4 and 31.8). The bottom of the groove had a sooty and hard (burnt?) surface. It is very likely that the groove in some way connected the hearth-pit with the dwelling.

Samples for phosphate-analysis was taken all over the site. The results confirm to some degree the interpretation made during the excavation, namely that there were a dump area north-west of the dwelling. There were also higher concentrations of phosphate further north, in an area that left few find and where cultural-layers were lacking. The dwelling itself had no higher concentrations of phosphate compared with adjacent areas.

Some concluding remarks

To judge from the size of the dwelling and the fact that there was just one fireplace situated in the centre, indicates that it was inhabited by a small unit, perhaps an extended family. It is likely that Timmerås was inhabited on seasonal basis for several years during the cold season. One argument for this is the fact that the dwelling had been dug into the ground. Other indications are the presence of hazelnuts and the sooty cultural layers with its mixture of fire-cracked stones. All together it shows that the inhabitants used a lot of fire for protection from the cold. Grøn has proposed that winter inland settlements from the Boreal period, regarding protection from the predominant wind directions, were oriented to the north (Grøn 1987:311, 1995:52). Since Timmerås was oriented towards the north this could also indicate a winter settlement.

Most of the terrace was excavated manually and the very last step involved stripping the rest of the terrace with the assistance of a power shovel. The entire terrace was therefore surveyed and just one single dwelling was found. This seems to indicate that the society was split into smaller units during winter. It is possible though, that there was at least one more small unit not too far away from Timmerås. These groups could have been in regular contact and may also have co-operated in different kinds of tasks, such as hunting-activities. Finally, it should be mentioned that the interpretation that a family-unit inhabited the site is not obvious. The author would not reject the possibility that Timmerås represents the remains of a task-group, e.g., a hunting camp, which was utilised on seasonal basis.

References

Braathen, H. 1980. Hvor gammel er "øksekulten?" In: Festskrift til Sverre Marstrander på 70-årsdagen. *Universitetets Oldsaksamlings Skrifter.* Ny rekke, Nr. 3, 113–118. Oslo.

Fredsjö, Å. 1955. *Studier i Västsveriges äldre stenålder.* Göteborg.

Grøn, O. 1987. Seasonal Variation in Maglemosian Group Size and Structure. *Current Anthropology* 28, No. 3, 303–318.

—— 1995. *The Maglemose Culture. The reconstruction of the social organisation of a Mesolithic culture in Northern Europe.* BAR International Series 616.

—— 2000. Etnoarkæologi. In: Eriksen, B.V. (ed.) *Flintstudier. En håndbog i systematiske analyser af flintinventarer,* 187–206. Aarhus.

Hernek, R. and Nordqvist, B. 1995. *Världens äldsta tuggummi? Ett urval spännande arkeologiska upptäckter som gjordes vid Huseby klev, och andra platser, inför Väg 178 över Orust.* Riksantikvarieämbetet UV Väst. Kungsbacka.

Jensen, O.L. 2002. A sunken dwelling from the Ertebølle Site Nivå 10, Eastern Denmark. (in this volume).

Kindgren, H. and Schaller Åhrberg, E. 1999. From Sandarna to Lihult. Fredsjö's Enerklev phase revisited. In: Boaz, J. (ed.) *The Mesolithic of Central Scandinavia.* Universitetets Oldsaksamling skrifter. Ny rekke 22, 217–233. Oslo.

Larsson, L. 1975. A Contribution to the Knowledge of Mesolithic Huts in Southern Scandinavia. *Meddelanden från Lunds universitets historiska museum 1973–1974,* 5–28.

—— 1985. Of House and Hearth. The excavation and interpretation and reconstruction of a Late Mesolithic House. *In honorem Evert Baudou. Archaeology and Enviroment* 4, 197–209. Umeå.

Liedgren, L. 1992. *Hus och Gård i Hälsingland. En studie av agrar bebyggelse och bebyggelseutveckling i norra Hälsingland Kr.f – 600 e.Kr.* Studia Archaeologica Universitatis Umensis 2. Umeå.

Lundberg, Å. 1997. *Vinterbyar: ett bandsamhälles territorier i Norrlands inland 4500–2500 f. Kr.* Studia Archaeological Universitatis Umensis 8. Umeå.

Nordqvist, B. 2000. *Coastal Adaptations in the Mesolithic. A study of coastal sites with organic remains from the Boreal and Atlantic periods in Western Sweden.* GOTARC Series B. Gothenburg Archaeological Theses, No. 13.

Rydström, G. 1986. Sovplatser i skärvstensvallar. In: Studier i norrländsk forntid II. *Acta Bothniensia Occidentalis. Skrifter i västerbottnisk kulturhistoria* 8, 100–105. Umeå.

Sørensen, S.A. 1995. Lollkhuse – a Dwelling Site under a Kitchen Midden. *Journal of Danish Archaeology* 11 (1992–93), 19–29.

32. A Sunken Dwelling from the Ertebölle Site Nivå 10, Eastern Denmark

Ole Lass Jensen

Since 1992 the Hørsholm Egns Museum has carried out excavations on a former inlet at Nivå, Northeastern Zealand, where many sites from the Kongemose and Ertebølle periods, 7400–5000 BP, have been located. Some of the sites contain a considerable number of settlement features in the form of dwellings, fireplaces, pits and graves. In the context of such structures the site of Nivå 10, which was located on a small island in the estuarine part of the inlet, must be considered to be the most informative. The site comprises two brief occupation phases from the Late Kongemose and the earliest Ertebølle period respectively, which, due to rising sea level, are horizontally separated. So far, the excavation has aimed at exposing coherent areas connected with the Ertebølle habitation and in this respect a well-preserved feature interpreted as the remains of a dwelling was investigated. The feature comprised a shallow pit surrounded by postholes, with a distinct occupation layer containing a fireplace and several separate activity areas. Outside the dwelling, activity areas and pits of varying function were found. The pits included dumps, cooking places and a grave. In the following, an outline of the settlement will be given and a number of spatial analyses of the dwelling will be presented.

Introduction

Despite 100 years of research, finds of convincing dwellings from the South Scandinavian Ertebølle culture (6600–5000 BP) are virtually unknown. This is in spite of the fact that many large-scale excavations have been carried out in recent decades. Several structures have been claimed to represent traces of dwellings, but in most cases these were either rather dubious or could be rejected on the grounds that they represented other kinds of structures, or were later features located over Mesolithic settlements (e.g. Sørensen 1995:26 pp). It is definitely also a problem that most of the postulated dwellings are so dissimilar. As is the case in many other prehistoric cultures, we must assume that the Ertebølle culture also had a kind of "type-house" or at least a restricted number of dwelling types.

In recent years, a number of structures found in Denmark and Southern Sweden appear to cast new light on this problem – although we still have to explain some differences between these newly found structures. This article will present one of the so far most convincing and thoroughly documented dwellings from the Danish Ertebølle culture and give an outline of the settlement as a whole.

The Stone Age inlet at Nivå

The settlement named Nivå 10 is located on the eastern coast of Northern Zealand (Figure 32.1). During the Late Mesolithic Kongemose and Ertebølle periods (7400–5000 BP) the surroundings of the settlement comprised an inlet (Figure 32.2). On the shores of this inlet, and more rarely on small islands in the inlet itself, there are a large number of settlements; 24 have so far been located from the periods in question.

Needless to say, the formation of the inlet was a dynamic process. Around 7200 BP the sea level rose from

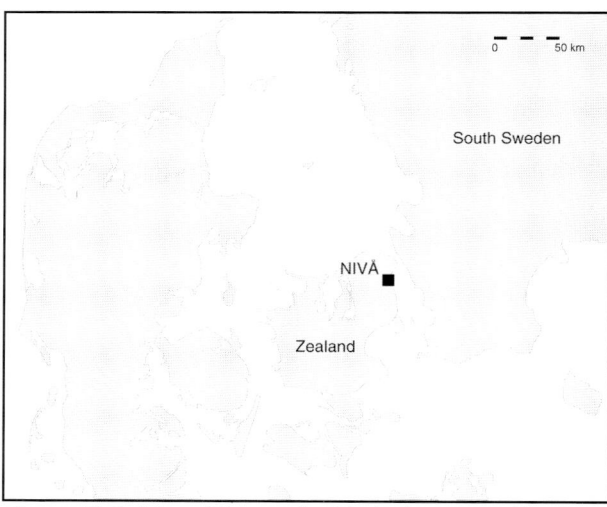

Figure 32.1 Map of Denmark with the location of the Stone Age inlet at Nivå.

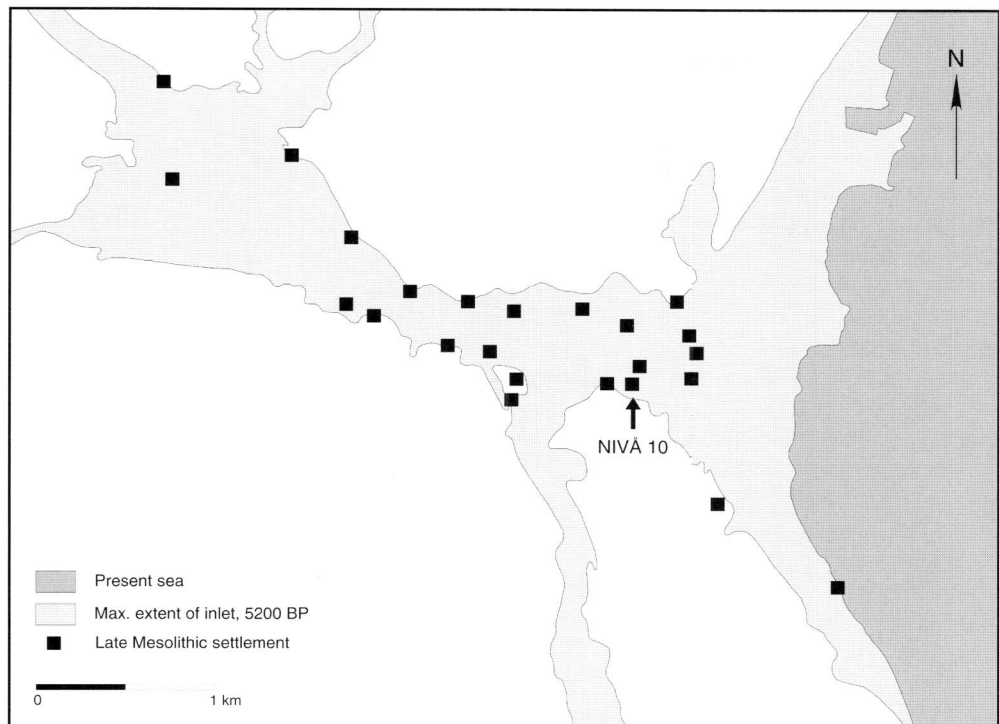

Figure 32.2 Map showing the maximum extent of the Stone Age inlet at Nivå, reconstructed on the basis of the 5 meter contour line, and the known late Mesolithic sites.

some metres below to 1–2 metres above the present level and at this point, the shoreline most likely had the form of a broad bay. The contemporary settlements from the Early Kongemose culture, which tend to be the easternmost sites, consist of thin, limited occupation layers, indicating rather brief occupation phases. After the settlements had been abandoned, the continuing transgression covered them with layers of sand several metres thick. The transgression apparently caused no erosion of the culture layers, and due to this and the short-lived nature of the occupations, the settlements appear very well preserved and temporally well-defined.

The rising sea level motivated the Mesolithic hunters and fishers to establish new settlements on higher ground. As a result of this, we generally find the settlements from the Late Kongemose and the Early Ertebølle phases (c. 7000–6000 BP) between 3 and 5 metres above present sea level. In contrast to the older settlements, the occupation layers are generally not covered with protective layers of marine sand, and the localities are thus very vulnerable, for instance to the intensive modern farming of the area. The threat from ploughing is the background against which the four seasons of archaeological excavations at the Kongemose- and Ertebølle settlements of Nivå 10 have been carried out. These intensive and systematic excavations have yielded quite a number of informative structures, including the sunken dwelling.

The settlement

Unlike nearly all the other settlements on the Nivå inlet, the settlement was located on a small island, measuring approximately 110 x 80 metres, and situated at the mouth of the inlet less than 100 metres from its southern shore. Judging from surface finds and test pits, the settlement originally covered some 600 m², but due to ploughing only about 50% of the occupation layers were more-or-less intact prior to the excavation. So far, a little more than 140 m² has been excavated (Figure 32.3). The occupation layers consist, on average, of 20 cm thick sandy layers mixed with stones, charcoal, animal bones and flint artefacts. These layers were deposited directly on glacial sand or clay and are covered either by marine sand or, more usually, the plough soil.

At the southern and lowest part of the island, a limited occupation layer from the Late Kongemose period has been partly excavated. The occupation layer, which is still unaffected by ploughing, seems to be preserved in its full extent of approximately 200 m². Between 5 and 8 m north of the occupation layer were two larger pits which can be assigned to the Kongemose habitation. The northernmost depression contained a dump which consisted primarily of larger pieces of flint debris and refuse comprising fish and mammal remains. The other pit contained mainly fish and mammal remains. Under the Kongemose layer itself, there were several smaller features, including cooking pits and a fireplace. Around

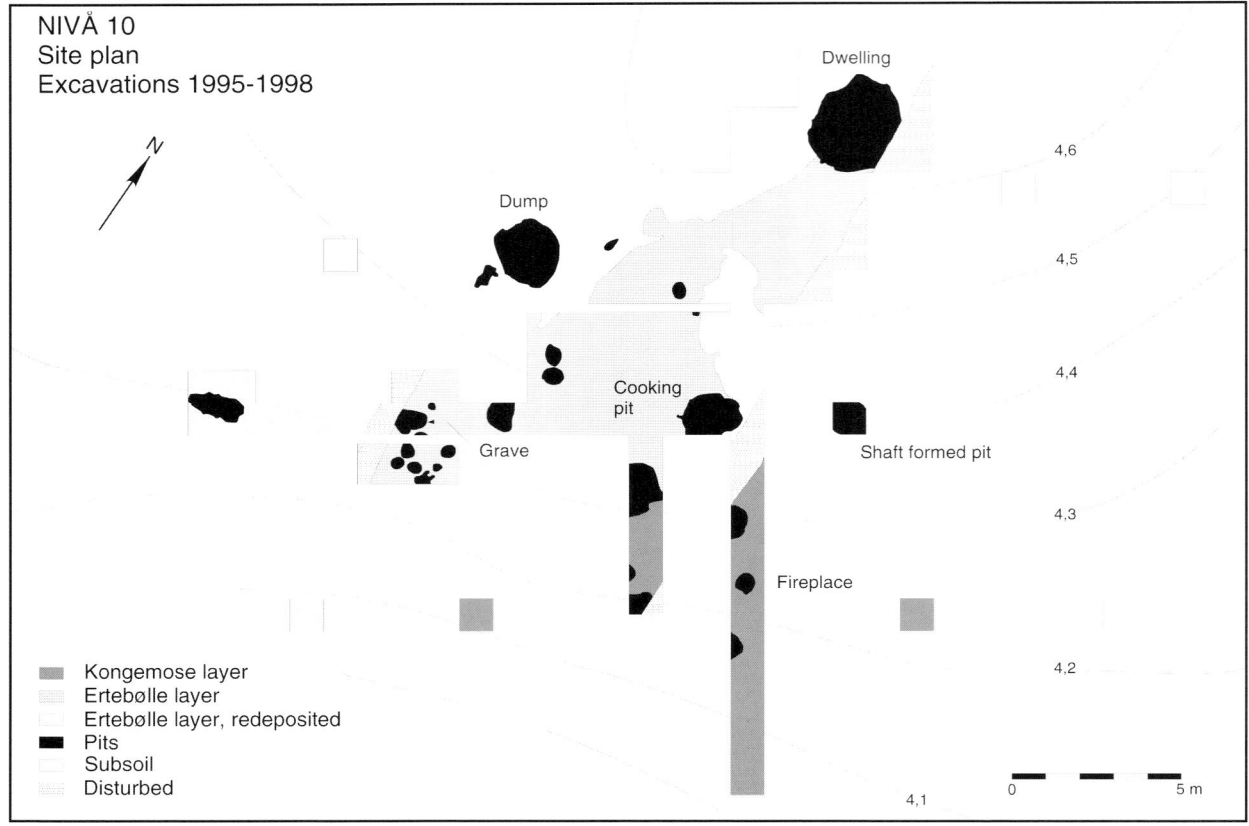

Figure 32.3 Nivå 10. General plan of the excavations 1995–1998.

the fireplace a distinct concentration of animal bones was uncovered. As was the case in the pits, the bones were mainly from red deer, roe deer, wild boar, flatfish and codfish. Immediately north of the fireplace there was a flint knapping area where microblades were produced from handle cores. So far, only a single ^{14}C date has been obtained from the Kongemose settlement. The sample, consisting of charcoal, comes from a small pit below the culture layer, and was dated to 6350 BP (K-7118), corresponding to the Kongemose-Ertebølle transition.

During the subsequent Early Ertebølle period, though probably after a period of several hundred years had elapsed, as indicated by both the typology and the ^{14}C dates, a new occupation took place on the island. Due to the rising sea level, this was situated to the north of the Kongemose habitation on the higher parts of the island. However, the southernmost 3–4 metres of the Ertebølle layer are clearly chronologically mixed, as they contain some lithic material of Kongemose type. The extent of the Ertebølle layer can be followed over an area of 15 × 15 m. The layer had originally extended at least a further 10 m to the north, where it has now been destroyed by ploughing. Underneath the culture layer there were about 25 features in the form mainly of pits but also stake- and postholes. These structures, with one exception, were all of Late Mesolithic date and belonged primarily to the Early Ertebølle period.

To the southwest, relatively far down the slope, a grave of Early Ertebølle date was excavated. The grave pit contained the bones of a man (Jensen 2000:25). Close to the grave a cluster of seven small, rather uniform pits forming a horseshoe-like pattern was excavated. These contained regular flint waste and animal bones. Pits of this small size were not commonly found at the settlement and they may be related to the grave. To the east of the grave two larger pits, dated to the Ertebølle culture, were investigated. One was probably used for cooking, while the other was a 75 cm deep, shaft-like structure with a paved stone base. This latter pit contained very few finds. One possible use for this structure could have been the storage of food. In the occupation layer north of the pits mentioned there were several more-or-less coherent activity areas. Especially the southern part of the culture layer contained abundant finds reflecting both flint knapping and butchering. Northernmost in the excavation area there was a well-defined structure interpreted as a sunken dwelling.

The dwelling

We mostly see Mesolithic dwellings either documented as latent structures, i.e. when characteristic spatial patterns occur in the distribution of lithics, or as more obvious structures, i.e. a definite cluster of postholes or a pit

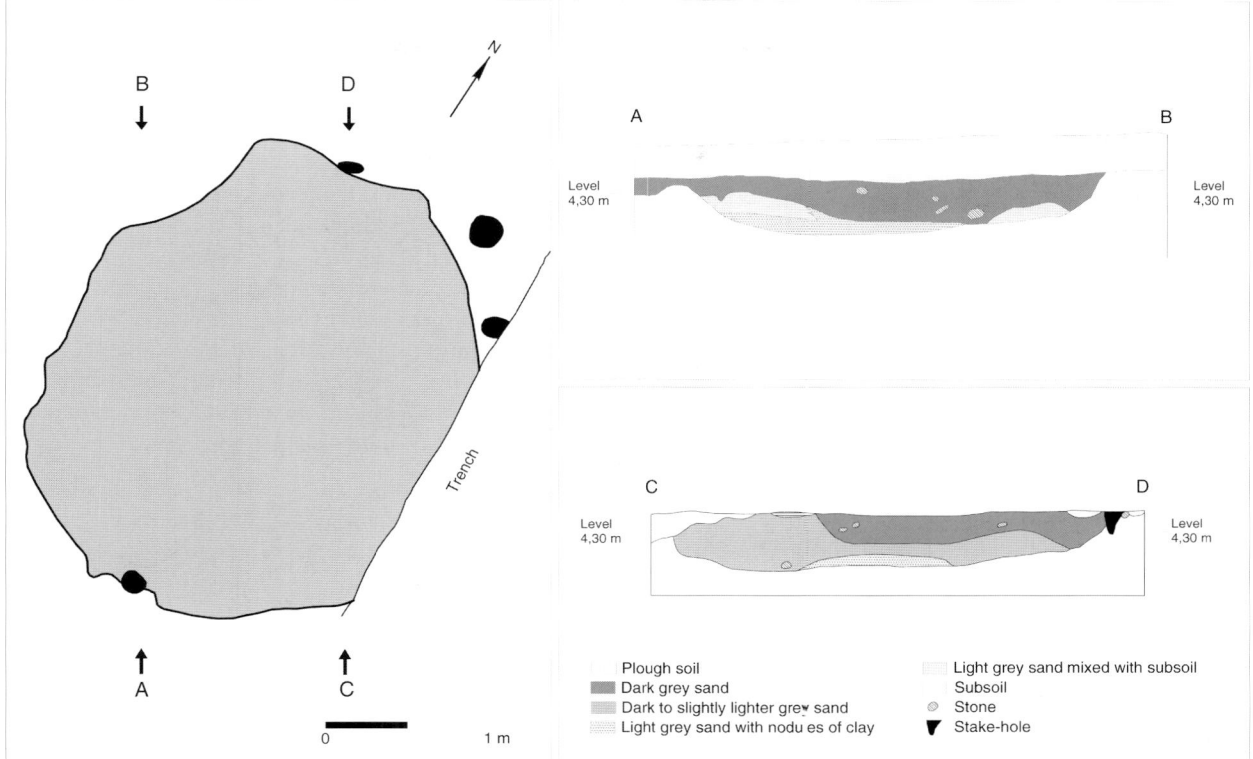

Figure 32.4 Plan and sections of the sunken dwelling.

associated with postholes, which very well could be regarded as the remains of a dwelling, but where the internal lithic distribution is very much disturbed. Only rarely are we fortunate enough to find a tangible structure combined with a well-preserved lithic distribution, allowing us to gain information about the layout of the interior. The sunken dwelling found at Nivå 10 is just such an example.

The pit

The dwelling pit was found in association with the Ertebølle layer and was partly covered by it. The pit was up to 3.2 m long and 2.4 m wide with a slightly irregular, oval outline and orientated N-S (Figure 32.4). The pit was cut by a trench to the east but this had only affected a minor part of the structure. The pit was dug up to 35 cm into the subsoil, which in the western part consisted of clay and in the eastern part of sand. The slopes of the pit were uniform and steep and the bottom was approximately flat. Along the edge, four stake-holes were found; these were probably traces of the wall construction. The stake-holes were 10–15 cm deep. Two of them had rounded bases, while the others were V-shaped in cross-section. Additional stake-holes may have been present, but later disturbed by ploughing or by the digging of the trench. As can be seen from section C-D (Figure 32.4), the northern stake-hole cuts the fill of the pit, which may indicate that the stake is later than the pit. However, the fill of the stake-hole indicated that the lower part of the stake had remained in place after the dwelling was abandoned. Possible later fill in the pit could therefore have built up against the stake.

The fill of the pit comprised dark grey, sandy soil of the same character as the culture layer elsewhere on the site. Some of the fill could possibly have originated from settlement activities after the dwelling was abandoned. One main task is therefore to determine at which level in the pit the actual occupation layer (or layers) can be found. In other words – which of the more than 11.000 artefacts found within the feature belong to the occupation phase of the dwelling and which do not, and is such a distinction possible?

Method of excavation

Before turning to the spatial analyses, it is necessary briefly to describe the method applied to the excavation of the pit. The fill was excavated in 5 cm thick horizontal layers respecting geologically discrete layers. In this way, six levels were excavated. At each level, the limits of the various layers were recorded as well as the positions of stones, larger animal bones etc. The finds from the separate levels were collected in squares of 1/4 m^2 and the fill was consistently dry-sieved.

Stratigraphy

If we turn our attention to the stratigraphic observations, it was clear that the composition of the fill changed from being rather homogenous to being more complex towards the middle levels of the excavation. Here there was an approximately 10 cm thick horizon, with the fill in the middle of the western part being clearly a darker grey due to a higher content of fragmented charcoal. At the same time, the amounts of both burned and unburned stones and animal bones increased markedly. An increase in the number of artefacts was also observed in these middle levels. These observations may indicate that we are dealing with the "floor-level" of the dwelling. One would expect the occupation layer to be found at the bottom of the pit as seen, for instance, in pit-houses from later prehistory, but this appears not to be the case here. The lower 10 cm of the fill consisted of lighter grey sand mixed with nodules of clay and containing a decreasing number of finds. Furthermore, two large stones embedded in the subsoil extended up into this basal layer. One would expect these to have been removed if the "floor-level" actually was situated at the bottom of the pit. More likely the light-coloured basal layer should be regarded as deliberate back-filling of the pit, eventually for the purpose of levelling or drainage.

Along the inside of the southern border of the pit, the culture layer was, to a considerable extent, mixed with light grey subsoil. This layer may be regarded as material which had fallen into the pit due to traffic through an entrance. An entrance here would have faced the shore-line, an orientation frequently observed in Mesolithic dwellings (e.g. Grøn 1995:57).

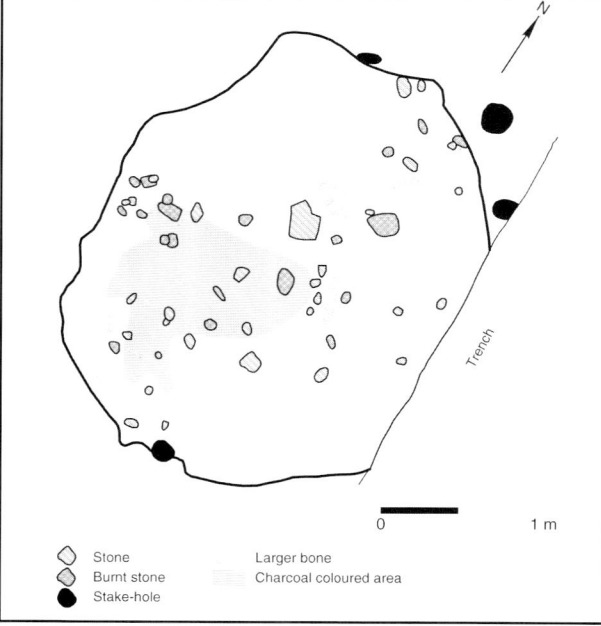

Figure 32.5 Plan of the supposed "floor level" of the sunken dwelling.

Figure 32.5 shows a plan of the dwelling with stones and larger animal bones from the 10 cm thick middle layer – the supposed "floor-level". The charcoal coloured area in the western part of the structure is indicated. This is coincident with the concentration of fire-shattered flint and most of the burnt stones were found in or close to this area. Without doubt it represents a fireplace. To the east of the fireplace a red deer antler and the unshed antlers of a roe deer were found.

As will become apparent, the previous interpretation of the structure as a sunken dwelling with a "floor-level" fits well with the spatial distribution of flint and animal bones. Thus, it is possible to divide the "floor-level" into different activity areas, in line with the activities expected to occur in a Mesolithic dwelling.

The spatial organisation

In order to obtain a picture of the interior spatial organisation, distribution plans for animal bones and the various categories of lithic material have been generated for each of the six excavated levels. In the following only a limited number of these plans are represented. However, the analyses show that the distributions in the two uppermost levels differ in general from the levels which supposedly represent the actual occupation of the dwelling. The distributions also differ in the lowermost level, the light-coloured "levelling-layer". Accordingly, only the three middle layers of the pit are presented in the following. Bioturbation has, of course, changed the original vertical position of many objects, so in this sense the distribution plans are incomplete.

The analyses of the spatial organisation began with the detection of the flint knapping area. To achieve this, the spatial distribution of small splinters, i.e. pieces of flint no larger than 10 mm, was mapped according to the methods described by Cziesla (1990:18 pp). Figure 32.6 shows the two upper levels of the "floor-horizon", levels 3 and 4. Here the main concentration lay in the easternmost part of the structure, to the east of the presumed entrance. A minor concentration is seen in the westernmost area. On figure 32.7A we see that the distribution in the lowermost of the levels, level 5, is quite similar to that of level 4. Mapping all three levels together generates the plan shown on figure 32.7B.

Flakes larger than 10 mm have a markedly different distribution. In levels 3 and 4, the main concentration lies in the western part of the structure, but there is also a clear scatter of flakes in the central and eastern parts (Figure 32.8). This distribution may very well indicate that the knapping area in the eastern part of the structure had, to some degree, been cleaned up. The lowest of the levels, level 5, shows a distribution of flakes which is very similar to the general distribution of small splinters (Figure 32.9A). If cleaning up of the knapping area did take place, one possible explanation for this distribution of flakes may be that those in the eastern part of level 5

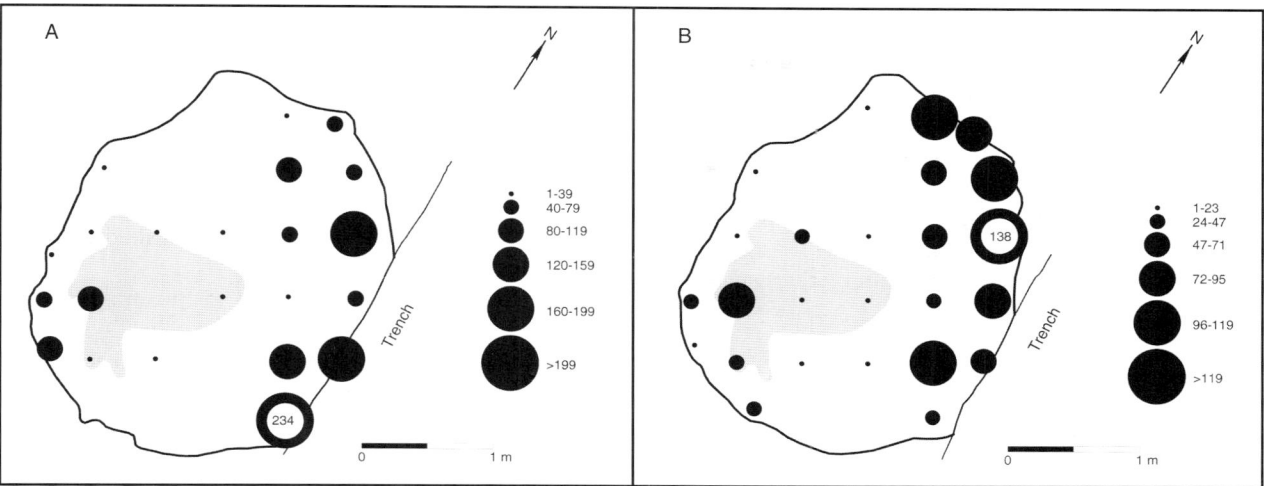

Figure 32.6 Distribution of flint splinters from excavation level 3 (A) and excavation level 4 (B). The number of splinters in the maximum quadrant is indicated separately.

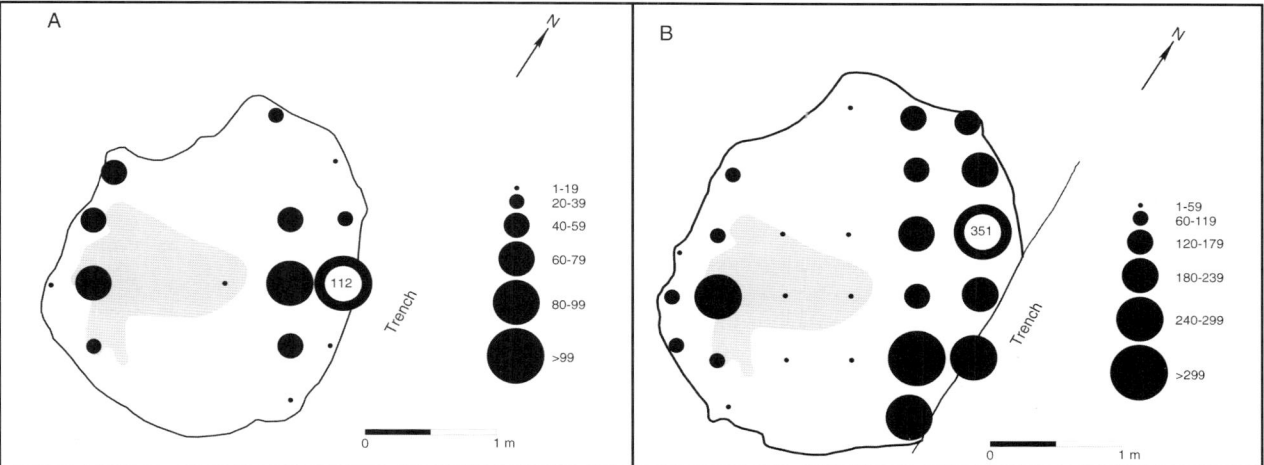

Figure 32.7 Distribution of flint splinters from excavation level 5 (A) and from excavation levels 3–5 concurrently (B).

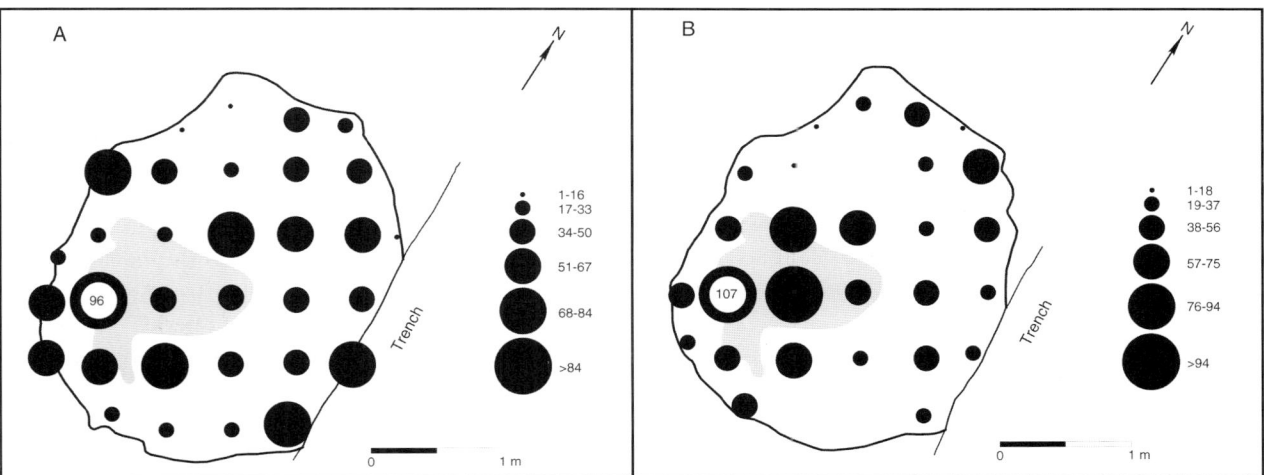

Figure 32.8 Distribution of flakes from excavation level 3 (A) and excavation level 4 (B).

represent, to some extent, pieces which were trampled into the floor layer and were thereby unaffected by any cleaning of the floor surface. Figure 32.9B shows the distribution of flakes for all three levels concurrently.

The cores and larger core fragments, 28 pieces in total, have a distribution almost identical to that of the flakes; only the eastern part of the structure shows a less dense concentration.

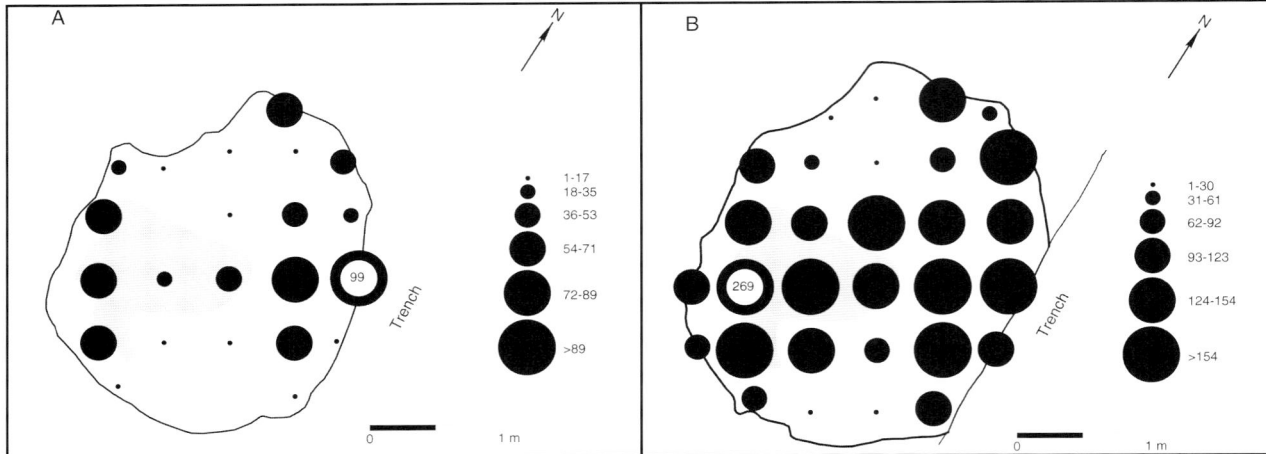

Figure 32.9 Distribution of flakes from excavation level 5 (A) and from excavation levels 3–5 concurrently (B).

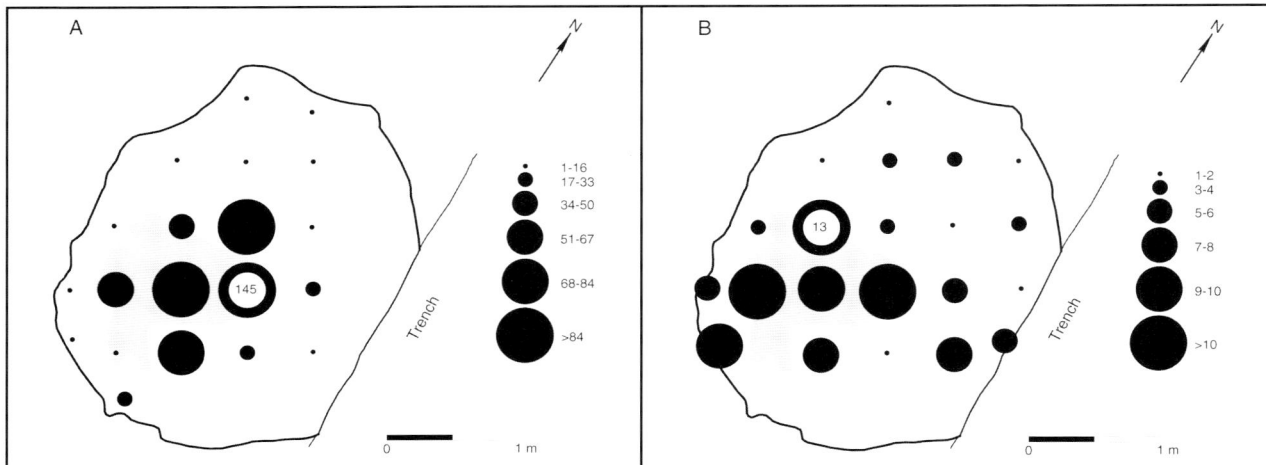

Figure 32.10 Distribution of animal bones from excavation levels 3–5 mapped as weight in grams per 1/4 m^2 (A) and distribution of unretouched blades, also from excavation level 3–5 (B).

The animal bones, mapped as weight in grams per ¼ m^2, are clearly concentrated close to the fireplace; this is the case for all three levels (Figure 32.10A). The bones total 817 pieces, primarily smaller fragments, which explains why the total weight is only 661gram. To this must be added the two large antlers previously mentioned. The species represented are red deer, roe deer, wild boar, birds (probably ducks), flatfish and codfish. This corresponds in general to the species composition found elsewhere on the site.

The unretouched blades, which total 98 pieces, are also concentrated around the fireplace and their distribution is to some degree similar to that of the animal bones (Figure 32.10B). This may indicate that many of the blades were used for the cutting of meat, but before use- and wear-analyses have been carried out, this cannot be confirmed.

The artefact assemblage, in the sense of "actual tools", totals only 30 pieces, comprising eight transverse arrowheads, six core axes, five backed blades and four truncated blades, two burins and a single blade borer. Two hammer stones and two bone points are also present. All of these artefacts, with the exception of the arrowheads, tend to be closely concentrated around the fireplace, or to the east of this, between the fireplace and the knapping area(s) (Figure 32.11A). This is also the case for the axe resharpening flakes and the burin spalls. The number of artefacts is too small to permit the detection of distinct activity areas of more limited size. The arrowheads show quite a different distribution, as they occur east or north of the fireplace (Figure 32.11B). However, unlike the other tool types, arrowheads were not as such part of the domestic activities taking place around the fireplace.

It is a characteristic of the distributions of stones, animal bones and flints that there are two small areas where there consistently are either no or very few finds; one area is in the north side, the other in the south side of the dwelling, where the entrance presumably was located. Perhaps these were cleaned-up areas in the dwelling used as sleeping quarters or for consumption of food or the like. A larger area along the eastern side of the pit also appears to be more-or-less free of large objects, except

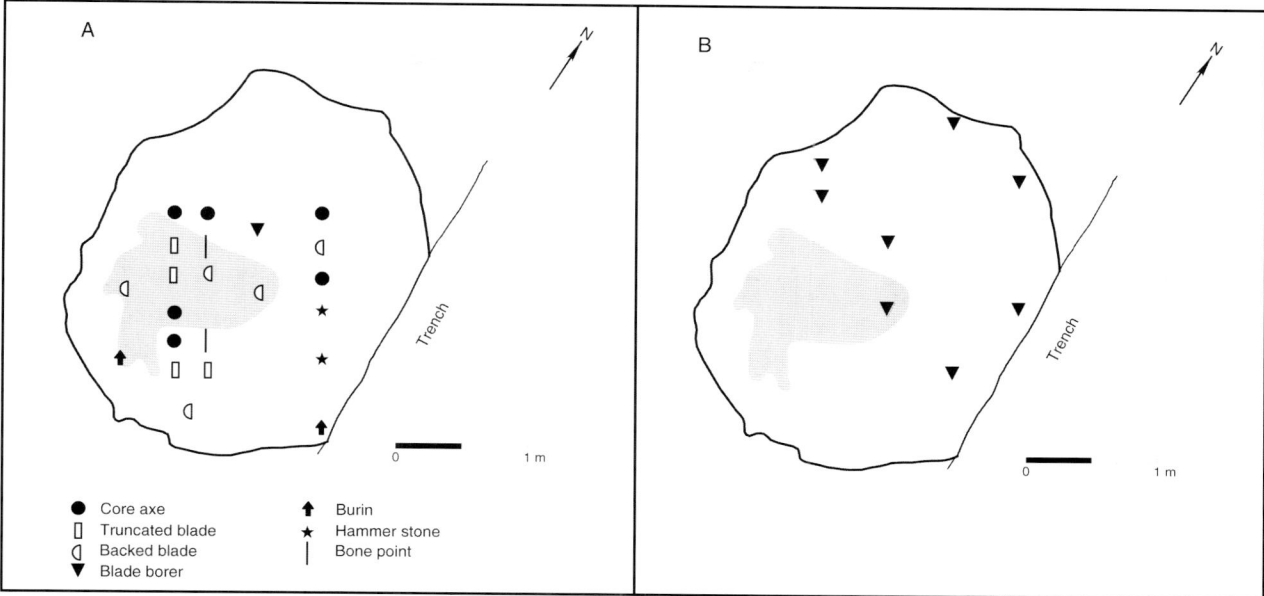

Figure 32.11 Distribution of "tools" from excavation levels 3–5 (A) and distribution of transverse arrowheads, also from excavation level 3–5 (B).

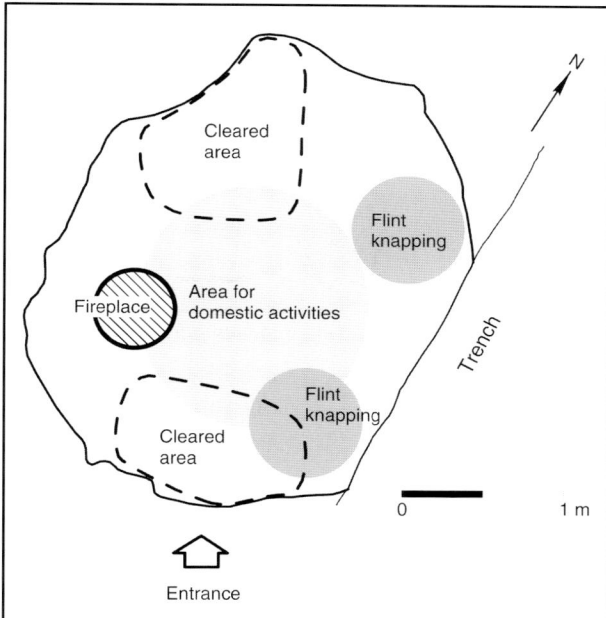

Figure 32.12 Plan of the proposed internal spatial organisation of the sunken dwelling.

for those possibly trampled into the "floor layer". Such maintenance of the floor could have been motivated by the occupant's use of this area only for flint knapping; although the area may also have been used for some other purposes.

Accordingly, it is now possible to outline the internal spatial organisation of the sunken dwelling excavated at Nivå (Figure 32.12). Some of the interpretations may appear debatable and more detailed analyses have yet to be carried out, for instance use- and wear-analyses and refitting. Similarly, further spatial analyses must in-corporate the layers and structures lying outside the dwelling.

Dating

Dating of the dwelling is based both on a typological dating of the artefacts from the fill and on a ^{14}C date. The types of transverse arrowheads and the hard hammer blade technology clearly date the dwelling to the Early Ertebølle Culture. A ^{14}C date for charcoal from the fireplace of 6000 BP (K-7116) supports this dating.

Parallels to the dwelling

A close parallel to the dwelling at Nivå 10 was excavated a few years earlier at Lollikhuse, also located in Northeastern Zealand (Sørensen 1995:19 pp). This dwelling, covered by a shell midden, comprised a shallow pit surrounded by postholes. The pit measured 5.5 x 4 m, thus covering an area three times larger than the Nivå pit. As at Nivå, a fireplace was located close to the western margin of the pit, but the Lollikhuse dwelling also contained an additional fireplace to the north. Unfortunately it has not yet been possible to identify a "floor-level" or occupation layer which would allow the interior spatial pattern to be studied in detail. However, apart from the size, many details of the construction are similar to those seen in the dwelling excavated at Nivå. In addition to the location of the stake-holes, a light-coloured basal layer is also characteristic of both dwellings. The dwelling at Lollikhuse is also dated to the Early Ertebølle period.

Finds of presumed sunken dwellings from beneath Ertebølle shell middens have also been recently reported from Western Denmark (Andersen 2000:37; Andersen, pers. comm.). Furthermore, a few sunken dwellings of

Kongemose and Ertebølle date have been found in Southern Sweden, but here the postholes are located *inside* the pit (Larsson 1975:5 pp, 1984:32, 1985:197 pp.). Recent excavations of Late Mesolithic settlements at the Nivå inlet itself have also yielded several large pits, of which some are surrounded by stake- or postholes. These structures, which are yet to be fully excavated, may be considered as sunken dwellings, and will be subjected to further research in the coming years.

Sunken dwellings are probably a common feature of Late Mesolithic sites in Southern Scandinavia, and they may very well represent the "type-house" of the Ertebølle culture. Clear examples of the interior spatial organisation are, however, still so uncommon that a valid comparison between the structures, and with it the drawing of valid conclusions, still cannot be carried out.

References

Andersen, S.H. 2000. Visborg. *Marinarkæologisk Nyhedsbrev fra Roskilde* 13, 36–37.

Cziesla, E. 1990. *Siedlungsdynamik auf steinzeitlichen Fundplätzen. Methodische Aspekte zur Analyse latenter Strukturen.* Studies in Modern Archaeology 2. Bonn.

Grøn, O. 1995. *The Maglemose Culture. The reconstruction of the social organisation of a mesolithic culture in Northern Europe.* BAR International Series 616.

Jensen, O.L. 2000. Nivå – gruber til liv og død. In: Hvass, S. (ed.) *Vor skjulte kulturarv. Arkæologien under overfladen*, 24–25. København.

Larsson, L. 1975. A Contribution to the Knowledge of Mesolithic Huts in Southern Scandinavia. *Meddelanden från Lunds universitets historiska museum*, 1973–1974, 5–28.

—— 1984. The Skateholm Project. A Late Mesolithic Settlement and Cemetery Complex at a Southern Swedish Bay. *Meddelanden från Lunds universitets historiska museum*, 1983–1984, New Series 5, 5–38.

—— 1985. Of House and Hearth. The Excavation, Interpretation and Reconstruction of a Late Mesolithic House. *Archaeology and Environment* 4. (In Honorem Evert Baudou), 197–209. Umeå.

Sørensen, S.A. 1995. Lollikhuse – a Dwelling Site under a Kitchen Midden. *Journal of Danish Archaeology* 11, 1992–1993, 19–29.

33. Some observations concerning the relationship between distribution patterns, floor size and social organisation

David Loeffler

The empirical base for this pilot study are two late Mesolithic semi-subterranean dwellings located in northern Sweden, one from Vuollerim which is affiliated with the quarts and slate tradition of northern Sweden and the other at Lillberget which belongs to the Finish Comb Ceramic tradition.

Independent cross cultural data is used to evaluate archaeological interpretations based on distribution patterns concerning social organisation as reflected in the division of floor space in response to family size and composition (one or two family dwellings) and functional or gender related work areas.

Introduction

If we accept the statement that houses are the physical manifestation of formal kinship relationships (Bodenhorn 1993:178) then one could assume that both floor size and its division (as represented by the distribution of features, artefacts and other cultural remains) might also reflect household size and composition as well as other types of social organisational factors such as the division of floor space based on either a functional or sexual division of labour.

This assumption is explored using the archaeological material from the floor area from two well preserved dwellings from the Late Mesolithic in combination with results from world wide comparative or cross cultural research (for a comprehensive discussion concerning the problems and possibilities confronting cross cultural research, see Ember 1991; Ember and Otterbein 1991; Ember *et al.* 1991; Ember and Ember 1995).

This paper will start with a presentation and analysis of the sites together with interpretations concerning distribution patterns and social organisation. These archaeological founded interpretations will then be compared and evaluated against independent data obtained from cross cultural studies.

Vuollerim–an archaeological presentation and interpretation

The site (Raä 1292, Jokkmokk Parish) is situated 13 kilometres S of the Arctic Circle between the Stora and Lilla Lule Rivers, 1 kilometre W of their present day confluence, on sandy soil with good drainage properties in a dry pine forest punctuated by peat bog deposits (Figures 33.1 and 33.2). With a distance of between 60–400 meters from each other are the remains of four semi-subterranean houses as well as numerous other traces of prehistoric activities which together cover an area of approximately 500x300 meters.

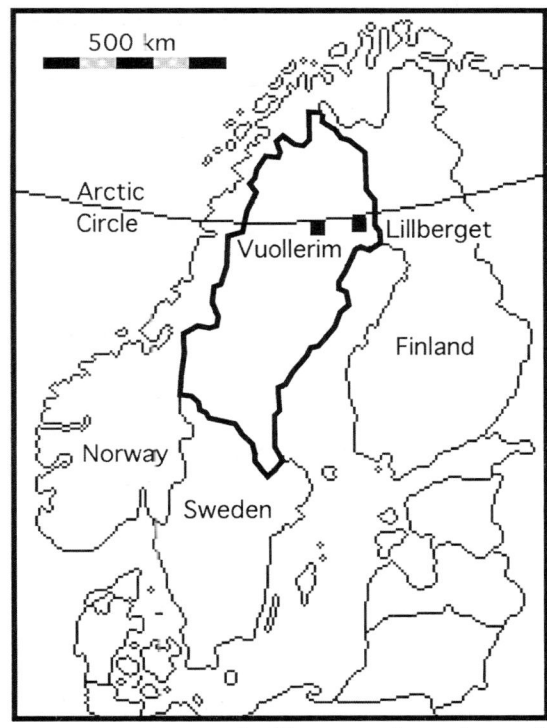

Figure 33.1 Vuollerim and Lillberget are located in northern Norrland. The boundary of Norrland is marked with a thick black line.

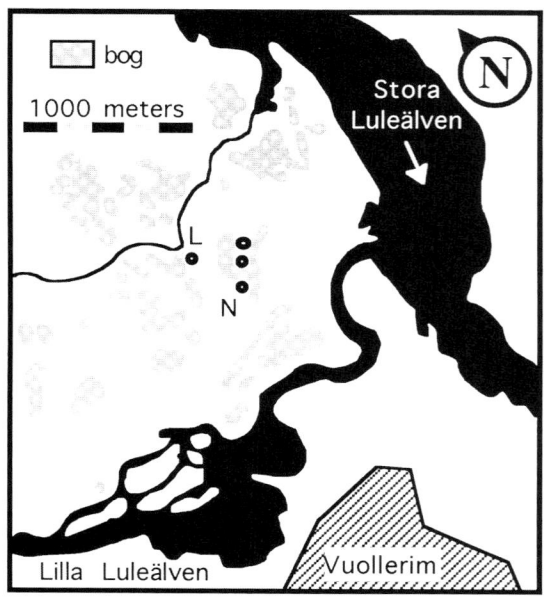

Figure 33.2 The four houses at the Vuollerim site. The dwellings Norpan 2 and Lasse's house are marked with N and L respectively.

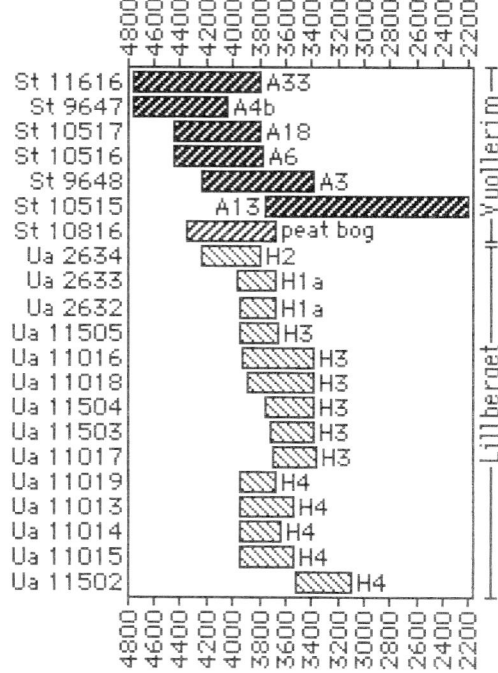

Figure 33.3 Calibrated 2 sigma C14 dates from Vuollerim and Lillberget (Stuiver et.al. 1998a). Dates from Norpan 2 include a rubbish pit (A3), storage pits (A13, 18 and 33), a hearth/cooking pit (A4a), a chimney like structure (A6) and the adjacent peat bog. H1a to H4 are dates from four of the houses at Lillberget.

At the time of the site's occupation the riverbed of the Lilla Lule River was situated ca 1 km N of its present channel, which means that the houses were located in a delta like landscape 5–20 meters from the waters edge.

On the surface all four houses appear as shallow depressions ca 12–19 meters long, 5–7 meters wide and 10–35 cm deep, surrounded by a low embankment ca 3–11 meters wide and 10–50 cm high. Two have been excavated, Norpan 2 completely, and Lasse's house partially.

So far only Norpan 2 has been C14 dated (Figure 33.3). The six dates span the period 4772–2207 cal BC 2 sigma (Stuiver *et al.* 1998). The date from feature A13 seems out of place. The sample was taken from a sooty layer which at first was conceived to be the remains of an internal component of this feature but might well belong to secondary filling of this storage pit and therefore not contemporary with its use. If such is the case the period of occupation would fall between 4772–3378 cal BC 2 sigma. This conclusion is supported by the C14 sample taken from the formative stage of the development of the adjacent peat bog, dated to 4348–3668 cal BC 2 sigma (Stuiver *et al.* 1998a). This peat bog was originally part of the river system that transversed the area at the time of occupation. This date indicates when the riverbed changed its course and might provides a clue to both why and when the site was abandoned.

At the present we do not know if any or all of the houses were contemporary. The discovery of a boot shaped knife of slate from Lasse's house, an artefact that is dated to the Early Neolithic (Eliasson and Joelsson 1989:38 p) would seem to indicate that these two houses could have been in use at the same time.

The floor area of Norpan 2 was 10.7–12 meters long and 4.2–4.7 meters wide. In and around the floor were a number of different features, the most predominate being cooking and/or hearth pits and storage pits. The storage pits were between 110–180 cm long, 80–145 cm wide and 35–60 cm deep. Three (A13, A14 and A33) were located in the western half of the floor area while one (A18) was found in the eastern half. Three cooking and/or hearth pits were found in the western half of the floor area. They measured between 54–69 cm long, 38–56 cm wide and 22–24 cm deep. The 8 cooking and/or hearth pits found in the eastern half of the house were 32–100 cm long, 24–44 cm wide and 15–42 cm deep. The filling consisted of either red to brown burnt material with soot and charcoal or brown-black sooty material with large amounts of charcoal. In all cases there was an abundance of burnt bones and fire-cracked stones in and around these features. One of these cooking/hearth pits (A8) was connected to a chimney like feature (A6), together they probably functioned as a small smoke curing device. Many of these features overlap each other, which would indicate that they were not all in use at the same time.

Immediately adjacent to and SW of the house was a round shallow depression, 2 meters in diameter and 5–10 cm deep which proved to be the remains of a small tent like structure (A23/27) which measured 3–3.8 meters in diameter and which contained relatively large amounts of red ochre. No traces of a hearth/cooking pit was found in this feature although a hearth pit (A9) which measured 130 cm long, 35–70 cm wide and 30 cm deep was found just 1.5 metes N of this floor area. Another tent like structure (A4a) was discovered just SE of the house. It was 4.5–5 meters long and 3.5–4 meters wide. Within this floor area the remains of one, possibly two, hearth/cooking pits (A4b and A10) were discovered, 44–65 cm long, 25–36 cm wide and 5–17 cm deep.

These three floor areas seem to be contemporary. The refitting of greenstone flakes found in the larger floor area with those found in the tent like feature A4a together with one C14 date clearly confirms this. The stratigraphical relationship between the tent like feature A23/27 and the larger floor area with its surrounding embankment is equivocal but would seem to indicate that this tent like feature was also in use at the same time as the other two floor areas (Loeffler 1998:87 pp).

Additional archaeological remains from the site as a whole consisted of ca 1600 litres of fire-cracked stones, large amounts of red ochre and ca 55 kg of burnt and unburnt bones. The bone material, which have yet to be properly analysed, seem to consist primarily of moose with smaller amounts of beaver, fish and birds. The 2349 stone artefacts and 38 131 flakes consist primarily of quartz (96.68%) with minor amounts of quartzite (0.41%), flint (0.14%), slate (0.56%), *strålstensskiffer* – a slate like greenstone (1.22%), sandstone (0.02%), *hälleflinta* – a fine grained acid igneous rock (0.07%), other unidentified rock materials (0.07%) and 1 flake of jasper. The most common artefact are the 975 scrapers of different types, followed by 734 scalar cores and 187 utilised flakes (Loeffler 1998).

Vuollerim appears to have many similarities with semi-subterrian dwellings (embankments of fire-cracked stone, Sw. *skärvstensvallar*) and related sites found scattered through out central Norrland. The types and frequencies of the stone materials and tool types, the presumed composition of the bone remains, the topographical location of the sites, their spatial relationship to other houses and other types of remains, the size of the floor area, the types and size's of the features found in and around the houses and sites are similar. The overall impression is that the houses at Vuollerim are affiliated with a cultural tradition which had its centre in central Norrland. This cultural tradition is distinguished by a technology based on quartz and slate with small amounts of greenstone accompanied by modest quantities of other imported stone materials, with settlements situated along the inland waterways and centred around permanent or semi-permanent base camps arranged into small villages with sparsely placed houses, characterised by a pronounced inland economy based on moose hunting, fishing and beaver trapping and a social organisation built up around a local group with long distance but presumably limited contacts with other areas and groups of people (Lundberg 1997:131; Loeffler 1998:101 pp; Loeffler 1999:102 p). Whether this affiliation is purely superficial, arising out of ecological, economic and/or technological similarities or is the result of deeper social and/or ideological interaction is unknown.

A spatial analysis of the different types of archaeological remains found on the large floor area of Norpan 2 shows a constantly reoccurring and persistent pattern (Figures 33.4 and 33.5). The spatial distribution of different tool types, flakes, the various lithic materials from which they are made, burnt bones, fire-cracked stones and red ochre all show two distinct concentrations of roughly equal proportions in the eastern and western half of the floor area. There are a few minor exceptions. For example, a majority of the slate (33 of 44) and *hälleflinta* (27 of 42) flakes are found in the western half of the house together with all 6 hammer stones, all 7 artefacts of flint, 7 of the 9 artefacts made out of *hälleflinta* and 6 out of 7 microblades, while greenstone flakes (177 of 188) and fragments of greenstone tools (133 of 142) are predominately found in the eastern half of the floor. These exceptions, although interesting, are both numerically and proportionately minor, the flakes from these three materials making up 0.7% and the artefacts 7% of their respective totals.

The number and types of features in the floor area are not as evenly distributed, but do not contradict the overall impression of a duel division of the floor area. In light of the archaeological evidence two explanations have been formulated which might explain this uniform spatial duality as revealed by the distribution of the different materials and features.

The first one is that the dwelling was inhabited by one household and the distribution pattern is either a result of the functional division of work space or a sexual division of labour resulting in the separation of the floor area into two different work spaces. If this were so then one would expect that different functional tasks or gender related work would require or involve dissimilar tool kits and/or features and would result in diverse accumulations in both the amount and types of features, tools and waste found distributed throughout the floor area .

The second explanation is that the dwelling was inhabited by two households, probably related, but with each procuring and providing basic necessities for its own members, with a certain amount of cooperation between households and possibly a certain amount of specialisation. In this case one would expect that both households required similar types and quantities of both tools and features and that this social arrangement would result in two clusters each containing comparable amounts of both types and frequencies of features, artefacts and waste with minor variations resulting from some degree of specialisation. One could also expect to find functional or gendered work related areas within each of the two households, and that this internal division would repeat itself in the distribution pattern within each household.

One could convincingly argue for a one household

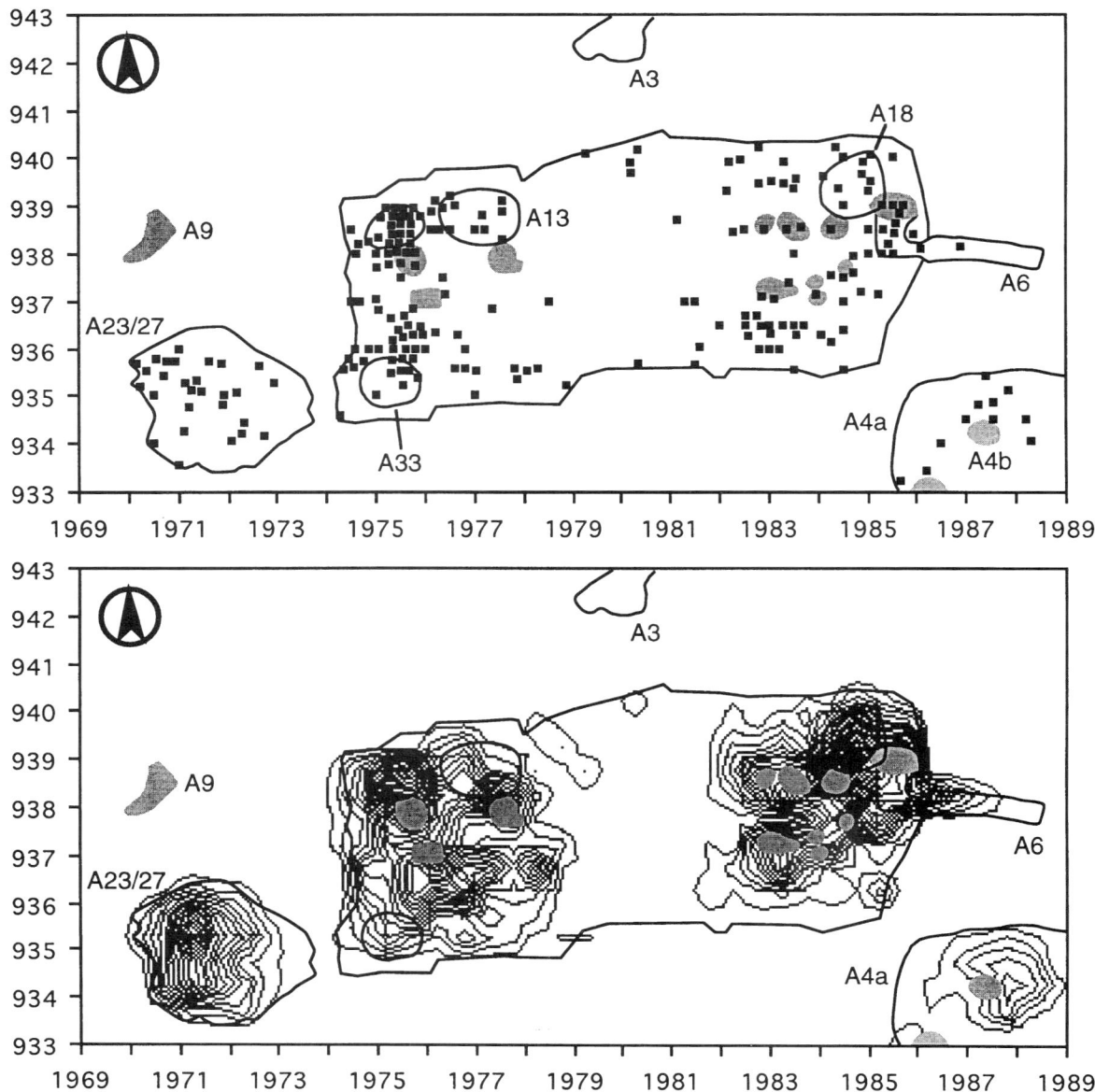

Figure 33.4 Norpan 2, Vuollerim. Spatial pattering of end scrapers (above) and quartz flakes (below), two examples of the reoccurring and uniform distribution of archaeological materials found on the floor area of the main dwelling and the two tent like structures. Hearths/cooking pits in grey hatching.

dwelling with either a functional or sexual division of labour based solely on the types, number and placement of the different features (Loeffler and Westfal 1985, 1986). This is not supported by the qualitative or quantitative distribution of different tools and waste materials. On the contrary, the distributions patterns of practically all tool and waste types would seem to support the two household explanation. There are exceptions but the distribution of these remains can be accounted for in the assumption that each of the two households would probably exhibit some degree of specialisation.

At this level of analysis gender specific activities or functionally prescribed work areas are not readily discernible. For the former this is partly due to the fact that we don't know what kinds of activities or which tools and waste products were gender specific, and in both cases any gender or functionally specific areas or activities that may have been carried out in the two half's of the floor area are inconspicuous in comparison to the vast majority of materials which constantly form dual distribution patterns. In any case, distinguishing between distribution patterns that are either the result of functional or gender related work, either within a one or two household dwelling, might be difficult or even impossible because the archaeological consequences of either of these two different social arrangements might well produce similar distribution patterns from which it would be difficult to choose.

	NW	NE	SW	SE	total
bones (grams)	2494/24.4%	3551/34.8%	2614/25.6%	1527/14.9%	10186/99.7%
fire cracked stones (liters)	84/21.9%	156/40.8%	83.1/21.7%	59.1/15.4%	382.2/99.8%
red ockre (counts)	91/22.9%	142/35.8%	86/21.7%	77/19.4%	396/9.8%
end scrapers	48/26.5%	47/25.9%	50/27.6%	36/19.8%	181/99.8%
side scrapers	11/24.4%	14/31.1%	10/22.2%	10/22.2%	45/99.9%
dubble scrapers	3/60%	1/20%	1/20%	0	5/100%
round scrapers	3/60%	0	2/40%	0	5/100%
frag. scrapers	16/35.5%	10/22.2%	13/28.8%	6/13.3%	45/99.8%
scraper blanks	11/25.5%	9/20.9%	15/34.8%	8/18.6%	43/99.8%
scalar cores	47/31.7	32/21.6%	43/29%	26/17.5%	148/99.8%
frag. scalar cores	28/26.9%	38/36.5%	19/18.2%	19/18.2%	104/99.8%
worked flakes	15/27.7%	23/42.5%	8/14.8%	8/14.8%	54/99.8%
micro blades	6/85.7%	1/14.3%	0	0	7/100%
points	0	2/40%	1/20%	2/40%	5/100%
whetstones	2/66.6%	1/33.5%	0	0	3/99.9%
hammerstones	5/83.3%	0	1/16.6%	0	6/99.9%
quartz artifacts	185/29.5%	184/29.3%	154/24.6%	103/16.4%	626/99.8%
quartz flakes	2252/25.1%	3073/34.3%	2418/27%	1202/13.4%	8945/99.8%
slate artefacts	8/28.5%	9/32.1%	7/25%	4/14.3%	28/99.9%
slate flakes	26/59%	7/15.9%	7/15.9%	4/9%	44/99.8%
hälleflinta artefacts	1/11.1%	2/22.2%	6/66.6%	0	9/99.9%
hälleflinta flakes	7/16.6%	1/2.3%	20/47.6%	14/33.3%	42/99.8%
flint artefacts	7/100%	0	0	0	7/100%
flint flakes	1/20%	2/40%	1/20%	1/20%	5/100%
greenstone artefacts	6/4.2%	110/77.4%	3/2.1%	23/16.2%	142/99.9%
greenstone flakes	6/3.2%	152/80.3%	5/2.6%	25/13.3%	188/99.9%
quartzite artefacts	1/100%	0	0	0	1/100%
quartzite flakes	10/29.4%	7/20.5%	8/23.5%	9/26.4%	34/99.8%
sandstone artefacts	1/33.3%	2/66.6%	0	0	3/99.9%

Figure 33.5 The numerical and proportional distribution of archaeological materials from the floor of Norpan 2, Vuollerim.

One can take the distribution analysis one step farther by sub-dividing the eastern and western halves of the house, breaking down the floor area from two into four areas, the NW, NE, SW and SE. The NW area contains the majority of the hammerstones, flint artefacts, microblades and slate flakes. The SW area contains a slight majority of tools and flakes of *hälleflinta*. A majority of the fragments of tools and flakes of greenstone are found in the NE area while the SE area shows slightly less proportions of all types of materials. At this level there is an inkling of differentiation which might represent a certain amount of specialisation between households, but the over all picture still remains the same even if details vary. Even at this level of analysis there seems to be no internal division of work space that repeats itself in each of the two household clusters which would could attribute to either functional or gender related causes.

The above analysis of the archaeological materials from the floor area would seem to indicate that the reoccurring distribution patterns are the result of activities carried out within a two household dwelling, each household occupying half of the house and utilising their own separate tent like construction, with each household carrying out similar activities and thus requiring and producing roughly equal amounts of both tools and waste with a certain, though minor degree, of specialisation.

Semi-subterranean houses in northern Sweden are primarily considered to be winter dwellings that functioned as either semi-permanent or permanent base camps (Lundberg 1997). This site, depending on how many of the four houses were occupied simultaneously, would therefore seem to represent a semi-permanent or permanent base camp for a local group consisting of either 4 or 8 households.

Lillberget-an archaeological presentation and interpretation

The Lillberget site (Raä 451, Överkalix Parish) lies about 18 km S of the Arctic Circle and 120 km E of Vuollerim (Figure 33.1). And like Vuollerim, it is the only site of its kind that has been documented and presented in any detail.

The Lillberget site lies on a gentle north slope composed of sand just above a bog at 58–64 m.a.s.l. At the time of occupation it was located near the beach on an island at the bottom of a fjord like formation about 35 km from the open sea.

There seems to be some doubt concerning how many semi-subterranean houses are present on the site (Figure 33.6). Halén has described ten while Färjare discounts house no. 4 and 9. In any case the houses are placed wall to wall in two groups. They vary in size from 3.5–13

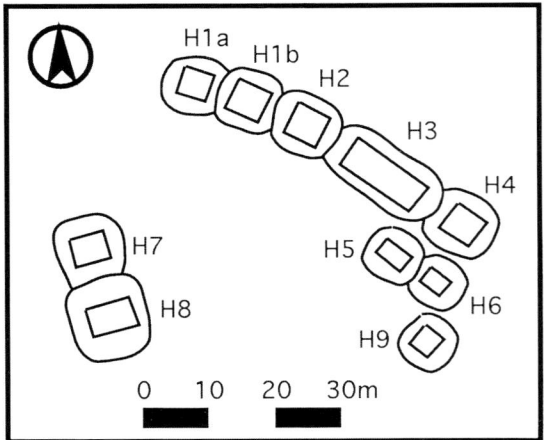

Figure 33.6 The ten houses at the Lillberget site. Adapted from Halén 1994.

meters long and 3.5–9.6 meters wide with the floor situated 40–60 cm below the surface of the ground. Each floor is surrounded by an embankment 2.5–3 meters wide and 40–60 cm high (Halén 1994:83 pp; Färjare 2000:11 pp).

The C14 dates, from both presumed and validated houses, range from 4246–3098 cal BC 2 sigma (Stuiver *et al.* 1998) and indicate that the dwellings could have been contemporary (Figure 33.3).

Three of the validated houses have been partly excavated (nos. 1a, 2 and 3) and one completely (no. 1b). Two hearths were found in each, located at opposite ends of the floor area. The hearths were rather large, being between 116–157 cm long, 57–124 cm wide and 5–25 cm deep, consisting of red burnt sand, burnt bones and charcoal but with only very small amounts of fire-cracked stones (Halén 1994; Färjare 2000).

At present the inventory of stone, ceramic and bone materials from only three houses is available (nos. 1a, 1b and 2). Quartz made up 79.5% of the stone material followed by flint with 11.7% and greenstone with 7.6%. The remaining 1.2% is made up of sandstone, slate, *hälleflinta*, quartzite and jasper. Ninety four tools of quartz were recovered: 65 scrapers, 12 blades, 10 cores, 5 drills, 1 knife and 1 transverse arrowhead. Of the 69 tools made from flint there were 33 scrapers, 14 bifacial (almond shaped) points, 13 blades and 2 transverse arrowheads. Nineteen tools of greenstone were recovered, 7 of these were axes or chisels and 4 were blades. Four scrapers and a number of flakes of red and green banded jasper were also found. One artefact of red slate was recovered, a small arrowhead with a wide tang and short straight barbs. In addition sixteen kilograms of Comb Ware ceramics were recovered (Halén 1994:99 pp).

An analysis of the 2106 grams of bone recovered these three houses shows that 81.1% were from different species of seal, 11.7% where either moose and/or reindeer and 4.1% where beaver (Halén 1994:164).

Additional material found at the site consists of a copper bead, stone fish hook sinkers, amber beads and pennants as well as small ceramic figurines or idols of both seal and humans. This material together with the relative abundance of both flint and jasper, the almond shaped bifacial arrowheads and the dating of the site would seem to place Lillberget within the Finnish Comb Ceramic tradition (Halén 1994; Färjare 2000).

The resulting distribution patterns from the spatial analysis of the archaeological materials from the floor area of house 1b shows some surprisingly similarities and contrasts to those from Vuollerim.

Once again we see that many of the different archaeological remains show a reoccurring and persistent dual pattern. The spatial distribution of the hearths, burnt bones, flakes/stone waste as well as tool types and ceramics, all show two distinct concentrations of roughly equal proportions in the eastern and western half of the floor area (Figures 33.7 and 33.8). The brunt bones are concentrated around the two hearths while flakes and stone waste together with stone tools and ceramics are distributed in roughly equal proportions between the eastern and western half of the house. This is similar to the pattern exhibited at Vuollerim and in like manner could be interpreted as resulting from a two household dwelling. The almost equal frequencies of materials present in the two half's of the house also indicates the absence of any pronounced specialisation between households.

When the analysis is taken a step further by subdividing the floor into four equal areas, the NW, NE, SW and SE, the resulting distribution pattern is quite revealing. The frequency of bone materials and flakes/stone waste show minor fluctuations in their spatial pattering but are more or less evenly distributed between the four areas. On the other hand both ceramics and scrapers, in roughly equal proportions, are found primarily within the NW and NE areas while cores, flint points and axes/chisels in more or less equal numbers are exclusively located in the SW and SE areas. The result from this analysis is consistent with the interpretation of the house as a two household dwelling, but it also clearly shows that there is a marked division of work space, not between households, but within each household which is practically identical. It remains to be explored if this division of work space is the result of a functional or sexual division of the floor area. At present there are no archaeological grounds on which to decide between these two explanations without arbitrarily assigning one or more of the archaeological remains as exclusively resulting from the activities of either men or women.

As in the case of Vuollerim the above analysis of the archaeological materials from this single floor area would seem to indicate that the reoccurring distribution patterns are the result of activities carried out within a two household dwelling, where each household carried out similar activities thus requiring and producing roughly equal amounts of both tools and waste. However, in contrast to Vuollerim, we can see that this entailed a high

	NW	NE	SW	SE	total
bone (g)	160/18.2%	300/34.1%	178/20.3%	241/27.4%	879/100%
ceramics (g)	1341/33.0%	2028/49.9%	211/5.2%	479/11.8%	4059/99.9%
stone waste (g)	1376/25.9%	751/14.1%	1765/33.2%	1417/26.7%	5309/99.9%
quartz scrapers	4/40.0%	4/40.0%	1/10.0%	1/10.0%	10/100%
flint scrapers	2/28.5%	3/42.8%	1/14.2	1/14.2	7/99.7%
flint points	0	0	2/50.0%	2/50.0%	4/100%
slate points	1/100%	0	0	0	1/100%
cores	0	0	2/66.6%	1/33.3%	3/99.9%
axes/chisels	0	0	1/25.0%	3/75.0%	4/100%

Figure 33.7 The numerical and proportional distribution of archaeological materials from the floor of house no. 1b at Lillberget.

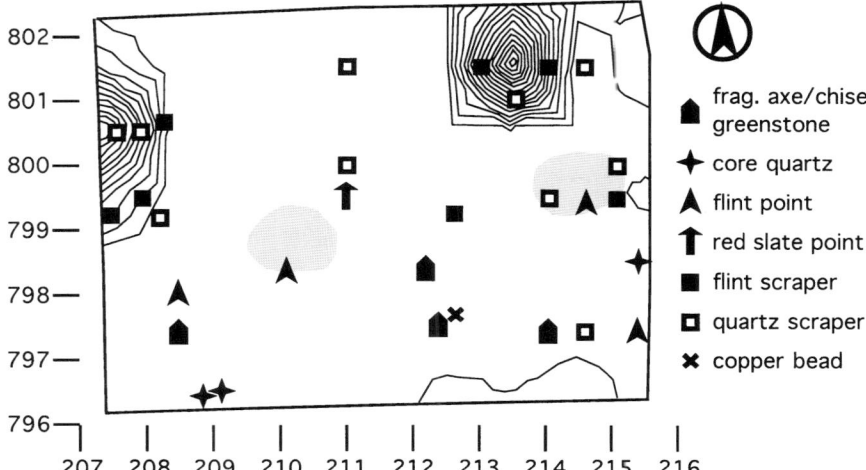

Figure 33.8 House 1b, Lillberget. Distribution of ceramics (isometric lines-71.4 gram interval) and artefacts on the floor area of house 1b at Lillberget. The two hearths are depicted in grey hatching.

degree of differentiation concerning the internal division and demarcation within each household in the use of the floor.

The site as a whole, depending on how many of the houses were occupied simultaneously, could represent a semi-permanent or permanent base camp for a local group consisting of 2 households per dwelling.

Cross Cultural Data-Floor and Population size

It would seem that the present archaeological analysis and resulting interpretations cannot be taken any further without additional and independent data from other sources. In this case cross cultural research concerning the relationship between floor and population size together with correlation's concerning the sexual division of labour will be employed in order to amend, illuminate or discredit the inference's drawn from the archaeological analysis.

Using a cross cultural ethnographic sample Naroll (1962) concluded that the relationship between settlement population and floor area is approximately 10 m^2 per person.

LeBlanc (1971) using a relatively small sample replicated Naroll's results but also pointed out that unless the sample is greatly increased the standard deviation of floor area in relationship to family size, which was rather large, will probably yield a poor indication of population size.

Wiessner's (1974) criticisms of Naroll's study summarise many of the problems encountered when using cross cultural comparisons. The first is that floor area may not represent population size if a group carries out many of their households tasks out of doors. The second problem follows from the first in that the remains of archaeological floor areas are difficult to estimate and concludes that the total settlement area might provide a more reliable measure of living space. A third aspect is that Naroll's constant did not take into account different settlement types with their corresponding differences in population density, such as short term hunter's sites or butchering stations. Wiessner also feels that Naroll did not account for cultural variation, that within one and the same culture interpersonal living space may vary (Wiessner 1974:343). Using the data from a number of Bushmen camps Wiessner presents an alternative model. Measurements of camp area include the entire settlement, which is defined as including the floor area of the huts, the major concentrations of material debris and the empty spaces between them. The resulting allometric model shows that area per person is 5.9 m^2 for camps with a population of

10 and that this increases to 10.2 m² for camps with a population of 25 people (Wiessner 1974:349).

In a restudy of population estimation from floor area Brown (1987) has provided comprehensive answers not only to the problems raised by Wiessner and others but also to problems of which he himself has noted from these and similar studies. Brown defines dwelling floor area as the roofed in area where the members of a household dwell and which is the typical dwelling of that culture or society (Brown 1987:12). From his cross cultural sample Brown arrives at a population estimation mean of 6.1 m² per person, which at a 95% confidence interval from one standard error gives a population mean of 4.7–7.5 m² per person (Brown 1987:31 pp). This estimation of population density is similar to both Naroll's, LeBlanc's and Wiessner's estimates as well of that of Casselberry (Brown 1987:32).

The cross-cultural studies concerning the correlation between floor and household size indicates that this relationship is not dependent on economic or social levels of development although Brown states that the results of his restudy are probably most appropriate when estimating the population of preindustrial and prehistoric cultures (Brown 1987:15). When calculating for floor area Brown not only measured that of the typical dwelling but also included, whenever possible, detached cookhouses, men's houses, adolescent dormitories, reception huts, porches and verandas. Not included were menstrual huts, sweat lodges, mortuary houses, sun shades, work huts, animal shelters and certain types of storage areas (Brown 1987:12).

The Population of Vuollerim

In light of the above one must make a decision whether to include or exclude the floor area of the two tent like features when calculating the total floor area for Norpan 2. To do this it would be helpful to know what they were used for. As seen above, one or possibly two hearths were found in feature A4a. It also contained, with few exceptions, the same types of archaeological remains (tool types, flakes, lithic materials, fire-cracked stones and possibly bone materials) as did the larger floor area. On the other hand no traces of a hearth were found in tent like feature 23/27. It also differed from the other floor areas and the site in general by the relatively large amounts of red ochre which where found within its boundaries. But like its companions it more or less contained the same types of archaeological remains that were found throughout the site. This does not answer the question concerning their function but one could hazard a guess that these two tent like structures do not fall into any of the categories that were excluded by Brown with the possible exception of having functioned as work huts. With these difficulties in mind they have never the less been included in the calculation for the total floor area of this site.

The floor area of Norpan 2 is about 51 m², while the two tent like features A4a and A23/27 had a floor area of about 18 m² for the former and 11.4 m² for the latter, which added together gives a living space of 80.4 m². Using Brown's constant one arrives at a population estimation of 13 people for the Norpan 2 site (Figure 33.9).

The floor area of Lasse's house is approximately 18 meters long and 5–7 meters wide or about 108 m2. This site is only partly excavated, so we do not know if this site contains any contemporary tent like structures. If not, then the population of this house would have been about 18 people.

At the present only the floor size of two of the four houses is known and we do not know if all four houses were contemporary. If only two houses were in use then the estimated population of the site would have been about 31 people divided into two groups composed of two households each with between 6–9 individuals in each household.

If we assume that the other two houses were also contemporary and that their floor area is similar to that of the excavated houses then the population of the site as a whole would have been somewhere in the vicinity of about 62 people.

The Population of Lillberget

We do not know the exact size of the floor areas of those houses which have not been excavated or are only partly sampled nor do we know if all of the houses were in use at the same time. Further more there is some doubt as to the authenticity of two of the houses, nos. 4 and 9. While Halén is convinced that they are houses, Färjare, who as excavated no. 4, is not (Halén 1994:93 pp; Färjare 2000).

If we assume that all features are contemporary and that they are either 8 or 10 in number then the total population of the site would have been either 48 or 53 people respectively (Figure 33.9).

The results from this analysis shows that the population estimate for some of the houses is so low that it is questionable if they functioned as two household dwellings or were even used as dwellings at all.

House no. 1a, 1b, 2, 3 and 8 would seem to clearly represent two household dwellings. This is either supported through the presence of two hearths in opposite sides of the dwelling and/or corroborated by the relative size of the estimated floor area. Together these five houses would represent a total population of 40 individuals.

House nos. 4, 5, 6, 7 and 9 seem too small to have functioned as two household dwellings. An alternative explanation is that they are either one household dwellings or served some other purpose equivalent to the tent like structures at Vuollerim and those noted by Brown, see above. Together they represent a population of between 8–13 people depending on whether or not one includes the two uncertain structures (nos. 4 and 9) as dwellings.

The houses seem to be structurally organised after size.

house no.	floor area m²	pop. estimate
Norpan 2	51.0	8.3
A4a	18.0	2.9
A23/27	11.4	1.8
Lasse's house	108.0	17.7
house 1a	44.3	7.2
house 1b	47.4	7.7
house 2	27.3	4.4
house 3	70.0	11.4
house 4	19.0	3.1
house 5	12.0	1.9
house 6	20.0	3.2
house 7	20.0	3.2
house 8	55.0	9.0
house 9	12.0	1.9

Figure 33.9 The known and estimated floor area of the houses at Vuollerim and Lillberget and the population estimate per house using Brown's constant.

With the exception of houses 7 and 8, all two dwelling houses are built wall to wall in a row while the smaller dwellings are grouped together in the SE area of the site.

In light of the above It would seem that we faced with two main alternatives. The first is that the site is composed of 5 two household dwellings together with 3–5 house like structures that functioned in some auxiliary capacity. In this case we are looking at 10 households organised into 5 two household dwellings where each household is made up of between 3–7 individuals.

The second alternative is that the site represents 5 two household dwellings in combination with 3–5 one household dwellings. In this case we are looking at 13–15 households organised into 5 two and 3–5 one household dwellings where each household is made up of between 2–6 individuals.

There is a third alternative. The one and two dwelling houses are not contemporary and not only represent different periods but two different social structures. It would seem that this impasse can only be resolved by further excavations.

Cross Cultural Data-Gendered Space

In accordance with Gero let us assume that half of all prehistoric populations consisted of women and that they actively engaged in various activities, including the making and using of stone tools and that women also were the active participants in household production and management. From this it is would follow that women's work, as represented by archaeological materials, would most likely be found and recognisable on the house floors located at base camps (Gero 1991:169 pp).

If we make a further assumption that both Vuollerim and Lillberget were base camps then one would be hopeful of finding evidence of gendered space in these dwellings. However, as we have already seen, the analysis of the distribution patterns from Vuollerim do not seem to support this assumption. Even though there are slight indications of occupational diversity within and between each of the two main household clusters, the overall and rather uniform distribution of the archaeological materials throughout the floor area makes it difficult to discern and delimit any functional and/or gender specific work areas which are duplicated in each of the two household clusters.

On the other hand, the results from Lillberget clearly show that within each of the two main household clusters there is a conspicuous demarcation in the use of the floor area as revealed by the distribution analysis. In each of these two household clusters we see similar amounts of ceramics and scrapers N of the hearths, with similar numbers of points, axes/chisels and cores S of the hearths while the bone and stone waste materials are more or less evenly distributed. The question remains if this is a result of a functional or gendered use of space. One could in part resolve this problem if one could, with any amount of probability, link any gender specific activities to one or more of the archaeological materials.

Murdock and Provost's (1973) cross cultural ethnographic study of 185 societies show that pottery production was not clearly linked to gender affiliation. The study did however show that there was a correlation between gender and pottery production in relationship to the level of economic and social complexity. Broadly speaking, in small scale societies where production is based on kinship, where there is no clear distinction between the domestic and public spheres of social life and where economic, social and political rolls are defined according to the participants life cycle or age, it is more likely that women are responsible for pottery production (Murdock and Provost 1973; Wright 1991).

If we accept that the societies under consideration here fall within the definition given above then one could conclude that the ceramics from Lillberget are gender specific and represent woman's work. From this one could argue that their distribution also represents separate and gender specific space with women situated N and men S of the hearths. If this is correct then one could further conclude from the distribution patterns of tools and stone waste that the majority of scrapers were made and used by women while the points, axes/chisels and cores were made and used by men. If one were to extent this line of reasoning one could speculate that many scrapers, from other northern Swedish sites, represent women's work. This in turn would entail, considering that scrapers are one of the most common tool types found on sites, that a large part of the archaeological record in this part of Sweden depicts women.

This chain of reasoning is highly speculative, based as it is on a number of highly tentative assumptions. Douglas Price (pers. com.) quite correctly points out that there may be a big difference between who makes something and who uses it. In other words, even if there is a sexual division of labour, does this automatically entail a differential, that is gendered, division of space? The answer to this is of course, no (Bodenhorn 1993). This brings us right back to were we started, we can clearly see that there is a division of work space within the two main household clusters at Lillberget but we can not determine with the data on hand if this is a result of a functional or gendered use of space.

Despite this present impasse it would seem feasible, with the further use of cross cultural data, to develop and advance a persuasive case that could support one of these two assumptions. This is a line of inquiry that will be more fully explored in a forthcoming paper.

Conclusions

The spatial patterns as reflected by the distribution of both features, artefacts and waste materials on the floor area's of both Norpan 2 and house 1b at Lillberget would seem to indicate that these dwellings were each occupied by two households. The estimation of population size is problematical. In this case households, not individuals, are of interest and therefore a fixed numerical value concerning the number of individuals that inhabited the sites is not essential. What is significant is that the archaeological interpretation is supported by independent cross cultural data concerning the relationship between floor and population size, showing that the floor area of both houses is large enough to have accommodated two households. It also indicates that the other 3 houses at Vuollerim and another 4 of the houses at Lillberget could have been inhabited by two households. It also clearly shows that the remaining 5 houses at Lillberget where not large enough to accommodate two households and that these may represent either one household dwellings or some type of auxiliary structures.

In the case of Vuollerim the spatial patterns shows that the two households used and produced relatively equal amounts of artefacts and waste. There are differences that indicate a certain amount of specialisation between households, but these are both numerically and proportionately minor. It is difficult to detect any discreet and reoccurring variations embedded within each of the two distribution or household clusters that could be attributed to a division of the floor area according to functional or gender division of labour. At this level of analysis the available cross cultural data did not provide any guidance concerning this question.

The spatial patterns exhibited on the floor area from house 1b at Lillberget, in contrast to those from Vuollerim, show a clearly marked and reoccurring variation embedded within each of the two main distribution or household clusters that might well be the result of a division of the floor area according to either a functional or gendered division of labour. The cross cultural data on hand was inadequate in that it could not provide conclusive grounds from which it would be possible to decide which of these two divergent organisational principles might have produced these patterns.

The method of employing independent cross cultural data to support or invalidate interpretations derived from archaeological data has met with mixed success. It none the less shows that this line of inquiry has potential and can be developed into a useful analytical tool.

References

Bodenhorn, B. 1993. Gendered Spaces, Public Places: Public and Private Revisited on the North Slope of Alaska. In: Bender, B. (ed.) *Landscape, Politics and Perspectives.*

Brown, B.M. 1987. Population Estimation from Floor Area: A Restudy of "Naroll's Constant". *Behavior Science Research* 21, 1–49.

Eliasson, L. and Joelsson, J. 1989. *Knivar och spetsar. En jämförande studie av skifferföremål från Västerbottens kust- och inland.* Unpublished paper from the Department of Archaeology. Umeå University.

Ember, M. 1991. The Logic of Comparative Research. *Behavior Science Research* 25, 143–153.

Ember, M. and Ember, C.R. 1995. Worldwide Cross-Cultural Studies and Their Relevance for Archaeology. *Journal of Archaeological Research* 3, 87–111.

Ember, M. and Otterbein, K.F. 1991. Sampling in Cross-Cultural Research. *Behavior Science Research* 25, 217–233.

Ember, C.R., Ross, M.H., Burton, M.L. and Bradley, C. 1991. Problems of Measurement in Cross-Cultural Research Using Secondary Data. *Behavior Science Research* 25, 187–215.

Färjare, A. 2000. *Variationer på ett tema. En studie av keramiska uttrycksformer och depositionsstruktur på den kamkeramiska boplatsen Lillberget.* C-uppsats i arkeologi, Umeå Universitet, Institutionen för arkeologi och samiska studier. Umeå.

Gero, J.M. 1991. Genderlithics: Women's Roles in Stone Tool Production. In: Gero, J.M. and Conkey, M.W. (eds.) *Engendering Archaeology. Women and Prehistory.*

Halén, O. 1994. *Sedentariness During the Stone Age of Northern Sweden.* Acta Archaeologica Lundensia. Series in 4:o. No. 20.

LeBlanc, S. 1971. An Addition to Naroll's Suggested Floor Area and Settlement Population Relationship. *American Antiquity* 36, 210–211.

Loeffler, D. 1998. *Arkeologisk Undersökning av Norpan 2 (J106A), Vuollerim, Raä 1292, Jokkmokks sn, Lappland, 1983–1987.* UMARK 13, del 1–8. Department of Archaeology, Umeå University. Umeå.

—— 1999. Vuollerim. Six Thousand and Fifteen Years Ago. *Current Swedish Archaeology* 7, 89–106.

Loeffler, D. and Westfal, U. 1985. A Well Preserved Stone Age Dwelling Site. Preliminary Presentation of the Investigations at Vuollerim, Lapland, Sweden. *Archaeology and Environment* 4, 425–434. Umeå.

—— 1986. En 6000-årig jägarbosättning. *Populär Arkeologi* 2, 12–14.

Lundberg, Å. 1997. *Vinterbyar. Ett bandsamhälles territorier i Norrlands inland 4500–2500 f.Kr.* Studia Archaeologica Universitatis Umensis 8.

Murdock, G.P. and Provost, C. 1973. Factors in the Division of Labour By Sex: A Cross-Cultural Analysis. *Ethnology* 12, 203–225.

Naroll, R. 1962. Floor area and settlement population. *American Antiquity* 27, 587–588.

Stuiver, M., Reimer, P.J., Bard, E., Beck, J.W., Burr, G.S., Hughen, K.A., Kromer, B., McCormac, F.G., v.d.Plicht, J. and Spurk, M. 1998. Calib. *Radiocarbon* 40, 1041–1083.

Wiessner, P. 1974. A Functional Estimation of Population from Floor Area. *American Antiquity* 39, 343–349.

Wright, R.P. 1991. Women's Labour and Pottery Production in Prehistory. In: Gero, J.M. and Conkey, M.W. (eds.) *Engendering Archaeology. Women and Prehistory.*

34. A recently discovered Mesolithic wet site at Riihimäki, South Finland

Heikki Matiskainen and Mikhail G. Zhilin

South of the Riihimäki city is a large bog basin, which was originally isolated from the Yoldia Sea. The basin was the source of the Vantaanjoki River discharging into the Gulf Finland. During the Stone Age the shores of this body of water, the river and the estuary were utilised and settled by the local population.

Archaeological research began in 1997 with the surveying of the site and with excavations in mineral soil sites in 1998 and 1999. The settlement dates to the Early and Late Mesolithic, Early and Late Comb Ware, and up to the end of the Bronze Age. Quartz artefacts and debitage were found in a field ditch beneath the organic layer in the turf. At this location a small trench was opened in 2000 to investigate the site. The data shows 1) that the lake had been transgressive on least tree occasions during the Holocene 2) and the artefacts (oblique-bladed quartz arrowhead, quartz scrapers, burins and striking debris) indicates the Litorina Mesolithic of the Finnish chronology.

The authors are collaborating in the study of Stone Age wet sites in Finland and the Upper Volga region in Russia. Investigations will continue during the following years.

Location, geology and the history of the basin

The City of Riihimäki is situated approximately 70 km north of Helsinki. Finland's present capital was established in the 16th century at the mouth of the Vantaanjoki River. The main branch of this river has its sources in small lakes to the south and east of Riihimäki. South of Riihimäki is a large sphagnum bog area known as Silmäkeneva through which the present-day Vantaanjoki River flows. The fringes of the bog have been cleared to create fields.

Riihimäki is located in an area between Finland's Salpausselkä I and II end moraine formations. The local soils consist of glacial clay as the fill of valleys, ablation moraines and minor glacial ridges: lengthwise moraines and de Geer annual moraines of short-term origin.

Silmäkeneva bog is a basin confined by such a short-term end moraine stage. According to diatom analysis by Professor Pentti Alhonen it was isolated from the Yoldia Sea during the latter's freshwater facies. The threshold elevation is ca. 84–85 metres above present sea level, and the Ancylus Lake transgression cannot be estimated to have reached this elevation in the 4–4.5 mm land-upheaval zone (Hyvärinen 1999:79 pp). The result was the formation of an ancient lake several square metres in area that remained an independent body of water until its paludification, which took place approximately after the beginning of the Common Era. The discharge threshold, the source of the Vantaanjoki River, remained in place unchanged, which means that the history of the lake was quite static.

The sedimentology of the lake consists lowermost of varved clay deposited on the moraine. The stratification of glacial clay came to an end around the time of isolation and a very thick, up to 6-metre, layer of clay gyttja accumulated during the Boreal and Atlantic period. The gyttja is overlaid by fine detritus gyttja, in turn covered by various limnothelmatic turfs that stratified during the paludification stage. The growth of sphagnum turf began approximately 1500 years ago and in places it is several metres thick, giving the site the nature of a raised Sphagnum bog. After the Second World War, the discharge threshold of the Vantaanjoki River has been deepened, the whole bog area was trenched and fields were cleared in its dried fringes. Extra land for developed was also thus obtained for the city.

The estuary of the Vantaanjoki River withdrew southward as the result of land uplift and shore displacement of the Baltic. At the time of the maximum elevation of the Ancylus Lake, the estuary was close to the lake's discharge threshold, but in the regression stage it withdrew to a distance of tens of kilometres. The eustatic Litorina transgression to some degree offset shore displacement, with the formation of rich complex of Comb Ware period sites in the Tikkurila area in the present-day City of Vantaa. During the Stone Age, the Vantaanjoki River formed a uniform social territory comparable to the postglacial prehistory of the Porvoonjoki River. (Matiskainen 1989b:55 pp).

Archaeological research at Silmäkeneva Bog

Silmäkeneva Bog is crossed by a group of islands consisting of transverse glacial moraines with sediments of stratified layers of sand and gravel as sediments. The archaeological survey conducted in 1997 focused on these islands and similar formations on the fringes of the basin. Evidence of approximately 15 dwelling sites was obtained.

Excavations were begun in 1998. The selected site proved to be Mesolithic but no precise date could be established. The quartz artefacts are most probably from the Early Mesolithic. The other excavation site (Arolammi 7 A) was chosen because of a concentration of finds on a moraine terrace extending into the bog layers near the discharge channel of the lake. The excavations were continued in 1999 and 2000, during which it could be observed that the terrace area was occupied during the Late Mesolithic, the early stage of Early Comb Ware (Comb Ware style I:2) and predominantly during the Late Comb Ware period (style III). There were also minor indications of Late Neolithic occupation.

A trial section (Arolammi 7 C) was excavated in the bog in front of the moraine terrace. The organic sediments at this location contained potsherds, a net float of pine bark, quartzes and a large number of stones that had disintegrated as the result of heating. Three samples were dated from the early Early Comb Ware level; the ceramic horizon gave the date 5330± 100 BP (GIN-10758), 4950 ± 150 BP (GIN-10759) and 5460±160 BP (GIN-10757). These dates broadly correspond to the known age of ceramics in Finland (cf. Asplund 1995:Fig.3).

During the summer of 2000 a larger excavation area was opened next to the trial section in the bog. Only a limited number of finds were obtained. The material here may be anthropogenic material deposited in the waters of the shore, possibly there by humans or washed there by the internal transgression of the lake.

It is an interesting fact that three transgression facies have been distinguished in the organic sediment. In the organic limnic or turf sediment they are distinguished as gyttja or even gyttja clay on the part of the uppermost transgression sediment. This phenomenon has been noted in several borings carried out in the shore zones of the lake. It has not yet been completely investigated to what degree the transgressions were caused by factors of climatic history or whether beaver colonies possibly damming the discharge channel could have caused the rises in water level.

Organic turf beneath the topmost thick gyttja clay was dated to 4460±210 BP (GIN-10760). In terms of the chronology of forest history this may attribute the transgression and the result accumulation of gyttja clay to the Sub-Atlantic climatic depression.

The refuse fauna from the mineral layer consists of fragments of burnt bone. Ms Pirkko Ukkonen, lic. phil., who carried out the osteological analyses, identifies the majority of fragments as fossils of elk, beaver and pike. Interestingly, the material includes a few fragments of pig bones and a bovine identified from a molar.

An interesting curiosity in terms of human subsistence is a layer of caltrop, or water chestnut *(Trapa natans* L.) discovered at a depth of approximately 20 metres in a bog field by the shore of the dwelling site. The layer is ca. 10–15 cm thick and possibly the richest fossil layer of its kind hitherto known in Finland. As an indicator of the post-glacial thermal maximum the water chestnut is dated to a period from the beginning of the Atlantic to the Sub-Atlantic. The southern boundary of this plant is currently in the South Baltic region. At the time of writing the connection of the water chestnut layer with the settlement horizon is still under investigation, above all with regard to possible explicit human exploitation or improvement of growth conditions. The layer is dated to 5360±120 BP (GIN-11035).

Arolammi 7D, a Mesolithic site

There is a drainage ditch at the edge of the mineral soil (forest zone) and the bog layer (field). Soil from the ditch initially revealed a few flakes of quartz, and in 1999 when the profile of the ditch was cleaned and prepared, quartzes were observed at a depth of roughly 80 cm beneath the surface of the field.

In 2000 a trial section measuring one metre by five metres was excavated at this location. The stratigraphy is as follows (see profile illustration):

1 Recent vegetation layer
2 Soil removed from the ditch
3 Brown peat
4 Grey-brown clayish gyttja
5 Brown lignosum peat, (lower part mixed with grey gyttja)
6 Coarse peat, mixed with sand and fine gravel and some boulders, (sandy stria between layers 5 and 6)
6a A mixture of peat with various forest products (bark, branches, pine cones, hazelnuts, etc)
7 Grey gyttja
8 Grey clay, with glacial varved clay at the bottom

The Mesolithic finds were in layers 6 and 6 a. They consisted of quartz artefacts and flakes, stones broken by heating and a piece of wood worked by man. The acidity of the sediment was measured at ca. pH 4.2 –4.5, which means that bone artefacts and bone refuse fauna cannot survive under these conditions.

An oblique-bladed quartz arrowhead is a datable artefact type; specimens were recovered in a trial section excavated in mineral soil above the trial trench opened in 1999 (Arolammi 7B) and in a mineral soil layer in the location Arolammi 7 A. In the Finnish material the oblique-bladed quartz arrowhead is dated to the Late Mesolithic (Luho 1948:5 pp). In the radiocarbon-dated shoreline displacement chronology of the Baltic, the zone

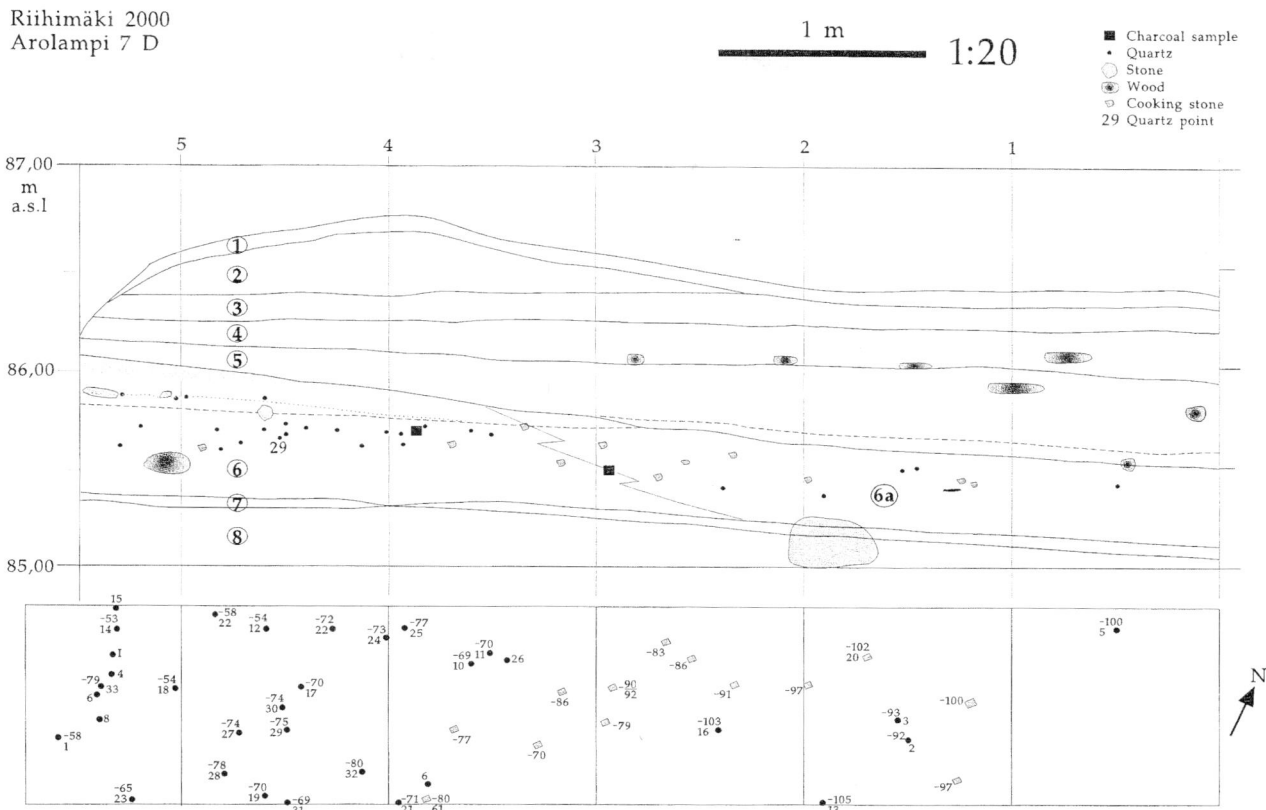

Figure 34.1 The profile of the trial section of the Mesolithic Site Arolammi 7 D, Riihimäki, South Finland.

of these finds is dated to the period 7700–6000 BP (Matiskainen 1986:91 p; 1989a:389).

Occupation layer 6 contained a large number of small pieces of charcoal. Two relatively large charred pieces of wood were selected for radiocarbon dating, which is believed to date the anthropogenic settlement horizon 6a as follows:

6630±70 (GIN-11042)   3rd sqm.   -75–80 cm
6050±40 (GIN-11037)   4th sqm.   -90 cm

The upper part of horizon 6 gave the date 5660+-60 (GIN-11038). The lowest horizon of layer 6 was dated to 7080+-120 (GIN-11039).

Arolammi 7D radiocarbon dates stays in good agreement with the previous shore-displacement chronology based dating of the oblique bladed quartz arrowheads in Finland: the end of the preceramic Litorina Mesolithic.

The quartzes (approximately 30 specimens) consist of a few scrapers, burins, cores and flaking debitage corresponding to material excavated from Mesolithic dwelling sites (Figure 34.1). There were no finds of ceramics. It is still unclear whether the uppermost quartzes were in situ in the sandy sediment of the upper part of layer 6 or whether they had been transported along with sand washed into the location by the transgression. The remainder of the material in the organic layer, however, was deposited through human action. The heated rocks were of such weight that any shore action that would have moved them would also have spread mineral sediments over a broader area in the finds layer, which in turn was not observed. The quartzes and other material were probably thrown from a higher location on the shore or were spread in the shallow water on the shore, or deposited in a drier stage through activities on the turf at the shore.

Figure 34.2 The Mesolithic Bog Site Arolammi 7 D. The find level is marked with white nails.

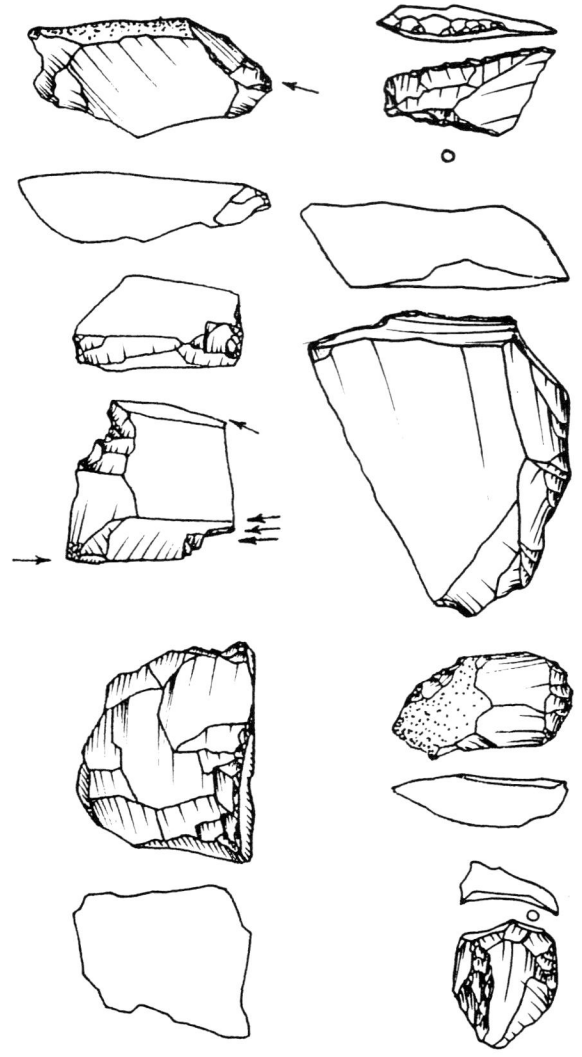

Figure 34.3 Quartz finds (obliqe arrowhead, scrapers, burin and core) of the Mesolithic Site Arolammi 7 D. Scale 1:1.

At a later stage, when the water level rose and the production of organic matter increased, the material was covered by limnic turf or detritus gyttja.

At the time of writing we must still rely on preliminary information and excavations will continued at the site in 2001 and 2002. Other dwelling sites dating from different periods of the Stone Age and covered with organic sediments have been discovered in the surroundings of the ancient lake of Silmäkeneva. Trial excavations and boring point to an interesting main feature in the settlement and the history of the lake. Owing to the rise of the surface the later sites of the ceramic period appear to be located in mineral soil at a higher shore elevation, while the Mesolithic quartz sites are at lower levels covered by organic sediments. This would suggest that the rise of the level of the lake would largely have taken place during the Sub-Boreal and with reference to the above gyttja clay date in more dramatic developments at the beginning of the Sub-Atlantic period.

Acknowledgements

The present study is part of the authors' broader project "Stone Age bog sites in Finland and Russia" which has received support from the Academy of Finland and the Russian Academy of Sciences. The excavations at Riihimäki have also received support over the course of several years from the EU fund. The authors wish to thank the multi-disciplinary experts who have participated in the project: Professor Pentti Alhonen and Pirkko Ukkonen, Lic. Phil., of the Department of Geology and Palaeontology of the University of Helsinki, Docent Terttu Lempiäinen of the Department of Botany of the University of Turku, Dr. Markku Mäkilä of the Geological Survey of Finland, Espoo, Mag. Phil. Kersti Kihno of the Estonian Academy of Sciences, Tallinn, Mag. Phil. Natalia Zaretskaya of the Russian Academy of Sciences, Moscow, MA Timo Jussila from "Microlith Ltd" and other participants and landowners. The English translation is by Jyri Kokkonen, MA.

References

Asplund, H. 1995. Radiocarbon Dating of Jäkärlä Ceramics – a Comment on Comb Ceramic Chronology and Typology. *Karhunhammas* 16. University of Turku, Dept. of Cultural Studies, Archaeology, 69–75.

Hyvärinen, H. 1999. Shore Displacement and stone Age Dwelling Sites near Helsinki, South Coast of Finland. In: Huurre, M. (ed.) *Dig it all.* Gummerus, 79–89. Jyväskylä.

Luho, V. 1948. Alajärven Kurejoen Rasin poikkiteräiset nuolenkärjet. *Suomen Museo LIV* 1947–1948, 5–22.

Matiskainen, H. 1986. Beiträge zur Kenntnisse der mesolithischen Schrägschneidepfeile und Mikrolithen aus Quarz. *Studia praehistorica fennica C F Meinander septuagenario decidata. Iskos* 6, 77–98.

—— 1989a. The Chronology of the Finnish Mesolithic. In: Bonsall, C. (ed.) *The Mesolithic in Europe. III Int. Mesolithic Symposium in Edinburgh 1985,* 379–390. Edinburgh.

—— 1989b. The Palaeoenvironment of Askola, Southern Finland. Mesolithic Settlement and Subsistence 10.000–6000 b.p. *Iskos* 8, 1–78

35. Liencres Revisited: the Significance of Spatial Patterning Revealed by Unconstrained Clustering

Christopher A. Papalas, Geoffrey A. Clark and Keith W. Kintigh

This paper re-examines spatial data from the open air Mesolithic site of Liencres, Spain using unconstrained clustering augmented by a procedure devised to assess the strength of patterning. Unconstrained clustering (UC) uses cluster analysis to group grid squares based on the similarity of artifactual contents rather than their spatial locations. The most readily interpretable results of UC come when the analysis reveals sets of spatially contiguous units with similar compositions. As traditionally applied, a significant weakness of the method is that it can be difficult to evaluate the strength of the spatial patterning. Here, we offer a Monte-Carlo technique that makes it possible to assess the strength of spatial patterning detected by unconstrained clustering. The technique is applied to reveal and interpret robust patterns in the spatial distribution of artifacts at Liencres.

Introduction

Spatial analysis can be viewed as a process of searching for behaviorally meaningful structure in spatial data (Kintigh and Ammerman 1982:31). Inasmuch as archeological data is intrinsically spatial, such pattern searches have been fundamental to archaeology since its inception. Many classic works by early archeologists had strong spatial components, usually involving the intuitive interpretation of distribution maps (e.g., Childe 1929; Adams 1974).

In the last few decades, there has been a growing interest in formal, mathematical methods of spatial analysis. This shift corresponds with our growing appreciation of the complexity of human behavior and with the quantity and precision of available archeological data. Although the human mind is adept at recognising spatial patterning, the complexity of some archaeological data defies intuitive interpretation. Formal methods can assist in untangling the intertwined behavioral and natural processes that produce the archeological record.

This paper uses a form of heuristic analysis to re-analyse spatial data from Liencres, an early Holocene site in Cantabrian Spain. The site represents a unique opportunity to examine the spatial organisation of a Mesolithic campsite. First, previous investigations of spatial patterning at Liencres will be reviewed. Next, Unconstrained clustering (UC) is used to explore the structure of the site. The results of this analysis are evaluated using Monte Carlo methods of probability estimation. The site is then interpreted and compared to archaeologically and ethnographically observed forager camps.

The Site of Liencres

Liencres is an open air site located on the coast west of the provincial capital of Santander and associated with the Asturian horizon of Cantabrian Spain. The immediate environs are characterised by heavily eroded limestone cliffs, stripped of vegetation by the action of wind and water. Sinkholes (*dolinas*) and other karstic phenomena are common. A survey of the area by Clark in 1969 revealed five aceramic lithic scatters in the process of being exposed by erosional processes. Four of these were characteristically Upper Paleolithic, but the fifth, called Liencres after a nearby town, was of Asturian affinity (Clark 1979a:249).

The Asturian is a relatively well-known Mesolithic assemblage characterised by a crude industry in quartzite and dated to the late Boreal and early Atlantic phases (Clark 1976; González-Morales 1982). Radiometric dates for the Asturian range from *c.* 9300 to *c.* 6500 BP (mean of 7 dates from 5 sites is 7817±223 BP) (Clark 1989:590). Liencres probably dates to the Boreal Period (rather than to the Atlantic), when a climate similar to that of today prevailed in the region. Pollen analysis at the site indicates a vegetational configuration similar to that of the present (Clark and Menéndez-Amor 1975:67 pp). Liencres is the only open site so far recorded for this horizon, and is located significantly east of the main concentration of Asturian sites. Perhaps most important, Liencres is the only Asturian site known to date that has a collection large enough for detailed analysis (Clark 1979a:251 p).

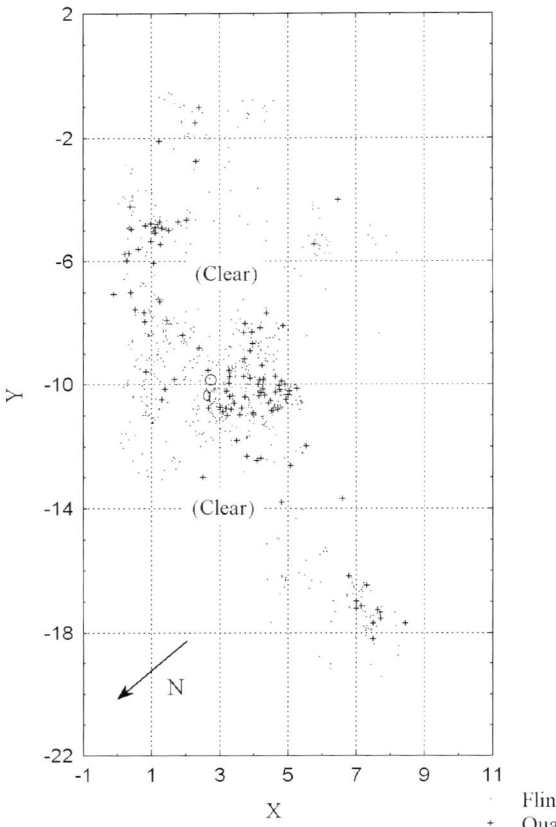

Figure 35.1 Liencres artifact locations.

of hypothetical functions for the stone tools and the materials they were used to work is also presented for heuristic purposes.

The distribution of all artifacts is given in figure 35.1, in which quartzite and flint have been differentiated. The quartzite boulders are depicted as open circles. It is evident that most of the artifacts are concentrated to the west of the quartzite boulders, almost as if someone had been sitting on them while knapping (Clark 1979a:263). Three smaller spatial clusters of artifacts are located east of the main concentration, in the upper portion of the map. Two conspicuous areas almost devoid of artifacts exist, centering at about X = 3, Y = -6 and southwest of X = 4, Y = -13. If Liencres is similar to many ethnographically observed camps, these areas might have been kept clear intentionally for the purposes of sleeping or resting and may even have been the locations of ephemeral structures.

Spatial Patterning at Liencres

It was immediately clear that the debris were highly structured, and numerous spatial analyses of the site contents have been conducted to elucidate that structure (Clark 1979a, 1979b). Clark's initial approach was to produce separate maps of different artifact classes, so that their distributions across the site could be compared visually. Although quartzite debris had a somewhat restricted distribution, flint and quartzite seem to have been knapped in spatially congruent or at least heavily overlapping areas. It also appeared that the secondary retouching of flint artifacts (resulting in tiny trimming flakes) was confined to the central portion of the site surrounding the cleared areas (Clark 1979a:263 pp).

Clark's next goal was to measure the degree of spatial aggregation within artifact classes, because he wanted to know if particular types were clustered. For this purpose, the Nearest Neighbour (NN) statistic was used to measure the spatial aggregation within artifact types. A complete description of this often useful but always problematic technique can be found in Blankholm (1991), Clark (1979a, 1979b), and Kintigh (1990). It was found that when, considered individually, many of the artifact classes under consideration were *not* strongly "clustered" in a way detectable by NN. Other artifact classes did exhibit degrees of spatial clustering, but the results were somewhat difficult to interpret.

After completing the conventional application of NN, Clark used various significance tests to evaluate the spatial association (or co-occurrence) between pairs of artifact types in a procedure first suggested by Whallon (1974). This procedure is somewhat complex, and space prevents a summary here. Strong associations between individual artifact types indicated three kinds of "tool kits" at Liencres. These are primary and secondary tool manufacture, light cutting, slicing, and shaving of animal and vegetal matter, and core preparation and primary manu-

When discovered in 1969, the site consisted of a scatter of lithic debris dispersed around the eastern edge of a large *dolina* situated on a rocky spine above an inlet. Surface materials consisted of quartzite and flint waste. Retouched flint tools, blades and bladelets were also common. Four large quartzite picks characteristic of the Asturian were also evident, and it is partly upon these that the association of the site with the Asturian horizon rests. Also noteworthy was a massive overturned quartzite grinding slab and a quartzite boulder in the middle of the site, both surrounded by chipping debris (Clark 1979a:250 p). The density of debris and the apparent lack of features suggest an occupation of short duration, possibly only a few days and probably for the specific purpose of exploiting the deposits of flint nearby (Clark 1979a:266).

The maximum surface scatter covered an area some 9 meters wide by 20 meters long, small enough for a sample approaching 100% to be collected. Although very sparse and sporadic, artifacts did occur up to 10 meters outside this area, these were of uncertain context and were not plotted on the final distribution maps (Clark 1979a:252). A total of 1,046 artifacts were recovered from the surface of the site. Of these, 249 were of uncertain context, were not plotted on the final distribution maps, and are thus not considered here. A list of all artifact types analysed in this paper with counts is presented in figure 35.2. A list

Type (Qz. = Quartzite)	n	Process	Raw Material	Hammer	Core Prep	Debris	Sec. Manufacture	Retouch	Cutting	Piercing	Sawing	Scraping	Stone	Nuts/Seeds	Wood, Antler/Bone	Vegetal Matter	Flesh	Hides	Other Uses
Flint core	15	Primary	X	X															
Qz. core	6	Primary	X	X															
Qz. lg. cobble	3	Primary	X	X															
Qz. sm. cobble	9	Primary	X	X									X	X					
Qz. split cobbble	14	Primary	X	X									X	X					
Flint core reduction flake	5	Primary			X	X													
Flint decort. flake	264	Primary			X				X						X	X	X	X	
Flint trimming flake	92	Secondary				X	X	X											
Qz. trimming flake	19	Secondary				X	X	X											
Flint flake	209	Secondary				X		X							X	X	X		
Qz. flake	68	Secondary				X		X							X	X	X		
Flint blade	48	Secondary				X		X							X	X	X		
Flint knife	3	Tool						X							X	X	X		
Flint perforator	8	Tool							X						X			X	
Flint bec	4	Tool							X						X				
Flint denticulate	6	Tool								X					X	X			
Flint burin	8	Tool									X				X				
Flint notch	4	Tool									X				X				Shaft straightening
Flint endscaper	7	Tool									X				X				Expended cores?
Qz. Pick	3	Tool	X												X				Digging
Flint point	2	Tool															X		Hunting

Figure 35.2 Summary of the artifact classes recovered from Liencres.

facturing activities (Clark 1979a:136). Tool manufacture, edge renewal, and core preparation were confined mainly to the southeastern (upper left) portion of the site, whereas cutting, slicing and shaving activities were primarily found in the center of the site (Clark 1979b:139).

Although Clark's work gives us some ideas as to which activities or artifact classes were associated, it would be helpful to apply other methods to clarify or refine this interpretation. Given the complex nature of artifact distributions at Liencres, a simplified description of the site revealing what was happening where without becoming lost in incomprehensible detail would be highly desirable. For this purpose, the approach known as Unconstrained Clustering was used (Whallon 1984).

Unconstrained Cluster Analysis

Unconstrained clustering is more of an analytical strategy than a specific technique, as it offers many options at each stage of analysis (Gregg *et al.* 1991). First developed by Whallon (1984), the approach was designed to be more congruent with the kinds of questions archeologists ask than more traditional techniques. It was explicitly developed to focus on the patterns of joint distributions of different materials and is free from consideration of cluster shape, size and density.

The first step of Whallon's UC is to accumulate smoothed compositional data (a vector of proportions of artifact classes) from the vicinity of each data point or, alternately, from even intervals across the site surface. These compositional data associated with the particular locations are then clustered with no consideration given to the locational information. Thus, the composition (i.e. type proportions) of artifacts for a particular spot is what is being clustered, and the analysis is "unconstrained" by any previous notions of cluster size or shape.

UC has been described as "probably the fastest, cheapest, and most elegant way of displaying the general nature of a spatial distribution" (Blankholm 1991:78), but it does have weaknesses. Although it is successful at revealing compositions, individual activities (represented by individual tools) are tough to spot (Blankholm 1991:87). At Liencres, where many artifact types are involved, this would be difficult in any case. Another weakness of Unconstrained clustering is that it is unable to distinguish overlapping activity areas. In these situations, the overlapping areas are assigned to a new "mixed" cluster (Blankholm 1991:76 p). By the very act of distinction, all cluster analyses mask similarities between clusters and hide differences within them, a feature they share with language itself.

Sampling and Data Preparation

UC is highly compatible with both the nature of data at Liencres and the questions we wish to ask of them. Before raw data are analysed, however, they must be "filtered" to remove unusual or extreme situations which will dominate subsequent analyses and obscure more subtle differences. This always entails a loss of data and the procedure must be tailored to specific archeological data sets and the questions being asked of them. Thus, it cannot be automated, although automation allows the rapid comparison of different filtering procedures. Filtering is usually a mixture of guesswork and experimentation and represents the most serious weakness in human analytical processes (Kintigh and Ammerman 1982:34).

Infrequent artifact classes can inordinately dominate many statistical analyses, and must be removed from the data to obtain robust results. Because there are no hard and fast rules for doing this, two different ad hoc rules were used here. In the first, all artifact classes with fewer than 3 objects were omitted. In the second approach, all artifact classes with frequencies less than 8 were omitted following Clark (1979). Although subsequent analyses were run on both data sets, the latter (all types < 8 occurrences omitted) gave the most interpretable results. It can be seen from figure 35.2 that this entailed the elimination of most classes of formal, retouched tools. Although the loss of data is always regrettable, this is a blessing in disguise. As Johnson persuasively argues, "we are more likely to obtain information about the spatial distribution of activities from waste products or expediently used tools than from tools that have been curated and used for a number of activities" (Johnson 1984:78).

On Grid Counts and Moving Templates

Before UC can begin, it is necessary to accumulate smoothed compositional data from across the site. Whallon (1984) originally advocated a "moving template" technique to smooth the data. Briefly, the technique moves a circular template from point to point, recording the local artifact composition (within a pre-set radius) for each point as percentages. Although the technique does smooth data, it can do so in a biased fashion. Some artifacts may count more than others in the density calculations. In a sparse area, this can have significant (and probably unpredictable) autocorrelative effects (Kintigh 1990:191).

While grid based approaches do entail some "blurring" of the data by the imposition of an arbitrary grid, it does remove these autocorrelative effects and is easily interpretable due to its simplicity (Kintigh 1990:196). As Blankholm puts it, "in most cases smoothing based on grid counts is to be preferred, both for clarity and simplicity" (1991:78). In grid analyses the contents of individual grid squares are statistically independent of each other, an enormous advantage. It will be argued that this property can be fruitfully exploited to evaluate the strength of clustering results.

The site was divided into a 1x1 meter grid, and the composition of each grid square was expressed as percentages. This was done in order to remove effects associated with artifact density. Some grid squares (especially those around the edges) had very low artifact counts. Because individual artifacts found in these low count squares were responsible for very high percentages relative to the other squares, they tended to dominate all subsequent analyses. Low densities are a ubiquitous problem in UC with two acceptable solutions. It is possible to increase the grid square size, but this entails a loss of resolution. It is also possible to exclude units below some threshold of counts per unit. The researcher is thus confronted with a three way trade-off between resolution, comprehensiveness, and robustness of results (Kintigh 1990:192). Because the size of the site and its potential for high-resolution results, it was decided to implement a density threshold. After some examination of the site maps and considerable experimentation, a minimum of 5 objects per grid square gave the most interpretable results.

K-Means Nonhierarchical Clustering

The next step was to cluster the grid square compositions using a clustering technique. Because the emphasis of unconstrained clustering is homogeneity of cluster composition, methods that minimise the sum of squared errors (SSE) and operate on Euclidean distances are appropriate. Whallon (1984) suggests Ward's Method, but k-means (Kintigh and Ammerman 1982) should work equally well or better for these purposes, and should usually give similar results (Blankholm 1991:81).

K-means analysis has the advantage of being intuitive and easy to understand because it is congruent with what our notions of what "clusters" are. The k-means program is a nonhierarchical divisive cluster analysis which attempts to minimise differences between members of the same cluster while maximising the differences between cluster centers. Mathematically, this entails trying to minimise the Euclidean distance from each point in a cluster to the cluster center, while maximising distances between clusters. In three or more dimensions, ideal clusters would appear as spherical concentrations of points. For a full discussion of k-means see Kintigh (1990) and Kintigh and Ammerman (1982).

K-means is a heuristic approach in that the appropriate clustering level (number of clusters) must generally be selected by the analyst from several choices. One reasonable way to proceed is to measure the distance from each point to the center of the cluster to which it is assigned, square these distances, and then add them together. This measure represents the global error of that clustering level and is called the sum of squared errors (SSE). Although the SSE must decrease as the number of clusters increases, clustering levels where the SSE lowers dramatically are good candidates. In the case of Liencres, no clear inflections existed and an alternative approach was used.

Departures from randomised data are another helpful way to select the best clustering level. If the points under consideration are well clustered, the SSE of the actual data decreases much more rapidly than that of the randomised data (Kintigh and Ammerman 1982:46). Figure 35.3 shows the difference between randomised and actual data for the site of Liencres for 250 random runs. As can be clearly seen, this difference is greatest at the nine cluster level. Other clustering levels were

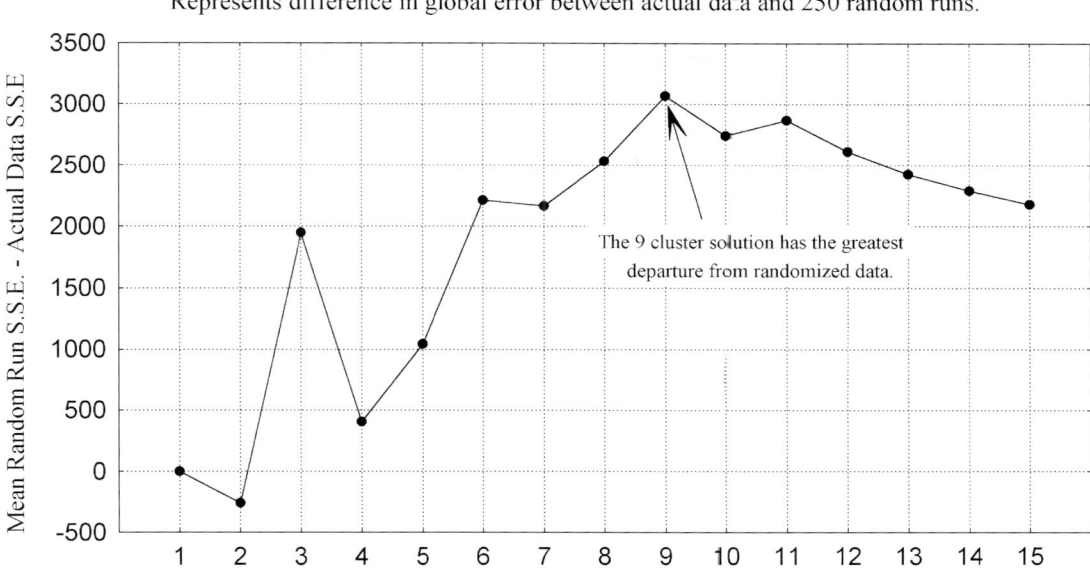

Represents difference in global error between actual data and 250 random runs.
Mean Random Run S.S.E. - Actual Data S.S.E
3500
3000
2500
2000
1500
1000
500
0
-500
1 2 3 4 5 6 7 8 9 10 11 12 13 14 15
The 9 cluster solution has the greatest departure from randomized data.
Clustering Stage (Number of Clusters)

Figure 35.3 K-Means sum of squared errors difference plot.

Cluster compositons are expressed in average percentages

		Primary Manufacture				**Secondary Manufacture**				**Tools**		
Cluster	N	**Fl. Core**	**Qz. Sm. cobble**	**Qz. split cobble**	**Fl. decort. flake**	**Qz. trim. flake**	**Fl. trim. flake**	**Fl. flake**	**Qz. flake**	**Fl. blade**	**Fl. perforator**	**Fl. burin**
1	10	0.86	**1.6**	1.17	50.27	0.77	8.71	27.26	2.68	2.08	1.33	**3.27**
2	2	0	0	0	0	0	**58.33**	41.67	0	0	0	0
3	8	0.51	0.23	**3.03**	22.81	4.58	15.79	27.45	17.96	6.41	0.23	0.99
4	*1*	*0*	*0*	*0*	*16.67*	*0*	*0*	*16.67*	*0*	*50*	*0*	*16.67*
5	3	4.44	0	2.78	41.67	**5**	0	10	**33.33**	0	**2.78**	0
6	*1*	*14.29*	*0*	*0*	*0*	*28.57*	*0*	*28.57*	*14.29*	*0*	*0*	*14.29*
7	4	0	1.32	0	32.06	1.32	37.89	10.13	6.67	10.61	0	0
8	9	0.62	0	1.83	28.71	1.23	10.38	**42.98**	1.53	**11.76**	0.65	0.3
9	5	**10.86**	0	2.86	**60.19**	2.86	6.19	8.86	0	8.19	0	0

Clusters 4, 6 Italicized (not discussed)
Column Highs Bold
Row Highs Underlined

Figure 35.4 K-Means cluster compositions, 9 cluster solution.

considered, but the nine cluster solution gave the best compromise between resolution and interpretability.

The locations of grid squares are presented in figure 35.5, and the cluster compositions are presented in figure 35.4. Many other procedures gave roughly similar results, suggesting that this solution was detecting robust patterning in the data. There are two clusters which only occur once each – clusters 4 and 6. Examination of these grid squares revealed that they had very low counts (5 and 7, respectively). Their compositions are presented in figure 35.4, but they are dropped from subsequent analysis.

Contiguity and Interpretability

There is no straightforward way to evaluate the statistical significance of clustering results. Unlike some methods,

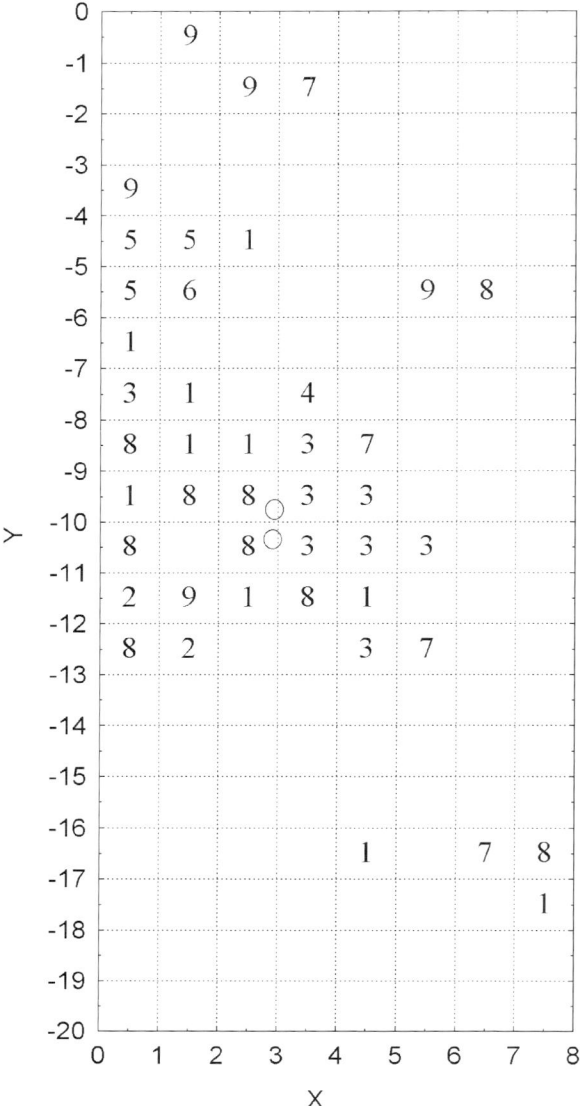

Figure 35.5 Nine cluster solution.

sense to look for broader or larger areas of spatial integrity or homogeneity. Indeed, a kaleidoscopic pattern may be very hard to handle and interpret" (Blankholm 1991:81). Given human body size, most human activities simply take more than a square meter to perform, and this should be reflected in the distribution of artifacts across the site surface. Given that each grid square is an independent sampling unit, large areas of *contiguous* grid units assigned to the same cluster would indicate robust structure in the data. With our approach, the relative contiguity of data can be statistically evaluated. This approach thus compares the data to a context driven model.

Contiguity is easily quantifiable. For a given square assigned to a particular composition-based cluster, it is possible to simply count how many adjacent squares are of the same type. In our implementation, squares meeting only at the corner count as half an adjacency. Thus, a square completely surrounded by ones of the same type has a contiguity (C) of exactly six. These measurements can be simply added to produce both cluster specific and global results. Using a DOS program written by Kintigh for this purpose (CONTIG) and available over the internet *(http:www/pages.prodigy.net/keith.kintigh)*, the adjacency counts for each grid square were summed by cluster assignment. For the observed configuration the overall total is 1065. Then, the specific cluster assignments of the occupied squares were randomised holding constant the occupied grid locations and the number of squares assigned to each compositional cluster. By comparing the aggregate contiguity measure of a large number of random runs with the original data, it is possible to assess the likelihood of getting as high a contiguity measure as was observed by chance. That is, the randomly generated adjacencies can be expressed as a one-tailed (directional) probability p(C) which can be used to assess the significance of the observed clustering results. In addition to evaluating the strength of clustering results, this probability measure may also be used as a proxy for describing the relative dispersion or aggregation of a particular cluster.

The results of this analysis are presented in figure 35.6 for 1000 random runs. In only three out of a thousand runs (mean 1047) did the overall contiguity match or exceed that of the original data (1065). This indicates a very high likelihood that our clustering results are robust and do reflect some aspects of the site's structure. Contiguity varies widely from cluster to cluster. Three clusters (2, 3 and 5) are highly contiguous, whereas two seem dispersed (clusters 7 and to a lesser extent, 9). In order to understand these differences, it is necessary to consider their relationship to the compositions of the clusters.

cluster analyses cannot fail. That is to say, they will always produce clusters regardless of the nature of the data to which they are applied. All cluster analyses impose their own order upon the data to a greater or lesser extent, a feature they share in common with language itself (Shennan 1988:228). In contrast to language, it is possible to develop formal methods that can evaluate the extent to which a particular classification is useful for interpretive purposes.

Aldenderfer argues that most cluster validation methods are best conceptualised as "methods which assess the compatibility of a clustering solution with a particular theoretical perspective on what constitutes a good classification" (1982:62). In this case, there is one independent criterion for evaluating UC results. As Whallon (1984:276) and Blankholm (1991:77) both note, there is no tendency inherent in the procedure to form spatially coherent clusters. "For interpretation, it makes

Interpretation of Cluster Compositions

Now that we are confident that our analysis has revealed significant aspects of the site's structure, we may move

1000 Random Runs

Cluster	Count (C)	Observed Contiguity	Mean Random	Std. Random	Min. Random	Max. Random	Estimated Prob. p(C)
All	43	1065	1046.77	0.16	1033	1071	**0.003**
1	10	7	6.73	0.1	0	21	0.478
<u>2</u>	2	1	0.15	0.02	0	2	<u>0.097</u>
3	8	16	4.29	0.08	0	17	**0.001**
4	1	0	0	0	0	0	1
5	3	5	0.44	0.03	0	5	**0.004**
6	1	0	0	0	0	0	1
7	4	0	0.98	0.04	0	8	1
8	9	8	5.55	0.09	0	19	0.214
9	5	1	1.63	0.05	0	11	0.697

Probability estimations < 5% are in bold type.
<u>Probability estimations < 10% are underlined.</u>

Figure 35.6 Grid contiguity computation for the nine cluster solution.

towards detailed interpretation of those results. We will begin by considering the center of the site and will work out towards the periphery. The two large open areas in the center of the site may have been intentionally kept clear for the purposes of resting or sleeping. Ethnographically observed forager camps often consist of a prepared area where a wide variety of tasks are carried out. Work which causes uncomfortable amounts of debris is carried out just outside this area (Spurling and Hayden 1984:232). Also, larger chipping debris is obnoxious, and tends to get "scuffled" towards the edges of prepared areas (Stevenson 1982, 1991).

Cluster One conforms closely to the edges of the clear areas and has a composition consistent with this interpretation. It can be characterised as consisting primarily of flint flakes with a smattering of other artifact types. Cluster one has the highest proportion of burins (3.3%) and small quartzite cobbles (1.6%) at the site. It also has a relatively high proportion of perforators, and is thus rich in all tool types that require extensive retouch (e.g., not blades). In ethnographic accounts, the fringes of intentionally cleared spaces are likely to be chosen for the caching of finished tools – where they are handy but out of the way (Carr 1991:241).

Various knapping episodes can be distinguished in the spaces between the cleared areas. It is likely that *Cluster Three* and *Eight* represent the overlapping debris from several chipping events. Although both are highly contiguous and consist primarily of knapping debris, cluster three has a significantly higher proportion of quartzite. It is of note that the interface between these clusters coincides with the final locations of the quartzite boulders. One could speculate that the knappers sat upon them and chipped quartzite facing west during a single or very few episodes. Because flint was worked more frequently at the site it does not show this restricted distribution. In contrast, *Clusters Two* and *Five* seem to represent spatially segregated individual knapping episodes. Both form discrete spatial clusters, and cluster five corresponds exactly to a spatial cluster of quartzite artifacts identified by Clark (1979a:262).

Finally, messy or obnoxious activities seem to have been carried out on the periphery of the site. This is also consistent with many ethnographically observed forager camps, where cooking, butchering, and some knapping (especially the initial stages of production) are carried out well away from cleared areas (Spurling and Hayden 1984:232). The spatial distributions of *Clusters Seven* and *Nine* support this general interpretation. These clusters are generally dispersed in discrete spatial clusters at the periphery of the site. Cluster seven is actually much less contiguous than would be expected by chance (p(C) = 0.98). Contiguity is one kind of spatial pattern, but not the only one. Dispersal represents a different kind of spatial patterning that is measured only indirectly with this method.

The compositions of these clusters also support this interpretation. Cluster seven has relatively high proportions of flint trimming flakes, flint decortication flakes, and blades. Blades found in these locations, and decortication flakes themselves, may have been used for butchery. Phosphate analyses at the site indicate concentrations of organic substances consistent with food preparation (Butzer and Bowman 1979). Finally, *Cluster Nine* clearly represents areas where the primary reduction of flint took place frequently and to the relative exclusion of other activities (Figure 35.4). This cluster has the highest relative abundance of flint cores and decortication flakes, which together comprise over 70% of all artifacts.

Conclusions

It appears that the deposition of artifacts during the brief use life of Liencres were structured in several important

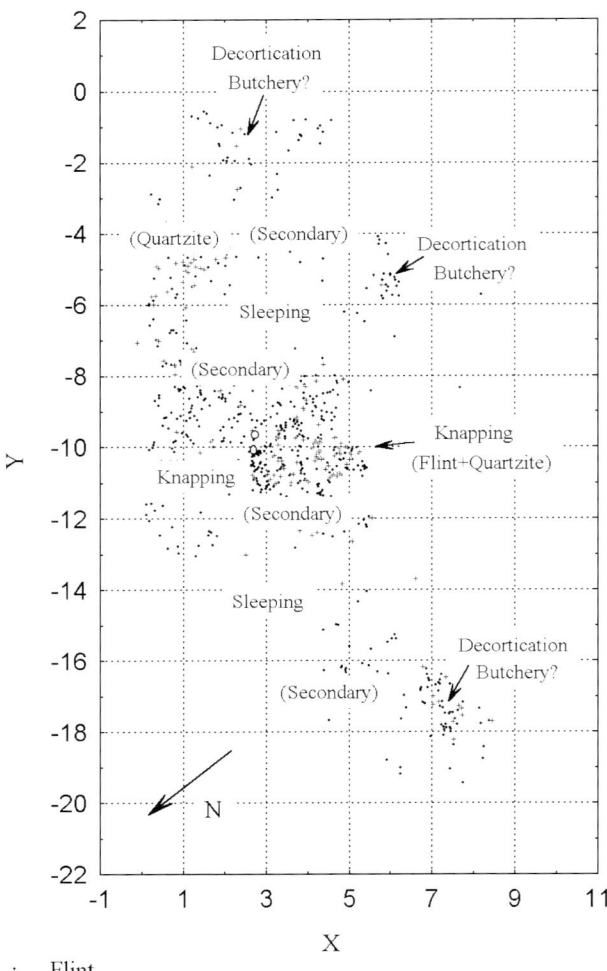

Figure 35.7 Activity areas at Liencres.

ways (Figure 35.7). The two large open areas may have been kept clear for the purposes of resting, creating a halo of "scuffled" artifacts and cached tools. Various overlapping knapping episodes can be distinguished in the spaces between the open areas. The quartzite boulders in the center of the site also structured the use of space, as evidenced by the differences between Clusters Three and Eight. Finally, messy or obnoxious activities seem to have been carried out on the periphery of the site. This overall interpretation is congruent with that forwarded for Pincevent by Leroi-Gourhan and Brézillon (1972), and supported by Carr (1991) and Lang (1992). It is also consistent with a many ethnographically observed short term forager camps (Brooks and Yellen 1987).

Unconstrained clustering has proven itself capable of quickly and easily isolating key aspects of pattern in the Liencres data. Like all analyses of any kind, this one entailed some subjective decisions. Subjective elements exist in all archaeological interpretation, and hypotheses should be tested independently whenever possible. In this case, independent assessments of clustering results were accomplished through the use of context driven models and simulation. Although they lack the sophistication and elegance of classical techniques of significance testing, Monte Carlo estimations are easy to conceptualise and are robust in that they make fewer *a priori* assumptions about data structure.

Optimistic early studies in spatial analysis made significant headway, but quickly encountered a past more complex than expected. Some researchers have used these difficulties to argue that all spatial analysis is doomed to failure. This is, in the words of George Cowgill, "logically akin to the drunk who loses his keys in a dark section of the street but hunts for them under the streetlight, because the light is better there" (Cowgill 1993:560).

Others have resisted formal techniques in general for philosophical reasons. These critics have been useful for pointing out biases in quantitative archaeology, but seemingly fail to realise that many of their objections apply to all forms of description. Quantitative techniques are themselves description and expression, and share characteristics in common with all symbols. In contrast to language, formal techniques can be invented, changed, or dismissed freely to suit the purposes of a community of researchers. Their utility lies in the strategically chosen and explicit nature of this description.

As Roy Rappaport noted, the very characteristics of language that provide the basis for humanity's astounding adaptive flexibility also give birth to confusion, and "threaten with chaos and babel the orders that groups do establish" (Rappaport 1979:202). Attempts within anthropology to define such ubiquitous concepts as "culture" or "household" clearly demonstrate how tricky even verbal description can be (cf. Hammel 1984). The greatest utility of quantitative methods is perhaps that they allow us to create new forms of description while forcing us to be precise about what we mean.

References

Adams, R.M. 1974. Patterns of Mesopotamian irrigation agriculture. In: Downing, T.E. and Gibson, M. (eds.) *Irrigation's Impact on Society*. Anthropological Papers of the University of Arizona No. 25, 1–6.

Aldenderfer, M.S. 1982. Methods of cluster validation for archaeology. *World Archaeology* 14 (1), 61–71.

Blankholm, H. 1991. *Intrasite Spatial Analysis in Theory and Practice*. Aarhaus.

Brooks, A. and Yellen, J. 1987. The preservation of activity areas in the archaeological record: Ethnoarchaeological and archaeological work in Northwest Ngamiland, Botswana. In: Kent, S. (ed.) *Method and Theory for Activity Area Research: An Ethnoarchaeological Approach*, 63–106. New York.

Butzer, K. and Bowman, D. 1979. Some sediments from Asturian archaeological levels from Cantabiran Spain. *Quaternaria* 21, 287–291.

Carr, C. 1991. Left in the dust: contextual information in model-focused archeology. In: Kroll, E. and Price, T.D. (eds.) *The Archaeological Interpretation of Spatial Patterns*, 221–256. New York.

Childe, V.G. 1929. *The Danube in Prehistory*. Oxford.

Clark, G.A. 1976. *El Asturiense Cantábrico (Bibliotheca Praehistorica Hispana No. 13)*. Madrid: Consejo Superior de Investigaciones Cientificas.

—— 1979a. Liencres: an open station of Asturian affinity near Santander, Spain. *Quaternaria* 21, 249–302.

—— 1979b. Spatial association at Liencres, an Early Holocene open site on the Santander coast, north-central Spain. In: Upham, S. (ed.) *Computer Graphics in Archaeology*. Arizona State University Anthropological Research Papers No. 15, 121–144.

—— 1983. *The Asturian of Cantabria: Early Holocene Hunter-Gatherers in Northern Spain*. Anthropological Papers of the University of Arizona No. 41.

—— 1989. Site functional complementarily in the Mesolithic of northern Spain. In: Bonsall, C. (ed.) *The Mesolithic in Europe*, 589–603. Edinburgh.

Clark, G. and Menéndez-Amor, J. 1975. Muestras de pólen de Liencres: niveles 1 y 2. *Cuadernos de Arqueología de Deusto* 3, 67–70.

Cowgill, G.L. 1993. Distinguished Lecture in Archaeology: Beyond Criticizing New Archaeology. *American Anthropologist* 95(3), 551–573.

González-Morales, M.R. 1982. *El Asturiense y Otras Culturas Locales*. Centro de Investigactión y Museo de Altamira Monografiás No. 7.

Gregg, S., Kintigh, K. and Whallon, R. 1991. Linking ethnoarchaeological interpretation and archaeological data: The sensitivity of spatial analytical methods to post-depositional disturbance. In: Kroll, E. and Price, T.D. (eds.) 1991 *The Archaeological Interpretation of Spatial Patterns*, 149–196. New York.

Hammel, E. 1984. On the *** of Studying Household Form and Function. In: Netting, R., Wilk, R. and Arnold, E. (eds.) *Households: Comparative and Historical Studies of the Domestic Group*, 29–43. Berkeley.

Johnson, I. 1984. Cell frequency recording and analysis of artifact distributions. In: Hietala, H.J. (ed.) *Spatial Analysis in Archaeology*, 75–76. Cambridge.

Kintigh, K.W. 1990. Intrasite spatial analysis: a commentary on major methods. In: Voorips, A. (ed.) *Studies in Modern Archaeology* 3. 165–200. Bonn.

—— 1994. *Tools for Quantitative Archeology 2000*. Tempe.

Kintigh, K.W. and Ammerman, A.J. 1982. Heuristic approaches to spatial analysis in archaeology. *American Antiquity* 47(1), 31–63.

Lang, S.A. 1992. *An Investigation of Image Processing Techniques at Pincevent, an Upper Magdalenian Site in Northern France*. Arizona State University Anthropological Research Papers No. 43, Tempe.

Leroi-Gourhan, A. and Brézillon, M. 1972. Fouilles de Pincevent: Essai d'analyse ethnographique d'un habitat magdelénien (la section 36). *Gallia Préhistoire* suppl. VII.

Rappaport, R.A. 1979. *Ecology, Meaning and Religion*. Berkeley.

Shennan, S. 1988. *Quantifying Archaeology*. San Diego.

Spurling, B. and Hayden, B. 1984. Ethnoarcheology and intrasite spatial analysis: A case study form the Western Australian Desert. In: Hietala, H.J. (ed.) *Intrasite Spatial Analysis in Archaeology*. Cambridge.

Stevenson, M.G. 1982. Toward an understanding of site abandonment behavior evidence from historic mining camps in the southwest Yukon. *Journal of Anthropological Archaeology* 1(3), 237–265.

—— 1991. Beyond the formation of hearth-associated assemblages. In: Kroll, E. and Price, T.D. (eds.) *The Archaeological Interpretation of Spatial Patterns*, 269–300. New York.

Straus, L.G. 1979. Mesolithic adaptations along the northern coast of Spain. *Quaternaria* 21, 305–327.

Whallon, R. 1974. Spatial analysis of occupation floors II: the application of nearest neighbor analysis. *American Antiquity* 39(1), 16–34.

—— 1984. Unconstrained clustering for the analysis of spatial distributions in archaeology. In: Hietala, H.J. (ed.) *Intrasite Spatial Analysis*, 242–277. Cambridge.

36. The function of the Mesolithic sites in the Paris basin (France). New data

Christian Verjux

Although the Mesolithic sites have been studied since the 19th century in the Paris basin, few of them have shown a spatial organisation of the artefacts. These data seemed to indicate short but successive occupations of hunters-gatherers. The sites excavated during the last twenty years have often revealed a more complex situation with graves and different kinds of pits. This may mean a possible reduction in the mobility of the human groups, during the Mesolithic, some millennia before the first meeting with farmers.

The Mesolithic sites in the Paris basin are well known by a great number of studies and excavations done since the 19th Century, often in the sandy areas. Some of these works, and especially the first ones, were not carried out with a method that allowed an understanding of the spatial organisation of the artefacts. During these early years, the main purpose was to establish chronological and typological frameworks of the Mesolithic occupations, based on the lithic industries, principally flint arrowheads, and sometimes on radiocarbon dates. A few of these sites have yielded structures, such as built hearths, hut or tent remains, but the organisation of the settlements has rarely been described (Rozoy 1978:1091 pp).

During the last twenty years new sites were discovered and studied in the Paris basin. They provided new data, especially in Auneau (Eure-et-Loir), where we have been studying a great number of Mesolithic structures since 1990 (Verjux 2000).

In this paper, we are first going to examine well-known sites, such as Montbani, Coincy and Sonchamp, and secondly the results of new excavations. Finally we will start a discussion about the status of the last hunters-gatherers in the Paris basin (Figure 36.1).

Figure 36.1 Location of the Mesolithic sites in the Paris basin. Black points indicate those described in the text (from Rozoy 1978, completed).

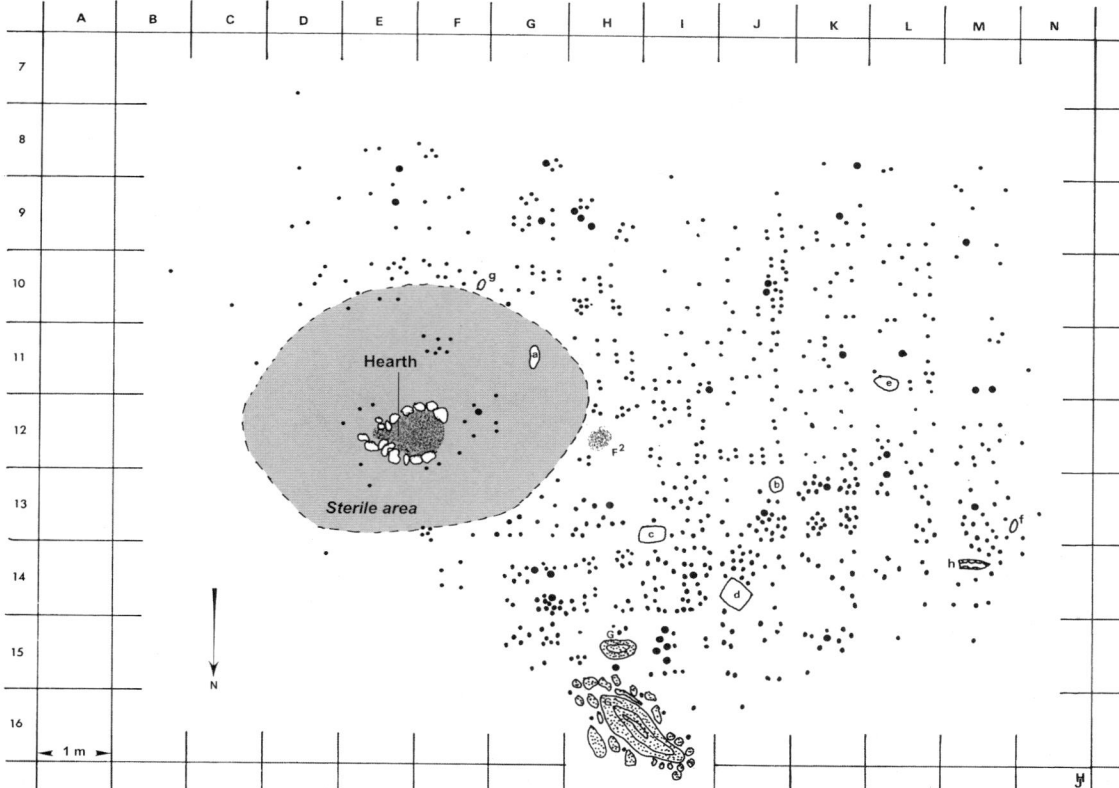

Figure 36.2 A possible vestige of a Mesolithic hut in Sonchamp III (from Hinout 1996).

Well-known sites

In the famous site of "Montbani" (Mont Notre Dame, Aisne) discovered in 1914, there have been many excavations up to the sixties. From 1963 to 1968, René Parent studied an area of 190 m² (Parent and Planchais 1972). The Middle Mesolithic levels (Tardenoisien) were well preserved, under about 1 meter of sterile sand. 22 hearths were found, most of them were between 20 and 30 cm in diameter, but some of them were wider. 7 fire-cracked sandstone and millstone mounds might be hearth dumps. Two fireplace dates suggested several occupations between 8060 ± 350 BP (Gif 356) and 6930 ± 170 BP (Gif 1106). The Mesolithic populations came back to this place several times. The spatial organisation is therefore difficult to understand.

Still in the sixties, René Parent dug at Coincy "La Sablonnière" (Aisne). The site had been known since 1885 and Raoul Daniel had begun to study it by sifting the sand to gather the Mesolithic artefacts. The Parent's excavation field was only in an area of 40 m² but 10 hearths were discovered (Parent 1973). The distribution of artefacts shows 2 denser sectors, in the centre and in the southwest. The hearths were at different depths, in the archaeological level. The deepest fireplace has been dated about 8190 ± 190 BP (Gif 1226), according to the flint industry of the Middle Mesolithic, namely Middle Tardenoisien.

The sites of Sonchamp "Le Bois de Plaisance" (Yvelines) were discovered in 1935 and many excavations were done up to 1952. In 1965, Jacques Hinout began to study several sites. The settlement of Sonchamp III covered about 80 m² (Hinout 1996). A 10 m² sterile area surrounded one hearth, dug through the ground down to 65 cm and built with millstones. This structure was interpreted as the location of a hut (Figure 36.2). Outside, flint waste, tools and arrowheads were found. No radiocarbon date is available, but, according to the flint industry, this site seems to belong to the end of the Middle Mesolithic, maybe around 7000 BP.

Also studied by Jacques Hinout, the site of "Bois de Chinchy", in Villeneuve-sur-Fère (Aisne), has shown hearths and flint workshops, over 250 m² (Hinout 1989). One hearth was made with millstones. All around this fireplace, an elliptic ashy area covering approximately 8 m² was interpreted as the remains of a tent or a hut. No similar organisations were identified near the other hearths. The only date of this site seems too young (Gif 6318: 6150 ± 100 BP).

Many Mesolithic sites were known in Fère-en-Tardenois (Aisne). They were first discovered in 1879 by Edouard Vielle (Parent 1967). More than 10 sites were recognised in the "Allée Tortue" and have been studied since 1952, specially by Rene Parent and Jean-Georges Rozoy over several hundred square meters (Rozoy 2000a). The spatial organisation shows concentrations of flint artefacts that are interpreted as different settlements. Several pits have been distinguished by studying the

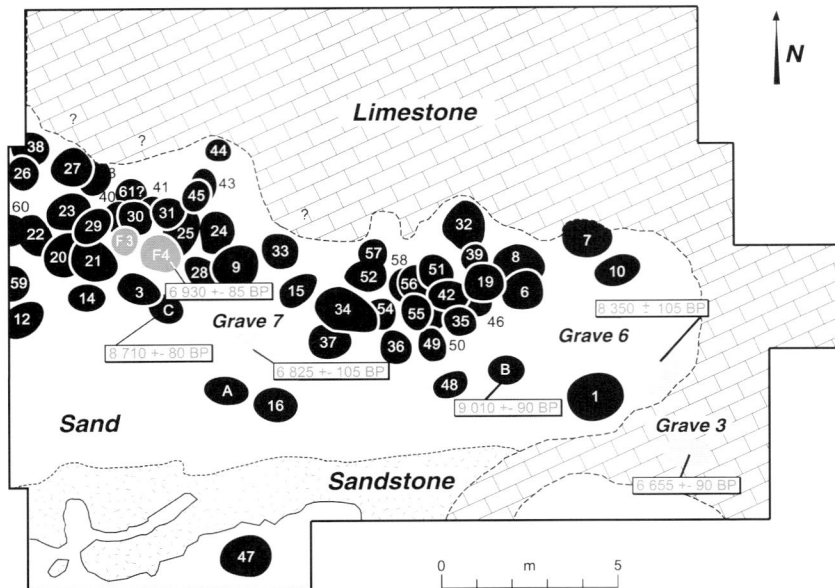

Figure 36.3 The Mesolithic pits in Auneau "Le Parc du Château" (Eure-et-Loir). Available radiocarbon dates are mentioned.

vertical distribution of the flints but it was difficult to identify them during the excavation (Rozoy and Slachmuylder 1990). The radiocarbon datings are not in relation with these late Mesolithic occupation.

Concerning the exploitation of raw materials, a so-called "factory" of sandstone tools was discovered in 1875 in the south of the Fontainebleau Forest (Villiers-sur-Grez "La Vignette", Seine-et-Marne). At the same time, since 1886, two researchers have begun excavations in the Montmorency Forest near Piscop and Bouffemont (Val d'Oise). Systematic prospecting and digs were carried out between 1940 and 1955 (Tarrête 1977). In this area, the bedrock is a tertiary marine sand, including sandstone benches, and the Mesolithic populations produced macrotools using this raw material. This original industry was called "Montmorencien" and the tools "prismatics" (cf. Figure 36.4). They are quite different from Neolithic axes. The dating was uncertain because sandstone tools were mixed with Tardenoisian industry. It was supposed to belong to the Mesolithic and following research has shown that these heavy tools were often present in the Middle Mesolithic sites.

Several sites have shown features. Hearths are known but only one was built with stones and many of them were shallow ones. 8 sites in the Montmorency Forest have given pits (Daniel 1957). At least 25 were certified but the actual number was probably greater. They have been filled with sandstone debitage and broken tools, but also with flint flakes, tools and arrowheads too. They were interpreted as extraction features and sometimes, especially the broadest ones, as interred dwellings. In Piscop M1, for instance, the best known site, at least 2 hearths and 14 pits have been dug. Some of them were 2 meters deep and were between 1,5 and 3 meters in diameter (Giraud *et al.* 1938).

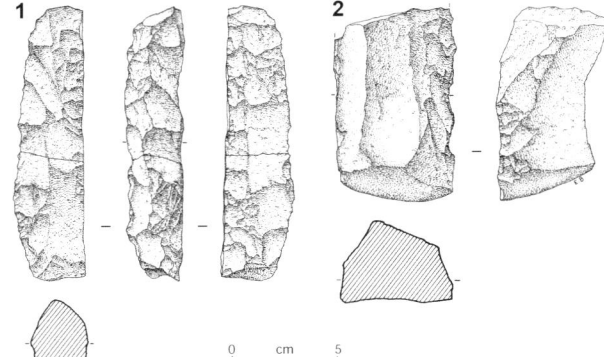

Figure 36.4 Auneau "Le Parc du Château" (Eure-et-Loir). Fontainebleau Sandstone heavy tools: 1. Prismatic ; 2. Sidescraper. (Eve Boitard del.)

In the Loire Valley, a culture of the Middle Mesolithic identified near Beaugency (Loiret) has been called "Beaugencien" (Rozoy 1978:825 pp). The sites are numerous and essentially known from the recovery of surface artefacts. These sites were often very large, for instance more than 10000 m² in "Les Hauts de Lutz", and seem to indicate many sequential or lasting occupations. Heavy tools, similar to Montmorencien artefacts, but made in tertiary flint, and rarely in sandstone, were found on these different places. Only one salvage excavation was carried out in 1971–1972 on a very small surface (30 m²) and no features were identified.

No grave was known in the Paris basin until very recently. Indeed most of the sites have been studied in sandy grounds, where bones are not preserved. Meanwhile, a few numbers of possible burials are mentioned: for instance, in Piscop M1, the edge of a wide pit was built with big stones and this structure was interpreted as a grave, like two shallow pits, recovered with flat stones (Giraud *et al.* 1938). In Fère-en-Tardenois (Allée Tortue X and XIV), two millstone mounds looked like the arrangements of Téviec or Hoëdic graves (Rozoy and Slachmuylder 1990).

Recent excavations

The site of Acquigny "L'Onglais" (Eure) was dug between 1980 and 1983 and covered 200 m^2 (Chancerel and Paulet-Locard 1991). Several Mesolithic occupations were discovered and many structures were identified, such as hearths, post-holes and areas covered with pebbles. The industry is typical of the Middle Mesolithic and two radiocarbon dates set it around 8150 ± 460 BP (Gif 7700) or 8020 ± 160 BP (Gif-Tan 88146). Ten macro-tools were collected ; three of them looked like Montmorencien sandstone implements.

J.G. Rozoy identified 11 camps in the site of Cires-les-Mello "Le Tillet" (Oise), that have been studied since 1987 on a surface about 250 m^2. The spatial organisation indicates little dwellings from 10 to 30 m^2, very close to each other (Rozoy 1996). Three hearths date from 9278 ± 60 BP (Lyon-842), 8895 ± 60 BP (Lyon-839) to 7980 ± 65 BP (Lyon-847), and confirm the successive occupations pointed out by the arrow-heads study (Rozoy 2000b). Some pits were probably present but were very difficult to recognise in this sandy ground, due to the lack of bones.

At La Chaussée-Tirancourt "Le Petit Marais" (Somme), Thierry Ducrocq began a rescue excavation in 1990 over about 150 m^2 (Ducrocq and Ketterer 1995). The Mesolithic levels and features are well preserved under Neolithic and more recent layers. Three pits and two graves were discovered. They date of the Middle Mesolithic, and at least two main occupancies are revealed from 8460 ± 70 BP (Gif 9329) or 8420 ± 70 BP (Gif 9330) to 7770 ± 80 BP (Gif 9331) or 7840 ± 90 BP (Gif 8913). The pits are wide and deep, filled with rubbish, but might be in relationship with the graves, because two of them contained faunal deposits. The first grave is a secondary burial of one person and the second one is a cremation, which contains several people. Other sites near La Chaussée-Tirancourt, often situated in valley bottoms, have been studied and have provided information about chronology and environment (Ducrocq 1997).

In Val de Reuil "Les Varennes" (Eure), an original grave discovered during a rescue excavation was recognised as a Mesolithic one by a radiocarbon analysis (Ly 6239: 8715 ± 310 BP). Bones of two or three people were identified, covered with many burned faunal remains, especially skulls of deer and aurochs (Billard *et al.* 1999).

In 1996, a very large site was studied in Rueil-Malmaison "Les Closeaux" (Hauts-de-Seine) during a salvage dig directed by Laurent Lang. Several sectors provided Mesolithic levels (Lang *et al.* 1997). The sector 4 was excavated on about 200 m^2. No structure was found, but 2 or 3 concentrations of lithic artefacts and faunal remains of Early Mesolithic were preserved. 3 sectors occupied during the Middle Mesolithic have revealed 7 hearths, a lot of fire-cracked stones and debitage, but they did not show obvious spatial organisation. Both in Late and Middle Mesolithic sectors macro-tools were found, in association with flint industry and faunal remains. The oldest were manufactured in flint, but the others were mainly made of sandstone. A burial, interred in a squatting position, was found in the same stratigraphic conditions, and about twenty meters around a pit filled with pieces of sandstone was identified. A cremation may have been also present on this site.

In Auneau "Le Parc du Château" (Eure-et-Loir), more than sixty pits, dug through the sand by the Mesolithic populations, between 9000 and 6500 BP, have been discovered since 1990 over about 150 m^2 (Verjux 1999, 2000). These features are very numerous and they often cut each other (Figure 36.3). Six main categories can be distinguished within these structures: rubbish and cooking pits, possible storage structures, post-holes with stones, burials and intentional deposits of faunal remains. In the sector already excavated, the Mesolithic archaeological layers have been almost entirely destroyed by a Neolithic occupation and by natural erosion. We can therefore study only the dug structures.

Several hearths contained fire-cracked limestone and sandstone rocks and sometimes charcoals patches. A few of them were cooking-pits, dug through the ground and filled with fire-cracked stones. A radiocarbon dating sets F4 to about 6930 ± 85 BP (Ly 7972). Despite the existence of sandstone bedrock, we did not disclose an actual exploitation of it, although some cores and bladelets were made with this raw material. Nevertheless a few heavy sandstone tools have been uncovered such as scrapers or prismatics (Figure 36.4).

Some pits have been filled with rubbish, such as faunal remains, which are very well preserved. Aurochs and roebuck are the most represented animals, with deer and wild boar. A few pits were almost cylindrical and deeper, up to 1,50 m, and showed vertical walls. Despite the absence of organic vestiges, except bones, they look like storage structures (Figure 36.5). Several pits are quite different and contained only big stones, probably to wedge vertical wood pieces. In one case, 200 kg of limestone and sandstone rocks have been laid in a pit. They seem to be post-holes, but no spatial organisation is apparent.

The oldest grave, from the Middle Mesolithic (Ly 5606: 8350 ± 105 BP), contained a man interred in a sitting position in a large pit, filled with about 300 kg of big stones (Figure 36.6). Two other burials date from the end of the Mesolithic. The first skeleton was lying on his chest upon a paving (Ly 4731: 6655 ± 90 BP). The second one was simply buried on his back in a single pit (Ly 7097: 6825 ± 105 BP). A bone point was found in each grave.

Finally, three pits contained original faunal deposits: a

skull of an aurochs was buried without other remains, except in one case, where an antler was placed upon the skull. Two available dates locate these pits as the most ancient vestiges of the site: 9010 ± 90 BP (Oxa 5643) and 8710 ± 80 BP (Oxa 5644).

These numerous structures in Auneau are related to several human occupations and sometimes chronological indications can be drawn from the lithic industry, microliths or sometimes stratigraphic data. The radiocarbon dates confirm these different periods during the middle and the late Mesolithic.

Discussion

The Mesolithic settlements have been studied in the Paris basin for more than a century but, as I tried to demonstrate, the information is quite incomplete and unequal. Many Mesolithic settlements seem to have been inhabited several times, sometimes throughout the successive millennia. It is always difficult to establish if people came back in the same place very often and to define their length of stay. The information about the dwellings is still rare, and recent excavations pointed out the difficulties of studying the spatial organisation of artefacts. Very few of these sites have revealed possible huts locations. Meanwhile, the identification of pits is the greatest difference with earlier research. A recent work (Verjux in press) disclosed at least a dozen sites with such features in the Paris basin (Figure 36.7).

When the conditions of preservation were quite good, several Mesolithic sites provided faunal remains with the lithic artefacts. It means that we can soon hope for new data in terms of hunting strategies and seasonality, because those available today are unfinished (Bridault 1997). Likewise, before 1990, no Mesolithic grave was known in the Paris Basin. Up to now four sites with burials have

Figure 36.5 Auneau "Le Parc du Château" (Eure-et-Loir). A cylindrical pit, about 1 m deep, which may be a storage feature.

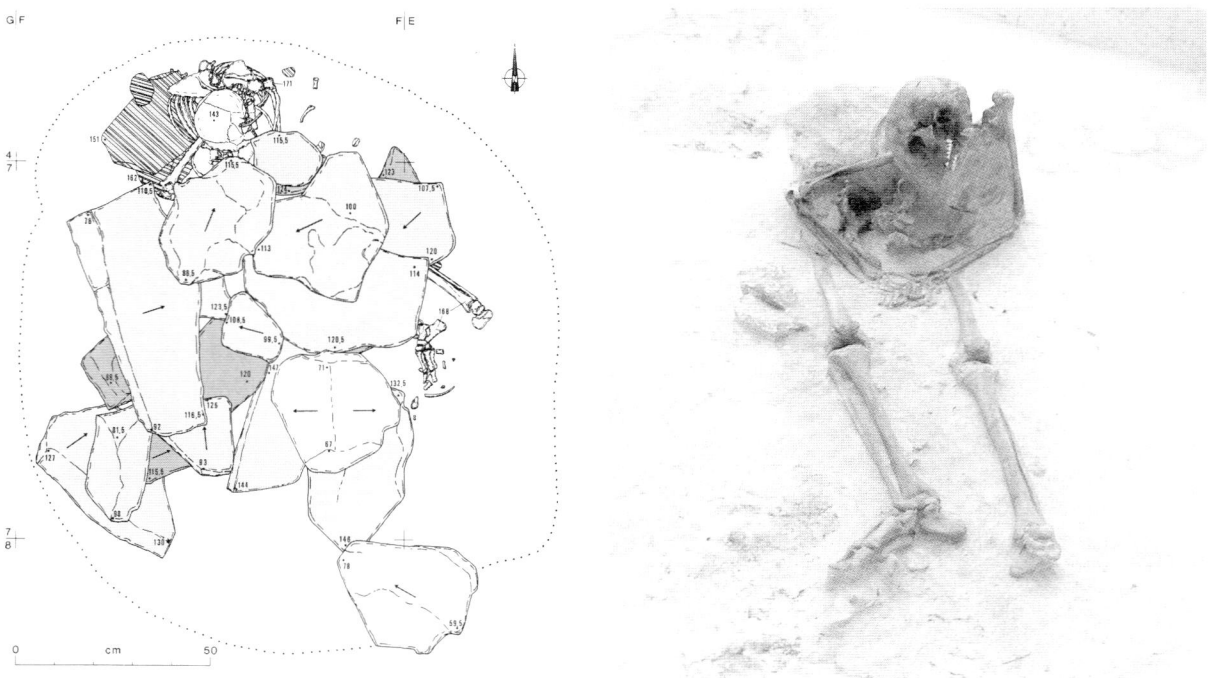

Figure 36.6 Auneau "Le Parc du Château" (Eure-et-Loir). Grave 6. The plan shows the distribution of stones upon the body. The skeleton clearly indicates the sitting position.

Figure 36.7 Sites with Mesolithic pits known in the Paris basin.

been identified and the great variability of these graves (inhumation, cremation, secondary burial ...) indicates the strong possibility of discovering new funeral sites during the following research.

Heavy tools like prismatics are certified in many sites of the Early and Middle Mesolithic. Their presence may have to do with forest clearance and suggests a special adaptation to the temperate forest. The Montmorencien sites in the centre of the Paris basin give evidence of a consequential exploitation of sandstone, quite different from usual hunter-gatherer behaviour.

In the Near East, permanent dwellings appeared before 10000 cal BC, associated with storage pits, ground-stone industry and graves, for example at Mallaha or Ouadi Hammah (Aurenche and Kozlowski 1999). The comparison with this developing sedentarity indicates large differences with western Europe, especially for climate and natural resources (cereals, game). Meanwhile, pits are widespread in late Mesolithic dwellings, particularly near the coasts, often in association with burials, and may indicate an increase in the degree of sedentism (Neeley and Clark 1990).

The presence in the same place of hearths, cooking and rubbish pits, and maybe storage structures and burials, could indicate that a few Mesolithic populations may have change their way of life. For instance, in Auneau, although the site has been inhabited several times during at least 3 millennia, features are too numerous and varied for wandering people. It could mean a possible reduction in mobility with a semi-sedentary or even a completely sedentary lifestyle, although this kind of sites was previously too little known in the Paris basin.

As the study has just begun with these recent data and these new hypotheses, it is now necessary to develop the research in directions to reconstruct the landscape and to estimate the human effects, to examine the question of seasonality (seasonal camps, specialised activities or the evolution toward becoming sedentary), and also to find a greater number of well preserved and stratified sites.

Acknowledgements

I thank particularly Emilie Lardenois and Simon Bryant for their help with the English language.

References

Aurenche, O. and Kozlowski, S.K. 1999. *La naissance du Néolithique au Proche Orient ou le paradis perdu*, 256. Errance Ed.

Billard, C., Arbogast, R.M. and Valentin, F. 1999. Dépôts animaux et crémation dans une sépulture mésolithique en Haute-Normandie. *L'Archéologue* no. 40, 50.

Bridault, A. 1997. Chasseurs, ressources animales et milieux dans le nord de la France de la fin du Paléolithique à la fin du

Mésolithique: problématique et état de la recherche. In: Fagnart, J.P. and Thévenin, A. (eds.) *Le Tardiglaciaire en Europe du nord-Ouest.* Actes du Colloque Chronostratigraphie et environnement des occupations humaines du Tardiglaciaire et du début de l'Holocène en Europe du Nord-Ouest, 26–30 octobre 1994, 165–176.

Chancerel, A. and Paulet-Locard, M.A. 1991. Le Mésolithique en Normandie: état des recherches. *Mésolithique et Néolithisation,* 113e Congrès National des Sociétés Savantes, 1988, 213–229. Strasbourg.

Daniel, R. 1957. Les gisements préhistoriques de la forêt de Montmorency (Seine-et-Oise). Troisième partie. *Bulletin de la Société Préhistorique Française,* LIV, 516–523.

Ducrocq, T. 1997. Contribution à la connaissance du Mésolithique du bassin de la Somme. In: Fagnart, J.P. and Thévenin, A. (eds.) *Le Tardiglaciaire en Europe du nord-Ouest.* Actes du Colloque Chronostratigraphie et environnement des occupations humaines du Tardiglaciaire et du début de l'Holocène en Europe du Nord-Ouest. Amiens, 26–30 octobre 1994, 107–121.

Ducrocq, T. and Ketterer, I. 1995. Le gisement mésolithique du "Petit Marais", La Chaussée-Tirancourt (Somme). *Bulletin de la Société Préhistorique Française,* t. 92, 2, 249–259.

Giraud, E., Vaché, C. and Vignard, E. 1938. Le gisement mésolithique de Piscop. *l'Anthropologie,* t. 48, 1–27.

Hinout, J. 1989. Le gisement tardenoisien final du Bois de Chinchy, commune de Villeneuve-sur-Fère (Aisne). *Revue Archéologique de Picardie,* no. 3–4, 15–26.

Hinout, J. 1996. Les sites mésolithiques de Sonchamp (Yvelines) lieu-dit "Le Bois de Plaisance". Le gisement sauveterrien moyen de Sonchamp III. *Revue Archéologique du Centre,* t. 34, 89–107.

Lang, L., Bridault, A., Gebhardt, A., Leroyer, C., Limondin, N., Sicard, S. and Valentin, F. 1997. *Occupations mésolithiques dans la moyenne vallée de la Seine. Rueil-Malmaison "Les Closeaux" (Seine-et-Marne).* DFS de sauvetage urgent, SRA Ile de France, 2 Vol.

Neeley, M.P. and Clark, G.A. 1990. Measuring social complexity in the european Mesolithic. In: Vermeersch, P.M. and Van Peer, P. (eds.) *Contributions to the Mesolithic in Europe,* 127–137. Leuven.

Parent, R. 1967. Le gisement tardenoisien de l'Allée Tortue à Fère-en-Tardenois (Aisne). *Bulletin de la Société Préhistorique Française,* t. LXIV, Etudes et Travaux, fasc. 1, 187–208.

Parent, R. and Planchais, N. 1972. Nouvelles fouilles sur le site tardenoisien de Montbani (Aisne) – 1964–1968. *Bulletin de la Société Préhistorique Française,* t. 69, Etudes et Travaux, fasc. 2, 508–532.

Parent, R., avec la coll. de Planchais, N. and Vernet, J.-L. 1973. Fouille d'un atelier tardenoisien à la Sablonnière de Coincy. *Bulletin de la Société Préhistorique Française,* t. 70, 337–351.

Rozoy, C. and Rozoy, J.G. 1996. Fouilles sur sable au Tillet. *Notæ Praehistoricæ,* 16, 123–144.

—— 2000 a. L'Allée-Tortue à Fère-en-Tardenois (Aisne): un site mésolithique complexe. *Bulletin de la Société Préhistorique Française,* t. 97, 5–56.

—— 2000b. Datations ^{14}C-AMS du Mésolithique du Tillet (Cires-les-Mello, Oise). *Bulletin de la Société Préhistorique Française,* t. 97, 305–306.

Rozoy, J.G. 1978. *Les derniers chasseurs. L'Epipaléolithique en France et en Belgique, essai de synthèse.* Bulletin de la Société Archéologique Champenoise, no. spécial, 3 Vol.

Rozoy, J.G. and Slachmuylder, J.-L. 1990. L'Allée Tortue à Fère-en-Tardenois (Aisne – France) Site éponyme du Tardenoisien récent. In: Vermeersch, P.M. and Van Peer, P. (eds.) *Contributions to the Mesolithic in Europe,* 423–433. Leuven.

Tarrête, J. 1977. Le Montmorencien. Xe Supplément à Gallia-Préhistoire, 218.

Verjux, C. 1999. Chronologie des rites funéraires mésolithiques à Auneau (Eure-et-Loir – France). In: Thevenin, A. (ed.) *L'Europe des derniers chasseurs, Epipaléolithique et Mésolithique,* Actes du 5e Colloque International UISPP, Grenoble, 18–23 septembre 1995, 293–302.

—— 2000. Les fosses mésolithiques d'Auneau (Eure-et-Loir – France). In: Crotti, P. (ed.) *Méso '97* Actes de la Table ronde "Epipaléolithique et Mésolithique", Lausanne, 21–23 Novembre 1997, Cahiers d'Archéologie Romande no. 81, 129–138.

—— in press. Creuser pour quoi faire? Les structures en creux au Mésolithique, *Approches fonctionnelles en Préhistoire,* XXVe Congrès Préhistorique de France, 24–26 Novembre 2000, Nanterre.

37. Mesolithic settlement structures in Reichwalde – Preliminary observations on Mesolithic sites

Jürgen Vollbrecht

The Landesamt für Archäologie Sachsen conducts archaeological investigations in the lignite mining area of Reichwalde, East Saxony; the project is financially supported by the LAUBAG (Lausitzer lignite mining company). Recent investigations resulted in the detection of several Mesolithic sites belonging to at least two phases of the Mesolithic, dating to the centuries around the transition Boreal/Atlantic. The potential for further analysis of the intra site spatial structuring of the sites is investigated in this article.

This report is based on recent excavations of Mesolithic sites in the lignite mining area of Reichwalde, in the state of Saxony, eastern Germany. Fieldwork is still in progress. At the present stage of analysis some dense distribution patterns and structural elements from excavated situations can be reported, but the preliminary character of the results has to be kept in mind; for more detailed interpretations, further analysis has to be awaited. Situated in Northeast Saxony, close to the Polish – German border and some 35 km north of the city of Bautzen, the lignite mine of Reichwalde is one of the most southern mines of the Lausitzer lignite region. Reichwalde is located at the southern rim of the Lausitzer Urstromtal, the most southern German ice marginal valley. Belonging to the southern part of the European lowlands, the pradolina formed during the second last glaciation and is cut into older glacial deposits (Wolf and Alexowsky 1994, 225 pp). The region destroyed by the lignite mining is situated between the Neiße and the Spree- river. It is part of a cultural landscape, rich in artificial lakes that has developed here on sandy grounds with intercalated peat deposits. The area under our recent investigation covers 12 km^2 and exhibits 5 major landscape elements: The southern border is formed by the rim of the ice marginal valley. North of it follows its sandy filling, the upper 20 m of which are fluvial sands of Weichsalian age that form a rather flat landscape. The flatness of the landscape was altered by moderate erosive activity and by dune- and coversand accumulations, partly during the Late Glacial, partly during the Holocene. To the north the bed of the river Weißer Schöps, a tributary of the Spree river crosses the area and in the south, a chain of peat deposits is present. More than 20 newly found Mesolithic find spots of variable size, as well as a group of undatable flint occurrences have been located in the course of systematic prospecting during the last years. Most of the Mesolithic occurrences are situated more or less close to the peat deposits in the southern part of the area under investigation. Further analysis of most of the sites has to be done, further field work has to be carried out as well, in order to clarify and evaluate the general distribution pattern. (Vollbrecht 1998/99; Ullrich *et al.* 1999; Vollbrecht 2001).

A closer look has been taken to the situation around one of the peat deposits, the former Großteich Altliebel. Below the north-western parts of the peat deposit, a late glacial soil was encountered, that contained an early Federmesser site, together with an *in situ* early Allerød- forest occurrence (Vollbrecht 1998/99; Elburg and van der Kroft 1999; Friedrich *et al.* 2001). Mesolithic finds are abundant along the northern margin of the peat deposit and in the adjacent parts of the landscape, where several morphological situations have been investigated; further works will follow. A coversand elevation and a part of the landscape south of it, closer to the peat deposit have the highest flint artefact occurrences (Figure 37.1). Especially on the coversand the flint occurrence is very dense. The total of the massive flint occurrence there covers about 1600 m^2, a bit over 900 m^2 has been investigated until now. South of the coversand elevation about 250 m^2 have been excavated so far with three dimensional recording of the finds. Field works in both situations are still not finished. Chronologically the finds from the two different morphological positions belong to two subsequent phases of the Mesolithic: on the coversand elevation, a Late Boreal occupation (see below) is present. This is further substantiated by the occurring microliths. Out of 146.000 artefacts registered so far, nearly 700 microliths have been identified. Besides various points, the dominating microlith type is the narrow scalene triangle. Just 5 trapezes were encountered there. South of the coversand elevation, an early Atlantic (see below)

Figure 37.1 Two major sites are located close to the peat deposit: On top of a coversand elevation, as well as south of it, closer to the former lake's edge dense traces of human presence during the Mesolithic have been encountered. View from the Southwest. Photo by Landesamt für Archäologie Sachsen, June 1999.

occupation site is under excavation: trapezes dominate the assemblage of about 100 microliths identified so far.

The Mesolithic on the coversand elevation

On top of the coversand elevation a small area of 50 m^2 (Figure 37.2), where a total of 29.095 lithics was registered three dimensionally, served as a test case for evaluating the preservation of the find horizon. Subsequently in the surrounding about 900 m^2 were sieved. Since counting of about 200.000 stone artefacts from the areas where sifting was conducted are not yet finished, the following observations are reported from the 50 m^2 test excavation.

During the last 100 years, trees were growing on top of the coversand, mostly pines that were cut down some 4 years ago, in the course of clearing of the area close to the lignite mining activities. The pine's roots were dragged out by a machine, and in the resulting holes many stone artefacts were found. There are no signs of prehistoric use of the coversand elevation after the Mesolithic and before medieval times.

The Mesolithic finds occur in the B- horizon of a sandy brown earth, the development of which did start in the late glacial and, according to our soil scientist A. Renno, was altered by the formation of an iron podsolic soil since the middle Holocene. The upper part of the soil was mechanically disturbed by ploughing some hundred years ago. The profile on top of the coversand elevation contains below the recent surface some 15–30 cm of plough

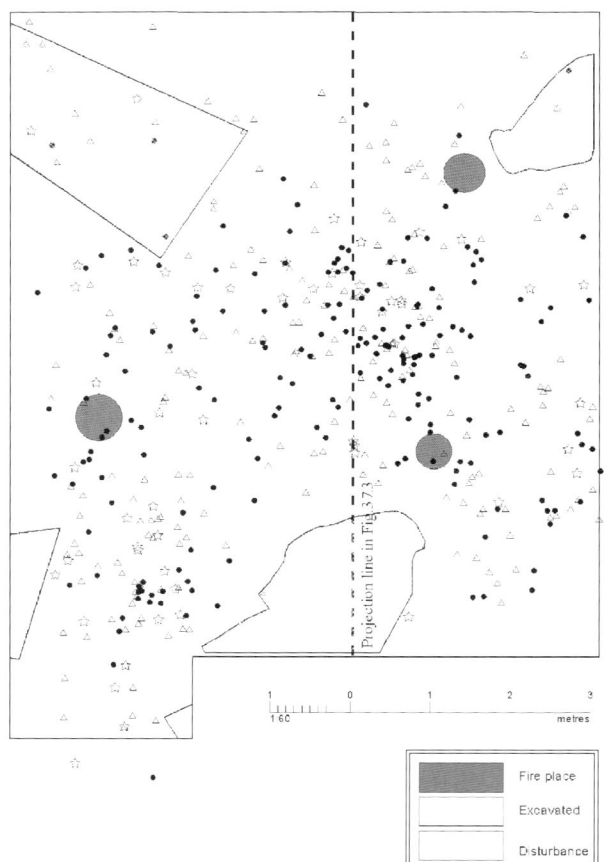

Figure 37.2 Plan of the 50 m^2 test excavation on the coversand elevation.

x = 705

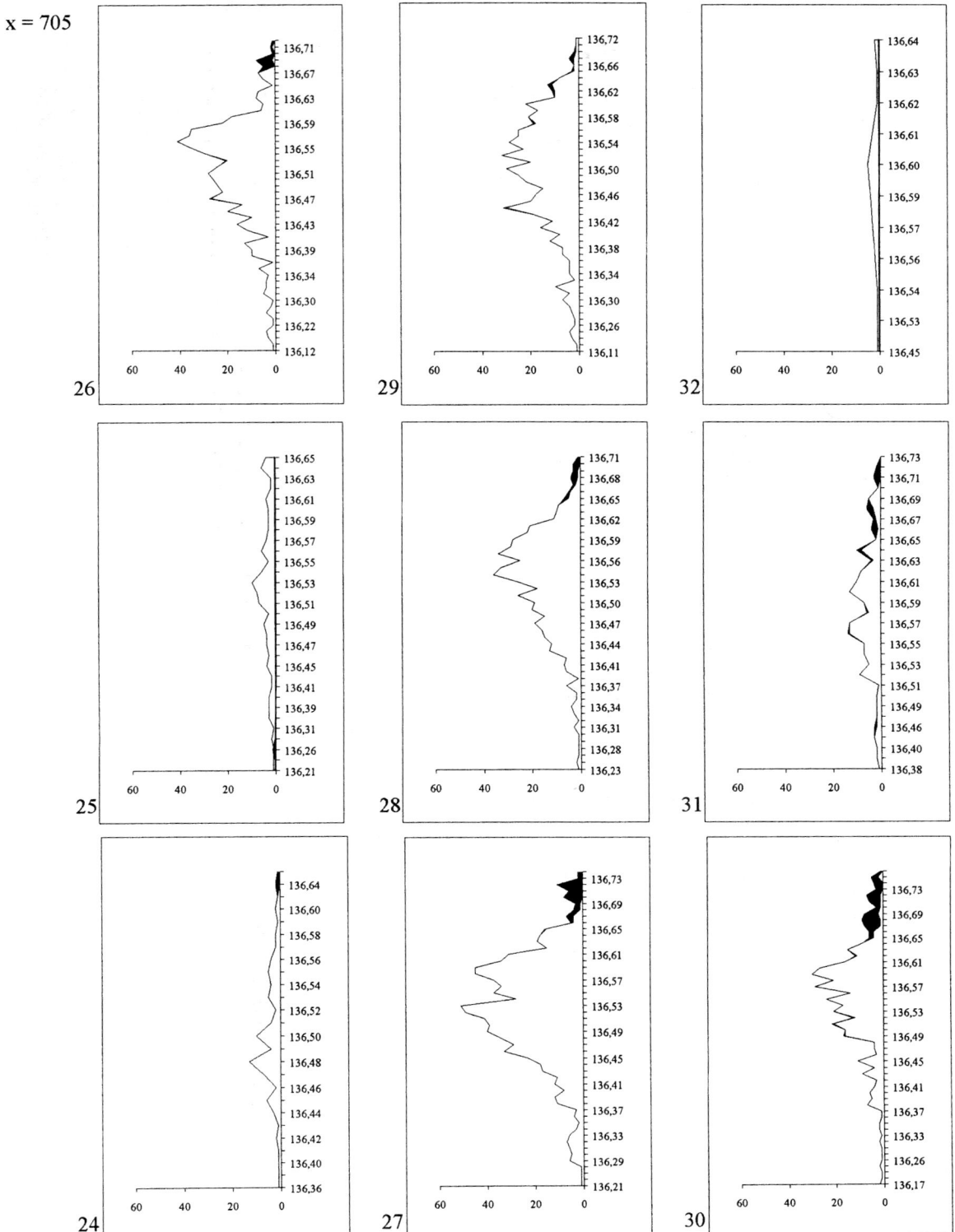

Figure 37.3 Projections of flint artefacts per square meter, along the row of squares east of the projection line shown in figure 37.2.

horizon, and below, the rest of the B- Horizon. Due to the soil development, ground features are hardly visible in that horizon. Of course in the flanks of the coversand elevation, the profile is more differentiated.

An example of vertical projections of the flint artefacts per square metre that were three-dimensionally recorded in the small test trench shows the squares running south to north in the middle of the excavated area (Figure 37.3).

Figure 37.4 Profile through the western hearth in the excavated trench. Infrared black and white photo, view from the south. The image demonstrates the difficulties in determination of the hearth's boundary below the stone fragments. Photo by Landesamt für Archäologie Sachsen, Autumn 1998.

In the plough horizon (black signature) just a minor amount of Mesolithic stone artefacts (about 6%) was encountered, while the mass of finds is lying well below it, within the B-horizon (white signature). Probably the majority of finds was already vertically dislocated to a depth, not reached or further dislocated by past agricultural activities (for further description of the vertical projections see Vollbrecht 2001).

The number of encountered flint microdébitage (chips and debris smaller than 1 cm) is about 54% of all flint artefacts (about 24.000). 53% of all flint artefacts encountered in the soil below the plough horizon are microdébitage. In the plough horizon covering and capping the soil however the occurrence of microdébitage is relatively high (61% of flint artefacts encountered in this horizon.)

Neither accumulation of aerial sands can be observed by our geological group (Renno and Ullrich in Friedrich *et al.* in press) nor can a conclusive sign of wind erosion be deduced from the profile. So at the present stage of work, as a working hypothesis, the amount of chips smaller 1 cm can be viewed as a number that is not highly affected by wind or water erosion. Probably we are dealing with a material more or less unaltered by natural agents that would result in some kind of size sorting, like wind or water activities. The taphonnomic significance of the counting of microdébitage is to be further substantiated in future, but measurements of artefact dimensions have not been finished yet. Moreover, the microdébitage is not the only group of artefacts smaller than 1 cm: for example many of the proximal, medial and terminal micro blade fragments (about 12% of the flint artefacts) are to be included in this group, so a higher number of small artefacts, probably well over 60% is to be expected. All excavated sediments were sieved with 2,5 mm mesh width. The inclusion of the remainders from the sift will also result in a higher proportion of small artefacts in this assemblage.

It may be correct that besides the fact of strong vertical movements, mostly due to rotten roots and bioturbation, the assemblage encountered is more or less intact, at least mapping of the horizontal distribution of the finds below the plough horizon would then mainly reflect the result of Mesolithic accumulation of material, and its post-depositional alterations as a result of treefalls for example.

Three distinct features were encountered in the course of the excavation. Although these features probably reflect different functions, they are collectively assigned as fire places in figure 37.2. The B- horizon exhibits a rather massive occurrence of flint and non flint material. The non flint objects, mostly fragments of pebbles of quartz, quartzite, siliceous slate, granite show a distinct density distribution. Especially not yet published results of refittings of the pebbles further substantiates the distribution pattern. In the area north-east of the centre and 5–6 m to the south-west relatively small areas of densely accumulated non flint fragments were encountered. The western accumulation is clearly connected to the most western fire place encountered. It is a hearth, that had a rather small diameter of 42 cm and was visible as a greyish charcoal rich discoloration of the light brown sand, that contained fragments of burnt pebbles and was surrounded by such fragments (Figure 37.4). The pebbles and pebble fragments were encountered lying in a rather unordered way, especially bigger pieces lying outside the hearths filling, that had a visible depth of 23 cm. Heating of the

Mesolithic settlement structures in Reichwalde – Preliminary observations on new Mesolithic sites

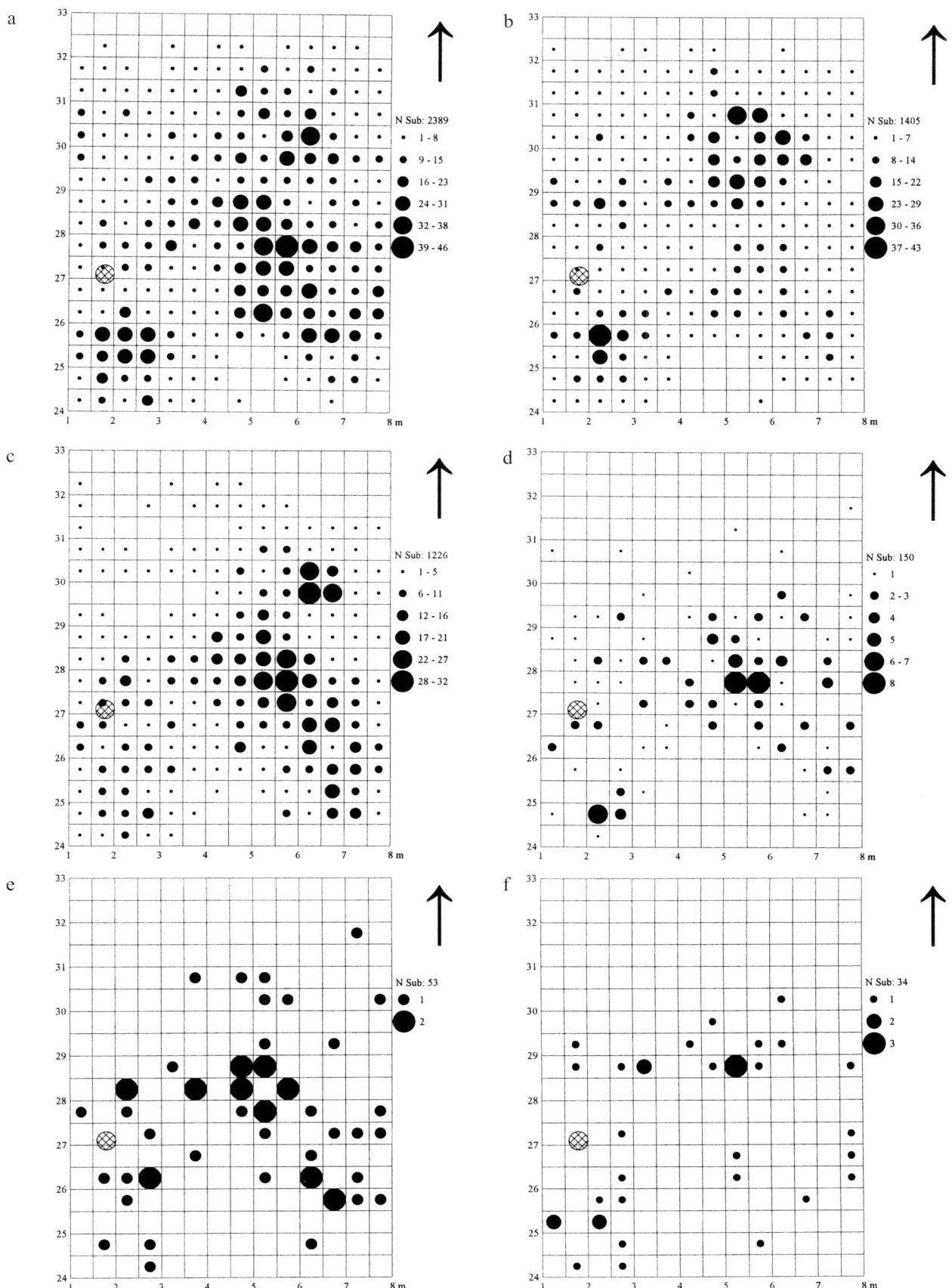

Figure 37.5 Density distributions in 50 m² test excavation. a) intact blades and flakes, b) flint debris > 1 cm, c) burnt microdébitage, d) microburins, e) scalene and isosceles triangles, f) endscrapers.

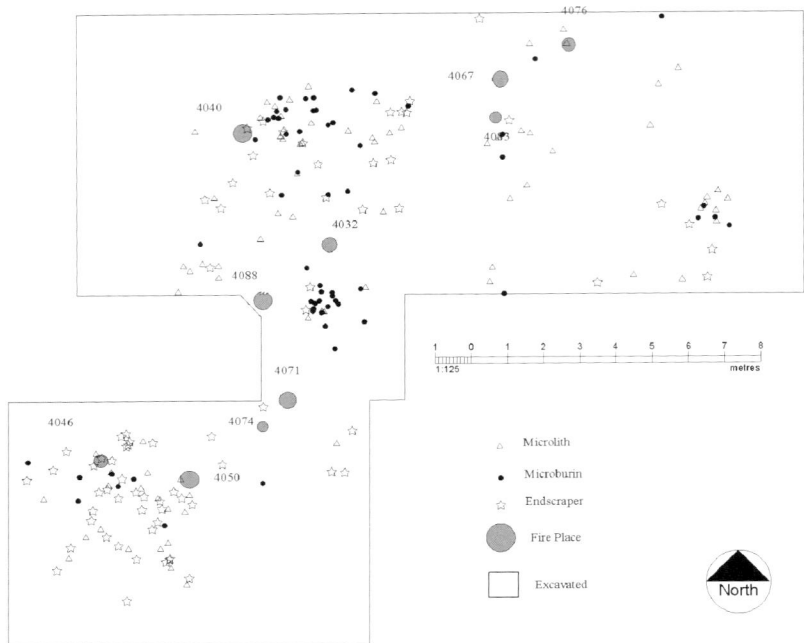

Figure 37.6 Plan of excavation in the younger Mesolithic find horizon. AMS- dates were obtained for the following hearths: 4032 (KIA 7963): 7445 ± 34 BP, 4040 (KIA 8527): 7411 ± 38 BP; 4046 (KIA 9665): 7499 ± 43 BP; 4050 (KIA 9664): 7042 ± 46 BP; 4071 (KIA 9662): 7033 ± 44 BP; 4076 (KIA 9666): 7410 ± 38 BP.

pebbles seems to be the past purpose of this hearth (Vollbrecht 1998/99; Vollbrecht in Friedrich *et al.* 2001). Charcoal from the hearth was sampled and AMS dated in Kiel, resulting in an age of 7926 ± 38 BP (KIA 7964), dating the hearth to the Late Boreal.

A density map (only the hearth is mapped in the density distribution maps, the northern fire place from figure 37.2 probably reflects a dump of burnt stones, while the eastern fire place in figure 37.2 did appear as a thin layer of charcoal) of all intact flakes and blades (Figure 37.5a) shows certain concentrations of material in the eastern and south-western parts as well as in the north-east. A contrasting density distribution is reflected by mapping of flint fragments and debris > 1 cm. It is especially abundant in the north-east, directly adjacent to the concentration of complete blades and flakes. Less frequently the bigger flint debris is also present in the south-western part (Figure 37.5b). Small pieces are regarded as objects that suffer little from centrifugal effects during the times of occupation. The density distribution of encountered microdébitage, meaning all pieces smaller than 1 cm, in this example the burnt microdébitage (Figure 37.5c), again reflects the concentrations seen before, the dense eastern one, separated of it a small dense occurrence in the north-east, and a less dense one in the south-west. In contrast the microburins (Figure 37.5d) are clearly restricted in their density distribution, lying inside the eastern and the south-western concentrations. Scrapers and microliths, in this case scalene and isosceles triangles (Figure 37.5e) are present in the eastern and the south-western concentrations. The

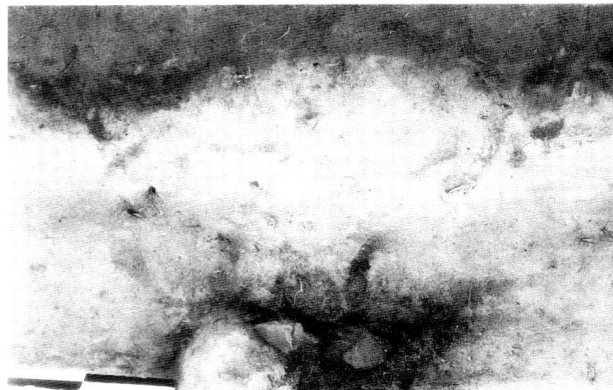

Figure 37.7 Mesolithic hearth pit 4032. Infrared black and white photo, showing the invisibility of the upper part of the pit. Photo by Landesamt für Archäologie Sachsen, winter 1998.

triangles closely accompany the restricted zone of higher microburin density, seen before for the eastern concentration; they occur relatively often around the hearth. Scrapers (Figure 37.5f) occur to closely accompany the triangles, but the densities do not fully coincide, instead occupying neighbouring squares.

The small test trench reported here indicates, that a certain differentiation of structures is possible. The boundaries of the encountered concentrations are partly lying outside the excavated and inside the surrounding sieved areas, where several further concentrations of stone artefacts and some 5 more hearths are located.

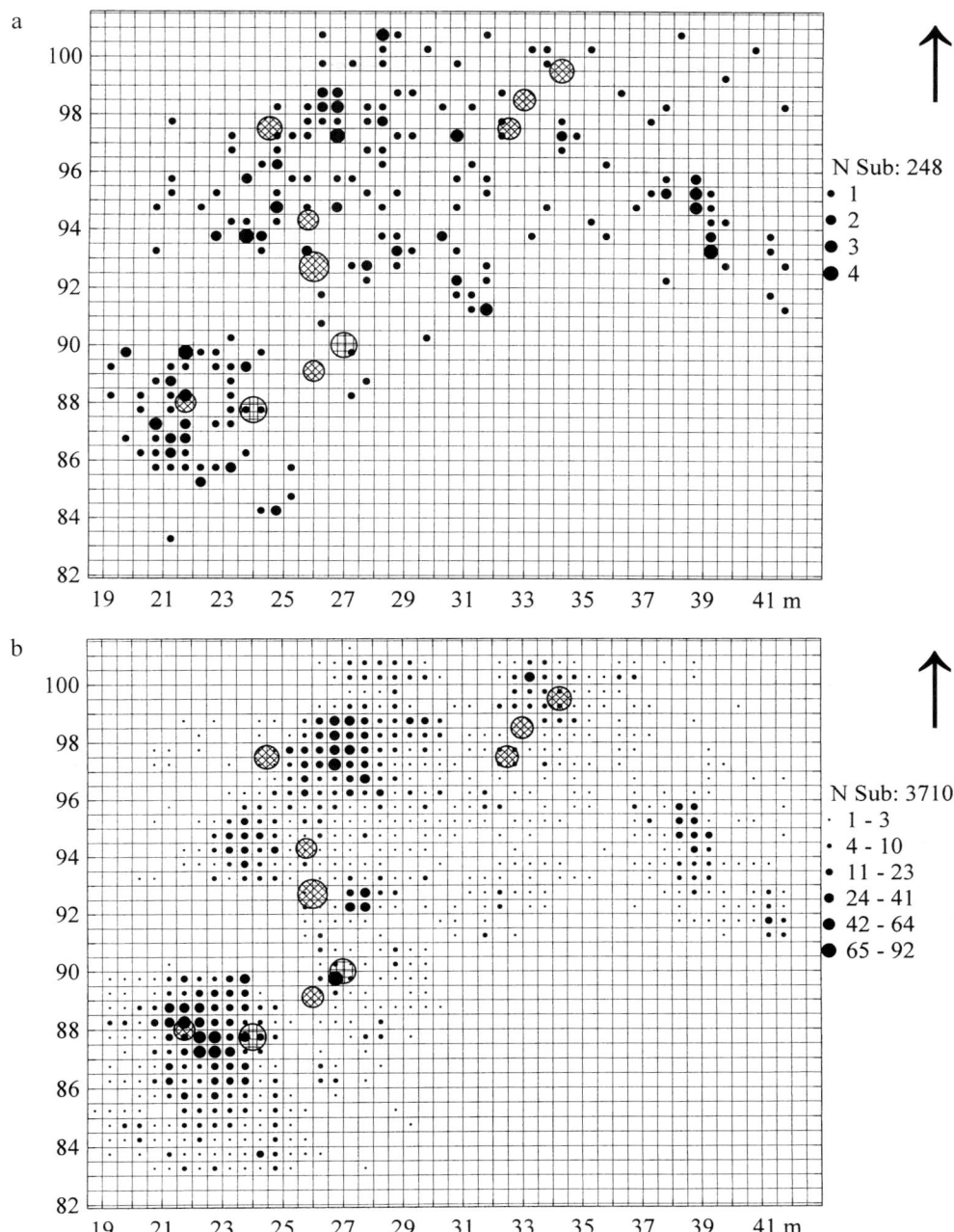

Figure 37.8 Density distributions in the younger Mesolithic find horizon. a) intact blades and flakes, b) microdébitage. Excavated part of the mapped area is indicated in figure 37.6.

The Mesolithic south of the coversand elevation

Southeast of the coversand elevation a 40–50 m wide, slightly southward inclined (Figure 37.1), relatively flat plain is running parallel to the peat deposit. Here another Mesolithic site is located west of a channel that enters into the former lake. About 300 m² of the find horizon are well preserved in a humic podsol, that exhibits some traces of water influence. The Ah- Horizon that formerly formed the lands surface is mostly missing, but the bleached Ae- horizon is present in all parts of the excavated area. In contrast to the situation on the coversand hill, a variety of pre- and post soil formation features has been observed here.

Until now, about 230 m² have been excavated, about 14.000 lithic objects were encountered, 80% of the finds are flint artefacts. About half of the finds from the soil occur in the bleached horizon, the other half lying in the B- horizon below.

10 hearth features (Figure 37.6) and further a number of Mesolithic pits were encountered during the excavation: Concerning the hearths, one hearth (4046 in Figure 37.6) is of the same type as the one reported from the

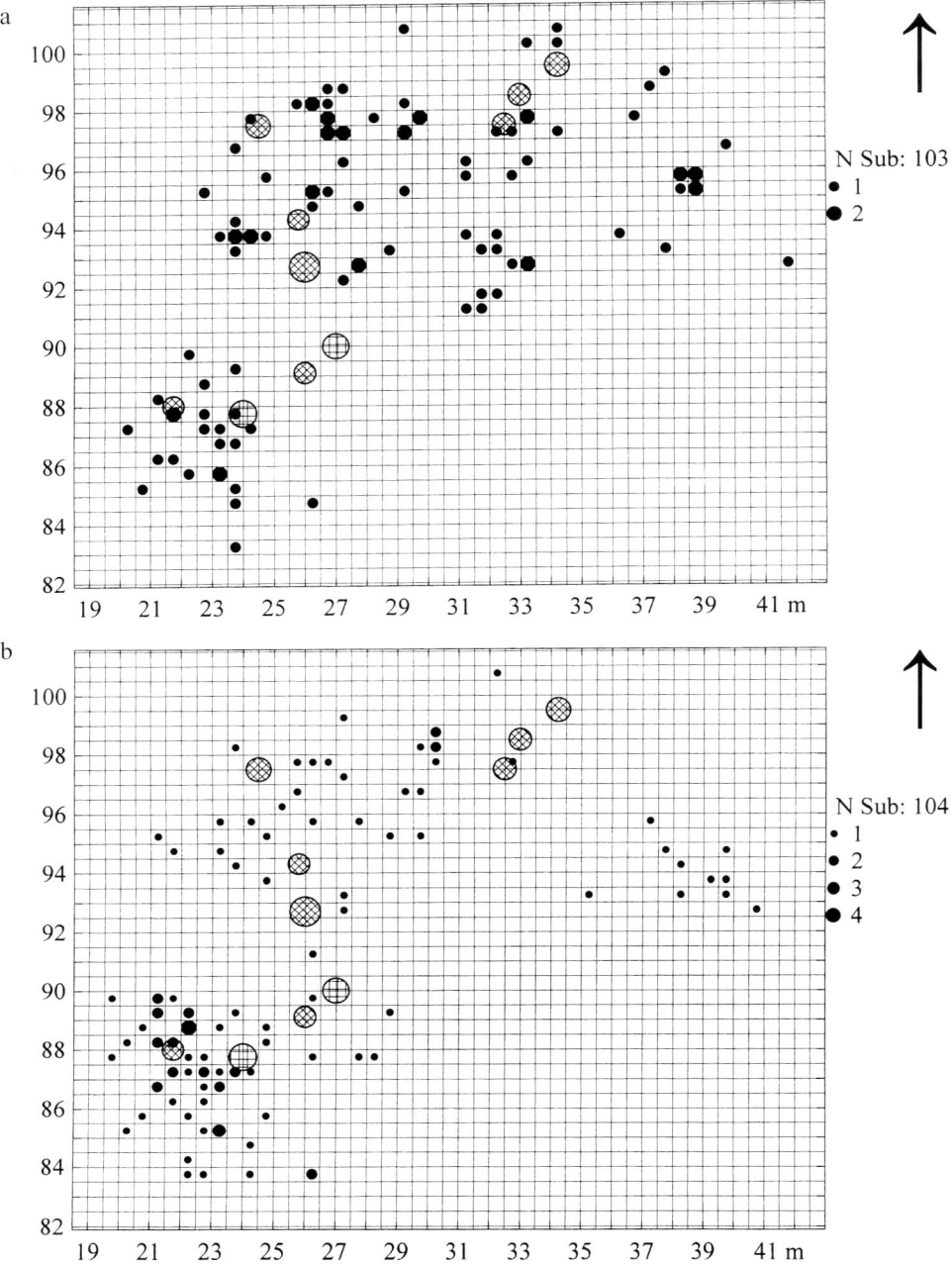

Figure 37.9 Density distributions in the younger Mesolithic find horizon. a) microliths, b) endscrapers. Excavated part of the mapped area is indicated in figure 37.6.

coversand elevation, the remaining 9 hearths are of a different type, which is related to relatively small fire-pits, with mean diameters of about 40 cm. The charcoal rich fillings are only visible in the B- horizon of the podsol, lying in pits that were deepened down into the former ground well below the find horizon. Sometimes burnt branches are to be found at the ground of the hearths. Up to now, no wood determinations are available. The pit´s boundaries mostly exhibit slight bioturbation. Since in the 15–20 cm thick bleached horizon no traces of the former pits are visible, experiments in refinding the upper limits of the pits by using Infrared black and white photography were conducted. The experiments did not bring further visible results: If the bleaching process would have altered charcoal rich deposits in the upper part of a filling, it should have been possible to detect the upper boundaries using infrared photography (Figure 37.7). Since this is not the case it may be concluded, that the hearths did only have charcoal in their lower parts, the upper parts being empty. After use they were filled with sand intentionally or the hearth´s walls broke down in relatively short time, until it was filled with sand. These sands inside the hearths, covering the filling were later transformed by soil formation processes.

The functions of the hearths remain unclear. A few small fragments of burned bone were encountered in two hearths. Stone artefacts or rock fragments are rarely to be found in the hearth´s fillings as well. Determinations of charred plant material from the fillings could, in analogy of the observations by Perry (1999) in the Netherlands result in the detection of edible plant remains, for example tubers of *Typha latifolia*, hence reflecting procurement of plant food resources from the nearby lake. Further analysis has to be awaited.

6 hearths were AMS- dated. With 2- sigma confidence 4 of them (4040, 4032, 4076, 4046, see Figure 37.6) fall in the early Atlantic time span around 6400 – 6200 cal. BC, while with the same confidence, the other two (4050, 4071, see Figure 37.6) are about 200 years younger. The younger hearths occurred in the southern part of the excavation.

Bigger fragments of all raw materials and debris >1 cm indicate concentrated occurrences in the central northern part, where mainly quartz debris was encountered, and in the western part around one of the hearths (4046), the one that is of the type encountered also on top of the coversand elevation, and in the southern part of the area excavated so far, where mainly bigger quartzite fragments are located in an area with several pits (not shown in these maps). A density map of the complete flint blades and flakes (Figure 37.8a) point again to a concentration in the northern central part, to the western and south-western parts, separated by a so far non excavated block (see Figure 37.6), and to a further concentration in the east, as well as to some smaller situations. The debris <1 cm (Figure 37.8b) perhaps gives the clearest impression of the encountered concentrations in the south-west, the west, the central north, in the east as well as a smaller situation east of the hearth 4088. The situation east of this hearth seems to be an area of microlith fabrication, according to the density of microburins, that appear to have quite restricted distributions. Beside the area just mentioned it is especially the northern central concentration that contains many microburins. All situations that contain microburins do also contain microliths (Figure 37.9a), maybe fabrication and/or retooling can be stated for these places. The density distribution of scrapers (Figure 37.9b) that are as numerous as the microliths does show a different pattern: while the microliths appear mainly in the northern and less frequently in the south-western concentration, and are also present in the parts around and south of the three northern hearths, scrapers do mainly occur in the south-western concentration, are less abundant in the northern one, and are mainly missing in the eastern part, just being present in the form of a loose stray of scrapers over an area restricted to 8–10 m².

Conclusion

The interpretation of both situations reported here has to await further fieldwork and further analysis. To me it seems probable, that the sandy environment of Reichwalde where bones are nearly not preserved, bears sites with a good potential for further analysis of settlement and activity structures.

References

Elburg, R. and van der Kroft, P. 1999. Überraschungen aus der Tiefe. Das Moorprojekt Reichwalde. *Archäologie Aktuell im Freistaat Sachsen* 5, 90–95.

Friedrich, M., Knipping, M., van der Kroft, P., Renno, A., Schmidt, S., Ullrich, O. and Vollbrecht, J. 2001. Dynamik in Siedlung und Landschaft an einen See in Reichwalde. *Arbeits- und Forschungsberichte zur sächsischen Bodendenkmalpflege* 43, 21–94.

Perry, D. 1999. Vegetative Tissues from Mesolithic Sites in the Northern Netherlands. *Current Anthropology* 40 (2), 231–237.

Ullrich, O., Vollbrecht, J. and Wirtz, D. 1999. Archäologische und Geowissenschaftliche Untersuchungen im Vorfeld des Tagebaus Reichwalde. *Sächsische Heimatblätter* 45 (1), 17–26.

Vollbrecht, J. 1998/99. Jäger am Waldsee. Das Moorprojekt Reichwalde II. *Archäologie Aktuell im Freistaat Sachsen* 6, 12–21.

—— 2001. Das Mesolithikum am Nordrand eines Moores bei Reichwalde, Ostsachsen. *Die Kunde* N.F. 52, 145–172.

Wolf, L. and Alexowsky, W. 1994. Fluviatile und glaziäre Ablagerungen am äußersten Rand der Elster- und Saale-Vereisung; die spättertiäre und quartäre Geschichte des sächsischen Elbgebietes. *Altenburger Naturwissenschaftliche Forschungen*, Heft 7, 190–235.

Session V

Territoriality – Regionalisation

38. Introduction

Berit Valentin Eriksen

Regional studies have a long tradition in the Mesolithic archaeology of Europe and with the present possibilities of computer aided processing of large and complex datasets, GIS analysis, etc., regional approaches are as popular as ever. In fact most of the papers presented at the MESO2000 conference would fit nicely within this heading.

Essentially, the region is an analytical construct associated with sub-division of space. In a regional scale approach, the extent and the delimitation of the study area depends first and foremost on the methodological approach, the questions addressed, and the chronological framework of the study. Together these issues determine the scale of analysis. A region may cover an area of a few hundred or several thousand square kilometers, and it may be circumscribed by more or less well-defined topographical, political, demographic, economic, or other natural or socio-cultural boundaries. The scale and the geographical delimitation of a region is highly dependent on the nature of its perceived or defined boundaries. Depending on the definition, regions may overlap, include, or eliminate each other and may even build up a hierarchy of behavioral universes – or territories. Thus, in prehistoric hunter-gatherer archaeology, *regionalisation* (or the study of regionality), essentially is a matter of investigating spatial structures, such as the distribution of settlements on the landscape *or* behavioral aspects relating to exploitation patterns within an area. *Territoriality*, generally is a much more loaded concept. The territory may be defined vaguely as a behavioral universe, but it may also be seen as a defended area, i.e. an area controlled by a specific ethnic group.

In the European Mesolithic regional studies have often been performed at a fairly local scale, i.e. usually a landscape approach with a geographical focus on areas varying from a few hundred up till a few thousand square kilometers. The object of these studies quite often is to establish the socio-economic and natural setting, such as the site catchment area, of a specific site or group of sites, or to delineate the settlement history of a particular area and period. Some researchers have also attempted a more generalised, macro-regional approach, with a geographical area of interest covering larger areas, such as the Northwest European lowland, the Iberian Peninsula, Great Britain, or Scandinavia. These endeavours have often been devoted to largely descriptive presentations with a main focus on questions pertaining to chronology and subsistence economy.

Most recent studies (independent of scale of analysis) acknowledge that the various Early Mesolithic hunter-gatherer groups of Europe as a rule were quite mobile. As regards the Later Mesolithic things get increasingly complicated and in many regions it seems perfectly reasonable to assume a semi-permanent settlement and exploitation pattern as time goes on. Accordingly, it would be a serious mistake to assume that man-land relationships and land-use patterns remained constant through time. In fact, many scholars have argued for an increased regionality in the course of the Mesolithic, thus obviously acknowledging important changes in man-land relationships through time. On the other hand, the analytical basis supporting these observations and accordingly their level of reliability may vary tremendously depending on the quality and quantity of the archaeological record.

South Scandinavian archaeology is for example blessed with a rich organic record from the Earlier as well as the Later Mesolithic. Considering the latter (i.e., the Ertebølle-culture) it is possible to discuss aspects of regionality with a very high level of reliability and accuracy, and it is even possible to assert questions of biological as well as cultural ethnicity. In other areas of Europe (e.g. southern Germany) regional groupings may be studied almost exclusively on the basis of analysis of lithic inventories. Conclusions are accordingly far more speculative and far less detailed. Obviously, any discussion of increased regionality depends on the region(s) studied and the quality of the archaeological remains involved.

The following papers clearly illustrate the marked spatial and temporal diversity in the archaeological record. They take us to various regions in mesolithic western Europe: from Cantabrian Spain over southern Germany to Scandinavia: Denmark, Norway and Sweden – and to

Great Britain: Scotland, the Isle of Man and northern England. Unfortunately there are no papers from eastern Europe, but despite the geographical bias this is nonetheless a very diverse group of papers. Evidently a *region* is a quite elastic concept, and a regional approach may be a matter of considerable variation with respect to scale and objective.

39. The spatial and chronological development of the Late Mesolithic Nøstvet period in coastal southeastern Norway from a lithic raw material perspective

Evy Berg

The results from recent excavations in the Follo region, Akershus County in southeastern Norway have provided renewed interest in the study of the processes of procurement and tool production from different locally available raw materials. The Oslofjord area appears to be the center for the classic coastal Nøstvet culture. The questions that are addressed in this paper are: When in the Mesolithic does the use of locally available raw materials for tool production begin in coastal southeastern Norway? Which raw material types are utilised, and how were they procured? For what purposes were the different raw materials utilised? The role of the continuous isostatic uplift and the patterns of utilisation of available raw material sources will also be addressed. Ideological aspects of the Mesolithic landscape are important for understanding the social frames that raw material procurement strategies operated within.

Introduction

The Oslofjord area is the center for the Mesolithic Nøstvet culture. The Follo region in Akershus County in Southeastern Norway, on the eastern side of the fjord has been intensively surveyed over the last 20 years, and more than 250 Mesolithic sites have been located in connection with plans for building new roads, railways and industrial areas (Figure 39.1). The results from recent excavations conducted by the National Museum of Antiquities, Oslo,

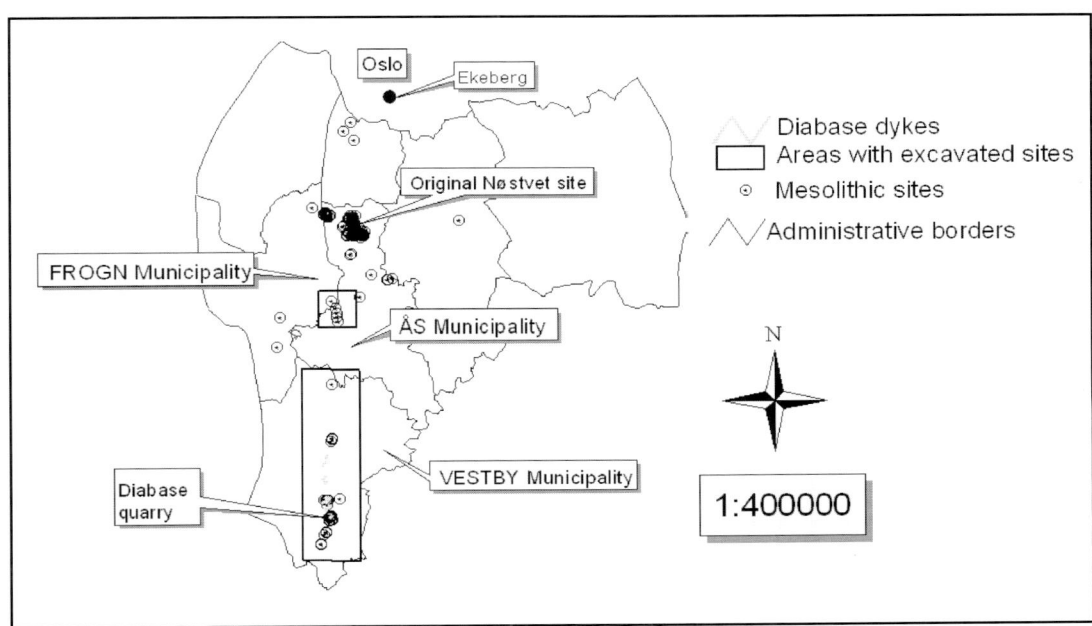

Figure 39.1 Oslo and the adjacent Follo region in Akershus.

in three of the municipalities in the Follo region provided renewed interest in the study of the processes of procurement and tool production from various locally available non-flint raw materials. Until 1993 very few Mesolithic sites had been excavated in the inner part of the Oslofjord. Between 1993 and 1997 twelve Nøstvet sites were excavated in Vestby, Ås and Frogn municipalities (Berg 1995, 1997, 1999). The new finds provide data regarding the use of the landscape over a 2–3000 year period, particularly the use of local raw materials for artifact production.

Geographic Limits of the Nøstvet Culture in Norway

The finds mostly occur along the coast. The Nøstvet axe is mainly restricted to coastal areas, and is rare in the interior. Only in rare cases have Nøstvet axes been found along the southwestern coast and never in numbers often encountered along the Oslofjord. The Lihult axe in Sweden is the equivalent of the Nøstvet type. The former is found along the Swedish coast and inland. Due to modern borders, Norwegian and Swedish archaeologists each have one piece of the Nøstvet/Lihult puzzle. Further west the composition of artifact assemblages varies, so that in the southwestern part of Norway the differences become so great that the Nøstvet label is no longer meaningful and the assemblage should be interpreted as an independent social territory (Ballin and Lass Jensen 1995:236). The Mesolithic sites in western Norway do not generally include any typical Nøstvet traits. What is common over large areas is a microblade technology, while the larger artifacts vary with respect to techniques used in manufacture and form. For example, axes in western Norway are completely ground, pecking is used occasionally, but rarely, and core axes like the Nøstvet axe are not part of the assemblage. A wide variety of local rock types were utilised for different purposes, and patterns in the utilisation of certain raw materials like the Hespriholmen greenstone and Stakaneset diabase have been recorded (Alsaker and Bruen Olsen 1984). Nøstvet artifact types are found in the interior of eastern Norway, although they lack axes and the large non-flint artifacts like the sandstone knife. There is a great deal of various non-flint rock types in use in the interior (Boaz 1999:131 pp). Classical Nøstvet therefore seems delimited to the coastal areas around the Oslofjord, stretching into the interior of eastern Norway and into Sweden where it is known as the Lihult culture.

Survey and registration in Follo, Akershus

These sites were recorded solely on the basis of the occurence of flint material and artifacts in test pits. No other rock types were searched for, and the only and main criteria for selecting spots for test-pits were old shorelines. Documentation of newly recorded sites in Vestby (1998–1999) show that cores and flakes from diabase are a relatively common phenomenon. The use of this dense volcanic rock is thus not restricted to axes, although axe production is the most common usage. As yet there has been no organised search for other types of Mesolithic sites other than dwelling sites. Unlike dwelling sites, small quarries/procurement sites are not necessarily located along the ancient shorelines.

The sites excavated 1993–1997

Both typologically and chronologically the sites are representative of, and illustrate the development of the Nøstvet period in the Follo region, which is at least partly relevant for adjacent areas as well. The Nøstvet culture is defined on the basis of typological elements: the Nøstvet axe, microblade technology and various large non-flint tools, for example the sandstone knife/saw. The dates and material from the sites makes it possible to construct a typological/chronological sequence for the whole of the Nøstvet phase (Figure 39.2). Dates according to shoreline displacement curves in Follo are based on Sørensen for uncalibrated dates (1979), Sørensen et. al. for calibrated dates (1996). The oldest sites date to around 7700–7800 years BP, uncalibrated or 6600–6460 BC calibrated date. They show that a wide variety of different lithic materials were used for the production of both big and small tools: flint, rock crystal and other quartz varieties, quartzite, sandstone, metarhyolite, diabase, hornfels and different syenites (Figure 39.3). The variety is enormous compared to earlier periods where flint dominated and where there are only very small quantities and types of other materials such as rock crystal and quartz. Sites lie at approximately 70 m a.s.l. down to 65 m a.s.l. In the middle Nøstvet between 7300–6900 BP, uncalibrated date, the rock materials selected and utilised are more restricted, flint is the most important, rock crystal is used for small tools while diabase and hornfels are common in axe production while diabase is used for various large tools with unknown functions. Sandstone knives develop from small specimens in the early part of the period into a large uniform type by the middle and later part. Sites are located between approximately 62–57 m a.s.l.. The late part contains the typical Nøstvet assemblage of axes, sandstone knives, large sandstone grinding stones and microblade technology. Sites lie at approximately 55–45 m a.s.l.

In Follo a wide variety of non-flint materials appears in the archaeological record from 7800 BP, uncalibrated. It is still uncertain if this development might have started even earlier, since few older sites have been excavated. There is an indication that something new happens around 8000–7800 BP, uncalibrated. From one excavated site in Frogn at 86 m a.s.l., large quantities of worked rhomb porphyry were discovered. Ballin dates the site to 8000 BP, uncalibrated (Ballin 1998: 30 pp). This might be the remains from one of the first attempts to utilise locally occurring non-flint, non-silicate rocks. Chemical wea-

Shoreline curves: Sørensen 1979 and 1996,: Follo, Danielsen 1970: Østfold

Loc. name	Meters above sea level	Years BP uncalibrated curve	Years BP calibrated curve	Years BC calibrated curve	14C-date BP uncalibrated	14C-date BC calibrated 1 sigma	Lab. No.
Loc. 1 Trosterud	70-65	8000-7700	8900-8600	6900-6600	7745+75	6600-6460	Tua-1549
					7435+75	6370-6175	Tua-1548
Loc. 3 Kvestad	65-60	7700-7300	8600-8400	6600-6400	7435+70	6370-6180	Tua-1547
Rød nedre R72	62-60	7500-7300	8600-8300	6600-6300			
Loc. 2 Kvestad	60-58	7300-7000	8400-8000	6400-6000			
Loc. 4 Horgen	59-57	7100-6900	8100-7900	6100-5900			
Knapstad R113	55-54	6800-6700	7800-7600	5800-5600			
Labu R1	49-50	6400-6000	7300-7100	5300-5100			
Knapstad R114	49-47	6400-6000	7300-7100	5300-5100			
Stavengåsen R121	48-45	6300-5900	7000-6700	5000-4700			
Stavengåsen R21	48-45	6300-5900	7000-6700	5000-4700			
Gjølstad R34	44-42	5800-5700	6600-6400	4600-4400			
Gjølstad R33 Phase 4	41-39	5600-5300	6300-6000	4300-4000	5330+70 5390+75	4310-4010 4335-4095	Tua-893 Tua-894

Figure 39.2 Chronological table over sites excavated in Follo

Typological elements and percentage of non-flint rock types

Loc. name	Round-butted Axes	Nøstvet Axes	Microblade cores: Conical cores	Microblade cores: Handle cores	Bipolar cores	Transverse arrows	Small sand-stone knives	Large sand-stone knives	Grind-stones	Non-flint Rock present % of total material	Microblades % of total blade material
Loc. 1 Trosterud	6	16	1	1	50				3	15%	47%
Lok. 3 Kvestad	1	5	11	10	29		3		9	13%	91%
Rød nedre R72	3	1	4	1	3			1	9	38.60%	78%
Loc. 2 Kvestad	1	2	1		15				1	43%	96%
Loc. 4 Horgen	1	2	1		4				8	35%	70%
Knapstad R113		1		1					1	84%	99%
Labu R1		11			1			6	3	76.20%	100%
Stavengåsen R21			1	1					1	0.30%	92%
Knapstad R114		10		1	1				8	80%	100%
Stavengåsen R121		5	2	3	1			1	2	16.60%	78%
Gjølstad R34									1	0.30%	63%
Gjølstad R33			1	2	6	44			6	0.50%	47%

Figure 39.3 Typological elements and frequency of non-flint rocks

thering processes affect this particular volcanic rock to a much lesser extent than they do diabase and particularly the hornfels. The surface of the diabase is affected so that it's color changes from it's original dark gray/black to green and brown hues, but the shape of the artifacts and flakes is rarely effected to such an extent that they cannot be recognised. Both the surface color and the shape of the artifacts made from metamorphic hornfels may be eroded to such a degree that it is sometimes questionable whether one is dealing with artifacts or with natural lumps. The weathering varies with the quality of the rock, which again is determined by the original composition of sediments, and the conditions in the soil where the material is deposited. The use of sandstone is restricted mainly to grinding stones and a particular kind of knife or saw, with ground edges. Metarhyolite and quartzite were used to a certain degree. The various non-flint raw materials were used for a wide spectrum of purposes. Typically micro crystalline, dense rock types like diabase, hornfels and other volcanic/metamorphic rock types were preferred for axes, both the Nøstvet type and the pecked round-butted axes. There are however a small amount of other artifacts, possibly used for cutting purposes, which are mostly made out of diabase. Flake and sometimes microblade cores are found made from varieties of quartz and metarhyolite. Retouched flakes made from these materials have been found on several sites (Berg 1999:277 p). Throughout the Nøstvet period the number of recorded non-flint raw materials drops from about 12 in the early stage, to 6–8 in the middle of the period, to 5–6 in the late part and vanishes completely at the end of the period, that is to say about 5800–5700 BP uncalibrated. Figure 39.3 shows that the percentage of recorded non-flint raw materials on the sites differs enormously. This is almost certainly due to different activities being performed on different sites, and is not necessarily chronologically relevant, although it might be. There seems to be a lot of experimentation during the earliest period in which a large number of different materials are tried out when making various artifact types.

Procurement of local non-flint rock types

The procurement and utilisation of local raw materials has been documented extensively in Western Norway, but until now there has been only minor interest in the coastal cultures in eastern Norway. One reason is that the coastal Nøstvet culture was thought to be more like contemporary Danish cultures, where flint dominates completely. Sites excavated on the outer coast of the southern most counties Østfold and Vestfold are rich in flint material compared to those excavated along the inner part of the Oslofjord. Comparison with other flint assemblages for the purposes of typology and chronology were considered important, but this interest led to the neglect of studies concerning local raw materials (Mikkelsen 1975; Lindblom 1984). Also, quarries were either unknown or were situated in the interior (Sjurseike 1994). It was believed for a long time that there were no organised procurement and utilisation strategies for locally available lithics in coastal eastern Norway, compared with the situation in western Norway. Whenever local rock types not native to a site or the area surrounding it were found, deposition by the glacier during the Ice Age was the general explanation used to account for the presence of exotic rocks.

The first Mesolithic quarry found in Norway was the huge Hespriholmen quarry in Bømlo municipality in western Norway, which was identified in 1922 (Shetelig 1925), nearly twenty years after Brøgger's various works on the Nøstvet culture (Figure 39.4a). This quarry was extensively described and analysed (Alsaker and Bruen Olsen 1984; Alsaker 1987). More recent research into the Mesolithic of southeastern Norway has largely focused on chronological concerns, as well as economic and ecological questions (Mikkelsen 1975a, 1975b; Lindblom 1984). Raw materials, their procurement and use have not been investigated since Brøgger's studies, almost 90 years ago. The bedrock in the Follo region consists of Precambrian material, mainly gneisses, with younger intrusive dykes and sills. The Oslo paleo-rift, which dates to the Permian period, lies to the north and west of the Follo area and contains a wide variety of volcanic and metamorphic rocks, as well as older Paleozoic rocks that have escaped metamorphosis. Most of the intrusive dykes in the Precambrian bedrock are of Permian age and are connected to rifting. Among the most common intrusive rock types are diabase, amphibolites, syenites and rhomb porphyry (Sundvoll and Larsen 1993; Berthelsen et. al. 1996). The availability of these different raw materials has varied greatly during the post-glacial period, due to the extreme isostatic uplift in this region. The marine limit in the inner Oslofjord varies between 200–225 m a.s.l., and during early post-glacial times this area was largely submerged. The changes in the landscape were rapid during the first centuries after deglaciation, when the uplift was most extreme (Sørensen 1979; Hafsten 1983). An important question is the degree to which this continuous uplift has affected the utilisation of the raw material sources available in bedrock outcrops. For example, these sources were first available along the shore zone, but the continued uplift eventually moved them away from the shore. The effect of isostatic uplift does not necessarily indicate that all activities in the Nøstvet society were confined to the shore bound areas. A diabase dyke originally discovered at sea level would over the course of a few generations lie far from the shore. The same applies to collections of erratics, where such exist and were used for raw material procurement.

During the excavations in the Vestby municipality a site with a large amount of diabase flakes was found, Knapstad R114 (Figure 39.4b). The site was situated on a diabase dyke that outcropped here. Compared to the large Hespriholmen quarry (Figure 39.4a) it is tiny. As a result of this discovery a survey was undertaken along the planned railway/motorway to map all diabase dykes. Thirteen dykes, all tiny in cross section, varying between 0,5–2 m, were found (Snilsberg 1995). The quality of rocks in a dyke varies. In the middle of a dyke, it is relatively coarse grained, while the outer parts are fine grained. A comparison based on visual traits between the diabase material, both axes and debitage, and samples taken from the dykes from all the sites indicates that the dyke on R114 may have provided raw material for the production of an axe found on the nearby site Stavengåsen R121. Diabase from the quarry is interpreted as having been used for axe production on the site, for producing blanks or small blocks for further use elsewhere. On the site R121, which lies on the other side of the island from R114, a limited number of diabase flakes were found. Some of the flakes were refitted and formed a negative image of an Nøstvet axe (Olstad 1995). The finds on R121 indicate that the removal of small blocks might be as common as finishing the axe at the procurement/quarry site R114. Here several unfinished specimens were found. Most showed faults of various kinds, relating to the quality of the rock. One piece was about to split along the middle when work on it was given up. This indicates that the rock quality was not the best and that other still unknown rock sources with better qualities probably exist. Further north, there was strong correlation between axes from the site Rød nedre R72 and a sample from a dyke a couple of

Figure 39.4a The Hespriholmen greenstone quarry. Photo by Evy Berg.

Figure 39.4b Small diabase quarry in Vestby. Photo: Evy Berg.

kilometers further to the south. These results are not conclusive since diabase from different sources can look quite alike on the macroscopic level. To get any further with correlations between artifacts and known rock sources, analyses of the geochemistry of the various diabases is necessary (Berg 1995:154 pp, 1999:267 pp).

Ideology as a factor in raw material acquisition

Ideology is influenced by landscape. The extreme isostatic uplift during the Mesolithic in Eastern Norway meant that change was happening constantly. This factor must be taken into consideration when dealing with questions of ideological production, symbolic behavior and the structuring of landscape rights among groups and individuals. This applies to fishing/hunting grounds or the right to utilise an outcrop of suitable rock for the procurement of raw material for an axe. Another factor operating in this area is the fact that diabase dykes and outcrops of contact-metamorphic rocks, such as hornfels, are relatively small. Diabase dykes normally only measure a few meters in cross section. They often appear as clefts and crevices among the more erosion resistant gneisses of the Precambrian bedrock. A comparison with the big Hespriholmen greenstone quarry in Bømlo, Hordaland on the West coast makes this clear. The change of sea level is very different between eastern and western Norway. Hespriholmen was, for all practical purposes, always available since the deglaciation. In southeast Norway, however, there were few diabase outcrops available some 9000–10000 years ago, but the uplift soon produced more land and thus more available rock. The dark color of diabase dykes makes them very easy to spot at sea level, but visibility would decrease with growing vegetation. A marker for such outcrops would be clefts and crevices.

The combination of many small dykes in the landscape with rapid uplift and landscape change could lead to an ideological situation where the people inhabiting and using this landscape continually updated their ideas, in ideological production, symbolic behavior and the structuring of rights of utilisation of resources. Quarry sites in Australia are often described as "powerful places". When a local rock source was discovered it was given special significance and associated with powerful and dangerous forces (Tacon 1991:199). A person who owns the right to use an outcrop has obligations to ensure that it is used correctly and is therefore responsible to other people who want to utilise it. There might therefore be a number of restrictions on access to an outcrop, depending on the strength of the myths connected with it. Some places will be more restricted than others due to the strength of myths (Paton 1994:178). In a Norwegian Mesolithic context such an approach is easy to visualise concerning the large Hespriholmen quarry, which according to Alsaker was used from 9000–4000 years BP, uncalibrated, from the Early Mesolithic to the beginning of the Late Neolithic (Alsaker and Bruen Olsen 1984; Alsaker 1987). Both Hespriholmen and the large Stakaneset quarry further north in western Norway were special places within the encultured landscape of the Mesolithic people (Uleberg 1999:43 p). The tiny dykes in the rapidly changing landscape of southeastern Norway might have been regarded as "power places". If so, for how long were they regarded as special places? Did their status as power places change depending on how long they were in use, and how did their movement away from the sea, as well as the growth of vegetation on and near them, effect this status? Is there any way we can see that these places were powerful and special?

A recorded quarry that has never been excavated may shed some light on this. On the hill of Ekeberg in the city of Oslo there is a quarry that has been known for some time. It was discovered by a resident in the area who found some intentionally struck flakes there and brought them to the attention of the National museum of Antiquities in Oslo (Archaeological Registry number 033664). The Ekeberg plateau sticks up above the city and is quite steep, but flat on top. On the north side, facing the city, is a dyke consisting of what appears to be diabase and scree containing intentionally struck flakes. A crevice in the rock about a meter wide shows traces of being worked. Further down a steep slope the terrain widens and here lies a large collection of flakes and unworked stone. The lower part lies at about 90 m a.s.l. while the crevice itself is between 105–110 m a.s.l. According to shoreline dates this quarry predates the Nøstvet period by at least a 1000 years. So far there are no certain indications that any kind of rock utilisation or tools such as rock axes were in use at 9000 BP uncalibrated in southeastern Norway. An alternative explanation is that this dyke was not utilised until later, and that its use had no direct connection to the shore level. This "powerful place" could have been used over a long period of time. Further along the Ekeberg plateau lies a Rock-art site with animals, which is dated to the Late Mesolithic (Mikkelsen 1976; Haukalid 1999). Ekeberg obviously was a "powerful place" in the Late Mesolithic. Oslo lies at the innermost part of the Oslofjord today. The fjord stretched a bit further inland during the Mesolithic due to the higher sea level. At the beginning of the Nøstvet period the sea level was 70–75 m a.s.l. Ekeberg had by this time emerged as a promontory in the landscape. Here the ocean ended and travel further inland could be undertaken along the rivers. It might have been a meeting ground for different groups, a ritual and ceremonial place for many purposes. The rock quarried or collected from the dyke may have had a special significance, and access to the quarry site, the right to collect/quarry here could have been restricted in accordance with stories embedding rules of conduct. Restrictions concerning access might not have applied to all quarries or outcrops of suitable stone that were in use at this time.

How does the interpretation of the Ekeberg dyke/quarry affect our understanding of the small dyke in Vestby? Ekeberg might have been utilised earlier than the Nøstvet period due to its location on a higher shore level than the dyke on R114 in Vestby, but the quarry activities could be far younger, thus not related to direct access from the shore. The Vestby quarry/procurement site is far more rigorously dated according to the sea level changes than Ekeberg. The same or different groups, depending on the rules attached to those places, could have utilised them at the same time. As new dykes became available for exploitation, individuals or groups discovered them, claimed rights, and wove the site into their symbolic landscape and social organisation. It is possible that access to this site was regulated by different restrictions than those governing the Ekeberg site. The Vestby site was probably not used very extensively. About 30 000 artifacts of diabase were found here during the excavation in 1993. It is the only coastal quarry/procurement site excavated so far, and it is very unlikely to be a unique occurrence, but this dyke/quarry just happened to be the first of its kind to be excavated. The relatively small amount of rock used here might indicate that rock procurement was a localised affair in this region, but this question has many aspects which will require more research before any secure interpretations can be formulated. The social and ritual landscape of the Nøstvet period is still poorly known, and these aspects are as important as the purely functional or technical considerations.

Many sites recorded in this area during the last few years have turned up non-flint artifact like cores, flakes and axes, indicating widespread use of diabase. The registration of dykes along the new motorway resulted in the discovery of 13 dykes along this short stretch alone, indicating that a large number of tiny dykes with good quality rock probably exist both within this region and in related areas. Flakes made from the metamorphic hornfels have also been recorded. W.C. Brøgger identified hornfels as a common material for making Nøstvet axes (Brøgger 1905b). No quarries or procurement sites have so far been found. Hornfels do occur in the bedrock within the Oslo paleo-rift, but they may also have been transported by ice as erratics to other areas. One possible argument against using erratics is that they may be of poor quality. The chemical weathering of hornfels is rapid, especially in acid soils, where the rock becomes soft and completely useless for artifact production. Fresh hornfels, on the other hand, is dense and almost as sharp as flint. It may no longer be possible to recognise a hornfels quarry, if such existed, due to chemical erosion.

Conclusion

So far quarry activities related to dykes have only been dated to the Late Mesolithic. Future surveys should increase our knowledge concerning both the number of small quarries and the number of specialised sites where raw material was worked. It should also improve our understanding of their chronological sequence and of various procurement strategies. The changes that occurred in raw material selection observed during the Nøstvet period shows that something happened. The earliest part of the Nøstvet period is characterised by the use of a wealth of different rock types. Later on in the period the number of utilised rock types seemingly drops to half the number used in the early phase and by the transition to the Early Neolithic the whole local tradition for using non-flint raw material has seemingly vanished. The situation in western Norway is completely different, here the utilisation of local raw materials continued until the Late Neolithic. The combined dates and material from all the sites makes it possible to construct a typological/chronological sequence for the whole of the Nøstvet phase that includes both small and big artifacts. The landscape changed continuously with the sea level dropping by about 30 meters during the period, creating more land, changing small islands into bigger ones, fusing some of the islands with the mainland, altering fishing grounds, oceanic streams and the conditions for both animals, plants and food sources in the sea, e.g. oyster beds. The landscape at the end of Nøstvet period was quite different from that at the beginning. In this area landscape change is an important factor in social and ritual production and must be taken into consideration. Surveys and documentation conducted in this landscape needs to include strategies for localising quarries and procurement sites that are not necessarily located along ancient shore levels. Since diabase dykes have a certain degree of visibility due to their dark color and the fact that they erode faster than the surrounding bedrock, thereby creating/forming natural crevices, it is possible to devise indicators and criteria that will facilitate their discovery and documentation through archaeological surveys.

References

Alsaker, S. 1987. *Bømlo-Steinalderens råstoffsentrum på Sørvestlandet.* Arkeologiske avhandlinger 4. Historisk museum, University of Bergen. Bergen.

Alsaker, S. and Bruen Olsen, A. 1984. Greenstone and Diabase Utilisation in the Stone Age of Western Norway: Technological and Socio-cultural Aspects of Axe and Adze production and distribution. *Norwegian Archaeological Review* 17, No. 2, 71–103.

Ballin, T.B. 1998. *Oslofjordforbindelsen. Arkæologiske undersøgelser ved Drøbaksundet.* Varia 48. Universitetets Oldsaksamling. Oslo.

Ballin. T.B. and Lass Jensen, O. 1995. *Farsundprosjektet-stenalderbopladser på Lista.* Varia 29. Universitetets Oldsaksamling. Oslo.

Berg, E. 1995. *Dobbeltspor/E6-prosjektet Steinalderlokaliteter fra senmesolittisk tid i Vestby, Akershus.* Varia 32. Universitetets Oldsaksamling. Oslo.

—— 1997. *Mesolittiske boplasser ved Årungen i Ås og Frogn, Akershus. Dobbeltspor/E6-prosjektet 1996.* Varia 44. Universitetets Oldsaksamling. Oslo.

—— 1999. Spatial and chronological variation of raw-materials within the coastal settlement in Akershus and Østfold, SE Norway. In: Boaz, J. (ed.) *The Mesolithic of Central Scandinavia.* Universitetets Oldsaksamlings Skrifter no. 22, 267–283. Ny rekke. Oslo.

Berthelsen, A., Olerud, S. and Sigmond, E.M.O. 1996. *Geologisk kart over Norge, berggrunnskart OSLO 1:250000.* Norges geologiske undersøkelse. Trondheim.

Boaz, J. 1999. Pioneers in the Mesolithic: The Initial Occupation of the Interior of Eastern Norway. In: Boaz, J. (ed.) *The Mesolithic of Central Scandinavia.* Universitetets Oldsaksamlings. Skrifter no. 22, 125–152. Ny rekke. Oslo.

Brøgger, A.W. 1905a. *Strandliniens beliggenhed under stenalderen i det sydøstlige Norge.* Kristiania.

—— 1905b. *Øxer av Nøstvettypen. Bidrag til kundskapen om Ældre Norsk Stenalder.* Norges Geologiske Undersøkelse No. 42. Kristiania.

Haukalid, S. 1999. *Menneskets bilde: en studie av 10 veideristningslokaliteter i Øst-Norge.* Cand. Philol thesis in Nordic Archaeology, University of Oslo. Oslo.

Mikkelsen, E. 1975a. Mesolithic in South eastern Norway. *Norwegian Archaeological Review* 8, No. 1, 19–35.

—— 1975b. *Frebergsvik. Et mesolitisk boplassområde ved Oslofjorden.* Universitetets Oldsaksamlings skrifter – ny rekke 1. Oslo.

—— 1976. Østnorske veideristninger–Kronologi og øko-kulturelt miljø. *Viking* 40, 147–201.

Olstad, O. 1995. Øksemakeren i dobbeltsporet. *Nicolay* nr. 65/66, 26–36.

Paton, R. 1994. Speaking through stones: a study from northern Australia. *World Archaeology* 26, no. 2, 172–184.

Sjurseike, R. 1994. *Jaspisbruddet i Flendalen. En kilde til forståelse av sosiale relasjoner i eldre steinalder.* Unpublished mag. art dissertation. University of Oslo. Oslo.

Snilsberg, P. 1995. *Kartlegging av diabasganger langs ny vei og jernbane, Vestby.* Jordforsk. Report nr. 40/95. Ås.

Sundvoll, B. and Larser, B.T. 1993. *Rb-Sr and Sm-Nd relationships in dyke and sill intrusions in the Oslo rift and related areas.* NGU Bulletin 425 Miscellaneous research papers. Trondheim.

Sørensen, R. 1979. Late Weichselian deglaciation in the Oslofjord area. *Boreas* 8, 241–246.

Sørense, R., Johansen, Ø.K. and Dørum, K. 1996. *Frogn bygdebokverk. Bind 1. Fra urtid til ca. 1550.* Drøbak.

Tacon, P.S.C. 1991. The power of stone: Symbolic aspects of stone use and tool development in western Arnhem Land, Australia. *Antiquity* 65, 192–207.

Uleberg, E. 1999. Cultural Landscape in Stone Age Research. In: Boas, J. (ed.) *The Mesolithic of Central Scandinavia* Universitetets Oldsaksamlings Skrifter no. 22, 39–45. Ny rekke. Oslo.

40. Mesolithic Ethnicity – Too Hard to Handle?

Knut Andreas Bergsvik

The first section of this paper critically evaluates the application of the concept of "ethnic groups" in Mesolithic research. It is argued that the basic understanding of ethnicity, as well as the way it is approached by archaeologists is problematic. The second section focuses on possible solutions. It is suggested that ethnicity should be seen first of all as a boundary phenomenon and as a result of interaction between groups that perceive each other as different. An attempt is made to develop methodological tools for identifying such boundaries from archaeological data.

Introduction

The problem of regional variation has received considerable interest among archaeologists dealing with the European Mesolithic. Over the last few years, regionally distinct distributions of artifact styles, technologies, or raw materials have been interpreted as indicating "social territories" and "ethnic groups". In this article, I will take a critical look at some of these interpretations. My main objections are that, for too long, archaeologists working with the Mesolithic have paid too little attention to the discussions of ethnicity in the social sciences, and that they have been too uncritical when relating particular material culture distributions to ethnic groups. Ethnicity was probably important during the Mesolithic, but rather than being a static, homogeneous phenomenon which coincided nicely with cultural values and which persisted across time and space, it was more likely situational and local, and a function of boundary processes between different groups. Taking this position, ethnic groups cannot be documented in a straightforward fashion by mapping the distribution of randomly chosen cultural traits, as is too often the case with many studies. This insight has rather depressing implications for archaeologists and has led many to take a pessimistic and restrictive position. Here, a carefully optimistic stand is taken. It is held that Mesolithic ethnicity is not beyond reach, but if the subject is taken up, the study should apply an explicit social theory that bridges the traditional dichotomy between individualism and collectivism in the social sciences. Such an approach is attempted here, one that critically considers whether ethnicity was a relevant identity among Mesolithic populations. This is done by investigating the variety of ethnic relations among hunter-gatherers of the recent past. On the epistemological side, the approach acknowledges the active role that material culture plays in human discourse. Furthermore, it advocates an archaeological methodology that draws attention away from circumscription of ethnic groups to the boundaries between them.

Mesolithic cultures, social territories and ethnic groups

In order to explore regional diversity, the prehistoric populations in Europe were traditionally divided into "cultures", on the basis of regional distributions of associated stylistic similarities in selected aspects of material culture (Childe 1929; Brøndsted 1938–40). In a much cited passage, Childe related these distributions to distinct social units:

> We find certain types of remains – pots, implements, ornaments, burial sites, house forms – constantly recurring together. Such a complex of regularly associated traits we shall term a "cultural group" or just a "culture". We assume that such a complex is the material expression of what today would be termed a "people". (Childe 1929: v–vi).

Childe's "culture-historical" approach had considerable impact on the interpretations of regional archaeological distributions for many areas and periods. One scholar influenced by this approach was Grahame Clark. Although the main body of Clark's research on the Mesolithic was concerned with economic processes, he also tried to explain the regional variation of styles and types. In order to interpret these differences, he introduced the term "social territories" by which he meant:

> ...the total territory drawn upon for supplies, including raw materials, and finished products as well as food

stuffs, by a given community by virtue of belonging to a larger social grouping (Clark 1975:22).

The social grouping Clark had in mind was above the household and band levels. It was the most extensive territory of which the ordinary individual would probably, at this time, be aware. Clark argued that social groups at this level could be identified archaeologically, because they had been knit together in two distinct ways; by sharing in the redistribution of materials and products and by displaying certain idiosyncratic styles (Clark 1975:22). Clark's approach to Mesolithic social differentiation influenced writers to relate distributions of artefact styles and raw materials to social territories in areas as different as Northern Africa, England, and Western Norway (Close 1978; Jacobi 1979; Olsen and Alsaker 1984). At the second "Mesolithic in Europe" conference in 1980, Douglas Price developed the term further, by relating it explicitly to anthropological terminology. He argued that distinct adaptive patterns might be coherent with circumscription of human mating networks. The specific type of demographic unit hinted at by Price was the "dialectical tribe" (Birdsell 1953; Tindale 1974). He held that:

> The region is thus an area that should contain a relatively integrated population involved in similar subsistence practices and in the exchange of mates and information. Such a region is also anticipated to share "traditional" patterns of behaviour and activity (Price 1980:233).

Price developed a predictive approach for the Mesolithic of the northern European Plain, arguing that regional studies of styles and lithic raw materials may be used to delimit the regions and territories within which the Mesolithic bands operated. Peter Gendel (1984) took up this lead for the Mesolithic of the Netherlands and Belgium. But Gendel went even further in his interpretations. Gendel's data consisted of discrete regional distributions of different, contemporary arrowhead styles. Influenced by Martin Wobst's (1977) discussion of style as symbols of identity and particularly by Polly Wiessner's (1983) ethno-archaeological studies of different arrowhead styles and ethnic groups in Botswana, Gendel argued that the stylistic differences of these arrowheads could have been used to actively communicate ethnic differences between people from the different social territories within his study area. Several other scholars suggested links between social territories and ethnicity for different regions and periods. Petersen (1984) argued that different distributions of late Mesolithic bone/antler artefacts in Jutland/Fyn and Zealand/Scania in Denmark and Southern Sweden could be interpreted as resulting from neighbouring ethnic groups. In a similar vein, Kindgren (1991) concluded that an ethnic group probably occupied northwestern Västergötland, Sweden, during the late Mesolithic. His conclusions were based on regionally restricted distributions of tools and flakes made of a particular Cambrian flint, as well as spatial discontinuities of the raw materials used for adzes of the Lihult type. Verhart (1990) found strong correlations between different regions in northwestern Europe and stylistic differences in Mesolithic bone antler points. Similar to other artefact types noted by others (e.g. Arora 1973; Gramsch 1973; Kozlowski 1975; Rozoy 1978), Verhart's diachronic study also found that there were increased regional stylistic differences over time. These he interpreted as indicating decreasing sizes of the social territories during the Mesolithic. Raymond Newell and his colleagues (1990) arrived at similar conclusions. In a comprehensive book on Mesolithic ornaments in Western Europe they were able to distinguish a number of different regional styles. These different ornaments are seen as reflecting different language groups and dialects and therefore different ethnicity. On the basis of these assumptions they distinguish a number of ethnic groups in Mesolithic Europe.

Problematic aspects

The above studies of Mesolithic "social territories" and "ethnic groups" are hampered by two fundamental problems. The first problem is ontological and concerns the basic understanding of the concept of ethnicity. The second problem is epistemological and concerns the relationship between ethnicity and archaeological data.

Ontological problems

I find that the concept of "social territories", as defined by Grahame Clark as late as 1975, largely corresponds to the way "culture" was defined before the 1960's. In this period archaeologists and anthropologists shared similar viewpoints regarding this field of research. It was generally held that a "culture", "tribe" and "ethnic group" had more or less corresponding significance and was composed of implicit and explicit patterns of behaviour. This behaviour constituted the distinctive achievement of human groups, which consisted of patterns of material culture, beliefs, myths, ideas and values, all of which could be delineated, compared and classified (Singer 1968:530). Ethnic identity was in this context seen as a passive reflection of cultural similarity and was therefore assumed to coincide with discrete, homogenous, integrated cultures (Jones 1997:48). During the late 1950's and 1960's, however, several important critiques were raised against this simple classification.

The critiques, which were most explicitly formulated by Fredrik Barth (1969), shifted the focus from passive representations such as language and material culture to self definitions of particular ethnic groups in opposition to other groups. According to Barth, ethnicity is a form of social organisation and a characteristic of self-ascription and ascription by others:

A categorical ascription is an ethnic ascription when it classifies a person in terms of his basic, most general identity, presumptively determined by his origin and background. To the extent that actors use ethnic identities to categorise themselves and others for the purposes of interaction they form ethnic groups in the organisational sense (Barth 1969:13 p).

Instead of being passive products of cultural differences, ethnic groups are instead seen as collective organisational strategies, formed as a result of competition over socio-economic resources. An important element of his model was that the boundaries usually do not stop people from interacting with one another. On the contrary, people frequently cross the boundaries, which in Barth's approach are metaphorical more than physical. This leads, according to Barth, to a complex situation with regard to cultural content:

> ...although ethnic categories take cultural differences into account, we can assume no simple one-to-one relationship between ethnic units and cultural similarities and differences. The features that are taken into account are not the sum of "objective" differences, but only those which the actors themselves regard as significant (Barth 1969:14).

In accordance with this new understanding of ethnicity several specialists on hunter-gatherers questioned the existence of "tribes" as meaningful units (this critique was not directed towards "tribes" in the sense of evolutionary stages in social organisation). First of all, it was argued that tribes are ethnographical constructions, mainly based on the distributions of linguistic differences. They held that even linguistic boundaries can seldom be delineated on a map. There is usually a large degree of overlap around the border areas where multilingualism and dialect fuzziness dominate. Another argument is that there is a constant flow of "cultural" traits such as artefacts, art styles and techniques across the "tribal" borderlines. Except for very broad trends, few correlations have been documented between cultural traits and linguistic boundaries. Furthermore, "tribes" are almost never politically and territorially unified. Even their names are imposed on them by traders or early colonists. Finally, few ethnographers are able to document in-group notions referring to a social unit at this level. It was therefore concluded that tribes are not homogenous demographic units about which the local populations are particularly conscious of or with which they systematically identify (e.g. Berndt 1959; Fried 1968; McKennan 1969; Riches 1982; Suttles 1987).

These critiques of the concept of the tribe affect the cited studies of Mesolithic ethnic groups in a fundamental way, because in these studies the notion of tribes and social territories are accepted as basic, monolithic units of social organisation among hunter-gatherers in general. They also generally accept the tribe as the most important source of ethnic identification at the outset. The recent discussions and critiques within social anthropology demonstrate clearly that such an understanding of ethnicity is no longer acceptable. Therefore, if the concept of ethnicity is to be applied for interpretations of Mesolithic data, it needs a ontological re-orientation.

Barth's critiques and insights have influenced later anthropological studies of ethnicity. But the critique also has deep consequences for archaeological epistemology, which brings us to the second problem: How do we *know* that we are dealing with Mesolithic ethnic groups and boundaries in the archaeological data?

Epistemological problems: archaeology

The "normative" perspective of the culture-historical approach was already the subject of massive attacks during the 1960's from archaeologists such as Binford (1965) and Clarke (1968). Clarke questioned the very existence of archaeological cultures as "monothetic" units and pointed out the arbitrary selection and crude classification of artifacts as representative of whole cultural entities (Clarke 1968:35 pp). Instead he presented the "polythetic" model, which embraced a much larger variety of artifacts and attributes. These often presented themselves as untidy nesting hierarchies of artifactual groupings. Nevertheless, Clarke, like Childe before him, still saw these groupings as representative of cultural traditions of human groups (Shennan 1989:13). Binford, on the other hand, held that there is no predictive relationship between archaeological cultures and ethnic groups. Binford's key argument was that variations in archaeological assemblages are more likely to be explained as individuals or groups of people performing different tasks at different locations, rather than as ethnic diversity (Binford 1965: 205). Binford and his followers did not altogether abandon the idea that such distributions could correlate with ethnic groups, but this could only be the case within the *stylistic* domain (Conkey 1990:10). However, Sackett (1985) later questioned this dichotomization between function and style. While adopting a similar basic premise concerning style and ethnicity as did other processualists, he introduced the term "isocrestic variation" ("isocrestic" meaning "equivalent in use"). He argued that there are several equivalent ways of doing things, but people choose those which are in accordance with their own cultural tradition. These "isocrestic choices" result in isocrestic variation, of which style is only a subset; "a butchering technique may potentially convey as much ethnically stylistic information as a pottery decoration" (Sackett 1986). He therefore held that functional and non-functional aspects of human behaviour should not be analytically separated because they may have the same relevance on interpretation of social boundaries. A similar argument was forwarded by Lechtman (1977), but in contrast to Sackett's more passive isocrestic variation, she considered her Andean textile artisans as instrumental in expressing ethnicity as well. Wobst (1977) also stressed the active role of the material culture in the context of ethnic signalling. While supporting the distinction between style and function, he predicted that some highly visible artifacts that entered social contexts probably carried stylistic messages about social status. In contrast, small artefacts were not actively used as media for this type of information exchange.

Epistemological problems: ethno-archaeology

Inspired by Wobst, Wiessner (1983) undertook an ethno-archaeological study of arrowhead styles among different Kalahari San language groups. A correlation between these groups and different styles lead her to conclude that these different arrowheads actively communicated ethnicity ("emblemic style") and that the individual ("assertory") styles were subordinate to this in order to ease mobility between the ethnic groups. These interpretations were questioned by Sackett (1985), who held that Wiessner's emblemic styles probably did not actively communicate ethnicity, and that they were rather examples of his "isocrestic variation". In an influential ethno-archaeological study from Baringo, Kenya, Ian Hodder (1982) further complicated archaeological study of material culture. Here he discovered that some items were reserved for members of particular ethnic groups, while other items crossed the ethnic boundaries. Based on this data, Hodder held that although material culture is often loaded with symbolic connotations, these are not necessarily related to *ethnic* identity (see also Håland 1977). Another point connected to this was made by Gould (1980). Gould's ethno-archaeological studies from Australia demonstrated that his archaeological styles made little sense to the aborigines. For them, the origin, colour and sizes of the tools were often more important for their symbolic properties than Gould's own classifications. These arguments and cautions were further elaborated by Lemonnier (1986) on data from the Anga groups in New Guinea. Lemmonier argued, in line with Sackett, that styles of technology and production processes are just as informative about ethnicity as the end products themselves. He acknowledged that some of the technological choices and items in his case were related to the distribution of ethnic groupings. However, similar to Hodder, he said that their particular significance is dependent on the context, and that it is not possible to predict beforehand which of these choices or products has ethnic significance.

These discussions, which expose a far from simple relationship between material culture and ethnicity, have considerable consequences for the interpretations of the Mesolithic ethnic groups and social territories referred to above (Gendel 1984, Petersen 1985; Newell *et al.* 1990; Verhart 1990; Kindgren 1991). A fundamental problem concerning all of these studies is that the chosen types, raw materials or ornaments in the analysis, are assumed to be *actively communicating* ethnicity. In order to delimit which artifacts might have been relevant, Verhart assumes a relationship between energy input in artefacts and ethnic significance and therefore chooses bone and antler points, while Newell and his colleagues choose ornaments in order to avoid the functional bias. The other studies do not explicitly formulate such criteria. However, as Hodder has effectively shown, archaeologists cannot *a priori* assume what kinds of objects or styles were used to signal ethnic identity by a prehistoric group. If ornaments, tools and raw materials were not related to such identities, they might easily have been distributed across ethnic boundaries. According to Sackett's discussion of style and function, neither the degree of energy input nor the lack of utilitarian value are sufficient arguments for *these* artefacts to be associated with ethnic identity. In fact *any* object or technological choice is likely to symbolize ethnicity. In my view the cited studies have therefore only characterised and described specific geographical distributions or distributions of particular raw materials. No convincing arguments have been presented that these should be interpreted as reflecting the distributions of prehistoric ethnic groups.

As a result of these problems many regard ethnicity as an impossible field of research for archaeologists. Social anthropologists remain largely negative (e.g. Lemonnier 1986:181), pointing to the interpretative problems that face them in *living* societies. A number of archaeologists also express scepticism. Relating to the ethno-archaeological discussions in particular, many take a restrictive stance (e.g. Clark 1994; Bågenholm 1996; Stark 1998). The most explicit example of such a restrictive attitude is Bruce Trigger, who states that although ethnicity *was* of importance for prehistoric peoples,

> ... it was a subjective concept that archaeologists cannot hope to study to any significant degree in the absence of relevant historical or ethnographic data. Fortunately, there are many more appropriate problems that archaeologists who lack access to other sorts of data are equipped to investigate (Trigger 1995:277).

Possible solutions

So where does this leave the study of Mesolithic ethnicity? Is it too hard to handle? Should archaeologists follow Trigger's recommendation and find easier and more adequate problems to discuss? In my view, Trigger's attitude to the problem is too restrictive. I agree in principle that some prehistoric social relations might be difficult to grasp, simply because they cannot be related to the archaeological data in any convincing manner. But I am not sure if ethnicity should be included among these at the outset. In my view, ethnicity is a relevant field, including periods and regions that are not covered by historical or ethnographic sources. But if the problem is taken up, the approach must be altered considerably in comparison with the studies that I have referred to above.

Here, an explicit social theory is considered, and the relevancy of ethnicity in a Mesolithic context is critically discussed. I will also attempt to develop an archaeological methodology which focuses on the boundaries instead of on the circumscription of prehistoric ethnic groups.

The social theory

I find it necessary to accept the consequences of Fredrik Barth's main thesis, and look upon ethnicity as a boundary phenomenon, primarily concerning how people think about themselves as groups and how they set themselves apart from other groups. Still, Barth's seminal work does not cover all aspects of ethnicity, and during the last few years sociologists, anthropologists and archaeologists have extended his approach.

One important aspect of Barth's approach is the active role of the individual as entrepreneur (cf. Barth 1966). In the context of interaction between ethnic groups who occupy different ecological or social niches, entrepreneurs may apply their ethnicity or even change ethnicity as a strategy in order to reach their social or economic goals. Ethnicity is therefore viewed as an "organisational vessel which may be given varying amounts and forms of content in different socio-cultural systems" (Barth 1969:14). Barth's approach proved to be very influential for the "instrumental" approaches, where ethnicity is regarded as "constituting the shared beliefs and practices that provide the groups with the boundary maintenance and organisational dimensions necessary to maintain, and compete for, socio-economic resources" (Jones 1997:74). Others have also pointed out the fluid and situational aspects of ethnicity. A person's ethnic identification, they argue, can vary in different situations depending on the context and scale of identification, resulting in a series of nesting dichotomizations of inclusiveness and exclusiveness (Cohen 1978:387). Later scholars have become increasingly aware that common interests and self maximising economic and political aspects have been over emphasised by the instrumentalists. Psychological factors and senses of self, myths of origin, common institutions, and cultural background, although acknowledged by Barth and others, are factors taken for granted and play secondary roles compared to economic and political relations in the formation and transformation of ethnicity. The ultimate implication of this perspective may therefore be that ethnicity is constantly changing and fluid; that it only comes into existence in order to serve the purpose of interest groups (Olsen and Kobylínski 1991:20 p; Jenkins 1997; Jones 1997:77 pp). Such an understanding of ethnicity may not seem very workable for prehistoric archaeology and may partly explain some of the scepticism of the concept. Olsen and Kobylínsky (1991:22) therefore call for an adequate theory of ethnicity applicable to archaeology; one which not only considers the function of ethnicity but also cultural factors of descent. Jones (1997) has recently published such an approach, and also the anthropologist Jenkins (1997). Here, I will mainly follow Jenkins' approach.

Jenkins maintains, in line with the instrumentalists, that ethnicity is socially constructed as a result of boundary processes. He therefore rejects that it is "primordial" in the sense of a fundamental, essentially unchanging and an unchangeable aspect of human existence. On the other hand, he admits that ethnicity under a number of circumstances can take on a "primary identity", along with gender, kinship and selfhood. It may therefore matter a great deal for the local populations and it may be more resistant to change than many of the instrumentalists are willing to admit. He points out, however, that ethnicity is first of all a local phenomenon: a product of local circumstances and situations. It is not likely to have the same force everywhere. Drawing mainly on the thinking of Handelman (1977), Cohen (1985), and Cornell (1996), but also on the practice-theories of Giddens and Bourdieu, Jenkins argues that, in addition to the transactional, one must also pay attention to the symbolic construction of similarity that goes on *within* the boundary: to the conjunction between the institutional and the cultural. The "cultural" as a concept needs some clarification here. Jenkins defines "culture" as a domain of symbols and meanings which is participated in unevenly across a population. Instead of a singular form, it is a model of different *cultures* of social differentiation based on language, religion, cosmology, symbolism, morality, and ideology (Jenkins 1997:14). This definition differs significantly not only from that of "culture" as an all-embracing characteristic of humanity, but also from "culture" in the traditional sense of a "people" as discussed in the above paragraph. Culture in Jenkins' sense is obviously an important part of the package of socialisation during the early stages of a child's life. It constitutes a basic and embodied "sense of self" which often goes unquestioned, but which is essential for understanding the world and for being understood by the world. Depending on the circumstances, and the salience of ethnicity, early socialisation is likely to include an ethnic component. Such a component will refer explicitly to common cultural aspects that characterise the ethnic group in contrast to other groups (the vast amount of cultural aspects that are *shared* with the opposing group in question will not be relevant for this purpose, but may be important in defining a third group). These common cultural aspects will be applied as symbols for group similarity in the context of early socialisation:

> Cognitively, if nothing else, the child will develop a point of view on a social world which is axiomatically organised in terms of ethnic classifications. She will learn not only that she is an 'X', but also what this means: in terms of her esteem and worth in her own eyes and in the eyes of others; in terms of appropriate and inappropriate behaviour and in terms of what it means not to be an 'X', what it means to be an 'Y' or 'Z' perhaps (Jenkins 1997:59).

According to Jenkins, the social construction of cultural difference is therefore dependent upon the social construction of cultural similarity. In fact, these two aspects are likely to strengthen one another: A cultural awareness or categorisation of the Other – relating to what others believe, how others do things and how others behave – may work back on the internal ethnic identifications, by creating stronger consciousness about own language, non-verbals, dress, food or structure of space. At the boundary, culture is made explicit and transformed from something that is *known* to something that is known *about* (Jenkins 1997:76).

Based on these considerations, Jenkins defines ethnicity as "collective identification that is socially constructed with reference to putative cultural similarity and difference" (Jenkins 1997:75). This definition is adopted here because it embraces the active personal element and therefore the changeable and situational nature of ethnicity. At the same time it takes the cultural content seriously without specifying the *nature* of this content. It is therefore applicable to different kinds of ethnicities. This brings us to the next point, which considers if ethnicity is an adequate concept for the study of small scale hunter-gatherer societies.

Is ethnicity a modern phenomenon?

Several writers hold that ethnicity is a relatively modern phenomenon and a product of colonialism and capitalist world systems (e.g. Fried 1968; Wolf 1982; Shennan 1989; Comaroff and Comaroff 1992). The authors of a recent collection of articles on the subject (Stark 1998) for example argue that social groups in the past may have been different from and more flexible than ethnic groups today. Rather than being a member of a bounded group, people may also have had networks of overlapping identities (Hegmon 1998:273). In line with this, MacEachern (1998:130) says that it would be a mistake to focus only on one level – the "ethnic"– at the expense of others. More neutral concepts are therefore presented, such as "social fields" (Welsch and Terrell 1998) or "social boundaries" (Goodby 1998).

There is no doubt that colonialism, trade and other western influences have contributed to a disintegration of pre-existing forms of ethnic identity. These factors have resulted in the creation of a number of new, strongly self-conscious groups who use their ethnicity as an argument in economic and political issues. But does this imply that ethnicity as a collective social identity was *not* at work before the colonists and traders arrived and that ethnicity was not embedded in the political relations among prehistoric populations? Today most anthropologists realise that hunter-gatherers cannot be seen as a "cultural type", and that basic social and psychological processes within such societies are not different from those found in humanity in general (e.g. Kuper 1988). Furthermore, modern as well as prehistoric hunter-gatherers lived under a variety of environmental. demographic, socio-economic and cultural conditions, creating diversity in the past as well in the present (Kelly 1995:340). This diversity is likely to have constituted an important background for ethnicity. I therefore agree with Jones when she maintains that:

> ...it is therefore no reason why ethnicity should be restricted to the context of European colonialism, or to any other macro socio-historical developments, if it is seen as the kind of group consciousness that is based on the dialectical opposition of different cultural traditions in the process of social interaction (Jones 1997:102).

Acknowledging that ethnicity is an effect of both isolation *and* interaction, I therefore find it a key concept for the analysis of prehistoric social life. Depending on the context, it can function as a "primary identity" (Jenkins 1996:65) and may thus have been crucial in determining the organisation of many other types of inter-group phenomena. Instead of escaping from the problem, by applying more general or neutral terms, I therefore consider ethnicity to be an adequate and important field of research for prehistoric archaeology. Still, one can not deny that some of the most influential models for how ethnicity works are taken from complex modern multi-ethnic societies like the City of London or the island of Mauritius (Cohen 1974; Eriksen 1992). The conditions constraining and enabling ethnic groups in such places (urban centres, extensive travelling, visual media) are obviously very different from those affecting the Mesolithic hunter-gatherers, even if basic social and psychological behaviours may have been the same. In order to modify and supplement these theories, but also to avoid a determinist view (e.g. Newell *et al.* 1990), it is therefore necessary to investigate the nature of socially constructed boundaries among hunter-gatherer groups in the recent past.

Ethnic relations among recent hunter-gatherers

One problem regarding many ethnographic accounts on ethnicity is that the fieldwork, the majority of which was conducted during the first half of the 20th century, was done within the "etic" or "scientific" paradigm, i.e. one was less occupied with actors notions than with one's own notions and classifications (Riches 1982:3). They are therefore subject to the critiques of Barth and others referred to above. On the other hand, more recent and "emic" studies (those more concerned with the actors notions) are usually society-centric and focused on locally distinct behaviour rather than on boundary processes and inter-regional relations (Wobst 1978:303). Considering that most, if not all, of the hunter-gatherers today are deeply embedded in the modern world, emic approaches on inter-ethnic relations cannot entirely replace the etic data today. On the other hand, it is argued that it is important to bridge the gap between etic and emic approaches anyway (Riches 1982:3). In the context of ethnicity, this means that data concerning how groups of people identify themselves and categorise others should be regarded alongside data on "scientifically" documented boundaries and interaction across boundaries. During the past few years, such issues have been addressed for hunter-gatherers of the Northwest Coast of America, in Northern Canada, Alaska and Australia.

Recent specialists on ethnicity downplay the topological and territorial overtones of the term "ethnic boundary", arguing that "boundary" instead should be seen as a metaphor for a process that takes place between members of different identities, and as something that can occur anywhere or in any context (Jenkins 1996:98). The critique of the "tribe" as a general, inclusive and territorial unit among hunter-gatherers can probably be seen as a consequence of this line of thinking. However, the abolishment of the "tribe" as a general, inclusive unit, does not mean that in-group identity related to territorial boundaries is absent among hunter-gatherers. On the contrary, there seems to be an agreement that such notions are important, but they are primarily found at lower levels, which also constitute the largest and most inclusive units in terms of kinship-ancestor relations, territorial rights, and political organisation. For North America it is argued that collective in-group notions are strongest at the level of the "locational band" or "regional band" (Helm 1968:118; McKennan 1969:105; Riches 1982:110). These political and territorial units are more or less equivalent to the "local groups" of the Northwest Coast of America, which serve as comparable reference points for in-group identities in this area (e.g. Drucker 1983:88). Peterson and Long (1986:26 p) hold that the "band" generally has a similar significance in Australia. But although in-group references to the "local group" or "band" may prove to be the most pronounced, it does not follow that in-group attitudes are exclusively found here. The case of the Australian clan-estate relationship (cf. Stanner 1965) demonstrates that strong in-group attitudes may cut across boundaries of hunting territories. In-group notions may also refer to larger alliances of several bands/ local groups against common enemies (Berndt and Berndt 1964; Burch and Corell 1972; Drucker 1983; Lourandos 1998:61). Furthermore, in-group identification sometimes refers to encompassing units such as "Eskimo" as opposed to "Indian" in Northern Canada and Alaska (e.g. Graburn 1979; Townshend 1979). Berndt and Berndt (1964:42) are therefore probably generally correct when they characterise the Australian Aborigines as having nesting ethnic identities depending on the context of the situation.

Data on out-group categories indicate that such attitudes flourish among hunter-gatherer groups. Often they relate to specific, named, often adjacent groups. In other instances, general, categorical terms are applied, like "mountain people" or "inland people" (Lourandos 1998:45). They may also refer to "strangers" in general, which is a much used term for people who are not band, kin, or allies. These are usually treated with hostility (Burch and Corell 1972). Although relations may be friendly in practice, negative attitudes are a typical feature of the out-group attitudes and categories. "Less-than-human", "half-human" or other derogatory remarks are popular, often used in opposition to the term "human" by which the local populations designate themselves (Helms 1988:22 pp). These prejudices are instilled in the members of the in-group at an early age. Ernest Burch illustrates this point very well: "Countless evenings of hearing about treachery and warfare, or hilarious renderings of other speech style could only reinforce such attitudes, serving to differentiate further the members of one's own society from all other human beings" (Burch 1980:278). Hostile relations notwithstanding, the situation is not generally characterised by isolation and lack of contact. Although mountain ranges or dry basins separate people, resulting in fairly endogamous populations (e.g. David and Cole 1990), natural boundaries usually do not prevent contact (e.g. McCarthy 1939–40; Burch 1988). The degree and nature of the inter-group relations, however, varies considerably. In the case of Australia, many groups participate in long distance social networks. Some of these networks are "open" and cut across linguistic groups and major drainage basins, involving exchanges of both spouses and artefacts (Tindale 1974:75 pp; Hamilton 1980:8 p; Lourandos 1998:56 pp). Such systems are, however, most common in the arid zone. In the Southwest, but also in the tropical north, more "closed" social networks operate, which usually involve only the neighbouring territorial bands (Lourandos 1998). In North America these more closed networks are most common in some parts of Alaska and on the Northwest Coast where they include trading partnerships, exchanges of marriage partners as well as aggregations, feasting, competitions and war (e.g. Burch and Correll 1972; Townshend 1979; Drucker 1983; Burch 1988). In arctic boreal Canada, on the other hand, the networks are more open (e.g. Damas 1963).

This brief account indicates that, similar to modern ethnic groups, hunter-gatherers have pronounced in-group identities as well as out-group categories. Hunter-gatherers also frequently interact with out-groups. In addition, it appears that, although most prominent at local levels, ethnic identity can be found at several levels of the social organisation at the same time. I will therefore hold that ethnic relations among recent hunter-gatherers are essentially the same as in "modern" societies. Still, there is one important aspect that separates hunter-gatherer ethnicity from that of populations in the industrialised world. Not only among modern ethnic groups, but also among groups related to early state formation, origin myths often refer to places far away from where people actually live (Eriksen 1992; Hedeager 1997). In reality, however, several of these ethnic groups are co-residential. With a possible exception for the clan-estate relationship in Australia (Stanner 1965), such a "melting-pot" situation generally does not fit the hunter-gatherers I referred to above. In these cases ethnic boundaries are "real" in the sense that they relate to territorial boundaries: the in-groups are usually co-residential while the out-groups live somewhere else. One might argue that I embrace here the "primordial" approach, and see particular hunter-gatherer groups always as descendants of the pristine occupants of a given territory, but this is not my position. I acknowledge that origin myths are quite as "invented" among hunter-gatherers as they are in the modern world and that migrations often take place. On the other hand, one should not always take for granted that ethnic identities constantly are constructed, re-invented and contested or that the group in question just recently formed such an identity and that the historical development in the region has been one of constant migration and flux. As Jenkins points out, "To say that ethnic identity is transactional and changeable, is really to say that it *may* be; it doesn't mean that it *always* is or *has* to be" (Jenkins 1997:51). In this context it should be considered that most of the Mesolithic populations lived in small-scale local arenas, detached from the globalised world as we know it today. They were certainly not confronted with powerful and aggressive colonist states. If they had ethnic identities, these were products of relations with other neighbouring groups on more or less similar socio-economic levels. Such relations may of course have been highly competitive, rapidly changing and fluctuating, but they may also have been stable over long periods of time.

Ethnic boundaries and material culture

Based on the ethnographic data, it is possible to assume that ethnic boundaries among hunter-gatherers often coincide with spatially defined or territorial boundaries. If this is the case I would expect that such spatially defined ethnic boundaries could also have been relevant during the Mesolithic period. However, bearing in mind the epistemological discussion on material culture and ethnicity, how can we possibly come to grips with such boundaries? A combination of broad geographical distribution studies and detailed studies of local contexts and circumstances is recommended here.

At the broad level, I find that the old method of documenting the regional variation in artefacts, styles and technologies still serves this purpose. What the early archaeologists saw was a tendency to regionalisation in the archaeological data: functionally similar tools were made differently in different areas. Raw materials and ornaments tended to vary in similar fashions. Over time these regions became smaller. Of course this is a perfect example of the "culture-historical" methodology that was criticised above. Stephen Shennan, for example, argues that an archaeological culture defined in this way is a pure analytical construct and the probability that it coincides with any socio-cultural unit of the past is very small (Shennan 1989). But I cannot agree with this. I agree with Shennan that it would be wrong, as Childe did, to interpret these regions automatically as reflecting ethnic groups, but I think it would be a mistake to abandon the methodological approach altogether. Instead I would like to take two steps back and ask, once again, what these distributions mean. In my opinion the regions which Newell *et al.*, Gendel, Verhart, Kindgren and Petersen were able to delineate are extremely interesting, first of all because they are very good examples of James Sackett's isocrestic variation (1985). If we follow Sackett's reasoning, this does not mean that we are dealing with different ethnic signalling. Instead it probably tells us something about increased regionality; that people move less than before and that they stay more permanently within smaller regions than before. Due to decreased inter-group contact and communication about cultural values, different styles and traditions develop independently of each other. Such traditions would not be restricted to particular raw materials or particular axe shapes. As Sackett points out, they would also include subsistence practices, hunting techniques, cooking techniques, architectural solutions, location of sites, rock-art styles, etc. Along with a large number of aspects lost for us today, these traits would constitute the culture (local meanings) of the populations. As many such cultural traits as possible should therefore be recorded.

Although we are able to map the distribution of all of these traits, we would still be far from our purpose, because neither isocresticism nor culture is equivalent to ethnicity (Shennan 1989:20). Culture may be shared unevenly, because different segments of the population participate in multiple and not always shared spheres of social interaction. As a result archaeological entities or isocrestic traits will not constantly be found together and the pattern is likely to be an untidy one (Clarke 1968:299). Clarke developed classificatory expedients in order to remove the untidiness in the cross-cutting distributions and to reach some kind of essence in the material culture, which he thought would be representative of a prehistoric ethnic group. But such a procedure is criticised by Shennan (1989:13) who argues that one should instead recognise untidiness *itself* as the essence of the situation. I believe Shennan is correct in that one should consider all archaeological traits, not only the ones that fit. On the other hand I find his critique unsatisfactory if it involves a rejection of every type of concurring spatial distribution of different archaeological traits as meaningful in terms of ethnicity. Instead one should focus more on another point made by Shennan, namely that culture or isocrestic variation provides the raw materials for the forming of ethnic identities by a local population and that it has the potential to be received as messages of ethnicity by another population (Shennan 1989:20; Conkey 1990:11). This implies that artefacts should be seen as more than passive reflections of ethnicity. They may rather, as

Wiessner points out in her discussion with Sackett, be activated into meaningful style in certain contexts and situations (Wiessner 1985:162). Still, an even more radical step should be taken here. It is argued that the very distinction between active and passive in this matter puts too much weight on humans as controllers of their life worlds and that it underestimates the role that material culture plays for human beings. Although we are conscious and purposeful actors, we are also continuously restricted and structured by the material world. We get new things and we change habits, but things and habits also work back on us and take part in constructing our selves. According to John Barrett (1994:36), such "structures" are in a sense pre-understandings; they are not questioned in day to day activities, but they orientate the subjects and enable them to act effectively. Tradition and memory thus become, according to Barrett, necessary conditions of agency.

In a context of ethnicity, one might argue that the more people have in common in terms of values, technology or subsistence practices, the more they are likely to recognise and acknowledge other people as similar to themselves. Conversely, the more different the material culture, the greater are the chances of perceiving them as different. As Jones (1997:125) points out, the choices of values and styles are not coincidental within the socio-historical context. Therefore, when groups enter into contact situations with people who have different habits and a different material culture they interpret their own traditions and habits anew; they strengthen them or they discard them. In such situations it is likely that people draw on traditional values, origin myths and learned technological styles that separate them from other groups and that they use these values and styles to signal their ethnic belonging. On the basis of these assumptions I would maintain that regional distribution studies of similarities and differences in the archaeological record are of some help because they would delineate areas with greater and lesser habitual or cultural overlap. In so doing they would indicate where possible ethnic boundaries might have been situated on the terrain.

At even more detailed levels of the archaeological analysis such possible boundaries should be investigated further. It is important, however, to stress that identification of boundaries between ethnic groups is not the same as *circumscription* of such groups. Although particular ethnic groups may have lived within single territories, it is not likely that boundary processes between neighbouring groups were of the same kind, either in terms of in-group/out-group relations or on the symbolic meaning of the material culture. *The boundary processes can therefore best be studied at a local level*, where the symbolic meaning of particular artefacts and practices are likely to be less equivocal than on a regional scale. Rather than trying to circumscribe groups by means of archaeological or other criteria, it is therefore much more fruitful to concentrate on local behaviour on both sides of possible boundaries of a more limited length. In the following I will discuss a set of archaeological criteria that may help distinguish between arbitrary boundaries and socially constructed boundaries during the Mesolithic period. The criteria that will be discussed here are historical continuity, co-variation, sudden fall-off and boundary crossing.

1. Historical continuity. One might expect that boundaries with deep traditions, going back to times immemorial, would be less changeable and more important than other more recently formed boundaries. Such "old" boundaries would provide spatial references for in-group/out-group attitudes. They would also, if the mobility across them traditionally were lesser than within, constitute a boundary between areas that people knew well and areas with which they were less familiar. A boundary indicated by distributions of styles, types or raw materials in one particular period should therefore coincide with a similar type of boundary in the preceding period(s).

2. Co-variation. Hunting techniques, architectural solutions, lithic industries, cuisine and other traditions are normally shared unevenly across space. One may therefore not expect to find a clear cut correlation of such traits. On the other hand, common culture may also be a powerful resource for ethnicity. If the distribution boundaries of many independent archaeological variables are coincidental, this might indicate that one is dealing with delineation of a group that has strong indigenous traditions.

3. Sudden fall-off in raw material distributions. In the case of the distribution of particular raw materials, gradual fading is the normal or expected, because increasing distance from the source will lead to increasing transportation costs and therefore more limited requests. Gradual fading towards a distribution boundary therefore says little about the social significance of such a boundary. On the other hand, if the disruptions of the raw material gradients are marked and if this boundary is not coincidental with natural boundaries such as mountain plateaus or long stretches of water that would prevent further spread, one might be dealing with a situation where the raw material was not permitted to cross or was not wanted across the boundary. In such cases the raw material may have carried ethnic significance.

4. Crossing. ethnicity is first of all a result of boundary processes. A discussion of the topic should therefore consider not only the archaeological traits that constitute the boundary but also the ones that go across. If there are no crossing items, this might be due to lack of contact (for example due to insurmountable natural boundaries) and the evidence for an ethnic relation would be weak. Distribution studies of lithic materials provide the best data on crossing.

Considering that the raw materials have to be moved physically, one would presume that a wide distribution of a particular stone would indicate the maintenance of contact between groups.

In addition to moving back and forth between these different levels of archaeological analysis, it is also necessary to investigate the socio-historical circumstances that would make ethnicity relevant in the first place. In my view, two types of circumstances are particularly likely to generate strong ethnic relations in hunter-gatherer societies: sedentism and contrasting subsistence patterns.

1   Sedentism. Although residentially mobile peoples may have ethnic relations with others, one may perhaps expect that sedentary hunter-gatherers would be more predisposed for developing this type of intergroup relations. Neighbouring sedentary hunter-gatherers usually exploit similar ecological niches. In a context of competition over resources (particularly at the border areas) between such groups, ethnicity is likely to appear as an organisational feature because it provides the ideological basis for boundary maintenance between the groups. In such situations local leaders are likely to make ethnicity an important issue, often in order to "mask" internal conflicts that are the results of increased circumscription (Ramstad 1998). The sense of being different may also have stronger cultural foundations among sedentary than among mobile peoples, because sedentism implies that people stay permanently around certain sites and territories. Groups therefore develop close attachments to the area itself and to locales within the area. Such attachments are likely to provide strong resources for in-group identity. Although sedentism may allow for task groups or individual messengers to be mobile over long distances, it generally implies restrictions on mobility for the groups as a whole. Most people who live outside the territory would thus be regarded as unfamiliar strangers, toward which negative out-group attitudes are likely to be most pronounced.

2   Contrasting subsistence patterns. In areas with major differences in subsistence practices, such as between neighbouring inland residential hunter-gatherers and coastal hunter-fishers, or between coastal hunter-fishers and inland farmers, ethnicity is likely to be an important factor. It is to be expected that the type of subsistence would have determined a major part of the cultural repertoire. In a case of coastal hunter-fishers vs. farmers, these different populations would eat different food and use different tools, but they would also most likely have quite different attitudes towards animals, landscapes and seasons. In the zones of interaction between populations (e.g. Zvelebil 1998), these attitudes are likely to have been perceived as very different. Between coastal hunter-fishers and inland hunter-gatherers the differences would not be that dramatic, but it is easy to imagine that inland elk-hunters would have different tool kits as well as different preferences for food compared to salmon-fishing groups on the nearby coast. From what is said about the "cultural stuff" being ethnically relevant, it is to be expected that such groups with contrasting subsistence patterns would easily mobilise the cultural differences as symbols of ethnic belonging in contexts of interaction between the two.

Obviously, these lists of criteria and circumstances are not exhaustive and are certainly not absolute in the sense that ethnicity is excluded if one or more of the criteria cannot be satisfied, or that ethnicity is proved if they all are. They should only be seen as working tools in the process of exploring the problem in a Mesolithic context. Hopefully, such a multi-level approach will produce plausible arguments for the spatial location of prehistoric ethnic boundaries. But it will never produce one single valid interpretation on the subject. Undoubtedly, an ethnic group only exists in the consciousness of those who include themselves within and exclude themselves from this group. It can therefore not be "found" in the archaeological data (Olsen and Kobylinsky 1991:12). When investigating the problem, one therefore must be open to a situation where several incompatible but potentially valid (multivalent) interpretations of the same data can exist side by side. Some archaeologists (e.g. Kohl 1993:15 p; Trigger 1995) see a number of dangers with such an open epistemological position, arguing that if we accept a plurality of interpretations particularly with regard to ethnicity, we may also be forced to accept a number of racist, chauvinist and nationalist readings. An alternative is that archaeologists, while pleading objectivity, present their interpretation as the only valid solution. However, this may lead to an even more dangerous situation for existing minorities (Härke 1995:56; Jones 1997:11). A third alternative is to avoid the problem altogether (Trigger 1995), but such a strategy leaves the field open to non-professionals, entirely beyond the influences of sound archaeology. The open position, which is advocated here, should not however, be seen as an excuse for launching badly supported hypotheses or for performing sloppy methodology. On the contrary, only careful quantitative and descriptive analysis will make it possible to delimit the number of potentially valid interpretations. The approach recommended here is to apply a multi-level approach which includes both regional and local levels of study. This implies that investigations of different contexts for both production, use and discard of the lithic tools should accompany distribution studies of stylistic elements, raw materials and other habitual traits. Such a shift of emphasis between different perspectives on the archaeological data is likely to improve the understanding of both ethnicity and contact between different ethnic groups in Mesolithic Europe.

Conclusion

To conclude, I think it is important that archaeologists who study the Mesolithic engage in the concept of ethnicity. But when dealing with the concept it is necessary to heed the consequences of the social anthropological insights and look upon ethnicity as a situational socially constructed phenomenon primarily concerned with how people think about themselves as groups and how they set themselves apart from other groups. It is a social construction of "us" and "them" which is marked in cultural terms. Archaeologically, it is important to get an overview of the empirical situation, over the variation of cultural aspects that are present in the current context, but also over the socio-historical circumstances that would make ethnicity relevant in the first place. When the concept is applied, it should therefore come as a result of thorough and broadly informed empirical studies, not from spatial distributions of randomly selected tool types or raw materials alone.

Acknowledgements

I would like to thank Randi Barndon, Hein Bjartmann Bjerck, Lars Forsberg, Gitte Hansen, David Loeffler, Morten Ramstad, David N. Simpson and Leif Inge Åstveit for valuable comments on earlier versions of the manuscript. I am also grateful to Sylvia Peglar, who corrected the English text.

References

Arora, S.K. 1973. Mittelsteinzeitliche formengruppen zwischen Rhein und Weser. In: Kozlowski, S.K. (ed.) *The Mesolithic in Europe*, 9–22. Warzawa.
Barrett, J.C. 1994. *Fragments From Antiquity*. Oxford.
Barth, F. 1966. *Models of Social Organisation*. Royal Anthropological Institute Occational Paper No. 23. Glasgow.
—— 1969. Introduction. In: Barth, F. (ed.) *Ethnic Groups and Boundaries. The Social Organization of Culture Difference*, 9–38. Oslo.
Berndt, R.M. 1959. The concept of "tribe" in the Western desert of Australia. *Oceania* 30, 81–107.
Berndt, R.M. and Berndt, C.H. 1964. *The World of the First Australians: an Introduction to the Traditional Life of the First Australians*. London.
Binford, L.R. 1965. Archaeological systematics and the study of culture process. *American Antiquity* 31, 203–210.
Birdsell, J. 1953. Some environmental and cultural factors influencing the structure of Australian aboriginal populations. *American Naturalist* 87, 171–207.
Brøndsted, J. 1938–40. *Danmarks oldtid 1–3*. København.
Burch, E.S., Jr. 1980. Traditional Eskimo societies in Northwest Alaska. *Senri Ethnological Studies* 4, 253–304.
—— 1988. War and trade. In: Fitzhugh, W.W. and Crowell, A. (eds.) *Crossroads of Continents: Cultures of Siberia and Alaska*, 227–240. Washington D.C.
Burch, E.S. Jr and Correll, T.C. 1972. Alliance and conflict: inter-regional relations in North Alaska. In: Guemple, D.L. (ed.) *Alliance in Eskimo Society*. Proceedings of the American Ethnological Society 1971, 17–39. Supplement. Seattle.
Bågenholm, G. 1996. *Etnicitet som problem i arkeologisk forskning*, Gotarc Serie C. Arkeologiska Skrifter No. 11. Göteborg.
Childe, V.G. 1929. *The Danube in Prehistory*. Oxford.
Clark, G. 1975. *The Earlier Stone Age Settlement of Scandinavia*. Cambridge.
Clark, G.A. 1994. Migration as an explanatory concept in Paleolithic archaeology. *Journal of Archaeological Method and Theory* 1, 305–343.
Clarke, D.L. 1968. *Analytical Archaeology*. Cambridge.
Close, A. 1978. The identification of style in lithic artifacts. *World Archaeology* 10, 223–237.
Cohen, A. 1974. Introduction: The lesson of ethnicity. In: Cohen, A. (ed.) *Urban Ethnicity*, ix–xxiv. London.
Cohen, A.P. 1985. *The Symbolic Construction of Community*. London.
Cohen, R. 1978. Ethnicity: problem and focus in anthropology. *Annual Review of Anthropology* 7, 379–403.
Comaroff, J. and Comaroff, J. 1992. *Ethnography and the Historical Imagination*. Boulder.
Conkey, M. 1990. Experimenting with style in Archaeoogy: Some historical and theoretical issues. In: Conkey, M. and Hastorf, C. (eds.) *The Uses of Style in Archaeology*, 5–17. Cambridge.
Cornell, S. 1996. The variable ties that bind: content and circumstance in ethnic processes. *Ethnic and Racial Studies* 19, 265–289.
Damas, D. 1963. *Igluligmiut Kinship and Local Groupings: a Structural Approach*. Anthropological Series 65, National Museum of Canada, Bulletin 196. Ottawa.
David, B. and Cole, N. 1990. Rock art and inter-regional interaction in northeastern Australian prehistory. *Antiquity* 64, 788–806.
Drucker, P. 1983. Ecology and political organization on the Northwest Coast of America. In: Tooker, E. (ed.) *The Development of Political Organization in Native North America*, 86–98. Washington.
Eriksen, T.H. 1992. *Us and Them in Modern Societies: Ethnicity and Nationalism in Mauritius, Trinidad and Beyond*. Oslo.
Fried, M.M. 1968. On the concepts of "tribe" and "tribal society". In: Helm, J. (ed.) *Essays on the Problem of Tribe*. Proceedings of the annual 1967 spring meeting of the American Ethnological Society, 3–20. Seattle.
Gendel, P.A. 1984. *Mesolithic Social Territories in North-western Europe*. BAR International Series 218. Oxford.
Goodby, R.G. 1998. Technological patterning and social boundaries: ceramic variability in southern New England. In: Stark, M.T. (ed.) *The Archaeology of Social Boundaries*, 161–182. Washington.
Gould, R.A. 1980. *Living Archaeology*. Cambridge.
Graburn, N. 1979. Indian-Eskimo relations. *Arctic Anthropology* 16, 184–195.
Gramsch, B. 1973. *Das Mesoliticum im Flachland zwischen Elbe und Oder*. Berlin.
Hamilton, A. 1980. Dual social systems: technology, labour and women's secret rites in the western desert of Australia. *Oceania* 51, 4–19.
Handelman, D. 1977. The organization of ethnicity. *Ethnic Groups* 1, 187–200.
Hedeager, L. 1997. *Skygger af en annen virkelighed: Oldnordiske myter*. København.
Hegmon, M. 1998. Technology, style and social practices: archeological approaches. In: Stark, M.T. (ed.) *The Archaeology of Social Boundaries*, 264–280. Washington.
Helm, J. 1968. The nature of Dogrib socioterritorial groups. In: Lee, R.B. and DeVore, I. (eds.) *Man the Hunter*, 118–125. Chicago.
Helms, M.W. 1988. *Ulysses' Sail: an Ethnographic Odyssey of Power, Knowledge, and Geographical Distance*. Princeton, New Jersey.
Hodder, I. 1982. *Symbols in Action. Ethnoarchaeological Studies of Material Culture*. Cambridge.

Härke, H. 1995. 'The hun is a methodical chap': reflections on the German pre- and protohistory. In: Ucko, P.J. (ed.) *Theory and Archaeology: a World Perspective,* 187–222. London.

Håland, R. 1977. Archaeological classification and ethnic groups. *Norwegian Archaeological Review* 10, 1–31.

Jacobi, R.M. 1979. Early Flandrian hunters in the South-West. *Devon Archaeological Proceedings* 37, 48–93.

Jenkins, R. 1996. *Social Identity.* London.

—— 1997. *Rethinking Ethnicity: Arguments and Explorations.* London.

Jones, S. 1997. *The Archaeology of Ethnicity. Constructing Identities in the Past and Present.* London.

Kelly, R.L. 1995. *The Foraging Spectrum. Diversity in Hunter-Gatherer Lifeways.* Washington.

Kindgren, H. 1991. Kambrisk flinta och etniska grupper i Västergötlands senmesoliticum. In: Browall, H., Persson, P. and Sjögren, K.-G. (eds.) *Vestsvenska stenålderstudier,* 33–70. Göteborg.

Kohl, P.L. 1993. Limits to a post-processual archaeology (or, dangers of a new scolasticism). In: Yoffee, N. and Sherratt, A. (eds.) *Archaeological Theory: Who Sets the Agenda?*, 13–19. Cambridge.

Kozlowski, J.K. 1975. *Cultural Differentiation of Europe From 10th to 5th Millenium B.C.* Warzawa.

Kuper, A. 1988. *The Invention of Primitive Society.* London.

Lechtman, H. 1977. Style in technology: some early thoughts. In: Lechtman, H. and Merrill, R.S. (eds.) *Material Culture: Style, Organization and Dynamics of Technology,* 3–20. New York and St. Paul, Minnesota.

Lemonnier, P. 1986. The study of material culture today: Toward an anthropology of technical systems. *Journal of Anthropological Archaeology* 5, 147–186.

Lourandos, H. 1998. *Continent of Hunter-Gatherers: New Perspectives in Australian Prehistory.* Cambridge.

MacEachern, S. 1998. Scale, style and cultural variation: technological traditions in the Northern Mandera mountains. In: Stark, M.T. (ed.) *The Archaeology of Social Boundaries,* 107–131. Washington.

McCarthy, F.D. 1939–40. "Trade" in Aboriginal Australia and "trade" relationships with Torres strait, New Guinea and Malaya. *Oceania* 9, 405–438 (part 1); *Oceania* 10, 80–105 (part 2), 171–195 (part 3).

McKennan, R.A. 1969. Athapaskan groupings and social organization in central Alaska. In: Damas, D. (ed.) *Contributions to Anthropology: Band Societies,* 93–114. Ottawa.

Newell, R.R., Kielman, D., Constandse-Westerman, T.S., Van der Sanden, W.A.B. and Van Gijn, A. 1990. *An Enquiry Into the Ethnic Resolution of Mesolithic Regional Groups.* Leiden.

Olsen, A.B. and Alsaker, S. 1984. Greenstone and diabase utilization in the stone age of Westen Norway: Technological and socio-cultural aspects of axe and adze production and distribution. *Norwegian Archaeological Review* 17, 71–103.

Olsen, B. and Kobyliński, Z. 1991. Ethnicity and anthropological and archaeological research: a norwegian-polish perspective. *Archaeologia Polona* 29, 5–27.

Petersen, P.V. 1984. Chronological and regional variation in the late Mesolithic of eastern Denmark. *Journal of Danish Archaeology* 3, 7–18.

Peterson, N. and Long, J. 1986. *Australian Territorial Organization.* Oceania Monograph 30. Sydney.

Price, T.D. 1980. Regional approaches to human adaptation in the Mesolithic in the North European plain. In: Gramsch, B. (ed.) *Mesoliticum in Europa,* 217–234. Berlin.

Ramstad, M. 1998. Common group identity with or without ethnicity? The Norwegian west coast during the late stone age. In: Anderson, A.-C., Gilberg, Å., Jensen, O.W., Karlsson, H. and Rolöf, M.V. (eds.) *The Kaleidoscopic Past: Proceedings From the 5th Nordic TAG Conference Göteborg, 2–5 April 1998,* 355–365. Göteborg.

Riches, D. 1982. *Northern Nomadic Hunter-Gatherers. A Humanistic Approach.* New York.

Rozoy, J.-G. 1978. *Les Derniers Chasseurs: L'Epipaléolitique en France et en Belgique,* Bulletin de la Société Archaéologique Champenoise, numéro espécial.

Sackett, J. 1985. Style and ethnicity in the Kalahari: A reply to Wiessner. *American Antiquity* 50, 154–159.

—— 1986. Style, function, and assemblage variability – a reply to Binford. *American Antiquity* 51, 628–34.

Shennan, S. 1989. Introduction: Archaeological approaches to cultural identity. In: Shennan, S. (ed.) *Archaeological Approaches to Cultural Identity,* 1–32. London.

Singer, M. 1968. The concept of culture. In: Sills, D.L. (ed.) *International Encyclopædia of the Social Sciences,* 527–543. London.

Stanner, W.E.H. 1965. Aboriginal territorial organization: estate, range, domain and regime. *Oceania* 36, 1–26.

Stark, M.T. 1998. Technical choices and social boundaries in material culture patterning. In: Stark, M.T. (ed.) *The Archaeology of Social Boundaries,* 1–11. Washington.

Suttles, W. 1987. Cultural diversity within the Coast Salish continuum. In: Auger, R., Glass, M.F., MacEachern, S. and McCartney, P.H. (eds.) *Ethnicity and Culture,* 243–249. Calgary.

Tindale, N.B. 1974. *Aboriginal Tribes of Australia.* Berkeley.

Townshend, J.B. 1979. Indian or Eskimo? Interaction and identity in Southern Alaska. *Arctic Anthropology* 16, 160–182.

Trigger, B.G. 1995. Romanticism, nationalism, and archaeology. In: Kohl, P. and Fawcett, C. (eds.) *Nationalism, Politics and the Practice of Archaeology,* 263–279. London.

Verhart, L.B.M. 1990. Stone age bone and antler points as indicators of "social territories" in the European Mesolithic. In: Vermeersch, P.M. and Van Peer, P. (eds.) *Contributions to the Mesolithic in Europe,* 139–151. Leuven.

Welsch, R.L. and Terrell, J.E. 1998. Material culture, social fields, and social boundaries on the Sepic Coast of new Guinea. In: Stark, M.T. (ed.) *The Archaeology of Social Boundaries,* 50–77. Washington.

Wiessner, P. 1983. Style and ethnicity in the Kalahari San projectile point. *American Antiquity* 48, 254–276.

—— 1985. Style or isocrestic variation? A reply to Sackett. *American Antiquity* 50, 160–166.

Wobst, M. 1977. Stylistic behaviour and information exhange. In: Cleland, C.E. (ed.) *For the Director: Research Essays in Honor of James B. Griffin,* 317–342. Ann Arbor.

—— 1978. The archaeo-ethnology of hunter-gatherers or the tyranny of the ethnographic record in archaeology. *American Antiquity* 43, 147–178.

Wolf, E. 1982. *Europe and the People without History.* Berkeley.

Zvelebil, M. 1998. Agricultural frontiers, Neolithic origins, and the transition to farming in the Baltic basin. In: Zvelebil, M., Dennell, R. and Domanska, L. (eds.) *Harvesting the Sea, Farming the Forest: the Emergence of Neolithic Societies in the Baltic Region.* Sheffield Archaeological Monographs 10, 9–27. Sheffield.

41. Between Quartz and Flint. Material culture and social interaction

Tom Carlsson, Göran Gruber, Fredrik Molin and Roger Wikell

Mesolithic settlements are known from several locations in the province of Östergötland, Sweden. In the central part of the town Motala large quantities of quartz and flint, as well as an impressive amount of organic material, have recently been found. The material sheds new light on the Late Mesolithic in the entire region.

Contacts during the Mesolithic in the western parts of Östergötland point in multiple directions. Artefacts indicate interaction with local Mesolithic societies to the south and on the west coast of Sweden, as well as on the east coast. The lithic waste from different raw materials and the artefacts give us opportunities to discuss different aspects of material culture, in terms of close contacts between the local (the home) and the interregional (the world).

The way Mesolithic man chose raw material is a good example of the dualism between the access to raw material and social strategies in the society. In the western parts of Sweden flint totally predominates. In the eastern parts of Sweden the settlements are completely dominated by quartz. Quartz represents about 85% of the material from the Motala settlement. This is clearly the local basic raw material for "the everyday artefact". Flint, on the other hand, is not available locally, but in the region, by crossing the great Lake Vättern. Accordingly, the flint in Motala generally originates from Kinnekulle in Västergötland and was definitely imported as a raw material for a specific purpose: making microblades. Artefacts were not just linked to specific actions, such as hunting or gathering, but also to different actors at different levels of Mesolithic society. The material culture represents an individual as well as a collective identification. The settlement in Motala sheds new light on cultural interaction in Late Mesolithic society: interaction on a local and interregional level.

E pluribus unum?

Is there a world beyond flint? What news from the periphery? In the very first speech at Meso 2000 conference, Stefan Kozlowski pointed out that the prevailing view of the European Mesolithic places all the regions on an equal footing in a shared material culture. When viewed from a very general perspective, this is true. The regionalisation that Kozlowski called for in his speech does naturally exist all over Europe (Kozlowski in this volume). The boundary between different raw material traditions in Scandinavia demonstrates with perfect clarity the presence of regional distinctiveness; where flint is no longer available, the European flint community ceases. Material culture is expressed regionally without any impoverishment of artefact types and with no loss of cultural complexity. In the border zone, the choices of the Mesolithic communities are instead accentuated. Regional access to different raw materials reveals influences from several different places in a cultural mix.

The chief aim of this article is to interpret a border zone, the province of Östergötland in central Sweden. Östergötland is on the boundary between two different lithic traditions, flint in the west and quartz in the east. The starting point for the discussion is a recently discovered settlement site in Motala, with a large and varied body of finds.

Theoretical points of departure

Societies should not be regarded as closed systems with relations only to their neighbours, but should be studied within a wider geographical and historical perspective. The material culture at any specific point in time is a historical product. The meanings of the objects are related to the structured content of the historical traditions (Hodder 1986:171). The exchanges of goods and ideas are in this perspective important components in any attempt to explain a particular cultural mixture. Diffusion and exchange, even between closely situated societies are not, however, self evident. The spread of objects and the adoption of new ideas, which create the conditions for changing patterns in the local society, reflect the activities and strategies of the individuals who inhabit the societies. The spread of objects and ideas is thus related to the kinds of attitudes and the role the artefacts played in the society. Society's attitude to different objects should have central importance (Carlsson 1995:44).

Our overall working method is to consider the area from four perspectives: the world, the district, the neighbourhood and the home. We believe that all these perspectives were part of Mesolithic people's consciousness. The geographical spaces were used in different ways depending on many different factors, such as seasonal use and social affiliation. The analytical method makes it possible to work with several parallel variables from different perspectives, for example, the find material considered in the light of the special geographical conditions of the place in a historical context.

1. The World. The distinctive geographical character of the nearby and distant surroundings. The world is also the traditionally known, mythical surroundings with their eschatological ideas. The world view of a society is included in this concept.
2. The District. The area known through one's own travels or those of other people, used within the model for seasonal migration. The district contains all the dimensions of the mental landscape.
3. The Neighbourhood. The immediate area for everyday movements within the district. This is a familiar space for everyday pursuits.
4. The Home. The hut/house and the habitation site, incorporating a spatial organisation, a disposition of space.

The different perspectives are linked through the movements of Mesolithic people in the landscape. The mental meanings of the different physical spaces are also interlinked. The spatial organisation of the home, for example, is created according to an idea, probably close to a Mesolithic world view. The world was represented in the home, and the home reflected the world.

A brief history of research – seeing is believing

In preparation for the international congress of archaeology in Stockholm in 1874, Oscar Montelius studied the collections at the Museum of National Antiquities. His aim was to discuss whether there had been a Stone Age population in central Sweden. Montelius had noticed a Stone Age culture that distinguished itself from the previously known ones, and he presented these new findings at the congress (Montelius 1870–1873). Among the stray finds in the museum there was nothing striking that could give its name to any new cultural group. The lack of flint made classification impossible, so the finds could not be linked to known chronologies. The collections mainly consisted of simple greenstone axes.

Quartz had not yet attracted any attention as a raw material. Settlement sites with nothing but quartz were first noticed in the 1930's (Engström 1932). Sten Florin worked with the waterside locations of quartz settlement sites and their dating (Florin 1948). A hundred years after Montelius' discovery of a Stone Age population in eastern central Sweden, the next attempt was made to divide the material chronologically. Stig Welinder suggested the name "flint and quartz group" after having conducted several small scale studies in the 1970's (Welinder 1973, 1977). The few flint artefacts were still necessary for imposing order on the material.

The difficulty of finding distinct types in the pieces of quartz still colours the view of this regional tradition. An attitude like "seeing is believing" impedes archaeological research. Quartz was for a long time ignored in surveys, and only the occurrence of flint was taken as evidence of human presence. Flint was synonymous with the Stone Age.

In the last few decades, however, archaeology has accepted quartz as source material. Through increased knowledge of the significance of quartz for Mesolithic people, archaeologists have once again been able to fill the earliest Stone Age of eastern central Sweden with people (see Åkerlund in this volume). Two worlds, one of flint and one of quartz, thus stand out in Scandinavia. The world of flint is linked to a Western European technological and material community. Areas with quartz

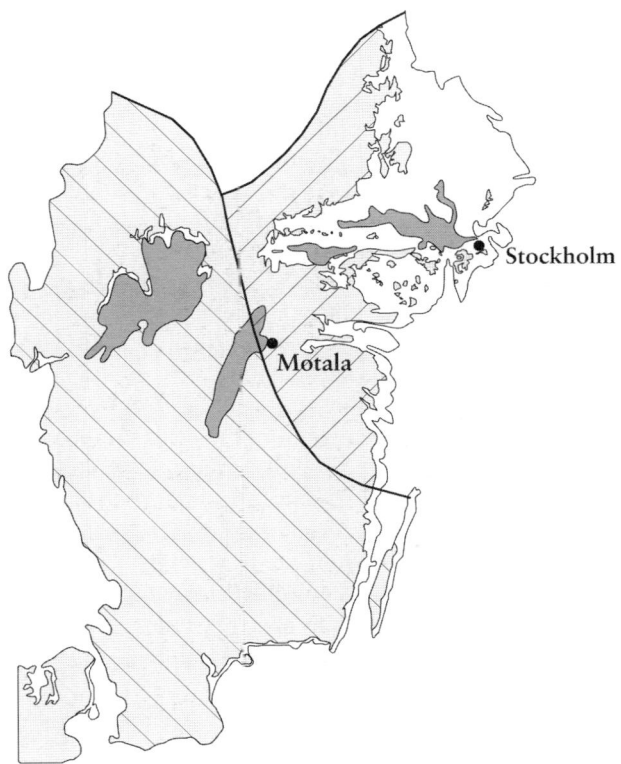

Figure 41.1 The two lithic worlds. From Åkerlund 1996. Digital drawings by Lars Östlin.

as raw material reflect a different community, another lithic culture. In the border zone between these two worlds there are regions with contacts in both directions.

The World

In general terms, the Swedish Mesolithic can be divided into different raw material regions. Flint totally dominates in the southern and western parts, while quartz is mainly found in eastern central Sweden and to the north. From this broad perspective, the regional availability of suitable raw materials stands out as a crucial factor (Åkerlund 1996). Geographically and culturally, Östergötland lies between a world of flint to the south-west and a world of quartz to the north-east.

The world of flint

In the world of flint in Scandinavia there are several different Mesolithic cultures named after archaeological find spots, for example, Maglemose and Kongemose. For the Late Mesolithic we know of the Ertebølle culture from southern Scandinavia and Lihult on the west coast of Sweden. In Norway the corresponding culture is called the Nøstvet (see Berg in this volume). The landscape on the west coast at this time was an archipelago with many islands. In this part of Scandinavia, Mesolithic people saw the sun setting in the sea.

Flint dominates the raw material, and the material culture displays both similarities and differences with respect to the areas to the south. The toolkit consists of several recognisable flint objects which, to the archaeologist's relief, can be divided into different types: core axes, blade scrapers and borers are guiding artefacts. Microblades were manufactured from handle cores. The culture also has a greenstone axe characterised by coarse scars left by the manufacture. It is primarily polished at the edge and it often has a triangular cross-section. The axe is called a Lihult axe.

The world of flint ranges from the coast on the west towards the interior. On the eastern shore of the large Lake Vänern is Kinnekulle, a high mountain with the only source of Cambrian flint. Mesolithic people were not slow to use this source. Cambrian flint has its physical limitations, however. It is not suitable for the manufacture of large objects and seems to have been mostly used for making microblades (Kindgren 1991).

The world of quartz

To the east and north of Vättern, the world of flint comes to an end. Unlike western and southern Sweden, the settlement sites here are dominated by quartz and other local rock types. In eastern Sweden some 90–100% of the finds are of quartz. The quartz was for a long time incomprehensible, since retouched pieces occur very rarely, and hence no tools can be registered. It has proved fruitless to try to find or translate defined tool forms of flint from different cultures in southern Scandinavia. This was pointed out back in the 1930's by Engström, who was one of the first to realise the significance of quartz at sites without pottery (Engström 1932). The anonymity of quartz meant that no type site was identified at an early stage of research, which in turn increased the anonymity. If any of the sites known today had been published a hundred years ago, we would probably now be finding concepts like "the Paradiset Culture" in the literature (Hammar and Wikell 1994). For the Late Mesolithic, perhaps one of Engström's sites would have given rise to a name, for example, "the Hult Culture" (Engström 1936).

The meaning-bearing elements in material culture are found at a different level than in the raw material or the purely technical aspect. There has been criticism of the interpretations of mass material in terms of typical objects and flint flakes (Knutsson 1998; Lindgren 1998). Similar criticism has long been heard in Finland (Siiriäinen 1969, 1975). Quartz, together with other locally occurring rocks, behaves in a way that corresponds to its nature and thus leaves different traces from flint. Artefacts were shaped according to the special properties of the material. People used what was available locally and regionally, working it into suitable "artefacts", within the framework of tradition and custom. The Mesolithic societies appear to have had a pragmatic view of lithic technology (Knutsson 1998).

Archaeologically investigated quartz sites are mainly found in the former eastern outer archipelago (Knutsson et al. 1999). The landscape was characterised by tens of thousands of islands and skerries. There were eskers running north-south for distances of tens of kilometres, with light coloured sandy beaches. Pine was a common tree on the poor soils, while mixed oak woods dominated the inland and the valleys on the larger islands. The settlements left by fishermen and seal hunters, who saw the sun rise in the sea, tended to face south on sandy beaches. This was an extremely rich environment with good opportunities for providing a livelihood. Many places were visited and used by the canoe borne population, and all these places contain worked quartz. A widespread system of small campsites and larger assembly places can be discerned through the varying quantities of quartz and the size of the habitation areas. At the campsites there may be only a handful of flakes while the assembly places, such as Eklundshov, may have hundreds of thousands of pieces of quartz (Lindgren 1996). The quartz was quarried from the veins that run through the Precambrian rock or was picked up as nodules along the beaches. The cores were mainly worked with hammerstones in three reduction methods: platform technique, anvil technique and bipolar technique (Callahan 1987). The stone axes are mainly pecked axes of rock which were pounded into a round shape, but there are also polished, almost square axes. A special find group from the archipelago consists of knives of different types of rock.

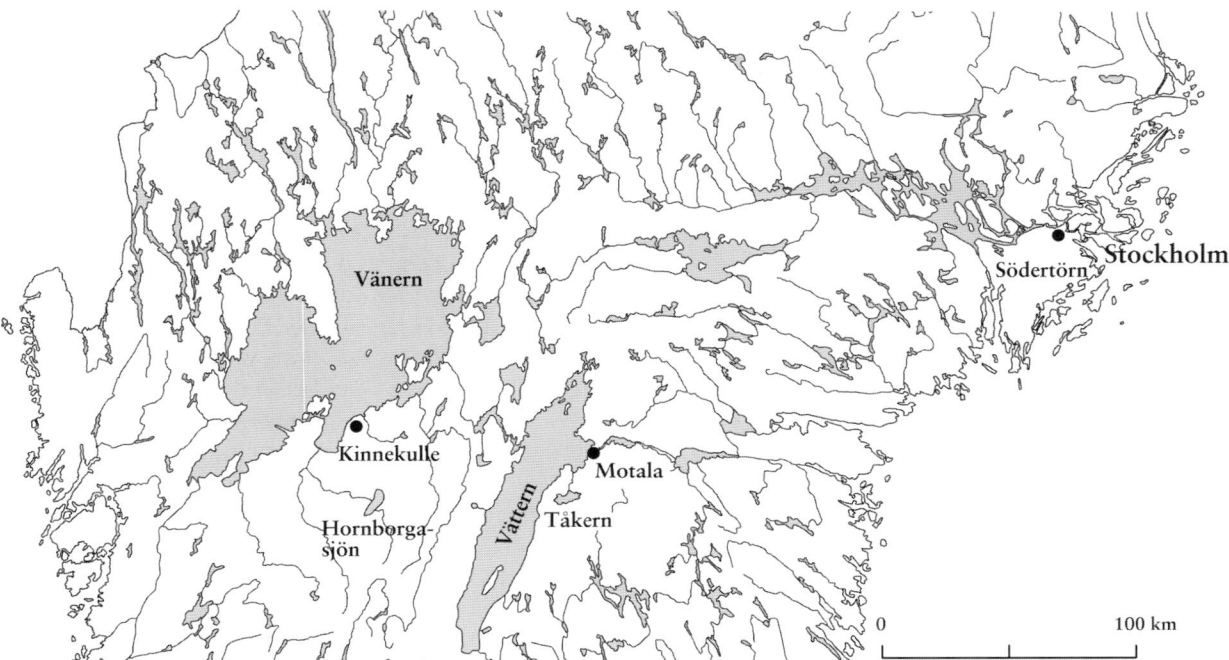

Figure 41.2 Map of Central Sweden with some sites and areas discussed in text. Digital drawings by Lars Östlin.

The use of microblades links the Late Mesolithic societies in much of Europe. We find the manufacture of microblades on the west coast of Sweden and in the interior, but not in the outer archipelago on the east coast. This difference is probably not only due to ecological factors; it is also a cultural expression. These material traces have been interpreted as reflecting two socially distinct groups (Lindgren 1997; Åkerlund 2000).

People probably did not feel the absence of flint. Quartz was not necessarily a replacement for flint. The regional groups have to be studied on their own terms, naturally bearing the neighbouring areas in mind. In central Sweden, in the area between quartz and flint, there are a number of settlement sites with great similarities to Motala. Quartz predominates, but there are also cores of quartzite and flint (Lindgren 1997:31). In Motala there are handle cores of both raw materials. This shows that the site was closely associated with the world of flint but that the choice of raw material also linked it to the world of quartz. The absence in eastern central Sweden of other indicative Mesolithic artefacts, such as microliths, indicates that something in the "European Mesolithic community" stops at the boundary between quartz and flint. At any rate, this applies to the lithic tradition.

The District

The landscape of Götaland consists of plains with fertile, clayey soils, separated by highlands where the stony moraine gives a rugged impression. Both landscape types contain thousands of small lakes and wetlands. There are also two large lakes which can be compared to small

Figure 41.3 The river in Motala (Motala Ström) and the Mesolithic settlement area. Photo by Tom Carlsson.

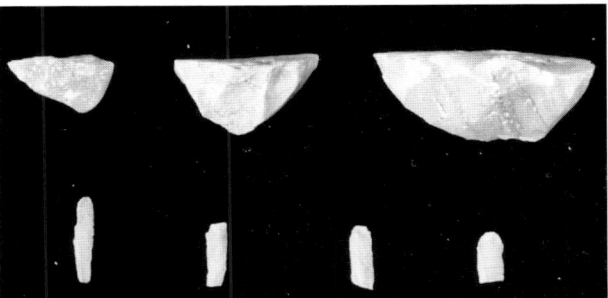

Figure 41.4 Handle cores and microblades in quartzite from Motala. Photo by Göran Gruber.

inland seas, Vänern and Vättern, whose name means "water", are lakes that people throughout the ages have referred to. The people in the inland were always close to shores, even if the salt sea was far away. Here the lowland plains were filled with dense Atlantic mixed oak woods. Paths wound between places of human occupation.

Västergötland

The interior of Västergötland is characterised by concentrations of Late Mesolithic settlement sites around the extensive water systems and on the shores of lakes of varying size. Around Hornborgasjön a large number of find spots and settlements have been registered (Kindgren 1991, 1996). The artefacts found on the settlement sites are almost exclusively of Cambrian flint from Kinnekulle.

The distribution of Cambrian flint shows a distinct core area within a limited region in a part of the plains district and around the nutrient rich lakes. Based on this distribution, it has been assumed that there was a distinct ethnic group in the area in the Late Mesolithic. The people here almost exclusively used Cambrian flint as raw material (Kindgren 1991:64). Find spots with quartz and eastern Swedish pecked axes also occur on the western side of Vättern, for example, at Svanvik (Cullberg 1975:44). These settlement sites have been viewed as a rather sharp boundary with the group that used Cambrian flint. What generally distinguishes the settlement sites in Västergötland from those in Östergötland is the use of quartz and other rocks at the latter and a higher proportion of pecked axes. Otherwise the stock of artefacts is similar, for example, with handle cores and microblades (Kindgren 1991:58).

Cambrian flint occurs to a lesser extent outside this area, but it is found in a small quantity to the east, for instance, in Närke at the settlement sites of Vallby and Skävi and at occasional settlement locations along the Baltic coast, for example, at Jordbro and Eklundshov (Kindgren 1991:47; Larsson *et al.* 1997:25 p.; Bergold and Holm 1999; Lindgren and Lindholm 1998).

Östergötland

The Mesolithic environment in Östergötland and Västergötland is similar in many ways: large forests, shallow bird lakes and in particular the proximity to the sea. In the Late Mesolithic the Baltic Sea was saltier than it is today, with the Litorina Sea about 40 m higher than the present sea level. Two bays cut deep into Östergötland, forming a narrow inner archipelago with large and small islands. In many respects the landscape resembled the outer Mesolithic archipelago, with a varied environment of skerries and forest. Lake Vättern today is perceived as a barrier marking the boundary between the eastern and western provinces of Götaland. Until recently it was claimed that there were no Mesolithic settlement sites around Vättern because the nutrient poor lake was not considered equally as attractive for settlement as the more nutrient rich lakes of the plains (e.g. Kindgren 1991:51 pp). It has now become obvious that this picture is mistaken, particularly since two lacustrine Mesolithic settlement sites were recently found north of Motala (Helander and Zetterlund 1998; Wikell pers. com.). Along the whole former shore of Vättern there are a great many stray finds of both pecked axes and the typically western Swedish Lihult axes. In the light of the newly discovered settlement sites, these may be assumed to represent settlements that are unknown today.

Lake Tåkern in western Östergötland is in many ways like the environment around Hornborgasjön (Browall 1999). Around Tåkern there are about 30 registered settlement sites from the Mesolithic and the Neolithic, with finds including flake axes and core axes (Arne 1905). The settlement site at Holmen stands out as one of the most interesting. Among the finds were pecked axes and Lihult axes and a number of antler tools, including a decorated chisel (Browall 1980:48 pp, 1999:297 pp). The antler tools can be linked on good grounds to the site of a probable Mesolithic burial (Browall 1999:301; Molin 2000:34). From Holmen we also have a blade of Cambrian flint. Isolated microblades of Cambrian flint have been found at several Mesolithic settlement sites in Östergötland. The majority are from the Early and Middle Mesolithic, for example, Storlyckan and Högby (Molin 2000).

Östergötland belonged to both the flint world and the quartz world by virtue of its geographical location in a border zone. The archaeological research tradition, however, has focused chiefly on flint. We still do not know, for example, how large a proportion of quartz there is in the material around Tåkern. Many quartz settlement sites have been discovered in recent years in eastern Östergötland (Åkerlund 1996; Ericsson *et al.* manuscript in preparation). Only a few of these have been excavated, however; examples are Leverstad and the Norsholm district (Nilsson 1976; Lindgren 1991).

A large number of pecked axes show the location of Late Mesolithic settlements around Linköping. Among the finds there are also a few axes of western Swedish Lihult type (Damell 1976:14 p). On the outskirts of the city there are also known settlement sites with worked quartz and microblades of flint (Molin 2000:35). Along the whole coast as it was in the Mesolithic, several similar find spots have been documented. These consist overwhelmingly of quartz and axes of both pecked and Lihult type. Handle cores also occur (e.g. Hellman 1970; Nilsson 1976; Åkerlund 1996). The majority of the sites give the impression of short term seasonal use. Certain sites distinguish themselves in this respect, however, Borgsmon or Hults Bruk outside Norrköping, where both occupation layers and about a hundred axes have been documented (Nordén 1932; Engström 1936:5 pp).

In the distribution of Late Mesolithic finds and sites one can suspect the seasonal movements in the landscape that are considered typical of Mesolithic societies. The geographical extent of these movements is still uncertain. A tendency of increasingly larger assembly places during the Late Mesolithic has also been detected. Some of the settlement sites along the coast and the one in Motala are examples of this. The movements in the landscape reflect the choice of raw materials. At many places in eastern central Sweden there are microblades of Cambrian flint. None of these sites, however, shows such a high proportion of Cambrian flint as the Motala site (Carlsson *et al.* 2000; Molin 2000). Nor do we find any traces of the manufacture of these microblades anywhere else. The microblades at the other settlement sites were probably mounted in finished tools. The distribution of these artefacts testifies to broad contact networks.

The Neighbourhood

Motala has a highly strategic location in the landscape, with favourable communication routes throughout the ages. The water route to the west goes over Lake Vättern. Via the river, Motala Ström, a narrow bay of the Litorina Sea could be reached about 30 km to the east. North of Motala there are deep, mountainous forests. To the south is today's fertile plain, which in Mesolithic times consisted of a woodscape with ample wetlands and small shallow lakes. The meeting place of the different physical geographical zones created good opportunities for communication and provision.

In the eighteenth century a stone bridge was built over the river in Motala. In earlier times there was a ford here, a natural place for humans and animals to cross the fast flowing water. Motala is in every respect the meeting place reflected in the meaning of the name: *mot* (meeting) and *ala*, from a Germanic word for sanctuary or temple (Franzén 1982:73).

In today's Motala it is no longer possible to see the Mesolithic landscape. The growth of the town has completely changed the appearance of the terrain. Motala was an important town as far back as the seventeenth century and was therefore mapped early on. With the aid of a map from 1639 and several eighteenth century maps we can recreate the original landscape. The area occupied by houses and streets today were once sandy heights covered by deciduous woods in the Mesolithic. The early maps also mark marshy and uncultivable areas. In the Mesolithic these were shallow lakes with partly open water, environments with a rich and varied animal life.

The Home

The archaeological investigation in Motala is a rescue excavation. In the first stage of the investigation, in the autumn of 2000, only a small part of the whole area was excavated. The project is being run by the National Heritage Board, Eastern Excavations Department (UV Öst). The results presented below are preliminary, being mainly based on observations made during fieldwork and in the initial work of registration and analysis.

The settlement site in Motala has been dated to 5915±60 BP, 4900–4720 cal. BC, 1-sigma (Ua-25375). It is located by a calm backwater after the first cataracts in Motala Ström. The area gives a good image of the Mesolithic environment, since the location today is virtually identical to what it was like 7000 years ago (Nilsson 1968). The settlement is situated on a gentle moraine slope giving protection against the westerly winds from Lake Vättern, which can be very strong in the winter half of the year.

The favourable location of the settlement is strengthened at the place where different geographical zones meet, along the course of Motala Ström. A favourable settlement location offering a varied diet all year round is in fact a criterion set up by Kristina Jennbert as characteristic of a permanent Mesolithic settlement. She proceeds from conditions in southern Scandinavia and also stresses the importance of large areas with room for different activities and the occurrence of cemeteries in the vicinity (Jennbert 1984). The Late Mesolithic settlements that have been investigated in eastern central Sweden in recent years vary in size from just a few hundred square metres to 5,000 m^2 and more (Larsson *et al.* 1997:26). The settlement by Motala Ström is estimated to have been at least 3,000 m^2 but was probably even bigger, since it has been partly destroyed by a modern house and a railway. Like several other places in southern Scandinavia, the settlement in Motala is a Late Mesolithic place of assembly for several family groups, probably a winter habitation or a stationary year round habitation.

The results of the excavation paint a good picture of the spatial organisation of the site. The finds show, among other things, that the area near the shore was mainly used for working stone. There were also waste pits containing large quantities of quartz, flint and bone. On the other hand, the area has no hearths or cracked stone, which is interpreted as showing that the actual dwelling, the huts, were placed away from the edge of the water, higher up in the terrain.

The assemblage

Quartz is the predominant find material. About 25,000 pieces have been found. The material mostly consists of flakes, debitage and debris. The reduction methods that occur are platform, bipolar and anvil techniques. In addition, 115 hammerstones were found within the excavated area of just over 100 m^2, which reinforces the interpretation of the site as an intensively used knapping place.

The amount of flint is also large by Östergötland standards: just over 1000 pieces of both south Scandinavian and Cambrian flint. Production residue and handle cores show that microblades were manufactured on the site. A third kind of stone found in considerable quantities is quartzite. This has a slightly denser structure than quartz, and the flakes are very similar to flint. Microblades and handle cores also occur in this material. Apart from quartz, flint and quartzite, there are reduction remains of several other types of stone, such as *hälleflinta*, porphyry and greenstone. The excavation also uncovered pecked axes and polished greenstone axes. In addition, there was a large number of axe fragments and damaged axe edges. Ten or so hammerstones of red porphyry may be associated with the pecking of the axes (cf. Lindgren and Nordqvist 1997:59). Other finds were three intact grindstones and a large number of grindstone fragments.

In the Mesolithic occupation layer and in the waste pits there are large quantities of burnt and unburnt bone. A preliminary osteological assessment shows the presence both of big game in the form of elk, deer, wild boar and fish, including both perch and pike. Motala Ström is an obvious food resource thanks to its fish, but it is also an important communication link to other areas. Several fragments of bone harpoons and a slate knife may be connected with marine hunting in the nearby sea. A few bone harpoons were previously known in the region, one of them having been found together with the skeleton of a seal (Olsén 1965:26). The harpoons and the slate knives reflect the movement of Mesolithic people in the landscape.

The finds also contain a very convincing west Swedish ingredient, for example, microblades of Cambrian flint and handle cores. A Lihult axe has previously been found in the neighbourhood. Despite the west Swedish elements, the material is predominantly quartz. In terms of both quantity and composition, the find material has clear parallels to the settlement sites excavated in the former outer archipelago at Södertörn (Larsson *et al.* 1997; Lindgren and Lindholm 1998; Drotz and Ekman 1998). The Late Mesolithic people in Motala had clear cultural bonds to the world of quartz.

Conclusion: Who are you calling peripheral?

Our aim has been to describe a Mesolithic border zone, Östergötland in central Sweden, a distinct geographical area, between two worlds. In terms of geography and culture, this is an intermediate zone, whose inhabitants were in contact with two different lithic traditions. These two adjacent traditions probably reflected partly differing world views. The world of flint starts on the west bank of Lake Vättern, while only quartz was used a couple of dozen kilometres east of Motala. Here the entire Western European lithic tradition changes shape within a short distance. The change in material culture affected the local society, the relationship of the world view to material culture can best be described as a symbiosis.

The world of quartz was not a low-technology, non-complex society on the periphery of the flint rich areas. Large settlement sites like those at Motala and Eklundshov reflect a society with a great need to organise the home.

Quartzite technology was appropriate for this purpose. The maker produced the pieces that were considered desirable. The raw material was not of crucial significance for the function of the object, and flint was not regarded as an absolute necessity: the meaning of the object did not lie in the raw material. If this had been the case, the local and regional networks would also have provided the neighbours on the periphery with flint. Mobility between the home, the neighbourhood and the district involved no problem. People in Östergötland had a wide network of contacts to both the south and west, as shown by the distribution of certain flint artefacts and Lihult axes. The bone harpoons found in Motala reflect movements in the district, as far as the Baltic coast 30 km away. Artefacts found at a great distance from their place of manufacture reflect the movements and social interaction of Mesolithic people more than they reflect a need for raw material.

Professor Kozlowski's desire to regionalise the Mesolithic may be said to be satisfied (Kozlowski in this volume). What the archaeological regions actually meant for Mesolithic people, however, is a question that has not been discussed here. Material culture should be a variable in the attempt to understand processes and people's actions in prehistoric societies, and not an end in itself to define archaeological geography. What we see from our archaeological distribution maps is several contemporary, parallel social relations. We detect traces of people's actions in relation to one another: material culture and social interaction.

References

Arne, T.J. 1905. Ett fynd från äldre stenåldern i Östergötland. *Meddelanden från Östergötlands Fornminnesförening* 1905, 31–32.
Bergold, H. and Holm, J. 1999. *Lämningar från mesolitikum till efterreformatorisk tid vid Skävi. E20. Närke, Viby socken, Skävi 1:81 och Brånntorp 1:6. RAÄ 222.* Dnr 3209/93. Riksantikvarieämbetet. Avdelningen för arkeologiska undersökningar. UV Mitt, Rapport 1998:72. Stockholm.
Browall, H. 1980. Mesolitisk stenålder vid Tåkern. Östergötland 1980. *Meddelanden från Östergötlands och Linköpings Stads Museum*, 47–59.
—— 1999. Mesolitiska mellanhavanden i västra Östergötland. In: Gustafsson, A and Karlsson, H. (eds.) *Glyfer och arkeologiska rum – en vänbok till Jarl Nordbladh*. Gotarc Series A, vol. 3, 289–303. Göteborg.
Callahan, E. 1987: *An Evulation of the Lithic Technology in Eastern Middle Sweden during the Mesolithic and Neolithic*. AUN 9. Uppsala.
Carlsson, T. 1995. Objects and Attitudes. Lusatian Impact Material and Mental Culture in South-East Sweden during the Late Bronze Age. *Journal of European Archaeology* 1995:3, 43–58.
Carlsson, T., Nielsen, A-L., Elfstrand, B., Molin, F., and Gruber, G. 2000. *Ett arkeologiskt linjeprojekt i västra Östergötland*. Riksantikvarieämbetet, Avdelningen för arkeologiska undersökningar. Rapport UV Öst 2000:12. Linköping.
Cullberg, C. 1975. Stenåldersboplatser i Västergötland. *Västergötlands Fornminnesförenings Tidskrift* 1975–1976, 43–84.
Damell, D. 1976. Linköpingsbygden under förhistorisk tid. In:

Kraft, S. (ed.) *Linköpings historia 1. Från äldsta tid till 1567*, 11–24. Linköping.

Drotz, M., Ekman, T. 1998. *Jordbromalm – säl- och vildsvinsjägare i Haninge*. Riksantikvarieämbetet, Avdelningen för arkeologiska undersökningar. Rapport UV Mitt 1998:48. Stockholm.

Engström, T. 1932. *Ett boplatsområde i Kvarsebo socken*. KVHAA handlingar 37:3. Stockholm.

—— 1936. Strandbundna fynd äldre än yngre Litorinamaximum (L II). *Från stenålderns boplatskultur vid Bråviken*. KVHAA 37:6, 3–23. Stockholm.

Franzén, G. 1982. *Ortnamn i Östergötland*. Stockholm.

Helander, A. and Zetterlund, P. 1998. *En mesolitisk boplats vid Nedra Lid. Arkeologisk förundersökning. Näs, Nedra Lid, UV 1, Västra Ny socken. Motala kommun, Östergötland*. Riksantikvarieämbetet. Avdelningen för arkeologiska undersökningar. Rapport UV Linköping 1997:24. Linköping.

Hellman, G.A. 1970. Ringarums forntida bosättning. In: Gärme, E. (ed.) *Bondebygd och bruksbygd. Ringarums socken genom tiderna*, 12–23. Norrköping.

Hodder, Ian. 1986. *Reading the Past. Current approaches to interpretation in archaeology*, 51–107. Cambridge.

Kindgren, H. 1991. Kambrisk flinta och etniska grupper i Västergötlands senmesoliticum. In: Browall, H., Persson, P. and. Sjögren, K.-G. (eds.) *Västsvenska stenåldersstudier*. Gotarc Serie C Arkeologiska skrifter 8, 33–69. Göteborg.

—— 1996. Stenålder vid Hornborgasjön. *Västergötlands Fornminnesförenings Tidskrift* 1995–1996, 215–223. Skara.

Knutsson, K. 1998. Convention and lithic analysis. In: Holm, L. and Knutsson, K. (eds.) *Proceedings from the Third Flint Alternatives Conference at Uppsala, Sweden, October 18–20, 1996*, 71–91. Occasional Papers in Archaeology 16. Uppsala.

Kozlowski, S. 2002. The Mesolithic; What do we know and What do we believe? (in this volume).

Larsson, M., Lindgren, C. and Nordqvist, B., 1997. Regionalitet under mesolitikum. In: Larsson, M. and Olsson, E. (eds.) *Regionalt och interregionalt, Stenåldersundersökningar i Syd- och Mellansverige*. Riksantikvarieämbetet, UV, Skrifter 23, 13–55. Stockholm.

Lindgren, C. 1991. En nyupptäckt stenåldersboplats i Östergötland. *Arkeologi i Sverige* 1. Ny följd 1, 61–66. Riksantikvarieämbetet. Uppsala.

—— 1996. Fyndkoncentrationer och aktivitetsytor – metodval och tolkningsproblem. In: Bratt, P. (ed.) *Stenålder i Stockholms län*. Stockholms läns museum, 29–37. Stockholm.

—— 1997. Östra Mellansverige. In: Larsson, M. and Olsson, E (eds.) *Regionalt och interregionalt, Stenåldersundersökningar i Syd- och Mellansverige*. Riksantikvarieämbetet, UV, Skrifter 23, 21–32. Stockholm.

—— 1998. Shapes of quartz and shapes of minds. In: Holm, L. and Knutsson, K. (eds.) *Proceedings from the Third Flint Alternatives Conference at Uppsala, Sweden, October 18–20, 1996*, 85–101. Occasional Papers in Archaeology 16. Uppsala.

Lindgren, C. and Lindholm, P. 1998. *En mesolitisk boplats vid Jordbro industriområde*. Riksantikvarieämbetet, Avdelningen för arkeologiska undersökningar, UV Mitt, Rapport 1998:73. Stockholm.

Molin, F. 2000. Mesolitikum i västra Östergötland – forskningsläge och aktuella problemområden. *Vetenskaplig verksamhetsplan för UV Öst, arkeologiskt program 2000–2002*. Riksantikvarieämbetet, Avdelningen för arkeologiska undersökningar, Rapport UV Öst 2000:21, 33–41. Stockholm.

Montelius, O. 1870–1873: Bronsålder i norra och mellersta Sverige. *Antikvarisk tidskrift för Sverige* III, 3–11. Stockholm.

Nilsson, C. 1976. *Fornlämningarna 149 och 150. Gravfält, äldre järnålder, boplatsrester, stenålder, stensträng. Skärslund, Bäckeby, Skärkinds sn. Östergötland*. Arkeologisk undersökning 1971. Riksantikvarieämbetet. Rapport. Stockholm.

Nilsson, E. 1968. Södra Sveriges senkvartära historia. *Geokronologi, issjöar och landhöjning*. Kungl Svenska Vetenskapsakademiens Handlingar, Fjärde serien. Band 12 nr 1, 11–117. Stockholm.

Nordén, A 1932. Östergötlands äldsta stenåldersboplats. *Stenåldersboplatser i Östergötland*. KVHAA 37, 3–15. Norrköping.

Olsén, P. 1965. Norrköpingstraktens fornminnen. In: Helmfrid, B. and Kraft, S. (eds.) *Norrköpings historia*, 1–39. Norrköpings stads historiekommitté. Stockholm.

Siiriäinen, A. 1969. *Uber die Chronologie der steinzeitlichen Kustenwohnplätze Finlands im Lichte der Uferverschiebung*. Helsinki.

—— 1975. *Quartz, Chert and Obsidian: A comparison of raw materials in Late Stone Age aggregate in Kenya*. Finskt museum. Helsinki.

Welinder, S. 1977. *The Mesolithic Stone Age of Eastern Middle Sweden*. Antikvariskt arkiv 65. Kungliga Vitterhets Historie och Antikvitets Akademien. Stockholm.

Åkerlund, A. 1996. *Human Responses to Shore Displacement. Living by the Sea in Eastern Middle Sweden during the Stone Age*. Riksantikvarieämbetet. Arkeologiska undersökningar. Skrifter 16. Stockholm.

Personal communication

Wikell, Roger. Riksantikvarieämbetet, Avdelningen för arkeologiska undersökningar, Stockholm. "Varamoboplatsen vid Vätterns strand".

42. Initial Evaluation of Grahame Clark's Model of Mesolithic Transhumance in Northern England: A Perspective from the Pennine Uplands

Randolph E. Donahue and William A. Lovis

Research in the English Pennines designed to test Grahame Clark's transhumant model of Mesolithic settlement, derived from his research at the site of Star Carr, demonstrates regular utilisation of upland habitats. One key expectation of Clark's model is the presence of residential sites in the uplands. Systematic subsurface sampling and site excavation in the Yorkshire Dales has revealed a series of earlier and later Mesolithic sites characterised by assemblages reflecting limited activity sets that suggest both logistic use of the uplands and consistency of location choice through time. Raw material selection and utilisation reveal both locally derived chert as well as flint from the eastern Yorkshire lowlands. Initial evaluation of this data suggests long distance logistic use of the Pennines by eastern lowland populations. These results are inconsistent with the expectations of Clark's model.

Introduction

Ever since Grahame Clark's (1954) study of Star Carr, archaeologists have offered alternative explanations for the function and seasonality of the site. With Clark's (1972) suggestion that Star Carr was a winter base camp and that summer camps would be found in the uplands, the issue expanded in importance. Re-assessment of the original data (e.g. Legge and Rowley-Conwy 1988), the collection of new site data from Star Carr (Mellars *et al.* 1998) and regional survey in the Vale of Pickering (Schadla-Hall 1989) provide further insights that generally contradict Clark's original interpretations. These new interpretations, however, provide no understanding of the role, if any, of the numerous upland sites in the North York Moors and Pennines. Whatever role Star Carr or other lowland sites may have had within a subsistence-settlement system, it has become clear that further research in the lowlands is unlikely to clarify either the situation in the uplands or its relationship to lowland contexts. We present here an initial evaluation of results from the Yorkshire Dales Hunter-Gatherer Mobility Project, which has as its aim to improve understanding of hunter-gatherer adaptive strategies in the region, and to evaluate Grahame Clark's hypothesis regarding long distance hunter-gatherer transhumance in Yorkshire during the Mesolithic. Specifically, this paper seeks to address issues of mobility and settlement as they relate to Clark's model whether or not the underlying reason for their mobility strategy relates to red deer, as Clark (1972) had proposed.

Star Carr and the Problem of Mobility

Grahame Clark excavated at Star Carr during the middle of the last century. Analysis of the material led him to the conclusion that this was a winter settlement site (Clark 1954). In 1972 Clark introduced the idea that Star Carr was located within the winter hunting territory of a hunting band. He proposed that complementary summer hunting territories were located in the uplands, primarily in the North York Moors, located a short distance north of Star Carr, and also in the Pennines, some 100 km to the west. This shift between lowland and upland hunting territories was presumably keyed to the seasonal migration of red deer (Clark 1972), which is why we invoke the term transhumance to characterise the seasonal mobility aspects of his model. In contemporary terms this proposition would be interpreted as residential mobility between different seasonal components of a larger settlement system, with the clear implication that residential sites would be present in both the lowlands and the uplands, each associated with a suite of logistical sites at a sub-regional level.

The dichotomy between residential and logistic sites (Binford 1982) is central to a test of this hypothesis. Expectations are that residential sites are of longer occupation duration, possess evidence of multiple activities, with larger population aggregates of mixed gender and age composition. As such, site sizes should be larger, artefact assemblages should reflect a broad range of subsistence and maintenance activities including evidence of investment in physical facilities and potentially display marked spatial structuring or partitioning of activity sets. These expectations contrast with those of logistic sites which are more activity specific, of shorter duration and often the consequence of use by smaller groups exhibiting more homogeneous age and gender composition. In this context, confirmation of Clark's model requires the presence of residential sites in the uplands, and such sites should be associated with others displaying logistic characteristics.

Clark (1972) cited numerous upland sites that he felt supported his model including some in the Pennines such as Warcock Hill and Windy Hill, Deepcar (Radley and Mellars 1964) and Stump Cross (Walker 1956). Although questioning Clark's model, Jacobi's (1978) report of two Mesolithic sites on the North York Moors apparently provided further upland support for Clark's seasonal transhumance model. These sites, Pointed Stone 2 and 3, consisted of artefacts of similar technology and raw material as those at Star Carr. Even so, given their location of less than a full day's walk from the Vale of Pickering this would still leave open the question of long-distance transhumance.

Meanwhile, reassessment of the original Star Carr site and re-analysis of the material finds have resulted in numerous reinterpretations of the site and the season of its occupation. Caulfield (1978) indicated that the dietary significance of red deer at Star Carr had been over-estimated, and that the site was more likely a butchering station or kill site. Jacobi (1978) argued that the site was a base camp and that its occupation extended at least into the early summer. Pitts (1979) argued for intermittent use of Star Carr year round. Andresen *et al.* (1981) rejected Clark's season of occupation and suggested that the site was occupied intermittently year round, but for a shorter duration than indicated by Pitts (1979). They also saw this as a butchering site with the kill site nearby. Grigson (1981) argued that Star Carr was occupied during the summer based on roe deer antler and some migratory avifauna. Price (1982) supported Clark's idea that this was a base camp, but that the area excavated was primarily a dump for large debris. He also rejected Clark's proposition of a winter settlement. In a significant contribution Legge and Rowley-Conwy (1988) re-examined the faunal material and produced estimates that the site was occupied minimally from May to July. Moreover, they suggest (1988: 69 pp) that the pattern of bone element frequencies matches that of Nunamiut hunting camps, not residential sites (cf. Binford 1978). Mellars and Dark (1998) provide the most recent discussion regarding seasonal indicators, and they conclude that an estimate of April through June, perhaps March to July, more accurately describes the principal period of occupation.

These results contradict both Clark's initial assessment of seasonality as well as his 1972 model of upland and lowland resource use. A detailed regional coring survey and excavations within the Vale of Pickering led by Schadla-Hall are leading to further insights regarding the relationship between Mesolithic sites and the margins of relict Lake Flixton (Schadla-Hall 1989). Based on excavated materials from these sites, Rowley-Conwy (1995) has produced a model indicating that winter base camps were located near the coast with summer base camps and winter procurement locations in the Vale of Pickering.

Despite what appears to be serious erosion of Clark's initial interpretations of Star Carr, it must be recognised that Star Carr is only one of numerous Mesolithic sites in the region. Further, reinterpretations of Star Carr have not, to date, resulted in more advantageous ways to understand the numerous locales of either the North York Moors or the Pennines. Thus, issues of site location and abundance, seasonal timing, function and regional relationships remain open. Clark's (1972) model is still the primary vehicle that assists these issues, although clearly his work must be cast in the context of contemporary hunter-gatherer theory.

Hunter-gatherer mobility theory (e.g., Kelly 1992) has advanced substantially since Grahame Clark originally proposed a seasonal transhumance model for the Mesolithic hunter-gatherers of northern England. Binford (1980) introduced the concept of logistical mobility. It not only complemented residential mobility, but could be shown to have major implications for the frequency of residential moves, on the distribution and kinds of sites in the landscape, the procurement and redistribution of materials and foods and the organisation, size and complexity of societies (Kelly 1995). In this instance, for example, we suggest that it is best to view the Pointed Stone 2 and 3 sites (Jacobi 1978) as resulting from short distance mobility and not as residential sites resulting from seasonal transhumance. These sites lie only 12 km from the Vale of Pickering (40 km from Star Carr) and contain archaeological assemblages that are strongly logistic in nature given the highly restricted range of artefact forms present. Mellars (1998:234) also views these as specialised sites occupied by (male) hunters.

Numerous studies have reassessed Clark's economic interpretations of Star Carr, leading many to suspect that Clark was either incorrect or, from the vantage point of 50 years, overly simplistic. Even if correct, these studies do not lead to the rejection of Clark's transhumant model, but at best they offer alternative models that may have operated contemporaneously.

Field Research in the Yorkshire Dales

The 160 km^2 study area of the Yorkshire Dales Hunter-Gatherer Mobility Project encompasses the Malham plateau and the adjoining river valleys or dales (Figure 42.1). The region is in the headwaters of three major drainages. The River Ribble, to the west, drains to the Irish Sea, while the River Wharfe and the tributaries of the River Aire, ultimately drain eastward to the North Sea. The plateau itself is a limestone karst formation with both extant and relict lakes, wetlands and several hundred caves. Within the uplands there are regionally available

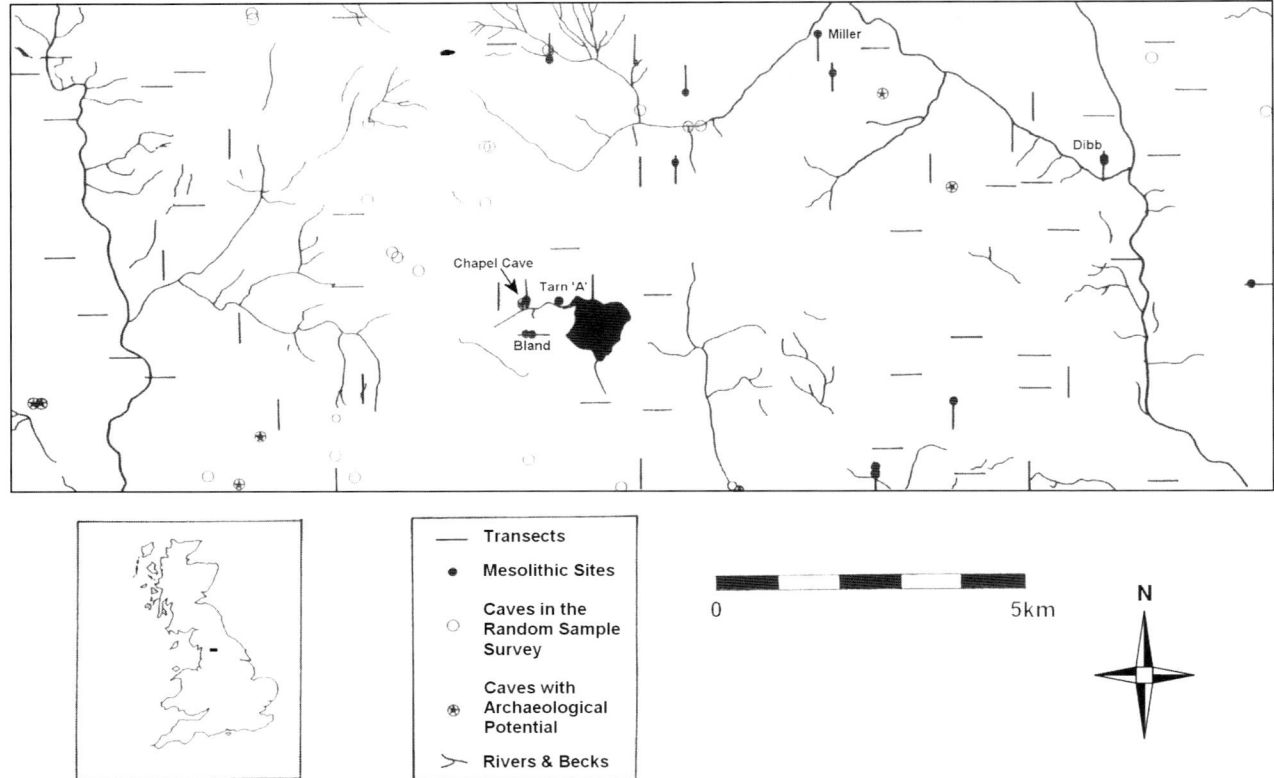

Figure 42.1 The research area showing the location of transects and sites.

cherts that are fundamentally distinct from the flints available in the eastern Yorkshire lowlands. The raw material distribution, coupled with assemblage characteristics, provides insights into the way individual sites and locations are integrated into a regional system of mobility.

The project research design includes two components: a probabilistic regional site survey and the excavation of a sample of open and cave sites. The project has surveyed sixty-four 500 metre transects that include subsurface systematic sampling at 50 metre intervals. Major excavations have been performed at the site of Chapel Cave and the open site of Malham Tarn Site A, both located near the wetlands of the Malham Tarn. Test excavations have also been conducted at five other sites, significant among these being Dibb I and Dibb II.

Initial Results of the Field Research

Fourteen Mesolithic sites have been intercepted by the transect survey and, although diverse in assemblage configuration, they appear to confirm the association of Mesolithic sites in the uplands (and dales) with wetland habitats.

There is a lower density of Mesolithic sites in the western part of the plateau (the Ribble drainage system) which is consistent with the activities and findings of amateur collectors and which suggests social and mobility ties with the eastern rather than western lowlands. This is counterintuitive given the closer proximity of western drainages to coastal lowlands (Figure 42.1).

The flaked stone recovered from the random regional survey sample indicates that there is a slight prevalence of chert overall, but that chert is more prevalent on the plateau than in the valleys (Figure 42.2). These results are supported by differential use of lithic raw material at upland sites and at sites located on river terraces of Wharfedale and Littondale, at lower lying elevations at the eastern and western margins of the project study area. At Dibb I, a late Mesolithic site located on an eight meter terrace of the River Skirfare, there occurs a high percentage of flint. At the site of Dibb II, located on a bench 13 metres above the River Skirfare, there is an assemblage dominated by flint artefacts typical of the earlier or transitional Mesolithic, specifically long, broad blades.

Open sites on the plateau display low percentages of flint, whereas the only cave excavated, also on the plateau, displays the highest percentage of flint of any site sampled. Malham Tarn Site A is one of a large series of Mesolithic sites identified on the northern, eastern and western margins of Malham Tarn (Williams *et al.* 1987). Tarn Site A is the most visible of these in terms of both topography and artefact density. Malham Tarn itself was a repetitive focus of Mesolithic upland use on the Malham plateau.

Our research at Tarn Site A reveals a dynamic and changing landscape with substantial shifts in local drainage

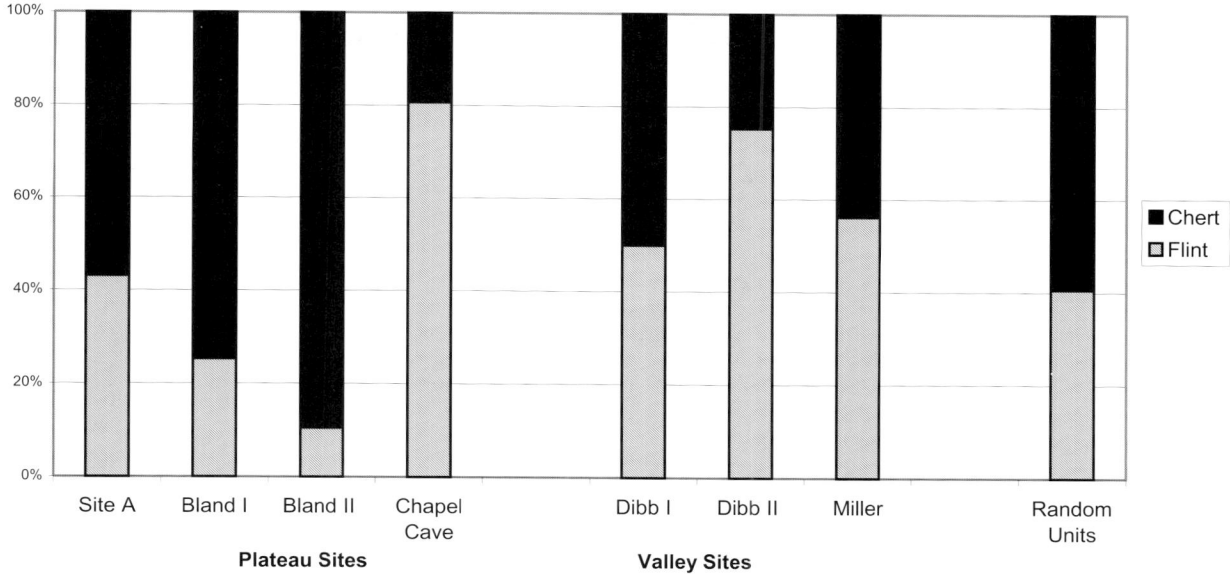

Figure 42.2 The percentages of upland chert and eastern lowland flint from excavated sites and the random sample of test pits in the research area.

and drainage features. Specifically, systematic geophysical prospecting reveals the presence of a series of relict ravines in-filled with primarily finer grained colluvial sediments. These features suggest that during the Mesolithic occupation of Tarn Site A that upland drainage may have been greater in volume with more channels than what is seen today. Mesolithic populations inhabited the higher and better drained elevations of this system, employing both the bases and margins of these drainage features. While Late Mesolithic artefacts dominate the Tarn Site A assemblage, the minority presence of broad blades reveals an Early Mesolithic onset of occupation which is consistent with the findings from Chapel Cave.

The lithic tool assemblage consists of numerous microliths, of which many show impact damage, abundant burins that might be indicative of bone and antler tool manufacturing and very few scrapers. We have identified hearth features associated with microliths and microburins and a rare gritstone technology. Gritstone, locally deposited in the glacial till, was transported to the site, aggregated in proximity to hearths and systematically reduced into slabs of varying thickness and size. Larger segments were employed as platforms adjacent to hearth features containing thermally altered stone, while smaller and thinner slabs, possibly reduced by marginal grinding, were found deposited within hearth features.

Chapel Cave bottomed out at over 2 metres below the surface. We have a radiocarbon date of 6575±50 BP (OxA-8837; 5620–5424 cal BC 2 sigma [Stuiver and Reimer 2000]) from charcoal near the top of the Mesolithic sequence and overlying an additional 0.70 metres of stratigraphy. The small macro-faunal assemblage has few identifiable specimens. Personal ornaments, including stone and bone beads, were recovered in the deeper Mesolithic layers. The raw material is primarily flint and the tool assemblage is comprised almost solely of microliths.

Discussion

The distribution of Mesolithic sites in the eastern drainages of the study area suggests stronger settlement and mobility integration with the eastern lowlands. Our assessment of data from Chapel Cave, Malham Tarn Site A and the Dibb I and II sites is that hunter-gatherers exploited the uplands using at least a long distance logistical strategy. None of these sites exhibits the expectations for residential sites articulated earlier in this discussion, a requirement for confirmation of Clark's model. The tool assemblages reveal a highly restricted range of activities; even at larger reoccupied locales such as Tarn Site A. Chapel Cave reveals that task groups visited the region coming with prepared tool forms and eastern lowland flint and utilised the natural features of the landscape for protection while practising hunting and possibly other resource procurement activities (Figure 42.3). These task groups then returned to their residential bases located in the lowlands of eastern Yorkshire. This said, we do not yet reject the possibility that residentially local hunter-gatherers were procuring flint through trade or exchange, or through task group procurement from the eastern lowlands.

Malham Tarn Site A amply demonstrates the potential complexity of the proposed seasonal logistic model. The flint and chert frequencies from this site suggest more intensive use of local raw materials consistent with longer term seasonal use by local or distant populations engaging in logistic activities.

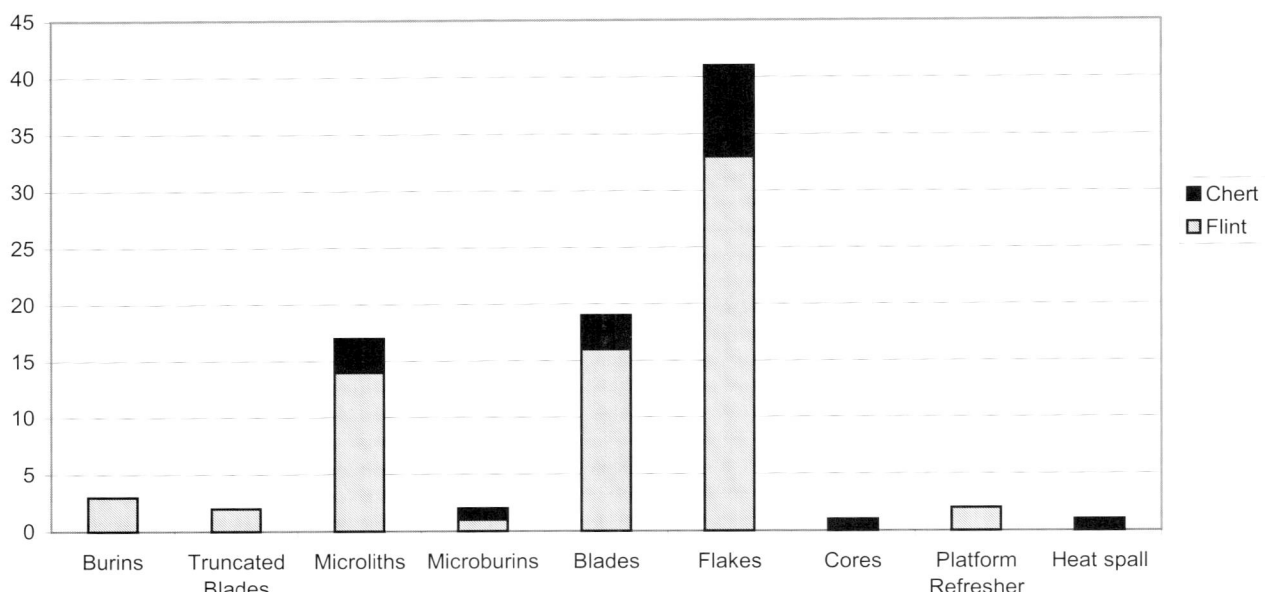

Figure 42.3 The frequency distribution of tool types and raw material categories from the Mesolithic deposit at Chapel Cave. Tool forms (accounting for 22% of flaked lithic material) include burins, truncations and microliths.

The temporal aspects of the Pennine data are also of import to this discussion, given that Clark's model was initially developed for the Early Mesolithic. There is a low incidence of Early Mesolithic occupation within the study area, including earlier components at Tarn Site A, Dibb II and the basal deposits at Chapel Cave, reflecting limited use of the uplands during this time period. Significantly, however, all of these locations were reoccupied during later Mesolithic periods, suggesting that the fundamental structure of location choice between the two periods is similar. The primary difference is that there are greater frequencies of Late Mesolithic sites, which suggests more intensive or more frequent use of the Malham Plateau and headwaters during that time. This may be simply the result of population increase in northern England. Assemblages from both time periods reflect that these sites are logistic and not residential in function. Therefore, both site frequencies and site functions lead to initial rejection of Clark's model.

Our data indicates that Clark (1972) was fundamentally correct in identifying long distance use of the uplands by populations associated with the eastern lowlands. His lack of access to current hunter-gatherer theoretical advances and detailed environmental data, however, prohibited his recognition of both the variability in hunter-gatherer mobility strategies and the complex changes in upland landscapes that occurred during the early Holocene.

Conclusions

In sum, the Yorkshire Dales Hunter-Gatherer Mobility and Subsistence Project suggests that Clark's model associating activities in the Pennines with hunter-gatherers of the eastern lowlands is fundamentally correct, although the nature of the mobility and social relationships may be more complex than initially imagined. The Pennine site data (and for that matter the North York Moors data) have not yet revealed the kinds of residential sites that Clark's model requires for confirmation. In fact, it is possible that most known sites in the Pennines are a consequence of extended logistic forays across several economic seasons. Re-interpretation of Star Carr and other sites in the Vale of Pickering can potentially assist in connecting the upland and lowland components of this system, although any such present or future re-interpretation must now account for the presence of logistic sites in the uplands.

Acknowledgements

This research has been funded by the Arts and Humanities Research Board, British Academy, the National Trust, Society of Antiquaries of London, Yorkshire Dales National Park, Michigan State University and the University of Bradford. J. Dodds, A. Evans, N. Sewpaul, T. Sparrow, C. Warren, and I. White assisted with data collection and the figures for this paper. Special thanks are given to M. Newman (National Trust) and R. White (Yorkshire Dales National Park) for their support of this research.

References

Andresen, J.M., Byrd, B.F., Elson, M.D., McGuire, R.H., Mendoza, R.G., Staski, E. and White, J.P. 1981. The deer hunters: Star Carr reconsidered. *World Archaeology* 13, 31–46.

Binford, L.R. 1978. *Nunamiut ethnoarchaeology*. New York.

—— 1980. Willow smoke and dogs' tails: hunter-gatherer settlement systems and archaeological site formation. *American Antiquity* 45, 4–20.

—— 1982. The archaeology of place. *Journal of Anthropological Archaeology* 1, 5–13.

Caulfield, S. 1978. Star Carr – an alternative view. *Irish Archaeological Research Forum* 5, 15–22.

Clark, J.G.D. 1954. *Excavations at Star Carr*. Cambridge.

—— 1972. *Star Carr: A case study in bioarchaeology*. Modular Publications 10. Reading.

Grigson, C. 1981. Fauna. In: Simmons, I. and Tooley, M. (eds.) *The environment in British prehistory*, 110–124. London.

Jacobi, R. 1978. Northern England in the eighth millenium BC: an essay. In: Mellars, P. (ed.) *The early postglacial settlement of northern Europe: an ecological perspective*, 128–140. London.

Kelly, R.L. 1992. Mobility/sedentism: concepts, archaeological measures, and effects. *Annual Review in Anthropology* 21, 43–66.

—— 1995. *The foraging spectrum*. Washington, D.C.

Legge, A.J. and Rowley-Conwy, P.A. 1988. *Star Carr revisited: a re-analysis of the large mammals*. London.

Mellars, P. 1998. Postscript: Major issues in the interpretation of Star Carr. In: Mellars, P. and Dark, P. *Star Carr in Context*, 215–241. Cambridge.

Mellars, P. and Dark, P. 1998. *Star Carr in Context*. Cambridge.

Mellars, P., Schadla-Hall, T. and Lane, P. 1998. Excavations in Trench A: 1985 and 1989. In: Mellars, P. and Dark, P. *Star Carr in Context*, 29–46. Cambridge.

Pitts, M. 1979. Hides and antlers: a new look at the gatherer-hunter site at Star Carr, North Yorkshire, England. *World Archaeology* 11, 32–42.

Price, T.D. 1982. Willow tales and dog smoke. *Quarterly Review of Archaeology* 3, No. 1, 4–7.

Radley, J. and Mellars, P.A. 1964. A Mesolithic structure at Deepcar, Yorkshire, England, and the affinities of its associated industries. *Proceedings of the Prehistoric Society* 30, 1–24.

Rowley-Conwy, P. 1995. Mesolithic settlement patterns: new zoological evidence from the Vale of Pickering, Yorkshire. *University of Durham and University of Newcastle Upon Tyne Archaeological Reports* 1994, 1–6.

Schadla-Hall, T. 1989. The Vale of Pickering in the Early Mesolithic context. In: Bonsall, C. (ed.) *The Mesolithic in Europe*, 218–224. Edinburgh.

Stuiver, M. and Reimer, P.J. 2000. *Radiocarbon calibration program CALIB rev. 4.3*. Quaternary Isotope Lab. University of Washington. Seattle.

Walker, D. 1956. A site at Stump Cross, near Grassington, Yorkshire, and the age of the Pennine microlithic industry. *Proceedings of the Prehistoric Society* 22, 23–28.

Williams, D.J., Richardson, J.A. and Richardson, R.S. 1987. Mesolithic sites at Malham Tarn and Great Close Mire, North Yorkshire. *Proceedings of the Prehistoric Society* 53, 363–383.

43. Mesolithic territorial behaviour in Central Scandinavia and adjacent regions

Per Falkenström

Territoriality among hunter-gatherers is often discussed against the background of stylistic variation. This method has been successfully applied to lithic artefacts in several studies. In central Scandinavia, however, style is a vague concept in Mesolithic contexts. Absolute datings are few, especially in Sweden, and re-occupations are evident on most sites. These circumstances offer no direct information about social boundaries, but additional methods give valuable information on territorial behaviour. Despite mixed artefact aggregations it is possible to identify territorial behaviour beyond merely stylistic characteristics. Settlement patterns, technology and choice of raw materials are assumed to reflect varying types of social relations. This information is also seen as a significant attribute when trying to identify local identities and territorial behaviour. It is suggested here that a combination of methods with different sorts of data contribute to the study of Mesolithic territories. Thus it is possible to either discern territorial consciousness or to detect an absence thereof.

Introduction

Prior to the mid 1990's few archaeologists paid attention to local lithic raw materials in central Scandinavia. Although artefacts from this region have been presented and interpreted they were compared to south Scandinavian artefacts and not regarded as remains of local traditions. Hence, territorial aspects have been touched upon only briefly, especially in a Mesolithic context.

The purpose of this paper is to draw attention to Mesolithic artefacts and social structure in central Scandinavia, a region encompassing the interior of middle Sweden and southeastern Norway (Figure 42.1). Adjacent regions are also considered but to a minor extent. In spite of limited investigations I will point out the possibilities of discerning territorial behaviour on the basis of the lithic artefacts that have been found there.

While flint is almost exclusively found in southern Scandinavia and along the Norwegian west coast, quartz, quartzite and volcanic rocks predominate in the interior.

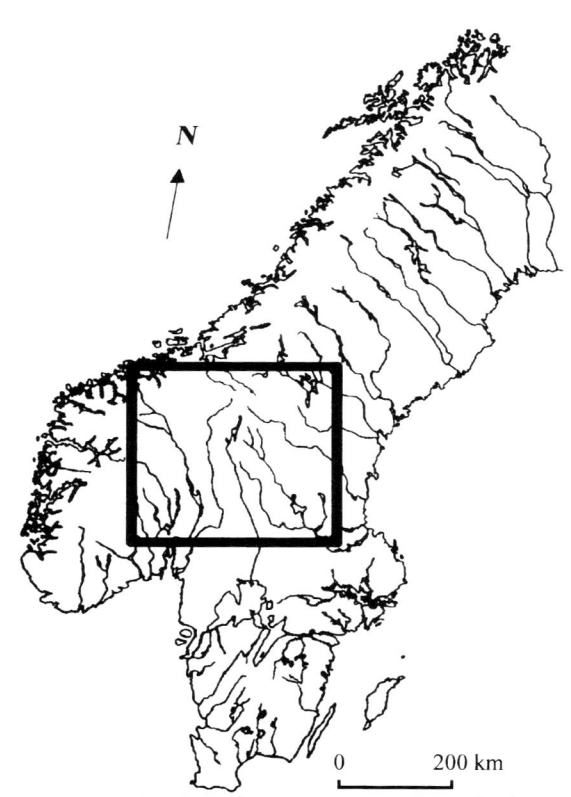

Figure 42.1 The Scandinavian peninsula with the main investigation area marked.

In central Scandinavia there are about 40 petrographically defined and locally available raw materials of which more than 70% have been chosen for tool manufacturing (Lannerbro 1976:29). Several tools are thought to be Mesolithic but the local availability and use of raw materials is characteristic of later periods as well.

Flint is often seen as an appropriate indicator of group identity. For example, territories in the Mesolithic have been recognised through flint distribution and stylistic variation (Gendel 1984). Unfortunately, artefacts of comparatively coarse raw materials have rarely been considered using stylistic standards. Such a neglect is apparently due to the irregularities and the less crystallised texture in comparison to flint. However, if it is difficult to identify stylistic attributes this issue has yet to be solved by other methods. There seems to be an increasing consciousness concerning Mesolithic territories in central Scandinavia, but most studies have not been problem oriented to the same degree as in other regions. Furthermore, most studies have been concerned with later periods and sedentary settlements.

In general, territoriality is associated with the growth of agriculture, settled populations and their properties. Nevertheless, permanent settlements are not necessary prerequisites for identity and territorial markers in mobile societies. Modern man is certainly aware of similar conditions whereupon territories can be relatively well defined. These may be strong reasons why approaches to hunter-gatherer's territories often seem to be vague or almost absent.

Mesolithic settlement patterns have been discussed in other works (for example Hyenstrand 1987:154; Boaz 1998:42) and are important contributors to these studies. Below, I will continue to compile relevant data on settlement patterns and raw material distribution. Accordingly, I hope to clarify what can be elicited from varying lithic artefacts concerning social territories.

Hunter-gatherer territoriality

When it comes to the organisation of space among hunter-gatherers many different approaches have been presented. This is an ambiguous task resulting from the nature of the archaeological record and varying sorts of methodological applications. Moreover, territoriality includes several aspects of both natural and cultural meanings. Therefore, territoriality must be defined specifically in order to understand prehistoric responses to ecological conditions and social networks.

Originally, studies on human territorial behaviour were derived from animal ethology. Biologically oriented scholars argued for aggression and defence of fixed areas. To some degree these are still essential behaviours in human societies. Anthropologists, on the other hand, have emphasised complexity and variety within the species of *Homo sapiens* (Malmberg 1980:47). As a consequence of this polarisation, territorial research is more or less concerned with either innate behaviour or distinct social organisation.

There seem to be many mechanisms that regulate territorial behaviour. Sufficient distances between groups of the same species prevent fighting and stress, limit the spread of disease and promote breeding behaviour. Petersen has suggested a number of adaptive strategies for hunter-gatherers. These may serve to adjust group size to resources, resolve conflict by fission and level out demographic variance. More flexible solutions also include division of labour and different levels of mobility depending on age of the group members (Petersen 1975:58 pp). There are of course several ways to co-operate within and between groups. It is interesting to note the reasons for the maintenance of such behaviours. Apart from the explanations just mentioned above, other significant approaches are often neglected.

From an archaeological point of view, hunter-gatherer territories have often been discussed in connection with land exploitation or technological similarity. These approaches can be relevant when dealing with subsistence or functional aspects but less useful concerning social relations. Additional and more adequate approaches such as social interaction should be included. Gendel defines a social territory as "an area occupied by a population of hunter-gatherers who participate in the exchange of mates and who share a distinct identity and language." (Gendel 1994:5). This definition gives no specific clues on how to identify social territories only from lithic assemblages. On the other hand, it is valuable as a framework on which further analyses can be based.

In recent years hunter-gatherer complexity and the formation of group identity have been of interest for archaeologists with particular emphasis on individual perceptions and social group relations. I think this view is important, since priority is given to the individual and his/her role in relation to group behaviour and the physical landscape. This should not be seen as a shift towards exclusively postprocessual views. Rather, I will go beyond external factors that seem to affect population dispersal. Demographic and ecological factors are not the only elements that affect territorial behaviour. Socio-economic stress and population growth are also important. As indicated in Petersen's discussion, group solidarity is maintained by various combinations of strategies. In my opinion this should be expressed through acts and behaviours which are then the characteristic traits of group identity. To a certain extent this should also be reflected in the visible remains from site occupations.

What are the potentials for reconstructing Mesolithic territories from only lithic artefacts? This possibility must be regarded as relatively limited but still possible to accomplish with an elaborate set of methods. One major problem is how to define the social units of interaction and their territorial markers. Most related studies on social structure have had different preconditions. Although proposed social units show differences regarding composition and complexity, an ethnoarchaeological compilation by Constandse-Westermann and Newell suggests a threefold division into social units. In band societies, the *band* is an independent and exogamous unit. A certain number of bands form a *dialectal tribe*, which forms a third social unit, the *language family* (Constandse-Westermann and Newell 1989:108 p).

Local bands can also be subordinated to a *regional band*. In comparison, this is a more flexible social unit where group fissions or kinship obligations are concerned. A number of regional bands form a tribe, the cohesive social unit with a common language and conscious group affiliation. This means that individual movements between local bands do not alter the individual's sense of tribal identity. Besides, additional units can be identified in specialised task groups and gender based division of labour (Lundberg 1997:129). Of course, cultural and natural change bring some inconsistency to the social units that make up territories. However, these concepts are still relevant in interpretations of archaeological assemblages.

Indications on Mesolithic territories

The cultural identity of hunter-gatherers has turned out to be very complex. As group identification requires some sort of contact with another group it is assumed that group identity can be expressed through acts and tools in everyday life. For instance, the rapid distribution of microblade technology across Scandinavia could hardly have occurred without established social networks. Hence, there should have been certain attributes related to specific groups and individuals during the Mesolithic period. Such identificational markers could be tools, knowledge or skills in lithic production. Additional markers such as raw materials and colours might have been chosen for symbolic values. These aspects will be further discussed below.

While Norwegian research on the Mesolithic provides much information, the Swedish part of central Scandinavia is badly known. This is partly due to few radiocarbon datings from the region. Under these conditions we can hardly confirm territorial change for longer periods of time. In spite of this chronological dilemma, we are still able to discuss territoriality from several alternative aspects.

Style

As stated above, stylistic determinations have not been sufficiently recognised in central Scandinavia. We must keep in mind that large assemblages remain to be classified, but so far there has been no successful way to attribute different raw materials according to certain styles. For instance, axes are very few or too irregular in order to attain relevant results from styles only. However, more distinct patterns appear in the coastal regions. The distribution of Mesolithic adzes and axes in southwestern Norway are interesting once the styles and raw materials have been determined. The choice of greenstone and dolorite correspond to two regions with additional separations of styles and raw material sources. The regions are thought to represent different territories as reflections of regional bands equivalent to one or two dialectal tribes (Nygaard 1987:151 p).

It must be stressed that the distribution of raw materials facilitates subsequent interpretations of stylistic attributes. In this way Gendel has observed stylistic variation among flint microliths in northwestern Europe. According to Gendel, the diagnostic styles seem to coincide with different social territories, mainly concentrated to river valleys. To large degree these territories overlap in the Early and Middle Mesolithic. When stylistic and raw material variation become more explicit in the Late Mesolithic, these changes can also be related to changing settlement patterns and increased territorial consciousness (Gendel 1984:155 p). Where flint or equivalent raw materials are absent or rare, the possibility of style categorisation are often limited. If possible, relatively coarse raw materials must be analysed together with other sources of information.

Lithic technology

Lithic technology should not be seen as an isolated part of any given population group. This has been confirmed through experiments by Callahan, using different raw materials. He emphasises the significance of functions in the tool making process. Reduction methods are performed with the final product in mind. Appropriate raw materials have been chosen to fit this purpose. When knapping, the reduction method is of course dependent on the limitations of the raw material, but technical skill also plays an important part in this process. As the core changes during reduction, different types can be produced, either through further shaping by retouche and/or use (Callahan 1987:61 p). In other words, the final product does not necessarily reflect the entire reduction sequence. Besides, applications of different reduction methods and techniques depend on a particular set of choices such as traditional values, individual skill and available raw materials.

It is interesting to study technological change and its implications concerning the introduction of polished axes and ceramics in hunter-gatherer societies. Hallgren has noticed a rapid distribution of Neolithic artefacts of the Funnel Beaker Culture in middle Sweden. He shows that ceramics, grinding stones and round-butted axes were acceptable innovations among Late Mesolithic bands, but only south of the river Dalälven. These groups are further supposed to have formed a larger ideological unity, probably consisting of a few dialectal tribes related through exogamous relations in southern Scandinavia and northern Europe (Hallgren 1996:20).

Generally, a new technology might fit the needs of Mesolithic populations irrespective of social borders. This could also include choices concerning the acceptance or rejection of technological innovations. Both sorts of behaviour can be discerned by comparing the widely distributed microblade technology in circumpolar regions and the more restricted production of macroblades. The macroblades are particularly well represented north and just south of the river Dalälven (Falkenström 1996:61). In this case, lithic technology reflects two different traditions. Probably, the less widespread macroblade technology would reflect group affiliation. No subdivisions of this group could be made by only studying the lithic technology.

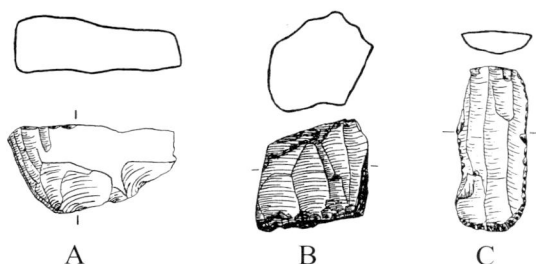

Figure 42.2 Mesolithic artefacts from the Swedish interior. A: Handle core of silicified tuff. B: Platform core of quartzitic silt stone. C: Blade scraper of flint. Scale 1:2 (after Lannerbro 1991:90, 127 p).

Lithic raw materials

Local raw materials in central Scandinavia seem to be of special interest since various bed rocks have been used in prehistoric times. Some are widely distributed while others are particularly rare. Local availability is naturally significant but imported materials – and consequently the maintenance of social relations – should not be underestimated. In spite of few Swedish studies on this subject some Norwegian investigations may shed light upon the Mesolithic on the Swedish side.

Boaz argues for oppositions between coastal and interior settlements during the Nøstvet period. To solve these tensions, intensified variability and specialisation did appear on Nøstvet settlements, especially after 7000 uncalibrated BP (Boaz 1998:29). During the Late Mesolithic there was not only a change in production, but also a shift in the choice of raw materials. In addition to traditional functional aspects of raw materials, such a choice must also be considered in relation to symbolic and aesthetic values (Bergsvik 1999:285).

Local bed rocks and/or moraine materials have been used to a large extent in central Scandinavia. Unfortunately there seem to be few connections between local quarries and raw materials found on archaeological sites. Natural formation processes such as chemical abrasion partly explain the difficulties in identifying prehistoric quarries. Furthermore, recognising microscopic differences between, for example, quartz and quartzite prevent reliable petrographical analyses. Despite failures, this method is still useful when illustrating general trends. On the whole, specific raw material locations correspond with artefact distribution in central Scandinavia. The same relationship can also be seen in corresponding parts of Norway.

In the Norwegian mountain region, microblades and contemporary Late Mesolithic artefacts reveal interesting communication routes. In contrast to low lying areas, mountain sites are small and apparently of temporary duration. In addition, the distribution of raw materials indicates occupations by two different groups. Gustafson thinks that the presence of flint shows that the interior was used by a coastal population. Another distribution pattern can be connected with quartz and quartzite using groups, presumably from low lying areas on the Swedish side (Gustafson 1980:9). There have been several attempts to locate a boundary in the Norwegian highlands. It should not be an end in itself to locate sharp boundaries as they often encompass large areas. These boundary areas must also be seen in relation to changing socio-economic conditions. However, the variability of lithic raw material still confirms that the interior was used differently.

The use of local bed rocks is a characteristic trait in central Scandinavia and raw material variability is particularly well represented on Mesolithic settlements (Figure 42.2). For instance, porphyries and quartzite often occur together with relatively rare raw materials such as flint and jasper. However, the distribution of red quartzite in the western parts of Sweden, close to the national border, seems to form a territory where local availability was of major importance. About 50 kilometres to the east, another pattern appears when one compares lithic artefacts and volcanic bedrock. The complicated geological conditions have created silicified tuffs and porphyries. In southern Norway, there are other local raw materials such as mylonite and rhyolite. These conditions do not indicate strictly limited concentrations but rather overlapping distributions, especially along water systems. Comparisons between the regions show distinct local production with a predominance of one sort of raw material.

Lithic colours

As parts of the whole symbol system, colours are used in everyday life. Anthropological studies mention black and white as the most significant colours that are used in connection with events of life and death, supernatural powers *etc*. Red is also mentioned and often used to reinforce and balance the power of specific symbols (Lundberg 1997:167). The significance of other colours is apparently dependent on their specific socio-historical context. The wide colour range of lithic materials in central Scandinavia could represent important symbols associated to different activities, though hitherto of unknown significance in prehistory.

The colours of lithic materials had probably some meaning to the groups, perhaps concerning quality or functional aspects related to certain raw materials. In addition, rarity might have affected their use as symbol markers. For example, the red lustre of jasper probably had exotic connotations since it is very rare in these latitudes. The quality of jasper is quite the same as flint and accordingly would have been attractive for functional, symbolic and aesthetic reasons. Flint also belongs to this group of so called exotic raw materials since it does not occur naturally in the interior but was imported. The frequency of both flint and jasper decreases from west to east in the interior regions. Both colour and lustre could have been used as identification markers for flint and jasper using groups. The groups could also have used certain colours and lustre in order to maintain social networks.

Settlement patterns

Ever since the deglaciation of central Scandinavia about 8000 uncalibrated BP, regional variation can be observed between different Mesolithic groups. These patterns are rather vague and it is not until the Late Mesolithic that more complex patterns seem to have emerged, at least in southeastern Norway, where there were complex socio-economic changes during this time. During the later part of the Nøstvet, between 7000 and 5000 uncalibrated BP, there is an increase of specialisation between coastal and interior territories (Boaz 1998:42). There are strong reasons to suggest similar changes in the Swedish interior. The Mesolithic settlements here have characteristic features with diagnostic artefacts and different raw materials, but re-occupation over thousands of years has resulted in mixed sites. This causes problems regarding contemporary and representative analyses for specific regions and even within single sites. On the other hand, mixed sites should be regarded as one significant aspect of territorial behaviour. If site variability can be associated to movements of a few bands or a tribe, then re-occupation should have encouraged group identity.

Varying site scales and artefact assemblages may give more information about group complexity and seasonal activities. Some patterns can be estimated on the basis of site attributes such as amounts, density, distribution and variability of artefacts. In addition, topographic features could have been significant markers in the formation of social territories (Forsberg 1985:270 p).

To a certain extent, some sites in central Scandinavia are concentrated to particular topographical regions but do not necessarily coincide with the social territories that have been suggested here (Figure 42.3). Thus, the settlement patterns can be interpreted as extended social networks across water systems as well as highland and lowland regions. Nevertheless, there are more significant topographical features. The natural boundary known as the *Limes Norrlandicus* roughly coincides with the river Dalälven. When using the social units discussed above, differences in material culture on both sides of the Dalälven River can be associated with separate dialectal tribes or maybe separate language families. A preliminary analysis shows a few bands belonging to these tribes along the coast in middle Sweden (Knutsson *et al.* 1999:115 pp). How did these bands differ from the bands in the interior? Were there any seasonal movement between the interior and coastal areas? So far, very few settlements have been identified in this region and territorial patterns are based on different find categories than those used to define the interior. For that reason we must be careful when comparing regions from different perspectives.

In northern Sweden, the coastal/interior opposition was previously thought to reflect settlement patterns with long distance movements on a seasonal basis. Recent research rather indicates pronounced territorial behaviour with fewer and more permanent occupations, at least during the Late Mesolithic and the Neolithic. In a region just north of the area under study here, Lundberg has analysed embankments of fire-cracked stones. These features have been interpreted as winter dwellings and date from the Late Mesolithic to the Middle Neolithic. In spite of their long chronological sequence, Lundberg concludes that they reflect semi-sedentary occupations and a durable social structure. What she calls a "village" is supposed to represent a local band with relatives in adjacent "villages" which together form a regional band. In this view a number of regional bands would represent a tribe whose members share the same language. The tribe would also be the social unit with possible marriage partners, belonging to different regional bands (Lundberg 1997:130 p).

Lundberg has observed divergences between interior and coastal regions, similar to those noted in southern and middle Sweden. The regional bands in the interior are interpreted as a tribe with seasonal movements between interior summer and winter settlements. Apparently, there were comparatively limited contacts with coastal tribes. Finds of Swedish flint and Norwegian slate artefacts would support this interpretation (Lundberg 1997:147).

Investigations in southern Norway together with the middle and northern parts of Sweden have contributed to our knowledge about interior regions in central Scandinavia. If we consider Mesolithic and Early Neolithic find contexts, another tribe can be discerned approximately north of the river Dalälven. Subdivisions into regional bands are also discernible with reference to characteristic artefacts from Mesolithic hunter-gatherers. It should be possible to detect local groups, but such a task demands more comprehensive research. So far, chronology is too uncertain and more radiocarbon dates are needed if we want detailed information about Mesolithic territories and the social units associated with them.

An ethnoarchaeological approach

From the discussion above we can now conclude that new territories are created along with changing social networks. Sometimes the changes create new kinship identities and territorial boundaries. Peterson mentions interesting events concerning these matters, which are barely observable in archaeological contexts. Among !Kung Bushmen in southwestern Africa and among aboriginal bands in Australia a few old people could affect the behaviour of the whole group. Because old members were as mobile as the younger members the territory was smaller than expected in relationship to archaeological estimations. Although no visible borders exist, defence of local group boundaries have been documented in Arnhem land, Australia. To be accepted by a local group, visitors are obliged to wait before the necessary ceremonies can be held (Peterson 1975:60 p). In this situation of ritualised behaviour, social borders are expressed and physical violence overcome. As long as they know how

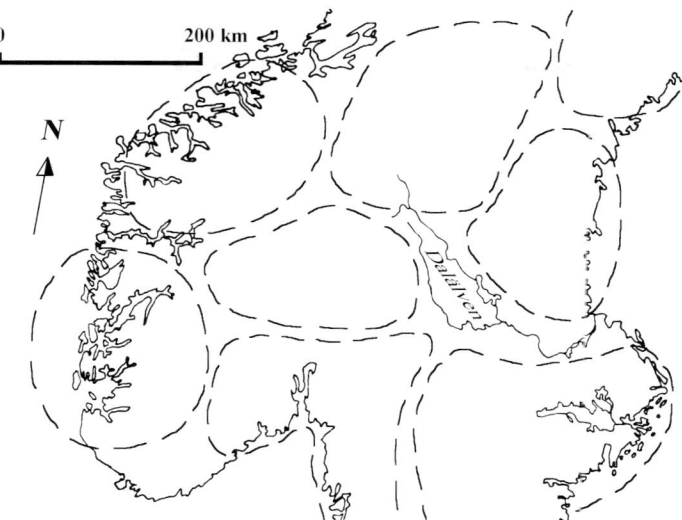

Figure 42.3 Suggested territories in central Scandinavia during the Mesolithic. Each territory refers to a regional band with similar group identity. These are further supposed to form a tribe approximately north of the river Dalälven.

to behave, the participants can confirm their membership with and to common social unit.

Conditions are different in Binford's study of the Nunamiut Inuits in Alaska. These bands occupy both coastal and interior regions. The settlements would be located according to established traditions and social relations where internal order is always maintained at the settlements. One exception to this was when mobile game caused irregular territorial patterns. Where conditions are suitable for hunting, winter settlements are small and scattered. Extended families live in separate tents and the distance between them is less than that between summer settlements. Several groups are reunited during the summer. This is also the time when hunting parties move to known aggregation points in the mountains for co-ordinated activities. Generally, there are small individual tents and major hearths on these locations. They are only temporary occupations for a few days but still within walking distance from residential settlements (Binford 1991:46 pp).

The behaviour of the Nunamiut shows that settlements may express local group identity, but extended relations are also present on almost every location occupied by the same local group. Similar events can hardly be reconstructed from archaeological remains, but this kind of ethnographic data is nevertheless an important framework for archaeological interpretation.

Ethnographic data often demonstrates interaction between topography, language, kinship alliances and social distance. Usually inter-marriages hold groups together through social and political obligations. However, the relations can change rapidly when large groups split into smaller social units. In time, geographical distance increases at the expense of social distance. In most mobile societies territorial overlapping cannot be avoided, but different social units may be more or less evident. Because people often feel secure in known regions, settlements are located accordingly: along river valleys and close to allied groups.

Similarly, Mesolithic settlements are located at major water systems and regional bands seem to have been grouped accordingly. However, ethnographic sources show extensive variety between groups of hunter-gatherers concerning their social structure and territorial behaviour. Moreover, the number of band members changes in relation to subsistence strategies, group fission, seasonal movements, post-marital events *etc*. If ethnographic models are relevant to Mesolithic conditions in central Scandinavia, we can assume that each regional band might consist of 1–5 local bands. Yet, without convenient data it is difficult to estimate adequate population numbers.

In this context, lithic artefacts offer relatively limited information. This does not mean that archaeological interpretations are based exclusively on artefacts. Reasonably, by combining different sorts of data more plausible patterns can be discerned. Usually, ethnographic studies tell us of more complex behaviours, often associated to kinship relations. Ethnographic studies may yield conventional data if these are used critically. In the ethnographic literature, territorial behaviour often has to do with short term change and unique events, often irrelevant for archaeological interpretations, but of valuable importance if we want to understand hunter-gatherer complexity. Reconsidering the use of lithic material in central Scandinavia, the artefacts reflect different ways of production, probably associated to group identity and territoriality. With an ethnoarchaeological approach, including Binford's and Peterson's studies, it can also be stated that the Mesolithic artefacts clearly demonstrate dynamic social networks.

Conclusions

In order to discern explicit territorial behaviour in central Scandinavia I have chosen relevant methods with regard to the lithic material in question. Technology, raw material distribution, colours and settlement patterns have yielded valuable information. Topography and ethnoarchaeological approaches have also been considered. Interpretations are further based on suggested territories in adjacent regions. Radiocarbon dates, mainly from the Norwegian interior, set the chronological framework to 7000–5000 uncalibrated BP, a period characterised by increasing territorial behaviour. These patterns reflect oppositions between coastal and inland regions and are similar to contemporaneous conditions among Mesolithic populations in Sweden.

The territories discussed here are seen to reflect regional bands with similar group identities and elaborate social networks. During the course of the Mesolithic two completely different traditions appear north and south of the river Dalälven. With regard to the increasing differences during the Mesolithic these traditions might represent tribes with different social structures and, possibly, languages.

Ethnoarchaeological data highlights the importance of kinship groups with overlapping social networks. The territories I have suggested could indicate related kin groups, distinguished by different behaviour with regard to the choice of raw materials, distinct settlement patterns *etc.* The significance of maintaining such behaviours are partly expressed in the re-occupation of sites. The territories might also be the result of an increasing need to express group identity, which had developed in the Late Mesolithic. Fortunately, refined chronological divisions will facilitate identifications of contemporary social groups and their inherent territorial behaviour.

Acknowledgements

Thanks to Elisabet Green for improving the English text. I am indepted to Kjel Knutsson and David Loeffler for their comments on the manuscript. Any shortcomings are of course mine.

References

Bergsvik, K.A. 1999. A new reference system for classification of lithic raw materials: A case study from Skatestraumen, western Norway. In: Boaz, J. (ed.) *The Mesolithic in Central Scandinavia.* Universitetets Oldsaksamlings Skrifter Nr. 22, 283–297. Oslo.

Binford, L.R. 1991. When the going gets tough, the tough get going: Nunamiut local groups, camping patterns and economic organization. In: Gamble, C.S. and Boismier, W.A. (eds.) *Ethnoarchaeological Approaches To Mobile Camp sites. Hunter-Gatherer and Pastoralist Case Studies.* Ethnoarchaeological Series 1, 25–138. Ann Arbor.

Boaz, J. 1998. *Hunter-Gatherer Site Variability: Changing patterns of site utilization in the interior of eastern Norway, between 8000 and 2500 B.P.* Universitetets Oldsaksamlings Skrifter Nr. 28. Oslo.

Callahan, E. 1987. *An evaluation of the Lithic Technology in Middle Sweden during the Mesolithic and Neolithic.* Societas Archaeologica Upsaliensis. Aun 8. Uppsala.

Constandse-Westermann, T.S. and Newell, R.R. 1985. Social and Biological Aspects of the Western European Mesolithic population Structure: a Comparison with the Demography of North American Indians. In: Bonsall, C. (ed.) *The Mesolithic in Europe.* Papers presented at the third international symposium, 106–115. Edinburgh.

Falkenström, P. 1996. *Spån och spånande. Mesolitiska storspånsindustrier i Dalarna och Härjedalen.* MA thesis. Department of Archaeology. Uppsala University. Uppsala.

Forsberg, L.L. 1985. *Site variability and settlement patterns. An analysis of the Hunter-Gatherer Settlement System in the Lule River Valley, 1500 B.C.–B.C./A.D.* Archaeology and Environment 5. Umeå.

Gendel, P.A. 1984. *Mesolithic Social Territories in Northwestern Europe.* BAR International Series 218. Oxford.

Gustafson, L. 1980. Om «vestgrensa» i høyfjellet. *Arkeo,* 1980, 6–10.

Hallgren, F. 1996. Sociala territorier och exogamirelationer i senmesolitisk tid. En diskussion utifrån boplatsen Pärlängsberget, Södermanland. *Tor* 28, 5–27.

Hyenstrand, A. 1987. Forntid i grännsland. In: Björklund, S. (ed.) *Lima och Transtrand – ur två socknars historia,* 109–166. Malung.

Knutsson, K., Lindgren, C., Hallgren, F. and Björck, N. 1999. The Mesolithic in eastern central Sweden. In: Boaz, J. (ed.) *The Mesolithic in Central Scandinavia.* Universitetets Oldsaksamlings Skrifter Nr. 22, 87–123. Oslo

Lannerbro, R. 1976. *Implements and Rock Materials in the Prehistory of Upper Dalarna.* Early Norrland 4. KVHAA. Stockholm.

—— 1991. *Det södra fångstlandet. Katalog. Del I. Vanån.* SAR Field Studies Nr. 3. Stockholm.

Lundberg, Å. 1997. *Vinterbyar. Ett bandsamhälles territorier i Norrlands inland 4500–2500 f. Kr.* Studia archaeologica universitatis umensis 8. Umeå.

Malmberg, T. 1980. *Human territoriality. Survey of behavioural territories in man with preliminary analysis and discussion of meaning.* Studies in the Social Sciences 33. Lund.

Nygaard, S.E. 1987. Socio-economic developments along the southwestern coast of Norway between 10.000 and 4.000 B.P. In: Rowley-Conwy, P., Zvelebil, M. and Blankholm, H.P. (eds.) *Mesolithic Northwest Europe: Recent Trends,* 147–154. Sheffield.

Peterson, N. 1975. Hunter-Gatherer Territoriality: The Perspective from Australia. *American Anthropologist,* 53–68.

44. Regionalism in the Mesolithic of Southern Germany

Michael Jochim

Social and regional groups among prehistoric hunter-gatherers are notoriously difficult to reconstruct. This paper explores these topics in the Mesolithic of southern Germany, where a considerable amount of research has been carried out. Various interpretive problems underscore the need for regional fieldwork as well as studies of artifact technology, typology, style and raw materials. These studies, in turn, must be integrated with theories of style and evolutionary ecology in attempts to reconstruct patterns of social interaction.

Introduction

With a few notable exceptions, research into the central European Mesolithic has focused largely on chronology, technology and subsistence (Taute 1967; Hahn 1983; Eriksen 1991; Cziesla 1992; Kind 1996; Jochim 1998). Much less primary attention has been given to fundamental social issues of exchange and interaction, social groupings, networks and boundaries. The result of such a research bias has been a growing knowledge of Mesolithic populations as ecologically situated economic beings, but only a vague appreciation of their social and cultural relations. This bias is certainly comprehensible in light of the nature of the available data: a large number of surface lithic scatters supplemented by a handful of excavated caves, rockshelters and open-air camps containing food refuse as the most obvious organic remains. Such a record provides few unambiguous indications of social relations. Whenever such topics are discussed, it is usually in the form of casual interpretations based on implicit assumptions. The presence of exotic stone materials in assemblages dominated by local stone, for example, may be seen as evidence of exchange relations with neighbouring groups or alternatively as an indication of the scale of normal seasonal movements. Social groups and their boundaries may be seen in the distribution of certain retouched tools (Kozlowski 1973) or of different methods of blade platform preparation (Tillman 1993).

If we are to expand our anthropological understanding of the Mesolithic in this area, we need to move beyond such casual interpretations to focus explicit attention on the social geography. We need to design research to address such topics as: 1) the scale of land use; 2) the organisation of land use; 3) the relationship between the social and the natural geography and 4) the nature of social boundaries. This paper represents a step in this direction, part of long term research into patterns of land use and culture change in the southwest German Mesolithic. It builds upon a long history of research in this area, but directs attention specifically to the above topics.

Evolutionary Ecology

An enormous amount of attention has been given to questions of land use among hunter-gatherers. In general terms, this literature can be characterised as emphasising either ecological and economic factors on the one hand, or social and ideological ones on the other. The ecological /economic approaches have a long and diverse history (Bettinger 1991), but have recently been united within the coherent theoretical framework of evolutionary ecology (Smith and Winterhalder 1992; Kelly 1995). Based on the fundamental assumption that land use behavior has been shaped by natural selection, evolutionary ecology employs a cost-benefit methodology to model such topics as range size, patch choice and territorial defense (Cashdan 1992). Within this framework, human foragers, like other animals, can be expected to demonstrate clear patterning between features of the natural environment and aspects of land use. By contrast, other approaches, by emphasising the active, creative nature of humans as cultural beings, stress the independence of behavior from what they perceive as ecological determinism. In these views, cultural landscapes are imposed upon the natural geography and may be informed as much by ideological considerations as by economic needs (Tilley 1994; Bradley 1998; Ucko and Layton 1999). In part because these approaches are not formally derived from an established body of coherent theory, they tend to approach explanation not through predictive modeling, but rather through interpretation aided by ethnographic analogies.

If one takes the view that humans are both ecologically and culturally situated, then studies of land use pose serious methodological challenges. A rather pragmatic approach is to use the ecological models as baseline expectations and to seek to explain deviations from such models in terms of social and ideological factors, in effect, to use the latter to explain the "residue" of patterns not in line with ecologically based predictions. A variation of this approach is to use (and expect) ecological models to predict only general, coarse patterns, while appealing to social and ideological factors to explain the fine details. Both approaches reflect a perception that ecological interpretations are more tractable and easier to develop. This is the approach that will be taken here, with the realisation, however, that this ease of application may be illusory; it is difficult to specify all of the relevant costs and benefits and, particularly in archaeological applications, to assign realistic numbers or weights to them. Initially, then, some general ecological predictions about various aspects of land use will be presented; problems and complications will be examined later in the proposal.

The Scale of Land Use

A large body of ecological literature suggests a strong set of relationships between the size of areas exploited by foragers and environmental and demographic variables. These can be phrased as simple predictive statements and include the following:
– Range size should decrease as resources become more abundant.
– Range size should decrease as resources become more homogeneously distributed and in phase.
– Range size should decrease as competition increases.

The Organisation of Land Use

Organisational aspects of land use include a variety of topics frequently investigated in archaeology, most commonly within an ecological framework. Among these topics are: settlement location, frequency of reoccupation, frequency of residential movement and the degree of logistical organisation. For each of these, the resource geography has been usually viewed as a critical determinant in developing the following predictions (eg. Kelly 1995).
– Locations are chosen so as to minimise resource acquisition costs.
– More stable and productive resource concentrations attract more frequent reoccupation.
– Residential moves are triggered by sufficiently declining marginal returns in accessible resource patches to make moves to new patches more efficient, despite the costs of the moves.
– The importance of logistical organisation increases as resources become more patchy and differentially distributed across the landscape.

The Relationship Between Cultural and Natural Geography

Foraging societies perceive, classify and compartmentalise the natural landscape in various ways, imposing a cultural order and distributing their activities accordingly. The common sense ecological proposition, bolstered by many ethnographic studies, is that there should be some correspondence between cultural and natural landscapes. Among the G/Wi, each band territory is said to contain "a nexus of resources which they require to fill a wide range of needs and in all seasons of the year" (Silberbauer 1972:294). In arid habitats, the distribution of water is a crucial factor in both the economic (Lee 1972; Silberbauer 1972) and ideological (Berndt 1972) use of the landscape. Seasonal changes in settlement and activities are often keyed to environmental changes, producing more or less repetitive seasonal rounds.

It is the existence of such strong ethnographic patterns and the support of ecological models that encourage so many archaeological studies to demarcate areas for investigation based on environmental features. Common archaeological study areas include river valleys and adjoining heights, strips of coastline and hinterland or transects up major mountain slopes. All have the benefits of including considerable environmental variation and therefore probably variation in activities and settlements as well. The following general propositions, therefore, may be put forward:
– Social territories will be situated so as to include a relatively large proportion of the ecological variation in the region.
– Ecologically similar portions of territories will be used in similar ways.
– Major discontinuities in the geographic distributions of overall resource abundance and travel costs will form the peripheries of social territories.

Social Boundaries

Based to a great extent on the ethnographic record, there has been a tendency for archaeologists to project a hierarchical and bounded model of prehistoric hunter-gatherers onto the past. From the bands and tribes of Aboriginal Australia (Birdsell 1953) to the microbands, macrobands and linguistic groups of the Canadian Subarctic (Helm 1972) and the settlement, local group and river group of the Ainu (Watanabe 1972), such a hierarchical arrangement of groups has been often described. Because each had a spatial correlate, a hierarchical nesting of increasingly socially inclusive areas could also be expected, and has guided interpretations of the archaeological record. Yet ethnographers have also been vocal in emphasising the fluid nature of hunter-gatherer social groups, the frequent changes of membership and shifts of residence and the variability among groups in the degree of fluidity and boundedness (Hiatt 1968; Lee 1972).

Ecological approaches to these issues have emphasised both economic defensibility and risk, tied ultimately to resource structure (Dyson-Hudson and Smith 1978; Wiessner 1982; Cashdan 1992). Three resulting predictions are that:
- Territorial defense and boundary maintenance should increase as resources become more abundant and predictable.
- Economic interdependence, exchange and visiting across social boundaries should increase as environmental variability and unpredictability increase.
- Social boundedness should increase with population density.

Problems with ecological models

The Scale of Land Use

Even within the ecologically based literature, problems in applying ecological predictions about the scale of land use have been recognised. Cashdan (1992), for example, points out the difficulty in quantifying an organism's resource "needs", and that such needs may be much larger than basic biological maintenance levels if the organism is an energy maximiser (that is, can use excess food to increase fitness). In light of this difficulty, it is easy to imagine the complications posed by hunter-gatherers, who may consider a variety of non-nutritional resources as "necessary" (such as high quality stone, ochre or particularly rare plants) and who may find a myriad of uses for foods beyond simply eating them (such as feasting, gifts, exchange items or offerings). Moreover, Binford (1983) stresses that the range size over the long term may be much bigger than that in any particular year, depending on the nature of resource depletion and renewability. In his example from the Nunamiut the lifetime range is five times as large as that used in one year.

As a result of such complications it is small wonder that so few archaeological studies have attempted formal predictions about the size of annual ranges from environmental features or that considerable disagreement can exist about the range of annual movement among specific groups of prehistoric hunter-gatherers. In reconstructions of the Upper Palaeolithic of southwestern France, for example, the range of yearly movement has been portrayed in a variety of ways at differing geographic scales (Sieveking 1976; Spiess 1979; Bahn 1979; Gordon 1988). Similarly, southwestern Germany during the Magdalenian has been variously seen as economically self-contained (Hahn 1979; Weniger 1982) or as part of a range that extended to the North European Plain (Sturdy 1972).

The Organisation of Land Use

Again, the ecological predictions may prove difficult to operationalise because of our inability to quantify past resource distributions, so that the best we might hope for is to be able to predict general rankings of different locations and habitats. However, these predictions also ignore various other factors of potential importance. The position of a location relative to others may encourage a use not easily predictable from its resources alone. For example, sheltered areas along streams might be generally selected for residential occupation, but if a subset of those locations lies close to prime lakeshore locations that are even more preferred, then this subset may see little residential use. Material factors other than resources may be significant to decisions about site location and reoccupation, both positive factors (such as obtaining a view, shade or winter sun) and negative (for instance, avoidance of mosquitoes or high wind). Non-material factors may also be crucial in such decisions, including the history of events at different locations (deaths, marriages) and the symbolic meanings attached to different locales (as the birthplace of ancestors or the location of spirit activities, for example).

The complexity underlying settlement decisions suggests that many current approaches to settlement studies, such as the development of predictive models with GIS, face serious challenges in identifying variables of significance and in giving meaning to patterns identified.

The Relationship Between Cultural and Natural Geography

Ecological study areas are often chosen, and interpreted, as if they corresponded to the ranges of prehistoric groups as well; the assumption is made that the natural units correspond to cultural units, primarily because they include some implicitly requisite resource variety in close proximity. Yet there are many possible ways to carve up a landscape and distribute activities across it. Lakes may form the center of one group's territory or the meeting point for many. Similarly, rivers may lie at the center or the boundary of territories. Lowland valleys and adjacent hills might be claimed and used by separate groups, or they might be combined in group areas as transects perpendicular to the valley. While it might well be that in each particular case the arrangement makes ecological sense, depending on very specific environmental data, it might also be the case that other factors entirely, such as history of occupation or actions of neighboring groups, are largely responsible for the configuration of space use. We need to be cautious in inferring cultural geography from the natural landscape.

Social Boundaries

Observations among Kalahari groups pose some contradictions to the ecological models, in that "the most territorial groups are located where resources are sparsest and most variable" (Cashdan 1992:264). In these cases, territorial perimeters are not actively defended, but in the potentially competitive context for scarce resources, people are reluctant to enter neighboring areas.

Moreover, it is clear that the distribution of material remains in the archaeological record may be affected by habitual use of areas, territorial defense, flexibility of residence and affiliation, exchange and visiting. Consequently, the inadequacies of simple, resource based territorial models to account for certain patterns in the ethnographic record insure that we are in a weak position to predict the nature of material distributions from features of the natural environment. Our position is further weakened by our only partial understanding of style in material remains and how it reflects both active manipulations and passive interactions (Sackett 1985; Wiessner 1985). Certainly, the fact that different material artifacts in the same society can pattern spatially in different ways should make us cautious about inferring social meaning from material patterns (Wiessner 1983, 1984).

As a result of the factors discussed above, it is difficult to generate robust predictions about prehistoric land use, predictions that are not *a priori* weakened by an awareness of their deficiencies. Consequently, an investigation of Mesolithic social geography cannot justifiably take the form of straightforward testing of hypotheses deductively derived from evolutionary ecology. Rather, from the outset it must combine prediction with pattern seeking and inductive inference, explicitly working back and forth between the two modes of research.

Southwest Germany in the Mesolithic

Southwest Germany has a long history of research and a comparatively rich archaeological record for the Mesolithic. A number of excavated cave, rockshelter and open-air sites are supplemented by numerous surface finds from early archaeological surveys around lakeshores as well as from the work of private collectors. Because large regional gaps in coverage existed, however, my colleagues and I have been conducting surface surveys since 1992 designed to create a more representative picture of the archaeological distributions (Jochim *et al.* 1998). Using the topographic map quads at 1:25000 as our framework, we have walked fields in a range of contexts from the limestone plateau of the Swabian Alb south across the Danube Valley and the moraines of Oberschwaben to the shores of Lake Constance. Although this survey still continues, and is being supplemented by testing and excavation of selected sites, some provisional regional patterns will be discussed here.

At this point we really know nothing about the social organisation and groupings in the German Mesolithic. We can assume that there were social groups and recognised affiliations, and perhaps shifting subgroups, but it seems dangerous to jump to the assumption of the existence of tribes, bands, and other ethnographic entities. The issues of social geography will have to be cautiously approached in two ways. First, ethnographic analogy can be used, primarily to develop ideas about the likely range of options of land use, if only to temper archaeological interpretations with some realistic constraints. Second, and more importantly, empirical studies of the archaeological record will be discussed as a first step toward reconstructing the social landscape of southwest Germany.

Ethnographic Patterns

Ethnographic data can be employed to suggest something about the likely patterns of range size, settlement distributions and boundaries. Their implications can be compared to the archaeological record, in full awareness, however, that prehistoric behavior in this area may have no modern correlates.

Range Size

It would be useful to know the area within which recognised hunter-gatherer social groupings can exist. What is a realistic size for social, cultural or linguistic networks? Given that local ecology and resources play a large role in the size of group territories, it makes sense to look to modern groups inhabiting environments similar to that of Mesolithic Germany. Since there are no such groups, a sample of 20 North American Indian societies occupying relatively forested environments of various sorts was examined. Location of these groups ranged from California to Canada, with coastal locations and high latitudes avoided (Figure 44.1).

TRIBE	AREA (SQ. KM)
CHILULA	426
WHILKUT	649
HUPA	930
KAROK	3123
ATSUGEWI	5344
SHASTA	11867
NIPISSING	12968
ACHUMAWI	13602
LILLOOET	17000
MENOMINI	21860
CHILCOTIN	32700
LAKE OKANAGAN	41000
SEKANI	44375
NEZ PERCE	45000
CARRIER	50000
BEAVER	52400
KOOTENAY	59500
SAULTEAUX	81250
NORTHERN OJIBWA	111875
ALGONQUIN	136468

Figure 44.1 Table showing a sample of Native American tribal areas.

The variety of "tribal" areas is astonishing, ranging from 426 to over 136,000 square kilometers. Much of this variation is certainly due to resource abundance, as there is a definite latitudinal trend in area size, with the smallest being in California, but I suspect that the differences among groups also reflect a considerable freedom, within ecological constraints, for historical and social processes to play a major role.

This sample might be used to generate reasonable upper and lower limits to the size of social areas in southwestern Germany during the Mesolithic. Converting the ethnographic territories to circles of different radii, we find that the radius can range from 12 to 208 kilometers. At the lower end, such a territory would encompass a lake such as the Federsee, or a portion of the Lake Constance shore, or a small strip of the Danube Valley. At the other extreme, a territory with a radius 208 kilometers would include all of southern Germany and part of central Germany, Switzerland, and eastern France. Our preferences between these two extremes could be influenced by knowledge of the abundance of various resources and of the human population density in Mesolithic Germany, but unfortunately, these are truly unknown.

Settlement Distributions

A review of the ethnographic literature makes clear that within such tribal territories, land use is not evenly distributed. There are both ecological and social reasons for this. Regions richer in resources clearly show much greater intensity of use and settlement. In addition, the landscape is often socially carved up in such a way that subgroups, focusing on their own resource concentrations, more intensively settle in small portions of the landscape, leaving the rest of the area open to more casual and extensive use. The pattern of settlement distribution, consequently, might be expected to be discontinuous across the landscape. Relatively empty areas might exist within an occupied territory. Such areas might, indeed, be poorer in resources than other areas, but even relatively rich areas might show such a pattern if they fell on the social interstices between subgroups.

Boundaries

The ethnographic record informs us that boundaries between groups (and subgroups) can take a variety of forms. Discrete, linear edges to territories, as depicted on most ethnographic maps, are rare. Much more common are two other forms. Frequently, territories of adjacent groups will overlap, claimed and used by both but not constantly defended by either. Another form of boundary is the no-man's land, an area empty of all but the most ephemeral settlement, used only sporadically by each group, but at great risk of attack. These latter two types of boundary would likely show a similar pattern in the archaeological record: overlap and no-man's zones would contain materials from both groups, and therefore the overall distribution of socially or ethnically distinct traits would show a clinal pattern with no abrupt edges. In addition, the likelihood of shifting boundaries through time would further blur any discontinuities in distributions, even in the rare case of discrete social boundaries.

Summary

Guidelines for interpretation that may be drawn from ethnographies include the following:

- Areas habitually used by groups might range tremendously in size and are likely to be unpredictable solely from ecology, except on a comparative and relative basis. I cannot assume *a priori*, for example, that the Upper Danube drainage corresponded to a social territory, despite the fact that this forms a convenient study area. Determination of range size must be largely an empirical endeavor.
- Settlement is likely to be discontinuous across the landscape and is likely to reflect both ecological and social factors. Even relatively rich areas may appear to be underused.
- The distribution of material traits is likely to be clinal with no discrete edges marking social boundaries. Large, quantified regional databases will need to be examined to determine the social patterns.

Empirical patterns

The assumption here is that social groups of various sorts existed during the Mesolithic and that they may be reflected in the distribution of material traits, whether in conscious or unconscious aspects of style. We can then turn to the archaeological literature and record to see what patterns have been identified and at what spatial scale. The major categories of material traits that have been examined are lithic typology (primarily of microliths) and types of ornaments.

Based upon shared typological traits, the most commonly recognised grouping in the Early Mesolithic of this area is the "Beuronien" as originally defined by Taute (1967), which is identified by Kozlowski and Kozlowski (1979) as one of the major culture areas of Europe, extending from eastern France, Germany, southern Belgium and northwestern Switzerland eastward into the Czech Republic and Austria. Its social correlate has been characterised by Tillmann (1993:173) as a trans-regional culture-group that must have consisted of numerous local groups. Affinities with areas of northern France have led to the inclusion of the Beuronien into a still larger entity, the Beuron-Coincy province. Both ethnographic analogy and common sense suggest that these two large groupings could not have corresponded to interacting societies, but rather to some larger entities, perhaps of shared history and culture.

The possible extent of smaller subdivisions has been seen in differences in proportions of various microlith types among areas. The Rheinland-Pfalz, southern Belgium and southern Lorraine, for example, have been distinguished from southwestern Germany both by Thevenin (1998) and by Cziesla and Tillmann (1984). Similarly, southeastern Germany has been seen to differ from southwestern Germany during the Early Mesolithic in the dominant types of microlithic points (Rieder and Tillmann1989). One final example is Thevenin's (1998) separation of northwestern Switzerland from Germany during the Boreal period.

A quite different approach was taken by Newell *et al.* (1990), who examined the distribution of various types of ornaments and jewelry in sites across Europe. Their interpretations rested explicitly upon an ethnographically-derived model of hierarchical, nested social groups consisting of language family, tribe and band. According to their results, during the Early Mesolithic, southwestern Germany was part of a language family that extended from Spain to Sweden, a tribal grouping that included parts of Spain, France, Germany, Switzerland, Austria, Italy and Slovenia, which also included portions of two separate bands, one confined to the upper Danube basin, the other also encompassing portions of France, Switzerland and Italy.

Most interesting about these various approaches is that the areas so defined are not isomorphic with one another. In particular, lithic approaches emphasise southwestern Germany's similarities east and west, while the study of ornaments reveals strong similarities with regions north and south. This lack of congruence calls to mind ethnographic studies in which recognised social groups such as clans have been found to share a bewildering array of different material traits with different sets of neighbors in patterns that make no ecological sense (Lemonnier 1986). Depending upon which traits are examined, a group may share greater similarities with different neighbors and material patterns may define different larger groupings.

What these studies do not do, and cannot do, is describe the finer distributions of sites and traits within these large regions. An understanding of land use requires examination of distributional patterns at a variety of scales and this is where regional survey can be of use. The nature of boundaries, for example, cannot be easily seen from a handful of sites; we need broad coverage across the landscape in order to detect the patterns of various material characteristics. Settlement concentrations cannot easily be recognised unless intervening areas have been examined.

Southwestern Germany has, indeed, been recognised to contain a number of site concentrations during the Early Mesolithic. Two of these in or near our study area are the Federsee and the western shores of Lake Constance. Both were originally detected through the focused surveys of Reinerth beginning in the 1920s. Not clear, however, was whether these clusters were real or were simply derived

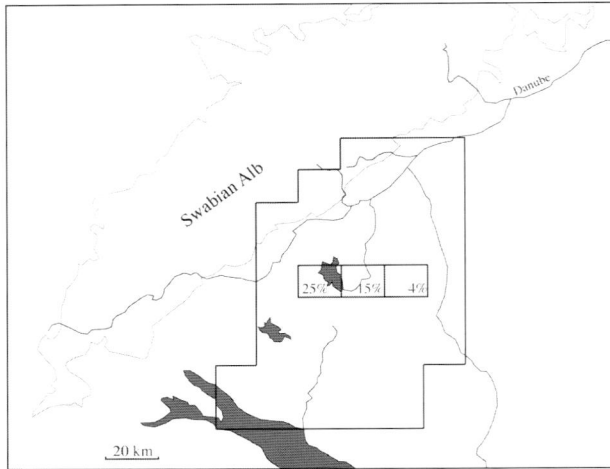

Figure 44.2 Survey area in southwestern Germany with east-west transect. Numbers reflect percentage of surveyed fields with finds.

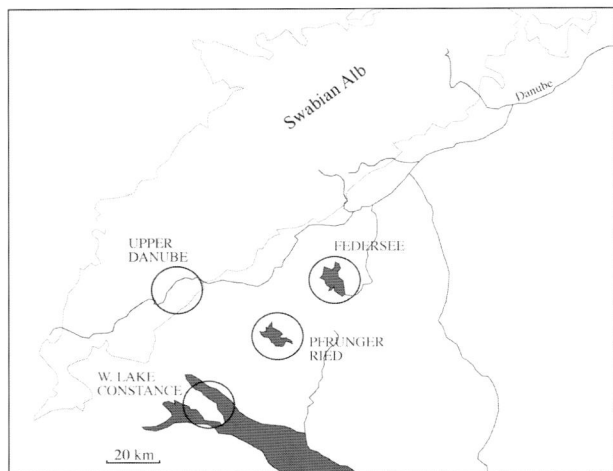

Figure 44.3 Four Mesolithic site concentrations in southwestern Germany.

from the survey bias toward large lakeshores. Our survey has now provided coverage for part of the area around these two concentrations and can address this issue. An 11 kilometer wide transect 25 km east of the Federsee, for example, reveals a dramatic dropoff in the number of sites and artifact density within sites (Figure 44.2). With few exceptions, rich surface sites in this area are confined to areas on or near the lakeshore.

To the south and west, there is a similar pattern of decreasing site numbers and richness, interrupted, however, by a new concentration around another lake, the Pfrunger Ried. It appears that the Federsee, the Pfrunger Ried and western Lake Constance, as well as the upper Danube Valley, are true concentrations of occupation, about 20–25 km from each other and that the intervening areas, including other lakeshores, saw much less intense use (Figure 44.3). As the survey expands, we hope to be able to further document the distribution of occupation intensity.

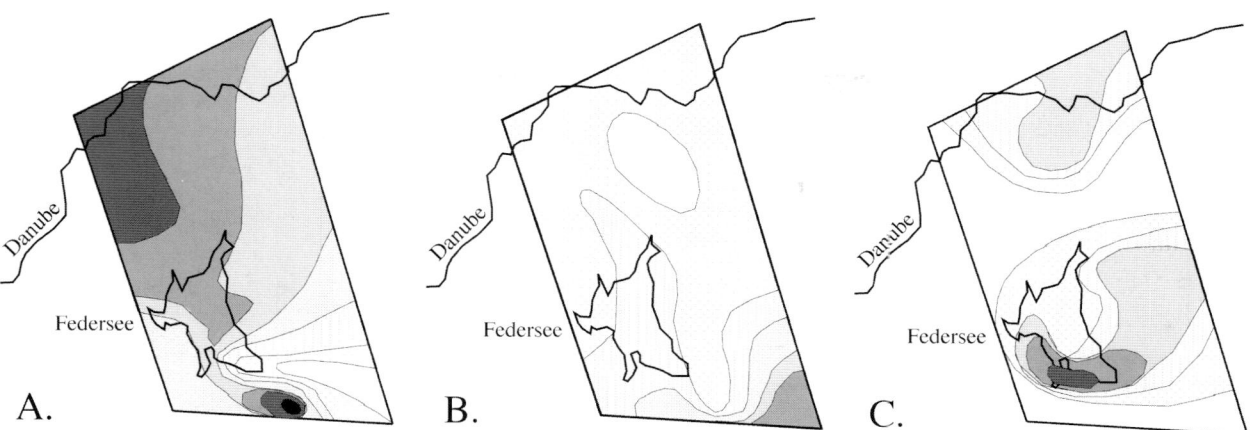

Figure 44.4 Distribution of stone raw materials as percentage of site assemblages; darker shades represent higher percentages. A) Jurassic chert; B) radiolarite and C) brown chert.

The relationship among these concentrations is another topic that can be addressed by survey at this scale. On going tests and excavations are designed to investigate the subsistence activities occurring around the different lakeshores in order to see if they form different economic components in a regional system, or are similar, redundant areas of land use. Stylistic characteristics of artifacts in the various concentrations can also be examined to see if variation at this scale exists. In a preliminary study, for example, samples of microlithic triangles and points from sites on the Pfrunger Ried (54), the Federsee (75) and the upper Danube (60) have been compared according to several traits: length of retouched and unretouched sides and right- or left-handedness. One attribute, the length of the longer retouched edge, shows a decreasing similarity with distance among the clusters or, in other words, a clinal distribution. The proportion of right-handedness, by contrast, shows a reverse pattern in this sample: the most significant difference measured (with $p < .001$) is between the Pfrunger Ried (72% right-handed) and the nearby Federsee (43% right-handed). It seems that at this scale the distributions of different attributes are not isomorphic and investing them with social meaning remains a challenge.

One other material characteristic that has been preliminarily examined is the distribution of stone raw materials. Jurassic chert from the limestone of the Swabian Alb is the predominant material throughout much of southwestern Germany, but others of significance include radiolarite of Alpine origin and a brown chert from a source in the moraine region of Oberschwaben. Examination of the distribution of these materials in a portion of the survey area shows some clear patterns of distance decay (Figure 44.4). Jurassic chert declines in frequency southward from the Alb; radiolarite decreases from south to north and brown chert shows two concentrations, apparently reflecting two sources, one in Oberschwaben and one in the Alb. It is interesting that deviations from a simple distance decay pattern occur at the Federsee, with both Jurassic chert and radiolarite somewhat more common than in adjacent areas at the same relative distance from the sources. This area of concentrated occupation apparently draws more heavily upon distant sources, perhaps reflecting something about the scale of mobility and the economic centrality of the lake.

Conclusions

Obviously, few concrete interpretations about the social geography of southwestern Germany can be made from the data at hand, but regional survey appears to offer a promising avenue to pursue. Local and regional patterns of distribution of materials and attributes over a broader area can be combined with ecological and economic information with the hope of ultimately informing us about the interrelationships among social interaction, mobility and subsistence. Interpretations will certainly need to make use of ethnographic analogy, but must first emanate from the empirical patterns that survey data can provide.

References

Bahn, P. 1979. Seasonal migration in south-west France during the late glacial period. *Journal of Archaeological Science* 4, 245–257.

Berndt, R. 1972. The Walmadjeri and Gugadja. In: Bicchieri, M. (ed.) *Hunters and Gatherers Today*, 177–216. New York.

Bettinger, R. 1991. *Hunter-gatherers: Archaeological and Evolutionary Theory* New York.

Binford, L. 1983. *In Pursuit of the Past*. London.

Birdsell, J. 1953. Some environmental and cultural factors influencing the structuring of Australian Aboriginal populations. *American Naturalist* 87, 171–207.

Bradley, R. 1998. *The Significance of Monuments*. London.

Cashdan, E. 1992. Spatial organization and habitat use. In: Smith, E. and Winterhalder, B (eds.) *Evolutionary ecology and human behavior*, 237–266. New York.

Cziesla, E. 1992. *Jäger und Sammler: die Mittlere Steinzeit im Landkreis Pirmasens*. Brühl.

Cziesla, E. and Tillmann, A. 1984. Mesolithische Funde der Freilandfundstelle "Auf'm Benneberg" in Burgalben/Waldfischbach, Kreis Pirmasens. *Mitteilungen des Historischen Vereins der Pfalz* 82, 69–110.

Dyson-Hudson, R. and Smith, E. 1978. Human territoriality: an ecological reassessment. *American Anthropologist* 80, 21–41.

Eriksen, B. 1991. Change and continuity in a prehistoric hunter-gatherer society. *Archaeologica Venatoria* 12. Tübingen.

Gordon, B. 1988. *Of men and reindeer herds in French Magdalenian prehistory.* British Archaeological Reports, International Series 390. Oxford.

Hahn, J. 1979. Essai sur l'ecologie du Magdalenien dans le Jura souabe. In de Sonneville-Bordes, D. (ed.) *La fin des temps glaciaires en Europe*, 203–214. Paris.

Hahn, J. 1983. Die frühe Mittelsteinzeit. In: Müller-Beck, H. (ed.) *Urgeschichte in Baden-Württemberg*, 363–392. Stuttgart.

Helm, J. 1972. The Dogrib Indians. In: Bicchieri, M. (ed.) *Hunters and Gatherers Today*, 51–89. New York.

Hiatt, L. 1968. Ownership and use of land among the Australian Aborigines. In: Lee, R. and DeVore, I. (eds.) *Man the hunter*, 99–102. Chicago.

Jochim, M. 1998. *A hunter-gatherer landscape: southwest Germany in the Late Palaeolithic and Mesolithic*. New York.

Jochim, M., Glass, M., Fisher, L. and McCartney, P. 1998. Mapping the Stone Age: an interim report on the south German survey project. In: Conard, N. and Kind, C. (eds.) *Aktuelle Forschungen zum Mesolithikum*, 121–132. Urgeschichtliche Materialhefte Band 12. Tübingen.

Kelly, R. 1995. *The Foraging Spectrum*. Washington.

Kind, C. 1996. Bemerkungen zur Diversität des südwestdeutschen Frühmesolithikums. In: Campen, I., Hahn, J. and Uerpmann, M. (eds.) *Spuren der Jagd – Die Jagd nach Spuren*, 325–330. Tübinger Monographien zur Urgeschichte 11. Tübingen.

Kozlowski, J. and Kozlowski, S. 1979. *Upper Palaeolithic and Mesolithic in Europe*. Warsaw.

Kozlowski, S. 1973. Introduction to the history of Europe in early Holocene. In: Kozlowski, S. (ed.) *The Mesolithic in Europe*, 331–366. Warsaw.

Lee, R. 1972. The !Kung Bushmen of Botswana. In: Bicchieri, M. (ed.) *Hunters and gatherers today*, 326–368. New York.

Lemonnier, P. 1986. The study of material culture today: toward an anthropology of technical systems. *Journal of Anthropological Archaeology* 5, 147–186.

Newell, R., Kielman, D., Constandse-Westermann, T., Van der Sanden, W. and Van Gijn, A. 1990. *An inquiry into the ethnic resolution of Mesolithic regional groups*. Leiden.

Rieder, K. and Tillmann, A. 1989. Das Mesolithikum im nördlichen Oberbayern. In: Rieder, K. (ed.) Steinzeitliche Kulturen an Donau und Altmühl, 93–107. Ingolstadt.

Sackett, J. 1985. Style and ethnicity in the Kalahari: a reply to Wiessner. *American Antiquity* 50, 154–159.

Sieveking, A. 1976. Settlement patterns of the later Magdalenian in the central Pyrenees. In: Sieveking, G., Longworth, I. and Wilson, K. (eds.) *Problems in economic and social archaeology*, 583–603. London.

Silberbauer, G. 1972. The G/Wi Bushmen. In: Bicchieri, M. (ed.) *Hunters and gatherers today*, 271–325. New York.

Smith, E. and Winterhalder, B. (eds.) 1992. *Evolutionary ecology and human behavior*. New York.

Spiess, A. 1979. *Reindeer and caribou hunters: an archaeological study*. New York.

Sturdy, D. 1972. Some reindeer economies in prehistoric Europe. In: Higgs, E. (ed.) *Palaeoeconomy*, 55–95. Cambridge.

Taute, W. 1967. Grabungen zur Mittleren Steinzeit in Höhlen und unter Felsdächern der Schwäbischen Alb, 1961 bis 1965. *Fundberichte aus Schwaben* 18/1, 14–21.

Thevenin, A. 1998. Les grandes lignes du Mesolithique en France et dans les regions limitrophes. In: Conard, N. and Kind, C. (eds.) *Aktuelle Forschungen zum Mesolithikum*, 1–14. Urgeschichtliche Materialhefte Band 12, Tübingen.

Tilley, C. 1994. *A Phenomenology of Landscape*. Oxford.

Tillmann, A. 1993. Kontinuität oder Diskontinuität? Zur Frage einer Bandkeramischen Landnahme im südlichen Mitteleuropa. *Archäologische Informationen* 16, 157–187.

Ucko, P. and Layton, R. 1999. *The archaeology and anthropology of landscape*. New York.

Watanabe, H. 1972. The Ainu. In: Bicchieri, M. (ed.) *Hunters and Gatherers Today*, 451–484. New York.

Weniger, G. 1982. *Wildbeuter und ihre Umwelt*. Archaeologica Venatoria 5. Tübingen.

Wiessner, P. 1982. Risk, reciprocity and social influences on !Kung San economics. In: Leacock, E. and Lee, R. (eds.) *Politics and history in band societies*, 61–84. Cambridge.

—— 1983. Style and social information in Kalahari San projectile points. *American Antiquity* 48, 253–276.

—— 1984. Reconsidering the behavioral basis for style: a case study among the Kalahari San. *Journal of Anthropological Archaeology* 3, 190–234.

—— 1985. Style or isochrestic variation? A reply to Sackett. *American Antiquity* 50, 160–165.

45. Mesolithic hunter-gatherers in the Isle of Man: adaptions to an island environment?

Sinéad B. McCartan

The archaeological evidence shows there to have been extensive Mesolithic activity on the Isle of Man, and similar to the evidence from elsewhere, the picture is neither uniform or simple. This paper summarises the history of Mesolithic studies on the island, presents the results of recent research and discusses some issues relating to the Mesolithic settlement of this island.

Introduction

The Isle of Man lies in the middle of the Irish Sea, is just over 53 km long and 21 km wide and has an area of 588 sq km. It lies about 60 km from the coasts of both Ireland and north-west England, some 70 km from Anglesey in Wales and just 20 km from the Mull of Galloway in south-west Scotland (Figures 45.1 and 45.2). Given the island's position in the middle of the Irish Sea, and its visibility from different parts of the western coast of Britain and the eastern coast of Ireland, it is hardly likely to have escaped the attention of Mesolithic hunter-gatherers. It will be argued that the Isle of Man, rather than being an isolated refuge or a convenient 'stop off' point enroute to more attractive areas within the Irish Sea basin, was the focus of long-term settlement by Postglacial hunter-gatherers.

A number of issues are raised by the artefactual evidence, such as the date of colonisation of the island, the nature of the use of the island and the variation in lithic artefacts that may be interpreted as indicating either insularity or contact with hunter-gatherers groups elsewhere.

Environmental Background

Separating the island's northern and southern uplands is the central valley that runs between Douglas and Peel (Dackombe and Thomas 1985:1; Dackombe and McCarroll 1990:10) (Figure 45.3). East and west of the uplands lie the coastal plateaux and on the east coast this plateau gives way to the plain of Malew which is overlooked, from the extreme south by the Mull Hill and the Calf of Man. At the northern end of the island the uplands stop abruptly, giving way to the northern plain, composed entirely of glacial drift, and broken at the extreme northern point by the Bride hills.

That the Isle of Man was ice-free by about 16,000 years ago is attested by a radiocarbon date of 15,150±350 BP (Birm-754) that was obtained from a kettle hole on the Jurby Ridge in the north-west of the island (McCarroll *et al.* 1990:55). Opinion differs radically over the existence and dating of landbridges within the Irish Sea basin (Eyles and McCabe 1989; Boulton 1990; Lambeck 1991; Wingfield 1995). Wingfield (1995:233), for example, has suggested that one existed between the Isle of Man and north-west England/north Wales at around 10,000 BP and another extended from the island to Ireland about 9700 BP. It is argued that the land-link with Ireland was broken by 9500 BP and that by about 9000 BP the link with Britain was severed (Wingfield 1995:233).

Little is known about the range and dating of the Isle of Man's Holocene vertebrate fauna. Early isolation as an island has led to a very restricted range of native fauna, similar to the situation in Ireland. Some insight into the Manx record, however, can be gleaned from recent research in Ireland where a broad chronology for its Pleistocene and Holocene faunal record has been established (Woodman *et al.* 1997). Auroch (*Bos primigenius*), brown bear (*Ursus arctos*), red deer (*Cervus elaphus*), wild pig (*Sus scrofa*), elk (*Alces alces*) and roe deer (*Capreolus capreolus*) are considered to be the largest land mammals available for exploitation by Mesolithic hunter-gatherers in Britain. In Ireland, however, auroch, elk and roe deer are unknown and it is uncertain if they ever reached the Isle of Man. The earliest archaeological record of roe deer in the Isle of Man is from the later prehistoric and early historic site of Chapel Hill, Balladoole, Arbory (McCarroll *et al.* 1990:76). In Ireland, brown bear was present during the Mesolithic, but its remains have not been found in association with cultural material (Woodman *et al.* 1997:138; McCormick 1999: 359). It is also possible that brown bear colonised the Isle of Man, although there is no evidence of its presence.

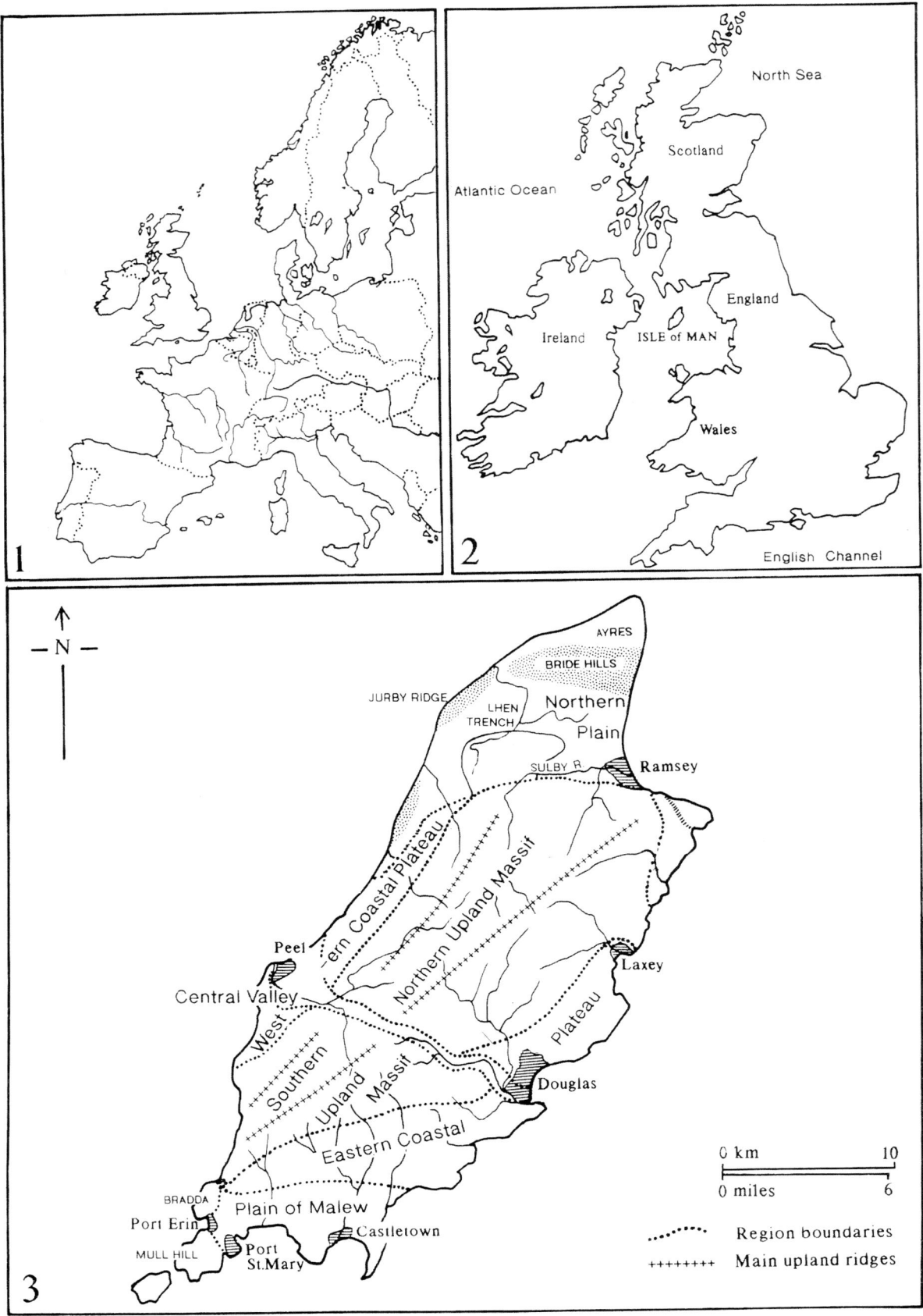

Figure 45.1 1. The Isle of Man within Europe. 2. Location map of the Isle of Man in the British Isles. 3. The Manx landscape divided into eight physiographic regions (after Dackombe and McCarroll 1990).

Mesolithic hunter-gatherers in the Isle of Man: adaptions to an island environment?   333

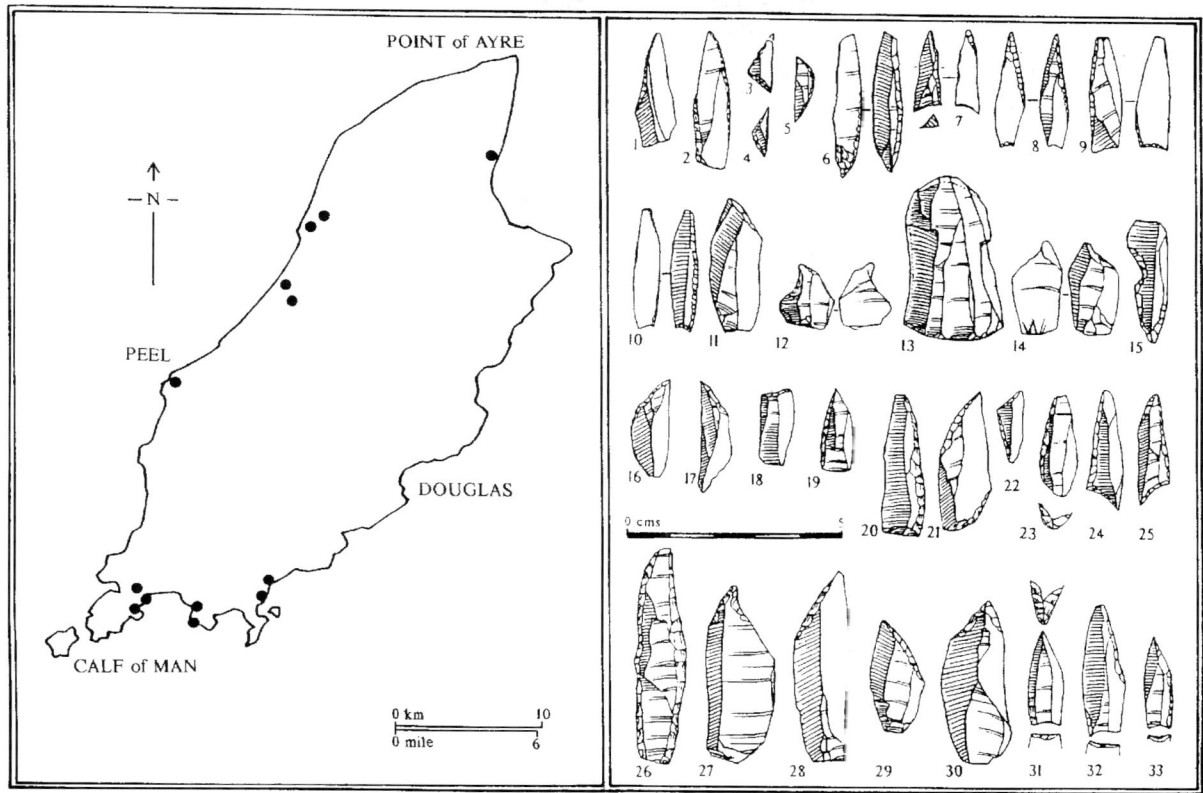

Figure 45.2 Distribution of Clark's 'Tardenoisian'sites; 'Tardenoisian'flints: 1–15 from Glen Wyllin; 16–33 from Port St. Mary (after Clark 1935).

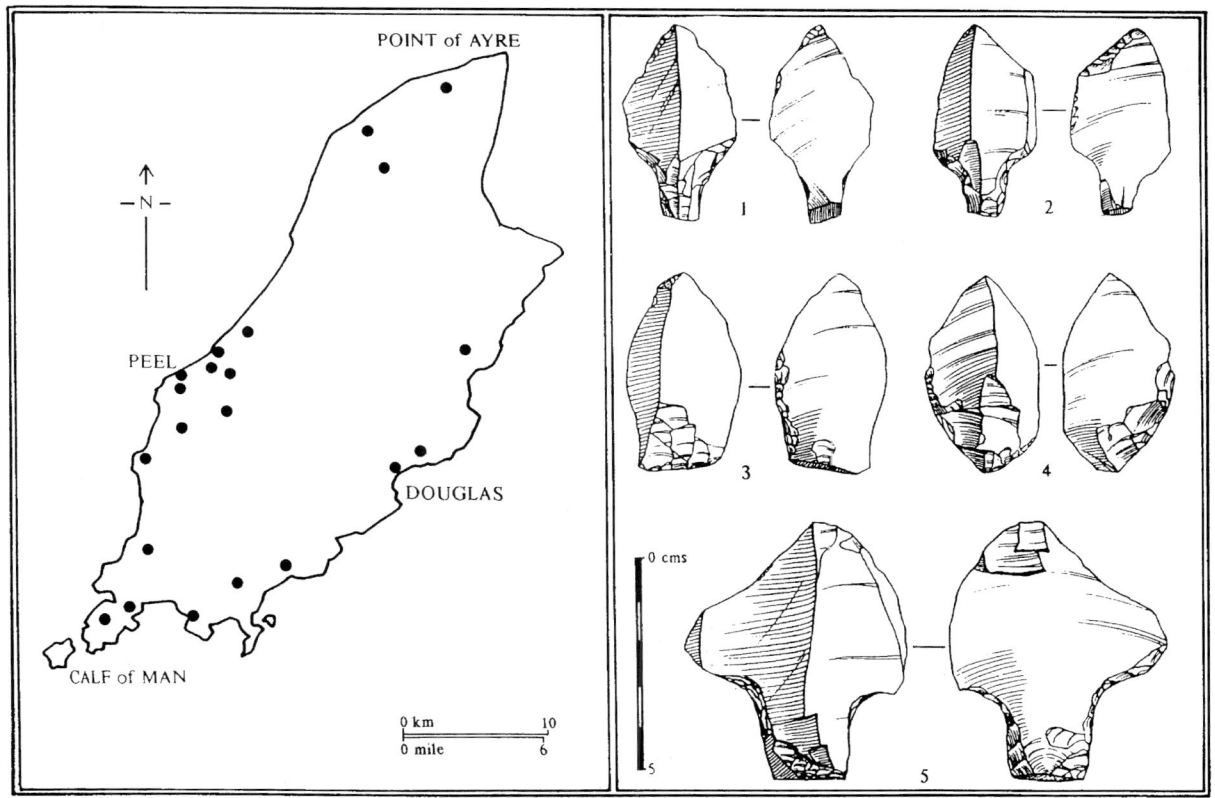

Figure 45.3 Distribution of Clark's 'Bann River Culture'; 'Bann River Culture' flints: 1, 3 and 4 from Kirkill, Rushen; 2 from Cronk y Chule, Lonan; 5 from Glencrutchery, Douglas (after Clark 1935).

Red deer has long been assumed to have been the main large mammal exploited during the British and Irish Mesolithic. In the Irish context, however, this assumption has now been seriously undermined since red deer is not known to occur between approximately 12,000 and 4000 BP (Woodman *et al.* 1997:152). On this evidence, it has been argued (McCormick 1999:360) that red deer was deliberately re-introduced into Ireland during the Neolithic. Van Wijngaarden-Bakker (1989:132) has also suggested that Mesolithic hunter-gatherers in Ireland may have used seal skins in place of red deer skins as they are similar in size and texture. It has not been established if red deer were present in the Isle of Man during the Mesolithic period, although if a landbridge did exist to north-west England and north Wales until around 9000 BP they might be expected to have colonised the island. A jawbone of red deer from the Lhen trench at the Guilcaugh, Isle of Man (McCarroll *et al.* 1990:76), has been reported, although recent work on the Holocene fauna has raised doubts over the initial identification of this material (Tomlinson pers. comm.). Wild pig, in contrast to the situation in Britain, appears to have been the primary mammal exploited during the Irish Mesolithic, accounting for 98% of the faunal assemblages from Mount Sandel, County Derry and Lough Boora, County Offaly (van Wijngaarden-Bakker 1989:127). The tusk of what has been described as wild pig is known from the shell midden at Port St. Mary, Isle of Man (Woodman 1987:20) and it might be assumed, by analogy, that this animal was also an important food resource for Manx hunter-gatherers. Preliminary examination, however, by Tomlinson (pers. comm.) suggests that this tusk may belong to domestic pig. Wild cat (*Felis silvestris*) bones have also been tentatively identified from the midden at Port St. Mary (Garrad 1978:68), although the contextual relationship between the bones and the midden is not entirely apparent from the original excavation report (Swinnerton 1889). Until more information is available on the range and dating of the Manx Holocene fauna, it may be assumed that the faunal range was no less than that for Ireland, and indeed it was possibly greater. In addition, given the island setting, the exploitation of marine rather than terrestrial food resources may have been much greater and the latter may have simply complemented a sea-based diet.

The study of the vegetation history for the Manx early Postglacial period is dependent on a limited number of published pollen cores, the most informative for the early Postglacial being those taken at Lough Cranstal in the north of the island. A date of 7825±120 BP (Hv-5226) marks the approximate beginning of the marine transgression and another of 7370±110 BP (Hv-5225) denotes the approximate end of the transgression. The Lough Cranstal pollen evidence indicates that by about 7400 BP a well-developed mixed oak woodland comprising alder (*Alnus*), elm (*Ulmus*), oak (*Quercus*) and hazel (*Corylus*) was established (Tooley 1978:22; McCarroll *et al.* 1990:67). Unlike Scotland, the Manx palynological evidence and charcoal record do not indicate disturbances in the landscape prior to the period of dated human colonisation (Innes pers. comm.).

Manx Mesolithic Studies

The early settlement sites of Port St. Mary and Glen Wyllin were the focus of investigations by the local antiquarian Frederick Swinnerton (1889; 1892). The chronological position of these sites was not fully appreciated, however, until the first collation and interpretation of the evidence for the Manx Mesolithic by Clark in 1935 when he identified two very distinct Mesolithic stone tool traditions on the island. The earliest, the 'Tardenoisian', was represented by a microlithic industry (Clark 1935:71) with eleven find-spots distributed in the extreme south, west and north-west of the island (Figure 45.2).

The later tradition was represented by a series of butt-trimmed and tanged forms and was called by Clark the 'Bann River Culture'. It had twenty-one find-spots distributed in the east and further north in Ayre (Clark 1935:74) (Figure 45.3). Clark drew attention to the similarity of this material to that found in Ireland, particularly along the River Bann. Clark (1935:75) noted that in the Isle of Man this material was sometimes found alongside Neolithic artefacts, such as leaf-shaped arrowheads, suggesting that although Mesolithic in origin, the tradition may have flourished at a later date.

Woodman's 1978 reappraisal of the Manx Mesolithic proposed a twofold chronological division of the microlithic tradition. The material from Port St. Mary that comprised large numbers of elongated scalene triangles and broad hollow-based points was considered by Woodman (1978:126) to represent the earliest sequence in the microlithic industries. The material from Glen Wyllin, which is characterised by small triangles, isosceles triangles, crescents and small needle points was considered to be later in the sequence (Woodman 1978:126). Woodman (1978:127) also suggested that the hollow-based point was an insular development, indicative of population continuity on the island, and that its resemblance to the British Horsham point was purely fortuitous.

Clark's 'Bann River Culture' was renamed by Woodman as the 'Heavy-Bladed Industry' and he concluded that the main similarity between the Manx and Irish Late Mesolithic material was in the primary knapping strategy, in particular the use of the so-called 'Larnian core'. Very distinct differences between the Irish and Manx material have, however, also been noted, such as the greater number of tanged points in the Isle of Man (Woodman 1978:133 p). These points have been divided into two main types, a very narrow form and a rather splayed form, and the latter is thought to be an insular development. Furthermore, barforms, points, picks and polished axes –

types present in Irish assemblages – are so far absent in the Isle of Man. The broad similarities between the two technologies, however, would seem to suggest that the origin of the Manx 'Heavy-Bladed' Mesolithic lies within the later phases of the Irish Mesolithic, although the Manx tradition appears to have subsequently developed independently (Woodman 1978:133).

Excavations at Cass ny Hawin, Malew, in the 1980's produced the first, and until recently the only, dates for the Manx Early Mesolithic. They date a microlithic industry between 7695±95 BP (UB-2660) and 7350±95 BP (UB-2593) (Woodman 1987). It was suggested by Woodman (1987:20) that this industry bridged the gap between the earlier Port St. Mary and later Glen Wyllin traditions, the implication being that the initial date for colonisation might be closer to 8000 BP. Excavations at a site at Rhendhoo in the Lhen Trench in 1989, in the north-west of the island, produced dates in association with 'Heavy-Bladed' material of between 6110±50 BP (BM-2694) and 5170±50 BP (BM-2695) (McCartan 1994). Butt-trimmed flakes, similar to those found at Rhendhoo, are associated with dates at the site of Newferry, County Antrim, of 5705±90 BP and 5415±90 BP (Woodman 1977:177 p). The Rhendhoo and Newferry dates suggest, therefore, a contemporaneous use of similar tools in both Ireland and the Isle of Man, but also a probable prolonged use in the latter. The dates from both Cass ny Hawin and Rhendhoo confirm that the microlithic industries were superseded by a 'macrolithic' tradition, and the latter site indicates additionally that, as in Ireland, a phase of the Mesolithic is represented by a non-microlithic stone tool industry (Woodman 1986).

In addition to the excavations at Cass ny Hawin and Rhendhoo, the 1980's witnessed a growth in fieldwalking activity in the Isle of Man that resulted in the accumulation of a large collection of archaeological material. The vast majority of the surface collections is extremely well provenanced and has consequently formed the basis for research by the author. Analysis of these collections has dramatically increased the known number of Mesolithic find-spots and has allowed a re-assessment of the evidence for the Mesolithic settlement of the Isle of Man.

In summary, there are now eighty-one known find-spots of Early Mesolithic microlithic material of which sixty-one (75%) are provenanced (McCartan 1990, 1999). Despite the more than seven-fold increase in the number of sites, the distribution of find-spots has not changed dramatically from that noted by Clark (1935) (Figure 45.4). The most obvious exceptions are those in the Lhen Trench, beside the Sulby River and those on the east coast at Ballavarkish, just north of Ramsey, Cronk y Chule near Laxey and Finch Hill in Douglas. The dense concentration of sites in the Lhen Trench undoubtedly reflects the activity of one particular field-walker in the locality. On a general level, the Early Mesolithic sites can be subdivided on the basis of an absence or presence of microliths in the assemblage. Fifty of the eighty-one sites

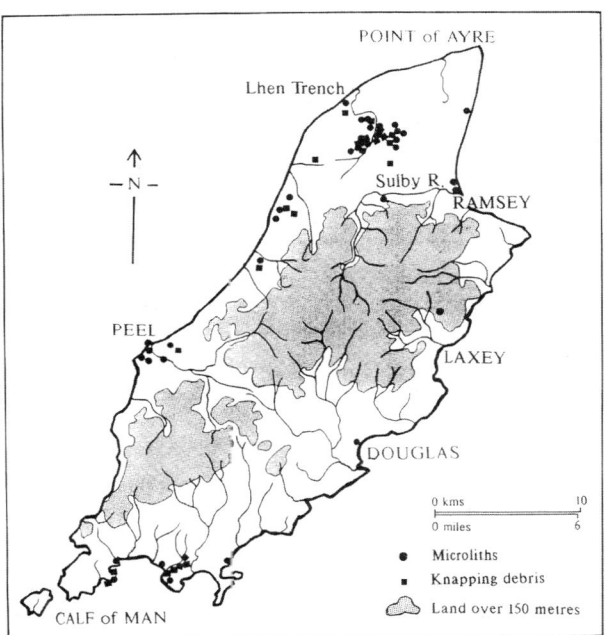

Figure 45.4 The current distribution of Early Mesolithic sites.

(of which thirty-seven are provenanced) have microliths. The remaining thirty-one sites (of which twenty-four are provenanced) are represented solely by knapping debris. It is possible to interpret these two groups as representing different site-types – where knapping debris represents a manufacturing site, as opposed to a domestic site or task-specific site with finished objects. Caution must be exerted, however, not to over-interpret surface-collected material given its many inherent problems.

The distribution evidence indicates a dense concentration of sites in the lowlands, although many have clearly been lost to rising Postglacial sea levels. It is possible that the lowlands, both coastal and riverine, were the focus of settlement with base camps, while other areas, including the uplands, were used to exploit specific resources on a more temporary basis. What is believed to be a Mesolithic clearance episode has been dated to 6925±55 BP (AA-29336) from Ballachrink, in the Lhen Trench. Both microlithic and macrolithic stone technologies have been found within a short distance from where the pollen core was taken, but it is currently impossible to determine which phase of the Mesolithic is associated with this clearance event. The scant evidence for the use of the uplands, however, most probably reflects the lack of opportunities to make discoveries, rather than avoidance by hunter-gatherers.

There has been a dramatic increase in the known number of Late Mesolithic find-spots. There are now some three hundred and twenty-five sites compared to Clark's twenty-one (Figure 45.5). Collections comprising solely knapping debris account for one hundred and sixty-eight of this number, and the majority of these are mixed with

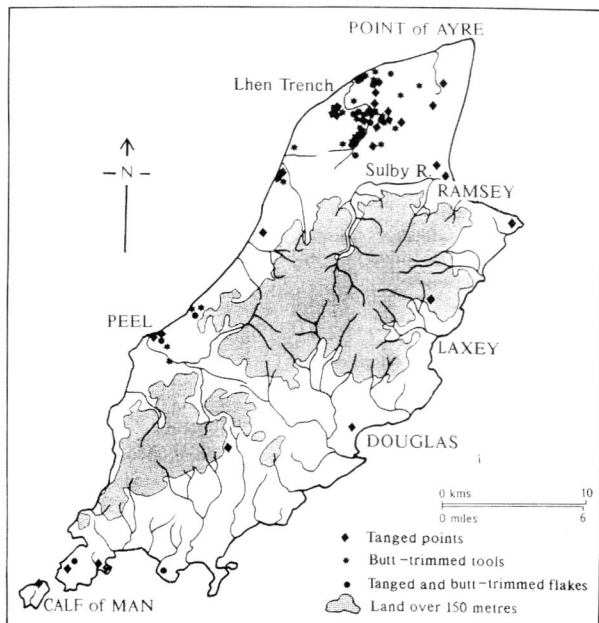

Figure 45.5 The current distribution of Late Mesolithic sites with tanged and butt-trimmed tools.

artefacts that span a number of chronological periods. One hundred and fifty-seven sites, of which eighty-six (55%) are provenanced, contain diagnostic Late Mesolithic artefacts. Of these, seventy-five have tanged points only, forty-nine sites have butt-trimmed only, and thirty-three have both types of artefact. The different compositions may reflect different activities, but may also reflect chronological differences. In the absence of more excavated and dated assemblages these differences remain unexplained. The distribution of Late Mesolithic findspots is widespread across the island and shows greater use of the interior. The uplands still show sparse activity, but a date from a pollen core from Beinn-y-Phott in the northern uplands indicates possible forest clearance at 6240±60 BP (Beta-81358) (Tomlinson 1997:60).

Issues for Consideration

Dating the Initial Colonisation

The dates from Cass-ny-Hawin, Malew, indicate Early Mesolithic settlement on the Isle of Man by at least 7600 BP. Until very recently (see below) the earliest Mesolithic dates from the Isle of Man were significantly later than those for Britain and Ireland. For example, in Wales, Nab Head has produced dates of 9210±80 BP (OxA-1495) and 9110±80 BP (OxA-1496) and Rhuddlan E, in north Wales, has produced a date of 8739±86 BP (BM-691). In Scotland, the island of Rum has produced settlement evidence dating to 8590±95 BP (GU-1873) and similar dates are known from a site at Fife Ness, in Fife (Wickham-Jones 1990; Wickham-Jones and Dalland 1998).

Dates spanning between 9000 and 8500 BP are also known from Daer in Clydesdale (SAN 1998; Finlayson 1999:879). In Ireland, Mount Sandel, County Derry, has produced dates ranging between 9000 BP and 7800 BP (Woodman 1985:148). Given the dating evidence from Britain and Ireland there seemed little reason why colonisation of the Isle of Man should not have taken place by 8000 BP.

Following the Stockholm conference the author co-directed a two-week excavation at Ballacregga, in the valley of Glen Wyllin, Kirk Michael, Isle of Man. The excavation revealed a site with microlithic material, and hazelnut shells produced dates of 8120±75 BP (GU-9193) and 8115±60 BP (GU-9192). These dates firmly place colonisation before 8000 BP and future work will hopefully elucidate the nature of this settlement.

The change or transition from a microlithic to a macrolithic stone tool tradition might imply that a second major colonisation took place sometime after 7000 BP. The macrolithic tradition that replaced the microlithic is found only in Ireland and the Isle of Man, and it is almost certain that it came to the latter from the former. The reasons for this change in technology are unknown, although environmental reasons are often muted as the probable cause. The apparent rejection of the use of the bow and arrow, for which the 'Bann flake' and tanged points were unlikely to have been intended, would have fundamentally affected the hunting strategies of hunter-gatherers. The bow and arrow, therefore, may have played a less important role in the tool-kit of the island hunter-gatherers.

Factors Influencing Colonisation

Both 'push' and 'pull' factors may have prompted the movement of hunter-gatherers across the Irish Sea. Increasing population density in Britain may well have pushed people towards new lands, but economic factors such as too much competition for too few resources may also have been important, as may have been social pressures.

Equally, the 'pull' factors may have included the perceived rich marine food resources available on a small island. Further attractions of this island environment may also have included the perceived security of the island setting, and its position as a 'stepping stone' to farther lands. Human curiosity as a motivating factor cannot be ruled out.

Whatever the factors influencing colonisation, a knowledge of, and access to, watercraft technology was essential in order to cross the Irish Sea. There is no doubt that boats were used, as attested by the large number of settlements on islands. The evidence, however, is limited and includes the Star Carr wooden paddle (Clark 1971:23) and the fragmentary wooden boat from the Shannon estuary at Carrigdirty, County Limerick (Lanting and Brindley 1996:88; O'Sullivan 1997:15). Skin boats would

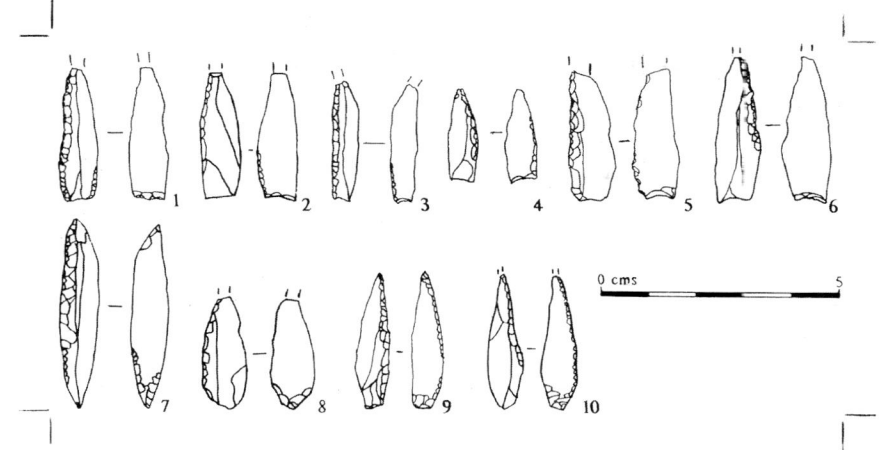

Figure 45.6 Manx hollow based (nos. 1–6) and inverse basally modified (nos. 7–10) points.

certainly have been more effective, and safer, in open sea conditions (Fry 1995:14).

The Nature of Island settlement

The characteristics of islands and their unique properties will be discussed in relation to the Isle of Man elsewhere (McCartan, forthcoming). It is too simplistic to consider that the nature of settlement was simply a question of either temporary or permanent. Although continuity of settlement is not easily demonstrated, the density of finds and the presence of local forms of artefacts would suggest that there had always been a continuous population.

Within the island context the distribution evidence (see above) seems to illustrate primarily lowland settlement. Base sites were probably sited in the lowlands with task-specific sites located in other areas to exploit certain resources. The Isle of Man offers a variety of lowland ecological niches including riverine and wetland habitats, in addition to the obvious coastal habitat. The majority of sites appear to be located close to or beside the main rivers, although there has been a loss of coastal sites. Evidence for upland activity is limited, but undoubtedly there was movement between the low-and uplands, as well as within the lowlands.

Subsistence strategies developed on the mainland required adaptation to cope with the limited resources of an island environment. Over-exploitation could result in the depletion of available resources, and without due care, the extinction of these resources. The underlying implication is that hunter-gatherers managed their environment in the full knowledge of maintaining the island's resources.

The island setting, however, does not necessarily mean isolation, and indeed, the sea was undoubtedly a means, rather than a barrier, to communication. Long-term sustainability, on health and breeding grounds alone, would have necessitated contact with hunter-gatherer groups from elsewhere.

A Question of Influences and Insularity

Clark (1935:70) stated 'the interaction of British and Irish influences and the occasional insular developments are the chief features of the prehistory of the island (*Isle of Man*)'. Britain was considered by Clark to have been the source of influence during the Early Mesolithic and Ireland during the Later Mesolithic. Woodman (1978), subsequently identified 'insular developments', namely the Early Mesolithic hollow-based microlith (Figure 45.6, 1–6) and the Late Mesolithic broad tanged point (Figure 45.2, 5). One of the challenges of the Manx Mesolithic is to identify and interpret both the influences and the insular developments.

Within the Early Mesolithic tradition two microlith types in particular illustrate influences from Britain: the hollow-based point and the inverse basally modified point. While Woodman has identified the hollow-based point as an 'insular' Manx development, most probably from the short edge scalene triangle, and dismissed any connections with the English 'Horsham Culture', the point of commonality between the two is the actual 'hollow base'. Additionally, the Manx inverse basally modified points are similar to those assigned to the English 'Honey Hill' assemblages (Figure 45.6, 7–10). Both the 'Horsham' and 'Honey Hill' assemblages share many characteristics, but are regarded as belonging to distinctly different stone technologies and their distribution is very different (Reynier 1997:531 pp). 'Horsham' assemblages appear almost exclusively in south-east England and Honey Hill assemblages in the English midlands and East Anglia. Reynier (1997:540) has postulated that these two assemblages may be part of two regional facies of a broader technology that may date to the early part of the 9th millennium and that their discrete spatial distributions may hint at some degree of social reorganisation.

The Manx hollow based and inverse basally modified points might initially have been the result of influences from elsewhere, but the former, in particular, appears to have subsequently evolved on a local basis. Local developments may have been a response to local needs, for example, an adaptation of tools for use on resources dictated by the island environment. The Manx hollow-based points have been dated to around 7600 BP at Cass ny Hawin which is a millennium later than the relevant 'Horsham' sites (Reynier 1997:535). The basally modified points have now been dated to just before 8000 BP at Ballacregga, Isle of Man. It is difficult to determine if both types of points in the Isle of Man represent a chronological development, an adaptation of hafting and tool technology to local needs, or a regional variant of a wider culture.

The fundamental similarities between the stone technologies of the Manx and Irish later Mesolithic technologies lie in the primary reduction strategy, and the production and use of butt-trimmed and tanged points. The differences between these two technologies are striking, as the Irish assemblages comprise a range of tool types additional to the butt-trimmed and tanged points – bar forms, points and polished axes – that are absent in the Manx assemblages. Knowledge of the full complement of the Manx assemblages is hampered, however, by the lack of excavated material and of evidence for organic tools. Nevertheless, the absence of a microlithic stone technology on the Isle of Man during the later part of the Mesolithic, when one was employed nearby in Britain suggests the existence of some form of barrier to influence from that direction.

Conclusions

There is evidence for the extensive settlement of the Isle of Man during the Mesolithic period which seems to have been initially colonised sometime before 8000 BP, with the Mesolithic way of life continuing to around 5000 BP. The island sustained a permanent hunter-gatherer population that was probably dependent on a maritime economy, supplemented by terrestrial resources. To avoid the over-exploitation of food supplies some form of regulation, and possibly management, of the environment and food resources would have been required. Assuming accessibility to and knowledge of watercraft technology, isolation from Ireland and Britain may not have been complete and economic and social needs probably required contact with these adjacent lands to be maintained. The archaeological evidence also suggests that the Isle of Man did not function within a closed system and understanding the nature of the contacts and influences between the island and mainland hunter-gatherer groups may help elucidate the role of the island within the Irish Sea province.

Acknowledgements

I would like to thank the Trustees of the National Museums and Galleries of Northern Ireland. Thanks to Richard Warner, Caroline Wickham-Jones and Philippa Tomlinson who commented on drafts of this paper and to Deirdre Crone who prepared the illustrations for publication. Philippa Tomlinson and Jim Innes very kindly allowed me access to results of unpublished research. Finally, I would like to thank the Centre for Manx Studies (Gustav Adolphs Acadamien), Douglas, Isle of Man, for a grant that enabled me to attend the Meso 2000 conference.

References

Boulton, G.S. 1990. Sedimentation and sea level changes during glacial cycles and their control on glacimarine facies architecture. In: Dowdeswell, J.A. and Scourse, J.D. (eds.) *Glacimarine Environments: Processes and Sediments*, 15–52. Geological Society, Special Publications 53. London.

Clark, J.G.D. 1935. The Prehistory of the Isle of Man. *Proceedings of the Prehistoric Society* 1, 70–92.

—— 1971. *Excavations at Star Carr*. Cambridge.

Dackombe, R. and McCarroll, D. 1990. The Manx landscape. In: Robinson, V. and McCarroll, D. (eds.) *The Isle of Man: Celebrating a Sense of Place*, 10–17. Liverpool.

Dackombe, R.V. and Thomas, G.S.P. 1985. *Field Guide to the Quaternary of the Isle of Man*. Cambridge.

Eyles, N. and McCabe, A.M. 1989. The Late Devensian (<22,000 BP) Irish Sea Basin: the stratigraphic record of a collapsed ice-sheet margin. *Quaternary Science Reviews* 8, 307–351.

Finlayson, B. 1999 Understanding the initial colonisation of Scotland. *Antiquity* 73, No. 282, 879–884.

Fry, M.F. 2000. *Coití: Logboats from Northern Ireland*. Northern Ireland Archaeological Monographs No. 4. Belfast.

Garrad, L.S. 1978. Evidence for the History of the Vertebrate Fauna of the Isle of Man. In: Davey, P. (ed.) *Man and Environment in the Isle of Man*, 61–75. British Archaeological Reports, British Series 54(i). Oxford.

Lambeck, K. 1991. Glacial rebound and sea-level change in the British Isles. *Terra Nova* 3, 379–389.

Lanting, J. and Brindley, A. 1996. Irish logboats and their European Context. *The Journal of Irish Archaeology* 7, 85–95.

McCarroll, D., Garrad, L. and Dackombe, R. 1990. Lateglacial and Postglacial environmental history. In: Robinson, V. and McCarroll, D. (eds.) *The Isle of Man: Celebrating a Sense of Place*, 55–76. Liverpool.

McCartan, S. 1990. The Early Prehistoric colonisation of the Isle of Man: Mesolithic Hunter-gatherers. *Proceedings of the Isle of Man Natural History and Antiquarian Society* 9, No. 4, 517–534.

McCartan, S.B. 1994. A Later Mesolithic site at Rhendhoo, Jurby, Isle of Man. *Proceedings of the Isle of Man Natural History and Antiquarian Society* 10, No. 2, 87–117.

—— 1999. The Manx Early Mesolithic: a story in stone. In: Davey, P.J. (ed.) *Recent Archaeological Research on the Isle of Man*, 5–11. British Archaeological Reports, British Series 278. Oxford.

McCormick, F. 1999 Early evidence for wild animals in Ireland. In: Benecke, N. (ed.) *The Holocene History of the European Vertebrate Fauna: Modern Aspects of Research*, 355–371. Archäologie in Eurasien, Band 6. Rahden.

O'Sullivan, A. 1997. Last foragers or first farmers? *Archaeology Ireland* 11, No.2, 14–16.

Reynier, M.J. 1997. Radiocarbon dating of Early Mesolithic stone technologies from Great Britain. In: Fagnart, J-P and Thévenin, A. (eds) *Le Tardiglaciaire en Europe du Nord-ouest*, 529–542. Paris.

SAN. 1998. The earliest site in Scotland? *Scottish Archaeological News* 28, 1.

Swinnerton, F. 1889. The early Neolithic cists and refuse heap at Port St. Mary. *Yn Liaor Manninagh* 1:1, 241–244.

—— 1892. Pre-Aryan remains at Glen Wyllin, Isle of Man. *Yn Liaor Manninagh* 1:2, 262–264.

Tomlinson, P. 1997. The Manx hill-land: the palaeoenvironmental resource. *Proceedings of the Man hill-land Seminar*, 57–64. Douglas.

Tooley, M.J. 1978. Flandrian sea-level changes and vegetational history of the Isle of Man: a review. In: Davey, P. (ed.) *Man and Environment in the Isle of Man*, 15–24. British Archaeological Reports, British Series 54(i). Oxford.

Van Wijngaarden-Bakker, L.H. 1989. Faunal Remains and the Irish Mesolithic. In: Bonsall, C. (ed.) *The Mesolithic in Europe*, 125–133. Edinburgh.

Wickham-Jones, C.R, 1990. *Rhum: Mesolithic and later sites at Kinloch. Excavations 1984–1986*. Society of Antiquaries of Scotland, Monograph series 7. Edinburgh.

Wickham-Jones, C.R. and Dalland, M. 1998. A small Mesolithic site at Fife Ness, Fife, Scotland. *Internet Archaeology* 5. http//intarch.ac.uk/journal.issues/wickham_index.html.

Wingfield, R.T.R. 1995. A model of sea-levels in the Irish and Celtic seas during the end-Pleistocene to Holocene transition. In: Preece, R.C. (ed.) *Island Britain: a Quaternary perspective*, 209–242. London.

Woodman, P.C. 1977. Recent excavations at Newferry, Co. Antrim. *Proceedings of the Prehistoric Society* 43, 155–199.

—— 1978. A Re-appraisal of the Manx Mesolithic. In: Davey, P. (ed.) *Man and Environment in the Isle of Man*, 119–139. British Archaeological Reports, British Series 54(i). Oxford.

—— 1985. *Excavations at Mount Sandel 1973–77*. Northern Ireland Archaeological Monographs No. 2. Belfast.

—— 1986. Problems in the colonisation of Ireland. *Ulster Journal of Archaeology* 49, 7–17.

—— 1987. Excavations at Cass ny Hawin, a Manx Mesolithic Site, and the Position of the Manx Microlithic Industries. *Proceedings of the Prehistoric Society* 53, 1–22.

Woodman, P., McCarthy, M. and Monaghan, N. 1997. The Irish Quaternary Fauna Project. *Quaternary Science Reviews* 16, 129–159.

46. Indications of regionalisation in Mesolithic Scotland

Alan Saville

Some of the difficulties of identifying regionalisation are considered, as are the limitations of the Scottish Mesolithic database. Two suggestions are made for recognising socially meaningful regionality: one on the basis of the localised exploitation of distinctive raw materials, the other on diversity of material culture between Ireland and south-west Scotland.

Introduction

In my conference version of this paper I began by summarising the nature and limitations of the evidence for the Mesolithic period in Scotland. The available database has expanded considerably since the overviews by Morrison (1980:154 pp) and Woodman (1989) in terms of known sites and findspots (Saville 1998). There have also been major new fieldwork campaigns (e.g. Mithen and Lake 1996), and in particular there are now many, more reliable, radiocarbon dates for this period (Bonsall *et al.* 1995; Bonsall 1996). However, the advances have mainly been quantitative rather than qualitative – Scotland has yet to produce a Friesack, Skateholm or Star Carr of its own – and the record is still dominated by lithic artefacts, supplemented by some significant finds of artefacts of bone and antler. Moreover, although the direct AMS radiocarbon dates on the latter give a span from the 9th to the 5th millennia BP for Mesolithic occupation (Bonsall 1996:Table 11.1), periodisation within this span has not been satisfactorily achieved. In part this is because the dated bone and antler artefacts have rarely been found in any contextual association with diagnostic lithic tools.

It has not even been possible to isolate successfully any precise correlates for the Early (*c.*10,000–8500 BP) or Later Mesolithic (*c.*8500–5500 BP) subdivisions of England and Wales (Jacobi 1973, 1976; Mellars 1974) on the basis of typologically coherent artefact assemblages from Scotland. This is an obvious hindrance to the exploration of questions of regionalisation, which naturally requires some confidence that any variation being examined is within a consistent time-frame.

In terms of the peopling of Scotland in the Mesolithic, there are as yet no concrete archaeological data, in the form of characteristic artefacts, to indicate occupation of the Outer Hebrides or Shetland before the Neolithic period. Otherwise Mesolithic people by the end of the Later Mesolithic were present throughout the Scottish mainland and most of the Inner Hebrides and the Orkney Isles (Saville 2000), though the extent to which the uplands were exploited remains problematic.

Scotland is of course a relatively recent political concept and strictly speaking is as such irrelevant to the study of Mesolithic regionalisation, since it is simply the northern part of the basic biogeographical zone of northern Britain, which arguably begins at the southern end of the Pennines/Peak District (Figure 46.1). There are many general links in terms of lithic typology between zones on either side of the modern border (Mulholland 1970:97; Bonsall 1980:457; Weyman 1984) and beyond, though no specific comparative analysis has been undertaken. One exceptional example of cross-border linkage is the antler harpoon-head from Whitburn on the Durham coast (Mellars 1970), which finds its closest British parallel in the harpoon head from MacArthur Cave, Oban, suggesting some reality to the notion that northern Britain was part of the same 'techno-territory' in the Later Mesolithic (see below).

A recent overview of the Mesolithic period in northern England has usefully demonstrated the distribution in gross terms of known Mesolithic findspots regardless of phase (Spikins 1999:Fig. 2.3). This provides two specific contrasts with the situation in Scotland. Firstly, the overall number of findspots is apparently far greater in northern England, which might, in crude terms, suggest regional divergence in the sense of less widespread settlement in Scotland, a smaller population, or a delay in colonisation, or a combination of all three factors. Secondly, the distribution of findspots in northern England shows a clear concentration on the upland zones, whereas in Scotland the known distribution is still predominantly coastal, esturine and riverine (though see Edwards *et al.* 1983:Figs. 1–2 for Mesolithic evidence from the interior of southwest Scotland).

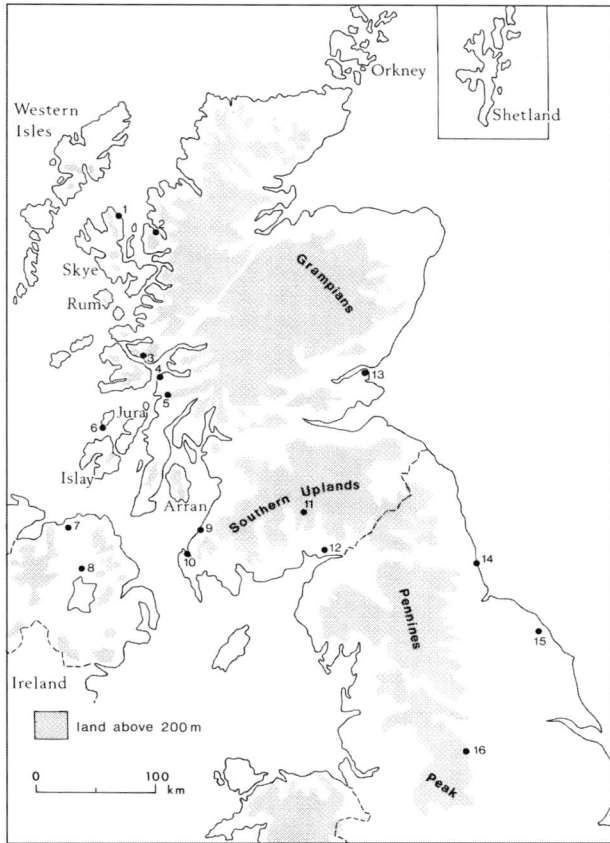

Figure 46.1 Northern Britain showing the location of sites and areas mentioned in the text. Key: 1. An Corran, Staffin, Skye; 2. Shieldaig, Loch Torridon, Highland; 3. Acharn, Morvern, Highland; 4. Oban, Argyll; 5. Kilmelfort Cave, Argyll; 6. Oronsay, Argyll; 7. Mount Sandel, County Londonderry; 8. Newferry, County Antrim; 9. Ballantrae, Ayrshire; 10. Kirkcolm, Dumfries and Galloway; 11. Daer Reservoir, South Lanarkshire; 12. Annan, Dumfries and Galloway; 13. Morton, Fife; 14. Whitburn, Tyne and Wear; 15. Star Carr, Seamer, North Yorkshire; 16. Deepcar, South Yorkshire.

At the moment these contrasts seem to stand up in overall terms as indicating a macro-regionally distinct pattern, but the validity of the existing database has to be seriously questioned (cf. Spikins 1999:28). Biasing elements include the amount and type of fieldwork undertaken in each area and the availability of the evidence due to, for example, the effects of afforestation, colluviation, peat cover, arable cultivation and past sea-level change.

In this paper I will look first at the concept of regionalisation and some ways in which it has been approached in the study of the Mesolithic period, then turn to a few cases where regionality may be the explanation for observed patterning. I am not concerned here with questions of initial postglacial colonisation in Scotland (Morrison and Bonsall 1989; Wickham-Jones and Woodman 1998) nor with the Mesolithic-Neolithic transition.

Mesolithic regionalisation

If anything more is to be meant by regionalisation in prehistory than the contemporaneous occupation of separate geographic zones, then archaeologists customarily point to diversity in the material record. In normative terms, such diversification would be assumed to be sufficient to have socio-cultural if not ethnic specificity. In other words, a recognisable archaeological contrast between adjacent geographic areas within the same chronozone would be taken to reflect, at the very least, some separate identity of social groups, at the most separate ethnic affiliation. For Mesolithic studies this concept of discoverable social territories now has a fairly long history (e.g. Clark 1975:22). Many archaeologists today, however, would demur from such assumptions, particularly in the matter of ethnicity, and recent overviews have rightly stressed the complexities and ambiguities involved (e.g. Jones 1997:106 pp). Nevertheless, as was apparent from numerous presentations at the Meso 2000 conference, there remains a conviction among many workers on the European Mesolithic that geographic patterning in archaeologically recovered material culture does have socio-cultural meaning.

Language, though not without its own complications, is probably the clearest manifestation of group affiliation and ethnicity, but in any direct sense it remains unrecoverable from remote prehistory. Ethnographically we can in some cases be persuaded that material culture provides an identifiable correlate to, or proxy for, linguistic distinction, though this is usually applicable to fuller cultural inventories than the archaeologist investigating the Mesolithic period can expect.

Moreover, in terms of ethnic identity, it is clothing, personal decorative ornaments, hairstyle, body decoration, burial custom, house style, settlement layout, and art, which can be the most informative about group affiliation. These aspects of material culture are precisely those among the most vulnerable to loss in archaeological terms. In fact, from Mesolithic Scotland, the only 'ethnic identity' category available from the above list as surviving evidence is that of personal decorative ornaments – and there are not many of these. Apart from a single, possibly artificially perforated, Pelican's Foot shell from the site of Morton B on the Fife coast (Coles 1971:347), the only ornaments are cowrie shell beads. These occur on several Mesolithic sites on the western seaboard of Scotland (Simpson 1996:Fig. 15.5), but they also occur in southern England (Barton 1994:Fig. 7, 1996:Fig. 5) and cannot be used on their own as ethnic indicators.

Newell et al. (1990) have recognised this and use the cowrie shell bead to help define a so-called western language family or area network in the Later Mesolithic. This means that the occurrence of cowrie shell beads among Mesolithic people in Scotland can only be said to situate them within a very broad cultural complex. Indeed, given the natural ubiquity of the cowrie in the north

Atlantic zone, it would be more significant if Mesolithic people in Scotland had not used these shells for beads. Newell *et al.* (1990) have proposed further social subdivision – to hypothetical tribe and band level – for parts of Europe where other types of ornament are more plentiful and more localised in distribution, but could not include Scotland because of the absence of relevant artefacts.

Given the limited database, archaeologists studying the Mesolithic period have seized on whatever other material culture is available and have suggested ethnic identity possibilities on that basis, encouraged by the few ethnoarchaeological studies which support socio-territorial or even ethnic interpretations of diversity in mundane material culture (e.g. Hodder 1982; Sampson 1988). Barbed antler points have seemed an obvious candidate for this kind of analysis (Verhart 1990) but the evidence so far suggests that these points are, like the cowrie shell beads, only indicators at a rather broad techno-complex level. While they may help to support the identification of broad 'language family' areas, they do not, at least in Scotland, appear to be relevant at the level of any smaller social entity. This is perhaps inevitable since there are so few of these artefacts and because they do not exhibit idiosyncratic characterisation in the form of decoration or typology.

The desire to see regionally distinct social territories on the basis of the lithic artefact repertoire alone has quite a long pedigree in Mesolithic studies. The best known example in Britain is Jacobi's (1979) use of variation in the occurrence of certain distinctive microlith types to suggest regional groupings, which could be interpreted as reflecting social territories in England and adjacent parts of the European mainland. Jacobi was writing before the major debates of the early 1980s concerning the identification and meaning of style in lithic artefacts, which Gendel (1984) was able to accommodate within his overview and still remain hopeful about the potential for visualising social territories. While Gendel (1987), cautiously, continued to be optimistic, Jacobi (1987) recanted, seeming to presage the general doubts of the post-processual era about any straightforward equations between material culture and society (Tilley 1989). Apart from the fact that in early prehistory there are always problems of chronological control – not knowing if one is seeing patterning through time rather than space – archaeologists are now aware that there are likely to be many other factors complicating the identification of 'assemblages' and their inter-comparison. Function is one such factor, especially relevant when it is often microlith types which are being compared, given all the problems of understanding how to interpret their use (Finlayson *et al.* 1996; Finlayson and Mithen 1997). There may also be ecological and raw material parameters, which could constrain the utility or even possibility of certain toolkits, as well as factors of seasonal variation.

One result of such developments in Britain, which for

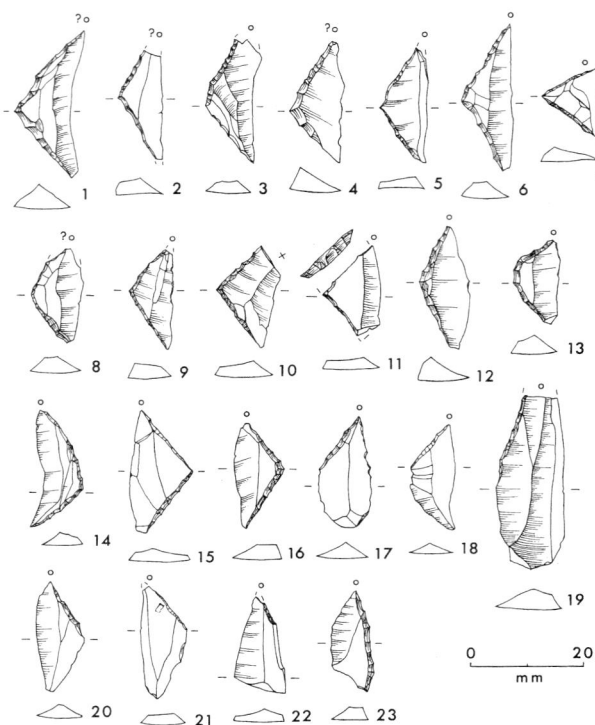

Figure 46.2 A selection of flint microliths from the excavations at Morton, Fife (Coles 1971). 1–16: 'broad' triangles; 17–22: obliquely blunted points; 23: edge blunted. Site A, trench 44: 9, 10, 12, 18, 20, 21, 22; Site A, trench 47: 3, 5, 6, 7, 8, 11, 17; Site A, trench 53: 2, 14, 16, 23; Site A, trench 55/56: 1, 4, 15, 19; Test-pits, trenches 48/49/52: 13. National Museums of Scotland collection (BNA). Drawn by Marion O'Neil.

the Mesolithic were crucially influenced by the late Grahame Clark's advocacy of economic prehistory or 'bioarchaeology' and his increasing disenchantment with lithic studies (Clark 1972a, 1972b, 1973), is that the ability to undertake studies of the kind of patterning in which Jacobi was initially interested have been compromised by the inadequacy of publication of the basic lithic artefact data. In Scotland, a classic example of this is provided by the 1970s excavation project on the island of Oronsay, which was so focused on the socio-economic aspects of the environmental data that the lithic artefacts recovered were not included in the publication (Mellars 1987). While admitting that Mesolithic studies in Scotland are challenged by the absence of a fuller range of material culture and that all opportunities to recover economic 'ecofacts' should be seized, it would on the other hand be foolish to turn away altogether from lithic artefacts – the one element of the record which is ubiquitous and abundant.

In those parts of Europe less influenced by the 'Cambridge school' of economic prehistory and less affected by the traumas of Anglo-American post-processual self-doubt, there is still considerable support for the detailed analyses of lithic inventories and the idea

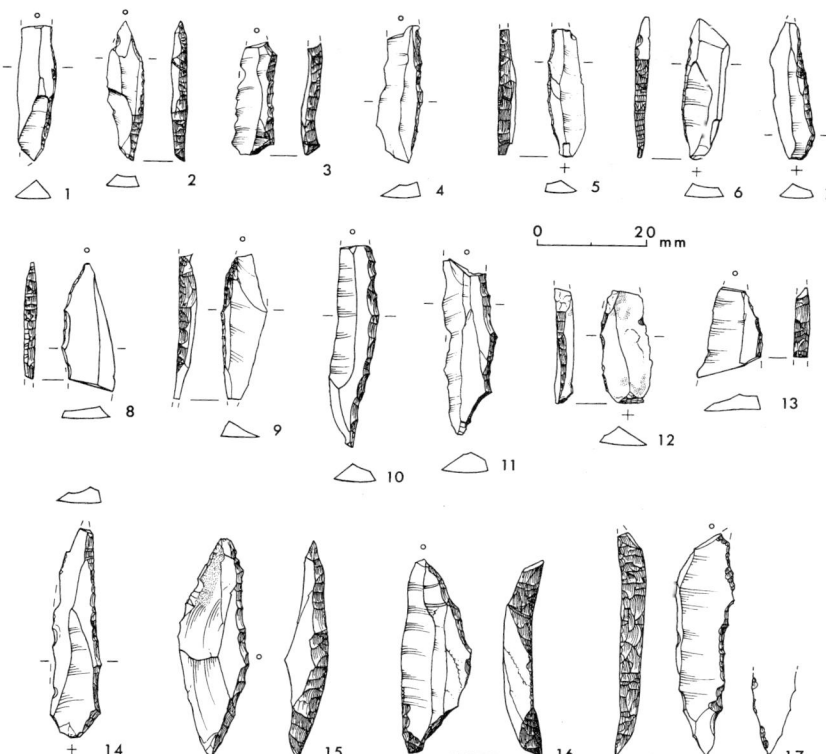

Figure 46.3 Flint microliths and backed bladelets from Kilmelfort Cave, Argyll (Coles 1983). National Museums of Scotland collection (HMA). Drawn by Marion O'Neil.

that lithic artefacts, and microliths in particular, can be stylistic indicators with socio-territorial implications (e.g. Rozoy 1997; Thévenin 1998). There are also some classic case studies of regional variation defined on the basis of diagnostic lithic artefacts which still seem valid (e.g. Vang Petersen 1984), so it is worth looking at what evidence there may be from the lithic database in northern Britain.

Lithic artefacts

Arguments are still unresolved on the question of an Early Mesolithic (c.10,000–8500 BP) in Scotland. Typologically, the best candidate for a parallel to the kind of lithic industry found at Star Carr (Clark 1954), at least in terms of microliths, is still the site of Morton A, Fife (Coles 1971), where relatively large isosceles triangles predominate, together with some plain obliquely-blunted points (Figure 46.2). Regrettably there are no entirely reliable dates associated with this material and much confusion has arisen about its chronological position (Myers 1988; Woodman 1989). This is partly because of conflation with the adjacent, but separate, Later Mesolithic site of Morton B, which now has reliable dates (on bone tools) in the 6th millennium BP (Bonsall *et al.* 1995:Table 1). The confusion has been compounded by the apparent association of mid-9th millennium BP radiocarbon dates (on carbonised hazelnut shells) with Later Mesolithic microlith types at Kinloch, Isle of Rum (Wickham-Jones 1990a), and the position has now been further confused by an even earlier date of 9075±80 BP (AA-30354) (Ashmore 1999) on charcoal in apparent association with Later Mesolithic microliths at an inland site at Daer Reservoir, South Lanarkshire, on the Scottish Southern Uplands.

Pronouncements on the Early Mesolithic in Scotland are therefore mostly a matter of faith rather than fact, but it does seem probable that an approximately Star Carr-type Early Mesolithic was present and is reflected in the assemblage from Morton A (cf. Reynier 1997), and perhaps in those from Lussa Bay (Mercer 1970a) and Glenbatrick G1 (Mercer 1974) on Jura, and less explicitly as elements from other mixed assemblages (Morrison and Bonsall 1989:141). The question thereafter arises as to whether there is any other early material from other parts of Scotland which might point to diversification during this period. Ignoring the problem of the 'tanged points' (Edwards and Mithen 1995), which are a rag-bag of undiagnostic forms probably irrelevant to the Early Mesolithic, there is only one feasible alternative at the moment, though again this hinges on typology in the absence of any absolute dates.

Over towards the west coast, near to Oban, the site of Kilmelfort Cave, excavated in the 1950s (Coles 1983), has produced an idiosyncratic assemblage with microliths and other backed forms (Figure 46.3). These artefacts do not fit readily with what is known of the Later Mesolithic in Scotland, nor do they, as a group, have any other obvious local parallels. Given the salvage circumstances under which they were recovered, it cannot be certain that the Kilmelfort Cave artefacts are coeval and part of an homogeneous assemblage. Purely on their own terms, however, the Kilmelfort Cave flints have a typologically 'early' aspect (Coles 1983:18). It is perhaps not too fanciful to see similarities here (Fig.3:11 and 17) with convex-backed and angle-backed points such as those from cave sites in Wales (David 1991).

This is the only tentative suggestion which can be made at present about differentiation within the Early Mesolithic of Scotland. In the absence of any chronological fix for the Kilmelfort Cave material, it is perhaps as likely that there is a time difference between Kilmelfort Cave and Morton A, with the Kilmelfort Cave microliths and backed bladelets representing an otherwise unrecognised strand of the Early Mesolithic. It is worth remembering, however, Jacobi's (1978:302 pp) recognition, on the basis of microlith types and varying raw materials, of two apparently contemporary Early Mesolithic social groupings in the Pennines, North York Moors and Lincolnshire. This distinction, between contemporary 'Star Carr' and 'Deepcar' assemblage types in both upland and lowland areas, has come to be generally accepted (Spratt 1993). It is now being refined through a closer scrutiny of the radiocarbon dates and it is being suggested that the 'Deepcar' assemblages, while they overlap with those of 'Star Carr' type, are on the whole slightly later and perhaps represent a settlement move inland (Reynier 1997, 1998). In the case of the Kilmelfort Cave assemblage, the temptation, purely speculatively, is to suggest an horizon earlier rather than later within the Early Mesolithic of Scotland.

Taking Scotland as a whole, however, there is clearly a contrast with northern England in terms of what is entirely absent from the artefact record. There are no Maglemosian-type barbed points of the kind so well represented at Star Carr, except for the totally unprovenanced uniserial barbed point, often erroneously listed as from Glenavon, Banffshire (Morrison and Bonsall 1989:Fig. 4). Nor are there any artefacts of elk or bovine bone, or any amber objects, and there are virtually no flint axe/adze/pick-type core-tools (see below). This is, however, the same for most of northern England apart from Star Carr, so we could be dealing purely with bias in the archaeological record, rather than regionalisation as such. On the other hand, the fact that so few indicators of broad-blade lithic technology have come to light in Scotland in comparison with such prolific findspots both on and outside the uplands within northern England (Radley and Mellars 1964; Buckland and Dolby 1973; Jacobi 1978) may, at the very least – and accepting all biases (Spikins 1999) – suggest less intensity of settlement.

Perhaps all that can be suggested on the basis of the evidence mentioned so far is that there is as yet no trace of Early Mesolithic presence further north within Scotland than Fife (Morton A) on the east and Argyll (Kilmelfort Cave) on the west. This leaves open the question of a time-lag in the Mesolithic occupation of the far north, which, if it were the case, would indicate a regionalised colonisation pattern, but the data are hardly sufficient to substantiate this, and rapid waterborne pan-coastal settlement of the Scottish mainland, analogous to the Norwegian pattern (Bang-Andersen 1996), is more probable.

The Later Mesolithic in Scotland can be caricatured as an undistinguished background of narrow-blade, 'geometric', microlithic industries, from which the 'Obanian' assemblages of the western seaboard (Mellars 1987), with their bone and antler artefacts and associated economic data from shell middens, seem to shine out like a beacon in the dark. However, the current consensus is that the 'Obanian' sites are merely the product of a combination of adaptation to a particular resource in a specific ecotone and the accident of archaeological survival, and that the 'Obanian' is only regional in this limited way and not in a sense which has implications for cultural grouping (Bonsall 1996). The shell-midden economy of the classic 'Obanian' can now be seen to extend for a distance of over 200 km up the west coast of Scotland from Oronsay to An Corran in north-east Skye (Saville and Miket 1994), and a similar distance from Oronsay to the east coast of Scotland if the site of Morton B is included in this designation. With the 'Obanian' we seem simply to be seeing a glimpse of a widespread adaptive mode in the Later Mesolithic, which was applicable to all Scottish and northern English coastal areas where the circumstances were suitable, but for which the evidence rarely survives.

A major part of the problem with being able to recognise any other patterning there is likely to be within the Later Mesolithic in Scotland is gauging the validity of the chronological homogeneity of industries and the lack of adequate analysis and publication of assemblages of any size (Saville 1998:215). The fullest publications of assemblages have been those by Mercer (e.g. 1974) resulting from his long-term personal project to study the Mesolithic on the Isle of Jura (Searight 1984). However, the lack of stratigraphy at these sites, the obvious admixtures from multi-period use of the same locations, the absence of reliable radiocarbon dates, and the idiosyncratic typology and illustration used in the publications, means that the Jura data are somewhat problematic for making wider comparisons within or beyond Scotland (cf. Woodman 1989:11 pp).

Elsewhere in Scotland the low numbers of adequately published microliths – to take the most ubiquitous and diagnostic tool-type – simply do not allow the necessary comparisons to be made. There are as yet unconfirmable hints that some thick, edge-blunted forms of microlith may be special to Orkney (Saville 1996:217) and that small crescentic microliths may have a particular currency in parts of Scotland (Wickham-Jones and Dalland 1998: 15), but this is clutching at straws. It is sad to reflect that the available database of well-published microliths or other lithic tools from the Scottish Later Mesolithic has increased little since the work of Lacaille (1954). I have already mentioned that the lithic finds from the Oronsay excavations (Mellars 1987) remain unpublished, and it seems the analysis and detailed publication of large lithic collections has just 'gone out of fashion' archaeologically. This current indifference to artefact typology often means that those few drawings which are published lack sufficient information, for example on the orientation and completeness of microliths (cf. Martingell and Saville 1988), which renders them both difficult to use in wider comparison and undermines confidence in the actual analysis of implement types in the accompanying reports.

Raw materials

While there may be problems with identifying variation in terms of typology or style among Scottish Later Mesolithic assemblages, this is certainly not, in the broad sense, the case with raw materials. Whereas flint, albeit sometimes in small quantities, seems to be used just about everywhere, in the form of beach or gravel pebbles which have no location-specific signatures, this is not true of most of the flint alternatives, whose use appears rather more localised. It is one of the features of the Scottish Mesolithic that a wide variety of silicious raw materials was exploited (Finlayson 1990; Saville 1994a). As many authorities have suggested (e.g. Gendel 1984), there would seem to be considerable potential for using the distribution of Mesolithic tools made of particular lithic raw materials to generate theoretical territories, which could then be investigated further. This is particularly so if the raw materials are source specific and can be readily identified from hand-held specimens without magnification.

Difficulties again arise in following this line of research at the moment because of the limitations of the database. The main problem here is that many of the assemblages of Mesolithic artefacts which contain non-flint artefacts are from excavations or surface collections at locations reused during the Neolithic and Bronze Age periods. Although more unusual non-flint materials were sometimes used for formal, diagnostic tools in the northern British Mesolithic, including microliths (e.g. made from baked mudstone at An Corran, Skye (Saville and Miket 1994), or from volcanic tuff in Cumbria (Cherry and Cherry 1973)), it is more often the case that the non-flint component of an assemblage comprises the less diagnostic artefacts. There is then uncertainty over whether the non-flint artefacts belong to the Mesolithic or to a later period.

This is less of a problem in much of southern Scotland where naturally occurring cherts, predominantly blue-green-grey or purple-grey in colour, were commonly used for all tool forms, including microliths. Some assemblages are exclusively of chert, others have varying mixtures of flint and chert, the flint usually being seen by analysts as the more valuable imported material (Mulholland 1970: 85; Finlayson 1990). Unfortunately, to return to what is becoming a sub-theme of this paper, there are no modern publications of these chert assemblages. The most recent detailed analysis and publication of a Scottish Mesolithic site with a strong chert component was over 50 years ago (Davidson et al. 1949). There are also unresolved issues as to the extent and accessibility of the geological occurrence of knapping-quality chert and investigations are on-going into the possibility of Mesolithic quarrying for chert in the Scottish Southern Uplands (Graeme Warren pers. comm.). Moreover, it is not yet possible to map the full extent of sites with chert utilisation in the Mesolithic, other than that they are likely to reflect the occurrence of usable cherts across a broad swathe of central and southern Scotland and into northern England (Wickham-Jones and Collins 1978).

Chert use in the Mesolithic seems primarily local to the area of its geological origin, which in northern England means the carboniferous limestone regions from Northumberland through to northern Lancashire and northern Yorkshire, and around the Derbyshire Peak District at the southern end of the Pennines (Radley 1968). However the use of this raw material was not uniform. For example, in the Mesolithic, unlike in later prehistoric periods, chert was not used in Weardale or on the Durham coast (Young 1984), whereas Hind (1998) has pointed to the Mesolithic import of chert into the central Pennines and elsewhere from sources in both the southern and northern Pennines. Chert is common in the Later Mesolithic assemblages from the limestone uplands of Cumbria, but flint was used preferentially for tools such as microliths (Cherry and Cherry 1987:70).

Quartz is a raw material even more readily available in Scotland than chert, particularly in the north and west, and it was certainly exploited for formal tools by Mesolithic people. Its ubiquity as a raw material makes it less useful in the study of regionality, especially as only rarely are chronologically diagnostic tools, such as microliths, found in quartz, so that there is often doubt about the Mesolithic date of quartz artefacts.

In principle, a material such as pitchstone (Thorpe and Thorpe 1984; Simpson and Meighan 1999), which seems only to have been obtainable in knapping quality from a few locations on the Isle of Arran, and which is readily identifiable from hand-held specimens, offers a much better opportunity for distributional analysis. However, while it is clear that pitchstone was exploited during the Mesolithic on Arran itself (Affleck et al. 1988), it is by no means certain that it was utilised outside Arran during this period (Wickham-Jones 1986). This needs to be said despite entrenched claims in the literature that Mesolithic artefacts of pitchstone have been found across southern Scotland, for distances of up to 160 km from Arran (Mulholland 1970:86; Morrison 1980:170; Morrison

1982:5; Thorpe and Thorpe 1984:Fig. 3). The occurrence of pitchstone in the form of non-diagnostic artefacts at multi-period locations, for example at Ballantrae, Ayrshire (Lacaille 1945:86) and at Bolsay Farm, Islay (Mithen 1995:269 p), does not necessarily establish a Mesolithic context. Nor does the widespread occurrence of pitchstone pyramidal single-platform bladelet cores and the bladelets struck from them need have any significance for the Mesolithic, since there is more reason to think that this is a Neolithic, if not also an Early Bronze Age phenomenon, with perhaps more symbolic than functional meaning. In fact, current evidence would suggest that pitchstone was not particularly valued during the Mesolithic period, either for tools or as an unusual 'magic' stone.

This contrasts with the case of bloodstone, a raw material available from the Isle of Rum, which, albeit not preferentially in respect to flint, was used by Mesolithic people both on the island of origin and on the surrounding islands and mainland. Research on the exploitation of Rum bloodstone has defined a relatively restricted distribution zone (Clarke and Griffiths 1990; Wickham-Jones 1990b), extending from Acharn, Morvern, in the south to Shieldaig on Loch Torridon and An Corran, Skye, in the north (Figure 46.1). This is a total north-south distance of $c.120$ km, or a radius of $c.60$ km from the source on Rum. Figures for Mesolithic "economic territories" have been analysed by Newell *et al.* (1990:47) to suggest a potential mean area of $c.67 \times 42$ km or 2849 sq km, and one can find comparable suggestions of territory size for Mesolithic groups in various parts of Europe (e.g. Jochim 1998:206). Imposing this kind of calculation onto the Scottish landscape – or rather 'seascape' on this part of the west coast – is needless to say tendentious, but the discernible pattern of bloodstone dispersal is within the same order of magnitude and is one of the few available pointers to what could be a genuine regional grouping. The distribution certainly appears local and regional, not inter-regional. Some further confidence may be provided by the fact that the bloodstone raw material is given no special treatment or use by Mesolithic people, it is merely an alternative, and possibly an inferior alternative, to flint or some other local equivalents such as chalcedonic silica. Thus it may not have been a raw material which was particularly sought after, but one which was exploited opportunistically. This mundane use of bloodstone makes it part of the background noise of material culture, and therefore perhaps more likely to be a genuine proxy indicator of a social or economic territory than it would be if it were a raw material invested with any special qualities.

There are hints that there may be other raw materials of localised occurrence which were used discriminately or opportunistically during the Mesolithic period, such as silicified limestone in the far north and Orkney (Saville 2000:95), but these are not yet as well documented as bloodstone.

Presence/absence and the Irish question

Perhaps the only other perceived patterning in the Scottish Mesolithic record which might be relevant to this inquiry is where an absolute contrast exists between regions by the presence of certain items of material culture in one and their absence in another. As we have seen, the fact that most elements of material culture present in the early Holocene at Star Carr are absent in Scotland and elsewhere in northern England is likely to be a factor of bias in the archaeological record. For presence/absence to be interpreted as socially meaningful there has to be an expectation that the archaeological record in each area is fundamentally comparable. This would seem to be the case with the Later Mesolithic in north-east Ireland and south-west Scotland. The Irish Later Mesolithic is characterised by the presence of relatively large butt-trimmed flakes, uniplane cores, stone axeheads, flint axeheads/picks, and an absence of microliths (Woodman and Andersen 1990). Given the fact that the sea crossing between Ireland and Scotland is so short and that contact between the two areas was clearly no problem in the Neolithic period (Saville 1999), the absence of Irish Later Mesolithic lithic artefact types in south-west Scotland and the abundance of microliths there, makes for a striking contrast. Until recently it could have been said with justification that the Mesolithic archaeology of south-west Scotland, though frequently discussed (Coles 1963; Morrison 1982), was disadvantaged by the lack of modern excavation. This is at least no longer the case on Islay (from the southern end of which Ireland, only 40 km away, is clearly visible, and vice-versa), where there has been extensive recent work (McCullagh 1989; Mithen *et al.* 1992; Mithen and Lake 1996). This work has shown no links with Later Mesolithic Ireland in terms of artefact type or raw material, confirming earlier conclusions based on work undertaken on Jura.

Elsewhere in south-west Scotland a new assessment of museum and private collections is needed, but I am currently aware of only two potentially relevant artefacts, both unfortunately isolated surface finds, which might reflect some contact across the North Channel. The first is the so-called 'Bann point' from Annan, Dumfriesshire (Coles 1966; Saville 1999:111). Broad flakes of roughly leaf-shaped form with a point formed by bilateral, partly invasive, retouch are not a feature of Scottish Mesolithic assemblages, while such implements do occur in the Irish Later Mesolithic (Woodman and Andersen 1990:378 p), particularly at Newferry, County Antrim (Smith and Collins 1971; Woodman 1977). However, the Annan example is by no means typical, especially since it lacks any trimming at the butt, and cannot anyway be seen as a clear-cut Mesolithic indicator, since similar forms occur in later periods.

The second artefact is a previously unpublished core-tool of generalised axehead/pick type, found at Kirkcolm, Wigtownshire (Figure 46.4), which has fairly close

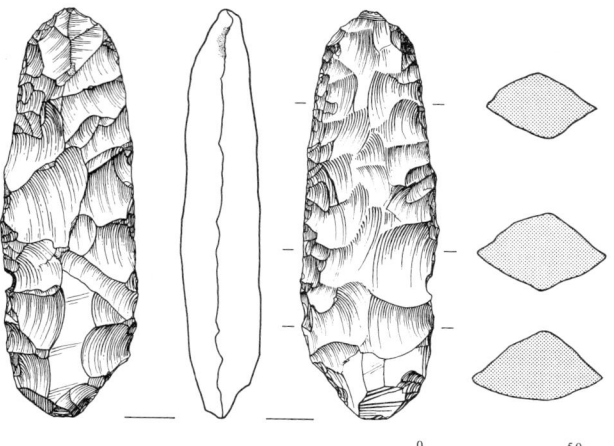

Figure 46.4 Flint core-tool from Kirkcolm, Wigtownshire. Dumfries and Galloway Museum Service: Stranraer Museum (1993.3). Drawn by Marion O'Neil.

parallels with numerous Irish examples of both Later and Early Mesolithic date (Movius 1953:Figs. 14–15; Woodman 1978:Figs. 14 and 36; Woodman 1985:Fig. 24; Sinéad McCartan pers. comm.). By contrast, it has virtually no parallels in Scotland, apart from the anomalous, and anyway typologically rather dissimilar, core-tools from Fair Isle (Saville 2000) and Morton, Fife (Coles 1971:314; Saville 1994b), and the possible core-tool fragment from Stairhaven, Wigtownshire (Coles 1963: 86). The same is true for northern England, where, other than at Star Carr, there seem to be extremely few examples (there is a *tranchet* axehead from West Hartlepool on the Durham coast (Trechmann 1936:plate 35); two others are listed from Durham (Wymer 1977:83 pp); none are recorded from Cumbria). This core-tool from Kirkcolm, therefore, despite its complete lack of archaeological context, does seem on typological grounds (cf. Woodman 1992:94) to be both 'Irish' and Mesolithic.

Thus the Kirkcolm implement could be the exception which proves the rule that there was virtually no complementarity in terms of material culture between the two regions in the Later Mesolithic. What could this mean? The implication is that a real social barrier of some kind existed, either in terms of there being absolutely no contact between the two zones, which would be very hard to believe since it does not appear the case at any subsequent period, or, perhaps more likely, in terms of separately established social systems with mutually exclusive material culture. If so, a rather extraordinary regional difference of population group, one which would have persisted for a millennium or more in the Later Mesolithic, is indicated. Recognition of this enigmatic situation is by no means new (Coles 1963:92; Woodman 1978:205 pp) but the anomaly is compounded by the evidence now available for some similarity of lithic repertoires earlier in the Mesolithic.

The excavated assemblages from Mount Sandel, County Londonderry (Collins 1983; Woodman 1985), which provide the typological basis for the Early Mesolithic in the north of Ireland, contain a range of microliths and other forms which can be matched among the assemblages from Islay (Mithen *et al.* 1992: 251) and Jura (Mercer 1970b). The greatest contrast again lies in the absence of flint core-tools or Mesolithic stone axeheads from Islay, Jura, or elsewhere in south-west Scotland (Saville 1994b). This may simply relate to the absence of suitable lithic material in the latter and its abundance in northern Ireland. However, there must of course have been an equivalent in terms of heavy-duty tools in Scotland, and the only possible substitute evinced by the available record are tools of antler. Antler-beam mattocks can be used to work wood, and are found in Scotland on Mesolithic sites where conditions of preservation allow (Mellars 1987). Thus the absence of red deer in Ireland during the Mesolithic (Woodman 2000:237), and therefore of antler for tool-making, could be the explanation for this element of the contrast.

Nevertheless, it would appear to be significant that, at an earlier stage in the Mesolithic period, when there was a certain equivalence of microlith types between north-east Ireland and south-west Scotland, there is still no evidence for contact. Unlike the case with Rum bloodstone, there is nothing to show that the flint of north-east Ireland was being used by Mesolithic people in Scotland who were living within a comparable distribution zone; these people made do with their own local beach flint, supplemented by alternatives such as quartz and non-lithic resources such as antler. From this initial position of equivalence *but* difference, there appears to have been a trajectory of separation which continued until the Neolithic period. Even then of course, while there is evidence for contact in the form of some aspects of material culture, there are numerous differences – for example in certain implement types (Saville 1999:110) and in tomb design – which suggest that contact may still have been more in the form of exchange between essentially separate communities.

The evidence thus far, therefore, would suggest that the separation of south-west Scotland and north-east Ireland during the Later Mesolithic provides a remarkable example of the reality of regionalisation as distinguishable from the archaeological record.

Acknowledgements

I am grateful to John Pickin, Curator of Stranraer Museum, for information on the Kirkcolm core-tool and for permission to publish it here. Sinéad McCartan kindly provided reference photographs of core-tools in the Ulster Museum collections. Marion O'Neil was responsible for the artefact illustrations (Figs. 2–4). My attendance at the Meso 2000 conference was funded by the National Museums of Scotland.

References

Affleck, T.L., Edwards, K. and Clarke, A. 1988. Archaeological and palynological studies at the Mesolithic pitchstone and flint site of Auchareoch, Isle of Arran. *Proceedings of the Society of Antiquaries of Scotland* 118, 37–59.

Ashmore, P.J. 1999. A list of archaeological radiocarbon dates. In: Turner, R. (ed.) *Discovery and Excavation in Scotland 1998*, 125–128. Edinburgh.

Bang-Andersen, S. 1996. Coast/inland relations in the Mesolithic of southern Norway. *World Archaeology* 27(3), 427–443.

Barton, R.N.E. 1994. Second interim report on the survey and excavations in the Wye Valley, 1994. *Proceedings of the University of Bristol Spelaeological Society* 20, No. 1, 63–73.

—— 1996. Fourth interim report on the survey and excavations in the Wye Valley, 1996. *Proceedings of the University of Bristol Spelaeological Society* 20, No. 3, 263–273.

Bonsall, C. 1980. The coastal factor in the Mesolithic settlement of north-west England. *Veröffentlichungen des Museums für Ur- und Frühgeschichte Potsdam* 14/15, 451–472.

—— 1996. The 'Obanian problem': coastal adaptation in the Mesolithic of western Scotland. In: Pollard, T. and Morrison, A. (eds.), *The Early Prehistory of Scotland*, 183–197. Edinburgh.

Bonsall, C., Tolan-Smith, C. and Saville, A. 1995. Direct dating of Mesolithic antler and bone artefacts from Great Britain: new results for bevelled tools and red deer antler mattocks. *Mesolithic Miscellany* 16, No. 1, 2–15.

Buckland, P.C. and Dolby, M.J. 1973. Mesolithic and later material from Misterton Carr, Notts. – an interim report. *Transactions of the Thoroton Society of Nottinghamshire* 77, 5–33.

Cherry, J. and Cherry, P.J. 1973. Mesolithic habitation sites at St Bees, Cumberland. *Transactions of the Cumberland and Westmorland Antiquarian and Archaeological Society* 73, 47–66.

—— 1987. *Prehistoric Habitation Sites on the Limestone Uplands of Eastern Cumbria*. Cumberland and Westmorland Antiquarian and Archaeological Society, Research Series, Volume II. Kendal.

Clark, J.G.D. 1954. *Excavations at Star Carr*. Cambridge.

—— 1972a. *Star Carr: a Case Study in Bioarchaeology*. Addison-Wesley Module in Anthropology 10. Reading, Mass.

—— 1972b. The archaeology of Stone Age settlement. *Ulster Journal of Archaeology* 35, 3–16.

—— 1973. Seasonality and the interpretation of lithic assemblages. In: de Motes, J.M. (ed.) *Estudios dedicados al Prof. Dr. Luis Pericot*, 1–13. Universidad de Barcelona, Instituto de Arqueologia y Prehistoria. Barcelona.

—— 1975. *The Earlier Stone Age Settlement of Scandinavia*. Cambridge.

Clarke, A. and Griffiths, D. 1990. The use of bloodstone as a raw material for flaked stone tools in the west of Scotland. In: Wickham-Jones, C.R. (ed.) *Rhum, Mesolithic and later sites at Kinloch: excavations 1984–86*, 149–156. Society of Antiquaries of Scotland Monograph 7. Edinburgh.

Coles, J.M. 1963. New aspects of the Mesolithic settlement of south-west Scotland. *Transactions of the Dumfriesshire and Galloway Natural History and Antiquarian Society* 41, 67–98.

—— 1966. A "Bann point" from Dumfriesshire. *Transactions of the Dumfriesshire and Galloway Natural History and Antiquarian Society* 43, 147.

—— 1971. The early settlement of Scotland: excavations at Morton, Fife. *Proceedings of the Prehistoric Society* 37(2), 284–366.

—— 1983. Excavations at Kilmelfort Cave, Argyll. *Proceedings of the Society of Antiquaries of Scotland* 113, 11–21.

Collins, A.E.P. 1983. Excavations at Mount Sandel, lower site, Coleraine, County Londonderry. *Ulster Journal of Archaeology* 46, 1–22.

David, A. 1991. Late Glacial archaeological residues from Wales: a selection. In: Barton, N., Roberts, A.J. and Roe, D.A. (eds.) *The Late Glacial in North-West Europe*, 141–159. Council for British Archaeology, Research Report 77. London.

Davidson, J.M., Phemister, J. and Lacaille, A.D. 1949. A Stone Age site at Woodend Loch, near Coatbridge. *Proceedings of the Society of Antiquaries of Scotland* 83 (1948–49), 77–98.

Edwards, K.J., Ansell, M. and Carter, B.A. 1983. New Mesolithic sites in south-west Scotland and their importance as indicators of inland penetration. *Transactions of the Dumfriesshire and Galloway Natural History and Antiquarian Society* 58, 9–15.

Edwards, K.J. and Mithen, S. 1995. The colonization of the Hebridean Islands of western Scotland: evidence from the palynological records. *World Archaeology* 26(3), 348–365.

Finlayson, B. 1990. Lithic exploitation during the Mesolithic in Scotland. *Scottish Archaeological Review* 7, 41–57.

Finlayson, B., Finlay, N. and Mithen, S. 1996. Mesolithic chipped stone assemblages: descriptive and analytical procedures used by the Southern Hebrides Mesolithic Project. In: Pollard, T. and Morrison, A. (eds.) *The Early Prehistory of Scotland*, 252–266. Edinburgh.

Finlayson, B. and Mithen, S. 1997. The microwear and morphology of microliths from Gleann Mor. In: Knecht, H. (ed.) *Projectile Technology*, 107–129. New York.

Gendel, P.A. 1984. *Mesolithic Social Territories in Northwestern Europe*. BAR International Series 218. Oxford.

—— 1987. Socio-stylistic analysis of lithic artefacts from the Mesolithic of northwestern Europe. In: Rowley-Conwy, P., Zvelebil, M. and Blankholm, H.P. (eds.) *Mesolithic Northwest Europe: Recent Trends*, 65–73. Sheffield.

Hind, D. 1998. Chert use in the Mesolithic of northern England. *Assemblage* 4. (http://www.shef.ac.uk/~assem/4/4hind.ht).

Hodder, I. 1982. *Symbols in Action: Ethnological Studies of Material Culture*. Cambridge.

Jacobi, R.M. 1973. Aspects of the "Mesolithic Age" in Great Britain. In: Kozlowski, S.K. (ed.) *The Mesolithic in Europe*, 237–265. Warsaw.

—— 1976. Britain inside and outside Mesolithic Europe. *Proceedings of the Prehistoric Society* 42, 67–84.

—— 1978. Northern England in the eighth millennium bc: an essay. In: Mellars, P. (ed.) *The Early Postglacial Settlement of Northern Europe*, 295–332. London.

—— 1979. Early Flandrian hunters in the South-West. *Proceedings of the Devon Archaeological Society* 37, 48–93.

—— 1987. Misanthropic miscellany: musings on British Early Flandrian archaeology and other flights of fancy. In: Rowley-Conwy, P., Zvelebil, M. and Blankholm, H.P. (eds.) *Mesolithic Northwest Europe: Recent Trends*, 163–168. Sheffield.

Jochim, M.A. 1998. *A Hunter-Gatherer Landscape: Southwest Germany in the Late Palaeolithic and Mesolithic*. New York.

Jones, S. 1997. *The Archaeology of Ethnicity*. London.

Lacaille, A.D. 1945. The stone industries associated with the raised beach at Ballantrae. *Proceedings of the Society of Antiquaries of Scotland* 79 (1944–45), 81–106.

—— 1954. *The Stone Age in Scotland*. London.

McCullagh, R.J. 1989. Excavation at Newton, Islay. *Glasgow Archaeological Journal* 15 (1988–89), 23–51.

Martingell, H. and Saville, A. 1988. *The Illustration of Lithic Artefacts: a Guide to Drawing Stone Tools for Specialist Reports*. Lithic Studies Society Occasional Paper 3/Association for Archaeological Illustrators and Surveyors Technical Paper 9. Northampton.

Mellars, P.A. 1970. An antler harpoon-head of 'Obanian' affinities from Whitburn, County Durham. *Archaeologia Aeliana* (4th series) 48, 337–346.

—— 1974. The Palaeolithic and Mesolithic. In: Renfrew, C. (ed.) *British Prehistory: a New Outline*, 41–99. London.

—— 1987. *Excavations on Oronsay: Prehistoric Human Ecology on a Small Island*. Edinburgh.

Mercer, J. 1970a. Flint tools from the present tidal zone, Lussa Bay, Isle of Jura, Argyll. *Proceedings of the Society of Antiquaries of Scotland* 102 (1969-70), 1-30.

—— 1970b. The microlithic succession in N. Jura, Argyll, W. Scotland. *Quaternaria* 13, 177-185.

—— 1974. Glenbatrick Waterhole, a microlithic site on the Isle of Jura. *Proceedings of the Society of Antiquaries of Scotland* 105 (1972-74), 9-32.

Mithen, S. 1995. Mesolithic settlement and raw material availability in the southern Hebrides. In: Fischer, A. (ed.) *Man and Sea in the Mesolithic*, 265-272. Oxbow Monograph 53. Oxford.

Mithen, S.J. and Lake, M. 1996. The Southern Hebrides Mesolithic Project. In: Pollard, T. and Morrison, A. (eds.) *The Early Prehistory of Scotland*, 123-151. Edinburgh.

Mithen, S.J., Finlayson, B., Finlay, N. and Lake, M. 1992. Excavations at Bolsay Farm, a Mesolithic settlement on Islay. *Cambridge Archaeological Journal* 2, No. 2, 242-253.

Morrison, A. 1980. *Early Man in Britain and Ireland*. London.

—— 1982. The Mesolithic period in south-west Scotland: a review of the evidence. *Glasgow Archaeological Journal* 9, 1-14.

Morrison, A. and Bonsall, C. 1989. The early post-glacial settlement of Scotland: a review. In: Bonsall, C. (ed.) *The Mesolithic in Europe*, 134-142. Edinburgh.

Movius, H.L. 1953. Curran Point, Larne, County Antrim: the type site of the Irish Mesolithic. *Proceedings of the Royal Irish Academy* 56,C, 1-195.

Mulholland, H. 1970. The microlithic industries of the Tweed Valley. *Transactions of the Dumfriesshire and Galloway Natural History and Antiquarian Society* 47, 81-110.

Myers, A.M. 1988. Scotland inside and outside of the British mainland Mesolithic. *Scottish Archaeological Review* 5, 23-29.

Newell, R.R., Kielman, D., Constandse-Westermann, T.S., Van der Sanden, W.A.B. and Van Gijn, A. 1990. *An Inquiry into the Ethnic Resolution of Mesolithic Regional Groups*. Leiden.

Radley, J. 1968. A Mesolithic structure at Sheldon, with a note on chert as a raw material on Mesolithic sites in the southern Pennines. *Derbyshire Archaeological Journal* 88, 26-36.

Radley, J. and Mellars, P. 1964. A Mesolithic structure at Deepcar, Yorkshire, England, and the affinities of its associated flint industries. *Proceedings of the Prehistoric Society* 30, 1-24.

Reynier, M.J. 1997. Radiocarbon dating of Early Mesolithic stone technologies from Great Briatin. In: Fagnart, J.-P. and Thévenin, A. (eds.) *Le Tardiglaciaire en Europe du Nord-Ouest*, 529-542. Paris.

—— 1998. Early Mesolithic settlement in England and Wales: some preliminary observations. In: Ashton, N., Healy, F. and Pettitt, P. (eds.) *Stone Age Archaeology: Essays in Honour of John Wymer*, 174-184. Oxbow Monograph 102/Lithic Studies Society Occasional Paper 6. Oxford.

Rozoy, J.-G. 1997. Territoires sociaux et environnement en France du Nord et en Belgique de 14000 à 6000 BP. In: Fagnart, J.-P. and Thévenin, A. (eds.) *Le Tardiglaciaire en Europe du Nord-Ouest*, 429-454. Paris.

Sampson, G.C. 1988. *Stylistic Boundaries among Mobile Hunter-Foragers*. Washington.

Saville, A. 1994a. Exploitation of lithic resources for stone tools in earlier prehistoric Scotland. In: Ashton, N. and David, A. (eds.) *Stories in Stone*, 57-70. Lithic Studies Society, Occasional Paper 4. London.

—— 1994b. A possible Mesolithic stone axehead from Scotland. *Lithics* 15, 25-28.

—— 1996. Lacaille, microliths, and the Mesolithic of Orkney. In: Pollard, T. and Morrison, A. (eds.) *The Early Prehistory of Scotland*, 213-224. Edinburgh.

—— 1998. Studying the Mesolithic period in Scotland: a bibliographic gazetteer. In: Ashton, N., Healy, F. and Pettitt, P. (eds.) *Stone Age Archaeology: Essays in Honour of John Wymer*, 211-224. Oxbow Monograph 102/Lithic Studies Society Occasional Paper 6. Oxford.

—— 1999. A cache of flint axeheads and other flint artefacts from Auchenhoan, near Campbeltown, Kintyre, Scotland. *Proceedings of the Prehistoric Society* 65, 83-123.

—— 2000. Orkney and Scotland before the Neolithic period. In: Ritchie, A. (ed.) *Neolithic Orkney in its European context*, 91-100. Cambridge.

Saville, A. and Miket, R. 1994. An Corran rock-shelter, Skye: a major new Mesolithic site. *Past* 18, 9-10.

Searight, S. 1984. The Mesolithic on Jura. *Current Archaeology* 90, 209-214.

Simpson, B. 1996. An analysis of the Mesolithic body ornament from the Scottish Western Isles. In: Pollard, T. and Morrison, A. (eds.) *The Early Prehistory of Scotland*, 237-251. Edinburgh.

Simpson, D. and Meighan, I. 1999. Pitchstone – a new trading material in Neolithic Ireland. *Archaeology Ireland* 48, 26-30.

Smith, A.G. and Collins, A.E.P. 1971. The stratigraphy, palynology and archaeology of diatomite deposits at Newferry, Co. Antrim, Northern Ireland. *Ulster Journal of Archaeology* 34, 3-25.

Spikins, P. 1999. *Mesolithic Northern England: Environment, Population and Settlement*. British Archaeological Reports, British Series 283. Oxford.

Spratt, D.A. 1993. The Upper Palaeolithic and Mesolithic periods. In: Spratt, D.A. (ed.) *Prehistoric and Roman Archaeology of North-East Yorkshire*, 51-67. Council for British Archaeology, Research Report 87. London.

Thévenin, A. 1998. Les grandes lignes du Mésolithique en France et dans les régions limitrophes. In: Conard, N.J. and Kind, C.-J. (eds.) *Aktuelle Forshungen zum Mesolithikum*, 1-14. Urgeschichtliche Materialhefte 12. Tübingen.

Thorpe, O.W. and Thorpe, R.S. 1984. The distribution and sources of archaeological pitchstone in Britain. *Journal of Archaeological Science* 11, 1-34.

Tilley, C. 1989. Interpreting material culture. In: Hodder, I. (ed.) *The Meanings of Things*, 185-194. One World Archaeology 6. London.

Trechmann, C.T. 1936. Mesolithic flints from the submerged forest at West Hartlepool. *Proceedings of the Prehistoric Society* 2, 161-168.

Vang Petersen, P. 1984. Chronological and regional variation in the Late Mesolithic of eastern Denmark. *Journal of Danish Archaeology* 3, 7-18.

Verhart, L.B.M. 1990. Stone Age bone and antler points as indicators for "social territories" in the European Mesolithic. In: Vermeersch, P.M. and Van Peer, P. (eds.) *Contributions to the Mesolithic in Europe*, 139-151. Leuven.

Weyman, J. 1984. The Mesolithic in north-east England. In: Miket, R. and Burgess, C. (eds.) *Between and Beyond the Walls: Essays on the Prehistory and History of North Britain in Honour of George Jobey*, 38-51. Edinburgh.

Wickham-Jones, C.R. 1986. The procurement and use of stone for flaked tools in prehistoric Scotland. *Proceedings of the Society of Antiquaries of Scotland* 116, 1-10.

—— 1990a. *Rhum: Mesolithic and Later Sites at Kinloch, Excavations 1984-86*. Society of Antiquaries of Scotland, Monograph 7. Edinburgh.

—— 1990b. The use of bloodstone on the Island of Rhum, Scotland, and beyond. In: Séronie-Vivien, M.-R. and Lenoir, M. (eds.) *Le Silex de sa Genèse à L'Outil*, 349-356. Paris.

Wickham-Jones, C.R. and Collins, G.H. 1978. The sources of flint and chert in northern Britain. *Proceedings of the Society of Antiquaries of Scotland* 109 (1977-78), 7-21.

Wickham-Jones, C.R. and Dalland, M. 1998. A small Mesolithic site at Craighead Golf Course, Fife Ness, Fife. *Tayside and Fife Archaeological Journal* 4, 1-19.

Wickham-Jones, C.R. and Woodman, P.C. 1998. Studies on the

early settlement of Scotland and Ireland. *Quaternary International* 49/50, 13–20.

Woodman, P.C. 1977. Recent excavations at Newferry, Co. Antrim. *Proceedings of the Prehistoric Society* 43, 155–199.

—— 1978. *The Mesolithic in Ireland*. BAR British Series 58. Oxford.

—— 1985. *Excavations at Mount Sandel 1973–77*. Northern Ireland Archaeological Monographs No. 2. Belfast.

—— 1989. A review of the Scottish Mesolithic: a plea for normality! *Proceedings of the Society of Antiquaries of Scotland* 119, 1–32.

—— 1992. Excavations at Mad Mans Window, Glenarm, Co. Antrim: problems of flint exploitation in east Antrim. *Proceedings of the Prehistoric Society* 58, 77–106.

—— 2000. Getting back to basics: transitions to farming in Ireland and Britain. In: Price, T.D. (ed.) *Europe's First Farmers*, 219–259. Cambridge.

Woodman, P.C. and Andersen, E. 1990. The Irish Later Mesolithic: a partial picture. In: Vermeersch, P.M. and Van Peer, P. (eds.) *Contributions to the Mesolithic in Europe*, 377–387. Leuven.

Wymer, J.J. (ed.) 1977. *Gazetteer of Mesolithic Sites in England and Wales*. Council for British Archaeology, Research Report 20. London.

Young, R. 1984. Potential sources of flint and chert in the north-east of England. *Lithics* 5, 3–9.

47. Early Mesolithic settlement patterns in Holmegårds Bog on South Zealand, Denmark. A social perspective

Henrik Schilling

The analysis of a large number of early Mesolithic sites in Holmegårds Bog shows a difference in settlement pattern between phase I and phase II–IV of the Maglemose culture. During the earliest phase (8750–7900 BC cal) only the northern part of the bog was exploited. The sites are small and structured in clusters. This pattern is similar to the settlement pattern in the Bromme culture more than 2000 years earlier. During the three following phases of the Maglemose culture (7900–6400 BC cal), a gradual intensification in the exploitation of Holmegårds Bog can be traced through time, as the number of sites in the bog increased dramatically (one settlement each 12 years on average to one each 1.3 years in later times). During this period sites spread to the whole area of the bog and a few sites became very large. The differences seen in the Maglemosian settlement patterns can also be traced to other bogs on Zealand, in Scania and northern Germany.

Natural causes as well as the nature of the landscape may explain some parts of this development, however a social explanation is more satisfying. Carbon isotopes suggest that the people who utilised the Holmegårds Bog lived in the inland year round and were part of an inland-based population. Holmegårds Bog was never permanently settled, but rather appears to have been one geographical element in the territory of a large social group. The large settlement complexes situated on the glacial deposits at the edge of the bog may be interpreted as winter base camps; the settlement complexes situated on the peat banks may be larger aggregation sites for social gatherings.

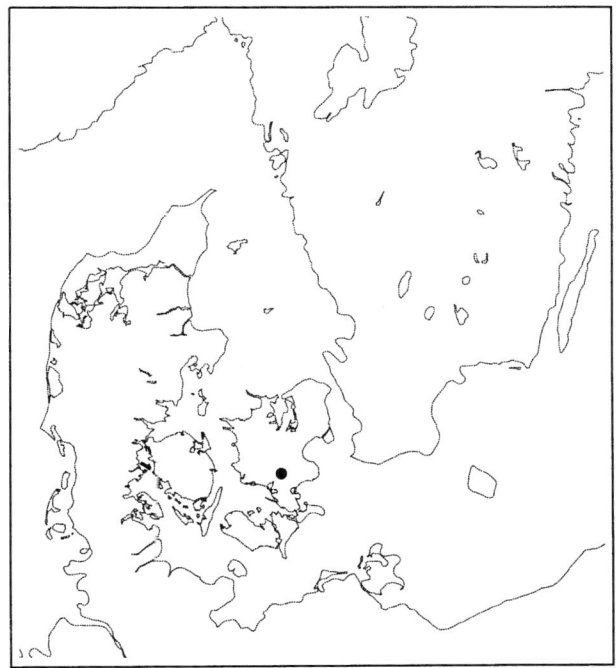

Figure 47.1 Map of Denmark showing Holmegårds Bog.

Introduction

Holmegårds Bog is situated on South Zealand, Denmark north of the city of Næstved (Figure 47.1) For almost a century the bog has been a laboratory for the study of late Paleolithic and early Mesolithic man in Denmark. From World War I until the 1950's the bog produced some very well preserved Maglemose sites of which Holmegård I, IV and V are considered classic examples (Broholm 1925; Becker 1945; Becker 1953).

Between the late 1950's and the late 1970's surveys were conducted that almost covered the total edge of the bog. Through systematic, extensive surface-collection, Anders Fischer, Bjarne Grønnow and Axel Johansson documented numerous late Paleolithic and Mesolithic sites from the glacial deposits around the edge of the bog (Fischer *et al.* 1978).

The excavated and surface collected data form the basis of the following analysis of the early Mesolithic settlement patterns of the Maglemose culture in Holmegårds Bog from 8750 to 6400 BC cal.

It should be stressed that the data is, in many ways, biased and the results are to be considered as a sketch rather than as a final study. Furthermore, the topic is still in many ways in a pioneer phase. This paper will not address the many problems facing further research, but it

Schilling 1999	Maglemose Phase	Calibrated years BC	Blade technology
I	Barmosegroup, Brinch Petersen M0	8750–7900 BC	Hard, direct percussion
II	Brinch Petersen M1-M2	7900–7200 BC	Direct, elastic percussion
III	Brinch Petersen M3	7200–6800 ? BC	Soft, indirect technique, conical microbladecores
IV	Brinch Petersen M4-M5	6800 ?–6400 BC	Soft, indirect pressuretechnique, handle cores

Figure 47.2 Chronology of the Maglemose culture.

will present some models that deserve testing and future consideration.

Holmegårds Bog – geology

Holmegårds Bog is a large complex of several basins comprising approximately 18 km^2 situated in a hilly landscape 30 m above sea level. The largest water course of Zealand, the Suså stream, runs through the bog. The bog complex is defined by two different geological formations. To the west the basins are large, deep kettle holes with steep sides, while the eastern and northern parts of the bog are shallow basins created by melt water.

The bog was once a large complex of lakes. Filling and overgrowing of the bog began in early post glacial times and ended in the early Atlantic about 5400 BC cal. In the late Atlantic, the area turned into a raised bog which existed until recently (Jessen 1925; Nilsson 1947; Andersen *et al.* 1984).

Unfortunately it is not possible to correlate the development of the settlement patterns with the changing shores of the former lakes in any detail. A general picture is, however, possible, and it shows elements of typical horizontal stratigraphy.

All sites from the late Paleolithic and the earliest phase of the Maglemose culture were situated at the edge of the bog on the firm glacial deposits. During the following phase of the Maglemosian, a few sites were situated on the peat. It is not until the last two phases of the Maglemose culture, however, that sites were generally situated on the peat. Man disappeared from Holmegårds Bog at about 6400 BC cal, more than 1000 years before the final closing of the bog. Settlements reappeared during the middle and late Ertebølle culture, and it is tempting to connect the reoccupation with the development of the raised bog during late Atlantic times.

The data

In total, 84 % of the sites are known only from extensive surface collections. The remainder are excavated or sifted sites, including the classic sites. Sites with more than two artefacts (135 sites), were included in the analysis and 109 sites date from the Maglemose culture. Though more than 25 000 artefacts were analysed, the material is very unevenly distributed. Sixty-five sites have less than ten artefacts and only eight sites have more than 1000 artefacts.

It is obviously not possible to perform any qualitative analysis on such a biased material. However, the data is suitable for quantitative analysis that provides a broad picture of the settlement patterns.

The data from the Maglemose culture was ordered in four different chronological phases based on a combination of blade technology and type fossils. Figure 47.2 shows how the relative chronology correlates with the established chronologies. At the moment the radiocarbon dates are too few to create a firm absolute chronology. The late Maglemose culture (phase III and IV) is especially difficult to date.

General picture

Without exception, all periods of the Danish Stone Age are represented in the Holmegårds Bog. However the utilisation of Holmegårds Bog shows three marked peaks (Figure 47.3). The first peak was during the late Paleolithic Bromme culture from about 11 500–10 500 BC cal. During the following Ahrensburg culture, the use of the area was very sporadic. The second and by far the largest settlement phase was during the Maglemose culture from 8750–6400 BC cal (Figure 47.3 Mag I – Mag IV). During the Kongemose and the early Ertebølle period from 6400–5000 BC cal man was almost absent from Holmegårds Bog. The third and last peak began around 5000 BC in the middle of the Ertebølle culture, continuing into the early Neolithic beyond 3900 BC.

The Maglemose settlement patterns in Holmegårds Bog

Phase I (8750–7900 BC cal)

Nineteen sites are known from phase I. These sites are concentrated in the northern most part of the bog (Figure

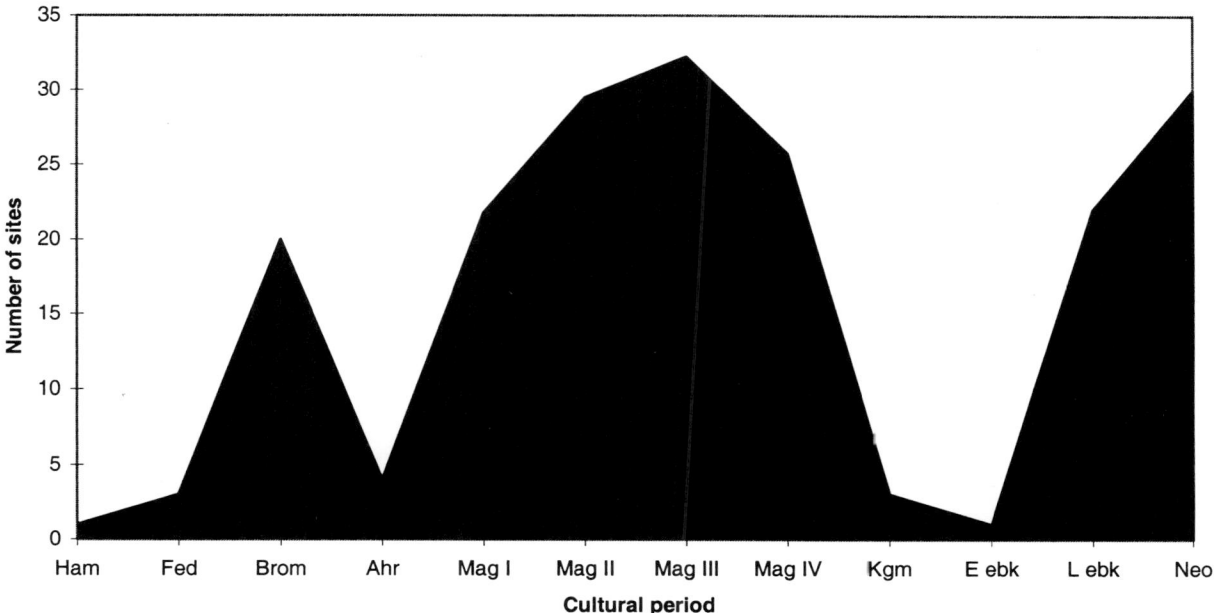

Figure 47.3 Distribution of sites according to date. Note the Maglemose culture Mag I–IV.

47.5) in an area where the former lake was shallow. The sites are situated on the glacial deposits at the edge of the bog or on small islands. All sites are quite small and the largest site (Nyskær 4) does not exceed 60 m. in diameter. Nyskær 4 was excavated by Anders Fischer who recorded 1700 artefacts.

The sites of this phase seem to reflect only one or a very few occupations at the same spot. The sites appear to be structured in clusters, very similar to the settlement pattern of the Bromme culture.

The distribution of sites from the Bromme culture illustrates this structural similarity (Figure 47.4). The Bromme sites show a very neat picture with four tight clusters of sites, similar to the clusters in Maglemose phase I. Excavated sites in Holmegårds Bog show that each Bromme site has from one to four different occupations more or less at the exact same spot (Johansson 1996). The Bromme settlement pattern shows, however, a different overall distribution in that the sites are concentrated in the southern parts of the bog.

Phase II (7900–7200 BC cal)

The settlement pattern changed dramatically in phase II (Figure 47.6). The 26 sites show a much more even distribution and settlements seem to cover much of the area. At least three sites grew very large. One of them is the well known site Holmegård V (Becker 1945; Fischer 1974). The largest site (Nyskær I) is 250 x 40 m. and has produced more than 1000 artefacts through surface collection alone (Johansson 1990).

Such large sites are termed settlement complexes. A settlement complex is a site that exceeds 100 meters and has produced more than 500 artefacts through surface collection. If excavated the total amount of artefacts must exceed 2000. The complexes reflect many occupations and later it will be argued that they may reflect several simultaneous occupations rather than materials accumulated from many small occupations through time.

Phase III (7200–6800? BC cal)

The settlement pattern of phase III is very similar to that of phase II (Figure 47.7). There are 27 sites which are mainly distributed in the western areas of the bog. This pattern may have been caused by the overgrowing of the shallow eastern and northern basins.

The number of designated settlement complexes increased to five during this period and they were situated both on the peat covered shores of the bog and on glacial deposits. Two close lying sites at Broksø are an example of the latter and are perhaps the largest Maglemose sites known on Zealand. Each site exceeds 250 x 100 meters and produced more than 5000 artefacts through surface collection alone.

Phase IV (6800?– 6400 BC cal)

The settlement pattern of phase IV is quite similar to that of phase II and is nearly identical to that of phase III (Figure 47.8). The 21 sites show an even, more markedly western distribution. There are five identifiable settlement complexes and like phase III they are situated both at the edge of the bog and on the peat covered shores of the former lakes. To some extent even the same locations produced complexes, as during phase IV. The largest

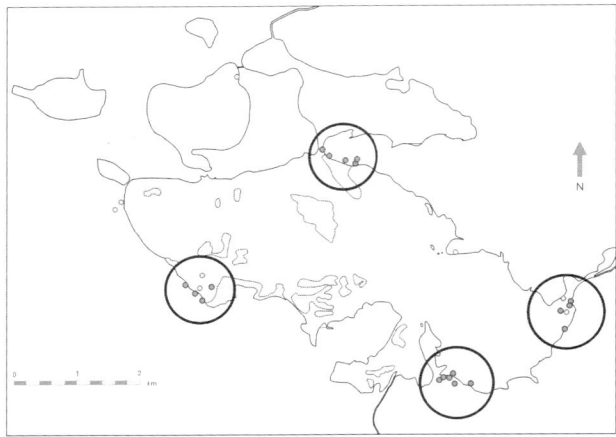

Figure 47.4 The settlement pattern of the Bromme Culture in Holmegårds Bog (11 500–10 500 BC calibrated).

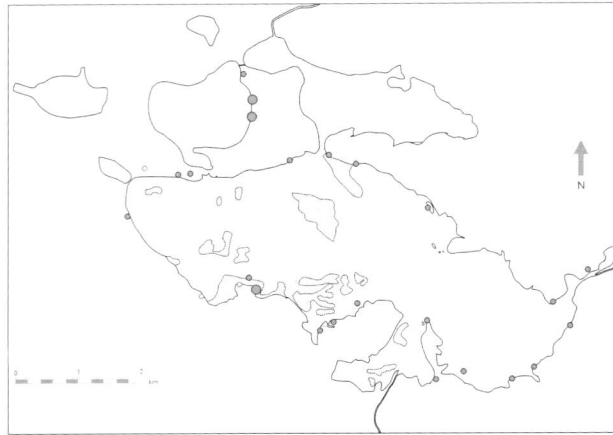

Figure 47.6 The settlement pattern of the Maglemose Culture phase II in Holmegårds Bog (7900–7200 BC calibrated).

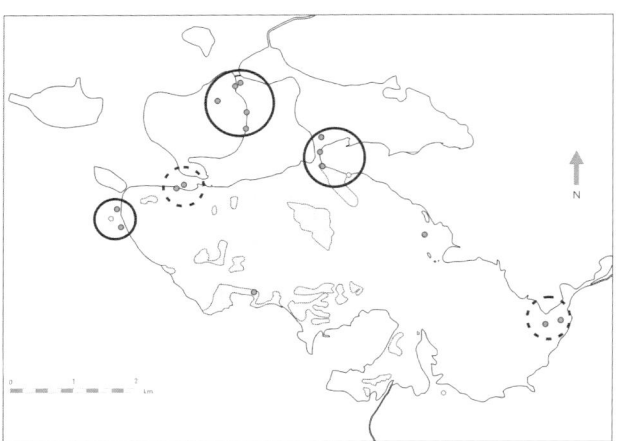

Figure 47.5 The settlement pattern of the Maglemose Culture phase I in Holmegårds Bog (8750–7900 BC calibrated).

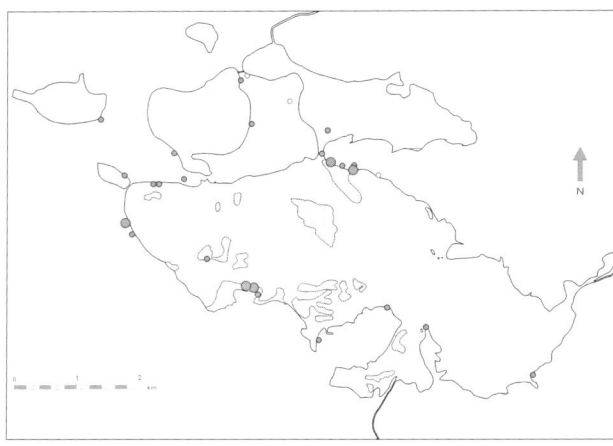

Figure 47.7 The settlement pattern of the Maglemose Culture phase III in Holmegårds Bog (7200–6800? BC calibrated).

settlement complex is Fensmark Skov which is 200 x 60 meters and produced 1600 artefacts through surface collection.

Conclusion

The analysis shows a clear difference between phase I the phases II–IV. All sites were relatively small in phase I and settlement complexes are unknown. During phase I the sites were distributed in clusters, while they were more evenly distributed during phase II–IV. The settlement pattern in phase I is more like the late Paleolithic Bromme culture than the later phases of the Maglemose culture.

Comparative analysis

The settlement patterns in Holmegårds Bog reflect a

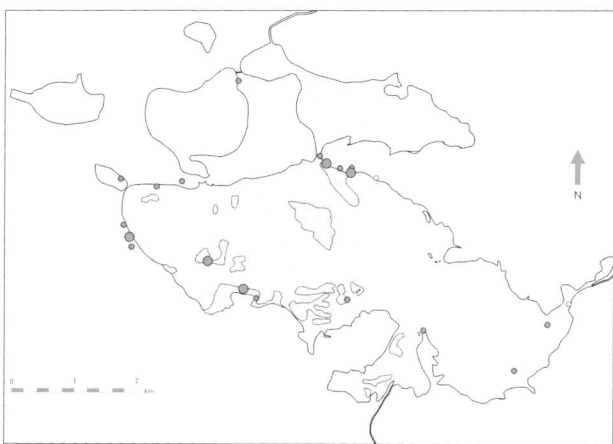

Figure 47.8 The settlement pattern of the Maglemose Culture phase IV in Holmegårds Bog (6800?–6400 BC calibrated).

general, early Mesolithic settlement pattern in south Scandinavia rather than just a local development. No Maglemose sites are known from phase I that can match the large settlement complexes of phase II–IV in Holmegårds Bog. Nothing comparable has been found, neither in Barmosen on South Zealand (Johansson 1990), Duvensee in north Germany (Bokelmann 1981), Draved Bog (Sobotta 1991) in South Jutland or at Bare Mosse in Scania (Welinder 1971). All of these bogs are all known for having intensive early Maglemosian settlement.

It is possible to find sites from phase I that are structured in clusters in the same way as those in the Holmegårds Bog. The best example is Barmosen on South Zealand, where the sites were clustered in the northeastern part of the bog in a restricted area (Johansson 1991). A similar pattern is also indicated in Sværdborg Bog (Schilling 1999).

It is possible to point out a number of large settlement complexes in south Scandinavia dating from phase II–IV. Mullerup on West Zealand, Denmark is a complex from phase II (Sarauw 1903). A site like Lundby II on South Zealand is very similar as well (Henriksen 1980). Sværdborg I (Henriksen 1976) and Lundby I on South Zealand (Henriksen 1980), Øgaarde in the Åmose (Mathiassen 1943) and Ageröd I in Scania (Larsson 1978) are settlement complexes from phase III and IV which either match or exceed the size of the settlement complexes from Holmegårds Bog during the same period. It is very important to notice that these complexes are from bogs with different histories and very different geological settings. This fact indicates that the development of settlement complexes was not primarily a product of a local geological development, and the large sites seem therefore to reflect more than just an adaptation to the local environment.

Interpretations

Thus, the question arises, what do the settlement patterns reflect and what caused the shift at the end of the first phase of the Maglemose culture? It has already been suggested here that the settlement patterns reflect an active population in charge of their own lives and destinies rather than a passive adaptation to environmental changes. The rest of this paper will argue in favour of this interpretation.

Landscape model

The similarity between phase I and the Bromme culture is interesting due to the way sites are structured in small clusters despite a difference of 2000 years in time and cultural discontinuity. On the other hand, it is also interesting that phase I is so different from phase II–IV despite both chronological continuity and continuity in material culture. It seems as if a Paleolithic way of life continued into the early Mesolithic. Unfortunately we have too few well excavated sites from phase I and no settlement sites with proper assemblages of faunal remains to evaluate this speculation.

The open forest landscape was a common feature for both the Bromme culture and phase I of the Maglemose culture, and the similarities may reflect the way hunter-gatherers in general exploited such an environment. The utilisation of the landscape seems to have been quite extensive during both periods.

It seemed that *how* to settle was the same between the Bromme and Maglemose, but that *where* to settle was different. The focus on the southern part of Holmegårds Bog during the late Paleolithic may be explained by the hunting of migrating reindeer (Jönsson 1983). The clusters of sites at both the inlet and outlet of the Suså stream are situated at typical geographical bottlenecks for migrating reindeer. The focus on the northern part of Holmegårds Bog during phase I of the Maglemose culture may be explained by an economy concentrated on fishing pike in the shallow waters in the springtime, a time when pike are abundant in these kind of places.

Calculations of the intensity in settlement suggest an increase in the number of occupations during the Maglemose culture. Such calculations are dangerous, and must be considered in light of the intensity of occupation at each site, the visibility and the duration of the different periods, and the potential number of undiscovered sites. Therefore the calculations must be considered as only rough estimates.

During the Bromme culture and phase I of the Maglemose culture, the size of occupation approximately was that of one single family occupation every 12 years. In phase II it increased to one occupation every 4 years, and during phase III and IV it increased to one occupation every 1.3 and 1.4 years.

Phase I clearly shows the fewest and smallest sites. However, the sites are most visible in phase I due to the limited influence of horizontal stratigraphy. Because of the same reason, phases III and IV may in fact be underrepresented because the peat areas have not been surveyed as intensively as the edges of the bog. Future research is therefore more likely to enhance this perceived difference in settlement intensity, rather than reduce it and therefore the suggested increase in settlement intensity seems real. Even though the calculations have tried to squeeze in as many people as possible, the settlement intensity was relatively low even at its highest level.

The increasing number of settlements during later phases could also be explained as a product of the development of the landscape. The early Mesolithic covers the Preboreal, Boreal and early Atlantic times. During these 3000 years the landscape changed rapidly. The forest became more dense, lakes filled in and sea level changes reduced the land area by two-thirds. This had a negative impact on the amount of resources and their availability. The overgrowing of lakes meant fewer good spots to settle near water, and settlements concentrated on fewer locations, hence the emergence of large complexes. This

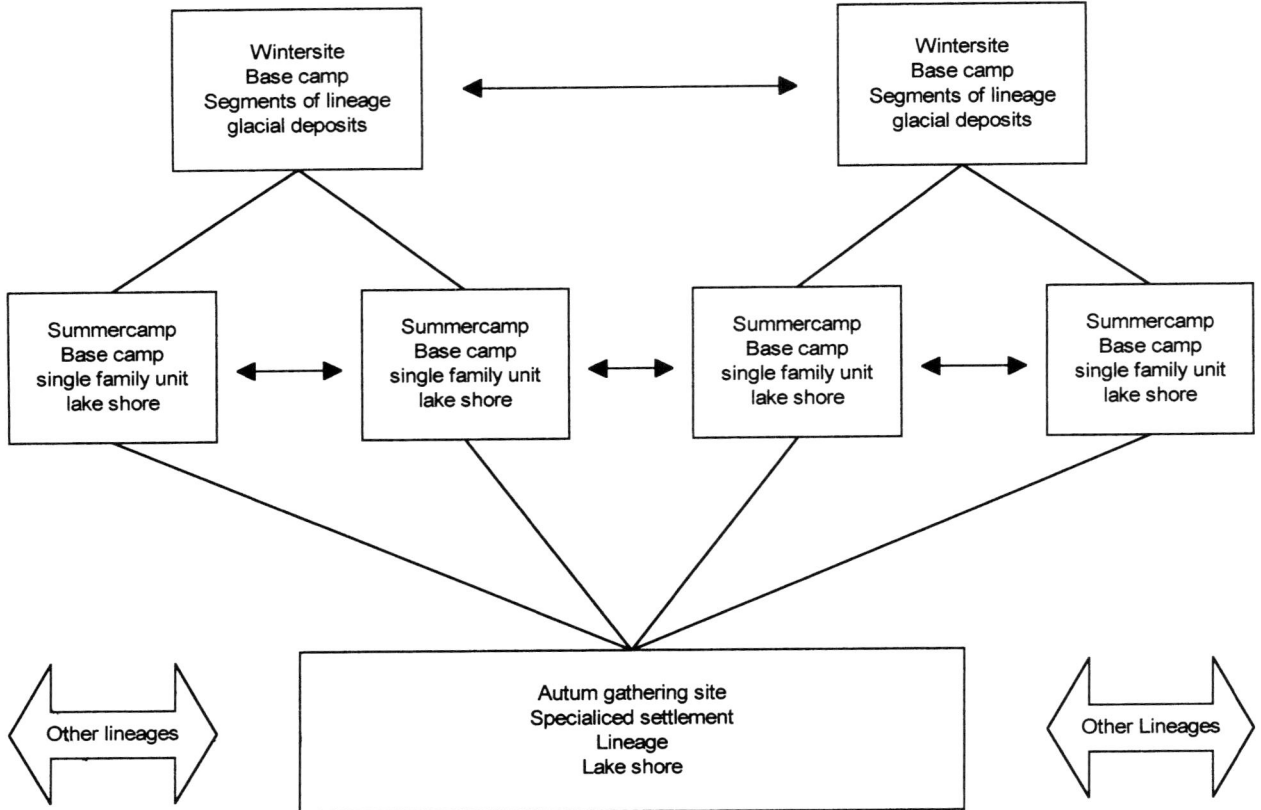

Figure 47.9 Model of the settlement concept of the Maglemose Culture phase II–IV.

may lead to the incorrect conclusion of a Maglemose inland population under pressure and a system on its way to a collapse. Some may also interpret this pattern as leading to the emergence of a coastal adaption at the end of the Maglemose culture, an adaptation that later evolved into the well known marine-adapted Kongemose and Ertebølle cultures.

Social model

Though it is possible to explain the settlement pattern as an adaption to environmental change, it is argued here that this is not necessarily the best explanation. One should not exclude the significance of the environment as a factor, but it is possible to explain the same data more sufficiently and completely through a social perspective.

There has been a considerable amount of debate regarding the use and limitations of carbon isotopes as an accurate indicator of prehistoric diets (Fischer this volume). If the method is accepted as accurate and unbiased, it therefore seems possible to get an idea of the general settlement pattern. The ^{13}C values of Danish Maglemose humans and dogs varies between $-25,22^{0/00}$ and $-14,7^{0/00}$ PDB. From the Holmegård Bog three ^{13}C values are known, they vary between -18 and $-19,5^{0/00}$ PDB. The isotope values from Holmegård cover Phase II–IV of the Maglemose culture.

The Radiocarbon Institute in Copenhagen recently changed the standard of fully terrestrial food intake from $-17^{0/00}$ PDB to $-19,8^{0/00}$. Following this, marine resources cannot be totally excluded from the early Mesolithic diet on Zealand. However, the ^{13}C values are far removed from the level of the marine adapted Ertebølle culture and it has turned out that aquatic food intake will pull the isotope values towards the marine spectrum (Day 1996). It is therefore possible that the people who settled in Holmegårds Bog lived in the inland area all year round, like much of the Maglemose population on central Zealand.

During the early part of the Maglemose period the coast was more than 100 kilometres distant as the crow flies. The sea transgressed the Great Belt area ca. 7200 BC cal, but the dog from Holmegård I shows an isotope value of $-18^{0/00}$ and dates from about 6500 BC cal. Although the sea and its rich resources was less than 40 kilometres away, people maintained an inland lifestyle for centuries, staying far below the carrying capacity of the land. The differences between phase I and phase II–IV in regards to site size, their location and the overall structuring of the settlement patterns reflect a changing social and cultural concept of settlement and not simply changes in environment.

It is not as yet possible to describe the settlement concept of phase I, so we must make due with the phase II–IV settlement concept (Figure 47.9).

The large settlement complexes may reflect winter base camps or late summer/early autumn gathering sites, depending on their location and inventories. The old theory that it is not possible to occupy the peat-covered shores of the lakes during wintertime because of a raised water table is supported by the seasonal indicators in the fauna remains on peat covered sites.

Becker (1953) and Fischer (1974) have suggested that Holmegård V was a winter camp. The site is located on the well-drained glacial deposits. The nearly total lack of fish spears may indicate a winter occupation. Pike was a mainstay of early Mesolithic man, but is out of reach of a fish spear during winter.

The tool inventory from Holmegård V consists of scrapers, burins, knifes, arrows, *etc.*, reflecting many different activities (Schilling 1999). Holmegård V may be the home of a group of families during the winter in phase II. Other settlement complexes situated like Holmegård V are known from both phases III and IV. Unfortunately they are only known through surface collection, thus reducing the reliability of their inventories.

The settlement complexes located on the peat covered shores of the former lakes in Holmegårds Bog have inventories very different from those of Holmegård V and are almost totally dominated by microliths. Excavated sites include Holmegård I, II and IV. Sites from other bogs like the Sværdborg I site show the same attributes. The sites reveal a dominance on hunting and may simply be accumulations reflecting centuries of hunting trips. The sites are huge though, and many also contain rare objects like ornamented bone artefacts and other exotica. These sites are therefore more likely be the social gathering sites of the Maglemose culture and housed large congregations in the late summer and early autumn when hazelnuts and game were plentiful. People were probably occupied by feasting, not working, which would explain the lack of scrapers, burins *etc.* The inventories show that hunting and meat played a major role, perhaps reflecting male social activities.

During the spring and early summer people split up into family groups and lived fairly isolated lifestyles. Numerous sites reflecting a single family occupation during spring and summer are known from phase II–IV in Holmegårds Bog. Holmegård VI is a particularly good example of this. In the Åmose Bog the famous Ulkestrup huts likely reflect the same phenomenon.

Territory and social groupings

A remaining question pertains to the size of the social grouping and the size of the territory. The analysis show that even at the height of settlement, Holmegårds Bog was only visited sporadically. It was never the fixed territory of a single, large social group. Instead the bog was part of a much larger settlement range. The carbon isotopes suggest that classic areas like the Åmose Bog and the Køng-Lundby-Sværdborg Bog were part of this

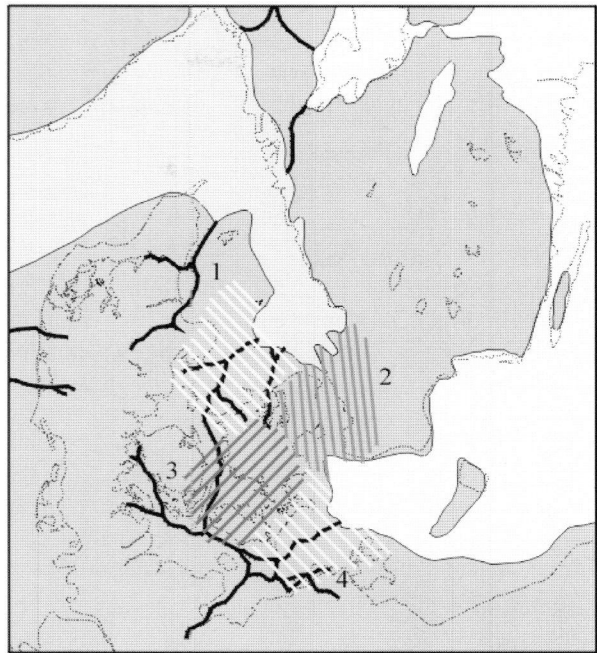

Figure 47.10 Possible social groupings in East Denmark during phase II–IV of the Maglemose culture.
1: Great Belt coastal group including Mullerup
2: Øresund coastal group including Køge Sønakke.
3: Central Zealand inland group includning Holmegårds Bog, Åmose Bog and Køng-Lundby-Sværdborg Bog.
4: Ancylus lake group. Still hypothetical.

same settlement system. Scholars have always focused on the classic areas but the central part of Zealand is rich in lakes and other bogs not yet researched. The central parts of Zealand could easily support a fairly large social group. This group could be an independent tribe, but it is more likely that the group was part of an even larger social network. Lacking a better word it could be termed a lineage and the population of most of eastern Denmark was possibly knit together in one related social unit.

The isotope values from Mullerup of $-16,5^{0/00}$ and from Køge Sønakke at $-14,7^{0/00}$ show a certain level of marine food intake. Both skeletons were found closer to the sea than the other early Mesolithic skeletons from central Zealand and may reflect other social groups/lineages within the tribe who lived closer to the sea and focused on a more mixed economy (Figure 47.10).

Objects of marine origin are known from several of the large inland settlement complexes. On Ageröd I and Sværdborg I seal bones were recovered (Larsson 1978). A deep sea mussel, *Cyprina islandica,* was found at Lundby II, and was probably used as a pendant (Hansen 1995). Amber is known from many Maglemose sites and was probably imported from coastal areas where it is easily found.

These indicators of coastal activity suggest that contacts may have been frequent with the neighbouring lineages of the tribe. People from the coastal area may have paid visits to their tribesmen, exchanging amber and exotica. If the lineages practised exogamy, the arrangement of marriages was a very obvious reason for occasional visits and was in addition an obvious way to circulate goods.

Conclusion

This paper has presented a very general view of the Maglemose settlement patterns in the Holmegårds Bog and has highlighted some clear differences within the Maglemose culture. On the basis of a large quantitative set of data from the Holmegårds Bog, it is possible to argue for the year round population of central parts of eastern Denmark, as well as to discern possible social groupings in eastern Denmark. This paper has argued that there can be little doubt that the settlement patterns in the Holmegårds Bog identified here reflect social configurations and not simply multiple adaptations to environmental changes.

References

Andersen, S.T., Aaby, B. and Odgaard, B. Vad 1984. Environment and Man. Current Studies in vegetational History at the Geological Survey of Denmark. *Journal of Danish Archaeology* 2, 184–196.

Becker, C.J. 1945. En 8000 årig stenalderboplads i Holmegårds mose. Foreløbig meddelelse. *Fra Nationalmuseets Arbejdsmark 1945*, 60–72.

—— 1953. Die Maglemosekultur in Dänemark. Neue Funde und Ergebnisse. *Congres Intern. des Sciences Prehistoire et Protohistoire; Actes de la III Session*, 180–183. Zürich.

Bokelmann, K. 1981. Neue Aspekte zur Sammelwirtschaft im frühen Mesolithicum. *Offa* 38, 21–40.

Broholm, H.C. 1925. Nye fund fra den ældste stenalder. Holmegård og Sværdborg fundene. *Årbøger for nordisk Oldkyndighed og Historie 1924*, 1–144.

Day, S.P. 1996. Dogs, Deer and Diet at Star Carr: a Reconsideration C-isotope Evidence from Early Mesolithic Dog Remains from the Vale of Pickering, Yorkshire, England. *Journal of Archaeological Science* 23, 783–787.

Fischer, A. 1974. An ornamented flintcore from Holmegaard V, Zealand, Denmark. *Acta Archaeologica* 45, 155–168.

Fischer, A., Grønnow, B. and Petersen, C. 1978. En bosættelses arkæologisk undersøgelse ved Holmegårds Mose – et projektoplæg. *Kontaktstencil 15*, 45–48. Umeå.

Hansen, K. Møller. 1995. Maglemosebopladsen Lundby II – Ny undersøgelse. *Kulturhistoriske Studier*. Vordingborg.

Henriksen, B. Bille. 1976. *Sværdborg I Excavations 1943–44. A settlement of the Maglemose culture*. Arkæologiske studier III. Copenhagen.

—— 1980. *Lundby-holmen*. Nordiske Fortidsminder 6. Copenhagen.

Jessen, K. 1925. De geologiske forhold ved de to nye bopladser i Holmegaards Mose. In: Broholm, H.C. (ed.) *Nye fund fra den ældste stenalder. Holmegaard og Sværdborg fundene. Årbøger for Nordisk Oldkyndighed og Historie 1924*, 14–28. Copenhagen.

Johansson, A.D. 1990. *Barmosegruppen. Præboreale bopladsfund i Sydsjælland*. Århus.

—— 1996. A Base Camp and Kill Sites from the Bromme culture on South Zealand, Denmark. In: Larsson, L. (ed.) *The earliest Settlement of Scandinavia, and its relationship with neighbouring areas*, 87–97. Acta Archaeologica Lundensia series in 8, no 24. Stockholm.

Jønsson, J.H. 1983. *Stoksbjerg Bro. En senpalæolitisk boplads i Porsmose-Holmegårds Mose, Sydsjælland*. Unpublished manuscript.

Larsson, L. 1978. *Ageröd I:B, Ageröd I:D. A study of Early Atlantic Settlement in Scania*. Acta Archaeologica. Lundensia ser. 4 in quarto, No. 12. Stockholm.

Mathiassen, T. 1943. *Stenalderbopladser i Åmosen*. Nordiske Fortidsminder III, h.3. Copenhagen.

Nilsson, T. 1947. A Pollen-Analytical Investigation in Holmegårds Bog with Considerations as to the Age of the Dwelling-Places of the Maglemosian Period in Denmark and surrounding Areas. *Dansk Geologisk Forenings Meddelelser* Nr. 11, 201–217.

Sarauw, G. 1903. En stenalderboplads i Maglemose ved Mullerup, sammenholdt med beslægtede fund. Bidrag til belysning af Nystenalderens begyndese i Norden. *Årbøger for Nordisk Oldkyndighed og Historie*, 148–315.

Schilling, H. 1999. *Maglemosekulturens bosættelsesmønstre i Holmegårds Mose – Miljøets diktat eller kulturelle valg*. Unpublished master thesis. University of Copenhagen.

Sobotta, J. 1991. Frühmesolitische Wohnplätze aus Draved Moor, Dänemark. *Archaeologisches Korrespondenzblatt* 21, 457–467.

Welinder, S. 1971. *Tidig postglacialt mesoliticum i Skåne*. Acta Archaeologica Lundensia. Series in 8^0 Minore N^0 1. Lund.

48. The Mesolithic in the Cantabrian Interior: Fact or Fantasy?

Lawrence Guy Straus and Manuel González Morales

Ever since the research of the Conde de la Vega del Sella at the beginning of the 20th century, it had appeared that the Mesolithic occupation of the Cantabrian region of northern Spain was confined to the narrow coastal strip and that the densely wooded montane interior had been abandoned by humans after the Azilian. Recent work (e.g., El Mirón and Los Canes Caves) indicates, however, that although sporadic and low in frequency, there were some incursions into and uses of the interior. Some of this occurred in the Preboreal, but especially late in the Boreal and early Atlantic phases, after which Neolithic sites begin to appear in the record. The exact nature of the relationship between Mesolithic and Neolithic systems in the period between c. 6000–5500 BP remains to be definitively clarified, although it seems that there was a fairly long period (at least several centuries) of contemporaneity between Neolithic occupations of the upper Ebro River Basin in Navarra and Alava and Mesolithic ones along the Atlantic facade of the Cantabrian Cordillera.

Introduction

The authors of this paper have in the past disagreed about the issue of early Holocene human occupation of the montane interior of Cantabrian Spain and have decided to explore the present state of our knowlege of Mesolithic settlement, its terminal Paleolithic precedents and Neolithic successors in this region, particularly in light of our ongoing excavation of El Mirón cave and other recent developments in research concerning the period between c. 10,000–6000 BP (all dates are given here in uncalibrated radiocarbon years) in north-central Iberia. In 1979, following the ideas of the late David Clarke (1976), Straus (see also Straus and Clark 1986; Straus 1991a; Clark 1995), among other things, suggested that the Asturian coastal midden sites of eastern Asturias and western Cantabria may have partly overlapped in time and been functionally complementary with late Azilian sites in the mountainous hinterland (i.e. foci mainly on mollusc collection and fishing versus hunting). Subsequent increases in carefully excavated and radiocarbon dated sites permitted González Morales (1989, 1992, 1995) to convincingly argue that the Azilian *sensu stricto* ended at just about the same time that the Asturian *conchero* phenomenon began, i.e. c. 9300 BP. Given Straus' acceptance of this fact, the purpose of this paper is to explore the question as to what (if anything) was going on by way of human occupation in the non-coastal parts of Vasco-Cantabria and how this may (or may not) relate to the (late) appearance of Neolithic technologies and subsistence in this sector of the Atlantic facade of Western Europe. This is related to the broader problem of human settlement of the Old Castilian uplands and upper Ebro basin during the terminal Pleistocene and early Holocene. The overall issue, of course, is that of the relative suitability of different biotopes for Mesolithic (i.e. foraging) versus Neolithic (i.e. farming and herding) types of adaptations.

The Cantabrian region, located between c. 2–6° W and 43°– 43°30' N, is a narrow coastal strip between the Bay of Biscay/Cantabrian Sea shore and the Cantabrian Cordillera/Picos de Europa (Figure 48.1). It is some 300 km long on the east-west axis from the western end of the Pyrenees to the Río Nalón, where there is a major lithological change to the Galician shieldrock, no more than 25–50 km wide. Summits along the Cordillera generally rise from east to west from c. 1100 m to 2600 m (the latter elevations being in the Picos de Europa, only c. 25 km from the present shore). The coast is steep, with a very narrow continental shelf, so the present shore was essentially established by early Holocene times. Administratively the area is divided from east to west among the two coastal Basque provinces of Guipżcoa and Vizcaya and the uniprovincial autonomous regions of Cantabria (formerly Santander) and Asturias. To the south of the Cordillera, the first two provinces are abutted by Alava – the third province of the Basque autonomous region (Euskadi) – and the separate Navarra region, much of both of which are in the upper Ebro valley, with elevations of no more than 400–600 m.a.s.l. In contrast, Cantabria and Asturias are adjoined by the northern meseta of Burgos, Palencia and León, which is generally

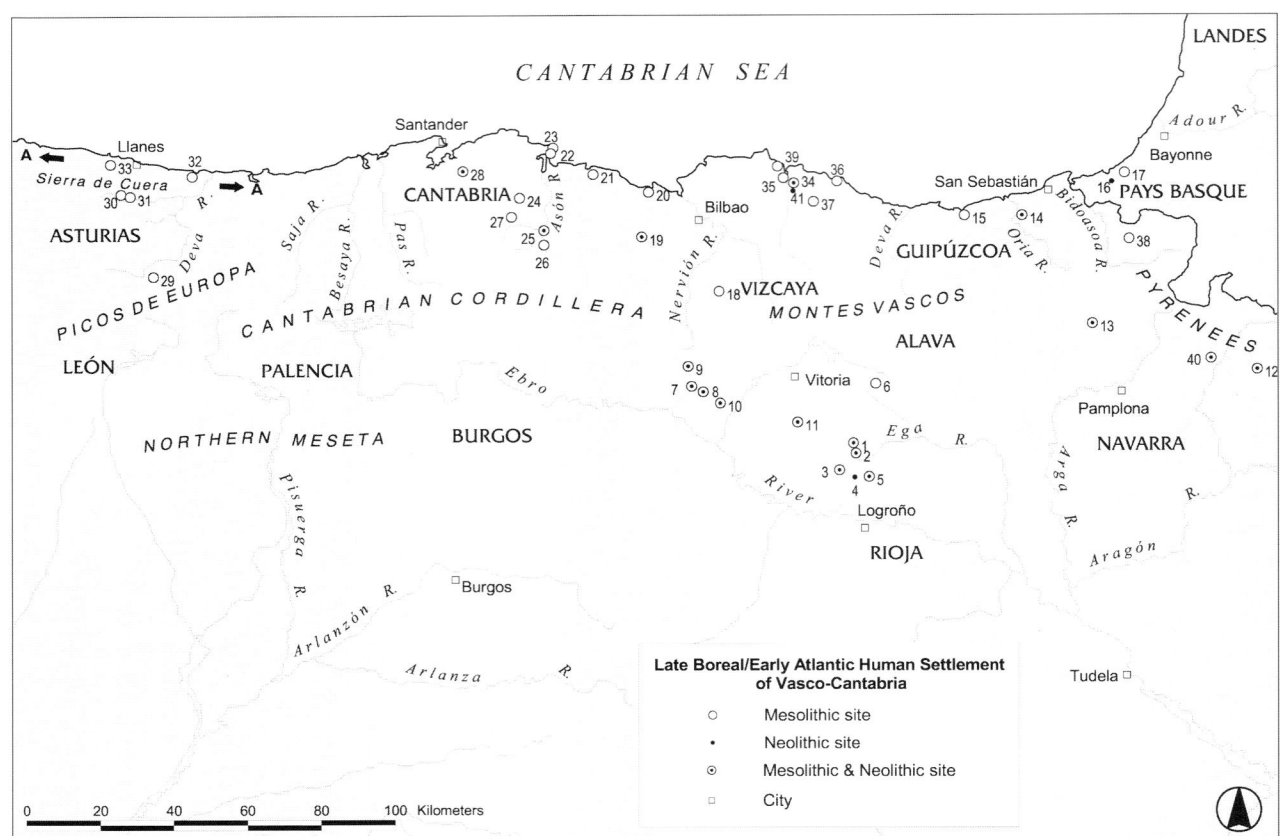

Figure 48.1 Human settlement of Asturias, Cantabria, Euskadi and Navarra during the Boreal and early middle Atlantic Phases. M=Mesolithic, N=Neolithic, A—A=main concentration of Asturian concheros.

1) Atxoste Kanpanoste M+N), 2) Kanpanoste Goikoa (M+N), 3) Montico de Charratu (M+N), 4) Peña Larga (N), 5) La Peña de Marañón (M+N), 6) Kukuma (M), 7) Socuevas (M+N), 8) Fuente Hoz (M+N), 9) Berniollo (M+N), 10) La Renke (M+N), 11) Mendandia (M+N), 12) Zatoya (M+N), 13) Abauntz (M+N), 14) Marizulo (M+N), 15) Herriko Barra (M), 16) Mouligna (N), 17) Moura (M), 18) Urratxa (M), 19) Arenaza (M+N), 20) Pico Ramos (M), 21) La Trecha (M), 22) La Fragua (M), 23) El Perro (M), 24) La Chora (M), 25) El Mirón (M+N), 26) Tarrerón and Las pajucas (M), 27) Cubio Redondo (M), 28) La Garma (M+N), 29) La Calvera (M), 30) Los Canes (M), 31) Arangas (M), 32) Mazaculos (M), 33) La Riera (M), 34) Santimamiñe (M+N), 35) Atxeta (M), 36) Lumentxa (M), 37) Kobeaga (M), 38) Berroberria (M), 39) Pareko Landa (M), 40 Aizpea (M+N) and 41) Kobaederra (N).

c. 1000 m high and mainly drained by the Duero. The coastal region normally has mild, equable temperatures (annual average: c. 14°C) and high precipitation (1000–1400 mm), mostly in form of rain, with snow generally restricted to the mountains. The meseta is much colder and drier. The Ebro Basin has a distinctly Mediterranean climatic regimen and biotic environment. The ecological boundry between the Atlantic coastal and respectively the mesetan or Ebro Mediterranean worlds is very sharply defined at the Cordilleran passes.

Terminal Paleolithic Precedents

During the Last Glacial Maximum, the Iberian Peninsula, along with southern France, was the refugium for human populations whose range had contracted drastically with the abandonment of NW Europe down to the latitude of the Loire (Straus 1991b). Solutrean settlement in Spain and Portugal was mainly concentrated in the coastal peripheries of the Peninsula (Straus 1991c), but there is now credible evidence (perhaps a half-dozen sites) for at least visits to and/or minor occupations of some areas in the interior (notably in Guadalajara, Madrid and Beira Alta, near the Portugal-Spain border), despite the cold conditions which existed on the mesetas, as well as the presence of glaciers on most of the mountain chains of the Peninsula from the Pyrenees and Cantabrian Cordillera south to the Sierra Nevada in Andalucía (Straus *et al.* 2000a, 2000b). Specifically concerning the Cantabrian region, there are few Solutrean sites in montane contexts, but they do exist: Bolinkoba (Sierra de Amboto, Vizcaya) and El Mirón (Sierra del Hornijo, Cantabria). And there are 3–4 Solutrean sites south of the Cordillera in the upper Ebro drainage of Navarra (Utrilla and Mazo 1994).

However, it was under the generally warming climates of the Tardiglacial that there was a marked movement (or "reconquest", to use the term that the late Louis Méroc applied to the Magdalenian of the Pyrenees) into the uplands, both in the Cantabrian Cordillera and in the mesetas of northern and central Spain (Straus *et al.* 2000a, 2000b). In the Magdalenian the evidence consists of numerous dated living sites in montane habitat along the north face of the Cordilleran crest, coupled with several cave art sites of probable Magdalenian age and a few living sites, notably La Dehesa in Salamanca (Fabián 1997) on the northern meseta (see Cacho and Pérez 1997 with references). The situation gets clearer in the latter region during the Epipaleolithic Azilian period, with several definite or probable sites in Burgos and León (see Corchón 1989; Bernaldo de Quirós and Neira 1996), in addition to the numerous Azilian sites up the valleys and on the steep northern slopes of the Cordillera, even in the Picos de Europa (Arias 1999; Díez 1999). Although the human population of the Cordillera or northern meseta was never as relatively dense as it was near or along the Cantabrian shore, it did become more significant (and thus quite visible archeologically) in the closing centuries of the Last Glacial and first centuries of the Postglacial.

Across that time, vegetational conditions were (presumably) still relatively open, but with increasing stands of pine, birch and ultimately, a mixed oak-associated deciduous tree communities, depending on the particular phase, elevation and habitat (see Dupré 1988; Watts 1986; Turner and Hannon 1988, all with references). The Tardiglacial and initial Holocene (i.e. Dryas I and Preboreal) constituted a time of rapid and profound environmental change, with correspondingly significant changes in human adaptations. The strategies for survival increasingly included fishing, shell-fishing, plant-gathering and the hunting of small, swift and/or dangerous game (i.e. roe deer, ibex, chamois, boar in addition to the standard red deer). Some coastal Azilian sites, e.g. La Riera in eastern Asturias (Straus and Clark 1986), in addition to having the characteristic flat-section antler harpoons and fish remains, also contain abundant marine molluscs, while others further inland, e.g. El Piélago in Cantabria (Garcia Guinea 1985) are similarly rich in landsnails. In Iberia, the harpoons are restricted to sites in the Cantabrian region, but similar non-geometric microlithic industries are found in mesetan sites, as well as, more generally, in Portugal and Mediterranean Spain (Bicho 1993; Aura and Pérez 1995).

The Vasco-Cantabrian Mesolithic

Following the Pre-boreal, the dense mixed deciduous forest, especially including oaks and hazel, took over the landscapes of north Atlantic Spain, under temperate, humid climatic conditions in the Boreal (see summary of vegetational evidence in González Morales 1982). Temperatures were even higher in the Atlantic period, coinciding with the Flandrian transgression *c.* 6000 BP, but with a continuation of the mixed deciduous forest (see Fano 1998). The coastal hills and lower mountainous terrain was densely forested with oaks, elm, lime and ash, while the high mountain slopes (especially the eastern Pyrenees) had more pine and birch (Zapata and Meaza 1998). It is likely that there were few clearings and that the ocean shore and the banks of the larger rivers, as well as rock cliffs, represented the only natural openings in the forest. New marshes were being created in inlets and along the estuaries of rivers, especially during the Flandrian. What was the nature of human settlement under these conditions?

First of all, there may be significant problems of archeological representativeness in a period of relatively high temperatures. Caves may not have been so generally used as occupation sites as they had been during the Last Glacial, there may have been many open-air Mesolithic sites, yet these are not present in the archeological record. Either these sites were swept away by subsequent erosion on the region's many steep slopes, especially as a result of the anthropic deforestation that first occured in the Neolithic, accelerated in the Chalcolithic (e.g. Zapata and Peña 1998) and was repeated in following millennia, such as in the 18th century, or they are deeply buried under colluvium and alluvium in the valley bottoms. The presence of a few open-air Asturian sites is suggested by the presence of cobble picks at a few coastal locations (e.g. Clark 1976,1983; Díez 1999), but is contested in terms of the specifics of some cases, e.g. Liencres (González Morales 1982). Other kinds of open-air sites of likely Mesolithic age are virtually absent, so if some or many of the Asturian *conchero* cave sites were in fact cold season occupations, we could be missing at least part of the warm season component or "pose" as a result of differential preservation and/or visibility.

Seasonality evidence related to this issue is both limited and seemingly contradictory: M. Deith's oxygen isotope analyses of marine shells (Deith 1983; Deith and Shackleton 1986; M. Deith unpublished data cited in González Morales 1995:75) show only cold season (notably winter) collection of molluscs at La Riera, Mazaculos and several other Asturian sites in eastern Asturias. On the other hand, mammalian faunal analyses by J. Altuna and K. Mariezkurrena (cited by González Morales 1995:75) for Mazaculos show that some young individuals of several species were killed in late spring/summer. (The mammalian evidence from La Riera is of scant utility: one red deer fawn was killed in spring and another in winter, see Altuna 1986:268). The interpretation preferred, especially by González Morales, is that people occupied the coastal zone year-round, concentrating their shellfishing in the cold months, perhaps when other food resources were scarce (e.g. plants) or in poor condition (e.g. game animals). But this would not preclude the existence of Asturian-age "expeditions" (e.g. logistical hunting parties or even residential moves in summer or other seasons) into the Cantabrian interior.

The Asturian phenomenon is characterised by a completely unprecedented density of sites. As of the mid 1980's there was a known total of 77 Asturian sites over the full geographic range of the "culture" (i.e. a 180 km stretch of coast between the cities of Avilés in central Asturias and Santander in central Cantabria (Clark and Straus 1986:362), but a recent, detailed study (Fano 1998) of the distribution of *concheros* just in the eastern most (cultural core) area of Asturias between the Bedón and Deva rivers (a 35 km long stretch of coast) enumerated 81 sites (only two of which are barely further than 4 km from the shore). Asturian sites, with their characteristic *concheros* and cobble picks, but otherwise impoverished artifact assemblages, date between 9300–6500 BP uncalibrated (i.e. Boreal and earliest Atlantic).

In central Cantabria, near the present day Bay of Santander, recent excavations in La Garma Cave A have produced evidence of a major shellmidden with a miniature cobble pick and several AMS dates between 7700–6900 BP (Arias *et al.* 1997,1999a). Further east, the evidence is less abundant, but recent research has been adding notably to the extant record of non-Asturian Mesolithic age sites on or near the coast of eastern Cantabria, notably González Morales' (e.g. 1990,1995, 1999) Lower Río Asón Project (El Perro, La Fragua and La Trecha sites, with dates for Mesolithic materials spanning the period between 9300–5500 BP). Shell-middens first with Azilian artifacts and later with scant, banal artifacts, but without Asturian cobble picks, range across the Pleistocene-Holocene boundary and the first four millennia of the Holocene. Coastal Mesolithic sites are even more scarce in the Spanish Basque Country. The most significant coastal site in Euskadi, Santimamiñe near Guernica, was unfortunately excavated early in the 20th century and remains radiometrically undated. Other minor, possibly Mesolithic components near the Vizcayan shore include Atxeta, Kobeaga and Lumentxa, all poorly-known, but with considerable evidence of marine resource exploitation. (The other significant sites are in coastal bogs near Biarritz in the French Basque Country). Compared to the relatively high numbers of Azilian sites both near the coast and in the mountainous interior of the Basque Country (even in and south of the Cordillera), dating up to *c.* 9500 BP, there seems to be relatively little evidence of Mesolithic occupation of this region especially when compared to eastern Asturias and western Cantabria. Such evidence as there is seems to be concentrated in Navarra and Alava (see below).

Mesolithic in the Cantabrian Interior?

Many sites with late Magdalenian and Azilian components in the hills and mountains throughout the whole Vasco-Cantabrian region were abandoned at about the end of the Pre-boreal. But some artifact assemblages in the uppermost levels in these sites, especially in the Basque Country, contained geometric microliths, typical of the Mesolithic despite their relatively great age (e.g. El Piélago, Zatoya and Ekain). Several of the most spectacular montane sites did cease to be occupied after the Azilian (e.g. Collubil, Los Azules, El Castillo, El Rascaño, El Salitre, Portugain and Abauntz). So what is the evidence for occupation of the upland interior after the Azilian?

Los Canes

This small cave is located on south face of the Sierra de Cuera (maximum elevation: 1375 m.a.s.l.) in the shadow of the Picos de Europa, above the Cares valley of eastern Asturias. The site itself is at only 325 m.a.s.l. and only about 13 air km from the present shore at Llanes up and over the Sierra de Cuera. The distance to the shore is *c.* 32 km via the valleys of the Cares and its confluent the Deva or *c.* 22 km via the valleys of the Cares and (over a low divide west of Cuera) the Bedón. Excavation of this site by Arias (1990, 1991, 1995, 1999a, 1999b) yielded human burials in a consequently rather mixed deposit (6) that cuts across Magdalenian levels. The human remains from the three graves (four individuals) have been AMS-dated to 6265±75, 6770±65, 6860±65 and 6930±95 BP. With all due caution because of the mixing by the grave digging, these burials seem to be associated with geometric microliths, microburins, a simple, undecorated perforated antler (*bâton*) and marine molluscs attesting to coastal visits. The *bâton* is similar to ones from the Asturian *concheros* of Fonfría and Tres Calabres near the shore of eastern Asturias. The graves are in turn overlain by Neolithic ceramic bearing deposit. (There are contradictions among Arias' various publications as to whether double bevel-retouched microliths occur in both the Mesolithic and Neolithic deposits or in only the latter). It would seem that Los Canes was used in Mesolithic times more as a burial chamber than as a living site, but the fact that at least four individuals died in the vicinity of this cave does seem to testify to a frequent (if not abundant) human presence in the montane interior. The as yet little published cave of Arangas, virtually adjacent to Los Canes, has yielded a series of levels with faunal remains (especially young caprids, birds, landsnails and even marine molluscs) and relatively scanty artifact assemblages, apparently without geometric microliths. These layers are dated by a series of precise AMS determinations ranging between 8300–8000 BP (plus a more recent conventional date of 7150±470 for a higher, pre-ceramic unit, see Arias *et al.* 1999a, 1999b). Since these deposits all pre-date the Los Canes burials, Arangas does not seem to have been a Mesolithic living site related to that sepuchral cave.

La Calvera

This rockshelter, at 1180 m.a.s.l. in the Picos de Europa of western Cantabria, is near La Mina rockshelter (1000 m.a.s.l.). The latter site (poorly excavated, sketchily published and undated) has been attributed to the Azilian, which, because of the supposed presence of geometric microliths, may be problematic although not impossible (see discussion in Díez 1999:80 p). La Calvera, in contrast, has been carefully excavated, but so far has yielded very limited cultural materials. There are several levels, the upper four of which have hearths. All except the top layer lack ceramics, but the lithics from the presumably early Holocene levels lack diagnostic artifacts. A pre-Atlantic Mesolithic age is suspected by the excavator (Díez 1999:81 p), but this interesting and extremely high site is in need of a larger excavation and radiometric dating.

El Mirón
This large cave is situated above the Ruesga valley of the upper Ason River at an elevation *c.* 280 m.a.s.l., although it is surrounded by summits and ridges of about and above 1000 m in a Cordilleran forerange, the Sierra del Hornijo, in eastern most Cantabria on the border of Vizcaya. El Mirón is *c.* 25 km from the Holocene shore at the mouth of the Asón. Sandwiched between a long Upper Paleolithic sequence that terminates with final Magdalenian/Azilian layers that date between *c.* 12,000–11,500 BP and the earliest Neolithic levels with well made (non-Cardial) ceramics, domesticated animals, especially ovicaprines (Altuna, J and Mariezkurrena, K. pers. comm.) and three radiocarbon dates of 5600–5800 BP, there is a deposit variously labelled Strata 101–102 at the rear of the cave vestibule, 304–305 in the center and 10.1 toward the front. Although there are lateral facies variations within this unit (now continuously exposed along a 15 m long transect), from sandier in the rear to siltier in the front, this deposit attests to very humid conditions with significant calcium carbonate precipitation, causing it to be locally cemented. Several radiocarbon dates place the formation of this deposit between *c.* 10,000–8500 BP, after which there was a major, 2500 year hiatus in the stratigraphic sequence of the El Mirón vestibule, whose cause (erosion or non-deposition) is still being investigated (González Morales and Straus 2000; Straus *et al.* 2001). Compared to the rich, underlying Magdalenian and Azilian layers, this deposit is decidedly very poor in cultural remains (both faunal and artifactual). Altogether, there 686 items of lithic debris and only 10 retouched tools (and no bone implements) from all the Mesolithic age units combined. Over two-thirds of the debris component is composed of microdébitage (trimming flakes and shatter of <1 cm in length). There are 93 larger flakes, 41 blades, 57 bladelets, 8 burin spalls, 2 cores and 21 chunks (large angular debris or core remnants). The presence of a hammerstone agrees with the other evidence for *in situ* flint knapping (including abundant microdebitage, the presence of cores, decortication items, a crested blade and two platform renewal flakes). The formal tools include 4 endscrapers, a simple burin on break, a pair of continuously retouched pieces, a retouched bladelet, a microgravette (backed) point and one miscellaneous item. There is also a possible grindingstone. The faunal remains are all of wild animals. All in all, it is a very meagre inventory, especially considering the large area excavated for this unit (*c.* 25 sq. m.). It is clear, however, that this is a non (pre-) geometric Mesolithic, probably evidence of several very ephemeral visits to this vast cave during the Pre-boreal and early Boreal period. (Preliminary pollen analysis shows significant arboreal representation dominated by hazel and oak, together with abundant ferns testifying to high humidity, Iriarte, M.J. pers. comm.). Either the cave was unused during the late Boreal and early Atlantic, or all evidence of any such occupations was totally eliminated by erosion prior to Neolithic occupation in the middle Atlantic.

That the upland interior of eastern Cantabria was at least sometimes occupied in the middle Atlantic period by people who either lacked or did not discard ceramics, is attested by the sites of Cubio Redondo, in a coastal hill range about 15 km NW of El Mirón and *c.* 20 km inland of the shore at the mouth of the Asón and Tarrerón, a small cave about 2 km upstream of El Mirón along the Río Calera, a montane tributary of the Asón. Both sites have yielded circle segments with double-bevel retouch (as at Los Canes), but no ceramics in the levels in question, which are dated to 6630 and 5780 BP (both ±50) at Cubio Redondo and 5780±120 BP at Tarrerón (González Morales *et al.* in press, with references). Interestingly, the latter two dates (and two dates from the upper aceramic shellmidden deposit in La Trecha on the coast *c.* 10 km east of the Asón estuary) overlap with the oldest Neolithic (ceramic associated) dates from El Mirón. The assemblage sizes in all cases are very small (see below for similar evidence of apparent temporal overlap between ceramic and aceramic assemblages *c.* 6000 BP in the nearby coastal Basque provinces. Las Pajucas, adjacent to Tarrerón (but on the Vizcayan side of the border with Cantabria) is undated, but contains a banal lithic industry without ceramics and only wild game, notably chamois, which is not surprising given its montane setting at 400 m.a.s.l. (Altuna 1980).

Urratxa
This cave is located at an elevation of 1015 m.a.s.l. in the Sierra de Gorbea on the border between Vizcaya and Alava. Recent archeological excavations revealed that Urratxa's contents had been completely mixed by clandestine diggings. However, radiocarbon dates on various human and mammal bones show that the site had contained Azilian and Mesolithic occupations, as well as Neolithic human burials. Microgravette and Azilian points, as well as thumbnail endscrapers, are relatively abundant in the homogenised artifact assemblage, but there is only one geometric microlith (a trapeze) and nothing else that is typologically characteristic of the Mesolithic (Muñoz and Berganza 1997). Thus it is really only the two dates of *c.* 6.9 kya that attest to the presence of at least ephemeral visits to this high mountain cave during the early-middle Atlantic phase. The (presumably) combined Azilian and Mesolithic stone artifact assemblages show that the flints brought to the site came from

c. 40 air km to the south (Condado de Treviño) and, in far lesser quantities from the Vizcayan syncline (c. 35 km to the north), and from the Sierra de Urbasa (c. 56 km to the east-southeast). The site seems to have been a fairly specialised ibex hunting locus, but there are also not insignificant quantities of red deer and boar in the non-domesticated component of the mixed assemblage. The contacts with the Ebro valley are particularly interesting in light of developments (i.e. the "spread" of the Neolithic) a few centuries later. Urratxa is truly a Cordilleran site with a Mesolithic component, albeit poorly known.

Other interior Mesolithic sites in the coastal Basque Country are few; one with radiocarbon dates (two at c. 8.5 kya) is Berroberría, located near the French border, c. 17 air km from the Holocene shore at Saint-Jean de Luz. Although it is at the western end of the Pyrenees, the peaks surrounding Berroberría only range between 700–900 m.a.s.l. At another site, Marizulo cave, the two undated "late" Mesolithic components have been characterised as "Tardenoisian". The cave at 260 m.a.s.l., in hilly country, is 12 air km due inland of San Sebastián in an area where the highest summits are at 650–800 m.a.s.l. The uppermost of the two aceramic levels is notable for the presence of dog remains (Altuna 1972). Otherwise the Mesolithic faunas are overwhelmingly dominated by red deer followed by boar and roe deer.

"Mesolithic"/"Neolithic" Temporal Overlap in the Coastal Basque Region

As with Tarrerón in the eastern Cantabria montane interior, there are dates of c. 5800–6000 BP associated with an aceramic artifact assemblage and a purely wild mammalian fauna (almost all red deer mainly hunted in the warm season) at the coastal Guipuzcoan open air site of Herriko Barra (Altuna et al. 1990; Alday 1998). The lithics include geometrics with double-bevel retouch. A similar aceramic assemblage dating to 6650±130 BP has recently been excavated at Pareko Landa on the coastal plain of central Vizcaya (López and Aguirre 1997). At the western end of the Vizcayan coast, near the border of Cantabria, the small cave of Pico Ramos has recently yielded a shellmidden at the base of its stratigraphic sequence. This *conchero* dates to 5860±65 BP and is poor in cultural remains, with no ceramics (Zapata 1995). On the other hand, the nearby cave of Kobaederra, also on the Vizcayan coasta plain, has recently yielded a seqence of early Neolithic levels dating to and greater than 5.8 kya, with geometric microliths (including ones with double-bevel retouch) and ceramics. Barley is present from the beginning and later in time wheat and millet appear (Zapata et al. 1997).

There is a controversial site, Arenaza (largely so because it is essentially unpublished, despite having been excavated intermittently since 1972), located in low hill country in eastern Vizcaya, about 12 km inland of the present mouth of the Río Nervión. The cave is at c. 120 m.a.s.l. The essential facts and new dates are summarised by Arias and Altuna (1999). Arenaza has yielded Azilian and non-geometric Mesolithic artifact assemblages from strata dated to c. 10,300 and 9.6 kya, the latter overlain by spits with geometric microliths. The overlying stratum, IC2, has ceramics and geometric microliths, but domesticated animal remains have not yet been identified from it, unlike overlying IC1, which is dominated by ovicaprines, followed by nearly equal quantities of pigs and cattle. There are also relatively small quantities of wild game (mostly red deer). This level has had several radiocarbon dates: a conventional one of 4965±195 BP and three new AMS determinations: 5755±65, 6040±75 and 10,860±120 BP (!). The AMS dates were all run on bones or teeth of supposedly domesticated cattle, but the Azilian age date is inexplicable, as there is said to be no evidence of disturbance. The most one can say is that the early Neolithic at Arenaza, not far from El Mirón, Tarrerón, Cubio Redondo or La Trecha, is possibly about the same as the early ceramic layers at the first site and the non-ceramic deposits at the latter three.

Holocene Forager Sites in the Upper Ebro Drainage of Navarra and Alava

If interior (and, for that matter, even coastal) Mesolithic sites are relatively scarce in the Atlantic-draining Basque provinces, they seem to be more abundant in the upper Ebro basin of Navarra and especially Alava, which may beg the question of their main sphere of social inter-relationships: Atlantic or Mediterranean. The sites are found at a wide range of elevations, but all are in Mediterranean habitats, which are clearly distinguished from those of the Atlantic side of the Cordillera.

The highest is Zatoya, at 900 m.a.s.l. on the southern face of the Pyrenees in NE Navarra, an area where the mountain summits range between 1400–1500 m, which is very definitely mountainous terrain. Sandwiched between Azilian (11,800–11,500 BP) and early Neolithic (6320 BP) levels, the Mesolithic (a.k.a. "non-geometric Epipaleolithic") deposit in this cave is dated by two radiocarbon determinations to c. 8200 BP (Barandiarán and Cava 1989) and was deposited under only partly wooded conditions, with only very low pollen percentages of pine, oak, hazel, alder and linden (Boyer-Klein 1989), presumably because of the sites high elevation. The nearby site of Aizpea (c. 730 m.a.s.l.) fills the gap between the Boreal and middle Atlantic phases in Zatoya, having geometric microlithic components dating to 7800–7200 and 6800–6600 BP and underlying an early Neolithic layer dated to 6370±70 BP (Cava 1997).

Abauntz, at 700 m.a.s.l. in north-central Navarra in the uppermost headwaters of an Ebro tributary, contains what is characterised as an Azilian assemblage that is radiocarbon dated to 9540±300 BP (Pre-boreal). This level is manifestly separated from a very early Neolithic layer dated to 6910±450 BP (Utrilla 1982).

The province of Alava, south of the Cordillera between Vizcaya and the upper Ebro, has a number of early Holocene (Pre-boreal and especially Boreal) forager sites, followed without interruption by several early Neolithic sites. In the western part of the province there is a cluster of sites. Berniollo is an open air site dated to 9940±490 BP with non-geometric microliths (Ibáñez and González Urquijo 1996). Fuente Hoz has a sequence that includes non-geometric (8100–7100 BP) and geometric Mesolithic and Neolithic (6120±280 BP) levels. Other Mesolithic sites with evidence of the early transition to the Neolithic in the western Alava area include Socuevas and Larrenke (Alday 1998). All these sites are on the order of c. 500 m.a.s.l. in elevation.

The Condado de Treviño (an administrative enclave of Old Castile in the south-center of Alava) has a couple of Mesolithic sites: Montico de Charratu and Mendandia, both with non-geometric followed by geometric components. The non-geometric assemblage from the latter site dates to 7800 BP. These sites lie at 600–700 m.a.s.l.

In eastern Alava, the site of Kanpanoste Goikea (740 m.a.s.l.) has a similar sequence: non-geometric (7700 BP), geometric (6500 BP) Mesolithic, an hiatus and finally a late Neolithic (Alday 1998). The geometric Mesolithic has a high arboreal pollen fraction, dominated by hazel, with lower amounts of pine and traces of beech, alder, oak and lime (Iriarte 1998); several of these trees (plus others) are represented among the wood charcoal samples, attesting to the forested surroundings of the site at the time of human use (Zapata 1998). The adjacent site of Atxoste has a similar sequence, but includes an early Neolithic (Alday 1998). Nearby Peña de Marañon in southern Navarra, but on the Alava border only 18 km north of the Ebro itself at c. 500 m.a.s.l., has a non-geometric Mesolithic component dating to 7900 BP. Finally, in NE Alava, the small cave of Kukuma, located at 715 m.a.s.l., was a fairly specialised caprid-hunting site. Although undated, it has a small lithic assemblage including both geometric and non-geometric armatures (Baldeón and Berganza 1997). Its pollen analysis indicates a dense mixed deciduous forest, probably of Boreal/early Atlantic age (Isturiz 1997).

In sum, the early (Pre-boreal/early Boreal) and late (late Boreal/early Atlantic) Mesolithic sites of the trans-cordilleran upper Ebro drainage in Navarra and Alava are quite numerous and seem to follow directly from the several highland Azilian sites that had existed in terminal Late Glacial times. There does not seem to have been any abandonment of this region, despite the growth of woods, ultimately to be characterised as dense, mixed deciduous forest, although more pine dominated and more open in the higher elevations. There were clearly two technological phases in the Mesolithic of the upper Ebro: non-geometric and geometric. The former is not dominated by backed bladelets/points as in Mediterranean Spain, but the "boom" in geometric microliths in the late Mesolithic is reminiscent of the situation just prior to the arrival of Neolithic technology in Mediterranean Spain. It also seems that there was a period of coexistence between aceramic (late Mesolithic) and ceramic (early Neolithic) technologies (and economies?) in the period between about 6700–6300 BP (uncal.) in the upper Ebro (Alday 1998).

The inescapable conclusion for this region, which is characterised by Mediterranean type climate and environment, is that there was continuity of human settlement and that Neolithic technologies and subsistence practices, brought up-valley from Mediterranean Spain, were adopted by pre-existing populations. The modes of transition may have included trade/exchange, diffusion in the context of social contacts (including marriage), *etc.* The geometric microlith components of the overall technology continued (with the addition of double-bevel or "Helwen" retouch on some circle segments) across the Mesolithic-Neolithic transition in the upper Ebro drainage and, at least at first, many of the same caves and rockshelters were occupied as before.

Summary and Discussion

After the plentiful record of Azilian occupation of the mountains (and even the trans-Cordilleran mesetas of León and Old Castile) up to around 9000 BP, between then and c. 6500 or 6000 BP, archeological evidence for human use of the montane interior of the northern face of the Cantabrian Cordillera is very scanty, both in numbers of sites and in assemblage composition (as in the exceptional cases of Arangas and El Mirón caves). Meanwhile, during the time of the formation of the classic Asturian *concheros* of the coast of eastern Asturias and western Cantabria (and of a few known coastal sites in eastern Cantabria and the Basque Country), the archeological record does seem to suggest a strong concentration of human settlement along the shore, with a mixed subsistence base that combined marine resource exploitation with hunting (red and roe deer, boar and smaller mammals), birding and plant collection. The steep interior was once again being visited more regularly after c. 6500–6000 BP, in some cases by groups which still did not use ceramic technology (or at least did not discard vessels or even sherds at their montane sites, e.g. sites of Los Canes, Cubio Redondo, Las Pajucas, Tarrerón, Urratxa). At about the same time, ceramics were being adopted at a few other sites, notably El Mirón, adjacent to the Basque area and in the mountainous interior, but with easy connections to both the south and the southeast (Los Tornos Pass and the Carranza Valley, respectively).

The situation was apparently somewhat more complex in the eastern (Basque) sector. Here too there was a significant Azilian occupation of the mountains, including the Navarrese uplands between the Pyrenees and the Cordillera, where human occupation seems to have continued throughout the Pre-boreal and into the Boreal. There are numerous Mesolithic sites (both early and late) in the upper Ebro drainage of Navarra and Alava, with no evidence pointing to regional human abandonment of this more Mediterranean environment. About a third of the way through the Atlantic phase (post-glacial optimum), ceramics (e.g. at Aizpea c. 6400 BP, see Cava 1997) and (haltingly and spottily at first) agricultural products are introduced into this region (for example, at Peña Larga in SE Alava, with domesticated ovicaprines, cattle and pigs in the early ceramic Neolithic at 6130±230 BP, see Fernández 1997), presumably via the Ebro from the Mediterranean coastal regions of eastern Spain, as seems to be demonstrated by a string of Neolithic sites with descending radiocarbon ages as one ascends this great valley corridor (Alday 1998). There was a period during which some groups seem to have acquired/adopted at least the new ceramic techology, while others had not. In some cases (e.g. Zatoya and Marizulo), ceramics preceeded domesticates except for the dog (Mariezkurrena 1990). Other coastal Basque sites (e.g. Herriko Barra and Pico Ramos) have Helwen retouched segments, but no ceramics or domesticates, while still others (e.g. Kobaederra) have evidence for cereal agriculture and ceramics, despite a continued high degree of dependence on foraging for subsistence in the mid-Atlantic vegetational phase.

The circulation of flints from both sides of the Cordillera in the late Mesolithic at Urratxa (Muñoz and Berganza 1997) and the presence of both Atlantic and Mediterranean shells in the Mesolithic and early Neolithic levels at Zatoya (Barandiarán and Cava 1989), for example, provide evidence of widespread contacts between the Atlantic and Mediterranean worlds. The "new" expansion of human settlement up into the Cordillera during the early Atlantic phase corresponds temporally (and, one could hypothesize even "purposefully") with the "arrival" of the Neolithic on the south face for the mountains. Was "news" of the new lifeway with its innovative goods and products something that attracted the more-or-less coastally bound Cantabrian Mesolithic people toward the mountains and southern uplands of the Ebro drainage? One could speculate that the pottery was seen as a desirable status item by foragers (as has been argued in other sectors of the Atlantic facade during the period of transition between the Mesolithic and Neolithic), hence a "pull" toward the south. Naturally, an additional incentive for moving up into and over the mountains, despite the dense forest obstacles and few clearings especially on the Atlantic face of the Cordillera, may have been the additional food source provided by agricultural products. These were notably, at first, domesticated ovicaprines, followed later by cattle, pigs and cereal crops.

An alternate scenario, however, is to contemplate extreme SW France (the coastal French Basque Country) as a possible intermediate source area for the Neolithic of the Cantabrian coast (e.g. the open air Neolithic site of Mouligna near Biarritz, with radiocarbon dates between 5800–5100 BP, see Chauchat 1974). Yet the dates for Neolithic sites in Lower Aragón are significantly older than Mouligna and the ramifications of the early Neolithic (>6000 BP) on the southern shore of the mouth of the Gironde estuary (at La Lède de Gurp), c. 220 km north of Biarritz (Marambat and Roussot-Larroque 1989), are not yet understood. This may make the direct route of Neolithic diffusion from Mediterranean Spain toward the Cantabrian region seem more likely, at least at present.

Tentative Conclusions

Marine resource exploitation began to become significant to prehistoric Cantabrian adaptations, at least situationally or seasonally, as long ago as the Solutrean and early Magdalenian (e.g. La Riera and El Juyo). The supplementary use of shellfish and fish in human diets clearly increased throughout the Magdalenian and its terminal phase, the Azilian. At the same time, the late Upper Paleolithic settlement pattern (as part of wider trends taking place throughout western Europe) included movement up into the Cantabrian Cordillera (as at El Mirón) and even onto the mesetas of Old Castile especially in its final phases. Thus took place in the context of the warming conditions of the late Tardiglacial and initial Holocene, but before dense, mixed deciduous forests dominated by oaks and beech had completely taken over the evironments of Vasco-Cantabria. No doubt the reforestation of the region, especially given its rugged terrain, made visibility and movement difficult. This may have "pushed" people to utilise the closed interior less and less in the Boreal phase, while the rich inlets, estuaries and marshes of the rising Holocene sea level certainly "pulled" them toward an ever greater utilisation of the littoral and exploitation of marine resources, especially along the most favored stretches of coast (e.g. eastern Asturias/western Santander, the Asón and Guernica estuaries). A combination of burgeoning population density along this narrow coastal strip and the "pull" of the new products associated with the Neolithic lifeway already present on the other side of the mountains for several centuries, seems to have impelled people to once again visit, use and even at least temporarily inhabit the interior. Some groups acquired ceramics quickly and brought them down to their sector of the shore, while others just learned of the double-bevel retouching technique for microliths, but went home empty handed as far as pottery was concerned, at least at first. Similarly, some groups acquired a few domesticated animals relatively quickly once contact had been made with the Neolithic world, while others did not. Thus the Atlantic phase cultural landscape of the Atlantic facade of Vasco-Cantabria was a mosaic of technologies and subsistence types during the late, gradual transition to the Neolithic in this peripheral region. Even once megalithic monuments began to dot the landscape, c. 5800–5500 BP, the economy of this region continued to depend heavily on hunting and gatherering, with major changes in overall lifeways only coming in the terminal Neolithic/Chalcolithic periods, c. 4500–4000 BP. But that is a different story, one that is also told in the uppermost levels at El Mirón. Meanwhile, there are hints that after a fairly brief and spotty incursion onto the northern Meseta of Old Castile in late Magdalenian/Azilian times, this high, inhospitable region was once again abandoned (or at least depopulated to the extent of reaching archeological invisibility) in the early Holocene. When late Neolithic settlements were eventually established there, this happened in the context of a demographic desert quite unlike the situation along the Cantabrian coast, where, to the contrary, there seems to have been continuity of human settlement throughout the Boreal and Atlantic phases. The significance of megalithic monuments in the two regions may therefore have been somewhat different, given the different social and economic contexts in which they were first erected, the Vasco-Cantabrian ones as early as 5800–5500 BP, roughly contemporaneously or slightly after the arrival of the first ceramics and domesticates along the northern face of the Cordillera.

Acknowledgements

Our excavations since 1996 in El Mirón Cave have been funded by grants from the Fundación Marcelino Botín, National Science Foundation, L.S.B. Leakey Foundation, National Geographic Society, Ministerio de Educación y Cultura, Gobierno de Cantabria and University of New Mexico. We thank all our excavation crew members and scientists collaborating in the study of this site, the stratigraphy of which (so far) spans the period between the Bronze Age and the Mousterian.

References

Alday, A. 1998. Kanpanoste Goikoa. *Memorias de Yacimientos Alaveses* 5. Vitoria.
Altuna, J. 1972. Fauna de mamíferos de los yacimientos prehistóricos de Guipúzcoa. *Munibe* 24, 1–464.
—— 1980. Historia de la domesticación animal en el País Vasco desde sus orignes hasta la romanización. *Munibe* 32, 1–163.
—— 1986. The mammalian faunas from the prehistoric site of La Riera. In: Straus, L. and Clark, G. (eds.) *La Riera Cave*. Anthropological Research Papers 36, 237–274 and 421–479. Tempe.
Altuna, J., Cearreta, A., Edeso, J.M., Elorza, M., Iriarte, M.J. and Mariezkurrena, K. 1990. El yacimiento de Herriko-Barra y su relación con las transgresiones marinas holocenas. *Actas de la 2ª Reunión del Cuaternario Ibérico*. Bilbao.
Arias, P. 1990. Adaptaciones al medio natural de las sociedades humanas de la región cantábrica durante el Boreal y el Atlántico. *The Late Quaternary in the Western Pyrenean Region*, 269–283. Universidad del País Vasco. Bilbao.
Arias, P. 1991. *De Cazadores a Campesinos. La Transición al Neolítico en la Región Cantábrica*. Santander.
—— 1995. La cronología absoluta del Neolítico y el Calcolítico de la región cantábrica. Estado de la cuestión. *Cuadernos de Sección, Prehistoria-Arqueología* 6, 15–39.
—— 1999a. La colonisation holocène des Monts Cantabriques: le cas de la région des Picos de Europa. In: Thévenin, A. (ed.) *L'Europe des Derniers Chasseurs*, 93–100. Paris.
—— 1999b. The origins of the Neolithic along the Atlantic coast of continental Europe: a survey. *Journal of World Prehistory* 13, 403–464.
Arias, P. and Altuna, J. 1999. Nuevas dataciones absolutas para el Neolítico de la Cueva de Arenaza. *Munibe* 51, 161–71.
Arias, P., Altuna, J., Armendariz, A., Gonzalez Urquijo, J.E., Ibanez, J.J., Ontarıon, R. and Zapata, L. 1999. Nuevas aportaciones al conocimiento de las primeras sociedades productoras en la región cantábrica. *Saguntum-PLAV* Extra 2, 549–57.
Arias, P., González Sainz, C., Moure, A. and Ontañón, R. 1997. El proyecto "Estudio integral del complejo arqueológico de La Garma". *II Congreso de Arqueología Peninsular* I, 147–162. Fundación Rei Afonso Henriques. Zamora.
Arias, P. and Pérez, C. 1995. Excavaciones arqueológicas en Arangas, Cabrales: las cuevas de Los Canes, El Tiu Llines y Arangas. *Excavaciones Arqueológicas en Asturias 1991-94*, 79–92. Principado de Asturias. Oviedo.
Aura, E. and Pérez, M 1995. El Holoceno incial en el Mediterráneo español. In: Villaverde, V. (ed.) *Los Ultimos Cazadores*., 119–146. Instituto de Cultura Juan Gil-Albert. Alicante.
Baldeón, A. and Berganza, E. 1997. *Kukuma*. Memorias de Yacimientos Alaveses 3. Vitoria.
Barandiarán, I. and Cava, A. 1989. *El Yacimiento Prehistórico de Zatoya*. Trabajos de Arqueología Navarra 8. Pamplona.
Bernaldo de Quirós, F. and Neira, A. 1996. Occupations de haute montagne dans la région cantabrique espagnole. In: Delporte, H. and Clottes, J. (eds.) *Pyrénées Préhistoriques*, 193–203. Paris.
Bicho, N. 1993. Late Glacial prehistory of central and southern Portugal. *Antiquity* 67, 761–775.
Boyer-Klein, A. 1989. Análisis polínico. In: Barandiarán, I. and Cava, A. (eds.) *Trabajos de Arqueología Navarra* 8, 231–234. Pamplona.
Cacho, C. and Pérez, S. 1997. El Magdaleniense de la Meseta y sus relaciones con el Mediterráneo español: el Abrigo de Buedía. In: Fullola, J.M. and Soler, N. (eds.) *El Món Mediterrani despres del Pleniglacial*. Centre d'Investigacions Arqueológiques, Serie Monogràfica 17, 263–274. Girona.
Cava, A. 1997. L'Abri d'Aizpea. *Préhistoire Européenne* 10, 151–72.
Chauchat, C. 1974. Datations C14 concernant le site de Mouligna. *Bulletin de la Société Préhistorique Française* 71, 140.
Clark, G.A. 1976. *El Asturiense Cantábrico*. Bibliotheca Praehistorica Hispana 13. Madrid.
—— 1983. *The Asturian of Cantabria*. Anthropological Papers of the University of Arizona 41. Tempe.
—— 1995. Complementariedad funcional en el Mesolítico del Norte de España. In: Villaverde, V. (ed.) *Los Ultimos Cazadores*, 45–62. Instituto de Cultura Gil-Albert. Alicante
Clarke, D. 1976. Mesolithic Europe: the economic basis. In: Sieveking, G., Longworth, I. and Wilson, K. (eds.) *Problems in Economic and Social Archaeology*, 449–481. London.
Corchón, M.S. 1989. Datos sobre el epipaleolítico en la Meseta Norte: la Cueva del Nispero. *Zephyrus* 41/42, 83–100.
Deith, M. 1983. Seasonality of shell collecting, determined by oxygen isotope analysis of marine shells from Asturian sites in Cantabria. In: Grigson, C. and Clutton-Brock, J. (eds.) *Animals and Archaeology: Shell Middens, Fishes and Birds*. British Archaeological Reports S-183, 67–76. Oxford.
Deith, M. and Shackleton, N. 1986. Seasonal exploitation of marine molluscs: oxygen isotope analysis of shell from La Riera Cave. In: Straus, L. and Clark, G. (eds.) *La Riera Cave*. Anthropological Research Papers 36, 299–313. Tempe.
Díez Castillo, A. 1999. *Utilización de los Recursos en la Marina y Montña Cantábricas*. Gernika.
Dupré, M. 1988. *Palinología y Paleoambiente*. Servicio de Investigación Prehistórica, Serie de Trabajos Varios 84. Valencia.
Fabián, J.F. 1997. La difícil definición actual del Paleolítico superior en la Meseta. El yacimiento de La Dehesa (Salamanca) como exponente de la etapa Magdaleniense final. In: de Balbín,

R. and Bueno, P. (eds.) *II Congreso de Arqueología Peninsular*, vol.I, 219–238 Zamora.

Fano, M. 1998. *El Habitat Mesolítico en el Cantábrico Occidental*. British Archaeological Reports 732. Oxford.

Fernández Eraso, J. 1997. *Peña Larga*. Memorias de Yacimientos Alaveses 4. Vitoria.

Garcia Guinea, M.A. 1984. Las cuevas azilienses de El Piélago (Mirones, Cantabria) y sus excavaciones de 1967–1969. *Sautuola* 4, 13–154.

González Morales, M. 1982. *El Asturiense y otras Culturas Locales*. Centro de Investigación y Museo de Altamira, Monografías 7. Santander.

—— 1989. Asturian resource exploitation: recent perspectives. In: Bonsall, C. (ed.) *The Mesolithic in Europe*, 604–606. Edinburgh.

—— 1990. La prehistoria de las Marismas. *Cuadernos de Trasmiera* 2, 13–28.

—— 1992. From hunter-gatherers to food producers in northern Spain. In: Clark, G. (ed.) *Perspectives on the Past*, 204–216. Philadelphia.

—— 1995. La transición al Holoceno en la Región Cantábrica: el contraste con el modelo del mediterráneo español. In: Villaverde, V. (ed.) *Los Ultimos Cazadores*, 63–78. Instituto de Cultura Juan Gil-Albert. Alicante

—— 1999. La prehistoria de Santoña. *Monte Buciero* 2, 17–28.

González Morales, M. and Straus, L. 2000. Excavaciones en la Cueva del Mirón (Ramales de la Victoria, Cantabria). Campañas de 1996–99. *Trabajos de Prehistoria* 57, 121–133.

González Morales, M., Straus, L., Díez, A. and Ruiz Cobo, J. in press. Postglacial coast and inland: the Mesolithic-Neolithic transition in Cantabrian Spain. In: Angelucci, D. and Milliken, S. (eds.) *Regional Approaches to Mesolithic Land Use in Europe*. International Monographs in Prehistory. Ann Arbor.

Ibáñez, J.J. and González Urquijo, J.E. 1996. *From Tool Use to Site Function*. British Archaeological Reports S-658. Oxford.

Iriarte, M.J. 1998. Análisis palinológico del deposito arqueológico de Kanpanoste Goikoa. In: Alday, A. (ed.) *Kanpanoste Goikoa*. Memorias de Yacimientos Alaveses 5, 85–94 Vitori.

Isturiz, M.J. 1997. Análisis palinológico del yacimiento arqueológico de Kukuma. In: Baldeón, A. and Berganza, E. (eds.) *Kukuma*. Memorias de Yacimientos Alaveses 3, 71–73

López Quintana, J. and Aguirre, M. 1997. Patrones de asentamiento en el Neolítico del litoral vizcaino. In: Rodríguez Casal, A. (ed.) *O Neolítico Atlantico e as Orixes do Megalitismo*, 335–351. Universidad de Santiago de Compostela. Santiago de Compostela.

Marambat, L. and Roussot-Larroque, J. 1989. *Bulletin de l'Association Française pour l'Etude du Quaternaire* 1989–2, 73–89.

Mariezkurrena, K. 1990. Caza y domesticación durante el Neolítico y Edad de los Metales en el País Vasco. *Munibe* 42, 241–52.

Muñoz, M. and Berganza, E. 1997. *El Yacimiento de la Cueva de Urratxa III*. Universidad de Deusto. Bilbao.

Straus, L.G. 1979. Mesolithic adaptations along the northern coast of Spain. *Quaternaria* 21, 305–327.

—— 1991a. The Epipaleolithic and Mesolithic of Cantabrian Spain and Pyrenean France. *Journal of World Prehistory* 5, 83–104.

—— 1991b. Human geography of the late Upper Paleolithic in western Europe. *Journal of Anthropological Research* 47, 259–278.

—— 1991c. SW Europe at the Last Glacial Maximum. *Current Anthropology* 32, 189–199.

Straus, L., Bicho, N. and Winegardner, A. 2000a. The Upper Paleolithic settlement of Iberia: first-generation maps. *Antiquity* 74, 553–566.

—— 2000b. Mapping the Upper Paleolithic regions of Iberia. *Journal of Iberian Archaeology* 2, 7–42.

Straus, L. and Clark, G. 1986. *La Riera Cave*. Anthropological Research Papers 36. Tempe.

Straus, L., González Morales, M., Farrand, W. and Hubbard, W. 2001. Sedimentological and stratigraphic observations in El Mirón, a Late Quaternary cave site in the Cantabrian Cordillera, northern Spain. *Geoarchaeology* 16, 603–630.

Turner, C. and Hannon, G. 1988. Vegetational evidence for late Quaternary climatic changes in southwest Europe in relation to the influence of the North Atlantic Ocean. *Philosophical Transactions of the Royal Society of London* B 318, 451–485.

Utrilla, P. 1982. El yacimiento de la Cueva de Abauntz. *Trabajos de Arqueología Navarra* 3, 203–358.

Utrilla, P. and Mazo, C. 1994. El Solutrense en el valle medio del Ebro. *Férvedes* 1, 89–104.

Watts, W. 1986. Stages of climatic change from full Glacial to Holocene in northwest Spain, southern France and Italy: a comparison of the Atlantic coast and the Mediterranean basin. In: Ghazi, A. and Fantechi, R. (eds.) *Perspectives on the Past*, 101–111. Philadelphia.

Zapata, L. 1995. El depósito sepulcral calcolítico de la Cueva Pico Ramos. *Munibe* 47, 33–197.

—— 1998. La explotación del medio vegetal en Kanpanoste Goikoa. In: Alday, A. (ed.) *Kanpanoste Goikoa*. Memorias de Yacimientos Alaveses 5, 95–104. Vitoria.

Zapata, L. and Meaza, G. 1998. Procesos de antropización y cambios en el paisaje vegetal del País Vasco atlántico. *Munibe (Ciencias Naturales)* 50, 21–35.

Zapata, L., Ibáñez, J. and González, J. 1997. El yacimiento de la Cueva de Kobaederra. *Munibe* 49, 51–63.

49. Scotland's First Settlers: an investigation into settlement, territoriality and mobility during the Mesolithic in the Inner Sound, Scotland, First Results

Karen Hardy and C.R. Wickham-Jones

This paper presents the preliminary results of a fieldwork project combining survey, test pitting and excavation to examine the Mesolithic settlement of the Inner Sound, on the west coast of Scotland. The project has taken the relationship between settlement and the sea as its focus and as such it concentrates on coastal sites within the study area. Work is still in its infancy, but it has already demonstrated the remarkable archaeological richness of the area. First results include the identification of many new sites, several of which include midden, though not all are Mesolithic. Excavation on one site has revealed a rich midden dated to the early eighth millennium BP. It is composed mainly of limpet shells and has been initially interpreted as a rapid accumulation of material, perhaps relating to a time of famine. The midden has yielded much worked bone, shell and antler as well as lithics including microliths and finds of debitage and partially made pieces show that activities on site included tool manufacture as well as food processing. Mesolithic finds continue below the midden as well as around it, so that the midden material may be placed in a wider context. Post-excavation work is only just starting, but initial information on the use and distribution of lithic raw materials shows that wider detail, for example on transport and social contacts may well be forthcoming. Though the study area is small, there is already evidence of variation from one part of the area to another in the type of site and site combinations that relate to the Mesolithic.

Background

Scotland's First Settlers (SFS) was set up in 1998 as a regional study of the Mesolithic around the Inner Sound, on the Atlantic seaboard, western Scotland. Given the importance of the sea in the Mesolithic, both as a resource and for transport, the project has taken for its focus the seascape defined by Skye and the mainland, an area with a large coastline incorporating many islands (Figure 49.1).

The initial aims of the project were to identify new Mesolithic sites within the study area, which would be followed by detailed excavation of one or more sites. Prior to SFS, three Mesolithic sites were known in the area, An Corran, in north east Skye (Hardy et al. forthcoming), Redpoint in Torridan (Gray 1960) and Shieldaig (Walker 1973), at the north end of the Applecross peninsula. Work at An Corran in the early 1990's had highlighted the potential for the survival of shell midden material in the area, something which was previously thought rare in Scotland. The Early Holocene in Scotland was a time of dynamic environmental change and this is something with which the Mesolithic population would have had to come to terms. Scotland's First Settlers is particularly interested in looking at shell middens in order both to reconstruct environmental change from surviving organic material and to examine their internal composition for information on the human lifestyle. The two can then be combined and further information drawn from related non midden sites in order to examine other issues such as the relationship between midden and non midden sites: something which has long troubled Mesolithic scholars in Scotland.

The landscape of the Inner Sound presented a variety of resources to its Mesolithic inhabitants. It is an area of deep and volatile sea speckled with islands of varying sizes. Much of the coastline is steep sided, mountainous and rocky, and slopes quickly downwards into deep water, but there are areas of more gentle coastline and in many places rocky foreshores are exposed for long periods. It is today a fertile area, both for fish and shellfish, and this was clearly the case in the past despite considerable sea level change. The deep sea lying so near the coast was clearly well used as attested by the number of deep water fish remains in the middens. At the point of writing, work has comprised a brief trial field season in 1999 and one full season in 2000. There are three main strands to the fieldwork:

1. coastal survey, to identify potentially Mesolithic sites, both rockshelters and caves as well as open sites,
2. test pitting to assess preservation and dating of sites, and finally
3. the detailed excavation of a few selected sites.

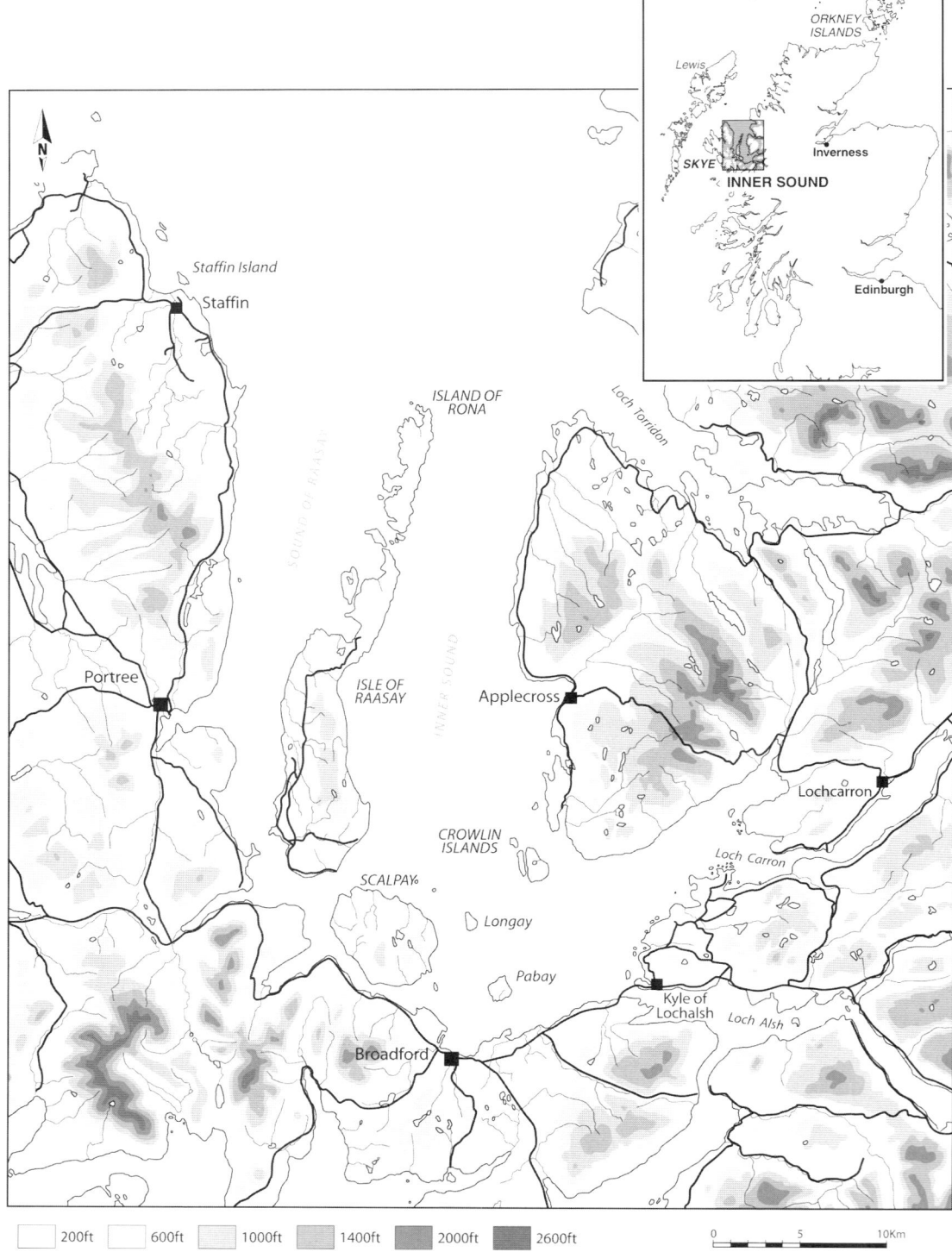

Figure 49.1 The study area, topography.

Survey and Test Pitting

To date (Nov 2000) the coastal survey has produced 104 new sites, of which 52 have been test pitted (Figure 49.2). Most of the newly found sites are rockshelters though a number of open middens and lithic scatters were also recorded. While it is as yet too early to identify how many of these sites date to the Mesolithic, a substantial number have been found to contain lithics (Figure 49.3). Four of the test pitted sites from 1999 have radiocarbon determinations (Figure 49.4), and two, as indicated by artefactual material (Finlayson *et al.* 1999:25 pp), date to the Mesolithic.

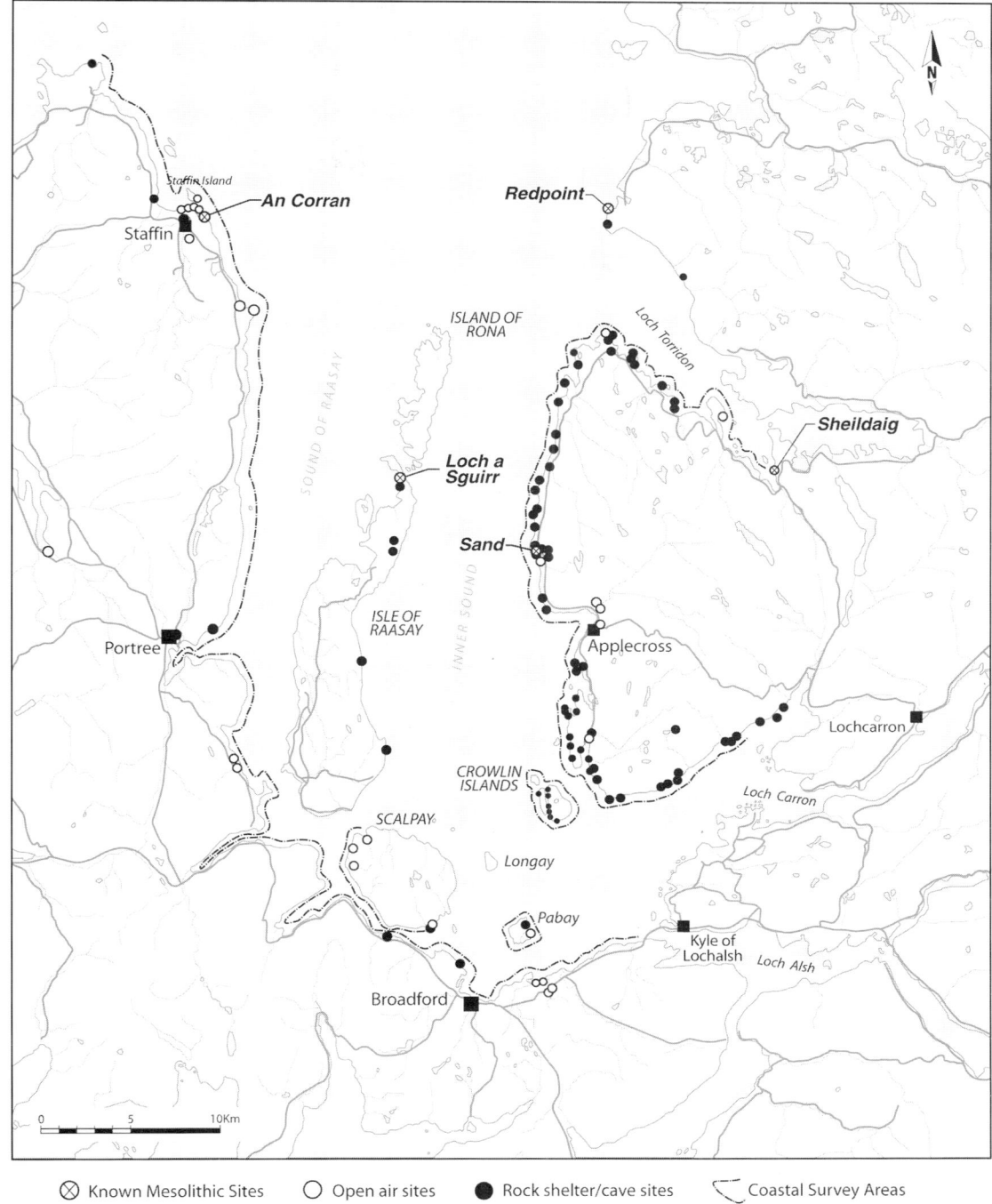

Figure 49.2 Surveyed areas and location of new sites.

The distribution of sites at present may reflect those areas where the most intensive fieldwork has taken place (Figures 49.1 and 49.2), but it is interesting that it seems to concentrate in three specific areas: around the site of An Corran at Staffin in the north; around the southern small islands such as Pabay and Scalpay; and on the Applecross peninsula. Several stretches of coast that have been surveyed and shown to reveal no sites: in some cases this may be due to the local geomorphology (eg: the west coast of Skye to the north of Portree), but in other cases it is more likely to be due to the destruction of archaeological sites by more recent development such as farming and building (eg: the southern coastal lands around Broadford, Figure 49.1).

An unexpected problem in finding Mesolithic sites has been that a large proportion of the rockshelters contain rockfall (probably related to early Holocene instability) and though it is often possible to see midden material below this, test pits do not allow for its proper examination (Figure 49.5). Larger scale excavation, for which the

Figure 49.3 Sites with lithics, by site type.

OxA no.	Trench and Spit	Sample ref	Radiocarbon age (BP)
Ashaig 1, NG 6866 2420			
OxA-9277	1/12	charcoal *(Betula)*	769±36
OxA-9278	1/4	charcoal *(Corylus avellana)*	771±32
OxA-9279	1/6	charcoal *(Betula)*	723±33
Crowlin 1, NG 691 338			
OxA-9250	3/4	charcoal *(Betula)*	1296±39
OxA-9251	1/11	charcoal *(Betula)*	1799±37
OxA-9252	1/6	charcoal *(Betula)*	477±35
OxA-9253	1/5 (artefact N11)	bone, deer (trapezoidal bone point)	316±39
Loch a Sguirr, NG 6084 5286			
OxA-9254	1/6	charcoal *(Betula)*	2055±39
OxA-9255	1/2 (artefact N25)	bone, deer (bevel ended tool)	7245±55
OxA-9305	1/3	charcoal *(Betula)*	7620±75
Sand NG 6841 4934			
OxA-9280	9/8	antler	7520±50
OxA-9281	9/8 (artefact N19)	bone, deer (bevel ended tool)	7715±55
OxA-9282	9/7 (artefact N18)	bone, deer (bevel ended tool)	7545±50
OxA-9343	9/8	charcoal *(Betula)*	7765±50

Figure 49.4 Radiocarbon determinations from sites tested in 1999.

Figure 49.5 The rockshelter at Crowlin 1 showing rockfall below which lies midden.

project does not have the resources, would be necessary to test for the presence of Mesolithic midden in these cases.

Excavation of a Shell Midden Site at Sand

So far, one major excavation has taken place, at Sand in the Applecross peninsula (Figures 49.1 and 49.12). This is a rockshelter site, where an extensive midden lay just below the turf. It proved to have very good organic preservation and the finds included bevel ended and pointed bone tools and a fragment of antler harpoon (Figure 49.6), as well as a narrow blade microlithic assemblage (Figure 49.7). The excavation was designed to look at the build up of archaeological material below the midden as well as at deposits away from the midden so that a broad picture of the whole site can be built up (Figure 49.8). Sand is the only site to have been looked at so far, and even this work is preliminary, the detailed post-excavation work has yet to be done, but there are already suggestions that it may challenge some accepted wisdoms.

The shell midden at Sand was a loose unconsolidated midden comprised mainly of limpets (Figure 49.9) with no stabilisation layers, deposits of non shell material or unconformities (Figure 49.10). Unlike many other middens in West coast Scotland (eg: Oronsay, see Mellars 1987:184 pp, 234 pp) it seems therefore to have accumulated within the space of one or a few short seasons. Beneath it lay a non midden layer containing a large quantity of bone and antler debris as well as debris from the manufacture of stone tools. The relationship of this layer to the midden has still to be investigated, and it is not yet dated, but it would seem to be a clear sign that activities at Sand comprised more than the deposition of midden alone. This point is reinforced by the presence around the midden of non-midden deposits which contain Mesolithic material including microliths and other stone tools.

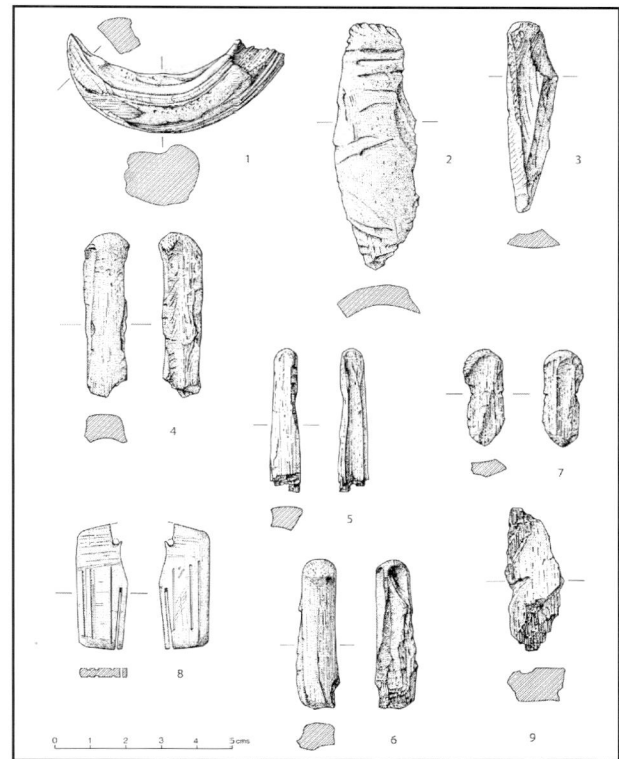

Figure 49.6 Sand, worked bone and antler. 1) boar's tusk; 2) bevel ended tool, roughout; 3) bevel ended and pointed tool; 4–7) bevel ended tools; 8, bone comb (from more recent rock shelter); 9) antler harpoon (broken).

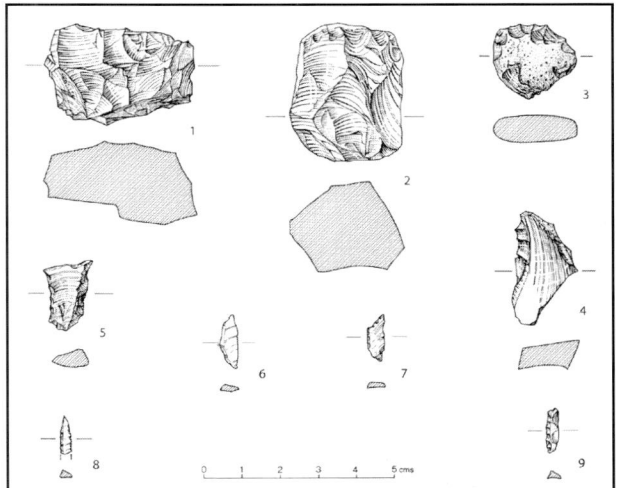

Figure 49.7 Sand, flaked lithics. 1–2) cores; 3) scraper; 4–5) edge retouched; 6–9) microliths.

Nevertheless, shellfish collection and processing was clearly central to the activities taking place at Sand. Shellfish were not the only food material in use: there were finds of both animal and fish bone in the midden, but the dominance of shells (in particular limpets which

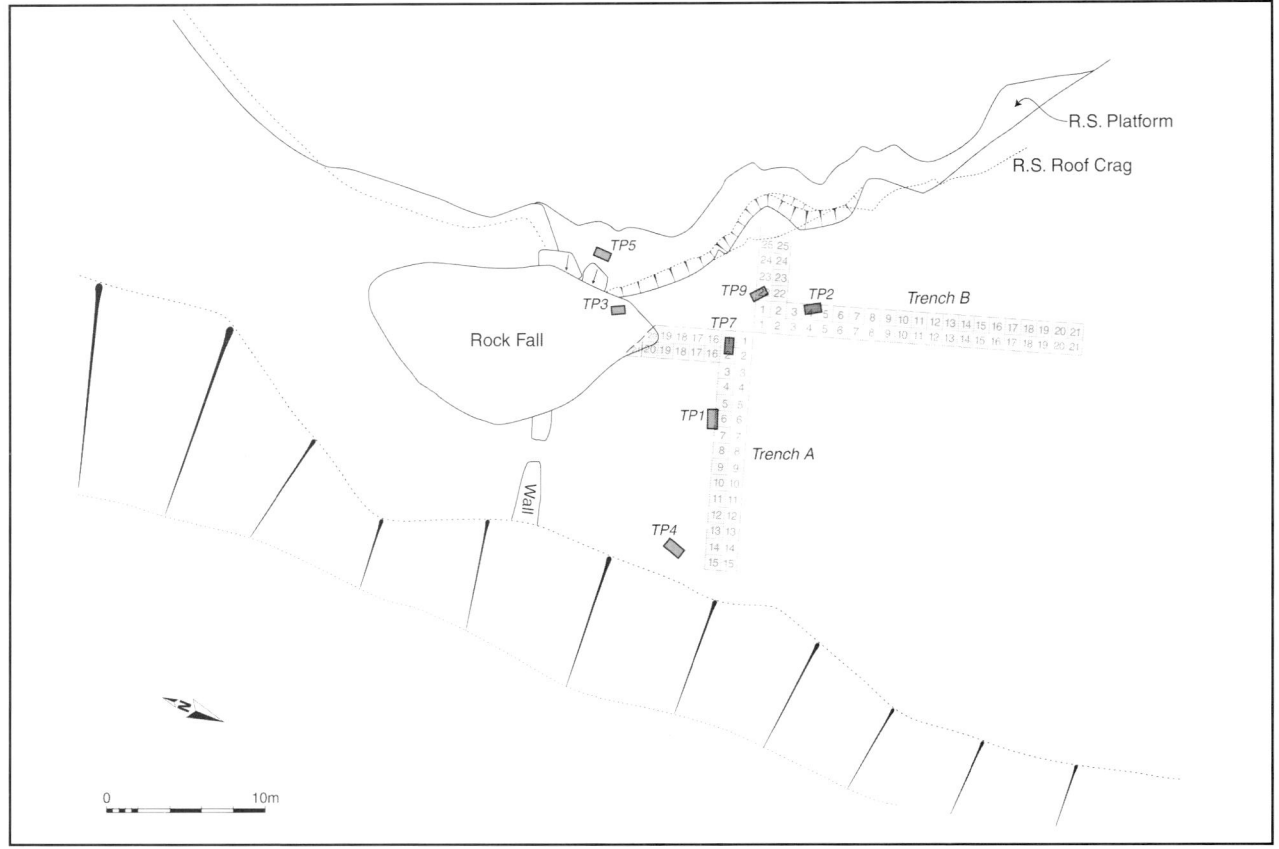

Figure 49.8 Sand, excavation plan.

Figure 49.9 Sand, view of the limpet midden during excavation.

comprise around 90% of all shells) suggest that they were the main food resource. The relative unimportance of fish bones in the midden also suggests that the limpets were directly consumed by the Mesolithic occupants of the Sand shelter and not, as has sometimes been suggested, used only for bait. Limpets were however, not the only shellfish. The midden contains a wide range of shells including winkles, cockles, mussels, crustacea and dog whelk.

With regard to the processing of food at Sand, the huge quantity of pot boilers and bevel ended bone tools suggest that both were integral. There is certainly abundant evidence of heat, not only in the fire-cracked stones, but also as small fragments of charcoal, though no certain in situ hearths were found. There were also fragments of charred hazelnut shell, presumably gathered from the surrounding woodlands, which suggest other diversity in the food resources.

Within the midden itself, there is also evidence of activities unrelated to food. There is some lithic debitage, and this, together with a fragment of harpoon that appears to have broken during manufacture (Figure 49.6), suggests tool production. A worked piece of scallop shell (Figure 49.11) shows that other activities, possibly relating to jewellery manufacture, were also taking place, and the presence of a perforated cowrie shell bead and small bone pieces with a double bevel end that have been tentatively

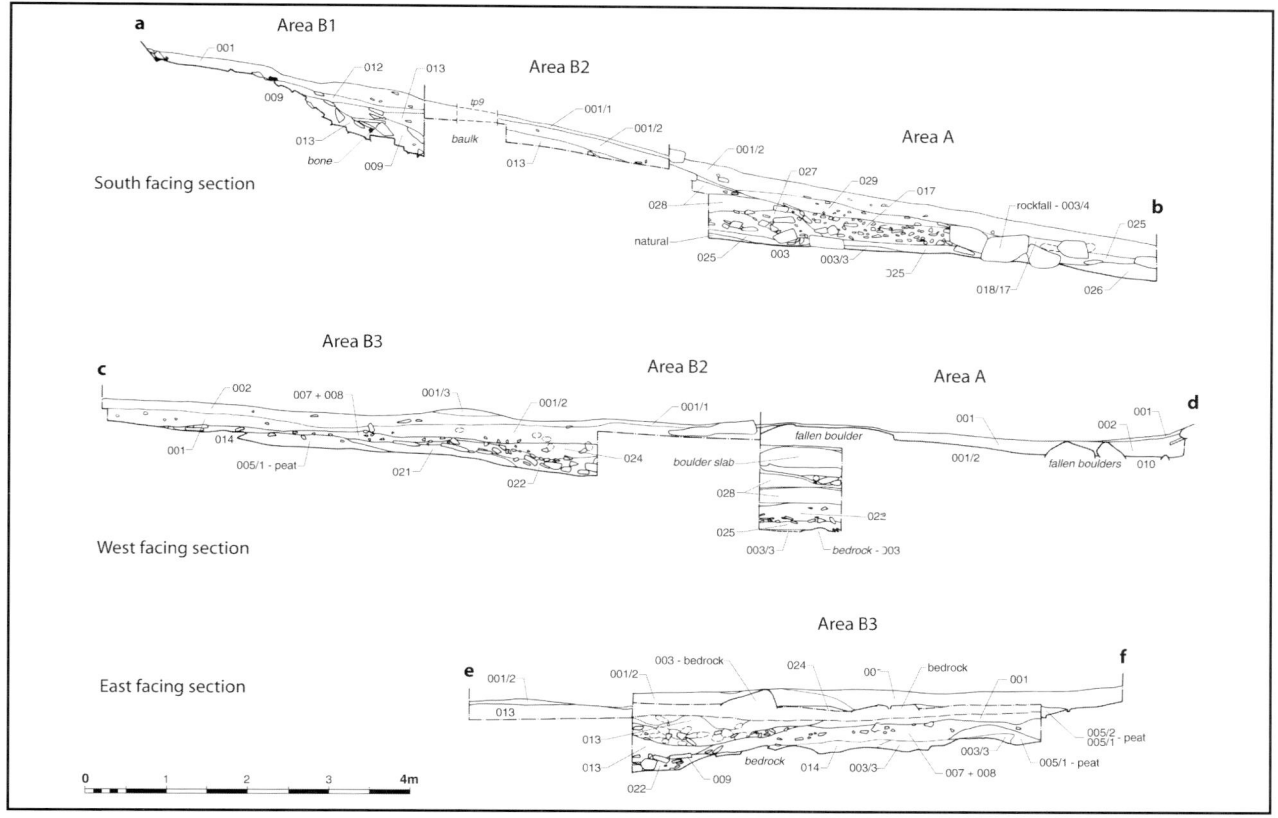

Figure 49.10 Sand, section drawing across midden.

interpreted as bone toggles (Figure 49.6) suggest information about clothing and decoration. In this respect, the presence of an inedible shell: dog whelk, is interesting. In later periods dog whelk was harvested for the extraction of a purple dye and recent work at Smoo cave has suggested that this took place on a large scale as far back as the Neolithic (Ceron pers. comm.). The harvesting of dog whelk at Sand is strongly indicative of the importance of some form of colour and art, in whatever form, to the Mesolithic inhabitants.

As the shell midden at Sand seems to have accumulated over a very short time it may have been a response to unusual conditions, such as a time of famine. If it were to represent a normal "winter's" occupation (for the sake of argument) we would expect the peninsula to be littered with similar shell middens from other years, but this is not the case (and our survey work has been very comprehensive). There are many midden sites certainly, but not all are Mesolithic, and they do not survive in the quantity to be expected if they were a normal part of the seasonal round for any substantial part of the Mesolithic in Western Scotland. Clearly, one of the lines that will be of crucial importance for the post-excavation interpretation is the investigation of seasonality. With this in mind the midden contains many otoliths which should be useful, and isotope analysis on shell samples is under discussion. Close dating of the site will also be useful.

In this respect the wider marine and environmental

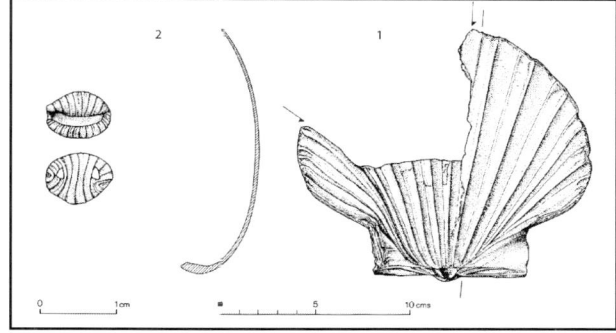

Figure 49.11 Sand, worked shell. 1) cut scallop shell; 2) perforated cowrie shell.

context of the site is very important. Geomorphological work around Sand has identified three new paleo-shorelines (Figure 49.12) which suggest that at 7700 BP the sea level reached up to just below the rockshelter with a brackish marsh leading to exposed rock pools at a walking distance of some 30 m. In addition, the project is working together with Professor Kevin Edwards to look at the early Holocene environment in the area, including both on-site and off-site pollen material, and with Dr Robert Shiel on soil micro-morphology. There is a possibility that the midden at Sand may date to the 8.2 kya environmental cooling episode (Edwards pers. comm.) and this is an intriguing suggestion in the light of its possible interpretation as a response to famine conditions.

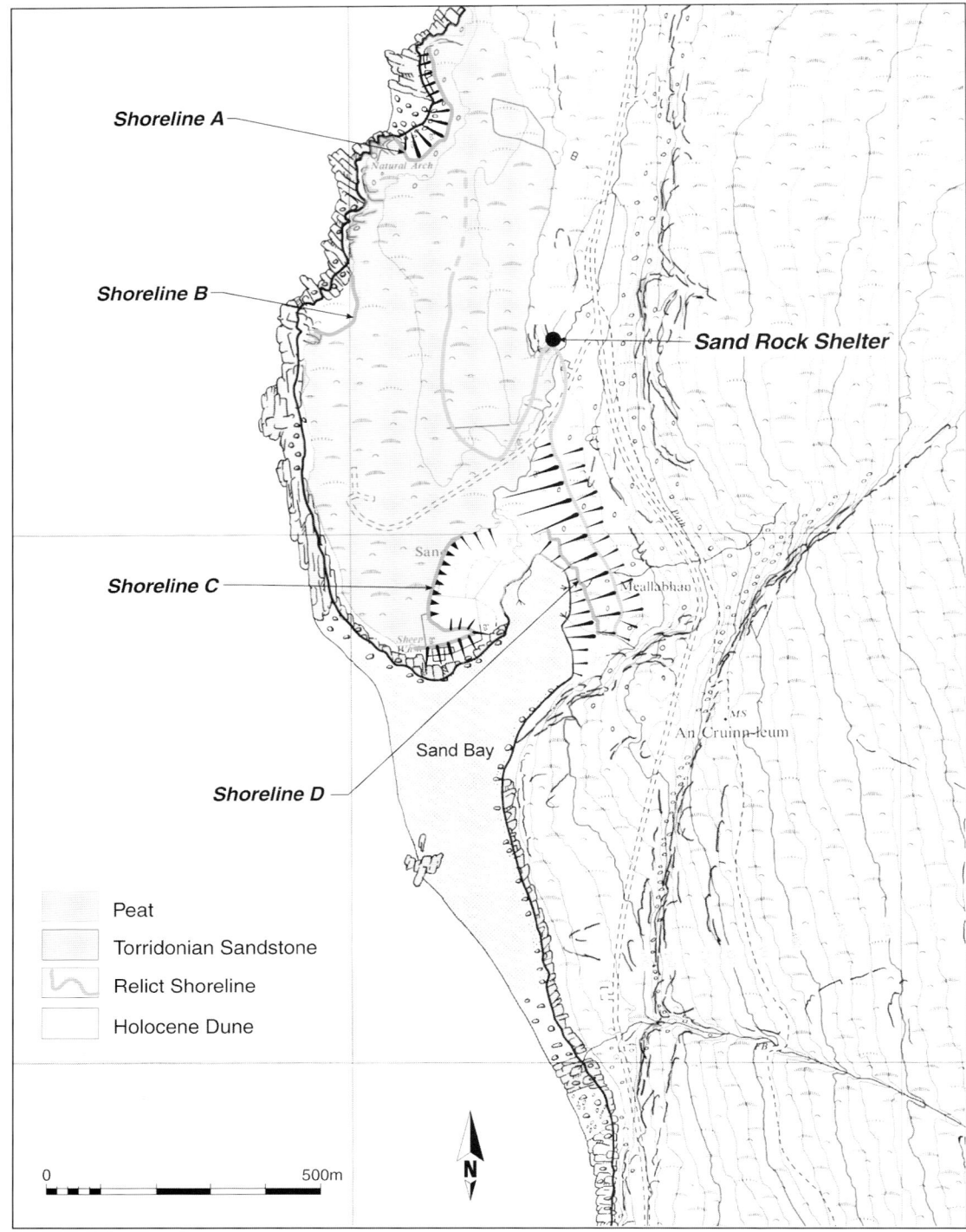

Figure 49.12 Sand, site location and palaeo-shorelines in the vicinity of the site.

The Mesolithic Around the Inner Sound: the Wider View

Midden sites, however, clearly formed only one part of the settlement suite of the Inner Sound in the Mesolithic. SFS survey has revealed other types of sites along the coastal strip, that may form a part of this suite: in addition to three definite Mesolithic midden sites (An Corran, Loch a Sguirr and Sand), there are 23 sites with lithic scatters as well as several other middens of uncertain date. The three Mesolithic shell middens are interesting in that each is very different. Each appears to answer different needs and provides clues as to the use of the area which need to be explored further.

An Corran (Figure 49.13) is a large, deep midden

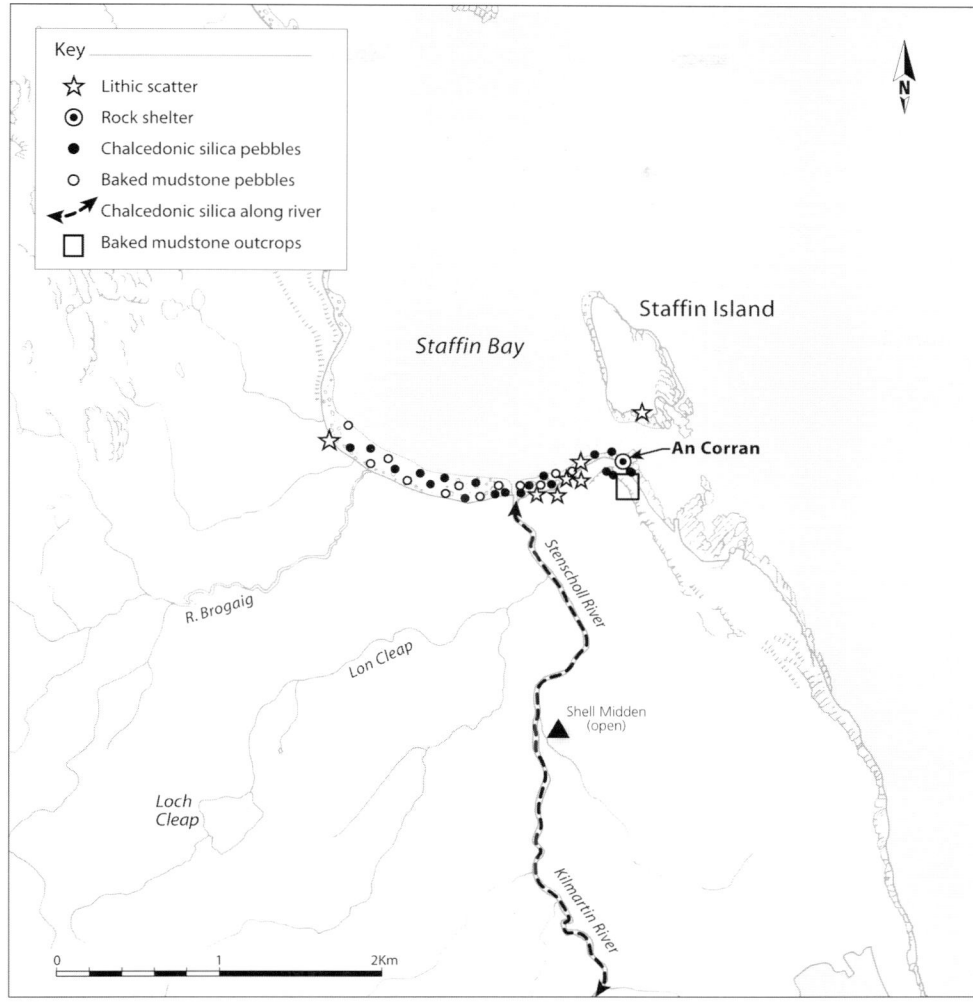

Figure 49.13 Staffin, location map of An Corran, local lithic scatters and lithic sources.

(Figure 49.14), which appears to have been occupied on and off over a long time at least into the Neolithic (Figure 49.15) (Hardy *et al.* forthcoming; Saville 1999). It is located beside two particularly good lithic sources (baked mudstone and chalcedonic silica), and as such may have been of central importance in the Inner Sound. Preliminary analysis of the use of lithic raw materials around the Inner Sound has shown that both of these were commonly used (below). SFS survey has revealed a cluster of lithic scatter sites close to An Corran (Figure 49.13) and these clearly merit further examination.

In contrast, the midden at Sand appears to be a short lived response to an extreme circumstance, such as a spell of famine. In this respect, it is well sited for shelter and to exploit a range of coastal resources including those of both shallow and deep water. Although there are other sites in the area, none are particularly close to the Mesolithic midden site which almost stands out in its isolation.

Loch a Sguirr, on Raasay (Figure 49.1) is yet another type of site, it lies at the top of a cliff well away from the

Figure 49.14 General view of An Corran, the site lies on the platform where a human figure may be seen.

type of shallow water deposits exploited elsewhere (Figure 49.16) (Finlayson *et al.* 1999:17 pp). The midden deposits here are shallow and it is unlikely to have been an intensive shellfish processing site. There are, however clear signs

Lab no.	Description of context	Sample	Radiocarbon age (BP)
AA-27743	Main shell midden	Human bone	3885±65
AA-27744	Black greasy midden	Human bone	4405±65
AA-27745	Basal layer of red clay, possibly disturbed	Pig bone	3120±60
AA-27746	Basal layer of red clay, possibly disturbed	Ruminant long bone	6420±75
AA-29311	Black greasy midden	Bevel ended bone tool on red deer metacarpus	4175±60
AA-29312	Main shell midden	Bone point on ovicaprid tibia	2045±60
AA-29313	Lower shell midden	Bevel ended bone tool on red deer metapodium	3660±65
AA-29314	Black greasy midden	Bevel ended bone tool on ruminant long bone	3975±50
AA-29315	Main shell midden	Bevel ended bone tool on red deer metatarsus	5190±55
AA-29316	Main shell midden	Bevel ended bone tool on ruminant long bone	6215±60
OxA-4994	Main shell midden	Bevel ended bone tool on red deer metatarsus	7590±90

Figure 49.15 An Corran: radio carbon determinations (Saville 1999).

Figure 49.16 General view of Loch a Sguirr.

of Mesolithic activity and one important factor may well have been its central location in the Inner Sound. From the hill above the site there are clear views around the Inner Sound on all sides (and some of the best mobile phone reception today). The vicinity of Loch a Sguirr has yet to be surveyed so that its Mesolithic context remains unknown, but this is a gap that the project plans to fill in 2001. Whether the central island chain, where Loch a Sguirr is situated, provided a hindrance to travel across the Inner Sound in the Mesolithic, or facilitated it, has yet to be determined, but the site at Loch a Sguirr is a clear indication that the Mesolithic seafarers made use of it.

One factor that stands out is that despite the relatively small size of the study area, in European terms, there is clear variation in the way in which this area was used throughout the Mesolithic. Not only is there variation among the sites themselves, as discussed above, but most of the midden and lithic sites to have been discovered, Mesolithic or not, lie in the northern half of the Inner Sound (Figure 49.2). Few sites have been found to the south. One reason may be that the southern area has a long history of agriculture and development. There are lithic scatters here and an open midden: all on the islands of Scalpay and Pabay (Figure 49.1). As these are not so well developed they may provide an indication of previous archaeological remains. There is also the complication of the effects of a higher sea level on the more gentle topography of the south. These are elements that the project plans to explore in the future.

Why the Inner Sound?

So far, the SFS project has demonstrated a remarkable density of survival of sites in the Inner Sound area. Whether or not this is representative of Mesolithic Scotland as a whole, it opens up certain issues for study. What were the attractions of this area in the early Holocene? The marine topography, with its numerous islands has already been touched upon: this, no doubt, facilitated both travel and settlement – both of which are central to the nomadic hunter-gatherer way of life, as commonly envisaged for the Scottish Mesolithic. This topography would also have provided a rich resource base from which various niches could be exploited including: salt and fresh/shallow and deep water; coastal; lowland and upland land units. Travel and contact outwith the area was also, of course, possible.

Movement is thus central to the interpretation of the way of life in the Inner Sound in the sixth – eighth millennia BP, but movement is a notoriously difficult thing to document archaeologically. Luckily for the SFS team, one of the other resources of the Inner Sound comes into play here, not only as an important resource in the Mesolithic, but also as an important resource for the archaeological researcher of today. This resource is stone (the archaeological use of stone in this way is something that was, of course, pioneered in Scotland by John Coles in his work at Morton, see Coles 1971:294 pp).

The Lithic Resources of the Inner Sound

Stone, suitable for tools, was vital to the Mesolithic population of Scotland but a general lack of good quality flint deposits meant that they had to search for, and use, a variety of other materials (Wickham-Jones and Collins 1978). The diversity of lithic materials used throughout prehistory in Scotland has been well documented elsewhere (Wickham-Jones 1986, 1990:51 pp), but previous studies have tended to focus on a fairly broad scale at the picture across the (modern) country as a whole. In general a lack of recent excavation and survey has meant that there has not been enough data from any one area for a detailed picture to be drawn. The work of Scotland's First Settlers is filling this gap for the Inner Sound and we are fortunate in that the area contains various good quality raw materials some of which are very restricted in their geographical source. What follows is a preliminary view, based on partial data, as it has not yet been possible to catalogue fully the extensive lithic collections.

There is no doubt that the lithic resources of the Inner Sound were of particular interest to its Mesolithic inhabitants. So far, the preliminary analysis of the lithic assemblages from sites round the Inner Sound has recorded the use of at least seven different lithic materials: Baked Mudstone; Rum Bloodstone; Quartz; Chalcedonic Silica; Flint; Chert and various Agates (Figure 49.17). The sources for some are spread generally across the area: quartz; and various cherts and agates, while others are much more restricted: baked mudstone; rum bloodstone and the siliceous chalcedonies.

One of the most distinct raw materials to have been used across the area in prehistory is baked mudstone which is found on most sites and is often the main component of a lithic assemblage. The outcrops of baked mudstone are very localised, however: so far it has only been recorded as isolated bands at Staffin in the north-west of the Inner Sound (Figure 49.13). Baked Mudstone is formed when pre-existing mudstones come into contact with newly formed igneous rocks and are baked in the process (Stevenson pers. comm.). It tends to occur as small, isolated, rafts which may form outcrops today. Mudstone cobbles are common in the area of the outcrops and it is likely that the Mesolithic community was collecting these to knap (Hardy *et al.* forthcoming). There is considerable variation in the outcrops, and baked mudstone generally degrades with time, but freshly obtained baked mudstone can be very hard and homogeneous, and of a shiny black

Material	Quantity
Chalcedonic Silica, Flint and Chert	1197
Baked Mudstone	945
Rum Bloodstone	233
Quartz and Quartzite	8771
Agate, Jasper and Rock Crystal	13
Coarse stone	9
Unknown	5

Figure 49.17 Breakdown of raw material use across the Inner Sound incorporating data from Clarke 1990 and SFS material as of 30.8.2000.

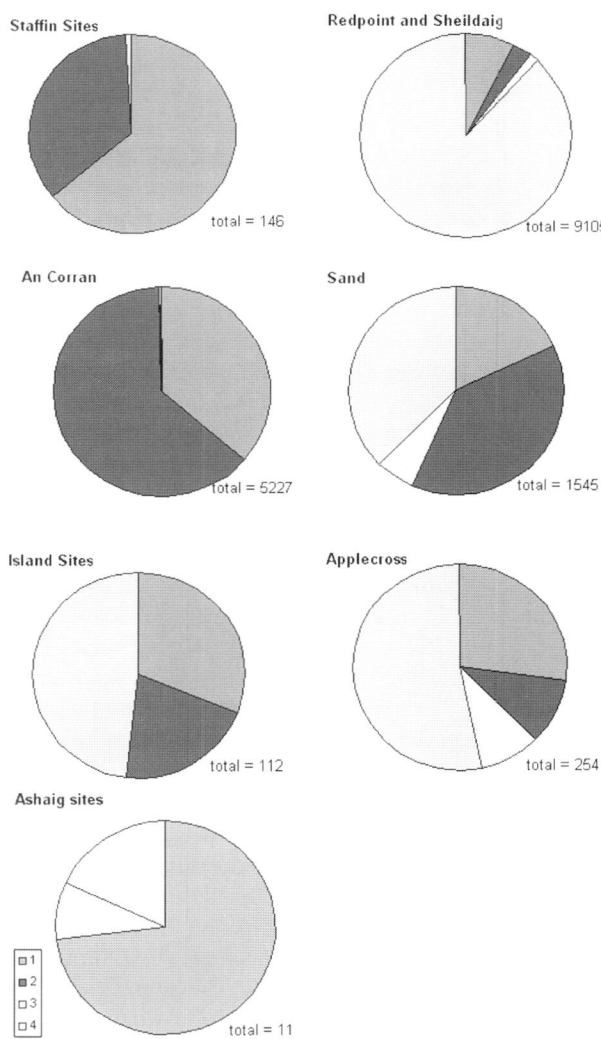

Figure 49.18 The use of different raw materials across the Inner Sound. 1: Chalcedonic Silica/flint/chert. 2: Baked Mudstone. 3: Rum Bloodstone. 4: Quartz and Quartzite

appearance. It would have provided a good quality material for tools and this is no doubt reflected in the Mesolithic preference for this material. It is notable that baked mudstone predominates at the sites where detailed excavation has taken place (Figure 49.18) such as Sand, in Applecross and An Corran (Hardy *et al.* forthcoming).

Chalcedonic silica is another material with a restricted source which again occurs at Staffin in the north (Figure 49.13) (Hardy *et al.* forthcoming). Here, it may be found as small nodules along the course of the Stenscholl river. Chalcedonic Silica was certainly an important raw material in prehistory, and it occurs on all sites, but visually it is indistinguishable to the naked eye from many of the local flints and cherty pebbles which are widely available throughout the area, especially in the east so that quantification of its use is difficult. Though further analysis is needed, the possibility remains that chalcedonic silica was transported from Staffin to other sites such as Sand in the east of the study area (especially in the light of the known movement of baked mudstone).

Implements of Rum bloodstone also occur on many sites, though in varying proportions. It seems to have been more common in the east and south of the study area and was never the main resource on any site (Figures 49.17 and 49.18). The preliminary analysis of the material catalogued to date shows that no bloodstone cores have been recorded, and that most bloodstone occurs as flakes and chunks, suggesting that the preliminary knapping of bloodstone cores was taking place outwith the Inner Sound. There are various sources of this material, but most would not have been of use in prehistory: previous research has shown that knappable bloodstone only occurs in one place, on the island of Rum, some 30 km to the SW (Figure 49.19). The existence of extensive Mesolithic activity on Rum is well documented (Wickham-Jones 1990) and work there confirmed that the material used for tools in prehistory was, indeed, likely to have come from Rum alone (Clarke and Griffiths 1990:149 pp). At the time it was not possible to document the nature of bloodstone exploitation in detail, but this is something which SFS hopes to investigate. At the same time, the presence at the south end of Skye of a Mesolithic site comprising an extensive scatter of bloodstone tools and debitage at Camas Daraich on the Point of Sleat, overlooking Rum, has recently been confirmed by excavation (Wickham-Jones and Hardy 2000). The use and distribution of Rum bloodstone is clearly worthy of further research.

Baked mudstone, Rum bloodstone and chalcedonic silica are all homogeneous rocks of relatively good quality. In contrast, other stones such as quartz, flint, chert and agate were of varied quality. The sources of these stones were all more widespread throughout the study area. They were used on many sites, but they rarely predominate and the impression is that most were mainly used to supplement other stones. The only exception to this is quartz which, perhaps surprisingly for its unpredictable quality, dominates many of the assemblages in the north and east of the area.

So far, quartz comprised around half of many assemblages, particularly of material recovered from surface collection or test pitting. To the north, however, at the sites of Sheildaig and Redpoint it seems to have been far more important. The excavations at Sheildaig have never

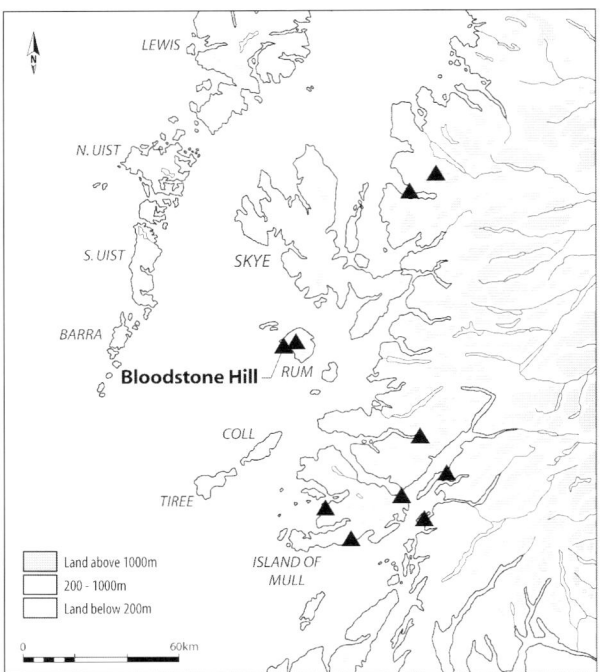

Figure 49.19 Sources of Rum Bloodstone, only that at Bloodstone Hill has yielded knappable material.

been fully published (Walker 1973) but preliminary work by Ann Clarke in the 1980s showed the quartz to be of good quality and some fine pieces were made, including several microliths (Clarke 1990:154 pp). Over 6000 lithics were recovered from Sheildaig, of which 88% were of quartz. Clarke also examined existing collections from Redpoint (Gray 1960; Clarke 1990:154 pp) where the assemblage amounted to 1356 pieces, of which 80% were of quartz. In 1999 Birch re-visited Redpoint as part of the SFS project and collected another 1748 pieces from the site of which 95% were of quartz (Birch 1999). As both sites lie within the study area work on these assemblages will be up-dated in the light of other local sites.

Flints and cherts are common across the area, perhaps unfortunately from our point of view, though they are mostly available only as small pebbles of variable quality. They occur in both till and gravel deposits as well as in the Applecross sandstone, and they seem to have been widely transported by both marine currents and rivers (Figure 49.20). Today, most appear to be of a corticated white or cream colour, though there are odd grey examples. It is impossible to distinguish most of them by the naked eye, nor can they be easily differentiated from the Chalcedonic silicas of Staffin. For the purposes of this paper they have, therefore, been lumped together with chalcedonic silica. Silicas like this do not dominate any assemblage, but they were clearly an important part of the Mesolithic knappers' repertoire.

Other stones like agates and jaspers are also widely distributed across the area, but were only infrequently used for tools, apparently to supplement the dominant

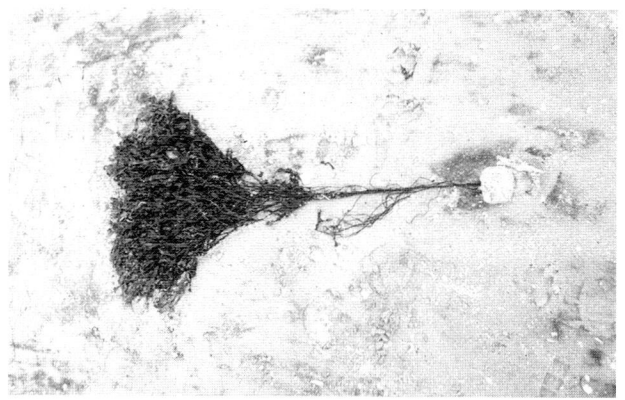

Figure 49.20 Marine transported flint: Sand beach.

raw materials. In general, the knappers preferred to use the better quality materials, even where they had to be transported from restricted sources. None of the journeys would have been long, but all involved some complex navigation around the islands that litter the Inner Sound, the waters of which are very susceptible to sudden squalls and prolonged bad weather conditions. The journey from Rum would have involved either the navigation of the narrow and fast flowing Kyles of Rhea or land transport for some 15 km along the peninsula of Sleat with a boat journey at either end.

The restricted sources of both Baked Mudstone and Rum Bloodstone, as well as the Chalcedonic silica, mean that some form of travel and contact has to have taken place. The lack of data in the past has meant that analysis of this transport remained largely conjectural, though some features have been noted previously, such as a general lack of cortical material away from the source areas (Clarke 1990:154 pp). SFS hopes to remedy this by providing information on a number of assemblages, all collected with the same rigour. As yet the work of the project is still in its infancy, but information on knapping technologies, core types and artifact types from each site should help to provide details of the movement of stones, and therefore of people around the Inner Sound.

Acknowledgments

Many people and organisations have helped this work to take place and all are due thanks. Acknowledgment should go first to our many funders: Historic Scotland, the Society of Antiquaries of Scotland, the Society of Antiquaries of London; the Prehistoric Society; The Russell Trust; Ross and Cromarty Enterprise; Leader II; The Munro fund, University of Edinburgh; many private donors; the Department of Archaeology, University of Edinburgh and the Applecross Estates Trust who have provided support in kind. Thanks go to those who put up with our intrusion into their lives and provided much support: DERA BUTEC and the Works Services department SERCO, Kyle of Lochalsh; RTB Applecross; the crew of LENIE from the RMAS; RJ Macleod Ltd; Highland Council Roads Department; Q Banting; Lorna Lumsden and Mike Summers. The illustrations for this paper have been prepared by Kevin Hicks and Sylvia Stevenson. In addition many people joined in to provide support and physical labour including especially the volunteers from Aberdeen University and Applecross village, the staff of the Centre for Field Archaeology, Edinburgh who provided both physical assistance and much help in kind, as well as Steven Birch; Mike Chase; George Kozikowiski; Fergus MacLeod; Martin Wildgoose and, of course, the children: Carmen; Victoria; Abi; Guille and Jamie!

References

Birch, S. 1999. *Scotland's First Settlers Interim Discovery Report: Redpoint.* Unpublished Report. Skye.

Clarke, A. 1990. The location and examination of archaeological sites and their associated assemblages. In: Wickham-Jones, C.R. (ed.) *Rhum: mesolithic and later sites at Kinloch, excavations 1984–86*, 154–156. Society of Antiquaries of Scotland Monograph Series no 7. Edinburgh.

Clarke, A. and Griffiths, D. 1990. The use of bloodstone as a raw material for flaked stone tools in the west of Scotland. In: Wickham-Jones, C.R. (ed.) *Rhum: mesolithic and later sites at Kinloch, excavations 1984–86*, 149–154. Society of Antiquaries of Scotland Monograph Series no 7. Edinburgh.

Coles, J.M. 1971. The Early Settlement of Scotland: Excavations at Morton, Fife, *Proceedings of the Prehistoric Society* 37, 284–366.

Finlayson, B., Hardy, K. and Wickham-Jones, C.R. 1999. *Scotland's First Settlers 1999, Data Structure Report.* Centre for Field Archaeology, University of Edinburgh, Unpublished Report. Edinburgh.

Gray, A.F. 1960. A collection of stone artefacts from Redpoint, Loch Torridon, Ross-shire. *Proceedings of the Society of Antiquaries of Scotland* 93 (1959–60), 236–237.

Hardy, K., Miket, R. and Saville, A. forthcoming. *An Corran, Staffin, Skye: a rockshelter with Mesolithic and later occupation.*

Mellars, P.A. 1987. *Excavations on Oronsay.* Edinburgh.

Saville, A. 1999. An Corran, Staffin, Skye. *Discovery and Excavation in Scotland* 1998, 126–127.

Walker, M. 1973. *Archaeological excavation of a microlithic assemblage at Sheildaig, Wester Ross, Scotland. Preliminary Report.* Unpublished Report. Edinburgh.

Wickham-Jones, C.R. 1986. The Procurement and Use Of Stone For Flaked Tools in Prehistoric Scotland. *Proceedings of the Society of Antiquaries of Scotland* 116, 1–10.

—— 1990. *Rhum: mesolithic and later sites at Kinloch, excavations 1984–86.* Society of Antiquaries of Scotland Monograph Series no 7. Edinburgh.

Wickham-Jones, C.R. and Collins, G.H. 1978. The sources of flint and chert in northern Britain. *Proceedings of the Society of Antiquaries of Scotland* 109 (1977–8), 7–21.

Wickham-Jones, C.R. and Hardy, K. 2000. *Camas Daraich.* Centre for Field Archaeology, Data Structure Report. Unpublished Report. Edinburgh.

Session VI

Exchange and Communication

50. Exchange: artefacts, people and ideas on the move in Mesolithic Europe

Anders Fischer

In the attempt to explain the functioning and development of Mesolithic societies, exchange has become a concept frequently referred to. Until recently, however, hard evidence for the existence of Mesolithic exchange has been lacking from most parts of the continent. The Northwest European examples of imported Danubian shaft-hole axes are probably the most celebrated exception (e.g. Fischer 1982; Jennbert 1984; Larsson 1988; Verhart 2000; Klassen, in press).

By announcing and organising a symposium session on the topic the organisers of MESO 2000 have successfully provoked the presentation of a series of new data on and approaches to Mesolithic exchange. At the same time the difficulty in distinguishing between the archaeological outcome of exchange as opposed to direct access through residential mobility or task group mobility has been exemplified.

The focus on exchange in the study of Mesolithic Europe is largely inspired by ethnography (e.g. Taffinder 1998; Verhart 2000). As an introduction I shall, therefor, recall the great geographical range and social importance often involved in trade and gift-giving among historically known foragers of other continents, irrespective of their highly diverse environmental and cultural setting.

Take, for instance, the North American Northwest Coast Indians, among whom long-distance trade and ceremonial gift-giving were decisive elements in the maintenance of power and prestige. These activities typically involved long sea voyages and contacts between linguistically and culturally different tribes (e.g. Suttles 1990:12 p; Halpin and Seguin 1990:80; Emmons 1991:53 pp). Marriage alliances over long distances were often arranged by the aristocracy to promote trade and power relations (Coles and Darling 1990:129 p). A most inspiring eye-witness account of these phenomena comes from John Jewitt (1815/1994:61 pp), who happened to live with a Northwest Coast chief for more than two years during the early part of the period of contact with European traders. This chief maintained regular and direct exchange relationships with high-ranking persons within a geographical range comparable to, for instance, the total area of the Late Mesolithic Ertebølle Culture.

John Jewitt reports on trade delegations from foreign tribes that came regularly by sea to the coastal summer residence of the chief. The identity and geographical location of these tribes is confirmed by modern anthropologists, and the journeyed distances cited by Jewitt are considered acceptable, on the reasonable condition that the route was not a straight line across sea and mountains, but followed the highly indented coastline (personal communication Roy Carlson, Canada). Most frequent were visitors from a northern tribe from which the chief's 'queen' came. According to Jewitt their journey was in the order of 300 km (corresponding to a good 100 km as the crow flies). Other regular exchange partners arrived from the south after having travelled by canoe about 500 km (c. 200 km, measured in a straight line). A third group, living to the east, is reported to have needed a specially long period of rest before their return journey. They faced not only travel by canoe but also travel over land (measured in a straight line across the mountains, the distance between the starting and the end points of their journey was c.130 km).

Other thought-provoking examples can be picked from the ethnographic record of Australia, which represents quite a different setting as concerns climate, population density and social complexity. From here we know of exchange networks reaching all the way across the continent. The exchange goods comprised a wide array of phenomena. Some, like large, decorated pearl shells (Akerman and Stanton 1994) had the potential of surviving in ordinary archaeological contexts. Others would be much less visible archaeologically, such as psychotropic bush tobacco (Mulvaney and Kamminga 1999:96 pp; Flood 2001:268 p), not to speak of ceremonial songs and dances distributed through these networks (Lourandos 1997: 43; Mulvaney and Kamminga 1999:95).

The papers of this session have their empirical bases in different parts of Europe. The potential exchange goods considered in these articles include the following:

- Greenstone and diabase axes from two quarry sites on the Norwegian West Coast (Bergsvik and Bruen Olsen)
- Western Swedish axes made of dolerite and related material, some of it possibly imported from southern Norway (Bengtsson)
- Flint blades found in northern Sweden as much as 1000 km from their sources in southern Scandinavia (Knutsson *et al.*)
- Cores and blades of cretaceous flint transported to Latvia, Estonia and Finland as much as 600 km from their source area in Lithuania and western Byelorussia, as well as finished tools of the same material brought to the Upper Volga region (Zhilin)
- Carboniferous flint items transported to Finland, Latvia and Estonia from source areas 400–500 km away, including the Upper Volga region (Zhilin)
- Weapons and ornaments of exotic faunal materials found on southern Scandinavian islands to which they were brought across the sea from other parts of the Baltic region (Fischer)
- Shaft-hole axes and pottery, which changed hands from central European farmers to foragers of north-western Europe (Fischer; Verhart)
- Flint from the Atlantic sea floor, found in the interior of Brittany, at least 15 to 40 km from the coast line of those days (Yven)
- Marriage partners exchanged between foragers of northern Europe (Knutsson *et al.*; Zhilin) and between farmers and foragers in western and northern Europe (Fischer; Schulting; Verhart).

As will appear from the subsequent papers, there were other actions than exchange, which could have been responsible for the transportation of artefacts from their source areas to the sites where they were found. The cyclical seasonal movements of mobile foraging populations are mentioned as a potential explanation of, for instance, the transfer of coastal flint into the interior of Brittany (Yven). It is argued, that in Late Mesolithic coastal western Norway, where a sedentary way of life is assumed, the procurement of material for axe manufacture took the form of direct access by task groups (Bergsvik and Bruen Olsen). The concept of task group operations may also be relevant in the interpretation of a number of Danish bones of humans and dogs, the C13-values of which are testimony to a significant consumption of marine food, even if they are found as far as 150 km up the rivers from the coast of their period (Fischer).

Several of the papers deal with the potential relations between exchange and the introduction of farming. In this connection, special attention is devoted to the possible transfer of marriage partners (Schulting; Verhart; Fischer). It should be noted, though, that the long-distance exchange of spouses may have been a widespread phenomenon long before the arrival of Neolithic economy (Knutsson *et al.*; Zhilin). In relation to the neolithisation, the possibility of exchange of brides or grooms provides us with an obvious explanation of how foragers could obtain the know-how needed for the adoption of husbandry and cultivation.

The papers of the present session generally tend to imply that Mesolithic exchange was part of peaceful negotiations to the benefit of both parties. It should, however, be recalled that the ethnographic record on foragers is rich in examples of recurring, non-peaceful inter-group activities conducted with the deliberate aim of getting access to wives and precious items (e.g. Burch 1988; Jedlickova 2000:54 ff.). The same may very well have been the case in the Mesolithic and in the transition from the Mesolithic to the Neolithic in Europe.

There were, no doubt, many transactions by which artefacts, people and ideas were moved around in Mesolithic Europe. The following papers clarify this to some degree and will, I hope, be an inspiration for further studies on these matters.

References

Akkerman, K. and Stanton, J. 1994. *Riji and Jakuli: Kimberley Pearl Shell in Aboriginal Australia*. Northern Territory Museum of Arts and Sciences. Darwin.

Burch, E.S. 1988. War and trade. In: Fitzhugh, W.W. and Crowell, A. (eds) *Crossroads of Continents. Cultures of Siberia and Alaska*: 227–240. Maryland.

Coles, D. and Darling, D. 1990. History of the Early Period. In: Suttles, W. (ed.) *Handbook of North American Indians 7, Northwest Coast*, 119–134. Washington.

Emmons, G.T. 1991. *The Tlingit Indians*. American Museum of Natural History. New York.

Fischer, A. 1982. Trade in Danubian shaft-hole axes and the introduction of neolithic economy in Denmark. *Journal of Danish Archaeology* 1, 7–12.

Flood, J. 2001. *Archaeology of the Dreamtime. A Story of Prehistoric Australia and its People*. Sydney.

Halpin, M.M. and Seguin, M. 1990. Tsimshian Peoples: Southern Tsimshian, Coast Tsimshian, Nishga, and Gitksan. In: Suttles, W. (ed.) *Handbook of North American Indians 7, Northwest Coast*, 267–284. Washington.

Jedlicková, D. 2000. *Exchange and First Contacts in Australia and Tasmania during the 1800s*. Kust Till Kust-Böcker. Department of Archaeology and Ancient History, Uppsala University, Uppsala.

Jennbert, K. 1984. *Den Produktiva Gåvan. Tradition och Innovation i Sydskandinavien för Omkring 5300 År Sedan*. Acta Archaeologica Lundensia, Series in 4°, No. 16. Lund.

Jewitt, J.R. 1815/1994. *White Slaves of the Nootka. Narrative of the adventures and sufferings of John R. Jewitt while a captive of the Nootka Indians on Vancouver Island, 1803–05*. Surrey.

Klassen, L. in press. The Ertebølle Culture and neolithic continental Europe: traces of contact and interaction. In: Fischer, A. and Kristiansen, K. (eds) *The Neolithisation of Denmark – 150 years of Debate*. Sheffield.

Larsson, L. 1988. Aspects of exchange in mesolithic societies. In: Hårdh, B., Larsson, L., Olausson, D. and Petré, R. (eds) *Trade and Exchange in Prehistory. Studies in Honour of Berta Stjernquist*. Acta Archaeologica Lundensia, 25–32. Series in 8°, No. 16. Lund.

Lourandos, H. 1997. *Continent of Hunter-Gatherers. New Perspectives in Australian Prehistory*. Cambridge.

Mulvaney, J. and Kamminga, J. 1999. *Prehistory of Australia*. St. Leonards.

Taffinder, J. 1998. *The Allure of the Exotic. The social use of non-local raw materials during the Stone Age in Sweden.* Aun 25. Uppsala.

Suttles, W. 1990. Introduction. In: Suttles, W. (ed.) *Handbook of North American Indians 7, Northwest Coast*, 12–13. Washington.

Verhart, L.B.M. 2000. *Time Fade Away. The Neolithization of the Southern Netherlands in an Anthropological and Geographical Perspective.* Archaeological Studies, Leiden University, Leiden.

Exchange and Communication

51. Knowledge and Interaction in the Stone Age: Raw materials for adzes and axes, their sources and distributional patterns

Lisbet Bengtsson

This contribution presents some results of an ongoing study within "From Coast to Coast: Stone Age Societies in Transition", a joint project between Göteborg University and Uppsala University.

The aim is to study the variety of raw materials used for the production of adzes and axes in western Sweden and to use this information to distinguish the sources and primary production areas, as well as to describe the way in which people interacted to gain access to the sources or to the tools themselves. This is being done so as to get a better idea of the knowledge that people had of good raw materials and how they used that knowledge.

The study is being carried out together with the geologist Ulf Bergström. Within the project, the so-called Lihult adzes are used as a basis. They are fairly well defined, both as a type and as a time indicator, and have a quite well-known distribution. For comparison, round-butted axes are also being studied, but to a less degree. These are also fairly well defined as a type but represent a longer time span and have a more general distribution. Debris from sites with such artefacts is also considered. The finds form part of collections in western Sweden and at the Museum of National Antiquities in Stockholm. Possible sources of the raw materials are being investigated by means of geological maps and surveys.

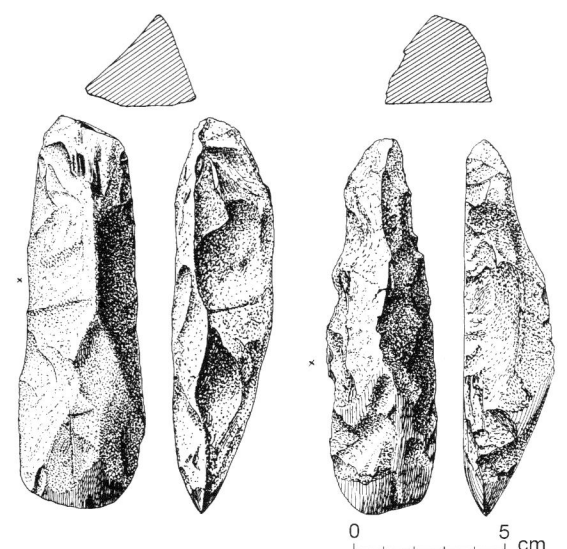

Figure 51.1 Lihult adzes from the Lihult type site. Original line-drawing by A. Hjelm, at the Gothenburg City Museum.

Figure 51.2 The Lihult type site. Original photograph by O. Frödin 1903–4, at the Gothenburg City Museum.

Introduction

This article deals with the so-called Lihult culture of the Late Mesolithic. It is considered a tradition that was present in western Sweden and has been dated to about 5800–5400/5000 BC there (Nordqvist 1997:65) (see figure 51.9 for a general view of the Scandinavian peninsula). Its most diagnostic object is the Lihult adze, named after finds from the type site at Lihult, north-east of Strömstad in northern Bohuslän (Figures 51.1 and 51.2). The site is located by Lake Lången, which was connected with the sea during the Mesolithic.

In an ongoing project, in which I am working together with the geologist Ulf Bergström, we are using the Lihult adzes as a basis for our study. The Lihult adzes are fairly well defined both as a type and as a time indicator and have a quite well-known distribution. We are also looking at the round-butted axes (Figure 51.3), which have apparently a longer time span (Mesolithic–Neolithic) and a more general distribution.

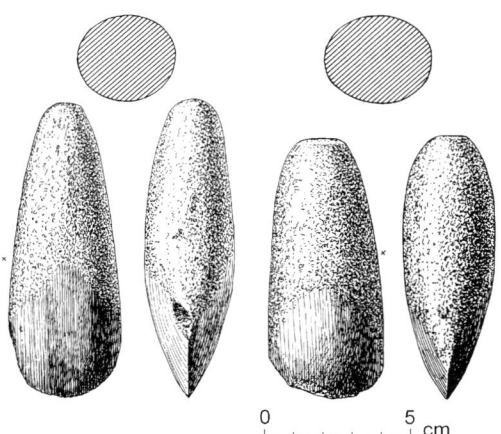

Figure 51.3 Round-butted axes from the Lihult type site. Original line-drawing by A. Hjelm, at the Gothenburg City Museum.

The distribution of Lihult adzes and possible reasons for their distribution

Most of the Lihult adzes have been found on, or close to, the coast of Bohuslän (Figure 51.4). There are several possible interpretations of this phenomenon:

1 The type represents a regional fashion, an identity marker.
2 The type represents a certain kind of work or production. In the region, it was used for purposes, such as kajak manufacture, that were not relevant, or were less relevant, in other regions.
3 The adze was made in the region, because that was where especially suitable raw materials were available, such as dolerites.
4 The type was really more widespread than we can confirm today but was made of other, perishable materials in other regions, such as bone or wood.

There is one more region in Sweden, where the Lihult adzes have been found in great numbers, namely close to the south-western corner of Lake Vänern. Close to the sites by the south-western corner of Lake Vänern are the Halle and Hunne mountains, both of which are known for their dolerite layers. This dolerite was used for the manufacture of Lihult adzes and for other tools in Mesolithic times (see, for example, Cedergen 1932). However, the adzes on the West Coast of Sweden were not necessarily manufactured by Lake Vänern and then taken to the West Coast. Dolerite predominates as a raw material for the Lihult adzes on the coast also, but there the inhabitants apparently exploited other sources.

For example, most of the adzes and round-butted axes from the Gossbydal site on the island of Hisingen within the municipality of Gothenburg were made of dolerite, but there the dolerite was not from the Halle or Hunne mountains but instead possibly came from local dykes (Bergström 1958). This indication is now under study by our group.

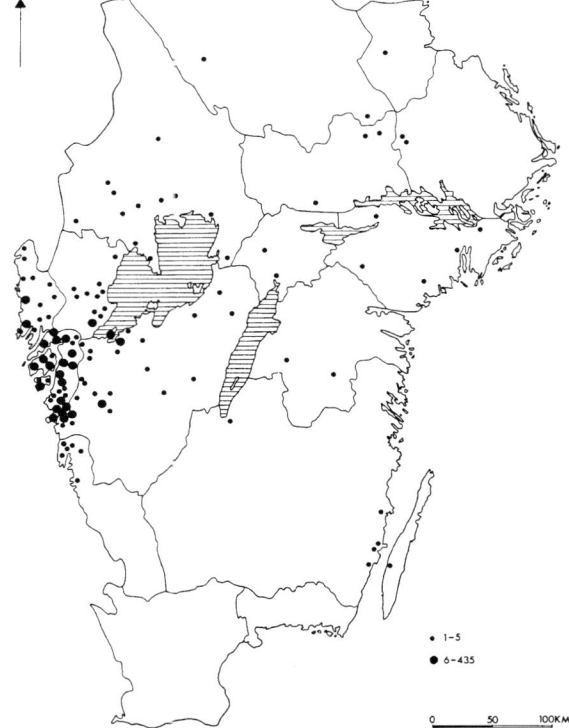

Figure 51.4 The distribution of Lihult adzes. Number per parish. Based on Welinder 1977:58.

In southern central Bohuslän, in the sector that lies within the range of ice movement from the Halle and Hunne mountains, people used glacial boulders from those mountains, boulders that they found in their neighbourhood (Bengtsson 1993).

If we turn inland, to the Lake Hornborga area, between Lake Vänern and Lake Vättern, that area lies outside the ice movement from the Halle and Hunne mountains (see figure 51.7 for the location of Lake Hornborga). There, the Lihult adzes were made of a variety of raw materials, including sandstone, and the same holds true for the round-butted axes from that area (Kindgren 1987; Kindgren 1991). This scheme seems to indicate a local tool production.

Water levels

In the Late Mesolithic, the water level was higher than it is today. The land uplift since the Late Mesolithic has been more accentuated in the northern part of the study area than in the southern. The map in figure 51.5 is based on a mathematical model that takes these differences into consideration. The model itself was presented by Leif Andersson at the MESO2000 conference. The map shows the calculated shore-level at about 5000 BC. Although the later part of the Late Mesolithic period is not yet sufficiently well dated in western Sweden (see Nordqvist 2000:213), 5000 BC should roughly correspond to the later part of the Lihult culture.

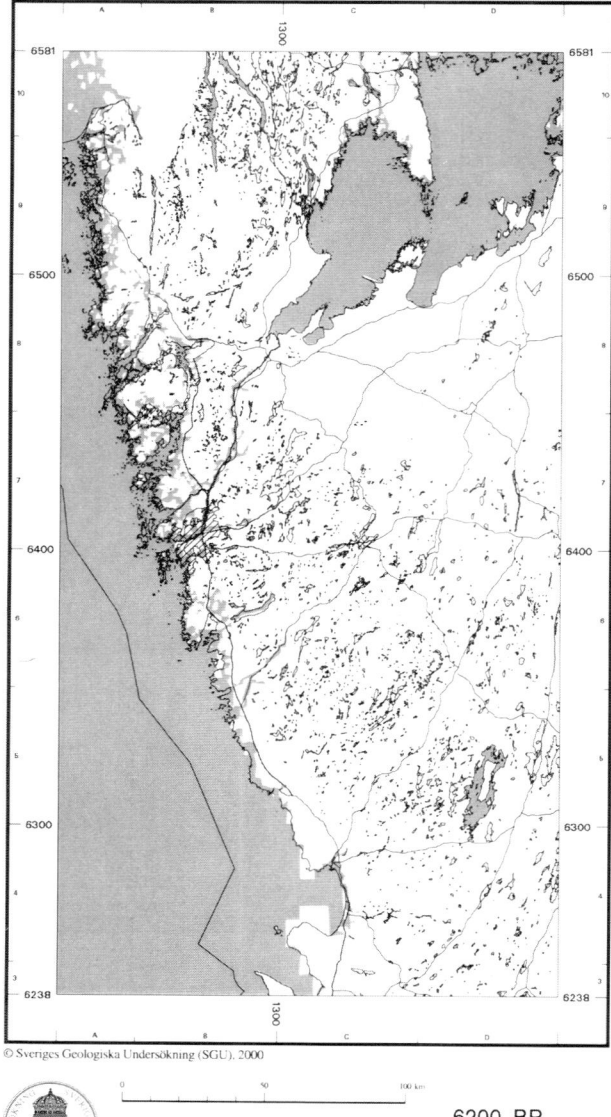

Figure 51.5 Shore-line about 5000 BC in western Sweden. Based on a mathematical model worked out by Tore Påsse and plotted by Leif Andersson, both at the Swedish Geological Survey.

Finds from the Lihult type site and their rock types

In our project we have, up to now, looked especially at the finds from the Lihult type site and their rock types. As far as possible, we wanted to correlate the finds with known occurrences of the different raw materials. Most of the finds from the Lihult type site are at the Museum of National Antiquities in Stockholm. The collection in Stockholm includes both Lihult adzes, round-butted axes and core axes, with a total of just over a hundred. Ulf Bergström has grouped the adzes and axes on the basis of a visual inspection (Figure 51.6).

As can be seen in figure 51.6, most of the adzes/axes from the Lihult type site are made of dolerite, but other rock types are also represented. They include specimens of rocks similar to dolerites, volcanites, andesite, rhomb porphyry and sandstones. Among the adzes and axes in the collection, Ulf Bergström selected 35 finds to test their density. For 28 of them, it was also possible to measure their natural, magnetic remanence. They clustered, so that those made of younger dolerites could be distinguished, as well as those of rhyolite and sandstone. One find yielded exceptional values and is possibly made of dacite. For the remaining seven adzes and axes, the magnetic remanence was so low that it could not be reliably measured. They were of sandstones and probably older dolerites.

The Lihult type site is located in an area with Bohus granite, but this rock was not used for tool production at the site. It is probable that at least some of the adzes and axes from Lihult were made of rocks from the Oslo field, which is across the Oslofjord, as seen from the Lihult type site. Those rocks include the rhyolite lava, the rhomb porphyry and the red sandstone present in the Lihult material.

It has been suggested that there was no ice movement from the Oslo field towards northern Bohuslän, and therefore no glacial boulders from the Oslo field would be present along the coast. However, boulders from the Oslo field *can* be found along the shores of Bohuslän. There are at least two options: either people chose boulders on the exposed shores of Bohuslän or they crossed the Oslofjord to choose – or to negotiate for – raw materials from there.

Routes used

It can be assumed that during the Late Mesolithic, people preferred to move over water whenever possible. To move over water along the coast was comparatively easy. The interior was, as far as we know, densely forested, so that when moving over long distances, people probably used the waterways as much as possible there as well. To walk across country would have been the last option, and a good guess is that, whenever they had to walk, they would try to do so, either along those waterways that were too shallow to be suitable for paddling or along the ridges of hills. In both instances, the natural features would help them to orient themselves.

The distribution of Lihult adzes indicates that the major movements were along the coast (Figures 51.4 and 51.8). Some sites, like the Lihult type site, were located somewhat inland but seem to have been oriented mainly towards the coast and the sea. To leave the Lihult type site, people could use three different routes during most of the time that the site was in use and would thereby reach the coast and the sea. One route was through the strait of Svinesund and the Idefjord, leaving the site towards the north-north-east, the other route was towards

Type	Dolerites	Rocks similar to dolerites	Volcanites (rhyolite, etc.)	Andesite	Rhomb porphyry	Sandstones	Total number
Lihult adzes	19	3	7		1	5	35
Round-butted axes	9					2	11
Core axes	1		1	1		1	4
Adze/axe fragments, not defined as to type	2						2
Adzes/axes, which do not fit into the Lihult-adze or round-butted-axe category							8
Adzes/axes, type and rock still to be correlated	29		7		1	9	46*

* I have information on 42 out of the 46 adzes/axes: 28 Lihult adzes; 5 round-butted axes; 8 adzes/axes, which do not fit into the Lihult-adze or the round-butted-axe category; 1 probably a natural stone, but possibly used as an adze/axe.

Figure 51.6 Adzes and axes from the Lihult type site in the Museum of National Antiquities, Stockholm, grouped according to type and rock, on the basis of a visual inspection.

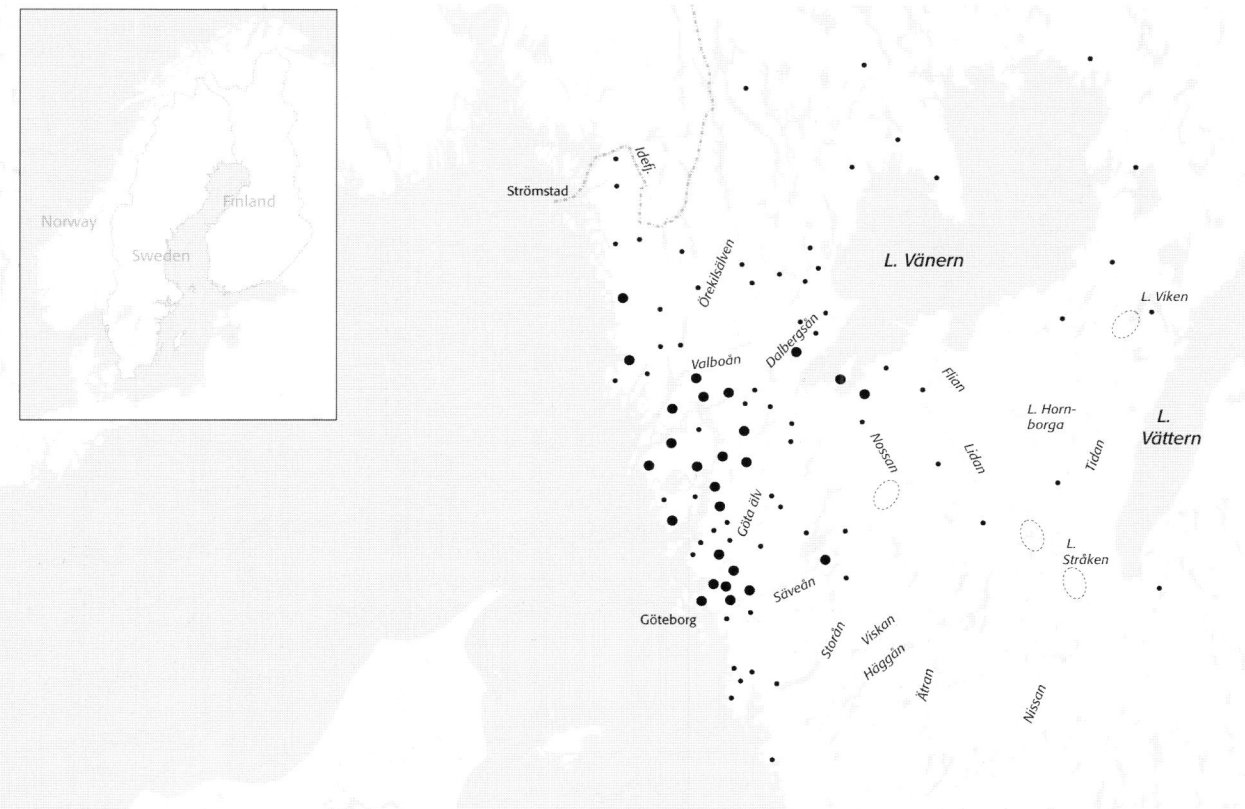

Figure 51.7 Navigable waterways and the distribution of Lihult adzes in western Sweden. Small dots mark 1–5 Lihult adzes, large dots mark 6–435 Lihult adzes, ellipses mark passages that were apparently little used by people using the Lihult assemblage or not used at all. Based on present-day navigability, according to Svenska Kanotförbundet c. 1990a; Svenska Kanotförbundet c. 1990b, and on Welinder 1977:58.

the south-west via Strömsvattnet, and the third was roughly towards the west via what is now a small lake called Sopperödsvattnet (Figure 51.7). A Lihult site located near the type site, Kasebacken, was situated by the same water system.

There are several waterways in western Sweden today that are navigable for the whole or part of the year (Svenska Kanotförbundet c. 1990a.; Svenska Kanotförbundet c. 1990b). These are marked on the map (Figure 51.7). All these were certainly navigable in the Late Mesolithic.

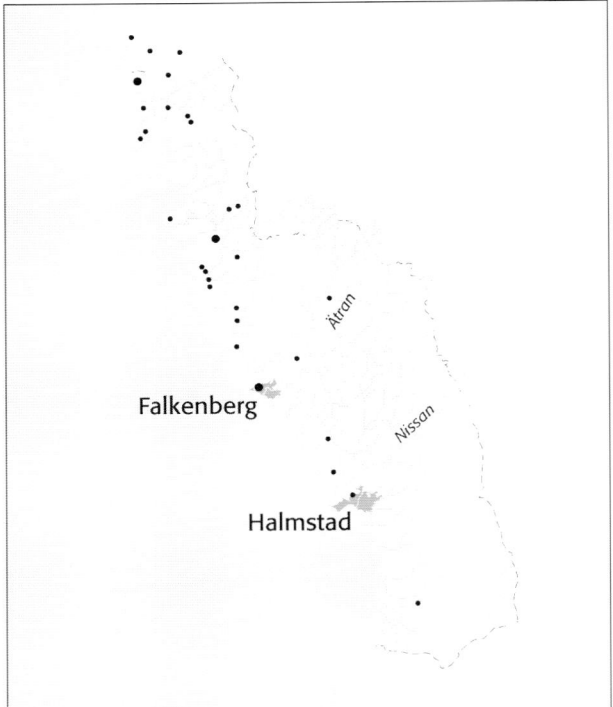

Figure 51.8 Distribution of Lihult adzes in Halland. The greater number of adzes, as compared with those in figure 51.4, can be explained by the fact that more private collections were used by Bramstång. The present-day shoreline. Based on Bramstång 1990:37.

For example, one of the routes that people used was to the west from Lake Vänern, up the Dalberg River, and from there to the south-west to the Hästefjord, where a number of Lihult adzes have been found (see Rex Svensson 1988) (Figure 51.7). From there, they could easily pass Lake Ellenö and then follow the Valbo River to the coast to the present town of Munkedal.

Routes little used or not used at all

If we consider that the presence of Lihult adzes in western Sweden indicates a region of contacts and interaction, then I am more concerned, in a way, by the signs of no contact within that region than by the signs of contact. One example of a route that they could have used but apparently did not, according to the spread of the Lihult adzes in the landscape, or used only very occasionally would have been to leave Lake Vänern's eastern side and go up the Tidan River (Figure 51.7). From one point, it is only 3 km from the Tidan River overland to Lake Viken, which is connected with the large Lake Vättern. Only a very few Lihult adzes have been found by Lake Vättern or further to the east.

Another example of a possible route, which does not appear to have been very much used or maybe was not used at all would have been to go up the Tidan River but further upstream, to Lake Stråken (Figure 51.7). From Lake Stråken, it is only 3.5 km overland to the upper reaches of the Nissan River. Going down the Nissan, one would reach the present town of Halmstad on the West Coast. Another option from Lake Stråken would have been to continue to the west, then cross overland to the Ätran River, with as little as 1 km between the Tidan River and the Ätran River systems, at Lake Lönern, and from there continue on the Ätran to the West Coast, reaching it close to where the present-day town of Falkenberg is located (Figure 51.7). There are only a few finds of Lihult adzes in these more southerly parts of the West Coast of Sweden. Furthermore, those that have been found were located close to the actual coast (Bramstång 1990), rather than along the river systems. In accordance with what has been mentioned above, their distribution seems to indicate that in the more southerly parts of the West Coast of Sweden, the major movements were *along* the coast, although with short trips inland, rather than up and down the rivers themselves (Figure 51.8).

Another question is, why the people apparently did not use the route from Lake Vänern, up the Nossan River towards the south-south-east, then overland to the Säve River and down to the West Coast (Figure 51.7). The overland stretch is short, only 4.5 km, and if they prepared a path and kept it open, that stretch would take only an hour. We have vestiges of visits from the lower reaches of the Nossan River (that is, close to Lake Vänern) and from Lake Mjörn (that is, close to present-day Alingsås) along the Säve River, but we have no vestiges from the higher reaches of these two systems. Of course, they may have taken this route without leaving any vestiges in the upper reaches, but it certainly does not appear to have been a "hot" route, in spite of the fact that it would have taken them only about 3 days from Lake Vänern to present-day Gothenburg taking that route.

Reflections

The distribution of the Lihult adzes as a fairly well-defined type indicates in itself that people met, exchanged ideas about tool production or tool use or exchanged the tools themselves for other goods. It would be more difficult to explain the spread of the adzes by, for example, seasonal movements of groups of people, as most of the adzes in Sweden have been found in rather similar settings, that is, along the West Coast. Of course, this does not in itself exclude the possibility that people moved between different localities during the year.

We have several indications that people used local sources for raw material. The most evident cases would be the many sites close to the Halle and Hunne mountains, where tools were manufactured. Other areas where tools were apparently produced from locally available, raw materials were around Lake Hornborga and in southern central Bohuslän, and possibly also on the island of Hisingen. It seems that the richness of the sources in the Halle and Hunne mountains also attracted people from other areas, as some of the sites near the mountains seem to have been used more specifically for tool production than for living. In the Hästefjord area, it appears that ready-made adzes were brought in from the area by the Halle and Hunne mountains.

At least some of the raw materials used at the Lihult type site were non-local. An interesting observation is the great number of grindstones from the type site. It seems reasonable to believe that the site was especially used for the finishing process in the production of adzes and axes. To my knowledge, no chips have been recovered from the site, and the adzes and axes themselves were apparently manufactured elsewhere. I suggest that the inhabitants manufactured the tools at the sources of the raw materials – that is, on the coast or across the Oslo fjord – and then brought them to the Lihult type site for the finishing process, before they passed them on to others or put them to use elsewhere. As the site has not been excavated, chips may lie in the ground, but it seems improbable that there would be enough chips to correspond to the manufacturing process of all or most of the adzes and axes from the site. When Ulf Bergström and I inspected the site, I saw no chips.

Some sources of raw material seem to have been exploited continuously from the Mesolithic and into the Neolithic, such as the Halle and Hunne mountains, while others were maybe used only once, such as specific glacial boulders. There may have been hindrances in the approach to some sources, either of a social or some other nature. For example, why were the three routes Lake Vänern → the Tidan River → Lake Viken → Lake Vättern or Lake Vänern → Tidan River → Lake Stråken → the Nissan River → the West Coast or Lake Vänern → the Tidan River → Lake Stråken → the Ätran River → the West Coast not included in their spheres of interaction or only rarely used? Hostile neighbours? Or simply because those routes were never included, by tradition?

There were probably gaps both in the knowledge among the people and in the social interaction between regions. Any change in economy probably affected both the patterns of travel and the circulation of tools, as well as the emphasis placed on the production and use of tools with different qualities. If we look at the West Coast of Sweden, the Lihult adzes are concentrated further to the north than both the town of Halmstad and the town of Falkenberg. On the Norwegian side of the border, there are similar adzes from the Late Mesolithic, the so-called Nøstvet adzes (see, for example, Brøgger 1905; Berg 1999). I have the impression that one central sphere of interaction was around the Skagerrak and the Oslofjord, rather than, say, between Lake Vänern and the West Coast of Sweden. As this sphere of interaction is split by a national border today, it has not been properly investigated.

We can assume that the people along the coast found no physical obstacles to remaining in direct contact with each other over considerable distances. As regards time

Figure 51.9 Route followed by a kajaker along the coast of the Scandinavian peninsula. Covering a distance of about 5,000 km, the trip took 71 days. Original map produced by Meloja, in Toolanen 2000:19.

spent in travelling, one paddles 30–40 km a day in a modern kajak, with normal speed and without straining oneself. That means that leaving the city of Gothenburg, one would reach the latitude of present-day Strömstad in 3–4 days (Figure 51.7). A strong person familiar with the sea and with paddling, on leaving Gothenburg, would reach Strömstad in 2 days, if the weather was good. I assume that, in the Late Mesolithic, the Oslofjord was criss-crossed by paddlers between the "Swedish" and the "Norwegian" sides.

As an example, in 1999, a paddler went offshore close to the border between Russia and Norway, paddled along the Norwegian coast and then continued along the Swedish coast to the border with Finland (Figure 51.9). The distance was about 5,000 km, and it took him 71 days (Toolanen 2000; Danielsson 2001). Even if we reckon with only half the speed, a paddler in the Late Mesolithic would have been able to cover the same distance in 4 ½ months.

It would probably have taken people in the Late Mesolithic only a couple of weeks to go from the Swedish to the Norwegian West Coast, to visit friends or relatives or for other reasons. If they did not go, it must have been for other reasons than mere distance.

In the literature, I have often received the impression that people in the Late Mesolithic are considered to have been exposed to, rather than to have been active participants in, their environment, and that they are considered counters in a game rather than creative, human beings. One point that I want to make here is that we should consider peoples' capacity to be in charge of their lives, their capacity to know their environment well, their capacity to explore and find new places, and their capacity to interact and negotiate with people living in their own, as well as in other regions. I believe that, in the instances in which members of groups did not move away from a very restricted area, they had their reasons. One reason may have been hostile neighbours; another may have been social and political agreements between different groups as to who was to be in charge of certain transactions, in certain areas, and with certain groups.

Acknowledgements

I wish to express my thanks to Ulf Bergström for his collaboration in the project and to the staff at the Gothenburg City Museum and the Museum of National Antiquities in Stockholm for their help. Stig Welinder and Carina Bramstång let me use their figures. The National Heritage Board facilitated my participation in the MESO2000 conference. The project is financed by the Bank of Sweden Tercentenary Foundation and by the Wallenberg Foundation.

References

Alin, J. 1955. *Förteckning över stenåldersboplatser i norra Bohuslän*. Göteborgs och Bohusläns Fornminnesförening. Gothenburg.

Bengtsson, L. 1993. Lihultyxor i Bohuslän: råmaterialen och deras härkomst. En diskussion. *Fornvännen* 88, 137–154.

Berg, E. 1999. Raw material use and axe production in the Mesolithic of Southeastern Norway. In: Boaz, J. (ed.) *The Mesolithic of Central Scandinavia*. Universitetets Oldsaksamlings Skrifter. Ny rekke. Nr. 22, 267–282. Oslo.

Bergström, L. 1958. *P.M. beträffande petrografisk undersökning av stenföremål från Gossbydal, Torslanda socken, Bohuslän*. Manuscript on file at the Gothenburg City Museum. Gothenburg.

Bramstång, C. 1990. *Lihult- och limhamnsyxor: en undersökning av senmesolitiska förekomster i Halland*. Unpublished examination paper. Göteborg University, Department of Archaeology. Gothenburg.

Brøgger, A.W. 1905. *Øxer av Nøstvettypen: Bidrag til kundskapen om Ældre Norsk Stenalder*. Norges Geologiske Undersøkelse No. 42. Kristiania.

Cedergren, K.G. 1932. *Bidrag till Vänersborgstraktens förhistoria: I. Stenåldersbebyggelsen*. Vänersborgs Söners Gilles årsskrift. Vänersborg.

Kindgren, H. 1987. *Material och kultur: spridningsmönster av kambrisk flinta och etniska grupper i Västergötlands senmesolitikum*. Unpublished examination paper. Göteborg University, Department of Archaeology. Gothenburg.

— 1991. Kambrisk flinta och etniska grupper i Västergötlands senmesolitikum. In: Browall, H., Persson, P. and Sjögren, K.-G. (eds.) *Västsvenska stenåldersstudier*. GOTARC Ser. C, nr 8. Göteborg University, Department of Archaeology, 33–69. Gothenburg.

Nordqvist, B. 1997. Mesolitiska grönstensyxor i Västsverige. In: Larsson, M. and Olsson, E. (eds.) *Regionalt och interregionalt: stenåldersundersökningar i Syd- och Mellansverige*, 64–70. Riksantikvarieämbetet, Byrån för arkeologiska undersökningar, Skrifter nr 23. Stockholm.

— 2000. *Coastal Adaptations in the Mesolithic: A study of coastal sites with organic remains from the Boreal and Atlantic periods in Western Sweden*. GOTARC. Series B, No. 13. Göteborg University, Department of Archaeology. Gothenburg.

Rex Svensson, K. 1988. *Hästefjorden under stenåldern: fynden berättar*. Älvsborgs Länsmuseum. Vänersborg.

Svenska Kanotförbundet (ed.). c. 1990a. *Kanotvatten. I: Blekinge län (K), Kristianstads län (L), Malmöhus län (M), Hallands län (N)*. Stockholm.

Svenska Kanotförbundet (ed.). c. 1990b. *Kanotvatten. I: Göteborgs och Bohuslän (O), Älvsborgs län (P)*. Stockholm.

Toolanen, G. 2000. Petri rundade Skandinavien. *Kanot-Nytt*, Year 50, 2000, No. 1, 18–19.

Welinder, S. 1977. *The Mesolithic Stone Age of Eastern Middle Sweden*. Antikvariskt arkiv 65. Stockholm.

52. Traffic in Stone Adzes in Mesolithic Western Norway

Knut Andreas Bergsvik and Asle Bruen Olsen

Stone adzes of greenstone and diabase from the quarries at Hespriholmen and Stakaneset were distributed throughout Western Norway. The main distribution areas of these two raw materials are restricted to a northern and a southern region. These regions overlap slightly in the district of Nordhordland. The aim of this paper is to investigate whether the adzes were the results of exchange or direct access. It is argued here that within these two regions, adzes were mainly acquired through direct access, while the more limited flow of adzes across the overlap-zone in Nordhordland were exchanged. The exchange relations were most likely organised in the context of ethnic relations in the boundary area.

Introduction

Exchange is an important concept in archaeology, but it is also a very broad one. In the general sociological sense, it involves all interpersonal contacts and includes transference of material as well as non-material goods, artifacts as well as information (Renfrew and Bahn 1996:335). Obviously, interpersonal transference of goods and information happened all the time during the Mesolithic. In this wide meaning of the concept, exchange was a part of daily social life. Traditionally, however, archaeologists specialising in the field of hunter-gatherers research have not applied the concept in such a general fashion. The term is usually applied to situations where an artifact or a raw material has not been acquired through direct access. Despite a growing interest in the subject (e.g. Clark 1965; Jennbert 1984; Larsson 1988; Chapman 1993; Nash 1998), Mesolithic finds are usually not interpreted as results of exchange. The main reason for this is probably the general view of prehistoric hunter-gatherers as procuring their own goods, foods or raw materials by means of residential mobility or task group mobility. As a result, when the topic of acquisition is brought up, direct access has traditionally been seen as a more likely option than exchange.

Exchange is only chosen for the rare cases when artifacts or raw materials originate so far away that direct access is considered an unrealistic alternative (Eriksen 2000). It may, however, also be relevant for cases when an implement has crossed an ethnic and territorial boundary, because such a boundary would have put restrictions on the mobility related to direct access. Still, this interpretative option is seldom preferred, because it requires a lot from the archaeological data: evidence for social or ethnic boundaries and exchange across those boundaries are difficult to secure at the same time (but see Fisher 1982). Sometimes we are able to identify social and territorial boundaries, but the data on crossing are weak. In other cases, long-distance distributions of goods are demonstrated, but we are at pains to establish social boundaries.

For Mesolithic Western Norway, these source-critical problems are as salient as anywhere else, but compared to many other regions, the area is characterised by extensive lithic raw material variation. Detailed analysis of this variation, particularly of the production and

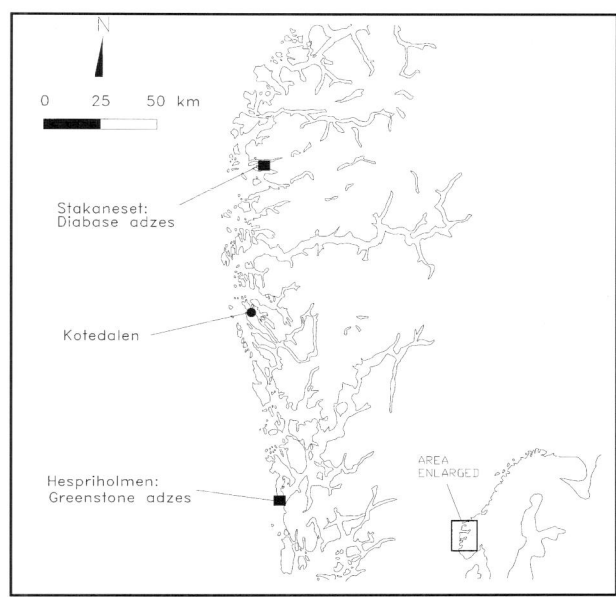

Figure 52.1 Western Norway.

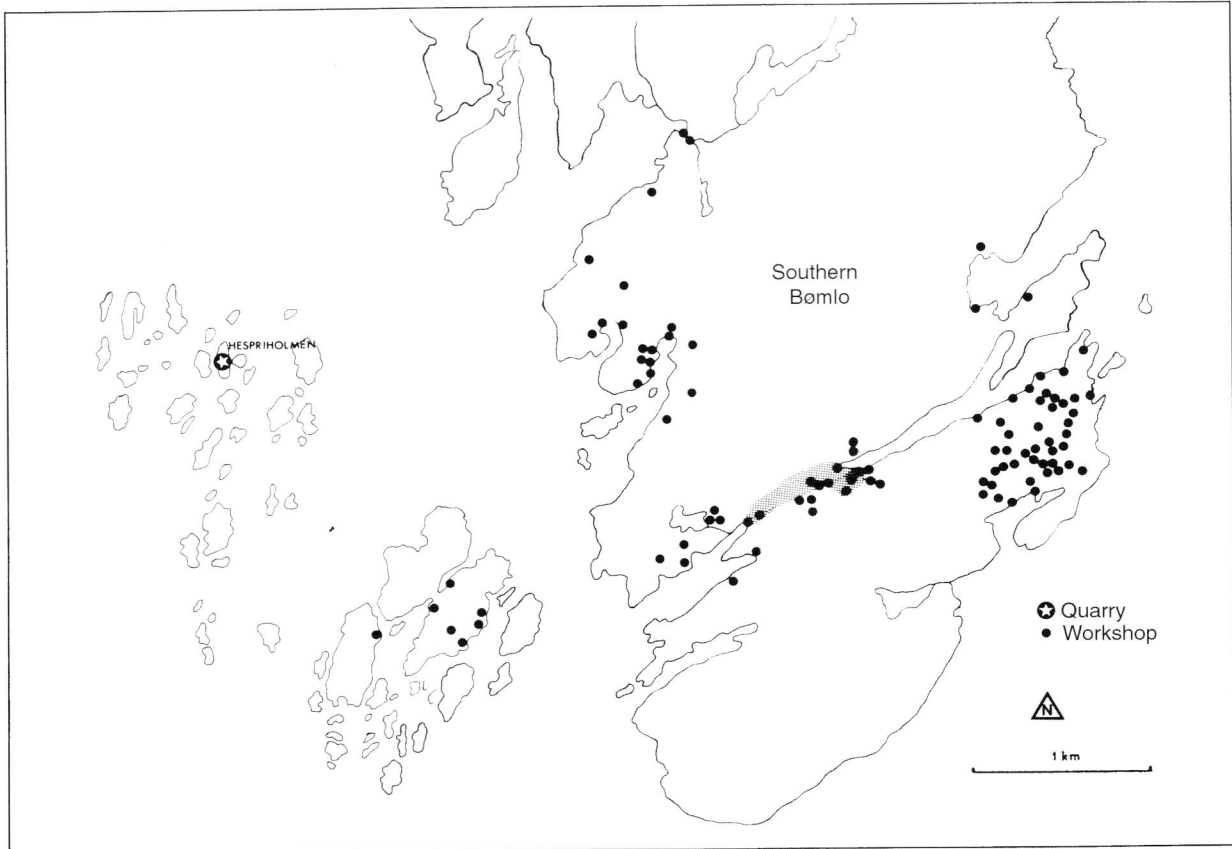

Figure 52.2 The quarry at Hespriholmen and workshop site distribution at Southern Bømlo (after Olsen and Alsaker 1984, Fig. 5).

distribution of diabase and greenstone adzes, has provided robust data on long-distance exchange as well as exchange across social boundaries. We will argue that the slightly overlapping distribution areas of Mesolithic diabase and greenstone adzes indicate the existence of an ethnic boundary in the district of Nordhordland, and that items were regularly exchanged across it. Within the main distribution areas, however, adzes and blanks were mainly acquired by direct access.

Manufacturing and distribution of greenstone and diabase

In Southern Norway, flint dropped by icebergs was the most common material used in lithic tool production during the first two millennia after deglaciation, but from around 9000 BP the pattern changed. Gradually a number of local rocks were utilised, most of which were quarried from bedrock outcrops. Among these were quartz crystal, quartz, mylonite and chert for struck stone tools, sandstone for grinding slabs, and soapstone for net sinkers. Mesolithic adzes were predominantly made of greenstone and diabase, and their quarries have both been identified. The greenstone quarry, which was identified by the geologist Kolderup in 1925, is situated on Hespriholmen, a small islet off the main island of Bømlo (Figure 52.2). The diabase quarry, found by Svein Brandsøy in 1978, lies about 250 km to the north, on the peninsula Stakaneset in the Flora district (Figure 52.3). Analyses of the adze production and distribution from these two quarries have been undertaken by Sigmund Alsaker and Asle Bruen Olsen in co-operation with geologists from the University of Bergen (Olsen 1981; Olsen and Alsaker 1984; Alsaker 1987). The results can be summarised as follows:

Both quarries were taken into use at the same time, about 9000 BP. A large number of radiocarbon dates from the quarries, workshop sites, and other site types strongly indicate that they were utilised continuously for 5000 years, not only through the middle and late Mesolithic, but also during the early and middle Neolithic periods.

Both outcrops were exploited by crack heating the bedrock. Blocks were then extracted using large hammerstones. A simplified model of the diabase and greenstone flow can illustrate the actual process of adze manufacturing in the production system (Figure 52.4.) Three main manufacturing stages (Figure 52.5) can be separated spatially within this system:

A Primary reduction of blocks in *the quarry area* (1). This stage involves a preliminary coarse flaking of the quarried blocks selected for adzes. The rough-

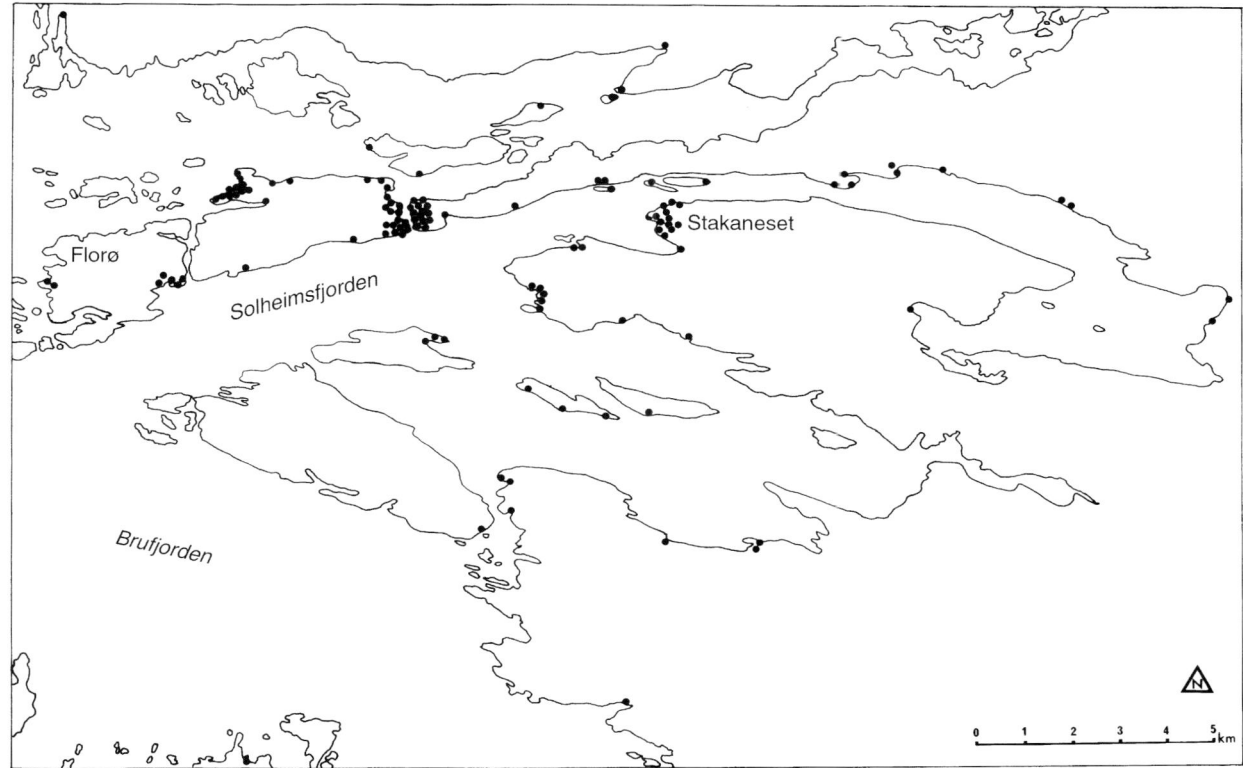

Figure 52.3 The quarry at Stakaneset and workshop site distribution in Flora (after Olsen and Alsaker 1984, Fig, 4).

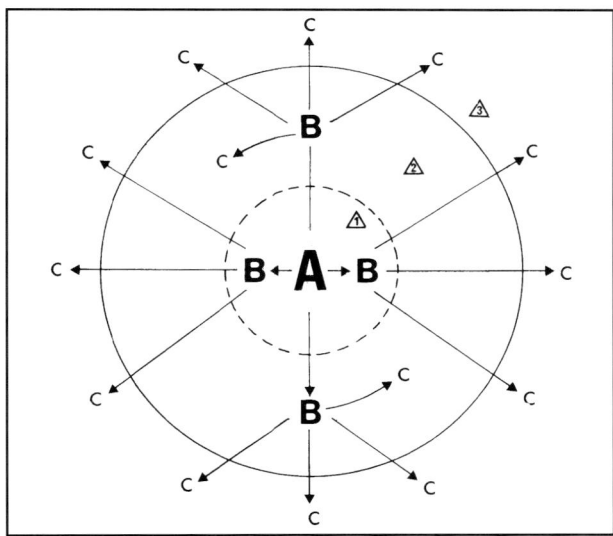

Figure 52.4 Simplified model of the greenstone and diabase flow in the production system. (1) Quarry area, (2) Production area, (3) Distribution area (reproduced from Olsen and Alsaker 1984, Fig. 8).

Figure 52.5 The three main stages in adze manufacture: A: rough out, B: blank, C: finished adze (after Olsen and Alsaker 1984, Fig. 7).

outs are large, more or less irregular cores, often cylindrical in form with platforms at the ends (A).

B Secondary reduction of rough-outs at workshops. The rough-outs were transported by boat to the workshop sites in the vicinity, defined as *the production area* (2) (Figures 50.2 and 50.3). Few workshop sites are found more than 10 km away from the quarries. In the production area, the rough-outs were reduced to blanks by secondary flaking (trimming) leading closely to the desired shape. The blanks have distinct edge and neck portions (B).

C Final grinding/pecking and polishing at living sites. The blanks were transported to living sites throughout *the distribution area* (3). At these sites, the final shaping into adzes took place by grinding/pecking of adze-bodies and polishing of edges (C).

The distribution patterns of greenstone and diabase adzes are identified on the basis of examination of the total collection of Mesolithic adzes found in southern Norway (Figure 52.6). The methods used are hand classification (diabase and greenstone are easy to recognise visually) combined with thin section and/or trace element analysis of random samples. The results of this examination were intriguing. The distribution shows an extensive spread of material, some specimens being found 600–650 km away from their source. However, only 1,2 % of the diabase specimens and 3,6 % of the greenstone specimens occur at a distance greater than 200 km from the quarries. On the basis of the distribution studies, it seems reasonable to conclude that greenstone and diabase from the Hespriholmen and Stakaneset quarries dominated the "adze-market" in Western Norway throughout the Mesolithic period. Here, as much as 60 % of all Mesolithic stone adzes were produced from one or another of these two raw materials. Not only the relative dominance of these raw materials, but also the impressing length of time of the manufacturing and distribution, indicate that the adzes made of Hespriholmen greenstone and Stakaneset diabase were highly valued goods. As such, they are particularly well suited for discussions of social boundaries and exchanges across boundaries. But before we address these questions, we will roughly outline the development of the settlement patterns of Mesolithic Western Norway so that the proposed inter-group relations can be understood in their proper socio-historical context.

The settlement patterns

During the early and middle Mesolithic sites are generally small and scattered, situated in different types of environment, often on harsh locations, indicating a community composed of residentially mobile, probably rather opportunistic groups (Nygaard 1990; Olsen 1992; Nærøy 2000). This pattern changes around the middle/late Mesolithic transition, at about 7500 BP, which corresponds chronologically with an observed marked increase in the exploitation of the greenstone and diabase quarries. The settlement structure of the late Mesolithic is mainly characterised by concentrations of large sites located in geographically restricted resource optimal areas, especially narrow channels with strong tidal currents. Several such channels along the coast have been thoroughly surveyed and investigated. Among them is Fosnstraumen in Nordhordland with the well-known site Kotedalen (Figure 52.1) (Olsen 1992, 1995; Warren 1994; Bergsvik 1995, 2001). These investigations have revealed marked late Mesolithic site clusters, which probably represent continuous occupations or highly frequent reoccupations of these areas, reflecting a sedentary life style. This development towards intensification and sedentism is observed in all the surveyed channel areas in the southern as well as northern regions, and is therefore considered to be a general development, probably triggered by group circumscription imposed by social restrictions on mobility in combination with demographic and climatic changes (Olsen 1995; Bergsvik 1999, 2001). The high degree of permanence and reoccupation suggests that such settlement areas were not accessible for all, but functioned as home bases for single local groups, independent of whether they were sedentary or semi sedentary. In our opinion, the sedentary life style in the late Mesolithic of western Norway was dependent on task group mobility (cf. Helm 1968) for the purpose of securing vital non-local resources and for the maintenance of inter-group social networks. Such a theory is supported by a variety of smaller sites of different types both within and outside the core areas, which in our model should be interpreted as task group sites.

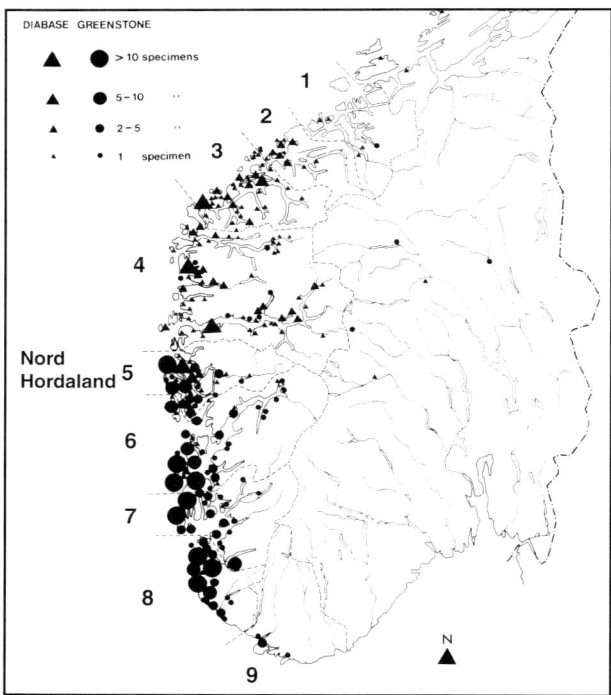

Figure 52.6 The distribution of greenstone and diabase adzes in Southern Norway. The area is divided into 9 sub-regions. The overlap-zone between the two raw materials is situated in the district of Nordhordland district (sub-region 5) (after Olsen and Alsaker 1984, Fig. 9).

A social boundary in Nordhordland

Since the concept of "social boundary" is almost as broad and general as that of "exchange" it needs a definition relevant for our approach. Here we define the term as a territorial boundary between ethnic groups who perceive each other as different. Ethnic identity is seen as a collective identification based on common institutions and putative cultural similarity and difference (Jenkins 1996). We realise that archaeological approaches to ethnicity based solely on archaeological sources are hampered by considerable epistemological problems (e.g. Trigger 1995). However, we believe that if the interpretations are supported by several independent archaeological variables, they should not be regarded as inadequate at the outset (Jones 1997; Bergsvik 2002). In the following, we will suggest that the district of Nordhordland is likely to have marked an ethnic boundary during the late Mesolithic period. This interpretation is based on discontinuities in the material culture distributions in this local area:

1. The distribution areas of greenstone and diabase are almost geographically exclusive, with the exception of a rather limited overlap zone in the Nordhordland district, situated about equal distance from the quarries (Figure 52.6). Such a barely overlapping distribution pattern might be explained as coincidental if the fall-off was gradual up to this point. However, when the relative Mesolithic diabase and greenstone frequencies are separated according to smaller sub-regions within the main distribution areas, both distributions show a marked fall-off just north and south of the overlap zone in Nordhordland (Figure 52.7). The boundary therefore cannot be explained as coincidental.

    We may add that there is a strong historical continuity in the distribution networks, indicated by a marked fall-off that is equally distinct for the subsequent early- and middle Neolithic adzes made from these particular raw materials (Olsen and Alsaker 1984:96). An almost identical fall-off can also be noted in this district for the early Neolithic rhyolite distributions (Alsaker 1987:60).

2. The finishing process (pecking vs. grinding) in the manufacturing of greenstone and diabase adzes is different north and south of Nordhordland. The vast majority of the northern adzes are finished by grinding, while the southern adzes are often worked by both grinding and pecking (types 1–2 and 3 respectively, Figure 52.8). The percentage ratios for these two categories are 81/19 in the northern region and 57/42 in the southern region (Olsen 1981; Alsaker 1987).

3. The greenstone and diabase adzes are also characterised by different shapes in the south compared to the north of Nordhordland. The greenstone specimens are predominantly long, slim adzes with pointed necks. The diabase specimens are generally short and blunt with rounded necks (types 1 and 2, Figure 52.8). This distinction has so far been tested by close examination of the material from two random areas in each of the regions, comprising the districts Hareid/Nordfjord in the northern region and Karmøy/Indre Hardanger in the southern region (Gjerland 1984). A comparison of the relative frequencies shows a

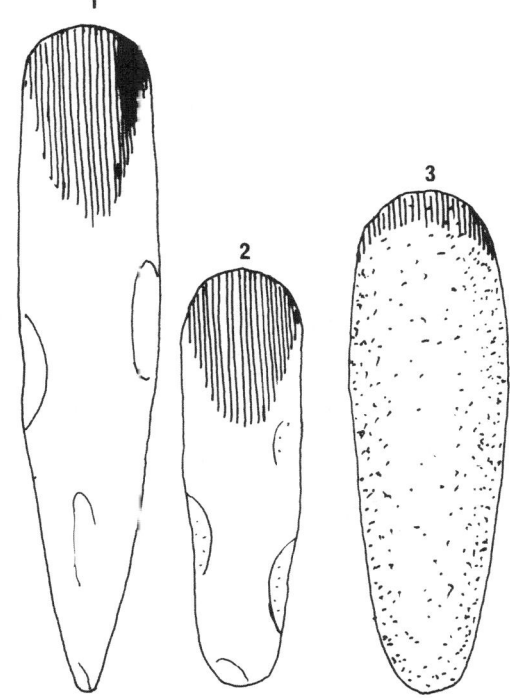

Figure 52.8 Different types of Mesolithic adzes. 1: Long, slim, with pointed neck, 2 and 3: Short, blunt with rounded neck. 1 and 2 are finished entirely by grinding, while 3 is finished by pecking of the body and grinding of the edge (after Olsen and Alsaker 1984, Fig. 12a).

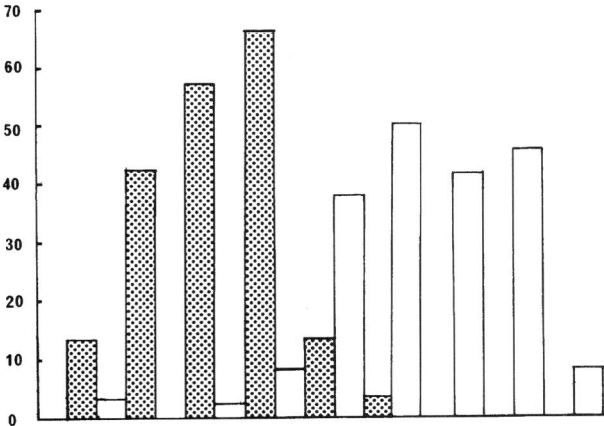

Figure 52.7 The Mesolithic greenstone and diabase percentages in the sub-regions shown in Figure 52.6. (after Olsen and Alsaker 1984, Fig. 15a).

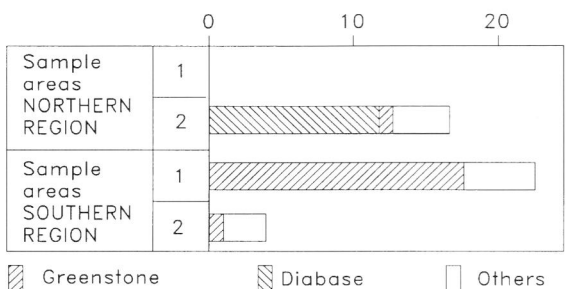

Figure 52.9 The percentages of long (type 1), and short (type 2) ground adzes in the data from two random areas in each of the regions (after Gjerland 1984, Fig 56).

Figure 52.10 Cross-shaped club (left) and star-shaped club (after Gjessing 1945, Fig. 70).

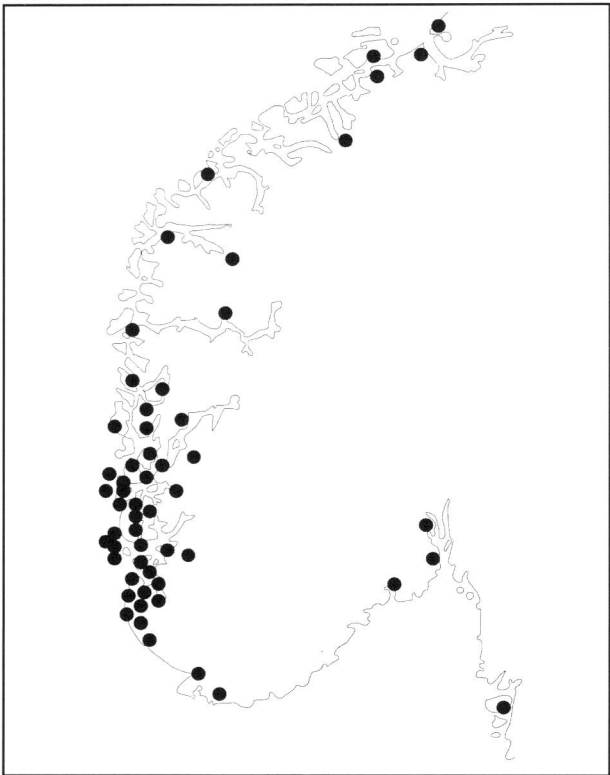

Figure 52.11 The distribution of cross-shaped clubs in Southern Norway (after Gräslund 1962, Fig. 3).

marked difference between the two regions (Figure 52.9), which is in accordance with the general tendency observed during Olsen's and Alsaker's raw material classification (Olsen and Alsaker 1984: 97). These differences may be due to different properties of the two raw materials. There are, however, some fine examples of "greenstone adze shaped" diabase adzes and vice versa. Besides, the form distinction is not only geographically significant for the greenstone and diabase adzes, but it also applies to other Mesolithic adzes found in the two regions.

4. The main distributions of cross-shaped clubs (type II) and star-shaped clubs correspond clearly with the main distribution area of Mesolithic greenstone adzes (Figures 52.10 and 52.11). These two artifacts are often decorated and are interpreted as having mainly served symbolic purposes (Solberg 1989; Glørstad 1999). Previously it was somewhat uncertain whether they were Mesolithic or Neolithic (Gräslund 1962; Solberg 1989), but recently published clubs from excavated contexts are all radiocarbon dated to the middle or early late Mesolithic (Olsen 1992; Glørstad 1999). Here, they are therefore considered Mesolithic.

5. The hunters' rock-art in Western Norway is almost exclusively situated in the Northern distribution area of diabase (Figure 52.13). Here, two large sites are known, Vingen (more than 2000 figures), and Ausevik (400 figures). Brandsøysund (4 figures) is situated between these large sites. In contrast, only three small sites are found in the greenstone distribution area, Rolland (1 figure), Rykkje (1 figure), and Vangdal (7 figures). The chronology of the rock art is not yet established, but there is a tendency to date it mainly to the Neolithic period (Walderhaug 1998). Recent archaeological investigations at Vingen, however, indicate that the site was mainly used during the Mesolithic (Lødøen 2002).

The distribution patterns of these five Mesolithic cultural practices in Western Norway are concentrated either in the northern or southern regions. Previously, these patterns have been interpreted as indicating Mesolithic "social territories" (Olsen and Alsaker 1984) in the sense of "the total territory drawn upon for supplies, including raw materials, and finished products as well as food stuffs,

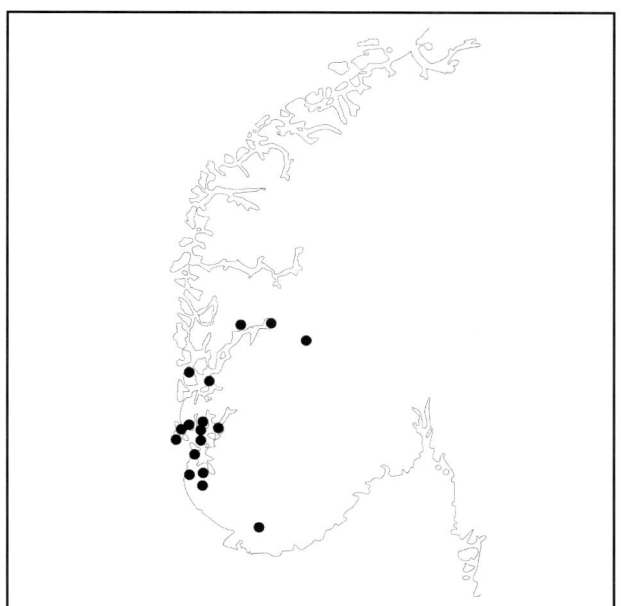

Figure 52.12 The distribution of star-shaped clubs in Southern Norway (after Gräslund 1962, Fig. 2).

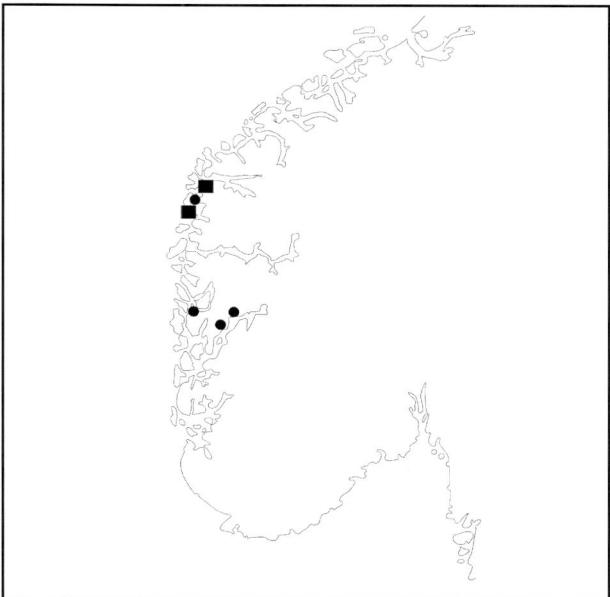

Figure 52.13 The distribution of hunters' rock-art sites in Western Norway. From top: Vingen (2000 figures), Brandsøysund (4 figures), Ausevik (400 figures), Rolland (1 figure), Rykkje (1 figure), Vangdal (7 figures) (Walderhaug 1998). Note that hunter's rock-art sites outside of Western Norway are not included.

by a given community by virtue of belonging to a larger social grouping" (Clark 1975:22). Such territories have generally been equated to the distribution of ethnic groups (e.g. Gendel 1984). This understanding of social territories and ethnic groups is, however, problematic on ontological as well as epistemological grounds (Bergsvik 2002). Rather than interpreting the main distribution areas of greenstone and diabase as representing distinct prehistoric social territories or ethnic groups, we prefer to consider these as examples of James Sackett's "isocrestic variation" (Sackett 1985). In our context, this means that, due to restrictions on mobility, sedentism and reduced contact, people developed different ways of doing things in the southern and northern regions. The patterns thus seem to justify that we are dealing with separate populations integrated in long-term, indigenous traditions.

Although ethnicity probably was an important factor at many levels among these populations, it is unlikely that all groups throughout these regions had similar concepts of it everywhere, either in terms of in-group notions and out-group categories, or in terms of the symbolic meaning of material culture. Ethnicity can therefore not be expected to appear as a homogeneous and monolithic "thing" to be described and analysed in a similar fashion on a large regional scale, but rather as a local and situational phenomenon, which needs local archaeological investigations. Thus, to justify the use of the concept of ethnicity, there has to be some empirical support for it in terms of marked local cultural differences – and more importantly – we need indications that these cultural differences were symbolically meaningful for the Mesolithic ethnic groups.

Currently it is exclusively the empirical situation in Nordhordland that may justify the use of the term ethnicity. As we have seen, the archaeological data here are characterised by concurring distribution boundaries of several cultural traits, but also by a marked raw material fall-off. This shows a dramatic local discontinuity, which indicates that mobility, and communication within the regions south and north of Nordhordland was much more extensive than across this district. The discontinuity is not determined by topographical conditions. There are no natural barriers in this area, such as mountain plateaus or long stretches of water that would hinder communication and prevent further spread of artifacts. As pointed out above, the Mesolithic subsistence patterns were similar along the entire coastline. Therefore, the discontinuity cannot be explained as a result of different subsistence practices in the north as opposed to the south. In this area we are therefore probably faced with a boundary that is not coincidental, but constructed and deliberate. In our view, we are dealing with a situation where some cultural features were not *permitted* to cross, or were not *wanted* across the boundary. Such a situation needs to be explained in social terms, and at the moment we find no better term than ethnicity: people to the north and to the south of this boundary perceived each other as different, and therefore used similarities and differences in material culture as symbols of similarity internally among the in-group members as well as difference in the contexts of social interaction with the out-groups. It is still unclear what particular historical circumstances could have led the construction of a social boundary just here. However, it appears that it was maintained and renewed for several thousand years among the local populations.

Direct access and cross-boundary exchange of adzes

There are several traits in the material culture that cut across the supposed social boundary in Nordhordland. Among these is the use of flat/oval adzes and chisels, regular stone clubs, soapstone net-sinkers, bipolar technique and microblade technique. These traits seem to be shared unevenly across space. Some of them occur frequently as far away as eastern Norway, middle Norway and Sweden. One might argue that such crosscutting distributions provide arguments against the existence of an ethnic boundary. However, an untidy and unsystematic distribution of cultural traits is not an argument in itself against the existence of social boundaries (Shennan 1989). It is rather a prerequisite for it, considering that ethnicity is a product of social interaction rather than isolation from other groups (cf. Barth 1969). Opposing ethnic groups should therefore be *expected* to share a number of cultural features. Nevertheless, sharing cultural features such as a technology or a style does not say anything about the maintenance of contact networks, or about continuing exchange relations between groups, considering that they are the ideas of how to make things rather than the things themselves. Technologies or styles may quite likely be the results of diffusion at single events. Exchange relations are therefore best studied in the distributions of raw materials. The issue of inter-group exchange networks is here exclusively dealt with on the basis of the diabase and greenstone distribution, since the distributions of other raw material categories have not yet been thoroughly analysed for this purpose.

Regional procurement

Firstly, we will address the problem of distribution *within* the southern and northern regions. The crucial question is whether the intra-regional greenstone and diabase dispersals are results of exchanges or direct access. We will argue that the adzes were mainly procured by direct access. First of all, we have not been able to establish any socially constructed boundaries *within* the main distribution areas of greenstone and diabase, which might have hindered mobility, related to direct procurement. Secondly, the distribution patterns do not reveal any clustering tendencies outside the production areas which would be expected if the distribution was based on directional trade from redistribution centres (Renfrew 1977). Thirdly, if the patterns were a result of the less complex down-the-line exchange from the quarries themselves, the distributions would be characterised by an evenly decreasing tendency in the distributions with the maximum centred around the production areas as the source locations. However, the dispersal does not match such a pattern, as the sub-regional distribution frequencies indicate that all parts of the main distribution areas except the overlap zone in Nordhordland are equally well supplied. Finally, if the sedentary groups that presumably lived in the production area controlled the quarries, worked the rough-outs and traded the blanks themselves, one would expect the manufacturing to be concentrated on one or a few large workshop sites. However, no such large Mesolithic workshop sites have yet been found (a possible exception is the large "Sokkamyro" site, which has both late Mesolithic and Neolithic phases (Alsaker 1987:29)). The production areas are instead characterised by high densities of small workshop sites spread within a close radius from the quarry suggesting that, rather than a tightly organised communal activity, many small, independent groups were involved in both quarrying and manufacturing as well as dispersal of the stone adzes.

From these observations it is reasonable to conclude that the populations of the northern and southern regions mainly secured their demands for greenstone and diabase adzes by direct access to the quarries based on a principal rule of equal rights attached to the sharing of a valued resource of limited abundance. As pointed out above, the Mesolithic local groups generally seem already to have subscribed to sedentism during the early phases of the late Mesolithic. Instead of being an activity involving the entire group, it is therefore likely that the quarrying was taken care of by smaller segments of the population. The spatial site differentiation indicates that task group mobility was an important factor in the procurement system in the late Mesolithic society. Therefore, here we therefore argue that procurement of diabase *within* the southern and northern regions was mainly made by task groups. These groups probably originated in smaller, sedentary local group territories within these regions. Acquisition of adzes may very well have been an important goal for such long distance task group moves. As we have tried to demonstrate above, the stone adze procurement involved a complex and time-consuming process that undoubtedly required special skills. It was not something that was done on the side. It is therefore not likely that the adze procurement can only be seen as embedded in the food procurement activity (cf. (Binford 1979). Visits to quarries may rather have been important *in their own right*, as a prime motive for long distance task group travelling.

Cross-boundary exchanges

The cross-boundary flow of greenstone and diabase should probably not be interpreted in terms of direct access. If the theory of a social boundary through the district of Nordhordland is accepted, this probably put restrictions on the task group mobility across it. Consequently, diabase adzes found in the northern region and the greenstone adzes in the southern region should be interpreted in terms of exchange.

In order to examine more closely the character and frequency of cross-boundary interaction, the contexts of consumption and discard of these adzes was examined closer at the boundary in Nordhordland. Nordhordland was chosen, because this area constitutes the presumed ethnic boundary area. As such, one would expect that local groups here were the ones that were practically engaged in inter-ethnic relations. From the data available, it seems that the southern connections were stronger than the ones that went to the north. This is indicated by the greenstone and diabase frequencies. For the sub-region of Nordhordland, the greenstone frequency is only slightly lower than in the sub-regions further south, while that of diabase is significantly lower than in the north. This may imply that the inhabitants of Nordhordland mainly had ethnic out-group relations with local groups north of the area.

In the last few years, several large base camps have been excavated in this district. One such site is Kotedalen at Fosnstraumen, which was inhabited almost continuously by sedentary groups during the late Mesolithic. Ten radiocarbon-dated phases were documented, representing a sequence of continuous occupation or re-occupation during the entire period (Olsen 1992). In the perspective of ethnicity one has to ask whether the local groups who occupied this site identified themselves as "southerners" or "northerners". Such a question is of course impossible to answer with any certainty. However, in addition to the general tendency of a southern connection in Nordhordland referred to above, the same southern affinity is indicated by the presence of several cross-shaped clubs from the Mesolithic layers in Kotedalen (Olsen 1992:98). If the ties towards the south were stronger, it is interesting to note that both greenstone and diabase adzes are found in the same layers: a total of 9 greenstone and 18 diabase specimens were collected at the site (Olsen 1992:77). From what is said about the regional social restrictions on direct access, the Kotedalen group would have had direct access to only one of the quarries, in this case presumably that at Hespriholmen. The diabase adzes in Kotedalen thus reflect some form of late Mesolithic exchange relations. Considering that these diabase adzes are present in all of the excavated layers, it is suggested here that cross-boundary traffic in stone adzes was not a sporadic or accidental affair. These exchange relations may rather be seen as a part of regulated and frequent social relations with out-groups.

In such a situation, the Kotedalen groups or individuals would have been an exchange link in the long distance distribution networks. Although the adzes probably meant different things to different people, it is easy to postulate that the prime motive for the long distance exchange of adzes was social and ideological more than utilitarian, since both regions were self-supplied with adzes of comparable raw material qualities. The penetration of greenstone adzes into the northern region, and vice versa, as well as the dispersal of greenstone and diabase adzes in the areas outside western Norway (Figure 52.2), is therefore likely to reflect exchanges of highly valued goods. There is no room here for discussing the social implications of this at any length, but one objective may have been to establish affiliations or to fulfil social obligations towards the neighbouring ethnic groups. Another objective – which is not incompatible with the first – may have been to generate symbolic power in order to create or maintain social status within the local group.

Conclusion

The point of departure of this paper was that specialists in the field of prehistoric hunter-gatherer research have seldom been able to discuss exchange relations. This void in the Mesolithic research is explained mainly as a result of source-critical problems. In order to discuss exchange, data on both social boundaries and flow of artifacts across those boundaries must be presented. However, these different types of data are often difficult to obtain at the same time. The specific purpose of this paper was to investigate whether the distributions of greenstone and diabase adzes in Western Norway could be explained as exchange-networks, or if they were the results of direct access. We have found that both exchange and direct access are indicated by the distribution patterns. In our view, the procurement of adzes within each region of distribution was secured by task groups who had direct access to the quarries, while the flow of adzes between these regions was based on exchange relations across a boundary in the district of Nordhordland. The boundary is indicated by co-varying distribution discontinuities of several independent cultural traits, as well as a marked fall-off in the southern distribution of diabase and a northern distribution of greenstone. Nordhordland constitutes an overlap area between these distributions, and is interpreted as a socially constructed ethnic boundary maintained and renewed throughout the Mesolithic period.

We believe that exchanges as well as ethnicity are important research fields, and this short article should only be seen as a first step in the process of exploring these themes in Stone Age Western Norway. We willingly admit that more detailed and refined analysis of the empirical material is likely to lead to a much better understanding of the nature of social boundaries as contexts of exchange and ethnic relations than has been presented here. But such an understanding may also improve if we expand the theoretical framework. Initially, we pointed out that "exchange" in the broad sense includes much more than passages of goods across social boundaries. One could, for instance, also apply such an expanded definition of exchange for the greenstone and diabase production and distribution *within* the southern and northern regions. As we have argued, the quarries themselves are likely to have been shared among many groups, some of them coming from distant places. In the contexts of quarrying, long distance task groups with immemorial rights and obligations to the quarries may also have used the opportunity to create new alliances and to strengthen kinship ties. Furthermore, such situations might also be important for the maintenance of common history and ideology. In other words, the extraction and working of greenstone and diabase may have been important social events in the lives of these people. At these events, exchange in such a wide sense would be particularly important.

Acknowledgements

We would like to thank David N. Simpson for his valuable comments on the manuscript and for his generous help in preparing this paper. We are also grateful to Sylvia Peglar, who corrected the English text.

References

Alsaker, S. 1987. *Bømlo – steinalderens råstoffsentrum på Sørvestlandet.* Arkeologiske avhandlinger 4. Bergen.
Barth, F. 1969. Introduction. In: Barth, F. (ed.) *Ethnic Groups and Boundaries. The Social Organization of Culture Difference,* 9–38. Oslo.
Bergsvik, K.A. 1995. Bosetningsmønstre på kysten av Nordhordland i steinalder. En geografisk analyse. In: Bergsvik, K.A., Nygård, S. and Nærøy, A.J. (eds.) *Arkeologiske skrifter 8. Steinalderkonferansen i Bergen 1993,* 111–130. Bergen.
—— 1999. Steinalderundersøkelsene ved Skatestraumen, Sogn og Fjordane. In: Dommasnes, L.H. and Mandt, G. (eds.) *Arkeologiske skrifter fra Universitetet i Bergen 10,* 5–26. Bergen.
—— 2001. Sedentary and mobile hunter fishers in stone age Western Norway. *Arctic Anthropology* 38, 2–26.
—— 2002. Mesolithic ethnicity – too hard to handle? (in this volume).
Binford, L.R. 1979. Organization and formation process: looking at curated technologies. *Journal of Anthropological Research* 35, 255–273.
Chapman, J. 1993. Social power in the Iron Gates Mesolithic. In: Chapman, J. and Dolukhanov, P. (eds.) *Cultural Transformations and Interactions in Eastern Europe,* 71–121. Aldershot.
Clark, G. 1965. Traffic in stone axes and adze blades. *Economic History and Review* 18, 1–28.
—— 1975. *The Earlier Stone Age Settlement of Scandianvia.* Cambridge.
Eriksen, B.V. 2000. "Squeezing blood from stones" – flintoldsagernes vidnesbyrd om social struktur, subsistensøkonomi og mobilitet i ældre stenalder. In: Eriksen, B.V. (ed.) *Flintstudier. En håndbog i systematiske analyser av flintinventarer,* 231–267. Århus.
Fisher, A. 1982. Trade in Danubian shaft-hole adzes and the introduction of Neolithic economy in Denmark. *Journal of Danish Archaeology* 1, 7–12.
Gendel, P.A. 1984. *Mesolithic Social Territories in Northwestern Europe.* BAR international series 218. Oxford.
Gjerland, B. 1984. *Bergartsøkser i Vest-Noreg. Distribusjon sett i forhold til praktisk funksjon, økonomisk tilpasning of tradisjon i steinalderen.* Unpublished mag.art. thesis, Historical Museum, University of Bergen. Bergen.
Gjessing, G. 1945. *Norges Stenalder.* Oslo.
Glørstad, H. 1999. Lokaliteten Botne II – Et nøkkelhull til det sosiale livet i mesolittikum i Sør-Norge. *Viking* LXII, 31–68.
Gräslund, B. 1962. Skafthålsförsedda spetsredskap av sten. *Tor* VIII, 105–150.

Helm, J. 1968. The nature of Dogrib socioterritorial groups. In: Lee, R.B. and DeVore, I. (eds.) *Man the Hunter,* 118–125. Chicago.
Jenkins, R. 1997. *Rethinking Ethnicity. Arguments and Explorations.* London.
Jennbert, K. 1984. *Den produktiva gåvan: Tradition och innovation i Sydskandinavien för omkring 5300 år sedan.* Acta Archaeologica Lundensia. Series in 4°. No. 16. Lund.
Jones, S. 1997. *The Archaeology of Ethnicity: Constructing Identities in the Past and Present.* London.
Larsson, L. 1988. Aspects of exchange in Mesolithic societies. In: Hårdh, B., Larsson, L., Olausson, D. and Petré, R. (eds.) *Trade and Exchange in Prehistory: Studies in Honour of Berta Stjernquist.* Acta archaeologica Lundensia. Series in 8°. No. 16, 25–32. Lund.
Lødøen, T.K. 2002. Late Mesolithic rock-art and expressions of ideology. (this volume).
Nash, G. 1998. *Exchange, Status and Mobility: Mesolithic Portable Art of Southern Scandinavia.* BAR International Series 710. Oxford.
Nygaard, S. 1990. Mesolithic western Norway. In: Vermeersch, P.M. and Van Peer, P. (eds.) *Contributions to the Mesolithic in Europe,* 227–237. Leuven.
Nærøy, A.J. 2000. *Stone Age Living Spaces in Western Norway.* BAR International series 857. Oxford.
Olsen, A.B. 1981. Bruk av diabas i vestnorsk steinalder. Unpublished mag. art. thesis, Historical museum, University of Bergen. Bergen.
—— 1992. *Kotedalen – en boplass gjennom 5000 år. Bind 1: Fangstbosetning og tidlig jordbruk i vestnorsk steinalder: Nye funn og nye perspektiver.* Bergen.
—— 1995. Fangstsedentisme og tidlig jordbrukspraksis i vestnorsk yngre steinalder belyst ved undersøkelsene i Kotedalen, Radøy, Hordaland. In: Bergsvik, K.A., Nygård, S. and Nærøy, A.J. (ed.) *Arkeologiske skrifter 8. Steinalderkonferansen i Bergen 1993,* 131–150. Bergen.
Olsen, A.B. and Alsaker, S. 1984. Greenstone and diabase utilization in the stone age of Westen Norway: Technological and socio-cultural aspects of axe and adze production and distribution. *Norwegian Archaeological Review* 17, 71–103.
Renfrew, C. 1977. Alternative models for exchange and spatial distribution. In: Earle, T. and Ericson, J.E. (eds.) *Exchange Systems in Prehistory,* 71–90. New York.
Renfrew, C. and Bahn, P. 1996. *Archaeology: Theories, Methods and Practice.* 2 edition. London.
Sackett, J. 1985. Style and ethnicity in the Kalahari: A reply to Wiessner. *American Antiquity* 50, 154–159.
Shennan, S. 1989. Introduction: Archaeological approaches to cultural identity. In: Shennan, S. (ed.) *Archaeological Approaches to Cultural Identity,* 1–32. London.
Solberg, B. 1989. Køller, klubber og hakker av stein. Lite påaktede gjenstandsgrupper i vestnorsk yngre steinalder. *Universitetets Oldsaksamlings Årbok* 1986–88, 81–102.
Trigger, B.G. 1995. Romanticism, nationalism, and archaeology. In: Kohl, P. and Fawcett, C. (eds.) *Nationalism, Politics and the Practice of Archaeology,* 263–279. London.
Walderhaug, E. 1998. Changing art in a changing society: the hunter's rock-art of western Norway. In: Chippindale, C. and Taçon, P.S.C. (eds.) *The Archaeology of Rock-Art,* 285–301. Cambridge.
Warren, J.E. 1994. *Coastal sedentism during the Atlantic period in Nordhordland, Western Norway?. The middle and late Mesolithic components at Kotedalen.* Unpublished MA thesis, Department of Anthropology, Memorial University of Newfoundland. St. John's.

53. Trapping up the rivers and trading across the sea – steps towards the neolithisation of Denmark

Anders Fischer

A series of C13-measurements of bone from humans and dogs from Danish inland sites demonstrates a high degree of coast-inland 'commuting' throughout the Mesolithic. Judging from the geographical distribution of sites, this traffic took place by boat. Likewise, trading across the sea was a reoccurring exercise at least during the Middle and Late Mesolithic. Through maritime exchange, attractive and prestige-enhancing objects were distributed all over the West Baltic region. In the Ertebølle period items of southern neolithic origin were incorporated into this trade system. The simultaneous intensification of coast-inland commuting is here suggested to be a response to an increasing demand for fur and skin to be exchanged with neolithic societies south of the Baltic. Fur trapping up the rivers and trading across the sea are thus considered as two connected phenomena which in the end established a situation where the introduction of farming was technically possible and socially profitable.

Transporting items within or across social boundaries?

Artefacts of non-local provenance are seen here and there within most of the European Mesolithic. In some cases a possible source of origin is so near that their transport may simply be a consequence of the local population's seasonal movements. Other items have been transported so far away from their cultural and geographic origins that exchange through many hands is the only realistic explanation.

This paper considers which of such exotic artefacts are the results of exchange and which have more likely been transported in connection with seasonal movements. The archaeological and zoo-archaeological records from Denmark form the empirical basis for these considerations.

Figure 53.1 gives the geographic distribution of the Ertebølle Culture. It was located around the western Baltic and was characterised by a uniform development of material culture over a period of nearly one and a half millennia. From the geographic distribution of settlements

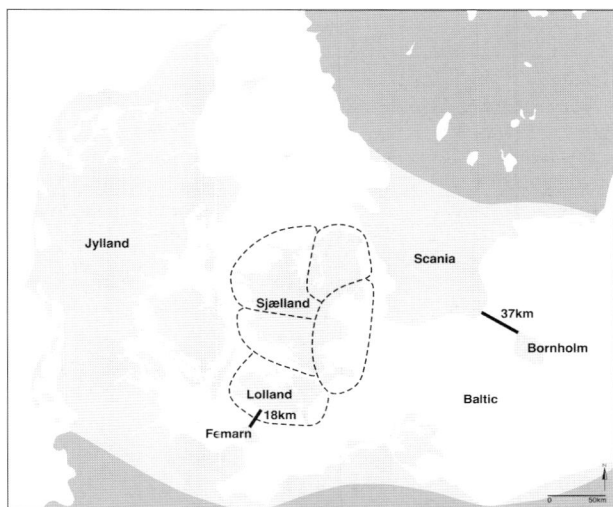

Figure 53.1 The geographical extent of the Ertebølle Culture and a provisional division into social territories of Sjælland and surrounding islands. The uniform development of the material culture implies frequent voyages across the open sea. Travelling from, for instance, Scania to Bornholm or from Femarn to Lolland would probably have implied entering the territories of foreign social groups.

it appears that this culture was highly dependent on the sea, the rivers and the lakes for subsistence and transport (e.g. Fischer 1997; Paludan-Müller 1978, in press).

Studies of stylistic details, primarily in the shapes of flake axes from Ertebølle sites on Sjælland and the surrounding islands, have demonstrated geographical variations which have been suggested to represent different social territories (Johansson 1999; cf. Petersen 1984). Taken at face value, each of these territories may be defined as a segment of land, measuring ca. 50 km parallel to the main orientation of the coast (Figure 53.1). It must be admitted, though, that these territories are still highly hypothetical, and it should be noted that the authors mentioned above have only studied the archaeological records from the coastal zone. The inland finds have not yet been taken into consideration.

Site name	Sample species	Date (C14 BP or typological)	uncertainty of the date	δ¹³C ‰	reservoire correction of C14 date	calibrated C14 date BC	Lab. No.
Koelbjerg	Human	9250	85	-20.7	0	8523-8476	K-4063
Holmegård V	Dog	8580	60	-17.7	109	7542	Ka-6999
Mullerup	Human	8410	90	-16.5	155	7316-7206	K-4151
Holmegård V	Human	8340	90	-19.7	34	7449-7350	K-4153
Holmegård V	Human	8220	190	-18.2	91	7079	K-4152
Kongemose 1979	Human	8060	65	-21.9	0	7058	AAR-6788
Holmegård I	Dog	7980	70	-18.0	98	6688	Ka-6998
Bodal K	Human	6275	50	-15.7	185	4994-4965	AAR-4765
Bodal AL	Dog	5765	45	-13.3	275	4340	AAR-4767
Ringkloster	Dog	5420	210	-18.8	68	4223-4169	K-4133
Bodal A	Dog	5380	50	-19.2	53	4221-4054	AAR-4769
Skolæstbo	Dog	5355	45	-14.9	215	3962	AAR-4766
Bodal E	Dog	5340	80	-20.1	19	4220-4053	AAR-4770
Præstelyng	Dog	5260	65	-21.6	0	4042	K-3773
Ringkloster	Dog	5230	70	-21.3	0	4038-3997	K-4132
Ulkestrup Lyng	Dog	Maglemose Culture	Context	-21.9			
Sværdborg I	Dog	Maglemose Culture	Context	-19.5			
Holmegård 1944	Dog	Maglemose Culture	Context	-17.4			
Kongemose	Dog	Kongemose Culture	Context	-17.0			
Kongemose	Dog	Kongemose Culture	Context	-14.0			
Kongemose V	Human	Kongemose Culture	Context	-22.9			
Ringkloster	Dog	Ertebølle Culture	Context	-20.0			K-386
Ringkloster	Dog	Ertebølle Culture	Context	-11.8			K-387

Figure 53.2 δ¹³C levels in bone collagen of Mesolithic humans and dogs from Danish inland sites. Each sample is provided with a date, either based on a direct AMS analysis of the bone in question, or based on the typological date of its context.

If the division into social territories suggested by A.D. Johansson (1999) is accepted as a relevant working hypothesis, the seasonal movements of these Ertebølle social groups must have taken place over relatively short distances, i.e. less than 50 km as the crow flies (cf. S.H. Andersen 1998).

C13-evidence on coast-inland commuting

The numerous Danish inland settlements are important for the discussion of the geographical extent of Mesolithic seasonal migration. For generations it has been evident that the well preserved swamp sites of eastern Denmark generally represent summer habitation. For an almost equally long period it has been discussed where the inhabitants of these sites lived the rest of the year (e.g. Fischer 1993). Did they live permanently in the inland (at the lake-side sites), or, did they spend the rest of the year by the sea?

Measurements of δ¹³C values in bone collagen from Mesolithic skeletal remains of humans and dogs found at inland sites are most relevant to this debate in as much as they provide a possibility for estimating the average proportion of marine food consumed by the individuals in question (cf. Noe-Nygaard 1988; Clutton-Brock and Noe-Nygaard 1990; data from these papers are included in figure 53.2). This topic is dealt with in an ongoing project aiming at absolute dates and stable isotope analyses (δ¹³C and δ¹⁵N) of Stone Age man and his four-footed companion (Fischer et al. in prep.).

At the moment, 23 C13-measurements of bones from humans and dogs, found at Mesolithic sites in the Danish inland, are available (Figure 53.2). Based on AMS dates of the bones themselves or on the typological date of their individual context, these samples can be sorted out in the following chronological categories: Maglemose Culture (ca. 9000–6400 BC), Kongemose Culture (ca. 6400–5400 BC) and Ertebølle Culture (ca. 5400–3950 BC) (all absolute dates in this paper are calibrated calendar years Before Christ).

Based on empirical data from Scandinavia, a 100% marine diet is estimated to result in δ¹³C values around –10,0‰. A 100% terrestrial diet seems to lead to δ¹³C values of approximately –20.6‰ (Johansen et al. 1986; cf. Richards and Hedges 1999; Fischer in press b). In the present paper focus is on samples where the marine signal is most significant, i.e. values in the intervals –10.0 to –15.0‰ and –15.1 to –17.5‰. They represent individuals whose average consumption of marine food over a period of several years prior to their death was in the scale of more than ca. 50% and more that ca. 25% respectively.

Inland finds of human and dog bones with δ¹³C values around –20.6‰ need not be taken as indications of the existence of a special category of around-the-year inland settlers. Some individuals found at coastal sites have similar C13-values. It is important to notice that fish and molluscs from rivers and lakes often have $\delta^{13}C$ values that are significantly more negative than terrestrial plants and animals (Lanting and van der Plicht 1996; Dufour *et al.* 1999). For instance, Stone Age fish bones from the Danish Åmose have values in the scale of –21 to –27‰ (Fischer and Heinemeier in prep.). Consequently a diet including a mixture of marine and fresh water resources may lead to bone collagen $\delta^{13}C$ values that appear terrestrial!

Figures 53.3a–c show the geographical distribution of the samples listed in figure 53.2. These maps also give a generalised outline of the location of the coast during the respective culture epochs.

From the classical site Mullerup (Sarauw's Island) we have an example of a Maglemosian human being whose diet included a considerable proportion of marine food. The $\delta^{13}C$ value of –16.5‰ implies that roughly 39% of this person's food came from the sea in case it was made up of marine and terrestrial organisms only. Considering the topographical location, the numerous remains of fresh water fish, the fish hooks and the leister prongs of most of the well preserved Maglemosian inland sites (including the one on Sarauw's Island) it is obvious that the individual in question also had a significant intake of fresh water food. Therefore, it is likely that nearly half of this person's diet was based on marine organisms. Consequently this human being probably spent most of the years prior to his/her death by the sea. The nearest coast was approximately 30 km away as the crow flies or at least 50 km by boat down the river (Figure 53.3a).

From Holmegård there are further examples of Maglemosian humans and dogs whose diet included a proportion of marine food. The apparently somewhat smaller share as compared with the Mullerup person may be explained by the much larger distance to the sea.

As far as we know from fauna remains, all the inland sites of the Maglemose Culture represent seasonal habitation, mainly or solely from the summer (e.g. Sørensen 1976; Rosenlund 1980; Richter 1982; Rowley-Conwy 1993; Fischer 1993).

At the present time we have no more than three inland samples from the Kongemose Culture. As can be seen from figure 53.2, two of the individuals in question have consumed marine food to a significant degree. The topography and the fauna remains of many of the Kongemosian inland sites suggest seasonal habitation, mainly in the summer, but there are also indications of short hunting visits during other seasons (Noe-Nygaard 1995).

Likewise, the C13-values of the inland samples from the Ertebølle Culture show great variation, and several of them represent a high proportion of marine food. The numerous Ertebølle sites from the inland area of the Åmose (Figure 53.3c) seem to be of seasonal character (K. Andersen 1983), and the same most probably applies to the huge Ringkloster site. The fauna remains indicate that this site was a hunting camp with special focus on the

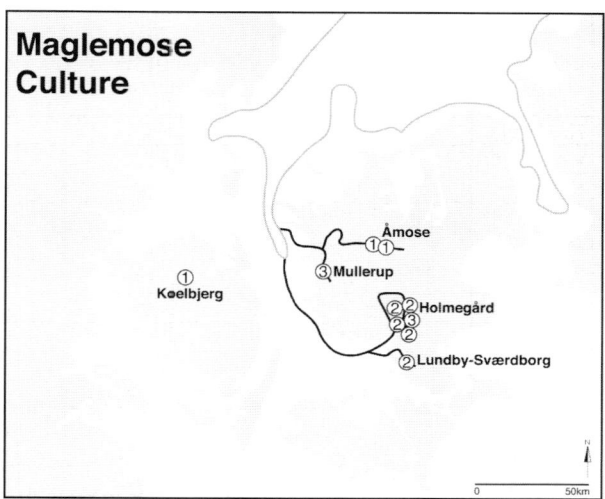

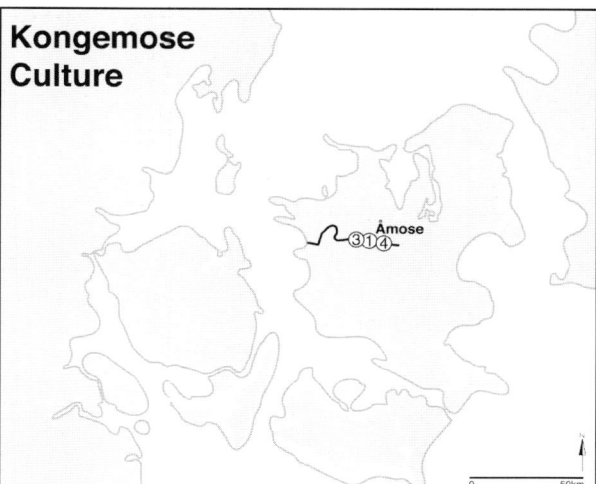

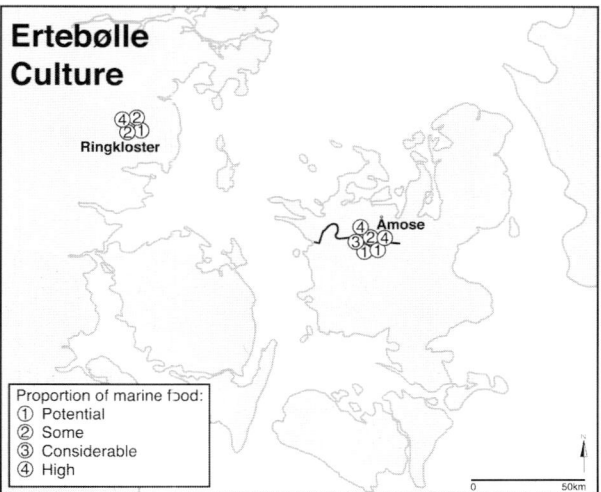

Figure 53.3 Evidence of Mesolithic coast-inland commuting based on $\delta^{13}C$ values of bone collagen from dogs and humans found at Danish inland sites. The symbols indicate the proportion of marine food consumed by the 23 individuals represented. Four categories are distinguished: ≥ -15.0‰ (high), –15.1 to –17.5‰ (considerable), –17.6 to –20.0‰ (some) and ≤ -20.1‰ (potential). The location of the coastline during each stage is to be taken as a rough generalisation only.

procurement of fur and skin (Rowley-Conwy 1993, 1998). Trapping also played a role of some significance on the contemporary sites in the Åmose. The bone material from the late Ertebølle summer site of Præstelyng, for instance, includes five very young calves of red deer and roe deer, which may have been killed mainly for their special quality hide. The site, furthermore, comprised the remains of at least three pine martens and two otters (Noe-Nygaard 1995). Owing to their high quality fur, these species have been much pursued by trappers in historical times.

One conclusion of the C13-evidence presented in figure 53.2 is that throughout the Mesolithic, inland Denmark was in all likelihood exploited seasonally by groups which lived much of the year by the sea. During the Kongemose and Ertebølle epochs, habitation sites evidently clustered around favourable fishing places along the coast, and the same may have been the case during the Maglemose epoch (Fischer 1997, in prep.). The large central places by the sea seem to have been inhabited around the year for generations and by many people. Considering the data presented above, the inland sites appear to be part of this coast-oriented settlement pattern: small groups from the coastal centres frequently moved into the interior for a variety of activities, including trapping.

Trapping also took place in the coastal zone as exemplified by two piles of bones representing 9 and 12 skinned individuals of pine marten respectively. They were found in the dump area of the Tybrind Vig site (Hans Dal, pers. com. 2001) which belongs to the early, middle and late Ertebølle Culture. The remains of fur-bearing animals at this site also include wildcat, fox, otter, badger and polecat. It is remarkable that the majority of bones from these species are found in the upper layers of the site, which means the time immediately prior to neo-lithisation (S.H. Andersen 1985).

Data from several Danish inland bog areas indicate intensified, seasonal settlement in these environments during the final centuries of the Ertebølle epoch (e.g. Troels-Smith 1967; S.H. Andersen 1977; K. Andersen 1983; Schilling 1997). This was earlier interpreted as a consequence of a food crisis among the coastal population of that period (Fischer 1974, in press a; Paludan-Müller 1978, in press). However, a recent status of data does not show obvious signs of intensification of food procurement during the relevant period (Fischer in press b). As an alternative explanation it is suggested that the intensified exploitation of the inland during the late Ertebølle period was to a high degree a response to changing conditions within the social sphere, including an increasing demand for high quality fur and skin (Fischer in press b).

Other indications of coast-inland connections

Figure 53.4 shows a pendant made of a non-fossilised shell of a marine mollusc, which was found at a Maglemosian site in Lundby bog, southern Sjælland (Møller Hansen 1995, 2001). In principle, it may have been

Figure 53.4 A testimony of contact between coast and inland during the Maglemosian epoch: a pendant made of the shell of the marine species black quahog (Cyprina islandica), found at the seasonal camp Lundby II. Scale in mm. Photo: K. Møller Hansen, Sydsjællands Museum.

Figure 53.5 Remains of Mesolithic provisions for the journey from the coast to seasonal camps in the Åmose? Femur of grey seal (Halichoerus grypus) from the site of Øgårde and spine bones of a small whale, probably a white-beaked dolphin (Lagenorhynchus albirostris) from the Kildegård site. Scale in cm. Photo: G. Brovad, Zoological Museum, University of Copenhagen.

brought in from the coast either through trade or through seasonal coast-inland commuting. Considering the seasonal indicators of this site (Rosenlund 1980) and the outcome of the C13-measurements mentioned above, the presence of this exotic find is most likely a result of seasonal movement.

During the Maglemose epoch a voyage from the coast to the bogs of Lundby-Sværdborg and Holmegård in southern Sjælland would most obviously be accomplished

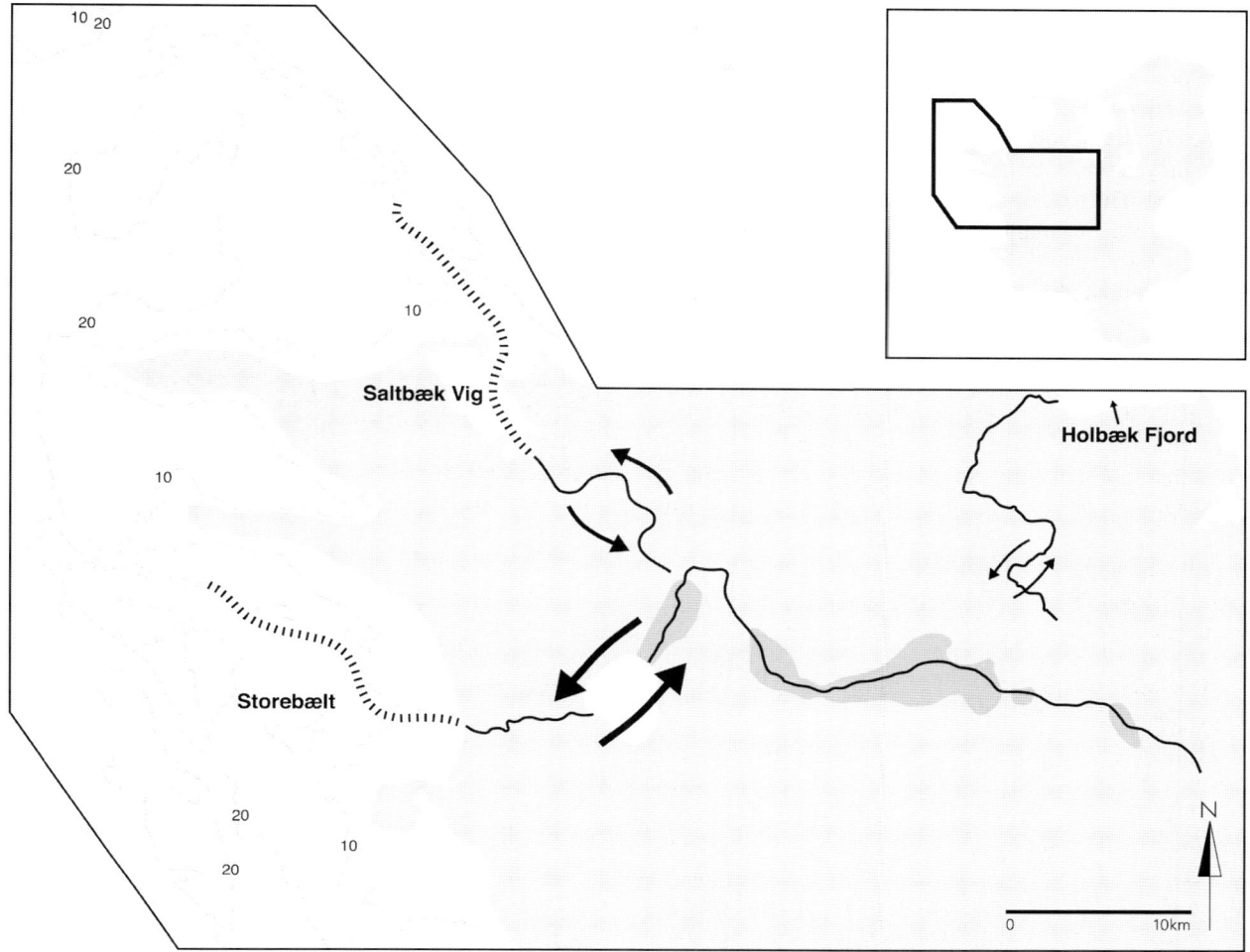

Figure 53.6 Model of seasonal 'commuting' between the Åmose and the coast. The main transport corridor is presumed to have been the Åmose river ending in the Storebælt, to the west. If luggage and vessels were carried over land for a short distance, the commuting may also have included a corridor towards the north-west. The distance between the Åmose river and the minor river running into Saltbæk Vig is only 0.8 km of almost level ground. Likewise seasonal movements primarily by boat may have taken place between Åmose and Holbæk Fjord to the north-east. The extraordinary density of Mesolithic settlements in the Åmose as compared for instance with that of Holmegård bog and Lundby-Sværdborg bog may be a result of its accessibility from various parts of the social (tribal) territory (cf. Figure 53.1)

by boat up the rivers. The distance would have been in the scale of 150–200 km and could easily be traversed in a week.

The bones of marine mammals shown in figure 53.5 were found at culturally mixed Mesolithic settlements in the Åmose. For generations it has been open to debate whether such remains of marine species from culture layers in the inland were the results of exchange or of seasonal movement. Considering the C13-analyses of human and dog bones from the Mesolithic sites in the Åmose (Figure 53.2), it now seems probable that these seal and whale bones are testimony of seasonal coast-inland commuting. They represent meaty parts of the animals and may be the remains of 'picnic packages' for the voyage from the coast.

During the Ertebølle epoch such journeys need not have involved much hardship. The distance from the sea to the Åmose was ca. 25 km as the crow flies (Figure 53.6). Travelling by boat up the Åmose river the voyage could probably be made in a day.

So, a number of exotic artefacts found at Danish inland sites should now be excluded from the list of indisputable trade items. They are, more likely, outcome of seasonal movements between coast and inland. This probably also applies to similar items found elsewhere in Europe at Mesolithic inland sites located less than 150–200 km from the coast of those days.

But, there are other kinds of exotic artefacts, which certainly are the outcome of exchange.

Mesolithic exchange

At the beginning of the Kongemose epoch the Danish islands were separated from the Continent (Fischer in prep.). Soon after, several of the large species of game became extinct on these islands (Sørensen 1988). Elk, for example, disappeared from Sjælland, but not from Scania. As demonstrated by P. Vang Petersen (1990), this fauna extinction allows us to distinguish a number of middle and late Mesolithic archaeological items that are of non-local origin. This, for instance, applies to a richly decorated weapon made of elk antler, stylistically dated to the Kongemose epoch (Figure 53.7). Its was found in north-eastern Sjælland, and may therefore derive from Scania.

Figure 53.8 shows the distribution of exotic Mesolithic fauna items from Denmark. They are all of spectacular character – weapons and ornaments of obvious prestige value. There are no finds of unmanufactured bones that may have been brought to the Danish islands as parts of hunted game meant for ordinary subsistence. Such none-spectacular bones (cf. Figure 53.5) would have been expected in case the remains of exotic fauna were the result of task groups' hunting in distant areas where these tasty species of game still survived. Therefore, this group of exotica is, most probably, the outcome of exchange across social boundaries.

The Danubian shaft-hole axes from Denmark and southern Sweden are well known examples of Mesolithic long distance trade (Fischer 1982; Jennbert 1984; Larsson 1988; Klassen and Jonsson 1999; Klassen in press). They are made of a distinctive kind of rock, which does not exist naturally in northern Europe. When new, these axes were very conspicuous with their shining smooth surfaces, varying between green-black and olive green (Figure 53.9). They were exotic, not just in their raw material, but also in their design, including their perfect shaft-holes made by means of a drilling technique that had not hitherto been seen in southern Scandinavia (Fischer in press b).

According to geological analyses, the Danubian shaft-hole axes from Denmark are made of a type of rock the source of which is probably Bulgaria or Slovakia (Schwarz-Mackensen and Schneider 1986; Pedersen *et al.* 1997). The shortest distance between the source areas and Denmark is 1000–1500 km (Figure 53.10).

The Scandinavian axes of this type are the outcome of exchange across many social territories. This conclusion is drawn not just on the long distance they have been moved. The main thing is that their producers and their

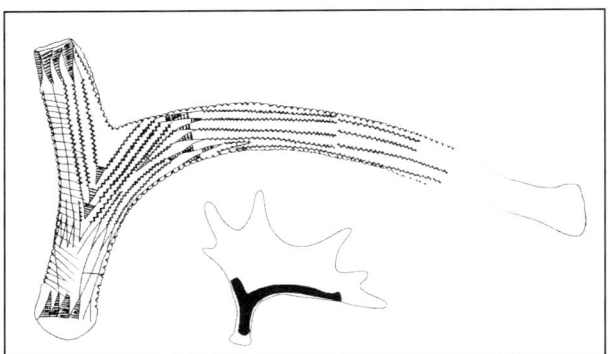

Figure 53.7 A probable trade item: a weapon made of elk antler. It was found near Maglemosegård, north-east Sjælland, to where it was imported from outside Sjælland. Its exotic and symbolic character was emphasised by striking engraved ornaments. Drawn on the basis of Vang Petersen 1990.

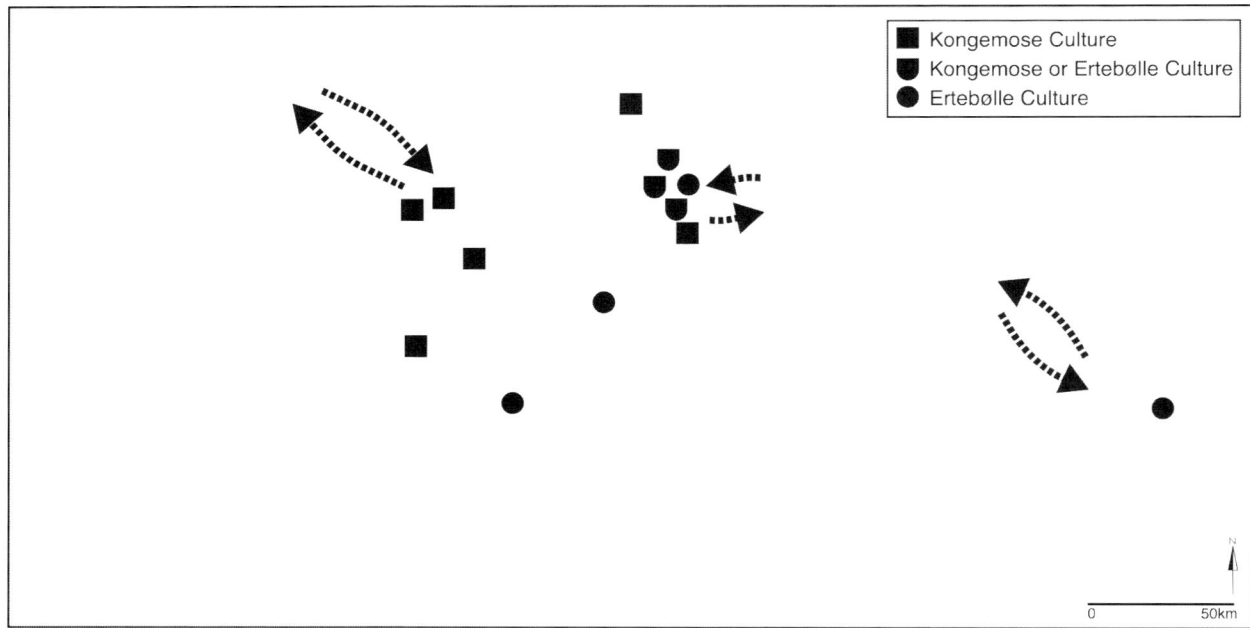

Figure 53.8 The location of exotic Mesolithic fauna remains from the Danish Middle and Late Mesolithic. They all represent weapons or ornaments of obvious symbolic value. Drawn on the basis of Vang Petersen 1990.

Figure 53.9 Danubian shaft-hole axe from Maglelyng in the Åmose. Scale in cm. Photo: A. Fischer.

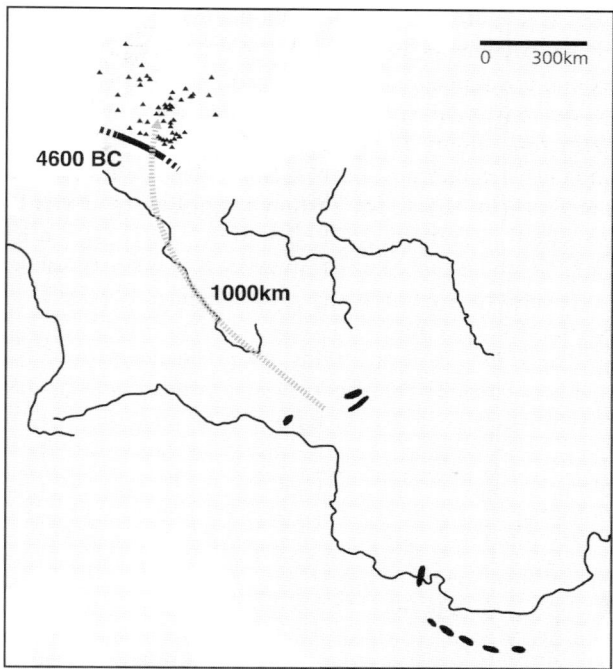

Figure 53.10 Distribution and hypothetical trade route of Danubian shaft-hole axes found in Denmark and Sweden. These axes were imported by the Danish Ertebølle Culture for a period of several hundred years prior to neolithisation north of the Baltic, which began ca. 3950 BC. The trade route passed the Ertebølle Culture south of the Baltic, where farming was practised from ca. 4600 BC. The hatched areas of Bulgaria and Slovakia mark the possible sources of the rock in question.

receivers were widely different concerning economy and material culture. The former were farmers of Central European Danubian Cultural tradition, while the latter were foragers of North European tradition.

The find contexts of the Danubian shaft-hole axes indicate that they arrived in Denmark in the middle and late stages of the Ertebølle Culture (Fischer 1982; Pedersen *et al.* 1997; Klassen in press). The absolute date of the middle stage of the Ertebølle Culture is ca. 4800–4300 BC. This means that these axes were already present at least 300 years before the introduction of farming, which took place in this region ca. 3950 BC (Fischer in press b).

The trade routes of the Danubian shaft-hole axes went through northernmost Germany, where farming was already being practised. The Ertebølle Culture south of the Baltic became neolithic not later than 4600 BC (Hartz *et al.* in press).

The Danubian shaft-hole axes found north of the Baltic are concentrated on the Danish islands (Figure 53.10). Thus, their distribution stresses the importance of maritime exchange. Judging from their geographical location, they probably arrived in Denmark by boat across the Baltic.

The existence of a maritime trade system helps to explain why farming, apparently, was introduced at least as early on the island of Sjælland as on the peninsula of Jylland, to which farmers and cattle from Central Europe could have arrived by land.

As appears from figure 53.10, the Åmose has the highest concentration of finds of Danubian shaft-hole axes in Denmark. This is not necessarily just a consequence of especially intense archaeological research. It may also be due to unusually intense cultic activity. During the Early Neolithic this fresh water system was a centre of ritual exercises, which led to a remarkable concentration of votive pottery, flint axes, boats, human bodies, *etc.* (Koch 1998; Fischer in press b). The many Danubian axes in the same bog may represent an initial stage of this tradition of votive deposition of artefacts of special symbolic value.

The neolithisation process

Long distance exchange of prestige items between Mesolithic groups in the West Baltic region was a common phenomenon during the Kongemose and Ertebølle epochs. In the middle and late Ertebølle periods, stone axes from neolithic societies in the south were incorporated into this exchange system. The intensified seasonal inland habitation seen at the same time may be the result of a growing demand for such assets as skin and fur, which could be exchanged with other regions, especially with the southern regions from which the Danubian stone axes were obtained.

It is easy to imagine that this exchange of prestige goods went hand in hand with the exchange of ideas and individuals. At the time when Danubian shaft-hole axes were introduced in Denmark, the Ertebølle Culture south of the Baltic was already practising small-scale farming.

The continued influx of objects from the Danubian cultures probably resulted in an inflationary process, in which it gradually became difficult to express wealth through personally portable material symbols alone. In such a situation socially ambitious groups north of the Baltic may have been inspired to engage in the production of cattle husbandry and cereal cultivation. Both activities offered exotic and attractive foodstuffs, which could be served profitably in the course of prestige-promoting feasts. The seeds and animals needed for such an innovation could be procured through the exchange system. Assuming that marriage exchange was practised to the same degree as in the most relevant ethnographic parallels, competence in the practising of farming could be acquired rather easily by marrying a person from the neolithic exchange partners south of the Baltic (Fischer in press b).

In conclusion, the introduction of farming in Denmark may be seen as part of a socio-economic process driven by a desire among socially ambitious individuals and groups to gain power and prestige. Exchange over long distances across the sea had a central role in this process. It generated the need for and it served as the medium for the introduction of livestock and cereals. The local basis for this exchange may, to a high degree, have been skin and fur procured through intensified seasonal trapping which included the interior parts of the region. Trapping up the rivers and trading across the sea may, thus, be seen as important and interconnected aspects of the neolithisation of Denmark.

Acknowledgements

The analyses of human and canine bones presented above, the production of graphics for the paper, and the revision of the language of the manuscript was supported by the Danish Research Council for the Humanities, case no. 9902642, registration no. 28812. Bendt Nielsen (Ry), who did the graphic set-up of the drawings, and Freddy Volmer Hansen (Jyderup), who corrected the English language are both thanked for their effective and sensitive assistance.

References

Andersen, K. 1983. *Stenalderbebyggelsen i Den Vestsjællandske Åmose*. Fredningsstyrelsen. Copenhagen.

Andersen, S.H. 1977. Ertebøllekultur på Vestfyn. En oversigt. *Fynske Minder* 1977, 7–36.

—— 1985. Tybrind Vig. A report on a submerged Ertebølle settlement on the west coast of Fyn. *Journal of Danish Archaeology* 4, 52–69.

Clutton-Brock, J. and Noe-Nygaard, N. 1990. New osteological and C-isotope evidence on Mesolithic dogs: companions to hunters and fishers at Star Carr, Seamer Carr and Kongemose. *Journal of Archaeological Science* 17, 643–653.

Dufour, E., Bocherens, H. and Mariotti, A. 1999. Paleodietary implications of isotopic variability in Eurasian lacustrine fish. *Journal of Archaeological Science* 26, 617–627.

Fischer, A. 1974. Introduktionen af korn og kvæg i Sydskandinavien – en befolkningspres-model. *Kontaktstencil* 8, 91–111.

—— 1982. Trade in Danubian shaft-hole axes and the introduction of neolithic economy in Denmark. *Journal of Danish Archaeology* 1, 7–12.

—— 1993. Mesolithic inland settlement. In: Hvass, S. and Storgaard, B. (eds) *Digging into the Past. 25 Years of Archaeology in Denmark*, 58–63. Aarhus.

—— 1997. People and the sea – settlement and fishing along the Mesolithic coasts. In: Pedersen, L., Fischer, A. and Aaby, B. (eds.) *The Danish Storebælt since the Ice Age – man, sea and forest*, 63–77. Copenhagen.

—— 2001 in press a. The introduction of cereals and cattle into Southern Scandinavia: a population-pressure model. In: Fischer, A. and Kristiansen, K. (eds.) *The Neolithisation of Denmark – 150 Years of Debate*. Sheffield.

—— 2001 in press b. Food for feasting? An evaluation of explanations of the neolithisation of Denmark and southern Sweden In: Fischer, A. and Kristiansen, K. (eds.) *The Neolithisation of Denmark – 150 Years of Debate*. Sheffield.

—— in prep *Stenalderens Havopslugte Bopladser og Skove på Bunden af Øresund*. Skov- og Naturstyrelsen. Copenhagen.

Fischer, A. and Heinemeier, J. in prep. *Reservoir effect in food residue on pottery*.

Fischer, A., Heinemeier, J. and Richards, M. in prep. *Coast-inland relations in Stone Age Denmark*.

Hartz, S., Heinrich, D. and Lübke, H. in press. Coastal farmers – the neolithisation of northernmost Germany. In: Fischer, A. and Kristiansen, K. (eds.) *The Neolithisation of Denmark – 150 Years of Debate*. Sheffield.

Jennbert, K. 1984. *Den Produktiva Gåvan. Tradition Och Innovation i Sydskandinavien För Omkring 5300 År Sedan*. Acta Archaeologica Lundensia, Series in 4°, No. 16. Lund.

Johansen, O.S., Gulliksen, S. and Nydal, R. 1986. 13C and diet: analysis of Norwegian human skeletons. *Radiocarbon* 28, 754–761.

Johansson, A. 1999. Ertebøllekulturen i Sydsjælland. *Aarbøger for Nordisk Oldkyndighed og Historie* 1997, 7–88.

Klassen, L. in press. The Ertebølle Culture and neolithic continental Europe: traces of contact and interaction. In: Fischer, A. and Kristiansen, K. (eds.) *The Neolithisation of Denmark – 150 Years of Debate*. Sheffield.

Klassen, L. and Jonsson, A. 1999. A unique shafthole axe from recent excavations in the Järavallen beach ridge. *Lund Archaeological Review* 5, 21–39.

Koch, E. 1998. *Neolithic Bog Pots from Zealand, Møn, Lolland and Falster*. Nordiske Fortidsminder. Serie B, Vol. 16. Copenhagen.

Lanting, J.N. and van der Plicht, J. 1996. Wat hebben Floris V, skelet Swifterbant S2 en visotters gemeen? *Paleohistoria* 37/38, 491–519.

Larsson, L. 1988. Aspects of exchange in Mesolithic societies. In: Hårdh, B., Larsson, L., Olausson, D. and Petré, R. (eds.) *Trade and Exchange in Prehistory. Studies in honour of Berta Stjernquist*. Acta Archaeologica Lundensia, Series in 8°, No. 16, 25–32. Lund.

Møller Hansen, K. 1995. Maglemosebopladsen Lundby II. Ny undersøgelse. *Kulturhistoriske Studier*, 5–12. Vordingborg.

—— 2001. Strandtur. *Skalk* 2001, No. 2, 16–17.

Noe-Nygaard, N. 1988. 13C-values of dog bones reveal the nature of changes in man's food resources at the Mesolithic-Neolithic transition, Denmark. *Chemical Geology (Isotope Geoscience Section)* 73, 87–96.

—— 1995. *Ecological, sedimentary, and Geochemical Evolution of the Late-Glacial to Postglacial Åmose Lacustrine Basin, Denmark*. Fossils and Strata 37. Oslo.

Paludan-Müller, C. 1978. High Atlantic food gathering in northwestern Zealand: ecological conditions and spatial representation. In: Kristiansen, K. and Paludan-Müller, C. (eds) *New Directions in Scandinavian Archaeology*. Studies in Scandinavian Prehistory and Early History, 120–157. Copenhagen.

—— in press. High Atlantic food gathering in northwestern Zealand: ecological conditions and spatial representation. In:

Fischer, A. and Kristiansen, K. (eds.) *The Neolithisation of Denmark – 150 Years of Debate.* Sheffield.

Pedersen, L., Fischer, A. and Hald, N. 1997. Danubian shafthole axes – long distance transport and the introduction of agriculture. In: Pedersen, L., Fischer, A. and Aaby, B. (eds.) *The Danish Storebælt since the Ice Age – man, sea and forest,* 201–205. Copenhagen.

Petersen, P.V. 1984. Chronological and regional variation in the Late Mesolithic of Eastern Denmark. *Journal of Danish Archaeology* 3, 7–18.

—— 1990. Eksotiske faunarester i Kongemose- og Ertebølletid – resultat af udveksling? *Hikuin* 16, 17–30.

Richards, M.P. and Hedges, R.E.M. 1999. Stable isotope evidence for similarities in the type of marine food used by late mesolithic humans at sites along the Atlantic coast of Europe. *Journal of Archaeological Science* 26, 717–722.

Richter, J. 1982. Faunal remains from Ulkestrup Lyng Øst. In: Andersen, K., Jørgensen, S. and Richter, J. 1982. *Maglemose Hytterne ved Ulkestrup Lyng,* 141–177. Copenhagen.

Rosenlund, K. 1980. Knoglematerialet fra bopladsen Lundby II. In: Henriksen, B.B. 1980. *Lundby-holmen. Pladser af Maglemose-type i Sydsjælland,* 128–142. Copenhagen.

Rowley-Conwy, P. 1993. Season and reason: the case for a regional interpretation of mesolithic settlement patterns. In: Peterkin, G.L., Bricker, H. and Mellars, P. (eds) 1993. *Hunting and Animal Exploitation in the Later Palaeolithic and Mesolithic of Eurasia.* Archaeological Papers of the American Anthropological Association no. 4, 179–188.

—— 1998. Meat, furs and skins: mesolithic animal bones from Ringkloster, a seasonal hunting camp in Jutland. *Journal of Danish Archaeology* 12, 87–98.

Schilling, H. 1997. På sporet af stenalderens jægere og fiskere i Sydsjællands indland. *Kulturhistoriske Studier* 1997, 27–37. Vordingborg.

Schwarz-Mackensen, G. and Schneider, W. 1986. Petrographie und herkunft des rohmaterials neolithischer steinbeile und –äxte im nördlichen Harzvorland. *Archäologisches Korrespondenzblatt* 16, 29–44.

Sørensen, K.A. 1976. Zoological investigation of the bone material from Sværdborg I – 1943. In: Henriksen, B.B. 1976. *Sværdborg I. Excavations 1943–44. A settlement of the Maglemose Culture.* Arkæologiske Studier III, 137–148. Copenhagen.

—— 1988. *Danmarks Forhistoriske Dyreverden.* Copenhagen.

Troels-Smith, J. 1967. The Ertebølle Culture and its background. *Palaeohistoria* 12, 505–528.

54. Appropriation of the Past. Neolithisation in the Northern Scandinavian Perspective

Kjel Knutsson, Per Falkenström and Karl-Fredrik Lindberg

In this paper the Mesolithic in Northern Sweden is discussed in relation to the neolitisation process in southern Scandinavia. It is argued that the late Mesolithic handle core tradition found throughout the region, spread from the south through people moving in the exchange networks and that it carried values important for the reproduction of these societies. A change in material symbolism that takes place at c. 4500 cal BC is seen as the result of an ethnic process whereby northern hunter-gatherers actively, as a response to the neolithisation, appropriated a new identity and thus new material symbols.

Introduction

The Mesolithic in Southern Norrland is poorly known. The region is especially interesting, as it borders on the northernmost part of what seems to have been a fundamental cultural change in the northern fringe of Europe in the middle of the fifth century cal BC, the Neolithisation. Hunter-gatherer groups inhabiting this region never took up the Funnel Beaker economy and ideology (Hallgren this volume). The social, economic and ethnic processes that must have been active here can be studied only if it is more actively included in the archaeological discussion.

Figure 54.1a Scandinavia with important regions mentioned in the text.

Figure 54.1b Scandinavia with Mesolithic sites north of the TRB border in Norrland. 7000–4500 cal BC.

The Mesolithic in Southern Norrland

Sites of Mesolithic character (with handle cores, keeled scrapers, blade cores, microblades, macroblades, *etc.*)in southern Norrland (Figures 54.1b, 54.2a and 54.2b), north of the Early Neolithic border of the TRB culture, have been found during archaeological surveys in a wide range of environments. Most of the sites are situated at 150–200 m. a. s. l., though altitudes of 50 m can be found at a few locations in south-eastern Dalarna. At the time of occupation, the latter were probably situated close to the former seashore. Towards the north-western parts of Dalarna and Härjedalen, there are several sites at altitudes up to 800 m. a. s. l. This sort of topography also naturally includes the Norwegian highland to the west. One should bear in mind that the environment during the Mesolithic some 9000–6000 years ago, was comparatively open and that the tree line was about 200 m higher.

There is variability regarding site locations and artefact compositions. Usually the sites with high variability are located on lakes or in river valleys in attractive biotopes. Low-variability sites are more spread out in the landscape.

The degradation of humus is a very slow process in Norrland. Consequently, stratigraphy is seldom useful for dating. These conditions, together with repeated visits to the sites, have contributed to the development of mixed sites. Furthermore, only a handful of Mesolithic sites have so far been excavated in the area, covering nearly 20 000 km², from Jämtland in the north to Dalarna in the south.

A few attempts have previously been made to place the archaeological assemblages in a rough time/space framework. Ragnar Lannerbro, who has surveyed the whole area for almost 40 years, has used southern Swedish typology in order to identify a Mesolithic horizon in the stray-find material. Apart from diagnostic, middle Mesolithic artefacts, such as handle cores, keeled scrapers and conical platform cores, he also mentions "chipping stones" and "pick-axe-like" tools (Lannerbro 1976:74). Lindberg (1994), on the same grounds as Lannerbro, defines three chronological phases in the Mesolithic. He suggests that parts of the blade and flake scrapers, core axes, irregular platform cores and some undefined cores should be dated before 6500 cal BC. During the following 500 years, handle cores were introduced. From 6000 BC, core axes and "axes" occur together with the Mesolithic diagnostic artefacts. After 4000 BC, Lindberg suggests that these types decreased, while typical Neolithic finds, such as polished axes and slate arrowheads, increased but still within the hunter-gatherer economy (Lindberg 1994:25).

To create an artefact typology in Norrland is difficult (especially when it is compared with the flint areas to the south), owing to the use of local raw materials such as tuffite and porphyry. Most of the typologically well-known, artefact types of western-Scandinavian origin mentioned above are exceedingly rare in the region. Big, prismatic blades, together with handle cores, microblade cores and microblades, made of local raw materials, are

Figure 54.2a Scandinavia with sites with macroblades in Norrland.

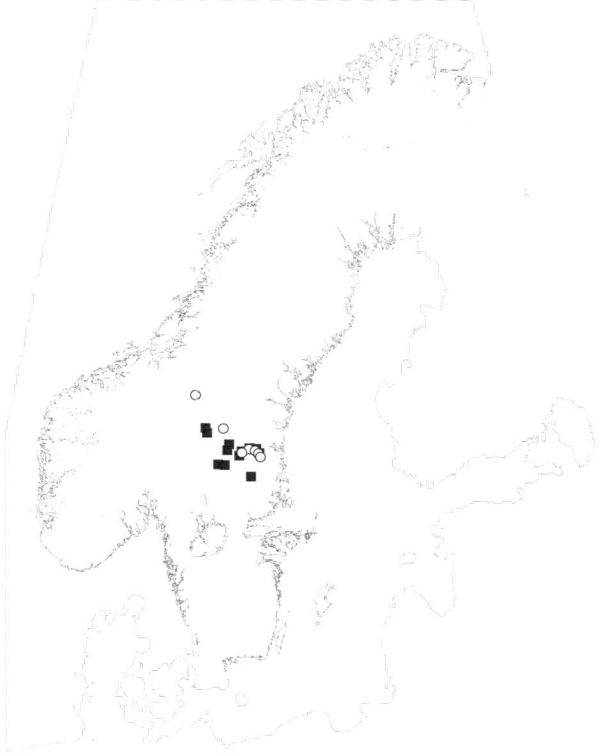

Figure 54.2b Sites with macroblade cores and sites with production debris from macroblade production.

Micro blades	93
Handle cores	76
Keeled scrapers	57
Micro blade cores	44
Blade cores	30
Platform cores	52
Blade scrapers	50
Flake scrapers	81
Axes	51
Line sinkers	26
Whet stones	26
Ceramics	7

Figure 54.3 Correlation between sites with macroblades and other types of finds of Mesolithic character.

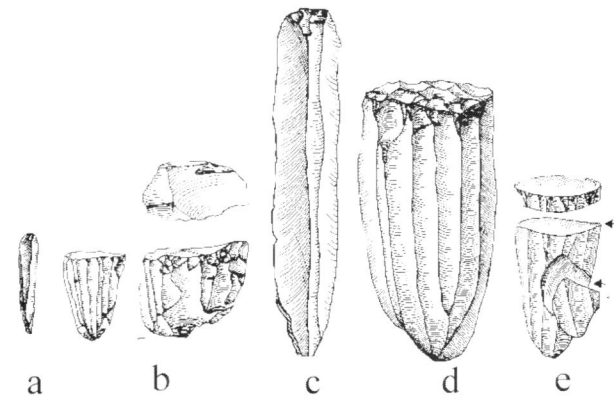

Figure 54.4 Diagnostic Mesolithic artefacts from southern Norrland.

the typical "mass material" of the region. Blades have been listed on 350 surveyed and excavated sites (Figure 54.2a) (Falkenström 1996). We started our investigations by trying to connect sites with blades with other diagnostic-find categories on the sites. An overview demonstrates that microblade technology is well represented among sites with blades. This relationship is expressed by the presence of microblades, handle cores and keeled scrapers on a large number of sites containing blades. This places the sites discussed here roughly in a middle/late Mesolithic context, compared with the find circumstances and typology on the Swedish west coast (Nordqvist 1999) and in south-eastern Norway (Ballin 1999) (Figure 54.3).

Of 350 sites with blades, no more than 100 show clear associations with the typical Mesolithic categories shown in figure 54.4. Our survey shows that there seems to be a differentiation between production and consumption areas in the landscape. Some sites have only blades, others have both blades, cores and production debitage. This may have been caused by a varied use of the landscape.

Finds of Neolithic character are few in the region. It is actually hard to define a Neolithic in the area. Certain types of polished axes, slate fragments, whetstones and line sinkers form a particular group of finds with few connections with the supposed Mesolithic industry but, since they are represented on most of the sites but to a very small extent, they indicate some sort of place related continuity over the Mesolithic-Neolithic border. In order to support the relevance of this conclusion, we have referred to a few excavated sites in southern Norrland where clear chronological horizons have been discovered (Figure 54.1b).

At Limsjön (Raä 405) in Leksand parish, one Mesolithic site was excavated in the early eighties. *The excavation yielded typical, Mesolithic, lithic artefacts made of different raw materials: handle cores, keeled scrapers, microblade cores, microblades, blade cores, blades, platform cores, blade scrapers and flake scrapers*

These finds are strikingly similar to those on the surveyed sites in southern Norrland discussed above. n recent years, further excavations of similar sites have been carried out on the coast of south-eastern Norrland (Gårdsjösund (Björck 1999; Björck *et al.* 2000), Valhalla (Raä 66), Ockelbo parish in the province of Gästrikland (Apel 1997)). This reflects, together with the stray finds, an extended settlement pattern across a varied landscape from the coast to the inland during the Mesolithic. Technology and tool typology shows strong connections to Southern Norway and the Swedish West-Coast Blade analyses (Ballin 1999; Nordqvist 1999).

In southern Norway, blades are found in large amounts on almost every site older than 4000 cal BC. In this respect, blades are suitable for a quantitative analysis of change and continuity during the Mesolithic, a fact deliberately used by Hein Bjerck in his analysis of the Mesolithic chronology in S-W Norway (Bjerck 1986). As the second step in our analysis, owing to the low frequency of formal tools and the large amounts of blades in the southern Norrland Mesolithic, we decided to analyse the blade industry specifically, on the basis of the in-depth analysis by Hein Bjerck. Thus, Bjerck begins by dividing his material into three periods.

1. The Fosna tradition, 8000 cal BC and earlier. Characteristic typological elements: flake adze, core adzes, coarse burins, single-edged, tanged points, microliths, unifacial blade cores and coarse macroblades.

2. The early microblade tradition, 8000–6000 cal BC. Characteristic typological elements: ground core adzes of greenstone, blade-fragment burins, blade borers/engravers, microliths, multifacial microblade cores, regular narrow macroblades and microblade-core preforms, previously interpreted as fragments of core adzes.

3. The late microblade tradition, 6000–4200 cal BC. Characteristic typological elements: ground core adzes of diabase, soapstone sinkers, blade borers/

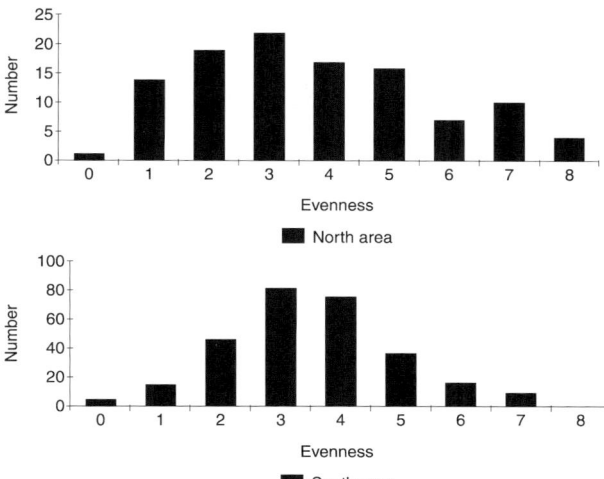

Figure 54.5a. Diagram showing the evaluation of blade evenness according to an intuitive 8 graded scale (based on criteria presented in Bjerck 1986).

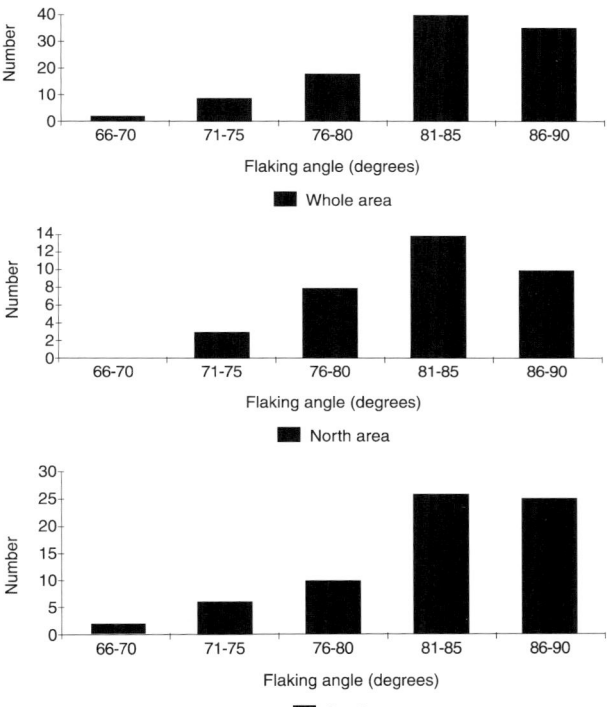

Figure 54.5b Diagram showing the flaking angle of blades in southern Norrland (based on Bjerck 1986).

engravers, anvil stones/hammer stones, multifacial microblade cores, regular microblades with platform remnants and irregular microblades without platform remnants. (ibid;107 pp).

In his analysis of the flint blade assemblages, Bjerck uses four variables, evenness, flaking angle, width and uniformity. (ibid;113). In our analysis, stress was laid on three of Bjerck's variables, evenness, flaking angle and width.

The main problem in applying this method to the blade assemblages in this region is that the raw material of the blades is variable. This makes it hard to evaluate evenness as between different parts of the region. Evenness is judged by the blade's dorsal, ventral and lateral sides. The evenness is graded between 0 and 4, and then the dorsal and ventral sides are graded between 0 and 4. These two grades are then added giving the blade a score between 0 and 8. The evenness, flaking angle and width were laid out in three bar charts each. If, for example, a bimodal curve could be found in the whole region, it would be pointing to two different populations representing either a time or space difference.

If we look at the graphs of the flaking angle all three are similar to each other, with a peak at 81–85° (Figure 54.5b). If that is compared with Bjerck's result, it will place them in the early microblade tradition (Bjerck 1986:115). When we come to the graphs of evenness, a difference between the northern part and the southern part of the region is visible (Figure 54.5a). If this is compared with Bjerck's investigation, the graphs of southern area could be interpreted as belonging to the late microblade tradition, while the graphs from the northern area shows a mixture of the early and the late microblade traditions. (ibid;115).

Correspondence analysis

The analysis above hinted at a possible spatial and/or temporal differentiation in the southern Norrland Mesolithic. This was also partly supported by an evaluation of artefact typology in general, conical microblade cores being more common in the north. As a third step in this first evaluation of the surveyed sites, we therefore decided to make a multivariate statistical analysis. Sixteen artefacts with some chronological significance in well-dated contexts on the Swedish west coast and Norway, were picked out from the southern Norrland database of 350 sites (Falkenström; 1996). 186 sites thus remained for the analysis (Lindberg 1998:27). The correspondence analysis (Lindberg 1999) of the data showed some differences between parts of the investigation area concerning the occurrence of artefacts and artefact-combinations. Figure 54.6 shows the distribution of types along the second axis of the analysis. Bladeknifes, blade cores and transverse arrowheads are placed to the left on the axis, followed by handle cores, keeled scrapers and blades. Farthest to the right on the axis, conical microblade cores and microblades occur. Note that blades occur on several sites where blade cores do not. Conical microblade cores are separated from handle cores and keeled scrapers. (Lindberg 1998:28 p)

As the next step in the analysis, we plotted the values from the correspondence analysis on a geographical map. There appeared to be a difference between the northern and southern parts of the region as already hinted at by the blade analysis. In the southern part, 77% of the sites

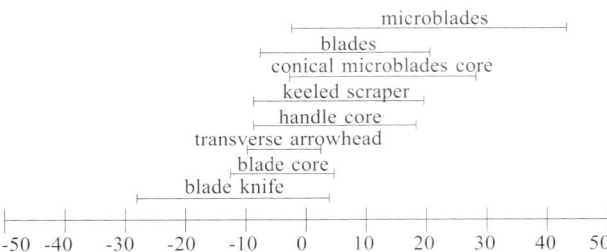

Figure 54.6 The multivariate analysis of 186 Mesolithic sites in Southern Norrland. The second axis.

were on the negative side of the correspondence axis and their average value was 0.69, while in the northern part, 54% of the sites were on the negative side and the sites had an average value of 4.02. The conical microblade cores are chiefly present in the northern part of the investigated area, around the township of Orsa. These cores are different also with respect to raw-material choice. They are made mainly of red jasper. Platform cores and blade cores are present almost exclusively in the southern part of the investigated area, while blades are found in the entire area. Transverse arrowheads are found only in the southern part. Of the bladeknifes, one was found in the northern part and three in the southern part. Handle cores, keeled scrapers, blades and microblades are also characteristic of the entire area. To sum up, we may say that the pattern found on the axis can also be found in the landscape, the southern part represented by the left side of the axis and the northern part by the right side of the axis.

A northern cultural border in the Mesolithic

Our analysis so far has shown that the Mesolithic in southern Norrland may tentatively be divided into a northern and a southern group. These may be separated in either time, or space or both. Here the dating of the early Norwegian mountain sites and the material that is found on them is of great interest, because an opening in the melting ice sheet during the Boreal made migration from present Norway into our investigation area possible as early as around 7000 cal BC (Forsberg 1996:243). A total of 29 sites from the mountain area in southern Norway have been 14C-dated to between 7600 ad 5000 cal BC (Indrelid 1975:4). These dates show that an early settlement of the area after the retreat of the ice sheet actually took place. The movement of the reindeer to the mountain area may have been the reason for the early sites in the region.

A common feature of the Mesolithic sites on Hardangervidda is the great number of well-formed microblades, conical microblade cores and handle cores. This may be connected with the MM B and LM A periods in southeastern Norway (Ballin 1999) or with Bjercks's Late Microblade tradition in the middle and late Mesolithic in western Norway. The concentration of conical microblade cores of the Late Microblade tradition type found in the north-western part of the research area in Dalarna and Härjedalen may thus be a result of an early migration over the mountains. The fact that the evenness measure in the blade analysis presented earlier in this paper showed the presence of two blade-making traditions in this northern region strengthens this proposal. What we see in our analyses is probably the result of mixed, middle and late Mesolithic sites in the north-west.

It must be mentioned, however, that the Mesolithic migration into this area may be explained by an early immigration from south-western Sweden or eastern Norway, where conical microblade cores of the same type were used in the Sandarna phase/ MM B phase, dated approximately between 6300 and 5600 cal BC (Sjögren, 1991:18 pp; Ballin 1999: 203 pp). However, the latter idea does not conform at all well to the spatial distribution of our material.

The settling of the area north of the TRB culture border some 3500 years before the introduction of a Neolithic economy in the area should thus be tentatively understood as a process in which the first groups of hunter-gatherers came in from the Norwegian mountain areas as the ice melted away north of the Hardangervidda around 7000 cal BC, opening a pathway through the mountains. The high mountain areas (over 800 m a..s. l.) in the north-western part of the area show evidence of this first settling, indicated by coarser blades and conical microblade cores made of local raw materials. The southern part of the area bordering on eastern central Sweden was under water by this time, but so far the small areas of dry land seem to have been settled later or possibly at roughly the same time by groups with a lithology reminiscent of the Sandarna culture on the Swedish west coast. This process seems to have created a cultural distinction between the southern and the northern group throughout the Mesolithic in the area, with the "border" somewhere in southern Jämtland. The southern group is characterised by a macroblade industry not found north of central Härjedalen and not south of southern Dalarna. Exchange of blades between the northern and the southern group seems, however, to have taken place (Figures 54.2a and b), since single finds of macroblades have been made up to southern Lapland. As we shall see later, this distinction between north and south seems to have lived on, and the important changes in settlement patterns and material symbolism at the onset of the Neolithic south of the area closely follow this "old border" established early in the postglacial period.

The handle-core tradition in northern Europé

The analysis of the blade assemblages in the southern part of Norrland informed us about the general structure of the Mesolithic in this region, with some preliminary observations on time/space structures related to the first settling of the area. We also noted the lack of excavated sites and also a lack of knowledge about the Neolithic components in this region. In pursuing our discussion of the preconditions for and the effects of the Neolithisation in the northern Scandinavian perspective we therefore extended our attention to the area north of southern Norrland. We initially chose to concentrate on the handle-core tradition, because this is the only lithic industry correlated to Mesolithic sites in the north. Today, we know of many surveyed sites with the handle-core tradition all over Norrland (Knutsson 1993; Olofsson 1995) and this is also where most of the excavated sites can be found to the north of the area discussed earlier in this paper (Figure 54.7). As will be shown, the handle-core tradition may be one important clue to the understanding of the processes leading to cultural change at the onset of the Neolithic, at least as regards Norrland.

The development of the handle-core tradition is to be found in southernmost Scandinavia around 7000 cal BC (Bille-Henriksen 1976; Larsson 1978, 1990; Sörensen 1995). The earliest datings from western Sweden, Norrland and Central Sweden can be set at roughly 6500 cal BC on the basis of sites such as Dammen and Genevad (Kindgren and Schaller-Åhrberg 1999; Nordqvist 2000) on the west coast; Lyttersta (Knutsson *et al.* 1999) in eastern central Sweden; Leksand (Larsson 1994) and Gårdsjösund (Björck 2000) in southern Norrland; Högland (Andersson 1999) and Nyluspen (Olofsson 1996) in northern Norrland. In southern Norway, Ballin (1999) has shown that the beginning of the handle-core tradition must be set at roughly the same time. The idea of producing narrow miniblades, using this special method or "schème opératoire" thus seems to have spread over a vast region stretching from northern Germany and western Poland (Sörensen 1995) to northernmost Lapland in Sweden within a period of 500 years or less.

Norrland was colonised by groups of hunter-gatherers following the retreating ice already in the early part of the Holocene (7500 cal BC) (Knutsson 1993; Forsberg 1996; Svensson and Lundqvist 1997; Forsberg and Knutsson 1999), possibly from western Norway or western Sweden. The introduction of the handle-core tradition into the area some 1000 years later should be seen as a social process of change within existing hunter-gatherer groups rather than as the result of groups migrating into new lands (compare Boaz 1999:125 pp) and above for a discussion of the colonisation of the southernmost highlands in Norway just to the west of and in the north-western part of our research area around 7000 cal BC by groups belonging to the Early Microblade tradition, and Lindberg (1994) and Olofsson (1996) and above for the arguments in favour of the presence of the late Boreal, Sandarna culture in central Scandinavia and southern Norrland (Dalarna)).

The handle-core tradition seems to have disappeared around 5200 cal BC in Skåne (Arlöv I) and Denmark (the beginning of the Trylleskov phase) (Sörensen 1995) (Figure 54.8 a) and *c.* 700–1000 years later within a vast region covering the central and northern parts of the

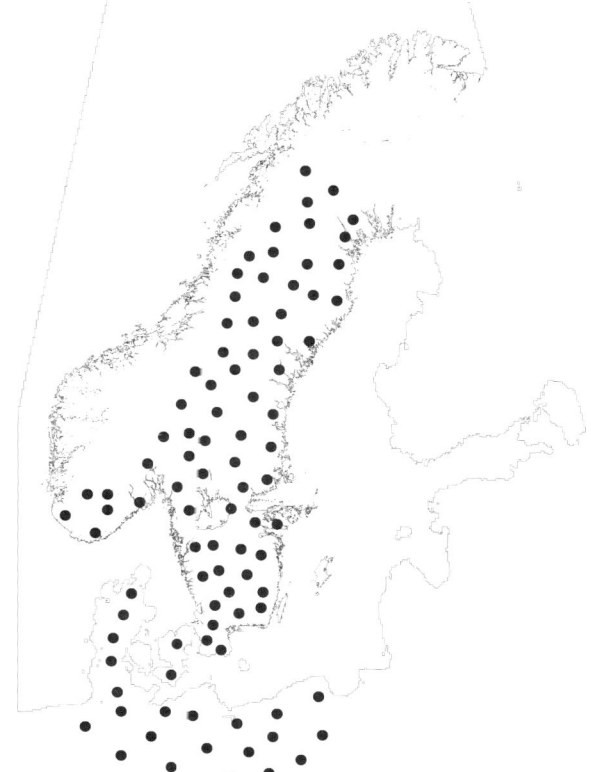

Figure 54.7 Generalised distribution of the handle-core tradition in Scandinavia 7500 cal BC- 4000 cal BC.

Scandinavian peninsula somewhere around 4500–4000 cal BC (see, however, Olofsson 1995:95 pp) for a discussion of some possibly later materials in Norrland), as new material symbols were appropriated from the Ertebölle sphere (Figure 54.8 b) (transverse arrowheads, polished greenstone axes, Limhamn axes, flakeaxes) in the south (Larsson 1973; Knutsson 1993; Olofsson 1995; Forsberg 1996; Nordqvist 1997:4; Ballin 1999; Knutsson et. al. 1999; Nordqvist 1999; Knutsson and Vogel 2000) and "northern" symbols (quartz, red slate, greenstone, *etc.*) in the northern part of the area (Baudou 1995; Lundberg 1997). On the Swedish west coast, the use of handle-core technology expands in intensity at the same time as the new symbols are appropriated (Nordqvist 1999:43) (recent analyses by Johan Wigforss at the Gothenburgh Archaeological Museum, however, seems to indicate a more abrupt change. Wigforss pers. com. 2001). In eastern central Sweden, it seems to be abandoned already at *c.* 4400 cal BC (however, see Sundström and Apel 1998 for a modified view). In southern Norway, Ballin mentions five (5) sites belonging to the late Mesolithic B phase (4500–4000 cal BC, significantly characterised by transverse arrowheads). The production of microblades in the early part of the phase (4500–4350 cal BC) probably indicates that there is a production of microblades alongside the transverse arrowheads but that this technology will disappear during this phase. Ballin also states that handle-cores are present on some of the

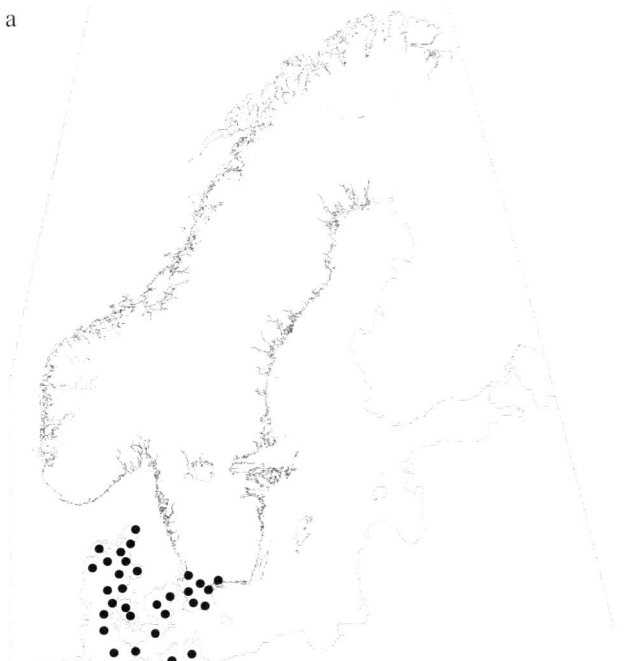

Figure 54.8a Distribution of the Ertebölle representing an interaction sphere between hunter-gatherers and farmers in southern Scandinavia.

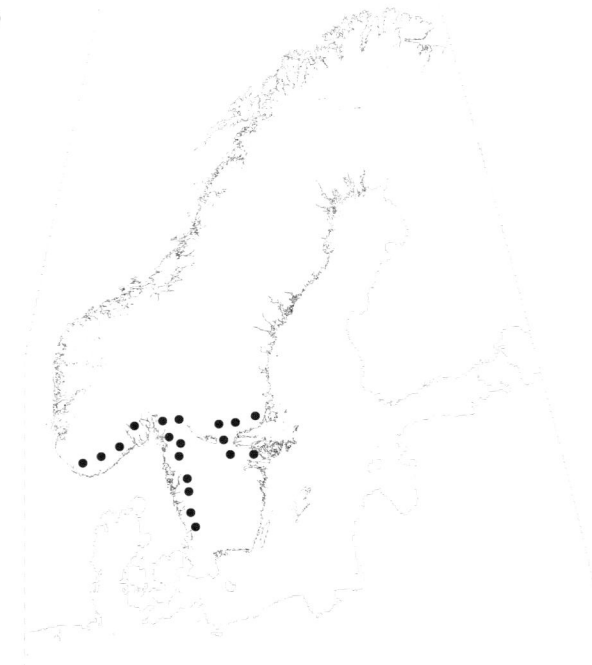

Figure 54.8b Areas in southern and central Scandinavia where Ertebölle material symbolism were introduced c. 4500 cal BC.

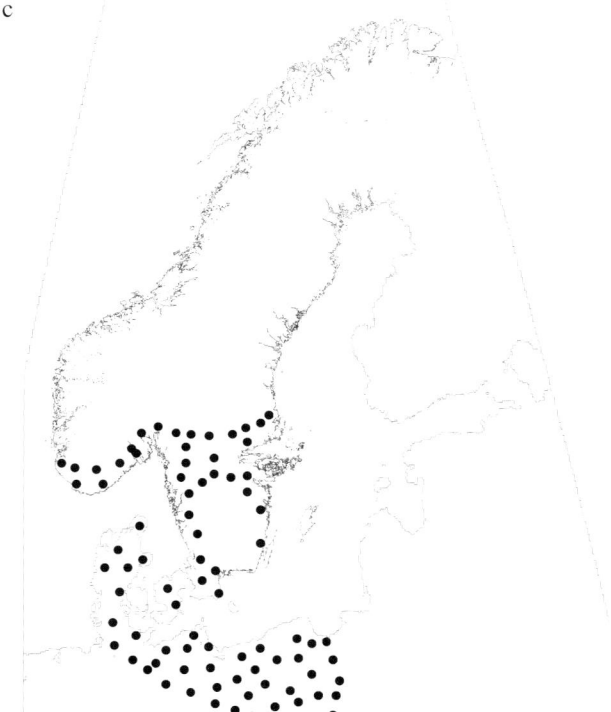

Figure 54.8c The expansion of the TRB idea c. 3900 cal BC in southern and central Scandinavia.

LMB sites in eastern Norway, but then only on sites dated to the earliest part of this period, i.e. c. 4500 cal BC or perhaps slightly later (Ballin 1999:287 pp).

This large-scale change in material culture disrupted the putative archaeological homogeneity over the Scandinavian peninsula represented by the handle-core tradition and, as it seems, resulted in a split between groups of hunter-gatherers in the north and hunter-gatherers in the south, along a line stretching from eastern central Sweden in the east to south-western Norway (Figure 54.8 b). This change in technology and tool design and thus material symbolism may be tentatively interpreted as the disintegration and simultaneously the creation of new social ties and world views communicated and carried by the material culture in this area, subsequently leading to the acceptance of a Neolithic way of life around 3900 cal BC in the south, and a different identity and social networks in the north (Figure 54.8 c). This picture, although brief and general, can be used as a meaningful setting for a discussion of the social processes leading to change in the human communities with special reference to the Neolithisation.

Exchange networks within and between late Mesolithic social units

Exchange is of vital importance to the reproduction of social ties in hunter-gatherer societies (Wiessner 1983) in the same way as "the gift" as a concept and as a strategy is of fundamental importance in any human society (Mauss 1972). Referring to interpretations of late Mesolithic burial customs in relation to an anthropological classification of the social organisation of cultural groups into three hierarchical levels (band, dialect tribe and language family) by Newell *et al.* (1989), Hallgren (1996: 20) presented a theory stating that the late Mesolithic dialect tribe called the "Sus tribe" found in southern Scandinavia as part of a proposed, pan-European, language group, in actual fact should be extended northwards up to the central Swedish region. Newell et.al. based their interpretation of the extension of the Sus tribe on ornaments found only on organic material from graves, and Hallgren correctly states that; "the northern limit of the Sus tribe is artificial because the ornaments that define its extension to the north consist of organic material, a find category seldom preserved on settlement sites in eastern central Sweden" (Hallgren 1996: 20) (translation by K.K.).

On the basis of the same line of argument, and, illustrated by the roughly contemporaneous spread and decline of the handle-core tradition in Scandinavia, we would like to propose that the social networks subsequently discussed by Hallgren should be extended to the northernmost part of Swedish Lapland. We are not thereby implying that the territory of the Sus tribe with its proposed marriage networks should be extended all the way to northern Lapland. But we propose that the social networks, represented by the handle-core tradition did so. As we have already shown above, the distribution of macroblades in Norrland indicates exchange networks within the region between southern and northern- Norrland groups.

Nuñez (1990:33 pp.), on the basis of the findings of Brjussow (1957) and Meinander (1961), has similarly proposed that the spread of the ceramic traditions (comb ceramic) into the forest regions of north-eastern Europe, including Finland, in Boreal times (starting *c.* 5500 cal BC in Finland), was a result of the spread of ideas resulting from exogamy and, although not explicitly stated, a virilocal, post-marital rule of settlement within the social and economic exchange networks of the hunter-gatherer groups inhabiting this area east of Scandinavia in Boreal/Atlantic times. To the south of this area, early LBK settlements can be found around 5500 cal BC and interaction between them and the hunter-gatherers to the north, brought the knowledge of pottery-making to the latter (Nunez 1990:35). Women, as a classificatory group, were supposed to be responsible for pottery-making. As they moved from the home territory after marriage, although they never discussed why this was done or accepted, they subsequently brought the knowledge of ceramic production with them.

A similar interpretation has been proposed by Hallgren for the above-mentioned spread of the Neolithic "idea" into central Scandinavia around 3900 cal BC (Hallgren 1996:18 p). In Accordance with this line of argument, Hallgren states that: "At the same time as the marriage network constitutes the forum for such a spread, it also constitutes the frame for how far it spreads. This means that the area within which the new feature is spread (in this case, the TRB culture) defines the extension of the marriage networks at this time" (Hallgren 1996: 21) (translation by K. K.). The extension of a late Mesolithic social unit held together by marriage networks based on a virilocal, post-marital settlement rule is, here hypothetically related to the proposed "*Sus tribe*". The development of the local ceramic traditions in the east discussed by Nunez (1990) must be understood in the same way.

Discussing the preludes to the Neolithisation in general and to southern Norway specifically, Fuglestvedt uses arguments related to change that touches on the same topic as Nunez (1990), Newell *et al.* (1986) and Hallgren (1996). By reference to the development of cemeteries and rock art in the late Mesolithic, she proposes that: "late Mesolithic societies in Scandinavia put religion into play in rituals, perhaps related to newly developed religious concepts (Fuglestvedt 1999:29). This in turn should point to the development of tribal groups in the area at this time, the late Mesolithic. The point made is that in tribal social organisation a person´s marriage becomes decisive for attachment to certain kin groups, that is, clans or lineages seen as special cultural categories (Keesing 1981:218 in ibid: 29) and that the relationships between relatives and in-laws will to a greater extent be ensured by normative standards for interaction. This in turn implies the existence of power in various types and degrees, i.e. a kin-group leadership in which exchange of goods and people (as objects of gift exchange) (Mauss 1972) is carried out on behalf of a lineage. Fuglestvedt therefore continues by proposing that in the late Mesolithic we have not only farmer and non-farmer interaction (responsible for change in southern Scandinavia) but also non-farmer and non-farmer interaction "that is, intermarriage between hunter-gatherer groups in east Norway/west Sweden and Scania/Zealand". This in then illustrated by female graves in Skåne and Denmark containing exotica like elk teeth, representing signs of long-distance contacts. This long-distance, intergroup exchange may, as has been proposed by Hallgren, have been decisive for the change in material symbolism, although differently staged in different regions, seemingly actively relating central Scandinavia to the south, where farmers and hunter-gatherers at this time were in close contact, as was illustrated by the development of a ceramic tradition and the exchange of goods like shoe-last axes and T- shaped antler adzes (Fisher 1982). It may be noted that the area where this "intensified exchange" is found corresponds exactly to the area where the handle-core tradition disappeared in 5300 cal BC, Skåne and Denmark, thus indicating that the "Neolithic idea" and "the handle-core tradition" somehow did not fit.

Local groups and exchange north of the TRB border

Within the large and materially variable area united by the handle core tradition, stretching from northern Germany to northern Lapland (Figure 54.7), earlier research has hammered out seemingly stable material patterns in the southern part of the region (Ertebölle, Lihult, *etc*.) which now tentatively interpreted as the material representations of local groups within the proposed territory of the *Sus tribe*. Although the question of the relation between technocomplexes, styles and the identification of meaningful, social/cultural, "ethnic" categories is more than problematic (Wobst 1977; Weissner 1984; Weissner 1989; Sackett 1990), it is theoretically interesting to interpret tentatively these material patterns as the representations of social units like local groups within a dialect tribe (Newell et. al. 1986). Leaving the details of the intensely discussed, southern region aside for a moment, we would like to return to these questions and refer to the result of our ongoing but so far highly preliminary and empirical work in the area north of the TRB culture border in Sweden.

Low formal variability, and thus also variability in artefact types, are characteristic of all of the northern-Swedish, Mesolithic assemblages which makes any identification and discussion of local groups using that type of information, at least for the present, exceedingly difficult. A large-scale pattern based on artefact variation, as already stated, divides Norrland into two halves.

In the northern part of this region the archaeological-source situation is, for the present, better, owing to the more intense excavation work carried out for the building of hydro-electric-power plants during the latter part of the last century. The sites belonging to this period (6500 – 4300 cal BC) are small: a hearth, a cooking pit, together with lithics and faunal refuse dumps (Forsberg 1989; Knutsson 1993; Forsberg 1996). Forsberg has, based on this, proposedl a settlement model of small family groups foraging in the landscape and a social organisation best described as non-complex (Forsberg 1989). The lithic material is formally simple, consisting of debitage, scrapers, microblades and handle-cores. The possibilities of defining local group identity based on lithic technology and style thus seem to be limited

Raw-material variation may, however, give us a further clue to the understanding of local groups and exchange networks in the region. In southern Scandinavia, the local groups in the late Mesolithic are found within the flint-using areas. Here, group variation is defined mainly by using stylistic traits in basically the same, lithic, raw material, flint. In northern Sweden, the formally simple materials are, on the contrary, characterised by a large variability in raw-material use. On the basis of the work of Olofsson (1995), Falkenström (1996) and Karlsson (2001), this fact can be used to make some preliminary observations concerning the local use of raw material as an expression of identity and as possible representations of sub groups and exchange networks.

Figure 54.9 represents the distribution of handle-cores and microblades made of two raw materials (tuffite and quartzite) found north of the TRB culture border. The distribution of the raw-material groups no doubt creates distinct sub-areas within the general handle-core tradition in the area. It would be easy to propose that each of these areas should be seen as the territory of a local group with its distinct and culturally constructed idea of raw-material use. If this is true, it also follows that the exchange of microblades between the local areas did not exist. The distribution of production areas (the handle cores) and the products (the microblades) co-vary spatially. This is true for the use of tuffite in the south and quartzite in the north (Figures 54.9a and b). At present, we cannot but give this spatial pattern a functional explanation, that is, that lithics were produced and used in relation to the physical presence of raw materials. Local groups may

Figure 54.9a Distribution of tuffite handle-cores and microblades in Norrland (After Olofsson 1995)

Figure 54.9b Distribution of quartzite handle-cores and microblades in Norrland (After Olofsson 1995).

very well have used several materials during the movement in annual cycles within their territory.

The presence of flint cores, flint microblades and some flint macroblades in the area also argues in favour of existing, large-scale, social networks using these artefacts as one component, and operating in the region as a whole (Figure 54.10); compare Ågetoft (1996). As stray-finds on excavated sites, the flint finds are actually exceedingly few but are present. In relation to the Scandinavian region as a whole, there is a typical "fall-off curve", with fewer finds the further one moves from the natural flint areas to the south-west.

The point that we want to make here, however, is that the whole region covered by the "handle-core tradition", from the south to the north, including the two or three, hypothetical northern-Scandinavian, local groups, at some level seems to have participated in this social network, that is, including a vast territory north of the proposed northern limit of the *Sus tribe*. We would to argue here that the handle-core tradition was part of a material symbolism in the hunter-gatherer communities within the social network, a symbolism that may have expressed some central values that were important for the social reproduction of these groups. The spread, it may be argued, was in the hands of people who knew the technology and moved their place of settlement, perhaps after marrying. The acceptance of the technology and the technological know-how was, however, adjusted to local raw materials. Nunez (1991) argued for a virilocal, post-marital rule and exogamy in the comb-ceramic groups of Finland and western Russia, and Hallgren (1996) had the same idea for the late Mesolithic groups of the Sus tribe, owing to an assumed connection between the type of innovation (ceramics and cultivation respectively) and the women. Newell and Condstandse-Westermann, for their part argued for the same thing on the basis of on variation in skeletal size among male and female material in graves during this period (1986:295). Size similarities among women over a large area indicated a "blending" of genetic materials so as to homogenise this group. A difference in stature among men was consequently interpreted as a result of men not moving between groups after marriage.

Before continuing there is thus reason to discuss the possible relationship between social categories and the handle-core tradition which, following Hallgren's (1996: 27 pp) and Fuglestvedt's (1999:31 p) interpretations of the "Sus tribe", would be spread by the hands of those who moved on marriage, the women. By reference to Fuglestvedt's idea of bringing ritual into play in the late Mesolithic as a response to or as a necessity for social change and thus changes in interaction between social institutions, we shall try to do this by taking a short look at the find contexts of handle-cores, microblades and related artefacts.

The handle-core tradition. The structure of find contexts

The find contexts for the handle-core tradition and the material culture related to it (bone points with flint insets)

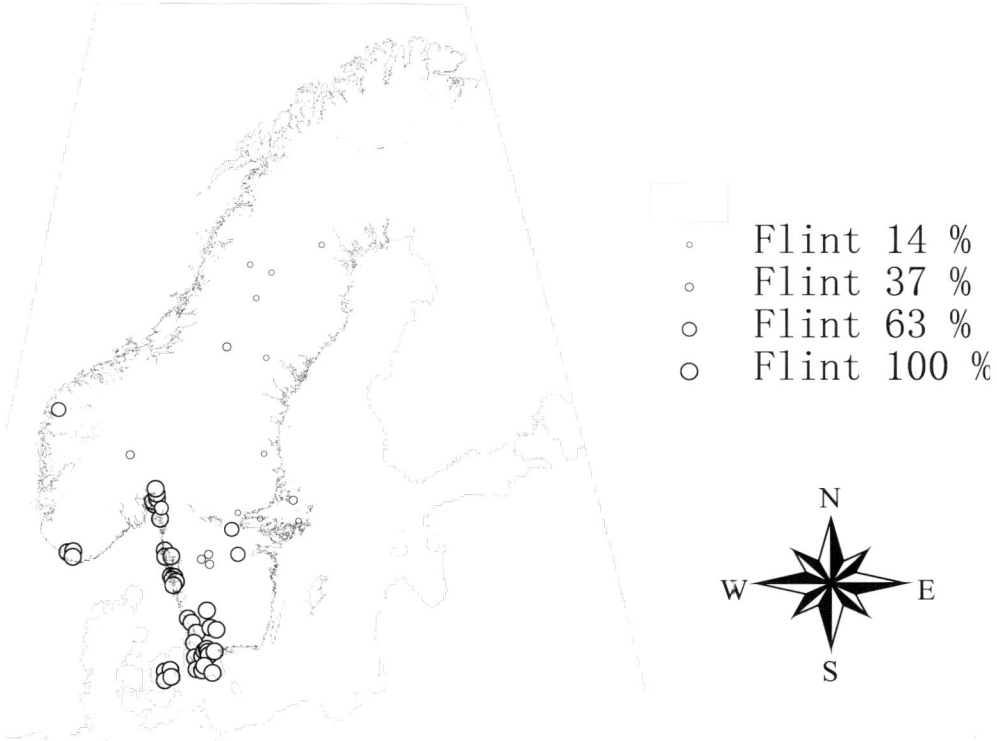

Figure 54.10 Relative proportion of microblades and handle-cores of flint on sites with handle core technology in Scandinavia.

are varied. Microbladecores, microblades and bone points with microblade insets are found in settlements, in graves and as moor deposits (Larsson 1973; Karlsson 2001), and finally what may be called "event contexts". Their presence in graves and in sacrificial contexts no doubt gives them the character of participants in rituals, but this may also be said about event contexts.

Moor contexts

The contexts of tools, slotted bone points, related to the production of tools with microblade insets in southern Scandinavia have been discussed by Ulla-Karin Larsson (1973) and their spatial relation to the southern-Scandinavian region by Verhart (1990). Archaeological finds on moors are traditionally related to offerings and rituals. Of a total of 274 slotted bone points, 24 pieces have on account of their good preservation, been classified as moor offerings (Montelius 1917; Liden 1942; Althin 1952). Although no detailed discussion of the find contexts of 124 stray, slotted bone points is presented in Larssons database, it must be assumed that most of these finds were found on moors as well. There is thus no doubt that the handle-core tradition, being part of the production of slotted bone points, must be seen as a technology intimately related to ritual contexts related to moor offerings in late Mesolithic Scandinavia.

Burial contexts

In a study of the burial practices of the late Mesolithic in southern Scandinavia, Strassburg has argued in a critical assessment of biological sexing by osteologists, that the five grave gifts in the form of slotted bone points (and a handle core) with microblade insets in late Mesolithic burials, the skeletons can be attributed to the female sex (Strassburg 2000:155 pp). Like the bone points on moors, the presence of slotted bone points in grave contexts thus relates them to rituals and – important for our line of argument – links both the points and the handle core itself to the biologically determined category of women.

Event contexts

Two instances of contexts with slotted bone points, microblade insets and the bones of animals have been found in the area. On Allerums moor in Skåne, a slotted bone point was found between the ribs of a dog (Lidén 1942:17) and on Orups moor close to Copenhagen, a slotted bone point was found in conjunction with a wild-boar skeleton (Mathiassen 1935:135). The slotted bone point with flint insets may therefore in certain cultural contexts have been used in rituals and was thus perhaps conceptually similar to the Australian death spear with quartz insets, used in ritual killing (Flood 1987:276 p).

We may thus tentatively propose that the handle-core tradition may have been part of important reproductive rituals or events during the Kongemose period in southern Scandinavia and that at some level it may also have been related to the biologically determined, female sex. Assuming a virilocal rule of post-marital settlement in the discussed area, the expansion of the handle-core tradition in middle Mesolithic times may then be tentatively interpreted as resulting from women moving within the hunter/gatherer marriage networks discussed here. With them, they took the know-how and the knowledge of the handle-core tradition. With this technological tradition may have gone a cultural value system or ideology that was metaphorically attached to it

Both moors and graves are acknowledged settings for rituals and thus for the interpretation, negotiation and construction of cultural values and categories and therefore also for the redefinition of these. The handle-core tradition may be understood as "political" (Edmonds 1990) and the proposed cultural values attached to it may have been decisive for its spread throughout the area in the late Boreal/Atlantic period. As a case in point, Anette Weiner has discussed the role of material culture in the negotiation of cultural values, and above all, related this to female agency and things used as mnemonic devices in the service of order. "Although possessions, through their iconographies and histories, are the material expressions of 'keeping', the most that such possessions accomplish is to bring a vision of permanence into a social world that is always in the process of change. The effort to make memory persist, as irrational as the combat against loss can be, is fundamental to change" (Weiner 1992:8). That is, the tension between structure and agency may foster the seeds of change, a tension that is not only played out in specific ritual contexts but also in everyday behaviour

How these people, through material culture, reproduced the past for the future is a key question, at least according to Weiner. Material symbols and technology are active in this process and the slotted bone points and the handle-core tradition found in explicit ritual settings argue in favour of seeing it as one active part in the structuration and change of a social order in what we may call the Scandinavian Sus tribe. This leads on to an evaluation of the character of the most common find context, "the settlement".

The settlement context

Over 126 slotted bone points have been found in settlement contexts in the southern part of the network covered by the handle-core tradition. In contrast to the well-preserved, grave and moor points, the finds from settlements are usually in a fragmentary state. They are mostly found in what are traditionally interpreted as refuse areas, that is, in former bodies of water close to settlements. The cosmological charging of garbage (Hodder 1982) in general and the liminal character of water (Strassburg 2000) have been discussed by archaeologists for quite some time. Apart from this, the actual living space of the settlement is of interest here. The discussion must now move from the slotted bone point to the lithics, the handle core technology itself.

In the same way as technological practice, illustrated here by the production and use of the slotted bone point with flint insets, may have been involved in the reproduction of social order in ritual settings and in exchange, the sites, the spaces in which production and use are staged, give meaning to these actions. Cosmology and social relations are recreated and negotiated through the organisation and use of space. (c.f. Bourdieu 1984; Giddens (1984: XXV; Ingold 1993; Hornborg 1994; Lawrence and Low 1990; Smith and David 1995).

Sites where the traditional archaeological materials, such as stone tools and debitage are found, may thus have been important social arenas for cultural reproduction. But the site is thus also a place of tension and therefore promotes cultural change. Material culture, functioning as vital parts of this communication, not least as references to the ancestral past, will then be active both in conserving structure and in inducing change (Weiner 1992), or as Mark Edmonds says in talking about lithics;

> "... The creation of technology, the form that it takes, and the manner of its subsequent deployment, serve as powerful media through which people reproduce some of the basic categories of their social and material world. For the same reason, traditions of making and using may also serve as a point of departure in the negotiation of new relations and new meanings."... (Edmonds 1990:56 p).

Thus, we have to situate and understand the activities (technological) within the larger, meaningful social practices of which they are part and, above all, link them to material representations. The change to a Neolithic "way of life" in the southern part of the area covering the proposed social network of the handle-core tradition, here called the "Sus tribe", must then be understood as an area where the seed of change is visualised in settlement contexts dated to the period 4500–4000 cal BC. Change in material symbolism was also taking place in the north at this time (Baudou 1993; Lundberg 1997; Hallgren 1998).

Let us take a look at some well-described context of which the handle-core tradition is part. We shall give examples from well-excavated sites in northernmost Lapland and eastern central Sweden. Here, we shall tentatively try to merge spatial structures with the material culture related to the handle-core tradition conceptualised as a "mnemonic device" used in negotiations about cultural values struggling for permanency and stasis in a world that, through messages and stories circulating in the social networks, brings news from afar about a changing world.

Vuollerim, Lapland

Excavated in the eighties, this Stone Age site with a well-preserved hut wall was recently published (Loeffler 1998 and in this volume). The site has been dated to 4500 and 3900 cal BC (Loeffler 1998: 95; Vogel forthcoming) and contained the handle-core technology. This makes the site the latest and one of the northernmost that shows the presence of the handle-core technology in Norrland (Olofsson 1996). An additional report from a hut wall, identical in form, size and site layout, partly excavated in the eighties, close to the first-mentioned, has also recently been compiled (Knutsson and Vogel 2000; Vogel, 2000), as well as a part of the settlement area in front of the entrance of the first mentioned hut (Vogel and Knutsson 2000).

The two sites consist of a hut wall containing cultural debris with an entrance facing the former bed of a stream, framing a floor area with faunal refuse and lithic debitage (Figure 54.11). The material is dominated by flaked quartz, but some other materials are present as well (quartzite, greenstone, slate and flint). The flint argues in favour of southern connections, but some finds in the hut point to northern exchange routes as well. Among other things, there is a slender slate arrowhead of the Nyelv type (Simonsen 1975:235; Helskog 1980:49 p) which is common in northern Norway and Finland. It is here dated to period two of the late Stone Age in Finnmark (Andreassen 1985:143; Schanche 1988:83 p), i.e. possibly to the later part of the Vuollerim settlement phase around 3900 cal BC.

The quartz debitage inside the huts forms two distinct and opposed concentrations in both huts. These have tentatively been interpreted as the living spaces for two family units (Loeffler 1998:76 pp). In the completely excavated hut, the handle-core tradition, in the form of quartz handle cores, quartz microblades and flint microblades, is found in only one of the concentrations. In the yard outside the hut entrance, this structural opposition is mirrored (Figure 54.11). The distinct pattern may, in Gidden´s words, be seen as the result of actions "routinely" being carried out over and over again according to a cultural logic.

The huts are variously oriented, but they have in common the fact that they lie in line with the flowing water of the Lule river. Thus, instead of the stars, the sun or the moon, the river seems to have been of importance in the local cosmology, at some level controlling the way in which social life on the site was structured. This is a common theme in many societies, and up-the-river and down-the-river have different connotations and are charged with various meaning. For example, up-the-river can be envisaged as the place of the ancestors (Metcalf and Huntington 1990). The handle-core tradition then, just like a figure of thought, may on this site be structurally related to up-the-river and thus to the ancestral past. Symbolically, bearing in mind, the ideas presented above, this opposition may be seen as a tension between the old (the handle-core tradition) and the new (the greenstone). "The ancestral pasts has to be continually brought into

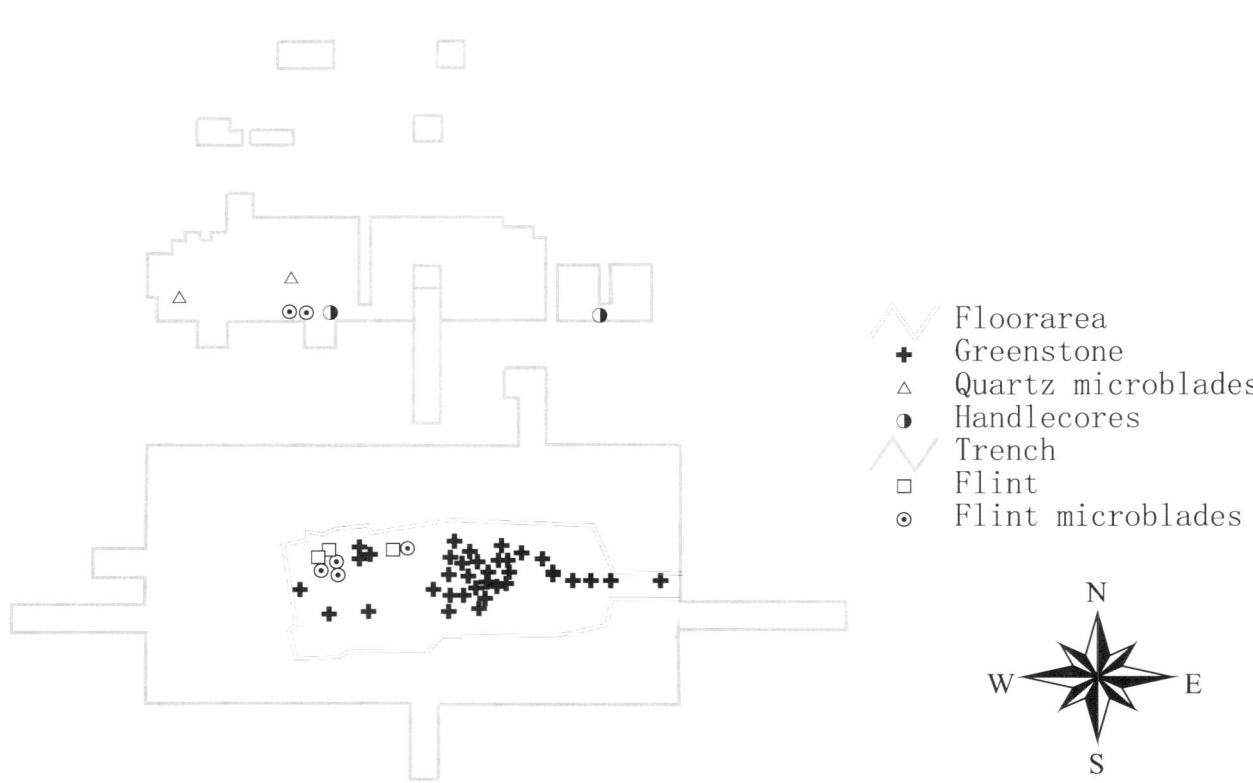

Figure 54.12 Find distribution at the Vuollerim site.

and related to activity in the present...because in songs, ceremonies and sacred objects, the land is remembered and cared for" (Tilley 1994). The handle core and the slotted bone points may thus perhaps symbolically be linked to ancestors through narratives of the ancestral past (compare Mauss 1972:61 ff.).

Skumparberget, eastern central Sweden

This site has been interpreted as a hunting stand (Binford 1989). Lithic debris was excavated beside a large boulder, at the time of the settlement c. 4500 cal BC facing a wide bay in the Littorina Sea. The spatial analysis of the lithic debitage showed that two individuals had been sitting next to each other, crouching behind the boulder, knapping, among other things, microblades from handle cores (Knutsson and Melchert, in the press). It can thus be approached analytically as a social setting. Squatting behind the boulder waiting for prey, the knappers thus, no doubt repaired their tools by the learned routines of their lithic craft but at the same time, by their technology and gestures, reproduced and negotiated some of their cultural values and/or categories (Figure 54.12).

The microblade technology at the site was based on two distinct raw materials, black schist and white quartz. A closer look at the distribution of the debitage reveals that one knapper primarily used black schist, and the other primarily white quartz One could as a starting-point, see the variable use of raw materials here as an imprint of a dynamic social situation in which the colour of the raw material was somehow involved. Symbolically uniting the two individuals, the handle-core tradition, as part of a technological tradition with its known gestures, at the same time helped to define the two knappers as individuals or as part of a socially distinguished subgroup within the society to which they belonged through the raw materials used. In the same area of eastern central Sweden, a black-and-white, spatial distinction within roughly contemporary sites has been noticed (Knutsson and Melchert, in the press), thus extending the structural opposition to other sites and technologies.

These two, very briefly presented sites have indicated that the handle-core tradition, although differently staged in different areas, may have been involved in the daily reproduction of cultural values, social institutions and cultural beliefs. Human agency within settlements is thus, compared with the grave and moor contexts discussed earlier, also part of the meaningful spectrum of the "handle-core tradition", a meaningful spectrum seemingly related to the dynamic reproduction and negotiation of cultural values through rituals and daily activities in "settlements". The disappearance of this technology at c. 4500 cal BC could have meant a fundamental break in cultural beliefs.

Figure 54.12 The Skumparberget site, features and find distribution.

Change

We started the first section of this essay by reference to the spread and disappearance of the handle-core tradition in Scandinavia and northern Germany. We proposed that the disappearance was correlated to a large-scale change in material symbolism within the hunter-gatherer groups living in the central Scandinavian region slightly before the change in material culture that we call the TRB culture. The TRB culture also seems to have involved a change in subsistence pattern towards domesticated animals/crop growing and thus in the relationship between culture and nature. The change in material symbolism at 4500 cal BC may thus have paved the way for the change in human-nature relationships and perhaps social structure. "if social relationships provide a conceptual model for human-nature relationships, a modification of the latter will generally begin with "prior mutation" of the former" (Descola 1994:330, in Hornborg, 1994:9). Actively involved in the reproduction of and perhaps the bearer of the hunter-gatherer world-view tied to the ancestral past during most of the Atlantic period, the handle-core tradition disappeared as "new gods" and associated symbols were appropriated.

We proposed above that the handle-core tradition was somehow linked to the female sex. In later grave contexts in the same area, the transverse arrowhead that showed up in eastern central Sweden *c.* 4500 cal BC was connected with the male sex. The change in the hunter-gatherer way of life. ideology or world view, approaching the fourth century BC, may thus have been related to a change connected with new roles of the sexes, perhaps reflected in the content and the organisation of exchange.

Late Mesolithic/early Neolithic change north of the TRB border in Norrland; Fire-cracked mound sites

To enable us to discuss cultural change in northern hunter-gatherer groups it is obvious from our study that the area immediately north of the TRB border must be archaeologically investigated more thoroughly. As our investigation has shown, we have a rich Mesolithic period in the area but a lack of excavations of sites and of chronological resolution. In accordance with the logic of the discussion in this paper, however, the area north of the less investigated "macro blade group" must have been part of and actively involved in a larger, social and economic network in the late Mesolithic. In this region (Jämtland, southern Lapland, Ångermanland, Medelpad), hundreds of archaeological sites belonging to the Mesolithic and Neolithic have been excavated, published and discussed as a result of the building of hydro-electric-power dams from the forties onwards (Baudou 1995; Forsberg 1996; Lundberg 1997). For studying change in the hunter-gatherer groups north of the TRB border forming the basis of and as a result of the Neolithisation, this area, 500 km north of the TRB border, is, for the present, probably the most fruitful place. Here, at the onset of the fundamental change 4500 cal BC in the south, new types of dwellings were built and new material symbols were appropriated. As we shall see, the distribution of fire-cracked, mound sites closely follows the central Norrland, cultural border (Figure 54.2a, b) with roots in the early Holocene.

Evert Baudou speaks of the change in material symbolism correlated to the establishment of the fire-cracked stone mounds in 4500 cal BC (Lundberg 1997) as "a peculiar Norrland", thereby implying some sort of ethnic distinction with connotations to the present-day, sociopolitical situation *vis-á-vis* the southern part of Scandinavia. This may, as we stated above, have been the result of an active reaction by the northern hunters-gatherers to the changes taking place in the southern part of Scandinavia (compare Hallgren 1998). Compared with the previous period here identified by the handle-core tradition discussed above, these sites are characterised by semi-subterranean huts surrounded by fire-cracked mounds with settlement debris, including finds of refuse fauna, flaked quartz, quartzite and polished, red-slate tools (Lundberg 1987). The new raw materials and tool designs were no doubt part of a new identity, perhaps an active identification with peoples living in the north, an appropriation of similar tool designs and choices of raw materials. Flint tools and flakes are found throughout the stratigraphy of the walls surrounding the hut floors (9 out of 19) thus indicating a continued exchange relationship with groups to the south and/or south west where flint occurs as ice transported beach nodules. It is further noticeable that handle cores and microblades are to be found at several of the sites (5 out of 19), implying a continuity from previous periods, a situation already hinted at in the analysis of the Vuollerim site. No detailed analyses of these settings have so far been carried out, however, but the find contexts, on account of their richness, will no doubt serve as an important setting for future discussions of hunter-gatherers in change, a change, at least partly, instigated by things, people and stories of remarkable events to the south circulating in the old exchange networks.

Acknowledgements

This research is part of the Coast to Coast project "Stone Age Societies in Change" financed by the Swedish Tercenary Foundation. The project is a collaboration between Uppsala, Göteborg, Stockholm and Lund Universities.

References

Althin, C-A. 1952. Bäckaskogs och Lummelundagravarnas ålder. *Fornvännen* 1951, 360–364.

Andersson, B. 1999. *Människan i Norrland under mesoliticum. En berabetning av tre boplatser med hjälp av sammanfogning av avslag och brukskadeanalys.* Arkeologiska studier vid Umeå universitet: 6. Umeå.

Ballin, T.B. 1999. *Kronologiske og regionale forhold i sydnorsk stenalder. En analyse med udgangspunkt i bopladserne ved Lundevågen (Farsundprosjektet).* Afhandling til Ph.D.-graden. Institut for Forhistorisk arkæologi, Moesgård, Aarhus universitet. Aarhus.

Baudou, E. 1993. Norrlands forntid – ett historiskt perspektiv. Höganäs.

Bille-Hendriksen, B. 1976. *Svaerdborg I. Excavations 1943–1944. A settlement of the Maglemose culture.* Arkaeologiska Studier. Vol. III. Köpenhamn.

Bjerck, H.B. 1986. The Fosna-Nøstvet problem. *Norwegian Archaeological Review* 19(2), 103–121.

Bloch, M. 1989. *Ritual, History and Power. Selected Papers in Anthropology.* Monographs on Social Anthropology 58. London and Atlantic Highlands, N.J.

Bloch, M. and Parry, J. (eds.) 1982. *Death and the regeneration of life.* Cambridge.

Boaz, J. 1999. Pioneers in the Mesolithic: The initial occupation of the interior of eastern Norway. In: Boaz, J. (ed.) *Th Mesolithic in Central Scandinavia.* Universitets Oldsaksamlings Skrifter, Nr. 22, 125–149. Oslo.

Bourdieu, P. 1977. *Outline of a Theory of Practice.* Cambridge

—— 1984. *Distinction: A Social Critique of the Judgement of Taste.* Cambridge.

Brjussow, A.J. 1957. *Geschicte der neolitischen stämme in europäischen Teil der UdSSR.* Berlin.

Clark, J.G.D. 1975. *The earlier Stone Age Settlement of Scandinavia.* Cambridge.

Descola, P. 1994. *In the Society of Nature: A Native Ecology in Amazonia.* Cambridge.

Edmonds, M. 1990. Description, Understanding and the Chaine Operatoire. *Archaeological Review from Cambridge* 9:1, 55–69.

Falkenström, P. 1996. *Spån och spånande. Mesolitiska storspånsindustrier i Dalarna och Härjedalen.* MA-thesis. Institute of Archaeology, Uppsala University, Uppsala.

Forsberg, L. 1989. Economic and Social Change in Northern Sweden 6000 B. C.–1000 A.D. In: Larsson, T.B. and Lundmark, H. (eds.) *Approaches to Swedish prehistory*. British Archaeological Reports. International Series 500, 55–82. Oxford.

—— 1996. The earliest settlement of northern Sweden- Problems and perspectives. In: Larsson, L. (ed.) *The earliest settlement of Scandinavia*. Acta Archaeologica Lundensia. Series in 4°, No. 24, 241–262. Lund.

Forsberg, L. and Knutsson, K. 1999. Converging conclusions from different archaeological perspecives: The early settlement of Northern Sweden. In: Binz, P. (ed.) *Epipaleolithique et Mesolithique en Europé*, 52–61. Grenoble.

Fuglestvedt, I. 1999. Inter-Regional Contact in the Late Mesolithic: The Productive Gift Extended. In: Boaz, J. (ed.) *The Mesolithic in Central Scandinavia*. Universitetets Oldsaksamlings Skrifter, Nr. 22, 217–233. Olso.

Giddens, A. 1984. *The Constitution of Society. An Outline of the Theory of Structuration*. Berkely.

Gräslund, B. 1971. En stenåldersboplats vid nedre Ransjön I Härjedalen. *Jämten* 64, 141–146. Östersund.

Hallgren, F. 1996. Sociala territorier och exogamirelationer i senmesolitisk tid. En diskussion utifrån Pärlängsberget, Södermanland. *Tor* 28, 5–28.

—— 1998. Etnicitet I Mellansverige och södra Norrland. In. Johnsen, B. and Welinder, S. (ed.) *Etnicitet eller kultur*, 61–78. Östersund.

Hodder, I. 1982. *Symbols in Action. Ethnoarchaeological studies of material culture*. Cambridge.

Hornborg, A. 1994. *Ecology as Semiotics. Outlines of a Contextualist Paradigm for Human Ecology*. Working papers in Human Ecology 1. Lund university, Human Ecology Division. Lund.

Indrelid, S. 1975. Problems relating to the early mesolithic settlement of southern Norway. *Norwegian Archaeological Rewiew* 8, No.1, 1975, 1–18.

Ingold, T. 1993. Technology, language, and intelligence: A reconcideration of basic concepts. In Gibson, K. and Ingold, T. (eds.) *Tools, Language and Cognition in Human Evolution*, 449–472. Cambridge.

Karlsson, B. 2000. *Identitet och tradition i Skandinavien under senmesolitikum*. C-D paper, institute of archaeology and ancient history, Uppsala university. Uppsala.

Karsten, P. and Knarrström, B. (red.) 2001. *Tågerup specialstudier*. Riksantikvarieämbetet. Lund.

Kindgren, H. and Schaller-Åhrberg, E. 1999. From Sandarna to Lihult. Fredsjö's Enerklev phase revisited. In: Boaz, J. (ed.) *The Mesolithic in Central Scandinavia*. Universitetets Oldsaksamlings Skrifter, Nr. 22, 217–233. Olso.

Knutsson, K. 1993. Garaselet-Lappviken-Rastklippan. Introduktion till en diskussion om Norrlands äldsta bebyggelse. *Tor* 25, 5–52.

Knutsson, K., Hallgren, F., Lindgren, C. and Björck, N. 1999.The Mesolithic in Eastern Central Sweden. In: Boaz, J. (ed.) *The Mesolithic in Central Scandinavia*. Universitetets Oldsaksamlings Skrifter, Nr. 22, 87–123. Olso.

Knutsson, K. and Vogel, P. 2000. *Arkeologisk undersökning av stenåldersboplats Lasses hydda (J106C), Vuollerim. Raä 1292, Jokkmokks sn, Lappland. Undersökningar 1986–1987*. Teknisk rapport sammanställd av Pierre Vogel and Kjel Knutsson. Vuollerim 6000 år- arkeologiskt museum och fornby. Arkeologiska rapporter 2. Vuollerim.

Knutsson, K. and Melchert, P. Manuscript. *Skumparberget II. Ett jaktpass för 7000 år sedan*. Uppsala.

Lannerbro, R. 1976. *Implements and Rock Materials in the Prehistory of upper Dalarna*. Early Norrland 4. KVHAA. Stockholm.

Larsson, L. 1978. *Ageröd 1:B-Ageröd 1:D. A study of early Atlantic settlement in Scania*. Acta Archaeologica Lundensia. Series in 4°. No 3. Lund.

—— 1990. The Mesolithic of Southern Scandinavia. *Journal of World Prehistory* 4 No 3, 34–52.

Larsson, M. 1994. Stenåldersjägare vid Siljan. En atlantisk boplats vid Leksand. *Fornvännen* 1994/4, 237–250.

Larsson, U-K. 1973. *De svenska fynden av flinteggade benspetsar*. C- paper institute of archaeology, Lund university. Lund.

Lawrence, D.L. and Low, S.M. 1990. The Built Environment and Spatial Form. *Annual Review of Anthropology*, 453–505.

Lechtman, H. 1993. Technologies of power: The Andean case. In: Henderson, J. and Netherly, P. (eds.) *Configurations of Power in Complex Societies*, 244–280. Ithaca N.Y.

Lemmonier, P. 1990. Topsy Turvy Techniques. Remarks on the Social Representation of Technology. *Archaeological Review from Cambridge* 9:1, 27–37.

Liden, O. 1942. *De Flinteggade benspetsarnas nordiska kulturfas*. Lund.

Lindberg, K-F. 1998. *Mesolitikum i Dalarna och Härjedalen*. MA-thesis. Institute of archaeology and ancient history, Uppsala University, Uppsaia.

Lindberg, U. 1994. *Vanån. Den förhistoriska fångstnäringens kronologi och kontakter*. MA-thesis, Institute of Archaeology, Stockholms University. Dupl. Stockholm.

Loeffler, D. 1998. *Arkeologisk undersökning av Norpan 2 (J 106 A), Vuollerim, Raä 1292, Jokkmokks sn, Lappland. Undersökningar 1983–1987*. UMARK 13: 1–8, Arkeologiska Rapporter från Institutionen för Arkeologi och samiska Studier. Umeå.

Lundberg, Å. 1997.*Vinterbyar. Ett bandsamhälles territorier I Norrlands inland 4500–2500 f. Kr*. Studia Archaeologica Universitatis Umennsis. 8. Umeå.

Mathiassen, M.J. 1935. Om Mullerup mose og Mullerup-kulturen. *Fra Holbaek Amt*, 38–53. København.

Meinander, K-F. 1961. De subneolitiska kulturgrupperna i norra Europa. *Societas Scientarium Fennica*. Årsbok XXXIX B 4. 2–20.

Metcalf, P. and Huntington, R. 1990. *Celebrations of Death. The Anthropology of Mortuary Ritual*. Cambridge.

Midgely, M. 1992. *TRB culture. The First farmers of the North European Plain*. Edinburgh.

Mikkelsen, E. 1975. Mesolithic in South-eastern Norway. *Norwegian Archaeological Review* 8(3), 19–35.

Montelius, O. 1917. *Minnen från vår forntid I*. Stockholm.

Newell, R.R., Kielman, D., Condstandse-Westermann, T.S., van der Sanden, W.A.B. and van Gijn, A.1990. *An inquiry into the ethnic resolution of mesolithic regional groups. The study of their decorative ornaments in time and space*. Leiden.

Nordqvist, B. 1997. Regionalitet under mesolitikum. Västkusten. In: Larsson, M. and Olsson, E. (eds.) *Regionalt och Interregionalt. Stenåldersundersökningar i Syd-och Mellansverige*. Riksantikvarieämbetet. Arkeologiska undersökningar. Skrifter nr 23, 32–46. Uddevalla.

Nunez, M., 1990. On Subneolithic Pottery and its Adoption in Late Mesolithic Finland. *Fennoscandia archaeologica* VII, 27–47.

Olofsson, A. and Olsson, H. 1999. The Mesolithic in Värmland. Research status. In: Boaz, J. (ed.) *The Mesolithic in Central Scandinavia*. Universitetets Oldsaksamlings Skrifter, Nr. 22, 73–86. Oslo.

Olofsson, A. 1995. *Kölskrapor, mikrospånkärnor och mikrospån*. Arkeologiska studier vid Umeå universitet, 3. Umeå.

Sackett, J.R. 1990. Style and ethnicity in archaeology: the case for isochrestism. In: Conkey, M. and Hastorf, C. (eds.) *The use of style in archaeology*. Cambridge.

Sjurseike, R. 1994 *Jaspisbruddet i Flendalen-enkilde til forståelse av sociale relasjoner i eldre steinalder*. Avhandling til magistergrad. Oslo.

Smith, A. and David, N. 1995. The Production of Space and the House of Xidi Sukur. *Current Anthropology* 36: 3, 441–471.

Strassburg, J. 2000. *Schamanic Shadows. One Hundred generations of Undead Subversion in Southern Scandinavia, 7000–4000 BC*. Stockholm Studies in Archaeology 20. Stockholm.

Sundström, L. and Apel, J. 1998. An Early Neolithic Axe Production and Distribution System within a Semi-Sedentary Farming Society in eastern Central Sweden, c. 3500 BC. In: Holm, L. and Knutsson, K. (eds.) *Proceedings from the Third Flint Alternatives Conference at Uppsala, Sweden, October 18–20, 1996* Occasional Papers in Archaeology 16, 155–191. Uppsala.

Sörensen, S.A. 1995. *Kongemosekulturen i Sydskandinavien.* Jægerpris.

Svensson, A. and Lundqvist, U. 1997. *Norrlands kolonisering.* Ma-thesis. Institute of archaeology and ancient history, Uppsala university. Uppsala.

Tilley, C. 1994. *A Phenomenology of Landscape; Places, Paths and Monuments.* Oxford.

Weiner, A.B. 1992. *Inalienable Possessions. The Paradox of Keeping-While-Giving.* Berkely.

Weissner, P. 1983. Style and social information in Kalahari San projectile points. *American Antiquity* 48, 253–276.

Verhart, L. 1990. Stone Age Bone and Antler Points as Indicators for "Social Territories" in the European mesolithic. In: Vermeersch, P.M. and Van Peer, P. (eds.). *Contributions to the Mesolithic in, Europé* 139–151. Leuven.

Wobst, X. 1977. Stylistic behavior and information exchange. In: Cleland, C.E. (ed.) *For the director: research essays in honor of James B. Griffin.* Anthropological Papers, Museum of Anthropology, University of Michigan 61. Ann-Arbor.

Vogel, P. and Knutsson, K. 2000. *Arkeologisk undersökning av stenåldersboplats Norpan 2-Framsidan (J106A), Vuollerim. Raä 1292, Jokkmokks sn, Lappland. Undersökningar 1993–1994.* Teknisk rapport sammanställd av Pierre Vogel and Kjel Knutsson. Vuollerim 6000 år- arkeologiskt museum och fornby. Arkeologiska rapporter 1. Vuollerim.

Ågetoft, B-O. 1996. *Territorialitet och utbytesrelationer i mesolitikums jägar-samlar samhällen.* MA-thesis. Institute of archaeology and ancient history, Uppsala University, Uppsala.

55. The marrying kind: evidence for a patrilocal postmarital residence pattern in the Mesolithic of Southern Brittany?

Rick Schulting

Stable isotope data on human bone from the Breton Mesolithic sites of Téviec and Hoëdic indicate that females consumed less marine foods than males. This is provisionally interpreted as the result of an exogamous marriage pattern, with women moving to the coastal sites from a variety of locations, including more terrestrially-focused communities. The implications of this pattern are explored for both the Mesolithic itself, and for the Mesolithic-Neolithic transition. Relevant factors include the presence of coastal and inland groups, population density and the process of hypergyny.

Introduction

The ability to maintain a viable population is a cornerstone of social as well as biological reproduction. In small-scale societies of the kind present in the Mesolithic of western Europe, marriage partners must have been more often than not sought outside the local community. While we know this to be the case, it is difficult to address the issue archaeologically. Consequently, when archaeologists speak of exchange, discussion is often limited to the acquisition and exchange of material resources; for earlier prehistory, this frequently means an emphasis on lithics (e.g. Jacobi 1979; Fischer 1982; Gendel 1989). The 'exchange' of people is undoubtedly more difficult to trace, and yet it would have been equally if not more essential, particularly in small-scale societies. How far did people have to travel to meet suitable marriage partners? Mobility has long been seen as an important, if not defining, characteristic of hunter-gatherer societies, but, with some notable exceptions (e.g., Wobst 1974, 1976; Mandryk 1993; MacDonald and Hewlett 1999) this has often been phrased in subsistence terms. Clearly the need to acquire marriage partners presents another motivation for mobility.

Marriages are exchanges between groups, rather than just between individuals. This is obvious enough, and continues to hold to some extent even in the individualistic societies of the modern West; in the past it would have been a far more powerful and pervasive aspect of marriage. Driving home the point is a large ethnographic literature on the topic of marriage, with discussions of wife-givers and wife-takers, bride-price, dowry, and so forth (Levi-Strauss 1969; Godelier 1986; Schlegel and Eloul 1988). These suffice to show the importance of the subject, as the kinds of social relationships and alliances that are formed through marriage have implications for many other aspects of society. Indeed marriage alliances often provide the conduit through which the exchange of materials and services flow (e.g., Burton 1987), in addition to being one of the primary avenues for the formation of political alliances. Whatever their own motivations, individuals involved in marriage exchanges in small-scale societies would have acted as fulcra for a complex web of social relations. In this sense it is legitimate to regard the person as an objectification of social relationships (Strathern 1988:313 pp).

This paper addresses the possibility that evidence for an exogamous, patrilocal marriage pattern in the Mesolithic of southern Brittany can be found in dietary stable isotope data on human remains from the sites of Téviec and Hoëdic. The implications of this possibility are explored, both for population density and regional interaction within the Mesolithic, and for the subsequent process of neolithisation. The interpretation put forward, it should be emphasised, is preliminary, and subject to revision in light of the results of an ongoing investigation.

Site background

Téviec and Hoëdic are Mesolithic cemeteries presently located on small offshore islands in Morbihan, south Brittany (Figures 55.1 and 55.2). The sites were excavated in the 1920s and 30s by the Péquarts (Péquart *et al.* 1937; Péquart and Péquart 1954), and are best known for their relatively elaborate mortuary practices. The ten graves found at Téviec held the remains of some 23 individuals, while the nine graves recovered from Hoëdic held 14 individuals. What have been interpreted as large ritual hearths, typically containing red deer and boar mandibles, were found immediately above a number of the graves.

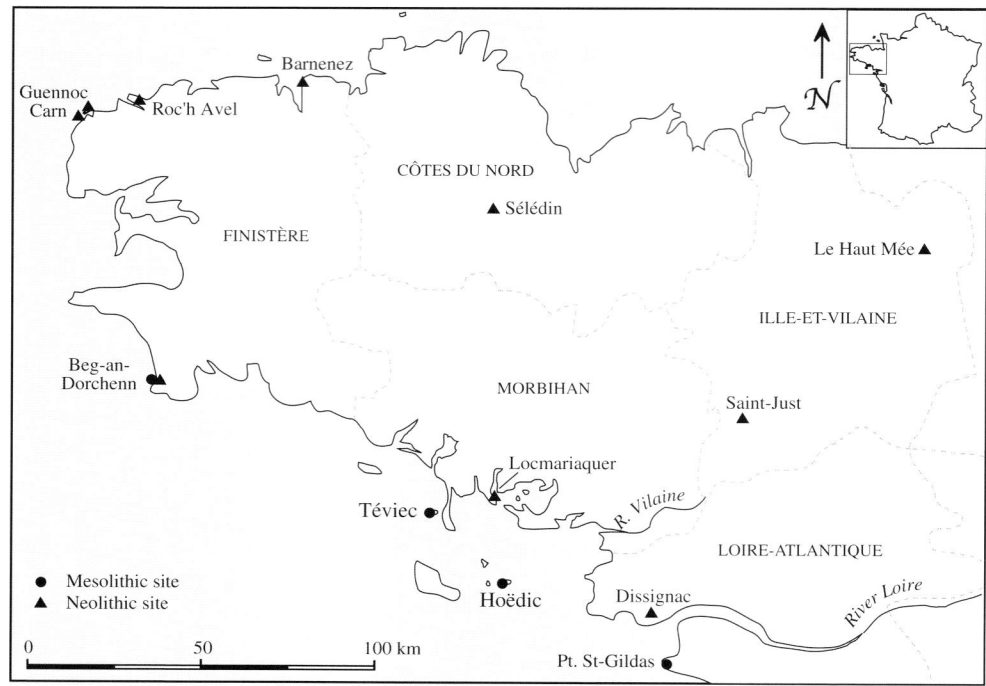

Figure 55.1 Map of Brittany showing key Mesolithic and Neolithic sites

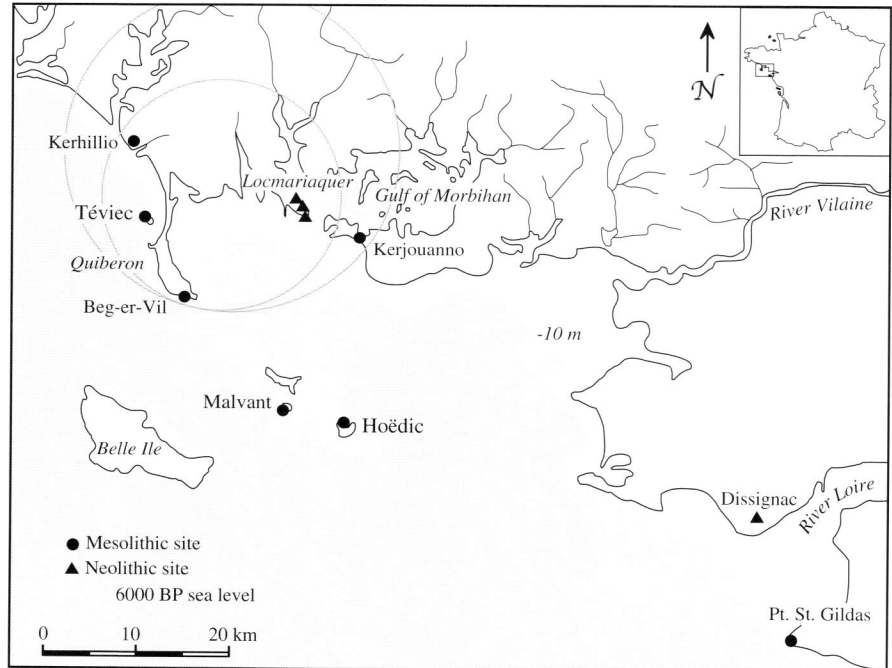

Figure 55.2 Map of coastal Morbihan showing locations of sites mentioned in text; the circles around Téviec refer to hypothetical 500 and 1000 km² maximum band territories

Grave inclusions, particularly in the form of marine shell beads and red deer antlers, were also numerous (Taborin 1974; Schulting 1996). But perhaps most important is the structure of the graves themselves, many of which show multiple interments that are clearly successive in the same tomb. This is reminiscent of the treatment of the dead seen in chambered tombs, and opens up the possibility that the Mesolithic graves were in some way precursors to the far larger and more elaborate burial monuments of Neolithic Brittany (Case 1976).

A series of 14 AMS dates on the human remains themselves indicate that the sites were used for burial over a surprisingly long time, on the order of some 2000 years. However, this range is exaggerated by two outliers, and the majority of the dates from both sites fall between 6500 and 6000 BP (Schulting 1999; Schulting and Richards 2001).

The isotopic evidence

The application of the stable isotope technique to prehistoric human diet has a relatively long history (Vogel and van der Merwe 1977). There are many available summaries, so details need not be repeated here (Schwarcz 1991; Schoeninger and Moore 1992). However, two key points are worth emphasising: 1) the measurement of bone collagen provides an estimate of some aspects of that individual's diet averaged over, in the case of an adult, a period of 5–10 years, and 2) measurements on bone collagen reflect only the protein component of the diet. While not all specific foods types can be discriminated, the difference between marine and terrestrial sources of protein is one that does show up very well.

After excavation, the human remains from Téviec and Hoëdic were divided between various institutions, and some material has been lost in the intervening years. A total of 25 individuals were available for analysis (presented in detail in Schulting and Richards 2001). The results (Figure 55.3) indicate that the inhabitants of both sites made considerable use of marine foods, ranging from 50 to 80% of the protein component of the diet. Such a wide range in a single population is unusual in stable isotope studies (cf. Schwarcz 1991), but is exaggerated by a number of factors. First of all and most apparent is the difference between the two contemporary sites, with the individuals from Hoëdic consistently showing higher $\delta^{13}C$ and $\delta^{15}N$ values, indicating greater use of marine foods (on the order of 70 to 80%). For Téviec, a somewhat more balanced use of marine and terrestrial foods seems to be indicated (60 ± 10% marine). Another possibility is that different kinds of seafoods were being exploited at Téviec, including a higher proportion of inshore and estuarine species that can show intermediate values between fully 'marine' and terrestrial signatures (Peterson et al. 1985). In either case, what this consistent difference does indicate is that those making use of the sites for burial were not part of a single homogenous group, but rather maintained separate subsistence adaptations over the long term.

The isotope values also show interesting variation along two other dimensions: age and sex. The five children analysed, ranging from neonatal to approximately four years of age, are distinguished by their elevated stable nitrogen values relative to the adults (importantly, stable carbon isotope values are not subject to this effect). This is not unexpected: in essence, breastfeeding infants are feeding off of their mothers, and so are raised above them by one trophic level, equating to about 3‰ ($\delta^{15}N$ measures trophic level) (Schurr 1997). The sample lacks a sufficient cross-section of children of different ages, and so it is not possible to address the question of weaning age in more detail at this stage. Of greater relevance for the purposes of this paper is the observed difference in stable isotope values between the sexes. Females at both sites show lower carbon and nitrogen values than males, i.e., they seem to show less use of marine foods (Schulting and Richards 2001). At first glance this difference is rather subtle, but nevertheless it is suggestive (Figure 55.4). In light of the low sample numbers, further investigation of the possible relationship between sex and diet requires that the measurements from both sites be combined into a single pooled sample. To facilitate this, the effect of the difference averages for the two sites must be cancelled out, achieved by standardising the values. The consistency of the difference becomes much more apparent at this point (Figure 55.5).

Age/sex	$\delta^{13}C$	sd	average $\delta^{15}N$	sd	n
Téviec					
adult male	-15.2	0.5	11.7	1.5	3
adult female	-15.9	0.8	10.2	2.7	4
subadult	-14.2	0.3	14.1	0.5	3
overall	-15.3	0.9	11.9	2.6	10
Hoëdic					
adult male	-13.8	0.5	13.4	0.8	4
adult female	-14.6	1.1	11.4	2.7	5
subadult	-14.5	0.3	14.5	1.4	2
overall	-14.3	0.9	12.6	2.1	11

Figure 55.3 Average $\delta^{13}C$ and $\delta^{15}N$ values for age/sex groups – note that sample size for the stable isotope analysis is further reduced by the exclusion of the values for two females and two males for which only ion-exchange values from the Oxford AMS dating system are available; such values show an offset and are not directly comparable with those undertaken specifically for palaeodietary purposes

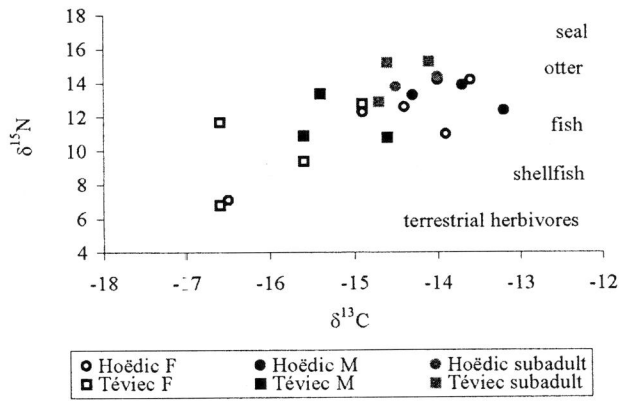

Figure 55.4 Plot of $\delta^{13}C$ and $\delta^{15}N$ values for age/sex groups at Téviec and Hoëdic; the fauna refer to $\delta^{15}N$ values only, showing respective tophic levels (human consumers would be elevated above food group by about 3‰)

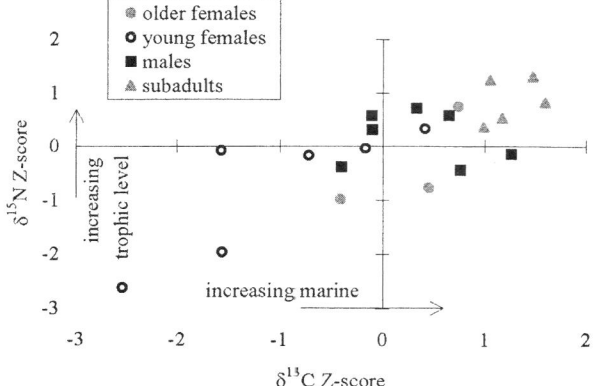

Figure 55.5 Plot of standardised $\delta^{13}C$ and $\delta^{15}N$ Z-scores for age/sex groups at Téviec and Hoëdic

Explaining the difference

The difference between male and female diet may be explained either in autochthonous or in allochthonous terms. Of course these need not be mutually exclusive, although for analytical purposes it is useful to treat them so in the first instance. An autochthonous account invokes differences in the diets of men and women spending their lives in the same community. One aspect of this could involve culturally imposed food restrictions ('taboos') for either men or women. Such restrictions are well known in the ethnographic literature, and could account for the relatively small differences observed. One especially suggestive example comes from the Wamira of New Guinea, among whom women are forbidden from consuming seafoods during pregnancy and nursing (Kahn 1986, cited in Hastorf 1991). Of course, a similar effect would be achieved if men were forbidden to eat a terrestrial protein source (most likely animal-derived, since indigenous plant foods in temperate Europe are typically low in protein, hazelnuts being a notable exception) and made up the balance by consuming proportionally more seafoods. The restrictions could operate either continually or only at certain times of the year. In the latter case, the restricted food/s would need to comprise a higher proportion of the dietary protein in order to have the same long-term effect on bone collagen stable isotope values.

A variation of the autochthonous account would involve differential food acquisition and consumption activities for men and women as an aspect of their daily lives. In a logistically organised subsistence/settlement system (Binford 1980, 1982), men and women may gather and consume separately a significant proportion of their daily food. For women this might include more terrestrial plant and animal foods and such marine foods as shellfish and other inshore species (cf. Moss 1993). The degree of difference seen in the isotopic results, and hence diet, is not great, and could be accounted for by occasional short trips away from a main settlement by single-sex task groups. As there would seem to be little means of distinguishing between these two variations on an autochthonous theme, they are for present purposes treated together.

An allochthonous explanation, on the other hand, proposes that the observed difference in stable isotope values results from residual dietary differences reflecting the origins of men and women in different communities. Since it can probably be safely assumed that no distinct communities were living closer to the coast than those using Téviec and Hoëdic, this scenario would involve women originating in communities with a somewhat more terrestrially-based economy (and hence probably more inland) moving to the coast, and remaining there, at some time prior to their deaths. The most likely reason for this would be as marriage partners. This is an explanation that has been suggested for similar observations in human bone collagen $\delta^{13}C$ values elsewhere, but has rarely been explored in any detail (cf. Schulting and Richards 2001). Interestingly, the mortuary treatment in one grave at Hoëdic differed sufficiently from the normative practice to lead the excavators to the suggestion that the individual buried there, an adult female, was a stranger to that community: 'était celle d'une femme étrangère à la colonie hoëdicaise?' (Péquart and Péquart 1954:32). This is of course very speculative, since non-normative mortuary treatment may arise for a number of reasons.

Since both the autochthonous and allochthonous accounts seem plausible, is there any way to choose between them? If the explanation is autochthonous, it might be expected that values for the sexually indeterminate infants and children would show a bimodal distribution of values, or at least a wider range of values than that seen in either adult males or females. But, in fact, the sub-adults clearly separate from the adult females and instead group with the adult males, showing an equivalent emphasis on marine protein. This evidence is not conclusive, as it is conceivable and indeed probable that any imposed food restrictions (or difference resulting from differential access to foods) would only come into effect upon reaching 'adulthood', however that was defined by the Mesolithic inhabitants of Brittany. Children might be considered gender-neutral with regard to food restrictions until adopting adult roles. Furthermore, as noted above, the five children available for analysis were all very young, ranging to neonate to approximately age four. It is unlikely that children of this age would be participating in the kinds of subsistence activities that would result in different diets. However, if the female diet is the 'base camp' diet, as seems reasonable, then, in an autochthonous account, it would be expected that very young children would group with them, rather than with the males. This is not the case. An alternative, that all five of the children measured happened to be male and so group with the adult male diet for this reason, is statistically very improbable. Nor does there seem to be any reason to suppose a cultural bias towards the burial of only male children at Téviec and Hoëdic.

Site	Grave	Sex	Age	Trivia	Littorina	Ratio	dominant
Téviec	E (11)	M	young adult	1130	520	2.17	*Trivia*
Téviec	K6 (16)	M	young adult	257	37	6.95	*Trivia*
Téviec	M (13)	M	young adult	300	2	150.00	*Trivia*
Hoëdic	F1 (5)	M	mid adult	1	1	1.00	-
Hoëdic	K (9)	M	young adult	442	99	4.46	*Trivia*
Téviec	B (2)	F	young adult	187	7	26.71	*Trivia*
Téviec	D (1)	F	young adult	24	38	0.63	*Littorina*
Téviec	H3 (15)	F	young adult	15	527	0.03	*Littorina*
Téviec	H1 (14)	F	young adult	0	64	0.00	*Littorina*
Téviec	K5 (6)	F	young adult	350	212	1.65	*Trivia*
Téviec	K4 (10)	F	adolescent	220	210	1.05	*Trivia*
Hoëdic	H (8)	F	mid adult	38	538	0.07	*Littorina*
Hoëdic	J (7)	F	young adult	134	604	0.22	*Littorina*
Hoëdic	L (10)	F	mid/old adult	0	248	0.00	*Littorina*

- data from Taborin 1974: Table 37
- note that individual in Téviec grave B has been re-assessed as female

Figure 55.6 Relationship between sex and shell bead species in graves

There is another, somewhat more direct line of inquiry focusing on the females themselves. Human bone collagen is slowly but continually replaced over the lifetime of the individual, so that over a period of five to ten years there is a complete turnover (Stenhouse and Baxter 1979). Thus the bone collagen of women would begin to change once they moved to communities closer to the coast and adopted a new diet. After a period of some years (the rate depending on how istopically different the new diet was from the old) this change would become detectable in their stable isotope values. This being the case, the bone collagen of younger women should retain more of their original inland 'terrestrial' isotopic signature than older women, whose bone collagen would have had longer to change over to reflect their new marine-oriented diet. While assessing age with any degree of precision from adult skeletal remains is fraught with difficulties, a division into broad categories such as 'young' and 'middle/old' adult is straightforward, as well as necessitated by the small sample sizes available. When the standardised values for the two age groups are compared, a striking pattern emerges (Figure 55.5). Older women clearly show greater use of protein from marine sources; in fact they are indistinguishable in this respect from the adult male group. Younger women, by contrast, separate out from all other age/sex classes. It might be added here that, while they have been omitted from the analysis, the two females from Téviec for which only ion-exchange values are available support the trend; the young adult female has the lowest value of either site, while the adolescent female has the second lowest ion-exchange value.

However, an autochthonous account of the observed patterning – the grouping of the children and the older women together with the males rather than the females, and the separation of the younger females – remains an intriguing possibility. Gender is not a simple either/or binary opposition, nor need it be stable throughout an individual's lifetime (Strathern 1988; Gilchrist 1999). For example, as noted above, children may be gendered neutral. And older women may come to be in many respects gendered 'male'. Social status may also play a role here, so that certain aspects of male roles would only be open to some older women (and limited to only some men as well for that matter). Some hint of this with regard to Téviec and Hoëdic specifically is provided by Taborin's (1974:171 pp) analysis of the abundant shell bead ornamentation found in the graves. Males were found to be predominantly associated with beads made of *Trivia europea* (cowrie) shells, while females were associated with beads made of *Littorina obtusata* (periwinkle) shells. But the distinction is not exclusive, rather it is one of degree. Thus females typically have ornaments comprising shells of both species, but with proportionally more *L. obtusata* (Figure 55.6). The association between sex and dominant shell species, while not invariant, is significant (Fisher's exact test, $p = 0.049$). Taborin also points to a tentative relationship between age and quantity of shell ornaments; young and middle-aged adults seem to have been interred with more ornamentation than both younger and older individuals (Taborin 1974:174 pp). In this case, however, the association is not statistically significant.

While neither scenario – autochthonous or allochthonous – can be ruled out, the balance of the evidence appears to favour the hypothesis that in-marrying women are responsible for the observed differences in male and female stable isotope values. This interpretation accounts for more aspects of the patterning in the isotope values than the alternative. In light of the small sample size and relatively small differences being discussed, this conclusion must remain tentative. Further isotopic analysis on teeth, currently underway, will help refine the interpretation put forward here (the dentine component of teeth forms during childhood and changes minimally thereafter). Oxygen, lead and strontium isotope analysis may offer other approaches to the problem, provided that geological sources are sufficiently distinct over the relatively short distances envisaged for the movement of people in southern Brittany.

The suggestion is not that all the women buried at Téviec and Hoëdic originated from inland communities. The situation was doubtless far more complex than this. Marriage partners could be exchanged between coastal communities, and no doubt this was often the case. Thus the proposition is that women were marrying in from a greater variety of locations, including some more inland communities. And these were themselves not necessarily reliant solely on terrestrial resources. Intermarriage would be facilitated between groups that shared a certain amount of basic knowledge concerning one another's economic practices, and lifestyle in general. If ethnographic accounts are any guideline, groups for a considerable distance inland may have made seasonal use of coastal resources, either directly and/or through trade. Indeed, use-rights to these may have been maintained partly through intermarriage with coastal groups.

The remainder of this paper will assume the validity of the allochthonous scenario, exploring some of its implications both for relationships between coastal and inland groups in the Mesolithic, and for the Mesolithic-Neolithic transition.

The existence of separate coastal and inland groups?

An apparent requirement of the argument presented here is that separate groups with settlement and subsistence foci on the coast and interior, respectively, did exist in the later Mesolithic of Brittany. Actually, this is not quite the case. All that is necessary is that some communities have diets that are more terrestrially oriented. Their focus of settlement might still be near the coast: the point is adequately made by the notable differences in diet between Téviec and Hoëdic themselves. What is required, however, is the existence of communities showing even less reliance on marine foods than seen at Téviec. In order to differentiate them from near-coastal mainland sites such as Téviec, I will refer here to such hypothetical communities as 'inland'. This is not to deny the possibility that some Mesolithic communities did have a predominantly inland settlement focus, and in fact there is some evidence to suggest that this may have been the case.

The Breton Mesolithic was long thought to be largely confined to the coast. Recent fieldwalking has radically changed this perception in the département of Finistère (west Brittany), where a large number of Mesolithic lithic scatters are now known from the interior (Gouletquer 1991; Kayser 1992; Gouletquer *et al.* 1996; Marchand 1999). (The continuing paucity of Mesolithic sites in the interior of Morbihan is probably due to lack of intensive field survey rather than actual absence.) While beach pebble flint is overwhelmingly preponderant in the coastal assemblages, there is much greater use of non-flint materials on the inland sites. Indeed, in Finistère, the lithic materials that completely dominate inland assemblages are entirely absent from the coastal zone, the separation occurring some 20 km inland from the present coastline (Yven 2000; see also Gouletquer *et al.*1996). The interpretation of this pattern, however, is not entirely straightforward. Scarre (2001) cites the same lithic evidence in support of his view that single groups were utilising both coast and interior in a structured seasonal round, with territories paralleling river courses. But given the degree of separation of lithic materials, it seems at least as plausible to argue for the presence of distinct coastal and inland groups. This also has the advantage of agreeing with the isotopic data (at least in Morbihan; no data are available for Mesolithic Finistère, which may of course present a different pattern), which suggests a population with a focus of settlement on or near the coast. The degree of reliance on marine protein, particularly in the case of Hoëdic, is too high to be consistent with only seasonal use of coastal resources.

Aside from the raw material itself, stone tool typology also appears to offer some support for the existence of separate groups. While many of the differences seen between lithic assemblages are due to change over time, there is clearly a synchronic spatial element as well (Marchand 1999). The question is at what scale this can be applied. The most striking stylistic division in the later Mesolithic occurs between a regional grouping, the Téviecien, covering Finistère and Morbihan on the one hand, and the Retzian group to the east of the mouth of the River Vilaine, on the other (Marchand 1995, 2000: Fig. 2; Tessier 1984). This is a larger scale than is envisaged for the movement of most individuals in marriage. However, as the border between these two lithic style zones occurs just to the east of the Gulf of Morbihan, its distance from Téviec and Hoëdic is not that great. Yet the fact that there is so little evidence for interaction suggests that this was a strongly maintained cultural boundary (none of the highly distinctive Châtelet points associated with the Retzian were found in any of the Téviecien assemblages west of the Vilaine). In any case, what is being argued here more generally is a scenario of marriage exchange predominantly between networks of local communities, not between larger and more distant social formations (although this would probably have occurred on occasion, especially among emergent high-status families – see below). While there are some indications of more local typological variation in lithic assemblages (Rozoy 1978; Marchand 1999), difficulties in dating render their interpretation problematic. An ongoing survey project in Brittany, concentrating on

Finistère, may provide additional information that could help resolve some of these issues (Marchand, personal communication 2000).

Marriage in the Mesolithic

Although there are a number of factors to consider, the need to acquire marriage partners from outside the local group is largely predicated on the size of that group. Endogamy is not a viable long-term option below a certain group size, variable but generally placed at about 500 individuals (Wobst 1974, 1976; Meiklejohn 1978; Mandryk 1993; MacDonald and Hewlett 1999;). Local communities, or 'minimum bands' (Steward 1969), in the European Mesolithic would likely be far below this. Thus, not surprisingly, local communities in small-scale societies *must* be exogamous in order to maintain biologically viable populations. Logically then, and as demonstrated with a cross-cultural ethnographic sample by MacDonald and Hewlett (1999; see also Mandryk 1993), as population density decreases, the mating network must encompass a larger area.

A key issue then becomes the population density of Mesolithic Brittany. It is improbable that population was sufficiently dense to permit the necessary concentrations either within single communities or within small clusters of immediately adjacent communities. To address the question in any more detail on the basis of the available archaeological data is difficult, and it is necessary to turn to other sources of information. Based largely on ethnographic analogy, a number of researchers have suggested an average figure of 0.1 persons/km^2 for temperate Europe in the Mesolithic (Jochim 1979; Rozoy 1978; see also Hassan 1981:Table 12.3). Others have favoured considerably lower estimates (e.g., 0.01 to 0.02 persons/km^2 [C. Smith 1992]). On a more local and regional basis, population densities would be highly variable; in particular, it can be suggested that coastal values would have been significantly higher, possibly by as much as an order of magnitude (i.e., 1.0 persons/km^2). Fisher-hunter-gatherers on the Northwest Coast of North America achieved comparable, or even higher, population densities (Kroeber 1939). By contrast, population density in some parts of the interior of Brittany may have been well below 0.1 persons/km^2.

These figures provide some basis on which to explore the implications of differing population densities in terms of the territory size required to maintain viable populations (Figure 55.7). Taking first an average value of 0.1 persons/km^2, an area the size of Morbihan would barely suffice for a single mating network. Obviously, under such conditions local groups would have to be exogamous over large distances. A high population density of 1.0 persons/km^2 on the other hand would result in nearly 14 endogamous mating networks, or maximum bands, in Morbihan. At this density, an area of only 500 km^2 (e.g., a circular territory with a diameter of just over 25 km – Figure 55.2) would be required to sustain a population of 500 individuals. Given lower sea-levels at the time, and the probable high productivity of the surrounding sea, the enlarged island group that would encompass the modern island of Hoëdic would in itself comprise about half the required area. The proximity of nearby Belle Ile and the mainland coast would then largely obviate the biological, if not the social, need for exogamy at a level that would incorporate more inland groups. In the case of Hoëdic, the isotopic data are in fact consistent with a network of inter-marrying communities relying primarily on coastal resources. Mainland coastal communities, with access to a larger interior hinterland and so more terrestrial and/or estuarine foods, could provide marriage partners with the slightly more terrestrial diets required to explain the isotopic results. At a lower population density, say 0.5 persons/km^2, the resulting territory (nearly 36 km in diameter) would require that marriage partners be sought further afield, either along the coast or into the interior.

Two points worth emphasising follow from this brief modeling exercise. The first is that the division between the groups making use of Téviec and Hoëdic – as indicated isotopically by their differing diets – may have been at the population level. In other words, although not a component of the original argument for their existence (Schulting and Richards 2001), it is conceivable that at high population densities (0.5–1.0 persons/km^2) the groups using the sites for burial were circulating in at least partly distinct mating networks. In reality, of course, there is likely to have been considerable interaction, including marriage exchange, between those living in such close proximity. Indeed, the similarity of the isotopic

Region	area (km^2)	Density .05		Density .10		Density .50		Density 1.0	
		Pop^n	Net^2	Pop^n	Net	Pop^n	Net	Pop^n	Net
Brittany	27208	1360	2.7	2721	5.4	13604	27.2	27208	54.4
Morbihan^1	6823	341	0.7	682	1.4	3412	6.8	6823	13.7

^{1} the various *départements* of Brittany are all approximately the same size
^{2} number of endogamous mating networks assuming a population of 500 individuals per network

Figure 55.7 Land areas and population estimates at selected population densities for Brittany and Morbihan

values for the young females at Hoëdic with the overall average at Téviec may provide a hint of this. If so, the relationship does not seem to be reciprocated at Téviec. The second point is that, given the substantially lower population densities posited for interior regions, the distances over which marriage partners needed to be sought by inland groups, should they even exist, would be greater than for coastal groups. This implies that it would be more to the interest of inland groups to instigate intermarriage with coastal groups than vice versa.

Mapping these models back onto the archaeological record is at present not possible. Sites like Beg-er-Vil, Malvant and Kerhillio would clearly be within the maximum band territory, and possibly within the local group territory, of either Téviec or Hoëdic (Figure 55.2). While neither Malvant nor Kerhillio have organic preservation, from their near-coastal locations they would be expected to share Téviec and Hoëdic's marine-oriented economy. The small faunal assemblage from the shell midden at Beg-er-Vil confirms this (Kayser 1991; A. Tresset pers. comm. 2000). In general it is at least a few kilometers further inland that communities with more terrestrial-based economies should occur, although, as noted above, even two sites located near the coast may exhibit a significantly different balance of resources. Unfortunately, the interior of Morbihan is basically unknown in terms of known Mesolithic sites. Kerjouanno comes closest to meeting the criteria, as it would have been at least 20 km from its contemporary coastline, but it dates typologically to an earlier phase of the Mesolithic (Rozoy 1978). The inundated area represented by the modern Gulf of Morbihan would be a prime candidate for a concentration of later Mesolithic settlement, and its rich estuarine conditions could produce the kind of intermediate isotopic values that are implicated for the postulated in-marrying women at Téviec and Hoëdic.

Many researchers would hold that coastal Mesolithic communities in northwest Europe were socioeconomically differentiated to a greater degree than the majority of hunter-gatherers of inland temperate Europe (e.g., Broadbent 1979; Price 1985; Rowley-Conwy 1986, 1998; Clark and Neeley 1987; Larsson 1989; Fischer 1995). If it can be assumed that this was the case for coastal Brittany, then perhaps it was predominantly high-status families that were marrying outside of the immediate area, seeking alliances with other socially elevated families further afield. The degree to which such families can be termed 'elite' and the longevity of their position are not really an issue here. The point is that, with rare exceptions, even small-scale societies are not fully egalitarian at the family level (Cashdan 1980; Wiessner 1996). Status differences, no matter to what degree, exist, and efforts are made to perpetuate, as well as to resist, them. Thus, families will often try to maintain and improve their position relative to other families through such strategies as arranged marriages. This is a pattern well-attested in the literature of the complex fisher-hunter-gatherer societies of the Northwest Coast of North America, where high-ranking families sought marriage alliances with other families of equal or higher standing, often outside the local area (Drucker 1951; Duff 1952; Boas 1966). The express purpose of such marriages was to acquire contacts in distant villages, providing potential trade contacts and allies. Perhaps, then, the cemeteries at Téviec and Hoëdic never held all the dead of the communities they served; certainly there are far too few individuals to indicate that they did. High social standing may have been one of the criterion of selection for burial at the sites. This would also help to account for several other features of the graves – their unusual richness in terms of grave goods, their relatively complex structure, and their repeated use (Schulting 1996).

Implications for the Mesolithic-Neolithic transition

Not surprisingly, the question of the Mesolithic-Neolithic transition in Brittany is a complex one. As is often the case, the two periods are for the most part approached by specialists focusing either on the Mesolithic or on the Neolithic. Then there is the added problem of the paucity of good radiocarbon dates from secure contexts for both periods. This situation is improving somewhat, with new investigations into the Mesolithic, together with new research and dating programmes on the major Neolithic monument complex at Locmariaquer in the Gulf of Morbihan. Currently, however, the earliest appearance of the Neolithic in southern Brittany remains uncertain, and may lie anywhere between 6000/5800 BP (Giot 1987; Giot *et al.* 1994), and 5500/5400 BP (Cassen 1993). In either case, dates obtained on human bone from Téviec and Hoëdic indicate the continued, if sporadic, use of both sites well into what would be chronologically defined as the Neolithic period (Schulting 1999; Schulting and Richards 2001). This is particularly so when a marine reservoir correction is applied (making them younger by 100 to 400 years), causing four or five burials to post-date 6000 BP, and one to post-date 5000 BP. Yet the stable isotope results from Téviec and Hoëdic show little indication of a concomitant change in diet.

If the early Neolithic dates are accepted, it seems that people with a 'Mesolithic' fisher-hunter-gatherer subsistence economy were living on the coast of southern Brittany at the same time that 'Neolithic' groups (as identified by the presence of pottery, monuments and domestic animals) were present in the same area. Supporting this view are recent investigations at Er Grah, Locmariaquer – less than 30 km distance from the Mesolithic sites and rich in Neolithic monuments (Lecornec 1987, 1994) – which revealed a pit containing two fully articulated domestic cattle, dating to around 6000 BP (Tresset and Vigne in press) (Figure 55.1). That the two 'cultures' may have nonetheless remained separate is shown by the complete absence of pottery from the midden levels at Téviec and Hoëdic. Nor, with one or two possible exceptions that are no longer possible to verify (due to the loss of the material), were the remains of any domestic species (other than dog) found at the sites (Péquart et al. 1937; Péquart and Péquart 1954; Rozoy 1978).

Whether the Neolithic appeared first on the coast or in the interior of Brittany remains largely an open question. The distribution of monuments, both long mounds (*tertres tumularies*) and passage graves, is strongly coastal, but there are some early inland sites as well, such as the monument complex of Saint-Just, Ille-et-Vilaine, dating to about 5600 BP (Briard et al. 1995; Le Roux et al. 1989). In fact there is increasing evidence for a relatively early Neolithic presence in the interior of Brittany (L'Helgouac'h and Lecornec 1976; Le Roux et al. 1989; Briard et al. 1995; Cassen and Hinguant 1996; Cassen et al. 1998; Cassen et al. 1999). The earliest (c. 6000 BP) and best documented example comes from the trapezoidal longhouse found at Le Haut Mée in northeast Brittany, some 125 km from the Morbihan coast. Clearly intrusive within the local context, the site shows strong links – both in pottery and in architecture – to the Villeneuve-St-Germain group of the Paris Basin Neolithic (Cassen and Hinguant 1996; Cassen et al. 1998). Isolated finds of Villeneuve-St-Germain pottery have also been made along the Loire in the Saumur region, some 100 km from the river's mouth (Cassen et al. 1999).

What, then, are the implications for the scenario outlined in this paper for the process of neolithisation in Brittany? If the exchange of marriage partners between different local Mesolithic groups was a long-standing practice – as indeed it must have been, regardless of the merits of the case for a patrilocal postmarital residence pattern that I have argued here – then it seems inevitable that at some stage communities following a more 'Neolithic' lifeway would have entered onto the scene. Whether such communities originated outside Brittany or represent indigenous adoption of new elements matters little in the present context. Similarly, whether the focus of settlement was initially inland or coastal is less important than the more terrestrially oriented basis of their subsistence economy (currently presumed rather than satisfactorily demonstrated through stable isotope analysis). The small size of these early Neolithic communities would have made it equally imperative for individuals to seek marriage partners outside the local group. No doubt contact and exchange with indigenous groups influenced the character of the Neolithic that eventually emerged. Interestingly, studies of forager-farmer interaction in the Kalahari indicate that Basarwa foragers more successfully negotiate the social and economic transition to becoming agro-pastoralists when they are linked through marriage with Bantu herders (Vierich 1982).

The concept of hypergyny may be relevance in understanding the process of neolithisation in Brittany (cf. Zvelebil 1996, 1998 for the Baltic region). Hypergyny refers to the tendency for women from low-ranked societies to marry into the lower echelons of higher-ranked societies. The pattern is a common one, seen repeatedly not only in ethnographic situations, as among the Okiek, Basarwa and others (Speth 1991; A. Smith 1998), but in recent Western society as well (Glass 1966). Whether this is a strategy employed at the level of the lineage, family, or individual is an interesting question, but one that lies beyond the scope of this paper. No doubt part of the answer is that the specifics of each situation are highly variable. While hypergyny may have been a factor even in the Mesolithic, with women from inland communities marrying into coastal groups perceived to be of higher standing, its expression may have become much more pronounced with the appearance of the Neolithic. As noted by Speth (1991), when the two societies in question are a hunter-gatherer society and a food producing society, the movement of women in marriage will usually be from the former to the latter. Indeed, marriages with indigenous women may have been sought out by young men from Neolithic communities as a means of bypassing the control by elders over the women of their own communities (cf. Dennell 1984; Patton 1993:64).

As the balance of power increasingly shifted in favour of new and at least partly introduced Neolithic lifeways, it is likely that fewer and fewer women would marry into those groups still following traditional 'Mesolithic' lifeways. That is, Neolithic groups would come to be perceived as being of higher status. Not only were they associated with new technologies and impressive large, fat domestic animals and a reliable source of carbohydrates, but, in the building of monumental tombs, they were capable of organising labour to an extent previously unimagined (cf. Sherratt 1995). Eventually, with a continuing dual process of hypergyny and the response of indigenous men, lifestyles and cultures may have converged and given rise to a distinct Breton Neolithic culture, albeit one emphasising novel over traditional elements. The Mesolithic way of life in coastal Brittany (and perhaps elsewhere) may have eventually disappeared not because it was not viable economically, which it clearly was, but because it became increasingly difficult to recruit marriage partners. If this were the case, then Mesolithic groups would be unable to reproduce themselves not only socially, but biologically as well.

Acknowledgments

I would like to thank the organisers for hosting a most enjoyable conference. Thanks also to Joanna Ostapkowicz and Alasdair Whittle for comments on an earlier draft of this paper.

References

Binford, L.R. 1980. Willow smoke and dogs' tails: hunter-gatherer settlement systems and archaeological site formation. *American Antiquity* 45, 4–20.

—— 1982. The archaeology of place. *Journal of Anthropological Archaeology* 1, 1–31.

Boas, F. 1966. *Kwakiutl ethnography*. Chicago.

Briard, J., Gautier, M. and Leroux, G. 1995. *Les mégalithes et les tumulus de Saint-Just, Ille-et-Vilaine*. Paris.

Broadbent, N.D. 1979. *Coastal resources and settlement stability*. Archaeolgical Studies 3. Uppsala.

Burton, J. 1987. Exchange pathways at a stone axe factory in Papua New Guinea. In: Sieveking, G.G. and Newcomer, M. (eds.) *The human uses of flint and chert*, 183–191. Cambridge.

Case, H. 1976. Acculturation and the earlier Neolithic in western Europe. In: De Laet, S.J. (ed.) *Acculturation and continuity in Atlantic Europe*, 45–58. Bruges.

Cashdan, E.A. 1980. Egalitarianism among hunters and gatherers. *American Anthropologist* 82, 116–120.

Cassen, S. 1993. Material culture and the earlier Neolithic in western France. *Oxford Journal of Archaeology* 12, 197–208.

Cassen, S., Audren, C., Hinguant, S., Lannuzel, G. and Marchand, G. 1998. L'habitat Villeneuve-Saint-Germain du Haut-Mée (Saint-Étienne-en-Coglés, Ille-et-Vilaine). *Bulletin de la Société Préhistorique Française* 95, 41–75.

Cassen, S. and Hinguant, S. 1996. Du Néolithique Ancien en Bretagne. *Bulletin de la Société Préhistorique Française* 93, 147–148.

Cassen, S., Marchand, G., Menanteau, L., Poissonier, B., Cadot, R. and Viau, Y. 1999. Néolithisation de la France de l'ouest: témoignages Villeneuve-Saint-Germain, Cerny et Chambon sur la Loire Angevine et Atlantique. *Gallia Préhistoire* 41, 223–251.

Clark, G. and Neeley, M. 1987. Social differentiation in European Mesolithic burial data. In: Rowley-Conwy, P., Zvelebil, M. and Blankholm, H. (eds.) *Mesolithic north west Europe: recent trends*, 121–127. Sheffield.

Dennell, R. 1984. The expansion of exogenous-based economies across Europe: the Balkans and central Europe. In: De Atley, S.P. and Findlow, F.J. (eds.) *Exploring the limits: frontiers and boundaries in prehistory*. BAR International Series 223, 93–115. Oxford.

Drucker, P. 1951. *The corthern and central Nootkan tribes*. Washington, D.C.

Duff, W. 1952. *The Upper Stalo Indians of the Fraser Valley*. Royal British Columbia Provincial Museum. Victoria.

Fischer, A. 1982. Trade in Danubian shaft-hole axes and the introduction of Neolithic economy in Denmark. *Journal of Danish Archaeology* 1, 7–12.

—— 1995. An entrance to the Mesolithic world below the ocean. Status of ten year's work on the Danish sea floor. In: Fischer, A. (ed.) *Man and sea in the Mesolithic*, 371–384. Oxford.

Gendel, P.A. 1989. The analysis of lithic styles through distributional profiles of variation: examples from the western European Mesolithic. In: Bonsall, C. (ed.) *The Mesolithic in Europe*, 40–48. Edinburgh.

Gilchrist, R. 1999. *Gender and archaeology*. London.

Giot, P.-R. 1987. *Barnenez, Carn, Guennoc*. Travaux du Laboratoire d'Anthropologie de l'Université de Rennes 1. Rennes.

Giot, P.-R., Marguerie, D. and Morzadec, H. 1994. About the age of the oldest passage-graves in western Brittany. *Antiquity* 68, 624–626.

Glass, D. 1966. *Social mobility in Britain*. London.

Godelier, M. 1986. *The making of great men: male domination and power among the New Guinea Baruya*. Cambridge.

Gouletquer, P. 1991. Les problemes posés par le "Mésolithique" de Basse-Bretagne: les moyens de les résoudre. In: Thevenin, A. (ed.) *Mésolithiques et Néolithiques en France et dans les régions limitrophes*. Comité des Travaux Historiques et Scientifiques, 177–196. Paris.

Gouletquer, P., Kayser, O., Le Goffic, M., Leopold, P., Marchand, G. and Moullec, J.-M. 1996. Ou sont passes les Mésolithiques cotiers Bretons? Bilan 1985–1995 des prospections de surface dans le Finistère. *Revue Archéologique de l'Ouest* 13, 5–30.

Hassan, F.A. 1981. *Demographic archaeology*. New York.

Hastorf, C.A. 1991. Gender, space, and food in prehistory. In: Gero, J.M. and Conkey, M.W. (eds.) *Engendering archaeology: women and prehistory*, 132–162. Oxford.

Jacobi, R.M. 1979. Early Flandrian hunters in the south-west. *Proceedings of the Devon Archaeological Society* 37, 48–93.

Jochim, M.A. 1979. "Catches and caches": ethnographic alternatives for prehistory. In: Kramer, C. (ed.) *Ethnoarchaeology*, 219–246. New York.

Kayser, O. 1991. Le Mésolithique Breton: un état de connaissances en 1988. In: Thevenin, A. (ed.) *Mésolithiques et Néolithiques en France et dans les Régions Limitrophes*. Comité des Travaux Historiques et Scientifiques, 197–211. Paris.

—— 1992. Les industries lithique de la fin du Mesolithique en Armorique. In: Le Roux, C.-T. (ed.) *Paysans et Bâtisseurs: L'émergence du Néolithique et les origines du mégalithisme*. Revue Archéologique de l'Ouest, Supplement 5, 117–124. Rennes.

Kroeber, A.L. 1939. Cultural and natural areas of Native North America. *University of California Publications in American Archaeology and Ethnology, 38*. Berkeley.

L'Helgouac'h, J. and Lecornec, J. 1976. Le site mégalithique de Min-Goh-Ru, près de Larcuste à Colpo (Morbihan). *Bulletin de la Société Préhistorique Française* 73, 370–397.

Larsson, L. 1989. Late Mesolithic settlements and cemeteries at Skateholm, southern Sweden. In: Bonsall, C. (ed.) *The Mesolithic in Europe*, 367–378. Edinburgh.

Lecornec, J. 1987. Le complexe mégalithique du Petit Mont à Arzon (Morbihan). *Revue Archéologique de l'Ouest* 4, 37–56.

Lecornec, J. 1994. *Le Petit Mont, Arzon-Morbihan*. Documents Archéologiques de l'Ouest. Rennes.

Le Roux, C.-T., Lecerf, Y. and Gautier, M. 1989. Les megalithes de Saint-Just (Ille-et-Vilaine) et la fouille des alignments du Moulin de Cojou. *Revue Archéologique de l'Ouest* 6, 5–29.

Lévi-Strauss, C. 1969. *The Elementary Structure of Kinship*. Boston.

MacDonald, D.H. and Hewlett, B.S. 1999. Reproductive interests and forager mobility. *Current Anthropology* 40, 501–523.

Mandryk, C.A.S. 1993. Hunter-gatherer social costs and the nonviability of submarginal environments. *Journal of Archaeological Research* 49, 39–71.

Marchand, G. 1995. Éléments pour la définition du Retzian. *L'Europe des derniers chasseurs*. 5e Colloque International UISPP, 213–224.

Marchand, G. 1999. *Le Néolithisation de l'ouest de la France. caractérisation des industries lithiques*. BAR International Series S748. Oxford.

—— 2000. Le Néolithisation de l'ouest de la France: aires culturelles et tranferts techniques dans l'industrie lithique. *Bulletin de la Société Préhistorique Française* 97, 377–403.

Meiklejohn, C. 1978. Ecological aspects of population size and growth in Late-Glacial and Early Postglacial north-western Europe. In: Mellars, P. (ed.) *The Early Postglacial settlement of northern Europe*, 66–79. London.

Moss, M.L. 1993. Shellfish, gender, and status on the Northwest Coast: reconciling archaeological, ethnographic, and ethnohistorical records of the Tlingit. *American Anthropologist* 95, 631–652.

Patton, M. 1993. *Statements in stone: monuments and society in Neolithic Brittany*. London.

Péquart, M. and Péquart, S.-J. 1954. *Hoëdic, deuxième station-nécropole du Mésolithique côtier Armoricain*. Anvers.

Péquart, M., Péquart, S.-J., Boule, M. and Vallois, H. 1937. *Téviec, station-nécropole du Mésolithique du Morbihan*. Archives de L'Institut de Paléontologie Humaine XVIII. Paris.

Peterson, B.J., Howarth, R.W. and Garritt, R.H. 1985. Multiple stable isotopes used to trace the flow of organic matter in estuarine food webs. *Science* 227, 1361–1363.

Price, T.D. 1985. Affluent foragers of Mesolithic southern Scandinavia, In: Price, T.D. and Brown, J.A. (eds.) *Prehistoric hunter-gatherers: the emergence of cultural complexity*, 341–360. New York.

Rowley-Conwy, P. 1986. Between cave painters and crop planters: aspects of the temperate European Mesolithic. In: Zvelebil, M. (ed.) *Hunters in transition*, 17–32. Cambridge.

—— 1998. Cemeteries, seaonality and complexity in the Ertebølle of southern Scandinavia. In: Zvelebil, M., Dennell, R. and Domanska, L. (eds.) *Harvesting the sea, farming the forest: the emergence of Neolithic societies in the Baltic region*, 193–202. Sheffield.

Rozoy, J.-G. 1978. *Les derniers chasseurs. L'Épipaléolithique en France et en Belgique. sssai de synthèse*. Bulletin de la Société Archéologique Champenoise. Charleville.

Scarre, C. 2001. Modelling prehistoric populations: the case of Neolithic Brittany. *Journal of Anthropological Archaeology* 20, 285–313.

Schlegel, A. and Eloul, R. 1988. Marriage transactions: labor, property, status. *American Anthropologist* 90, 291–309.

Schoeninger, M. and Moore, K. 1992. Stable bone isotope studies in archaeology. *Journal of World Prehistory* 6, 247–296.

Schulting, R.J. 1996. Antlers, bone pins and flint blades: the Mesolithic cemeteries of Téviec and Hoëdic, Brittany. *Antiquity* 70, 335–350.

—— 1999. Nouvelles dates AMS à Téviec et Hoëdic (Quiberon, Morbihan). rapport préliminaire. *Bulletin de la Société Préhistorique Française* 96, 203–207.

Schulting, R.J. and Richards, M.P. 2001. Dating women and becoming farmers: new palaeodietary and AMS data from the Breton Mesolithic cemeteries of Téviec and Hoëdic. *Journal of Anthropological Archaeology* 20, 314–344.

Schurr, M.R. 1997. Stable nitrogen isotopes as evidence for the age of weaning at the Angel site: a comparison of isotopic and demographic measures of weaning age. *Journal of Archaeological Science* 24, 919–927.

Schwarcz, H.P. 1991. Some theoretical aspects of isotope paleodiet studies. *Journal of Archaeological Science* 18, 261–276.

Sherratt, A. 1995. Instruments of conversion? The role of megaliths in the Mesolithic/Neolithic transition in north-west Europe. *Oxford Journal of Archaeology* 14, 245–260.

Smith, A.B. 1998. Keeping people on the periphery: the ideology of social hierarchies between hunters and herders. *Journal of Anthropological Archaeology* 17, 201–215.

Smith, C. 1992. The population of Late Upper Palaeolithic and Mesolithic Britain. *Proceedings of the Prehistoric Society* 58, 37–40.

Speth, J.D. 1991. Some unexplored aspects of mutualistic Plains-Pueblo food exchange. In: Spielmann, K.A. (ed.) *Farmers, hunters, and colonists*, 18–35. Tucson.

Stenhouse, M.J. and Baxter, M.S. 1979. The uptake of bomb 14C in humans. In: Berger, R. and Suess, H.E. (eds.) *Radiocarbon dating*, 324–341. Berkeley.

Steward, J.H. 1969. Postscript to bands: on taxonomy, processes, and causes. In: Damas, D. (ed.) *Contributions to anthropology: band societies*, 228–295. National Museums of Canada, Bulletin 228. Ottawa.

Strathern, M. 1988. *The gender of the gift*. Berkeley.

Tessier, M. 1984. Les industries préhistorique à microlithes du pays de Retz. *Etudes Préhistorique et Protohistorique des Pays de la Loire* 7, 73–132.

Tresset, A. and Vigne, J.-D. in press. Le dépot d'animaux de la structure e4 d'Er Grah: une illustration de la symbolique des bovins à la charnière de Mésolithique et du Néolithique Bretons? *Gallia Préhistoire* supplément.

Vierich, H.I.D. 1982. Adaptive flexibility in a multi-ethnic setting: the Basarwa of the southern Kalahari. In: Leacock, E. and Lee, R. (eds.) *Politics and history in band societies*, 213–222. Cambridge.

Vogel, J.C. and van der Merwe, N.J. 1977. Isotopic evidence for early maize cultivation in New York state. *American Antiquity* 42, 238–242.

Wiessner, P. 1996. Levelling the hunter: constraints on the status quest in foraging societies. In: Wiessner, P. and Schiefenhövel, W. (eds.) *Food and the status quest: an interdisciplinary perspective*, 171–191. Providence.

Wobst, H.M. 1974. Boundary conditions for paleolithic social systems: a simulation approach. *American Antiquity* 39, 147–178.

—— 1976. Locational relationships in Palaeolithic society. *Journal of Human Evolution* 5, 49–58.

Yven, E. 2000. The deposits of raw material and the quarry sites at the Mesolithic in the Trégor in Brittany (France). (In this volume.

Zvelebil, M. 1996. The agricultural frontier and the transition to farming in the circum-Baltic region. In: Harris, D.R. (ed.) *The origins and spread of agriculture and pastoralism in Eurasia*, 323–345. London.

Zvelebil, M. 1998. Agricultural frontiers, Neolithic origins, and the fransition to farming in the Baltic basin. In: Zvelebil, M., Dennell, R. and Domanska, L. (eds.) *Harvesting the sea, farming the forest: the Emergence of Neolithic societies in the Baltic region*, 9–27. Sheffield.

56. Mesolithic Economic and Social Changes in the Southern Netherlands

Leo Verhart

Due to study of sites in a site-related context examples from abroad have long been the model for research into the Mesolithic of the Netherlands. In recent years a regional approach have been adopted in studying relationships and context between sites. Two examples are presented: the early Mesolithic of the Vlootbeek region and the Late Mesolithic of the Venray region.

Northwestern Europe is assumed to have developed in a similar way, characterised by a decrease in mobility, more permanent settlements, more intensive exploitation of food resources, increasing complexity, more pronounced territoriality, an increase in stress and violence. In the Netherlands developments in Mesolithic society appear to have a different, almost reversed direction than the traditional model influenced by the Ertebölle example in Scandinavia. Not from simple to increasingly complex, but perhaps even from complex to less complex.

If the Ertebölle based model cannot be applied in the Netherlands, the question arises how the transition from Mesolithic to Neolithic should be considered. Within the framework of ethnographic and archaeological data a number of possible neolithisation models may be formulated. A major social factor appears to be increased competition within or among hunter-gatherer groups starting with the arrival of Neolithic (Bandkeramik) groups in the southern part of the Netherlands. The main elements in these models are the concept of stages in contact. A first stage of contact with increasing social competition, followed by a second stage that eventually would have led to the disappearance of a lifestyle essentially based on hunting and gathering. Archaeological data illustrating these models is presented.

Introduction

Examples from abroad have long been the model for research into the Mesolithic in the Netherlands. Both theoretically and in studies of the material culture, developments in other countries were kept in mind. Research results were fitted to suit celebrated examples from elsewhere, for example the Anglo-American theoretical approach of Lewis Binford (1978, 1982, 1990, 1991) and Michael Jochim (1976) and for the material culture Scandinavia in particular was the guiding light. In addition the typological approach reigned supreme for a long time (Bohmers/Wouters 1956).

The background to this approach was mainly practical. The Dutch Mesolithic is characterised mainly by thousands of sites consisting almost exclusively of concentrations of flint. Sites with organic remains are very rare. This 'poverty' forced us to look to the infinitely greater Scandinavian potential. There was another reason as well. The Mesolithic has mainly been studied in a site-related context. Excavation results of one individual site were compared to the results of other Dutch sites or to examples from abroad. Only relatively recently has a regional approach been adopted in studying relationships and context between sites, yielding unexpected and surprising results.

In this article the results of this regional investigation will be discussed and the conclusions will be used as materials for the reconstruction of the transition from Mesolithic to Neolithic in the southern Netherlands.

Regional research

Site-related research reigned supreme well into the sixties. Whereas in Scandinavia regional Stone Age research had long been practised (Mathiassen 1943, 1948, 1959) and regional research was popular in the Netherlands in a different context (Waterbolk 1962), the arrival on the scene of Ray Newell and Douglas Price caused a change in views on the Mesolithic. Important factors were the theoretical ideas of the New Archaeology, but also the application of regional research.

Newell started a regional project on the shores of the Bergumermeer in Friesland (Newell 1973, 1980), but the most extensive study was that of the Mesolithic on the Drents Plateau (Price 1980, 1981). This approach was not to be pursued due to the unmanageable nature of the Dutch material. The Dutch Mesolithic has grappled with the dilemma of a wealth of sites that are relatively easy to

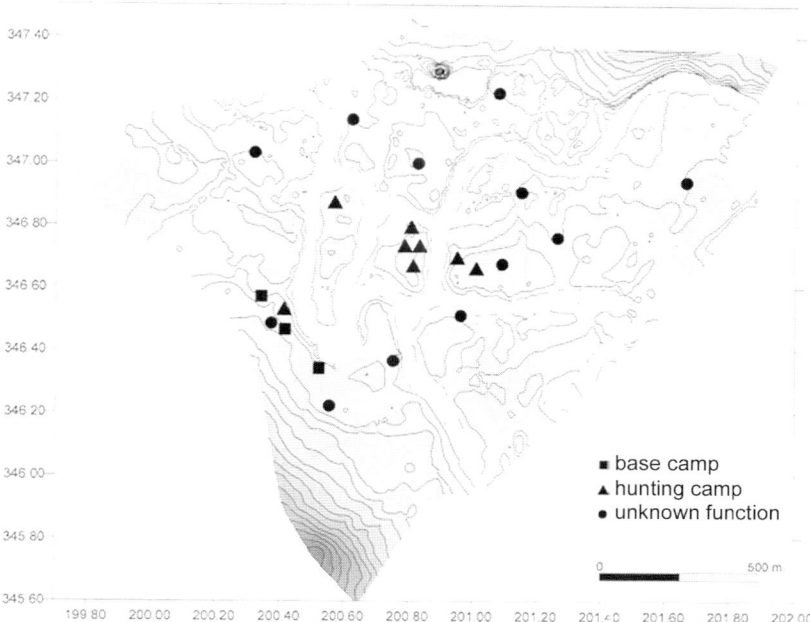

Figure 56.1 A palaeogeographic reconstruction of the Vlootbeek valley and the distribution of Early Mesolithic sites. Legend: quadrate: base camp, triangle: hunting camp and circle: site with unknown function.

find, but an overall picture created by these thousands of sites that is highly distorted. This distortion is caused by 4 factors:

1. In the eastern part of the Netherlands Pleistocene deposits are on the surface. In the west these have been covered by Holocene deposits. In the east finds can be collected easily on the surface, resulting in an overrepresentation in the distribution pattern.
2. As Mesolithic man did not dig much, all finds are located in the top 30 centimetres of the soil profile and are therefore highly susceptible to disturbance, in particular by agricultural activities.
3. Location and intensity of archaeological research determine distribution patterns to a great extent. Clusters in the distribution pattern are the result of research intensity and do not reflect habitation intensities.
4. Mesolithic man appears to have favoured the same localities over long periods of time, so chronologically separate activities are almost impossible to find. This severely impedes research into settlement typology and settlement patterns.

After Price's disappointment, some Dutch researchers returned to this approach in the eighties. In the north of the Netherlands research was carried out in Groningen (Groenendijk 1993), Friesland (Huiskes 1988) and in the southern Netherlands two projects were started. Arts and Deeben concentrated mainly on the Late Palaeolithic (Arts 1989), whereas the Mesolithic and the transition from Mesolithic to Neolithic was studied by the University of Leiden (Verhart 2000; Wansleeben/Verhart 1990). The latter investigation, referred to as the Meuse Valley Project, was aimed at localising as many sites as possible that had been used only once and for short periods of time only, in order to provide a clear picture of the activities hunter-gatherers engaged in. The results of this project will be emphasised here.

Early Mesolithic: the Vlootbeek region

Starting in 1986, fieldwork was carried out in the valley of the Vlootbeek, near Posterholt, southeast of Roermond (Verhart 1995). As agricultural activities were limited in this area, most sites are quite undamaged. Field reconnaissance has yielded so far 23 Early Mesolithic sites. Younger Mesolithic sites are absent. This phenomenon is unique in the Netherlands. Sites, however small they may be, have therefore not been mixed and offer excellent opportunities to gain insight into the behaviour of Early Mesolithic hunter-gatherers.

In studying the surface finds it soon became apparent that there were relatively small find complexes with a preponderance of projectile points and large find complexes yielding a wide range of tools. The location of the sites, too, shows significant differences. The small sites are located on old sand and gravel banks in the valley, whereas the larger sites are situated on the higher embankments (Figure 56.1). This was suggestive of a functional split between hunting camps in the valley and base camps on the embankments. To test this hypothesis two sites have been excavated.

In 1993–1995 a small camp, with an overall surface of 400 m2, was investigated. Approximately 6000 pieces of

Excavated square	Lab.	Material	Age BP		Error Cal.
59.50/203.00 B1	UtC-4918	charcoal	237	31	1651-1953AD
56.75/198.50 B2	UtC-4919	charcoal	22.570	150	
61.00/200.75 B1	UtC-4915	charcoal	28.020	220	
61.00/202.75 B2	UtC-4921	charcoal	40.100	800	
61.25/200.00 B2	UtC-4914	hazelnut	8.800	60	7946-7705 BC
56.75/198.50 B2	UtC-4920	hazelnut	9.080	50	8091-8035 BC
59.50/203.00 B1	UtC-4917	hazelnut	9.100	50	8095-8041 BC
61.75/201.00 B1	UtC-4916	hazelnut	9.160	80	8333-8078 BC

Figure 56.2 Posterholt C-14 results

Tool type	Hunting camp		Base camp	
	n	%	n	%
points	61	54.0	15	21.7
micro burins	31	27.4	1	1.5
scrapers	3	2.7	11	15.9
burins	3	2.7	20	29.0
retouched blades/flakes	15	13.3	22	31.9
total	113	100.1	69	100.0

Figure 56.3 Posterholt tools.

flint have been recovered from undisturbed subsoil, only 1400 of which are larger than 15 mm.

The find spread shows a distinct small concentration, with a diameter of approximately 6 metres, containing two small clusters, each only a metre in diameter. Finds consist mainly of debris of flint production: several hammer stones, cores, fragments, flakes and blades. The flint used was of good quality and comes partly from deposits in the Meuse bed, but another part appears to stem from the Belgian province of Hainault. Some pieces of Wommersom quartzite have been found as well. The ratio among the tools is remarkable. Scrapers – so numerous on Stone Age sites – are almost non-existent, whereas points and micro burins have a strong presence with 81%. Among the points A- and B-points dominate. Many points are broken, with a predominance of base fragments, and show traces of use. There is a small number of scrapers and the number of flakes and retouched blades is not very large either. There were copious amounts of charcoal in the find layer, but there was no dug hearth. From the distribution pattern of the burned flint the presence of a surface hearth can not be ascertained either. The presence of a hearth can however be inferred from several burned hazel shells.

In order to determine the age of the site, a series of C-14 datings was executed, yielding surprising results (Table++ 1). From identical find locations four hazel shells and four pieces of charcoal have been dated. The results demonstrate the unreliability of charcoal for site dating on sandy soils. This site turns out to contain recent charcoal as well as old charcoal carried along with the river sediments. Only the hazel shells can be used to reliably date the site to approx. 9100 BP.

The acuity of the various distribution patterns indicates that the site has been well preserved. There are differences in the distribution of cores and tools. The retouched tools, including the scrapers, are located in the southwestern part. The points and micro burins relics overlap and can be distinguished into two separate clusters: one concentration in the west and another in the centre. The presence of a hut or tent on this site does not appear likely. The find spread is not indicative of that kind of shelter. An open air sojourn appears most likely.

Excavation data are still being processed, so the interpretation has to be tentative. Some observations may already be made. The overall find spread, the acuity of the pattern and the finds all suggest the area was used only once and for a short time only. Due to the large number of points, the many micro burins and the small number of scrapers this site may be described as a hunting camp.

Various activities appear to have occurred in spatially distinct areas. Most conspicuous is the overlap between points and micro burins. This is indicative of the manufacture of points and repair of hunting gear in situ. The presence of two clusters might signify the presence of two people performing these activities, or at least two chronologically separate occasions. The small size of the site is an indication that the group staying here must have been small. If ethnographic data from recent hunter-gatherers apply to the Dutch Mesolithic as well, it is likely that a small band of hunters, made up of men and boys, stayed here.

In 1996–1999 a larger camp was investigated. In an area of 90 by 70 metres three concentrations were found. Within each concentration clusterings could be discerned. One of these has been investigated in more detail; the area turned out to have been used repeatedly in the Early Mesolithic and various activity zones could be distinguished within the excavated area. An old tree fall proved to contain numerous burins and burin spalls, a small hunting camp was located in the western part and the centre yielded an accumulation of material suggestive of a number of overlapping activities. The tool composition is entirely different from that of the hunting camp. Points are much less numerous and micro burins are almost completely absent. In addition, tools that can be related to domestic activities are present in large numbers. Within the excavated area at least five deeply dug hearths have been found.

The investigation is still in progress, but these data are indicative of a base camp. The split into hunting camps on islands in the valley and on embankments and base camps on the higher embankments may be explained in two ways. The encampments may have been used in a yearly cycle, which would require us to demonstrate 'synchronicity'. This appears to be impossible. The second possibility is that the encampments represent two exploitation stages of the valley. These stages may be 50 years apart, but this can also not be substantiated due to the limitations of the C-14 method and our typological framework.

It is remarkable that there exists such a strong differentiation in encampments within a small area in the Early Mesolithic.

Late Mesolithic: the Venray region

Within the framework of the Meuse Valley Project an area of approximately 150 km² was investigated around Venray in the period 1988 to 1992. By way of making an inventory of amateur collections, executing field reconnaissances and an excavation the materials have been collected for reconstructing the behaviour of Late Mesolithic hunter-gatherers.

Geographically the terrain is characterised by three large features: in the east a narrow zone with Late Pleistocene and Holocene Meuse sediments, in the middle the coversands and in the west the peat moors of the Peel, nowadays mostly cut. From the Peel two brooks run east and flow into the Meuse.

The distribution of Late Mesolithic sites is remarkable (Figure 56.4). Sites are concentrated on the transition between coversand and the Meuse valley to the east. A second cluster lies in the west where the brooks rise, at

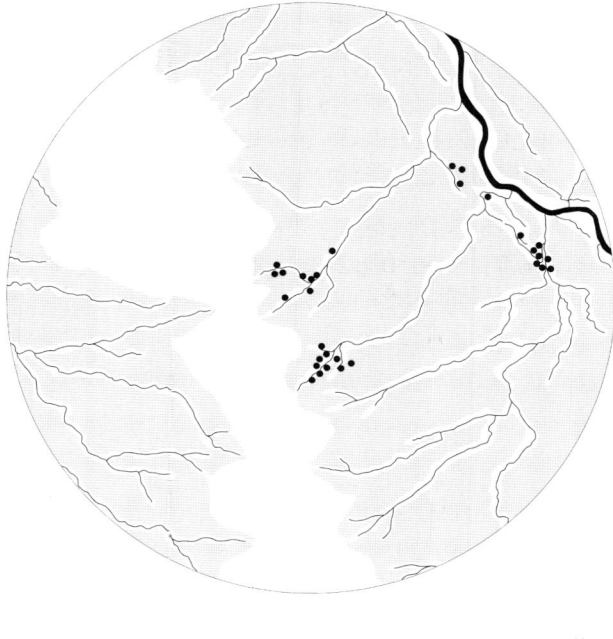

Figure 56.4 Simplified reconstruction of the terrain in the Late Mesolithic with the location of sites known to date in the core region Venray. White: peat and open areas along brooks and rivers; grey: forest.

the exact transition between Peel marshes and the coversand area.

The tool composition of the surface sites dating from the Late Mesolithic is almost identical. On all sites the ratio between the categories: points, scrapers, backed blades and retouched blades/flakes is almost identical. Points are often present in somewhat greater numbers. No single tool category is dominant.

In order to gain insight into the nature of the activities on a site, an excavation was executed at Merselo-Haag. Within an area with a low find density three clusterings could be ascertained. Two clusters were almost identical in artefact composition, with numerous small flakes, cores and a limited number of tools, indicative of small flint production sites. The third cluster contained many tools as e.g. retouched flakes and blades, trapezes, scrapers and a remarkable amount of backed blades. Analysis of the distribution of the various raw material groups and refitting reveal that the three clusters belong to a single occasion of use.

This was a relatively small camp where a wide range of activities occurred. The presence of a large number of points is indicative of the importance of hunting at that location, but domestic activities may be inferred from the remaining find material as well. It was concluded that this was a small base camp that had not been in long-term use. The similarity in tool composition and size make it plausible that the other sites in the region had a somewhat similar function (Wansleeben and Verhart 1998). This means that the larger settlements, inhabited for longer periods, that have been assumed for this period (Newell 1973; Price 1980, 1981), do not occur in this region. These might possibly be outside the region, but it is much more likely that many of the larger base camps from the Late Mesolithic are actually accumulations of various habitation activities at a single site over time.

In this respect the settlement pattern differs markedly from that in Denmark. On the eve of the arrival of colonising farmers hunter-gatherers lived in relatively small encampments.

Models of transformation from Mesolithic to Neolithic

The results of the regional research lead to other conclusions than generally assumed for the Late Mesolithic. The picture of the Late Mesolithic is traditionally strongly influenced by the Ertebølle-model. Large parts of northwestern Europe are assumed to have developed in a similar way, characterised by a decrease in mobility, more permanent settlements, more intensive exploitation of food resources, increasing complexity, more pronounced territoriality, an increase in stress and violence (Rowley-Conwy 1983; Price and Brown 1985; Zvelebil 1986, 1996; Price and Gebauer 1992; Price 2000; Zvelebil and Lillie 2000). It is easy to envisage the transition to a new, Neolithic way of life in this setting. After all, the prerequisites for this new way of life, in particular a decrease in mobility and larger and more permanent settlements, are already in place. The sole new factor is the introduction of domesticates.

In the Netherlands developments appear to have a different, almost reversed direction. Not from simple to increasingly complex, but perhaps even from complex to less complex. So if the Ertebølle model can not be applied in the Netherlands, the question arises how the transition should be considered.

Signs of the traditional explanations for the transition from Mesolithic to Neolithic, such as economic superiority, violence, a deteriorating climate and population growth are absent or can not be demonstrated. Ethnographic comparisons between modern and prehistoric hunter-gatherers are not feasible either. In order to gain insight into the processes surrounding this transition it was decided to study the contacts between socially and economically highly divergent societies. A literature study was conducted for the contacts between local populations and new arrivals in New Guinea, Greenland, America and Australia (Verhart 2000). Despite individual differences two things stand out. Two stages of contact can be distinguished. In the first stage there are contacts that do not lead to structural changes, but do have important social implications. The most important features are:

1. The results of first contacts appear to affect mainly the social subsystem, as opposed to the economic subsystem.

Figure 56.5 Wabag man from New Guinea wearing a biscuit bag. (Photo Collection M.J. Leahy, National Library of Australia)

2. The meaning an outsider attaches to an object often does not match the meaning of the local population (Figure 56.5).
3. The value these objects represent appears to be highly subject to inflationary developments. This results in a quantitative increase in the number of objects or the rise of other valuable objects in the exchange system.
4. The flow of commodities between two different sociocultural systems is widely divergent. The local population is interested in objects, almost never in food. Their own food is adequate for their daily subsistence; only food that may be re-used in the prestigious system is exchanged. The outsiders on the other hand are exclusively interested in food, sexual favours and useful raw materials, never in artefacts which are often considered inferior.
5. Only at a much later stage – what I called the second stage of contact with modern hunter-gatherers – economic motives will play a part, in the form of the possibilities for 'delayed prestige'.

After the first contact three main types can be distinguished in the further development of the relations in the process of acculturation and/or adaptation to the newcomers. Although presented as separate, in reality they often blend to some degree or other.

1. Dependent

There are two possible degrees of dependence. First, the native inhabitants are totally integrated, acculturated and no longer recognisable as a distinct socio-cultural group. As a second possibility the native population group is still identifiable. In such a situation there is a disruption of their traditional way of life and social and economic breakdown. In this phase the standards and values of the hunter-gatherers change, there are no longer any fixed rules and characteristics and they are unable to preserve their traditional economy any longer. Often societies in this kind of situation are despised and discriminated by the group they depend on. Their material culture degrades, artefacts from outside the culture come into use, standards and values of the other society are adopted, prostitution raises its head, as well as alcohol abuse and slavery. In short, the traditional hunter-gatherer society goes to seed, people are exploited and excluded. The final result is that they are often a negligible minority, underprivileged if they should manage to integrate into society.

2. Symbiotic

Both societies, hunter-gatherers as well as farmers, develop relations that meet the mutual needs, depending on the pressure of one group on the other. In such a situation the farmers are the dominant group that may impose change, wittingly or unwittingly, on the hunter-gatherers. Geographically speaking the two groups are close. Depending on the impact of one group on the other, the characteristics of the main adaptations are a.o.: changes in the settlement system, larger settlements, a longer habitation period, an increasingly sedentary lifestyle and attendant lower mobility, often the adoption of artefacts by the weaker partner, changes in diet and economy, continuous interaction between groups, exchange of marriage partners, in particular of the weaker symbiotic partner, competition among the groups in contact with outsiders and an increase in violence.

3. Independent

The third main type that can be distinguished among hunter-gatherers may be characterised as the aim to be as independent economically and socially as possible. In essence this is a kind of prolonged first contact stage. As a reaction all contact is resisted. This may be culturally inspired, mixed with spiritual/religious reasons, but a fear of losing one's own identity may play an important part as well. As a result of this kind of attitude they seek refuge in areas not exploited before. These should also be areas which are unsuitable for the economy of the outsiders they wish to avoid, or which the outsiders for some reason do not dare to enter and exploit. Hunter-gatherers will settle in areas unfit for agriculture or livestock. The existing settlement system and pattern will therefore change.

The archaeological implications

These developments and characteristics, as described above for the first stage of contact, are evident in northwestern Europe. From the data of the Meuse Valley Project and other investigations – mainly excavations – it may be inferred that in the south of the Netherlands the presence of Bandkeramik settlers and their successors, the Rössen Culture, seems to have had hardly any economic effects on the local population. The general impression is that the transition to a farming way of life did not occur until the end of the Rössen phase. In the succeeding Michelsberg phase a farming economy does exist, with strong Mesolithic overtones

When comparing distribution maps of LBK and Rössen artefacts it is apparent that objects of low value (pottery and sherds) have a limited distribution, exclusively in the area of contact. The more valuable adzes (Figure 56.6) and perforated adzes (*Breitkeile*) (Figure 56.7) are distributed over a much wider area, in the LBK phase still limited to a thin scattering, but in the Rössen phase much denser and extensive. The explanation that these objects were left behind by LBK or Rössen farmers is not very plausible; exchange is much more likely (Verhart 2000). The differences in distribution patterns point to intensifying contacts and indicate the growing importance of these implements in the prestige system.

As mentioned before, it is hard to separate first and second stages of contact in archaeological time. Moreover, at the moment second-stage contacts are less tangible archaeologically than first-stage contacts. The archaeological knowledge of the second stage of contact is based mainly on data from excavations in the west and middle of the Netherlands. In this stage economic transformations become apparent as demonstrated by the use of pottery, culture crops and animals in combination with hunting, gathering and fishery. The Mesolithic characteristics still visible in certain parts of the material culture, the settlement pattern and settlement type, lead to the conclusion that these are originally Mesolithic groups in a specific transformation phase with an increasing importance of agricultural elements in the economy.

Similar well-documented data are not available for the coversands in the south. There is a lack of organic elements of the food economy and material culture. It is possible, with some effort, to demonstrate Mesolithic origins in the flint industry. The few data on the settlement pattern and settlement types suggest a still highly Mesolithic way of exploiting the terrain, in combination with farming and husbandry.

From ethnography a number of correlates may be deduced for a second stage of contact. There are quite a number of characteristics present for a symbiotic relationship. Due to the small number of sites in the Dutch löss area, it is not possible to obtain an impression of the degree of influence of the farming communities and the effects on those communities themselves. Based on the

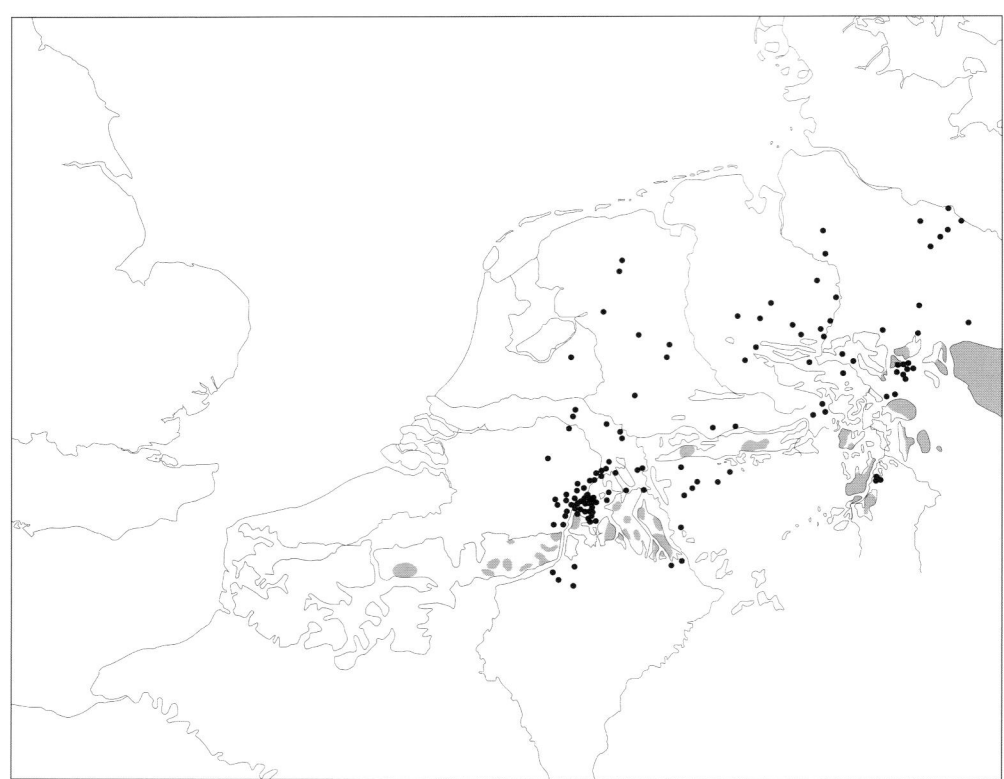

Figure 56.6 Distribution of LBK adzes in the northwest of Europe outside the löss area. Light grey: löss, dark grey: distribution of LBK settlements.

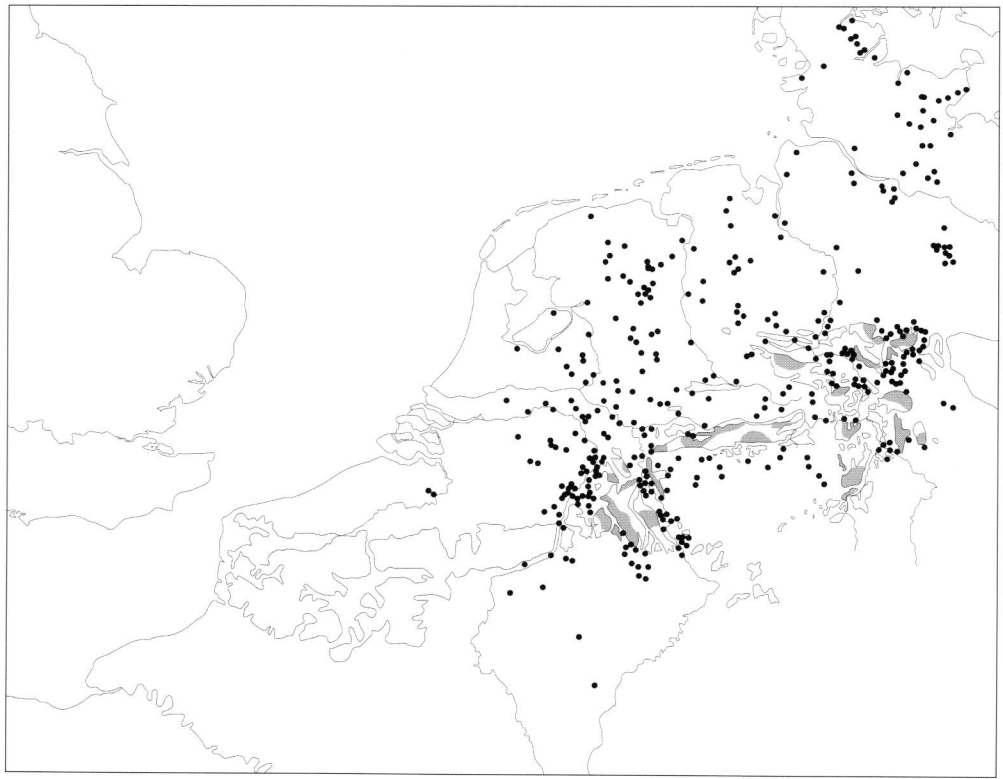

Figure 56.7 Distribution of perforated adzes (Breitkeilen) in the northwest of Europe outside the löss area. Light grey: löss, dark grey: distribution of Rössen settlements.

ethnographic data the flow of goods moving from hunter-gatherers to farmers will have been mainly organic in the Netherlands. As organic matter is hardly ever preserved, it is doubtful whether these relations would be archaeologically discernible. The changes should be most apparent in the hunter-gatherers. Excavations in the west and middle of the Netherlands demonstrate an increasingly sedentary lifestyle, larger settlements and changes in diet and economy. Ethnography makes it apparent that in such groups mutual competition increases and violence occurs. The small cemeteries of Swifterbant, Zoelen, Urk and Rijswijk-Ypenburg might be indications of territoriality and increasing competition.

We do not get a clear picture of the sandy areas. Indications for a similar development are provided by the settlement pattern in the core region of Venray. There we see a shift in location to areas more suitable for agriculture.

Conclusions

Within the framework of ethnographic and archaeological data a number of possible neolithisation models may be formulated. The main elements in this model are the ideas on a first stage contact, followed by a second stage that eventually would have led to the disappearance of a lifestyle essentially based on hunting and gathering.

Mesolithic society was not static, but continuously subject to changes within social, economic and ecological constraints. At present there are no signs that there were complex hunter-gatherer communities in the Netherlands. Indications such as status differences, specialisation, a richly ornamented ('emblematic') material culture, cemeteries and a sedentary lifestyle are absent. In the Netherlands we encounter a primarily egalitarian society. Competition on an individual level between members of the small mobile groups of hunter-gatherers should of course be allowed for. In seasons of plentiful and clustered food supply, aggregation may be expected, but (semi) sedentary settlement as is known from Denmark is not very likely. There are no indications that internal factors like population growth or external factors like climatologic or ecological changes have defined the neolithisation process. The arrival of Central European settlers marks the moment of change in Mesolithic society.

In the southeast of the Netherlands hunter-gatherers first encounter people settling inside a marginal zone of the hunter-gatherer territory – the löss area. The location of their settlements did not cause conflicts or intense competition for food. In a first contact stage there is a mutual exchange of goods (Figure 56.8). At first this flow is opportunistic and there is hardly any structural interaction. Analogous to several ethnographic instances, both groups attempt to exchange objects that are less valuable to them for more valuable items. As a result inflation and devaluation occur, where the number of objects may increase, but other objects, representing a higher value,

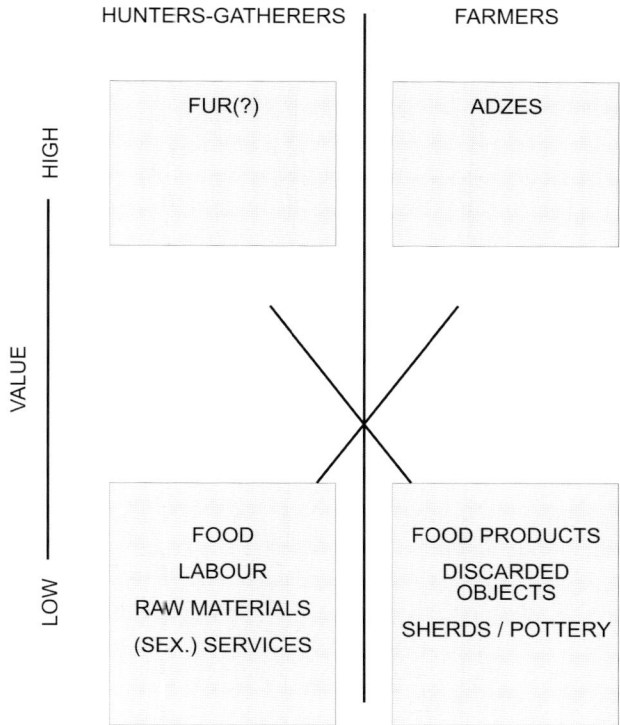

Figure 56.8 Model for exchange between hunter-gatherers and farmers in relation to changing value of exchange objects.

come into circulation as well. Several factors may start and reinforce this process. A major social factor appears to be competition within or among hunter-gatherer groups. Possession may play a part, as does the control over means of production as suggested by Bender (1978, 1981, 1985) (Bender and Morris 1988). A continuously reinforced intergroup competition may be involved as well, translated into rituals as is customary in Australia, but which will hardly be discernible archaeologically.

Other elements may stimulate these ever-intensifying contacts as well. For instance the possibility of a more sedentary lifestyle or the chance to fall back on your agrarian contacts in times of hardship. Innovations that can have important economic implications are often not recognised as advantageous in a first contact situation and will not play a major part at that stage.

Another element in this disregard for innovations, particularly agriculture, is the fact that in a first contact stage the contacts are made by men, who traditionally play this part, but often also have a higher status. Agriculture appears to be adopted only after a lengthy process of contacts, as it is the women who are active in this domain both among hunter-gatherers and among farmers. Gradually – in a sudden break or over a long period of time – the exchange will become less opportunistic and more structured. This is the beginning of a second stage contact that may have three different outcomes. The hunter-gatherer community becomes dependent, develops a symbiotic relationship with the farmers or dissociates itself from the newcomers and goes its own way. In this stage structural economic changes occur as well, when a decision is made to make contact. An example of this is the basic structure of the economy that has to change from an immediate return system to a delayed return system. The settlements will gradually become more permanent in character and the mobile lifestyle loses ground to a sedentary way of life. The advantages of a sedentary lifestyle are, despite its disadvantages, economically and socially great. An agrarian way of life can be extended, food resources are predictable and children may contribute their labour. Socially more mundane matters are involved, like more personal contact and sociability, but it also becomes possible to exercise control over people, gather possessions and have a more complex society. These are the seeds of a socially stratified society, a society fundamentally different from the free, unrestrained, egalitarian and mobile existence of the hunter-gatherers.

As a final consequence of the decision to make contact and to continue interaction, the hunter-gatherer way of life is doomed to disappear and from then on an agrarian economy will be the basis for life and economic development in prehistory.

References

Arts, N. 1989. Archaeology, Environment and Social Evolution of Later Band Societies in a Lowland Area. In: Bonsall, C. (ed.) *The Mesolithic in Europe*, 291–312. Edinburgh.

Bender, B. 1978. Gatherer-hunter to farmer: a social perspective. *World Archaeology* 10, 204–222.

—— 1981. Gatherer-hunter intensification. In: Sheridan, A. and Bailey, G. (eds.) *Economic archaeology*. British Archaeological Reports, Int. Ser. 96, 149–157. Oxford.

—— 1985. Prehistoric Developments in American Midcontinent and in Brittany, Northwest France. In: Price, T.D. and Brown, J.A. (eds.) *Prehistoric Hunter-Gatherers. The Emergence of Cultural Complexity*, 21–58. New York.

Bender, B. and Morris, B. 1988. Twinty jears of history, evolution and social change in gatherer-hunter studies. In: Ingold, T., Riches, D. and Woodburn, J. (eds.) *Hunter-gatherers I: History, evolution and social change*, 4–14. New York/Oxford.

Binford, L.R. 1978. *Nunamiut Ethnoarchaeology*. New York.

—— 1982. The Archaeology of Place. *Journal of Anthropological Archaeology* 1, 5–31.

—— 1990. Willow's Smoke and Dog's Tails: Hunter-Gatherer Settlement Systems and Archaeological Site Formation. *American Antiquity* 45, 4–20.

—— 1991. When the going gets tough, the tough get going: Nunamiut local groups, camping patterns and economic organisation. In: Gamble, C.S. and Boismier, W.A. (eds.) *Ethnoarchaeological Approaches to Mobile Campsites. Hunter-Gatherer and Pastoralist Case Studies*, 25–137. Ann Arbor.

Bohmers, A. and Wouters, A. 1956. Statistics and graphs in the study of flint assemblages III. A preliminary report on the statistical analysis of the Mesolithic in northwetern Europe. *Palaeohistoria* 5, 27–38.

Groenendijk, H. 1993. *Landschapontwikkeling en bewoning in het herinrichtingsgebied Oost-Groningen 8000 BC–1000 AD*. Ph.D. Thesis. Groningen.

Huiskes, B. 1988. Tietjerk-Lutse Geast I: A reconstruction of a Mesolithic site from an anthropological perspective. *Palaeohistoria* 30, 29–62.

Jochim, M.A. 1976. *Hunter-Gatherer Subsistence and Settlement: A Predictive Model*. New York.

Mathiassen, T. 1943. *Stenalderbopladser in Åmosen*. Nordiske Fortidsminder III.Bind 3.Hefte. Copenhagen.

—— 1948. *Studier over Vestjyllands oldtidsbebyggelse*. Nationalmuseets Skrifter, Arkæologisk-Historisk Række II. Copenhagen.

—— 1959. Nordvestsjællands oldtidsbebyggelse. Nationalmuseets Skrifter, Arkæologisk-Historisk Række VII. Copenhagen.

Newell, R.N. 1973. The Post-Glacial Adaptations of the Indigeneous Population of Northwest European Plain. In: Kozlowski, S. (ed.) *The Mesolithic in Europe*, 399–441. Warschaw.

—— 1980. Mesolithic Dwelling Structures: Fact and Fantacy. *Veröffentlichungen des Museum für Ur- und Frühgeschichte Potsdam* 14/15, 235–284.

Price, T.D. 1980. The Mesolithic of the Drents Plateau. *Berichten Rijksdienst voor het Oudheidkundig Bodemonderzoek Amersfoort* 30, 11–63.

—— 1981. Regional Approaches to Human Adaptation in the Mesolithic of the North European Plain. *Veröffentlichungen des Museum für Ur- und Frühgeschichte Potsdam* 14/15, 217–234.

—— 2000. *Europe's First Farmers*. Cambridge.

Price, T.D. and Brown, J.A. 1985. *Prehistoric Hunter-Gatherers. The Emergence of Cultural Complexity*. New York.

Price, T.D. and Gebauer, A.B. 1992. The Final Frontier: Foragers to farmers in Southern Scandinavia. In: Gebauer, A.B. and Price, T.D. (eds.) *Transitions to Agriculture in Prehistory*. Monographs in World Archaeology no. 4, 97–116. Madison.

Rowley-Conwy, P. 1983. Sedentary Hunters: the Ertebølle Example. In: Bailey, G.N. (ed.). *Hunter-Gatherer Economy. An European Perspective*, 111–126. Cambridge.

Verhart, L.B.M. 1995. An Early Mesolithic Hunting Camp at Posterholt, Municipallity of Amt Montfort (The Netherlands). *Mesolithic Miscellany* 16, 20–29.

—— 2000. *Times fade away. The neolithization of the southern Netherlands in an anthropological and geographical perspective* Archaeological Studies Leiden University 6. Leiden.

Wansleeben, M. and Verhart, L.B.M. 1990. Meuse Valley Project: the Transition from Mesolithic to Neolithic in the Dutch Meuse valley. In: Vermeersch, P.M. and Van Peer, P. (eds.) *Contributions to the Mesolithic in Europe*, 389–402. Leuven.

—— 1998. Geographical analysis of regional data. The use of site typology to explore the Dutch Neolithization process. *Internet Archaeology* 4.

Waterbolk, H.T. 1962. Hauptzüge der eisenzeitliche Besiedlung der nördliche Niederlande. *OFFA* 19, 9–46.

Zvelebil, M. 1986. *Hunters in transition. Mesolithic societies of temperate Eurasia and their transition to farming*. Cambridge.

—— 1996. What's in a name: the Mesolithic, the Neolithic and social change at the Mesolithic-Neolithic transition. In: Edmonds, M. and Richards, C. (eds.) *Understanding the Neolithic of North-West Europe*, 1–35. Glasgow.

Zvelebil, M. and Lillie, M. 2000. Transition to agriculture in eastern Europe. In: Price, T.D. (ed.) *Europe's First Farmers*, 57–92. Cambridge.

57. The deposits of raw materials and the quarry-sites during Mesolithic in the Trégor in Brittany

Estelle Yven

Flint is missing in the Armoricain massif. During the Middle and Recent Mesolithic, lithic local materials were used in order to make up for this lack.

With the help of a team, we prospected two regions in Brittany and pinpointed many deposits of stones fit for knapping. All were not exploited ; using varied criteria, certain places, described as "quarry-sites", were selected. The supply in lithic raw materials does not result from a random and opportunistic management.

A pattern of Mesolithic space organisation emerges within this, technical spaces are different between themselves, but, are also separate from the central residences at the spatial and functional levels.

The stones were used within restricted territories, which reveal different strategies of procurement of the lithic resources.

The method

For the past few years, we have studied how men exploited and managed the raw material sources in Mesolithic Brittany. This work is a result of a collaboration involving fifty other volunteer-prospectors and Pierre Gouletquer.

That researcher has developed a method of «archéologie extensive» (extensive archaeology) which consists in trying to analyse the functioning of not only one site but of all that make up a network. Thus he can delineate patterns which tell us how space was organised and managed (Gouletquer 1978:5; Gouletquer 1993:84 p). Our study was conducted after that method.

The work's original feature lies in a systematic search for the deposits of raw materials fit for knapping and also in checking which ones were used. Our next step is to try to understand how men organised their exploitation during the different periods of the Mesolithic.

Raw materials are stable by nature and we can approach the issue raised by the mobility of those hunters-gatherers (Féblot-Augustins 1999:193), by demarcating the raw material distribution areas and their movements. These distribution areas can be considered as territories of stones utilisation.

After studying the nature of the sites where the raw materials are found and how large they are, we will conduct a study as to their destination. The greater part of the information is collected through field-walking prospecting. Using this method, the lack of exhaustiveness is an inherent problem. All fields cannot be prospected, due the presence to houses, meadows, fallows and woods. Also, the thickness of the soil can be harmful to the site detection.

The picture of the material culture remains very partial and all the sites cannot be known. This method will never allow us to obtain an exhaustive and definitive inventory.

The collections which were picked assemble tools coming from mixed stratigraphic strata. There is no certainty as to the homogeneity of the sites. Typology and technology give some ideas about the chronological position of the gathered objects. They allow a careful distinction between the major sequences (Early Mesolithic, Middle Mesolithic and Recent Mesolithic) but the details within them cannot be distinguished.

Even so, field-walking enables us to collect some information within a very large geographic sector. Thus, the geographic questions can be approached, particularly those which concern the management of raw materials. Using our experience, we can say that collecting about a hundred objects is enough to obtain some significant proportions as to the representation of different materials.

Differences in occupation intensity within those units, those networks are known to have existed. Only a thorough study of poor areas could tell us more about it.

Field-walking is a good way of knowing the different types of sites favoured by Mesolithic men. Quite naturally we chose to work on these sectors but we also cross-checked our assumptions by studing areas which we thought would prove unsuccessful as such an action would comfort our assumptions. If our work consisted in discovering sites only, all we would have to do would be to study certain sorts areas known to have frequently hosted Mesolithic men. A thorough understanding of the occupation and management of a territory can only be reached through an exhaustive study.

The final results are less prestigious and more uncertain, more open to criticism. One sector might look poor because we were unable to find important sites. The numerous search operations conducted in the Morlaix and Callac areas allow us to state that if one of those areas lacked important sites, the reason is that proportionally, we had fewer opportunities to find occupation marks there. One sector considered as lacking in marks of occupation can only be called so in comparison with another sector previously studied in exactly the same conditions. There must be an agreement beforehand on what intensity is and what an important site is.

A site may be considered as important when a crew of four or five people find about a hundred or more objects in a field after one or two hours of sampling. We never forget that sometimes, we cannot find artefacts because of the thickness of the soil.

The map of the Morlaix region shows an intensive work of prospection that we think is good enough (Figure 57.1).

Geological reminder

When approaching the petrographic study of the Mesolithic industry of Brittany, it should be borne in mind that this region has no flint in its subsoil. Men had to use those pebbles which were carried along by marine streams and could be found on the shore. They result from the destruction of chalky areas which are thought to have existed near the shore. The southern most cretaceous outcrops are to be found at the bottom of the sea and spread from Guernsey to Ushant (Monnier 1982:100).

Men would use other siliceous materials to make up for the lack of flint. In the Massif Armoricain, macroscopic studies are enough to distinguish the various sorts of stones in use.

Sustained field walking operations allowed us to locate those deposits of raw materials fit for knapping.

The facies of rocks used during the Prehistoric periods display certain characteristics, whose origins are the results of few geological incidents. Those incidents have not been of interest to geologists, so they don't appear on geological charts. Their presence in the deposits is always justified by the geology of the area, but it is the research work of archaeologists to analyse the aptitudes of a stone for knapping (Pétrequin and Jeunesse 1995:24 ; Simonnet 1999:73).

Three types of stones will be studied in this work: microquartzite-calcedonic, "ultramylonite de Mikaël" and phtanite.

Microquartzite-calcedonic is the result of the metamorphism of a very fine grained sandstone confronted with important pressures that existed during landslides of granitic masses. It shows varied facies which can be studied according to colour and grain. Colours range from white to black with intermediate shades such as brown, pink and green. The stone itself may be translucid or may look like certain quartzites (Chauris and Garreau 1983: 140 pp).

Mylonites line the chief systems of faults. Ultramylonites can be cut up in bars and are characterised by tightly arranged grains (Chauris 1985:601). In the Morlaix region, ultramylonite displays an easily recognisable facies, black to dark green. The stone is made up of an amorphous paste and contains grains of quartz that have been partially digested.

M.P. Dabart, geologist at the university of Rennes (France), has agreed to examine certain archaeological samples. Her work allows us to say that the black stone found in the region of Callac *is* phtanite. This stone can only come from a geological formation called the "Briovérien à phtanites".

Three facies of phtanite have been noticed in various collections. The first one, which is temporarily known as the "Kerannou type" looks like flint and has the same knapping characteristics. Its colour ranges from black to dark grey with occasional small white veins. More seldom can we see blue, yellow or reddish small streaks. The samplings that look like flint are very black, translucid and consequently are fit for knapping according to the reference of J. Tixier (Inizan *et al.* 1995:21).

The second type of facies, called "Kerrunet 2", is not translucid, but its smooth appearance certainly allowed debitage conceived in advance. It ranges from dark grey to light grey, seldom black, and shows quartz veins that are deeper and bigger. That makes exploitation of part of the blocks impossible.

The last facies corresponds to the common phtanite used in the area for building walls, roads, etc. Local people call it « men gleiz » or « blue stone » and think it is the hardest stone in the area. In those blocks, quartz is ever present and takes the shape of thick and long veins. That facies is not fit for knapping and it is assumed that it was not systematically exploited in prehistoric times.

All the deposits evidenced by the geological map were systematically prospected in order to locate and to list the potentially used facies and to appraise the importance of the potential resources.

Reconnaissance and description of the deposits

In Brittany, the fieldwork has resulted in classifying the deposits into three kinds of sites : the deposits of raw materials fit for knapping but which, to date, remain unexploited whether they were known or not in the Mesolithic, explored deposits and exploited deposits also called "quarry-sites".

The quarry-sites

In Brittany, collections from some Mesolithic sites don't look like the usual collections. Sites are always situated on raw material deposits that contain facies fit for knapping.

Good quality crude blocks are fairly frequent. The collections of artefacts are characterised by a large number

The deposits of raw material and the quarry-sites during Mesolithic in the Trégor in Brittany

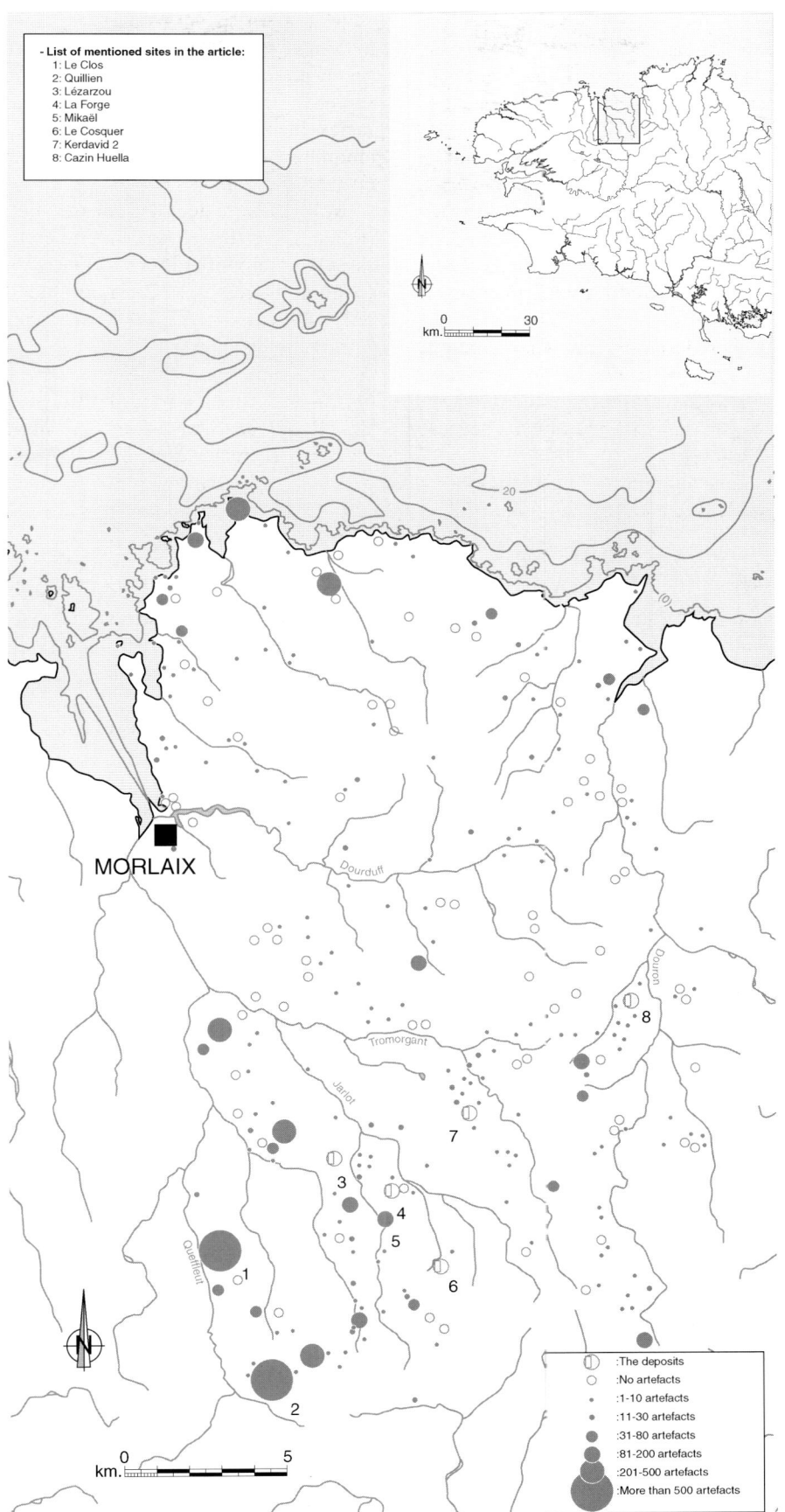

Figure 57.1 The Mesolithic occupation in the Morlaix region.

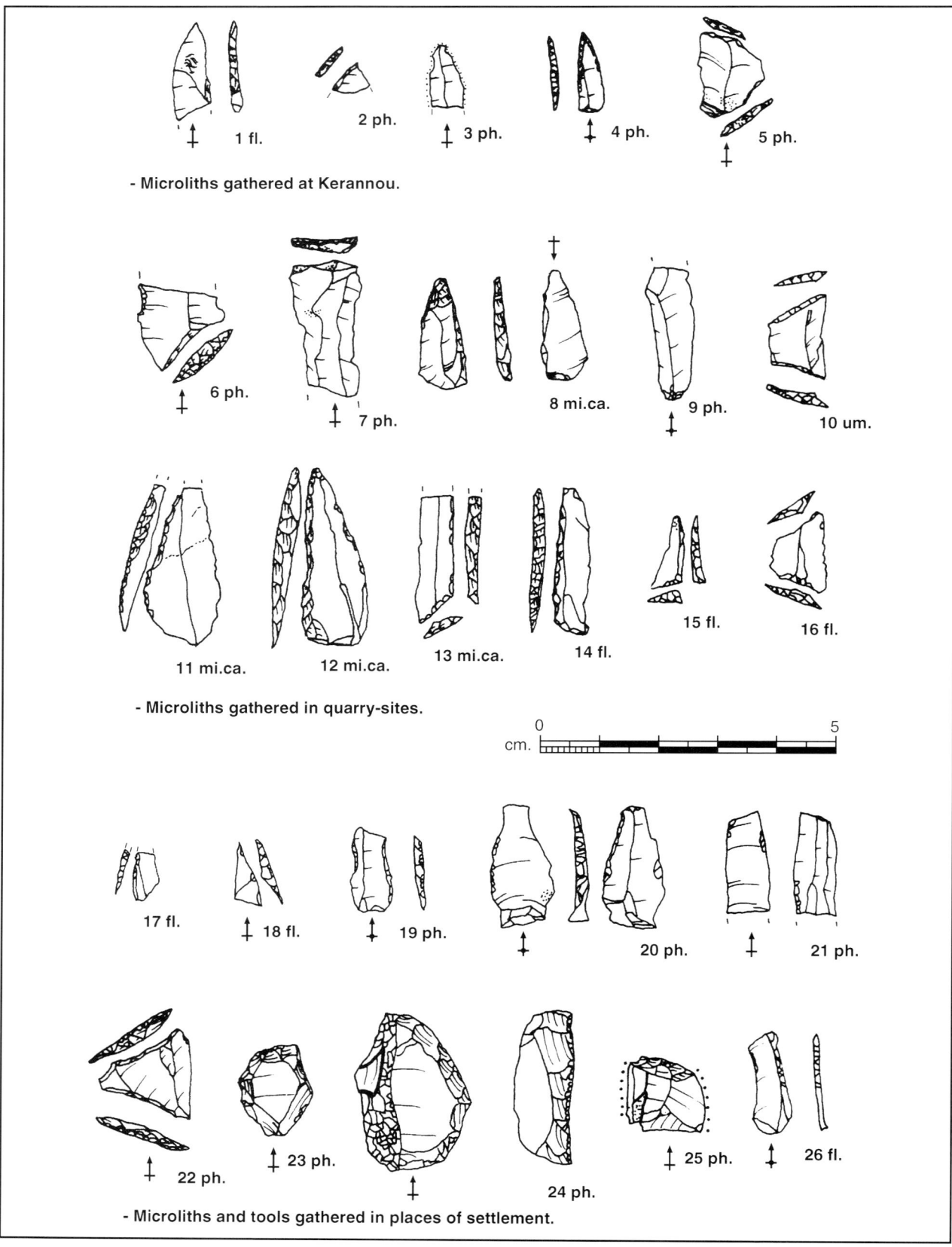

Figure 57.2 Microliths and tools gathered in Brittany: 1–5: site called Kerannou, 6–9: quarry-site called Kerhuellan, 10: quarry-site called Mikaël, 11–16: quarry-site called Le Clos (Gouletquar et al. 1996:20), 17–21: site called Keristen, 22: site called Pont-ar-Gwin, 24–26: site called Landujen ; fl: flint, mi.ca.: microquartzit-calcedon, ph.: phtanit, um.: ultramylonite de Mikaël. Drawing E. Yven.

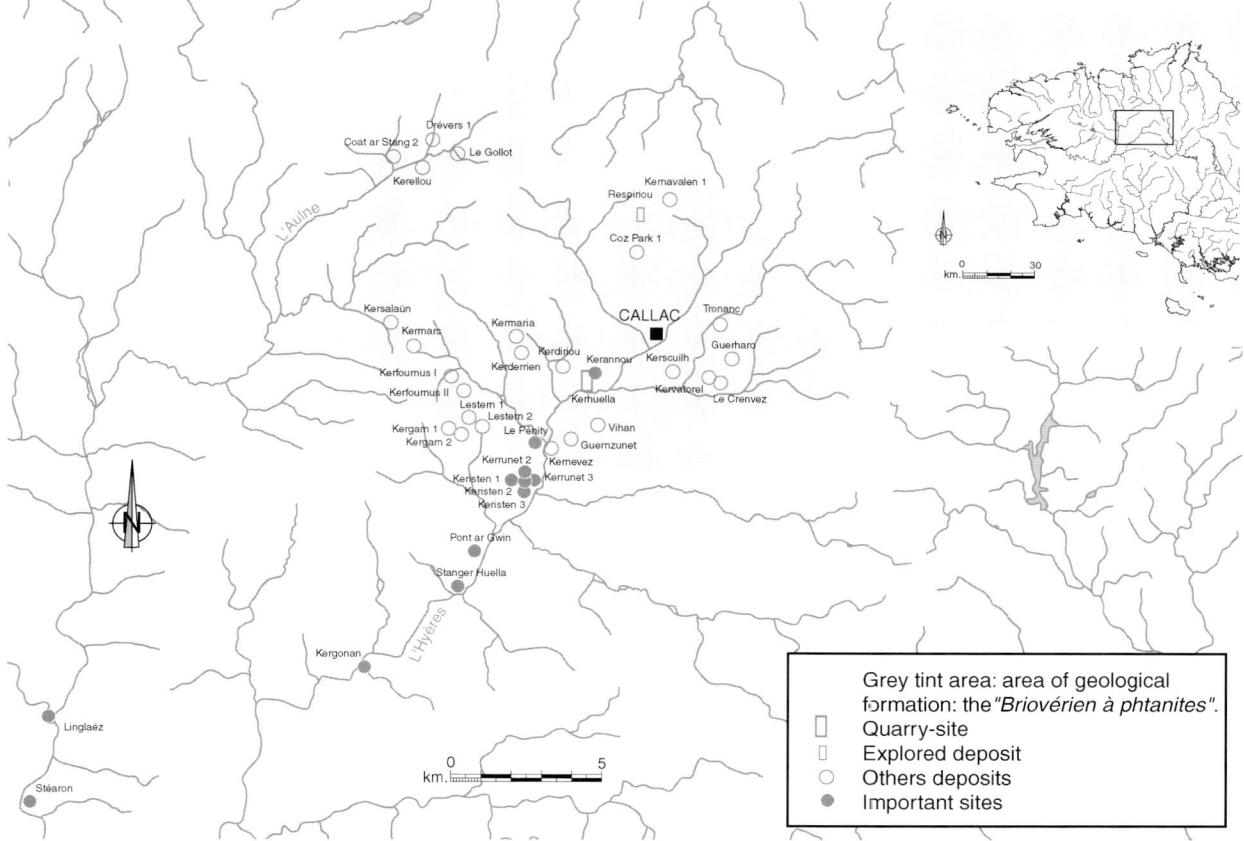

Figure 57.3 The Mesolithic occupation in the Callac region.

of blocks that were tested and left there after two or three removals, big flakes derived from the first phases of the "chaîne opératoire de débitage" and hammers in hard stones. The rate of pieces in local raw material is always high and is quite often over 80%. Conversely, those collections are characterised by a near total absence of elements coming from the full "débitage" of the cores, common tools and microliths. Traces of daily life are too few to regard those sites as places where people actually lived, nor can they be regarded as hunting resorts.

Those sites cannot be considered as real quarries as no sign of extraction has been attested today. However, they were supply places in lithic raw materials and they did function as real quarries. That is why we chose to emphasise that function by calling them "quarry-sites". Those were places where specialised and technical activities took place and they should not be taken for those central settlements where all the socio-economic activities were going on. The artefacts are characterised by their primary stage of manufacture.

In the Morlaix region, two quarry-sites have been located: le Clos (Plourin-lès-Morlaix, Finistère) and Mikaël (Plougonven, Finistère) (Figure 57.1).

The archaeological site of Le Clos is situated on a deposit of microquartzite-calcedonic. Men exploited this local stone in an intensive way and many objects were produced. The hammers which were the first products of the "chaîne opératoire de débitage" are numerous among the gathered artefacts. The site called « le Clos » was used as a source of supply during several periods. In the course of a planigraphy, different concentrations were located. They were characterised by the presence of various sorts of microliths : large pointed pieces characteristic of the Epipaleolithic, scalene triangles and backed bladelets, probably dating back to the middle period of the Mesolithic and also a few trapezes used during the recent period of the Mesolithic. (Gouletquer and Léopold 1994:47 p) (Figure 57.2).

At Mikaël, prospectors found a lot of objects. 75% of them were in an ultramylonite and some of them were large flakes (Gouletquer *et al.* 1996:19 pp). Only one trapeze was found along with a few common tools (Figure 57.2). Mikaël was an exploited deposit of ultramylonite Several studies showed that microquartzite-calcedonic was more in use during the Epipaleolithic and Middle Mesolithic while "ultramylonite de Mikaël" was more in use during the recent period of the Mesolithic.

In the Callac region, only one quarry-site has been located, Kerhuellan (Plusquellec, Côtes d'Armor). That archaeological site is located in the geological formation called "*Briovérien à phtanites*" (Figure 57.3).

Kerhuellan was a source of supply for a facies of phtanite. 85% of the objects came from that stone. They are characteristic of the description of quarry-sites.

Microliths are rare in this category of sites. At Kerhuellan we just have a point with a retouched base, characteristic of the Middle Mesolithic and also some bladelets with one arris (Figure 57.2).

Indirectly, a study of the sites around Kerhuellan provides some dating information.

A planigraphy was carried out on a site called Kerannou and located about fifty metres from Kerhuellan. The method consists in using an orthogonal grid of six metres to walk the fields. An intensive removal of objects then takes place which enables prospectors to have a much closer look at the soil. So that tiny pieces such as microliths can be picked up, as those are rather difficult to locate in the course of routine prospections. The study is in progress but we can already notice than several points going back to the Middle Mesolithic and a few trapezes were found using that method (Figure 57.2). This site was occupied on several occasions. It probably was a strategic position.

On other site, Keristen 2 (Carnoët, Côtes d'Armor), bladelets and microliths (an oblique flint point, a fragment of flint microlith and a backed bladelet in phtanite) testify to an occupation during the Middle Mesolithic. At Pont ar Guin (Carnoët, Côtes d'Armor), a trapeze knapped in phtanite demonstrates the utilisation of this material during the recent period of Mesolithic (Figure 57.2). Those sites are a proof that phtanite was used during the Middle and the Recent Mesolithic but there is no evidence that Kerhuellan was the only supply site. We will never be able to say that such deposit was used as a quarry-site for the whole area where phtanite was in use.

The explored deposits

In other deposits, some "débitage" products and hammers testify to the knowledge of other raw materials sources which have been explored but not exploited. There are not many objects in them, they were not often frequented. So they cannot be called "quarry-sites".

In the Morlaix region, three deposits of microquartzite-calcedonic belong to this category, Cazin Huella, Kerdavid 2 and Lézarzou, and two deposits of ultramylonite, la Forge and Cosquer. They are all situated in the parish of Plougonven (Finistère) (Figure 57.1).

Two places with « débitage » traces have been located on the Lézarzou site and a temporary occupation. We assume that the site was never exploited intensively because the raw material was not of good quality (Gouletquer *et al.* 1997:301). Also, the Cazin Huella deposit must have remained unexploited for the same reasons but the Kerdavid 2 deposit shows several bars of microquartzite-calcedonic fit for knapping and that look fairly homogeneous (Yven 1998:23). They show thick siliceous strata and they vary in colour. In the course of three sampling tests, three areas were found where those objects had been distributed on that site. In the first area, there were mainly large blocks and bars, most of which were untreated. In the second sector, there were tested samples and larger flakes. The third area contained a few objects characteristic of the final steps of the "chaîne opératoire de débitage ». The presence of bladelets and an oblique truncation point on that site testifies to the fact that the Kerdavid 2 deposit was known during one part of the Mesolithic. However, that site was not exploited either systematically or intensively. (Yven 1998:24).

On La Forge and Cosquer sites, some large flakes and hammers testify to an exploration, not an exploitation.

In the Callac region, the deposit of phtanite of Respiriou (Callac) is an explored site (Figure 57.3).

On the Respiriou and Kerhuellan sites, we find blocks of phtanite of the « Kerannou type » in the same proportions, along with tested blocks, large flakes and a few hardstone hammers. Yet, after three sampling tests only 72 artefacts were gathered on the first deposit, 63 of which were in phtanite, as opposed to 397 artefacts on the second one, 339 of which were in phtanite. The raw material, at Kerhuellan and Respiriou, has identical properties but prehistoric men had chosen just one quarry-site.

The unexplored deposits

According to M.P. Dabart, the phtanite deposits exist only in a geological formation, called the "*Briovérien à phtanites*". Three campaigns of field-walking were organised in that sector in order to pinpoint some potential exploited or unexploited deposits. As a result, we found many deposits such as Coz Park 1, Kernavalen 1, le Crenvez, Respiriou in the parish of Callac, Kerfournus I, Kerfournus II, Kergarn 1, Kergarn 2, Lestern 1, Lestern 2 in the parish of Carnoët, Guernzunet, Kernevez 1, Vihan in the parish of Duault, Coat ar Stang 2, Drévers 1, Kerellou, Le Gollot in the parish of Lohuec, Kersalaün, Kermarc in the parish of Plourac'h, Kerderrien, Kerdiriou, Kerhuellan, Kermaria in the parish of Plusquellec, Guerharo, Kerscuilh, Kervatorel and Tronanc in the parish of Saint-Servais. We chose to map all those places to check whether some were used more than others (Figure 57.3). Blocks of good quality phtanite were gathered on most of those sites but never in a big quantity. According to M.P. Dabart, that is a common feature characterising the deposits of that particular stone (Dabart 1997:50 pp). They were not exploited either because men did not know they were there or because they did not want to use them.

It is impossible to conduct a thorough study concerning the accessibility to those deposits that remained unexploited. Mesolithic populations lived in very dense primary forests and the conditions in which deposits could be pinpointed were completely different from those experienced by geologists and archaeologists at the end of the XXth century.

However it is useful to point out that all those sites that were explored and exploited are situated near rivers or streams, probably for easier location. P. Pétrequin has observed that in the primary forest of New-Guinea, men used to go up rivers testing pebbles with a hammer, till they found raw materials that would be fit for knapping (Pétrequin and Jeunesse 1995:25).

However, not all those deposits situated near streams were exploited, so, there must be other reasons than the mere accessibility to justify the choice of the sites that supplied in raw materials.

A selection of deposits

Such examples as Kerdavid 2 and Respiriou show that the quality of the raw materials was not the only reason for choosing one deposit rather than another. Some of them, that had blocks fit for knapping, were known in the Mesolithic but were not exploited. Technical and practical reasons alone cannot justify why given deposits of raw material were chosen. They do not constitute a determining factor of choice although, they may well have had some importance. Other factors such as the geographical situation and the position in the migration progression might also explain the choices.

In the Morlaix region, a field walking campaign was organised in a triangle-shaped area bordered by three brooks, the Tromorgant, the Jarlot and the Douron. No important Mesolithic site, no deposit exploited at prehistoric times could be discovered. However, the area that was prospected by P. Gouletquer and his group, between Queffleuth and Jarlot, revealed many sites and also two quarry-sites, the Clos and Mikaël (Figure 57.1). Yet, both areas offer the same pedological and geomorphological characteristics. (Yven 1998:32 p).

All the important sites discovered in the Callac region were located west of a stream called the Hyère. It is the same for Kerhuellan but Respiriou is situated further North, along an other stream (Figure 57.3).

The exploited deposits were selected. Each geographical sector would include a very restricted number of quarry-sites or, even most, a single place of supply in lithic raw materials. During the Mesolithic, inhabitants did not exploit all the resources that were available, nor did they make use of the potentialities offered by their environment. They did not get their supplies on all the smallest deposits available. They would operate to « *fréquents rejets d'utilisation systématique des possibles environnementaux*» (they did not systematically use all the possibilities of their environment) (Pétrequin 1991: 103).

That expression would hint at a farming population according to its author. Yet, it is in keeping with the Mesolithic territorial organisation described in this chapter.

The geographical distribution of artefacts

The utilisation territories of the stones

In Brittany, the Mesolithic populations did not live near the coasts all the time but we can assume they would migrate seasonally inland. Their migration followed certain routes along which certain rivers acted as borders (Gouletquer *et al.* 1996:15 p). According to A. Beeching, the number of sites linked with the migration orientation is important in structuring the landscape (Beeching 1989:334).

During their seasonal migrations, the Mesolithic populations that lived in Brittany would use various materials to make up for the absence of flint or to evade their dependence on coastal resources. So, some territories saw an intensive use of local stone like, for example, microquartzite-calcedonic in the Middle Mesolithic and "ultramylonite de Mikaël" in the Recent Mesolithic in the Morlaix area or the area where phtanite was used in the Callac sector.

The migration progression did not depend on whether those raw material deposits were there or not. They were not attractive enough to decide on the migration progression. On the other hand, the orientation of the migration could justify the use of a given deposit. The quality was just a secondary factor for their selection.

Sectors of occupation, sectors of exploration

In the Morlaix area, no important Mesolithic site was found East of the Jarlot brook despite numerous and intensive searches. We could assume that the Jarlot could have been a sort of limit between the sector of occupation (common territory) and the sector of exploration visited during occasional activities such as hunting expeditions. Small and various traces left in that sector testify to such an exploration (Figure 57.1). Those two sectors were parts of those territories where microquartzite-calcedonic and "ultramylonite de Mikaël" were used and they were probably occupied by the same groups.

In the Callac region, we find the same distinction between the sectors of occupation and the sectors of exploration. The second map shows only the more important sites and the different sorts of deposits but the whole area was prospected with the same intensity (Figure 57.3). As we have already mentioned before (cf. *supra*), all the important sites known to date were to be found in a valley and its west slopes: the Hyère valley. In spite of our investigations, we were unable to find a significant trace elsewhere. The common territory seems to be rather limited to a stream, the Hyère. As to the sector of exploration, we can think it lay in the vicinity of its valley. Our prospecting revealed a use of phtanite in this latter area but very few objects. There were about one to five artefacts per field and sometimes there was none.

The signification of those territories

During the Mesolithic, men only occupied some restricted areas of their territories, the sectors of occupation. The examples of the Morlaix and Callac regions enable us to think that those sectors were limited by streams whose functions were varied.

They were used as means of travelling but they also contained fish. It is thought that salmon fishing, which is still very popular in Central Brittany, was quite common during the Mesolithic. Unfortunately, bone traces are almost non-existent on archaeological sites.

Knapped stones followed their users and, to this day, testify to their presence. They show a very faint utilisation of microquartzite-calcedonic and "ultramylonite de Mikaël" in the Callac region with a ratio of 0 to 5%. In return, with only 2% of phtanite at the Clos and 1% at Mikaël, the latter material exists in the Morlaix region but in a very faint proportion.

The question is : do those ratios result from distribution and circulation logics or from the presence of different groups of people?

With the sites of Kergonan (Carhaix-Plouguer, Finistère), Linglaëz (Plouyé, Finistère) and Steraon (Cleden-Poher, Finistère), we can have some parts of the answer (Figure 57.3).

Kergonan corresponds to a very compact place and, probably, goes back to the Middle Mesolithic, which is obvious if we consider the shape of a fraction of microlith and a few bladelets with one arris. It is placed relatively far from the geological formation, the "*Briovérien à phtanites*" around twelve kilometres as the crow flies. Yet, the gathered collection includes 187 objects, 79% of which are in phtanite. The streams, especially the Hyère, did not carry those materials to the site. The sandy cover or wake that covers the phtanite blocks do not show any trace of erosion due to the action of water on those artefacts gathered at Kergonan. Those blocks cannot have a "secondary site" as their origin, like, for example, a fluvial deposit.

Only about ten kilometres away of Kergonan as the crow flies, the sites at Linglaëz and Steraon show a minor use of phtanite with respectively only 4% and 14% of that material among the gathered artefacts (Gouletquer *et al.* 1996:26). The proportions of phtanite increase significantly between those two sites. Stereon could well correspond to a stage beyond which the phtanite zone of influence began.

Those two categories of implantation might well belong to two different migrating routes. The first one being along the Hyère and the second one by the river, the Aulne. We are not sure those sites were contemporaneous but some traces that were discovered in the area corroborate the hypothesis of the existence of two routes, at least during the Middle and the Recent Mesolithic. In the first, we find some phtanite, in the second, more microquartzite-calcedonic and "ultramylonite de Mikaël".

The proportions show a clear cut difference between those two areas. It would appear that the management of raw materials was totally different depending on the sector. The proportions do not match the system of the different areas where the stones were distributed. These ones would be marked by a progressive drop of proportions of local stones depending on how far they were from the quarry-sites.

Such a difference in behaviour could testify to the existence of two neighbouring human groups, one travelling along the Hyère, and the other along the Aulne.

The distribution of the stones shows a regular process up to a certain stage. After that, there is a change in behaviour which could account for the existence of two groups not far from one another. These groups could have lived in limited and very restricted territories for strictly nomadic hunters-gatherers.

We will try and verify and define the nature of that hypothetical stage by studying the raw materials and typology through different forms of microliths and technology. They could well show that the borders of use of one raw material and technological borders are related. If that is the case, we will develop the idea of two different groups. Their differences would result, among other things, from the use of a certain type of local stone. Those stones would be considered as traditional for certain groups of people. From now on, they will be called usual materials.

The function of the other raw materials

Flint is present in every important Mesolithic site in the Callac region known to this day. A link with the coasts is ever present and needs to be defined and studied.

That region is about forty kilometres away from today's nearest coasts. One day's walk is enough to cover such distances. Mesolithic groups known to be nomads were able to walk those distances. Thus, flint may have been considered as one local material carried inland during seasonal migrations. Yet, flint occupies only a small proportion in the known collections. At Kergonan, 10% of artefacts are produced in this material, at Pont ar Guin, only 5%. Such small proportions tend to make us think that flint was exogenous to the Callac region for the group(s) who lived there. According to the study conducted on seven Mesolithic sites (Figure 57.3), Kerannou (Plusquellec), Kerhuellan, Keristen 1 (Carnoët), Keristen 2, Pont ar Guin and Stanger Huella, men did not select flint to produce bigger objects or tools. At Kerannou, for example, four of the five drawn microliths are in phtanite (Figure 57.2). Flint does not behave as an additional material. It is not used to make objects that cannot be produced by using phtanite. In the Callac region, the procurement and exploitation of flint never testify to an important technical investment. It cannot be regarded as a prestigious material exogenous to the territory. Also, flint does not correspond to the definition of a local material as its presence is not very important in the collections that were studied.

Within one or several ill-defined territories, flint was accepted as an usual material. It was used in the same situations as phtanite, it fulfilled the same functions.

Proportions change because of the distance of the sources. During the Middle and the Recent Mesolithic, in Western Brittany, local materials were not exploited instead of flint so as to do without it. They made it possible for men to get supplies in well defined areas. These areas could be equivalent to different places of occupation of a same territory or to territories of different groups.

We do not know exactly where flint came from, perhaps from the North, the South or the West coasts. Typological and technological studies should contribute to distinguish the places of supply. Perhaps were they selected too.

The important sites discovered in the Morlaix region are located about fifteen kilometres from the present coastline.

Flint holds an important place in all the constituted collections and the majority of microliths are produced from this material. So flint played an essential part in this sector despite the presence of microquartzite-calcedonic and of "ultramylonite de Mikaël".

Whereas the Callac groups did not necessarily maintain a straight link with the coasts and, perhaps, obtained flint in exchange systems, the Morlaix groups certainly came back cyclically near the seaside.

These different terms of the exploitation of flint testify to different strategies of procurement and of management of lithic resources. They could result from geographic problems linked with the distances from the coasts but also from distinct cultural traditions. Perhaps they will contribute to define the different Mesolithic groups of Brittany.

As far as we know, raw materials from distant origins did not exist in Brittany, at least during the Early and the Middle Mesolithic. We can just notice a circulation of local and usual materials between the various areas of distribution of the stones.

Conclusion

For the past few years, we have been trying to locate and make an inventory of as many potential and available lithic resources as we could, so as to get to know the local deposits of stones exploited during the Mesolithic. Next, we have been trying to determine why those people selected some deposits and how they organised the distribution and circulation of the raw materials from those sites. The whole of the "chaîne opératoire" related to the use of the raw materials is thus taken into account from the search for supply places to the use of the stones.

The results of our studies show that the supply in lithic raw materials did not ensue from a random and opportunistic management. Those men did not get their supplies on whichever small deposits they came across but they chose a restricted number of supply places or "quarry-sites". Those quarry-sites constituted structuring elements of their territories. Those territories were positioned along their migration routes and were limited to the sectors of occupation. They could testify to the existence of neighbouring human groups. Indeed, the study of the strategies of procurement of lithic resources reveals different modalities of management from one area to another. These modalities are limited by a hypothetical stage, at least for materials other than flint.

All the questions pertaining to the control of those limited and indispensable subsistence resources remain unanswered to this day.

A system of Mesolithic organisation stands out which is different from the ones noticed in the Palaeolithic and Neolithic. During the Early and Middle Palaeolithic, men used to live where the deposits worth exploiting existed (Monnier 1982:102 p; Monnier 1991:49 p). A recent inventory of lithic raw material sources of Sarladais and Gourdonnais verifies that major Palaeolithic sites were found exactly where the deposits of raw materials existed or very close to them (Turq et al. 1999:156). On the other hand, during the Recent Palaeolithic, the deposits were situated, at least, about ten kilometres away from the settlements (Demars 1982:155). In that period, men privileged tools made from bones and did not maintain the same relations of dependence with the lithic resources. During the Neolithic, men made a difference between " *l'outillage expédient(...) manufacturé sur des matériaux locaux et d'extraction aisée (...) des outillages qui témoignent d'investissements techniques importants* " (the expedient tools made from local materials and easy to quarry and the tools that implied important technical investments).These tools were always made from materials with a prestigious character, sometimes gathered a few hundred kilometres from the central settlements. They did not belong to the domestic "chaîne opératoire" (Binder and Perlès 1990:258 p).

In Brittany, such objects did not exist generally during the Mesolithic nor did the regular use of exotic materials.

During the Mesolithic, the places of settlement were set up near the raw materials supply sites. Yet, they were different at the spatial and functional levels. Lithic collections show that quarry-sites, places of settlement and hunting resorts were separated. A study of various Mesolithic sites in Western Brittany shows that most untreated blocks of raw materials were not carried straight from the supply site to main residences. The first technical gestures took place on the selected deposits which were used as quarries.

Men had invented a complex and structured way of managing their environment. Each element of their territory had a precise and specific function. They did not have much contact with distant regions and they were, on the whole, quite content with exploiting the resources they found on their restricted territory. At least that is the way things seemed to be in Brittany.

Acknowledgments

I want to thank all the people who gave their holiday time

to come and prospect the cornfields in Central Brittany and especially : I. Adelis, Y. Arnaud, D. Bernard, Y. Bougio, E. Castel, S. Colin, E. Condron, G. Corbin, F. Doucen, P. Forré, B. Ginet, J.M. Guldes, E. Ihuel, J.M. Lacot, A. le Bot, F. le Personnic, A. Leroy, P. Louédec, P. Léopold, J. Meslin, G. Monperus, Y. Pailler, A. Pello, J. Perry, P. Pottier, S. Quintel, A. Raoult, C. Stévenin, Y. Sparfel and R. Van Thielen. Without them the present research could not have been achieved. Philippe Forré has accepted to computerise certain data. I also want to thank Jean Abolivier for his important work of translation, Patrick Galliou for his help and Pierre Gouletquer for his advice.

References

Beeching, A. 1989. Sépultures, Territoire et Société dans le Chasséen méridional. L'exemple du bassin rhodanien. *Actes du Colloque International de Nemours*, 327–341.

Binder, D. and Perlès, C. 1990. Stratégies de gestion des outillages lithiques au Néolithique. *Paléo* 2, 257–283.

Chauris, L. 1985. Les mylonites: Pièges pour la tourmalisation deutérique. *Compte rendu de l'Académie des Sciences. Paris. T. 301, Série II*, 599–602. Paris.

Chauris, L. and Garreau, J. 1983. Le massif granitique de Plounéour-Ménez et les minéralisations associées. *Bulletin de la Société des Sciences Naturelles. Ouest-France. Nouvelle série 5*, 134–154.

Dabart, M.P. 1997. Les formations à cherts carbonatés (phtanites) de la chaîne cadomienne : genèse et signification géodynamique. Exemple du segment armoricain. *Documents du B.R.G.M. 267*. Orléans.

Demars, P.Y. 1982. L'utilisation du silex au Paléolithique supérieur: choix, approvisionnement, circulation. L'exemple du bassin de Brive. *Cahiers du Quaternaire, no.5*. Paris.

Féblot-Augustins, J. 1999. Raw material transport patterns and settlement systems in the European Lower and Middle Palaeolithic : continuity, change and variability. In: Roebroeks, W. and Gamble, C. (eds.) *The Middle Palaeolithic occupation of Europe*, 193–214. Leiden.

Gouletquer, P. 1978. Géographie humaine et archéologie en Basse Bretagne. *Norois* 97–98, 5–24.

—— 1993. Essais de synthèse. *Archéologie du paysage », Pen-ar-bed* 148–149, 83–92. Brest.

Gouletquer, P. and Léopold, P. 1994. Autopsie d'un site mésolithique – Le Clos (Plourin-lès-Morlaix, Finistère). *Revue archéologique de l'Ouest* 11, 31–51.

Gouletquer, P., Kayser, O., Le Goffic, M., Léopold, P., Marchand, G. and Moullec, J.M. 1996. Où sont passés les Mésolithiques côtiers bretons? Bilan 1985–1995 des prospections de surface dans le Finistère. *Revue archéologique de l'Ouest* 13, 5–30.

Gouletquer, P., Kayser, O., Le Goffic, M. and Marchand, G. 1997. Eléments pour une esquisse géographique du Mésolithique de la Bretagne occidentale. *Le Tardiglaciaire en Europe, Amiens 26–30 octobre 1994*, 293–307. Paris.

Inizan, M.L., Reduron, M., Roche, H. and Tixier, J. 1995. Technologie de la pierre taillée. Meudon.

Monnier, J.L. 1982. Le Paléolithique inférieur et moyen en Bretagne. Habitats et économie des matières premières. *Bulletin de l'Association française pour l'étude du Quaternaire*. 93–104.

—— 1991. Les matériaux lithiques du Paléolithique du Nord-Ouest de la France: choix et utilisation. *La Pierre Préhistorique – Actes du séminaire des 13 et 14 décembre 1990*. Laboratoire de Recherche des Musées de France, 45–52. Paris.

Pétrequin, P. 1991. Etude des terroirs : présentation. 116ième Congrès national des Sociétés savantes. Chambéry, 1991. *Préprotohistoire*, 103–106.

Pétrequin, P. and Jeunesse, C. 1995. *La hache de pierre : carrières vosgiennes et échanges de lames polies pendant le Néolithique*. Paris.

Turq, A., Antignac, G. and Roussel, P. 1999. Les silicifications coniaciennes du Sarladais et du Gourdonnais: inventaire et implications archéologiques. *Paléo* 11, *Décembre 1999*, 145–160.

Simonnet, R. 1999. De la Géologie à la Préhistoire: le silex des PréPyrénées, Résultats et Réflexions sur les perspectives et les limites de l'étude des matières premières lithiques. *Paléo* 11, *Décembre 1999*, 71–88.

Yven, E. 1998. *Variantes et constantes dans la gestion des ressources lithiques de l'Epipaléolithique au Mésolithique moyen en Basse Bretagne*. Mémoire de D.E.A, Université de Bretagne Occidentale Brest.

Session VII

Ritual and Symbolic Behaviour

58. Introduction

Lars Larsson

In comparison with the previous five conferences that have been held concerning the "Mesolithic in Europe" one can clearly see that the there was not great attention paid to "Ritual and Symbolic Behaviour".

This is probably due to the discipline's historical development. Mesolithic research was deeply influenced by the theoretical and methodological aims of "New archaeology" during the 1960's and 1970's (Binford and Binford 1968; Binford 1972). Its focus on social studies, the structures of societies and their clear links to the natural sciences were well in line with Mesolithic research in the Anglo-Saxon area of interest.

With the introduction of the post-processual or contextual archaeology in the mid 1980's research interests shifted towards the individual within any given social sphere together with the symbolic importance of material culture, lines of research that in some aspects stood in clear contrast to earlier work (Hodder 1982, 1986). Even if not all archaeologists have accepted these new theoretical concepts, they have never the less influenced the archaeological community.

Contextual archaeologists have mainly concerned themselves with the Neolithic period while "New archaeology" has continued to have a firm grip within Mesolithic research. After almost twenty years of existence, postpocessual archaeology is still controversial, but most researchers would agree that it has widened our understanding about relationships between human beings together with their mental and physical environments.

With the above in mind, a session devoted to ritual and symbolic behaviour was deemed appropriate. That this session also attracted the largest number of presentations must be taken as an indication of the heightened appreciation and interest that has taken place concerning these questions. This view is further confirmed by the variety of subjects covered by the papers presented, which were highly divers in content.

Burial research

The Mesolithic research of the 1960's and 1970's interpreted burials as social markers. The 1975 excavation of the Bøgebakken cemetery close to Vedbæk in eastern Denmark (Albrethsen and Brinch Petersen 1977) had a large impact within Mesolithic research despite the fact that Mesolithic cemeteries in other parts of Europe had been known since the 1930's (Pequart *et al.* 1937; Pequart and Pequart 1954; Gurina 1956; Roche 1972). The reason for this attention was probably due to the fact that a cemetery had now been found in southern Scandinavia, that is to say, within the "classical" region of Mesolithic research.

Interest in graves were to a very large extent influenced by the conceptions of mortuary practices developed within the theoretical framework of the New Archaeology, in which complex mortuary practices were assumed to reflect a complex social system (Saxe 1970; Binford 1971), an idea that has now been critically challenged (Parker Pearson 1999).

The excavation at Vedbæk, eastern Denmark, initiated a major project involving the habitation around a former lagoon, where several settlements and cemeteries were found. *Erik Brinch Petersen* and *Christopher Mejklejohn* presented some very interesting cremation graves from a complex of sand ridges that protected the lagoon from the open sea. Cremation has shown itself to be an important aspect of the mortuary practice, especially during an earlier period of the Late Mesolithic.

One of the best preserved sites to have been discovered in southern Scandinavia during recent years is Tågerup, located on the Swedish side of the Öresund Strait opposite Vedbæck, which contains abundant traces of both settlement activities and graves (Karsten and Knarrström 2001). *Torbjörn Ahlström* presented the skeletal material from the graves, which are dated to the Kongemose and Ertebølle Cultures. Based on results from isotope analyses he concludes that there was a clear division between inland and coastal settlement systems by about 7000 BP.

Graves and mortuary practices may also reveal a variety of social aspects and customs. *Marian Vanhaeren* and *Francesco d'Errico* have researched the rich grave goods deposited with interred children that date to the Late

Palaeolithic and Early Mesolithic from France and Italy. The grave goods consist of a large number of spool shaped beads made from shells. Practical experiments show that many hours of work have been invested into reshaping the shells. These beads are smaller than those made for adults, thus they have been intentionally shaped and sized for children. From this Vanhaeren and d'Ericco conclude that the intensity of work invested for the embellishment of these children is evidence for their conclusion that children were highly regarded in this society.

The cemetery at Zvejnieki in north-western Latvia is one of the largest of its kind in Europe. Radiocarbon dates show that its initial phase of its use begain in the seventh millennium B.C. and that it continued to be utilised into the Neolithic. The dating of specific graves has made it possible for *Guntis Gerhards, Gunita Zariņa* and *Ilga Zagorska* to recognise diachronic changes in the mortuary practice concerning both body position and the combination of grave goods. The number of grave goods is greater in children's graves than it is in adult graves. Almost half of the interred during the Mesolithic period were children, a situation that sets this cemetery apart from other cemeteries in Northern Europe.

The presentation by *Liv Nilsson* is based upon a new approach to mortuary archaeology, exploring the underlying structures of the conceptions of death in Mesolithic mortuary practices. The analysis is based on a French method, *Anthropologie de terrain*, a taphonomically based technique which uses knowledge concerning the biological processes of the decomposition of the human body after death in order to reconstruct mortuary practices in the past. She then takes a new look at the burials from Skateholm and Vedbæk. Instead of focusing on the type of social organisation these graves reflect, emphasises is placed on mortuary practices and ritual acts, thus introducing a complementary approach to the study of these burials, highlighting their ritual and religious content.

There is a need to complement our traditional categorisations with new ones. By doing so we can extract more information from them while developing methods of excavation, documentation and analysis, which will meet all of the demands from the theoretical frameworks we are using.

Aesthetics and Society

Mesolithic art has been a theme that has attracted researchers ever since Graham Clark made the Mesolithic carvings and engravings (in bone, antler and rock) well known to a wider archaeological audience (Clarke 1936). To link these aesthetical presentations to the society that produced them by encoding the reasons behind them has been the basis for several studies.

Thomas Terberger has worked on the many decorated artefacts from an area south of the Baltic. Decorated material from the younger and final Mesolithic, the Kongemose and Ertebølle periods, is limited in this area. He therefore concentrates on the older Mesolithic material. The area east of the Oder is characterised by single finds of richly ornamented *bâtons percés*. His study shows that decorated objects are a normal component on rich sites that show different phases of occupation and that stray finds probably originate from similar sites now destroyed.

If we compare categories of finds, e.g. bone mattocks, daggers or points and "bullroarers", the dominance of *bâtons percés* becomes apparent, together with their complexly of decoration. The decoration of objects might have had some special relevance in connection with their use. Finally, he sees no basis for, nor any necessity in trying to explain the distribution of these motifs as resulting from a formalised exchange system.

Bengt Nordqvist uses the structural principle of the conjunction of oppositions as his point of departure, in which totemism is only an expression, whose nomenclature is created by the names of animals and plants. The key to the understanding of this is the cross shaped adze from Stala and the rock painting at Tumlehed. The rock painting shows numerous pairs of oppositions, such as the contrast between culture and wild nature. The right and the left part of the rock painting are related to each another. The painting, with its two parts, is an expression of a common world, portrayed through the use of figures and symbols. The symbols depicted in the rock painting would seem to be placed in strategic positions with reference to one another. There is a social element, signifying a connection between a species of animal or plant and a group as defined by that society. The cross shaped adze from Stala is of interest because, once again, we see a mixture of figures and abstract symbols. Even if the differences or conjunction of opposites are made conspicuous through figures and symbols, they are all of them placed together on the same adze or rock painting, a condition which conveys the sense of a strong and/or united community.

In an attempt to approach religious aspects more closely, *Trond Klungseth Lødøen* deals with rock art, an archaeological category which has largely been underestimated within Mesolithic research. At the Vingen site in Western Norway, where more than 2000 rock carvings are located, archaeological surveys and excavations are exploring the relationship between rock art and other archaeological remains. What is of specific interest here is the presence of highly visible, circular depressions, interpreted as houses or some other kind of dwelling feature, together with a thick midden. Analyses of all the excavated and collected archaeological material clearly demonstrates that the main activity in this area took place during the Late Mesolithic. It is argued that the carvings at Vingen were produced by hunter-gatherers during periods when their ideology changed or shifted during the Late Mesolithic. This is a period when a change from a mobile to a more sedentary social structure occurred in Western Norway. The long term or permanent location of increasing numbers of people in a small area made incidental conflicts more likely, thus requiring some kind of mechanism for reducing this pressure on society. The rock art in Vingen might therefore reflect ritual activity as a result of a growing sedentary structure in the Late Mesolithic, and the different carvings might express collective discussions or negotiations among members of society.

Maria Hinnerson Berglund aims at another aspect of the cultural perspective that she defines as style, which is based on aesthetic norms of value. But in these circumstances style differs from typology, because style presupposes a form giving personality behind the object. Style always reflects an attitude. She bases her studies on conditions in prehistoric Greenland. The landscape and the changes of the season are manifest in human lives. The available raw material used in order to form the material culture was varied according to minerals and colours.

One way of capturing these aesthetics is based on a scheme which involves co-ordinating and interpreting a whole range of observations, and looking for underlying principles which reveal fundamental attitudes.

Rubbish or Symbols?

Contextual archaeologist's assume that almost all activities include both physical and metaphysical aspects. This means that the reason or intentions behind any kind of remains resulting from different kinds of activity might be multiple, that is to say, above and beyond ordinary every day, bread and butter concerns.

Helene Ahlbäck, using a combination of finds from Late Palaeolithic and Early Mesolithic sites, especially the bone and antler material, offers a reinterpretation of these localities. Previously they have been classified as ordinary settlements. Ahlbäck's study of the spatial and contextual relationship of different artefacts shows that some sites diverge or distinguish themselves from what is usually considered to be an ordinary settlement. By comparing these sites with ethnographic examples she finds certain similarities between them and the sacrificial sites of circumpolar peoples, as well as with those animal species that are usually involved in the shamanic thought systems of these peoples.

Keld Møller Hansen presents some new discoveries from the well known Danish bog site at Lundby Mose. At the edge of a kettle hole three assemblages consisting of elk bone were found. Similar finds have been made earlier at other sites. The bones show indisputable traces of human activity, extraction of marrow, cut marks, etc. Every assemblage represents a single incident. It seems that the finds clearly do not belong to any category that can be described as ordinary rubbish. Complete bones can be reconstructed from several of the split and broken pieces, which in turn can be show to have come from one single individual. The usual admixture of bones from other game species, so characteristic of settlement debris, is lacking. The remarkable breaking of the scapulae together with other signs of butchering and their subsequent deposition could be regarded as a type of ritual or hunting magic. These assemblages are considered to represent a number of singular hunting events that ended so far away from the settlement that it was not feasible to transport the pray back to the home site.

In exploring the relationship between nature and culture, *Bengt Nordqvist* asks if the refuse found on early Mesolithic sites in Western Sweden were treated in any special way. The question is, if a certain type of behaviour does play a signifigent role for these groups of hunters-gatherers, can these activities in turn be connected to different rituals?

Scientific Rituals

In contrast to most of the other Mesolithic research and researcher's, the final presentation by *Jimmy Strassburg* has a clear polemic undertone. He is very critical of his colleagues, whom he views as lacking theory and having a un-defined view of the Mesolithic. He considers that what is called the Mesolithic is still, to quite a considerable degree, an arbitrary Western construct and, as such, its boundaries and definitions hamper alternative analyses and perspectives. He considers that most presentations were delivered with none or an obscured socio-theoretical awareness. He is of the opinion that nothing much has happened in almost four decades of Mesolithic research as regards to basic theoretical responsibility and reference availability. He argues that the conference at Stockholm made it clear that the Mesolithic system of accepted concepts and interpretations are imposed on the particularities of prehistoric residues. Even the structuralist approach is denounced. These pairings are considered to be unabashedly painted with modernist colours, hues which transmit ideas of gender and kinship that belong to the Western ideals of the 1950's, or worse.

Strassburg contends that most of the Mesolithic archaeologist's who presented a paper at the conference retain and discussed normative relations in Mesolithic communities. Queer relations and non-normative relations of whatever kind that would disrupt the standard or excepted social divisions, were roughly removed in order not to disturb proper analysis and interpretation. Finally, he wants us to recognise that ritual is nothing but basic socio-cultural activity and that it ought to be acknowledged as such.

It should be possible to explore rich ideas and alternative avenues of research along different directions without recourse to stifling sarcasm and without having to sneer at or ridicule earlier results and/or older colleagues. Only then can one expect a meaningful exchange of ideas to occur. On the other hand, it is not uncommon that new ideas are often presented in an assertive and bellicose manner with a certain air of polemic and superiority in relation to earlier research. Apparently this is itself a type of ritual behaviour which, indeed, might well be a necessary perquisite in order for them to be noticed.

References

Albrethsen, S.E. and Brinch Petersen, E. 1977. Excavation of a Mesolithic cemetery at Vedbæk, Denmark. *Acta Archaeologica* 47, 1–28.

Binford, L.R. 1971. Mortuary Practices: their Study and their Potential. In: Brown, J.A. (ed.), Approaches to the Social Dimensions of Mortuary Practices. Memoirs of the Society for American Archaeology 25, 6–29.

—— 1972. *An Archaeological Perspective.* New York.

Binford, S.R. and Binford, L.R. (eds.). *New Perspectives in Archaeology.* Chicago.

Clarke, J.G.D. 1936. *The Mesolithic Settlement of Northern Europe. A Study of the Food-Gathering Peoples of Northern Europe during the Early Post-Glacial Period.* Cambridge.

Gurina, N. 1956. *Olneostrovski mogilnik.* Materialy i issledovaniya po arkheologgi SSSR 47. Moskva.

Hodder, I. 1982. *Symbols in Action.* Cambridge.

—— 1986. *Reading the Past. Current approaches to interpretation in archaeology.* Cambridge.

Karsten, P. and Knarrström, B. 2001. Tågerup fifteen hundred years of Mesolithic occupation in western Scania, Sweden. *European Journal of Archaeology* 4:2, 165–174.

Parker Pearson, M. 1999. *The Archaeology of Death and Burial.* Phoenix Hill.

Pequart, M. and Pequart, S-J. 1954 *Hoîdic. Deuxime station-nécropole du mésolithique cotier Armoricain.* Anvers.

Pequart, M., Pequart, S-J., Boule, M. and Vallois, H. 1937. *Téviec. Station-nécropole mésolithique du Morbihan.* Archives de l'Institut de Paléontologie Humaine 18. Paris.

Roche, J. 1972. *Le gisment mésolithique de Moita do Sebastião, Muge, Portugal.* I. Archéologie.

Saxe, A.A. 1970. *Social dimensions of mortuary practice.* Ann Arbor.

59. Art: Context and Tradition in the Paleolithic-Mesolithic Transition in Northern Europe

Helena Ahlbäck

This paper deals with the find contexts for Late Palaeolithic and Early Mesolithic portable art. The site analysed is mainly the Late Boreal/Early Atlantic site Sværdborg I situated on Southern Zealand, Denmark. Included for comparison are the Early Boreal Lundby I och II situated in the same area and the North German Stellmoor, with one Hamburg and one Ahrensburg level. The author argues that the classification of these sites as "settlements" have affected the interpretations of the material and thus our perception of the Older Stone Age in a desacralised manner. The sites should instead be read as purely ritual and sacrificial sites, where protective and purifying objects incised with symbols of shamanic guardian spirits have been used and thereafter left in place. It is also argued that the cosmological background to these acts show common features with a general circumpolar pattern as seen e.g. in Siberian and Saami ethnography. The possibility of an unbroken continuity of ideas from Palaeolithic times is suggested.

The Classification and Interpretation of Archaeological Material from the Palaeolithic–Mesolithic Transition

Portable art; meaning and find context

> Whirlpools in rivers on earth serve as entrances to the shamans' rivers. (Vasilevich 1963:57.)
>
> In concepts connected with the shamanistic river, the functions of the shamanistic tree are taken over by the islands where there live spirits – female shamans, the guardians and proprietesses of the clan's mythical road, the river. (Anisimov 1963:88).

This work is an attempt to understand Mesolithic portable art through looking at it in the light of its find context and its historical roots in the Palaeolithic era, with a particularistic approach. The criteria for the choice of sites for a detailed study were: 1.The sites should have some sort of dating and each represent a relevant time period, 2. They should possess preserved organics and 3. The material must be published in a fairly informative manner. The sites chosen were the North German *Stellmoor*, published in 1943 by Alfred Rust, containing one Hamburg and one Ahrensburg level; the Early Boreal *Lundby I and II*, and the Late Boreal/Early Atlantic *Sværdborg I*.

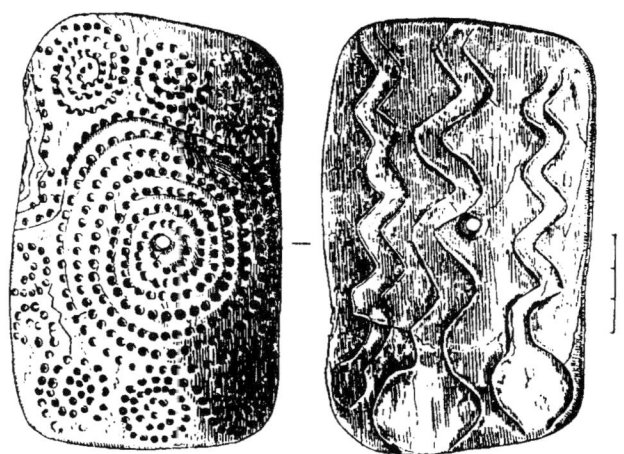

Figure 59.1 Ivory disc from the Siberian site Malta, dated to 14.750 BP. 14,1 X 8,5 cm. Abramova 1995 Fig. 108–4.

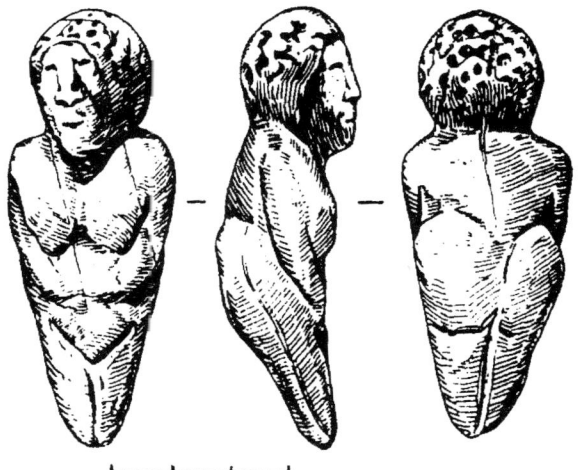

Figure 59.2 Ivory figurine from Malta, 14.750 BP. Height 8 cm. Abramova 1995 Fig. 105–5.

Working on the original archaeological sources, problematic for both linguistic and research historical reasons, I became increasingly puzzled by the material I met, by how it was classified in the publications and by the image of the Older Stone Age the interpreters painted.

I had learnt in the A-level lectures on the Mesolithic at Stockholm University that when Mesolithic "art objects" are not stray finds, they are connected with "settlement debris". They had sometimes been broken, and then "thrown away". This behaviour appeared utterly strange to me in the light of my previous studies in the history of religions. Why would an object of this kind be thrown away with the household garbage, especially if it was intact? It was of course by no means impossible, but gave an eccentric impression of the Mesolithic human. Perhaps this meant that it was the act of making the object that expressed meaning to the maker, rather than the object itself. Was the act of "throwing away" essential in some respect?

It was however this classification of the find context that I came to question during the study of the material, as we shall soon see.

The site Sværdborg I

This site is situated on Southern Zealand, Denmark, in an area where many Maglemose art objects are clustered. It was discovered in 1917 in the process of peat cutting in the extensive bog area Sværdborg Mose, and soon excavated by Friis-Johansen who published the material in 1919. Further excavations took place in 1923 under the direction of H.C. Broholm (Bille Henriksen 1976:9). Three areas from excavations in 1943–44 by C.J. Becker were published by Birgitte Bille Henriksen in 1976.

We find in the original publication from 1919 that the finds were immediately interpreted as a settlement, despite the fact that there were no trace of any huts or constructions. It is of course doubtable whether such traces would have been detected with the rough methods of excavation that were practiced at the time. Again according to Friis-Johansen 1919 the site had been situated on a humid meadow, stretching out as a tongue in a prehistoric lake connected with the Ancylus Lake. He states that the same was probably valid for other bog finds containing Maglemose art. Holmegaards Mose was a peninsula or small island in a prehistoric lake. Mullerup Mose has been a small island, where on the highest point the artifact carrying layer was found in peat deposited under dry conditions. Down along the sides of the island, they were found in "liver peat", formed under water. This is believed to indicate that the settlers have been throwing out "waste" in the water. Another island at Mullerup, excavated by Sarauw, was more problematic in the view of Friis-Johansen. Here, also the artifacts on top of the island were deposited in "liver peat".

The finds were large amounts of animal bones, deer antler and flint. There were also fragments of wooden twigs, charcoal particles, and here and there larger pieces of charcoal. The site appeared to cover an area of 140 metres north-south and 110 metres east-west. The main part of the animal bones and deer antler were found in the central part of this area.

A considerable amount of the animal bones and some of the flint was burnt. Concentrations of burnt flint and bones were intermeshed with a greyish substance mixed with charcoal. The excavator's impression was one of huge bonfires similar to the ones on the kitchen middens. The wood and charcoal was from pine, hazel, alder, birch and elm. Animal species were: roe deer (abundant, represented amongst others by 45 antlers and 28 left shoulderblades. Most are from fully grown animals), red deer (many antler pieces had been cut off as opposed to naturally thrown off; among the finds were the lower ends of 10 left and 8 right shoulderblades), elk (lower ends of 9 right and 8 left shoulderblades, and other), aurochs (both grown and young specimen), wild boar, fox, wild cat, dogs (at least three), wolf, bear, badger, otter, beaver, an animal in the publication classified as bull, water-vole, sea eagle, goosander, mute swan, duck (three different species), greylag goose, crane, cormorant, pike, heron, black-backed gull, squirrel, and tortoise.

The bird species indicate a summer "settlement". There were 8.300 flint "tools" and about 100.000 pieces of flint waste that were discarded after counting. About half of the "tools" were broken, some were worn, some were fresh and new. There were 776 "tools" of worked bone and antler.

Bille Henriksen (1976) interprets the area as a refuse area belonging to a settlement not yet found, situated slightly northwest of area A in the 1943–44 excavation. Here, microliths were broken in the flint concentration, (towards northwest), but intact in the bone concentration (towards southeast). This is interpreted (by her) as indicating an area of daily use, as opposed to a moist peripheral area (Bille Henriksen 1976:108).

Flint axes were evenly distributed in area A, sparse but oriented westwards in area B, and divided in two concentrations in area C, with core axes dominating over flake axes as one would expect (Bille Henriksen 1976:40, 57, 75). Area B yielded among many other finds a round butted axe of amphibiolite, a type mainly associated with Kongemose and Ertebølle cultures. There was also a tooth from a human individual aged 30–40. A small piece of rolled birch bark was the only wood material, according to Bille Henriksen due to bad preservation conditions. A so called "foreign element" is the water-worn metatarsus of a reindeer. The artifact category of facet-scraped metacarpus and metatarsus bones of aurochs, red deer and roe deer occur commonly in the "big sites" from the Maglemose culture. (A specimen from this site is depicted in Figure 59.3.)

They are not present in the Ertebølle culture. A parallell has been found in a grave in the Polish site Janislawice. It is (here) classified as a "bone smoother" (Bille

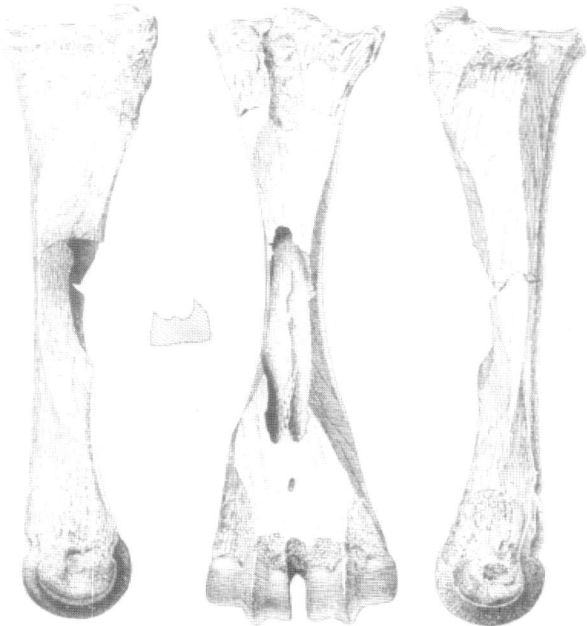

Figure 59.3 A facet-scraped metatarsus bone from aurochs. 27 cm. Svaerdborg I-1943, area B. Bille Henriksen 1976:68.

Figure 59.4 "Axe" from perforated deer antler. 20 cm. From Svaerdborg I-1917. Friis-Johansen 1919:165, fig. 35.

Henriksen 1976:95). Similar artifacts have been found in Neolithic contexts in Eastern Central Europe (Bille Henriksen 1976:106).

Area B yielded the entire skeleton of a wolf, with parts of the cranium and the claws missing. The ostheologist believes that the fur has been removed. (Bille Henriksen 1976:108). In the bone concentration in area A, parts of an otter has likewise been deposited after skinning (Ibid.).

According to the analysis by Kim Aaris-Sørensen of the 1943–44 material, the bones have been pollen dated to Early Atlantic times. The marrow has been removed from nearly all the bones already in prehistoric times. Figure 59.4 depicts an "axe" made from perforated deer antler from the 1917 excavation.

The "settlement" classification

I would like to stop here for a while and reflect on the material. If I was part of a hunting/gathering group, would I choose to camp on a humid meadow? If the site is Early Atlantic, in use at a time when the Litorina transgression had been going on for some time, it might even have been an island, to which the group would have had to ship over large game.

Presume then, that I would. If I was camping on an island in summer, would I build up a huge refuse area, covering almost the entire island, where I put bones in separate heaps, flint in others and lit bonfires in them? Without meaning anything in particular? Would I walk around in this refuse area and throw perfectly working, beautifully shaped stone axes around me until they were evenly distributed? My answer is no. These finds must be read in a different way.

Sacred space

Clive Gamble (Gamble *et al.* 1984:98) states that

> "Ethnographic studies of modern 'hunter-gatherers' have shown that there is a positive correlation between increase in latitude and dependence on meat. It would be surprising if Early Post-Glacial communities did not exploit the increasingly abundant plant resources of their environment, from the seed-bearing grasses of Southern Europe to the root plants, fruits and nuts of temperate Europe. The direct evidence, however, is sparse. Hazel nuts are common, sometimes in pits or even layers. Wild chestnuts were found on several north European sites, and yellow water lily at the Holmegaard site. The residue of several edible species were recovered at Starr Carr, including the latter, bog-bean and nettle."

This statement illustrates the view that all the finds at Mesolithic sites represent the food staples of base-camp-like settlements, a view rooted in processual positivism, materialism and obsession with food procurement. A certain variation in space is recognised, but only along an economic axis; some sites are "catch sites", others "butchery sites". It is my impression from the MESO 2000 conference in Stockholm that these research ideals are still the dominant ones in this particular field, for some reason. Some scholars appeared to cling to the idea that every archaeological interpretation rooted in the notion that religious conceptions influence human behaviour, is to be considered "New Age" and "not founded in the material". A "return to the data" was called for, and interpretational inspiration from anthropological and sociological writings was ridiculed.

As the last 15 years of theoretical development in archaeology has made clear, it is evident that the processual classification system of sites and artifacts is based on ethnography aswell, but not on reflective inquiries into the human mind and the complex and richly varied social workings of human societies, but on large scale neo-evolutionistic statistics. It projects the materialistic and economy oriented tunnel vision of industrial societies on prehistory.

In my eyes it is obvious that ethnographically studied peoples have a differentiated conception and use of space and the landscape. It might be so, that most of the Palaeolithic and Mesolithic base camps are never found, but what catches our eye archaeologically is places charged with religious significance, perhaps only visited for a short period of time every year, where ritual activities of e.g. sacrifice make artifacts accumulate in visible amounts. If this theory has any substance at all, the finds have to be read differently. In that case, the finds may tell us more about the world view and ritual life of Mesolithic humans, than about daily life at the base camp. What would the yellow water lily mean, if the site in question was a ritual ground? Why are certain animal species present, if not mainly for their content of proteines? What does the wolf mean? The otter? The swan?

Now, finally, a quotation from Mircea Eliade and his 1957 work "The Sacred and the Profane", where he elaborates on the differences between the secularised and the religious attitude towards time, space, nature and human existence.

> For religious man, space is not homogenous. He experiences interruptions, breaks in it; some parts of space are qualitatively different from others. […] For it is the break effected in space that allows the world to be constituted, because it reveals the fixed point, the central axis for all future orientation. […] …for nothing can begin, nothing can be done, without a previous orientation – and any orientation implies acquiring a fixed point. […] [This] is equivalent to the creation of the world. (Eliade 1987:20 p.)

The above quotation is Eliades interpretation of the meaning of an extra-sacred place, based on an extensive ethnographic material.

Lundby Mose

For a brief comparison, I would like to present the Early Boreal site Lundby, situated 2 km north of Sværdborg I. Lundby I has been situated on the western side of a small island in a prehistoric lake. The Lundby II material was found 70–80 m to the east, representing the eastern side of the island. At Lundby I, bones and barbed bone points

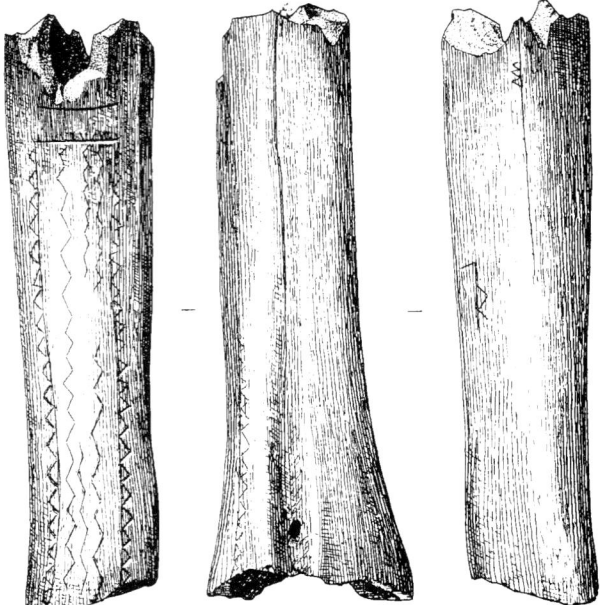

Figure 59.5 Ornamented metacarpus bone from aurochs, 16 cm, gathered from Lundby II. Bille Henriksen 1980:92, fig. 69.

were found to the west and south, and flint to the west and north.

Now – if I was a hunter living on this island, would I pile up bones and tools on what appears to have been the shore of the island? There was birch bark, shells from hazelnuts and a dog's excrement; almost 7.000 pieces of flint waste; bones from pike, swan, black stork, beaver, wolf, dog, bear, badger, otter, wild cat, polecat, wild boar, red deer, roe deer, elk and aurochs. Most common were wild boar. In general the bones came from young specimen. The ages of the animals indicate a time of visit between April and October. According to the ostheological analysis, the neonatal wild boar must have been killed in April or May. The 1–2 weeks old roe deer, the 13 months old roe deer, the 1½ to 2 months old wild boar and the 3–4 weeks old roe deer cluster in June–July. The 3 months old wild boar must have been killed in July–August. The about 6 months old badgers and some of the swans end up in August–September; and the 4 months old elk accompanied by the rest of the juvenile swans somewhere in September–October (Bille Henriksen 1980:132). There were also parts of a human cranium from an individual aged 40–60. The scraped metatarsus bones were present, here interpreted as spoons or containers. (See Figure 59.5.) A round butted axe was found (Bille-Henriksen 1980).

Stellmoor

With the Late Glacial site Stellmoor we are down in the Palaeolithic research tradition and thus liberated from Mesolithic materialism. The site was excavated in 1935 and published in 1943 by Alfred Rust.

The Hamburg level contained bones from snow grouse, little stint, swan, goose, wild duck, hare, lemming and reindeer. (The nearby Meiendorf had also wild horse.) Least number of individuals were for most species 1–2, but for reindeer 41. There were 190 flint "tools" of types listed on page 126. Furthermore 15 presumed wetstones of sandstone, 25 round sandstone pieces of unknown function, two hammerstones, one of quartzite and one of flint. Two sandstone discs measuring 30x30x2 cm and 33x22x3 cm. Some of these objects were incised. Worked reindeer antler and bone was abundant, types listed on p. 129. A number of reindeer shoulderblades were perforated by arrowshots.

The (later) Ahrensburgian level yielded pike, roach, frog, snow grouse, blackbacked gull, several other variants of gull, polar grebe, whooper swan, goose, wild duck, eagle, owl, lark, crow, musquash shrewmouse, wild horse, wild boar, wolf, red or polar fox, lynx, hare, beaver, elk, badger, lemming, reindeer and bison. The least number of individuals is for most species 1–5, but for reindeer 650. One of the finds is referred to as a "cult pole cranium". A 2 m long pole of pine wood was found, and close to the end pointing towards the center of the lake lay almost all the parts of a reindeer cranium. The teeth were quite worn indicating one of the oldest specimen of the site (Rust 1943:68). The presence of intact skeletons of reindeer containing large stones are interpreted as the remains of a sacrifice. There were two sacrificial reindeer in the Hamburgian level and 12 in the Ahrensburgian. Prominent in the Ahrensburgian level are the variety of differently shaped reindeer antler, grouping into a set of defined categories. Also about 1,000 bone "tools", amongst others 34 well preserved so called Lyngby axes, made from reindeer antler. The larger ones had "*Schlagmarken an den Nackenpartien*". The lengths varied between 23 and 57 cm. There were wooden tools, all made from pine wood. Arrows, 4 intact and over a hundred broken, 3 with inserted flint points. There were also the remains of two bows. The motifs of the incisions on some of the objects are mainly V-signs, zig-zag ribbons, angled lines and single lines. A 15 cm long elk rib is decorated in this manner. Concerning the sacrificial animals, only about two-year-old female specimen were sacrificed in both culture layers.

The publisher suggests an activity area used in winter (Rust 1943:197). He speculates on the meaning of the cult pole: "The landmark is raised at the foot of the hill in an inlet of a small lake". It might be meant to scare away evil spirits from the settlement, or a cult symbol. He interprets the entire site as a possible sacrificial site, quoting the ethnographer Nordenskiöld's discriptions from his late 19th century travels in North Siberia.

Nordenskiölds Russian host told him that the Samoyeds came there in pilgrimage from far away to their holy places, to make sacrifices and promises. The sacrificial site was situated on the highest point of the southwestern tip of Waigatsch Island and formed a natural mound. On

Figure 59.6 "*Sacrificial site at Falmai*". Rust 1943, fig. 31.

the site he found reindeer craniums, a large amount of other reindeer bones, bear bones, iron fragments, (axes, pieces of iron beakers, old knives, the metal parts of a broken harmonica, etcetera). On the eastern side of the mound were wooden sticks measuring from 15–20 cm up to 370 cm stuck down into the ground, carved to the shape of human faces representing deities. Close by were the remains of hearths where the sacrificial meals had been prepared (Rust 1943:218 p). (See Figure 59.6.)

Rust even put the spotlight on the problem of the difference in artistic language between the Siberian Samoyeds and the Ahrensburg material. He presents the very progressive thought that the abstract imagery of Ahrensburg leaves no space for individual expression, apart from the construction of the composition (Rust 1943:220). He rejects the idea of degeneration, and instead suggests the concentration and summary of complex concepts into one symbol (Ibid:221).

The striking likenesses in behaviour between Mesolithic populations and the Aboriginal tribes of the circumpolar area opens the possibility of an unbroken continuity of ideas over an enormously long time-span. Similar ideas have been presented by Josephine Flood in her work on Australian archaeology (Flood 1983). The settlers have been cut off from the mainland by the rising sea around 10.000 BP. Numerous myths discribe this event and ascribe it to the actions of both mythical people and real people with special gifts. Clive Gamble supports her ideas in *Timewalkers* (1995). New inter-disciplinary research on the prehistory of the Saami' was presented in a series for Swedish television in the spring of 2001 (2nd, 3rd and 4th of January, possible to watch at Statens Ljud- och Bildarkiv, Stockholm, Sweden). Björn Ambrosiani, head of the Excavations' Department at Riksantikvarieämbetet during the greater part of the period between 1959 and 1973, argued that, if the long period of isolation suggested by Lars Bäckman's genetic analysis of the Saami population is relevant, the Palaeolithic tradition economic and social matters of the clan. The assemblies were usually timed to coincide with the rituals. The clan shamans were also present at them. The anthropologists however do not believe this, but state that their background is instead that of a "patriarchal clan". Later they are discribed as "blood related" clans headed by "senior people". We also learn that "there was a strict division of labor", but in the next sentence that "If there were several women in the family, the younger ones also went hunting". The cosmogony was male oriented and incorporated active animals.

My main interest, for the possibilities of archaeological interpretation, is whether there is any correlation at all between the different parts of a cultural configuration (sexual division of labour, gender dynamics of the cosmology, gender dynamics of the ritual life, of social ideals and practices, kinship structures, etc). Peggy Reeves Sanday argues that there is a correlation between the agents in the cosmogony (the world creation mythology) and the perception of gender in social ideals and practices. (Sanday 1981). I do not believe her, since I do not trust ethnographers, nor later interpretations of their writings, enough to trust a large scale statistic analysis of their material. I also find that her own results prove her wrong. This is a pity, since if there was such a correlation, one could estimate one (unknown) part of the configuration on the basis of the archaeologically "known" parts, like one finds the answer to a mathematical equation through knowing the relationship between the known and unknown figures.

There are contexts where the parts appear to have been fairly analogous, as e.g. the Navajo (See Stone 1997:118 pp). Most social units however, are complex patchworks of contradictions, power play and active conflicts. (And, as Ian Hodder finds in his 1991 article, there is not only one form of power.) It is striking, though, how common it is in ethnographic interviews that informants refer to the "old days" when "things were different". They were almost always different in gender dynamics, and almost always in a less male dominated way; sometimes as recently as one generation back, or when old informants interviewed in the 1920's were little, which would put us somewhere in the 1850's. (See e.g. Popov 1966:104). Eleanor Leacock (1978) argues that many of these changes among hunting peoples were inferred by colonialism and the fur trade.

One possible interpretation of this phenomena is that things were more in balance in the 1800's, and that the contradictions in the 20th century sources are due to *recent change*. The Siberian Evenks were classified as patrilineal at the time of study. In the thought systems surrounding shamanism, however, traces of matrilineal religious concepts are visible (from which the opening quotation is taken). This can be interpreted along the above line of argument. The shamanic thought system would thus be an older layer in mythology, that is no longer analogous with the social dynamics at the time of study. This would be a neo-traditionalist approach, as opposed to the functionalist understanding of religion.

On the other hand, we see clearly in the archaeological material that things were not a static *status quo* for hunting peoples before 1800 either.

Concerning the gender configuration in shamanism, we find that in most tribes shamans are both male and female, sometimes with more males than females at the time of study, sometimes with more females. A few tribes have a gender exclusive pattern in one direction or the other (only males or only females). For some reason, the extremely few contexts where there is a theoretical decision that only males can shamanise get all the attention in synthetic literature and in the scolarly community in general.

Ritual among hunting peoples
If the archaeological material in this study is to be read as the result of one, simultaneous event, a communal hunting ritual might be the background to the more abundant remains of animal bones. Park (1938:62 pp) recorded such a ritual from the Californian Paviotso people.

The success of the undertaking was dependent on a shamanistic performance, which preceded the actual drive. The shaman directed the construction of a sagebrush-bark rope corral at a place he/she selected. That night a dance was held either at the camp established nearby or within the corral. Early in the morning the drive started. Each individual was considered the owner of what he or she killed. A woman or an older child who did not have the strength to kill an antelope touched or held some part of it until a man could offer assistance. During the ceremony, the antelope shaman went into trance and imitated the call of the antelope. The heads of all antelope killed were collected and roasted in communal pits and shared by all. When the skull had been cleaned of all flesh, the bones, together with the jaw-bone, were hidden in a clump of sage-brush. This was believed to assure the success of future drives.

The material might also be the result of long term accumulation of sacrifices in connection with shamanistic rituals. The shamanistic performances of the Evenk tribe are well documented. The shaman's tent of the Evenks was loaded with symbolic material culture, forming a miniature model of their cosmological universe (Anisimov 1963:84–174). In the center of the tent was the shamanistic world tree, the *turu* larch, on which the shaman climbed on his/her journey to the upper world. It was also percieved as a mythical clan tree to which the fate and life of the clan and the clansmen were connected. This idea was connected with the idea of the half-animal, half-human ancestor-spirits of the shaman. The ancestor-spirits of the shaman were imagined as living at the base of the clan tree associated with its roots, the beginning. These spirits were conceived as feminine spirits and were reflected in the form of the mother-mistress of the clan tree. The circle of ground occupied by the tent symbolised the middle world, or in other cases was interpreted as *the shaman's island in the middle of the mythical shamanistic clan-river that connected the upper, middle and lower worlds. Before the entrance to the tent were two huge pike figures, each with a square opening in the mid portion symbolising the entrance to the upper world.* Figures of birds (owl, loon, goldeneye, mallard goose) burbot and elk cow guarded the clan's road to the lower world. There was also a large figure of the mythical shamanistic elk, flanked by images of Siberian stags. The pole was thought of as the road to the upper deities. Here were also images of the sun and the moon. In the *anang* performance (to conduct the souls of the dead to the world of the dead) and in memorial feasts (the feeding of the souls of the ancestors) blood sacrifices were brought to the beings of the lower world and, accordingly, the head of a sacrificed reindeer was placed on a pole among the spirit images of the *onang* (western gallery of the tent). The clan fire represented the unity and communal beginnings of the clan. It was regarded as the dwelling place for the mistress of the clan hearth, who was also the spirit of the tent and the camp, the provider for the clan and the guardian of the souls of the dead. To this concept was linked an image of birth as a totemistic act of reincarnation. The first shamans, the progenitors of later shamans, were thought to have been women, mythical old women, the guardians of the road to the world of the dead. The drawings on the drum were executed by women. Cosmological conceptions of mother-animals were essential.

The shaman climbed up the *turu* to the supreme god. Back in the tent he began to divine by means of his rattle and reindeer scapula. He took the shoulder blades of sacrificed reindeer, laid hot coals on them, and predicted the future lead by the cracks formed. *At the end of the performance the shaman's tent was abandoned. The reindeer-skin covering was taken from it, but everything else remained in place.*

Interpretational Conclusions

In the light of the history of religions, then, what has taken place on the sites chosen for this study?

All the discribed locales can be read as extra-sacred spots where shamanistic rituals including sacrifice have been conducted. The prescence of shamanism in pre-history can of course never be proved in a positivist sense. Lewis-Williams (1997) simply argues for its presence in the Magdalénien on the basis of its widespreadness among hunter-gatherers. The surrounding thought system has probably been fairly constant, and perhaps similar to the one of the Siberian Evenk tribe. The choice of place transforms in the Palaeolithic-Mesolithic transition from the sacred hill near a lake (Late Palaeolithic Stellmoor) to an actual island or peninsula (Mesolithic Lundby I and Sværdborg I). Interestingly, the shamanic thought system of the Siberian Evenk tribe shows traces of two parallel concepts of the connecting path between the upper, middle and lower worlds; one land-oriented centered around the shamanistic tree (a larch) on which the shamans climb (a possible background to the frequent "fishbone" patterns in Mesolithic art), and one water oriented focussing on a sacred island in a connecting river where there lived female shaman guardian spirits. The clustering of Maglemose "art objects" to prehistoric lakes on Southern Zealand is interesting. Has this been a ritual center, later transgressed by the Litorina Sea?

What does the material mean? The deposited flint might have been believed to scare away hostile attacks on the clan territory, similar to the perception and use of metal in Siberia. Stray finds of incised objects around lakes may have been placed there by the clan shaman/shamaness to protect the clan against spirits harmful to humans. Concerning the holes in the pierced staffs, a symbolism of passage to other parts of cosmos, and/or tools of a shaman sucking out the disease spirit are two suggestions. The presence of certain animal species can be read as the remains of sacrificial acts; the more abundant species resulting from a communal drive hunt followed by a ritual sacrificial meal, and other species perhaps only indicating that the assignment of a new shaman has taken place here as well as the manufacture of his/her costume and paraphernalia, where animals considered spirit helpers were used as materials. The animal species of course shift in the Palaeolithic-Mesolithic transition due to the change in climate and landscape. The deer appears to have taken over the previous cosmological rôle of the reindeer. It is possibe that some tribes have followed their traditional animal spirit helpers on their migration to colder latitudes.

The purpose of the rituals has been the well being and renewal of the universe and the clan, a will to express gratitude to sky deities and the curing of a specific person. The "cult pole cranium" from the Ahrensburg level of Stellmoor is probably the remains of acts similar to the *anang* performance among the Evenks (to conduct the souls of the dead to the world of the dead) and their memorial feasts (the feeding of the souls of the ancestors), where blood sacrifices were brought to the beings of the lower world and, accordingly, the head of a sacrificed reindeer was placed on a pole among the spirit images of the *onang* (western gallery of the shamanic tent). The incised bone objects found on the sites have been shaman's paraphernalia, used for curing and marking his/her identity and importance for the well being of the clan, deposited here either as a sacrifice or after the death of the shaman. The incisions are motifs connected with the shamanic thought system, made to help the shamanic journeys and activities in the mental space.

The most common objection to this paper is that one cannot separate religion spatially from everyday life at the settlement. This objection is based on the misconception that this is what I am arguing – which it is not. The traditional separation of archaeological material in categories like "settlement debris" and "artifacts with magical function" is not useful at all. What I have found in the original ethnographic sources is however, that some places had a special meaning to the hunting peoples of the northern hemisphere. They were referred to as "sacred places" and charged with an even stronger supernatural power than the world in general. They were approached and acted upon carefully and according to stricter regulations than usual. What I have *not* found in the sources, though, is people living on a mountain of bones, antler, new and worn hunting tools and axes, on the shore on which they have chosen to camp. Hunters do not leave any trace, which is part of their problem in conflicts with colonial administration. Therefore, I choose to interpret Sværdborg, Lundby and Stellmoor as sacred sacrificial sites of a type frequently recorded in the ethnography of Saami and Siberian tribes. A holm is especially suitable for this purpose due to its natural spatial seclusion. The archaeological remains are the result of active and creative choices by prehistoric humans, inspired by their worldview and cosmology, and not the only possible response to an environmental situation or a hunting strategy.

Seen in the light of the processual worldview, focussing traditionally on strictly physical aspects of food procurement, a sacrificial site can perhaps be called a "settlement". People have been here, probably several times, and they have probably been eating. It is possible to count the resulting intake of calories and proteines. But one would miss what is really relevant, namely why people have been there, why they have been eating/sacrificing exactly these animal species at this particular time of year, what the carvings on the polished bones they left there mean, and what really happened here. It is my conviction that the answers to these questions are not the ones traditionally presented by processual research. The material achieves a different meaning than the material from a supposed base camp, also if the base camp was only a place to where the group returned to continue with other types of rituals around the hearth of the tent. Ceremonial tents are sometimes erected on the place where a communal ritual is held, but this does not make the site a settlement in the eyes of the performers.

Summary

The main problem in this paper has been the research traditional classification of large (Late Palaeolithic) Hamburg, Ahrensburg and (Mesolithic) Maglemose sites as "settlements". Three locales were chosen for a detailed study: the Late Palaeolithic, North German Stellmoor with one Hamburg and one Ahrensburg level, the Early Mesolithic Lundby I and II on Southern Zealand, Denmark, and the Late Mesolithic/Early Atlantic Sværdborg I. Since these locales are also find contexts for art objects, this classification also affects our reading and interpretation of art in the Palaeolithic-Mesolithic transition. The author has found that the archaeological material as it is presented in the original publications does not really support this classification. The counterarguments are: 1. There are no huts or constructions, 2. The Mesolithic sites show a common pattern of being situated on islands or peninsulas in lakes, Sværdborg I on a "humid meadow". These places do not seem like convenient choices for a camp. 3. The size of the sites, the distribution patterns and general character of the material (worked, unworked and incised bone and antler where the marrow has been removed in prehistoric times, concentrations of abundant flint and flint debris in parts fire damaged to some extent separated from the bone material, charcoal in concentrations giving the impression of "huge bonfires similar to the ones on the kitchen middens") does not apply to what one would expect from a gather-hunter-camp. The animal species in the bone material, however, as well as the material itself, does connect to what is known about the sacrificial sites of circumpolar peoples and the animal species usually involved in the shamanic thought systems of these peoples. The sites are therefore, in the light of a deep particularistic enquiry into the ethnography of hunting peoples, interpreted as arenas for communal shamanistic performances involving the curing of a sick person and a sacrificial ritual. The incised objects, and probably also many insignificant artifacts usually classified as "tools", were conciously placed there for protection, or were deposited after being used for curing and purification. The pattern of action seems strikingly similar all through the Palaeolithic-Mesolithic transition – apart from the fact that the animal species of course change with the flora and fauna of the changing environment. Many of the animal remains from Lundby II renders associations to the making of a shaman's costume.

References

Abramova, Z.A. 1995. *L'art paléolithique d'Europe Orientale et de Sibérie.* Grenoble.
Anisimov, A.F. 1963. The Shaman's tent. In: Michael, H. (ed.) *Studies in Siberian Shamanism,* 84–123. Arctic Institute of North America. Anthropology of the North: Translations from Russian Sources/No. 4. University of Toronto Press.
Bille Henriksen, B. 1976. *Sværdborg I. Excavations 1943–44. A Settlement of the Maglemose Culture.* Arkæologiske Studier Volume III. Copenhagen.
—— 1980 *Lundby-holmen. Pladser av Maglemose-type i Sydsjælland.* Nordiske Fortidsminder Serie B – in quarto, Bind 6. Det Kongelige Nordiske Oldskriftselskab, København.
Eliade, M. [1957] 1987. *The Sacred and the Profane. The Nature of Religion. The Significance of Religious Myth, Symbolism, and Ritual Within Life and Culture.* Orlando, Florida.
Flood, J. 1983. *Archaeology of the Dreamtime.* Sydney.
Friis-Johansen, K. 1919. En Boplads fra den ældste Stenalder i Sværdborg Mose. *Aarbøger for Nordisk Oldkyndighed og Historie.* III Række, 9 Bind, 106–235. Det Kongelige Nordiske Oldskrift-Selskab. Copenhagen.
Gamble, C., Champion, T., Shennan, S. and Whittle, A. 1984. *Prehistoric Europe.* London.
Gamble, C. 1995. *Timewalkers.* Middlesex.
Guss, D.M. 1993. Yekuana myths of the origins of artifacts. In: Anderson, R.L. and Field, K.L. (eds) *Art in Small Scale Societies. Contemporary Readings,* 150–157. New Jersey.

Hodder, I. 1991. Gender representation and social reality. In: Walde, D. and Willows, N. (eds) *The Archaeology of Gender. Proceedimgs of the Twenty-Second Annual Chacmool Conference,* 11–16. Calgary.

Holmberg, U. 1915. *Lapparnas religion.* Uppsala Multiethnic Papers 10. Uppsala.

Katz, R. 1976. Education for Trancendence: !Kia-Healing with the Kalahari !Kung. In: Lee, R. and De Vore, I. (eds) *Kalahari Hunter-Gatherers. Studies of the !Kung San and Their Neighbors,* 281–301. Cambridge, Massachusetts, and London.

Kroeber, A. 1925. *Handbook of the Indians of California.* Bureau of American Ethnology, Bulletin.

Leacock, E. 1978. Women's Status in Egalitarian Society: Implications for Social Evolution. *Current Anthropology* 19, 247–245.

Lee, R.B. 1993. *The !Kung San: Men, Women and Work in a Foraging Society.* Cambridge.

Lewis-Williams, J.D. 1997. Harnessing the Brain: Vision and Shamanism in Upper Palaeolithic Western Europe. In: Conkey, M.W., Soffer, O., Stratmann, D. and Jablonski, N.G. (eds) *Beyond Art: Pleistocene Image and Symbol,* 321–339. San Francisco.

Ohnuki-Tierney, E. 1973. The Shamanism of the Ainu of the Northwest Coast of Southern Sakhalin. *Ethnology* 12 (1), 15–29. Pittsburgh.

Park, W.Z. 1938. *Shamanism in Western North America. A Study in Cultural Relationships.* Northwestern University Studies in the Social Sciences No. 2. Nortwestern University, Evanston and Chicago.

Popov, A.A. 1966. *The Nganasan. The Material Culture of the Tavgi Samoyeds.* Indiana University, Bloomington.

Popov, A.A. and Dolgikh, 1964. The Nganasan. In: Levin, M.G. and Potapov, L.P. (eds) *The Peoples of Siberia.* The University of Chicago Press, Chicago.

Prokofyeva, Y.D. 1963. The Costume of an Enets Shaman. In: Michael, H.N. (ed.) *Studies in Siberian Shamanism,* 124–156. Arctic Institute of North America. Anthropology of the North: Translations from Russian Sources/No. 4. University of Toronto Press.

Rust, A. 1943. *Die Alt- und Mittersteinzeitlicher funde von Stellmoor.* Neumünster in Holstein.

Sanday, P.R. 1981. *Female Power and Male Dominance. On the Origins of Sexual Irequality.* Cambridge.

Stone, L. 1997. *Kinship and Gender. An Introduction.* Washington State University, Washington.

Vasilevich, G.M. 1963. Early concepts about the universe among the Evenks, In: Michael, H.N. (ed.) *Studies in Siberian Shamanism,* 124–156. Arctic Institute of North America. Anthropology of the North: Translations from Russian Sources/No. 4. University of Toronto Press.

Vasilevich, G.M. and Smolyak, 1964. The Evenks. In: Levin, M.G. and Potapov, L.P. (eds) *The Peoples of Siberia.* Chicago.

60. Mesolithic Human Skeletal Remains from Tågerup, Scania, Sweden

Torbjörn Ahlström

In 1998 six Mesolithic graves – one double grave and five single graves – were excavated at the site Tågerup, Scania, Sweden. Based on associated artifacts and radiocarbon datings of the charcoal in the fillings of the graves, it was concluded that three of the graves – containing four adult individuals – belonged to the early Kongemose culture, ca. 7400 BP. The remaining three graves – one adult and two subadults – were dated to the Ertebølle culture ca. 5800 BP. Disarticulated human skeletal remains were found in the waste deposits as well. These finds are dated to both the Kongemose and Ertebølle occupational phases. The five adults from Tågerup probably represent the remains of two males and three females. Apart from the two subadult individuals – one belonging to the age category infans I, the other to infans II – it is concluded that the five adult individuals belongs to the mature age category (i.e. 40–59 years). With the exception of one case of periapical periodontitis and a probable case of porotic hyperostosis (grave 1), there is no other paleopathological condition to report. No caries could be detected on the exposed teeth. At least two diametrically opposed models has been presented regarding the foraging behaviour of the Kongemose culture. One model assumes one population that was mobile and foraged from both terrestrial and marine environments.

The other model assumes that there exist two populations, one population living by the sea and foraging from a marine environment, the other population living in the hinterland and foraging from a terrestrial environment. Although Tågerup is situated close to the former shore and hence one would expect to find a marine signature, the two stable carbon isotope measurements are low, indicating a terrestrial subsistence base. The measurements from Tågerup do not support the model that there were two separate populations. The present database concerning stable carbon isotope measurements suggests that a marked shift in foraging behaviour, from terrestrial to maritime, occured at 7.000 BP.

Introduction

In retrospect, the profound environmental changes that comes along with the Postglacial period of southern Scandinavia, appear radical and might very well supply archaeology and anthropology with ultimate causes as to the variation with regard to foraging strategies, technology, settlement patterns and social systems etc. The evolution of diverse ecosystems in south Scandinavia – from the relatively open Preboreal forests to the dense canopies of the Atlantic forest – are encapsulated within the Mesolithic period (10.000 – 5.200 BP). Whatever transpired in the region during the Mesolithic period, south Scandinavian populations pursued a trajectory towards an increasing dependence on domesticated animals and plants following the end of the period. Human skeletal remains constitutes one important source to the illumination of this development. Although Mesolithic human skeletal remains are scarce, the situation in south Scandinavia has changed notably in recent years. Along with an increasing number of single finds, two large late Mesolithic burial grounds has been found: Bøgebakken on Zealand (Albrethsen and Brinch Petersen 1977) and Skateholm in Scania (Larsson et al. 1988). Now we are about to introduce a third burial ground: Tågerup.

The Mesolithic site Tågerup is located four kilometers east of Landskrona, Scania, Sweden (Figure 60.1).

Figure 60.1 Map of southern Scandinavia – with the Tågerup site marked (dot).

Today, a sandy embankment demarcated by two smaller streams – Saxån and Braån – marks the location of a former isthmus. During an excavation in the summer of 1998, six graves were unearthed. Disarticulated human bones were found in the waste deposits as well. Five graves were concentrated within an restricted area, whereas the sixth grave were located at a distance from the others. The graves emerged on the edge of the excavation area, towards the ridge of the embankment. The full extent of the burial ground has yet to be determined. It is likely that the higher grounds of the embankment will embrace more graves. The archaeology of the Tågerup area is affluent, with the archaeological excavations in 1998 concentrated to a Mesolithic site dated to the Atlantic Chronozone. At least two cultural phases can be noticed in the archaeological material encountered: the Blak- and Villingebæk-phases of the Kongemose culture (ca. 8.000–6.500 BP) and the Ertebølle culture (ca. 6.500–5.200 BP) (Karsten and Knarrström in prep). The purpose with this paper is to briefly describe the anthropological material excavated at the Tågerup site. Technical information regarding the skeletal remains is to be found elsewhere (Ahlström 2001).

Human Skeletal Remains from Tågerup

Except for the human bones retrieved from the waste deposits, the skeletal remains are brittle and lack cohesion. This is manifested in a severe fragmentation of the material. Several samples from the skeletons in the graves were recovered for ^{14}C-dating, but none contained datable samples of collagen (see below). The majority of the graves were recovered *en bloc*, i.e. still embedded in the sand with mostly the anterior surfaces of the skeletons exposed. Due to the fragile nature of the bone material, the skeletons were consolidated as they were lying. Needless to say, only the exposed surfaces of the skeletons were available for osteological analysis. The assessments of sex and age followed standards in the field, i.e. Ferembach, Schwidetzky and Stoukal (1980) and Buikstra and Ubelaker (1994). Stature were estimated on the basis of the regression formulas presented by Sjøvold (1990). Technical details and data are given in Ahlström (2001).

A direct dating of the human skeletal remains in the graves proved unrealisable, as there was no retrievable collagen. However, charcoal fragments in the filling of grave 1 gave the radiocarbon date 7495±75 BP (Ua-9946). A similar dating of charcoal in grave 5 yielded 7245±60 BP (Ua-9945). Based on these datings, and associated artifacts in the graves, it is argued that grave 1, grave 2, and grave 5 belongs to the Kongemose culture. Further, a fragment of a human parietal bone and a femur found disarticulated in the waste deposits gave the dates 7480±80 BP (Ua-9941) and 7415±80 BP (Ua-25197), respectively. The δ^{13}C-measurements of these Kongemosian finds are to be discussed below. Three graves are younger. Stratigraphically, grave 3 is positioned above grave 4. Charcoal in the filling of grave 4 was dated to 5820±100 BP (Ua-25218), i.e. belonging to the Ertebølle phase. The sixth grave, based on the finding of a transverse arrowhead, is dated to the Ertebølle culture as well (Karsten and Knarrström in prep). The results of the osteological analysis of the Tågerup are presented in figure 60.2.

Sexing human skeletal remains from the Mesolithic period has been proven difficult, in fact the sexual assessments of two of the most complete skeletons – Bäckaskog and Koelbjerg – has changed twice. By and large, this has to do with the input of cultural bias in the sexing procedures, i.e. the supposed correlation between biological sex and a slotted bone point with flint insets in the case of the Bäckaskog skeleton (cf. Gejvall 1970). As Mesolithic females were not supposed to engage in hunting activities, the artifacts found in the grave were interpreted as indicating male sex (Stenberger 1979). A similar fate may be ascribed to the Koelbjerg find. The Koelbjerg skeleton, found in a peat bog in 1941 on Funen, Denmark, represents the oldest and most complete individual from the Maglemose culture (Bröste and Fischer-Møller 1943; Tauber 1986). The original publication advanced the view that the remains represented a female, notwithstanding a robust cranium. Although the authors did not dwell at length regarding the morphology of the pelvic bones, it seems that the gracile postcranial bones along with a minute stature – 157.8 cm according to Manouvriers method – favored female sex. Here, the bias centers around the notion that Mesolithic males were supposed to be tall. However, the original determination did not gain wide acceptance. The Norwegian anthropologist Schreiner (1946) questioned the original sexing, drawing attention to the lack of correspondence between the Koelbjerg and Oberkassel finds. It is important to

Grave number	Affinity	Sex	Age category	Stature
1	Kongemose	Female	Mature (45–49 y)	148.6 cm
2	Kongemose	Male?	Mature (40–60 y)	159.7 cm
3	Ertebølle	–	Infans I (6–7 y)	–
4	Ertebølle	Female	Mature (40–44 y)	152.9 cm
5a	Kongemose	Male?	Mature (40–60 y)	–
5b	Kongemose	Female?	Mature (40–60 y)	163.5 cm
6	Ertebølle	–	Infans II (9–10 y)	–

Figure 60.2 Summary of results.

note that innominate bones were associated with both the Bäckaskog and Koelbjerg finds. The morphology of the Koelbjerg innominate fails to meet the female phenotype, and in the following, the Koelbjerg skeleton is referred to as a male (cf. Petersen 1998). The lessons that may be learned from this is first and foremost, that sexing ought to be based on morphological features of the innominate bones. Needless to say, assigning biological sex on the basis of artifacts reflects cultural bias and have no bearing whatsoever on human biology.

Sexing the individuals in graves 1 and 4 was straightforward. The pelvic characters indicates female sex, along with the morphology of the mandible and the gracile morphology of the nuchal crest, mastoid process and supraorbital margin. Although the glabella region must be characterised as being prominent, the majority of the traits studied suggests a female sex. Prominent glabella is a feature of the Bäckaskog skeleton as well. Given the relatively good preservational conditions of both skeletons, these individuals are assessed as females. The skeletons from graves 2 and 5 are more problematic due to the poor preservation. This is acute with regard to grave 2. Apart from the broad greater ischiadic notch – which could be due to postdepositional factors – all other characters imply male sex. A robust mandible with flared angels and a protuberant mental process is not a feature of the Bäckaskog skeleton, but is present with regard to the Koelbjerg skeleton. Due to the general void of informative characters and the robust features of the mandible, the skeleton in grave 2 is assessed as a probable male. The same assessment – probable male – is attached to individual 5a in grave 5. The only aspect that shed light on this individuals sex is the robust mandible. Somewhat more data is available for individual 5b. The list of sexually dimorphic traits of the cranium and innominate bone signals that we are confronting the skeleton of a gracile female. In comparison with the Bäckaskog cranium, this individual is apparently more gracile. Based mainly on the sexually dimorphic features of the skull and mandible, the skeleton is assigned as a probable female.

It is only for two individuals that we have reliable estimates concerning the ages at death. Portions of the auricular facets are preserved for both individuals in graves 1 and 4 respectively. In this context, it is important to make comparisons with the much better preserved skeleton of the Bäckaskog female. The auricular facets of all three individuals – 1, 4 and Bäckaskog – corresponds in the sense that there is no transverse organisation involving striae and billows. The surfaces of the facets are flat and dense with no granularity. Further, there is no macroporosity. Based on these findings, we are able to eliminate the possibility of younger adult ages (< 35 years), as granularity and transverse organisation is lacking. Further, we are able to eliminate advanced ages (> 50 years), as there is no macroporosity present. Based on the morphology of the auricular facets, the Bäckaskog skeleton was assigned to phase 5 (40–44 years), Tågerup 1 to phase 6 (45–59 years), and finally Tågerup 4 to phase 5 (40–44 years). These findings suggests that we are confronting three mature females: Tågerup 1 being somewhat older than Tågerup 4 and Bäckaskog. With respect to the adult individuals 2, 5a and 5b, the informations regarding the age at death are more circumstantial. Based on the attrition of the second molar in the upper and lower jaws respectively, the following sequence can be defined, from the least attrition to the most: Tågerup 4, Tågerup 2, Tågerup 5b, Tågerup 5a, and Tågerup 1. Thus, it may be inferred on the basis of attrition, that none of the individuals in grave 2, grave 5a and grave 5b are younger or older than the skeletons in graves 1 and 4 respectively. These findings suggests that the poorly preserved individuals in graves 2, 5a and 5b fit into the same age category as individuals 1 and 4, i.e. mature. There is no evidence to suggest that younger ages is relevant (i.e. adult), neither is there any evidence for older assessments (i.e. senile). Apart from two subadult individuals – one belonging to the age category infans I (grave 3), the other to infans II (grave 6) – it is concluded that the five adult individuals are mature (i.e. 40–59 years).

In the filling of grave 4, a concentration of teeth, traces of a mandible and red-ochre marked the existence of a grave (grave 3). The material from this grave represents a mixture of deciduous and permanent teeth. Only crowns were preserved, nothing of the roots. Based on the dental development chart of Gustafson and Koch (1974), the following may be relevant as to the assessment of the age of the individual. All deciduous teeth show signs of attrition with an exposure of dentine, stating that they have been in occlusion for some time. The first permanent molars of the upper and lower jaw shows no signs of attrition, stating that these teeth were obviously not in occlusion. The sequence of eruption of the first upper molar commences at the age of five years and ends at the age of eight years, with a peak at 6.5 years. Thus, the lack of attrition for the permanent first molars gives a *terminus ante quem* at 6.5 years for the individual. Assessing the *terminus post quem* may prove to be difficult as there is no roots preserved. However, the degree of dentine exposure reveals that the deciduous teeth has been in occlusion for some time. By all means, this individual belongs to the age group Infans I (1–7 years), and most probably to the later phase of this interval. Fragments of a subadult skeleton in a semiflexed position were found at a distance from the rest of the graves. The find of a transverse arrowhead in the vicinity of the pelvic region, may suggest that the cause of death was violent. Only traces of bone may be discenerd. The length of the femoral diaphysis is ca. 280 mm, suggesting an age around 9–10 years (Stewart 1968). The individual is brought to the age-category infans II.

The disarticulated skeletal remains from Tågerup are concentrated to two locations. Layer 4 represents activity dated to the Kongemose culture, and consists of a fragmented femur, where both the proximal and the distal epiphysis are dissipated, and a parietal bone. The two radiocarbon dates of this material (see above) suggests that the two bones may very well derive from one and the same individual. In the same layer, there is evidences of a burned individual. The following anatomical locations may be identified: the upper part of the squamous part of the occipital bone, a fragment of the left frontal bone with parts of the orbit, a fragment of a tibia immediately adjacent to the nutrient foramen and finally, a root of a premolar that is severely affected by attrition. With regard to suture closure, only the site lambda may be scored on the occipital fragment, where closure is minimal (1). Both cranial and postcranial elements are present, but the anatomical representation is far from complete. All burned bone fragments are white and calcined, suggesting that they have been subjected to a temperature over 800°C (Herrmann 1988). Cremations are known from South Scandinavia during the Mesolithic (cf. Brinch Petersen 1990; Larsson et al. 1988), and the burned bones from Tågerup could represent an early example of this burial custom. However, cremations involving fleshed bone usually produces characteristic, elliptic fractures due to the warping of the long bones (Thurman and Willmore 1981; Herrmann 1988). As no bone fragments displaying elliptic fractures has been identified in the burned bones from Tågerup, it cannot be ruled out that the bones were charred in an already defleshed and dry state. Layer 8 is considered – on archaeological grounds – to reflect activities during the Ertebølle culture. Here, human skeletal remains were found as well, all unburned. These remains represents at least two individuals. An inferior first deciduous premolar indicates an subadult individual, and the collar bone, mandible, zygomatic bone, temporal bone, and the upper first molar indicates an adult individual. The upper first molar shows attrition, stating that it has been in occlusion for some time and is not belonging to the same individual as the deciduous premolar. The disarticulated skeletal remains from Tågerup represents at least four individuals. Two of them – one unburned and one burned – belongs to the Kongemose phase, the other two to the Ertebølle phase. However, it should be emphasised that deciduous teeth are shed naturally and may not indicate the presence of a fourth decomposed body.

With the exception of one case of periapical periodontitis and a probable case of porotic hyperostosis (grave 1), there is no other paleopathological condition to report. No caries can be substantiated on the exposed teeth.

Paleodiet

Instrumental to any analysis of a prehistoric society is the reconstruction of the subsistence pattern. There are two stable isotopes of carbon, ^{12}C and ^{13}C. The concept of reconstructing prehistoric diets based on stable carbon isotopes rests on the discrimination and thus, the depletion of the heavier isotope (^{13}C) in food-chains (cf. Katzenberg 2000 for a review). This discrimination is not homogenous. The depletion of the heavier ^{13}C will depend on how carbon enters the food-chain involving a number of pathways and different sources. During photosynthesis, a fractioning of the isotopes occurs as plants discriminates against the heavier isotope (^{13}C). The difference between terrestrial plants and the standard amounts to -22 to -30‰, as there is relatively less of the heavier isotope. Terrestrial animals feeding on these plants will take on more or less the same isotopic signature. However, the marine environment is enriched with the heavier isotope resulting in a fractioning of the isotopes that is less compared with terrestrial plants. As there will be relatively more of the heavier isotopes in marine environment, the difference with respect to the standard is smaller.

A list of ^{14}C-datings and associated measurements of $\delta^{13}C$ has been compiled for southern Scandinavia (based on data presented in Tauber [1986], Persson [1999], Nordqvist [1999], and Lindqvist and Possnert [1999]) (Figure 60.3). A linear regression analysis with the $\delta^{13}C$ measurements as the dependent variable is presented below (Figures 60.4 and 60.5).

The Pearson correlation between $\delta^{13}C$ measurements and the ^{14}C-datings is -0.723, and significant. The coefficient of determination is 0.528, implying that 53 % of the variation with regard to the ratio of stable carbon isotopes may be explained by the decay of the radioactive isotope. The regression coefficient is significantly different from zero, implying that an increased decay of radioactive carbon is followed by a depletion of the heavier isotope. The general conclusion is that, as the Mesolithic period progresses, human skeletons became more enriched with respect to the heavier isotope 13. In the absence of a C4 photosynthesis, this is indicative of a shift from a terrestrial subsistence towards a more marine subsistence, at least with regard to the procurement of protein.

From 9.500 to 7.000 BP, the majority of the measurements indicate a terrestrial foraging behavior, with the exception of the sample from Huseby Klev that is definitely marine. Three measurements are certainly terrestrial (Koelbjerg and the two from Tågerup), and the others falling in between -19‰ and -18‰. However, some important points need to be addressed. At this time, the Baltic basin was successively transformed from the Ancylus-lake filled with sweet water, to the salty Litorina Sea. Thus, we cannot really expect a marine signature in the Baltic basin at this time. Formally, it cannot be known on the basis of stable carbon isotopes whether the populations present on Gotland (Stora Förvar, Kams, Stora Bjers) represents terrestrial foragers that occasionally visits the island, or permanent foragers living on the island, the archaeological context suggests the latter (Lindqvist and Possnert 1999). With respect to the finds from Hanaskede, Bredgården, and Bäckaskog, they are all evidently

Site and province	Lab #	^{14}C BP	δ^{13}C ‰
1. Koelbjerg, Funen	Tauber (1986)	9250±85	-20.7
2. Huseby Klev, Bohuslän	Ua-6411	9105±100	-15.63
3. Huseby Klev, Bohuslän	Ua-6410	9040±80	-15.25
4. Huseby Klev, Bohuslän	Ua-6407	8965±75	-15.63
5. Hanaskede, Västergötland	Ua-10295	8835±90	-19.09
6. Bredgården, Västergötland	Ua-6629	8645±95	-19.09
7. Stora Förvar, Gotland	Ua-3132	8555±135	-19.2
8. Stora Förvar, Gotland	Ua-13555	8380±85	-18.1
9. Stora Förvar, Gotland	Ua-13554	8360±95	-18.9
10. Stora Förvar, Gotland	Ua-3789	8340±100	-18.9
11. Stora Förvar, Gotland	Ua-2918	8270±75	-19.2
12. Stora Förvar, Gotland	Ua-13407	8260±95	-18.4
13. Stora Förvar, Gotland	Ua-3788	8220±95	-18.0
14. Kams, Gotland	Lu-1983	8050±75	-18
15. Stora Bjers, Gotland	Ua-10426	7970±80	-17.8
16. Bäckaskog, Scania	Ua-10667	7895±75	-19
17. Stora Förvar, Gotland	Ua-13406	7830±90	-17.7
18. Tågerup, Scania	Ua-9941	7480±80	-20.5
19. Stora Förvar, Gotland	Ua-2930	7440±85	-17.7
20. Tågerup, Scania	Ua-25197	7415±80	-21.1
21. Korsør Nor, Zealand	K-4262	6760±75	-14.90
22. Tybrind Vig, Funen	K-3558	6740±80	-15.70
23. Rønbjerg, Zealand	AAR-832	6680±140	-14.30
24. Uleberg, Bohuslän	Ua-7838	6630±100	-17.3
25. Bøggebakken, Zealand	K-2782	6290±75	-13.40
26. Holmegaard, Zealand	K-3559	6200±130	-11.90
27. Korsør Nor, Zealand	K-4185	6180±95	-14.50
28. Møllegabet II, Funen	K-6040	6170±85	-12.50
29. Bøggebakken, Zealand	K-2781	6050±75	-15.30
30. Melby, Zealand	K-1776	5830±110	-14.00
31. Bøggebakken, Zealand	K-2784	5810±105	-14.10
32. Norsminde, Jutland	K-5199	5790±95	-12.10
33. Vængesø, Jutland	K-3921	5540±65	-11.20
34. Vængesø, Jutland	K-3920	5500±70	-11.10
35. Stora Förvar, Gotland	Ua-3130	5500±95	-16.3
36. Ertebølle, Jutland	K-4933	5340±70	-16.50
37. Alby, Öland	Ua-2333	5260±70	-15.4
38. Dragsholm, Zealand	K-2224	5160±100	-12.00
39. Dragsholm, Zealand	K-2224	5160±100	-11.40

Figure 60.3 Specimens, radiocarbon dates and estimates of $\delta^{13}C$ from the Mesolithic of Southern Scandinavia.

Dependent variable	N	Correlation coefficient	Constant	Regression coefficient	Coefficient of determination	t-Ratio	P
δ^{13}C	39	-0.7268	-4.9505	-0.00157	0.528	-6.437	<0.001

Figure 60.4 Results of linear regression analysis of ^{14}C-datings and of $\delta^{13}C$ measurements.

terrestrial, but with some marine influence. The Bäckaskog female was found close to the former shore of the Litorina Sea. If her subsistence base was similar to that of the population of Gotland, we would expect a δ^{13}C -value close to -17.7‰. As this is not the case, it is safe to assume that her foraging behavior did incorporate a terrestrial component. The contrast between the Bäckaskog skeleton and the measurements derived from the parietal bone and the femur from Tågerup is nevertheless clear.

Noe-Nygaard (1988) advanced the view that during the Kongemose period, there were at least two populations with specialised foraging behaviors in south Scandinavia, one maritime and one terrestrial. Her analysis was based on measurements of bones from humans as well as dogs. Based on analogies of the present relationship between man and dog, it was assumed that measurements on dogs – which were more plentiful in the material – could be used as a proxy for human diets. If her model is correct,

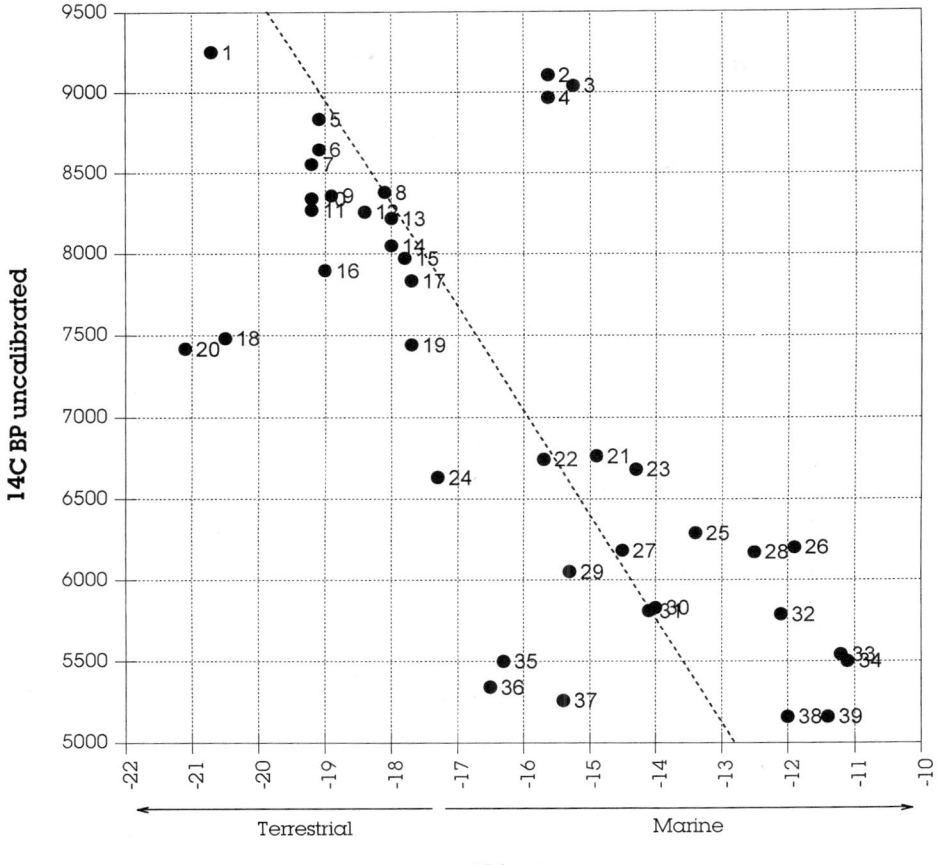

Figure 60.5 Results of regression analysis of stable carbon isotopes (x) and uncalibrated ^{14}C-dates (y) (cf. Figure 60.3).

we would have expected a marine signature with regard to Tågerup. This is not the case. Apart from Koelbjerg, measurements as low and terrestrial as the ones recorded for Tågerup is not present in the database. If we contrast this finding with the refuse from kongemosian sites from south Scandinavia, it is evident that terrestrial game dominates. Red deer, Roe Deer and Wild Boar constitutes 72.6 % of the identified fragments from Segebro (Lepiksaar 1983) and 97.3 % of the identified fragments from Argusgrunden (Møhl 1987). These sites are located close to the former shoreline, but substantiates a terrestrial presence. The analysis of the animal bones from the earliest occupational phase at Tågerup presents us with a similar picture: Red deer, Roe Deer and Wild Boar constitutes 85 % of the identified mammalian fragments (Eriksson and Magnell 2001). Maybe the shore-bound Kongemosian sites reflects other facets of the society than the immediate procurement of nutrition. An alternative explanation would be, that the location of the Tågerup settlement is not ultimately based upon the close vicinity to the sea, but rather on the strategic bifurcation of two streams that provides avenues to the foraging of the hinterland. Nevertheless, the Tågerup finding provides an interesting point of departure for the assessments of measurements from the younger Mesolithic period. On the basis of the scant evidence at hand today, there is nothing to suggest that this transformation was smooth. After 7000 BP, there is a distinct shift towards a marine subsistence. In fact, all measurements dated after 7000 BP may be considered as marine.

Acknowledgements

I would like to thank Per Karsten and Bo Knarrström of the National Heritage Board for placing the skeletal remains from Tågerup at my disposal.

References

Ahlström, T. 2001. De dödas ben. In: Karsten, P. and Knarrström, B. (red.) *Tågerup specialstudier*. Skånska spår. Arkeologi längs västkustbanan. Riksantikvarieämbetet. Avd. för arkeologiska undersökningar, UV-Syd, 70–81. Lund.

Albrethsen, S.E. and Brinch Petersen, E. 1977. Excavation of a Mesolithic cemetery at Vedbæk, Denmark. *Acta Archaeologica* 47, 1–28.

Brinch Petersen, E. 1990, Nye grave fra Jægerstenalderen. *Nationalmuseets Arbejdsmark*, 19–33.

Bröste, K. and Fischer-Møller, K. 1943. Koelbjerg skelettet. Et fund fra tidlig Maglemosetid. *Aarbøger for nordisk Oldkyndighed og Historie*, 211–231.

Buikstra, J.E. and Ubelaker, D.H. 1994. *Standards for data collection from human skeletal remains*. Arkansas Archaeological Survey Research Series No. 44. Fayetteville.

Eriksson, M. and Magnell, O. 2001. Det djuriska Tågerup. In: Karsten, P. and Knarrström, B. (red.) *Tågerup specialstudier*. Skånska spår. Arkeologi längs västkustbanan. Riksantikvarieämbetet. Avd. för arkeologiska undersökningar, UV-Syd, 156–27. Lund.

Ferembach, D., Schwidetzky, I. and Stoukal, M. 1979. Empfehlungen für die Alters- und Geschlechtsdiagnose am Skelett. *Homo* 30, 1–32.

Gejvall, N.G. 1970. The Fisherman from Barum – Mother of several children! *Fornvännen*, 281–289.

Gustafson, G. and Koch, G. 1974. Age estimation up to 16 years of age based on dental development. *Odontologisk Revy* 25, 297–306.

Herrmann, B. 1988. Behandlung von Leichenbrand. In: Knußmann R. (Hrsg.) *Anthropologie. Handbuch der vergleichenden Biologie des Menschen*. Band I, Teil 1, 576–585. Stuttgart.

Katzenberg, M.A. 2000. Stable isotope analysis: A tool for studying past diet, demography and life history. In: Katzenberg, M.A. and Saunders, S.R. (eds.) *Biological Anthropology of the Human Skeleton*, 305–327. Wiley-Liss.

Karsten, P. and Knarrström, B. in prep. *The Mesolithic Space. The Tågerup excavations*. The National Hertiage Board. Lund.

Larsson, L. (ed.) 1988. *The Skateholm Project. I: Man and Environment*. Skrifter utgivna av Kungl. Humanistiska Vetenskapssamfundet i Lund LXXIX. Stockholm

Lepiksaar, J. 1983. Djurrester från den tidigatlantiska boplatsen vid Segebro nära Malmö i Skåne (Sydsverige). In: Larsson, L. (ed.) *Segebro. En tidigatlantisk boplats vid Sege ås mynning*. Malmöfynd 4, 105–128. Malmö.

Lindqvist, C. and Possnert, G. 1999. The first seal hunter families on Gotland. On the Mesolithic occupation of the Stora Förvar cave. *Current Swedish Archaeology* 7, 65–87.

Møhl, U. 1987. Faunalevn fra Argusgrunden: en undersøisk boplads fra tidlig Atlantisk tid. *Antikvariske studier* 8, 59–90.

Noe-Nygaard, N. 1988. $\delta^{13}C$ values of dog bones reveal the nature of changes in Man's food resources at the Mesolithic-Neolithic transition, Denmark. *Isotope Geoscience* 73, 87–96.

Nordqvist, B. 1999. *A study of the Mesolithic on the West Coast of Sweden*. Gothenburg University. Diss. Göteborg.

Persson, P. 1999. *Neolitikums början*. Gothenburg University. Diss. Göteborg.

Petersen, H.C. 1998. Nyt lys over skelettet fra Koelbjerg: Et menneske fra tidlig Maglemosetid. *3. Nordiske Seminar om Biologisk Antropologi*. Anatomisk laboratorium. Retsmedicinsk Institut. Københavns Universitet, 42–44. København.

Schreiner, K.E. 1946. *Crania Norvegica II*. Instituttet for sammenlignende kulturforskning. Oslo.

Sjøvold, T. 1990. Estimation of stature from long bones utilising the line of organic correlation. *Human Evolution* 5, 431–447.

Stenberger, M. 1979. *Det forntida Sverige*. Stockholm.

Stewart, T.D. 1968. Identification by the skeletal structures. In: Camps, F.E. (ed.) *Gradwohl's Legal Medicine*, 123–154. Baltimore.

Tauber, H. 1986. Koelbjerg-kvindens alder og ernæring. *Fynske Minder* 28–33.

Thurman, M.D. and Willmore, L.J. 1981. A replicative cremation experiment. *North American Archaeologist* 2, 275–283.

61. Three Cremations and a Funeral: Aspects of Burial Practice in Mesolithic Vedbæk

Erik Brinch Petersen and Christopher MeikleJohn

Apart from the "simple" inhumation burials there is also evidence for the use of cremation as a burial type at Vedbæk. Even if only three such burials from two different sites have been identified, there is additional evidence for the use of cremations throughout the entire Mesolithic occupation at Vedbæk, i.e. from the older Kongemose to the end of the Ertebølle. Examination of the cremated bones points to the practice of a preceding scaffolding of some individuals. Scaffolding structures might indeed be present, whereas only indirect evidence has been found of the pyre itself. As seen from the calcined state of pendants, flint knives and amber pieces, other individuals must have been cremated fully dressed. Among the cremated persons, both sexes are represented, as well as newborns, adolescents and adults.

Despite the present tendency to regard sites with burials as central places with adjacent cemeteries, the evidence from Vedbæk is diametrically opposed to this opinion. Not only are burials here located under living floors, but they are also a common phenomenon on different types of sites. Thus cremations can be found not only on the year round occupations in the more protected part of the fjord, but can also be found on an exposed, but seasonally occupied site on the beach ridge itself. On both types of sites, however, cremations are used together with inhumations.

The Vedbæk fjord is of major significance for the Mesolithic prehistory of southern Scandinavia, in part due to a history of investigation spanning at least a century, aided by excellent preservation conditions. Work at Vedbæk over the past quarter century has also demonstrated a considerable diversity in Mesolithic burial patterning (Brinch Petersen and Meiklejohn in press). In this paper we will explore one aspect of this diversity, the primary and secondary evidence for Mesolithic cremation. Until recently, cremation was effectively unreported for the Mesolithic though, paradoxically, the poorly known cremation from Vedbæk Boldbaner was the first reported example from Mesolithic Europe (Mathiassen 1946), though some doubt as to its real affinity was expressed by local workers (i.e. Kunwald 1954). However, two cremation features have been recently excavated from the site of Gøngehusvej 7, (Brinch Petersen 1990, 1996; Kannegaard and Brinch Petersen 1993) both overlain by a stratified cultural horizon two meters below the present surface, one of which is directly dated by ^{14}C to the cultural horizon in which it is located. As a result, there can no longer be any doubt as to the Mesolithic affinity of cremation burials at Vedbæk. Furthermore, charred human loose bones from both older and younger sites in the region point to an expanded chronological range for cremations (Figure 61.1). Cremation must therefore be regarded as an integrated burial mode during most, if not all, of the Scandinavian Mesolithic.

Until the late 1980's cremation seemed to be of very limited distribution in the European Mesolithic. Prior to 1990, reported cases other than Vedbæk Boldbaner were restricted to Holland (Verlinde 1974; Arts and Hoogland 1987) and Scania (Larsson 1988). In the last decade this has rapidly expanded and now includes western Sweden (Schaller-Åberg, pers. comm.) and Gotland (Lindquist and Possnert 1999), Poland (Marciniak 1993), Belgium (Cauwe 1998), northern France (Ducrocq 1999), Serbia (Roksandic 2000), and Greece (Cullen 1995).

The description of material from sites in the Vedbæk fjord sequence must be considered preliminary. Some aspects of the material have been reported elsewhere, as noted. The complete descriptions of these materials will be included in the final report on the skeletal material from Vedbæk.

Material

Gøngehusvej 7, excavated between 1987 and 1990, is situated on the raised beach ridge that gradually closed the opening of the Vedbæk fjord into the Øresund (figure 61.1). It has been argued that sites on this beach ridge should be regarded as settlement displacement from the deeper part of the fjord towards the open shores of the sound following closure of the original opening (Vang Petersen 1982). In contrast, we now know that, beginning somewhere in the Kongemose period, seasonal occu-

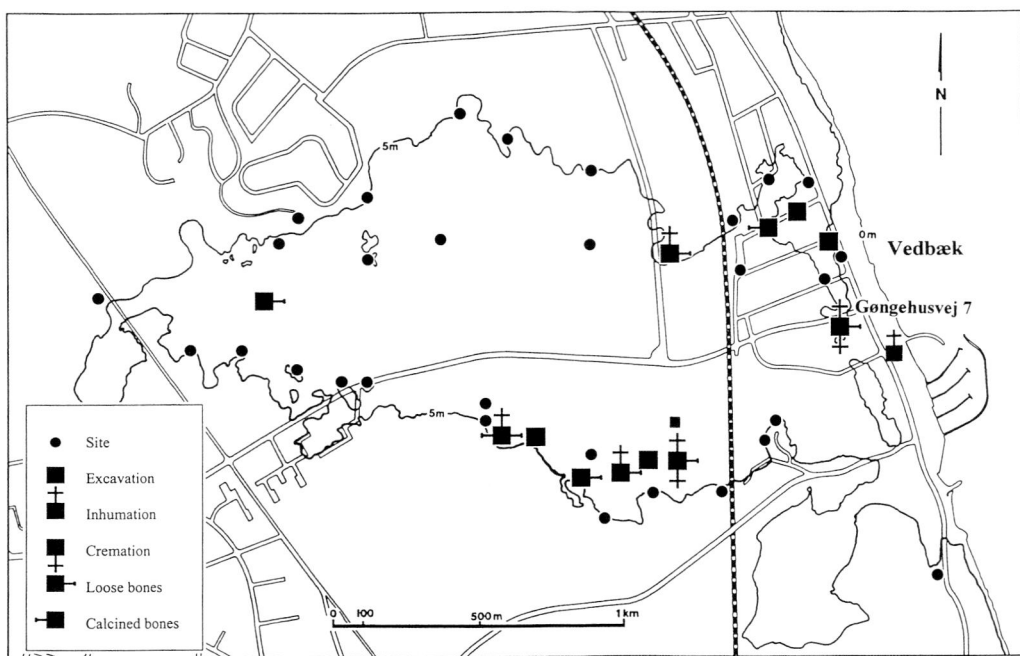

Figure 61.1 Distribution of human remains from Mesolithic Vedbæk.

pations, including one of three shellmiddens known from the fjord, took place on the beach ridge. The beach ridge gradually grew upwards and ahead of the ongoing rise in sea level (Christensen 1982, 1995).

The excavation of Gøngehusvej 7 uncovered some hundred square meters without reaching the limits of the site, except at the eastern seaward side, where later erosion by the sea truncates part of the original site (Brinch Petersen 1990, 2000). We concentrated the investigation on an undisturbed cultural horizon, situated two meters below the surface at an absolute level of 3 m asl, dating from the youngest phase of the Kongemose period (Brinch Petersen 1993). The layer immediately below the primary one consists of lithic scatters made up primarily of débitage from the production of core axes. Below this level only abraded and redeposited lithics were found indicating that, somewhere in the neighbourhood, even older occupational levels may still be located on the beach ridge (Fryd Koot 2000; Leen Jensen and Kjems 2000; Møller Nielsen 2000; Nordahn Frederiksen 2000; Vennersdorf 2000).

Given the limited time available due to the rescue nature of the excavation, Mesolithic and later levels above the primary occupation were mechanically removed, the exception being the Mesolithic double inhumation burial (feature CÆ) partly dissected by the northernmost section, and dug down from a higher level (Brinch Petersen et al. 1993). This site is unique with Mesolithic burials located in stratigraphic context from at least two levels. The Mesolithic occupation is, in turn, overlain by a level with some Bronze age features, confirmed by ^{14}C, and by limited remains indicating a landing site from the younger Iron Age (Ulriksen 1998).

Apart from the burials a number of features were recorded from the occupation layer (Figure 61.2). Whether there is a hut structure in the northern part of the excavation is still open for some debate. However, as we see it, the outline of the hut is made up of several stake holes, and in the center is a simple hearth with a few cooking stones. Also a child inhumation (feature CN) is located here. Just north of the hearth, but still within the hut, is a flaking area for a greenstone axe. The rest of the greenstone flakes are found outside and further to the north, with a grinding stone next to this dump. Inside the hut was a concentration of arrowheads, while the supposed door entrance was marked by several refitable elements of what resembles the so-called side-blow blade-flakes (Braidwood 1961).

Other features include pits with charcoal and cooking stones, pits with faunal remains, mostly of fish, and post- and stake-holes, unfortunately not always delineating clear structures, but in two cases marking burials. A small lithic hoard of a dozen flint blades was found. The lithic refitting, still in progress, ties the excavated area together, but also marks out different functional areas. An internal relative chronology among areas and features can be deduced from some of the refitted sequences (Figure 61.3).

In brief, based upon the structures, absence of dispersed cookingstones, fauna, dominated by fish, and the lithic composition, technological as well as typological, Gøngehusvej 7 differs in many respects from sites situated in the inner and more protected part of the fjord, all of which seem to reflect several all year round occupations. These are Stationsvej 17–19 (Bøttiger et al. 1999), Vænget Nord (Juel Jensen and Brinch Petersen 1985;

Three Cremations and a Funeral: Aspects of Burial Practice in Mesolithic Vedbæk 487

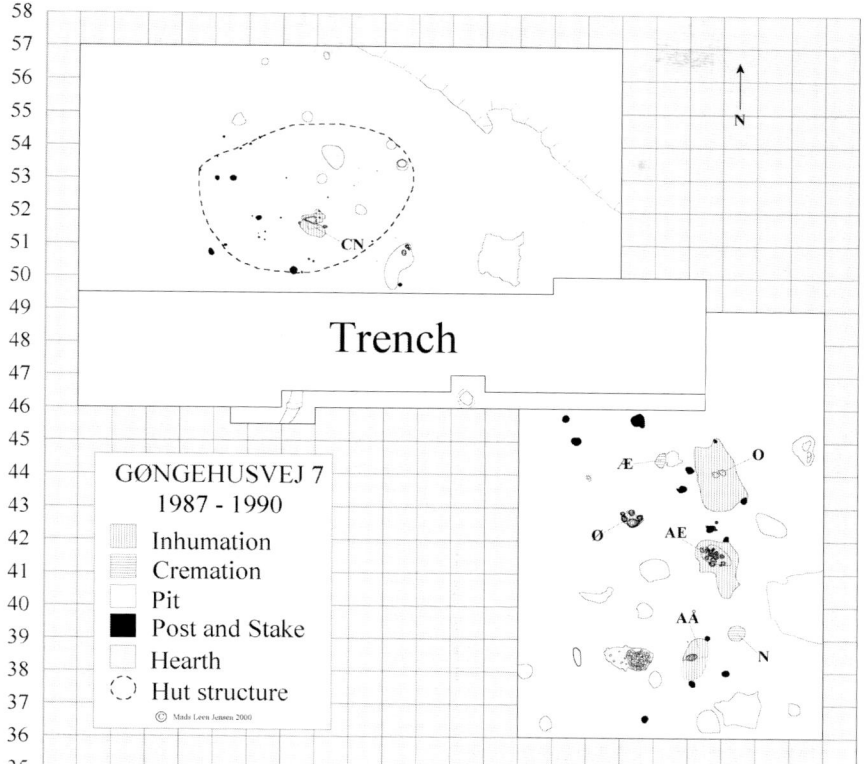

Figure 61.2 Gøngehusvej 7: Plan of features and burials.

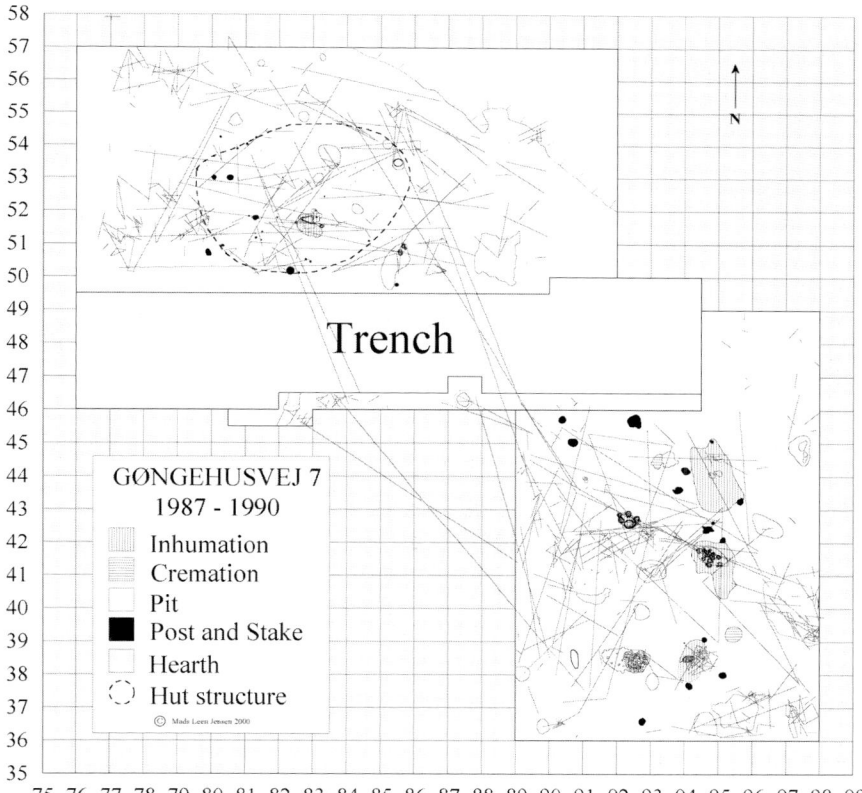

Figure 61.3 Gøngehusvej 7: features and burials and lithic refits.

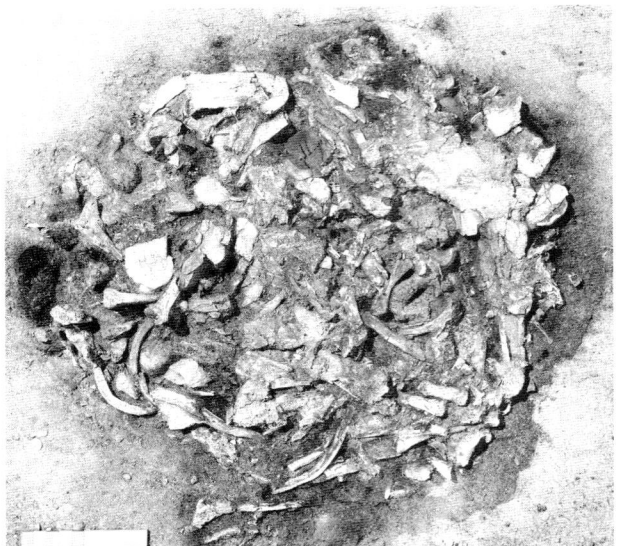

Figure 61.4 Gøngehusvej 7: Cremation N. (Photo by G. Brovad, Zoological Museum).

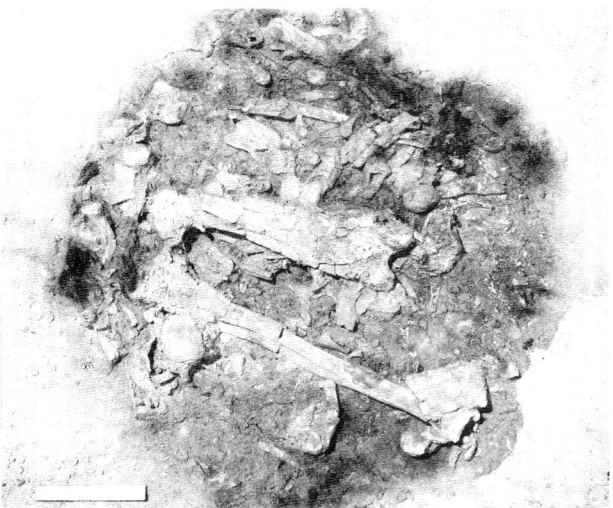

Figure 61.5 Gøngehusvej 7: Cremation N. (Photo by G. Brovad, Zoological Museum).

Figure 61.6 Gøngehusvej 7: Cremation N. (Photo by G. Brovad, Zoological Museum).

Price and Brinch Petersen 1987; Brinch Petersen 1989; Johansen 1998), Vedbæk Boldbaner (Mathiassen 1946; Vang Petersen 1977), Maglemosegårds Vænge (Vang Petersen 1979), Henriksholm-Bøgebakken (Albrethsen and Brinch Petersen 1977), Maglemosegård (Brinch Petersen et al. 1976 ; Aaris-Sørensen 1983), and Magleholm (Avnholt 1944).

Due to good preservation conditions in one feature (Ø), two others (AE, CN) have been interpreted as inhumation graves of children, while a couple of others (O, AÅ) might originally have contained adults, on the basis of their size (Brinch Petersen 1990). The complete skeleton of a dog, Canis familiaris, was found just below the cultural horizon. No traces of red ochre nor signs of skinning were seen so, unfortunately, it was not possible to determine if it had been placed in a pit and consequently should be regarded as a canine burial. However, the dog lies next to a burial pit, feature O. Finally, among the burials were two separated cremation features, N and Æ. The latter was excavated in the field, while the former, N, was lifted, left to dry and subsequently investigated under laboratory conditions at the Zoological Museum, thus ensuring better preservation, observation and documentation.

Cremation N – A shallow, bowl like pit, 40 cm across and 15 cm deep, was packed with uncleaned bones, identified as the remains of at least five individuals found together with lumps of charcoal from the original pyre and some small personal belongings (figures 61.4–61.6). Red ochre staining was still visible on some of the bones. A packing order of the bones could be observed with long bones placed next to and on top of each other across the center of the pit. The artifacts were recovered here and there among the bones. No superstructure was observed nor was there any lining of the pit. The top of the pit was relatively high, perhaps indicating a late construction within the occupational history of the cultural horizon. It should be noted that the pit was certainly not the original place of the cremation proper. The pyre could, however, have been an on-site phenomenon similar to Skateholm I (Larson 1989), due to the presence of calcined pieces of gravel among the bones, the same sediment that is found in the beach ridge.

The presence of charcoal remains among the bones indicates that these had not been cleaned before deposition. An identification of the charcoal shows that the wood used for the pyre consisted primarily of oak, while the fuel used in the nearby hearth, feature Q, shows branches of wild apple and the like, as seems to be normal for a domestic hearth. From a pyrotechnological perspective this is a clear and logical illustration of the difference between a small domestic fire and a pyre intended for several corpses.

As seen from the skeletal diagram (Figure 61.7), at least five individuals are represented in the pit (Meiklejohn and Wyman 1993). This skeletal diagram must be read though with some caution, as there were quite a

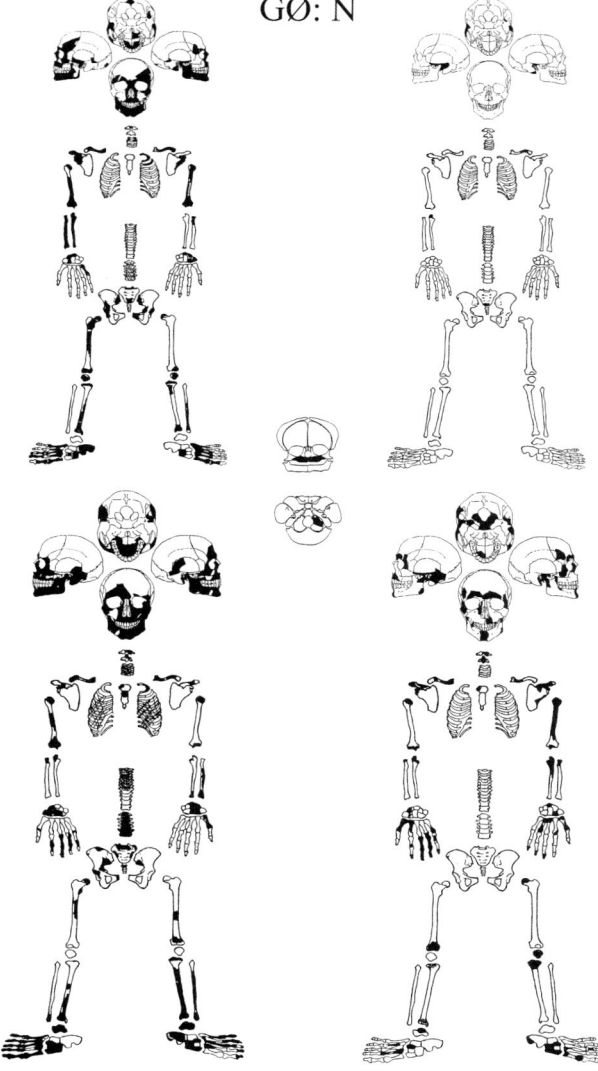

Figure 61.7 Gøngehusvej 7: Cremation N, skeletal diagram.

number of small fragments, that could not be identified as to the individual type of bone. We have, however, the impression, that most of the cremated bones from the five individuals had originally been placed in the pit. These are identified as two adults, one slightly older than the other but both in their twenties, and perhaps representing a male and a female due to a difference in bone size, a young teenager, a five year old child and an infant, less than one year of age. Whether the five originally shared a single pyre in the same state of decomposition, and thus initially shared the same time of death is a difficult question. However, they were all deposited in the same pit at the same time.

The calcination of the bones varies from a dark blue to white. Individual bones from a single individual show differences in the degree of calcination, as do different parts of the same bone, apparently depending on local exposure to heat. A fish scale-like patterning has been observed on some bones. On different pieces patches of red ochre have melted onto the calcined bones. Some bones show the characteristic patterning suggesting cremation of dry, green, bone, while other bones show signs of having been cremated in a fresh state (Buikstra and Swegle 1989; Schutkowski 1991; Mays 1998). Only one bone shows cutmarks, the mandible of the adult female. This occurs on the interior (medial) face of both condyles. Taken as a group, there is a possibility that some of the individuals had been through a preceding scaffolding before cremation.

The following further pieces, including artifacts, burned and calcined, were recovered from the pit: two fragmented flintblades and a small microblade; a lump of unworked amber; five front teeth from a young dog or a fox; five tooth pendants, front teeth from red deer; a set of bird wings, the size of a crow; and, finally, at least three duck feet. Unfortunately we are unable to individualise any of the tools, pendants or amulets.

A sample of charcoal from the original pyre and recovered from among the deposited human bones in the pit was subjected to a ^{14}C-date, and has given the following result: (K-6857) 6530 ± 60 bp or 5480–5390 cal BC with 1 st.dev. The corresponding layer has been dated on charcoal from a nearby hearth, feature Q, to (K-6856) 6720 ± 65 bp or 5620–5530 cal BC with 1 st.dev. (Rasmussen 1999). The non-overlapping of the two dates might indicate that feature N could have been intrusive from the uninvestigated layer above, despite the fact that no such observations were made in the field.

Cremation Æ – This feature was found closer to the supposed hut structure. It actually truncates neighbouring feature T, thus being younger than this small pit which contains a few dispersed cooking stones and some charcoal. The pit, 40 to 50 cm across and 70 cm deep with straight sides, had no visible superstructure, but in the westernmost side some sort of lining is seen (Figure 61.8). At the bottom was a clearly visible black lens, indicating a sort of wooden platter, or similar structure, as was the case with some of the other inhumations, [features Ø, AE, CN and AÅ] (Brinch Petersen 1990). Whether or not this burial pit remained open after construction, as was the case with inhumation Ø from the same site, is hard to say, but the infill of the pit, light sandy sediment, could be a hint in that direction.

In the middle of the supposed wooden plate was a small bundle of cleaned bones of one person. No charcoal from the original pyre, but a fire cracked fragment of flint blade, was recovered among the human bones. Between the bundle with the bones and the dark plate a fresh, unburnt, flint blade had been placed. Covering the plate and the bundle were the unburnt remains of an apparently complete corpse of a roe deer faun, about three months old. This indicates a time of burial around the first of September. To the best of our knowledge this is the first Mesolithic burial to be given a clear seasonal date.

Only one individual has been identified in this burial. The cleaned bones were all small fragments (Figure 61.9).

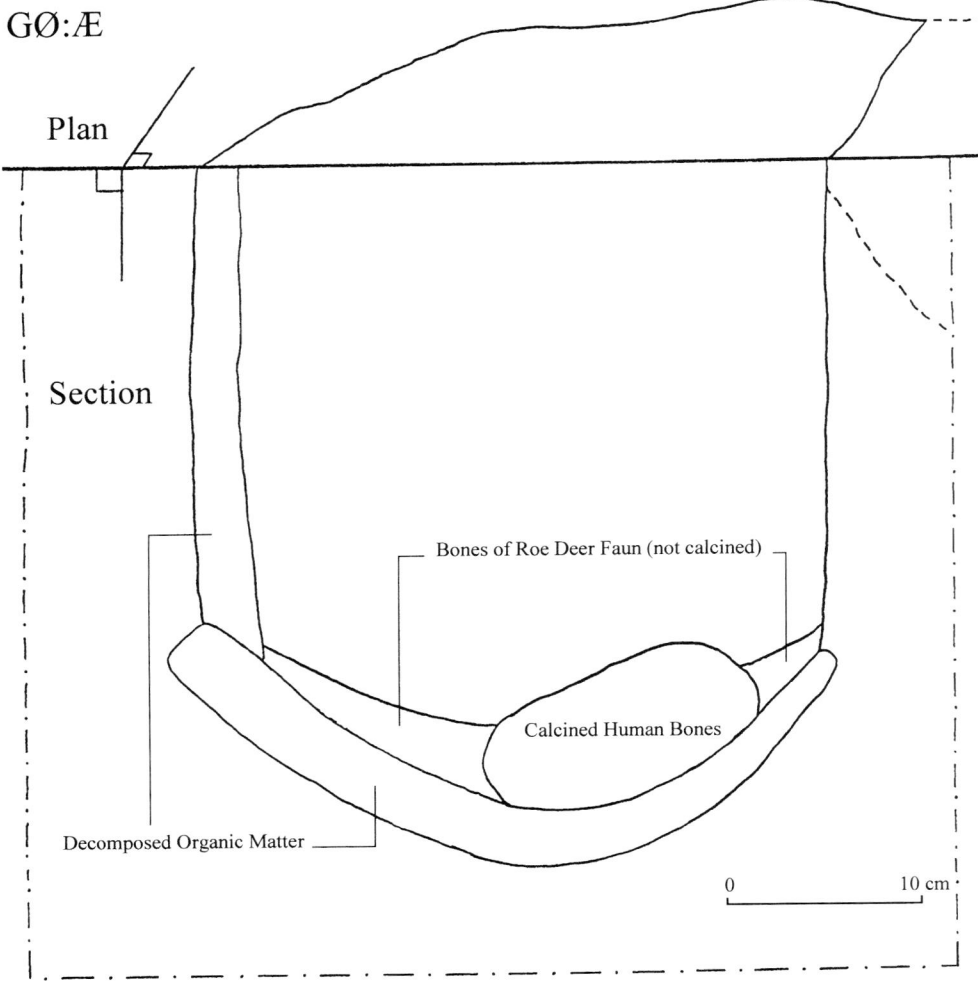

Figure 61.8 Gøngehusvej 7: Cremation Æ, section.

The individual was a young adult, probably in her twenties. The sex assessment is based on a gracile appearance. The single burnt flint knife on the pyre does not contradict this assessment (Brinch Petersen in press). It should be noted that the second flint knife, being unburnt, had not been on the pyre but only placed on the plate during the burial process. Finally, there were no traces of red ochre nor any cut marks. This feature clearly dates to the initial occupation of the cultural horizon in question. Due to the lack of charcoal among the human bones we do not have a ^{14}C date for the burial yet.

Vedbæk Boldbaner

This site was officially excavated by the National Museum in 1944–45, yielding an inhumation grave (Mathiassen 1946). The cremation was later discovered in 1946 by the local amateur A. Avnholt. There is no photograph of the cremation nor any drawing, but the provenience within the site has been determined. As well, based on Avnholt's report, a reconstruction of the original situation has been put forward (Vang Petersen 1977). Neither artifacts nor gravegoods have been reported, and unfortunately we do not know whether the human bones were originally cleaned.

The human remains suggest a single adult, perhaps female, as with feature Æ from Gøngehusvej 7 (Figure 61.9). Due to lack of charcoal from this cremation there is so far no direct ^{14}C date. However the site has yielded three dates on wood: (K-3167, K-3166 and K-1303) spanning a period from 6,180 to 5,320 cal BC with 1 st.dev. The evidence suggests that the cremation from Vedbæk Boldbaner is either contemporaneous with those from Gøngehusvej 7 or slightly older. Taken together, the three cremations should therefore be placed within the middle and latest part of the Kongemose period.

Stationsvej 17–19, Vedbæk

Rescue excavation from 1983 and 1984 has yielded what is, so far, the oldest Kongemose site from Vedbæk. Two ^{14}C-dates on charcoal from features below the cultural

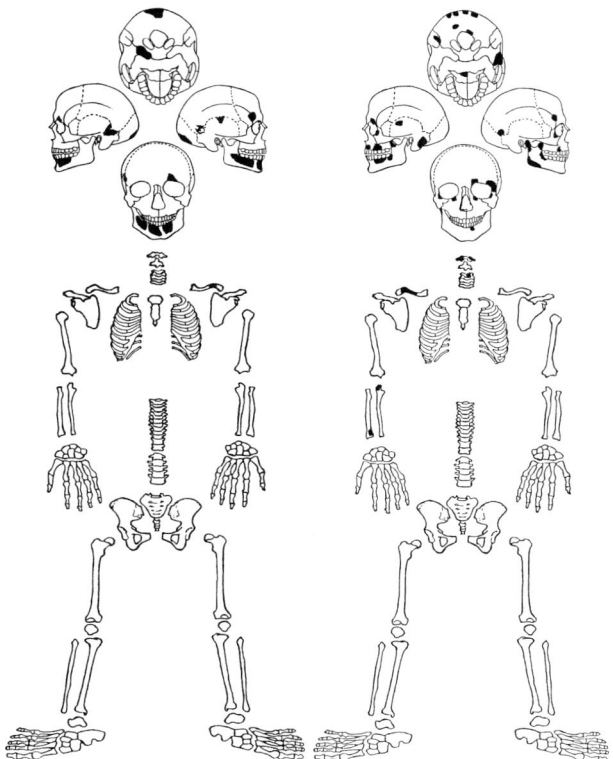

Figure 61.9 Vedbæk Boldbaner and Gøngehusvej 7, cremation Æ: skeletal diagram.

horizon span the period of (K-4959 and K-4714) 6,370 to 5,590 cal BC with 1. st.dev. (Tauber 1988). Three charred pieces of a human calvarium were found dispersed over several meters of the cultural horizon. Two of these fragments have been refitted. These fit within the category of "loose human bones" (see Meiklejohn and Denston 1987), but indicate that somewhere in the neighbourhood a pyre as well as a cremation burial could be hidden. Unfortunately, the central part of the site had been disturbed previously, due to the construction of a house in downtown Vedbæk (Bøttiger *et al.* 1999).

Maglemosegaard, Vedbæk

This site was excavated between 1975 and 1979 and shows a sequence of late Mesolithic, Ertebølle, layers terminating in an Early Neolithic horizon (Brinch Petersen *et al.* 1976). From this extensive excavation, only a single child's inhumation was recovered (Alexandersen 1979; Brinch Petersen 1979) together with some loose human bones, one of which had been charred. We can take this as evidence of an on-site cremation process, but this time dated to the Ertebølle period.

Møllegabet I

From this submarine site in the archipelago of southern Fyn, a single charred human femur has been reported among many other human ones, some of which had even been broken for marrow. The excavator suggests cannibalism, under which heading even the calcined femur has been placed (Skaarup 2000). We, on the other hand, take this as additional evidence for cremation during the Ertebølle period, but this time in a different settlement system than the ones at Vedbæk and Skateholm.

Chronological Results

With evidence in Denmark of three primary cremations from Vedbæk, two secondary ones from the same area and a further secondary case from Møllegabet, the chronological range of cremations in southern Scandinavia must now be enlarged to circumpass all of the Kongemose as well as the Ertebølle periods. This also extends the evidence from Skateholm. In addition, the new evidence from Stora Förvar appears to expand this chronological range further backwards in time (Lindquist and Possnert 1999). It must also be accepted that cremations and inhumations are found next to each other during the Mesolithic of Vedbæk, southern Scandinavia, and several other areas of Europe.

Cremational Scenarios

From later prehistoric periods the significance of cleaned versus uncleaned human bones within a cremation often has chronological significance. That is not the case here, where both modes of cremation occur in the same cultural horizon at Gøngehusvej 7. Feature Æ contained cleaned bones neatly wrapped in a bundle within a lined pit. The single personal object was charred. As gravegoods there was a single unburnt flint knife and the fresh corpse of a roe deer faun. In contrast, feature, N had uncleaned bones in a simple pit together with the remains of some personal belongings.

Perhaps the key question, probably unanswerable at present, is how cremation fits within overall burial practices in the Mesolithic (Brinch Petersen in press). When somebody dies, there is a problem. To bury or not to bury, that is the question. However, the nature of some finds is problematic. At sites such as Argusgrunden (Fischer *et al.* 1987), and Bergmansdal (Vang Petersen and Brinch Petersen 1979) there are examples of partly complete skeletons, but in both cases the allusion has been drawn to skeletons coming from non-observed burials. The first is a submarine dredging, while the other was a rescue excavation, where most finds had been recovered before the official investigation. So who can provide a meaningful picture? Or could we indeed have a situation, where human corpses or major parts of corpses were simply left behind to rot on the surface somewhere within the settlement?

What decides the first initial problem we simply do not know. If the decision has been taken to bury the dead, there comes the question of method, inhumation or cremation? The current record shows that in most cases it is inhumation, but in rarer cases a cremation is decided. The evidence to date does not suggest that this is obviously related to either sex or age. The cremation may then be either immediate or delayed. If immediate, a pyre is built and the cremation goes on with the corpse being placed here either dressed or not. Evidence from Danish inhumation burials suggests that corpses were usually buried in their clothes, a situation supported for some of the cremations discussed here in the form of personal belongings. In some cases, however, the process had to await until another time. The reasons are unclear but could include season of the year. When the time comes for the cremation, the corpse is taken down and put on the pyre. Either during the scaffolding period or during removal of the body from the scaffold there is the possibility for some of the human bones to be lost or spilled. This process could lead to the dispersion of what archaeologists call "loose human bones", though this is almost certainly not the only process behind the loose bones. The exhumation of corpses in the past (Albrethsen and Brinch Petersen 1977; Lass Jensen 2000) might add to the same phenomenon, and so could the use of human bones as remembrance of a deceased or an enemy, or even the accidental disturbance of graves by animals such as pigs (Rausing 1991), although no example has been recorded so far.

When one or more corpses have been successfully cremated, some of the bones from that pyre are recovered in order to be formally placed in a burial pit. The incomplete nature of some of the cremations suggests that there is apparently no need to recover them all in every case, though some recoveries may be more complete than others (e.g. Gøngehusvej 7, feature N). Remaining bones from the pyre may then be cleaned out and hidden away in an inconspicuous pit. Again during the cleaning up, some charred bones may be accidentally deposited in the cultural horizon. The difference among the two types of pits may be subtle, but the proper burial should be more elaborate, showing more concern from the survivors than the digging of an informal pit merely to hide away the superfluous bones. What seems unclear at the present time is the reason for the difference between recovered features with partial remains, such as Gøngehusvej 7, feature Æ or Vedbæk Boldbaner, and more apparently complete examples such as Gøngehusvej 7 feature N. Or could the difference in pit construction and accompanying grave-goods, feature Æ versus N and Vedbæk Boldbaner, indicate the dichotomy among formal versus informal inhumation?

Conclusion

This paper provides a preliminary report on the previously undescribed cremation features from Kongemose levels at the sites of Gøngehusvej 7 and Vedbæk Boldbaner, together with loose burnt bones from other sites in the Vedbæk area and elsewhere in Denmark. These findings extend the known distribution of cremation burial in both time and space. The Danish examples seem to be found throughout the Kongemose and Ertebølle periods, and Swedish evidence from Stora Förvar may push the practice back into the Maglemose. This confirms two elements of South Scandinavian burial practice that we have stressed earlier, that there is a considerable diversity within the patterns of burial, even within single sites, and that this diversity is not simply a feature of the late or terminal periods of the Mesolithic. In addition, we have provided some thoughts on the possible relationship between cremation, and other burial forms, and the generalised phenomenon of "loose bones" in the settlement debris of Mesolithic sites.

References

Aaris-Sørensen, K. 1983. An Example of Taphonomic Loss in a Mesolithic Faunal Assemblage. In: Clutton-Brock, J.C. Grigson (eds.) *Animals and Archaeology: 1. Hunters and their Prey*. BAR International Series 163, 243–247. Oxford.

Albrethsen, S.E. and Brinch Petersen, E. 1977. Excavation of a Mesolithic Cemetery at Vedbæk, Denmark. *Acta Archaeologica* 1976, 47, 1–28.

Alexandersen, V. 1979. Beskrivelse af et barn – ud fra 23 tænder. *Søllerødbogen*, 30–39.

Arts, N. and Hoogland, M. 1987. A Mesolithic Settlement Area with a Human Cremation Grave at Oirschot V, Municipality of Best, The Netherlands. *Helinium* XXVII, 172–189.

Avnholt, A. 1944. Oldtidsminder og oldtidsfund i Søllerød Kommune. *Søllerødbogen*, 41–72.

Braidwood, L. 1961. The General Appearance of Obsidian in Southwestern Asia and the Microlithic Side-blow Blade-flake in Obsidian. *Bericht Über den V. Internationalen Kongress für Vor- und Frühgeschichte Hamburg*, 142–147.

Brinch Petersen, E. 1979. Vedbækprojektet. Udgravningerne i sommeren 1978. *Søllerødbogen*, 21–29.

—— 1989. Vænget Nord. Excavation, Documentation and Interpretation of a Mesolithic Site at Vedbæk, Denmark. In: Bonsall, C. (ed.) *Proceedings of the 3rd International Mesolithic Symposium 1985*, 325–330. Edinburgh.

—— 1990. Nye grave fra jægerstenalderen. Strøby Egede og Vedbæk. *Nationalmuseets Arbejdsmark*, 9–31.

—— 1993. Ældre stenalder. In: Hvass, S. and Storgaard, B. (eds.) *Da Klinger i Muld... 25 års arkæologi i Danmark*, 46–49. Det Kgl. Nordiske Oldskriftselskab and Jysk Arkæologisk Selskab. Århus.

—— 1996. Danmarks ældste Brandgrave. In: Mahler, D.L.D. and Brandt Povlsen, L. (eds.) *Red Hvad Reddes Kan. Arkæologi i Københavns Amt 1982–95*, 14–15. Københavns Amtsmuseumsråd. København.

—— 2000. Under den gamle strandvej i Vedbæk. In: Hvass. S. and Det Arkæologiske Nævn (eds.) *Vor Skjulte kulturarv. Arkæologien under overfladen. Festskrift til Dronning Margrethe II*, 30–31. Det Kongelige Nordiske Oldskriftselskab and Jysk Arkæologisk Selskab. København.

—— in press. Mesolitiske grave og skeletter. In: Lass Jensen, O. (ed.) *Status og Perspektiver inden for dansk mesolitikum*.

Brinch Petersen, E., Christensen, C., Vang Petersen, P. and Aaris-Sørensen, K. 1976. Vedbækprojektet. Udgravningerne i Vedbæk-området. *Søllerødbogen*, 97–122.

Brinch Petersen, E. and Meiklejohn, C. in press. Paradigm Lost? Intensification, Sedentism and Burial Practice in Southern Scandinavia: some Questions and Suggestions. In: Janik, L.,

Kaner, S. and Rowley-Conwy, R. (eds.) *From Jomon to Star Carr: Holocene Hunters and Gatherers in temperate Eurasia.*

Brinch Petersen, E., Meiklejohn, C. and Alexandersen, V. 1993. Vedbæk. Graven midt i byen. *Nationalmuseets Arbejdsmark,* 61–68.

Buikstra, J.E. and Swegle, M. 1989. Bone Modification Due to Burning: Experimental Evidence. In: Bonnichsen, R. and Sorg, W.H. (eds.) *Bone Modification,* 247–258. Institute for Quaternary Studies. Orono.

Bøttiger Mørck, P., Casati, C., Hansen, F., Moberg Riis, K., Sørensen, L. and Tang Kristensen, J. 1999. Vedbæks ældste stenalderboplads. *Søllerødbogen,* 7–31.

Cauwe, N. 1998. *La grotte Margaux à Anseremme-Dinant. Étude d'une sépulture collective du Mésolithique ancien.* ERAUL 59. Liège.

Christensen, C. 1982. Stenalderfjorden og Vedbækbopladserne – havspejlets svingninger 5500–2500 f. Kr. *Nationalmuseets Arbejdsmark,* 169–178.

—— 1995. The Littorina Transgressions in Denmark. In: Fischer, A. (ed.) *Man and Sea in the Mesolithic. Coastal settlement above and below present sea level,* 15–22. Oxbow Monograph 53. Oxford.

Cullen, T. 1995. Mesolithic mortuary ritual at Franchthi Cave, Greece. *Antiquity* 69, 270–289.

Ducrocq, T. 1999. Le Mésolithique de la Somme (Nord-de-France). In: Thévenin, A. and Bintz, P. (eds.) *L'Europe des derniers chasseurs Épipaléolithique et Mésolithique. Peuplement et Paléoenvironment de l'Épipaléolithique et du Mésolithique,* 247–262. Documents préhistoriques 12. Paris.

Fischer, A., Møhl, U., Bennike, P., Tauber, H., Malmros, C.J., Schou Hansen, J. and Smed, P. 1987. *Argusgrunden – en undersøisk boplads fra jægerstenalderen.* Fortidsminder og kulturhistorie. Antikvariske Studier 8.

Fryd Koot, H. 2000. *Gravene på Gøngehusvej 7. En gennemgang og analyse, med speciel fokus på brandgraven N.* Unpublished BA-project. Department of Archaeology and Ethnology, University of Copenhagen. Copenhagen.

Johansen, L. 1998. Refitting Analysis of the Mesolithic Site at Vænget Nord in Denmark. In: Conard, N.J. and Kind, C.-J. (eds.) *Aktuelle Forschungen zum Mesolithikum.* Urgeschichtliche Materialheft 12, 186–188.

Juel Jensen, H. and Brinch Petersen, E. 1985. A Functional Study of Lithics from Vænget Nord, a Mesolithic Site at Vedbæk, NE Zealand. *Journal of Danish Archaeology,* 40–51.

Kannegaard, E. and Brinch Petersen, E. 1993. Grave, mennesker og hunde. In: Hvass, S. and Storgaard, B. (eds.) *Da klinger i Muld... 25 års arkæologi i Danmark,* 76–81. Det Kgl. Nordiske Oldskriftselskab and Jysk Arkæologisk Selskab. Århus.

Kunwald, G. 1954 De ældste Vidnesbyrd om Ligbrænding i Danmarks Oldtid. *Dansk Ligbrændingsforenings Beretning for 1954,* 71–112. København.

Larsson, L. 1988. *Ett fångstsamhälle for 7000 år sedan.* Kristianstad.

Lass Jensen, O. 2000. Nivå – gruber til liv og død. In: Hvass, S. and Det Arkæologiske Nævn (eds.) *Vor Skjulte kulturarv. Arkæologien under overfladen. Festskrift til Dronning Margrethe II,* 24–25. Det Kongelige Nordiske Oldskriftselskab and Jysk Arkæologisk Selskab. København.

Leen Jensen, M. and Kjems, S. 2000. *Menneskelige Adfærdsmønstre på Gøngehusvej 7 – en mesolitisk boplads i Vedbæk.* Unpublished BA-project. Department of Archaeology and Ethnology, University of Copenhagen. København.

Lindquist, C. and Possnert, G. 1999. The first Seal Hunter Families on Gotland. On the Mesolithic Occupation in the Stora Förvar Cave. *Current Swedish Archaeology* 7, 65–68.

Marciniak, M. 1993. Mesolithic Burial and Dwelling Structure from the Boreal Period Excavated at Mszano site 14, Torun District, Poland: Preliminary Report. *Mesolithic Miscellany* 14, 1–2, 7–11.

Mathiassen, T. 1946. En boplads fra ældre stenalder ved Vedbæk Boldbaner. *Søllerødbogen,* 19–35.

Mays, S. 1998. *The Archaeology of human Bones.* London.

Meiklejohn, C., Brinch Petersen, E. and Alexandersen, V. 1998. The later Mesolithic Population of Sjælland Denmark, and the Neolithic Transition. In: Zvelebil, M., Domanska, L. and Dennel, R. (eds.) *Harvesting the Sea, Farming the Forest: The Emergence of Neolithic Societies in the Baltic Region and Adjacent Areas,* 203–212. Sheffield.

—— 2000. The Anthropology and Archaeology of Mesolithic Gender in the Western Baltic. In: Donald, M. and Hurcombe, L. (eds.) *Gender and Material Culture: from Prehistory to the Present,* 222–237. London.

Meiklejohn, C. and Denston, C. 1987. The human skeletal material. In: Mellars, P. (ed.) *Excavations on Oronsay,* 291–300. Edinburgh.

Meiklejohn, C. and Wyman, J.M. 1993. *The skeletal Material from Feature N. Gøngehusvej 7 Vedbæk, North Sjælland, Denmark; A preliminary Report.* Department of Anthropology, University of Winnipeg. Winnipeg.

Møller Nielsen, M. 2000. *Blokkene på Gøngehusvej nr. 7.* Unpublished BA-project. Department of Archaeology and Ethnology, University of Copenhagen. København.

Nordahn Frederiksen, H. 2000. *Pilene på Gøngehusvej 7.* Unpublished BA-project. Department of Archaeology and Ethnology, University of Copenhagen. København.

Price, D.T. and Brinch Petersen, E. 1987. A Mesolithic Camp in Denmark. *Scientific American,* March, 90–99.

Rasmussen, K.L. 1999. 14C-dateringer, København 1998. *Arkæologiske udgravninger i Danmark* 1998, 310–326. Det arkæologiske Nævn. København.

Rausing, G. 1991. Bears, boars and burials. *Fornvännen* 86, 73–77.

Roksandic, M. 1999. *Cranial non-metric variability in the Djerdap skeletal series, Serbia: implications for the transition to agriculture.* Unpublished Ph.D. Thesis, Department of Archaeology, Simon Fraser University. Vancouver.

Schutkowski, H. 1991. Experimentelle Befunde an Brandknochen und ihre Bedeutung für die Diagnose von Leichenbränden. *Archäologische Informationen* 14, nr. 2, 206–218.

Skaarup, J. 2000. Jægerliv i sejlløbet til Ærøskøbing. In: Hvass, S. and Det Arkæologiske Nævn (eds.) *Vor Skjulte kulturarv. Arkæologien under overfladen. Festskrift til Dronning Margrethe II,* 36–37. Det Kongelige Nordiske Oldskriftselskab and Jysk Arkæologisk Selskab. København.

Tauber, H. 1988. Danske arkæologiske C-14 dateringer 1987. *Arkæologiske udgravninger i Danmark* 1987, 227–244. Det arkæologiske Nævn. København.

Ulriksen, J. 1998. *Anløbspladser. Besejling og bebyggelse i Danmark mellem 200 og 1100 e. Kr.* Roskilde.

Vang Petersen, P. 1977. Vedbæk Boldbaner – endnu en gang. *Søllerødbogen,* 131–170.

—— 1979. Træ til jægernes redskaber. *Søllerødbogen,* 56–80.

—— 1982. Jægerfolket på Vedbækbopladserne – kulturudviklingen i Kongemose- og Ertebølletid. *Nationalmuseets Arbejdsmark,* 179–189.

Vang Petersen, P. and Brinch Petersen, E. 1978. Bergmansdal – for 7000 år siden. *Helsingør Bymuseums Årbog,* 5–28.

Vennersdorf, M. 2000. *En sammensætningsanalyse af Gøngehusvej 7.* Unpublished BA-project. Department of Archaeology and Ethnology, University of Copenhagen. København.

Verlinde, A.D. 1974. A Mesolithic settlement with cremation at Dalfsen. *Berichten van de Rijksdienst voor het Oudheidkundig Bodemonderzoek* 24, 113–117.

62. Childhood in the Epi-Palaeolithic. What do personal ornaments associated with burials tell us?

Marian Vanhaeren and Francesco d'Errico

Taphonomic, technological and morphometric analyses of shell beads from a child burial in La Madeleine (Dordogne, France), dated to circa 10,190 BP, and those from a double child burial in the Grotte des Enfants (Ligury, Italy), dated to circa 11,130 BP, are used to reconstruct bead manufacturing techniques and discuss the significance of children's ornaments in the Epi-Palaeolithic. Beadwork from these burials was made by adults, involved a substantial investment of time in production and resulted in an ostentatious display on the child's body. The present study and data from contemporary burials shows that children wore tiny versions of adult beads. This at the very least indicates that children were considered as a distinct social group. The richness and variety of La Madeleine beadwork may be a function of the child's high status conferred by a hereditary ranking system.

Introduction

Personal ornaments are seen variously as objects used to beautify the body, as "dallies", amulets, exchange media, expressions of individual and group identity, markers of age class and gender and signs of power, wealth or social status. Given their polysemic nature, one might wonder whether archaeologists can use personal ornaments successfully to investigate issues such as ethnicity, language, exchange networks, and social hierarchy in prehistoric societies. Studies in ethnicity (Jones 1997) reveal that ornaments may have one or many of these functions and that to untangle them is difficult, even in cases where the study is of living people. Ethnography also shows that these functions change in time and that, to express self and group identity, the same members of a group may wear different types of personal ornaments according to the social context of use (war, feast, ritual, funeral, aggregation events, etc.). However, identifying these contexts in the archaeological record may be difficult. Ethnographic data also indicate that individual beads, the most common occurrence in excavations, rarely convey meaning. It is the combination and arrangement of several different beads, and their positioning on the body that is important (for example, in the hair, on bonnets, chokers, necklaces, pendants, bracelets, belts, anklets, garment decoration, etc.). Such associations only are available to archaeologists through the study of purposeful deposits such as pit contents, occasionally lost complete ornaments and primary human burials. Primary burials offer the advantage of being intentional, virtually instantaneous, deposits that often preserve the spatial arrangement of beads. Thus complex ornaments, composed of a large number of beads can be isolated and compared with others found on the same skeleton and we can investigate associations with anatomy, gender and age.

Primary burials guarantee that the associated type of beads (raw material, colour, species, shape, size, etc.) found therein and the techniques used to manufacture these objects were all part of the material culture of the mourners. Combinations of data on the choices, source, production, assembly, manner of wearing and degree of use of beads from one burial and from contemporary burials in the same or different sites may suggest the predominant functions of personal ornaments in a given society. The main question, of course, is how to integrate these data in a reliable framework of inferences to guide our interpretation, i.e. what kind of analogy should we adopt to proceed from beads to the individual and perhaps to her/his society.

Cross-cultural studies of mortuary practices usefully dismissed commonly held archaeological preconceptions embedded in the culture-history approach (Ucko 1969) and suggested the existence of some regularity among human groups following similar subsistence modes (Saxe 1970; Binford 1971; Brown 1971; Carr 1995; Testart 2000). These studies, however, did not provide concrete middle range theories applicable to the interpretation of ornaments associated with primary burials (Pearson 1999). One probable reason for this failure is that ethnographic literature rather than ethnoarchaeological fieldwork provided the data. Fieldwork could have involved a first-hand analysis of the technical and morphological variability of the ornaments to establish to what extent each

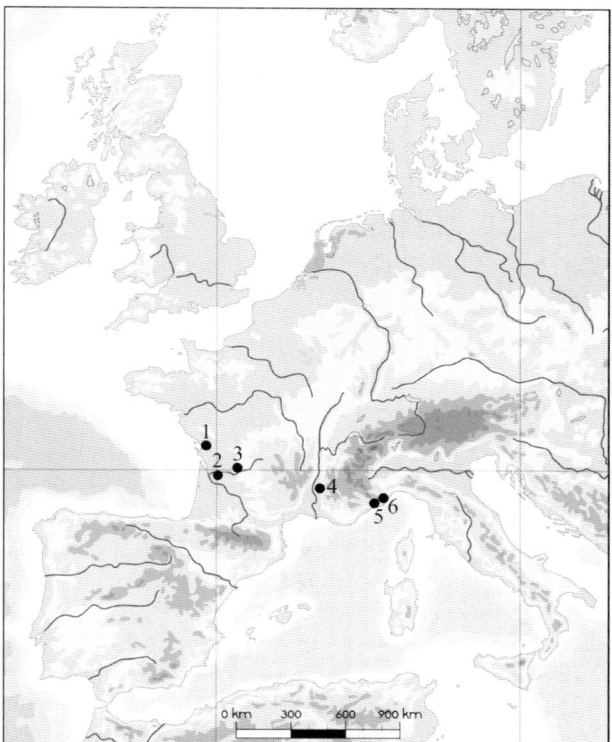

Figure 62.1 Map with the location of the Epi-Palaeolithic burial sites mentioned in the text. 1: La Vergne (Charente-Maritime), 2: Houleau (Gironde), 3: La Madeleine (Dordogne), 4: Aven des Iboussières (Drôme), 5: Grotte des Enfants (Ligury), 6: Arene Candide (Ligury).

of these variables provided information about the production, exchange and symbolic functions of the objects among the living in a known cultural context.

Analysis of ornament variability in cemeteries that we can assume confidently were used by the same human group provides a different approach to the problem. This may allow discovery of features that are common to all members of the group and those that identify gender and age classes. Comparison of contemporaneous cemeteries from different regions may reveal features peculiar to each group that are likely to represent cultural identity markers.

With this last aim in mind, we recently analysed grave good variability from two Epi-Palaeolithic – Early Mesolithic cemeteries from Southern Europe (Figure 62.1) (d'Errico and Vanhaeren 2000) – La Vergne in Western France (Duday and Courtaud 1998; Dupont 1998) and Arene Candide in Northern Italy (Cardini 1980; Bietti 1987). Dated around 11,700 and 9,000 BP respectively, each cemetery included approximately ten individuals with associated ornaments and grave goods. In each site, some categories of ornaments are common to all, or almost all, of the deceased and equally associated with adults and children irrespective of sex. However, the most abundant types of beads are different in each site. The deceased at La Vergne share ornaments made from shells of *Dentalium* and *Nassa* and the canines of red deer and fox, whilst at Arene Candide fragments of Lamellibranchia and shells of *Patella* and *Cyclope* fulfil this role. This led us to conclude that the materials used in the main personal ornament categories project aspects of group identity. Integration of this interpretation with a detailed analysis of grave goods associated with the 10,210 ± 80 year old (OxA-5682) Aven des Iboussières burial site in the South East of France, further refined the model. Our study made clear that not only the type and source of ornaments, but also the manufacturing techniques, size choices, forms of decoration as well as modes of suspension and wearing of the ornaments are relevant in conveying the cultural identity of neighbouring groups.

Ethnicity however, constitutes only one element in the construction of social identities. Regrettably, the poor archaeological context of the graves at Aven des Iboussières meant that our analysis could not establish if the documented features characterised the gender, age, and social status of the deceased. The aim of the present study is to investigate whether personal ornaments found in Epi-Palaeolithic child burials from Southern Europe are different from those associated with adults and, if so, to explore whether these differences help define how this age class was perceived in this period. To this end, we submit the personal ornaments from the La Madeleine child burial and those from the double child burial of the Grotte des Enfants to a taphonomic, technological and morphometric analysis. The result of these analyses are interpreted in the light of actualistic and experimental data, which enable us to highlight the capital role played by bead size and time consuming embroidery in Epi-Palaeolithic child burials, and discuss the implications of these features.

La Madeleine child burial

Peyrony discovered the La Madeleine child in the eponymous site in 1926 (Capitan and Peyrony 1928), located near Tursac in the Dordogne region of France (Figure 62.1). The skeleton is from a 3 to 7 year old child and recently was dated directly by AMS to 10,190 ± 100 BP (GifA-95457) (Gambier *et al.* 2000). Personal ornaments include perforated canines (2 red deer, 2 fox), perforated marine shells (176 *Neritina*, 42 *Turritella*, 24 *Cyclope*, 1 *Glycymeris*) and 1314 *Dentalium* shells (Taborin 1993; Vanhaeren and d'Errico 2001). Ochre heavily stains both the skeleton and the personal ornaments. The single drawing of the burial made during the excavation (Figure 62.2) shows that the child lay straight on her/his back and that the ornaments were located on the head and around the neck, elbows, wrists, knees and ankles. However, the precise location of each personal ornament is unknown.

Grotte des Enfants double child burial

Emile Rivière (1874; 1887) discovered this burial in 1874

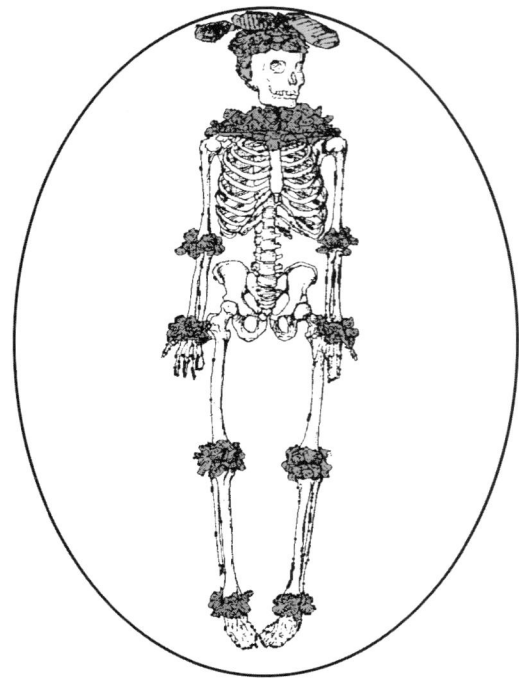

Figure 62.2 Sketch of the La Madeleine burial with location of the personal ornaments. The depression in which the child lay measures 2.6 by 0.9 m. After Capitan and Peyrony (1928: 122).

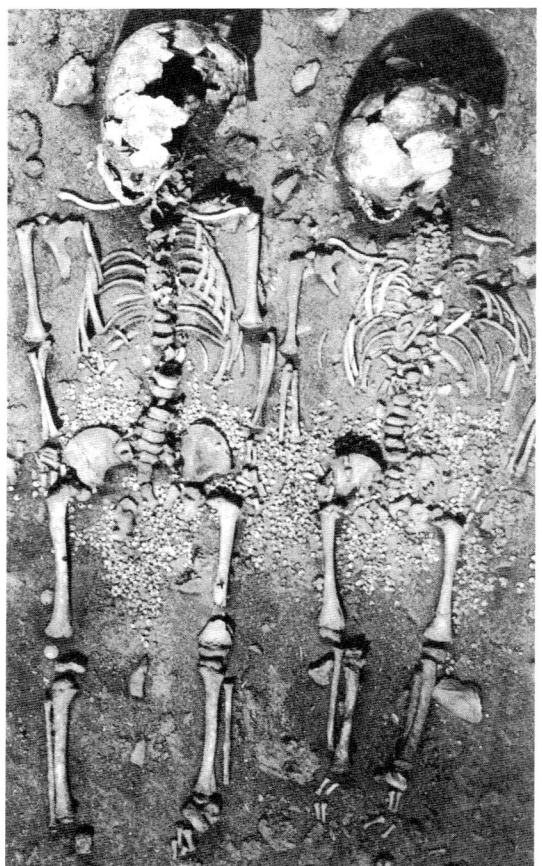

Figure 62.3 Grotte des Enfants double child burial with in situ location of the associated Cyclope beads. Photo MAN.

Figure 62.4 Cyclope shells found on the Grottes des Enfants skeletons. Scale: 1 cm. Photo MAN/L. Hammon.

in the Grotte des Enfants, one of the Grimaldi caves located in Ligury near the French-Italian border (Figure 62.1). Two children lay on their back, side by side (Figure 62.3). One of them (GE1) is dated directly by AMS to 11,130 ± 100 BP (GifA 94197) (Gambier et al. 2001). The ornaments consist of more then 1426 *Cyclope* shells (Vanhaeren in prep.) (Figure 62.4) found around their pelvii and a few shells of other species (*Patella, Pectunculus, Mytilus* and *Trivia*) (Taborin 1993). A recent study (Gambier 2001), involving the excavation of the *in situ* sediment on which the skeletons lay in the museum and an anthropological analysis, revealed that one child (GE1) was about 2 to 4 and the other (GE2) 1 to 2 years old. The latter has a flint point embedded in a thoracic vertebra, which may well have been the cause of death. No ornaments came from the sediment under skeleton GE2 and this suggests that just the front portion of the clothing had applied beads. The arrangement of some beads within the grave suggests they were strung in vertical lines. We cannot exclude the possibility that the children also wore bracelets as the infants' hands lay within the bead clusters near their hips. Two red deer third phalanges found in the waist region of GE1 may have completed her/his garment.

Methodology

Study of the personal ornaments associated with the La Madeleine and the Grotte des Enfants burials took place at the respective repositories of the Musée National de Préhistore (Les Eyzies-de-Tayac) and the Musée des Antiquités Nationales (Saint-Germain-en-Laye). We recorded the length, maximum and minimum diameter of the *Dentalium* shells from the La Madeleine burial (Figure 62.5) and the length of the *Cyclope* shells from the Grotte des Enfants. Shells were identified to the species level where possible using criteria proposed by Poppe and Goto (1993). Due to their small size and fragility, the measurements on the La Madeleine *Dentalium* were taken off high resolution digitised images. A sheet of graph paper was used to measure the *Cyclope* shells from the Grotte des Enfants. We examined the *Dentalium* shells with a low power optical microscope, recording the end morph-

Childhood in the Epi-Palaeolithic. What do personal ornaments associated with burials tell us?

Figure 62.5 Dentalium shells associated with La Madeleine child.

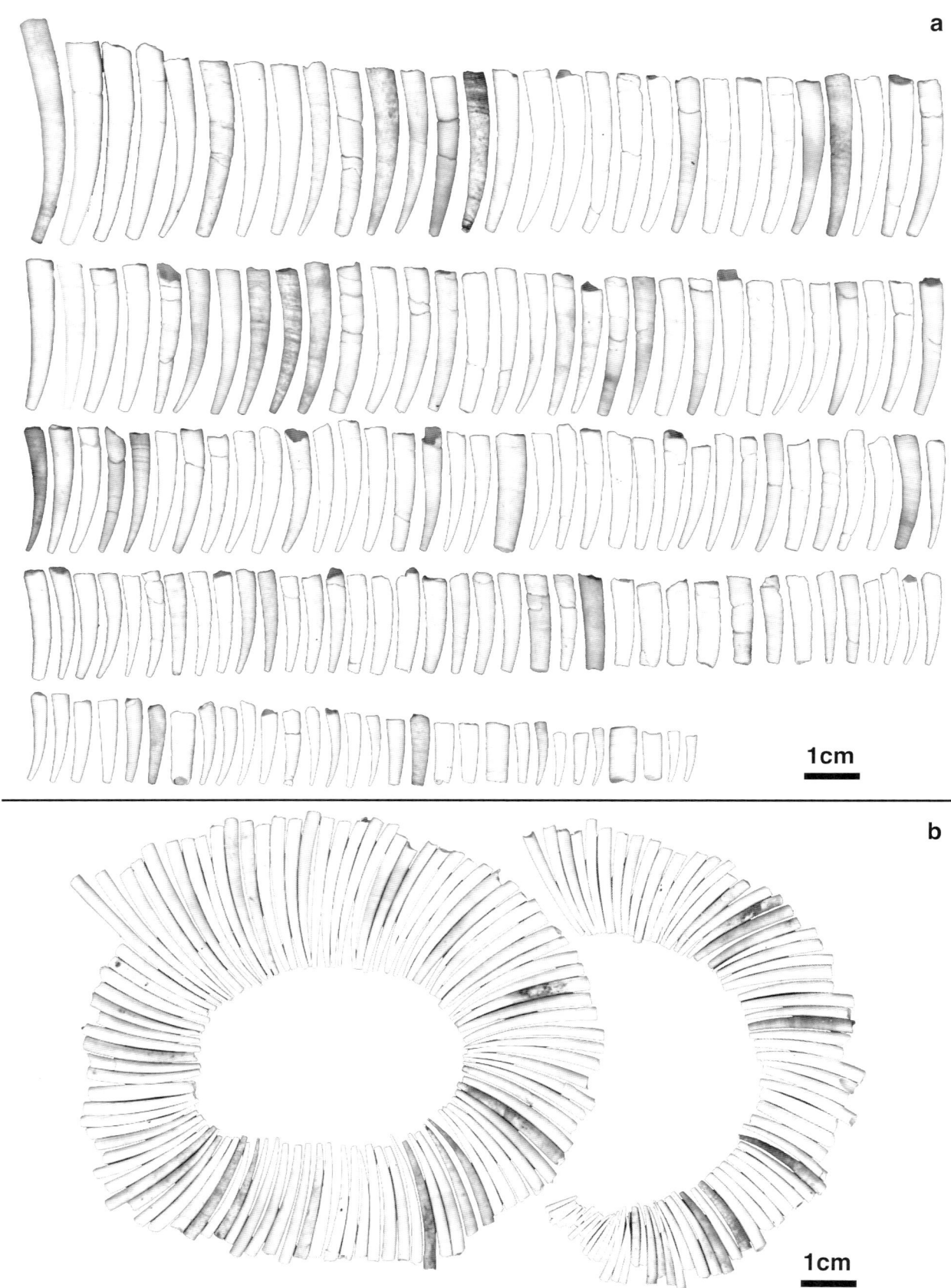

Figure 62.6 Dentalium shell reference collections from the beach (a) and from the Miocene palaeontological site of Saucats-La Brède (b).

ology and the presence of possible natural or anthropic traces.

Our reference collections include 339 modern *Dentalium*, most of them identified as *Dentalium entalis*, gathered on the Atlantic coast of the South West of France (Figure 62.6a), 244 *Dentalium sp.* from the Miocene fossil site of Saucats-La Brède (Cahuzac and Cluzaud 1999) (Figure 62.6b) and 203 modern *Cyclope* collected on the Mediterranean coast of the South East of France (Figure 62.7). Five persons collected the *Dentalium* from the beach in two hours; one person gathered the *Dentalium* from Saucats-La Brède in approximately two hours; one person collected the *Cyclope* shells in 3 hours. All encountered shells of these species were collected whether complete or fragmentary.

The variables recorded on the archaeological specimens were also taken on shells of the reference collection. Examination of the end morphology of the *Dentalium* characterised natural breakage morphologies. We experimentally split seventy modern and fossil *Dentalium* by snapping or sawing and observed the broken ends to characterise the diagnostic features of these techniques. We also used, for comparative purposes, measurements taken on 1112 *Dentalium*, mostly identified as *Dentalium dentalis* and *Dentalium mutabile inaequicostatum*, from the Aven des Iboussières cemetery (d'Errico *et al.* 2000b; Dupont in press).

Results

Unbroken *Dentalium* shells have a conical, slightly curved shape (Figure 62.6) and a length that is between 7 and 12 times their maximum diameter, depending on the species (Pope and Goto 1993). Almost all tubular beads from La Madeleine have a cylindrical rather than conical shape, a length of less than 12 mm (Figure 62.8a), and a length/maximum diameter ratio that varies between 1 and 5 (Figure 62.9a). Unbroken anterior openings described in the malacological literature are, like those in our comparative sample, always narrower than 1 mm (Figure 62.9d). The minimum diameter of the archaeological beads, in contrast, is always wider that 1.7 mm and mostly cluster between 2 and 3 mm (Figure 62.9b). It appears then, that in the archaeological specimens the thinner portion close to the anterior opening is missing. These observations lead us to conclude that 97% of the La Madeleine child tubular beads are short fragments of originally longer *Dentalium* shells and that a mere 3% are relatively long fragments (between 12 and 25 mm).

The beads are unlikely to result simply from a random or even selective collection of naturally fragmented and thus shortened *Dentalium* shell from a beach or a palaeontological site. Lengths of more than 85% of the La Madeleine *Dentalium* beads are less than the lengths of *Dentalium* in the beach and Miocene samples (Figure 62.8). Where the lengths of *Dentalium* shells from both comparative assemblages fall within the size range of the

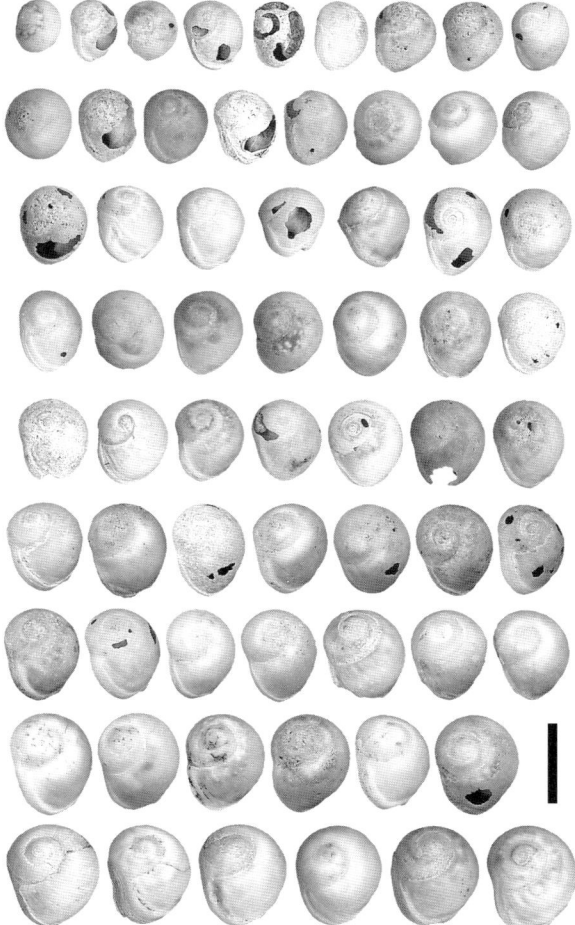

Figure 62.7 Cyclope shell reference collection collected on a Mediterranean beach. Scale: 1cm.

La Madeleine beads, the diameters generally are smaller than those measured on the archaeological specimens (Figure 62.9 g–h). The archaeological beads are short segments coming from the central and, to a lesser extent, from the posterior (i.e. widest) portion of massive *Dentalium*. Such segments, which seem to be rare in nature, result from the deliberate sectioning of longer shells to produce cylinders of around 6 mm length. The few longer fragments accounting for 3% of the La Madeleine collection also have sizes that are incompatible with shells from the reference collections. Diameters present in the archaeological sample are absent among fossil *Dentalium* and, when present in specimens from the beach, they are associated with much longer shells. Clearly, the La Madeleine beads do not result from a collection and use of *Dentalium* shells from a beach or a paleontological site without modification. Interestingly, the frequency distribution of the *Dentalium* lengths from the Aven des Iboussières burials (Figure 62.8d) significantly differs from that of La Madeleine (P<0.0001) as well as from that of both reference collections (P<0.0001).

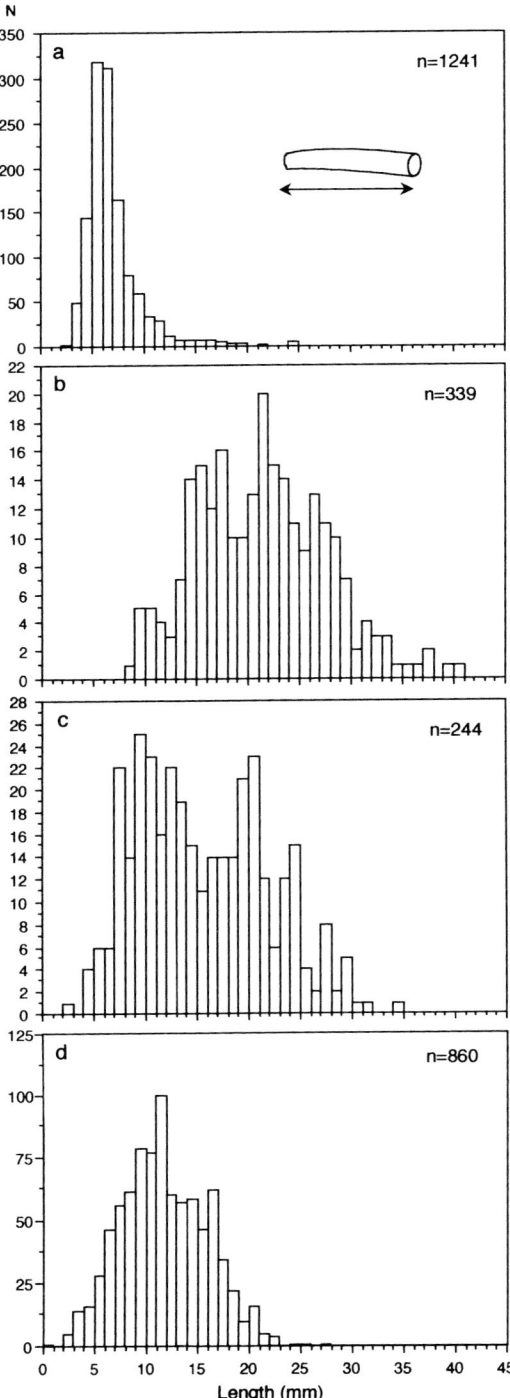

Figure 62.8 Frequency distribution of the Dentalium lengths measured on the La Madeleine (a), beach (b), fossil (c) and Aven des Iboussières (d) collections.

The morphology of La Madeleine *Dentalium* ends supports the conclusion that they were modified. It is possible to distinguish between intact openings of *Dentalium* shells, naturally broken ends, and ends created by humans using two techniques. Openings on unbroken *Dentalium* have regular edges and typically, the posterior openings are thin and sharp (Figure 62.10 a–d). Fractured *Dentalium* from modern and fossil thanatocenoses often have irregular edges created by microchipping. Fractures are either perpendicular or oblique to the main axis of the fragment and often show a lip-like morphology (Figure 62.10 e–f). The Miocene *Dentalium* assemblage provided two additional breakage morphologies. These are linear, regular fractures running perpendicular into the shell cylinder (Figure 62.10h), and fractures displaying a differential breakage of the inner and outer layers of the shell (Figure 62.10j). The former are similar to fractures produced by experimental snapping, whatever the form of this action (Figure 62.10k). Sawing produces ends with two facets. One is oblique and covered with traces left by the to-and-fro movement of the cutting edge. The break off resulting from the sawing leaves a facet perpendicular to the shell main axis that is morphologically similar to one produced by snapping the shell (Figure 62.10l).

Six types of end morphologies were identified on La Madeleine beads: 1) few intact posterior openings often affected by a slight smoothing (Figure 62.11a); 2) a similar proportion of equally smoothed lip-like fractures, found only on the posterior end of the fragments and comparable to fractures from the reference collections (Figure 62.11 b–d); 3) a large number of straight regular fractures, most commonly on the anterior end and similar to those produced by experimental snapping and found occasionally in the Miocene control assemblage (Figure 62.11 e–f); 4) rounded ends sometimes showing clear traces of post-depositional abrasion and/or microchipping (Figure 62.11 g–h); 5) few examples of ends with morphologies compatible with sawing (Fig.11i); 6) many rounded edges with undulating profiles and deep notches of a sort absent in natural assemblages (Figure 62.11l). The presence of cut marks (Figure 62.11 j–k) confirms that some shells were sectioned by sawing.

Sawing traces are the only unequivocal sign of human reduction of the shell length. A large number of straight fractures probably result from intentional breakage, as they are identical to those produced experimentally by snapping, and they occur on the beads in a much higher proportion than they do in the palaeontological control assemblage. In sum, the La Madeleine beads show at least two end types resulting from human manufacture. Undulating profiles and deep notches on the other hand, are likely caused by use wear. A flat longitudinal facet on the side of the bead, recognisable at microscopic level, is often associated with the notch (Figure 62.11l). This suggests that the beads were applied singly to material and friction from thread and cloth produced the notches and facets respectively. The recorded position of the beads on the body seems to confirm this interpretation since they were found, amongst other places, on the elbows and the knees where bracelets would be inappropriate.

The morphometric analysis of the Cyclope beads associated to the double child burial of the Grottes des Enfants shows that more than 90% of the archaeological

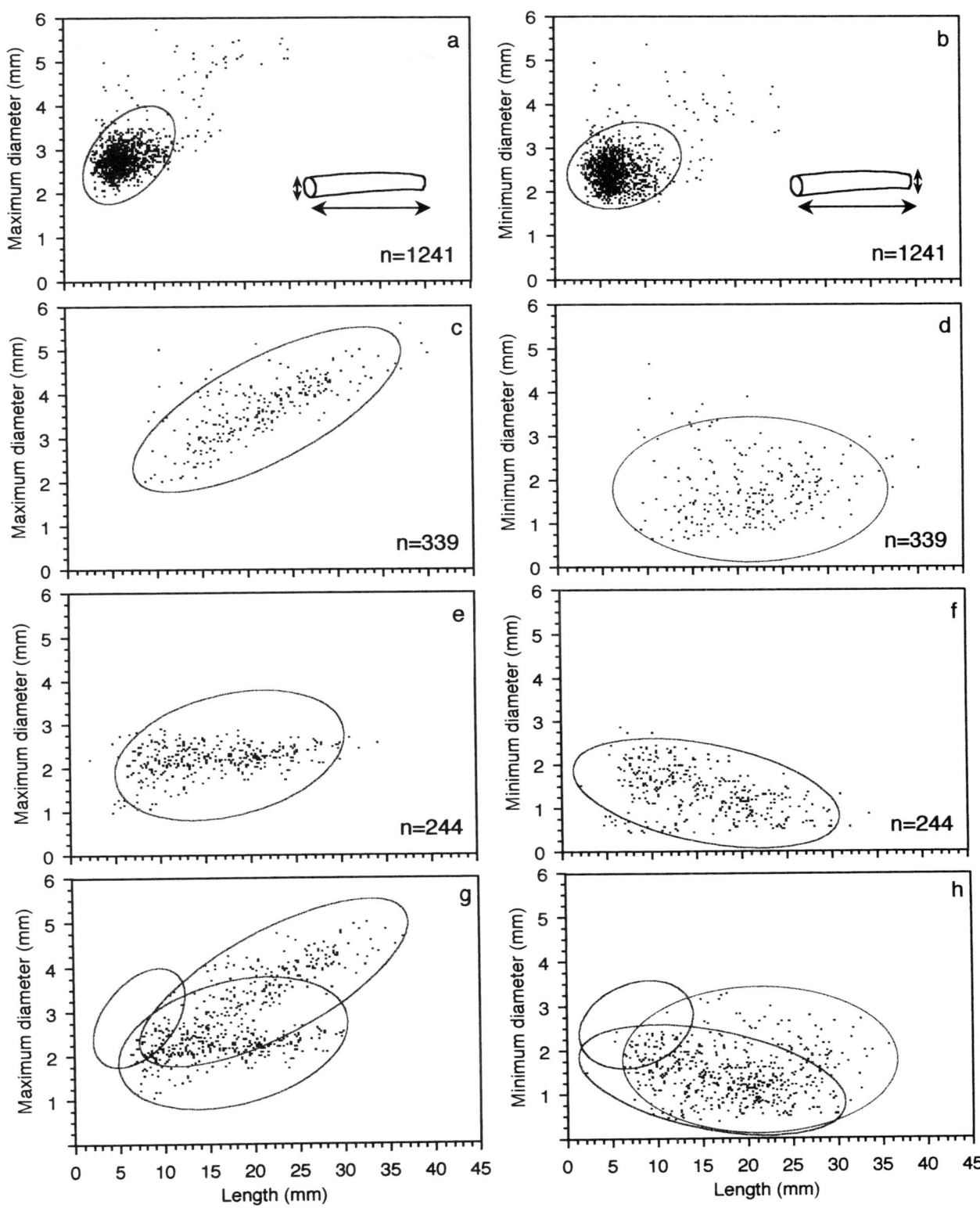

Figure 62.9 Correlation between length and diameters of Dentalium shells from La Madeleine (a,b), an Atlantic beach (c,d), and Saucats-La Brède collection (e,f). Diagram at the bottom (g, h) compares the confidence ellipse of the archaeological beads with scattergrams and confidence ellipses of reference collections (confidence ellipses = 95%).

shells are smaller than those naturally occurring on a modern Mediterranean beach (Figure 62.12). We cannot establish, however, whether archaeological and modern shells belong to the same species. Malacologists traditionally include larger Cyclope shells in the species Cyclope neritea while assigning the smaller ones to Cyclope

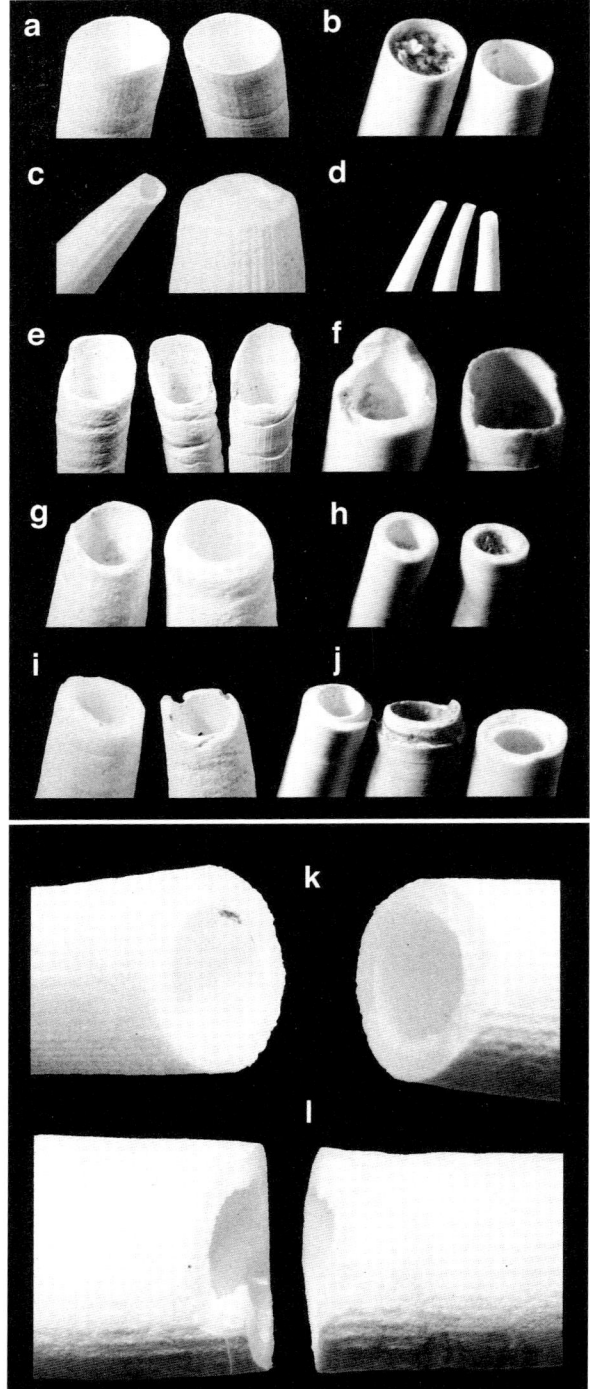

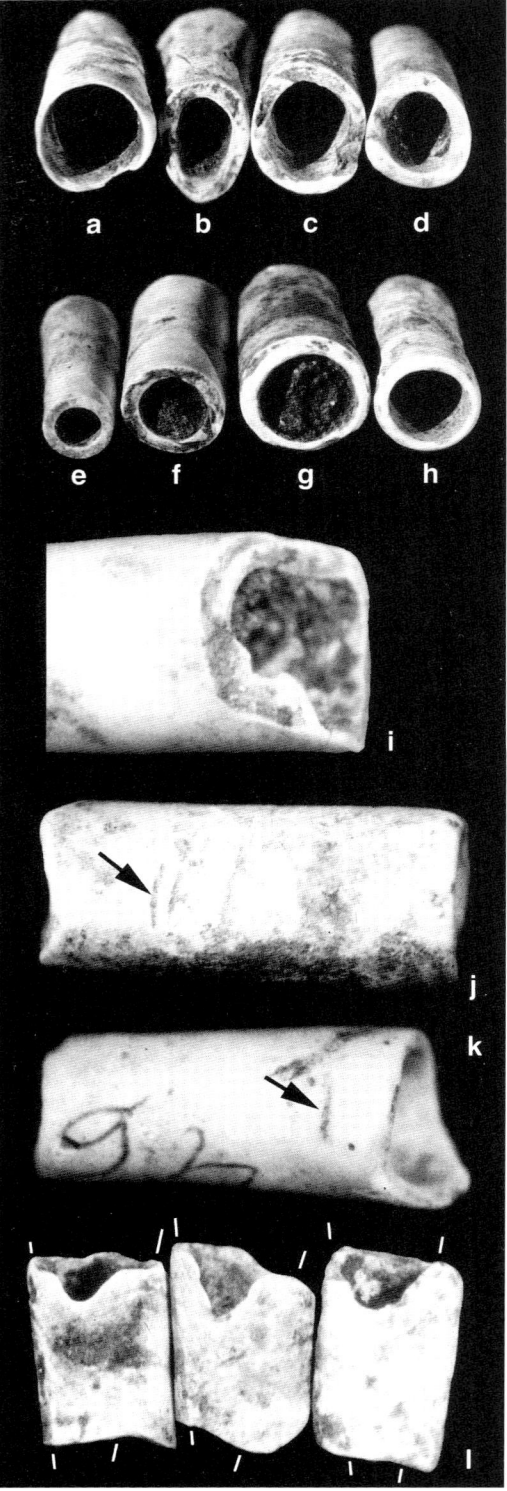

Figure 62.10 Top: end morphologies observed on Dentalium from the beach (left) and from the palaeontological site (right). a–b: unbroken posterior openings; c–d: unbroken anterior openings; e–f: lip fractures; g: rounded ends, h: straight fractures, i: irregular fractures, j: "step" fractures. Bottom: end morphologies produced by experimental snapping (k), and sawing (l).

Figure 62.11 End morphologies observed on the La Madeleine Dentalium beads. a: unbroken posterior end; b–d: lip fractures; e–f: straight fractures; g: post depositional damage; h: rounded end; i: end morphology probably produced by sawing; j–k: cutmarks (arrows) probably produced by the accidental side-slipping of the lithic tool during sawing; l: undulating end morphologies and notches associated to longitudinal facets interpreted as resulting from rubbing against threads and clothes. a–h: Photo MNP/Ph. Jugie

donovania although it is unclear whether size differences provide a reliable criterion for identifying species within this genus (Poppe and Goto 1993).

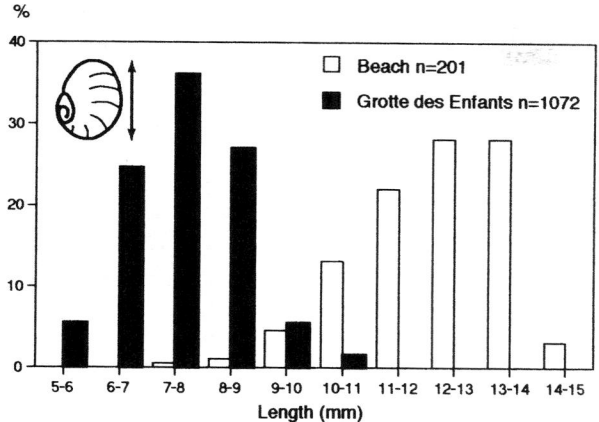

Figure 62.12 Frequency distribution of the Cyclope shells length from the Grotte des Enfants and from a Mediterranean beach.

Discussion and conclusion

The life history of La Madeleine tubular beads may shed light on their function in the community responsible for the burial of the child. Our comparative morphometric analysis indicates that most of the beads are of sizes that do not occur in natural assemblages and so must result from the deliberate and careful breakage of *Dentalium* gathered from a beach or fossil site. Since most of the *Dentalium* we collected in natural sites each can produce two beads of the size found in La Madeleine, we estimate that the assembly of sufficient number of shells to make the La Madeleine beads required between 5 to 20 hours, depending on the source of the material. We do not know whether the artisan, or members of her/his group collected the shells, or if they arrived by exchange. The existence of exchange networks involving shells is well attested at the end of the Upper Palaeolithic (Bahn 1982; Taborin 1993; Floss 2000). The presence of Mediterranean shells in the burial (20 *Cyclope*) indicates that at least some of the *Dentalium* may have the same origin.

The minimum diameter of the beads and the absence of natural anterior openings indicate that the bead maker systematically removed the pointed end of the shells, perhaps to produce tubes with openings large enough to admit the thread and to achieve the desired bead length of between 6 and 7 mm. Longer shells were probably broken twice or, more rarely, three times to produce two or three beads of standardised length from just one *Dentalium*. Fragments too short to be snapped readily were probably sawn to reduce the length. The size homogeneity of the small beads, composing 97% of the collection, strongly suggests production by one individual or at most a few group members for use together in a specific beadwork. It is very unlikely that these beads were acquired by a series of separate exchanges in their present sizes. In contrast to the smaller ones, the few long *Dentalium* associated with the burial are much more variable in size and certainly, they were employed in a different kind of beadwork. Their total length (75 cm) is compatible with a use as a doubled necklace.

Use wear patterns indicate embroidery rather than stringing of the small beads. A cumulative length of the beads of more than 9 m reveals the minimum length of thread required to complete the garment. This task also required the making of 2,400 holes in the garment with needles as thin as 1.5 mm (smallest diameters of the beads). Needles of this diameter come from the late Magdalenian layers of the site (Vanhaeren and d'Errico submitted). The material to which the beads were sewn was probably soft leather since experimental piercing of skins with bone awls indicates that thin needles break easily when used on robust skin (d'Errico et al. 2000a). It is difficult to evaluate precisely the amount of time needed to apply the beads, as it depends on the ability of the person. Nonetheless, as the task involved maintaining and replacing needles and the production of thread aside of the sewing itself, the work must have taken a considerable amount of time – we estimate a minimum working time of 30–50 hours. Use wear also indicates that the decorated cloth was worn by someone, probably the deceased child, and therefore cannot be interpreted as special purpose funerary dress.

The double burial from the Grotte des Enfants reveals a similar attitude towards child dress. Experimental gathering of *Cyclope* shells indicates that currently it is difficult to find shells as small as those with the double burial. If the size variability of this genus during the Late Glacial did not differ significantly from that of today, it took at least 30 hours – and probably much more, to collect the number of shells found on the two children. These small beads are difficult to manipulate when piercing and threading them in beadwork. The perforation size, ranging from 2 to 4 mm, and the number of shells involved suggest that the application of these beads on clothes was a time consuming activity, just as at La Madeleine. In the future, *Cyclope* shells found in contemporary burials and other archaeological contexts will be measured to verify whether the use of small shells results from selective gathering or from environmental changes. Available information suggests that big *Cyclope* shells existed at the time, for example at Arene Candide (Cardini 1980), but reliable data can only come from first-hand analysis. Another similarity with La Madeleine is that the beadwork in Grotte des Enfants was used during life, as indicated by smoothing on the perforation edge of many shells that we interpret as use wear (d'Errico et al. 1993).

The presence of few long *Dentalium* beads associated with the La Madeleine child and the predominance of long *Dentalium* beads in contemporary adult burials such as Aven des Iboussières and Houleau (Vanhaeren in prep.) as well as in settlement sites, demonstrates that small tubular beads are not a general feature of this time period. The indications from La Madeleine and provisionally, from Grotte des Enfants finds support at Sungir, where two infants wore about 10,000 ivory beads that on average, are one third smaller than those associated with an adult male burial in the same site (White 1993). We propose from this data that Epi-Palaeolithic people consciously associated small beads with children.

It is difficult to imagine that made to small size, embroidered onto a child's garment and worn for a long while, the *Dentalium* beads later might be redeployed in an ornament designed for adult use. Such a costly investment by adults in ornamentation for children needs an explanation. Is this just the symptom of a parent's "affection" for their child? Parental affection is a common feature of all human societies but the way in which it is embodied in material culture is peculiar to each society and generally bound by rules guaranteeing the conformity of dress with the social world view (Langer 1953, Leach 1976).

The specific form of children's beadwork potentially highlights a special status accorded to all or some members of this age grade among Epi-Palaeolithic societies. The youth of the La Madeleine and Grotte des Enfants children rules out the possibility that they achieved such a status through distinguished personal acts. Thus, is the investment in time and material embodied in beadworks a manifestation of hereditary rank or does it simply mark out children as a distinct social grade?

Available evidence is ambiguous and does not allow clear-cut interpretation. The similarity of the position, number, morphology and size of the beads associated with the Grotte des Enfants burials might support the latter hypothesis of a distinct social grade for children, unless these individuals were siblings or belonged to equally important lineages. A lack of variability in child grave goods at the contemporary and nearby cemetery of Arene Candide (Ligury, Italy) also conveys an impression of equality, althought these children were older in age than the Grotte des Enfants ones and might have achieved social adulthood. On the other hand, a Magdalenian/Azilian child burial without grave goods in Rochereil (Dordogne region), not far from the La Madeleine site (Jude 1960), potentially sustains the alternative hypothesis of hereditary ranking. Unfortunately, there is no radiocarbon date to confirm that Rochereil is contemporary with La Madeleine.

If rich ornamentation in child graves is due to hereditary rank, logically we should find evidence of status difference in adult burials, unless this was expressed only in children and not in adults, which would be rather unusual. Substantial variation in the amount and type of associated grave goods certainly is characteristic of Epi-Palaeolithic adult burials (May 1989; Binant 1991; d'Errico and Vanhaeren 2000). However, the dispersed distribution of such graves over Europe and within the time span of the Epi-Palaeolithic makes it difficult to establish if this variation is due to hereditary ranking or other causes (cultural affiliation, cultural change, acquired status).

Clearly, the small number of burials and even fewer interments of children found in the rare cemeteries complicates reaching certainty in this field. What is clear is that Epi-Palaeolithic people invested a surprising degree of attention, time and specific skills into the specific manufacture of ostentatious beadwork for children. This effort is comparable to that observed in more recent societies. Combining taphonomic and technological analysis of these objects provides a robust means of identifying the behaviours and by extension, the intentions behind the recovered archaeological remains.

Acknowledgements

We thank Royden Yates for very helpful comments on an earlier version of this manuscript and Dominique Gambier for interesting discussions on Upper Palaeolithic child burials and for sharing results of her analysis of the Grotte des Enfants burials. We thank Jean-Jacques Cleyet-Merle (Director), André Morala (Chief Technician) and the staff of the Musée National de Préhistoire, Les Eyzies-de-Tayac for facilitating our study of the La Madeleine material. We are also grateful to Marie-Hélène Thiault, former curator of the Palaeolithic section of the Musée des Antiquités Nationales, Saint-Germain-en-Laye, for permission to study the Grotte des Enfants shell beads. Philippe Jugie and Loïc Hamon, photographers at the Les Eyzies and Saint-Germain-en-Laye museums respectively, kindly provided some of the photographs used in this paper. Yves Gilly, Philippe Rocher and Cédric Beauval facilitated access to the Saucats La-Brède palaeontological collections. Modern reference collections were gathered with the help of several PhD students of the Institut de Préhistoire et de Géologie du Quaternaire (University of Bordeaux I). This research was funded by the OHLL CNRS program and by a fellowship given to Marian Vanhaeren by the Belgium Ministry of the Flemish Community and the Italian Ministry for Foreign Affairs.

References

Bahn, P.G. 1982. Inter-site and inter-regional links during the Upper Palaeolithic: the Pyrenean evidence. *The Oxford Journal of Archaeology* 1, 247–68.

Bietti, A. 1987. Some remarks on the new radiocarbon dates from the Arene Candide Cave (Savona, Italy). *Human Evolution* 2, 185–190.

Binant, P. 1991. *Les sépultures du Paléolithique.* Paris.

Binford, L.R. 1971. Mortuary practices : their study and their potential. In: Brown, J. (ed.) *Approaches to the Social Dimensions of Mortuary Practices*. Memoir of the Society for American Archaeology 25, 6–29. Washington, DC.

Brown, J. (ed.) 1971. *Approaches to the Social Dimensions of Mortuary Practices*. Memoir of the Society for American Archaeology 25. Washington, DC.

Cahuzac, B. and Cluzaud, A. 1999. Bilan scientifique et synthèse des données bibliographiques sur le Miocène moyen (Serravallien) de Saucats (Gironde, Bassin d'Aquitaine). *Bulletin de la Société Linnéenne de Bordeaux* 27 (2–3), 95–111, 113–133.

Capitan, L. and Peyrony, D. 1928. *La Madeleine : son gisement, son industrie, ses oeuvres d'art*. Paris.

Cardini, L. 1980. La necropoli mesolitica delle Arene Candide. *Memoria del Instituto Italiano di Paleontologia Umana* 3, 9–31.

Carr, C. 1995. Mortuary practices: their social, philosophical-religious, circumstantial, and physical determinants. *Journal of Archaeological Method and Theory* 2, 105–200.

d'Errico, F. and Vanhaeren, M. 2000. Mes morts et les morts de mes voisins. Le mobilier funéraire de l'Aven des Iboussières et l'identification de marqueurs culturels à l'Epipaléolithique. *Les derniers chasseurs-cueilleurs d'Europe occidentale*. Actes du colloque international de Besançon, octobre 1998, 325–342. Besançon.

d'Errico, F., Jardon-Giner, P. and Soler Major, B. 1993. Etude des perforations naturelles et artificielles sur coquillages. *Traces et fonction: les Gestes Retrouvés*, 243–254. Liège.

d'Errico, F., Baffier, D. and Julien, M. 2000a. Technologie et fonction des poinçons en os des couches châtelperroniennes de la Grotte du Renne à Arcy-sur-Cure. *XXVème Congrès de la Société Préhistorique Française, Approches fonctionnelles en Préhistoire,* 19. Nanterre.

d'Errico, F., Vanhaeren, M. and Dupont, C. 2000b. Le mobilier funéraire de la nécropole de l'Aven des Iboussières (Malataverne, Drôme) et l'identification de faciès culturels à la charnière Tardiglaciaire-Holocène. *Séminaire international "Représentations préhistoriques"*, 17ème Session, Art Préhistorique, Musée de l'Homme. Paris.

Duday, H. and Courtaud, P. 1998. La nécropole mésolithique de La Vergne (Charente-Maritime). In: *Sépultures d'Occident et genèses des mégalithismes (9000–3500 avant notre ère,* 27–37. Paris.

Dupont, C. 1998. *La malacofaune des sépultures de Ò La Grande Pièce Ò (La Vergne ; Charente-Maritime)*. DEA d'Anthropologie option Préhistoire, Institut de Préhistoire et de Géologie du Quaternaire. University of Bordeaux I. Bordeaux.

—— in press. The shell beads of the Aven des Iboussières (Malataverne, Drôme). In: Vanhaeren, M. and d'Errico, F. (eds.) *The language of the dead. New insights into Upper Palaeolithic and Mesolithic burials and Grave Goods*. Leuven.

Floss, H. 2000. Le couloir Rhin-Saône-Rhône: axe de communication au Tardiglaciaire? *Les derniers chasseurs-cueilleurs d'Europe occidentale*. Actes du colloque international de Besançon, octobre 1998, 313–321. Besançon.

Gambier, D. (ed.) 2001. *La sépulture des enfants de Grimaldi (Baoussé-Roussé, Italie)*. Documents préhistoriques 14. Paris.

Gambier, D., Valladas, H., Tisnérat-Laborde, N., Arnold, M. and Besson, F. 2000. Datation de vestiges humains présumés du Paléolithique supérieur par la méthode du carbone 14 en spectrométrie de masse par accélérateur. *Paléo* 12, 201–212.

Gambier, D., Valladas, H. and Tisnérat-Laborde, N. 2001. Datation absolue et attribution culturelle. In: Gambier, D. (ed.) 2001. *La sépulture des enfants de Grimaldi (Baoussé-Roussé, Italie)*. Documents préhistoriques 14, 27-29. Paris.

Jones, S. 1997. *The Archaeology of Ethnicity. Constructing identities in the past and present*. London, New York.

Jude, P.E. 1960. *La grotte de Rochereil. Station Magdalénienne et Azilienne*. Mémoire de l'Institut de Paléontologie Humaine 30. Paris.

Langer, S. 1953. *Feeling and Form*. New York.

Leach, E. 1976. *Culture and communication*. Cambridge.

May, F. 1989. *Les sépultures préhistoriques*. Paris.

Pearson, M.P. 1999. *The Archaeology of Death and Burial*. Phoenix Mill.

Poppe, G.T. and Goto, Y. 1993. *European Seashells. Volume II (Scaphopoda, Bivalvia, Cephalopoda)*. Wiesbaden.

Rivière, E. 1874. Sur trois nouveaux squelettes humains découverts dans les grottes de Menton. *Matériaux pour l'Histoire primitive* 9, 94–98.

—— 1887. *De l'Antiquité de l'Homme dans les Alpes-Maritimes*. Paris.

Saxe, A.A. 1970. *Social dimensions of mortuary practices*. PhD thesis. University of Michigan.

Taborin, Y. 1993. *La parure en coquillage au Paléolithique*. XXIXe supplément à "Gallia Préhistoire". Paris.

Testart, A. 2000. Que peut dire aujourd'hui l'anthropologie sociale des chasseurs-cueilleurs d'hier?. *Les derniers chasseurs-cueilleurs d'Europe occidentale*. Actes du colloque international de Besançon, octobre 1998, 343–349. Besançon.

Ucko, P.J. 1969. Ethnography and the archaeological interpretation of funeral remains. *World Archaeology* 1, 262–90.

Vanhaeren, M. in prep. *De la parure à l'identification des unités culturelles du Paléolithique supérieur. Application de nouvelles méthodes d'analyse*. PhD thesis. University of Bordeaux I.

Vanhaeren, M. and d'Errico, F. 2001. La parure de l'enfant de La Madeleine (fouilles Peyrony). Un nouveau regard sur l'enfance au Paléolithique supérieur. *Paléo* 13, 201-240.

White, R. 1993. Technological and Social Dimensions of "Aurignacian-Age" Body Ornaments across Europe. *Before Lascaux: The Complex Record of the Early Upper Paleolithic*, 277–299. Boca Raton.

63. Mobility and Aesthetics. On the Palaeo-Inuit style in the Nuuk Fjord area of Greenland

Maria Hinnerson Berglund

The situation

Mobility and Aesthetics is the name of a project that studies the Palaeo-Inuit in Greenland. Its point of departure is that archaeology is an activity of today, and that man, then as now, has always been a non-static being with a body and soul that are profoundly deeply interrelated. Before dealing with this I would like to say a few words about Greenland's prehistory and the term 'Palaeo-Inuit'.

Greenland's prehistory goes back more than 4500 years. The direct ancestors of today's Greenlanders are called the Thule people, Neo-Eskimos or Inuit. When they came to the country after 1200 AD (McGhee 2000:181 p) the Norse Greenlanders were already there; and before these there had been the Dorset, Saqqaq and Independence peoples, all with roots in North America. The common designation for these groups is Palaeo-Eskimos. However, in Greenland, where I live, the word 'Eskimo' is not used to categorise Greenlanders, and since 'Inuit' simply means 'human beings' I prefer to apply this term to the prehistoric inhabitants too. In other words I wish to call them the Palaeo-Inuit.

The Greenlandic archaeological landscape

The project *Mobility and Aesthetics* is about the Palaeo-Inuit, about their stone artefacts and site structures, and about the landscape in which their remains are found. Here, on the world's largest island, there are today not more than 55,000 people living in very small communities with no roads connecting them, so most of the country is untouched by modern times. It is a world in constant motion and rich in contrasts: sea and mountain, ice and flowers, storm and calm. Sometimes it is full of sounds, sometimes intensely quiet. How the Palaeo-Inuit perceived all this we do not know. We know a little about how far they travelled – inland and seaward – to hunt and survive. But we know nothing of how they viewed the space in which they moved around; for instance, whether there were any limits to concepts such as 'home' and 'away' (Clark 1996:40 p).

In Greenland as elsewhere, the archaeological 'landscape' is space and place (Tilley 1994; Heimann 2000) and consequently experiences and feelings. It is time, and thus motion, but this motion is also evident from the landscape itself: as geophysics. Here nature determines everything, including the archaeology.

Here we are still in the Ice Age. The inland ice is never far away, and in my investigation area (Figure 63.1) the ice flows out into the inner reaches of Kangersuneq, one of the fjord's many arms. It breaks off, and large icebergs sail out into the fjord. Sometimes they run aground, gather in bays and block off parts of the fjord before the tidal action pushes them out to sea.

The ice cap extends as far today as it did approximately 8,000 years ago (Weidick 1988:38). Its retreat culminated some thousand years later, but after that the ice advanced, and since then the ice margin has moved ahead and backwards several times. Local signs of the cold in the Nuuk area include various cryoturbations (Figure 63.2) (Schweger, C. University of Alberta, pers. comm.), while indications of the melting of the inland ice are found in the form of large moraines by the edge of the ice. The stabilisation of the spread of the inland ice meant that the land already stopped rising around 3,000 BC (Weidick 1995:265). There have been a number of displacements between land and sea since then (Figure 63.3) and evidence of this is often found at archaeological localities (see Weidick 1995:62; Philbert 1999:12 p). Indeed, a couple of the sites included in my project are located more or less underwater (Figure 63.4). The ongoing global warming is thus an increasing threat to the evidence of Greenland's prehistory. Apart from the gradual heightening of the relative sea level, sometimes called 'the sinking of Greenland' (Egedal 1947), stones deposited by stranded icebergs are also an archaeological problem – as are the tides (Figure 63.5). In the Nuuk area the tide raises the fjord by more than four metres, so transgression and erosion are constantly changing the coastlines.

Mobility and Aesthetics. On the Palaeo-Inuit style in the Nuuk Fjord area of Greenland

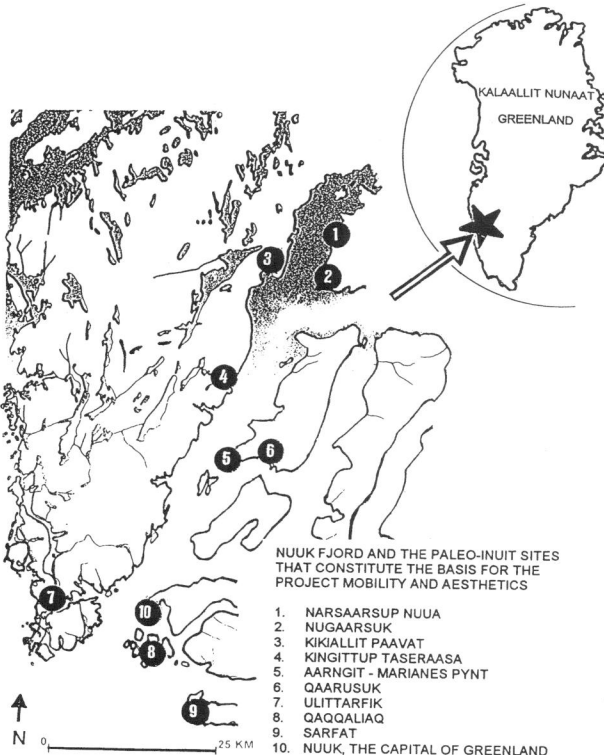

Figure 63.1 *The Nuuk fjord area of Greenland; the basis for the project* Mobility and Aesthetics.

Figure 63.2 *Cryoturbation, Nuuk district 1994. Photo Joel Berglund*

Palaeo-Inuit remains in the Nuuk Fjord area

Nuuk Fjord is characterised by several prominent mountains such as Sermitsiaq with its large glacier (Figure 63.6). Many of the mountains drop very steeply down into the fjord. It is impossible to land there, but there are other places – welcoming bays or points of varying size – which are suitable for settlement (Figure 63.6). The traces of such settlements blend in with nature, and some "ordinary stones" could turn out when excavated to be a fireplace – a box-hearth for instance – in the middle of a paved floor. Box-hearths are one type of Palaeo-Inuit

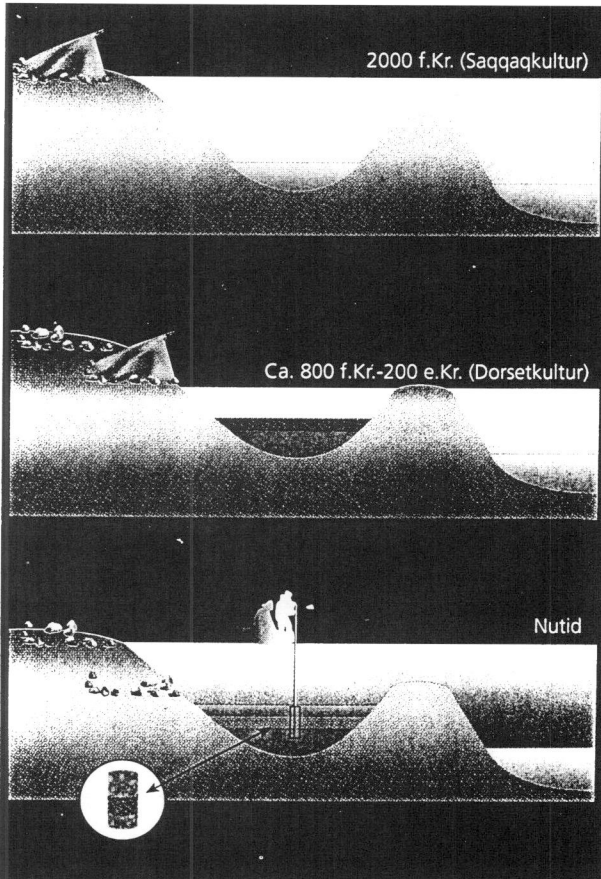

Figure 63.3 *Displacements between land and sea. Graphics: Irene Seiten in Philbert 1999.*

Figure 63.4 *From the excavation at Marianes Pynt, July 2000. Photo Maria Hinnerson B.*

settlement evidence in the Nuuk Fjord area; another is "the mid-structure" (Figure 63.7); and a third is "the outdoor fireplace". One of the sites is situated 15 m above sea level, others slightly more than 4 m a.s.l., while some of them, because of the tide, are completely submerged.

The stone tools found at these sites vary considerably (Figure 63.8). The raw material is usually *killiaq* (silica slate) in various colours and shades; from nearly black

Figure 63.5 Fuuja Larsen in the tidal ice at Narsaarsup Nuua, July 1999. Photo Maria Hinnerson B.

Figure 63.8 Samples of Paleo-Inuit tools from Marianes Pynt, Aarngit, Nuuk Fjord. Photo Maria Hinnerson B.

Figure 63.6 Mount Sermitsiaq and the site Marianes Pynt. Photo Maria Hinnerson B.

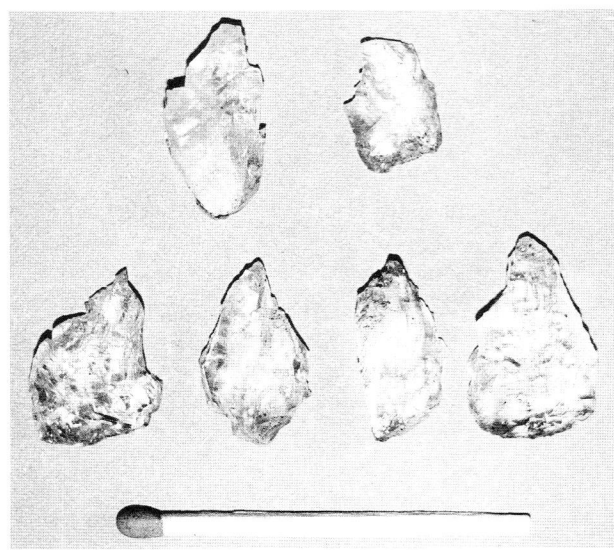

Figure 63.9 Burins of rock crystal.

Figure 63.7 The mid-structure fireplace at Narsaarsup Nuua during excavations, 1999. Dated to 3605 +-50 BP/2030–1885 cal BC 1-sigma (AAR-5589). Photo Maria Hinnerson B.

and blue to yellow and off-white. Chalcedony is common too. It is found in many colours, from purple and green to brilliant white, just like quartz. Some artefacts are made of the clearest rock crystal and sometimes we find jasper and chert too. The Palaeo-Inuit are included in "the Arctic Small Tool Tradition" but their tools are not always small. Points and knives vary in shape, from slender to round, from paper-thin to relatively thick. Some tools are ground to some degree, others not at all. Burins are a common find, as is burin spall. The burins are often of killiaq, but can also be of rock crystal (Figure 63.9).

Aesthetics as a tool in Palaeo-Inuitology

The tools of the Palaeo-Inuit are often strikingly beautiful, as is the environment in which they are found. In Greenland 'the experience' is always very much at hand – in the archaeological field work as well as in everyday life. In the field, once in a while, you wake up with your tent totally covered with new-fallen snow. You have large groups of jumping seals or giant whales passing by the excavation area. You see the same sights from your kitchen window, and when you go to work you might see a newly shot polar bear being winched ashore in the harbour. In these surroundings 'objectivity' along itself tends to fall flat. 'Hard facts' are simply not sufficient. Sensory impressions as well as feelings become a natural part of archaeology as well as life. This does not mean that I advocate a less stringent archaeological science. On the contrary, I believe that subjective things must be given more conscious attention in an attempt to find useful ways of conveying this qualitative aspect in a professional fashion. I think there are many ways of doing this. I have chosen to use the archaeological tool style.

The Palaeo-Inuit in Greenland are characterised by motion and beauty. This is their style. Traditionally, style is a technical term related to typology. But style differs from typology, inasmuch as style presupposes a form-giving personality behind the object. Style always reflects an attitude (Riis 1972:92), which means that style also has an emotional side. In style one finds the things one senses and feels – the aesthetics, a concept that stands for more than just beauty. Violence has its aesthetics too for example (Hinnerson Berglund 2000:67 p). An aesthetic perspective means that one must dare to start discussing value-laden concepts and one must be prepared to admit that subjectivity (Adorno 1997:356) and feelings are always part of the archaeological discourse – also in work like the identification of artefacts, for instance. The identification process is often perceived as a 'purely' intellectual activity, but it also involves emotional recognition, intuition (Adams and Adams 1991:39 p), creativity and so called 'tacit knowledge' (Polanyi 1966), that is the 'implicit' background knowledge that builds up our different mental maps and directs our attention towards a certain focus (Rolf 1995:63). Tacit knowledge is thus part of what is covered by the concept of 'perception', a term that involves epistemology as much as ontology. Very briefly, it is about becoming aware of something, becoming conscious. An important factor here is perceptual organisation, that is how one orders what one sees. Thus perception is not just about what we see, but also about what we wish to see – for example whether we are at all interested in seeing the potential inherent in a qualitative approach like aesthetics in archaeology. If an aesthetic approach is to be fruitful, we must open both eyes and try to see what is not immediately obvious, and we must *allow* ourselves to look at new perspectives in our work.

Using aesthetics as tool in Palaeo-Inuitology, I think we can bring our subject new or complementary knowledge. The extreme precision in the working of a slender denticulated projectile point, and the careful choice of material reflected in a brilliant burin of rock crystal, or in a scraper of red chalcedony can tell us many things about the Palaeo-Inuit world to which we have not yet paid attention. So to demonstrate the aesthetics of the Palaeo-Inuit material, I am now building up a practicable method and a precise terminology. It is not enough to describe the aesthetic value in simple terms like 'good' or 'poor'; or whether the object is aesthetically satisfying or not (Meynell 1997:78 p). It is a matter of bringing out, giving shape to and putting words to the qualities of the investigated material, and to do this work I have drawn on many different sources – from geology to wine-tasting.

Some of my fundamental concepts are surface, structure, value, balance, warmth and cold – i.e. the specific characteristics that can strengthen the aesthetic value; but I also work with terms like physicality, movement and direction. One way of capturing aesthetics is based on a scheme drawn up by Erwin Panofsky (1955:40 p) which involves coordinating and interpreting a whole range of observations, and looking for underlying principles which reveal fundamental attitudes. Another is to "morellicise" like Carlo Ginzburg (from Giovanni Morelli – see Ginzburg 1989:8; see also Hinnerson Berglund 2000). This is analogous to Sherlock Holmes' method of looking for clues. It is the apparently marginal or irrelevant details that reveal the distinctiveness of an artist, in this context the implement maker.

Material and meaning

I have found a source of inspiration for this qualitative approach in the Scandinavian Mesolithic literature on quartz and other so-called flint alternatives. It is clear that that sort of tool material receives more attention today than in the past, even outside the mountain regions (see Holm and Knutsson, 1998). It seems that more and more researchers are becoming interested in quartz and rock crystal as such. That is, quartz is not considered simply as a necessary evil, a substitute for flint, but as something that was selected for the sake of the material itself. Here I would like to recall Noel Broadbent's *thesis Coastal Resources and Settlement stability* (1979) where he emphasises the special qualities of quartz, both as a mineral and as "meaning". For instance he writes that rock crystal was used in California to cut the umbilical cord of newborn infants (ibid. 1979:48 p). For Aborigines in Australia, quartz tools are also particularly potent. Brightness and iridescence are highly valued, and objects that shimmer and 'emit' light like quartz are charged with spiritual power (Tilley 1994:53). Among Inuit, quartz is believed to be the coldest, hardest form of ice (Broadbent 1979:53) and in Greenland, where the massive Inland Ice is always close by, it is easy to imagine that ice and rock crystal may have meant something very special to people in prehistoric times.

My work deals with landscape, movements and experiences, and with tools, minerals, shapes and colours. We seldom find carvings and the like, but during excavations this summer we made one extraordinary find. It was a fragment of a point of ground killiaq, with diagonal lines across the surface. I have found the same pattern just once before, on a burin of killiaq, that is a Saqqaq

Figure 63.10 The Saqqaq burin, the Dorset figurine and the ground point fragment with diagonal incisions. Photo Erik Holm.

object. What makes this particularly interesting is that these diagonal notches resemble the "décor" on small wooden sculptures from the *late* Dorset, found both in Greenland and in Canada. These human-like figures have a clearly ritual meaning (Gulløv 1998:8). So perhaps we are on the track of a world of symbols that was common to Saqqaq and Dorset for several thousand years (Figure 63.10).

Summary

With an increased understanding of the qualitative aspect of human life, we can complement our scientific tool kit and try to reach below the surface of the archaeological discourse. In this way we can open up an avenue for new discussions; for example of present-day and past 'logics'.

One could, for instance, assume that mankind, then as now, lived in a multilogical world (Kapuscinski 1996:207) – perhaps in the same mixture of conflicting logics as today's archaeologists.

In combination with terms like experience, reflexivity and perception this becomes possible. With them it is natural to employ qualitative aspects like aesthetics in archaeology. The effect of aesthetics is "to train and extend the capacity of our levels of consciousness, experience, understanding and judgement" (Meynell 1997:75). A more aesthetic style in archaeology should then affirm pleasure and improve our ability to make stone live, when we as archaeologists create the image of mankind.

References

Adams, W.Y. and Adams, E.W. 1991. *Archaeological typology and practical reality*. Cambridge.

Adorno, T.W. 1997. *Aesthetic Theory*. Minneapolis.

Broadbent, N. 1979. *Coastal Resources and Settlement Stability*, AUN 3, Archaeological Studies. Uppsala.

Clark, G. 1996. *Rummet, tiden och människan*, Stockholm.

Egedal, J. 1947. The sinking of Greenland. *Meddelelser om Grønland* 134, 7. Copenhagen.

Ginzburg, C. 1989. *Ledtrådar*. Häften för kritiska studier. Stockholm.

Gulløv, H.C. 1998. *Kunst og Magi*. Nyt fra Nationalmuseet. Copenhagen.

Heimann, C. 2000. *Neolitiseringen i Västvärmland*. Institutionen för Arkeologi, Göteborgs universitet. Gothenburg.

Hinnerson Berglund, M. 2000. Style as Aesthetics – An attempt at a qualitative approach in Paleo-Inuit research in Greenland. In: Appelt, M., Berglund, M. and Gulløv, H.C. (eds.) *Identities and Cultural Contacts in the Arctic*, 64–70. Danish National Museum and Danish Polar Center. Copenhagen.

Holm, L. and Knutsson, K. (eds.) 1998. *Third Flint Alternatives Conference at Uppsala*, Opia, Dept. of Arch. and Ancient History, Uppsala University, Uppsala.

Kapuscinski, R. 1996. *Imperiet*. Stockholm.

McGhee, R. 2000. Radiocarbon Dating and the Timing of the Thule Migration. In: Appelt, M., Berglund, M. and Gulløv, H.C. (eds.), *Identities and Cultural Contacts in the Arctic*, 181–191. Danish National Museum and Danish Polar Center. Copenhagen.

Meynell, H.A. 1997. *En fråga om smak*. Nora.

Panofsky, E. 1955. *The History of Art as a Humanistic Discipline*. New York.

Philbert, P-E. 1999. Vand på modellerne. *Polarfronten 1999. Nr. 4*, Danish Polar Center. Copenhgen.

Polanyi, M. 1966. *The tacit dimension*. London.

Riis, T.J. 1972. *Arkeologi och klassisk konst*. Copenhagen.

Rolf, B. 1995. *Profession, Tradition och Tyst Kunskap*. Nora.

Tilley, C. 1994. *A phenomenology of landscape*. Oxford.

Weidick, A. 1988. *Gletschere i Sydgrønland*. Grønlands Geologiske Undersøgelser. Copenhagen.

—— 1995 *Grønlands Fysiske Natur*. Copenhagen.

64. Late Mesolithic Rock Art and Expressions of Ideology

Trond Klungseth Lødøen

The paper presents preliminary results from an ongoing research project at the site Vingen in Western Norway, where more than 2000 rock carvings are located. The relationship between rock art and other archaeological material both in Vingen and its surroundings are being explored by archaeological surveys in the area and excavations in the vicinity of panels with carvings. Based on this research a new dating framework for the rock art, and a new approach for the interpretations of Late Mesolithic ideology is suggested.

Background

Although new directions in archaeology during the last decades have opened our eyes and legitimised such areas of research as religion and beliefs in the Mesolithic, we are still left with interpretations, and suggested datings of archaeological material, which reflect attitudes from times when archaeologists rarely believed that people were occupied with such aspects during this part of the Stone age. On the basis of the existing literature, one might almost conclude that it was the introduction of agriculture in the Neolithic that opened prehistoric peoples' eyes to the concept of religion! Of course, some authors from time to time have argued for the presence of ritual activity in the Mesolithic and even in the Paleolithic, but I will argue that these efforts are exceptions from the general trend. While researchers of past agricultural societies have been occupied with the identification of social stratification and religious expression, it is no secret that researchers of prehistoric hunter-gatherer societies have been more concerned with issues such as adaptation to the environment, exploitation of resources, technology, and raw material procurement.

To investigate expressions of religion in the Mesolithic and to penetrate deeper into these issues, all categories of Mesolithic material must be included. To investigate such a topic, the most obvious material to start with, is probably archaeological remains representing mortuary practices, but as the geographical point of departure for my research is Western Norway, where Mesolithic graves are almost completely absent, this possibility is hardly available to me. I have, however, recently argued for significant ritual practice among hunters in the Middle and Late Mesolithic and in the Early and Middle Neolithic in Western Norway by the interpretation of deposited axes beneath flagstones or boulders, as votive offerings (Lødøen 1995, 1998). In light of this work it has been interesting to note how identically deposited, but chronologically separated artefacts, have been interpreted in previous research according to the current ideas; Late Neolithic deposits as votive offerings, Mesolithic, Early Neolithic and Middle Neolithic deposits as lost items, hidden treasures, or that these artefacts are from habitation sites that have not yet been located or investigated (Lødøen 1998:195, 199 p). In an attempt to approach religious aspects more closely, this paper will deal with rock art, an archaeological category which, I claim, has largely been underestimated in Mesolithic research. In order to demonstrate its potential for the understanding of Mesolithic religion, beliefs, and also ideology, I will present new interpretations of archaeological material from the Vingen site, which is known mainly for its rock art (Bøe 1932; Hallstrøm 1938:415 pp; Fett 1941; Bakka 1973:151 pp, 1979:115 pp; Mezec 1989; Mandt 1998:201 pp, Lødøen 2001). The material presented and the interpretations suggested are preliminary results of an ongoing project undertaking a more thorough investigation of the meaning of the rock art.

A substantial problem in rock art research is that of uncertain chronology. Rock art is difficult to date, and no direct dating methods have yet proved satisfactory. The result of this uncertainty has been that different researchers have claimed that one and the same site could be linked to periods widely separated in time. A fundamental aim of the project is therefore to develop a more accurate chronological framework for the rock art of Vingen, and to try to separate different chronological phases. The different phases will then be analysed in relation to contemporaneous archaeological material in order to reveal the contemporary context of the rock art and to create a better understanding of the social practices

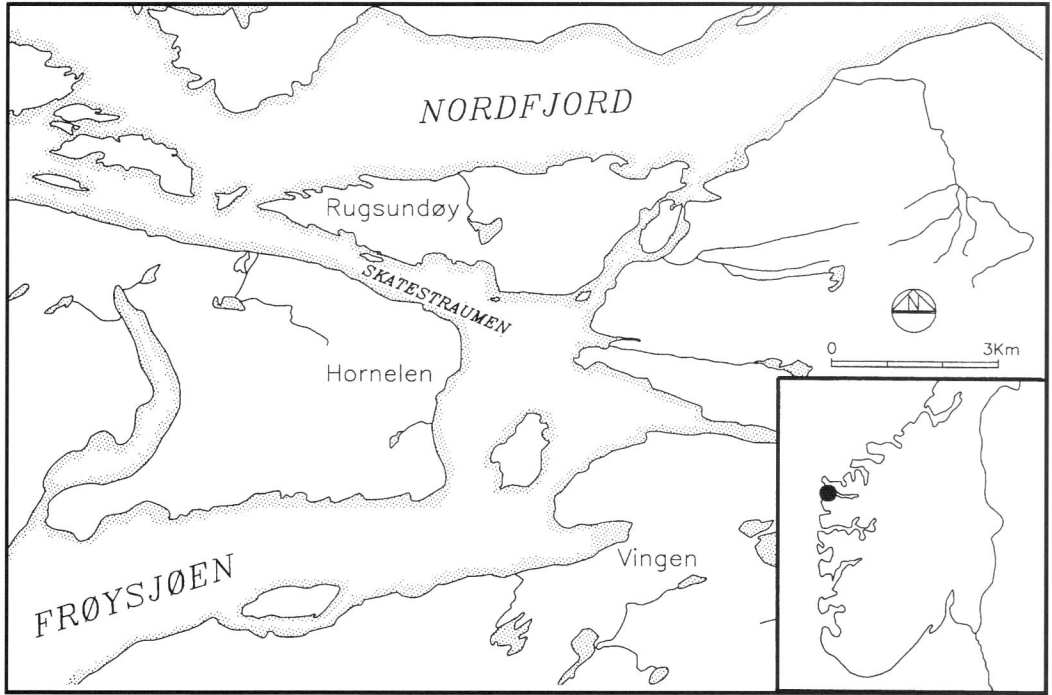

Figure 64.1 The locality of Vingen, in the Nordfjord area, Western Norway (Illustration by Knut Andreas Bergsvik).

associated with its production, and the meaning of the rock art.

Against the background of recently documented material it will be argued that the carvings at Vingen were produced by hunter-gatherers during periods of changing ideology within the Late Mesolithic period; 7500–5200, uncalibrated years B.P.

Vingen

Vingen (Figure 64.1) is located in a narrow fjord in the municipality of Bremanger in the northwestern part of the County of *Sogn og Fjordane*. Steep barren mountains rise up to 800 meter above sea level around the fjord, with slopes scattered with screes and numerous debris fans. Some more level areas exist, covered with thin layers of soil and vegetation. Large boulders and small piles of stones lie spread over the more level areas, but the bedrock is regularly and conspicuously exposed. More than 2000 rock carvings have been found around the fjord, on rock panels as well as on boulders and smaller stones. Most of these were produced by pecking, which leaves numerous pecking marks. Red deer are the most common motif, followed by other animals, anthropomorphic figures, and what can be described as abstract geometric figures. The carvings occur alone, as single depictions (Figures 64.3a, 64.3b), or in groups, as visualised scenes from the past (Figure 64.4). Most carvings are located on the southern side of the fjord on a terrace between the shoreline and the steep mountains, which will be the main area of focus in this paper (Figure 64.2).

Figure 64.2 The Vingen fjord and the coastal setting. The southern terrace where most carvings are located is seen in the centre of the picture. (Photo Trond Klungseth Lødøen).

Chronology

Since methods for direct dating of pecked or carved rock art are not available, most efforts at dating have been made by comparison with the results from geological shoreline displacement studies and the prevailing assumption that the rock art was produced at the shore. In Vingen the question of chronology and dating of the rock art has been a central issue for many years. One of the most commendable attempts was made by Egil Bakka in the 1970s. This was done on the basis of stylistic comparison of the variations in the animal motifs, the presence of stylistic similarity with other archaeological material, and

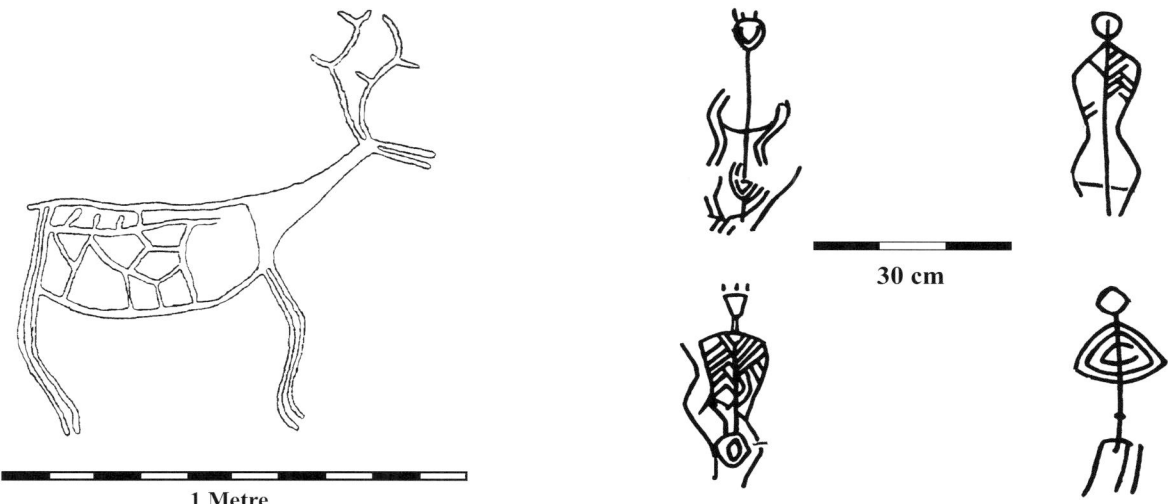

Figure 64.3 Tracing of red deer (a) and representations of anthropomorphic figures (b) (Tracings by Egil Bakka).

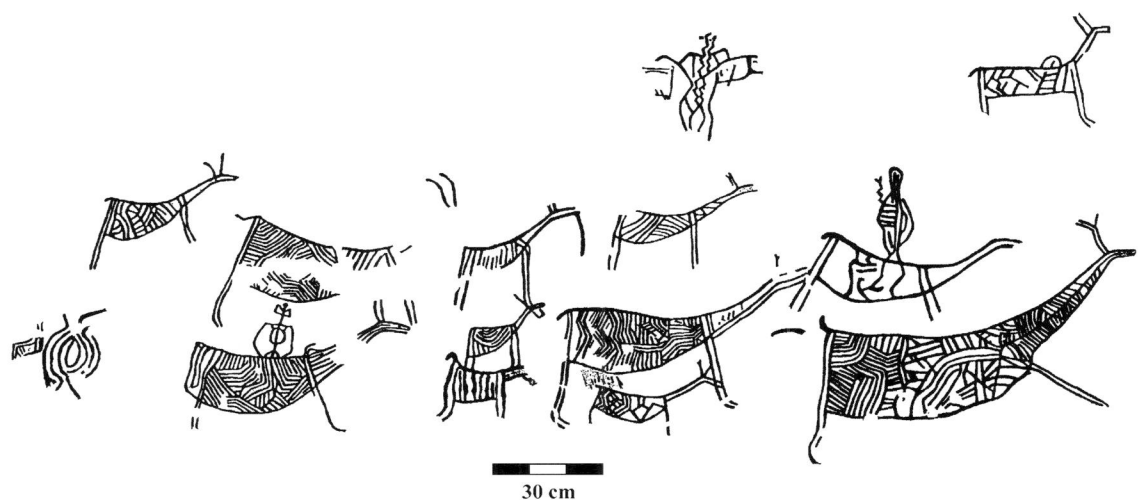

Figure 64.4 Segment of a rock panel with the visualisation of red deer and humans.

the relation to shorelines (Bakka 1973:156 pp, 1979:115 pp). He suggested a possible timespan for the rock art from the beginning of the Early Neolithic until the end of the Middle Neolithic, with a possible origin in the Late Mesolithic. Further, he developed a relative typological-chronological sequence from detailed studies of several hundred carvings on the basis of their superpositions. On the basis of this work he separated four different categories of red deer carvings. (Figure 64.5). At the time when he was working with these questions little archaeological material had been excavated or otherwise collected from the Vingen area, and the number of known carvings was far less than today.

Inasmuch as shoreline dating is a crucial aspect of Bakka's analysis of Vingen, and also because it has been used by numerous other researchers, it is important to understand its assumptions and limitations. Since the beginning of the 19th century archaeologists and historians have argued for a strong relation between rock art and prehistoric shorelines. Several researchers have pointed out that the locations of hunters' rock art in the inland areas of Scandinavia have a remarkably strong correlation with the shorelines of lakes and rivers (eg. Gjessing 1937:64 p; Mikkelsen 1977:181 pp). It has been argued that the location factors affecting the inland sites were the same as those for the coastal sites. While the watercourses along which the inland shorebound rock art sites are situated have been relatively stable since the last ice age, isostatic activity has continuously changed the elevation of the shorelines along the coast. However, due to a lack of sampling sites for the appropriate geological data, many of these shoreline curves, and by implication the dating of rock art, are very approximate, sometimes with hundreds of years of deviation. In addition, despite the strong correlation observed between the inland rock art and the shorelines of lakes and rivers, in reality the inland rock art varies by many meters in relation to the water level along the river and lake shorelines. They might

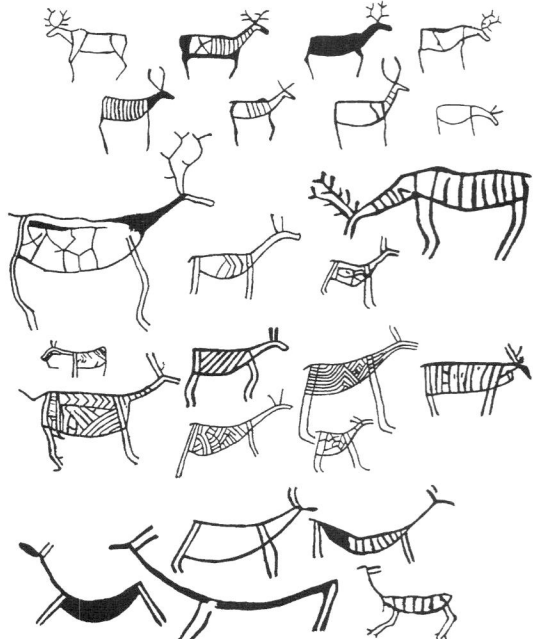

Figure 64.5 Egil Bakka's suggested typological-chronological sequence of red deer carvings. The Hammaren type (1–8), the Hardbakken type (9–12), the Brattebakken type (13–19) and the Elva type (20–24).

Figure 64.6 Excavation in the immediate vicinity of a rock art panel (Photo Trond Klungseth Lødøen).

have been produced many meters above the shore or even below maximum water level as argued by some authors (eg. Lindquist 1994: 24). If these uncertainties are taken into account, the dating of the rock art might vary within timeframes of several thousand years. At the time Bakka was dealing with these questions, the data on shoreline displacement were limited, but even today almost 30 years later this is still true. Despite the fact that new geological results have been provided for this area (e.g. Aksdal 1986), archaeological investigations in the vicinity of Vingen have highlighted the problem, where radiocarbon-dated Late Mesolithic sites have been excavated far below the supposed contemporaneous level of the shoreline (Bergsvik 2002).

The contemporary context of the rock art

Several investigations seeking to sample and collect archaeological material of importance for the rock art have been undertaken in the Vingen area. In addition to test pit surveys, test excavations and palaeobotanical sampling, a systematic examination of brooks, unvegetated soil, and debris have been carried out. Hollow spaces in the many scree slopes in the area have also been explored. Some of these investigations have been conducted because it has been necessary to remove the abrasive turf and soil that partly covers surfaces with rock art, in order to complete primary documentation of the many carved panels and reduce weathering. All these investigations have provided valuable stratigraphic information and led to the discovery of substantial numbers of artefacts of importance for the interpretation of the rock art and its context.

Test excavations have been undertaken in the immediate vicinity of some of the rock art panels, that is, immediately below or adjacent to the carvings (Figure 64.6). However, these have not resulted in any clear pattern of a regular deposition of archaeological material linked to the different rock art localities, since some investigations led to the discovery of stone artifacts or cultural layers and some did not. But of course, this does not rule out the possibility of deposition of perishable artefacts of wood or bone etc. The striking result from these investigations is that all the rediscovered archaeological material, including radiocarbon dates of charcoal from cultural layers, dates to the Late Mesolithic (Figure 64.7).

Dwelling features

What is of specific interest in this area, apart from the rock art and the other collected archaeological material, is the presence of highly visible, circular depressions, interpreted as houses or other dwelling features. A total number of nine certain dwelling structures have been documented. These have a diameter of less than 5 meters, and are constructed of surrounding stone and gravel walls. They are located between boulders and rock art panels, some in clusters (Figure 64.8a), others more isolated

Context	Radiocarbon dating results	Lab. reference
Dwelling feature	5825±75 B.P	(Tua-2189)
Dwelling feature	5530±70 B.P	(Tua-2190)
Dwelling feature	5870±80 B.P	(T-13697)
Dwelling feature	5665±80 B.P	(T-13695)
Midden	5960±70 B.P	(Tua-2281)
Midden	5970±105 B.P	(T-13979)
Midden	6220±105 B.P	(T-13980)
Midden	6830±70 B.P	(Tua-2282)

Figure 64.7 Uncalibrated dating results of charcoal samples from cultural layers in different dwelling features and from a midden at Vingen.

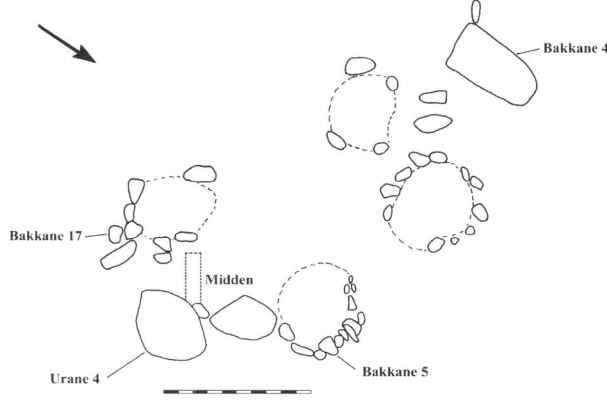

Figure 64.8 A cluster of 4 dwelling features surrounded by several stones and boulders with rock art (Names with numbers refer to different carvings) (a). A single dwelling feature located in the vicinity of a rock art panel (b).

(Figure 64.8b). None of these have yet been completely excavated, but test excavations have revealed the presence of cultural layers and provided highly homogenous archaeological material, clearly indicating a Late Mesolithic origin. In addition to the presence of waste flakes, blades, and conical cores, microblades struck from conical cores are common, which is in accordance with material documented elsewhere in Vingen. The dating is further substantiated by the dominance of characteristic Late Mesolithic raw material categories such as quartz, quartzite, rock crystal, mylonite, and flint (Nærøy 1988:209, 1993:89 pp; Olsen 1992:84 pp; Bergsvik 1999). The highly permanent character displayed by these features of stone and gravel walls is unknown elsewhere in lowland Western Norway. Only a limited number of radiocarbon dates exist from their cultural layers. They, however, support the dating of these structures to the Late Mesolithic period (Figure 64.7).

Midden

Recent test excavations in the vicinity of some of the dwelling structures have revealed a considerably thick midden among other archaeological material. With its extensive amount of fire-cracked rocks (Figure 64.9), this midden differs from Late Mesolithic middens found elsewhere in Western Norway. The artefacts from the midden are similar to those of the dwelling structures and there is reason to believe that the midden deposits are related to the structures. However the percentage of artefacts seem a little low compared to other Late Mesolithic middens.

Preliminary analyses of the midden and some of the dwelling features point strongly towards patterns of occasional occupation. The limited thickness and unstratified character of the cultural layer inside the dwelling features indicates that they were used during repeated short-term occupation or over a limited period. This is supported by radiocarbon datings of these layers which are clustered over a short time period. Occasional use of the dwelling features is further strengthened by the nearby located midden where radiocarbon datings, on the contrary, cover a considerable period of time through the later and middle part of the Late Mesolithic, indicating that the dwelling features were emptied or cleared from time to time (Figure 64.7). The content present in the different dwelling features today must therefore be seen as remains from the final occupation phase. However, more analyses will be necessary to support the process of delimiting different phases of use, represented by the midden and the nearby dwelling features.

Palynological investigations

As a means of providing more independent data for the contextualisation of the rock art and the dating of the

Figure 64.9 Investigated midden with fire-cracked rocks (Photo Trond Klungseth Lødøen).

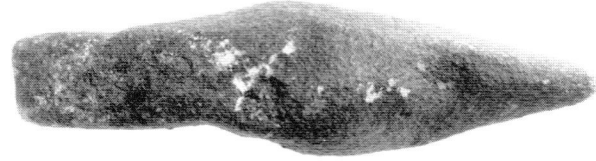

Figure 64.10 Pecking tool of diabase, from the Stakaneset quarry (Photo Svein Skare).

activity in Vingen, palynological investigations have been undertaken (Hjelle and Lødøen in prep). Core samples have been collected from two different bogs. One of these bogs has a highly central location in relation to the carvings and is assumed to contain data that reflects both local patterns of vegetation history and human impact on the environment. The other investigated bog is located on the fringe of the rock art area and is expected to reflect the general vegetation development in the area. In addition, material for palynological investigations has been collected from the midden presented above. These analyses are in progress, and are promising, as the bogs have been found to be undisturbed by modern activity and the bottom sediments have been dated to the Early Mesolithic and Middle Mesolithic, respectively. They are, therefore, fairly older than the earliest conceivable dating of the rock art and the activity at Vingen. However, these bogs reflect not only vegetation history. The basins where found to contain many layers of highly fractioned, probably windblown charcoal, which might reflect the nearby occupation, involving fire. Of course, one cannot exclude the possibility that some of these layers reflect natural forest fires, but it is highly probable that the dating of these layers will provide us with more information regarding the occupation history of the area. By comparing radiocarbon datings from the investigated dwelling features, the midden, and the results from the palynological studies, including the imbedded charcoal layers, a better background for further work on the dating of the rock art and the separation of phases will be developed. This will create a stronger basis for interpretations of the meaning of the rock art.

Rock art and archaeological material

There are of course many problems involved in the process of relating cultural layers and the deposited artefacts to the rock art at Vingen. Analyses of all the excavated and collected archaeological material clearly demonstrate that the main activity in the area took place during the Late Mesolithic. The alternative explanation is that the dwelling features and the deposited archaeological material predate the period of rock art production, that the major period for the production of the carvings was the beginning and middle part of the Neolithic as previously argued (Bakka 1973:170 pp, 1979:118). This explanation however is difficult to prove since there is a striking absence of Neolithic artefacts, such as cylindrical cores and tanged points made from blades struck from cylindrical cores. Even raw material categories related to the Neolithic periods, such as rhyolite and slate, are missing.

All the dwelling features are in close proximity to rock art localities and some even have carvings on the stones and boulders that make up their surrounding walls, thus indicating contemporaneity and unity (Figure 64.8a). In the course of surveys between the dwelling features, a new discovery of importance for the interpretation of the dwelling features and the rock art was made. In an eroded section of a cultural layer, an elongated artefact of diabase (Figure 64.10) with a pointed end was found together with flakes of the same character and made from the same raw material as from the dwelling features, and is therefore probably related to the occupation of the dwelling features. What is important here is that the diameter of the pointed end of this artefact tallies with the diameter of the pecking marks on most of the carvings at Vingen, and it is therefore probably a pecking tool used for the production of rock art. Despite the fact that this is a completely new discovery in Western Norway, the tool type is in accordance with proposals made by Bakka after examinations of the production technique and pecking marks at many sites (1975:15 p). One of the implications of this discovery is that it relates the dwelling features at least indirectly to the rock art, and contributes toward a dating of the carvings to the Late Mesolithic. Geological thin-section analyses and further classification have concluded that the raw material of the artefact undoubtedly comes from Stakaneset, in the municipality of Flora, not far from Vingen, where a quarry, in use during both the Mesolithic and the Neolithic, is located (Olsen and Alsaker 1984:71 pp; Skjerlie 1999).

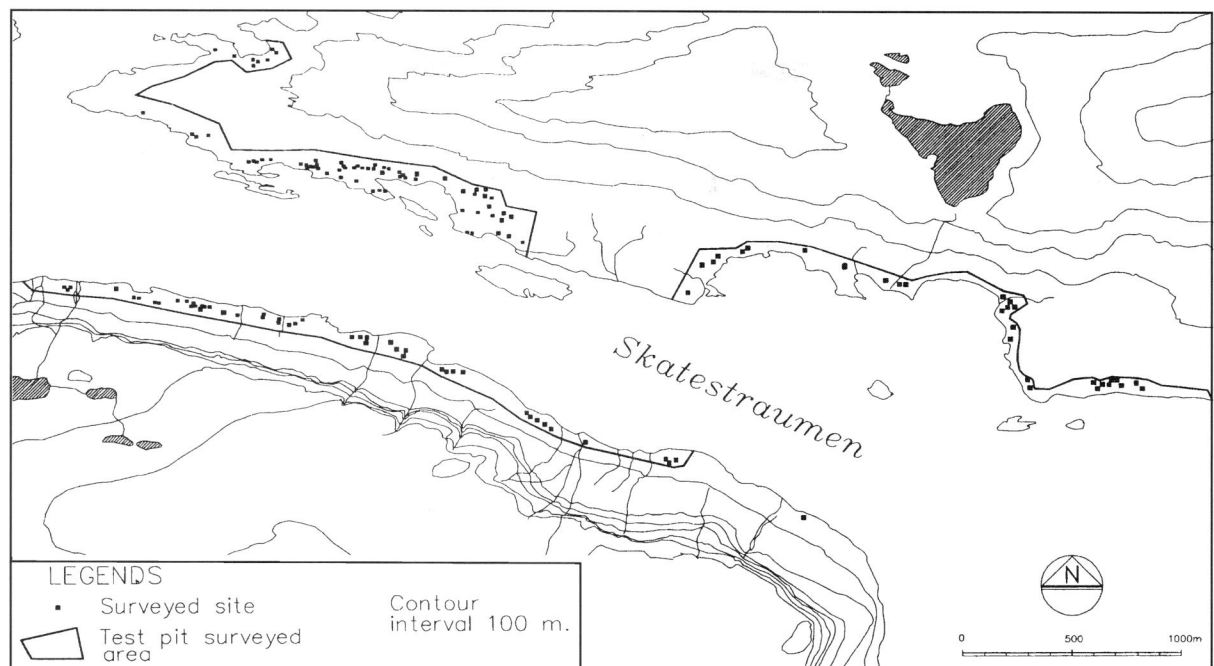

Figure 64.11 The tidal current with the location of excavated and surveyed Stone Age sites (Illustration by Knut Andreas Bergsvik).

Previous work on the exploitation of diabase and distribution of axes and adzes in Western Norway has argued for a close cultural relation between Vingen and this quarry (Olsen and Alsaker 1984:99 p), without any direct evidence for such a contact. The discovery of the above presented provinence-determined artefact has now strengthened this hypothesis. Due to its character, location, and its function as a raw material source, the Stakaneset quarry has been regarded as a sacred site by several authors (Olsen and Alsaker 1984:100; Lødøen 1995). It is therefore interesting to note that hardly any flakes or chipped pieces of diabase have been found in Vingen in comparison to the vast numbers of flakes on contemporaneous sites elsewhere. It is also striking that no Mesolithic axes have been found here as opposed to the many axes and chisels on contemporaneous sites in Western Norway (eg. Bjørgo 1981:50 pp; Bjerck 1983:20; Nygaard 1989:83 pp, 1990:230 pp; Olsen 1992:89 pp). This points towards a strongly regulated distribution of the raw material from the Stakaneset quarry, and might indicate that this material was treated with caution and respect in Vingen, thus supporting the interpretations of the Stakaneset quarry as a sacred site.

As shown, in addition to the large amount of rock art, the remainder of the archaeological record at Vingen – such as the midden with the high content of fire-cracked rocks, and the character of the dwelling features – point toward the existing set of activities as special and specific to Vingen. A forthcoming analysis will attempt to link rock art to contemporaneous archaeological material as a means of creating a better basis for analyses of the social practices associated with rock art production and analyses of its meaning. Separation of phases and the construction of a relative chronology for the rock art are under progress.

Rock art as expressions of ideology

What is striking about the results from all these investigations is that the dating of the activity coincides with changes of a general character in the Late Mesolithic. It has been claimed that towards the end of this period a change from a mobile to a more sedentary social structure occurred in Western Norway (eg. Warren 1994:89 pp). Archaeological material supporting this hypothesis has been documented in the Skatestraumen area a few kilometres north of Vingen (Figure 64.1) (Bergsvik 2002). Here more than 120 Stone age sites concentrated along both sides of a tidal current have been documented, and several of these have been partly or completely excavated. More than 40 of these sites have been dated to the Late Mesolithic (Figure 64.11). What is interesting about the sites in Skatestraumen, apart from their proven contemporaneity with the archaeological material at Vingen, is that these two areas are interrelated by the presence of archaeological material made from the same lithic raw material. They are also linked by the presence of raw material categories which are very limited. There is therefore reason to believe that the Late Mesolithic people responsible for the deposition of archaeological material and the production of carvings in Vingen were based along the Skatestraumen current. The concept of sedentism is still highly debated, but many results from excavations and surveys clearly point toward settlement patterns where the habitation sites were in use during longer periods of time or more frequently in the Late Mesolithic than in previous periods (Bergsvik 2002). In addition the limited distribution of raw material and tool types towards the end of the Mesolithic demonstrates a closer attachment to regions and places than earlier (Olsen and Alsaker 1984:94 pp; Bergsvik) and following from this, reduced mobility.

One of the interesting issues with this comprehensive material is to explore the religious and ideological implications of a change from a mobile to a sedentary social structure. It is likely that such a fundamental alteration of society, however gradual, would have led to substantial changes in ideology, religion, and beliefs. The long-term or permanent location of increasing numbers of people in a small area such as Skatestraumen made incidental conflicts more likely requiring some mechanisms for reducing this pressure on society. While mobile Mesolithic societies were able to split up into smaller segments in order to avoid or reduce conflicts, sedentary societies adopted different mechanisms to deal with such matters. Among other aspects sedentism is associated with higher degrees of social stratification, manipulation, and societal strain. In order to reduce such strain rituals were adopted to solve, mask, or negotiate possible conflicts, and to legitimise social roles. There is therefore reason to believe that the Vingen area was adopted as such a ritual site. Its location, between steep hillsides, provided the ideal seclusion for hidden ceremonies, rituals or esoteric activity.

Since the ideology of a society is reflected in all its different segments and levels, connotations mirroring social practice will be reflected in religion and in archaeological material suggesting religious activity. The rock art in Vingen might therefore reflect ritual activity as a result of a growing sedentary structure in the Late Mesolithic, and the different carvings might express collective discussions or negotiations among members of society, associated with thorough changes in society. Radiocarbon datings, not only from the dwelling structures, but all available datings from Vingen, restricted to a short time period before the Mesolithic – Neolithic transition from when sedentism seems to be more consolidated, support this hypothesis.

Many contextual studies of iconography through history have convincingly demonstrated that by the use of different procedures in the selection of represented subjects and the organisation of the pictorial space, images were used in persuasive or manipulating processes (eg. Tansey and Kleiner 1996:7 pp). Despite the fact that the depictions only represent a possible reality or even a misrepresentation of reality, they have a convincing character as the images look clear and natural. By transferring this knowledge to rock art studies it is clear from the way images are depicted that they had the power of ideological conviction. The way images were given permanency in stone or solid rock, locked in time and space, made them the only alternative among many possible representations of reality.

Against the background of the above discussion I will suggest that the rock art at Vingen is the remains of legitimising rituals triggered by societal strain related to increasing sedentism in the Late Mesolithic. At relatively earlier rock art sites in Northern, Middle and Western Norway, carvings of humans are generally absent (Gjessing 1932, 1936; Bakka 1973:162 pp). Big game, such as cervines, bears, and sea mammals predominate, which might reflect highly egalitarian mobile societies with strong associations to the natural world and no distinction between humans and the animal kingdom, also implying that the animal carvings might just as well have represented humans (eg. Hesjedal 1990:178 pp). The presence of a considerable number of anthropomorphic figures at Vingen, and its chronological contemporaneity with growing sedentism in Western Norway, could, on the contrary, be understood as the separation between animals and humans – between nature and culture, as society is changing from a mobile egalitarian form to one which is more sedentary and hierarchical.

It will be interesting to try to explore these issues further in the future and try to reconstruct what processes and social mechanisms the production of rock art underwent, whether it was a collective process or only associated with exclusive rights or roles in society held by ritual leaders or shamans. It is however thrilling to note that many figures show such astonishing similarity to each other, both in form, technique and expression, that there is reason to believe that they were produced by the same person or by individuals under the same influence. That only a few individuals at the time during the rock art production period were active in the process of producing carvings, is in accordance with the restricted number of artefacts and the limited thickness of the cultural layers in the dwelling features.

Another interesting circumstance is that so many carvings seem to have been deliberately hidden, under boulders, in the hollow spaces of screes, and under flagstones (Mandt and Lødøen in prep). These express a clear contrast to the many conspicuous and accessible panels and boulders with carvings. This might indicate patterns of conflict or opposition, or it might express different levels of publicity. Despite the clear tendency for only a few persons to have been involved with the production of the rock art and occupation of the area, other members of society could have had access to different panels or locations with rock art during ritual visits to Vingen, according to their positions or roles in society.

Conclusion

Even though Bakka's dating (1973) of the Vingen rock art is disputed in this paper, his four-stage typological-chronological sequence (Figure 64.5) might still be valid only pushed further back in time to the Late Mesolithic. Further work with these questions may reveal whether the suggested four-phase typology of red deer representations can be associated with chronological phases in the Late Mesolithic record both at Vingen and at other related areas in Western Norway. On the contrary, it might be that the differences in depiction of red deer reflect different meanings or various Late Mesolithic groups in the area. However, the above presented discussion clearly demonstrates that the prehistoric activity at Vingen predates the transition to the Neolithic in Western Norway. Previous datings of the rock art predominately to the Neolithic with an origin in the Late Mesolithic seem unlikely since the rock art appears to have continued to be produced in the same undisturbed manner, unaffected by the extensive cultural changes in the societies during the transition to the Neolithic. The archaeological record demonstrates that the Mesolithic – Neolithic transition implied, among other aspects, a thorough change in technology, the introduction of new dominating raw materials, changes in both the settlement and mobility patterns and associated changes in the society. Dating of the activity at Vingen exclusively to the latter part of the Late Mesolithic gives us a more understandable explanation of why the site was abandoned. This explanation might be further developed in future research and understanding of the triggering of the transition to, and the character of, the Neolithic in Western Norway.

In order to embrace rock art in culture historical approaches a more thorough investigation of its dating and chronology should be carried out. Too often rock art is excluded in culture historical synthesis because of the uncertainties regarding its dating. On the other hand archaeological excavations in the vicinity of rock art panels have rarely been carried out. The purpose of this paper is therefore both to present archaeological material from recent investigations at Vingen, to discuss possible chronological and cultural implications of the rock art, and to present an approach for the further analyses of the meaning of the rock art.

References

Aksdal, S. 1986. *Holocen vegetasjonsutvikling og havnivåendringer i Florø, Sogn og Fjordane*. Unpublished. Cand. Scient thesis. University of Bergen. Bergen.

Bakka, E. 1973. Om alderen på veideristningane. *Viking* 37, 151–187.

—— 1975. Geologically dated Arctic rock carvings at Hammer near Steinkjer in Nord-Trøndelag. *Arkeologiske skrifter* No 2. Historisk museum. University of Bergen, 7–48. Bergen.

—— 1979. On Shoreline Dating of Arctic Rock Carvings in Vingen, Western Norway. *Norwegian Archaeological Review* 12:2, 115–122.

Bergsvik, K.A. 1999. A new reference-system for classification of lithic raw materials. A case-study from Skatestraumen, Western Norway. In: Boaz J. (ed.) *The Mesolithic of Middle Scandinavia*, Universitetets Oldsaksamlings Skrifter. Ny rekke no 22, 283–297. Oslo.

Bergsvik, K.A. 2001. Sedentary and Mobile hunter-fishers in Stone Age Westren Norway. *Arctic Archaeology* Vol. 38 No. 1, pp. 2–26.

Bergsvik, K.A. 2002. Aekeologiske undersøkelser ved Skatestraumen. Bind I. *Arkeologiske avhandlinger og rapporter fra Universitetet i Bergen* 7. Bergen Museum. Bergen.

Bjerck, H.B. 1983. *Kronologisk og geografisk fordeling av mesolittiske element i vest- og midt-Norge*. Unpublished mag. art. thesis, University of Bergen. Bergen.

Bjørgo, T. 1981. *Flatøy et eksempel på steinalderens kronologi og livbergingsmåte i Nordhordland*. Unpublished mag. art. thesis, University of Bergen. Bergen.

Bøe, J. 1932. Felszeichnungen im westlichen Norwegen I. Vingen und Hennøya. *Bergens Museums Skrifter* 15. Bergen.

Fett, P. 1941. Nye ristningar i Nordfjord. Vingelva og Fura. *Bergens Museums årbok* 1941. Historisk-antikvarisk rekke. Nr. 6.

Gjessing, G. 1932. *Arktiske helleristninger i Nord Norge*. Instituttet for sammenlignende kulturforskning. Oslo.

—— 1936. *Nordenfjeldske ristninger og malinger av den arktiske gruppe*. Instituttet for sammenlignende kulturforskning. Oslo.

—— 1937. Veideristningen på Stein i Ringsaker. *Universitetetets Oldsaksamlings Årbok* 1935–1936, 52–68.

Hallström, G. 1938. *Monumental art of Northern Europe from the Stone Age*. I. The Norwegian localities. Stockholm.

Hesjedal, A. 1990. *Helleristninger som tegn og tekst. En analyse av veideristningene i Nordland og Troms*. Unpublished. Mag. Art. Thesis. University of Tromsø. Tromsø.

Hjelle, K. and Lødøen, T.K. in prep. *Vegetasjonshistoriske analyser av borekjerner fra Vingeneset og Djupedalen, Bremanger kommune, Sogn og Fjordane*. Report. Topographical files, Department of Archaeology, University of Bergen. Bergen.

Lindquist, C. 1994. *Fangstfolkets bilder. En studie av de nordfennoskandiska kustanknutna jägarhällristningarna*. Thesis and papers in Archaeology N.S A5. Stockholm.

Lødøen, T.K. 1995. *Lanskapet som rituell sfære i steinalderen. En kontekstuell studie av bergartsøkser fra Sogn*. Unpublished Cand. philol. thesis, University of Bergen. Bergen.

—— 1998. Interpreting Mesolithic axe deposits from a region in Western Norway. In: Kazakevicius, V., Olsen, A.B. and Simpson, S. (eds) *The Archaeology of Lithuania and Western Norway: Status and Perspectives*. Archaeologica Baltica 3, 195–204. Vilnius.

—— 2001. Interpretation of Stone Age Ideology based on Rock Art, Structures and Artefacts in the Vingen area, Western Norway. In: Helskog, K. (ed.) *Theoretical Perspectives in Rock Art Research*. The Institute for Comparative Research in Human Culture. pp 211–223. Oslo.

Mandt, G. 1998. Vingen Revisited. A Gendered Perspective on "Hunters" Rock Art. In: Larsson, L. and Stjernquist, B. (ed.) *The Worldview of Prehistoric Man*. KVHAA Konferenser 40, 201–224. Stockholm.

Mandt, G. and Lødøen, T.K. In prep. *Vingen – «... et naturens kolossalmusæum for helleristninger»*. Dokumentasjonsrapport 1993–99.

Mezec, B. 1989. *A Structural Analysis of the Late Stone Age Petrolygyphs at Vingen, Norway*. Unpublished MA dissertation. University College. London.

Mikkelsen, E. 1977. Østnorske veideristninger – Kronologi og økokulturelt miljø. *Viking* 40, 147–201.

Nygaard, S.E. 1989. The Stone Age of Northern Scandinavia: A review. *Journal of World Prehistory* 3, No. 1. 71 – 116.

—— 1990. Mesolithic Western Norway. In: Vermeersch, P. and van Peer, P. (eds.) *Contributions to the Mesolithic in Europe*. Papers presented at the Fourth International Symposium "The Mesolithic in Europe", 227–237. Leuven.

Nærøy, A.J. 1988. Teknologiske endringer ved overgangen fra eldre til yngre steinalder på Vestlandet. *Arkeologiske Skrifter*, No. 4, 205–213. Historisk Museum. University of Bergen. Bergen.

—— 1993. Chronological and Technological changes in Western Norway 6000–3800 BP. *Acta Archaeologica* 63 (1992), 77–95.

Olsen, A.B. and Alsaker, S. 1984. Greenstone and Diabase Utilization in the Stone Age of Western Norway: Technological and Socio-cultural Aspects of Axe and Adze Production and Distribution. *Norwegian Archaeological Review* 17, No. 2, 71–103.

Olsen, A.B. 1992. *Kotedalen – en boplass gjennom 5000 år*. Bind I, Fangstbosetning og tidlig jordbruk i vestnorsk steinalder: Nye funn og nye perspektiver. Historisk Museum, University of Bergen. Bergen.

Skjerlie, F. 1999. *Geologisk vurdering av steinredskap (B 15582) fra Vingen i Bremanger, Sogn og Fjordane*. Report. Topographical files, Department of Archaeology, University of Bergen. Bergen.

Tansey, R.G. and Kleiner, F.S. 1996. *Gardner's Art Through the Ages*. Fort Worth.

Warren, E.J. 1993. *Coastal sedentism during the Atlantic period in Nordhordland, Western Norway? The middle and late mesolithic components at Kotedalen*. Unpublished Master of Art Thesis. Department of Anthropology Memorial University of Newfoundland. St.John.

65. Pre-Boreal elk bones from Lundby Mose

Keld Møller Hansen

In 1999 the Museum of south Zealand, Denmark excavated parts of a kettle hole where three concentrations of marrow fractured elk bones were found. The bones are dated to the Pre-Boreal period, and with other similar findings from the Skottemarke and Favrbo sites, they constitute an exceptional find group in Denmark which may help us to unveil technological as well as ritual aspects of Pre-Boreal hunting.

The bones have multiple cut marks and most are marrow fractured. All the shoulder blades from this kind of finds are modified in a similar fashion: The crests have been removed and they either have a hole or they are fractured with parts of the shoulder blade missing. This deliberate destruction of the shoulder blades can not result from the hunt or marrow extraction since there are no marrow in the shoulder blades. Presumably the modification of the shoulder blades are the result of rituals, that were part of hunting magic or subsequent feasting. The finds from Lundby Mose have been C14 dated to rthe period between 9860 – 9930 BP and they are thus the oldest C14 dated Mesolithic find from Denmark.

Skottemarke and Favrbo

The elk bones from Skottemarke at Lolland were found in 1902 during digging in a bog for peat (Figure 65.1). The find was reported to the National Museum, which completed the excavation where no less than 275 bones, all elks, were collected. The zoologist Ulrik Møhl determined that the bones consist of one juvenile cow, four adult cows and a bull.

The excavation at Skottemarke also yielded 16 finely barbed points and a flint assemblage including some flake axes. These were mostly found at a higher level in the peat, whereas the elkbones were deposited close together in the detritus mud, under the peat, at the bottom of the former lake.

The Favrbo find in Zealand also was discovered during peat digging, but 18 years later (Figure 65.1). Here bones from an elk, a full-grown young bull, and a cow, approximately 1 year of age, were found.

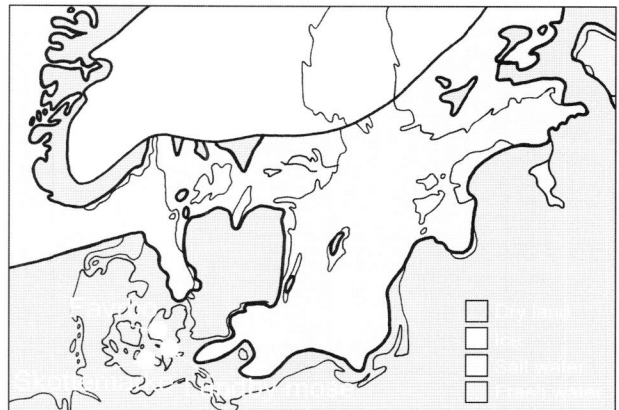

Figure 65.1 Map showing the Pre-Boreal landscape in Scandinavia and the three elk bone assemblage sites in Denmark.

The pollen analytical datings of the skeletons correspond with the radio-carbon determinations, which give a date of 9.400 BP for the Skottemarke find, while the two elks from Favrbo are dated to approximately 9.500 BP. The two finds have been carefully investigated and published by Møhl from Zoological Museum in Denmark in 1978 (Møhl 1978).

Lundby Mose (Lundby Bog)

The new find from Lundby Mose is situated in the south western part of an approximately 6000 square meter kettle hole (Figure 65.2). This sites is situated on the edge of the internationally known bog near Lundby, which through the years has revealed several settlements from the Maglemose culture. The most famous of these are the Lundby sites from the early Maglemose period.

It was two agricultural students who, in their digging frenzy, discovered the new find. These two students had dug a deep hole in the field where they found the well-preserved bones of an elk. Unfortunately, they had almost dug out the whole find before someone from the Museum

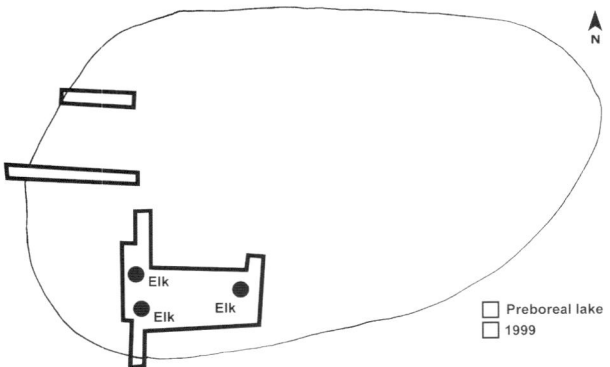

Figure 65.2 Map of the kettle hole showing excavation areas in 1999 and the three elk bone assemblage.

Figure 65.3 Elk bone assemblage number 1. Lundby Mose. Photo by Geert Brovad.

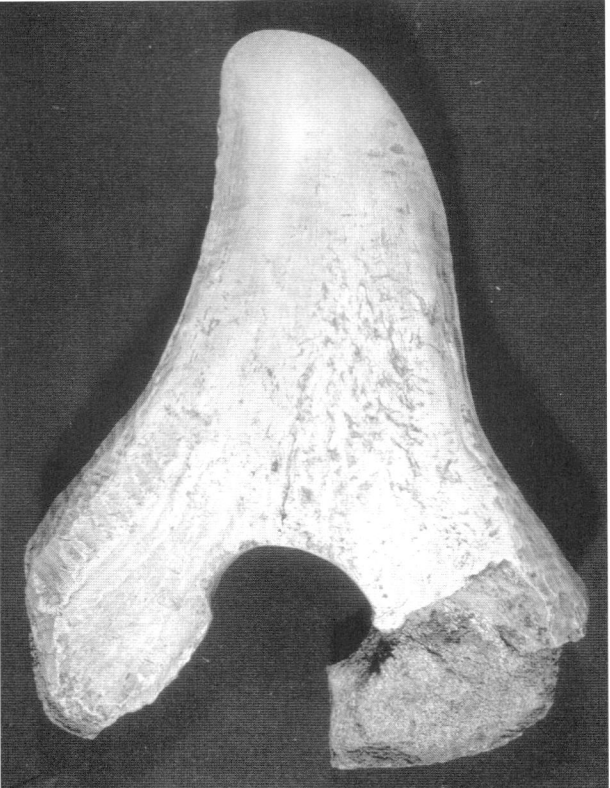

Figure 65.4 Elk antler mattock-head. Lundby Mose. Photo by Henrik Dahl.

Figure 65.5 Elk bone assemblage number 2. Lundby Mose. Photo by Geert Brovad.

arrived. So only a few bones remained (Figure 65.3), but interestingly, along with these was an axe of elk antler or a so called elk antler mattock-head.

The axe was broken in the neck, but apart from this, extremely well preserved (Figure 65.4). In Denmark there are about 25 of this particular type. The elk antler mattock-head from Lundby Moor is the first species found in situ, and consequently the first which with certainty can be dated to the Pre-Boreal period in Denmark. This dating was expected and does not come as a big surprise, as the type also is dated to this period at Starr Carr.

Elk-bone assemblage number two was situated a few meters from the first one and was not quite as well preserved as the bones were situated a bit higher up in the ground (Figure 65.5). It was remarkable that the bones were nicely gathered, almost inside a square meter.

The third elk-bone assemblage was situated 10 meters east of the two other finds (Figure 65.6). These bones were also more or less gathered inside a square meter and extremely well preserved. During the excavation of this lot, it was discovered that neither more nor less than 3 animals were situated here. Among the bones were found three small flakes and more exciting a sternum with a fragmented arrowhead (Figures 65.7 and 65.8): Notice that the arrow has come angled from left, and if the elk had trodden a step forward, the shot would have been lethal, as the arrow would have penetrated either the heart or the lungs.

Discussion of the finds

There is no doubt, that the finds from Skottemarke, Favrbo and Lundby Moor are to be seen in the same light. There

Figure 65.6 Elkbone assemblage number 3. Lundby Mose. Photo by Geert Brovad.

Figure 65.8 The fragmented arrowhead. Lundby Mose. Photo by Geert Brovad.

Figure 65.7 Sternum with a fragmented arrowhead. Lundby Mose. Photo by Geert Brovad.

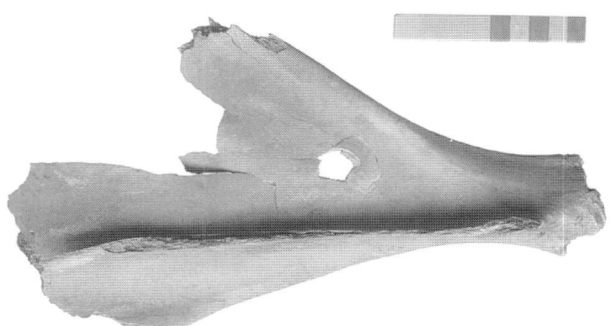

Figure 65.9 Scapulae with a ritual hole?. Lundby Mose. Photo by Geert Brovad.

are remarkable similarities between the finds, not only in time but also in their type. The state of the bones shows indisputable traces of human activity – splitting for marrow, cut marks etc.

The Lundby Mose finds have made it obvious that all the bones were deposited at the same time. Every find represent a secluded incident. It seems that the finds clearly do not belong to any category that can be described as ordinary "settlement debris" or maybe not even debris. Several of the split and broken bones can be reconstructed to whole bones, belonging to the same skeletons; furthermore, the usual admixture of bones from other game species, so characteristic of settlement debris, is lacking. The question is therefore asked, can the setting out of these elks remains be seen as a practice typical of the time – a culturally determined trait following the successful hunting of these Pre-Boreal big game animals?

A row of peculiarities associated with the finds show, that sometimes a seclusion has been made. Certain bones are missing – in particular cannonbones. In elk assemblage number 3 at Lundby Moor there could have been 12 cannonbones but only one was present. At Skottemarke, where there could have been 24 cannonbones, they are totally missing. As well at Favrbo cutmarks showed that antler points were removed. The removal of the bones and antler is undoubtedly for later use as raw materials for weapons and implements.

Concerning the marrowbone split technique, there are no significant differences between the bones in the three finds and those from the later Boreal settlement find in e.g. Zealand. A closer look at especially the shoulder blades from these finds, show that they are all modified in a similar fashion: They either have a hole or are fractured with parts of the shoulder blade missing (Figure 65.9). This deliberate destruction of the scapulae can in some cases be explained as a result of the hunt, but in other cases this cannot be the explanation. One of the scapulae from Lundby Moor and similar ones from Skottemarke show that some of the injuries may have another explanation. Here it is certain that the breaks did not occur until after the meat was removed from the animal. This is most obvious on two scapulas where, like on most of the others, you can see scrapingmarks (on the inside as well as the outside of the bone). This is the result of meat removal. Fortunately, some of these marks cross the break and can be found on the removed section of the bone, and indicate that the breakage took place after the butchering.

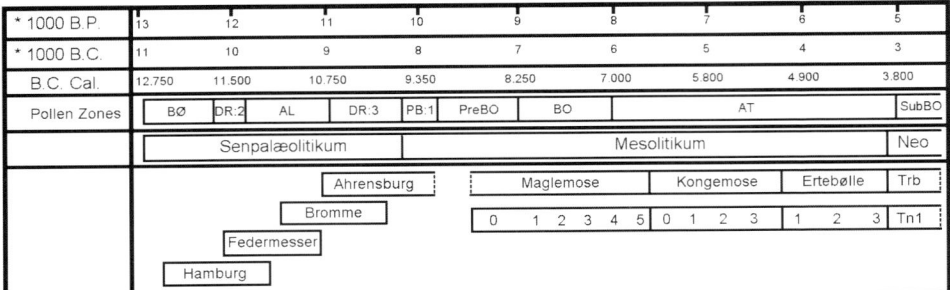

Figure 65.10 The C14 date from Lundby Mose, Skottemarke and Favrbo placed in the Danish Palaeolithic and Mesolithic chronology.

As in several other cases the spine on the scapulae in Figure 65.9 is broken off, which is remarkable because it has no culinary worth such as marrow.

The remarkable breaking of the scapulae together with the marrow spliting of the bones and their subsequent deposition together could be regarded as a type of ritual or hunting magic. Ritual and hunting magic take place in almost all hunter societies. From Lapland for instance, the Sami can tell about cultic places where this were still used in the 20th century to bring the marrow split bones of reindeer. After the end of the meal, which included splitting the bones for marrow, the various bones were collected and put in a particular place in the forest. It was an old custom and a rule that the animals' remains must not be divided but kept together. Such places where bones were placed can be found today still lying on the surface in the forest. After the end of the meal, it was custom to drive ones knife through the shoulder blade or just to crush it with stones. The old Sami who told the story did not remember why it was done, but only that it was (Møhl 1978).

It is possible that hunting magic might also have taken place in the settlements, but in this case it is very difficult to demonstrate. Shoulder blades of elk from the well known Danish Boreal settlements of Holmegaard, Svaerborg and Mullerup of central Zealand confirm the observance of this home settlement custom, where the rubbish is concealed under the surface of the life-giving and regenerating water. Ethnographic parallels show that hunting people often create myths about the animals they hunt. The primary target of these myths is to explain the connection between beast and man. In the Eskimos and Siberian societies, the basis of the myths are man and beast live in tribes and visit each other. An alliance, on which they both depend, exist between these two parties. The hunters have the understanding that the animals let themselves be killed in order to be able to visit the people's world. In this interaction it is essential that people understand that it is only a visit, and therefore act accordingly. They have to help the animals to be reborn. In this context, the most common thing to do is to collect the bones from the animals and deposit them in the re-creative nature, over or under water. The reward from the animals is then returned, to give again later their lives to the hunters. Often a long row of rituals and customs, which have to be followed, are also attached to this.

C 14 datings

The three finds from Lundby Mose have been radiocarbon dated with remarkable results (Figure 65.10). Bone assemblage number 1 can be dated to 9930 ±70 BP (AAR-5470), bone assemblage number 2 to 9950 ±75 BP (AAR-5469) and bone assemblage number 3 to 9860 ±70 BP (AAR-5471). The finds from Lundby Moor is at this point almost 500 years older than the parallel finds from Skottemarke and Favrbo.

For the first time we are able to document finds in Denmark from the very early part of the Pre-Boreal period, between the Ahrensburg culture and the Maglemose culture. The two cultures are considered as the reindeer and forest hunter cultures, respectively. It is still not certain which one of the cultures covers the early part of Pre-Boreal time. So was it the Maglemose or Ahrenburg hunters who killed and sacrificed the elks at Lundby Mose?

Radiocarbon datings show that apparently the oldest Maglemose sites only appear in the late period of the Pre-Boreal. Among these is the well-known south Zealand settlement Barmose, which is radiocarbon dated to approximately 9240 ± 150 BP and about 700 years younger than the Lundby Mose finds (Johansson 1990). However the elk antler mattock-head from Lundby Mose indicates that the Lundby Mose finds have to be considered from the Maglemose culture as axes of this type are dated only to this culture.

On the other hand, radiocarbon dates from the well known north German settlement Stellmore date the end of the Ahrensburg culture to be younger than 9810 ± 100 BP (Fischer and Tauber 1986), which is the start of the Pre-Boreal period and even later than the Lundby Mose finds.

The arrow in the chest bone could determine if it was the Ahrensburg hunters who had shot the animals. Unfortunately, the arrow head was broken and therefore impossible to identify. To determine the characters of the arrowhead an X-ray examination of the bone and the arrowhead also was made, but without succes.

The proceeding examinations

There is still a lot of information to be gained from the bones at Lundby Mose. Zoologists in the near future will try to find out the size, sex, age and at what time of the year the elks were killed. Finally it has to be clarified if there was a pattern in how the animals were cut up and the meat was removed. Moreover the marrow split bones open a unique opportunity for composition not only within one heap but also to possibly establish if the heaps are to be seen in connected.

There is additional information hidden in the bones. An example is a skull with animal bite marks in each end (Figure 65.11). According to the zoologists is likely they are dog bite marks and in that case the oldest traces from dogs in Denmark and probably in the Northern Europe.

It is quite possible that one or several dogs have been involved in the hunt of elks. Elk hunts today in Norway and Sweden are often carried out with tracker dogs, who after a shorter or a longer pursuit can tire the elks so that the hunter can come close enough to shoot.

The excavations in 1999 did not clarify how the finds should be considered. Are they part of a settlement and if so, what kind of settlement? Only a small part of the Kettle hole has been examined and therefore a settlement could easily be hidden along its border. Only a few meters from the 500 years younger Skottemarke find were traces found from a settlement of the same age!

Numerous Pre-Boreal settlements occur in south Zealand, but it is not possible to regard one of these as the source of elk bones to the Kettle hole (Figure 65.12).

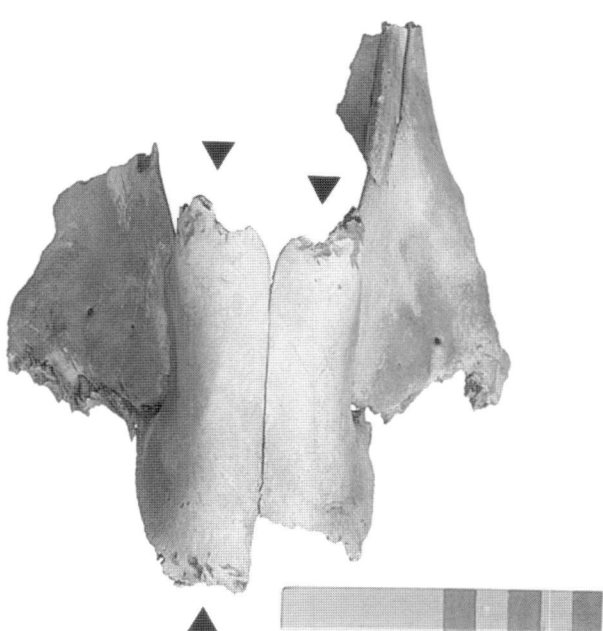

Figure 65.11 Cranium with animal bite marks, probably from a dog. Lundby Mose. Photo by Geert Brovad.

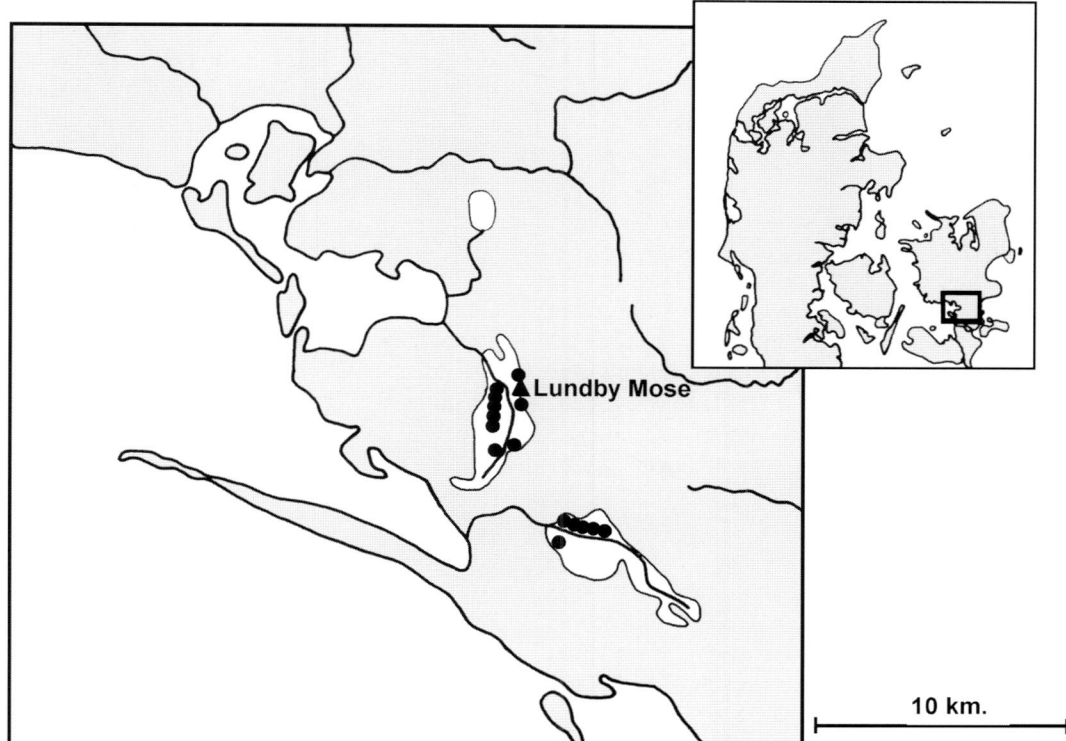

Figure 65.12 Pre-Boreal Sites in south Zealand.

Figure 65.13 A look into the future. Excavation in progress at Lundby Mose 2000. Photo by Keld Møller Hansen.

All these Pre-Boreal settlements are dated typological by their content to the last part of the period and therefore can not be connected.

Systematic investigations in the surroundings near the kettle hole have produced two inhabited sites. One of these can be dated to the late part of the Pre-Boreal period or early Maglemose culture, while the inventory from the other site suggest a Pre-Boreal or maybe even earlier age. All finds from the sites were recovered only as results of soil cultivation and are very limited in extent. These sites nead to be investigated in order to get a more exact dating.

Epilogue

The Lundby Moor finds are explained as a number of hunting events ending so far away from the settlement that it was not possible to get the pray home.

After one or several successful hunts, the elks were butchered over a period of maybe several days. Then the bones were broken and the hunters made a feast with the marrow. The shoulder blades were perforated and the spine chopped off as a part of a ritual, which ended by collecting all the bones and throwing them into the lake – except the bones that they needed for raw material.

The investigation in kettle hole at Lundby Moor will continue in September 2000 (Figure 65.13). The main purpose will be to clarify if there was a settlement at the edge of the kettle hole and to determine how many elkbones are in the kettle hole.

References

Fischer, A. and Tauber, H. 1986. New C-14 Datings of Late Palaeolithic Cultures of Northwestern Europe. *Journal of Danish Archaeology* 5, 7–13.

Henriksen, B.B. 1980. *Lundby-holmen. Pladser af maglemosetype i Sydsjælland.* Nordiske Fortidsminder Bind 6. København.

Johansson, A.D. 1990. *Barmosegruppen. Præboreale bopladsfund I Sydsjælland.* Århus.

Møhl, U. 1978. Elgsdyrskeletterne fra Skottemarke og Favrbo. Skik og brug ved borealtidens jagter. *Aarbøger for nordisk Oldkyndighed og Historie* 1978, 5–32.

66. A Taphonomy of Ritual Practice, a "field"-anthropological study of late Mesolithic burials

Liv Nilsson Stutz

As a complement to more traditional archaeological analyses of the late Mesolithic burials at Vedbaek and Skateholm, this paper presents a new approach to mortuary archaeology, exploring the underlying structures of the conceptions of death in Mesolithic mortuary practices. The analysis is based on the French approach Anthropologie de terrain, *a taphonomically based method which uses knowledge of the biological processes of decomposition of the human body after death in order to reconstruct mortuary practices in the past. This approach, which renders visible the treatment of the body of the dead, is combined with contemporary ritual theory which emphasises the role of practice. Ultimately, reconstructing the detailed taphonomic history of the burials from Skateholm and Vedbaek not only provides new information not previously recovered by traditional archaeological excavation and analytical techniques; it also deepens our understanding of the mortuary features as the traces of ritual practice, potentially allowing us to identify basic symbolic structures underlying the mortuary practices in late Mesolithic society.*

Introduction

Burials are valuable sources of insight into the past, whether the archaeological inquiry is concerned with social organisation, gender roles, ritual, religion, or cosmology. Throughout the history of our discipline, burials have also played a central role in the development of the epistemological bases of our interpretive frameworks. The privileged role burials play in the view we get of a past society as a whole is very clearly illustrated by the case of the European Mesolithic, for which the discoveries of the cemeteries in Vedbaek in eastern Zeeland, Denmark (Albrethsen and Brinch Petersen 1976), and Skateholm in southern Scania, Sweden (Larsson 1980, 1981, 1982, 1983, 1984, 1988), in the mid-1970's and early 1980's, not only led to changes in the way Mesolithic sites were excavated and surveyed, but actually contributed to inspire a reevaluation of the entire period. From having been regarded as representing foraging societies governed mostly by ecological conditions, the Mesolithic now became the stage for complex symbolic and ritual activities, leading archaeologists to revise their view of these groups as strictly egalitarian hunter-gatherers. These conceptions were to a very large extent influenced by the conceptions of mortuary practices developed within the theoretical framework of the New Archaeology, in which complex mortuary practices were assumed to reflect a complex social system (Saxe 1970; Binford 1971), an idea that may be critically challenged today (Parker Pearson 1999:32). Still, the late Mesolithic burials of Scandinavia have not come to rest easily in the categories expected from the New Archaeology's analysis of ranked and egalitarian groups (Price 1985:358 pp). As a more complete picture is constructed, drawing in other sites and other categories of finds, the debate about the social organisation of these Mesolithic societies is ongoing. With archaeologists voicing different opinions on the matter, the issue of complexity in the late Mesolithic has become entangled in the debate over the process of neolithisation, now a central question for Mesolithic research.

In this paper I will put these traditional "Mesolithic issues" to the side, but I still suggest that the Mesolithic cemeteries can offer valuable insight into the Mesolithic society as a whole. I present an additional perspective on the burials at Skateholm and Vedbaek. Instead of focusing on the pattern of social organisation reflected by the graves, this analysis looks at the mortuary practices and ritual acts *per se*, as important objects of study. Obviously, this does not imply that I consider the questions concerning the social organisation of the Mesolithic society irrelevant or uninteresting. Rather, I wish to introduce a complementary approach to the study of these burials, highlighting their ritual and religious content. After all, as Julian Thomas put it, "there is more to human sociality than ranking," (Thomas 1991:127). What I wish to focus on are the ideas that structured the mortuary ritual and explore what these might reveal about conceptions of death in Mesolithic society. In my search for these aspects of the Mesolithic, I want to go back to the archaeological sources and systematically explore their potential to reveal some basic sets of symbols and some basic concepts that structured the mortuary rituals in practice.

My analysis is based on the French approach *Anthropologie de terrain*, i.e. "field anthropology," a cross-disciplinary method which uses knowledge from biology about the process of decomposition of the human body after death in order to answer questions about the mortuary rituals. I combine this approach with contemporary ritual theory and practice theory. In presenting illustrative examples of the results from Skateholm and Vedbaek, I aim to outline both the methodological strength and the theoretical possibilities of combining rigorous taphonomic analysis of burials with the elucidation of fundamental cultural conceptions offered by a close analysis of ritual practice.

The Archaeological Study of Mortuary Rituals

When studying mortuary practices in the past, archaeology faces extensive challenges. Through our main source of information, the archeological record, we get only a very fragmented picture of the mortuary rituals. Moreover, we often only get a glimpse of the last stage (e.g., the final deposition of the body) in a long sequence of meaningful activities.

However, having access to the archaeological traces of the ultimate interment of the body, I believe that we can still get at some fundamental aspects of the mortuary ritual. If we want to reduce human death to its very basic facts, we might say that two things occur. First of all, a social individual vanishes. This is the dimension of death on which we, as archaeologists, typically focus. Second of all, at the moment of death something else occurs; a cadaver, a dead body, comes into being. Mortuary practices, however variable they might be from one society to the next, handle these two aspects: the body and the soul. Ethnography and social anthropology provide a very rich record that indicates clearly to us that these two aspects always are intertwined. Studies from the beginning of the century (Hertz [1907] 1960), as well as more recent work (Huntington and Metcalf 1979; Thomas 1980; Bloch and Parry 1982), have illustrated that the way in which the body is handled in the mortuary practices takes care of the needs of the soul – the souls of the dead according to the belief systems, but also the spiritual needs of the survivors. The dead body thus becomes a vehicle for the mythological and spiritual conceptions of life and death, and this is carried out, through ritual practice, according to structured and structuring principles. If we can study how the body was taken care of after death, we might get a glimpse of some of these principles. It thus seems clear that what people were *doing* with their dead is as important an object of study as other topics that have been developed in the archaeology of death over the last thirty years, such as the relationship between the individual's status in death and her or his social position in life (Saxe 1970; Binford 1971; Brown 1971; Tainter 1975, 1977, 1978), the form and location of the place for the dead in the site (Goldstein 1981) or its landscape context (Chapman 1981, 1995; Goldstein 1995), or the symbolic meaning and content of the mortuary feature (Pader 1982; Shanks and Tilley 1982; Tilley 1984; Parker Pearson 1999).

Contemporary ritual theory also emphasises the concept of practice. In her book *Ritual Theory Ritual Practice* Catherine Bell (1992) has deconstructed the category "ritual," emphasising that it is the very *ritualisation* of certain actions, marking them as separate from everyday life, that gives ritual its identity and underlies its transcendent effects. Ritual, according to Bell, proceeds through the structured and structuring production of ritualised actions, operating in three phases. First, it creates categories of binary oppositions. Second, these oppositions are placed into a hierarchical system. Finally, they are intertwined with other couples of oppositions into a complex chain of associations. This chain of associations generates a feeling of a logical system with clear, hierarchically organised order. Still, ritual practice generates only a "loose sense of totality and systematicity" (Bell 1992:104), perhaps because the set of symbolic associations may be augmented in individual thought and through opportunities for discussion and reflection with others during certain phases of a ritual or before or after the ritual event. Ritual, then, comes to encompass the entire world without developing a rigidly fixed structure of meanings that could be rejected as whole. On many levels of experience, from the feeling of participation in the present ritual to a lifetime of practice, ritual dynamics "afford an experience of 'order' as well as the 'fit' between this taxonomic order and the real world of experience" (Bell 1992:104). Ritual practice creates a world, and thus, ritual *is a world*, a reality experienced as natural, and objective.

Ritual is practice. In general, as a category of social practice that is logically marked from everyday life according to fundamental aspects of the culture's symbolic system, ritual practice provides an example *par excellence* of the inextricability of thought, relations of symbols, and action, as these elements work in dialectic oscillation in the unfolding of human social life (Bourdieu 1977). A theory of practice – in ritual or any other situation – allows the anthropologist to connect subjective lived experience to objectively documented patterns of social action, including sequences of verbal and physical gestures (Bourdieu 1977). Practice theory situates structures of social relations and power in the context of cultural and historical processes. Thus, it can potentially aid the archaeologist in envisioning not only how cultural practices persist in time, but also how they change historically. The bases of practice theory, in which meaning and action are always intertwined, are highly relevant to archaeologists. What we study are the material traces of practice. In the case of mortuary ritual, if we can recover the gestures carried out in the treatment and interment of the body, even if we cannot retrieve the full set of symbols which structured and were structured by ritual practice in the past, then we should be able to establish some basic sets of meaningful, symbolic oppositions about life and death, the individual and the group, the living and the dead, and purity and decay.

Yet, if we want to use the theoretical notion of practice to elucidate aspects of the structuring and structured symbolic systems of past societies, then it is obvious that our archaeological methods must provide a tie between the material remains *per se* and the gestures that produced them. I have suggested that practice theory already wraps together physical human actions with all of the structured factors that influence them and give them meaning. Human actions always have a meaningful dimension. Thus, the critical methodological development must focus on reconstructing actions in detail; when considered in the archaeological context of mortuary features, these actions may then be analysed as ritual gestures.

I contend that a major problem in the archaeology of death today is that while theoretical awareness has increased dramatically over the past thirty years, the methods of excavation and analysis have not seen a similar evolution. While we ask new questions, we tend to continue to use the same material and the same categorisations of the archaeological record. While the traditionally emphasised information, such as sex and age of the deceased, the level and form of energy spent (which ultimately connects not only to material wealth but also to aspects such as monumentality), and spatial distribution (which concerns relations between burials as well as landscape analysis of visibility) may still be very useful for many of the questions we are asking, they fail to completely capture the notion of practice. Moreover, although commonly employed field and laboratory techniques can securely document these categories of archaeological interest, we do not worry whether new theoretical concerns about ritual practice may be addressed with the research methods at hand. Our methods and theories are not sufficiently synchronised.

We need to begin by complementing our traditional categorisations with new ones. Yet, in order to do this we have to develop our methods of investigation in order to come closer to the archaeological material. If we understand our material sources better, then we can extract more information from them, and in doing so, we will have established methods of excavation, documentation, and analysis which meet all of the demands of the theoretical frameworks we are using. As I will attempt to demonstrate, a methodologically careful search for traces of the acts and gestures carried out as meaningful constituents of mortuary ritual in the past will also constitute a tool for a much better understanding of the taphonomical history of archaeological mortuary features. I contend that this will more thoroughly link a range of theoretical approaches to the archaeology of death to the material record itself. This represents a connection that theoretical archaeology has frequently been criticised for not making.

Anthropologie de terrain has the potential for meeting all of these demands. This method for researching mortuary sites has been presented in depth elsewhere (Duday and Masset 1987; Duday *et al.* 1990; Nilsson 1998; Crubézy 2000), and here I will only review some of the basic ideas. *Anthropologie de terrain*, or field anthropology, combines detailed observation of the position of the bones in the field, with knowledge about the processes involved in the natural decomposition of the human body after death. The situation that we encounter as archaeologists when we excavate a grave is influenced by taphonomic factors that are both natural and non-natural, and which, at different moments in the taphonomic history of the deposit, may have altered its appearance. Among the natural factors must be counted the decomposition of the organic material in the grave feature; this includes the soft tissues of the human body as well as perishable grave goods, clothing, body decoration, and components of the grave architecture. Among the non-natural factors we include the practices that produced the ritual treatment of the body and the grave. As Lee Lyman has pointed out, taphonomy is commonly misconceived as the study of how natural processes destroy information originally present in the archaeological record. In fact, taphonomy plays just as important a role in rendering visible the human agents who structure the material remains (Lyman 1994:33). *Anthropologie de terrain* achieves this by viewing the human body after death and the grave structure as a dynamic entity. The basic analytical tools of *Anthropologie de terrain* rely on the relative chronology of the decomposition of the articulations of the human body and the dynamic creation and filling of "empty spaces" as soft tissues decompose. These basic factors will strongly influence the way in which the human bones will scatter during the process of decomposition of the body in the grave. Moreover, since the process of equilibration between decomposition and infilling is highly dependent on the immediate environment of the body, the arrangment of bones uncovered by the archaeologist can reveal much additional information about the initial arrangement of the body in the grave structure. Thus, *Anthropologie de terrain* aims to reconstruct a taphonomic history of the grave, and in doing so, it yields as detailed as possible a document of the mortuary ritual. In general, while mortuary practices vary, the biological processes remain the same across cultural boundaries. By identifying the natural factors contributing to the taphonomic history of a mortuary feature, we can separate them from the intentional, ritualised gestures we ultimately seek to apprehend. The better understanding of these natural taphonomic processes more specifically allows us to extract information which gives us certain details of the mortuary practices; we can see how the grave and the body were prepared and how the body was positioned in the grave. The aim is basically to figure out what living people were doing with their dead. I have chosen to call this integration of practice theory with a detailed, taphonomically oriented methodology a "Taphonomy of Ritual Practice." The constant focus on what people were doing with their dead helps us connect to the structured and structuring aspects of ritual as it operated in a past human society. Because the ritual gestures and the symbolic schemes that give them meaning are so tightly, dialectically related, we should actually be able to get at the world that past mortuary practices created and structured. This should be very interesting to archaeology, social anthropology, history and the study of religion because in the long run, we might be able to discuss variability of ritual practice in space and time and the role of ritual in contextualising and contributing to the structured conflicts or the development of historical events that comprise the processes of social change. For now, though, I focus only on the analysis of ritual practice in the Late Mesolithic societies for which the cemeteries of Skateholm and Vedbaek were ritually significant.

The field excavation and documentation techniques of *Anthropologie de terrain* involve detailed drawing, photography, and description of the grave feature, with each individual bone recorded not only with three dimensional coordinates but also with the orientation of its anatomical landmarks (Duday *et al.* 1990; Courtaud 1996). This offers the most systematic and careful approach to the excavation, analysis and interpretation of burials in archaeology. The recovery of ritual practice will be maximised by the rich taphonomic information provided by such methods. In the case of Skateholm and Vedbaek, the excavation and documentation occurred only as *Anthropologie de terrain* was in its first years of development in France. Yet, the drawings, photographs, and field notes from Skateholm and Vedbaek are of excellent quality, and these documents have allowed me to carry out considerably detailed analysis of the taphonomic history of these late Mesolithic burials. As its name implies, *Anthropologie de terrain* has been developed as a complete field methodology for mortuary archaeology, but its principles do facilitate reanalysis of burials for which adequate information has been recorded.

Dealing with the Dead in the Mesolithic

My reanalysis of the Mesolithic burials at Skateholm and Vedbaek has mainly confirmed previous, basic interpretations of the mortuary practices, in some cases replacing more speculative arguments with stronger ones. Moreover these results have contributed new information and new perspectives. The complete results will be presented elsewhere. For this paper, I have chosen some examples which I think can illustrate the level and nuance of information we can obtain through a taphonomic analysis of ritual practice. I also touch on new questions suggested by this view of ritual in the Mesolithic. The examples I have chosen to discuss deal with the nature of the burials, the space of decomposition and the architecture of the structures.

The great majority of the burials at Skateholm I and II, and at Vedbaek are so called "primary burials." The term "primary" refers to the deposition of a fresh cadaver in the mortuary structure. In the field, the positive identification of a primary burial is most reliably made when labile articulations are preserved. These are anatomical connections which undergo decomposition of binding soft tissues at a relatively early stage. The most labile articulations are those of the bones of the hands, the phalanges of the feet, and the connections between cervical vertebrae (Duday *et al.* 1990:31 pp). These articulations are typically very well preserved at Skateholm and Vedbaek. In graves without preserved labile articulations, the overall preservation of the grave was so poor that the pattern of bone distribution could be better explained by post-depositional disturbance.

The notion of "primary" burial is opposed to that of secondary burial or burials/funerals "in multiple episodes". This term denotes the deposition of human remains that have undergone processes of natural decomposition or artifical reduction prior to the final burial (Duday *et al.* 1990:43 p). These processes can consist of cremation, active removal of the soft tissues or natural decomposition in a different location than the final burial. At Skateholm and Vedbaek we have evidence that strongly suggests burial/funerals in multiple episodes for some of the individuals. The most obvious cases are the few burials containing cremated remains of the individual.

There are also other examples of treatment of the body prior to burial. In one case at Skateholm I, a cadaver which was subjected to artificial disarticulation was subsequently buried in grave 13 (Larsson 1981:23). The skeletal parts were placed in a pit 1m long and 0.5 m wide. Overall, the skeleton was not found in an anatomically correct arrangement. However, some connections were intact, including those of the left fore-arm, wrist and hand, as well as those of the right foot (Persson and Persson 1984:20). Other anatomical units were totally lacking. The right hand and the left foot were completely missing (Persson and Persson 1984:20). The hypothesis that the body would have decomposed naturally somewhere else before its interment in grave 13 can be eliminated, because we have found the labile articulations of the left hand and the right foot properly intact. Moreover, bones joined at more resistant articulations were found separately in this grave. Clearly, this is not a matter of the common multiple episode type of burial, where the body decomposes in one or several places before the final deposition. On the contrary, for grave 13 it is clear that the cadaver must have been fairly fresh at the time of burial. This would thus represent a quite intensive artificial treatment of the cadaver before the burial. However, I emphasise that with only one isolated case like this, it is difficult to affirm whether this treatment was part of a ritualised mortuary practice. Because the

Figure 66.1 Burial 28, Skateholm 1. In this grave we have evidence for a reopening of the burial and a retrieval of bones after the process of decomposition was either in an advanced stage or terminated.

disarticulated, partial cadaver in grave 13 is unique at Skateholm I, some other explanation may apply. The interpretation of a similar treatment of that found in grave 13, or alternatively a secondary bundle-burial has been put forward for grave 60 at Skateholm I (Larsson 1984:54 pp). This conclusion was based on the fact that the burial pit was small compared to the size of an adult human being, with the limbs in tight contraction. My field-anthropological analysis does not support the interpretation of a secondary bundle burial. This conclusion is based on the fact that some of the phalanges of the hand are preserved in loose articulation. Most of the bones of the individual buried in grave 60 appear to be preserved in anatomically correct position. Because of the very poor state of preservation of the bones it is difficult to argue in favor of a treatment similar to that in grave 13, and the case remains ambiguous.

In terms of the nature of the burial overall, the dominant practice at the Skateholm and Vedbaek sites is that of primary interment. We have also seen that cremation of the body occurs in a small number. These two types of burial practices may appear as extreme contrasts. The former involves burying the dead intact, still resembling the individual in life, while the latter rapidly destroys the body. Yet, when looking at how these two practices handle the decomposition of the body, we observe that they actually have one thing in common: they both avoid the inevitable process of decomposition. In neither case are the survivors confronted with the biological and chemical processes that alter the appearance of the cadaver after death. We can note that these two ways of dealing with decomposition have a parallel in our society today, where we either cremate our dead or bury them intact. This attitude toward the corruption of the body contrasts highly with practices that permit decomposition to play out, rendering them visible as part of the process of death (for examples see Thomas 1980; Huntington and Metcalf 1979 or Bloch and Parry 1982).

One burial at Skateholm I contrasts highly with the predominant pattern that denies decomposition after death. In grave 28 at Skateholm I (Figure 66.1), it appears that the survivors have exploited their awareness of the decomposition of the soft tissues after death. This conclusion is based on evidence that individual bones were removed from the grave structure after decomposition of the soft tissues was more or less terminated. In this grave, the individual was positioned on the back with the limbs in extension. The grave pit can be described as rather shallow, but the field-notes indicate that no trace of post-depositional disturbance whatsoever was recorded during excavation. What is unusual about this burial is the remarkable absence of certain bones on the left side of the skeleton: the left radius, the left ulna, the left os coxae and the left femur are missing. All adjacent bones, however, are not only present but also well preserved and undisturbed. For the upper left limb we notice that the left humerus is lying in extension parallel to the medial axis of the body. It is slightly rotated inward so that its anterior and lateral sides face toward the surface. The limb was probably initially projected upward, following the rotation upward and outward of the scapula. Several of the carpal bones are present and appear to be perfectly articulated. The metacarpals and phalanges also appear to be fairly well articulated, and their position indicates that the segment decomposed in a filled volume. For the left lower limb we observe a very similar situation. The patella is present and its anterior side is exposed, lying immediately adjacent to the proximal extremity of the tibia. The left tibia and the fibula are lying in extension. This position indicates that the entire limb initially was in extension. The tibia and the fibula, as well as the bones of the foot expose their lateral side, and this indicates that the limb was rotated inward. Overall, the position of the bones clearly indicate that the burial is a primary deposition. The perfect articulation of the hands and the feet is a sure indicator of this. The missing bones, the left radius and ulna, the left *os coxae* and the left femur, have been removed after the deposition of the body in the grave, and probably after the process of decomposition was either advanced or terminated. Especially strong indication that these bones were removed after decomposition is the fact that the left carpal bones are still in articulation, the humerus appears as undisturbed and the left patella has remained in the burial structure. The bones must have been removed after the articulations at the elbow, wrist and knee had decomposed naturally. It is difficult to "date" the interference in the grave, but since it involves both labile (radius-scaphoid and lunate) and more resistant (humerus-ulna, femur-tibia) articulations, the body was probably either in a very advanced stage or terminal stage of decomposition, or alternatively, completely skeletonised at the time of the intervention. It *could* thus be a matter of up to a couple of years.

Further questions are raised by the space of decomposition in grave 28. These are relevant to understanding the intervention in the grave. The very minor disturbance of the adjacent bones suggests that the body was allowed to decompose in a way that allowed virtually direct access to the bones. This could have been facilitated by a coffin or a "sealed" pit. However, the analysis does not provide any support for this (for details about the analysis of the volume of decomposition, please see below). There are slight movements of some bones that could point to an empty space of decomposition. However, these movements are minor, and an empty space does not correspond with the facts that the right patella is balanced on its lateral border, and the position of the hand bones indicate that the segment decomposed in a filled space with immediate penetration of sediment. Based on these observations, I suggest that the body was buried intact and the pit was then filled with sediment. To explain the easy access to the bones I propose that when the body was buried, it was covered on top with a hide or maybe some wood that easily could be lifted away and expose the body. This would allow people to come back after a certain time, carefully remove the coverage and clear off the sediment above the body. The body would then be exposed enough to allow the removal of the left radius, the left ulna, the left *os coxae* and the left femur. The minor disturbances of the left side of the rib cage could probably be dated to the same intervention. If this hypothesis is correct, then the survivors buried the remains of the individual in grave 28 with the intention of coming back and retrieving the bones. Since this is a unique case at the sites analysed it remains difficult to evaluate the ritual significance of these gestures. Finally, it does not appear likely that the absences can be explained by the activity of burrowing animals since the entire bones are missing and there is no indication of fragmentation or splinter of the bones. Moreover, the hypothesis that a disturbing non-human agent may have worked from the surface and down is difficult to sustain since there are no visible traces of such disturbance in the soil. It also seems strange that the small bones of the left hand would remain untouched by such a disturbance.

This contrast in practices illustrated by grave 28 points to a dichotomy in Mesolithic conceptions of death and decomposition. While the dominating mortuary practices at Skateholm and Vedbaek seem to avoid confronting decomposition, the removal of the bones in this grave indicates that the process of decomposition was not only known, but also used and played out. Considered together with the large number of human bones in non-burial contexts at Mesolithic settlements (Larsson *et al.* 1981), the mortuary practices carried out for grave 28 provoke questions about how the removed bones were perceived, what or whom they represented: individuals, death, the dead as a collective, or all of these simultaneously. Maybe the ritual practices for grave 28 will provide an interesting lead in exploring the gradual change in burial practices in the Neolithic, when manipulation of the human remains became a dominant aspect of mortuary ritual.

The methods of *Anthropologie de terrain* also offer the possibility of reconstructing the space in which decomposition took place, providing a basis to establish how the grave structure was prepared. For instance, field anthropological analysis can identify whether the dead was placed in, for example, a coffin or whether it was interred simply in a filled in pit. Criteria for identifying these various practices have been outlined by several authors (Duday *et al.* 1990:34 pp), who base their determinations on the spatial relationships among the bones in the grave structure. Most basically, they argue, if the body decomposes in an empty space, at least some bones will tend to fall outside of the initial volume of the body during decomposition. This will not be the case in a filled space. In a filled grave, sediment which surrounds the cadaver tends to replace the soft tissues progressively. As a result, even the most labile anatomical connections will be preserved when sedimentary filling is gentle and constant. For the large majority of the burials at Skateholm and Vedbaek, the bodies decomposed in filled spaces, which is indicated by the very limited realm of movement exhibited by the bones in most of the graves. The bodies were probably placed in the grave pit and quite immediately covered by sediment. For a couple of burials at Skateholm II (graves IV and XX), traces of wood have been identified along the body (Larsson 1982:29, 1984: 68). Nevertheless, the field-anthropological study, provides no indication that decomposition occurred in an empty space. This means that wood in graves IV and XX was not part of a coffin or other enclosed structure that could have prevented the penetration of infilling sediment while the body decomposed. The wood probably originates from some other structure or arrangement in the pit, for example, wood or bark lining. Importantly, being able to establish the structure of the grave when the body was placed in it and buried gives us a concrete basis for envisioning a more detailed range of gestures associated with the mortuary practices. We can then develop new categories of interpretation and we could in the future look for comparisons with burials containing linings, coverages or other presence of wood.

Interestingly, the traces of organic and now vanished materials have been detected in other graves than the ones that were supposed to have coffins. A quite spectacular example of this can be seen in grave 8 in Vedbaek (Figure 66.2). Here a young woman has been buried on her back with the limbs in extension. To her lateral right side lay a new born child on a swan's wing. A closer examination of the female's skeleton reveals that this body may also have been placed on top of something – in this case, a material that has completely decomposed. For the thoracic cage of the female in grave 8, we note a very unusual pattern of spatial distribution of the bones. On both sides we note that for the first several ribs, the pattern is the usual one for the decomposition of a body lying on the back; the anterior parts of the ribs are projected downward and forward. For the majority of the ribs, however, we observe a totally atypical pattern of distribution. There is a lateral "expansion" of the rib cage. The posterior ends of the ribs are dislocated from the vertebral column and are projected forward, while the rest of the length of these ribs – continuing to their anterior ends – extends laterally. In fact, in several instances, particularly on the right side, we note that the anterior portions of ribs lie in front of (on top of) the humerus. Thus, a significant number of ribs moved outside the initial volume of the body during decomposition. It seems impossible to explain this pattern of spatial distribution unless a secondary empty volume developed beneath the thorax as the body decomposed. This dynamically forming empty space would have permitted the expansion of the thoracic cage as it became disarticulated. Most likely, the body was placed on top of some organic material that also decomposed. The movements of most of the ribs upward and outward is dramatic enough to indicate that this perishable material supporting the body formed a quite thick layer, lifting up the torso from the grave pit floor quite distinctively. The normal movement of ribs during decomposition in a filled grave is downward (caudal) and inward (medial). The pattern of decomposition of the pelvis also indicates the existence at one time of a secondary empty space. The *os coxae* have fallen laterally, slightly disarticulated from the sacrum, and the pubic symphysis has thus disarticulated, too. Morevoer, we note a slight rotation upwards of the whole right side of the pelvis. In fact, the sacrum has rotated, with its right side projecting upward. This movement must have taken place after the dislocation of the sacro-iliac joints. Meanwhile, the position of the bones of the perfectly articulated hands and feet, as well as the position of the upper limbs, contradicts decomposition in an empty grave structure. Overall, we may interpret the distribution of the bones of the female skeleton in grave 8 as reflecting the influence of a secondary empty space limited to the area beneath the upper body, including the pelvic region. Such a space could have formed if the body

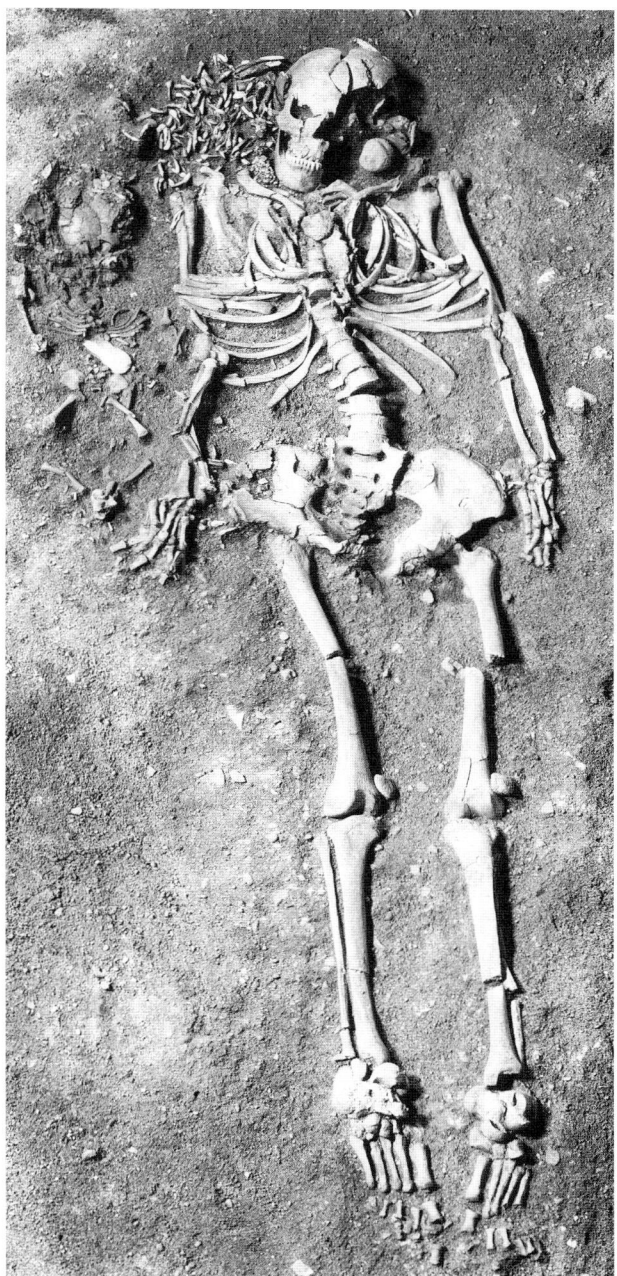

Figure 66.2 Burial 8, Vedbaek. The unusual pattern of distribution of the ribs of the adult individual in this grave indicates the presence of a secondary empty space behind the body during the process of decomposition. It is possible that the individual was placed on top of some perishable organic material that separated the body from immediate contact with the pit floor.

was placed on top of some organic material that decomposed relatively early and thus left a volume into which the skeletal elements could fall, but alternatively the body could have been placed on wooden beams that would have separated it from immediate contact with the bottom of the burial pit.

This naturally puts the practice of placing deer antler

or stones under the bodies of the dead in several graves at both Skateholm and Vedbaek into a new light. Maybe it was more common than we had previously thought that bodies were placed on top of some kind of material or structure on the grave floor. The swan's wing, deer antlers and stones have been directly observed in several grave structures, but wood or other organic materials that have not been preserved might also have been used to separate the body from the bottom of the grave pit. A less evident example of the same phenomenon can be seen in at least one case at Skateholm II, where we have a very similar evidence of a secondary empty space behind the right hemi-thorax of the individual in grave IX (Nilsson 1998). Once again, the detailed taphonomic analysis leads us to break up our traditional categorisations and start to reflect over the material in a new way. We can propose hypotheses about what this practice of placing some medium between the body and the grave floor may symbolise. The analysis also hints at an interesting pattern of ritual practice that might advance our understanding of the variation in the mortuary practices at the sites.

Conclusion

Through these examples from the Mesolithic cemeteries of Skateholm I and II and Vedbaek, I have aimed to show the methodological gains and the theoretical potentials of *Anthropologie de terrain*. Through its rigorous taphonomic approach, we retrieve more detailed, richer information about the graves. The method allows a more secure reconstruction of the nature of the burial and the initial position of the body in the grave. We can document organic material which has left no other trace than its influence on the distribution of the bones, as demonstrated by the indication of now-perished material supporting the upper body of the adult female in grave 8 at Vedbaek. In some cases, as in grave 28 at Skateholm I, we can make detailed inferences about several stages in the mortuary ritual. All of this new information is in itself very valuable. It gives us a new sense of the variability in the mortuary practices at the sites, and it suggests new categories for our interpretations. Yet, the methodology of *Anthropologie de terrain* also meets the demands of additional theoretical perspectives, including those of practice theory. By constantly trying to reconstruct what people were doing with their dead, *Anthropologie de terrain* may have a natural affinity with the concept of practice. Its taphonomic results do not simply reveal actions; practice theory provides a base to view these actions as meaningful gestures, which are structured in large part by sets of symbolic oppositions that link death and decomposition to other aspects of the culture's world. Thus, I have suggested that a taphonomy of ritual practice is a way to get at some of the underlying, structuring ideas of the Mesolithic mortuary practices. The analysis has highlighted the interesting dichotomy in the Mesolithic conceptions about death and decay through the pattern in which the decomposing body was ritually treated at the sites. My analysis of the taphonomic history of the graves at Skateholm and Vedbaek is currently ongoing. As we advance our knowledge about how death was conceived in relation to other symbolic categories – life, social order, individual identity, nature – we can further work toward a deeper understanding of Mesolithic society.

Acknowledgements

I would like to thank Erik Brinch Petersen and Lars Larsson for so generously having given access to their material and provided me with help and information throughout my analysis. I want to thank Henri Duday for the help he has provided throughout the analyses of these burials. I also want to thank the foundation Ebbe Kocks Stiftelse in Lund for financially supporting my participation in the conference "Mesolithic 2000." Thanks also to Aaron Stutz for his valuable comments and editorial assistance.

References

Albrethsen, S.E. and Brinch Petersen, E. 1976. Excavations of a Mesolithic Cemetery at Vedbaek, Denmark. *Acta Archaeologica* XLVII, 1–28.

Anderson Beck, L. 1995. (ed.) *Regional Approaches to Mortuary Analysis*. New York and London.

Bell, C. 1992. *Ritual Theory Ritual Practice*. New York and Oxford.

Binford, L.R. 1971. Mortuary practices: their Study and their Potential. In: Brown, J.A. (ed.) *Approaches to the Social Dimensions of Mortuary Practices. Memoirs of the Society for American Archaeology* 25, 6–29. Washington DC.

Bloch, M. and Parry, J. 1982. (eds.) *Death and the regeneration of life*. Cambridge

Bourdieu, P. 1977. *Outline Of a Theory Of Practice*. Cambridge.

Brown, J.A. 1971. The dimensions of status in the burials at Spiro. In: Brown, J.A. (ed.) *Approaches to the Social Dimensions of Mortuary Practices. Memoirs of the Society for American Archaeology*, No 25, 92–112. Washington DC.

Brown, J.A. and Price, T.D. 1985 (eds.) *Prehistoric Hunter-Gatherers: The Emergence of Cultural Complexity*, 435–42. San Diego.

Chapman, R. 1981. The emergence of formal disposal areas and the "problem" of megalithic tombs in prehistoric Europe. In: Chapman, R., Kinnes, I. and Randsborg, K. 1981 (eds.) *The Archaeology of Death*, 71–81. Cambridge.

—— 1995. Ten years After – Megaliths, Mortuary Practices, and the Territorial Model. In: Anderson Beck, L. (ed) *Regional Approaches to Mortuary Analysis,* 29–51. New York and London.

Chapman, R., Kinnes, I. and Randsborg, K. 1981. (eds.) *The Archaeology of Death*. Cambridge.

Courtaud, P. 1996. "Anthropologie de sauvetage": vers une optimisation des méthodes d'enregistrement. Présentation d'une fiche anthropologique. In: Castex, D., Courtaud, P., Sellier, P., Duday, H. and Bruzek, J. (eds.) *Les ensembles funéraires du terrain à l'interprétation*. Actes du Colloque du GDR "Méthodes d'Etudes des Sépultures." *Buletins et Mémoires de la Société d'Anthropologie de Paris*, n. s., t. 8, 3–4, 157–167.

Crubézy, E. 2000. L'étude des sépultures, ou du monde des morts au monde des vivants. Anthropologie, archéologie funéraire et anthhropologie de terrain. In: Ferdière, A. (ed.) *L'Archéologie Funéraire*, 8–54. Paris.

Duday, H., Courtaud, P., Crubézy, E., Sellier, P. and Tillier, A.-M. 1990. L'anthropologie "de terrain": reconnaissance et interprètation des gestes funéraires. *Bulletins et Mémoirs de la Société d'Anthropologie. de Paris*, n.s., tome 2, no. 3–4, 29–50.

Duday, H. and Masset, C. 1987. (eds.) *Anthropologie physique et archéologie. Métodes d'étude des sépultures*. Paris.

Goldstein, L. 1981. One dimensional archaeology and multidimensional people: spatial organisation and mortuary analysis. In: Chapman, R., Kinnes, I. and Randsborg, K. (eds.) *The Archaeology of Death*, 53–70. Cambridge.

—— 1995. Landscapes and Mortuary Practices. A Case for Regional Perspectives. In: Anderson Beck, L. 1995. (ed.) *Regional Approaches to Mortuary Analysis*, 101–121. New York and London,

Hertz, R. 1960. A Contribution to the Study of the Collective Representation of Death. *Death and the Right Hand*, 27–86. Oxford,. [first published 1907 in *L'Année Sociologique*, Vol. X, 48–137].

Huntington, R. and Metcalf, P. 1979. *Celebrations of death: the anthropology of mortuary ritual*. Cambridge.

Larsson, L. 1980. Stenåldersjägarnas boplats och gravar vid Skateholm. *Limhamniana*, 13–39.

—— 1981. En 7000-årig sydkustboplats. Nytt och gammalt från Skateholm. *Limhamniana*, 17–46.

—— 1982. Skateholmsprojektet. Nya gravar och ett nytt gravfält. *Limhamniana*, 11–41.

—— 1983. Skateholmsprojektet. Jägare – fiskare – bönder. *Limhamniana*, 7–40.

—— 1984. Skateholmsprojektet. På spåren efter gravsedsförändringar, ceremoniplatser och tama rävar, *Limhamniana* 49–84.

—— 1988. The Skateholm Project. Late Mesolithic Settlement at a South Swedish lagoon. In: Larsson, L. (ed.) *The Skateholm Project I. Man and Environment*. Acta Regiae Societatis Humaniorum Litterarum Lundensis, LXXIX, 9–19. Stockholm.

Larsson, L., Meiklejohn, C. and Newell, R. 1981. Human Skeletal material from the Mesolithic Site of Ageröd I:HC, Scania, Southern Sweden. *Fornvännen 76*, 161–168.

Lyman, R.L. 1994. *Vertebrate Taphonomy*. Cambridge.

Miller, D. and Tilley, C. 1984. (eds.) *Ideology, Power and Prehistory*. Cambridge.

Nilsson, L. 1998. Dynamic cadavers. A field anthropological analysis of the Skateholm II burials. *Lund Archaeological Review*, 5–17.

Pader, E.-J. 1982. *Symbolism, Social Relations and the interpretation of Mortuary Remains*. BAR International Series 130. Oxford.

Parker Pearson, M. 1999. *The Archaeology of Death and Burial*. Phoenix Mill.

Persson, O. and Persson, E. 1984. Anthropological Report on the Mesolithic graves from Skateholm, Southern Sweden, I. Excavation season 1980–1982. *University of Lund, Institute of Archaeology, Report series no. 21*.

Price, T.D. 1985. Affluent foragers of Mesolithic southern Scandinavia. In: Brown, J.A. and Price, T.D. (eds.) *Prehistoric Hunter-Gatherers: The Emergence of Cultural Complexity*, 341–363. San Diego.

Saxe, A.A. 1970. *Social Dimensions of Mortuary Practices*. Ph D thesis, Univerity of Michigan.

Shanks, M. and Tilley, C. 1982. Ideology, symbolic power and ritual communication: a reinterpretation of Neolithic mortuary practices. In: Hodder, I. (ed.) *Symbolic and Structural Archaeology*, 129–154. Cambridge,

Tainter, J.A. 1975 Spatial inference and mortuary practices: an experiment in numerical classification. *World Archaeology 7*, 1–15.

—— 1977. Modeling change in prehistoric social systems. In: Binford. L.R. (ed.) *For Theory Building in Archaeology*, 327–351. New York, San Francisco and London.

—— 1978. Mortuary Practices and the Study of Prehistoric Social Systems. In: Schiffer, M.B. (ed.) *Advances in Archaeological Method and Theory*, Vol. 1. New York, San Fransisco and London, 105–141.

Thomas, J. 1991. *Understanding the Neolithic*. London.

Thomas, L.V. 1980. *Le Cadavre. De la biologie à l'anthropologie*. Bruxelles.

Tilley, C. 1984. Ideology and the legitimation of power in the middle neolithic of southern Sweden. In: Miller, D. and Tilley, C. (eds.) *Ideology, Power and Prehistory*, 111–146. Cambridge.

67. To Touch the Mind

Bengt Nordqvist

An attempt is made to go beyond the material remains and instead try to understand the way of thinking. By analysing different images like rock-carvings and ritual behavior extracted through the refuse from the sites it seems possible to understand some of the general word of ideas connected to the early Mesolithic man.

Is it possible to reach beyond the flint flakes, the microliths, the chronologies and see anything else than material deposits? Is it possible? Can we reach so far in our research that we pass over the counting of the width of the blade, the extension of microliths? Can we go so far that we touch the mind of the Mesolithic man?

As a start, or as an example, I will try to reach beyond my way of looking at artefacts, carvings and images. As an attempt I will study remains from these early hunter-gatherers from a totemistic view. Similar attempts have been done on rock-carvings (for example Tilley 1991 pp; Wennstedt Edvinger 1993 pp). Lévi-Strauss suggests that it is about joining institutions of symbols on one hand and myths on the other hand (Lévi-Strauss 1969:112 p). Archaeologists don't have the myths from these Mesolithic hunters and gatherers, so instead it will be a discussion about connecting form and content.

The name totem comes from Algonquin language. The word totem means "it is a relative to me" (Lévi-Strauss 1969:29 p). We also know that the most common thought is that a person is related to a species of animal. The point of departure, as Lévi-Strauss points out, is the structural principle of the conjunction of oppositions, where the totemism only is an expression, whose nomenclature is created by names of animals and plants. He means that the most general principle is from China, with Ying and Yang. In this model there is an association of male/female, day/night, summer/winter in an organised entirety (Tao), which is reflected in concepts as the group, the day and the year. In this case the totemism shows how opposite pairs are conjunct. Even Radcliffe-Brown saw the oppositions and the integration as an important part of totemism (Lévi-Strauss 1969:128 p). This model with opposite pairs seems to be a direct expression of the structure of thoughts and probably even the structure of the brain (Lévi-Strauss 1969:117 p).

During early Mesolithic, what indications do we have about the way of thinking of the coastal living groups in Western Sweden? There are very unique images like decoration patterns, carvings and pictures that has been found in Western Sweden. These pieces of evidence could be looked upon separately or be related with another. A key to the understanding is the painting of Tumlehed and the cross-shaped adze from Stala. We also have several examples where food remains have been treated in a special way. The latest research about how these coastal groups were utilising their environment is also important in this discussion. So, what have these different traces from early Mesolithic in common? In this article I would like to show how these remains are pointing in the same direction and that they just are different expressions of the general world of ideas.

Remains from the Mesolithic man

The rock painting at Tumlehed is not dated and we don't know if all figures were made at the same time. It has always been connected to a hunter-gatherer society and mostly to the Mesolithic period (Nordbladh 1975:82 p; Sjöberg 1980:154 p; Fischer 1995:146 p). The painting is situated on the top of a mountain on a vertical rock surface, facing a former strait (Cullberg 1975:75 p). Today the rock painting is situated close to the town Gothenburg (Figure 67.1). During early Mesolithic it was placed far out in the existing archipelago as well in the periphery in the relation to the sites from the time period.

The painting content five different types of elements (Figure 67.2). Three of them can be described as reproductions and are expressed as figures. These are boats marked with human figures as well as the small whales and the large deer (maybe a red deer). Except these reproductions there are symbols. Beneath the small whales (probably white-beaked dolphins) there are zigzags (angle-lines) and above the red deer there is a net.

When the painting is divided it seems obvious that it consist of two main parts (Figure 67.3). On the right we have the red deer. It doesn't seem to present a hunting scene. The animal is not hurt and we don't see any arrows

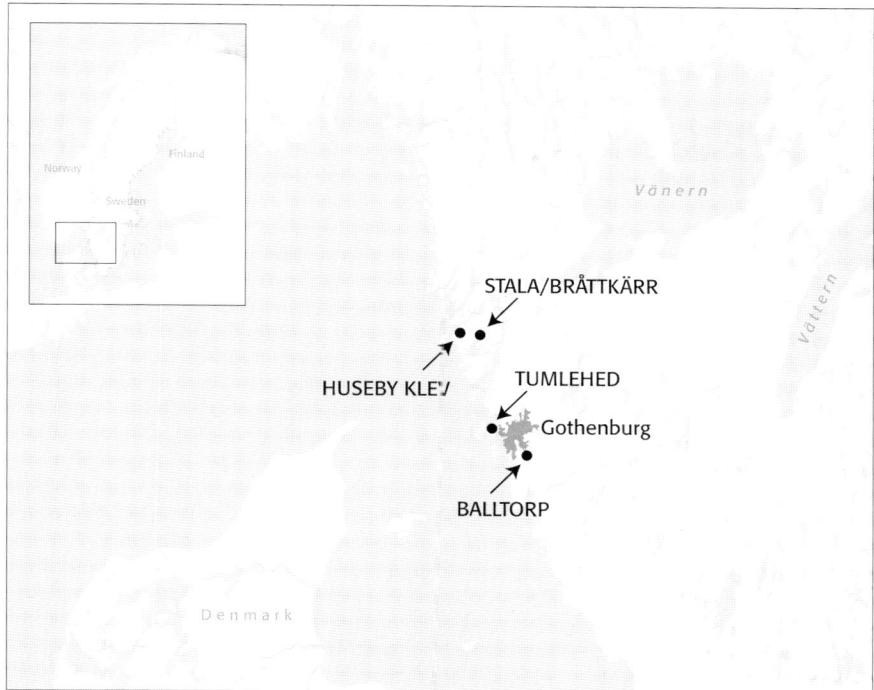

Figure 67.1 A map over the West Coast of Sweden.

or spears pointing at the body. The red deer seems rather to be standing in a position of being cautious and listing. From the neck and horns of the red deer there are a net growing up. The net stretches upwards and consists of more or less irregular "cells". Above the back of the red deer, the net transforms into a boat.

There is a figure that hasn't been understood. The figure can be described as having a T-shaped form and in its down part transforms between a mixture of a boat and an animal or a pit dwelling (Strassburg 2000:124 p).

In the upper part, to the left, there are three figures that have been interpreted as boats with humans. Beneath the three ships there are at least two small whales. The upper one is seen in full appearance and the other are only half-visible. It seems as the upper one is jumping above the surface of the sea and the other are only stretching the upper part above sea level. All together it express very well the annually returns of herds of small whales who each season pass through this coastal landscape. At the bottom of the rock painting, beneath the whales, there is a zigzag pattern. At the top, of this group of zigzags, the lines are somewhat wave-like. In the bottom there are strictly zigzags. So it seems like this group of symbols change from waves to zigzags.

The right and the left part of the rock painting are related to each another. Through the painting, with its two parts, all together express a common world of figures and symbols. And it is this combination of symbols and figures that make it possible to go further in the analysis. The right side represents the land living animal and can be seen as a symbol for the resources that is possible to

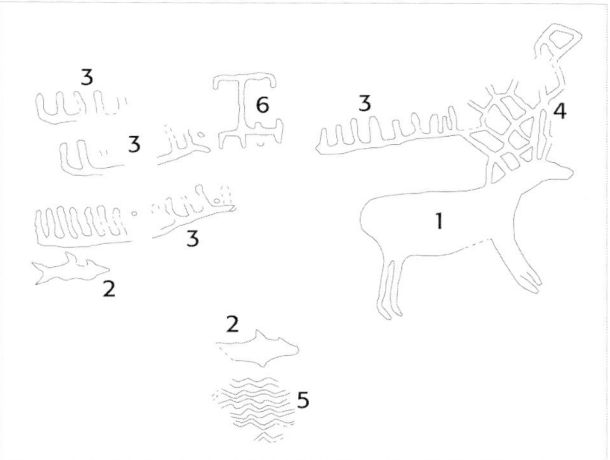

Figure 67.2 An outline of the rock painting at Tumlehed. It measures 2 x 2 m and it is facing to the south-east. It is painted in a red colour (hematite?) on a vertical rock surface. The painting consists of a large deer, maybe a red deer (1); small whales such as white-beaked dolphins (2); boats with humans (3); net pattern (4); zigzag pattern (5); and unknown figure (6).

find in the terrestrial environment. On the left there are figures that can be connected with the other counterpart in the coastal area and it is the marine environment. The whales are representing this resource as well as the red deer were for the land living. All together these two parts of the painting act for the surrounding resources these groups of hunter-gatherers actually where living in

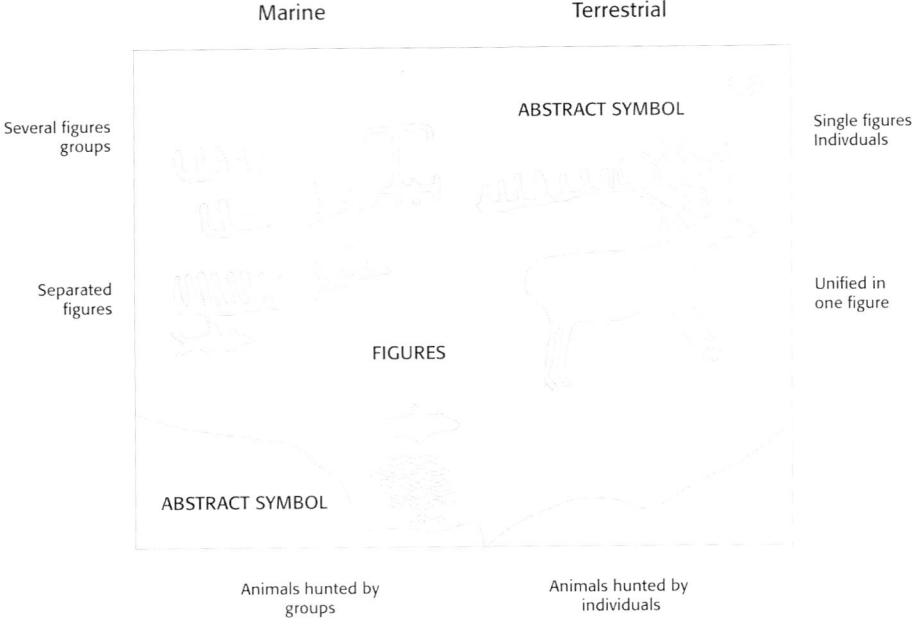

Figure 67.3 The painting of Tumlehed divided in parts and presented with different oppositions of pair.

(Nordqvist 2000:121 pp). For these groups of hunter-gatherers living in the coastal area, the terrestrial environment was important as the marine biotope. This conclusion is interesting in relation to how Rivers define totemism. He means that it is a unification of three elements. The first is a social element, which means a connection between a species of animal or plant and a group defined by the society (for example a clan). The second is a psychological element. This faith consists of an existent blood relation between group members and the animal. The third is a ritual element that assumes a respectful relation to the animal and the artefact. This was often expressed by a taboo to eat the animal, or to use the artefact, except on special occasions (Lévi-Strauss 1969:17 p). Also to emphases is that one basic phenomenon in totemism is the dualism. This dualism is valid for the whole nature and as a consequence of this outlook; all creatures and phenomena are divided in two halves. In relation to totemism such apprehension results in placing the surrounding world in categories (Lévi-Strauss 1969:55 p). Totemism also includes relations. The basic relations are nature-culture and individual-collective (Lévi-Strauss 1969:26 p). Bergson means that the individuality is dissolved within a species. To recognise one human being from another means that you can distinguish her from other persons. To recognise an animal means normally that you can distinguish the species. We recognise it as a class or category (Lévi-Strauss 1969:122 p). It seems as the individual is dissolved within the clan. Characteristic is also that social groups are distinguished by certain species from nature, as well as social groups are identified by symbols or symbolic artefacts (Lévi-Strauss 1969:111 p). In this rock painting there are numerous pairs of oppositions. One of these pairs of oppositions is the culture and the wild nature. On the upper part we have the humans and ships representing the culture. Below we have the wild nature represented by the terrestrial as well as the marine environment. Where the small whales and red deer consist of groups of animals that is eatable and tasty as well as they are seen as symbols – "We are what we eat". The wild are something positive, a surviving condition for the group or the tribe. Radcliffe-Brown as well as Malinowski consider that an animal become a totem because it first of all is "good to eat" (Lévi-Strauss 1969:81 p). Lévi-Strauss means that it has wider contents than that. Totemism is not just about metaphor relations; it is also a way of thinking or even a part of reflection (Lévi-Strauss 1969:44, 135 p).

Elkins propose that it exists materialistic symbols as well as nonmaterialistic symbols (Lévi-Strauss 1969:71 p). The first is the totem of the "meat". It is related to the organic and materialistic environment as well as to the matriarchal. The last is the totem of the "dreams". It is patriarchal and represents the spiritual and the non-materialistic. In the rock painting there is a tension between the nonmaterialistic and materialistic. In the center part of the painting there are naturalistic reproductions of whale as well as red deer (materialistic). Outside this center part, the figures change to schematic pictures of boats with humans. In extreme, these figures transforms just to symbols (non-materialistic). We see it as the net that is woven together with the red deer and the zigzags beneath the whales. These symbols seem to be each other's counterparts. Probably these different patterns symbolise both types of environments that these groups of hunter-gatherers actually were living in. It is a reason for returning to these symbols later on when the symbols of the adze of Stala are discussed.

It seems like the symbols of the rock painting are placed in strategic position. The pattern of the net is placed at the top on the right and the zigzags on the opposite position (down to the left). On the right side it changes from figure-motif to symbol in a perspective of "down to up". The left side shows opposite image. Another aspect is that the upper whale is jumping above the sea level and the other is partly under. To sum up, the right side is pointing upwards and the left is pointing down. All showed as an additive effect. We will see this additive effect a couple of times. It seems like the net stretches towards the sky (upper world) and the position of zigzags gives you a thought of the great depths (underworld). It could also be interpret as they represent life and death.

Another aspect deals with the amount – one or more. On the left side there are several boats with humans. There are also two or more whales as well as several zigzags. On the right side we have one red deer, one net and one boat. To pronounce it even clearer, they are woven all together in a single figure. On the left side we have the opposite conditions. We have several figures of each type. They are placed in groups, separated from each other. Each group consists of several figures that are presented as individual figures separated from each other. The zigzags are separated to individual lines even if they were placed in a group. We can also see that the represented groups of animal distinguish from each other. If we first look at how they live we can see that the small whales lives in large herds and they move over large distances. The red deer lives as single individuals or in minor herds. These animals live quite steady in a small regional area. If we consider how these different kinds of animals were hunted we can also recognise large differences. The small whales were hunted by several humans in a large amount of boats (collective hunting) and the red deer were hunted in the opposite way by individual hunters (individual hunting). Once again we see this repeating, additive effect, which seems to be important.

The cross-shaped adze from Stala was found at Bråttkärr in Stala Parish. The site is situated on the island of Orust, approximately 60 km north from the rock painting of Tumlehed (Sjöberg 1980:145 p; Hernek and Nordqvist 1995:26 p). This item gives us further information about their world of beliefs. With the presented interpretation of the rock painting of Tumlehed there are several angels of incidence concerning the adze with its different decorations. The cross-shaped adze has four arms and is made of stone (Figure 67.4). It has a well-polished surface. In the center, where the arms meet, there is a picked hole. There are decorations on all four arms. On the other hand, the types of decoration-elements vary. Some of the arms seem to be partly damaged, maybe caused by knocking.

A closer look shows that the adze has an upper- and a down part. It is also clear that even if there are several

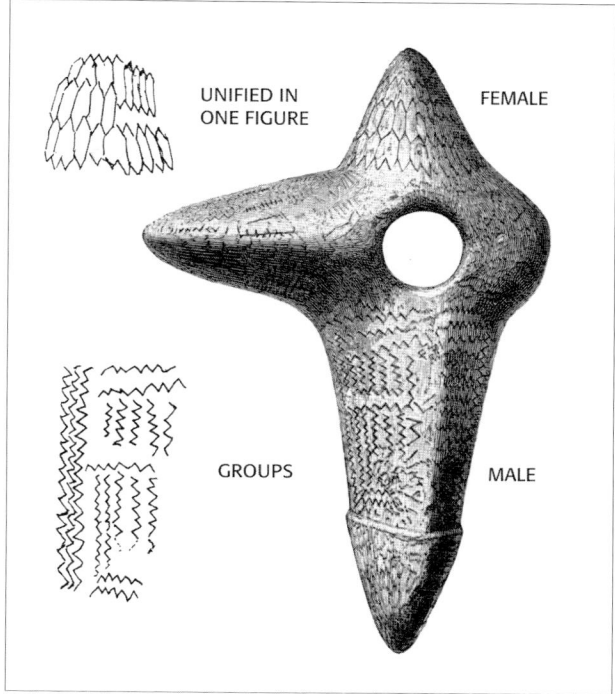

Figure 67.4 The cross-shaped adze from Stala. The upper part of the adze has decoration patterns of a net (hexagons) and zigzags.

different types of decorations, none of them are mixed. Each type of element of decorations is placed within the same group. The cross-shaped adze from Stala is very interesting, because once again we see a mixture of figure and abstract symbols. The largest arm on the adze has a figure-shape of a phallos. Once again there are abstract symbols and figures placed in special relation to each other. But in this case you can also read on to gender perspective. There are examples from Australia of totems and sexes. Within these groups the totem artefacts were acting as objects connected to sexes. The function of the totem was based on beliefs that there was a relation to certain species of animals connected to each sex (Lévi-Strauss 1969:52 p).

Elkins also propose three criteria's as definitions of systems of totemism. It is form, it is implications and it is function (Lévi-Strauss 1969:50 p). Concerning form it is about how the objects of totem are distributed between individuals and groups (concerning sexes, membership in the clan etc.). The role the totem is acting for the individual has done with the implication (as helper, protector, companion or as a symbol for the social group). The function consists of the role the totem has within the group (roles for marriage, social and moral sanctions etc). Another aspect concerning the individual and the group is how the society secures the perpetual and unity of the clans within the society (Lévi-Strauss 1969:79 p). For keeping this unity of the society (which actually consists of a multiple of individual feelings) require collective expressions that could be connected to concrete objects or artefacts. Lévi-Strauss propose a relationship as follows (in following order); Individual feelings of solidarity-collective, ritual behaviour-artefacts representing the group. This explains the place the symbols as the flag, the king and president have in modern societies. Similar expressions could be seen at the rock painting at Tumlehed but also at the cross-shaped adze from Stala.

Once again it is the zigzag- and the net pattern that plays the important role. Also in this case we have an example when patterns and real figures are woven together into a language of symbols. A clear example is the arm shaped like a phallos. It is the longest arm and zigzags cover the whole surface. Even at this time we see zigzags not linked into each other. Instead they are formatted in groups that form a community. The opposite arm is decorated with a pattern of net. This time it is the smallest arm. This arm has the shape of a young woman´s breast. Once again shape is connected to a certain decoration motif – the net (hexogram). The net pattern is carved only on the upper part of the adze. Here we have the same upper positions as on the painting from Tumlehed. The net is made up by three separated rows of nets. Contrary to the zigzags, the net is made up by "single cells" that are linked into one other and creates a woven row of "net cells". The whole net consists of three separated rows or groups. Should net patterns be interpreted as a reflection of the relation between females, it could be seen as the net is expressing three different lines of kinship. Each row of lines should in this sense reflect separate kin of kinship. It also shows that the women are woven together and creates a common line of kinship. They are not one single field, rather three single lines woven together. And they are all placed on the same arm.

It seems like the arms of the adze represent the different gender, as well as the symbolic power connected to the different sexes. The sexes are placed in opposite position to each other, with contrary size of the adze arms (once again this additive effect), all to pronounce female-male as a conjunction of oppositions. At the same time they are unified in one object, the cross-shaped adze or the rock painting. Even if the differences or conjunction of oppositions are pronounced in figures and symbols, it also pronounce the strong community. We se them all placed on the same adze or rock painting. Differences are important but at the same time the strength are placed in the community. We can see the sexes unified through the shafting hole of the adze. It seems like the shafting hole has a special power, which has been discussed concerning shamanism (Strassburg 2000:89 p). The cross-shaped adze from Stala could be seen as a tool for the shaman. The powerful idiom of symbols could be an expression of a tool or symbol for the special quality of the bearer. The in-carved human figure on the adze from Stala pronounces the aspect of shamanism (Nordqvist in press), but this aspect will not be discussed further in this article.

Refuse and conception

It is obvious that the refuse found at the early Mesolithic sites of Western Sweden were treated in a special way. The question is, if a certain behavior could play a role in these groups of hunters-gatherers activities, and if these activities presumably could be connected to different rituals?

At the site Balltorp, in the Göteborg area, there were found burned as well as unburned bones from animals. These bones had been treated in different ways. After the osteological analysis it was possible to conclude that it is only the bones from the marine environment that were burned (Jonsson 1996:42 p). The bones from the terrestrial environment had not been treated in this way. They were left unburned. After the analysis of the flint material as well as after the analysis of the settlement pattern it was obvious that Balltorp was a special site. The site of Balltorp was deviating in that sense that it was situated at the seashore of the mainland. But at the same time the dominating activity that has been done from this site were related to hunting terrestrial mammals. There was a pronunciation on the hunting activities concerning larger mammals as auroch, red deer, boar etc (Jonsson 1996:28 pp; Nordqvist 2000:134 pp).

How should the burned bones be interpreted? It seems reasonable that the food that were brought to the site and were originating from another environment had to be treated in a special way. It seems like the basic thought has been the contradictions between the marine and terrestrial environment. The contradictions require that the food from the marine area has to be treated or consumed concerned to a special ritual (Jonsson 1996:42 p). In this case it seems like the relation to the sea has to be destroyed. The most powerful act has been to use fire as such ritual power.

At the site Huseby klev, on Orust island, an important activity has been to hunt small whales (White Beaked dolphins). In the bone refuse there were a lot of different bone parts from different species. Concerning the small whales some interesting observations were made. For example, a disc with a hole in the center and with incisions made of a vertebra from a small whale. There are also found a shoulder blade from a dolphin with incisions (Hernek and Nordqvist 1995:87 pp; Nordqvist 2000:208 p). But once again the bones were treated in a special way. All bones from the whale were found except from the skull. It seems like the skull was treated in such a way that we couldn't found it together with the other bones. The skull must have been treated in another way than the normal refuse. And once again, it points out that the animals were treated in a way which could be seen as a scheme of ritual behavior. Concerning ethnographical records from North America, animals were treated with respect and were buried in their natural surroundings (as in the water or on the ground). Particular care was taken when the bones of the skeleton where arranged in anatomical order, although the skull was disposed separately. This ritual behavior is known in the Bear-ceremonies and is known from the Saami, or Lapps (in northern Scandinavia), in the west, and to the Lenape (Delaware) on the Atlantic coast in the east (Hultkrantz 1982:167 p). The skull of the bear was placed in a tree and the bones were laid out of reach for dogs and wild animal. The bear's soul was supposed to travel to the lower world to be reborn (Hultkrantz 1982:173 p)

To sum up

When considering the evidence from these coastal adapted groups it seems like it is possible to get a small glimpse of their way of thinking. We can observe that it is certain behavior related to how they looked up on the surrounding environment and society. This were expressed in different ways depending on if this view would be expressed on a rock painting, cross-shaped adze or if it was on the bones from the hunted animal.

Some of the elements that could be interpreted as ritual behavior are repeated. One of these is the contradiction between marine and terrestrial. This contradiction represents different parts of the natural surroundings as well as their world of ideas. In this environment it seems to exist tension between the different biotopes. If the conclusions of the analysis of the cross-shaped adze from Stala are included we can also see that there are a perspective of sexes. That view from a gender perspective shows us that there are a connection between sexes and the surrounding environment. Relating to that they represents as conjunctions of pairs it seems reasonable to assume that it existed a tension even between sexes, but at the same time it was the basic element for survival for the hunting-gatherer group. It seems like the female is closely connected to each other, woven together in groups and is expressed as a collective. The males are presented as singles, separate connected to each other, singularity within the group and they express individuality. It seems well fit in Elkins ideas concerning totemism and sexes. The matriarchal totemism generates the biological continuity of the clan. The patriarchal totemism is an expression for the herds' local unity in a geographic perspective (Lévi-Strauss 1969:71 p). So, the first is a diachronic and the second is a synchronic conjunction of the clan members. Elkins also propose that totemism has a double function. It expresses kinship and collaboration between individual and nature as well as continuity between the past and the present.

This Mesolithic society that were connected to the coastal adaptations were expressed, as well as at the rock painting at Tumlehed, with idioms of symbols as well as strongly complex abstract symbols. The behavior of burning food remains originating from the marine environment as well as the special treatment of dolphin skulls, fits also into the general world of ideas.

References

Bergen, H. 1958. *Les deux sources de la morale et de la religion*. Paris.
Cullberg, K. 1975. Tumlehed, Torslanda 216, Hällmålning, Stenålder/bronsålder. *FYNDrapporter* 1975, 73–76.
Fischer, A. 1995. *Man and Sea in the Mesolithic – coastal settlement above and below present sea level*. Oxbow Monograph 53. Oxford.
Hernek, R. and Nordqvist, B. 1995. *Världens äldsta tuggummi? Ett urval spännande arkeologiska upptäckter som gjordes vid Huseby Klev, och andra platser, inför väg 178 över Orust*. Riksantikvarieämbetet UV Väst. Kungsbacka.
Hultkrantz, Å. 1982. Religion and Experience of Nature among North American Hunting Indians. In: Hultkrantz, Å. and Vorren, Ø. (eds) *The Hunters. Their Culture and Way of Life*, 163–186. Bergen.
Jonsson, L. 1996. *Fauna och landskap i Göteborgstrakten under boreal tid. Djurbensfynden från den boreala kustboboplatsen vid Balltorp*. Mölndal kommun, Västergötland. Riksantikvarieämbetet Arkeologiska Resultat. *UV VÄST RAPPORT 1996:25*. Kungsbacka.
Lévi-Strauss, C. 1969. *Totemismen*. Uppsala.
Nordbladh, J. 1975. Tumlehed, Torslanda 216, Hällmålning, Stenålder/bronsålder. Beskrivning, Datering, Utvärdering. *FYNDrapporter* 1975, 79–84. Göteborg.
Nordqvist, B. 2000. Coastal Adaptations in the Mesolithic. A study of coastal sites with organic remains from Boreal and Atlantic periods in Western Sweden. *Gotarc. Series B. Gothenburg Archaeological Thesis*.Göteborg.
—— in press. Den huvudlösa gubben från Stala. En nypåträffad människofigur på Stalahackan. *In Situ*. Västsvensk Arkeologisk Tidsskrift.
Sjöberg, J–E. 1980. Konst eller Magi? Funderingar kring inventarienummer 127. In: Andersson, S. and Kaelas, L. (eds) Vid älven, fångst och odling. *Göteborgs arkeologiska museum, årstryck* 1979–1980, 144–156.
Strassburg, J. 2000. *Shamanic Shadows. One Hundred Generations of Undead Subversion in Southern Scandinavia, 7,000–4,000 BC*. Stockholm Studies in Archaeology 20.
Tilley, C. 1991. *Material culture and text. The art of ambiguity*. London.
Wennstedt Edvinger, B. 1993. *Genus och djursymbolik*. Arkeologiska studier vid Umeå Universitet 1. Umeå.

68. Rituals at the Meso 2000 Conference and the Mesolithic-Neolithic Terminological Breakdown

Jimmy Strassburg

In this article, the concept of ritual is criticised, along with insistent trends in Mesolithic research of today that may be described as ethnocentric, gender-biased and naively functionalist. Furthermore, it is claimed that the latent definitions of the two all-overriding archaeological concepts 'Mesolithic' and 'Neolithic' have a hampering effect on interpretations of prehistoric contexts that happen to fall within the chronological limits to which the two concepts in question supposedly apply. Nowhere is the power of the hierarchical Mesolithic-Neolithic differentiation scheme more conspicuous than in the case of an allegedly Mesolithic practice mixing with a context that is labelled 'Neolithic'.

This article is primarily based on my paper presentation at the 6th International Conference on the Mesolithic in Europe (Meso 2000, Nynäshamn, Sweden). Only at the last minute it came to my attention that I was to end, most involuntarily, the archaeological meeting in question. From having been a paper mainly devoted to the issue of the 'constructedness' of the Mesolithic and the Neolithic and some of the absurd effects thereof, such as indefensibly different interpretative practices within the two fields of expertise, it transformed. Indeed, it turned in part into a critical summary of what kinds of assumptions that had proliferated in the conference readings, where the latest research trends of the Mesolithic project ought to be present, loud and clear.

There has never been a Mesolithic. However, there *is* a Mesolithic, right here, right now, a monolithic scientific legacy of Western modernism and of the early formation of the archaeological *Wissenschaft* (*cf*. J. Thomas 1996:6), strangely situated like a living fossil in the interregional and global multiplicity of postindustrialist power structures. The Mesolithic is no more alive than in the heads and texts of the people attending the Meso 2000 jamboree. The secure sense of 'home' issues from that very multi-headed source.

Although ultimately based on observations of ancient remains of material culture forming patterns of various kinds, what is called the Mesolithic is still, to quite a considerable degree, an arbitrary Western construct. It is an academic-structural straight jacket and a rigid interpretative system rolled into one. As such, its boundaries and definitions hamper alternative analyses and perspectives. The awareness of such an epistemological myopia, merely rarely considered by speakers at the Meso 2000 conference, such as Victoria Mary Cummings (2000), is not new. The Swedish archaeologist Mats Malmer noted similar problems already 40 years ago (1963:11). He stood startled before an ever-growing situation of blunt divisions of the past taking on distinct and almost exclusive research features and interpretative responsibilities, a situation that created sectarian fields of specialists in its wake.

It goes without saying that the criticisms delivered above are not directed against the basis of the Mesolithic as such, *i.e.*, the bulk of subject materials that sorts under that suspiciously broad category of meaning production. Studying the materials concerned is thoroughly enjoyable and worthwhile. Rather, it is researchers' persistent leaning towards taken-for-granted academic structures, moulds and ready-made category slots that is worrisome (*cf*. Strassburg 1997). For instance, the Neolithic, the next rung on the archaeological cultural-evolutionary ladder, equals the Mesolithic project in every conceivable way as regards its constructedness. What extends the attention span of anyone delving deeper into the matter is not the fact that the archaeological projects discussed are products of a certain cultural setting. It is the fact that the Mesolithic and the Neolithic, as academic projects, are so notably different, a circumstance that results in peculiar interpretative preferences. At least such a description of dissimilarity is valid for the south-Scandinavian versions of these projects until today, the ones with which I am best familiar (Strassburg 2000). In a most generalising manner, the trends of difference have been summarised in two diagrams, Figure 68.1 and Figure 68.2.

The Mesolithic-Neolithic differences suggested in the diagrams are admittedly somewhat outdated. Today, they mainly live and thrive when one sets the early Mesolithic, such as the Maglemose, against the allegedly fully developed Neolithic. The late Mesolithic, such as the

Mesolithic	Neolithic
Life is essentially...	**Life is essentially...**
biological	psychostructural
ecological	economical
non-social	social
Mesoliths are repeatedly referred to as...	**Neoliths are normally called...**
primates	humans
foragers	domesticators
hunter-fisher-gatherers	farmers
bands	chiefdoms and tribes
They tend to be preoccupied with...	**They tend to be preoccupied with...**
environmental adaption	sociopolitical strategies
survival	surplus production
mobility	sedentism
animals and plants	ancestors
spirits and animism	deities and religion

Figure 68.1 Stereotypic Mesolithic-Neolithic dissimilarities.

Mesolithic	Neolithic
Habitats and niches	Landscapes
Site catchment circles	Territories
Huts	Houses
Families	Lineages
Flat graves	Monuments
Waste zones	Sacrificial bogs
Toss zones	Land depositions
Occupation zones	Living structures
Flint procurement	Mining
Plant procurement	Agriculture
Hunting	Herding

Figure 68.2 Institutions, living areas and other kinds of pivotal structures are usually differently termed for the Mesolithic and the Neolithic.

Kongemose or the Ertebølle, and the early Neolithic are nowadays described in such a way that the two terminologies are occasionally jumbled. However, they are not truly integrated but rather juxtaposed, a fact that ironically implies that the various contrasts between the Mesolithic and the Neolithic shine at their brightest when the two are forcedly combined in texts covering both the late Mesolithic and the early Neolithic. Notably weird effects occur in the twilight zone, as it were, effects that may be depicted as a war between new and powerful Neolithic essences slowly but surely shattering a supposedly stable, sleepy millennia-old world of Mesolithic phenomena of peace. If an object labelled 'Neolithic', such as a certain axe, is encountered in what is perceived as an otherwise Mesolithic context, it is somehow assumed that the artefact still retains its Neolithic meaning. Hence it creates a metaphorical embassy of the Neolithic inside the Mesolithic, not much unlike the Romans' tactics when infiltrating and converting cultures to the supremacy of Rome. The concept of foreign objects essentially changing as they move from one context to the next, as seen in anthropological studies (*e.g.*, N. Thomas 1991), is disregarded.

However, the characterisations of the Mesolithic and the Neolithic propelled here should not be mistaken for bygone caricatures. Although some archaeologists have in recent times claimed them to be under serious extinction, anybody attending the Meso 2000 conference would definitely question the validity of such optimistic remarks, at least as regards the Mesolithic. Already a simple, quick and incomplete listing of observations of overt research themes and hidden agendas revealed in surprisingly many of the presentations held in the intensive week of Mesolithic expertise would be a cause of alarm and disbelief.

Apart from an exceptionally small number of talks, such as the radiant exception of Nyree Finlay (2000), who discussed multiple authorship of androgynous objects and Strathern's partibility theory, the presentations have amazingly been delivered with none or concealed socio-theoretical awareness. Concepts that ought to be incredible in any text dealing with prehistoric lives, such as 'truth', 'reconstruction' and 'sociocultural fact', have repeatedly been used by the majority of researchers, often with no reservations whatsoever. Lévi-Strauss, who attended the Man the Hunter conference in the late 1960s, complained about the same problem (1968:351). How come that nothing much has happened in almost four decades in the Mesolithic field of research as regards basic theoretical responsibility and reference availability? As things stand now, joining the Mesolithic may at the extreme end mean entering into one of the last havens for delivering social bigotries with impunity. After displaying a limited set of scientific data concerning prehistoric fragments, such as a distribution map, a statistical graph or a find table, it is accepted custom and preferred ritual to drastically open the Pandora box of common-sense explanations and speak the words of wisdom. Having entered the third millennium, this is simply not an acceptable standard, especially given the perspective of a research field that regards itself as particularly scientific among the various archaeological branches.

The sociocultural contexts in which the Mesolithic have been and still are construed are typically conspicuously absent. Too many Mesolithic specialists have in their personal presentation chosen to voice their institutionally sanctioned opinions as if they were serving as unapproachable analytic judges, transparent and objective in capacity. Politics and awareness of interpersonal pressures regrettably fail to appear in the accounts.

Furthermore, the conference made clear that the Mesolithic system of accepted concepts and interpretations is still too much imposed on the particularities of prehistoric residues. It is apparently relaxed in its continuous generation of generalisations, a top-down approach without conscience, a macro-level framework unable to yield pictures of the past that are differentiated on the basis of, say, social identities and power relations. As Kristina Jennbert orally remarked at one of the early presentations that was performed in the Enculturing-the-landscape session on Thursday at the Meso 2000 meeting – serious investigations of even the most basic social differences are avoided or grossly simplified. The most common variety of the latter case at the conference was the division of a prehistoric context or phenomenon into ridiculously reified conceptual pairings, such as Male-Female or external 'ethnic' relations *contra* internal task-differentiation relations. These pairings are unabashedly painted with modernist colours, hues which transmit ideas of gender and kinship that belong to the Western 1950s or worse. An example of outmoded gender thinking that has flourished in the Meso 2000 meeting is the utterly androcentric vision of women as supreme gifts in marriage transactions.

Lastly, most Mesolithic archaeologists reading a paper at the meeting insisted on only discussing and picturing normative relations in Mesolithic communities. Queer relations, non-normative relations of whatever kind that seemingly disrupt the standard social divisions, were roughly removed in order not to disturb proper analysis and interpretation. As a consequence, the societies presented became inhumanly static and solid, instead of dynamic and in part potentially subversive. Far more than one Mesolithic expert had primates and alpha males in her or his mind when telling the audience how 'Stone Age' life was led.

The ritual Mesolithic-Neolithic asymmetry

Below, a handful of examples of the power of the Mesolithic and Neolithic categorisation schemes will be briefly presented. The cases may be said to involve rituals, and then funerary rituals in particular. Nonetheless, the constant choice and use of the concept of ritual is not satisfactory. Indeed, for the most part, it is outright unfortunate and uninformative.

As has been pointed out by several archaeologists (*e.g.*, Bahn 1989:62), when it comes to defining ritual in archaeology, it has for the most part been an all-purpose explanation used where nothing else comes to mind. It has been used in order to handle evidence that was not immediately accountable in modern common-sense words. Without exploring its meanings, it has been a painless way to finally settle feelings of bewilderment felt in relation to certain finds (Orme 1981:218). Prehistorians tend to employ the concept when standing clueless or listless before behaviour that they describe as symbolic or, in functionalist terms, as 'inefficient'. Moreover, all archaeological understandings of ritual have one thing in common; they set up ritual, however subtle, as having reference to mythical beliefs in mystical beings or powers, to sacred places, as something that is apart from the profane sphere of daily routine. Rituals somehow compose a world outside the everyday and the ordinary, a time out in the standard course of events (Strassburg 2000:35). Supposedly, there is a supernatural realm full of symbols overarching the natural, functional and normally efficient world of daily living. Such assumptions of prehistoric contexts being divisible according to binary pairs such as 'functional-symbolical' or 'natural-supernatural' have no support in the anthropological literature. The very idea that the bulk of actions in any given ancient past were bereaved of symbolic meaning and spiritual considerations is wishful thinking steeped in modernism.

Normally, for the Mesolithic specialist, phenomena that qualify as 'ritual' are characterisable as funerary, liminal, performative and sacrificial. Typically, they involve burials, depositions, offerings, manifested representations ('art'), special objects ('exclusive exchange') and special foodstuffs ('feasting events'). Funerary practices especially are regarded as fraught with strange ritualistic actions, following routinised authoritative predispositions long forgotten.

In order for such practices, as well as most other supposedly ritual courses of action, to be more specified and contextualised, they must be freed from the Durkheimian distinctions of ritual-non-ritual and religious-secular. Regularisation, repetition and routinisation lie at the basis of human life itself (Strassburg 2000:37). Ritual is nothing but basic sociocultural activity and ought to be acknowledged as such (Staal 1975:9; Rappaport 1979:174). Why, then, not use the term 'practice' instead and specify the interpretations concerned. Rather than extracting ritual as important in the power-practice complex, as something that is conservative and rigid, it is enough to admit 'a hierarchy of organised skills and processes', which includes all kinds of practices, Goffmanesque small encounters, extraordinary procedures and large-scale ceremonies (Goody 1977:28). The degree and amount of ontological friction, cosmological dramatisation, symbolic elaboration, emotional tension and social competition in any performed action vary, just as its tempo and timing (Strassburg 2000:37). In this way, descriptions of resistance and change are paved way for. In short, drawing the line between what is ritual and what is not in the complex realm of sociocultural action is hardly meaningful.

The obsession with the imagined Mesolithic-Neolithic transition and the supposedly dramatic shifts that occur in that 'zone' can go to great lengths of absurdity. For instance, Richard Bradley has recently noted for the pair of Dragsholm burials, which was unearthed a few decades ago in a late Mesolithic-early Neolithic shell midden on the north-west coast of Zealand, that the two were worlds apart (1998:35). One grave, the double burial with two individuals osteologically interpreted as women, lingers in the retarded Mesolithic, and the other, the single burial containing the skeleton of what has been judged as a young man, starts off fresh as part of the newly arrived Neolithic package. He bases this stark difference on two observations. Firstly, the double grave has been radiocarbon-dated to the end of the late Mesolithic, while the single grave has been dated to the very beginning of the Neolithic. Secondly, whereas the double grave contains objects that he will not perceive as Neolithic, the single grave does – a polygonal axe and a ceramic pot. However, should we consider Meiklejohn's and others' recent findings that the stable C 13 isotope plays a chronological role, affecting the C 14 dates of skeletons (1998), the double grave should be dated to the same date as the single grave. The individuals in the double grave exhibit a marine diet, whereas the single individual does not.

> Marine systems have a time lag or reservoir effect in their circulation of atmospheric carbon, resulting in overall C 14 levels that are lower than in the terrestrial system. Therefore, humans who utilise marine-based food will incorporate impoverished levels of C 14 into their systems. If such skeletal remains are dated they will have lower C 14 levels than predicted, and will thus appear older than they really are.
> (Meiklejohn *et al.* 1998:204 p)

Thus, the two sets of burials are not worlds apart, but two metres apart. Even if they actually are separated by a century or two, there is no *a priori* reason to assume great dissimilarities in the meanings induced by making the two burials. An axe or a ceramic pot does not bring with it a Neolithic package of ideas. A grave with such objects is not *per se* 'hotter' than a grave without. These items are nearly always internalised in a local social context and should be treated accordingly.

Another example of how a so-called Mesolithic burial form can be degraded in relation to a similar Neolithic burial is created when the Ertebølle boat burial from Møllegabet II, south of Fyn, is compared with the Funnel Beaker Øgårde boat burial, found in Åmose, on north-west Fyn. Although similar in almost every respect, the Møllegabet burial has by at least some Mesolithic researchers been described in purely functionalist terms (*e.g.*, Grøn 1992, 1993, 1995; Grøn and Skaarup 1993; Skaarup 1988, 1993, 1995; Skaarup and Grøn 1991, 1994). Using an old dugout for burial is practical, because in that way you do not have to build a coffin. Keeping it in place by surrounding it with stakes is useful in so far that the rotting corpse will not float away and spread diseases. The slight burning of the corpse was hygienic. Antlers and bows found right next to the corpse may have been employed as weight in order to weigh it down, a way to increase the deadlock, so to speak. By contrast, the Øgårde boat burial has been reconstructed in drawings and texts in much more vivid and exciting ways (*e.g.*, Christensen 1990, 1997; Skaarup 1995). The recently deceased individual was solemnly placed on the dugout, as if it was a floating bier. A fire was lit in order to expel evil forces and foods and tools were set into the aft for use in the afterlife journey. Interestingly, despite the fact that the Øgårde burial is also hemmed in by poles, it is going somewhere, to an imagined realm of the dead in the mythic distance. In brief, the older burial is described in passive functionalist terms, the younger in active eschatological terms. These acclaimed differences are completely unwarranted and show how strong the influence of the Mesolithic-Neolithic dichotomy really is.

A final example of how a burial practice of the Mesolithic immediately receives higher status and complexity when sorted into the Neolithic academic project is graves covered by wooden superstructures. When the question of a wooden construction standing over a burial in Mesolithic times arises, it soon becomes a matter of distrust. Are the shady patches actually the remains of a wooden structure? (Svend-Åge Tornbjerg, pers. comm.). Excepting Christopher Tilley's book from 1996, I have never observed that such funerary constructions are delineated in terms of mortuary houses. For the Neolithic cases, the situation is the reverse. The wooden superstructures are since decades gladly reconstructed as ancestral homes (*e.g.*, Madsen 1972; Glob 1975). The only debate that is running seems to be what the funerary houses looked like in detail. It is as if people living within the constructed confines of the Mesolithic are not allowed concepts such as home and house, because archaeological specialists have already sentenced them to a more or less animal-like life, imprisoned in fleeting mobility, or to a colonialist neverneverland with tribal 'camps' and 'huts'. Such automatons have no ceremonies or ceremonial structures. Features that seemingly scream 'spiritual and ancestral complexity' are still dismissed by some pre-historians as accidental (*e.g.*, Knutsson 1995). The things that they did and made were manifestations of instinct, emotion and finding-subsistence-in-nature issues (*ibid.*). Funnily enough, when people in the Neolithic of southern Scandinavia led mobile lives, which they typically did, they are portrayed as homesick, ancestral devotees, not ecology-bound dopes.

References

Bahn, P. 1989. *Bluff Your Way in Archaeology*. London.
Bradley, R. 1998. *The Significance of Monuments: On the Shaping of Human Experience in Neolithic and Bronze Age Europe*. London and New York.
Christensen, C. 1990. Stone Age Dug-Out Boats in Denmark: Occurence, Age, Form and Reconstruction. In: Robinson, D.E. (ed.) *Experimentation and Reconstruction in Environmental Archaeology*, 119–141. Oxford.
—— 1997. Både og sejlads i stenalderen. In: Pedersen, L. *et al.* (eds.) *Storebælt i 10.000 år*, 282–289. Copenhagen.
Cummings, V.M. 2000. Myth, Memory and Metaphor: Mesolithic Worldviews of Landscapes in Western Britain. (in this volume).

Finlay, N. 2000. Making Microliths: Multiple Authors in the Mesolithic. (in this volume).
Glob, P.V. 1975. De dødes lange huse. *Skalk* 1975:6, 10–14.
Goody, J. 1977. Against 'Ritual': Loosely Structured Thoughts on a Loosely Defined Topic. In: Moore, S.F. and Myerhoff, B.G. (eds.) *Secular Ritual*, 25–35. Assen and Amsterdam.
Grøn, O. 1992. 174. Møllegabet II. *Arkæologiske udgravninger i Danmark* 1991, 155.
—— 1993. 414. Møllegabet II. *Arkæologiske udgravninger i Danmark* 1992, 219.
—— 1995. Research in Stone Age Sites at Submerged Shore Zones. In: Fischer, A. (ed.) *Man and Sea in the Mesolithic*, 403–8. Oxford.
Grøn, O. and Skaarup, J. 1993. Møllegabet II. *Journal of Danish Archaeology* 10, 18–50.
Knutsson, H. 1995. *Slutvandrat?* AUN 20. Uppsala.
Lévi-Strauss, C. 1968. The Concept of Primitiveness. In: Lee, R.B. and DeVore, I. (eds.) *Man the Hunter*. 349–52. Chicago.
Madsen, T. 1972. Grave med teltformet overbygning fra tidligneolitisk tid. *Kuml* 1971, 127–50.
Malmer, M.P. 1963. *Metodproblem inom järnålderns konsthistoria*. Acta Archaeologica Lundensia in 8°; 3. Lund.
Meiklejohn, C., Petersen, E.B. and Alexandersen, V. 1998. The Later Mesolithic Population of Sjælland, Denmark, and the Neolithic Transition. In: Zvelebil, M., Danell, R. and Domanska, L. (eds.) *Harvesting the Sea, Farming the Forest*, 203–212. Sheffield.
Orme (Coles), B. 1981. *Anthropology for Archaeologists*. London.
Rappaport, R.A. 1979. *Ecology, Meaning and Religion*. Berkeley.
Skaarup, J. 1988. 464. Møllegabet ud for Æroskøbing. *Arkæologiske udgravninger i Danmark* 1987, 197.
—— 1993. Submarine bopladser. In: Hvass, S. and Storgaard, B. (eds.). *Da klinger i muld*, 70–75. Århus.
—— 1995. Stone-Age Burials in Boats. In: Crumlin-Pedersen, O. and Munch Thye, B. (eds.) *The Ship as Symbol*, 51–58. Copenhagen.
Skaarup, J. and Grøn, O. 1991. Den våde grav. *Skalk* 1991:4, 3–7.
—— 1994. 232. Møllegabet II. *Arkæologiske udgravninger i Danmark* 1993, 154.
Staal, F. 1975. The Meaningless of Ritual. *Numen* 26:1, 2–22.
Strassburg, J. 1997. Inter the Mesolithic – Unearth Social Histories: Vexing Androcentric Sexing Through Strøby Egede. *Current Swedish Archaeology* 5, 155–178.
—— 2000. *Shamanic Shadows. One Hundred Generations of Undead Subversion in Southern Scandinavia, 7,000–4,000 BC*. Stockholm.
Thomas, J. 1996. A Précis of *Time, Culture and Identity*. *Archaeological Dialogues* 3:1, 6–21.
Thomas, N. 1991. *Entangled Objects*. London.

69. Decorated objects of the older Mesolithic from the northern lowlands

Thomas Terberger

The following text discusses decorated objects from the continental northern lowlands of the earlier Mesolithic period. Antler and bone were first choice materials but in rare cases we have evidence of use of stone, amber and tortoise carapace. The finds are often connected with bigger sites. Bâtons percés, bone mattocks and points/daggers were preferred objects for decoration. The more important motifs show a wide distribution and compare with southern Scandinavian findings. The combination of barbed line-motif and zigzag line exemplifies the great similarities of decoration on a broader geographical scale. Possibilities to identify regional groups on the basis of motifs have to be seen critically. First evidence of decorated objects belong to the Preboreal (Friesack, Rothenklempenow), but an increasing number originates from the later Boreal/early Atlantic. Direct AMS-dating conducted at Verchen (Mecklenburg-Vorpommern) for the first time will help create a more reliable basis for interpretation.

Introduction: Towards Mesolithic art

There is increasing evidence for the development of art from the Magdalenian to the Mesolithic in western Central Europe. Red coloured pebbles with geometric pattern were found for example in a Magdalenian context at Abri Cabônes, French Jura, and recently at Hohle Fels, Swabian Alb (David *et al.*1998; Conard and Floss 1999). They demonstrate the gradual introduction of the Azilian style of ornamentation. An abrupt change at the beginning of the Alleröd-interstadial is not detectable. At the same time we can now recognise more evidence for figurative art in the Alleröd: Besides the well known sandstone smoother (Pfeilschaftglätter) engraved with schematic female figures from Niederbieber in the Rhineland (Loftus 1982), new radiocarbon dates for the double-burial at Bonn-Oberkassel provide a date for a cervid representation close to the beginning of the Alleröd (Baales and Street 1998:83). More important for the northern lowlands is an amber sculpture – probably a horse – discovered in the Federmesser context some years ago at Weitsche (Veil and Breest 1997; Terberger and Ansorge 2000). Evidence for the Younger Dryas is scarce and it is a matter of discussion how these finds fit in with the idea of a continuos development of art towards the Mesolithic period.

There are numerous examples of portable art dating from the Mesolithic of southern Scandinavia, but there are quite a lot of sites with decorated objects located on the mainland northern lowlands too. For the younger/final Mesolithic knowledge of decorated material of the Kongemose- and Ertebölle-periods from the area south of the Baltic Sea is limited. A bâton percé from Lübeck-Travemünde and finds from the sites of Travenort and Ralswiek-Augustenhof represent some of the more important examples (Jestrzemski 1987; Klinghardt 1924; Schwantes 1939), however, in the following I will concentrate on the older Mesolithic.

Material cannot be discussed in detail here. Work on this subject is restricted by information only being available on a preliminary level for sites like Friesack and Rothenklempenow. Additionally new decorated finds from Mecklenburg-Vorpommern and Brandenburg are not published yet (personal communication by B. Gramsch) and thus the ideas outlined here have to be taken as first summarising results.

The evidence: a short overview

The older Mesolithic is here defined as the period of the Preboreal, Boreal and early Atlantic and can be paralleled with the Maglemose Culture (in a broad sense). In the absolute time scale the beginning of the Preboreal can be attributed to 9600 cal BC (Jöris and Weninger 2000), although the earliest evidence of the Mesolithic is found to be somewhat later. The end of the older Mesolithic is less well defined. The beginning of the younger or late Mesolithic is connected with the first evidence of trapezes. In the more southern regions this phase is dated to 7000–6700 cal BC (plateau !; Gronenborn 1997). Recently Bokelmann (1999) argued for the date of the introduction of the trapezoid microliths in the northern lowlands being

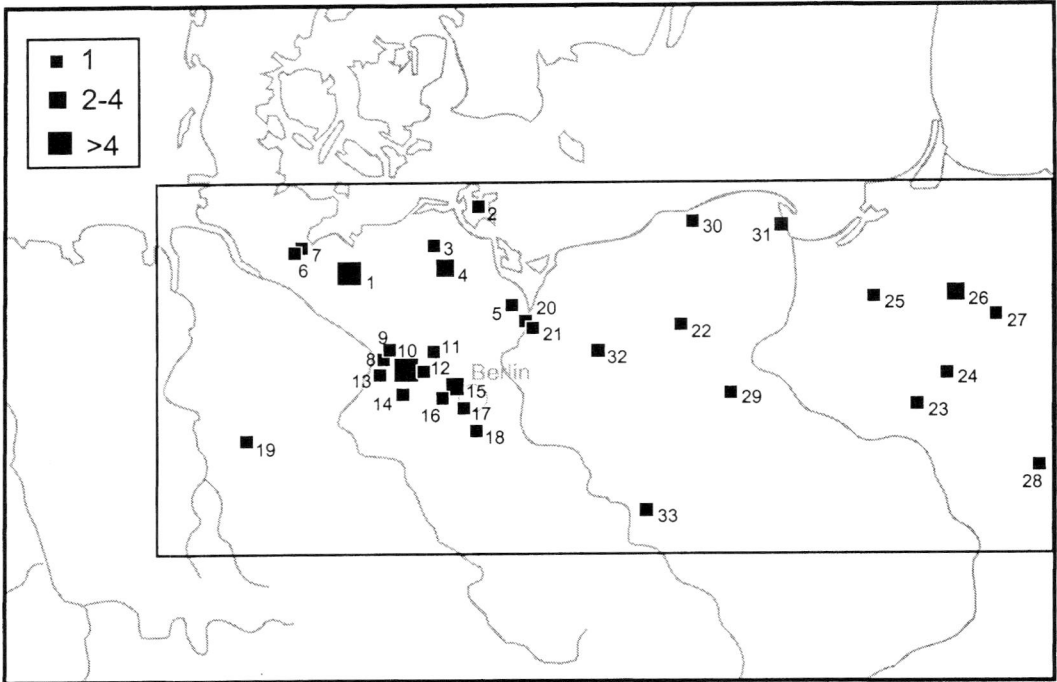

Figure 69.1 Location of sites with decorated objects of the older Mesolithic (see List). 1 Hohen-Viecheln. 2 Bergen-Tetel. 3 Tribsees. 4 Verchen. 5 Rothenklempenow. 6–7 Trave. 8 Siegrothsbruch. 9 Garz. 10 Friesack. 11 Bützsee-Altfriesack. 12 Wagenitz. 13 Strodehne. 14 Pritzerbe. 15 Wustermark 22. 16 Fernewerder. 17 Kleinmachnow. 18 Mellensee. 19 Langelsheim. 20 Stettin-Grabow/Sczcecin-Grabowo. 21 Stettin-Podejuch/Sczcecin-Podjuchy. 22 Trudna. 23 Pułtusk. 24 Ostrolęka. 25 Tłokowo. 26 Dudka. 27 Nitki. 28 Wozniki. 29 Biskupin. 30 Stolp/Słupsk. 31 Danzig/Gdansk. 32. Woldenberg/Dobigniew. 33 Pobiel 10 (all Poland).

some hundred years later at ca. 6200 cal BC. Thus we are missing a well defined beginning of the younger Mesolithic. Discussion on this point is ongoing, but we are dealing with a time-span of roughly 3000 years.

The area of interest is concentrated on the lowlands of northern Germany and northern Poland. Mapping the sites with decorated objects (Figure 69.1) a concentration in the wetland areas, with favourable conditions for preservation of organic material, becomes clear. Especially the Havel/Spree region (Berlin-Brandenburg) is well known for the richness of Mesolithic organic material. These finds show different examples of bâtons percés with variations of the barbed line-motif from Kleinmachnow, Strodehne and Friesack (Figure 69.2:1–2, 27–8; Gramsch 1973; 1979; 1987). Research at Friesack 4 is of outstanding importance (Gramsch 1987; Gramsch and Kloss 1990), but information for twelve decorated objects and their motifs – such as a tortoise carapace with engraved triangles (Gramsch and Larsson 2001) – is in part preliminary (see List). Other motifs are represented by two so called "bullroarers" (Schwirrhölzer) (Figure 69.2:6). Intensive work throughout the last decade in this area has contributed new finds for example from Bützsee-Altfriesack or Wustermark, site 22 (Cziesla *et al.* 1998:86; Beran 1999), but context, dating and style of these finds have to be established.

More to the Northwest evidence is restricted to two single finds from the Trave (Schleswig-Holstein) including a well known bâton percé dominated by rows of hatched triangles (Schwantes 1939) (Figure 69.2:10). At Mecklenburg-Vorpommern the excavated site of Hohen-Viecheln is of major interest (Schuldt 1961). There are two bone mattocks, a bâton percé and an antler mattock – probably itself a fragment of a bâton percé – quite richly ornamented (Figure 69.3:2–4). Other categories of finds show very limited decoration (Figure 69.3:1). Some years ago dredging at the river Peene close to lake Kummerow has delivered new ornamented material at the site of Verchen (Terberger in press). Irregular rows of lines on the first bâton percé give the impression of signs manufactured step by step. A second bâton percé from Verchen with various motifs illustrates well the probable process of ornamentation (Figure 69.3:9): On the central part of the object we can recognise the transformation of rows of short lines into a row of hatched triangles. Some form of composition is without doubt reflected by the "melting" of different motifs, but in relation to the other motifs there seems to have been no overall plan in mind. I would therefore prefer to interpret the piece as a reflection of a process of manufacture during the period of its use.

Excavations at Rothenklempenow of different layers of the Mesolithic are still in progress. A bâton percé is preliminary presented, but further objects have not been published yet (Schacht 1993). With its figurative represen-

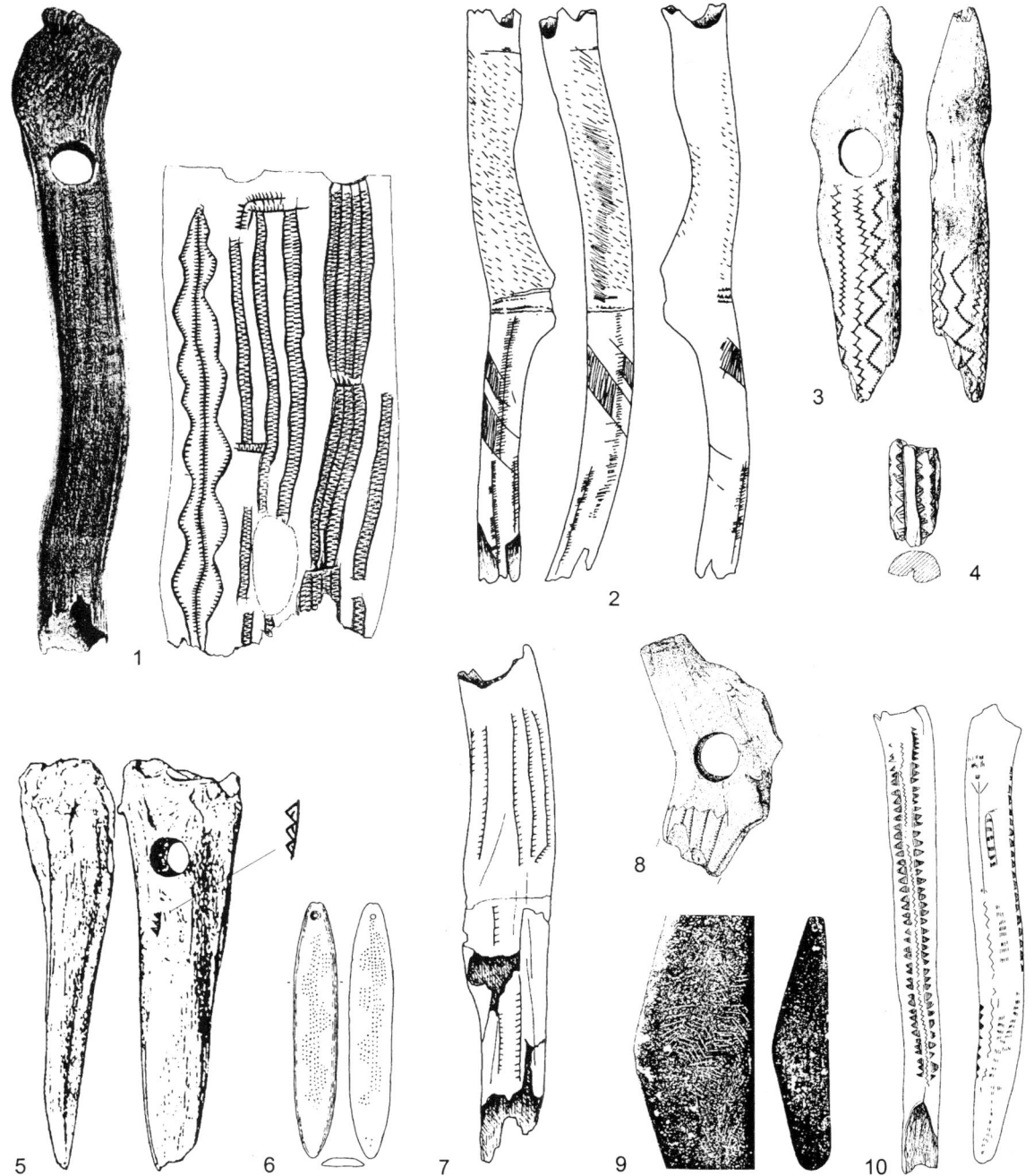

Figure 69.2 Decorated objects (see List). 1 Kleinmachnow. 2 Strodehne. 3 Wagenitz. 4 Siegrothsbruch. 5 Mellensee. 6 Pritzerbe. 7–8 Friesack 4. 9 Langelsheim. 10 Trave near Lübeck. – 1–5, 7–10: scale ca. 1:4; 6: scale ca. 1:3. – 2, 7, 10: drawing M. Wieczorek after Schwantes 1939; Gramsch 1987; Zotz 1941.

tation the bâton percé from Stettin-Podejuch (Sczcecin-Podjuchy) is one of the most beautiful objects and its surface reflects longer usage (Figure 69.4:2). Together with a lost piece from Stettin-Grabow (Sczcecin-Grabowo) it underlines the importance of Mesolithic settlement near to the river Oder (Galiński 1992) (Figure 69.4:1).

In the area East of the Oder the picture is characterised by single finds with a dominance of richly ornamented bâtons percés (Figure 69.1, 69.4:3, 69.4:5–7). New excavations in the Masurian Lakeland begin to alter the picture with finds such as an ornamented antler hoe showing an X-shaped mark from Dudka and a wonderful slotted bone point with groups of parallel incisions from Tłokowo (Figure 69.4:8) (Fiedorczuk 1995; Gumiński 1995; Sulgostowska 1996; 1998). The barbed line-motif (Stettin-Podejuch, -Grabow, Wozniki) and the line of small hatched triangles (Stettin-Grabow, Ostrolęka, Pułtusk) are the most common patterns of ornamentation. Besides

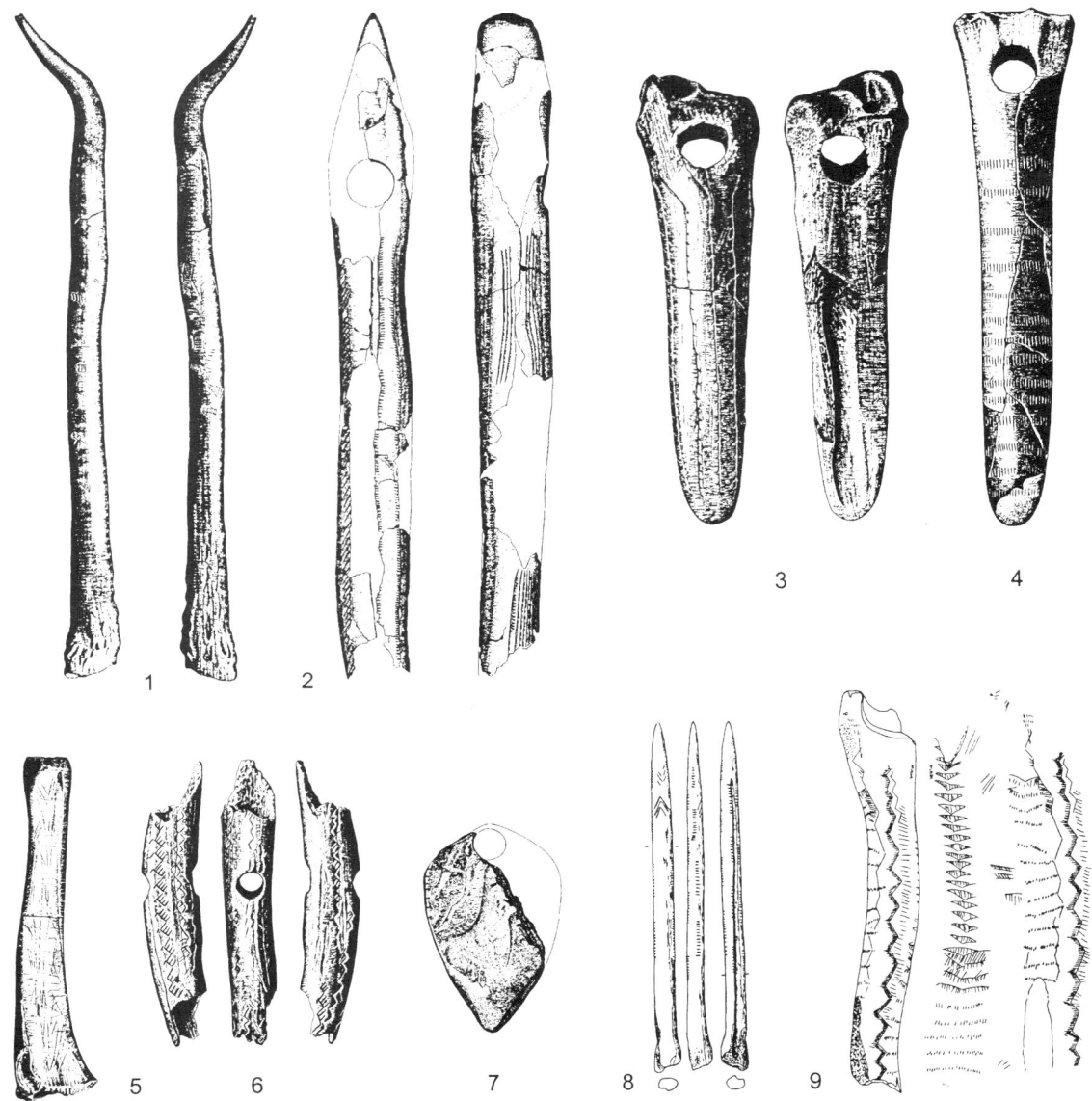

Figure 69.3 Decorated objects (see List). 1–7 Hohen-Viecheln. 8 Bergen-Tetel. 9 Verchen. – 1–10: scale ca. 1:4. – 9: drawing Ms. Felgenhauer.

organic finds where the connection with the Mesolithic is established quite safely on the base of typology and style, three amber objects have to be discussed. Besides the late glacial find from Weitsche mentioned above, the figurines of Stolp (Słupsk), Woldenberg (Dobigniew) and Danzig (Gdansk) are isolated evidence of high quality zoomorphic amber sculptures in the northern lowlands (Figure 69.4:9–11). The use of this material in the context of Mesolithic sites is only reported in isolated cases. A re-examination of the well known amber bear from Stolp established that the sculpture has only been slightly polished after its discovery. The shape and detail of the head belong to the original composition (Terberger and Ansorge 2000). In accordance with other colleagues (Kozlowski 1989, 1992) we see the closest parallels for the amber bear and probably for the horse and pig from Woldenberg and Danzig in the Mesolithic amber sculptures from Jutland. As Vang Petersen (1991) already pointed out, the strong bear played a major role for Mesolithic man.

Preliminary 57 ornamented objects can be attributed to the area of discussion (see List). On closer analysis we realise that a large number of objects are single finds (Figure 69.5). More contextual information is given by the sites of Hohen-Viecheln (9 objects) and Friesack (12 objects). However, the number of decorated artefacts has to be treated with caution, because at Friesack only five objects were found by excavation and at both sites there are artefacts with very minimal decoration.

A comparison illustrates that decorated objects are a normal component at rich sites with different phases of occupation like Friesack (Gramsch 1987) and single finds should often derive from such destroyed places (Figure

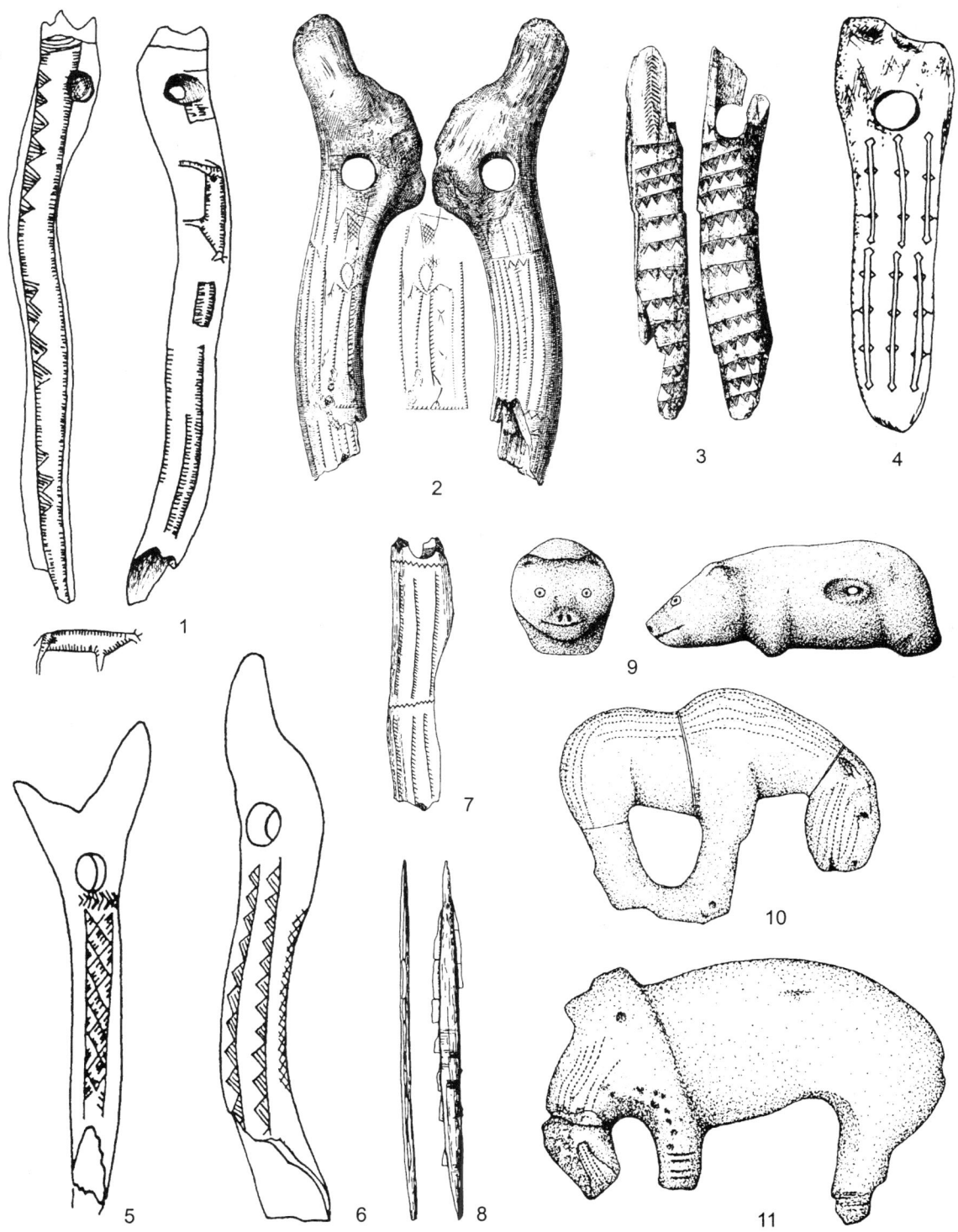

Figure 69.4 Decorated objects (see List). 1 Stettin-Grabow/Sczcecin-Grabowo. 2 Stettin-Podejuch/Sczcecin-Podjuchy. 3 Pułtusk. 4 Trudna. 5 Nitki. 6 Ostrolęka. 7 Wozniki. 8 Tłokowo. 9 Stolp/Słupsk. 10 Woldenberg/Dobigniew. 11 Danzig/ Gdansk. – 1–7: scale ca. 1:4; 8: scale ca. 1:3; 9–11: scale ca. 1:2. – 1 drawing M.Wieczorek after Kunkel 1936.

69.6). At the dredging site Verchen small bone points are under-represented, but the number of recovered mattocks argues for the presence of a bigger site here, too. The question remains whether these places reflect some kind of aggregation site where larger groups of people gathered and ritual behaviour was important, a concept which is proposed for the period of the Magdalenian (Conkey 1992).

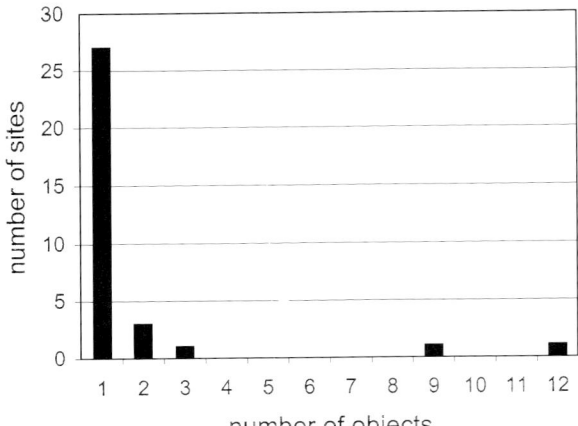

Figure 69.5 Frequency of decorated objects per site.

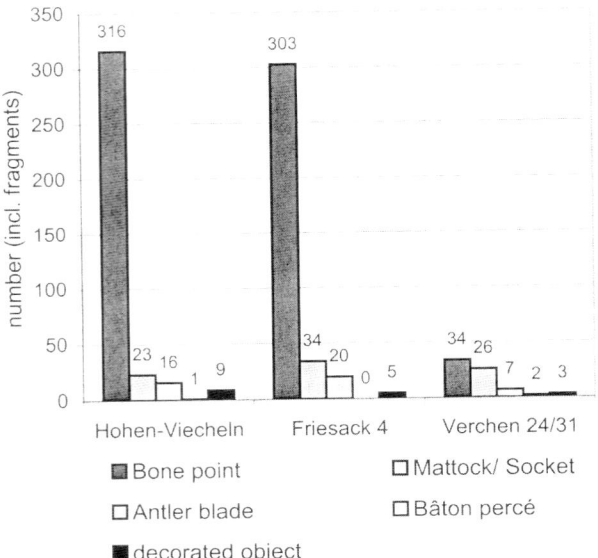

Figure 69.6 Frequency of different categories of organic material at Hohen-Viecheln, Friesack 4 (excavation only, until 1987) and Verchen 24/31 (after Schuldt 1961; Gramsch 1987; Terberger in press).

Materials and techniques

We recognise a variety of materials: As in southern Scandinavia cervid antler and sometimes elk antler and bone were the materials of choice, but exotic materials, such as a tortoise carapace from Friesack were also decorated. Evidence for wooden artefacts is limited to the younger/final Mesolithic with an ornamented paddle from Rüde 2, Schleswig-Holstein (Hartz and Lübke 1999). A pebble with geometric pattern from Langelsheim (Lower Saxonia) is an isolated example for the choice of stone (Grote 1979) (Figure 69.2:9). It is interesting to note that the site lies outside of the wetland areas housing the classical sites. Decorated flint nodules sometimes found in Zealand and Scania (Fischer 1975; Althin 1950; Larsson 2000) are not known to appear in the southern Baltic. If we accept the zoomorphic figurines to be of Mesolithic age, the use of amber is another shared feature with southern Scandinavia.

The latter ones also demonstrate the more complex manufacturing process of sculptures. Normally the decoration was conducted by simple engravings, but especially richly ornamented bâtons percés show intensive traces of altering and smoothing of the antler surface before decoration. Drilling technique was only used in very few cases. Some evidence seems to suggest, that the motifs were probably filled with a dark resinous material to emphasise the decoration. It is planned to gather more information about the amount of labour invested in manufacturing such objects by means of experiments. Evidence for painting is missing, although a red coloured stone with a possible bovine representation from Felsställe in southern Germany demonstrates that this technique was known at that time in Central Europe (Kind 1987:234 pp).

Categories and motifs

If we compare the categories of finds, the dominance of bâtons percés becomes apparent and they are often complexly decorated (Figure 69.7). Bone mattocks, daggers or points and "bullroarers" are further preferred categories. This result is certainly influenced by the nature of dredging sites, which favour the discovery of larger finds, but if we look at the excavated material of Hohen-Viecheln and Friesack the picture does not fundamentally change.

It is not intended to discuss the function of bâtons percés in this paper, but the decorated examples are worn by use and often broken and I therefore do not consider an exclusively ritual function a feasible explanation. This view is supported by the re-use of material which does not respect the ornamentation already present on the piece (Figure 69.2:8) (Andersen 1995–96:Fig. 14–15). The decoration of objects might have had special relevance in connection with their use-life, but once broken or discarded, they became a normal part of the waste material. A special context for the ornamented bâtons percés recovered during excavations was not reported. This view is supported by finds of Mesolithic cervid masks. At the site of Bedburg-Königshoven in the Rhineland the interpretation of two masks as relicts of ritual, chamanistic behaviour is widely accepted and these objects were found in a layer of normal discarded material (Street 1989).

Based on work by Clark (1936, 1975) and Gramsch (1989) it is possible to develop a list of motifs for the northern lowlands. Besides simple rows of short lines, the barbed line-motif is the most popular one (Figure 69.8). Further quite important patterns are lines of hatched small triangles and vertically hatched triangles normally arranged in a row.

Mapping the barbed line-motif (and variations; Clark 1936:169) shows that it is a widespread phenomenon

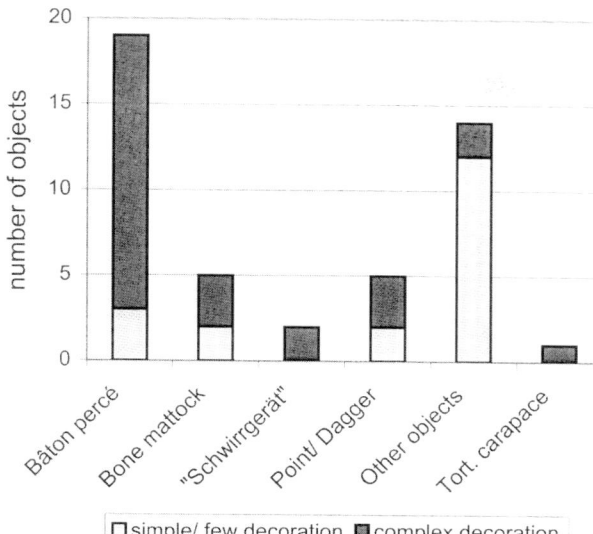

Figure 69.7 Frequency of decorated categories (bâtons percés with secondary used objects).

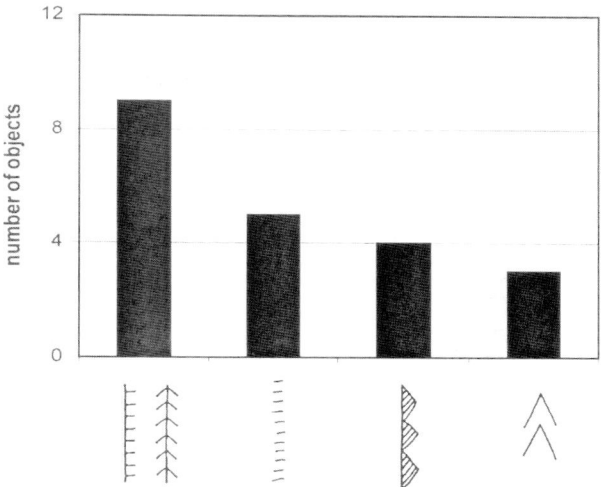

Figure 69.8 Frequency of some important motifs (barbed line with variations, see Clark 1936:169 motif a–d).

(Figure 69.9). This is not surprising because it is a quite well known Maglemosian motif in southern Scandinavia and it is represented as far as middle Sweden on a spatulate bone from Sollerön, Dalarna (Clark 1975:238). Furthermore the barbed line-motif seems to be routed in the Azilian of southwestern Europe where several engraved objects have been found at the cantabrian coast (d'Errico 1994:264), but there is evidence in eastern Europe, too (Kozlowski 1992:176 pp). Going into more detail we can observe that the barbed line-motif and a vertical zigzag line is represented in a very similar fashion on the objects of Wozniki (Figure 69.4:7), Mullerup, Højby (David 1999:203) and Sollerön. Another combination of these motifs with the zigzag at the end of the barbed lines is nearly identically presented in Friesack, Podejuch and Holmegaard (Brinch Petersen 1990) (Figure 69.9). But these consistencies must not be overestimated because they find a close parallel on an engraved bone fragment found in the Azilian layer of the French Grotte de Tai, Drôme (Art et Civilisation 1984:391) and on a bone from the Magdalenian level of Grotte du Placard (Bahn 2001). Other patterns of ornamentation, such as the row of hatched triangles, show a broad distribution from West to East, too (Sigrothsbruch – Pułtusk; Figure 69.2:4, 69.4:3).

We are obviously dealing with a repertoire of patterns shared by Mesolithic people in a broader territory (Clark 1975; Gramsch 1979) and the barbed line-motif is traceable to the Azilian in a far distant region. So the possibility of distinguishing territories of people by means of decorative motifs has to be seen critically. One of the earlier attempts to identify Mesolithic regional groups was based on personal adornment (Newell *et al.* 1990), a source which is to some degree dependent on raw material availability. The distribution of some categories of finds from the younger/final Mesolithic gives more promising results for this question (Vang Petersen 1984; Andersen 1995–96). Recently Cziesla (1999) suggested establishing a Mesolithic group territory in Northeast Germany using a point type. We do not want to rule out, that special motifs of ornamented objects, like for example the vertical hatched triangle as represented at Verchen and Friesack, or combinations of motifs possibly offer the chance to contribute to the identification of regional groups. For the younger/final Mesolithic specific distribution patterns of motifs can be observed (Jestrzemski 1987). To tackle this problem in more detail reliable dating of as many objects as possible is highly desirable.

Stettin-Podejuch and -Grabow are well known examples of figurative art and may represent special sites in a favourable environment. Despite the simple technique of ornamentation the lively character of the figure on the Podejuch-bâton percé (Figure 69.4:2) is striking and resembles examples from Jordløse, Veksø Mose and Sindalgaard on Zealand (Brøndsted 1960:102; Liversage 1966; Brinch Petersen 1990:209). Simple lines on the bâton percé from the Trave possibly represent another figure (Figure 69.2:10). Gramsch discusses the triangles and especially some connected triangular motifs on the fragment of a tortoise carapace from Friesack as evidence of anthropomorphic representations (Gramsch 1987:88; Gramsch and Larsson 2001). They show some similarity to the figures on the bone from Ryemarksgaard (Brøndsted 1960:85), but decisive details are missing. A different style of abstract figures is represented by two pieces from the more southern site of Pobiel (Bagniewski 1993).

Chronological aspects

The calibrated timescale of the older Mesolithic spans about 3000 years; however, information on the chronological context of portable art is limited in the northern lowlands (for example Gramsch 1979:48). 14 objects (9x

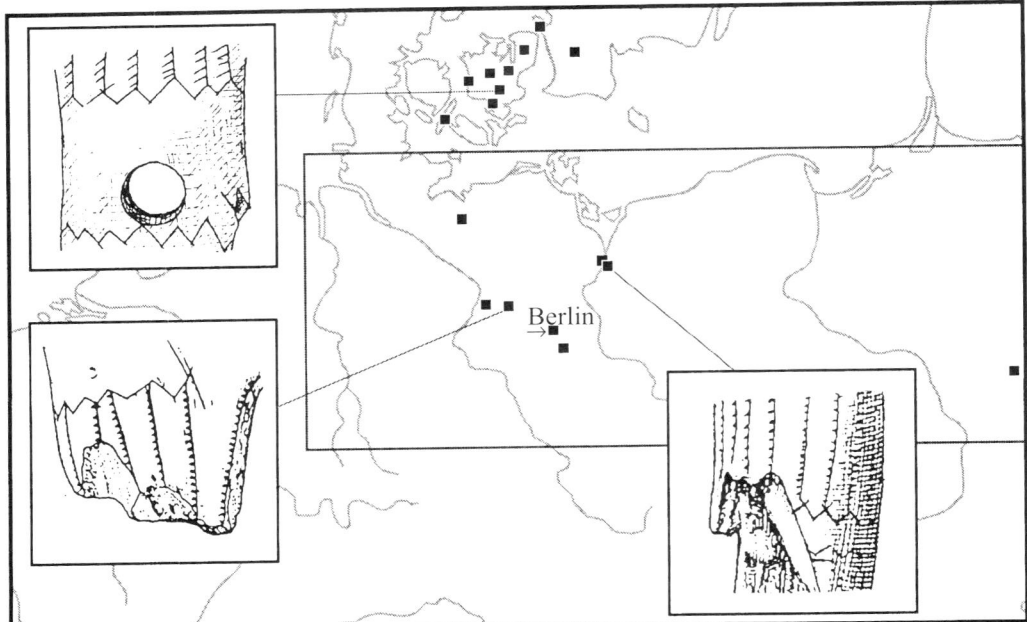

Figure 69.9 Mapping of the barbed line-motif (with variations) (southern Scandinavia with selected sites).

Hohen-Viecheln, 1x Friesack, 2x Wustermark 22, 2x Dudka) were found in excavated layers but only dated approximately, eight finds (1x Rothenklempenow, 5x Friesack, 2x Pobiel) have a more reliable stratigraphic context. Direct AMS-dating of an ornamented object was now conducted for the first time by the Landesamt für Bodendenkmalpflege Mecklenburg-Vorpommern.

First evidence is available for the mid to younger Preboreal: At Friesack a bone with a double zigzag-motif and a fragment of a bone mattock with a net-motif belong to this phase (Gramsch 1987:88). At the site of Rothenklempenow a bâton percé from the younger Preboreal is said to be decorated with a simple ladder-motif (Schacht 1993), but by my own impression the small decoration is composed of two elements similar to the barbed line-motif (personal communication with S. Schacht 3/2001).

A date of 8820 ±60 BP (UtC-9739) or ca. 8000 cal BC was obtained for a fragment of a bone mattock from Verchen depicting two hatched triangles and suggests an early Boreal context. It is probable that the bâton percé from Verchen with the identical triangle-motif belongs to the same period. At Friesack the early Boreal is represented by a bone with three short lines (Gramsch 1987:88).

We recognise increasing evidence for the younger Boreal/early Atlantic. At Friesack an awl/dagger is ornamented with parallel short lines and a re-used fragment of a bâton percé shows the barbed line-motif. The fragment of a tortoise carapace with hatched triangles is also dated to this period by pollen analysis (Gramsch 1987:88). The decorated finds from Hohen-Viecheln were connected with the later settlement phase by Schuldt (1961) and we may expect a variety of motifs for that period of time. However, we have to concede that the find layers for that phase at Hohen-Viecheln are not very well defined. Therefore it is intended in co-operation with the Landesamt für Bodendenkmalpflege Mecklenburg-Vorpommern to re-date important finds of this site. This could be a starting point to obtain more information by direct AMS-dating on objects from neighbouring regions to achieve a more reliable basis for the interpretation of this important information source of the Mesolithic.

Concluding remarks

I can not present many new ideas on the function and meaning of decorated objects at this moment. But the evidence from the northern lowlands points to a very clear preference of bâtons percés, which generally show more complex ornamentation, sometimes with zones of very different motifs. This is perhaps due to a longer use-life of these massive objects. If we follow this line of argument we have to expect a process of a "growing" presentation on this category.

Bone mattocks have a less distinct program and may have normally, as well as the smaller daggers/points and Schwirrhölzer, been decorated in one single step. The preferred categories are well suited for prestigious functions as elements/weapons of personal equipment and may have played a role in rituals. It is unclear whether their use was restricted to a special group of persons (see Larsson 2000, 33). Besides the richly ornamented objects we have evidence for some pieces with few signs or only very limited ornamentation and they are expected to reflect a less pronounced function.

There are a considerable variety of motifs and they do not seem to be connected with special categories. They normally have a wide geographical distribution and therefore I see no chance to propose neither a model of personal or clan signs nor limited group territories at the moment. They are a common feature of the Maglemose territory in a broad sense reaching from the Masurian Lakeland to Schlewig-Holstein (ca. 1000 km) and to (southern) Scandinavia in the North. Furthermore it could be demonstrated, that the barbed line-motif – even in details – finds clear parallels in the late Palaeolithic of southwestern Europe. Further investigation is needed to prove the possibility that special motifs may reveal a function as territory markers.

The possible meaning of the decoration is of course a very difficult aspect. If we assume that the motifs had (different) meanings we may ask whether these programs were understood in the same way in the area outlined above. Simultaneously we have to consider the aspect of time: Could the barbed line-motif reflect a continuity of meaning for a time span of ca. 4000 years or more? It is well possible that there was a long-term tradition in a formal sense and the level of meaning. Mesolithic people may have shared ritual beliefs on the background of common, late Palaeolithic ancestors and a similar way of life.

Without doubt we have to expect that social networks played an important role with the exchange of information, gifts and people. A decorated antler of Ageröd in Scania was proposed to be an example of long distance exchange (Larsson 1976), but the determination as Reindeer is not fully accepted (David 1999:353). Finally I see no basis or necessity to propose a model of a formalised exchange system to explain the distribution of motifs like Nash (1998:58 pp) has suggested for the younger/final Mesolithic of the Danish territory.

Acknowledgements

For the permission to publish finds of Verchen and the corresponding AMS-date I would like to thank Dr. F. Lüth, Ch. Jantzen M.A. and Dr. U. Schoknecht, Landesamt für Bodendenkmalpflege Mecklenburg-Vorpommern. I have to thank B. Gramsch, Potsdam, and S. Schacht, Lübstorf, for helpful informations. K. Terberger, Brighton, and Dr. M. Street, Neuwied, kindly organised corrections on the text. For some drawings I have to thank M. Wieczorek, Stralsund.

List of decorated objects, older Mesolithic (see Figure 69.1)

The list is preliminary, new objects will be published by B. Gramsch (personal information 7/2001).

Germany

Bergen-Tetel, single find: 1 bone dagger with rows of lines and chevrons; Gramsch 1973.

Bützsee-Altfriesack, dredging site: 1 tool fragment with few decoration, probably Mesolithic; Cziesla et al. 1998:86.

Fernewerder, single find: Schwirrgerät ("bullroarer") with complex decoration; Gramsch 1973.

Friesack, excavation (5 objects), dredging (6 objects) and old Reinerth-excavation (1 object, lost): 1 bone fragment with double zigzag line, 1 bone mattock fragment (?) with net-motif (Preboreal), 1 bone (Phalanx) with 3 short lines (early Boreal), 1 antler socket made of bâton percé fragment (Figure 69.2:8), 1 awl/dagger with 2 rows of short lines, 4 fragments of bâtons percés (Figure 69.2:7), 1 antler tine with barbed line, 1 fragment of tortoise carapace with hatched triangles and possible anthropomorphic figures (all late Boreal/early Atlantic), 1 object with hatched triangles (old excavations); Gramsch 1987; Gramsch and Kloss 1990; Gramsch and Larsson 2001.

Garz, dredging site: 1 bâton percé fragment (?) with few decoration, probably older Mesolithic; Zotz 1939–1940; Gramsch 1973:Anm. 69.

Hohen-Viecheln, excavations, 9 objects of the "younger settlement phase": 2 bone mattocks (Figure 69.3:3–4), 1 bâton percé (Figure 69.3:2), 1 antler mattock (probably bâton percé fragment) (Figure 69.3:6), 1 antler with some decoration (Figure 69.3:1), 1 perforated antler fragment with few short lines, 1 mattock of elk antler with marginal decoration (Figure 69.3:7), 1 bone point with short lines, 1 bone with rows of lines (Figure 69.3:5); Schuldt 1961, p 140, Taf. 43c,51–52. 55.60–62.64.

Kleinmachnow, single find: 1 bâton percé (Figure 69.3:1); Schoetensack 1903.

Langelsheim, surface find concentration: retoucheur with zigzag lines (Figure 69.3:9); Grote 1979.

Mellensee, single find: 1 bone mattock with short line of triangles (Figure 69.3:5); Gramsch 1973.

Pritzerbe, single find. Schwirrgerät ("bullroarer") (Figure 69.3:6); Gramsch 1973.

Rothenklempenow, excavations, >1 object: 1 bâton percé with simple ladder-motif, other objects not published yet; Schacht 1993, personal information S. Schacht 3/2001.

Siegrothsbruch, dredging site: 1 fragment of bâton percé (Figure 69.3:4); Gramsch 1979.

Strodehne, dredging site: 1 bâton percé fragment (Figure 69.3:2); Zotz 1939–1940.

Trave near Lübeck-Travemünde, dredging site: 1 bâton percé (Figure 69.3:10); Schwantes 1939.

Trave near Lübeck-Travemünde, dredging site: 1 fragment of bâton percé with 5 zigzag lines; Schwantes 1939.

Tribsees, dreging site: 1 bone with row of lines; Keiling 1987.

Verchen Fp. 24 u. 31, dredging site, 3 objects: 1 bâton percé (Figure 69.3:9), 1 bâton percé with few lines,

1 bone mattock fragment with vertically hatched triangle; Terberger in press.

Wagenitz, dredging site: 1 bâton percé fragment (Figure 69.2:3); Gramsch 1979.

Wustermark Fp. 22, excavation, 2 objects: 1 bone point/ dagger with groups of short lines, 1 elk antler fragment of mattock (?) with two fields of dense zigzag lines; Beran 1999.

Poland

Biskupin, excavation: 1 bone awl/dagger with ladder-motifs; Rajewski 1958.

Danzig (Gdansk), single find: 1 amber sculpture (pig), probably Mesolithic (Figure 69.4:11); Terberger and Ansorge 2000.

Dudka, excavation, 2 objects: 1 antler socket with an X-shaped mark, 1 tooth-pendant fragment with X-motifs; Fiedorczuk 1995.

Nitki, single find: 1 bâton percé (Figure 69.4,5); Gaerte 1929.

Ostroleka, single find: 1 bâton percé (Figure 69.4:6); Clark 1936; Kozlowski 1989.

Pobiel 10, excavation, 2 objects: 1 antler fragment with zoomorphic motif, 1 bone fragment with zigzag lines and anthropomorphic motif (both probably Boreal); Bagniewski 1993.

Pułtusk, single find: 1 antler mattock, probably fragment of bâton percé (Figure 69.4:3); Sulgostowska and Polak 1989.

Stettin-Grabow (Sczcecin-Grabowo), dredging site: 1 bâton percé (Figure 69.4:1); Kunkel 1936.

Stettin-Podejuch (Sczcecin-Podjuchy), dredging site: 1 bâton percé (Figure 69.4:2); Kunkel 1935.

Stolp (Słupsk), single find: 1 amber sculpture (bear), probably Mesolithic (Figure 69.4:9); Terberger and Ansorge 2000.

Tłokowo, single find with following excavations. 1 slotted bone point with groups of lines (Figure 69.4:8); Sulgostowska 1996.

Trudna, single find: 1 bone mattock (Figure 69.4:4); Galiński 1992.

Woldenberg (Dobigniew), single find: 1 amber sculpture (horse), probably Mesolithic (Figure 69.4:10); Terberger and Ansorge 2000.

Wozniki, single find: 1 bâton percé (Figure 69.4:7); Clark 1936.

References

Althin, C.H. 1950. New finds of Mesolithic Art in Scania (Sweden). *Acta Archaeologica* 21, 253–260.

Andersen, S.H. 1995–96. Ertebølle harpoons and killer whale teeth. Aspects of marine hunting in the Ertebølle period. *Kuml* 1995–96, 97–100.

Art et Civilisations des Chasseurs de la Préhistoire 34000–8000 ans av. J.-C. 1984. Paris.

Baales, M. and Street, M. 1998. Late Palaeolithic Backed-Point assemblages in the northern Rhineland: current research and changing views. *Notae Praehistoricae* 18, 77–92.

Bagniewski, Z. 1993. Untersuchungsergebnisse aus der mesolithischen Torfstation Pobiel 10 (Niederschlesien). *Prähistorische Zeitschrift* 67, 141–162.

Bahn, P. 2001. Palaeolithic weaving – a contribution from Chauvet. *Antiquity* 75, 271–272.

Beran, J. 1999. Wagenspuren und verzierte Jagdwaffen. Ein stein- und bronzezeitlicher Moorfundpltz bei Wustermark, Landkreis Havelland. *Archäologie in Berlin und Brandenburg* 1999, 46–47.

Bokelmann, K. 1999. Zum Beginn des Spätmesolithikums in Südskandinavien. Geweihaxt, Dreieck und Trapez, 6100 cal BC. *Offa* 56, 183–197.

Brinch Petersen, E. 1990. L'Art et les Sepultures mesolithiques en Scandinavie meridionale. In: *5 Millions D'Annees L'Aventure Humaine*, 118–125. Bruxelles.

Brøndsted, J. 1960. *Nordische Vorzeit I. Steinzeit in Dänemark*. Neumünster.

Clark, J.G.D. 1936. *The Mesolithic Settlement of Northern Europe*. Cambridge.

—— 1975. *The Earlier Stone Age Settlement of Scandinavia*. Cambridge.

Conard, N.J. and Floss, H. 1999. Ein bemalter Stein vom Hohle Fels bei Schelklingen und die Frage nach paläolithischer Höhlenkunst in Mitteleuropa. *Archäologisches Korrespondenzblatt* 29, 307–316.

Conkey, M. 1992. Les sites d'agrégation et la répartition de l'art mobilier, ou: y a-t-il des sites d'agrégation magdaléniens? In: *Le Peuplement Magdalénien*. Colloque Chancelade 1988. Documents Préhstoriques 2, 19–28. Paris.

Cziesla, E. 1999. Zur Territorialität mesolithischer Gruppe in Nordostdeutschland. *Ethnograhisch-Archäologische Zeitschrift* 40, 485–512.

Cziesla, E., Eickhoff, S. and Husmann, H. 1998. Neue Untersuchungen zum Mesolithikum in Brandenburg. In: Conard, N.J. and Kind, C.-J. (eds.) *Current Mesolithic Research*. Urgeschichtliche Materialhefte 12, 77–88. Tübingen.

David, E. 1999. *L'Industrie en Matières dures Animales du Mésolithique ancien et moyen en Europe du Nord*. Thèse de Doctorat. Paris.

David, S., d'Errico, F. and Thévenin, A. 1998. L'art mobilier de Ranchot (Jura) et de Rochedane (Doubs). In: Cupillard, C. and Richard, A. (eds.) *Les Derniers Chasseurs-Cuilleurs du Massif Jurassien et de ses Marges*, 192–200. Lons-le-Saunier.

D'Errico, F. 1994. *L'art gravé Azilien. De la technique à la signification*. Supplément à Gallia Préhistoire 31. Paris.

Fiedorczuk, J. 1995. Mesolithic finds at Dudka 1, Great Masurian Lakeland, and their chronological-taxonomic relations. *Przegląd Archeologiczny* 43, 47–60.

Fischer, A. 1975. An Ornamented Flint-Core from Holmegard V, Zealand, Denmark. *Acta Archaeologica* 45, 155–168.

Gaerte, W. 1929. *Urgeschichte Ostpreussens*. Königsberg.

Galiński, T. 1992. *Mezolit Pomorza*. Stettin.

Gramsch, B. 1973. Das Mesolithikum im Flachland zwischen Elbe und Oder. *Veröffentlichungen des Museums für Ur- und Frühgeschichte Potsdam* 7.

Gramsch, B. 1979. Zwei neue mesolithische Hirschgeweih-Lochstäbe mit Verzierung aus dem Bezirk Potsdam. *Veröffentlichungen des Museums für Ur- und Frühgeschichte Potsdam* 12, 39–50.

Gramsch, B. 1987. Ausgrabungen auf dem mesolithischen Moorfundplatz bei Friesack, Bezirk Potsdam. Veröffentlichungen des Museums für Ur- und Frühgeschichte Potsdam 21, 75–100.

Gramsch, B. 1989. Archäologische Kulturen des Mesolithikums. In: Herrmann, J. (ed.) *Archäologie in der Deutschen Demokratischen Republik. Denkmale und Funde 1*, 55–64. Leipzig.

Gramsch, B. and Kloss, K. 1990. Excavations near Friesack: an

Early Mesolithic Marshland Site in the Northern Plain of Central Europe. In: Bonsall, C. (ed.) *The Mesolithic in Europe. Third International Symposium Edinburgh 1985*, 313–324. Edinburgh.

Gramsch, B. and Larsson, L. 2001. Zwei ornamentierte Rückenpanzer der Sumpfschildkröte aus dem Mesolithikum des zirkumbaltischen Raumes. In: Gehlen, B., Heinen, M. and Tillmann, A. (eds.), *Zeit-Räume. Gedenkschrift für Wolfgang Taute*. Archäologische Berichte 14, 455–464. Bonn.

Gronenborn, D. 1997. Sarching 4 und der Übergang vom Früh- zum Spätmesolithikum im südlichen Mitteleuropa. *Archäologisches Korrespondenzblatt* 27, 387–402.

Grote, K. 1979. Ein verzierter Retuscheur des Mesolithikums vom Nordharzrand. *Nachrichten aus Niedersachsen Urgeschichte* 48, 159–165.

Gumiński, W. 1995. Environment, economy and habitation during the Mesolithic at Dudka, Great Masurian Lakeland, NE-Poland. *Przegląd Archeologiczny* 43, 5–46.

Hartz, S. and Lübke, H. 1999. Paddelfunde aus der Mittel- und Jungsteinzeit Schleswig-Holsteins. In: Cziesla, E., Kersting, T. and Pratsch, S. (eds.), *Den Bogen spannen ... Festschrift für Bernhard Gramsch*. Beiträge zur Ur- und Frühgeschichte Mitteleuropas 20, 147–160. Weissbach.

Jestrzemski, D. 1987. Eine verzierte mesolithische Geweihaxt aus der Trave bei Lübeck-Travemünde. *Offa* 44, 53–73.

Jöris, O. and Weninger, B. 2000. ^{14}C-Alterskalibration und die absolute Chronologie des Spätglazials. *Archäologisches Korrespondenzblatt* 30, 461–471.

Keiling, H. 1987. Baggerfunde von einem ältermesolithischen Rastplatz im Trebeltal bei Tribsees, Kr. Stralsund. *Bodendenkmalpflege in Mecklenburg*, Jahrbuch 1987, 29–46.

Kind, C.-J. 1987. *Das Felsställe*. Forschungen und Berichte zur Vor- und Frühgeschichte in Baden-Württemberg 23. Stuttgart.

Klinghardt, F. 1924. Die steinzeitliche Kultur von Lietzow auf Rügen. *Mitteilungen aus der Sammlung vaterländischer Altertümer der Universität Greifswald* 1, 5–43.

Kozlowski, S.K. 1989. *Mesolithic in Poland. A new approach*. Warschau.

Kozlowski, J.K. 1992. *L'Art de la Préhistoire en Europe Orientale*. Milano.

Kunkel, O. 1935. Ein mittelsteinzeitlicher Lochstab von Podejuch, Kr. Greifenhagen. *Monatsblätter der Gesellschaft für Pommersche Geschichte und Altertumskunde* 49, 57–61.

—— 1936. Ein mittelsteinzeitlicher Lochstab von Stettin-Grabow. *Monatsblätter der Gesellschaft für Pommersche Geschichte und Altertumskunde* 50, 47–52.

Larsson, L. 1976. A Mattock-head of Reindeer Antler from Ageröd, Scania. *Meddelanden från Lunds universitets historiska museum* 1975–1976, 5–19.

—— 2000. Expressions of Art in the Mesolithic Society of Scandinavia. In: Butrimas, A. (ed.) *Prehistoric Art in the Baltic region*, 31–61. Vilnius.

Liversage, D. 1966. Ornamented Mesolithic Artefacts from Denmark. Some New Finds. *Acta Archaeologica* 37, 221–237.

Loftus, J. 1982. Ein verzierter Pfeilschaftglätter von Fläche 64/74–73/78 des spätpaläolithischen Fundplatzes Niederbieber/Neuwieder Becken. *Archäologisches Korrespondenzblatt* 12, 313–316.

Nash, G. 1998. *Exchange, Status and Mobility. Mesolithic portable art of southern Scandinavia*. British Archaeological Reports International Series 710. Oxford.

Newell, R.R., Kielmann, D., Constandse-Westermann, T.S., van der Sanden, W.A.B. and van Gijn, A. 1990. *An Inquiry into the Ethnic Resolution of Mesolithic Regional Groups*. Leiden.

Rajewski, Z. 1958. New Discoveries in Western Poland. *Archaeology* 11, 40–47.

Schacht, S. 1993. Ausgrabungen auf einem Moorfundplatz und zwei Siedlungsplätzen aus dem Mesolithikum/Neolithikum im nördlichen Randowbruch bei Rothenklempenow, Kr. Pasewalk. *Ausgrabungen und Funde* 38, 111–119.

Schoetensack, O. 1903. Der durchlochte Zierstab (Fibula) aus Edelhirschgeweih von Klein-Machnow. *Globus* 84, 107–110.

Schuldt, E. 1961. *Hohen Viecheln. Ein mittelsteinzeitlicher Wohnplatz in Mecklenburg*. Schriften der Sektion zur Vor- und Frühgeschichte 10. Berlin.

Schwantes, G. 1939. *Die Vorgeschichte Schleswig-Holsteins I. Stein- und Bronzezeit*. Neumünster.

Street, M. 1989. *Jäger und Schamanen. Bedburg-Königshoven – ein Wohnplatz am Niederrhein vor 10000 Jahren*. Mainz.

Sulgostowska, Z. 1996. The Earliest Mesolithic Settlement of North-East Poland. In: Larsson, L. (ed.) *The Earliest Settlement of Scandinavia and its Relationship with Neighbouring Areas*. Acta Archaeologica Lundensia 8/24, 297–304. Stockholm.

Sulgostowska, Z. 1998. Continuity, change and transition: The case of Northeastern Poland during the Stone Age. In: Zvelebil, M., Domańska, L. and Dennell, R. (eds.) *Harvesting the Sea, Farming the Forest. The Emergence of Neolithic Societies in the Baltic Region*. Sheffield Archaeological Monographs 10, 87–94. Sheffield.

Sulgostowska, Z. and Polak, Z. 1989. Ornamentowana motyka rogowa z Narwii Pułtuskiem, woj. ciechanowskie. *Wiadomości Archeologiczne* 49, 1983 (1989), 191–196.

Terberger, T. in press. Drei verzierte mesolithische Funde aus der Peene nahe Verchen, Lkr. Demmin. *Bodendenkmalpflege in Mecklenburg-Vorpommern*, Jahrbuch 2000.

Terberger, T. and Ansorge, J. 2000. Der Bernsteinbär von Stolp (Słupsk, Polen) – ein mesolithisches Amulett? *Archäologisches Korrespondenzblatt* 30, 335–352.

Vang Petersen, P. 1984. Chronological and Regional Variation in the Late Mesolithic of Eastern Denmark. *Journal of Danish Archaeology* 3, 7–18.

—— 1991. Bjørnejagt. *Skalk* 1991/5, 3–6.

Veil, S. and Breest, K. 1997. La figuration animale en ambre du gisement Federmesser de Weitsche, Basse-Saxe (Allemagne) et son contexte archéologique: les résultats de la fouille de 1996. *Bulletin de la Societé Préhistorique Française* 94, 387–392.

Zotz, L. 1939–1940. Neue mittelsteinzeitliche "Lochstäbe" aus Norddeutschland, ihre altsteinzeitlichen Vorläufer und ihre Verwandtschaft zu den Spitzhauen. *IPEK* 13–14, 2–22.

70. Burial traditions in the East Baltic Mesolithic

Guntis Gerhards, Gunita Zariņa and Ilga Zagorska

Studies of burial traditions are of great importance for understanding hunter-gatherer society as a whole. The characteristic feature of the East Baltic cemeteries is the long duration of use, beginning in the Mesolithic and continuing into the Neolithic. New radiocarbon data, obtained during the last ten years, have confirmed this assumption. Now it is possible to single out Mesolithic burials more clearly, describe the characteristics of burial practices, obtain a first insight into demography, perform paleoanthropological reconstructions, and approach a little closer to the social and spiritual world of the ancient Stone Age inhabitants.

Introduction

There are only three burial places in the East Baltic where the Mesolithic burial traditions may be observed (Figure 70.1). The first is the well known Zvejnieki burial ground in northern Latvia, containing 315 graves in total, part of these belonging to the Mesolithic. The other two are smaller burial places in the north-western Lithuania – Spiginas and Duonkalnis, also containing some Mesolithic graves (Butrimas 1989:10 pp, 1992:4 pp). All of these burial grounds are inland cemeteries, connected with water-bodies, situated on islands or peninsulas. They occur together with adjacent corresponding settlement sites (as at Zvejnieki) or else were established within the settlement area (as at Spiginas and Duonkalnis). In Zvejnieki archaeological complex only one grave, the oldest, was found in the territory of the Mesolithic site, all others being located in a specially established burial area close to the site.

The main problem concerning East Baltic burials was chronological division of the graves. F. Zagorskis, who directed excavations at Zvejnieki burial ground, based his chronology on: 1) the archaeological typology of the grave goods; 2) the territorial distribution of the burials; 3) the changing burial traditions (Zagorskis 1987: 83 pp). The whole area of the burial ground was divided into smaller groups, following each other, as it was thought, in chronological order (turn of the 5th millennium until the early 2nd millennium b.c.). The radiocarbon dates that have been obtained at Uppsala and Oxford laboratories have introduced some corrections (Figure 70.2). The beginning of use of the Zvejnieki burial site has been pushed back to the 7th millennium b.c., and the latest graves, belonging to the Corded Ware Culture, have been dated to the end of the 3rd millennium. Also, it has been established that the highest, central section of the gravel ridge was used as a burial ground for an extended period of time, while the slopes of the elevation were mainly used for burial during one particular period – the Late Mesolithic (first half of the Atlantic) (Larsson and Zagorska 1996:3 pp; Zagorska 1997:42 pp.). Radiocarbon dates have also confirmed the Late Mesolithic age of the two graves from Spiginas, and singled out some Mesolithic burials at Duonkalnis, earlier proposed as the bearers of Mesolithic traditions into Neolithic cultures (Bronk Ramsey et al. 2000: 244).

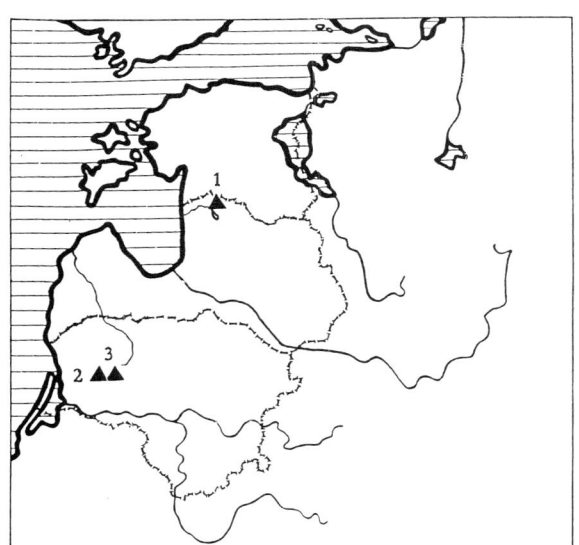

Figure 70.1 East Baltic territory with Mesolithic burial places: 1-Zvejnieki, Latvia; 2- Spiginas;, Lithuania; 3- Duonkalnis, Lithuania

Site	Lab. no.	Grave	^{14}C Age BP	Year Cal BC
Zvejnieki	Ua-3634	305.	8240±70	7412 – 7360*
Zvejnieki	OxA-5969	170.	8150±80	7260 – 7034
Zvejnieki	Ua- 3644	154.	7730±70	6594 – 6460
Zvejnieki	Ua- 14688	76.	6900±75	5806 – 5670
Zvejnieki	Ua – 3638	2.	6900±65	5806 – 5670
Zvejnieki	Ua- 3636	57.	6825±60	5702 – 5604
Zvejnieki	Ua- 3635	39.	6775±55	5675 – 5590
Zvejnieki	Ua- 3637	85.	6460±60	5434 – 5332
Spiginas	OxA-5925	3.	7780±65	6750 – 6460**
Spiginas	GIN- 5571	4.	7470±60	6440 – 6220
Duonkalnis	OxA-5924	4.	6995±65	5590 – 5720

* – For Latvian data OxCal v 3.3, Bronk Ramsey et al. 1999 is used; 1-sigma;

** – For Lithuanian data Ox Cal version 4.1 is used, Stuiver et al. 1993 –sigma.

Figure 70.2 Mesolithic graves from East Baltic, dated by radiocarbon (^{14}C) method;

Now, based on radiocarbon dates, the typology of the grave goods and some burial traditions, for archaeological purposes corresponding to some 60–70 burials from Zvejnieki, may be described as Mesolithic. For palaeo-anthropological studies a smaller number of graves was used, as human bones were not preserved sufficiently well for all measurements.

Mesolithic burial practice

The oldest burials in the Eastern Baltic are from Zvejnieki. They belong to Middle Mesolithic, the Boreal climatic period. The oldest, grave 305, was unearthed in the cultural layer of Zvejnieki II Mesolithic site. The interred person (male) was buried in a layer of ochre, with a fish spear and a vertebra of pike as grave goods. Part of the right leg of the skeleton was missing, perhaps deliberately removed. Two other graves (Nos. 154, 170) were situated on the highest part of the gravel ridge. They were strewn with ochre, but the grave fill consisted of light gravel. One grave (154) was partly covered with a stone setting. The burial of an elderly man, Grave 170, was one of the richest in the whole burial ground. It was decorated with a 167 animal teeth, forming splendid strings of pendants, an ornament at the hips and decoration of the footwear. For this adornment, wild boar tooth pendants were selected only. More interesting, however, was the headdress, consisting of 412 wild boar, elk and aurochs tooth pendants. This layout of the teeth is very reminiscent of a similarly decorated burial from Duonkalnis (Grave 4). Judging by the striking headdresses and the richness of the rest of the decoration, as well as the intensive layer of ochre, these burials may in fact represent the leaders and prominent members of the community.

The graves from the Late Mesolithic (first half of the Atlantic) were more numerous and showed some variety in burial practice. They were located at the very top and on the slopes of the gravel ridge. The deceased were placed in elongated graves in an intensive ochre layer, and in the grave fills light gravel as well as black earth was used. The latter was perhaps taken from the settlement area, containing bone and flint flakes. At Zvejnieki burial ground, all possible orientations of the graves were discovered, with a slight dominance of the SW and NE directions. The burials mainly consisted of single graves (85%), only some being double, triple or multiple burials. In these cases some adult person, male or female, had been placed together with children.

A trait that singles out Zvejnieki burial ground from all other North European Stone Age cemeteries is the great number of child and adolescent burials. These formed half of all the excavated Mesolithic graves. They were arranged with great care, always being strewn with ochre, and very often stone settings were created. Two thirds of child and adolescent burials were furnished with grave goods (Figure 70.3). The main forms of decoration were animal tooth pendants, bone spearheads and daggers, awls decorated in rhythmic sequence, and stone chisels. Offerings were often observed, consisting of animal and bird bones (*Anas platyrhynchus*).

Among the burials of adults, only some female graves were more richly adorned (Nos. 74, 76), and exceptionally rich in terms of inventory was the burial of an elderly woman (No. 57), with an elk-head staff made from bone, tooth-pendants, a bone spearhead, a stone chisel and grave goods of organic material that were not preserved.

The main animal species used for the tooth-pendants during the Late Mesolithic period were elk, wild boar, roe deer, aurochs and wild horse (Lõugas 2000). It must be mentioned that wild horse tooth ornamentation was not observed earlier, but was very common in the Late Mesolithic graves.

Thus, we may conclude that Mesolithic burial traditions were quite homogenous, bearing archaic features and revealing the hunter-gatherer way of life. Particular importance was attached only to some outstanding members of community, the main attention being given to children and juveniles. This phenomenon, as has already been mentioned in connection with the Skateholm burials (Larsson 2000:89 pp), indicates a complex worldview among the ancient Mesolithic inhabitants.

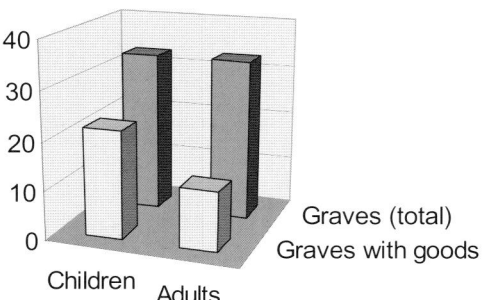

Figure 70.3 Zvejnieki burial ground, grave goods from Mesolithic graves.

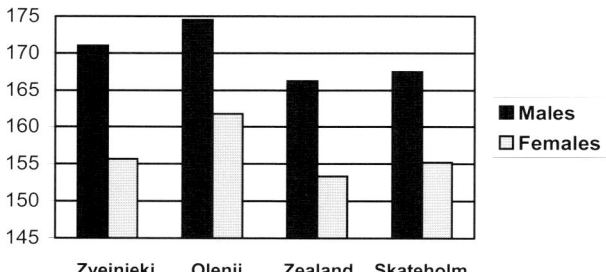

Figure 70.4 Mean body stature for the Mesolithic inhabitants at Zvejnieki and comparative data from Olenii Ostrov (Jacobs, 1993), Zealand (Jacobs, 1993; Formicola, 1999) and Skateholm (Persson and Persson, 1988). Reconstruction of body stature conducted according to unified methodology on the basis of published data).

Paleoanthropological reconstructions of the Mesolithic inhabitants of Latvia

Standard methods were used for age and sex determination (Brothwell 1981; Ubelaker 1989). Tooth eruption and degree of epiphyseal union according to Ubelaker were used to establish the age of subadult individuals. The form of the pubic symphysis was used for assignment of adults to age groups. Such features as cranial suture closure, osteoporosis, tooth wear and loss provide a basis for broad age groupings. Demographic indicators have been calculated from tables of mortality (Ascadi and Nemeskeri 1970).

Of the burials at Zvejnieki cemetery included in the study, sex and age could be determined for 28 individuals. 42.9% of these were children. The proportion of children among the Mesolithic burials at Zvejnieki is noticeably higher than among burials of the same period in Denmark or at Skateholm and Olenii Ostrov cemeteries (Meiklejohn et al. 1997:319) (Figure 70.5). However, this indicator is thought to be reduced by the poor preservation of bone material, and possibly also as a consequence of particular burial practices.

The highest child mortality was observed at ages 0–4 years, connected with the adaptation of the newborn child to the surrounding environment and characteristic of any population. The proportion of 5–6 year-olds is thought to be reduced as a result of the fragmented character of the material. The absence of burials of 15–19 year old juveniles in the Zvejnieki Mesolithic population can possibly be taken as evidence that the population was not subject to extreme stress situations and can generally be regarded as stable. Life expectancy for newborns, according to the data at our disposal, is 21.8 years (Figure 70.6), probably lower in reality, because data on infant mortality is missing. Among the Mesolithic burials at Zvejnieki cemetery, only one infant has been found.

The juvenile:adult ratio is 0.22 (Bocquet and Masset 1977: 65 pp). Out of 16 adult burials, 11 are male and 5 female. The sex ratio is 1.8. Research has also shown a significant male dominance in the Mesolithic populations of Vasilyevka I, Vasilyevka II and Olenii Ostrov cemeteries (Kozlovskaja 1996:105). In particular cases this tendency is a very marked one.

The number of adult individuals among the Mesolithic

Site	Age groupings				
	0–4	5–9	10–14	15–19	Total
Zvejnieki	8.5 (30.4)	1.5 (5.4)	2 (7.1)	0 (0.0)	12 (42.9)
Denmark	13 (20.3)	3 (4.7)	1 (1.6)	5 (7.8)	22 (34.4)
Skateholm	6 (10.3)	0 (0.0)	0 (0.0)	8 (13.8)	14 (24.1)
Olenii Ostrov	15 (14.6)	4 (3.9)	4 (3.9)	1 (1.0)	24 (23.4)

Figure 70.5 Subadult age structure of Mesolithic skeletal samples.

x	D_x	d_x	l_x	q_x	L_x	T_x	e^0_x
0	1.0	3.6	100	0.036	98.2	2176.2	21.8
1–4	7.5	26.8	96.4	0.278	332.1	2078.0	21.6
5–9	1.5	5.6	69.6	0.077	334.8	1746.8	25.1
10–14	2.0	7.1	64.3	0.111	303.6	1411.7	22.0
15–19	0.0	0.0	57.1	0	285.7	1108.1	19.4
20–24	1	3.6	57.1	0.063	276.8	822.4	14.4
25–29	4.9	17.7	53.6	0.330	223.7	545.6	10.2
30–34	4.1	14.5	35.9	0.403	143.3	321.9	9.0
35–39	1.5	5.4	21.4	0.250	93.8	178.6	8.3
40–44	2.0	7.1	16.1	0.444	62.5	84.8	5.3
45–49	2.5	8.9	8.9	1.000	22.3	22.3	2.5
Total	28	100					

Figure 70.6 Life table of Zvejnieki Mesolithic population.

burials in Zvejnieki cemetery is small, so the observed sex ratio might be fortuitous. As is known, male bone material is more robust and better preserved, and consequently is more commonly found in excavation. Also, particular mortuary practices cannot be excluded, which might have led to a dominance of male burials. There is no reason to consider that the sex ratio in the real Mesolithic population at Zvejnieki would not have been more or less equal.

Life expectancy for males at least 20 years old, e^{20}, is 14.7 years, a comparatively low figure (Piontek et al. 1996:307 pp). This is thought to be connected with the small number of adult individuals and the fragmented state of the material. Age could be determined only up to 50 years. Of 11 males, 6 (54.5%) had died aged 25–34, and 22.7% had died aged 45–49. A high mortality of young males may indicate possible stress situations in the Mesolithic population at Zvejnieki.

For adult females, e^{20}, was 13.7 years, lower than the figure for males. High female mortality (45.7%) was found in ages 25–29, probably connected with childbirth problems. It should be noted that there were only 5 females among the Mesolithic burials in Zvejnieki cemetery, so the results are not very significant statistically, and it was not possible to calculate reproduction figures for the Mesolithic population. The small quantity of data also prohibits calculation of the size of the Mesolithic population at Zvejnieki. The short lifespan for adults and the high mortality among young men and women may indicate a high level of biological and social stress in the Mesolithic population at Zvejnieki.

The body-build data for the Mesolithic population was reconstructed from bone material of 21 adult individuals (16 males and 5 females). Osteometric measurements were conducted in accordance with standard methodology (Martin and Saller 1957). Stature was calculated from regression equations, obtained in the study of anthropological material from Latvia (Gerhards 1999).

The oldest (7th–6th millennium BC) burials at the Zvejnieki site (male burials 305, 170 and 154) are characterised by long linear measurements of the long bones of the limbs, but with small circumferences. Thus, the Middle Mesolithic males are characterised by tall mean stature – 171.84 cm – and fairly gracile body-build. Particularly interesting among the body-build data is the relationship between the femur and tibia, the so-called crural index. The value of this index (84.3) is indicative of an extended tibia in relation to the femur. Such body proportions are found in present-day populations in the tropical belt. Thus, the anthropological literature has seen over 50 years of discussion on the question of the origin of such 'tropical' proportions among the Palaeolithic and Mesolithic populations of Europe (Biassutti 1951: 97 pp; Frayer 1981: 357 pp; Holliday 1999: 549 pp). The bone material of the people buried at the Zvejnieki site fully confirms the presence of such 'tropical' body proportions for the Mesolithic inhabitants of northern Europe as well.

The Late Mesolithic (5000–4000 BC) people buried in Zvejnieki cemetery are characterised by tall mean stature (170.83 cm for males; 155.65 cm for females) and medium robustness of body-build. The crural index has declined in comparison with the people of the Middle Mesolithic (82.0 for males; 83.1 for females). This may be connected with human biological adaptation in a progressive transition to a sedentary lifestyle, changing the character of physical stress on the lower limbs as compared to a foraging way of life.

Comparative studies on European Mesolithic populations show that already from the Late Palaeolithic onwards there were differences in stature between the inhabitants of Western (including Scandinavia) and Eastern Europe (Formicola and Giannecchini 1999: 319 pp). Western European Mesolithic populations (Teviec and Hoedic cemeteries in France; Muge in Portugal; El Collado in Spain; Uzzo and Molara in Italy; the cemeteries on Zealand in Denmark, such as Bogebakken, Vedbæk, Fannerup; Skateholm in Sweden) are characterised by relatively low stature (162–165 cm for males; 150–153 cm for females), while in all of the Mesolithic cemeteries in Eastern Europe (Vlasac in Serbia; Popovo and Olenii Ostrov in Karelia; Vasilyevka and Voloshskoye in Ukraine) the burials are characterised by tall mean stature (172–174 cm for males; 160–163 cm for females). The Mesolithic inhabitants of Zvejnieki fall within the Eastern European group, both in geographical terms and in terms of stature, and thus in terms of body-build are closer to the Mesolithic inhabitants of Karelia (Olenii Ostrov cemetery) than to Scandinavia (cemeteries on Zealand, Skateholm) (Figure 70.4). The reason for this difference in body stature between the Mesolithic inhabitants of Western and Eastern Europe is unclear. However, in discussing this question, chronological differences between different Mesolithic cemeteries should be taken into account. Thus, for example, the Mesolithic burials at Olenii Ostrov, and also a proportion of those at Zvejnieki, are a millennium or even several millennia older than the burials of the Zealand cemeteries or Skateholm. If, for example, we compare the Skateholm population with those burials at Zvejnieki that are contemporaneous with them (6500–6400 BP), then the differences in stature are not so marked. Thus, mean male stature at Zvejnieki in the Late Mesolithic-Early Neolithic transitional zone is 164.1±2.47 cm, and 167.51± 4.42 cm for the males buried in Skateholm cemetery.

Figure 70.4. Mean body stature for the Mesolithic inhabitants at Zvejnieki and comparative data from Olenii Ostrov (Jacobs, 1993), Zealand (Jacobs, 1993; Formicola, 1999) and Skateholm (Persson and Persson, 1988). Reconstruction of body stature conducted according to unified methodology on the basis of published data).

Figure 70.5. Subadult age structure of Mesolithic skeletal samples. Note: Data given as both row numbers of individuals and as percentages of total subsample.

Figure 70.6. Life table of the Zvejnieki Mesolithic population. x – age class groupings; D_x – numbers of individuals in each age class; d_x – proportion of individuals dying in each age class; l_x – number of individuals surviving in age class of an original cohort of 1000; q_x – probability that an individual in an age class will die before attaining the next age class; L_x – total number of years lived in an age class of all surviving people per 1000 individuals born; T_x – total number of years lived by the population from age x; e^0_x – life expectancy while belonging to the age group.

References

Acsadi, G. and Nemeskeri, I. 1970. History of human life span and mortality. Budapest.

Biassutti, R. 1951. Radio – humeral and tibio – femoral indexes in fossil and living man. *Homo* 2, 97–99.

Bocquet, I.P. and Masset, C. 1977. Estimateurs en paleodemographie. *L'Homme*, XVII (4), 65–90.

Bronk Ramsey, C. et al., 2000. Radiocarbon dates from the Oxford AMS system : Archeometry datelist 29. *Archeometry* 42, No.1, 244–245.

Brothwell, D.R. 1972. *Digging up bones*. London.

Butrimas, A. 1989. Mesolithic graves from Spiginas, Lithuania. *Mesolithic Miscellany* 10, No. 2, 10–11.

—— 1992. Spigino mezolito kapai. *Lietuvos archeologija* 8, 4–10.

Butrimas, A. and Kazakevicius, V. 1985. Ankstyvieji virvelines keramikos kulturos kapai Lietuvoje. *Lietuvos archeologija* 6, 30–49.

Formicola, V. and Giannecchini, M. 1999. Evolutionary trends of stature in Upper Paleolithic and Mesolithic Europe. *Journal of Human Evolution* 36, 319–333.

Frayer, D.W. 1981. Body size, weapon use, and natural selection in the European Upper Paleolithic and Mesolithic. *American Anthropologist* 8, 357–373.

Gerhards, G. 1999. *Stature reconstruction in Latvian Paleo-osteological Samples (comparison of methods)*. Manuscript.

Holliday, T.W. 1999. Brachial and crural indices of European Late Upper Paleolithic and Mesolithic humans. *Journal of Human Evolution* 36, 549–566.

Jacobs, K. 1993. Human Postcranial Variation in the Ukrainian Mesolithic – Neolithic. *Current Anthropology* 34, No. 3, 311–324.

Kozlovskaja, M.V. 1996. *Ekologija drevņih pļemen ļesnoi polosi Vostočnoi Evropi*. Moskva (in Russian).

Larsson, L. 2000. Cemeteries and mortuary practice in the Late Mesolithic of Southeren Scandinavia. *Muinasaja teadus* 8, 81–102. Tallinn.

Larsson, L. and Zagorska, I. 1996. New data on the chronology of the Zvejnieki Stone Age cemetery. *Mesolithic Miscellany* 10, No. 2, 10–11.

Lõugas, L. 2000. *Report on the analyses of tooth and bone pendants from the Zvejnieki burials, Latvia*. Manuscript in Institute of history of Latvia. Riga.

Martin, R. and Saller, K. 1957. *Lehrbuch der Anthropologie in Systematischer Darstellung*. Band 1. Stuttgart.

Meiklejohn, C., Wyman, I.M., Jacobs, K. and Jackes, M.K. 1997. *Issues in the Archaeological Demography of the Agricultural Transition in Western and Northern Europe: A View from the Mesolithic in Integrating Archaeological Demography Center for Archaeological Investigations*. Southern Illinois University at Carbondale. Carbondale.

Persson, O. and Persson, E. 1988. Anthropological report concerning the interred Mesolithic populations from Skateholm, southern Sweden. In: Larsson, L. (ed.) *The Skateholm Project*, vol. I , Man and environment, 89–105. Stockholm.

Piontek, J., Wiercinska, A. and Wiercinski, A. 1996. Mortality structure in Mesolithic, Neolithic and early Bronze age populations of Central Europe and Ukraine: A new methodological approach. *Anthropologie* XXXIV, No. 3, 307–313.

Ubelaker, D.H. 1978. *Human Skeletal Remains*. Chicago.

Zagorska, I. 1997. The first radiocarbon datings from Zvejnieki Stone Age burial ground, Latvia. *ISKOS* 11, 42–46.

Zagorskis, F. 1987. *Zvejnieku akmens laikmeta kapulauks* (Zvejnieki Stone Age Burial ground). Riga (in Latvian).

Session VIII

Hunter-Gatherers in Transition

71. Introduction

T. Douglas Price

This section of the Meso2000 conference proceedings focuses on changes in the Mesolithic, from the Paleolithic and to the Neolithic, in various parts of Europe. These transitions are critical phases of the Mesolithic and define its beginning and its end. These transitions also provide important perspectives from which we can examine those features that distinguish the Mesolithic from earlier and later periods.

The majority of the papers concern the end of the Mesolithic, the replacement of hunter-gatherers by farmers. This transition is arguably the most important in the whole of European prehistory. For that reason, I outline current evidence for this transition below, prior to a brief introduction of the papers in this section and their significance.

The end of the Mesolithic period in Europe is a time-transgressive phenomenon as the Neolithic, and its accoutrements, gradually spreads across the continent. Beginning shortly before 7000 BC, the first farmers make their appearance on the Aegean islands and the shores of mainland Greece. These earliest Neolithic groups arrived quickly after the end of the Pleistocene and the passing of the Paleolithic. In much of southeastern Europe, the Mesolithic is a short-lived era, if at all present, in this brief interval between the Old and New Stone Age.

From the Aegean region, the Neolithic expanded in two directions and two very different forms during the Seventh Millennium BC, north into the Balkans, and west along the northern shore of the Mediterranean. The Balkan Early Neolithic is characterised by large sedentary communities, a wide range of decorated ceramics, and diverse crops and herds. The Cardial Culture along the Mediterranean shore is known from scattered cave deposits containing distinctive ceramic vessels, sheep bones, and occasional evidence for wheat.

In the Sixth Millennium BC, the first farmers of Central Europe have been recognised in the Linearbandkeramik (LBK) Culture, which spread from Hungary across most of North Central Europe after 5500 BC. There is some evidence for limited cultivation and herding in this area prior to the arrival of LBK, but the sequence of events is not yet clear. At the same time, Early Neolithic groups were spreading from the Mediterranean and Atlantic coast into the interior of Iberia, France, Germany and the Low Countries.

After 3000 years, the Neolithic reached northwestern Europe, reaching the British Isles and Scandinavia at the beginning of the Fourth Millennium BC The evidence from Britain and Ireland is scanty and difficult to interpret, but suggests that the Neolithic was carried there by new groups of people (Woodman 2000). In Scandinavia, farming was adopted by indigenous Mesolithic groups and spread very quickly from the German border across Scandinavia within the limits of cultivation (Price 2000).

This process of transition is examined from a number of different angles in the articles that follow. The geographic coverage ranges from the Mediterranean and Atlantic coast of Iberia in the south and west, to the Ukraine in the east and Scandinavia in the north. The temporal range is from 9000 to 3500 BC, from the end of the Pleistocene to the end of the Mesolithic. Topical concerns involve change over time in technology, subsistence, organisation, and interaction. The order of the papers is generally geographic and chronological, beginning in southern Europe at the close of the Pleistocene and ending in central Sweden during the Subboreal climatic episode in the middle Holocene.

Laurent Costa, Denis Vigne, and their colleagues look at the early settlement of the Tyrrhenian islands and specifically the evidence for Mesolithic inhabitants on Corsica and northern Sardinia. Their work is critical in documenting the presence of pre-Neolithic inhabitants on the western Mediterranean Islands. Twenty years ago it was generally accepted that the islands of the Mediterranean were largely uninhabited prior to the Neolithic (Cherry 1990, Lewthwaite 1985). Today it is becoming clear that Mesolithic groups sailed to these islands and left visible traces of their presence early in the Holocene. Costa *et al.* have uncovered archaeological deposits from both Corsica and Sardinia with well-dated evidence of

Mesolithic occupation in the Eighth Millennium BC, shortly after the end of the Pleistocene.

The evidence suggests that the inhabitants were coastally adapted groups likely from the mainland, at least 50 km distant, who stayed for brief periods and utilised local foods and raw materials available on the islands. Interestingly, there were no large game hunted on the islands; subsistence was based completely on small game, primarily rabbits, and seafood. At the one large site in northern Sardinia, the bones of 75,000 –150,000 rabbits are estimated to have accumulated. The evidence documents both collecting and the coastal focus of the Mediterranean Mesolithic and suggests that pre-Neolithic voyagers may have utilised many islands.

The paper by *Maria Rosa Iovino* takes us south in the central Mediterranean to eastern Sicily in an examination of the Mesolithic and Early Neolithic. The focus here is on microwear analysis of stone tools from several layers in the deposits at Corruggi Cave. The analysis documented plant-working activities among the various tasks undertaken at the site. Cutting of siliceous plants was a significant part of the plant related activities but the evidence suggests that reeds rather than cereals were the primary target of these tools.

Further west, on the Atlantic coast of the Iberian Peninsula, *Ana Christina Araujo* writes about two transitions in the Mesolithic Portugal: from the Pleistocene to the Holocene and the beginning of the Atlantic episode. This discussion is put in the context of major pan-European environmental changes, including postglacial warming and the rise of sea level that continuously transformed the coastline during the first half of the Holocene. This first transition, from Pleistocene to Holocene, is accompanied by evidence for increase in population, in economic territories, and in the importance of aquatic resources. The second transition, coinciding with the Atlantic climatic optimum, witnesses a reorganisation of human settlement focused on the great riverine estuaries of southern Portugal. Shell middens and cemeteries suggest territorial definition and more permanent and substantial settlements. This pattern is witnessed along most of the Atlantic and North Sea coast of Europe during the Holocene and again emphasises the essential nature of coast adaptations in the Mesolithic.

Portugal continues to be the focus of interest in the paper by *Fiona Bamforth, Mary Jackes, and David Lubell*. This study takes the Mesolithic directly into one of the latest advances in archaeological research – ancient DNA studies of prehistoric bone. In this case, the application concerns samples from Mesolithic and Neolithic skeletal remains in Portugal and focus is on mitochondrial DNA. This study fits in a larger, and important, debate on the nature of the transition to agriculture in prehistoric Portugal and more generally in Iberia. One side in this debate has argued strongly that the Neolithic is brought to the shores of Portugal by colonists between 7200 to 8000 years ago (Zilhao 1998, 2000). The other side argues for continuity between the Mesolithic and Neolithic and the indigenous adoption of agriculture (Lubell *et al.* 1994; Jackes *et al.* 1997).

The authors have previously examined characteristics such as cranial size and shape, dental traits, and argued for continuity across the Mesolithic-Neolithic boundary. This evidence remains controversial, however, and they turn to ancient DNA. It is important to note, as the authors do, that this report is preliminary and more samples are needed before perceived patterns can be confirmed. The present study is based on the analysis of 28 tooth and bone samples from three Mesolithic and five Neolithic sites. Initial results suggest continuity between the Mesolithic and Neolithic samples. Without question ancient DNA is going to play a major role in our understanding of the prehistory of Europe, particularly in regard to the end of the Mesolithic.

We move next to the east and the question of the transition to the Neolithic in the Ukraine. *Malcolm Lillie* considers the Late Mesolithic and Early Neolithic communities in the Dneiper Rapids. The evidence for his study comes largely from the human skeletal remains in several cemeteries in this region. Detailed examination of the transition in terms of chronology (new radiocarbon dates), dental pathology, and stable carbon isotopes for information on diet indicates that the term Neolithic is basically a descriptive chronological development in this area rather than representing a major shift in subsistence, economy, or organisation. The archaeological and human osteological evidence all suggests that fisher-hunter-collectors continued their basic way of life across the Mesolithic-Neolithic boundary in this part of eastern Europe.

To the north, three papers consider the nature of the transition from the Mesolithic to the Neolithic in Poland, northern Germany, and central Sweden, in the classic area of the Early Neolithic Funnel Beaker Culture.

Lucyna Domanska looks at the relationship between hunter-gatherers and farmers in the Polish lowlands during the later part of the 6th millennium BC. Focus is on the Kuiavia district where early Linearbandkeramik communities appear ca. 5000 BC Interestingly, two different, geographically separate Mesolithic groups are recognised in this region at the end of the 6th millennium BC, known at the Chojnice-Pielki and Janislawice cultures. Chojnice-Pielki materials appear around 6000 BC and are related to north European lithic traditions. The Janislawice sites come later; their flint industry appears to be more closely related to southeastern Europe. Evidence of contact between the Chojnice-Pielki culture and the first LBK settlers appears in the form of exchange in raw materials, lithic technology, and tools. Evidence for contact between these LBK farmers and the Janislawice culture is suggested by the site of Deby and the shared use of chocolate flint. The site of Deby contains Mesolithic stone artifacts and domesticated animals, although the possibility of mixing cannot be ruled out at this site. Although the evidence for interaction between Mesolithic hunters and Neolithic farmers in this region is scanty, it nevertheless documents the contemporaneity of these groups and aspects of the interaction that took place.

Harald Lübke reports on submerged sites in the Wismar Bay region of the Baltic in northeastern Germany. Underwater survey and excavation in this area over the last three years has exposed several important sites and documented the presence of the latest Mesolithic Ertebølle in this region. The evidence from this region demonstrates that the Funnel Beaker Culture did not appear in northern Germany until 4100 BC. This date contradicts earlier arguments by Schwabedissen (1994) and others (e.g., Hoika 1994) that the Mesolithic-Neolithic transition took place much earlier in northern Germany than in southern Scandinavia. Intriguingly, however, the inland areas of Schleswig-Holstein remained Mesolithic until 3500 BC. It also fascinating to think that LBK groups were likely at the mouth of the Oder, no more than 100 km distant, by 4500 BC. In fact, today it appears that the spread of Funnel Beaker was almost instantaneous, reaching the Stockholm area by 3900 BC (see Hallgren, this volume).

The site of Timmendorf-Nordmole in the Wismar Bay is a large, coastal settlement from the latest Ertebølle, dating from 4400–4100 BC. The site stretches 250 x 100 m on the seafloor. Conditions for preservation are excellent. The actual settlement area of the site has been heavily eroded, as is often the case. The outcast layers, however, were well preserved with large pottery sherds, bone and antler loots, and wooden implements. Much of the artifactual equipment was related to fishing and the exploitation of marine species; terrestrial animals are only lightly represented. To date, evidence for the Early Neolithic is missing in the Wismar Bay, but excavations at a newly discovered site only 1 km from Timmendorf-Nordmole may change that situation in the coming years.

Leendert Louwe Kooijmans tours us through the excavations of two new waterlogged sites in the Rhine/Meuse delta in the Netherlands. These important excavations provide a first glimpse of wetland Mesolithic and early Neolithic sites outside of northern Europe. The deposits date from 5500 BC to 4500 BC and span the transition from the Neolithic transition in this area. The two sites, known as Hardinxveld 3 and 4 (De Bruin and Polderweg), were situated on the tops of sandy river dunes, The deposits extend from the dune tops down into the surrounding wetland deposits to depths up to 10 m below modern sea level. The presence of ceramics around 5000 BC at the site documents the existence of a ceramic Mesolithic. Subsequent connections with the Linearbandkeramik to the east are evidenced in typical LBK projectile points and later with pottery and imported stone tools and the faunal remains of cattle, sheep, goat and pigs. No cereal grains were found at the site.

Excellent conditions of preservation have meant that all manner of remains are preserved including wood, antler, bone, and other organic materials. The settlement area of the site contained relatively few artifacts but a number of pits, postholes, and a few burials. Some of these pits appear to be structures ranging in size from 3 x 3 m to 4 x 6 m with shallow convex bottoms.

The finds in the waterlain toss zone at the edge of the settlement include a complete dugout canoe of lime wood, four paddles of ash, two bow fragments of elm, a fish trap fragment of red dogwood and several decorated antler artifacts. Faunal remains include a diversity of species of large and small game, terrestrial and aquatic fowl and fish. Fishing focused on pike and the Cyrpinidae (roach, bream, tench). Plant remains document the importance of hazelnut, acorn, waternut, apple, and various berries.

Such wetlands sites are critically important for understanding the nature of subsistence and settlement in the late Mesolithic and during the transition to agriculture. The Hardinxveld sites are all the more remarkable as the first such sites to be recovered outside of Scandinavia and northern Germany. The remains emphasise the very gradual nature of the transition in terms of changes in technology, settlement, and subsistence.

Fredrik Hallgren looks at the evidence for the earliest Neolithic in east-Central Sweden in a large-scale perspective, considering the nature of social organisation and interaction in the Late Mesolithic and Early Neolithic, before and after 3900 BC. Noting that the transition from the Mesolithic to the Funnel Beaker culture was sudden and almost simultaneous across all of southern Scandinavia, Hallgren argues that its rapid spread and subsequent development resulted from changes in late Mesolithic society. Hallgren argues that the distribution of TRB was determined by the extent of existing Mesolithic social groups sharing exogamous marriage rules. Similar types of raw materials and stone tools are distributed across this broad area. Such marriage rules insured that interaction between groups was rapid and maintained over long distances in the Mesolithic.

This network, Hallgren suggests was responsible for the rapid spread of the Neolithic, likely through the movement of individuals making pottery and cultivating fields to new villages in marriage. As the Neolithic begins, distinctly local pottery traditions emerge which Hallgren links to a change in post-marital residence rules. Now, those individuals responsible for making pottery and cultivating the fields remain in their birth village and their spouses shift residence for marriage. In this perspective, social organisation and interaction are critical for an understanding of the transition to agriculture in Europe.

In Summary

There are a number of lessons to be learned from hunter-gatherers in transition.

It is clear that the Mesolithic of southern Europe was short-lived and only marginally distinguishable from the late Paleolithic. Coastal manifestations in the western Mediterranean islands and Portugal indicate the importance of marine resources. In the eastern Mediterranean and southeastern Europe the evidence for Holocene foragers is particularly scanty. Outside of a handful of sites in Greece and the Iron Gates region of the Danube, there are very few Mesolithic settlements.

Further to the east, in the Ukraine, Mesolithic groups accumulated large burial grounds and changed little if at all in terms of settlement and subsistence as a few Neolithic traits such as pottery and distinctive lithics filtered into their culture sometime after 5500 – 5000 BC. The paper by Lillie reminds us that distinction between Mesolithic and Neolithic remains unclear in some parts of Europe. Neolithic does not always imply an immediate and total shift to the utilisation of domesticated plants and animals. It is particularly the case in eastern Europe that this transition is highly variable and may or may not involve domesticates, pottery, and sedentary villages (Zvelebil and Lillie 2000).

Interaction and change with the arrival of the Neolithic are witnessed in northern Europe. What is perhaps most striking here is the information on the rate of change that is taking place. On the one hand, Mesolithic groups around the coast of the Baltic and North Sea resist the spread of Neolithic groups for more than 1000 years. Although there is some exchange of raw materials and finished products, the boundary between Mesolithic and Neolithic remains firm. This is the case in spite of the fact that distances between these two groups could likely be measured in tens of kilometers, as seen in the studies by Domanska and Lübke. This complete halt in the advance of the Neolithic is remarkable and points strongly to human choice as a major factor in the spread of the Neolithic. On the other hand, once the barrier is raised, the Neolithic moves across northern Germany and southern Scandinavia like wildfire. Funnel Beaker ceramics are first found in Mecklenburg after 4100 BC and by 3900 BC in the Stockholm area of east-central Sweden, a distance of more than 700 km. Such rapid rates for the transition are generally thought to be associated only with demic diffusion associated with the Cardial or LBK expansion (Price 2000).

Farming was apparently not an option; it eventually replaced Mesolithic foraging almost everywhere in Europe within the limits of cultivation. This transformation took place over a period of 3000 years, relatively brief period in archaeological time. This expansion seems to have taken place in a series of rapid moves and long stays over much of the continent. Clearly the Neolithic represented a successful new arrangement that changed human society forever. The European Mesolithic continued in a diminished state at the margins of cultivation: in the icy northlands of Scandinavia, in the marshes and steppe of White Russia and the Ukraine, and further east to the Urals and in a few of those places has only recently disappeared. This story of the end of the Mesolithic is told in greater detail in the following pages.

References

Cherry, J.F. 1990. The first colonisation of the Mediterranean Islands: a review of recent research. *Journal of Mediterranean Archaeology* 3, 145–221.

Hoika, J. 1994. Zur Gliederung der frühneolithischen Trichterbecherkultur in Holstein. In: Hoika, J. and Meurers-Balke, J. (eds.) *Beiträge zur frühneolithischen Trichterbecherkultur im westlichen Ostseegebiet* 1, 85–131. Neumünster.

Jackes, M., Lubell, D. and Meiklejohn, C. 1997. Healthy but mortal: human biology and the first farmers of western Europe. *Antiquity* 71, 639–658.

Lewthwaite, J. 1985. The Lacuna in the Lagoon: An Interdisciplinary Research Frontier in West Mediterranean Holocene Palaeoecology and Prehistory. *Extrait des: Cahiers Ligures de Prehistoire et de Protohistoire* 2, 253–264.

Lubell, D., Jackes, M., Schwarcz, H., Knyf, M. and Meiklejohn, C. 1994. The Mesolithic-Neolithic transition in Portugal: isotopic and dental evidence of diet. *Journal of Archaeological Science* 21, 201–216.

Price, T.D. 2000. The Introduction of Farming in Northern Europe In: Price, T.D. (ed.) *Europe's First Farmers*, 260–300. Cambridge.

Schwabedissen, H. 1994. Die Ellerbek-Kultur in Schleswig-Holstein und das Vordringen des Neolithikums uber die Elbe nach Norden. In: Hoika, J. and Meurers-Balke, J. (eds.) *Beiträge zur fruhneolithischen Trichterbecherkultur im westlichen Ostseegebiet*, 1, 361–381. Neumünster..

Woodman, P.C. 2000. Getting Back to Basics – Transitions to Farming in Ireland and Britain. Europe In: Price, T.D. (ed.) *Europe's First Farmers*, 219–259. Cambridge.

Zilhão, J. 1998. On logical and empirical aspects of the Mesolithic-Neolithic transition in the Iberian Peninsula. *Current Anthropology*, 1–14.

— 2000. From the Mesolithic to the Neolithic in the Iberian Peninsula. In: Price, T.D. (ed.) *Europe's First Farmers*, 144–182. Cambridge.

Zvelebil, M. and Lillie, M. 2000. Transition to Agriculture in Eastern Europe In: Price, T.D. (ed.) *Europe's First Farmers*, 57–92. Cambridge.

72. Long term change in Portuguese early Holocene settlement and subsistence

Ana Cristina Araújo

The Pleistocene-Holocene transition in Portugal features several climatic fluctuations that follow the general worldwide trends. As a result of the establishment of post-glacial conditions, biotopes and biomes were transformed. There was a significant rise in sea and land temperatures, as well as a major change in the shorelines, with large areas of the continental platform becoming submerged as the waters rose. Without necessarily being determinant, these transformations conditioned the settlement and subsistence strategies of human groups. During the early stages of the Holocene, corresponding to the Pre-Boreal and Boreal periods, a certain continuity in the exploitation of lithic raw materials and in the distribution of the human groups in the landscape is apparent. Still, there are major changes: aquatic resources become critical, economic territories seem to become larger, and overall population appears to decrease. The Atlantic climatic optimum brings about a second reorganisation of human settlement, which becomes focused on the estuaries of the larger rivers: the first burial grounds appear at this time, suggesting group identification with specific territories and a certain stability and permanence of habitation.

Introduction

The Mesolithic is a critical moment for understanding the adaptations of hunters and gatherers to the environmental transformations that occurred between the Pleistocene and the Holocene. For the period of time in question, which encompasses the second half of the Tardiglacial and the beginning of the Holocene, there occurred the range of bioclimatic fluctuations in the Portuguese territory that also took place on a global scale: the establishment of post-glacial conditions created by climatic warming, with repercussions on biomes and on the configuration and evolution of the coastline. Without necessarily being determinant, these two aspects are fundamental to understanding the settlement strategies and subsistence adopted by human groups at the time.

The archaeological sites that are situated in this spatial and chronological framework have characteristics that, in some cases, demonstrate continuity and, in others, show a marked break when viewed in a diachronic perspective. In order to make direct comparisons, it is important to recognise the time period being considered here – that is, the period immediately prior to and after the Dryas III, between 10.700 and 10.000 BP, and the beginning of the Atlantic, between 7500 and 6000 BP.

Palaeoenvironmental and palaeogeographic framework

Despite the scarcity of palaeoenvironmental data, the pollen sequences obtained for the Alentejo coast, together with wood charcoal analyses carried out on sites located on the limestone massif of the Estremadura, allow us to understand the impact on human settlement of the major changes that occurred between the end of the Allerød and the Atlantic:

– the significant rise in temperatures, both of the sea as well as on land, and the resulting repercussions on biomes;
– the rise in sea levels, resulting from the melting of the polar ice caps, with substantial modification of the configuration of the coastlines through the submersion of extensive areas of the continental platform.

The results obtained by Mateus and Queiroz (Mateus and Queiroz 1993, 1997; Queiroz 1999) point to the existence, during the Tardiglacial, of forests along the coast of the Alentejo dominated by Scots pine (*Pinus sylvestris*), which colonised the Pleniglacial sand dunes. From the Allerød onwards, regional biodiversity increased and was accompanied by an expansion of Maritime pine (*Pinus pinaster*) and the temperate forest. Following a short interregnum of these interglacial conditions during the Dryas III, with the temporary return of a cold climate and the regression of the forest and the vegetational cover in general, the early stages of the Holocene feature the maximum expansion of Maritime pine woods, along with extensive bush-like formations adapted to a wetter and

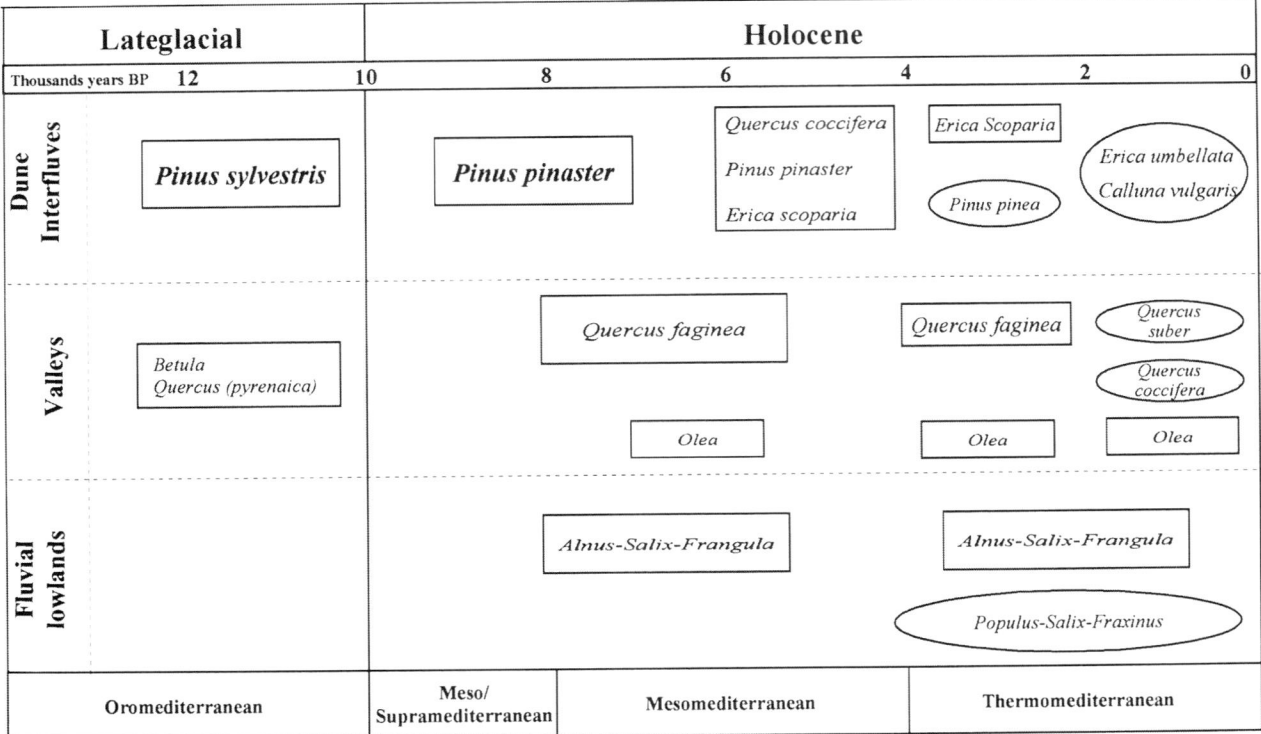

Figure 72.1 Main forest and shrubland vegetation in SW Portugal – Late glacial and Holocene (Queiroz 1998).

more temperate climatic regime. From the Atlantic onwards, the climate becomes gradually drier, and vegetation of a Mediterranean character develops (Figure 72.1). In the Estremadura, the anthracological data (Figueiral 1993, 1995) indicate that the Bølling/Allerød interstadial corresponds to a phase of expansion of the Maritime pine, which covered the sandy formations of the Rio Maior basin. Recent analyses carried out on charcoal from hearths identified at the site of Ponta da Vigia (coast of the Estremadura), dated to the Boreal, confirm the almost exclusive presence of Maritime pine on coastal dunes, similar to that which occurs in the south of the country (Van Leeuwaarden and Queiroz 2000). The Maritime pine, thus, appears to have been the dominant vegetal formation in this type of habitat during the first millennia of the Holocene. The relief of the adjacent calcareous massif, on the other hand, would have already been recolonised by oak forests. The impact of the Dryas III on these biomes is still unknown in its details, but it must have been as significant as that which is verified on the Alentejo coast, where one can detect clear climatic degradation and consequent diminution of taxonomic biodiversity (Queiroz 1999).

With the thawing of the polar ice caps, the sea level rose rapidly between 13.000 and 11.000 BP; this was the period during which water temperatures of the Atlantic reached values close to those of the present day (Duplessy et al. 1992). There was a brief reversion in Dryas III times, and peaks around 6 000 BP, when the estuaries of large rivers like the Tejo and Sado penetrated deeply into the interior. The stabilisation of present-day coastlines took place around 5500 BP.

The changes in climate and vegetation had a major impact on animal populations. The biomass of large mammals was drastically reduced, and species which required large territories – such as chamois and ibex – retreated to the higher mountains, or, as was the case with the horse, saw their habitat reduced to the fluvial plains. From the end of the Dryas III onwards, the composition of hunted mammalian fauna was dominated by red deer, along with aurochs, roe deer, wild boar, and lagomorphs.

Pre-Boreal and Boreal Settlement, Subsistence and Technology

The diminution of animal biomass and the restriction of catchment territories, owing to the expansion of the forest and the retreat of the coastline, must have had a considerable impact on human settlement and subsistence strategies.

The location and setting of Pre-Boreal and Boreal sites do not differ much from the final Magdalenian pattern (Zilhão 1997). There are several examples of stratigraphic sequences spanning both sides of the transition, both in the open-air and in caves. The majority of sites are located in the Estremadura (Figures 72.2–72.4), either along the coast or in the central limestone massif, suggesting the absence of significant structural variations in the distribution of human groups in the landscape throughout this period. In southern Portugal, however, the relative

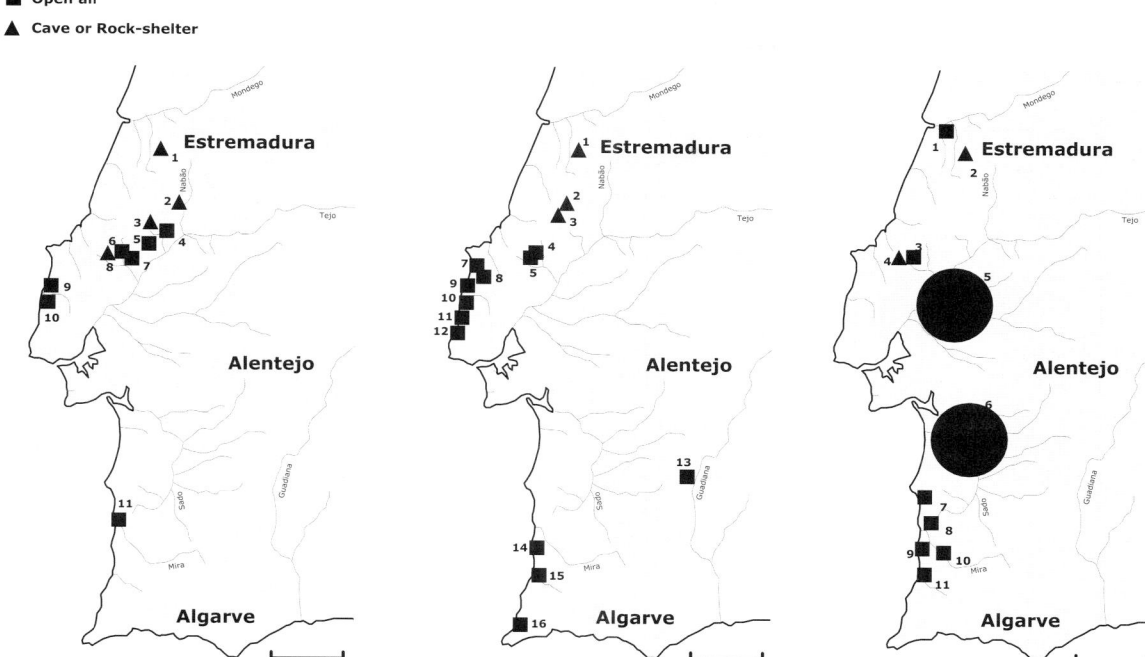

Figure 72.2 Allerød and Dryas III sites: *1: Gruta da Buraca Grande; 2: Gruta do Caldeirão; 3: Picareiro; 4: Bairrada; 5: Cabana da Horta; 6: Cabeço de Porto Marinho; 7: Carneira; 8: Abrigo Grande das Bocas; 9: Rossio do Cabo; 10: Vale da Mata; 11: Pedra do Patacho.* Pre-Boreal and Boreal sites: *1: Gruta da Buraca Grande; 2: Gruta do Casal do Papagaio; 3: Abrigo da Pena de Mira; 4: Areeiro III; 5 – Fonte Pinheiro; 6: Abrigo Grande das Bocas; 7: Vale Frade; 8: Toledo; 9: Ponta da Vigia; 10: Cabeço do Curral Velho e Pinhal da Fonte; 11: S. Julião; 12: Magoito; 13: Barca do Xerez de Baixo; 14: Palheirões do Alegra; 15: Montes de Baixo; 16: Castelejo.* Atlantic sites: *1: Forno da Cal; 2: Buraca Grande; 3: Forno da Telha; 4: Abrigo Grande das Bocas; 5: Concheiros do Vale do Tejo; 6: Concheiros do Vale do Sado; 7: Samouqueira e Vale Pincel; 8: Vidigal; 9: Medo Tojeiro; 10: Fiais; 11: Montes de Baixo.*

abundance of Pre-Boreal and Boreal sites stands in marked contrast to the virtual absence of evidence for the Upper Palaeolithic. This is due to two factors:

1. The episodic character of field research carried out so far, which has not been directed to the identification of Upper Palaeolithic sites;
2. The greater visibility of Mesolithic sites, which in most cases feature easy-to-detect shell-middens.

The result of systematic surveys which have recently been carried out in the zone of the backwater of the Alqueva (the southern interior of the Alentejo) clearly demonstrates the relevance of these reservations. This work, carried out by a team with a great deal of previous experience in the detection of Pleistocene open air sites, brought to light the discovery of various sites of the Upper Paleolithic and Early Mesolithic, in a region where, until two years ago, sites of these periods were completely unknown.

The analysis of the areas occupied and of the size of the assemblages retrieved in the Pre-Boreal and Boreal sites allows us to recognise the existence of three major types of sites, with certainly some functional significance (Figure 72.5):

1. The first group comprises very extensive open-air sites, generally containing a significant and diverse lithic component, and tool-kits that include different types of armatures. Subsistence activities must have been mainly connected with the exploitation of terrestrial resources. Most of these sites are located in interior areas around or inside the central limestone massif.
2. The second group comprises smaller sites containing scarce and less diverse lithic remains but featuring an abundance of molluscs. These open-air contexts are located close to the shoreline.
3. The third group comprises rock-shelters and caves located in the interior or on the periphery of the limestone massifs. These sites feature organic remains related to the exploitation of food resources of terrestrial and coastal origin, and tool assemblages that include several types of armatures.

These differences do not seem to be related to chronological or geographical factors. The data currently available suggest that the most reasonable explanation is functional complementarity. Although yet to be con-

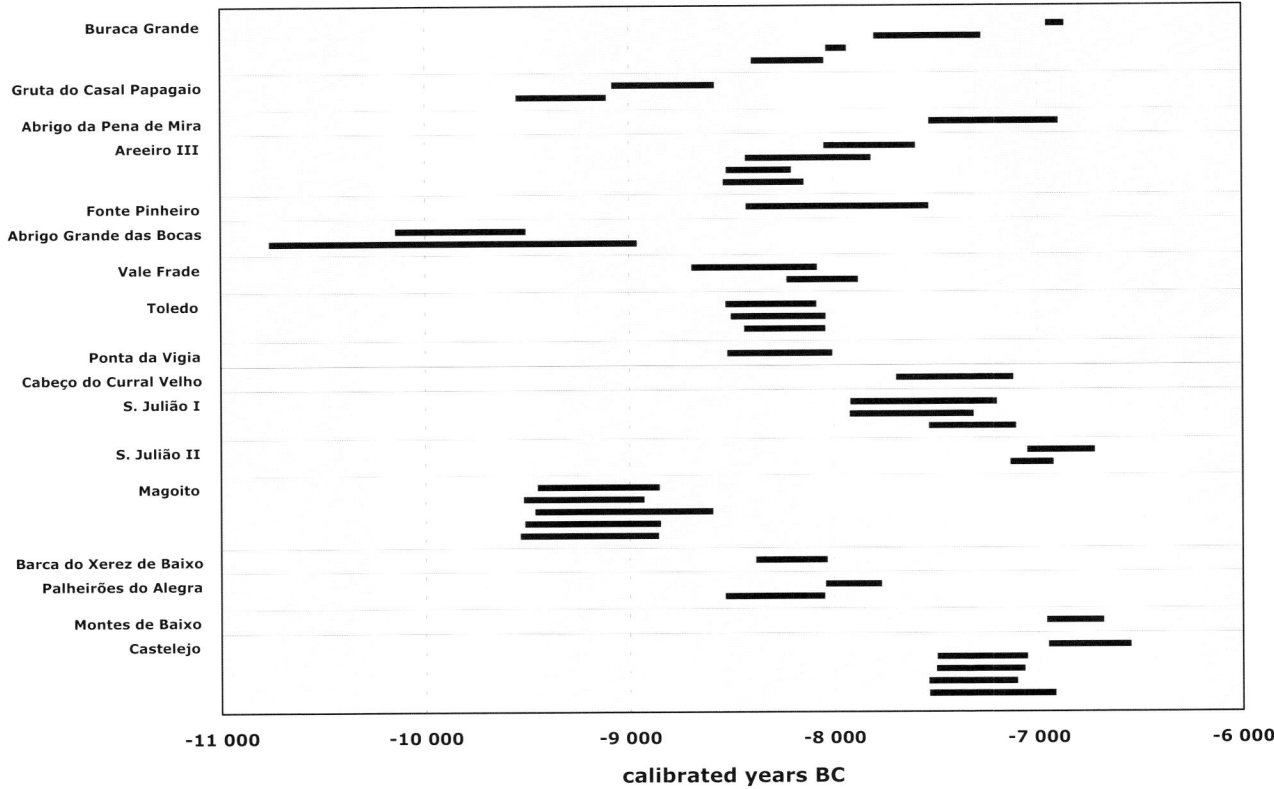

Figure 72.3 Radiocarbon dates for Portuguese early Mesolithic sites (calibrated years BC, 2 s). See Figure 72.4.

firmed, the emergence of this differentiation would constitute an element of rupture from the preceding period; in the Magdalenian, the variation in the functional characteristics of the sites appears to occur along a continuous spectrum (Zilhão 1997). Zilhão interpreted such an absence of internal differentiation as representing a settlement system characterised by a high degree of mobility; this was also reflected in the stone tool economy by the miniaturisation of the lithic tool assemblage, associated with the circulation of raw material exclusively or almost exclusively in the form of nuclei, without supports.

The characteristics of the lithic materials found in sites of the first group, namely the presence of diverse types of microlithic armatures, together with the absence of mollusc remains, suggest that subsistence activities must have been primarily focused on the exploitation of terrestrial resources. Otherwise, the accumulation of shells would have created a carbonaceous environment favorable to the preservation of organics. The sites in this group do not differ in a significant way from the sites of the Magdalenian that existed in these same regions. They could correspond, thus, to residential sites that were repeatedly occupied by small groups, organised around hearths and forming palimpsests of horizontal stratigraphy.

Recently, several Pre-Boreal and Boreal rock-shelter or cave contexts located on the central limestone massif, very far from the shoreline, have been found. They contain remains associated with the exploitation of estuary and coastal habitat resources. These sites, included in the third group, feature tool-kits including different types of microlithic armatures. The presence of resources of aquatic origin in these contexts probably indicates the occasional discard of food items carried from the coast in the framework of the logistical use of these sites, mostly for hunting and plant gathering.

The sites included in the second group, characterised by a more restricted distribution of remains, by low artifact density, and by an elementary and straightforward technology, feature an abundance of mollusc remains. The remains in these contexts suggest that they correspond to episodic occupations, probably of a seasonal nature, relating to the intensive exploration of subsistence resources of aquatic origin, that functioned as a fundamental complement in the diet of human communities in the beginning of the Holocene. The lithic industries present in these sites reflect a basic and expedient technology, and reinforce the interpretations previously advanced regarding the role played by these locations in the settlement and subsistence systems of the post-glacial.

The site of Pedra do Patacho, located at the mouth of the Mira river and radiocarbon dated to the Dryas III period (see Figure 72.2), is perhaps the best example known that demonstrates the importance that aquatic resources came to have in the diet of populations of this

Site	Sample	Lab. number	Age BP	Cal. BC 1 σ	Cal. BC 2 σ
Buraca Grande	Charcoal	Gif-9707	7580±30	6423-6382	6456-6367
Buraca Grande	Charcoal	Gif-9679	8120±70	7244-7009	7298-6775
Buraca Grande	Charcoal	Gif-9939	8445±20	7501-7446	7535-7434
Buraca Grande	Charcoal	Gif-9708	8680±40	7857-7580	7898-7544
Gruta do Casal Papagaio	Estuarine shells	ICEN-372	9270±90	8410-8097	8582-8081
Gruta do Casal Papagaio	Charcoal	ICEN-369	9710±70	9035-8935	9051-8610
Abrigo da Pena de Mira	Charcoal	ICEN-966	7810±120	6757-6465	7031-6398
Areeiro III	Charcoal	ICEN-548	8380±90	7499-7305	7546-7097
Areeiro III	Charcoal	ICEN-546	8570±130	7697-7489	7929-7314
Areeiro III	Charcoal	ICEN-494	8850±50	7968-7745	8023-7705
Areeiro III	Charcoal	ICEN-547	8860±80	8010-7737	8038-7644
Fonte Pinheiro	Charcoal	ICEN-973	8450±190	7583-7292	7927-7033
Abrigo das Bocas	Estuarine shells	ICEN-903	9880±80	9243-9041	9644-9006
Abrigo das Bocas	Bone	ICEN-900	9880±220	9756-8955	10262-8462
Vale Frade	Shells	Sac-1577	8710±80	7937-7603	8195-7581
Vale Frade	Shells	Sac-1586	8530±70	7599-7525	7729-7379
Toledo	Estuarine shells	ICEN-1529	8820±80	7967-7705	8028-7585
Toledo	Estuarine shells	ICEN-1533	8740±90	7928-7584	8002-7540
Toledo	Estuarine shells	Sac-1587	8620±70	7729-7581	7937-7541
Ponta da Vigia	Charcoal	ICEN-51	8730±110	7932-7576	8020-7508
Cabeço do Curral Velho	Estuarine shells	ICEN-270	8020±70	7037-6725	7195-6621
São Julião I	Charcoal	ICEN-179	8120±100	7259-6828	7420-6702
São Julião I	Estuarine shells	ICEN-109	8170±80	7291-7036	7423-6817
São Julião I	Estuarine shells	ICEN-153	7960±50	7005-6666	7035-6608
São Julião II	Charcoal	ICEN-73	7610±80	6466-6375	6553-6224
São Julião II	Estuarine shells	ICEN-107	7750±60	6600-6464	6636-6426
Magoito	Charcoal	ICEN-52	9490±60	8847-8433	8951-8355
Magoito	Shells	ICEN-80	9590±80	8980-8531	9020-8430
Magoito	Shells	ICEN-81	9410±120	8841-8270	8964-8094
Magoito	Estuarine shells	ICEN-82	9530±100	8948-8435	9013-8349
Magoito	Charcoal	GrN-11229	9580±100	8989-8523	9036-8360
Barca do Xerez de Baixo	Charcoal	Beta-120607	8640±50	7696-7546	7883-7535
Palheirões do Alegra	Charcoal	ICEN-136	8400±70	7500-7327	7543-7268
Palheirões do Alegra	Charcoal	GX-16414	8802±100	7967-7696	8033-7548
Montes de Baixo	Shells	ICEN-720	7530±70	6419-6230	6461-6183
Castelejo	Charcoal	Beta-2908	7450±90	6381-6177	6452-6048
Castelejo	Charcoal	ICEN-215	7880±40	7656-6604	6998-6556
Castelejo	Charcoal	ICEN-213	7900±40	6991-6610	7002-6568
Castelejo	Charcoal	ICEN-211	7970±60	7008-6667	7039-6605
Castelejo	Shells	BM2276R	7840±120	6994-6474	7036-6418

The dates on shell were calibrated with the curve for continental samples after subtraction of 380± 30 years (apparent age of this material in the archaeological sites from this time range, Soares 1993)

Figure 72.4 Radiometric results for the Early Mesolithic of Portugal.

period. This archaeological context, which we can situate in the transition from the Pleistocene to the Holocene, has as a principal characteristic the presence of a shell level dominated exclusively by shell species of coastal and estuarine habitats (Soares and Silva 1993). This fact suggests that the explanation for the appearance of this

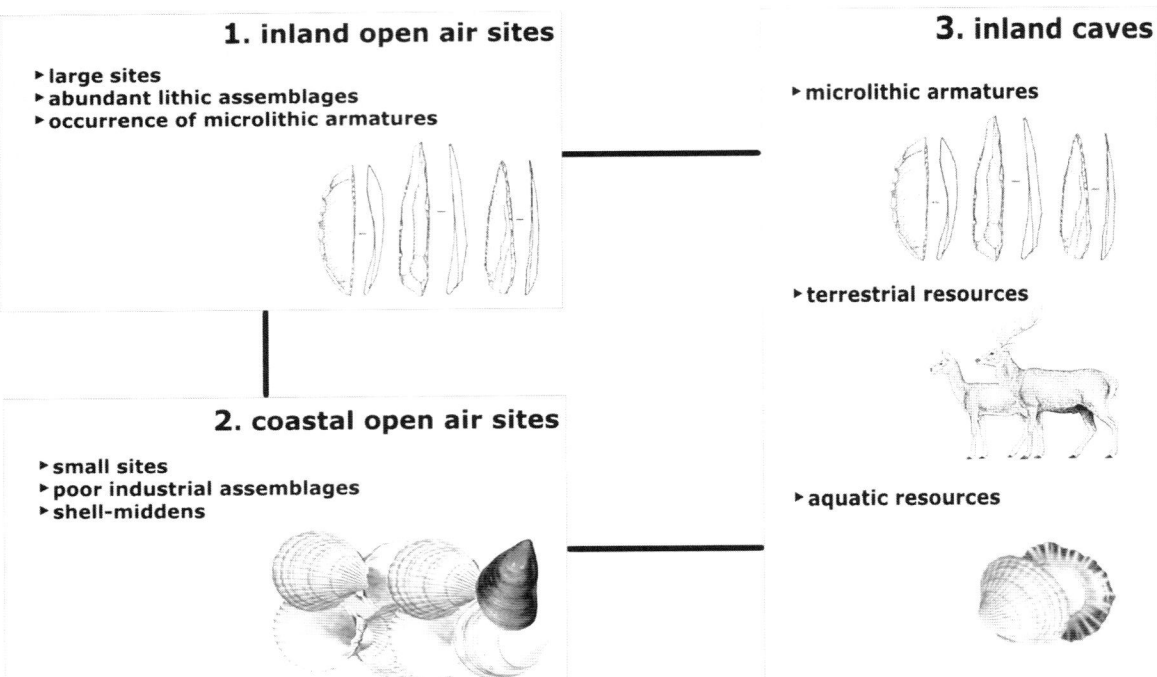

Figure 72.5 Early Mesolithic of Portugal: a hypothetical model of the settlement and subsistence system.

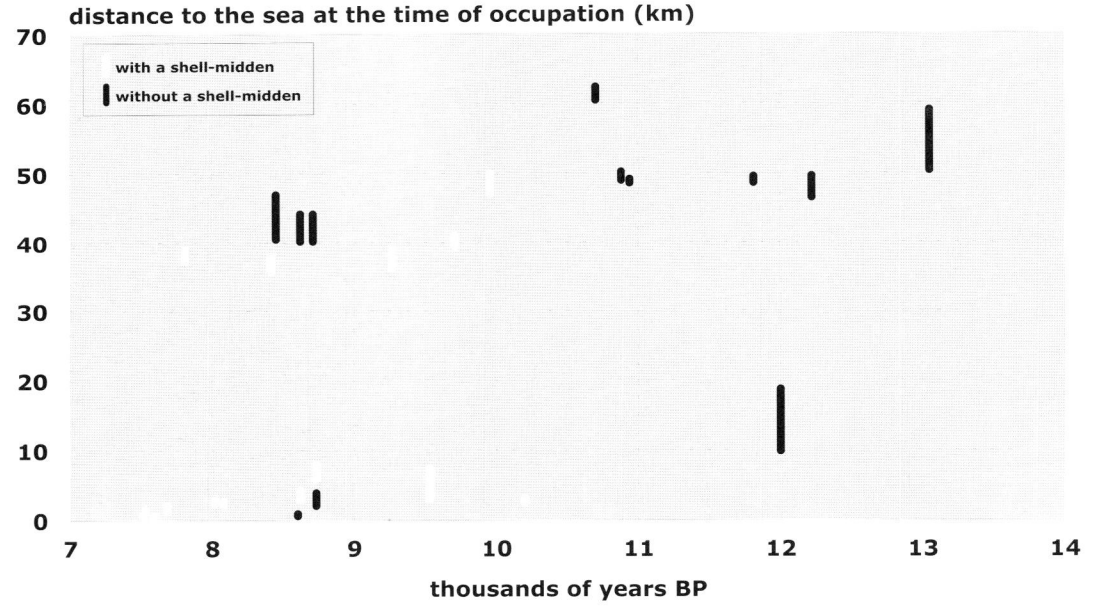

Figure 72.6 Site location versus time (across the Pleistocene-Holocene boundary, from Bølling to Boreal). A graph showing that the distance of a site from the sea did not determine the presence or absence of aquatic resources. See Figure 72.8.

new kind of site in the archaeological record should be found in the domain of subsistence. In other words, the formation of this new type of site is due to the significantly greater role of aquatic resources in the subsistence of human populations, from the Pre-Boreal onwards.

The submersion of the continental platform does not allow us to exclude the possibility that the exploitation of marine resources was already important in subsistence of the Final Magdalenian. But the fact remains that this importance was considerably increased between the end of the Dryas III and the Boreal, and it is demonstrated by the absence of any sites prior to 10.000 BP featuring an economically significant consumption of aquatic foods, regardless of distance to shoreline (Figures 72.6–72.7). Pre-Boreal and Boreal sites located, at the time of their occupation, quite far from the shoreline – around 30 to 50 km – contain significant amounts of molluscs, including both estuarine and coastal species; by contrast,

Site	Age BP	Distance to the present coastline	Isobathic		Distance to the ancient coastline		Notes
			Maximum	Minimum	Maximum	Minimum	
Castelejo 4	7510	175	-20	-10	750	525	C
Montes de Baixo 4	7530	2250	-20	-10	1575	1275	C
Castelejo 5	7590	175	-20	-10	750	525	C
S. Julião II	7680	120	-21	-13	2100	1275	C
Pena de Mira	7810	36700	-24	-14	39100	37150	C
Cabeço do C. Velho	8020	1025	-28	-16	2850	2400	C
S. Julião I	8030	20	-28	-17	2700	2100	C
Buraca Grande 8C	8415	31850	-33	-20	38000	35750	C
Fonte Pinheiro	8450	35825	-33	-22	46925	40475	S
Palheirões do Alegra	8600	30	-33	-21	900	600	S
Areeiro III - área 2	8620	36025	-31	-21	44125	40150	S
Vale Frade	8620	225	-31	-22	4275	2700	C
Areeiro III - área 1	8710	36025	-31	-21	44125	40150	S
Ponta da Vigia	8730	175	-32	-22	3825	2025	S
Toledo	8730	3800	-32	-22	7950	5850	C
Casal Papagaio (M)	9270	34300	-51	-26	39400	36100	C
Magoito	9530	70	-58	-33	7350	2925	C
Casal Papagaio (B)	9710	34300	-61	-51	41050	39400	C
Bocas (base)	9960	33950	-63	-51	50000	46925	C
Pedra do Patacho	10200	50	-62	-53	3075	2475	C
Caldeirão EB-topo	10700	56250	-53	-41	62400	60450	S
Pinhal da Carneira	10800	37050	-54	-44	50175	48900	S
CPM III T - sup.	10940	40500	-52	-40	49125	48525	S
CPM IIIS - méd.	11810	40500	-58	-40	49500	48525	S
Vale da Mata	12000	725	-63	-46	18675	9825	S
Picareiro G	12220	41000	-72	-55	49550	46400	S
Buraca Grande	13050	31850	-100	-80	59000	50300	S

Figure 72.7 Site location versus time (across the Pleistocene-Holocene boundary, from Bølling to Boreal). This table shows that the distance of a site from the sea did not determine the presence or absence of aquatic resources. Distances (in meters) are given to the present day and ancient shorelines. Isobathic values were taken from the variation curve of the relative average sea level, as established by Dias et al. 1997. Absolute dates were calculated from the average results obtained for contemporary samples from each archaeological context, excluding the standard deviation. C – with shell midden; S – without shell midden.

no such sites exist in the Magdalenian. This suggests that the influence of global climate change was responsible for two major transformations of settlement and subsistence systems:

1. The creation of a structural dependence on the exploitation of aquatic resources, both coastal and estuarine, while the same faunal species of terrestrial origin continued to be hunted (red deer, wild boar, roe deer, aurochs, horse, lagomorphs);

2. A significant enlargement of economic territories, related to changes in the mobility of the human groups.

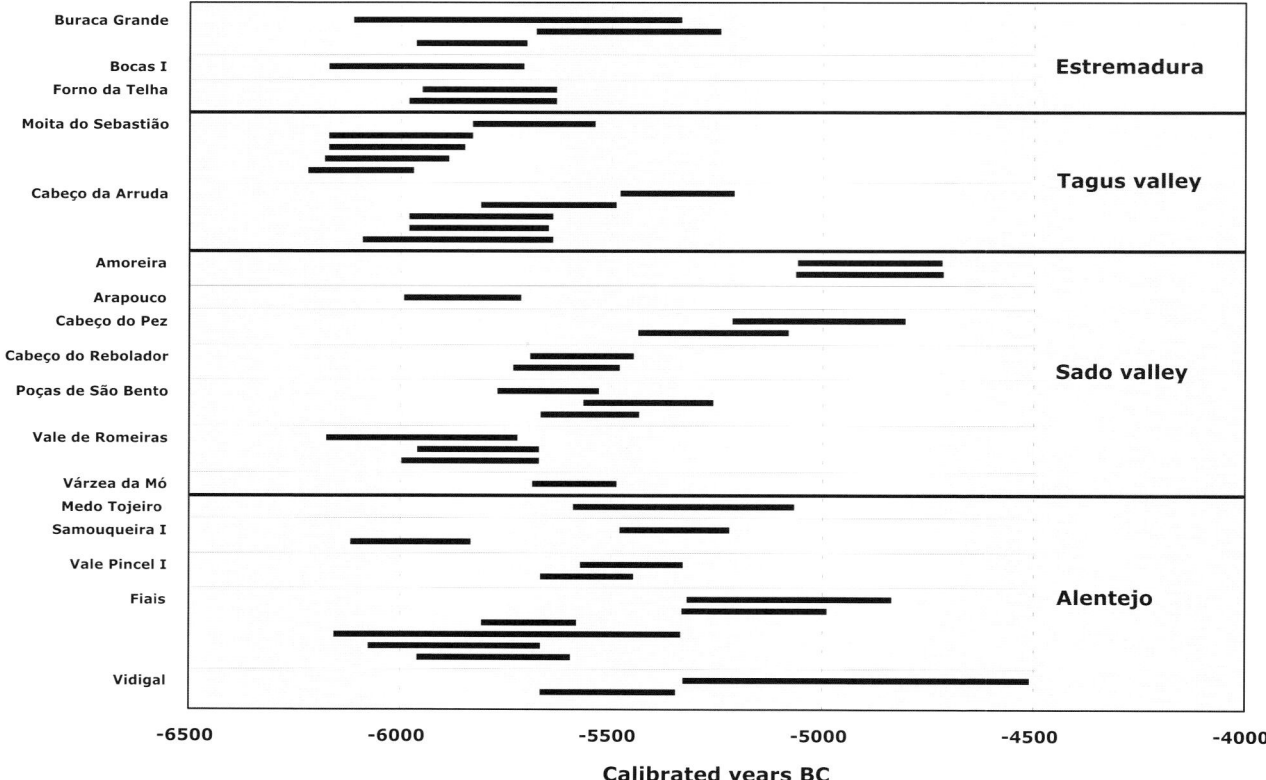

Figure 72.8 Radiocarbon dates for Portuguese Late Mesolithic sites. (calibrated years BC, 2 s). See Figure 72.9.

This being the case, and taking into account that, simultaneously, there was a decrease both in the available area for habitation and in the biomass of large mammals, I suggest that the passage to the Holocene was accompanied by an important demographic crisis, with an accentuated decline in the human population of the region. It is more difficult to assess the point at which this decline would have been gradual or abrupt. Taking into account the rapidity of the transition from the Dryas III to the Pre-Boreal, the second hypothesis, however, appears more likely. Furthermore, the palaeoclimatic indicators recently published by Taylor, based on the studies of ice cores in Greenland (Taylor 1999), suggest that this climatic change occured in only 20 years. That is, in less than a generation, the mean annual temperature rose between five and ten degrees, and the consequent melting of the polar ice caps precipitated a catastrophic rise in sea levels. As is obvious, these occurrences could only have had drastic consequences on human populations, and especially those living in coastal regions.

In conclusion, the remains found in Pre-Boreal and Boreal sites seem to have been accumulated by groups of highly mobile hunter-gatherers, probably organised in smaller and more dispersed units. They would have moved between the coast and the interior, using as pathways the numerous rivers and streams flowing from the periphery of the massifs; in the more humid climate of the beginning of the Holocene, these waterways, which were more regular and more voluminous, must have been easily navigable up to the sources with canoes that were capable of transporting a family group. The subsistence of these populations was based upon the exploitation of different ecological niches, depending on the time of year, and their technology was of a late Upper Palaeolithic tradition.

The changes in the Atlantic

The Atlantic period has long been known for its large sites (Figure 72.2; Figures 72.8–72.9). One might conclude from this fact that the climatic optimum would have brought about an increase in the population and, consequently, that population densities might have equaled or even outgrown the estimated Upper Palaeolithic levels. Still, everything seems to indicate that the appearance of these sites is related to a reorganisation of the settlement systems.

The territories favored by the last hunter-gatherers of the Holocene are the more interior areas, in ecotones of the ancient estuaries of the large rivers: the Tejo, Sado and Mira. This is obviously connected to the Flandrian transgression, which led to the formation of large estuaries, very rich in terms of their floral and faunal abundance and diversity. Their human exploitation resulted in the formation of large concentrations of bivalve molluscs, true mounds of organic garbage, the extension of which (both in area and in height) significantly transformed the original topography of the terrain.

Site	Sample	Lab. number	Age BP	Cal. BC 1 σ	Cal. BC 2 σ
Amoreira	Charcoal	Q-(AM85B2a)	5990±75	4944-4789	5060-4718
Amoreira	Estuarine shells	Q-(AM85B2b)	5990±80	4946-4787	5064-4715
Arapouco	Estuarine shells	Q-2492	7040±70	5959-5779	5992-5715
Bocas I	Estuarine shells	ICEN-899	7490±110	6017-5836	6170-5709
Buraca Grande	Charcoal	Sac-1461	6850±210	5943-5525	6112-5336
Buraca Grande	Shells	Sac-1459	6560±140	5583-5332	5680-5243
Buraca Grande	Charcoal	Gif-9940	7000±60	5944-5753	5964-5702
Cabeço da Arruda	*Homo*	TO-356	6360±80	5380-5235	5480-5210
Cabeço da Arruda	*Homo*	TO-355	6780±80	5732-5573	5810-5490
Cabeço da Arruda	*Homo*	TO-359a	6960±60	5960-5734	5980-5640
Cabeço da Arruda	*Homo*	TO-354	6970±60	5960-5740	5980-5650
Cabeço da Arruda	*Homo*	TO-360	6990±110	5980-5730	6090-5640
Cabeço do Pez	Estuarine shells	Q-2496	6150±70	5064-4908	5214-4805
Cabeço do Pez	Estuarine shells	Q-2497	6450±80	5373-5229	5437-5081
Cabeço do Rebolador	Estuarine shells	ICEN-278	6720±70	5627-5526	5693-5448
Cabeço do Rebolador	Estuarine shells	ICEN-277	6760±80	5680-5529	5733-5481
Fiais	Bones	ICEN-141	6180±110	5252-4946	5321-4836
Fiais	Bones	TO-706	6260±80	5270-5076	5333-4990
Fiais	Charcoal	TO-705	6840±70	5725-5609	5807-5582
Fiais	Bones	ICEN-110	6870±220	5953-5526	6156-5336
Fiais	Charcoal	TO-806	7010±70	5973-5750	6075-5668
Fiais	Estuarine shells	ICEN-103	6930±90	5924-5679	5960-5597
Forno da Telha	Estuarine shells	ICEN-416	6940±70	5847-5697	5950-5632
Forno da Telha	Estuarine shells	ICEN-417	6980±90	5947-5710	5981-5632
Medo Tojeiro	Estuarine shells	BM-2275R	6440±140	5448-5256	5590-5067
Moita do Sebastião	*Homo*	TO-135	6810±70	5739-5629	5830-5540
Moita do Sebastião	*Homo*	TO-134	7160±80	6091-5966	6170-5830
Moita do Sebastião	*Homo*	TO-132	7180±70	6097-5974	6170-5848
Moita do Sebastião	*Homo*	TO-133	7200±70	6108-5886	6180-5886
Moita do Sebastião	*Homo*	TO-131	7240±70	6129-5993	6219-5970
Poças de São Bento	Charcoal	Q-2494	6780±65	5726-5584	5770-5530
Poças de São Bento	Estuarine shells	Q-2495	6470±80	5443-5313	5566-5259
Poças de São Bento	Estuarine shells	Q-2493	6660±80	5595-5448	5668-5435
Samouqueira I	*Homo*	TO-130	6370±70	5382-5238	5480-5220
Samouqueira I	Estuarine shells	ICEN-729	7140±70	6011-5889	6117-5833
Vale de Romeiras	Bones	ICEN-144	7130±110	6043-5854	6175-5723
Vale de Romeiras	Estuarine shells	ICEN-146	6970±70	5936-5716	5960-5672
Vale de Romeiras	Estuarine shells	ICEN-150	7010±90	5956-5732	5997-5672
Vale Pincel I	Charcoal	ICEN-723	6540±60	5520-5389	5573-5331
Vale Pincel I	Charcoal	ICEN-724	6700±60	5601-5525	5668-5448
Várzea da Mó	Estuarine shells	ICEN-273	6730±60	5628-5528	5687-5488
Vidigal	Bones	GX-14557	6030±180	5220-4770	5330-4510
Vidigal	Bones	Ly-4695	6640±90	5593-5443	5668-5348

The dates on shell were calibrated with the curve for continental samples after subtraction of 380± 30 years (apparent age of this material in the archaeological sites from this time range, Soares 1993)

Figure 72.9 Radiometric results for the Late Mesolithic of Portugal.

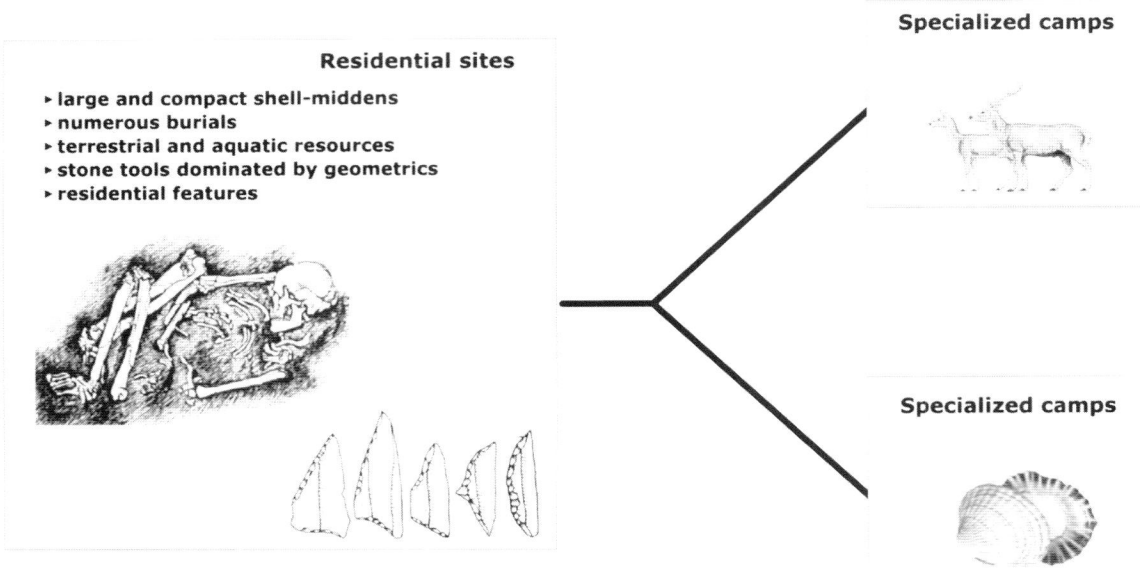

Figure 72.10 Late Mesolithic of Portugal: a hypothetical model of the settlement and subsistence system.

In Portugal, the shell middens of Muge and Magos are the best examples of this type of site. The accumulation of these remains is related to the adoption of a food regime for which resources of aquatic origin contributed about 50%, as shown by the analyses of stable isotopes performed on skeletons exhumed from these sites (Lubell and Jackes 1988; Lubell *et al.* 1994). As far as the animal component is concerned, the terrestrial resources are, like before, red deer, aurochs, roe deer, wild boar, and lagomorphs, with occasional remains of horse also occurring.

This type of location does not differ from the one that may be reconstructed for some Boreal sites currently located along the shoreline. In fact, at the time of their occupation, those places also corresponded to the interior of ancient estuaries. The real difference thus resides in the following aspects:

1. in the interior of the Pre-Boreal and Boreal estuaries, there are no sites as large as those found on the same ecotonal locations during the Atlantic period;
2. on the estuaries of the small rivers that were occupied during the Pre-Boreal and the Boreal there are no archaeological sites from the Atlantic;
3. only during the Atlantic were the shell-middens simultaneously used as cemeteries;
4. no sites dated from the Atlantic are known in the interior areas of the Estremadura limestone massif, except for some isolated peripheral cave or open-air sites;
5. all sites from the Atlantic are located within the limits of the major estuaries or in areas easily accessible by boat, suggesting the abandonment of the interior of the country in this period.

The abandonment of the limestone massifs and of the interior regions, or their logistic exploitation from the main settlement nuclei, must be related to the growth of the forests. Together with the appearance of favorable conditions in riverine areas, this growth must have originated processes of fusion between formerly dispersed groups, now joining in the banks of the large and very productive estuaries during the Atlantic climatic optimum. The characteristics of the sites known therein, namely the presence of numerous burials – the first real prehistoric cemeteries, suggest they were residential sites occupied in a more or less permanent way (Figure 72.7). Some smaller sites, however, are also known, and may represent temporary camps focused on the exploitation of very specific seasonal resources. The selection of estuarine zones as the ultimate refuges of Holocene societies of hunter-gatherers is, without a doubt, related to the faunal and floral diversity of these ecological niches. Although of a role proportionally less well represented, in caloric terms, than the molluscs of Mesolithic diets, this component was, certainly, a determinant in this process of establishment of populations on the estuaries. Constituting perhaps the most permanent and available resource, it would not be logical to conceive of a system in which communities were forced to travel large distances to the mollusc beds and immediately transport these to their respective camps, in order to make up for dietary deficiencies in periods of the year that were poorest in terms of available resources, especially taking into account the unfavourable relationship between the real weight represented by this component and the respective caloric component. If factors of distance and time are determinant in a system centered on mobility in the exploration of different types of resources, seasonal in nature, technology cannot function as a constraint on this system. The "microlithisation" and standardisation in the types and dimensions of supports and tools, easily substituted anywhere and, probably, in any context of resource acquisition, demonstrates the efficiency of the lithic technology of the final hunters of the Holocene. The proliferation and the reduced typological variability of the tools, with the almost overwhelming domination of very standardised geometric forms (triangles, trapezes, and segments), constitute, perhaps, the first great rupture, from the point of view of material culture, with the earlier systems of exploitation and use of stone.

These hunter-gatherer adaptations of the Holocene persisted in these ecological niches for more than one millennium, even after the introduction, in other regions of the country, of a new way of life based on food production. It was not until Neolithic deforestation that the large intermediate areas were inhabited, and only then did the country's settlement become as dense as it had been during the maximum of Upper Palaeolithic hunter-gatherer groups.

References

Almeida, F., Maurício, J., Souto, P. and Valente, M.J. 1999. Novas perspectivas para o estudo do Epipaleolítico do interior alentejano: notícia preliminar sobre a descoberta do sítio arqueológico da Barca do Xerez de Baixo. *Revista Portuguesa de Arqueologia* 2 (1), 25–38.

Araújo, A.C. 1994a. O concheiro epipaleolítico do Cabeço do Curral Velho, Cambelas, Torres Vedras. *Actas das V Jornadas Arqueológicas* 2, 43–51. Lisboa.

—— 1994b. A estação mesolítica do Forno da Telha, Rio Maior. *Trabalhos de Antropologia e Etnologia* 33 (1–2), 15–44.

—— 1998. O concheiro de Toledo, Lourinhã, no quadro das adaptações humanas do Pós-Glaciar no litoral da Estremadura. *Revista Portuguesa de Arqueologia* 1(2), 19–38.

—— 1999. A indústria lítica do concheiro de Poças de S. Bento, vale do Sado, no seu contexto regional. *O Arqueólogo Português* 4 (13–15), 87–159.

—— in press. O Mesolítico Inicial da Estremadura. *2º Colóquio Internacional sobre Megalitismo*. Actas.

Arnaud, J.M. 1993. O Mesolítico e a neolitização: balanço e perspectivas. In: Carvalho, G.S., Ferreira, A.B. and Senna-Martinez, J.C. (eds.) *O Quaternário em Portugal: balanço e perspectivas,* 173–184. Lisboa.

Arnaud, J. and Bento, J.D.A. 1988. Caracterização da ocupação pré-histórica da gruta do Casal Papagaio, Fátima, Vila Nova de Ourém. *Algar* 2, 27–34.

Arnaud, J. and Pereira, A.R. 1994. S. Julião. *Informação Arqueológica* 9, 62–63.

Aubry, T. and Moura, M.H. 1994. O Paleolítico da Serra de Sicó. *Trabalhos de Antropologia e Etnologia* 34, 43–60.

Aubry, T. and Moura, M.H. 1995. Nouvelles données sur les occupations paléolithiques de la Serra de Sicó. *Actas da III Reunião do Quaternário Ibérico,* 439–449. Coimbra.

Aubry, T., Fontugne, M. and Moura, M.H. 1997. Les occupations de la grotte de Buraca Grande depuis le Paléolithique Supérieur et les apports de la séquence Holocène a l'étude de la transition Mésolithique – Néolithique au Portugal. *Bulletin de la Société Préhistorique Française* 94 (2), 182–189.

Bicho, N.F. 1991. Areeiro III, an open air site dated to 8850 BP. Rio Maior, Portugal. *Mesolithic Miscellany* 12 (2), 1–10.

—— 1993. Late glacial prehistory of central and southern Portugal. *Antiquity* 67, 61–75.

—— 1994. The end of the Paleolithic and the Mesolithic in Portugal. *Current Anthropology* 35 (5), 664–673.

—— 1999. A ocupação epipaleolítica do Abrigo Grande das Bocas, Rio Maior. *O Arqueólogo Português* 4 (13–15), 53–85.

Bowman, S.G.E., Ambers, J.C. and Leese, M.N. 1990. Re-evaluation of British Museum radiocarbon dates issued between 1980 and 1984. *Radiocarbon* 32 (1), 59–79.

Daveau, S., Pereira, A.R. and Zbyszewski, G. 1982. Datation au C14 du site archéologique de la plage de Magoito, Portugal, scellé par une dune consolidée. *Clio* 4, 133–136.

Dias, J.M.A. 1985. Registos da migração da linha de costa nos últimos 18 000 anos na plataforma continental portuguesa setentrional. *Actas da I Reunião do Quaternário Ibérico* 1, 281–295. Lisboa.

Dias, J.M.A., Rodrigues, A. and Magalhães. F. 1997. Evolução da linha de costa, em Portugal, desde o último máximo glaciário até à actualidade: síntese dos conhecimentos. *Estudos do Quaternário* 1, 53–66.

Duplessy, J.C., Labeyrie, L., Arnold, M., Paterne, M., Duprat, J. and Van Weering, T.C.E. 1992. Changes in surface salinity of the North Atlantic Ocean during the last deglaciation. *Nature* 358, 485–488.

Figueiral, I. 1993. Cabeço de Porto Marinho: une approche paléoécologique. Prémiers résultats. *Estudios sobre Cuaternario,* 167–172.

—— 1995. Charcoal analysis and the history of *Pinus pinaster* (cluster pine) in Portugal. *Review of Palaeobotany and Palynology* 89, 441–454.

Gonzalez Morales, M. and Arnaud, J. 1990. Recent research on the Mesolithic in the Iberian Peninsula: problems and perspectives. In: Vermeersch, P. and Van Peer, P. (eds.) *Contributions to the Mesolithic in Europe – Papers presented at the fourth international symposium The Mesolithic in Europe,* 451–461. Leuven.

Lubell, D. and Jackes, M. 1985. Mesolithic-Neolithic continuity: evidence from chronology and human biology. In *Actas da I Reunião do Quaternário Ibérico* 2, 113–133. Lisboa.

—— 1988. Portuguese Mesolithic-Neolithic subsistence and settlement. *Rivista di Antropologia* Suplemento ao 66, 231–248.

Lubell, D., Jackes, M., Schwarcz, H., Knyf, M. and Meiklejohn, C. 1994. The Mesolithic-Neolithic transition in Portugal: isotopic and dental evidence of diet. *Journal of Archaeological Science* 21, 201–206.

Mateus, J.E. and Queiroz, P.F. 1993. Os estudos de vegetação quaternária em Portugal: contextos, balanço de resultados, perspectivas. In: Carvalho, G.S., Ferreira, A.B. and Senna-Martinez, J.C. (eds.) *O Quaternário em Portugal: balanço e perspectivas,* 106–130. Lisboa.

Mateus, J.E. and Queiroz, P.F. 1997. Aspectos do desenvolvimento, da história e da evolução da vegetação do litoral norte alentejano durante o Holocénico. *Setúbal Arqueológica* 11–12, 49–68.

Pereira, A.R. 1983. Enquadramento geomorfológico do sítio datado por C14 na praia de Magoito, concelho de Sintra, Portugal. *VI Reunión del Grupo Español de Trabajo del Quaternario,* 551–563. Vigo.

Queiroz, P.F. 1999. *Ecologia histórica da paisagem do Noroeste Alentejano.* University. Unpublished Ph. D. Thesis. Lisbon.

Raposo, L. 1994. O sítio de Palheirões do Alegra e a "Questão do Mirense". In: Campos, J.M., Pérez, J.A. and Gómez, F. (eds.) *Arqueología en el entorno del Bajo Guadiana,* 55–59. Huelva.

Silva, C.T. and Soares, J. 1997. Economias costeiras na Pré-história do Sudoeste Português. O concheiro de Montes de Baixo. *Setúbal Arqueológica* 11–12, 69–108.

Soares, A.M. 1989. *O efeito de reservatório oceânico nas águas costeiras de Portugal Continental.* Unpublished. Lisboa.

—— 1993. The ^{14}C content of marine shells: evidence for variability in coastal upwelling off Portugal during the

Holocene. *Isotope Techniques in the Study of Past and Current Environmental Changes in the Hydrosphere and the Atmosphere*, 471–485. Vienna.

Soares, J. and Silva, C.T. 1993. Na transição Plistocénico-Holocénico: marisqueio na Pedra do Patacho. *Al-madan* 2 (2), 21–29.

Taylor, K. 1999. Rapid climate change. *American Scientist* 87, 320–328.

Van Leeuwaarden, W. and Queiroz, P.F. 2000. *Estudo arqueobotânico do sítio da Ponta da Vigia (Torres Vedras)*. Unpublished Report.

Zilhão, J. 1992. Estratégias de povoamento e subsistência no Paleolítico e no Mesolítico em Portugal. In: Romanillo, A.M. (ed.) *Elefantes, ciervos y ovicaprineos*, 149–172. Santander.

—— 1997. *O Paleolítico Superior da Estremadura Portuguesa*, 2 vols. Lisboa.

Zilhão, J. and Lubell, D. 1987a. Concheiro do Pinhal da Fonte. *Informação Arqueológica* 8, 55.

—— 1987b. Concheiro de Pandeiro. *Informação Arqueológica* 8, 45–46.

Zilhão, J., Carvalho, E. and Araújo, A.C. 1987. A estação epipaleolítica da Ponta da Vigia, Torres Vedras. *Arqueologia* 16, 8–18.

Zilhão, J., Marks, A., Ferring, C.R., Bicho, N.F. and Figueiral, I. 1996. The Upper Paleolithic of the Rio Maior basin, Portugal. Preliminary results of a 1987–1993 Portuguese-American research project. *Trabalhos de Antropologia e Etnologia* 35 (4), 69–88.

73. Mesolithic-Neolithic population relationships in Portugal: the evidence from ancient mitochondrial DNA

Fiona Bamforth, Mary Jackes and David Lubell

Analyses of Mesolithic and Neolithic samples from Portugal have led to the formulation of an hypothesis that the population increased during and after a protracted period of shift in subsistence, during which there were biological responses to changing lifestyles. We report here on bioarchaeological analyses that support the hypothesis of change within a population which was not subject to marked gene flow, and provide preliminary information on the analysis of aDNA from Mesolithic and Neolithic skeletal samples.

Bioarchaeological background

The attempt to clarify relationships among Iberian populations using osteological data has a long history, particularly because of interest in Basque origins.

The initial attempts were based on craniometry M size and shape of skulls. While the method may be questioned, particularly with regard to environmental effects on skull size, it is not obsolete. For example, de la Rúa published "The craniofacial factors of the Basque skull, a comparative study" in 1992, and Lalueza Fox (1996; Lalueza Fox *et al.* 1996) has also recently published on Iberian craniometry. Our analyses have shown that, craniometrically, the Basques are northern Iberians, and that the Neolithic and Mesolithic Portuguese samples group together. We have, in fact, noted the near identity of the Neolithic Melides sample, which is craniometrically small, with the Portuguese Mesolithic (Jackes *et al.* 1997b).

Figure 73.1 suggests that size would indeed be a critical factor in discriminating among the geographical areas and chronological periods of Iberia based on these craniometric variables, and this was demonstrated using discriminant function analysis with the grouping variable indicated in figure 73.1. Although the craniometric variables are very well distributed in their correlations over the multiple extracted functions, generally interpreted as indicating that shape rather than size determines the clustering, size must remain a concern.

We have experimented with methods of reducing the effect of size on the discrimination, thus putting more weight on skull shape, using both Howells (1973) C scores and division by geometric means (DGM: see Jungers *et al.* 1995). The two methods of reducing the effect of size give similar results. However, there is a reduced spread over the major axis when using C scores, so that S.E. Spain groups with N. Spain. Because of this reduced discrimination, and following the lead of Collard and Wood (2000), we illustrate the DGM method of size-effect reduction in Figure 73.2.

Figure 73.2 shows the major functions resulting from a direct discriminant function analysis on the pooled sex means of a variety of adult skull samples (Figure 73.3)

	Mesolithic Portugal	Neolithic Portugal	Basques	S. Spain	N. Spain	SE. Spain
M1(GOL)	180.3	180.1	183.4	181.8	185.1	180.1
M5(BNL)	94.7	96.0	98.1	98.0	99.6	97.2
M8(XCB)	133.9	136.3	141.1	136.4	138.2	134.4
M9(WFB)	92.6	94.4	96.0	94.3	96.1	94.5
M45(ZYB)	122.7	121.4	125.7	124.6	126.9	120.8
M48(NPH)	69.5	65.1	69.9	68.3	68.9	65.3
M52(OBH)	29.2	31.3	33.8	32.1	32.9	31.3
M54(NLB)	23.9	23.4	22.7	23.9	23.7	22.5

Figure 73.1 Mean values (in mm.) of cranial measurements (Martin and Saller 1957–66; Howells 1973) by grouping variable.

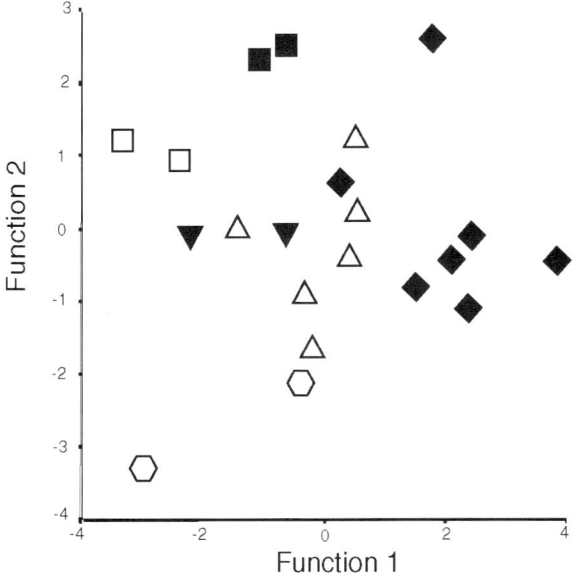

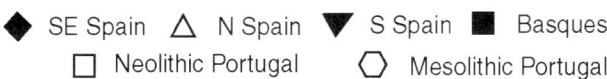

Figure 73.2 Direct discriminant function analysis of cranial measurements (size-effect adjusted): the grouping variable is as shown in the legend. The X axis illustrates the first canonical discriminant function which expresses 49.7% of the variation; the Y axis represents the second canonical discriminant function and 25.5% of the variation. Moita lies at the lower left.

from Mesolithic to modern times. As is common with archaeological data, the samples are varied, but we have used cranial measurements for which there are no missing data, and we have used only basic measurements that are standardised over two systems of measurement (Martin and Saller 1957–66; Howells 1973), and generally taken without error.

Figure 73.2 shows a clear differentiation between the two Portuguese Mesolithic sites, with Moita do Sebastião as an outlier, though separated from the Portuguese Neolithic sites only on the Y axis (with which orbital height is significantly correlated). The separation of Moita from Arruda is an unexpected result of size-effect reduction (compare with Jackes *et al.* 1997b, Fig. 1, male skulls only), but confirmation of a consistent finding in our research into other areas of Portuguese Mesolithic skeletal biology (Jackes and Lubell 1999a, 1999b).

Cranial size is at least partly determined by environmental factors: the separation of Moita and Arruda suggests that shape is also controlled by non-genetic factors, to some extent at least. On the other hand, we may assume that dental morphology, which is more genetically controlled, provides a more reliable method for determining population relationships.

In Jackes *et al.* (2001) Portuguese Mesolithic teeth, dated to around 7450 cal BP, are compared with teeth from several sites dated to the period 4500–5500 cal BP, and with a twentieth century Portuguese dental sample. [Calibrated dates are calculated at 1-sigma ranges. For the Mesolithic dates, we use $\Delta R = 250\pm35$ as suggested by Stuiver and Braziunas (1993:155), but see also Monge Soares (1993)]. The characteristics of premolar and first and second molar crowns are stable, and provide a method of examining genetic affinity, when outlier data provide scale, allowing for a more adequate interpretation of results. In Jackes *et al.* (2001) Canadian Iroquoian material provides the required outlier data, suitable because it is from an area in which unusually detailed archaeological work has been undertaken (e.g. Finlayson 1998). The conclusion, preliminary and based on a small number of traits, is that there is no evidence of any discontinuity in Portuguese dental morphology. The various Portuguese samples cluster closely, relative to the relationships between dental samples from the two Iroquoian sites.

Figure 73.4 shows the results of an analysis of the frequencies of 22 dental traits, representing aspects of the crowns of first, second and third mandibular and maxillary molars and distal mandibular premolars. The pooled left and right side incidences of the 22 traits are reduced to a matrix of Z values generated by an Anscombe transformation mean measure of distance (MMD) (the methods are outlined in Jackes *et al.* 1997a). Multidimensional scaling allows us to visualise the matrix, here in a three-dimensional form; the earlier (Mesolithic) samples are somewhat differentiated from the other later samples on the major (X) axis, but are themselves not identical.

In fact, analysis indicates that there is a statistically significant difference between the two Mesolithic sites, Moita do Sebastião and Cabeço da Arruda, despite their geographical contiguity and overlap in time. Two of the later samples, Paimogo I and São Paulo, are also significantly different from each other. All but one (Abrigo da Carrasca) of the post-Mesolithic Portuguese sites are significantly different from Arruda, but only Paimogo I is significantly different from Moita.

The dental trait analysis suggests that there is genetic heterogeneity within the Mesolithic of Portugal, which would be expected on the basis of small exogamous groups in which drift may occur. The dental trait analysis further suggests continuity across the Mesolithic/Neolithic boundary, with increased heterogeneity expected as a result of increasing population and greater sedentism. From the patterning of the significance of the MMD (mean measure of distance) statistics, Moita, especially, cannot be seen as representing a different population from that living in the same general area 2000 to 3000 years later. Analyses of more extensive data collected by Ana María Silva (pers. comm. 17/08/00) for the Late Neolithic and Chalcolithic (5500–4500 cal BP) sites indicate that even among these there are some differences which are marginally significant, and that finding is supported here.

In summary, then, we see little evidence for population

Samples	Source	Grouping variable
Moita do Sebastião	Meiklejohn	Mesolithic Portugal
Cabeço da Arruda	Meiklejohn	Mesolithic Portugal
Melides	Meiklejohn	Neolithic Portugal
Casa da Moura	Jackes	Neolithic Portugal
Guipuzcoan Basques (Aranzadi study)	Morant 1929	Basques
Basques (19th century)	de la Rúa 1992	Basques
Mediaeval Granada Muslims	Fox et al. 1996	S. Spain
Bronze Age Granada (mainly)	Fox et al. 1996	S. Spain
Visigothic North Meseta	Fox et al. 1996	N. Spain
Mediaeval Christian Cantabria	Fox et al. 1996	N. Spain
Bronze Age Central Catalonia	Fox et al. 1996	N. Spain
Mediaeval Barcelona Jews	Fox et al. 1996	N. Spain
Illot des Poros (Talayotic Majorca)	Fox et al. 1996	N. Spain
Mediaeval Christian Central Catalonia	Fox et al. 1996	N. Spain
La Bastida (Totana, Murcia)	Walker 1985	S.E. Spain
Cova del Palanqués (Novarrés, Valencia)	Walker 1985	S.E. Spain
Cueva de las Lechuzas (Villena, Alicante)	Walker 1985	S.E. Spain
Cova de les Llometes (Alcoy, Alicante)	Walker 1985	S.E. Spain
Cova del Morro de la Barsella (Torremanzanas, Alicante)	Walker 1985	S.E. Spain
Cova de la Pastora (Alcoy, Alicante)	Walker 1985	S.E. Spain
Cova de Beni Sid (Vall d'Ebro, Alicante)	Walker 1985	S.E. Spain

Figure 73.3 Samples used for craniometric analysis.

discontinuity between the Mesolithic and the Neolithic in western Iberia. In fact, we have also argued for a certain degree of continuity in broader terms of biological change M that is, in terms of trends through time rather than abrupt alterations with some sort of "revolution" in diet and lifestyle.

While our published stable isotope data appear to provide a clear differentiation in terms of diet, we draw attention to the heterogeneity of the Mesolithic data despite the minimal sample representation.

Figure 73.5, illustrates samples analysed by Schwarcz for our project (Lubell et al. 1994), for Cunha (H. Schwarcz, pers. comm. 20/04/99), and for the Los Canes Mesolithic material (P. Arias Cabal pers. comm. 23/12/99; Arias Cabal and Garralda 1996). It indicates that evidence for clear differentiation of Mesolithic and Neolithic may well be eroded as more data appear.

Our analyses over the last 16 years started from an hypothesis of a change in health with the introduction of domesticates, but with no prejudgement on the question of whether immigration would complicate our research on the Portuguese Mesolithic-Neolithic transition. We have found little evidence for a decline in health (Jackes et al. 1997a), and what there is contradicts previous ideas (Lubell et al. 1994). Our attempts to understand the transition based on studies of skeletal and dental morphology are limited by the geographical concentration of the Mesolithic material, and by taphonomic factors resulting from Neolithic ossuary burial, but we see a repeated pattern of gradual change beginning in the Mesolithic, with no sign of immigrant genes. While dental morphology may well provide some basis for clarifying genetic affinities, dental traits are not inherited in a simple fashion, and may not provide definitive answers. Nevertheless, there is now interest in the inclusion of anthropological data within an increasingly sophisticated archaeological approach to questions of migration and culture change (Sutton 1996; Burmeister 2000; Shennan 2000).

While proliferating studies of modern European Y chromosome and mtDNA can suggest the shape of the past (Richards et al. 2000; Rosser et al. 2000; Semino et al. 2000) there is no adequate control of the time-scale, and thus it is not possible to rely on the accuracy of reconstructions of past population affiliations based on the present-day gene frequencies.

In the light of all this, it is obvious that the analysis of aDNA is essential to the clarification of relationships among Iberian archaeological samples.

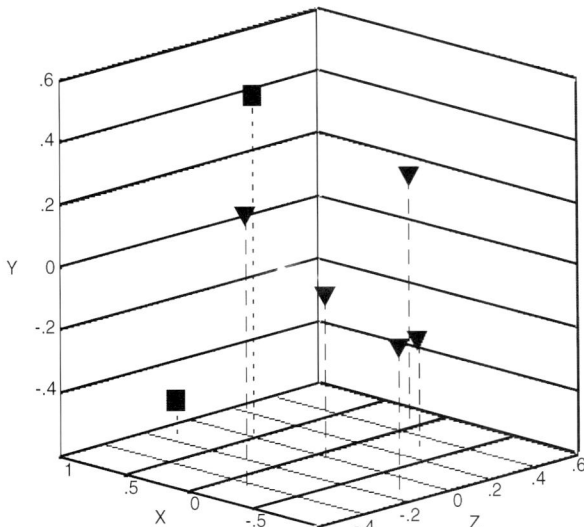

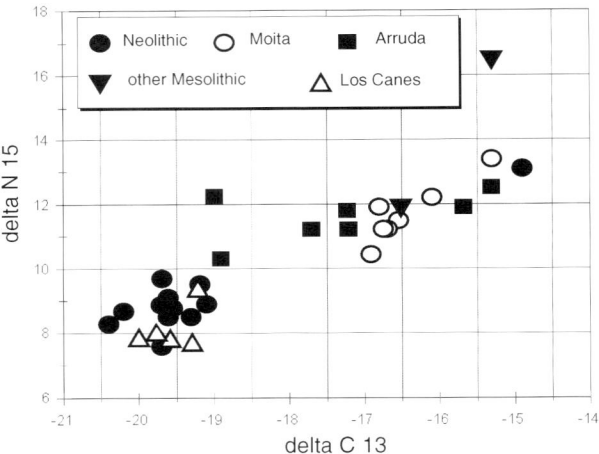

Figure 73.4 Multidimensional scaling of dental trait incidences: Mesolithic (squares) are somewhat differentiated from the Late Neolithic/Chalcolithic (triangles) samples on the first dimension (X). Note that the Late Neolithic/Chalcolithic samples are broadly spread along the X axis, which accounts for 47% of the displayed variation. The second dimension (Y) expresses 28% of the variation, and separates Moita (above) from Arruda (below). The third dimension (Z) covers 25% of the variation, which occurs among the Late Neolithic/Chalcolithic samples.

Figure 73.5 Scatter of stable isotope values for Portuguese Mesolithic and Neolithic individuals, and for five individuals from the Spanish site of Los Canes. In general the Neolithic diet is based on terrestrial components (bottom left), while Portuguese Mesolithic people have a more marine-based diet. Two individuals from Arruda are tending towards a more terrestrial diet, while the Spanish Mesolithic individuals have a diet indistinguishable on stable isotopes from the Portuguese Neolithic.

DNA analysis

The rapid development of new technologies for analysing DNA has led to increasing interest in DNA as a tool for examining population origins. There are two approaches – examination of DNA from large numbers of modern individuals from diverse populations with statistical analysis to predict population origins and secondly, examination of DNA extracted from ancient remains. In this paper we attempt to use DNA analysis to examine the degree of genetic continuity between the Mesolithic and Neolithic populations in Portugal.

Cells contain both nuclear and mitochondrial DNA (mtDNA) and both are valuable for examining prehistoric populations. With the exception of most of the Y-chromosome, nuclear DNA undergoes recombination, and nuclear encoded genes may be subject to positive or negative selection in a population because the proteins they code for may confer an advantage or disadvantage for survival. DNA which does not undergo recombination and which does not code for proteins is therefore of particular interest in this respect. Regions of the mitochondrial genome and Y-chromosome DNA have these characteristics and both may undergo mutations resulting in sequence changes that accumulate along the paternal lineage (Y-chromosome) and maternal lineage (mitochondrial DNA) (Lell and Wallace 2000). As these sequence changes accumulate they give rise to population specific sequence variations or haplotypes. Sequence variants sharing a common ancestor are designated as haplogroups.

Despite the common feature of non-recombination, there are important differences between mtDNA and Y-chromosomal DNA. In addition to the difference in parent of transmission, mtDNA has a higher mutation rate than nuclear DNA and permits fine distinction between populations. The Y-chromosome has a lower mutation rate and there are fewer informative sequence changes. However, the presence of both slow and fast evolving markers (de Knijff 2000) has facilitated the designation of ancestral haplogroups and haplotypes within Europe (Rosser *et al.* 2000; Semino *et al.* 2000) based on the examination of Y-chromosome material from a large number of modern Europeans.

Mitochondria are unique organelles because they have their own DNA (about 16,000 bases) coding for a few of the mitochondrial proteins and the machinery required to make those proteins. The entire mtDNA genome has been sequenced (Anderson *et al.* 1981). Each mitochondrion has 2–6 copies of its DNA, so there are many copies of mtDNA per cell whereas there is only one copy of the nuclear DNA. This provides an advantage when working with prehistoric samples because the mtDNA yield per sample is much higher than nuclear DNA. European mtDNAs fall into a number of broad haplogroups determined by sequence changes specific to a population.. Many of these sequence changes occur in the control region of mtDNA. Each haplogroup can be further subdivided into haplotypes. Based on examination of mtDNA from large numbers of modern Europeans, the major European haplogroups have been designated H, I, J, K, T, U3, U4, U5, V, W and X (Torroni et al. 1994; Richards et al. 1996, 2000; Simoni et al. 2000).

In this study, our approach was to examine Mesolithic and Neolithic remains from Portugal to determine whether there was evidence of genetic continuity between the two populations.

Haplogroups can be analysed by restriction fragment length polymorphisms (RFLPs), a technique where the sequence change causes either a loss or gain of recognition site for an enzyme that will cut DNA at a specified sequence of bases. Some workers have taken an alternative approach and sequenced the control region, a sequence of about a thousand bases where many of the population specific sequences occur. This analysis broadly correlates with the RFLP analysis.

There are several challenges in ancient DNA analysis. The material may be poorly preserved, but there is an approximate correlation between collagen content and success of DNA extraction. The yield of DNA is poor, and it is highly degraded. There may be mutations in the DNA caused by contact with chemicals, heat and ultraviolet irradiation that have accumulated with time. A major problem is that of contamination by extraneous DNA (Handt et al. 1996) which may occur at any time from initial excavation to laboratory analysis. Obsessive attention to laboratory technique is required to both avoid contamination, and to detect it should it occur.

Hypothesis

Our hypothesis was that evidence of continuity of the Neolithic and Mesolithic in Portugal would be demonstrated if the same distribution of mtDNA haplogroups were present in the Mesolithic and Neolithic samples examined. The appearance of new haplogroups or a difference in distribution of haplogroups in the Neolithic samples might be evidence migration from outside.

Samples available for analysis were from Neolithic and Mesolithic sites in central Portugal. The Mesolithic sites are Moita do Sebastião, Cabeço da Arruda and Cabeço da Amoreira, three shell middens located very close to each other near Muge on a small tributary of the Tagus. The Neolithic sites represent a larger geographic area and include the caves of Casa da Moura, Feteira, Furninha, Fontainhas (all located in the Estremadura northwest of Lisbon), and Melides (to the south of the Tagus near Sines). In total, we analysed 13 Neolithic samples (10 teeth, 3 bone) and 15 Mesolithic samples (all bone), ranging in date from 7200–8000 cal BP (see Lubell et al. 1994). We were also able to analyse a sample of Late Pleistocene wolf bone from Casa da Moura, which proved to be a valuable control.

Methods

The remains were visually well preserved. Great care was taken to avoid contamination by extraneous DNA at all stages of the analysis. All samples were extracted and analysed in duplicate. The second extraction was done on a separate occasion from the first. The sample was cleaned and the outer layer was scraped away. It was then soaked in bleach to destroy any remaining surface DNA (contaminating DNA is most likely on the surface), then immersed in liquid nitrogen, which allows the bone or tooth to be easily reduced to powder using a pestle and mortar. DNA was extracted from 500 mg aliquots of bone powder using guanidine thiocyanate to release DNA which was then adsorbed to a silica resin, then purified and eluted (Boom et al. 1990).

We opted to look at all Caucasian haplogroups so that the haplogroup of each sample could be identified. A limiting factor to this approach may be the amount of DNA available from each sample. Overall, H, I, J, K are the most common Caucasian haplogroups encompassing more than 60% of the population. The remainder are more recently described and tend to be the more minor. Based on analyses of modern Portuguese populations (Corte-Real et al. 1996; Simoni et al. 2000; Torroni et al. 1998), we expected the predominant haplogroups to be H, K, T U4 and V. We used the polymerase chain reaction to amplify about 100 bp of mtDNA which is about the largest fragment size that can be analysed for ancient DNA. DNA haplogroups were assigned after restriction enzyme digestion and electrophoresis. Only one key sequence which identifies each haplogroup was analysed. All analyses were validated by including a negative control for the amplification reaction, and a negative control for the extraction procedure, in this case, wolf bone. These controls are a check for DNA contamination during these procedures.

Results and conclusions

Haplogroup I was excluded from all the Neolithic samples and six of seven Mesolithic samples. One sample failed to amplify. None of 21 samples, both Neolithic and Mesolithic, belonged to haplogroup U6. For the haplogroup V, four samples failed to amplify, and none of the remainder belonged to this haplogroup. Thirteen samples have been analysed to date for the haplogroup K. Eleven (seven Neolithic and four Mesolithic) were not haplogroup K. To our surprise, we found two individuals who, using the K specific primers, have a larger than expected amplified product. Although we have not excluded an artifact, the result is reproducible for one sample. The second sample has not yet been re-analysed. The fragment is not cleaved by restriction enzymes used to detect the haplogroup K. We plan to sequence this DNA fragment to gain more information. One sample is from Arruda (Mesolithic) and the other from the Feteira (Neolithic), and the only sample we have so far analysed from this site.

This is interesting because these sites are separated by about 2,500 years, and represent different palaeoeconomic patterns and distinct burial practices. Feteira is a Neolithic ossuary cave in karstic limestone containing disarticulated human skeletal remains (Zilhão 1984). Arruda is an open-air Mesolithic shell midden occupation site on the terrace of a tributary to the Tagus estuary, and the human remains there are predominantly individual, and sometimes multiple, burials of complete bodies (Roche 1967, 1989). Thus, in view of the current discussion about the ways in which the Neolithic was introduced to western Iberia, this preliminary evidence is most intriguing because it suggests biological continuity along the female line (at least) between Mesolithic and Neolithic populations (for contrasting interpretations of what this might imply for the archaeological record (see Jackes et al. 1997a, 1997b; Zilhão 1998).

The absence of haplogroup V is notable as it is prevalent in Southwest Europe, particularly in the Basque population. However, a study of 121 Neolithic and Bronze Age Basque samples by Izagirre and de la Rúa (1999) has also shown absence of haplogroup V individuals. Haplogroup V is a derivative of haplogroup H, and has been calculated from data on modern samples to have arisen in Southwest Europe about 12,500 years ago. Izagirre's conclusions are that the Iberian population might have been heterogeneous and subject to a founder effect, or that the polymorphism arose at a later date than calculated. The absence of haplogroup I and U6 in our samples is not surprising. Haplogroup I is predominantly found in North and East Europe (Simoni 2000) and U6 is mainly North African (Macaulay et al. 1999).

In conclusion, our results to date demonstrate the feasibility of DNA analysis from Iberian skeletal remains. However, sample size is critical in this kind of analysis, and we would probably need 50 samples from each period to draw valid conclusions about this population. The polymorphism amplified using the haplogroup K primers is of interest, particularly as the samples come from two distinct sites. We will continue our analysis, but results at present suggest genetic continuity between the Neolithic and Mesolithic populations of Portugal.

Acknowledgements

The research reported here was funded by a Social Sciences Research Grant from the University of Alberta (to DL). Continuing research is now funded by a grant from the Social Sciences and Humanities Research Council of Canada (to DL, MJ, FB and others). Our samples come from previous work by DL and MJ in Portugal (funded by SSHRC), from Eugénia Cunha (Departamento de Antropologia, Universidade de Coimbra; new samples from Moita and Arruda), and from João Zilhão (Faculdade de Letras de Lisboa; Feteira samples).

We thank Christopher Meiklejohn (University of Winnipeg) for data collected during our joint work in Portugal; Pablo Arias (Departamento de Ciencas Históricas, Universidade de Cantabria) for permission to use the stable isotope data for Los Canes; and Dr. M.M. Ramalho (Serviços Geológicos de Portugal, Lisbon) for permission to work on materials under his care. Sample preparation and processing was done by Ann O'Neill and Kerri Albertson in Bamforth's laboratory. Participation at MESO2000 was made possible by our SSHRC grant (for DL) and the Department of Laboratory Medicine and Pathology, University of Alberta (for FB).

References

Anderson, S., Bankier, A., Barrell, B., de Bruijn, M., Coulson, A., Drouin, J., Eperon, I., Nierlich, D., Roe, B., Sanger, F., Schreier, P., Smith, A., Staden, R. and Young I. 1981. Sequence and organisation of the human mitochondrial genome. *Nature* 290, 457–465.

Arias Cabal, P. and Garralda, M.D. 1996. Mesolithic burials in Los Canes cave (Asturias, Spain). *Human Evolution* 11, 129–138.

Boom, R., Sol, C., Salimans, M., Jansen, C., Wertheim-van Dillen, P. and van der Noordaa, J. 1990. Rapid and simple method for purification of nucleic acids. *Journal of Clinical Microbiology* 28, 495–503.

Burmeister, S. 2000. Archaeology and migration: approaches to an archaeological proof of migration. *Current Anthropology* 41, 539–567.

Collard, M. and Wood, B. 2000. How reliable are human phylogenetic hypotheses? *Proceedings of the National Academy of Sciences* 97, 5003–5006.

Côrte-Real, H., Macaulay, V., Richards, M., Hariti, G., Issad, M., Cambon-Thomsen, A., Papiha, S., Bertranpetit, J. and Sykes, B. 1996. Genetic diversity in the Iberian Peninsula determined from mitochrondrial sequence analysis. *Annals of Human Genetics* 60, 331–350.

de Knijff, P. 2000. Messages through bottlenecks: on the combined use of slow and fast evolving polymorphic markers on the human Y chromosome. *American Journal of Human Genetics* 67, 1055–1061.

Finlayson, W.D. 1998. *Iroquoian Peoples of the Land of Rocks and Water, AD 1000–1650: A Study in Settlement Archaeology*. London Museum of Archaeology, London. Ontario.

Handt, O., Krings, M., Ward, R. and Pääbo, S. 1996. The retrieval of ancient DNA sequences. *American Journal of Human Genetics* 59, 368–376.

Howells, W.W. 1973. Cranial variation in man: a study of multivariate analysis of patterns of difference among recent human populations. *Peabody Museum Papers* 67, 1–259, Boston.

Izagirre, N. and de la Rúa, C. 1999. An MtDNA analysis in ancient Basque populations: implications for haplogroup V as marker for a major Paleolithic expansion from Southwestern Europe. *American Journal of Human Genetics* 65, 199–207.

Jackes, M. and Lubell, D. 1999a. Human skeletal biology and the Mesolithic-Neolithic transition in Portugal. In: Thévenin, A. (ed.) *Europe des derniers chasseurs Épipaléolithique et Mésolithique: actes du 5ᵉ colloque international UISPP, commission XII, Grenoble, 18–23 septembre 1995*, 59–64. Paris.

—— 1999b. Human biological variability in the Portuguese Mesolithic. *Arqueologia* 24, 25–42.

Jackes, M., Lubell, D. and Meiklejohn, C. 1997a. Healthy but mortal: human biology and the first farmers of Western Europe *Antiquity* 71, 639–658 (also http://intarch.ac.uk/antiquity/jackes).

—— 1997b. On physical anthropological aspects of the Mesolithic-Neolithic transition in the Iberian Peninsula. *Current Anthropology* 38, 839–846.

Jackes, M., Silva, A.M. and Irish, J. 2001. Dental morphology – a valuable contribution to our understanding of prehistory. *Journal of Iberian Archaeology* 3, 97–119.

Jungers, W.L., Falsetti, A.B. and Wall, C.E. 1995. Shape, relative size, and size-adjustments in morphometrics. *Yearbook of Physical Anthropology* 38, 137–161.

de la Rúa, C. 1992. The craniofacial factors of the Basque skull, a comparative study. *Homo* 43, 135–161.

Lalueza Fox, C. 1996. Physical anthropological aspects of the Mesolithic-Neolithic transition in the Iberian Peninsula. *Current Anthropology* 37, 689–695.

Lalueza Fox, C., Gonzalez Martin, A. and Vives Civit, S. 1996. Cranial variation in the Iberian Peninsula and the Balearic Islands: inferences about the history of the population. *American Journal of Physical Anthropology* 99, 413–28.

Lell, J. and Wallace, D. 2000. The peopling of Europe from the maternal and paternal perspectives *American Journal of Human Genetics* 67, 1376–1381.

Lubell, D., Jackes, M., Schwarcz, H., Knyf, M. and Meiklejohn, C. 1994. The Mesolithic-Neolithic transition in Portugal: isotopic and dental evidence of diet. *Journal of Archaeological Science* 21, 201–16.

Macaulay, V., Richards, M., Hickey, E., Vega, E., Cruciani, F., Guida, V., Scozzari, R., Bonné-Tamir, B., Sykes, B. and Torroni, A. 1999. The emerging tree of West Eurasian mtDNAs: a synthesis for control-region sequences and RFLPs. *American Journal of Human Genetics* 64, 232–249.

Martin, R. and Saller, K. 1957–66. *Lehrbuch der Anthropologie in systematischer Darstellung, mit besonderer Berücksichtigung der anthropologischen Methoden.* Stuttgart.

Monges Soares, A.M. 1993. The ^{14}C content of marine shells: evidence for variability in coast upwelling off Portugal during the Holocene. *Isotope techniques in the Study of Past and Current Environmental Changes in the Hydrosphere and Atmosphere (Proceedings) Vienna*. IAEA-SM-329/49, 471–485. Vienna.

Morant, G.M. 1929. A contribution to Basque craniometry. *Biometrika* 21, 67–84.

Richards, M., Côrte-Real, H., Forster, P., Macaulay, V., Wilkinson-Herbots, H., Demaine, A., Papiha, S., Hedges, R., Bandelt, H-J. and Sykes, B. 1996. Paleolithic and Neolithic lineages in the European mitochondrial gene pool. *American Journal of Human Genetics* 59, 185–203.

Richards, M.B., Macaulay, V., Hickey, E., Vega, E., Sykes, B., Guida, V., Rengo, C., Sellitto, D., Cruciani, F., Kivisild, T., Villems, R., Thomas, M., Rychkov, S., Rychkov, O., Rychkov, Y., Gölge, M., Dimitrov, D., Hill, E., Bradley, D., Romano, V., Calì, F., Vona, G., Demaine, A., Papiha, S., Triantaphyllidis, C., Stefanescu, G., Hatina, J., Belledi, M., Di Rienzo, A., Novelletto, A., Oppenheim, A., Nørby, S., Al-Zaheri, N., Santachiara-Benerecetti, S., Scozzari, R., Torroni, A. and Bandelt, H.-J. 2000. Tracing European founder lineages in the Near Eastern mtDNA pool. *American Journal of Human Genetics* 67, 1251–1276.

Roche, J. 1967. Note sur la stratigraphie de l'amas coquillier mésolithique de Cabeço da Arruda (Muge). *Communicações dos Serviços Geológicos de Portugal* 52, 221–242.

—— 1989. Spatial organisation in the Mesolithic sites of Muge, Portugal. In: Bonsall, C. (ed.) *The Mesolithic in Europe. Papers Presented at the Third International Symposium, Edinburgh 1985*, 607–613. Edinburgh.

Rosser, Z.H., Zerjal, T., Hurles, M.E., Adojaan, M., Alavantic, D., Amorim, A., Amos, W., Armenteros, M., Arroyo, E., Barbujani, G., Beckman, G., Beckman, L., Bertranpetit, J., Bosch, E., Bradley, D.G., Brede, G., Cooper, G., Côrte-Real, H.B.S.M., de Knijff, P., Decorte, R., Dubrova, Y.E., Evgrafov, O., Gilissen, A., Glisic, S., Gölge, M., Hill, E.W., Jeziorowska, A., Kalaydjieva, L., Kayser, M., Kivisild, T., Kravchenko, S.A., Krumina, A., Kuinskas, V., Lavinha, J., Livshits, L.A., Malaspina, P., Maria, S., McElreavey, K., Meitinger, T.A., Mikelsaar, A.-V., Mitchell, R.J., Nafa, K., Nicholson, J., Nørby, S., Pandya, A., Parik, J., Patsalis, P.C., Pereira, L., Peterlin, B., Pielberg, G., Prata, M.J., Previderé, C., Roewer, L., Rootsi, S., Rubinsztein, D.C., Saillard, J., Santos, F.R., Stefanescu, G., Sykes, B.C., Tolun, A., Villems, R., Tyler-Smith, C. and Jobling, M.A. 2000. Y-chromosomal diversity in Europe is clinal and influenced primarily by geography, rather than by language. *American Journal of Human Genetics* 67, 1526–1534.

Semino, O., Passarino, G., Oefner, P.J., Lin, A.A., Arbuzova, S., Beckman, L.E., de Benedictis, G., Francalacci, P., Kouvatsi, A., Limborska, S., Marcikiæ, M., Mika, A., Mika, B., Primorac, D., Santachiara-Benerecetti, A.S., Cavalli-Sforza, L.L. and Underhill, P.A. 2000. The Genetic legacy of Paleolithic *Homo sapiens sapiens* in extant Europeans: a Y chromosome perspective. *Science* 290, 1155–1159.

Shennan, S. 2000. Population, culture history, and the dynamics of cultural change. *Current Anthropology* 41, 811–835.

Simoni, L., Calafell, F., Pettener, D., Bertranpetit, J. and Barbujani, G. 2000. Geographic patterns of mtDNA diversity in Europe. *American Journal of Human Genetics* 66, 262–278.

Stuiver, M. and Braziunas, T. 1993. Modeling atmospheric ^{14}C influences and ^{14}C ages of marine samples to 10,000 BC. *Radiocarbon* 35, 137–189.

Sutton, R.E. 1996. The Middle Iroquoian colonization of Huronia. Unpublished Ph.D. thesis, McMaster University, Hamilton. Ontario.

Torroni, A., Bandelt, H-J., D'Urbano, L., Lahermo, P., Moral, P., Sellitto, D., Rengo, C., Forster, P., Savontaus, M-L., Bonné-Tamir, B. and Scozzari, R. 1998. mtDNA analysis reveals a major Late Paleolithic population expansion from southwestern to northeastern Europe *American Journal of Human Genetics* 62, 1137–1152.

Torroni, A., Lott, M., Cabell, M., Chen, Y., Lavergne, L. and Wallace, D. 1994. mtDNA analysis and the origin of Caucasians: identification of ancient caucasian-specific haplogroups, one of which is prone to recurrent somatic duplication in the D-loop region. *American Journal of Human Genetics* 55, 760–776.

Walker, M.J. 1985. *Characterising local Southeastern Spanish populations of 3000–1500 BC*. BAR international series 263. Oxford.

Zilhão, J. 1984. *A Gruta da Feteira (Lourinhã)*. Trabalhos de Arqueologia 1, Instituto Português do Património Cultural, Lisboa.

—— 1998. On logical and empirical aspects of the Mesolithic-Neolithic transition in the Iberian Peninsula. *Current Anthropology* 39, 690–698.

74. Interactions between the late Mesolithic hunter-gatherers and farming communities in Northern Poland

Lucyna Domańska

The aim of this paper is to discuss the problem of contacts between hunter-gatherers and farming communities during the second half of the VII mill. bp on the Polish Lowland. In this discussion special attention will be paid to the differences in the interactions between the Linear Pottery culture and the hunter-gatherers of the Chojnice-Pieńki and Janisławice cultures.

Introduction

In my paper, I intend to outline the interactions between the late Mesolithic hunter-gatherers and farming communities on the part of Polish Lowland called Kuiavia (Figure 74.1). This region seemed to be an especially suitable area for such investigation on account of its very early colonisation by the farming communities belonging to the Linear Pottery culture. The beginning of this process is confirmed, among other things, by materials from the site Grabie 4, contemporary with Flomborn-ačkova-Zofipole phase (Czerniak 1994:40 pp). In this area, therefore, hunter-gatherer settlement is recognised to a large extent (Figure 74.1). These investigations confirmed the complexity of the indigenous Mesolithic society (Domańska 1985:447 pp, 1989:25 pp, 1991:7 pp, 1995:93 pp, 1998:129 pp).

I will use the concept of the agricultural frontier to trace the interactions between these communities. This concept was introduced by M. Zvelebil to study the transition to farming in the lands adjoining the Baltic Sea (Zvelebil 1998:9). The agricultural frontier is understood as a zone of interaction between foragers and farmers, marked by various forms of contact and exchange (Dennell 1995:113 pp; Zvelebil 1998:10).

The late Mesolithic of the Kuiavia region

Kuiavia includes three geographical districts: pre-valley of the Vistula-Noteć rivers, Kuiavian Plateau and Kuiavian Lake District. The sandy soils dominate in the pre-valley, whereas the black soils are characteristic feature of the Kuiavian Plateau (Figure 74.1).

The late Mesolithic settlement of the discussed zone was mainly located in pre-valley of the Vistula-Noteć rivers. This is territory of a very low agricultural usefulness, with the landscape marked by ranges of dune ridges and abundant marshy areas. The sandy soils dominate there. In the parallel stretch of the pre-valley settlement of the Chojnice-Pieńki culture distinctly predominated, while in the meridian one settlement of the Janisławice culture.

For our studies the concentrations of the Chojnice-Pieńki sites discovered in the pre-valley of the Noteć river at the Kuiavian Plateau border and the concentration found on the sandy island inside the area of the black soils are the most important (Figure 74.1). These two concentrations of the hunter-gatherer settlement were located in close neighbourhood of the early farming landscape, which is characterised by the gently shaped river valleys covered with black soils.

The actually available C14 dates for the Chojnice-Pieńki in Poland are not earlier than the beginning of the VII millennium bp (Kozłowski 1989:112).

According to S.K. Kozłowski in the VI millennium bp there occurs a peculiar cultural uniformisation in Poland (Kozłowski 1989:122). This process is characterised by a gradual replacement of slim microlithis by increasingly more numerous trapezes and dominant irregular micro-side-scrapers among the tools on flakes. Such taxonomic change is visible among the materials discovered on the borderline between the pre-valley of the Noteć river and Kuiavian Plateau. This seems to confirm additionally the late chronology of the sites from the discussed zone.

The Janisławice settlement is connected with the south-eastern part of Kuiavia and exemplified by sites in Wistka Szlachecka (Schild *et al.* 1975:127 pp) and Dęby (Domańska 1991:7 pp). This part of Kuiavia is characterised by two types of landscape (Figure 74.1). The first one is connected with a part of so-called black and white Kuiavia and is distinguished by areas of black soil and also extensive areas covered with sandy soil. The second type of landscape is typical for the pre-valley of the Vistula river and characterised by dunes and marshy areas.

So, in the late Mesolithic two different cultural

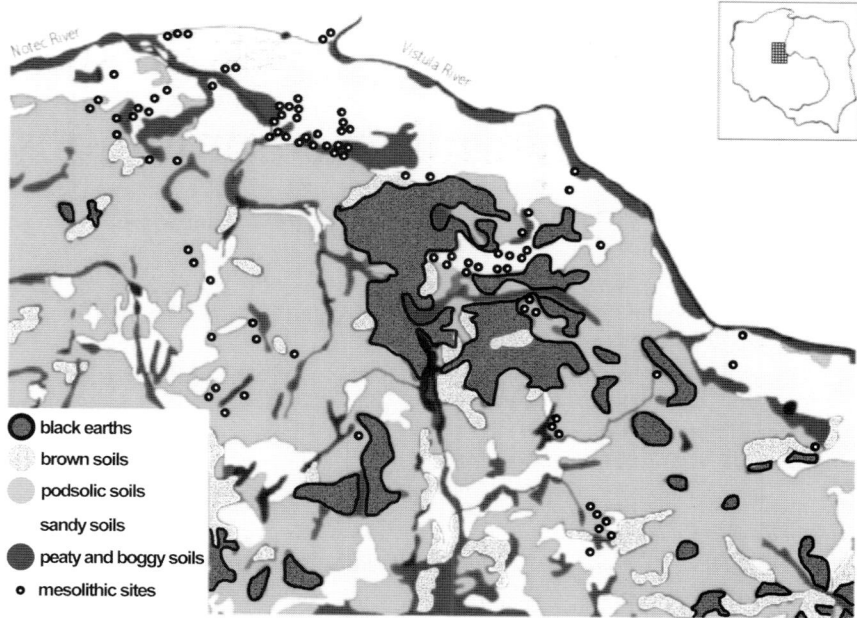

Figure 74.1 Distribution of the Mesolithic sites on the Kuiavia, Poland.

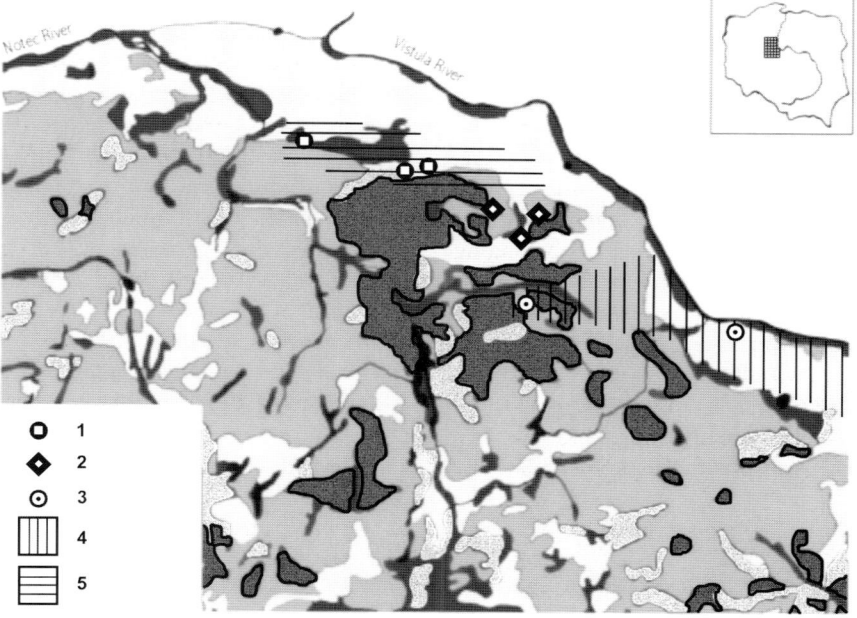

Figure 74.2 Contacts zones between hunter-gatherers and LBK farmers of the Kuiavia, Poland. 1. The Chojnice-Pieńki sites dated to the turn of the VII and VI mill. bp, 2. The LBK sites of the Podgaj type, 3. Sites of the Janisławice culture, 4. The Janisławice-LBK contact zone and 5. The Chojnice-Pieńki-LBK contact zone.

traditions were developing on Kuiavia territory: the Chojnice-Pieńki and Janisławice. The first one continued the north European tradition in tool production (Domańska 1985:447 pp) while Janisławice flint industry must be genetically related to the south-eastern Europe (Domańska 1998:130 pp).

Evidences of the contacts between the Chojnice-Pieńki hunter-gatherers and LBK

As the first group of people of the LBK appeared in the Kuiavia a process of information exchange between the early farming and gathering-hunting communities was initiated (Czerniak 1994:194 pp). However, the traces of their contacts in the Kuiavian materials are poorly legible.

They are confined to an exchange of raw flint materials, technology and tools.

1 Exchange of raw flint materials

The Mesolithic hunter-gatherers and early farming communities of Kuiavia used both local and imported flint raw materials, mainly from the south of Poland. As for the latter, chocolate and Jurassic Cracow flints were of the predominant importance (Domańska 1995:151).

The Chojnice-Pieńki communities used mainly local flint resources obtainable on river beaches and processed on the terrain of settlements. Though several artefacts of the chocolate flint are registered at the site Kolankowo 5, which is located in the pre-valley of the Noteć river at the Kuiavian Plateau border (Domańska 1995:103). The artefacts seem to correspond with LBK tradition and their presence at this site may confirm contacts of these two populations.

2 Exchange of working techniques

Exchange of the experience in local flint processing was confirmed by the LBK sites of the Podgaj type. Three sites of this type were investigated, all being small camping sites situated at the sandy bottom of the river valley (Figure 74.2). The characteristic feature of the materials from these sites is the specific technological structure of pottery (domination of the so-called kitchen ware: Czerniak 1994:57) and flint materials, which are distinguished by the use of the local and lack of the imported raw material and by reference to the Mesolithic tradition in the flint processing (Domańska 1985:452).

3 Exchange of ready tools

Exchange of ready tools is confirmed by the finds of shoe-last adzes discovered on the sites lying outside the Kuiavian concentration of the LBK sites. Many such products have been registered, among others, in Pomerania (Zvelebil 1998:18). Dates from this region indicate that Mesolithic settlement probably continued there even until the Early Bronze Age (Bagniewski 1998:111).

Evidences of the contacts between the Janisławice hunter-gatherers and LBK

In the layer of the fossil soil of the Dęby site from Kuiavia, flints of the Janisławice culture and bones of domestic animals were discovered (Domańska 1998:129 pp). These results have provoked discussion on the contacts between the Janisławice hunter-gatherers and LBK farmers on the Polish Lowland. Unfortunately, in the light of stratigraphic and chronological analyses, the unambiguous interpretation of these materials is impossible. The main question is, whether the flints and the bones of domestic animals in the layer of fossil soil are contemporaneous or not. Different analyses undertaken at this site did not solve the problem. So, at the present stage of investigation these materials cannot be an evidence for contacts between communities under discussion.

Although, it should not be ruled out that people of the Janisławice culture had some impact on LBK colonisation of the Kuiavia region, first of all by providing the colonists with the information about the geography of new-settled terrains (Czerniak 1994: 194 p). This supposition may be supported by the similarities in the chocolate flint distribution on this territory (Domańska 1995:151 pp).

On the Kuiavian Plateau the chocolate flint from southern Poland played a primary role in production process among the groups of the Janisławice, Linear Pottery and the early Funnel Beaker culture (Domańska 1995:152). The concentration of this raw material at the FBC sites near the Vistula river is clearly evident, whereas never does it dominate in technological process in other parts of the Kuiavian zone. Yet, a system of distribution of chocolate flint among Janisławice and LBK groups seems to be different. It reached equally the LBK settlements from different parts of Kuiavian Plateau. Probably, the same situation took place among Janisławice camps. The last statement seems to be confirmed by the Dęby site located on the Kuiavian Plateau. At this site the chocolate flint was the element of an essential technological importance and must have been imported in large amounts to the encampment. In the Janisławice culture, therefore, some mechanisms must have functioned providing an access to this kind of material in sufficient quantities to sites lying far from deposits (250–300 km).

Similarities between the Janisławice and LBK system of chocolate flint distribution may indicate that in the Kuiavian region the Danubian colonists distribute this flint by routes formed still in the Janisławice culture period.

Conclusions

A long history of contacts between the hunter-gatherers and LBK communities is scarcely legible in an archaeological record from the Kuiavian region. However, geographical spread of the evidences of the interactions between these communities permits to distinguish two contact zones.

First zone can be situated in the northern part of the Kuiavia (Figure 74.2), on the border between two types of landscapes. One of these landscapes is characteristic for the pre-valley of the Noteć river and was inhabited by the Chojnice-Pieńki. The second landscape is typical for the Kuiavian Plateau and is distinguished by the appearance of black soils. This territory was very early colonised by Danubian communities. Within discussed zone exchange of technological innovations and imports took place. The development of the contacts between the Chojnice-Pieńki hunters and the LBK farmers within this zone is characteristic, according to R. Dennell or M. Zvelebil, for the stationary frontier (Dennell 1985:113 p; Zvelebil 1998:16 p). This type of the agricultural frontier develops in stable or slowly changing situations, allowing for the development of communication and exchange between foragers and farmers.

The second frontier of contacts was arisen between the LBK and Janisławice populations. Exchange of information about new-settled terrains was the main reason for the contacts. Such situations corresponds with mobile frontier, which develops during periods of agricultural expansion (Zvelebil 1998:16). The Janisławice communities settled the area, through which the LBK expansion to the north took place.

The differences between the Chojnice-Pieńki-LBK zone and the Janisławice-LBK zone of contacts in the Kuiavia are probably connected with the different settlement network of these hunter-gatherers. The Chojnice-Pieńki groups stemmed from local tradition and they settled almost all sandy areas of Kuiavia while Janisławice communities were newcomers (Kozłowski 1989:22) who tried to colonise the southern part of this region.

References

Bagniewski, Z. 1998. Later Mesolithic settlement in Central and Eastern Pomerania. In: Zvelebil, M., Domańska, L. and Dennell, R. (eds.) *Harvesting the sea, farming the forest*, 111–119. Sheffield.

Czerniak, L. 1994. *Wczesny i środkowy okres neolitu na Kujawach, 5400–3650 p.n.e.* Poznań.

Dennell, R. 1995. The hunter-gatherer/agricultural frontier in prehistoric temperate Europe. In: Green, S. and Perlman, S.M. (eds.) *The archaeology of frontiers and boundaries*, 113–140. New York.

Domańska, L. 1985. Elements of a food-producing economy in the Late Mesolithic of the Polish Lowland. In: Bonsall, C. (ed.) *The Mesolithic in Europe. Papers presented at the third International Symposium*, 447–455. Edinburgh.

—— 1989. Cultural development of Kuiavian communities in the Late Mesolithic. *Archaeologia Interregionalis* 10, 25–39.

—— 1991. *Obozowisko kultury janisławickiej w Dębach woj. włocławskie, stanowisko 29.* Poznań-Inowrocław.

—— 1995. *Geneza krzemieniarstwa kultury pucharów lejkowatych na Kujawach.* Łódź.

—— 1998. The initial stage of food-production in the Polish Lowlands – the Dęby 29 site. In: Zvelebil, M., Domańska, L. and Dennell, R. (eds.) *Harvesting the sea, farming the forest*, 129–133. Sheffield.

Kozłowski, S.K. 1989. *Mesolithic in Poland. A new approach.* Wydawnictwo Uniwersytetu. Warszawskiego.

Schild, R., Marczak, M. and Królik, H. 1975. *Późny mezolit. Próba wieloaspektowej analizy otwartych stanowisk piaskowych.* Ossolineum.

Zvelebil, M. 1998. Agricultural frontiers, Neolithic origins, and the transition to farming in the Baltic Basin. In: Zvelebil, M., Domańska, L. and Dennell, R. (eds.) *Harvesting the sea, farming the forest*, 9–27. Sheffield.

75. My place or yours?

Fredrik Hallgren

In the beginning of the Scandinavian Early Neolithic (c. 3900 cal BC), the agricultural economy and the material culture of the Funnel-beaker Culture appeared in the whole of Southern Scandinavia, up to and including Mälardalen. The change seems to be simultaneous in the whole region. It is argued that the appearance of the Funnel-beaker Culture was the result of a change within the Late Mesolithic society. Thus, the geographical extent of the Scandinavian Funnel-beaker society was determined by the geographical extent of an already existing Late Mesolithic social unit. Exogamous relations between different Mesolithic local groups, within this larger social unit, contributed to spread the knowledge of the new way of life. It is further suggested that the nature of the marriage networks, and the rules of postmarital residence changed as society changed, when the way of life of the Funnel-beaker Culture was created.

Introduction

A basic thought that has shaped my reasoning, is something that have been discussed at previous Mesolithic conferences by among others Constandse-Westerman and Newell (Constandse-Westerman and Newell 1989): When people marry, one spouse leaves his/her parents home and moves to his/her mate. In a region with a low population density, as I believe was the case in the Stone Age of central Sweden, the move in connection with marriage could sometimes be made over considerable distances (Newell *et al.* 1990; Jacobs *et al.* 1996). This means, that people with knowledge of specific technological traditions often happened to move to areas where these traditions were not practised. Depending on the circumstances, these foreign traditions were or were not allowed in the new social environment.

The area discussed here is Mälardalen (the Mälaren valley), the region around the lakes Mälaren and Hjälmaren in eastern central Sweden (the countys Uppland, Västmanland, Närke and Södermanland). During the Stone Age the sea level along the east coast of central and northern Sweden was considerably higher than today (Åkerlund 1996, this volume), and the plains around the lakes Mälaren and Hjälmaren were covered by a large bay of the Littorina sea (c.f. Figure 75.2).

The Late Mesolithic (5400-3900 cal BC)

During the Late Mesolithic Mälardalen was characterised by sites situated by the seashore, with an economy geared mainly towards the exploitation of marine resources, such as seal and fish (Knutsson *et al.* 1999:105). Two things dominate the preserved material culture: greenstone axes, and knapped quartz. The greenstone axes are both pecked and polished, sometimes the polish is limited to the edge, but surface-covering polish also occur (Figure 75.1). Axes with a roundish section are the most common, but square section and polished narrow sides, similar to the later thinbutted axes are also frequent. There is a tendency for polish being more widespread in younger assemblages (Lindgren and Nordqvist 1997).

Figure 75.1 Greenstone axes characteristic of the Late Mesolithic in Mälardalen. (The axe to the left is actually from a site dated to 7000 cal BC, but the type is also frequent during the Late Mesolithic). After Lindgren and Nordqvist (1997:59 p).

taken as an indication that some experiments with cultivation of cereals were taking place (Hallgren 1996).

The Mesolithic of Mälardalen can also be described as lacking several traits of material culture, which neighbouring foraging groups displayed. The most conspicuous is the lack of pottery (Figure 75.2), which was present both on the nearby Åland-islands and in mainland Finland to the east and north-east in the form of Comb Ware ceramics (Dreijer 1941; Nuñez and Storå 1992; Edgren 1993; Andrén et al. 1995), on the southeastern side of the Baltic in the form of Narva and Neman pottery (Kempisty 1986; Kriiska 1996; Sulgostowska 1998; Timofeev 1998), and in southernmost Sweden and Denmark, in the form of Ertebølle pottery (Gebauer 1995; Persson 1999:118 pp). Another tradition that is absent, as shown by Kjel Knutsson, is a macroblade-industry, present both to the south and to the north of Mälardalen (Knutsson et al. 1999).

In my research I discuss these different traditions as tied to social units, partly by an unconscious process of learning a tradition that is reproduced within the unit, but also as part of a conscious communication of symbolic meaning, in the attempt to create the categories "us" and "them" (Sackett 1990; Wiessner 1990; Stark 1998).

The period discussed here is roughly contemporary with the Linear Band Pottery (LBK) tradition in a large sense, which appears just to the south of the map in Figure 75.2 around 5400 cal BC. The border between the LBK in the south and the hunter and gatherers to the north is stable for more than a millennia, and it is not until with the creation of the Funnel-beaker Culture way of life that agriculture appears in the southern parts of Scandinavia (Bogucki 1988, 2000; Price and Gebauer 1992; Rowley-Conwy 1995; Zvelebil 1998; Persson 1999a: Price 2000).

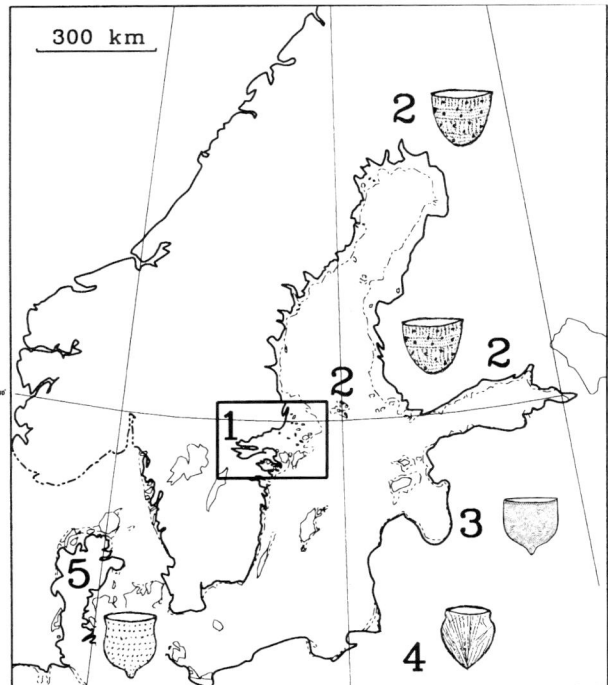

Figure 75.2 During the Late Mesolithic, pottery manufacture was practised by several hunter-gatherer groups around the Baltic (2–5), but was not adopted in Mälardalen (1) until with the creation of the Early Neolithic Funnel-beaker Culture. Caption: 1, the region Mälardalen; 2 Comb Ware Culture; 3, Narva Culture; 4, Neman Culture; 5, Ertebölle Culture. The shoreline map is adopted from Munthé (1940).

The Early Neolithic (3900–3300 cal BC)

The new traditions and subsistence strategies are adopted, or created, at pretty much the same time in the whole area from Denmark in the south to Mälardalen in the north around 3900 cal BC (Figure 75.3).

The Funnel-beaker Culture (TRB) in Mälardalen is characterised by two types of sites. Coastal sites dominated by remains from fishing and seal-hunting, and inland sites dominated by remains from domestic animals such as cattle and sheep/goat, and cultivated plants such as wheat, barely, peas, beans and vine-grapes (Florin 1958; Schiemann 1958; Hulthén and Welinder 1981; Welinder 1982, 1998; Kihlstedt et al. 1997; Hallgren et al. 1997:93 pp; Segerberg 1999). The same type of material culture (funnel-beakers, polygonal battle axes, thinbutted axes etc.), occur in both contexts. It is my belief that the inland sites, which typically covers several 10 000 of square meters, were used as basecamps, and that the coastal sites were used on a seasonal basis by the inland farmers (Apel et al. 1995:87 pp; Hallgren et al. 1997:104 pp). The relative dietary importance of domesticated products

Quartz was the main material used for small tools (c.f. papers by Knutsson, Lindgren and Åkerlund in this volume). Unretouched flakes were frequently used as tools, but a few formal types also occur such as microblade cores, scrapers and transverse arrowheads of quartz. The same formal types are also present in small numbers made in flint imported from southern Scandinavia. Slate tools are known from a several Late Mesolithic sites, and there is evidence of local manufacture of arrowheads in grey slate (Taffinder 1998:122 pp; Artursson in press). Imported slate tools also occur, recognisable by the non-local design (e.g. knifes with notches on the handle) and/or non-local raw material (red slate). The latter are imports from the middle part of Norrland (northern Sweden) several hundreds km to the north (Blomqvist and Åhman 1999; c.f. Lundberg 1997). As the presence of flint indicates long distance contacts with the south, so does the slate knifes point to the north.

On one Late Mesolithic site a saddle shaped grinding stone has been found (Hallgren et al. 1995; Hallgren 1996; Lidström-Holmberg 1998). The type is typical for the only slightly younger early Funnel-beaker sites, where they were used for the grinding of cereals, as have been demonstrated by Lidström-Holmberg (1993, 1998). The presence of such a tool at a Late Mesolithic site, may be

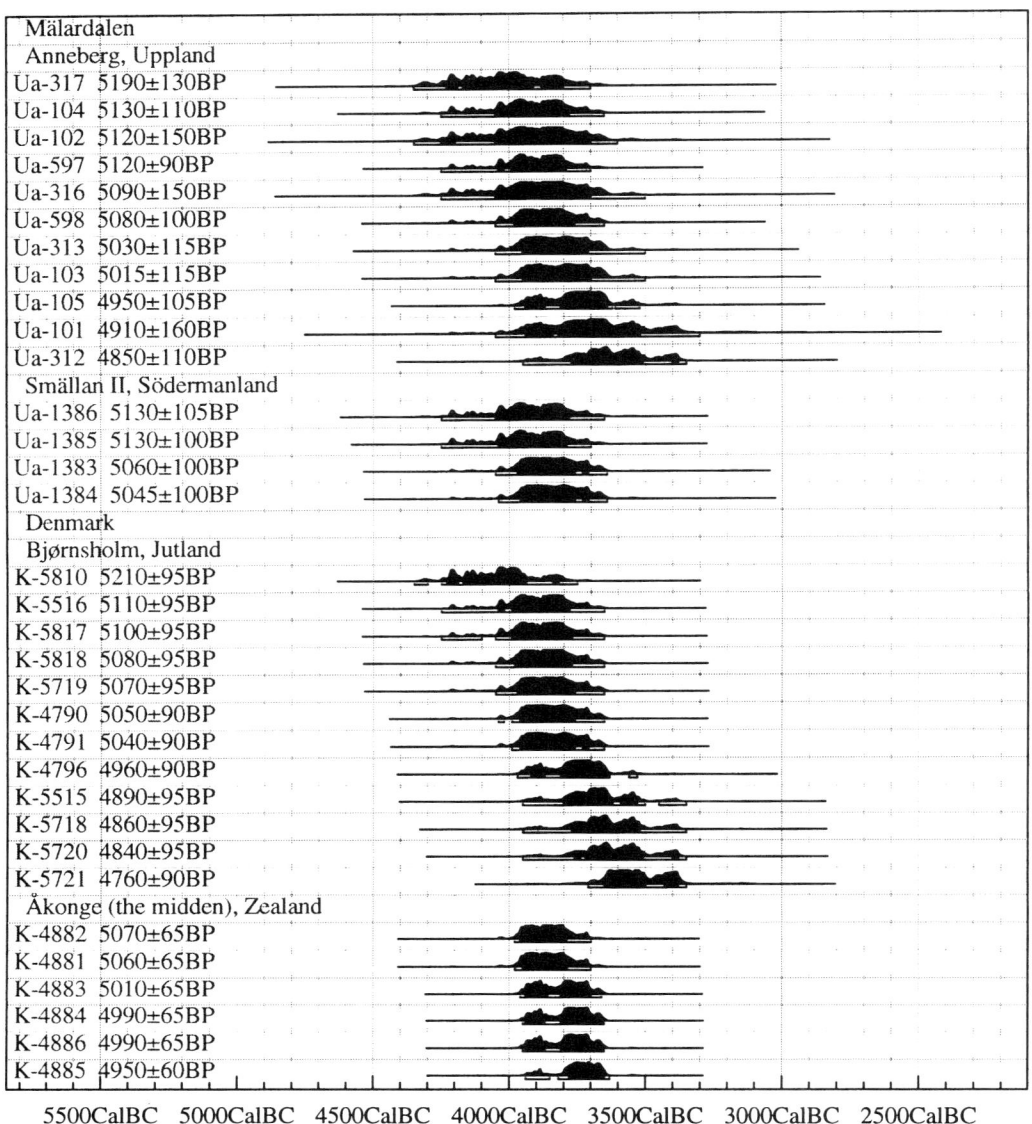

Figure 75.3 *14C-dates from early Funnel-beaker Culture sites in Mälardalen and Denmark. The samples from Anneberg consists of hazelnut shells, charcoal and food-crust on potsherds (Segerberg 1999:110 pp), the samples from Smällan II consists of charcoal (Kihlstedt et al. 1997:126). For information on Björnsholm see Andersen (1993) and Rasmussen (1993). For information on Åkonge see Fischer (1993), Koch (1998:337) and Stafford (1999).*

compared to wild resources can not be estimated on the basis of present data.

The material culture shows several traits of continuity with the preceding Late Mesolithic, for example in quartz reduction strategies, and the continued use of transverse arrowheads and pecked axes (Callahan 1987; Callahan *et al.* 1992; Kihlstedt *et al.* 1997). The thinbutted greenstone axes have clear predecessors in the local polished Mesolithic axes with a square section (Florin 1958). The new types of material culture, for example the pottery, show some direct parallels with funnel-beakers from other parts of northern Europe (c.f. Koch 1998), as seen in Figure 75.4c, but local designs appear right from the start of the local funnel-beaker sequence (Figure 75.4a–b)

(Hallgren and Possnert 1997; Hallgren 2000). The polygonal battle-axes of the region have a design that is peculiar to Central Sweden and southern Norway (Zápotocký 1992; Hallgren forthcoming).

The fast spread, the continuity in several technological traditions, and the local design of the new forms of material culture indicates that farming and new traditions were adopted within a local context, rather than being carried by a gradual wave of advance of an intruding new population.

The specific location of the northern border of the Funnel-beaker Culture, on both the west and the east side of the Baltic, has sometimes been explained by ecological and climatic factors (e.g. Hulthén and Welinder 1981:153

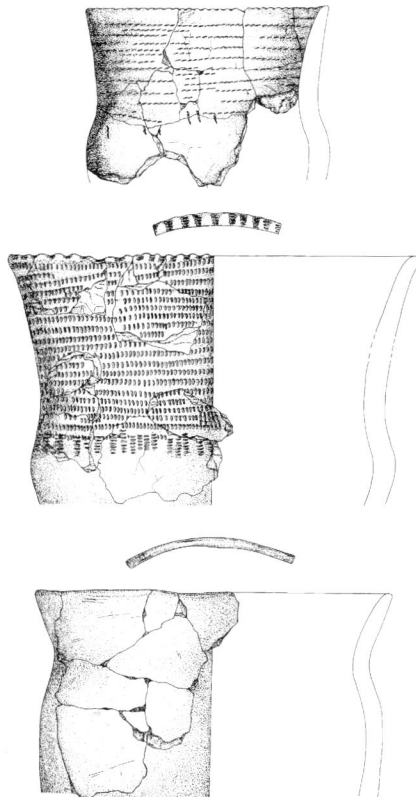

Figure 75.4 Funnel-beakers from Mälardalen. These three pots represent contemporary types, dated to the first half of the Early Neolithic. Scale 1:4. Reconstructions and drawings by Gunlög Graner. After Graner and Hallgren (forthcoming).

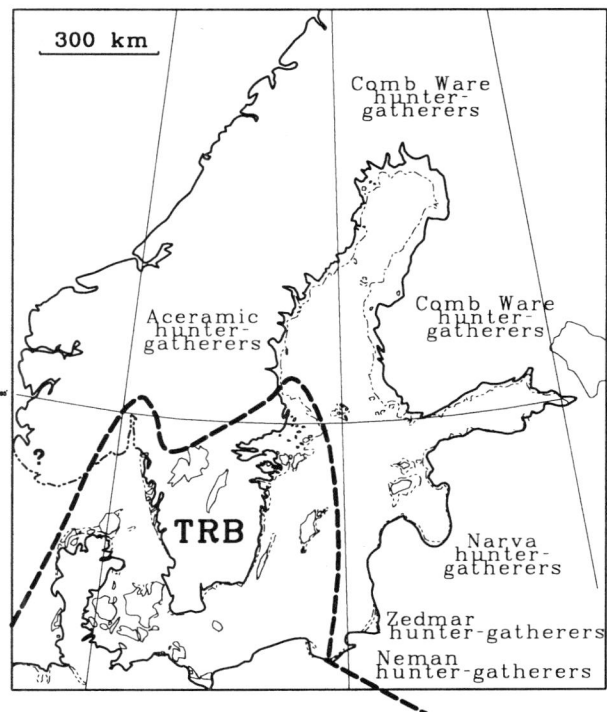

Figure 75.5 The Funnel-beaker Culture has a markedly different geographical extent on the western side of the Baltic as compared to the eastern side. Thus, the northern border of the Funnel-beaker Culture does not conform to a climatic or vegetational zone. The shoreline map is adopted from Munthé (1940).

pp; Sulgostowska 1998:92). There are several problems with this theory, the biggest being that the northern border does not follow any common ecological boundary. This is evident if one compares the northern border of the TRB in Scandinavia, with the northern border on the other side of the Baltic, which in this case is not to be found on the eastern but on the southern shore, in Poland (Figure 75.5). To the north of the Funnel-beaker Culture on the eastern side of the Baltic, there lived several hunter-gatherer groups, characterised by the material culture of the Neman-, Zedmar-, Narva- and Comb Ware Cultures (Kempisty 1986; Timofeev 1988, 1998; Timofeev *et al.* 1995; Kriiska 1996; Asplund 1998; Sulgostowska 1998; Pesonen 1999), people that choose not to adopt agriculture nor the material traditions of the Funnel-beaker Culture, even though the climatic and ecological conditions were just as good as those of Mälardalen.

Late Mesolithic marriage networks

As stated above, I believe that the local Funnel-beaker culture was created by a change within the Late Mesolithic society. As such, the change was structured by the structure of the Late Mesolithic social configurations.

The social organisation of modern hunter-gatherers has been described by Newell *et al.* (1990) as based on the stepwise larger social groupings: family, band, dialect tribe and language family, a division I have adopted as analytical concepts in my research. This structure can be viewed as a forum for different types of contact within and between societies. Marriage is an example of contact that is related to this structure as it most commonly is arranged between persons that originate from different bands, but often belong to the same dialect tribe or language group (Adams and Kasakoff 1975; Newell *et al.* 1990).

Most marriages are arranged between people within the same geographical region, but there are also examples of persons moving great distances in connection with marriage. Newell *et al.* mentions an example where persons moved from Alaska to Labrador within the span of a few generations of marriage (Newell *et al.* 1990:8). An example that concern shorter geographic distances, but is illustrative since it involves both farmers and hunter-gatherers, is the region of Torres Strait, where there was frequent intermarriage between horticulturists and hunter-gatherers of different language groups (Figure 75.6).

A rather different example is provided by the Wanano-Tukano of the Amazon, who are organised in exogamous dialect groups, and always marry persons belonging to other language dialect groups. These marriages are

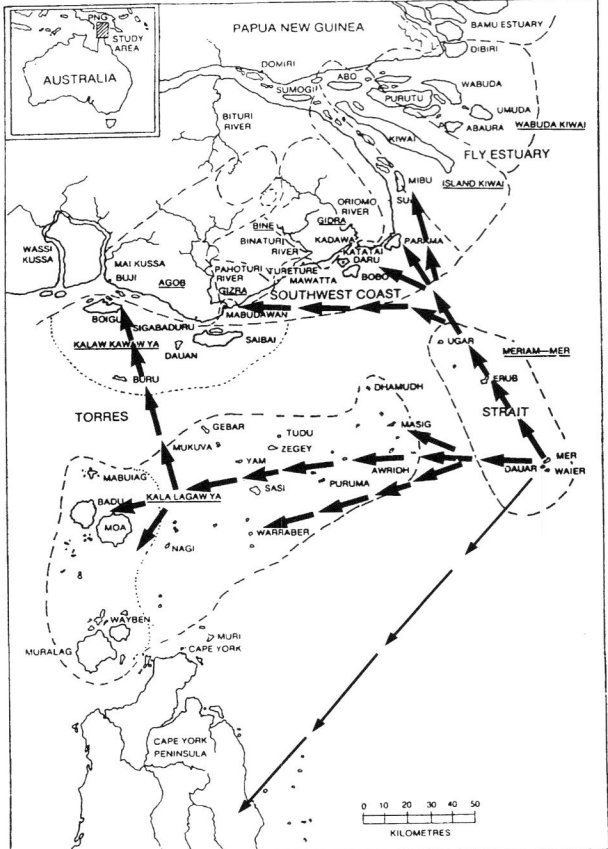

Figure 75.6 Marriage alliances in relation to language areas of the Torres Strait. The figure displays the situation as seen from the Meriam-mer speaking swidden-agriculturists of the island Mer. Most of their marriages were arranged with persons within their own language group. But distant marriages were also regularly arranged with people from the agricultural populations of New Guinea, as well as with horticulturists and hunter-gatherers of the central and western islands of the Strait, and with hunter-gatherers on the Australian continent. After Lawrence (1994).

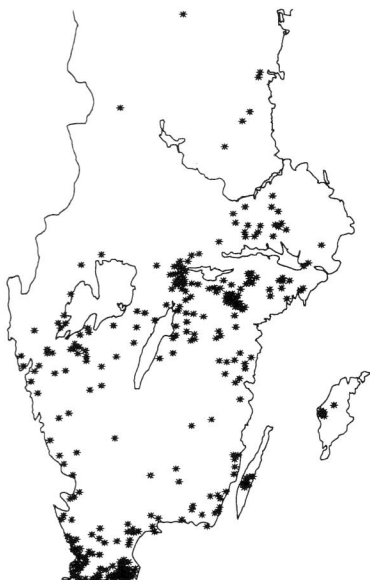

Figure 75.7 The distribution of polygonal battle-axes of the Early Neolithic Funnel-beaker Culture. After Florin (1938).

frequently arranged between people who live at a distance of 10 days of travel (Chernela 1992). 10 days of travel by canoe would have brought a Late Mesolithic traveller from Mälardalen to Denmark, or to the Comb Ware hunter-gatherers of northernmost Sweden (estimated speed in wooden canoe: 3.5-4 knots, 10 hours a day, c.f. Österholm 1988; Hallgren 1993:19).

One thing that characterise the spread of new ideas or traditions through exogamy, is that there is a difference in how knowledge associated with gender-specific tasks is transferred, depending on what postmarital rule of residence was applied. The question *My place or yours?* is therefor relevant if the spread of the TRB is seen as the result of contacts and moves within a marriage network.

The new traditions that appear in Mälardalen in connection with the neolithisation process are cultivation and the craft of pottery. Imported point- and thinbutted flint axes also appear as finished products, but when these tools were reworked it was done in accordance with the local stone napping tradition (Sundström and Apel 1998:181). This would seem to suggest that the new traditions were carried to these parts by in-moving spouses, who in accordance with the prevailing rule of residence, belonged to one specific gender. Which in this case would be the gender responsible for pottery craft and cultivation, but not the production of flint-tools. This scenario is discussed further in Hallgren (1996).

The already existing Late Mesolithic social network, would therefore contribute to that certain elements of the new phenomena, the Funnel-beaker Culture, were spread over a large area. At the same time, the extent of this marriage network also limited how far the new mode of life was spread in this way. According to this line of reasoning, the extent of the early Neolithic Funnel-beaker Culture in Scandinavia, defines the area of a Late Mesolithic social network. The northern border thus delimited, here illustrated by the occurrences of TRB polygonal battle-axes (Figure 75.7), coincides with the northern border of the distribution of pecked greenstone axes of the Mesolithic (Figure 75.8). It is suggested that this social unit consisted of several Late Mesolithic bands and/or dialect tribes, participating in the same marriage network (Hallgren 1996, 1998), the latter corresponding either to a group of dialect tribes, or a language family, sensu Newell *et al.* (1990).

To the north of this border there lived people that choose no to make and use pecked axes during the Mesolithic, and choose not to adopt agriculture nor the material culture of the Funnel-beaker Culture in the Early Neolithic (Boaz 1997; Lundberg 1998, Hallgren forth-

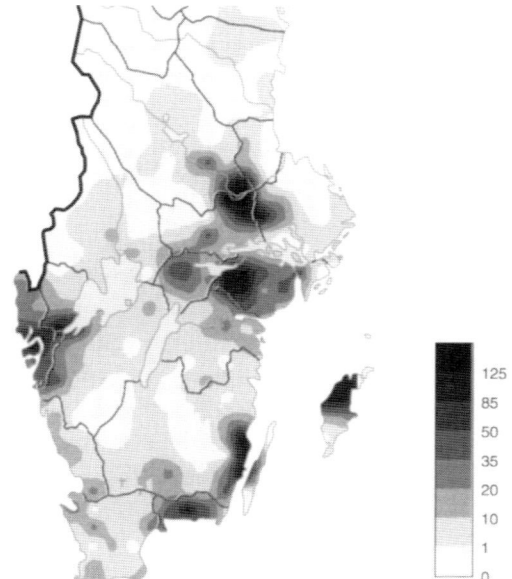

Figure 75.8 The distribution of Mesolithic pecked greenstone axes. After Selinge (1994).

coming). And while marriage networks among hunter-gatherers to some extent always overlap (Adams and Kasakoff 1975, Newell *et al.* 1990, Lawrence 1994), the people living to the north of this border may have belonged to a social network that rather faced north than south, and who expressed this orientation in their material culture.

Changing rules of residence and lineage formation

Soon after the appearance of the Funnel-beaker Culture in central Sweden, local ceramic traditions appear (Figure 75.4). These local traditions seem to be tied to, and reproduced within single settlements (e.g. Figure 75.4 a–b), while neighbouring settlements display quite different designs during the very same period (Figure 75.4 c). In my thesis, I discuss this as an indication of a formation of a lineage identity tied to specific settlements, and a change in the rules of postmarital residence, so that the gender responsible for the pottery craft from this point on stays at their place of birth. As such, they were also responsible for the re-creation of the lineage, the identity of which they manifested in the local design of their funnel-beakers (Hallgren 2000, Hallgren forthcoming).

In conclusion, when the Early Neolithic farmers of central Sweden asked: My place or yours, the answer was quite different compared to when their grandparents had as asked the same question only a few generations before, in Late Mesolithic times.

References

Adams, J.W. and Kasakoff, A.B. 1975. Factors underlying endogamous group size. In: Nag, M. (ed.) *Population and social organisation,* 147–174. Paris.

Andersen, S.H. 1993. Bjørnsholm. A stratified køkkenmødding on the central Limfjord, north Jutland. *Journal of Danish Archaeology* 10, 1991, 59–96.

Andrén, E., Veski, S. and Storå, J. 1995. Biostratigraphical investigations in connection with archaeological dwelling sites at Jansmyra, northeastern Åland. *Pact* 50, 355–365. Rixensart.

Apel, J.E., Bäckström, Y., Hallgren, F., Knutsson, K., Lekberg, P., Olsson, E., Steineke, M. and Sundström, L. 1995. Fågelbacken och trattbägarsamhället. Samhällsorganisation och rituella samlingsplatser vid övergången till en bofast tillvaro i Östra Mellansverige. *Tor* 27, 47–132.

Artursson, M. in press. *Lysinge I och II.* Arkeologiska rapporter från Arkeologikonsult AB, No 15. Upplands Väsby.

Asplund, H. 1998. Cultural groups and ethnicity. A Comb Ceramic case. In: Johnsen, B. and Welinder, S. (eds.) *Etnicitet eller kultur,* 79–99. Östersund.

Blomqvist, M. and Åhman, S. 1999. Skifferspetsar och kvartsavslag. Senmesolitikum på östra Södertörn. UV Mitt, Rapport 1998:95. Stockholm.

Boaz, J. 1997. *Stenalderundersökelsene på Rødsmoen.* Varia 41. Oslo.

Bogucki, P. 1988. *Forest farmers and stockherders. Early agriculture and its consequences in North-Central Europe.* Cambridge.

—— 2000. How agriculture came to north-central Europe. In: Price, T.D. (ed.) *Europe's first farmers,* 197–218. Cambridge.

Callahan, E. 1987. *An evaluation of the lithic technology in Middle Sweden during the Mesolithic and Neolithic.* Aun 8. Uppsala.

Callahan, E., Forsberg, L., Knutsson, K. and Lindgren, C. 1992. Frakturbilder: Kulturhistoriska kommentarer till det säregna sönderfallet vid bearbetning av kvarts. *Tor* 24, 27–63.

Chernela, J.M. 1992. Social meaning and material transaction: the Wakano-Tukano of Brazil and Colombia. *Journal of Anthropological Archaeology* 11, 111–124.

Constandse-Westerman, T.S. and Newell, R.R. 1989. Social and biological aspects of the Western European Mesolithic population structure: a comparison with the demography of North American Indians. In: Bonsall, C. (ed.) *The mesolithic in Europe. Papers presented at the third international symposium,* 106–115. Edinburgh.

Dreijer, M. 1941. Ålands äldsta bebyggelse. *Finskt Museum* XLVII, 1–63.

Edgren, T. 1993. Den förhistoriska tiden. In: Edgren, T. and Törnblom, L. (eds.) *Finlands historia 1.* 9–270. Helsingfors.

Fischer, A. 1993. Mesolithic inland settlement. In: Hvass, S. and Storgaard, B. (eds.) *Digging into the Past. 25 years of Archaeology in Denmark,* 58–63. Aarhus.

Florin, S. 1938. Vråkulturen. En översikt över de senaste årens undersökningar av sörmländska jordbrukarboplatser från äldre neolitisk tid. In *Kulturhistoriska studier tillägnade Nils Åberg,* 15–51. Stockholm.

—— 1958. *Vråkulturen. Stenåldersboplatserna vid Mogetorp, Östra Vrå och Brokvarn.* Stockholm.

Gebauer, A.B. 1995. Pottery production and the introduction of agriculture in Southern Scandinavia. In: Barnett, W.K. and Hoopes, J.W. (eds.) *The emergence of pottery. Technology and innovation in ancient societies,* 99–114. Washington.

Graner, G. and Hallgren, F. forthcoming. The pottery from a sacrificial fen at the Funnel-beaker Culture settlement Skogsmossen, Central Sweden (preleminary title).

Hallgren, F. 1993. *Bosättningsmönster i gränsland, Gästriklands stenålder.* Seminar paper, Uppsala University. Uppsala.

—— 1996. Sociala territorier och exogamirelationer i senmesolitisk tid. En diskussion utifrån boplatsen Pärlängsberget, Södermanland. *Tor* 28, 5–27.

—— 1998. Etnicitet under stenåldern i Mellansverige och Södra Norrland. In Johnsen, B. and Welinder, S. (eds.) *Etnicitet eller kultur,* 61–77. Östersund.

—— 2000. Lineage identity and pottery design. In; Olausson, D. and Vandkilde, H. (eds.) *Form, function, context,* 173–191. Lund.

Hallgren, F., Djerw, U., af Geijerstam, M. and Steineke, M. 1997. Skogsmossen, an Early Neolithic settlement site, and sacrificial fen, in the northern borderland of the Funnel-beaker Culture. *Tor* 29, 49–111.

Hallgren, F., Bergström, Å. and Larsson, Å. 1995. *Pärlängsberget, en kustboplats från övergången mellan senmesolitikum och tidigneolitikum.* Tryckta rapporter från Arkeologikonsult AB, nr 13. Upplands Väsby.

Hallgren, F. and Possnert, G. 1997. Pottery design and time. The pottery from the TRB site Skogsmossen, in view of AMS-datings of organic remains on potsherds. *Tor* 29, 113–136.

Hulthén, B. and Welinder, S. 1981. *A Stone Age economy.* Theses and papers in North-European archaeology 11. Stockholm.

Jacobs, K., Wyman, J.M. and Meiklejohn, C. 1996. Pitfalls in the search for ethnic origins: a cautionary tale regarding the construction of "anthropological types" in pre-indo-european Northeast Europe. In: Jones-Bley, K. and Huld, M.E. (eds.) *The indo-europeanization of Northern Europe,* 285–305. Washington.

Kempisty, E. 1986. Neolithic cultures of the forest zone in northern Poland. In: Malinowski, T. (ed.) *Problems of the Stone Age in Pomerania,* 187–213. Warsaw.

Kihlstedt, B., Larsson, M. and Nordqvist, B. 1997. Neolitiseringen i Syd-, Väst- och Mellansverige – social och ideologisk förändring. In: Larsson, M. and Olsson, E. (eds.) *Regionalt och Interregionalt. Stenåldersundersökningar i Syd- och Mellansverige.* Riksantikvarieämbetet Arkeologiska Undersökningar, Skrifter nr 23, 85–133. Stockholm.

Knutsson, K., Lindgren, C., Hallgren, F. and Björck, N. 1999. The Mesolithic in Eastern Central Sweden. In: Boaz, J. (ed.) *The Mesolithic of Central Scandinavia.* Universitetet Oldsaksamlings Skrifter, Ny Rekke, Nr. 22, 87–123. Oslo.

Koch, E. 1998. *Neolithic bog pots from Zealand, Møn, Lolland and Falster.* Nordiske Fortidsminder, serie B, Volume 16. København.

Kriiska, A. 1996. The Neolithic pottery manufacturing technique of the lower course of the Narva River. *Pact* 51, 373–384. Rixensart.

Lawrence, D. 1994. *Customary exchange across Torres Strait.* Memoirs of the Queensland Museum 34/2. Brisbane.

Lidström-Holmberg, C. 1993. *Sadelformade malstenar från yngre stenålder. "Grind my dear one, let her grind".* Rapport 2, Flatenprojektet. Statens Historiska Museum/Institutionen för Arkeologi, Uppsala Universitet. Uppsala.

—— 1998. Prehistoric grinding tools as metaphorical traces of the past. *Current Swedish Archaeology* 6, 123–142.

Lindgren, C. and Nordqvist, B. 1997. Lihultyxor och trindyxor - Om yxor av basiska bergarter i östra och västra Sverige under Mesolitikum. In: Larsson, M. and Olsson, E. (eds.) *Regionalt och Interregionalt. Stenåldersundersökningar i Syd- och Mellansverige.* Riksantikvarieämbetet Arkeologiska Undersökningar, Skrifter nr 23, 57–72. Stockholm.

Lundberg, Å. 1997. *Vinterbyar – ett bandsamhälles territorier i Norrlands inland, 4500 – 2500 f.Kr.* Umeå.

Munthe, H. 1940. *Om Nordens, främst Balticums senkvartära utveckling och stenåldersbebyggelse.* Kungliga Svenska Akademiens Handlingar 3:e ser, 19:1. Stockholm.

Newell, R.R., Kielman, D., Constandse-Westermann, T.S., van der Sanden, W.A.B. and van der Gijn, A. 1990. *An inquiry into the ethnic resolution of mesolithic regional groups. The study of their decorative ornaments in time and space.* Leiden.

Nuñez, M. and Storå, J. 1992. Shoreline chronology and economy in the Åland Archipelago 6500–4000 BP. *Pact* 36, 143–161. Rixensart.

Persson, P. 1999. *Neolitikums början.Undersökningar kring jordbrukets introduktion i Nordeuropa.* Kust till Kust Böcker Nr 1. Göteborg.

Pesonen, P. 1999. Radicarbon dating of birch bark pitches in Typical Comb Ware in Finland. In: Huurre, M. (ed.) *Dig it all. Papers dedicated to Ari Siiriäinen,* 191–200. Helsinki.

Price, T.D. 2000. The introduction of farming in northern Europe. In: Price, T.D. (ed.) *Europe's first farmers,* 260–300. Cambridge.

Price, T.D. and Gebauer, A.B. 1992. The final frontier: foragers to farmers in southern Scandinavia. In: Gebauer, A.B. and Price, T.D. (eds.) *Transitions to agriculture in Prehistory.* Madison.

Rasmussen, K.L. 1993. Radiocarbon datings from the Bjørnsholm site, north Jutland. *Journal of Danish Archaeology* 10 (1991), 93–96.

Rowley-Conwy, P. 1995. Wild or domestic? On the evidence for earliest domestic cattle and pigs in South Scandinavia and Iberia. *International Journal of Osteoarchaeology* 5, 115–126.

Sackett, J.R. 1990. Style and ethnicity in archaeology: the case for isochrestism. In: Conkey, M. and Hastorf, C. (eds.) *The uses of style in archaeology,* 32–43. Cambridge.

Schiemann, E. 1958. Die pflanzenfunde in den Neolitischen siedlungen Mogetorp, Ö. Vrå und Brokvarn. In: Florin, S. *Vråkulturen. Stenåldersboplatserna vid Mogetorp, Östra Vrå och Brokvarn,* 249–311. Stockholm.

Segerberg, A. 1999. *Bälinge mossar. Kustbor i Uppland under yngre stenålder.* Aun 26. Uppsala.

Selinge, K-G. 1994. *Kulturminnen och kulturmiljövård.* Sveriges Nationalatlas. Stockholm.

Stafford, M. 1999. *From forager to farmer in flint. A lithic analysis of the prehistoric transition to agriculture in Southern Scandinavia.* Aarhus.

Stark, M. (ed.) 1998. *The Archaeology of social boundaries.* Washington.

Sundström, L. and Apel, J. 1998. An Early Neolithic axe production and distribution system within a semi-sedentary farming society in Eastern Central Sweden, c. 3500 BC. In: Holm, L. and Knutsson, K. (eds.) *Third Flint Alternatives Conference at Uppsala.* Opia 16, 155–191. Uppsala.

Sulgostowska, Z. 1998. Continuity, change and transition: the case of North-Eastern Poland during the Stone Age. In; Zvelebil, M., Denell, R. and Domanska, L. (eds.) *Harvesting the sea, farming the forest. The emergency of Neolithic societies in the Baltic region.* Archaeological Monographs 10, 87–94. Sheffield.

Taffinder, J. 1998. *The allure of the exotic. The social use of non-local raw materials during the Stone Age in Sweden.* Aun 25. Uppsala.

Timofeev, V.I. 1988. On the problem of the Early Neolithic of the East Baltic area. *Acta Archaeologica* 1987, 58, 207–212.

—— 1998. The beginning of the Neolithic in the Eastern Baltic. In: Zvelebil, M., Denell, R. and Domanska, L. (eds.) *Harvesting the sea, farming the forest. The emergency of Neolithic societies in the Baltic region.* Sheffield Archaeological Monographs 10, 225–236. Sheffield.

Timofeev, V.I., Zajcevo, G. and Possnert, G. 1995. Neolithic ceramic chronology in the South-Eastern Baltic Area in view of ^{14}C accelerator datings. *Fornvännen* 1995, No. 1, 19–28.

Welinder, S. 1982. The hunting-gathering component of the Central Swedish neolithic Funnel-beaker Culture [TRB] economy. *Fornvännen* 77, 153–160.

—— 1998. Neoliticum - Bronsålder 3900-500 f.Kr. In: Myrdal, J. (ed.) *Det svenska jordbrukets historia. Jordbrukets första femtusen år,* 11–236. Stockholm.

Wiessner, P. 1990. Is there a unity to style?. In: Conkey, M. and Hastorf, C. (eds.) *The use of style in archaeology,* 105–112. Cambridge.

Zápotocky, M. 1992. *Streitäxte des mitteleuropäischen Äneolihtikums.* Weinheim.

Zvelebil, M. 1998. Agricultural frontiers, neolithic origins, and the transition to farming in the Baltic Basin. In: Zvelebil, M., Denell, R. and Domanska, L. (eds.) *Harvesting the sea, farming the forest. The emergency of Neolithic societies in the Baltic region.* Sheffield Archaeological Monographs 10, 9–27. Sheffield.

Åkerlund, A. 1996. *Human responses to shore displacement. Living by the sea in Eastern Middle Sweden during the Stone Age.* Riksantikvarieämbetet Arkeologiska Undersökningar, Skrifter nr 16. Stockholm.

Österholm, S. 1988. I utriggarkanot över Östersjön. *Populär Arkeologi* 1988, Nr. 1, 26–30.

76. The Transition from Mesolithic to Neolithic in eastern Sicily: A microscopic point of view

Maria Rosa Iovino

Previous discussions on the transition from Mesolithic to Neolithic in Sicily have generally taken place within a typological framework. The Mesolithic life-style as can be determined by the remains of the lithic industry and fauna, is generally associated with hunting-gathering activities. The Neolithic life-style, regarded as a "pottery and agricultural period", is essentially defined according to the "Neolithic package" which includes impressed and incised ware (such as the so called Stentinello pottery), ditched settlements, domesticated cereals and animals, grinding-stones always connected with the processing of cereals. Because of this typological approach, radiocarbon dates of most of the investigated sites are still lacking.

The only paleo-environmental and multidisciplinary approach in this region has been carried out in Uzzo's Cave, a Mesolithic- Neolithic site located on the north-western coastline, close to Trapani. But the data gathered there can not be extrapolated to explain specific features relating to other sites. This contribution, part of a more extensive research on the transition to Neolithic in eastern Sicily, is an attempt to better understand the archaeological context, focus on environmental exploitation connected with subsistence practices and with forms of economical activities, by determining tool function and by understanding the methods of works and productivity of tools.

Introduction

Research into the transition from foraging to food production is still in a very pioneering and speculative phase in Sicily. As in many areas where a long antiquary tradition has been followed by fairly extensive work in the 19th and early 20th centuries, the recognised sites are numerous but the majority of them lack the modern scientific documentation necessary for a detailed assessment. Until today the study of Sicilian prehistory is still conducted without a proper understanding of paleo-ecological contexts and human activities taking place at the locations. Most of the publications are still directed towards typo-chronological studies of pottery. Only from the Mesolithic/Neolithic site of Uzzo's Cave on the north-western side of Sicily have we information about the exploitation of plants and animals but this data cannot be automatically extrapolated to interpret contemporary sites. The transition to farming in Sicily has been discussed in recent years largely on the basis of the evidence from Uzzo's Cave. It needs to be emphasised that still material's taphonomy and involved factors of the deposit formation processes should be clarified.

At Uzzo's Cave a very early transitional phase (7000–6500 cal B.C.) is attested to (Meulengracht *et al.* 1981). The start of the Neolithic (around 6500 cal B.C.) is followed by an impressed ware stage which predates Stentinello's style pottery (Tusa 1997:182 p). It is still not possible to compare Uzzo's dates with those of eastern Sicilian Neolithic "impressed ware" settlements but it is interesting to note that the Stentinello phase in contexts of Calabria starts in the early 6th millennium B.C (Leighton 1996). The possibility of cultural change as a result of social and economic pressures and/or environmental circumstances has to be considered.

It might be suggested that many transformations in material assemblages from the Mesolithic to the Neolithic can be connected, inter alias, with changing alignments in an exchange system. Models set as elucidation for the passage from a hunting–gathering to an agricultural-pastoral economy (diffusionist or evolutionary-gradualist/ local processes) does not explain the transformation adequately but give only a generalised idea of the development in question. Besides, it should be remembered here that modelling will become even more important to anthropology and history, but only in concert with high-quality data from fieldwork.

Selection of sites to be studied

To better understand the Mesolithic-Neolithic transition in eastern Sicily, the following sites (Figure 76.1) have been selected: three Mesolithic sites (Grotta Corruggi, Perriere Sottano and Riparo della Sperlinga), respectively located in a coastal plain, an inner plain and a hill area. Diversity in site location will be of main importance to a

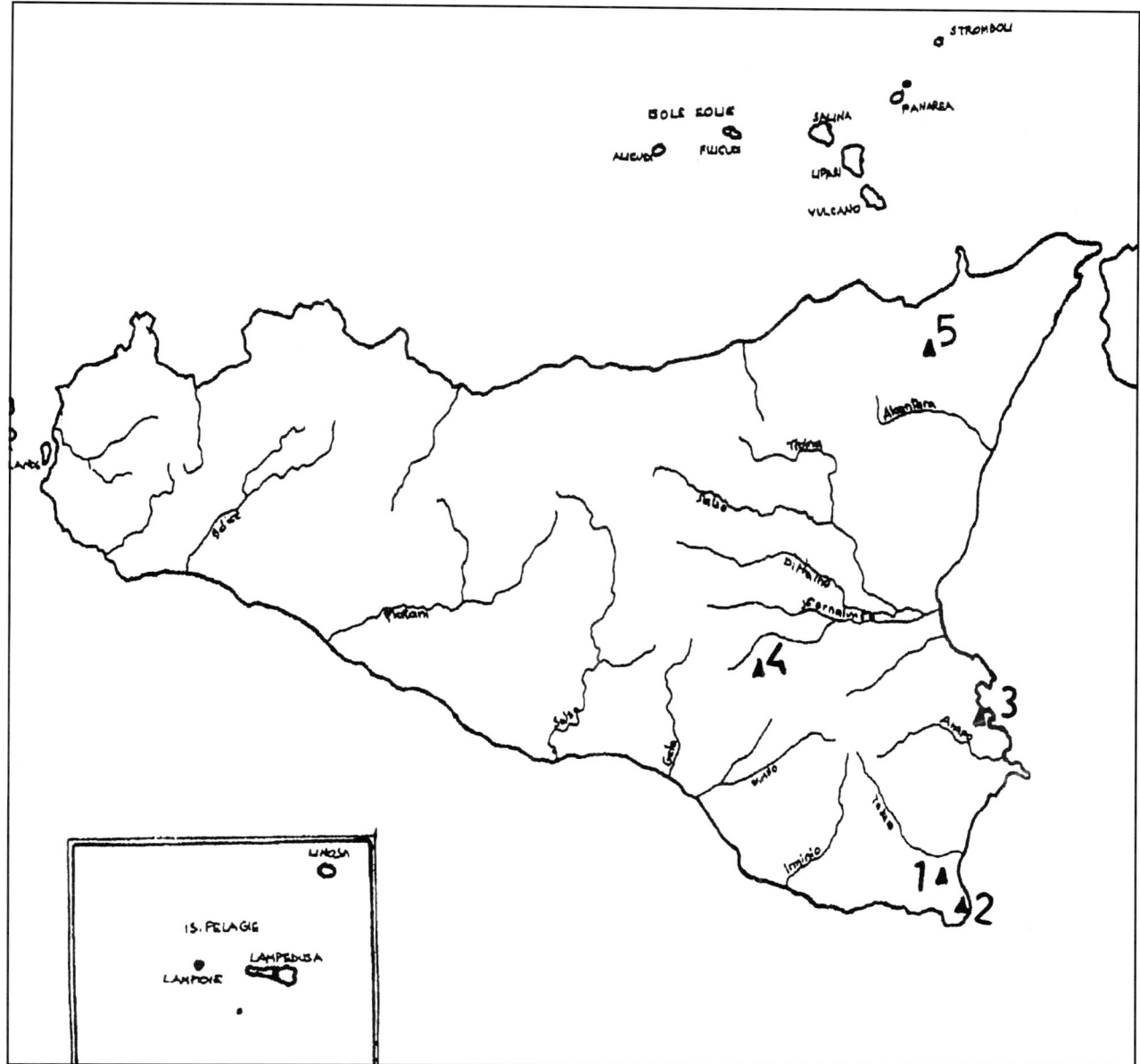

Figure 76.1 Location of the archaeological sites selected for this research: 1-Grotta Corruggi, 2- Vulpiglia, 3- Stentinello, 4- Perriere Sottano, 5- Riparo della Sperlinga di S. Basilio

better understanding of how natural resource exploitation is related to site location and highlight the peculiar advantage of different environments.

Two Neolithic sites:

a   The village of Stentinello has been interpreted by the pottery, the fauna remains, the presence of grinding stones and the presence of sickle blades as an already advanced stage of farming system (agriculture and animal husbandry).

b   Vulpiglia, only 1 km from Corruggi's Cave. It will be extremely important to verify the *spectrum* of resource exploitation on this site. Study of the activities carried out will help to clarify whether the inhabitants adopted the whole farming system or a specific life-style related to the coastal environment resources (fishing activities, for example).

Method

This study is carried out through functional analysis based on use-wear traces (Keeley 1980; Hurcombe 1992) in order to derive a variety of information about the use and rejection of these tools. This is in order to take into account changes in the use and nature of implements, in the light of potentially related transformations in social and other practices during the transition to farming and in order to examine whether supposed continuities and discontinuities in the surviving material may inform us about environmental, structures and social changing during this period.

Functional analysis can help to observe the shift between different daily practices attested to by lithic implements, as well as any changes or transformation involved the practices which took place. Functional analysis, integrated with residue analysis, in absence of botanical evidence, can also help to understand both plant resource exploitation and seasonality, giving further information for reconstructing the past landscape.

Experimental activities (Figure 76.2) addressed by the ecological and by the archaeological context, help in understanding use-wear traces formation in relation to executed actions and worked materials and permit a detailed analysis of the component of lithic assemblages.

Corruggi Cave

Corruggi Cave, nearly two miles northwest of Cape Pàssero, is situated over a rock bench that delimits the depression of the marsh of Marghella, approximately 50 m. from the beach of Vulpiglia (Figure 76.3), in the territory of Pachino (Syracuse). The cave (Figure 76.4), probably developed by marine erosion during the Interglacial of Riss/Wurm, was discovered by P. Orsi in 1898 (Orsi 1898:35 p). The first excavation was conducted by an assistent of Orsi without any attention for the stratigraphy. Excavations were resumed in 1945 by Luigi Bernabò Brea, who understood the presence of Neolithic and Mesolithic levels (Bernabò Brea 1949:1 pp). Two stratigraphic excavations (Trench A, in the western part: ca. mt 2 x mt 2; trench B, next to the northern wall of the

Figure 76.2 Experimental harvesting activity

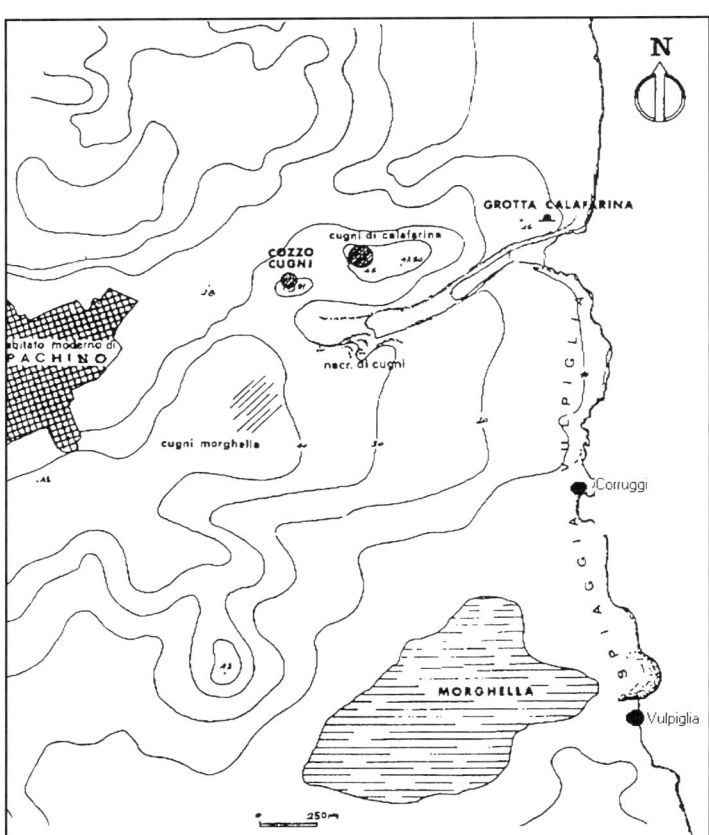

Figure 76.3 Location of Corruggi Cave (Pachino, Siracusa, Sicily)

cave near trench A,: ca. mt.1,50 x mt.1,50) were opened in the part of the cave that had been preserved from the previous diggings (Figures 76.5 and 76.6).

From these excavations, fewer lithic tools (flint mostly, and only 20 obsidian implements) were found than during the first excavation. Laplace (Laplace1964:25 pp) conducted a typological analysis of this complex and interpreted the industry of layers from 3 to 9 as final Epigravettiano, while those from layers 1 to 2 were Neolithic ones.

Very little is known about the prehistoric climate and vegetation of eastern Sicily and still less about the role of plant foods. Laboratory examination of wood carbons collected by Luigi Bernabò Brea (Bernabò Brea 1949:5 pp) during his excavation are now finally being carried out. For comparative purposes and for radiocarbon dating it may be necessary to take new samples from the preserved deposit of this cave. The analysis of the actual environmental elements suggest that Corruggi Cave was located inside a "coastal damp area". The area in which this cave is positioned is still very rich in spring water, even if now affected by high salinity, and corresponds to a classic *ecotone*: a boundary zone at the junction of two major ecosystems: coastal and wet terrestrial. A deciduous forest, that has been eroded by the degeneration to grassland, must have been in the surroundings because of the presence of certain animal species even if red deer could arrive close to the coast shore or on the banks of the Vulpiglia's marsh during the winter.

The composition of vegetation from coastal line to the inner place is, up to today, dominated by rock alophitos plants: *Crithmum maritimum, Cicorium spinosum, Limonium syracusanum e L. virgatum.*

Very close to these plants there is a line of low vegetation (*gariga*): *Timus capitatus, Sarcopoterium spinosum, Chamaerops humilis, Thymelaea hirsuta, Teucrium fruticans, Mandragora autunnalis, Iris planifolia.* This climax changes going towards the inner area where others are more common: *Pistacia lentiscus, Olea europea sylvestris, Phyllirea angustifolia, Myrtus communis, Urginea maritima, Ampelodesmos mauritanicus* and *Asphodelius ramosus* (Figures 76.7 and 76.8)

The coastal line is covered by *Cakile maritima; Salsola kali, Euphorbia peplis, Polygonum maritimum, Agropyrum junceum mediterraneum, Sporobolus arenarius,*

Figure 76.4 Actual vision of Corruggi Cave (Pachino, Siracusa, Sicily)

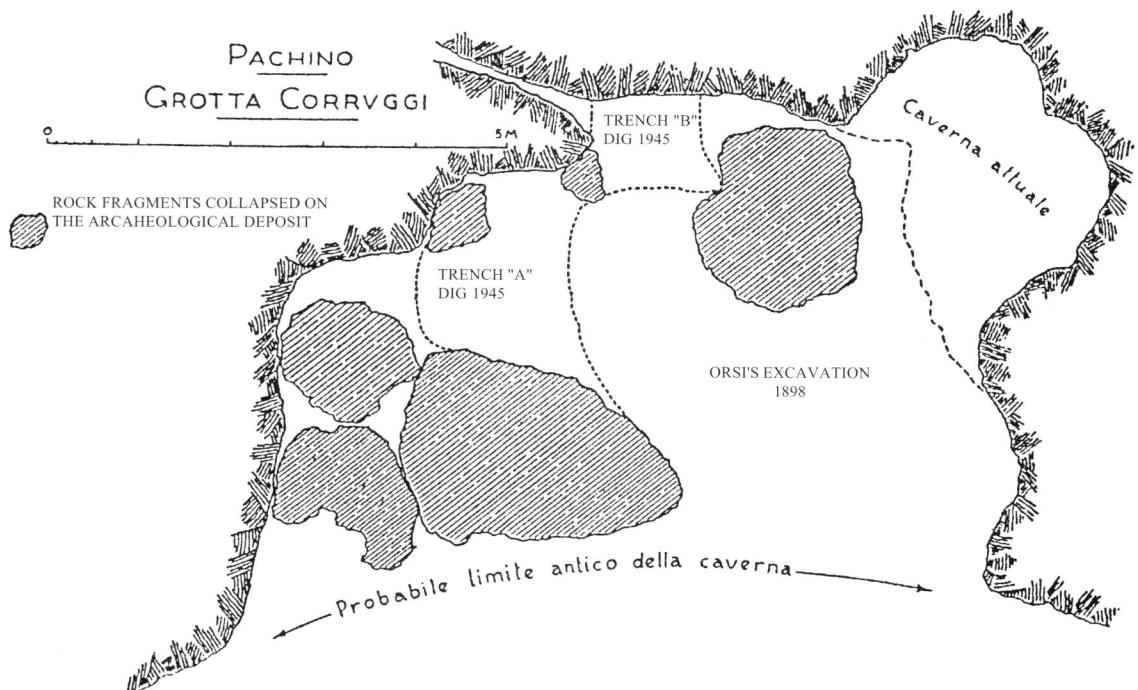

Figure 76.5 Plan of excavations made by Orsi and Bernabò Brea (after L. Bernabò Brea, 1949).

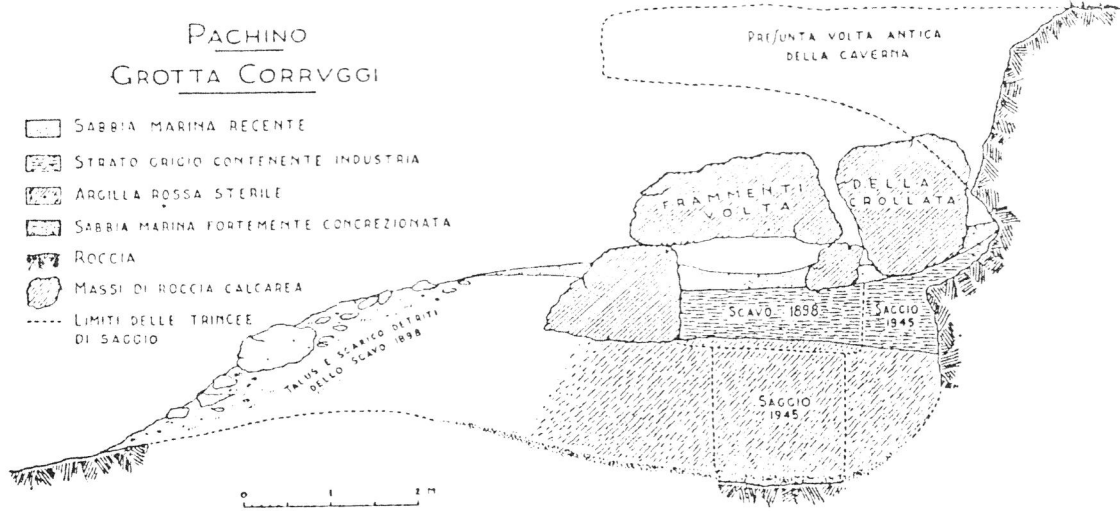

Figure 76.6 Plan of excavations made by Orsi and Bernabò Brea (after L. Bernabò Brea, 1949).

Figure 76.7 Asphodelius ramosus, whole plant.

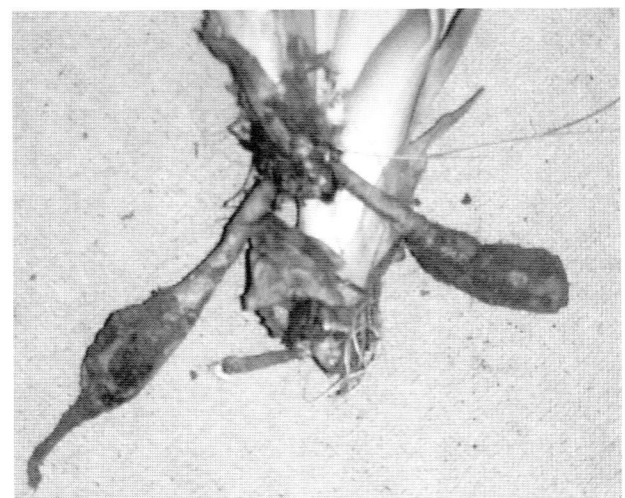

Figure 76.8 Asphodelius ramosus, rizomes.

Eryngium maritimum, Echinophora spinosa, Cyperus callii, Cutandia maritima, Ammophila arenaria arundinacea, Medicago marina, Larenea resedifolia, Pancratium maritimum.

Behind these plants, in a protected position from the sea, there is a very distinctive vegetation: *Juniperus macrocarpa, Ephedra fragilis, Pistacia lentiscus, Phyllirea angustifolia, Clematis cirrhosa,* and *Rosmarinus officinalis.*

Further away from the sea and closer to the marsh the vegetation becomes hygrophilous: *Salicornia fruticosa e S. radicantis, Hyparrhenia hirta, Lotus edulis, Stipa retorta, Trifolium stellatum, Iris sisyrinchium, Arthrocnemum glaucum, Juncus subulatus, Limonium serotinum, Suaeda vera.*

On the central part of Vulpiglia's marsh, that is under water for long period, there are water plants: *Ruppia maritima, Potamogeton pectinatus,* and *Lamprothamnium papulosum.*

Close to the banks of Vulpiglia's Marsh there are some other synanthropic species whose ecology is somewhat dependent on moist soils: *Phragmites australis* and, where the water is sweetest, *Arundo donax,* a domesticated reed.

It is still not well known if this composition of plant life corresponds with the botanical evidence from the archaeological context, because of the lack of pollen analysis. However, most of these plants can theoretically be a fuel supply and an important food resource. Young and green plants are edible and contain plenty of minerals and vitamins. Green leaves, starch-rich rhizomes, water lilies, berries, young inner bark could be eaten raw or cooked as well as algae.

This coastal zone had to be highly dynamic. Neolithic farmers, probably had, without having to destroy the landscape, a relatively simple agriculture utilising a system of shifting agriculture in which land was roughly cleared of vegetation, cultivated for a few years and then abandoned. Carbonised seed analysis from Uzzo's Cave

(Trapani) have confirmed that Early Neolithic man cultivated barley, wheat, leguminous plants and were gathering fruits (Costantini 1981:233 pp; Costantini *et al.* 1995: 225 p)

From the Neolithic levels of Corruggi there is no evidence of cereal cultivation but there is such evidence at the Vulpiglia settlement, and it could be that both settlements were occupied in the same period and Corruggi could represent a sort of *"hamlet"* of the Vulpiglia village.

From the Mesolithic context various mammalian species [*Equus (asinus) hydruntinus, Reg.Equus sp, Bos primigenius Boj, Bos sp., Cervus elaphus L., Sus scrofa ssp. L., Canis lupus L., Canis familiaris L, Vulpes vulpes (L.), Felis silvestris Schr., Oryctolagus cuniculus huxleyi Haeck., Erinaceus europaeous L., Microtus (terricola) sp.*], reptiles (*Emys orbicularis L., Testudo Hermanni Gm., Lacerta viridis L.*) and amphibian *(Bufo Sp.)* have been identified. The fauna species population from this deposit suggests that the climate during the Holocene period was a Mediterranean one similar to that prevailing today, the climate was slightly more cold and moist than at the present day. There is a notable absence of domesticated fauna from levels A 1–2 (Villari 1995:27), classified by Laplace as Neolithic period. The lack of fauna remains from levels B does not permit us to have an ulterior confirmation of this absence. Domesticated animals are found at the Neolithic Vulpiglia village.

Seafood resource exploitation, fishes as well as shellfish, is well attested to in Sicily since the Mesolithic time (Tagliacozzo 1993). Access to marine resources is an substantive advantage because of the supply of protein and trace elements such as iodine, that mean improved nutrition, growth and resistence to deficiency diseases such as kwashiorkor and goitre. Evidence of seafood exploitation is also testified to by the fauna remains of Corruggi's Cave (Cardini 1949:137 pp; Villari, 1995:27 pp), Vulpiglia (Guzzardi pers. comm.) and Stentinello (Villari 1995). At Corruggi's Cave, while fish bones (those found were probably related to the sgombride family) were a rarity, a wide range of shellfish were collected: *ostraca edulis, glycimeris glycimeris, acanthocardia tubercolata, arca noae, patella ferrugginea,, patella caerulea var. subplana, monodonta turbinata* and *cassidaria echinophora*. However, it is probable that shellfood is over-represented in relation to preserved fish bones. A typical fracture due to detachment of the shell from the rock by the means of a tool is visible on the edge of many patella shells. Without doubt a high contribution to the understanding of the environmental condition at that time could be acquired by the physical and chemical analysis of these shells.

Mesolithic and Neolithic people carried out some detailed and limited functional activities, such as shells gathering and hunting of wild fauna, as is testified by the archaeological record (Villari 1995: 27 pp). According to the thermodynamic Principle of Least Effort, people will preferentially seek to engage in those productive activities which result in the largest margin of return per unit of input of labour. Thus if possible the distance travelled to work in the fields will be reduced , foraging sites offering a variety of resources will be chosen locally, and resources like big-game or shoals of fish or seashells will be exploited in preference. If the environmental context is optimum a whole mode of life could be preferred to a settled farming system.

The close relation between fishing and basketry activity can be identified by the evidence that typical plants were collected (such as *Fragmites* and *chamarehops humilis* – dwarf palm- as well as *Amphelodesma mauritanicus*) to produce fishing equipment (for instance: fish containers, *creels* – for fishing- and fishing nets.). The same connection is also known from various ethnographic contexts such as Sri Lanka, where a primitive fishing system is still in use (Gerhard Kapitän, pers. comm.).

Functional analysis: preliminary results

The evaluation of the lithic industries coming from trenches A and B has evidenced that the implements show an high incidence of post-depositional surface alteration: patina, abrasion, bright spots (Levi Sala, 1986:229 pp) and traces of firing.

Consequently the lithic assemblage is difficult to analyse and thus the identification of a meaningful number of use traces will be important.

Considering the incidence of these alterations, I have decided to base my interpretation on an integrate data system based on micro wear traces, macro wear traces, residues and tool morphology.

This paper shows some preliminary data on micro wear analysis related to the implements from Corruggi's Cave. Of the 100 flint artefacts (débitage and instruments) coming from the Trenches A and B (Bernabò Brea excavation, 1949) of Corruggi's Cave I have selected 60 implements (60%) which show traces of use as more suitable for functional analysis. In total I observed diagnostic micro wear traces on 37 used edges of the initial sample. These micro wear traces are related to different types of actions on different materials. Most of the observed micro wear traces (22%) come from the Mesolithic levels. These traces indicate processing of plant fibres in varying states of dampness, working of bone/antler (Figure 76.9), hide processing activity, fish scaling, presence of stone working and activities related to the exploiting of soft, medium-hard and hard materials. I did not observe any micro wear traces relating to the gathering or working of shells even if some tools show macro wear traces that could be connected to the gathering of shells as is seen by comparing them to the experimental tools.

The contact with siliceous plants is widely testified to but in the majority of cases the traces of use look like *Fragmites* (as for instance *Arundo donax*) or *Juncacee* (as for instance *Juncus maritimus*) and vegetal fibres

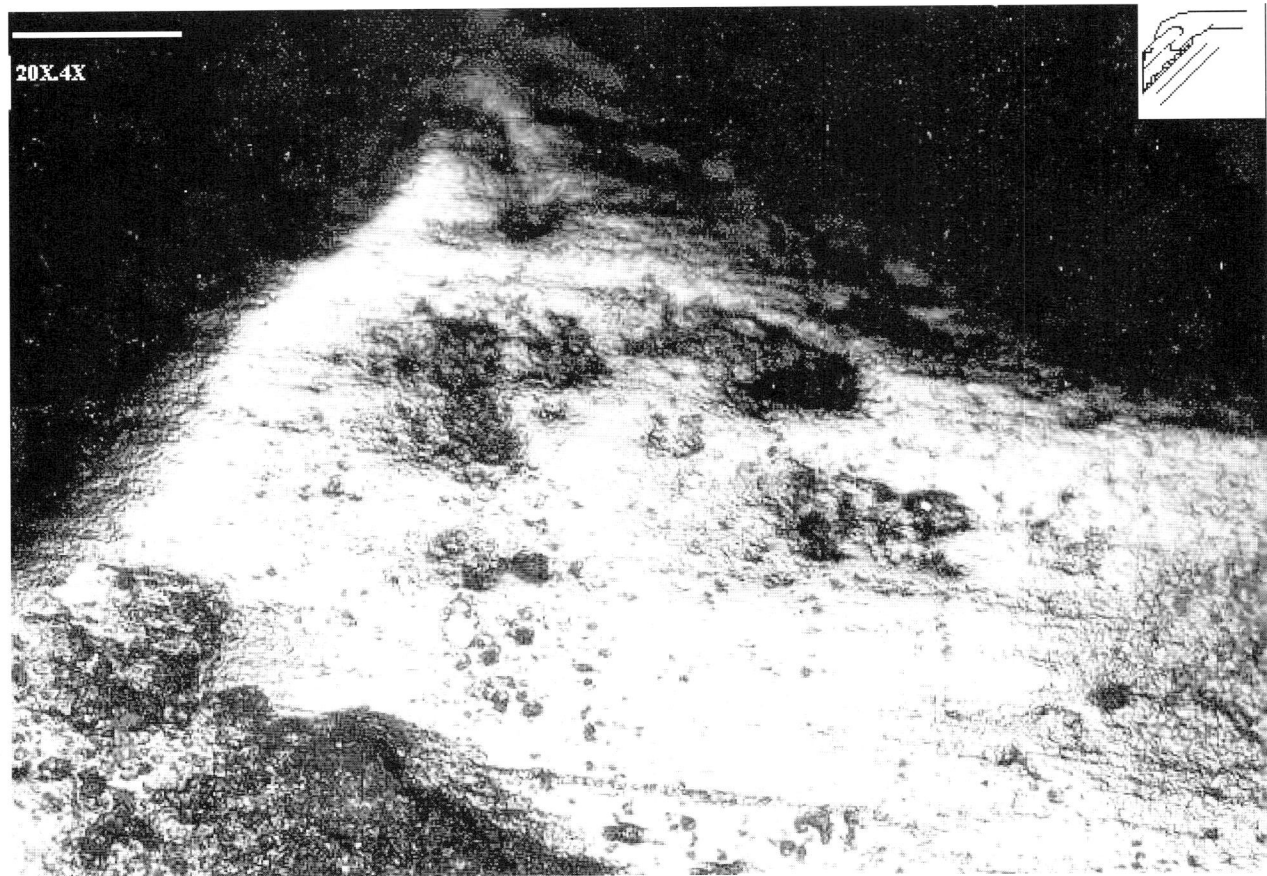

Figure 76.9 Polish interpreted as cutting bone. Drawing shows a schematic illustration of executed action.

whose polish has very distinguishable morphologic characteristics. However, there is little evidence of processing of non siliceous plants. The macro traces of use that identify the working of "soft" materials could be associated with these plants, but also to other soft substances. Generally, the actions involved are both cutting and scraping actions, and in some cases the two actions are associated, mostly when connected to resistant materials like dried reeds.

From levels between A and B micro traces related only to siliceous plants and woodworking have been identified. Macro wear traces connected with soft and medium hard materials could be related to these same materials. The working of the plant by scraping and cutting with a bladelet, not longer than 3,6cm, has been fairly frequently observed.

Interpretable micro wear traces from the Neolithic levels (A1, A2) show less variety in the kinds of resource exploitation and also here the micro wear traces relating to the exploitation of siliceous plant are interpretable as the processing of *Fragmites*.

The exploitation of non siliceous plants (such as roots, bone/antler and most frequently wood) are present too.

In any case, the degree of development of most of these use-wear traces suggests that many of these tools were not used for long before being discarded. It has also been observed that a high quantity (40%) of tools of this assemblage was not used even if they show a useful "typological" shape. This last evidence could mean that the people who used Corruggi's Cave were thinking about using these tools to do something in the future. This evidence could be in a way related with the periodic abandonment of the cave. If for any motive they had to abandon this cave for months (the winter period for instance, that can be extremely windy in this area) it could be that some implements were obliterated by soil deposits and that they were not longer visible when people went back to the cave. The observed micro wear traces relating to the working of bone/antler, hide processing and scaling give us a picture of people who fully exploited the hunted animals: they were producing bone/antler tools, working hide to obtain a more resistant material and scaling fish for consumption or stock processing (salting, smoking, or drying).

The use of the cave was connected with working activities for a long time since, but probably after its disuse, it became a little cemetery, as the abundance of human remains from trench B, not yet studied, suggestes. Forthcoming 14C data will give clearer vision of the levels of this cave and a future comparison of the data with the nearby Vulpiglia settlement will give more detailed suggestions about the differences of resource production, exploitation and consumption.

Any 16C analysis on the human remains found at Corruggi compared to any analysis of the human remains found at Vulpiglia could give a comparison reference for the human diet and related change.

The interpretations presented here are not final because they are based on work in progress. This means that the results of future analysis will be used to verify and refine patterns that have emerged.

Acknowledgements

This work and my research has benefited from the advises and discussions with Dr. AnneLou van Gijn, director of the Lithic laboratory of Leiden University. I gratefully acknowledge Prof. Leendert Louwe Koojimans for his support and interest in my research. Thanks are due to the Lithic laboratory of Leiden University, to the "Paolo Orsi" Archaeological Museum of Syracuse and to the "Museo delle Origini" of University "La Sapienza" of Rome. I wish to thank Mr. Ian Pauptit for the graphic realisation of the poster presented at the Meso 2000 Conference and last, but not least, Mr. Nigel Lengdon for scanning drawings and offering me cups of decaffeinated coffee. I thank Dr. Susanna Kimbell for the revision of the language of this paper. Needless to say, I am the only one responsible for any shortcomings of this paper.

References

Bernabó Brea, L. 1949. La cueva Corruggi en el territorio de Pachino. *Ampurias*, 11, 1–23.

Cardini, L. 1949. Appendice in L. Bernabó Brea: La cueva Corruggi en el territorio de Pachino, *Ampurias* 11, 137–139.

Costantini, L. 1981. Semi e carboni del Mesolitico e Neolitico della grotta dell'Uzzo, Trapani, *Quaternaria* 23, 233–247.

Costantini, L., Costantini Biasini, L. and Aleo, M. 1995. Le testimonianze archeobotaniche della Grotta dell'Uzzo, Trapani, *Giornale Botanico Italiano* 129, 225.

Hurcombe. L.M. 1992. *Use Wear Analysis And Obsidian: Theory, Experiments And Results*. Sheffield Archaeological Monographs 4. Sheffield.

Keeley, L.H. 1980. *Experimental Determination Of Stone Tool Uses*. Chicago.

Leighton, R. 1996. Research traditions, chronology and current issues: an introduction. In Leighton, R. (ed.) *Early Societies in Sicily*, 1–19. London.

Levi Sala, I. 1986. Use wear and post-depositional surface modification: a word of caution. *Journal of Archaeological Science* 13, 229–244.

Laplace, G. 1964. Les subdivision du Leptolithique italien. *Bullettino di Paletnologia Italiana*, S. 15, 73, 25–64.

Meulengracht, A., McGovern, P. and Lawn, B. 1981. University of Pennsylvania radiocarbon dates XXI. *Radiocarbon* 23, No. 2, 230–231.

Orsi, P. 1898. Pachino. Abitazioni di cavernicoli presiculi, e costruzioni di età bizantina riconosciute nel territorio del comune. *Atti dell'Accademia Nazionale dei Lincei. Notizie degli scavi di Antichità* 35.

Tagliacozzo, A. 1993. Archeologia della Grotta dell'Uzzo, Sicilia. Da un'economia di caccia ad un'economia di pesca ed allevamento. *Bullettino di Paletnologia Italiana*, Supplemento 84. Roma.

Villari, P. 1995. *Le faune della tarda preistoria della Sicilia orientale*, Siracusa.

Tusa, S. 1997. Origine della società agro-pastorale. In: Tusa, S. (ed.) *Prima Sicilia. Alle origini della società siciliana*, 173–191. Palermo.

77. The Hardinxveld sites in the Rhine/Meuse Delta, the Netherlands, 5500–4500 cal BC

Leendert P. Louwe Kooijmans

This paper is a brief account of the results of the excavation of two Late Mesolithic sites, situated in the wetlands of the Rhine/Meuse delta in the Netherlands. The sites are the first wetland complexes of this period west of Denmark-Schleswig and offer a wealth of new information on non-lithic material culture, subsistence, settlement function and settlement system. The stratigraphic sequence covers the period from the first contacts with the earliest agrarian communities of the loess zone (LBK) up till the first introduction of domestic animals, a thousand years later.

Introduction

This paper is intended to provide a brief account of the results of the partial excavation of two Late Mesolithic sites, situated in the wetlands of the Rhine/Meuse delta (Figure 77.1). The sites are the first wetland complexes of this period outside the Boreal zone, west of Denmark-Schleswig and offer a wealth of new information on societies of this period, especially on non-lithic material culture, subsistence, settlement function and settlement system. The stratigraphic sequence covers the period from the first contacts with the earliest agrarian communities of the loess zone (LBK) up till the first introduction of domestic animals, a thousand years later, or the 'availability phase' of the neolithisation process according to Zvelebil (1986).

The Dutch versions of the contractual reports on both sites are in print (Louwe Kooijmans (ed.) 2001a, 2001 b). English translations are planned. These are the result of the joint efforts of a large team that has worked intensively together during the actual excavation, the analysis and the writing of the report. This paper could only be written thanks to their expertise and dedication.

Discovery

Both sites are situated in the municipality of Hardinxveld-Giesendam and were named De Bruin (site 3) and Polderweg (site 4). They were discovered in 1994 on two buried Late Glacial dunes, locally called *donken*, during the systematic hand coring prospection of a new rail track linking Rotterdam with its German hinterland.

The discovery of the sites was not fully unexpected. Younger sites were known from the *donken* since the sixties, dating back to 4000 cal BC (Hazendonk). In large scale hand coring prospections Meso- and Neolithic remains appeared to be a regular feature of the dunes and to go back to 5500 cal BC, the lower limit of the standard coring depth. These sites were, however, beyond normal archaeological reach (Verbruggen in prep.; Louwe Kooijmans 1999).

Excavation

Excavation of the Hardinxveld sites appeared necessary since it was calculated that the foundation of the new rail would do serious damage to the soft archaeological deposits. Two carefully selected sections of the rail track were excavated on a contract basis by the Leiden University firm ArchOL as a part of the large scale archaeological rescue programme, coordinated by the State service for Archaeological Investigations (ROB) and financed by Dutch Rail. The trenches measured 16 x 24 m and 16 x 28 and in both cases covered a part of the top, slope and adjacent marsh deposits. The excavations lasted from September 1997 to July 1998 (Figure 77.2).

Preservation

The former living conditions along the water edge and the later accumulation of clastic deposits and peat under the influence of the Holocene rise of the sea level guaranteed optimal conservation and all favourable research conditions wetlands might offer. Organic remains are preserved, the complexes are uncontaminated, so all associations can be ascertained and the original spatial patterns are preserved. The Holocene sedimentary stratigraphy offers good opportunities for dating and phasing and for the reconstruction of the palaeogeography in the successive phases.

The Hardinxveld sites in the Rhine/Meuse Delta, the Netherlands, 5500–4500 cal BC

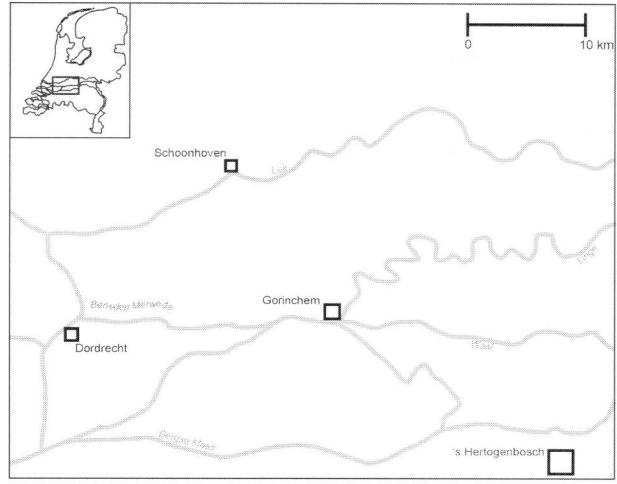

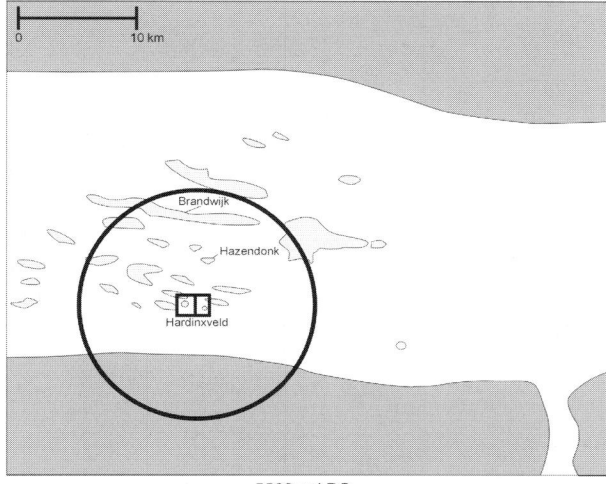

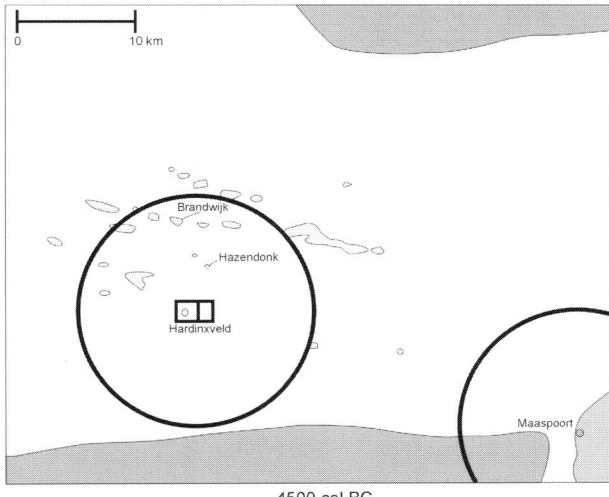

Figure 77.1 Location of Hardinxveld and Maaspoort. Palaeogeography 5500 and 4500 cal BC. Upland dark shading, donken *light shading, alluvial plain white.*

Main research questions and problems

We should realise that our image of the Mesolithic – at least for the greater part of NW-Europe – is dominated by the overwhelming evidence from southern Scandinavia.

Figure 77.2 Hardinxveld site 3 during excavation.

Whether we like it or not the Dutch Mesolithic as currently perceived, is very much a Danish clone. So a main research task was to profit from the opportunity to develop a new and independent sociocultural model for the Lower Rhine Basin.

A second task was to overcome the site-bound, anecdotal information and to reflect on the community the sites might be representative for, in a cultural respect. Third, the site would add essential new information to the badly known initial stage of the neolithisation process. The main problem in this field is the exceptional, non-representative environmental situation of the sites and the samples obtained.

Setting and Age

Geology and palaeoecology (Figures 77.1, 77.3)

The sites are located in the wetlands of the Rhine/Meuse delta, on the tops of two Late Glacial river dunes, 1 km apart. Such dunes are a characteristic feature of the submerged Late Glacial river valley. They are for the greater part covered by Holocene clay and peat deposits and only the tops of the larger dunes still appear at the surface. The *donken* of site 3 and 4 are fully concealed, with tops at 4 m and 5 m below Mean Sea Level respectively. The refuse levels on their slopes and in the surrounding marsh deposits reach down to –10 m as a result of the former low water table and later compaction.

The former landscape differed considerably from the present day embanked and drained meadow land with its many parallel ditches (Van der Woude 1983). A hand coring programme was undertaken to establish the overall Holocene stratigraphy and the palaeogeography of the subsequent physical landscapes in the various phases. The stratigraphy shows two stages of extensive clastic sedimentation, reflecting lakes and water courses, with small patches of peat formation in phases 1 and 3. During phase 2 peat bogs, mainly alder brushwood peat, prevailed. The dune tops were the only dry refuges in this extreme wetland environment.

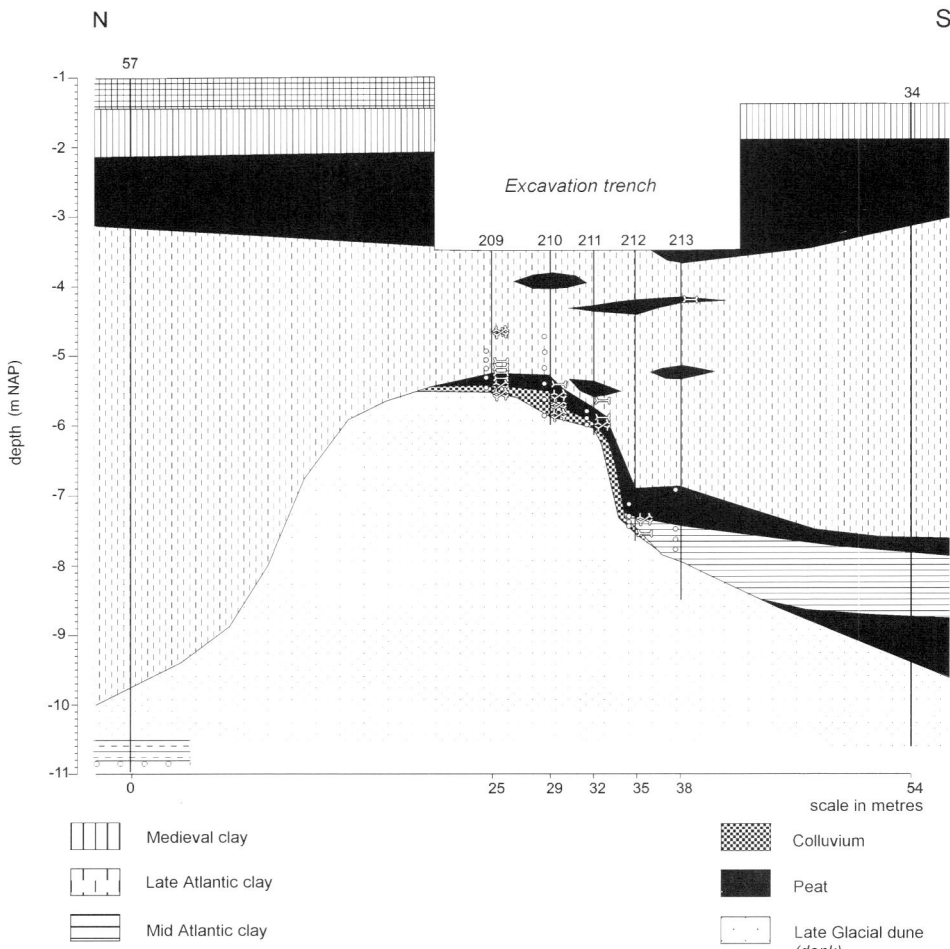

Figure 77.3 Hardinxveld site 3. Cross section based on hand corings. Excavation trench shown in its initial stage. The trench went down to the dune surface.

Vegetation was reconstructed with the aid of pollen diagrams, identification of macroremains and of the wood of twigs, branches and trees. The lakes were bordered by reed marshes. The dunes were widely visible due to the growth of high deciduous trees like oak, elm, ash and lime, with a varied shrub along the woodland edges. Alder and willow dominated the marshland. Altogether the landscape resembled that of the present day nature reserves in the peat zone of the western Netherlands, except that nowadays no large free flowing rivers dominate the water regime and link the marshes with the sea and the middle courses upstream as they did in prehistoric times.

The sites and their intrasite zonation (Figures 77.4–77.6)

The extent of the settlements (or better: of the refuse levels around the dunes) during the various phases has been established by means of the mapping of 'archaeological indicators' (like charcoal, bone fragments, wind blown sand grains) in the hand coring programme. The dimensions according to this definition vary between 20 x 80 m (site 4 phase 1) to 25 x 25 m (site 3, phase 3). We should realise that these dimensions relate to activities over a period of 200–300 years and as such are an accumulation or palimpsest of possibly smaller areas. For each phase roughly 20% of the archaeological levels were excavated and we cannot do otherwise than consider these sections as representative for the site as a whole.

Three depositional zones could be made out in the excavation trenches, zones that shifted upslope during the occupation as a result of ground water rise.

The relatively flat top of the dune can be considered as the settlement location proper. The dune top corners excavated showed a dense concentration of features: large and shallow pits, tree falls, some post holes and burials. Finds are relatively scarce and fragmentary.

The slope is covered by slope wash deposits or colluvium, presumably partly related to the digging of the wide pits. This colluvium contained masses of small and fragmentary finds, especially fish remains, bone fragments, flint and charcoal. In view of the occurrence of distinct concentrations at both sites this material has to

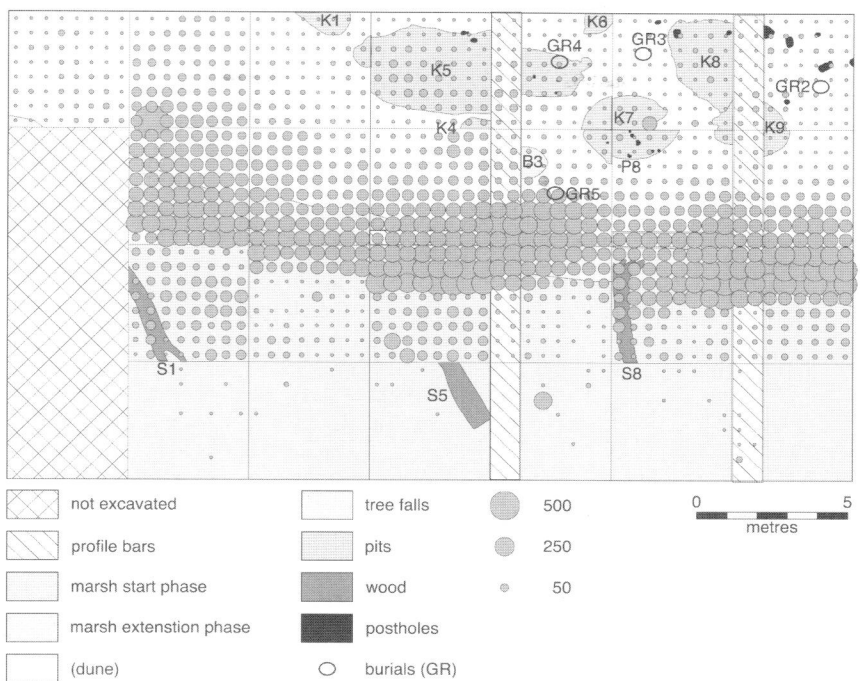

Figure 77.4 Hardinxveld site 4 phase 1. Landscape zones and features. Charcoal weight plotted for 50x50 cm squares as an indication of the occurrence of the colluvial deposits.

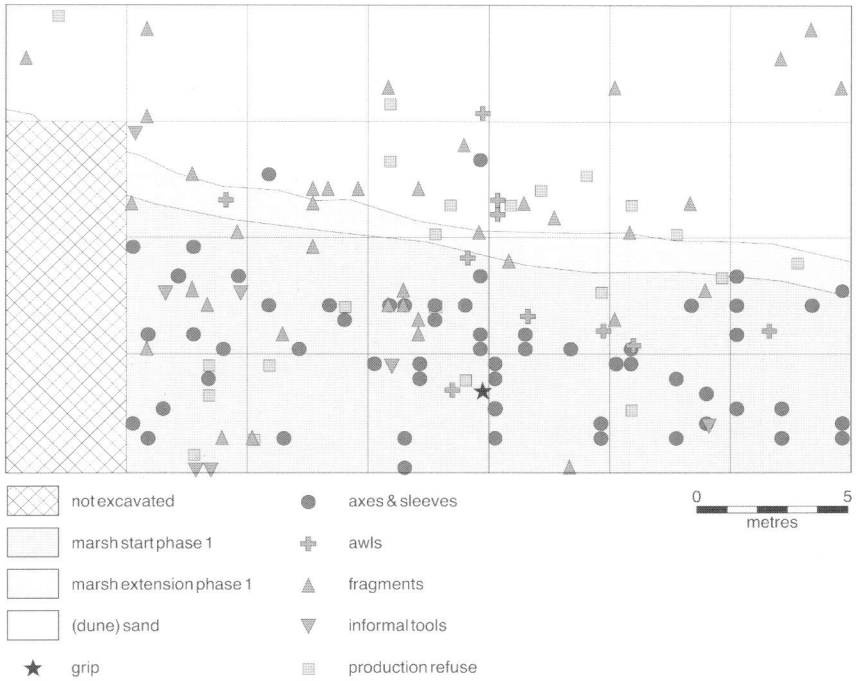

Figure 77.5 Hardinxveld site 4 phase 1. Landscape zones in the excavation trench. Individual antler artifacts plotted, showing the drop-and-toss zone in the marsh deposits.

be considered as reflecting primary activity areas along the former marsh margins, the material of which had been redeposited over only short distances.

The surrounding marsh deposits are to be considered as a toss and drop zone. Large objects, worn and broken implements, waste pieces of artefact production, and larger bones were found up to a distance of over 10 m from the dunes' water edges.

Dating and phasing (Figures 77.7, 77.22)

The sites 3 and 4 are dated 5500–4500 and 5500–5000

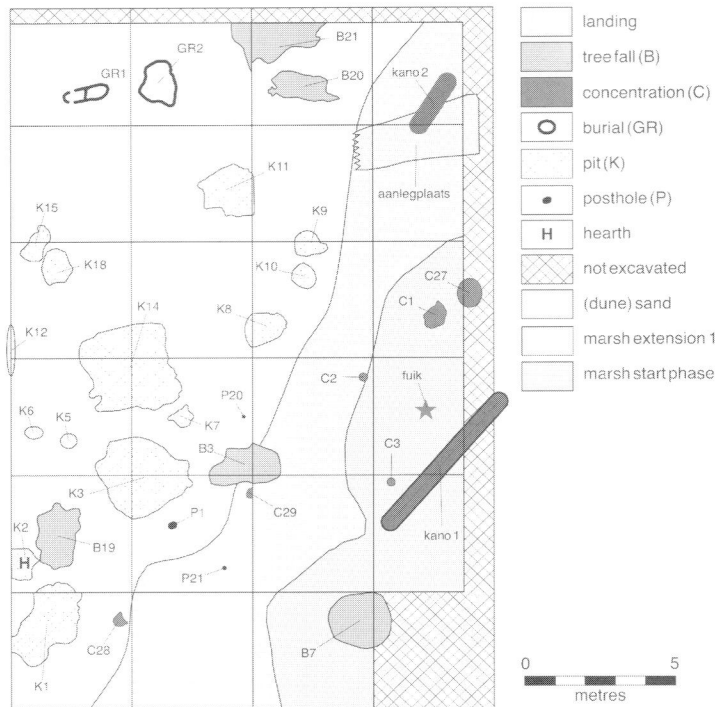

Figure 77.6 Hardinxveld site 3 phase 1. Landscape zones, features and large objects.

cal BC respectively on the basis of 30 radiocarbon dates, or contemporaneous with the Early and Middle phases of the Ertebølle Culture. The dates could be checked on the curve of the ground water level rise. Both sites were taken into use at about the same time and left when the top of the dune became submerged, which happened earlier at the lowest of the two (site 4). Between 5500 and 5300 the main occupation took place at site 4, with a complementary use of site 3. The main activities shifted to site 3 around 5300, but site 4 was visited as well up till 5000. So in the first centuries the dunes seemed to have been a kind of twin site with either a shifting or a complementary use. In view of the short distance one should not think of competing, but of cooperating groups or even just one community.

Three main phases could be made out. Phase 1 (5500–5300 cal BC) at site 4 precedes the earliest farming communities in the Rhineland-Belgian loess zone, 125 km to the south. The later phases 2 (5100–4800) and 3 (4700–4450) are contemporaneous with the Rhineland Bandkeramik (5300–4900), the Rössen and Blicquy cultures (circa 4900–4300) on the loess belt, 125 km to the south (Louwe Kooijmans 1993a, 1998).

Pottery was made and used from the beginning of phase 2 (5000 cal BC at site 4) onward, which can be used as an argument to consider this stage as the beginning of the Swifterbant Culture. Modest remains of domestic animals appear not before (the end of?) phase 3, which makes the complete sequence Mesolithic and the attested first phase of Swifterbant a ceramic Mesolithic.

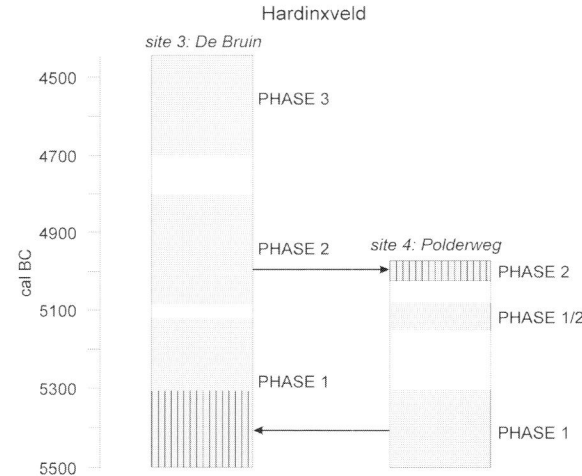

Figure 77.7 Hardinxveld chronology of sites 3 and 4 and their interpretation as a twin site. Grey shading = occupation. Vertical shading = relatively modest remains.

Features

Dwelling structures (Figures 77.4, 77.8)

Features comprise large round and oval pits, measuring 3 x 3 to 4 x 6 m, with shallow convex bottoms. Some are associated with post or stake holes and the most likely option is that these are the relics of small huts with sunken floors, comparable to those that recently came to light in southern Scandinavia (e.g. Larsson, L. 1985; Larsson,

Figure 77.8 Hardinxveld site 4 phase 1. Section across large pits 8 and 9.

M. 1986; Sørensen 1992; Jenssen this volume). The Hardinxveld pits, however, lack any internal structuring. They are dated to the main phases of occupation at the sites, to phase 1 at site 4 and to phase 2 at site 3.

Burials and isolated human remains

At both sites human burials were discovered. On site 4 an adult woman (*c.* 50 years of age) was buried on her back in a stretched position (Figure 77.9); a second interment of an adult person was severely disturbed. On site 3 one adult person was buried stretched on its back and later partly disturbed by the digging of a large pit, another adult must have been buried in a sitting posture in view of the layout of the preserved bones, similar to the well-known Bäckaskog burial, Skåne (Stenberger 1964:34), but found more widespread in Central Europe (Grünberg 2000, Abb. 47). Most remarkable are three dog burials at site 4, one in full anatomical articulation (Figure 77.10), another only partially preserved and a third only inferred from a concentration of unbroken bones, belonging to one animal. All burials date from phase 1. If we relate this type of formal disposal to a certain permanency of settlement, then the lack of burials from the later phases might indicate a shift in settlement function towards a more subordinate function of a (semi)permanent site elsewhere.

Among the masses of finds from the slope and clay deposits next to the *donk* quite a number of isolated human skeletal remains were identified: 80 at site 4, 10 at site 3. Among these are several almost complete crania, some found at site 4 at a distance of 10 m from the former dune edge in the area considered as a 'toss or drop zone'. It seems that these cannot simply be considered as disturbed burials, but must relate to a different and complex body treatment.

Intentional depositions

At site 3, phase 3 seven small pits were dug close together at the margin of the marsh, several meters from the dune's edge and at least partly used for intentional deposition: a pot, a piece of bone and of antler of red deer, three wooden sticks (one of these the exotic *Euonymus*) and a block of

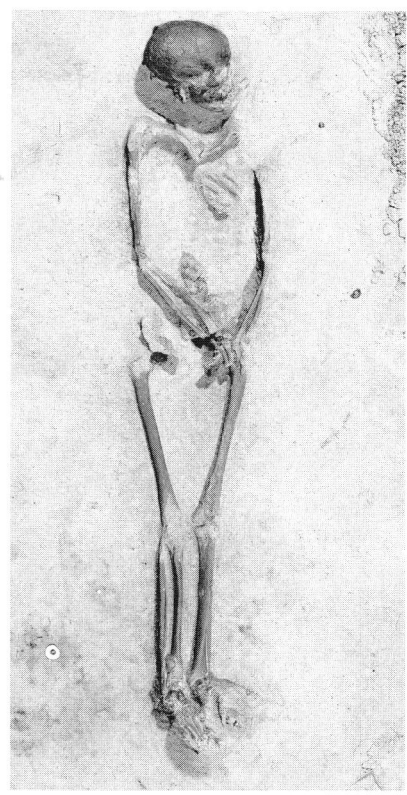

Figure 77.9 Hardinxveld site 4 phase 0, circa 5600 cal BC. Burial of a female of 40–60 years of age.

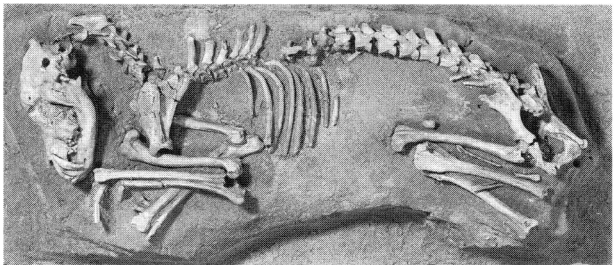

Figure 77.10 Hardinxveld site 4 phase 1. Articulated burial of a dog.

trunk wood were found below their fills. Nearby a suckling pig had been buried and selected bones of domestic animals were found deposited on the peat marsh. These are all interpreted as offerings comparable to those of the Scandinavian Early Neolithic (Koch 1996, 1999). The occurrence of such a specific cult location just in this phase of initial animal husbandry and the absence of any similar activity in the earlier phases might be no co-incidence. It might reflect a change of attitudes and ideas in the course of the neolithisation proces and of new relations between men and animals, between men and nature.

Artifacts (Figure 77.11)

Our view on the Mesolithic tool kit and technology is

site	4	4	3	4	4	3	3	3 total**	4 total**
phase	ph 0	ph 1	ph 1	ph 1/2	ph 2	ph 2	ph 3		
cal BC	>5500	5500 5300	5500 5100	5100	5000	5100 4800	4700 4450		
artifacts									
pottery	–	–	5	–	77	261	767	**1033**	77
flint	52	17640	384	1052	192	10798	1061	**12263**	18938
stone	1	58	22	3	1	1536	179	**1737**	63
bone/antler/tooth	6	239	25	13	15	192	46	**270**	327
wood	–	38	21	8	11	37	21	**79**	57
fibres (rope)	–	3	–	1	25	–	–	–	29
macroremains (samples)	–	30	11	–	12	63	17	**92**	42
wood *	53	495	93	125	165	167	121	**381**	859
bone:									
large mammals *	422	50356	2056	4669	767	12561	5265	**21594**	56214
microfauna	1	315	2	5	–	7	1	**10**	321
birds	7	530	47	69	37	578	319	**954**	643
reptiles	–	161	73	4	–	22	51	**147**	166
fish remains	1382	55929	3404	323	252	7159	4050	**14622**	57886
arthropods (samples)	–	4	–	–	2	–	–	–	6
human remains (isolated)	–	77	3	1	2	5	2	**10**	80
burials (dog/human)	1	4	2	–	–	–	1	**3**	5

* artifacts included
** non-phased objects included

Figure 77.11 Hardinxveld 1997–'98, sites 3 and 4, quantitative overview of recovered artifact categories and identifications of biological remains, according to site and phase.

mainly through refuse and discarded waste, but some objects give a glimpse of a more advanced technology and artifactual sophistication. These are objects that can be interpreted as accidentally lost or deliberately left: a complete dug out canoe, the two bow fragments, a decorated antler hand grip, the head of a small, carefully shaped bone pin, the decorated antler sleeves, the large, thin-walled and well-finished pot, deposited in a small pit in phase 3. They warn us not to underestimate the native knowledge system and the technical capacities of this society.

Flint and stone

The flint and non-flint stone are very informative about the contact lines of the former communities, since the delta and the site territory are devoid of any stone and so all lithics were brought in from the upland. The flint needs a more careful follow-up study, but it is clear that the bulk is derived from Meuse terrace gravels, 50 to 100 kms to the east. A few pieces from site 4, phase 1 are from Wommersom Quartzite and link the groups that used the *donken* to the exchange community of this specific highly rated type of stone (Gendel 1982). Hardinxveld is its northernmost occurrence. Site 4, phase 1 also produced a 4 kg precore of Rijckholt flint, that must have come straight from eluvial deposits in the South of Limburg. Long blades of the Rijckholt type of flint – considered to be made on mined flint – first appear with a few pieces in site 3, phase 2 and more frequently in phase 3.

The non-flint gravels do not comprise any characteristic Rhine material, but exclusively Meuse gravel and material of unknown provenance. A few large blocks – which if found in upland context would have been considered intrusive! – have their sources in South Limburg or even further south and one angular block must have come straight from the Ardennes, more than 150 km away. This is the most realistic option for two small fragments of pyrite as well.

It is only in site 3, phase 2 and 3 that erratic flint from a northern origin has been attested in any numbers, but we have to be alert for misidentifications and it has yet to be confirmed how prominent this presumed shift in orientation really was. Overall the contact lines appear to be southbound.

Antler industry (Figures 77.12–77.14)

The antler industry has many original aspects. It was focussed on the production of a wide range of *un-*

perforated axes on beams and tines, which might have been hand-held. Cut-off bases and some crowns and tines testify local production, mainly from collected, shed antlers. Heavy unperforated T-axes were used on hard material, presumably wood, and discarded after severe damage. Shaft hole axes are remarkably rare. Perforated T-axes of heavy and of slender make are an innovation of phase 3, more or less synchronous with their introduction in the later Ertebølle phase (Andersen 1973, 1994a). Sleeves from sections of beams to be mounted on hooked shafts are an original type of artefact and present in some numbers. Three, relatively long specimens have a shaft hole, a type of implement also uncommon to Scandinavia. Small adze blades, made on wild boars' tusks will have been inserted in sleeves, as demonstrated by a perforated specimen dredged up from the Meuse, near 's-Hertogenbosch. These insets were mounted perpendicular to the shaft and so the implement was used as a light adze, presumably for the finer type of woodworking, like finishing dug-out canoes. Their importance is demonstrated by the scratched and drilled decoration on two of the three sleeves. Points of tines were made into awls with a bevelled base.

A unique object is a small, decorated handgrip suitable for an inset of flint. The identification as a handgrip is based on the intensive traces of use at one of the sides. It

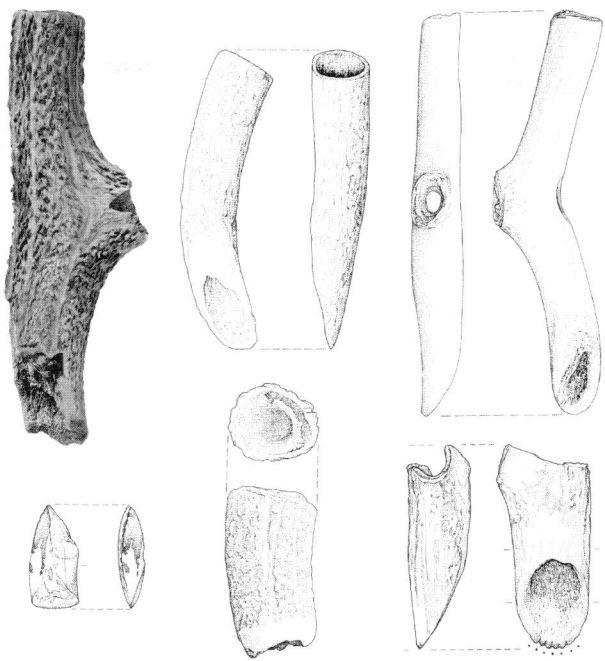

Figure 77.12 Hardinxveld site 3 and 4. Selection of antler and boar tusk implements, scale 1:2. Unperforated T-axe, T-axe fragment with toothed cutting edge, sleeve, tine axe, wild boar tusk adze inset (all phase 1), slender T-axe (phase 3).

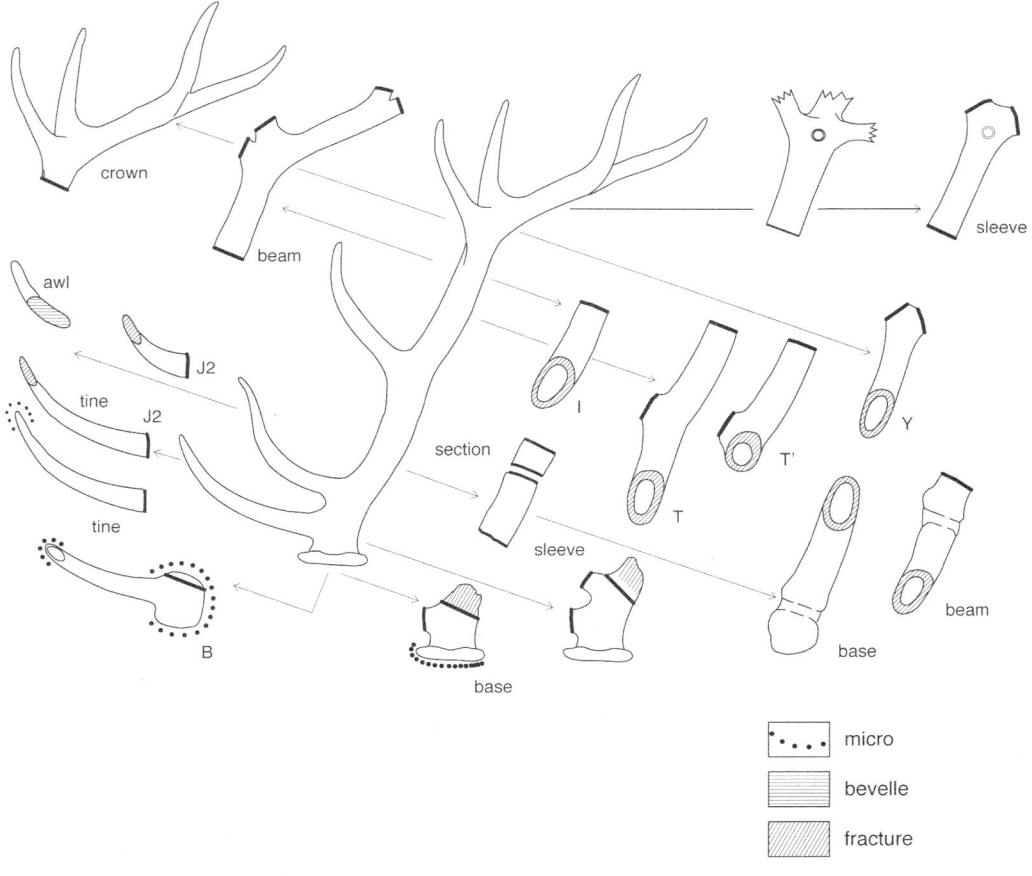

Figure 77.13 Hardinxveld site 3 and 4. Provisional production diagram of red deer antler implements.

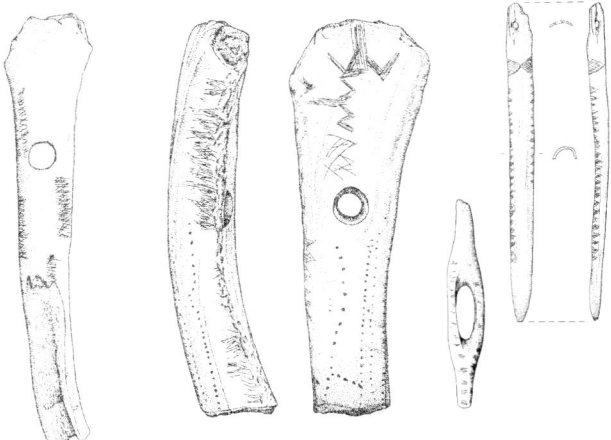

Figure 77.14 Hardinxveld, decorated antler and bird bone implements, scale 1:4. Two perforated sleeves and an object interpreted as a hand grip (all site 4 phase 1). Hollow gouge on ulna of Mute Swan (Cygnus olor), site 3 phase 2.

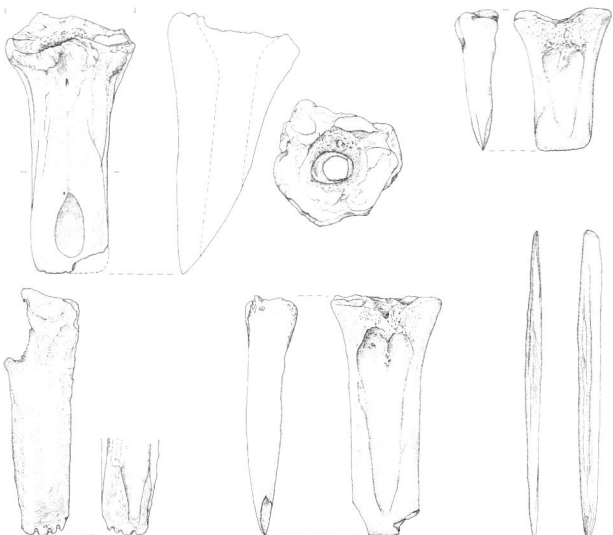

Figure 77.15 Hardinxveld, selection of aurochs metapodial implements, scale 1:4. Socketed adze, three heavy chisels (one with toothed cutting edge), all site 3, phase 2. Awl on unidentified long bone.

has formal characteristics in common with the younger wooden Neolithic handgrips from the Swiss lake side dwellings, like those from Egolzwil (Wyss 1983).

Bone industry (Figures 77.15–77.16)

The bone working is mainly based on metapodials, especially *metatarsalia*. Those of aurochs and elk were made into heavy socketed adzes and equally heavy chisels, always on the proximal part and after removal of the distal articular end. Less heavy implements, especially lighter chisels and a range of sharp and blunt awls were produced on red deer metapodials, split lengthwise several times.

The socketed adze appears to survive till a much later date in the west than in the north, since it was not any more in use in Scandinavia in post-Maglemose times. This type of metapodial industry with its production of chisels and awls appears to continue in the Rhine delta communities up till the Vlaardingen culture, where it is well-documented at the site of Hekelingen, with intermediate finds at the Hazendonk (Van den Broeke 1982; Maarleveld 1985).

A few implements were made on other long bones, like *radii*, or in an opportunistic way on broken pieces.

Wild boars tusks were not only worked into adze-insets, but also were lamellae of tusk enamel were also carved into enigmatic objects. Incisors of beavers were bevelled at their bases, not unlike the antler tine awls. Two red deer incisors with perforations were found.

Bird bones, especially the long bones of swan and white tailed eagle were worked into sharp awls. A speciality of site 3 phase 2 are blunt hollow gouges made on long bird bones, split lengthwise, one of these carefully decorated along one rim with a series of hatched triangles. This is again an implement with no parallels.

Wooden artefacts (Figures 77.17–77.18)

Most spectacular are the artefacts made of wood. We count 4 paddles made of ash, 2 large fragments of bows (elm), one of these modestly decorated, one haft made of ash, 1 complete dug-out canoe (lime), a large and several smaller canoe fragments (lime and alder) and a fish trap fragment made from red dogwood twigs. Less spectacular but equally interesting are presumed digging sticks, pointed sticks, an unfinished rough out for a paddle and refuse (split wood) of woodworking. The objects reflect the rational and functional choice of wood species also known from the northern Mesolithic sites. They inform us about wood technology. It seems that the traditional tangential splitting of especially ash and lime was supplemented in site 3, phase 2 with the 'Neolithic' technique of the radial splitting of oak.

Interestingly the implements differ in shape from their Scandinavian counterparts: the canoe has an elegant banana shape and no inserted board at the stern. Its interior seems to have been shaped using fire, unlike the Danish examples. In both aspects the canoe has more in common with the slightly younger dug-outs from the Central Paris Basin and Lake Neuchâtel (Arnold 1995–'96). The paddles are unique for their long, pointed shapes, bu have counterparts in two later examples from Swifterbant, dated c. 4000 cal BC.

The axe haft (site 4, phase 1) stands out by the form of its head, not fully perforated, but made for an insert. The haft is older than any other perforated handle. It, again, seems to have more in common with the axe handles of the Cortaillod tradition than with those from later contexts in Scandinavia (Müller-Beck 1965; Andersen 1981: 136 pp).

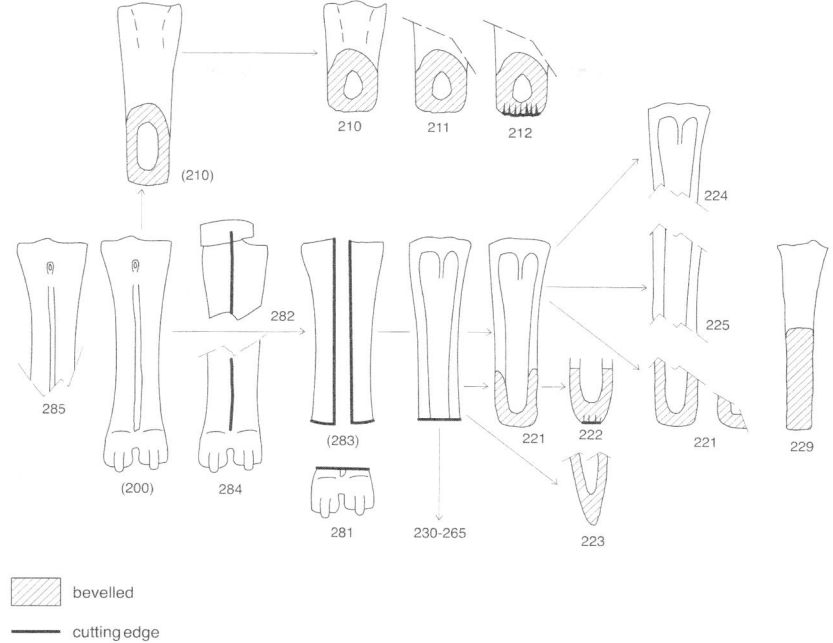

Figure 77.16 Hardinxveld site 3 and 4. Provisional production diagram of heavy metapodial implements. In a subsequent production stage lengthwise split metapodials were worked into a wide range of light duty implements, especially awls.

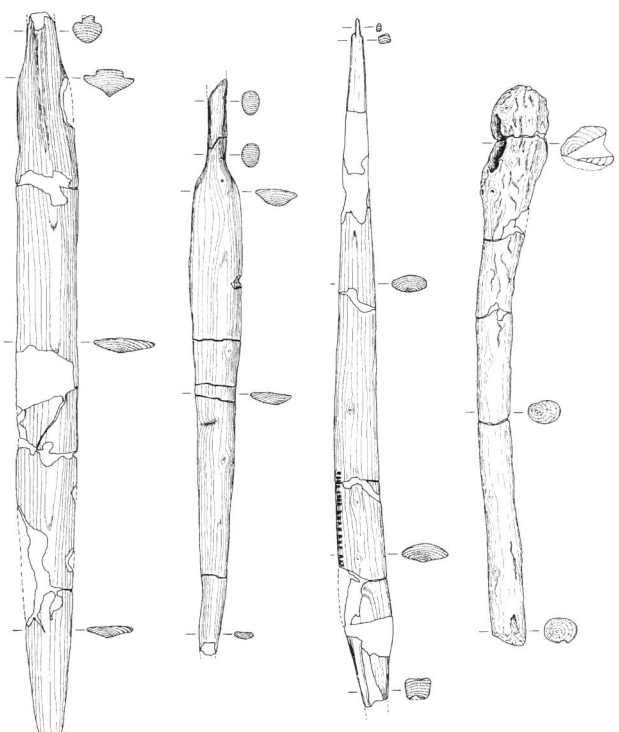

Figure 77.17 Hardinxveld site 4 phase 1, wooden implements, scale 1:8. Two paddle blades, half a (decorated) bow and a complete axe haft.

Figure 77.18 Hardinxveld site 3 phase 1, complete dug-out canoe made of lime.

Pottery

Simple coiled and pointed-based pottery makes its appearance in site 4, phase 2, around 5000 cal BC. It is a general aspect of site 3 phases 2 and 3. The forms develop from low-rimmed towards the well-known flaring rim forms of the 'classic Swifterbant'. In site 3, phase 2 a second type of pottery was found. It is tempered with small fragments of burnt bone and partially decorated with triangles filled with hatchings executed with a dentated spatula. This 'ware' is clearly related to some pottery from the Blicquy group of the Belgian loess zone (Hauzeur and Constantin 1993), but its source might not be that far away. The specific hatched 'Maltese cross motif' is considered there 'intrusive' as well, probably from the north. So an origin in the intermediate area, the southern sand region, is most likely.

Subsistence (Figure 77.19)

The large quantities of refuse testify that a wide diversity

site		4	4	3	4	4	3	3	3	4
phase		ph 0	ph 1	ph 1	ph 1/2	ph 2	ph 2	ph 3	total	total
beaver	*Castor fiber*	15	1174	107	144	194	808	294	**1209**	**1527**
otter	*Lutra lutra*	18	1159	44	121	26	451	118	**613**	**1324**
wild boar	*Sus scrofa*	5	977	101	63	10	65	5	**171**	**1055**
red deer	*Cervus elaphus*	3	183	12	9	2	65	18	**95**	**197**
roe deer	*Capreolus capreolus*	–	14	1	1	–	17	4	**22**	**15**
elk	*Alces alces*	–	–	1	–	–	12	3	**16**	–
aurochs	*Bos primigenius*	–	9	1	1	–	8	2	**11**	**10**
wild cat	*Felis silvestris*	–	24	22	2	–	19	7	**48**	**26**
pine marten	*Martes martes*	1	23	–	–	1	22	1	**23**	**25**
marten	*Martes sp*	1	13	1	1	–	9	–	**9**	**15**
polecat	*Putorius putorius*	–	–	1	1	–	1	–	**2**	**1**
fox	*Vulpes vulpes*	–	–	–	–	–	–	1	**1**	–
squirrel	*Sciurus vulgaris*	–	–	–	–	–	–	1	**1**	–
common seal	*Phoca vitulina*	–	1	1	–	–	6	–	**7**	–
grey seal	*Halichoerus grypus*	–	3	2	–	–	7	1	**10**	**3**
dog	*Canis familaris*	1	312	15	23	–	26	28	**69**	**336**
sheep	*Ovis aries*	–	–	–	–	–	–	2	**2**	–
goat	*Capra hircus*	–	–	–	–	–	1	1	**2**	–
sheep/goat	*Ovis/Capra*	–	–	–	–	–	1	8	**9**	–
swine	*Sus domesticus*	–	–	–	–	–	1	3	**4**	–
cattle	*Bos taurus*	–	–	–	–	–	–	15	**15**	–
swine/wild boar	*Sus spec.*	–	–	23	–	–	136	53	**212**	–
aurochs/cattle	*Bos spec.*	–	–	–	–	–	2	7	**9**	–
total		44	3892	331	366	233	1657	572	**2560**	**4535**

Figure 77.19 Hardinxveld 1997–'98, sites 3 and 4, identifications of large mammal remains, antler excluded, artifacts included, according to site and phase. NB 1 The 3 domestic animal bones in site 3 phase 2 are all derived from in the top of the phase 2 deposits and considered to be intrusive. NB 2 Wild boar is underrepresented in site 3 phases 2 and 3 as a result of the large Sus spec. *scores.*

of food resources was exploited, characteristic of a broad-spectrum subsistence strategy: large and small game, terrestrial and aquatic, fowl and fish, nuts and berries.

A main activity in all phases was fishing. From site 4, phase 1 alone circa 2 million fish remains have been collected in the large scale wet sieving programme. This means (20% is excavated) that 10 million fish bones are preserved from a 200 year use of the site. This gives an impression of the importance of fishing for the local community. The dominance of pike (*Esox lucius*, roughly 50% of the remains) and the composition of the fossil pike population (in calculated lengths) is such that specialised winter fishing during the spawning season is by far the most plausible explanation. This season is estimated as January/February for the warmer mid-Atlantic, slightly earlier than nowadays. Second were species of the family of Cyprinidae (the roaches, bream and tench) while all other fishes (eel, catfish, Salmonidae) were caught only in small quantities.

It is no surprise that the trapping of water mammals was another core business in this landscape: beaver and otter dominate in numbers of remains in all phases. Otters seem to have been killed selectively, but beavers were killed without distinction. The presence of large ungulates and of woodland fur animals can be understood when we realise that quite extensive dune complexes were still from sediment cover at that time. Wild boar and red deer were the main large game, complemented by an occasional roe deer and elk. Frequently captured fur animals were pine marten, wild cat and polecat. Common seal and grey seal must have occasionally penetrated into the intracoastal zone and been shot locally, in view of the occurrence of a large skull fragment.

Fowling concentrated mainly on ducks, but a wide

range of other waterfowl was shot as well. Pond tortoises were most probably collected in their winter hiding places.

The botanical component of the diet is as always underrepresented. Documented are acorn, hazelnut, waternut, wild apple and various berries.

Although two major landscape changes have been attested in the geological survey, these are hardly or not reflected in the faunal spectra. The inhabitants apparently carefully selected the ecological zones of their interest within their territory independent of the conditions in the immediate surroundings of the sites or the more general wooded or open lacustrine character of the river plain.

Social Aspects

Site function

We should realise that this part of the wetlands was within relatively easy reach from the southern upland for animals and man, at least during phase 1. The dunes were mere stepping stones into the wetlands in front of the main upland, that was only 5–7 km distant. This would change dramatically in the course of the time period under discussion, in which the ground water rose for several meters (from –7,5 to –4 m), the upland margin was drowned and shifted to the south for many kms, the river plain widened and the dunes grew smaller in number and in dimensions (Figure 77.1). At the same time society changed through the introduction of domestic animals and (perhaps) the introduction of a fully agricultural subsistence, crop cultivation included. Any shift in function of the sites should be viewed in this context of the dramatic synchronic changes in physical geography and society.

Although the site location on small dune tops in the middle of very extensive marshes is suggestive for a special function of the sites in the former settlement system, there are ample arguments for the status of base camp for complete households, at any rate for site 4, phase 1. These are the presence of some remains of women and children in the human skeletal material, the presence of formal burials and a considerable number of fixed settlement structures, even in the small section of the former settlement excavated. This interpretation is further supported by the dimensions of the site, by the range of functions established in the microwear study of the flint artefacts and not least by the wide range of bone and antler implements that were produced, used and discarded. A group of up to ten households, up to about 50 people, or a microband seems the most likely local group in view of the extent of the sites.

Most of these arguments hold for the succeeding main occupation on site 3, phase 2 as well, except for the absence of burials and the more restricted number of human remains. The presence of young children is, however, attested by two milk teeth.

In phase 3 the dune top had become very small and was fully covered by the site, the refuse density is less and the range of the antler and bone tools is considerably more restricted. The site function might very well have changed to that of a more subordinate special camp, which would fit to a supposed restructuring of the settlement system when domestic animals were adopted. The intentional deposition or offering at site 3 during this phase might be viewed in connection with a change in man-animal relationships, or as a wider, more fundamental change in world view in this early stage of neolithisation.

Seasonality (Figure 77.20)

Site 4, phase 1 was at any rate used in mid winter, in the spawning season of the pike. Winter occupation is confirmed by the remains of typical hibernating water fowl such as Red-throated Diver (*Gavia stellata*), Whooper and Bewick's Swan (*Cygnus cygnus and C. bewickii*), Goosander (*Mergus merganser*), Wigeon (*Anas penelope*), and Goldeneye (*Bucephala clangula*). A presence in Early Autumn is attested by collected waternuts (*Trapa natans*), hazelnuts (*Corylus avellana*) and (possibly) collected acorns. Age determinations of young beaver, otter and red deer gave no clues to seasonality. Although it is generally assumed that beaver and otter trapping is typically a winter activity, in view of the quality of the fur, we simply cannot confirm this for these sites. A main objection to a full winter presence are the antler ratios: 80 % is shed antler and only 20% is from hunted deer at both sites. In the case of a full winter occupation this ratio can only be explained if one refrained from shooting male red deer in the period September-December, which is not impossible if all attention was focussed on beaver and otter in this period. The conclusion must be that we cannot decide whether site 4, phase 1 was in use only in mid winter, with additional visits in early autumn, or for the full half year September-March.

Summer absence is mainly based on the absence or quasi-absence of remains of several anadromous fish species that would be expected as a result of summer fishing: Grey Mullet (*Mugil ramada*), Sturgeon (*Acipenser sturio*), Salmon (*Salmo salar*). The low numbers of eel (*Anguila anguila*) and catfish (*Siluris glanis*) can be explained by the fact that these animals hide in the mud during wintertime.

In contrast to phase 1, summer indicators are present in all assemblages from phase 2 and 3: a few remains of juvenile red deer, some bones of Purple Heron (*Ardea purpurea*). Two concentrations of adult Sturgeon dermal bone plates and skeletal parts in site 3 phase 2 are interpreted as reflecting incidental summer catches. Since the general composition of the faunal remains is not fundamentally different from that of site 4, phase 1, we consider the evidence too modest to conclude year round use but more likely to indicate an additional incidental summer use of the location in these later phases.

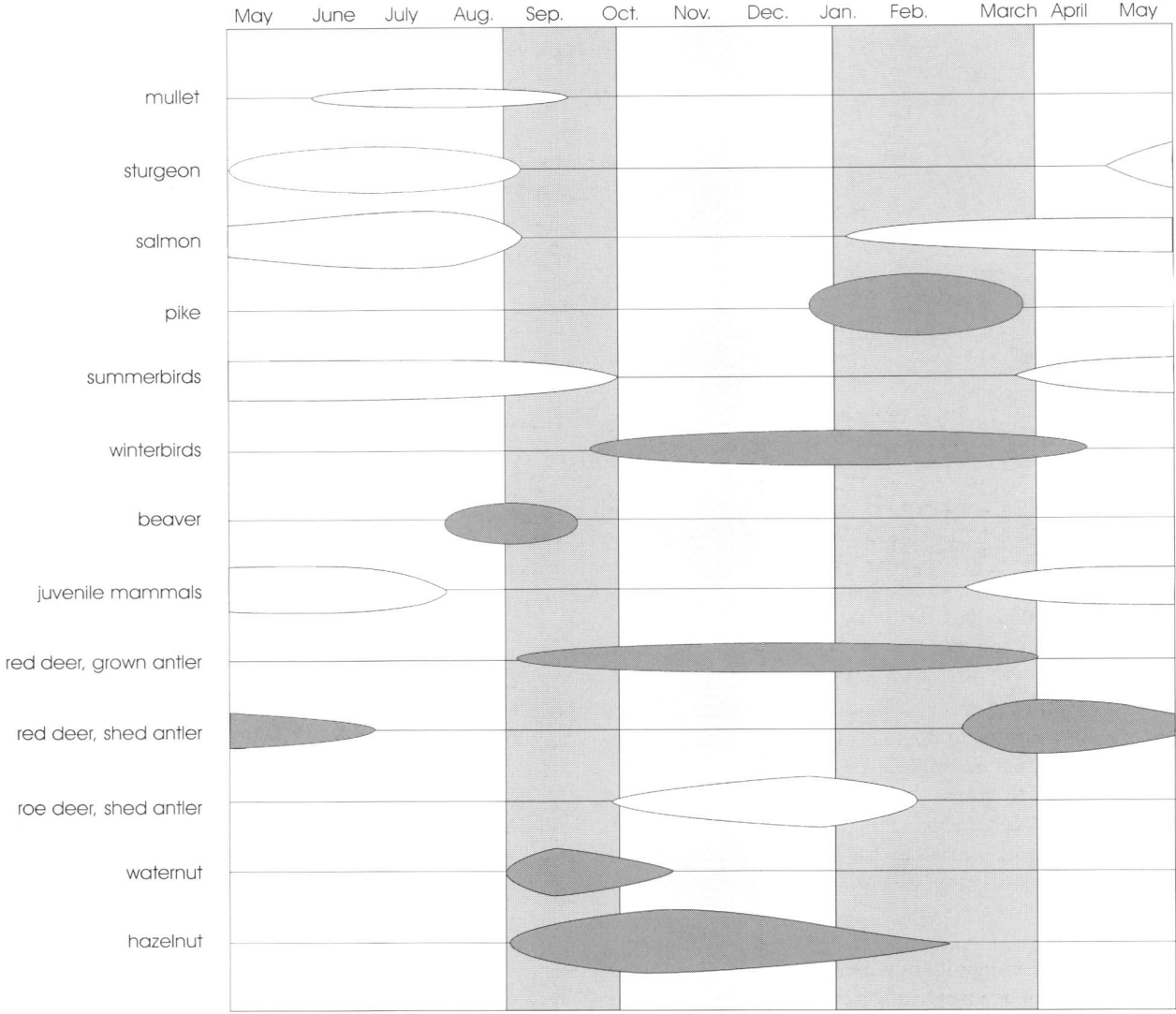

Figure 77.20 Hardinxveld site 4. Seasonal indicators and two interpretational options. Dark symbols: positive evidence, white symbols: negative evidence. Dark shading: option 1, winter base camp and additional early autumn use. dark and light shading: option 2, full autumn and winter occupation.

Specialisation

The dominance of beaver, otter and pike give the faunal remains an aspect of specialisation, seemingly contradicting the well-established base camp function.

This type of specialisation is, however, to be expected in a selective seasonal scheme as generally supposed for these communities, in combination with the exceptional, but very strategic site location. The remarkable scarcity – for the Late Mesolithic – of broad trapezes in the flint inventory might result from the restricted range of hunting activities. The well-known assemblages dominated by broad trapezes might therefore be considered to relate to the complementary activities of the other seasons.

The fact that such pronounced patterns can still be seen in the faunal composition, in spite of the long-term palimpsest character of the assemblages of all phases, implies that the sites were used in a recurrent way within a fixed yearly schedule over many centuries. This is considered as indicative of a stable 'resource use schedule' and of sustainable environmental relationships.

The wider cultural and social group (Figures 77.1, 77.21)

The function of the *donken* as locations of winter base camps implies the existence of complementary base camps for the other seasons in different palaeoecological settings, directed to the exploitation of another set of resources. A possible candidate is the site of Maaspoort, at the northern margin of the southern cover sand landscape, circa 30 km east of Hardinxveld. The site is documented by a small but highly distinctive assemblage of dredged-up bone and antler implements: a heavy Aurochs metapodial chisel and two perforated antler sleeves, one with a wild boar

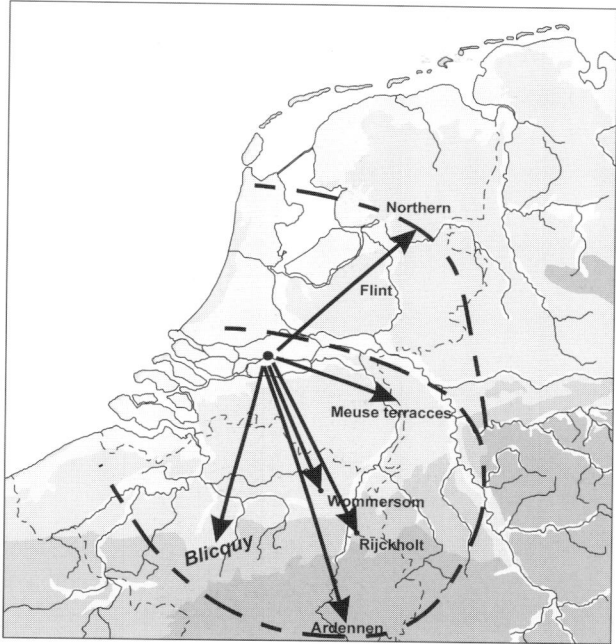

Figure 77.21 Hardinxveld site 3. External contacts as demonstrated by raw material and imported pottery.

Interaction sphere

In their stylistic differences both groups can be seen as representing a wider western and a northern tradition. But in spite of this they are connected as well by traits they have in common, reflecting common aspects of ideology and common native knowledge systems. As such we can point to the tradition of extended burial, of dog burial, of specific wood selection for special tool types, including dug-out canoes and of geometric decoration of specific implements (Andersen 1980, 1994b; Kannegaard Nielsen and Brinch Petersen 1993).

Neolithisation (Figure 77.22)

Apart from the general southern raw material contacts there is a modest number of finds that document direct connections with the farming communities of the loess zone. These are one typical and several atypical Bandkeramik (LBK) arrow heads from site 4, phase 1 (5500–5300 cal BC). These reflect direct or indirect contacts with the initial Rhineland LBK or even the preceding phase of the *ältesten Bandkeramik* that occurs not closer than the surroundings of Frankfurt-am-Main (Lüning *et al.* 1989; Lüning 2000). The first production of pottery around 5000 cal BC might have been inspired by that of the late LBK, be it that the technology and style is fully native.

In phase 2 contacts are proven by the Blicquy pottery and the first long blades of mined Rijckholt type flint. The first Rössen perforated Breitkeil wedges must have been exchanged to the north in this phase all over the country. Not a single whole specimen and no fragments were found at the Hardinxveld sites, but an indirect indication of their use might be the introduction of radial cleaving of oak in this phase as documented in some larger pieces of wood.

Rijckholt flint blades are more common in phase 3 of site 3 and it is also in this phase that the first remains of domestic animals are found. A modest number of bones of cattle, pig, goat and sheep occur in separate small concentrations within the general spread of refuse. Apart from the pig these are all limb bones, that are thought to be brought to the site as quarters and more likely to be connected with the supposed cultic deposition in the adjacent pits of the same phase than part of local subsistence. The site seems after all not suited for cattle, goat and sheep. It is a question whether these bones really document the introduction of domestics in the community or whether we should take some time lag into account, in view of the context of these bones and of the function of the site in the settlement system. However it may be, these are at any rate the first domestic animal bones north of the loess zone, dated earlier than expected, in the late Bischheim phase of the Rössen Culture. Charred cereal grains were not attested in spite of a large scale sampling and identification programme.

tusk inset, the other with a similar *décor pointillé* as the Hardinxveld specimen (Verhagen 1991). The site is ideally located for a combination of summer river fishing of salmon and large game hunting on the sand. So the yearly territory of the bands that used the *donken* can be conceived as the combination of both types of site territories: that on the sand margin and that on a *donk* in the marshland.

The wider community of which the Hardinxveld band formed part can be visualised on the basis of the rock and flint sources of phase 1 and of the imported Blicquy-type of pottery in phase 2. It stretched as far south as the loess zone and the northern fringe of the Ardennes, approximately coinciding with the Middle and Late Mesolithic spatial group (Gendel 1990), characterised not only by the use of Wommersom Quartzite but also (in the Boreal Middle Mesolithic) by surface-retouched points. Indeed the material culture – technology, tool types, style in general – of Hardinxveld must be considered as representative for this, western Mesolithic social entity. All obvious contrasts with contemporaneous southern Scandinavian assemblages are indications of a cultural differentiation of the Mesolithic as a whole already suggested on the basis of microlith spectra (Newell 1973; Kozlowski 1975). If we consider 'style' of material culture an expression of social identity then the Danish early Ertebølle and the Wommersom-Hardinxveld material-spatial units can be considered as separate and contrasting social entities on the level of a tribe. The 'empty' space in between, covering the total North German Plain to the west of the river Elbe might have been the territory of a separate, third Lower Saxon unit.

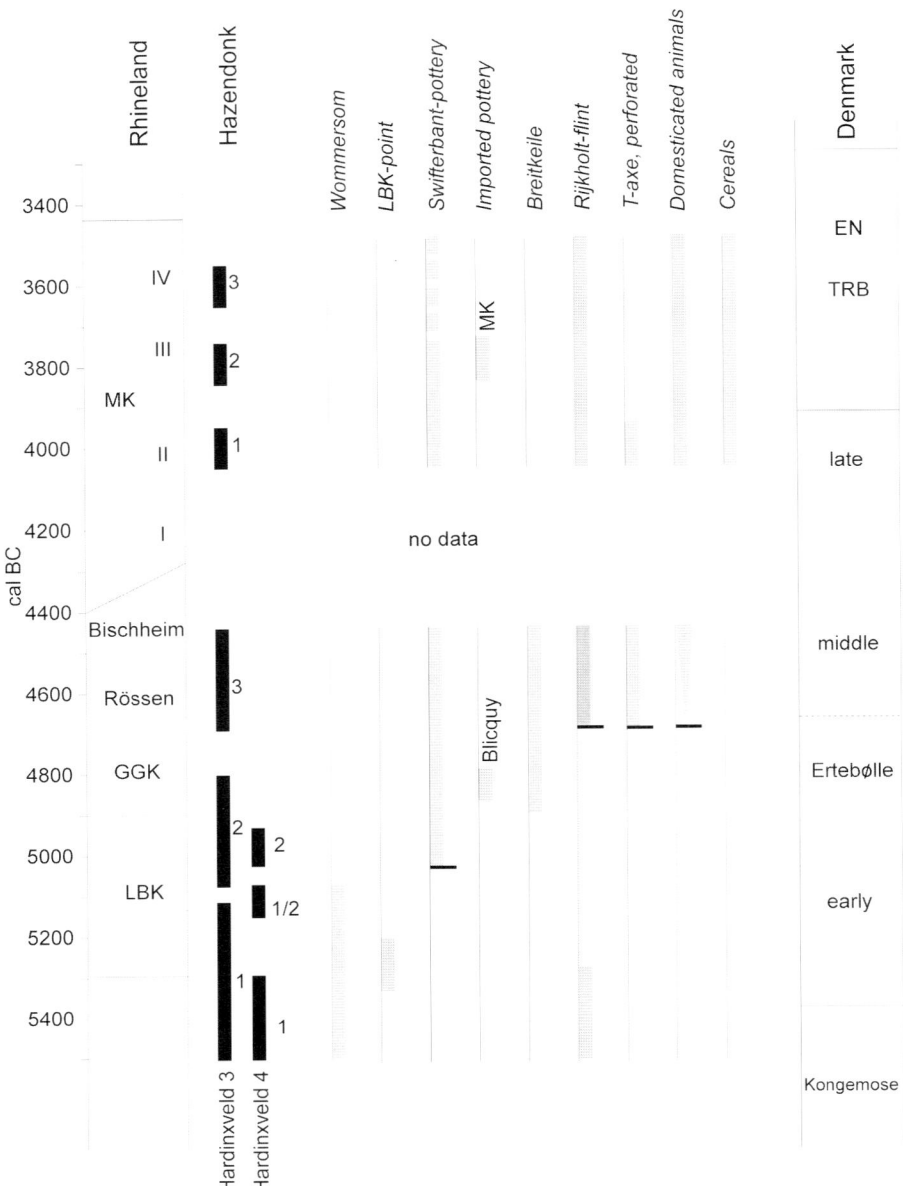

Figure 77.22 Gradual process of neolithisation as documented at the river dune sites of Hardinxveld and Hazendonk. Breitkeile: general evidence, not on the sites.

The period 4500–4000 cal BC is still a gap in our knowledge. At some moment in this period the first cereals must have been introduced into the north, since remains of emmer and einkorn are attested on all sites from 4000 onward, as at Hazendonk phase 1 and Swifterbant S3 (Bakels 1981; Van Zeist and Palfenier-Vegter 1981; Louwe Kooijmans 1993b). The domestic:wild bone ratio at the sites, however, never exceeds the 50% domestic in the wetlands up till the end of the Neolithic.

The neolithisation process had a different course in the Lower Rhine Basin than it had in Southern Scandinavia (Louwe Kooijmans 1993a, 1998; Raemaekers 1999). Although the 'export horizon' of Rössen Breitkeile covered both areas the subsequent sequence was different. The introduction of other Neolithic elements started much earlier in the Lower Rhine Basin than in Denmark, fully embedded in the Swifterbant Culture and completed at least some centuries before 4000 cal BC. We should, moreover, realise that most probably we do not see the Neolithic aspect at the wetland sites in their maximum expression. Fully Mesolithic Ertebølle in contrast, was rather abruptly replaced as late as 3950 cal BC by Neolithic EN TRB, in a distinct culture change.

The successive period, the first half of the 4th millennium is a period of contrast as well. In the Dutch river district the Swifterbant pottery continues to end up in the Hazendonk 3 style around 3600 cal BC. Society is, however, documented as agrarian by means of micro wear analysis of flint, artifact categories (sickle blades, quern stone fragments) and a domestic faunal assemblage at coastal Wateringen c. 3600 cal BC. (Raemaekers et al. 1997; Raemaekers 1999). To the north, as far as the Elbe, any documentation is lacking, with the exception of a few enigmatic assemblages from the central Dutch polder district.

The twin site of Hardinxveld 3 and 4 is a very welcome new source of information on all aspects of the Later Mesolithic of the Lower Rhine Basin and on the initial stage of neolithisation in that region. There are many similarities with the ever dominant Scandinavian data in social, economic and ideological respect. The artifact typology demonstrates, however, many differences and is an argument for considerable cultural differentiation. The same holds for the process of agropastoral transformation that followed a separate and distinctly different trajectory. In this way Hardinxveld helps us to reveal the cultural mosaic that lies hidden behind the microliths.

Acknowledgements

I would like to thank Joanne Mol for the use of figure 77.3, Louise van Wijngaarden-Bakker and Jacqueline Oversteegen for the use of figure 77.19, John Bintliff for reading and correcting the English.

References

Andersen, S.H. 1973. Ringkloster, en Jysk inlandsboplads med Ertebøllekultur. *Kuml* 1973–1974, 11–108.
—— 1980. Ertebøllekunst, nye østjyske fund af mønstrede Ertebølleoldsager. *Kuml* 1980, 7–62.
—— 1981. *Danmarkshistorien – Stenaldern – Jægerstenaldern*. Kopenhagen.
—— 1994a. Ringkloster, Ertebølle trappers and wild boar hunters in eastern Jutland, a survey. *Journal of Danish Archaeology* 12, 13–59.
—— 1994b. New finds of Mesolithic logboats in Denmark. In: Westerdahl, C. (ed.) *Cross roads in ancient Shipbuilding, Proceedings of the Sixth International Symposium on Boat and Ship Archaeology, Roskilde 1991*. Oxbow Monograph 40, 1–10. Oxford.
Arnold, B. 1995–1996. *Les pirogues monoxyles d'Europe centrale, construction, typologie, évolution*. Archéologie neuchâteloise 20/21. Neuchâtel.
Bakels, C.C. 1981. Neolithic Plant Remains from the Hazendonk, Province of Zuid-Holland, the Netherlands. *Zeitschrift für Archäologie* 15, 141–148.
Broeke, P. van den. 1982. Neolithic bone and antler objects from the Hazendonk near Molenaarsgraaf (prov. South Holland). *Oudheidkundige Mededelingen uit het Rijksmuseum van Oudheden te Leiden* 64, 163–195.
Gendel, P. 1982. The distribution and utilisation of Wommersomquartzite during the Mesolithic. In: Gob, A. and Spier, F. (eds.) *Le Mésolithique entre Rhin et Meuse*, 21–50. Luxembourg.
—— 1990. The Analysis of lithic styles through distributional profiles of variation: examples from the Western European Mesolithic. In: Bonsall, C. (ed.) *The Mesolithic in Europe*, 40–47. Edinburgh.
Grünberg, J. 2000. Mesolithisch Bestattungen in Europa. Ein Beitrag zur vergleichenden Gräberkunde. *Internationale Archäologie* 40. Rahden.
Hauzeur, A. and Constantin, C. 1993. Nouveaux éléments dans le Grupe de Blicquy en Belgique: le site de Vaux-et-Borset 'Gibour' et 'à 'La Croix Marie-Jeanne', II La Céramique. *Helinium* 33, 168–252.
Kannegaard Nielsen, E. and Brinch Petersen, E. 1993. Burials, people and dogs. In: Hvass, S. and Storgaard, B. (eds.) *Digging into the Past, 25 Years of Archaeology in Denmark*, 76–81. Aarhus.
Koch, E. 1996. *Neolithic bog pots from Zealand, Møn, Lolland and Falster*. Nordiske Fortidsminder B16. Copenhagen.
—— 1999. Neolithic offerings from the wetlands of eastern Denmark. In: Coles, B. and Schou Jørgensen, M. (eds.) *Bog bodies, sacred sites and wetland archaeology*. WARP Occasional Paper 12, 125–132. Exeter.
Kozlowski, S.K. 1975. *Cultural differentiation of Europe from the 10th to the 5th millenium B.C.* Warsaw.
Larsson, L. 1985. Of house and hearth. The excavation, interpretation and reconstruction of a Late Mesolithic house. *Archaeology and Environment* 4, 197–209. Umeå.
Larsson, M. 1986. Bredasten, an early Ertebølle site with a dwelling structure in South Scania. *Meddelanden från Lunds Universitets Historiska Museum* 1985–86, New Series 6, 26–49.
Louwe Kooijmans, L.P. 1993a. The Mesolithic/Neolithic Transformation in the Lower Rhine Basin. In: Bogucki, P. (ed.) *Case Studies in European Prehistory*, 95–145. Boca Raton.
—— 1993b. Wetland exploitation and upland relations of prehistoric communities in the Netherlands. In: Gardiner, J. (ed.) *Flatlands and Wetlands: Current Themes in East Anglian Archaeology*. East Anglian Archaeology 50, 71–116. Norwich.
—— 1998. Understanding the Mesolithic/Neolithic Frontier in the Lower Rhine Basin, 5300–4300 cal BC. In: Edmonds, M. and Richards, C. (eds.) *Understanding the Neolithic of northwestern Europe*, 407–427. Glasgow.
—— 1999. Shippea Hill and after: wetlands in North European prehistory and the case of the donken. In: Coles, J.N. and Mellars, P. (eds.) *World Prehistory, Studies in memory of Grahame Clark*. Proceedings of the British Academy 99, 107–124. London.
—— (ed.) 2001a. *Hardinxveld-Giessendam, Polderweg. Een jachtkamp uit het Laat-Mesolithicum, 5500–5000 v. Chr*. Rapporten Archeologische Monumentenzorg 83. Amersfoort.
—— (ed.) 2001b. *Hardinxveld-Giessendam, De Bruin. Een jachtkamp uit het Laat-Mesolithicum en het begin van de Swifterbant-cultuur, 5500–4450 v. Chr*. Rapporten Archeologische Monumentenzorg 85. Amersfoort.
Lüning, J., 2000. *Steinzeitliche Bauern in Deutschland. Die Landwirtschaft im Neolithikum*. Universitätsforschungen zur prähistorischen Archäologie 58. Bonn.
Lüning, J., Kloos, U. and Albert, S. 1989. Westliche Nachbarn der bandkeramische Kultur: La Hoguette und Limburg. *Germania* 67, 355–393.
Maarleveld, T.J. 1985. *Been en tand als grondstof in de Vlaardingen-cultuur*. Internal report Leiden University, Faculty of Archeology. Leiden.
Müller-Beck, H. 1965. *Seeberg-Burgäschisee-Süd, Teil 5, Holzgeräte und Holzbearbeitung*. Acta Bernensia II. Bern.
Newell, R.R. 1973. The Post-Glacial Adaptations of the Indigenious population of the Northwest European Plain. In: Kozlowski, S.K. (ed.) *The Mesolithic in Europe*, 399–440. Warsaw,
Raemaekers, D.C.M. 1999. *The articulation of a 'New Neolithic'. The meaning of the Swifterbant Culture for the process of Neolithisation in the Dutch-North German Plain*. Archaeological Series Leiden University 3. Leiden.
Raemaekers, D.C.M., Bakels, C.C., Beerenhout, B., Gijn, A. van., Hänninen, K., Molenaar, S., Paalman, D., Verbruggen, M. and

Vermeeren, C. 1997. Wateringen 4, a coastal settlement of the Middle Neolithic Hazendonk 3 Group. *Analecta Praehistorica Leidensia* 29, 143–191.

Sørensen, S.A. 1992. Lollikhuse, a dwelling site under a kitchen midden. *Journal of Danish Archaeology* 11, 19–29.

Stenberger, M. 1964. Det forntida Sverige. Stockholm.

Verbruggen, M. in prep. *Neolithicum op de donken.* PhD thesis Leiden.

Verhagen, A.J.C.E. 1991. 'De Hoogaard', een kultusplaats in Maaspoort, Den Bosch. *Archeologie* 3, 99–129.

Woude, J.D. van der 1983. *Holocene Palaeoenvironmental Evolution of a Perimarine Fluviatile Area.* Analecta Praehistorica Leidensia 16. Leiden.

Wyss, R. 1983. *Die jungsteinzeitlicher Bauerndörfer von Egolzwil 4 im Wauwilermoos, Band 2 Die Funde.* Archäologische Forschungen. Zürich.

Zeist, W. van and Palfenier-Vegter, R.M. 1981. Seeds and fruits from the Swifterbant S3 site. *Palaeohistoria* 23, 105–168.

Zvelebil, M. 1986. Mesolithic prelude and Neolithic revolution. In: Zvelebil, M. (ed.) *Hunters in transition, Mesolithic societies of temporate Eurasia and their transition to farming,* 5–15. Cambridge.

78. Late Mesolithic to Early Neolithic communities in the Dnieper Rapids region of Ukraine: chronology and socio-economic continuity?

Malcolm Lillie

Considerable new research has shown that the sequence of cultural developments pertaining to the Mesolithic-Neolithic transition in Ukraine is in need of significant revision (Lillie 1996, 1998a and b, Telegin et al. 2000). In addition to this new evidence a consideration of the dental pathology (Lillie 1998b) and stable isotope analyses (Lillie and Richards 2000), has shown that there is little anthropological evidence to support any major socio-economic shifts across these periods.

The Mariupol-type cemeteries of the Podnieprovie steppe region, and associated monuments, provide a significant resource from which to interpret the trajectory of socio-economic developments in terms of the populations themselves and their associated artefactual inventories. This study provides a summary of the new dating from in excess of 60 radiocarbon determinations from the Mariupol-type cemeteries.

Revisions to the periodisation of the Mesolithic and Neolithic periods, alongside observations on the evidence for continuity and a consideration of the potential resource procurement strategies employed by the populations of this region, all confirm that the later Mesolithic populations produce the foundations of the subsequent Neolithic (cf. Telegin 1987). There is little evidence to support the notion that the 'Neolithic' represents anything more than a 'descriptive' chronological development in this region. In essence we have secure, well-established populations that are exploiting fisher-hunter-gatherer subsistence strategies in a resource-rich riverine environment. In reality there is little to denote these populations as anything other than Mesolithic in character; if we take this term to imply predominantly resource-extraction as opposed to -production economies.

The clarification of the specific attributes of the Mesolithic-Neolithic transition in the Podnieprovie region, afforded by the new radiocarbon and palaeo-dietary evidence, has been facilitated by close collaborative links with colleagues in Ukraine, Russia and England. The evidence suggests that a degree of caution needs to be employed when approaching the Mesolithic-Neolithic transition from the perspective of ill-defined chronologies and limited studies of the populations in terms of their palaeopathology and isotopic signatures.

Introduction

The Dnieper Rapids region of Ukraine contains a significant number of cemeteries (termed Mariupol-type after the type site of Mariupol on the river Donets) dating from the earliest Holocene through to about 3000 cal. BC (Lillie 1998a) and beyond (Figure 78.1). As this chronological span encompasses what are traditionally perceived as the Mesolithic and Neolithic periods, and hence the Mesolithic-Neolithic transition, the cemeteries assigned to these periods form the basis of the current study. Originally, these cemeteries were reported as having contained in excess of 800 inhumation burials (Telegin and Potekhina 1987), of which about 310 were sufficiently well preserved to facilitate analysis. The term cemetery is used, due to the fact that these burial grounds are characterised as discrete areas set away from any associated settlement evidence, and are used solely for the purpose of burial from the Epipalaeolithic onwards.

During the initial stages of the research, 26 radiocarbon determinations were obtained, in order to more accurately define the chronological development of these cemeteries (Lillie 1998a, 1998b). The evidence provided by these dates indicated that the traditional seriation, focussing on typological considerations and based on assumed associations with the adjacent Tripolye farming culture and only limited absolute dating, were wholly unreliable in the sequencing of these monuments (cf, Telegin et al. 2000). In general, the Ukrainian Mesolithic cemeteries were dated to the 9th–7th/6th millennia uncal. BC, according to Telegin and Potekhina (1987), with the transition to the Neolithic being predicated on the appearance of pottery in the artefact inventories of sites in this region.

This categorisation appears in contrast to the more conventional understanding of 'the Neolithic' as a shift from 'wild' to 'domesticated' resource exploitation. Traditionally Telegin (1982) viewed crouched inhumations as representing a Mesolithic burial rite, with

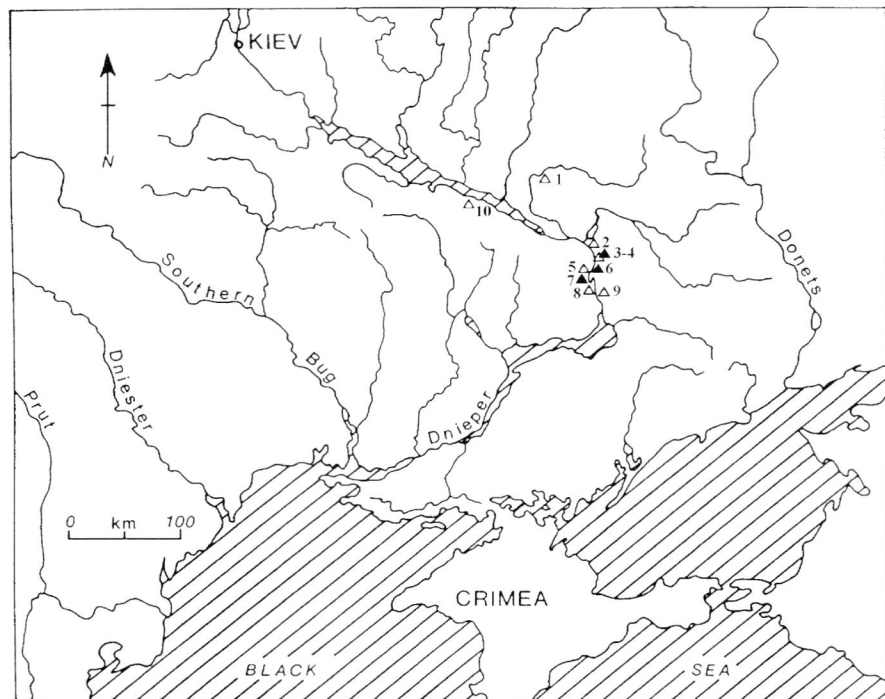

Figure 78.1 The Dnieper Rapids region, showing location of cemeteries discussed in text. 1. Osipovka, 2. Igren VIII, 3. Vasilyevka V, 4. Vasilyevka III, II, and 1, 5. Nikolskoye, 6. Marievka, 7. Voloshkoe, 8. Vovnigi II, 9. Yasinovatka, 10. Derievka I and II. Filled triangle = Mesolithic, unfilled triangle = Neolithic.

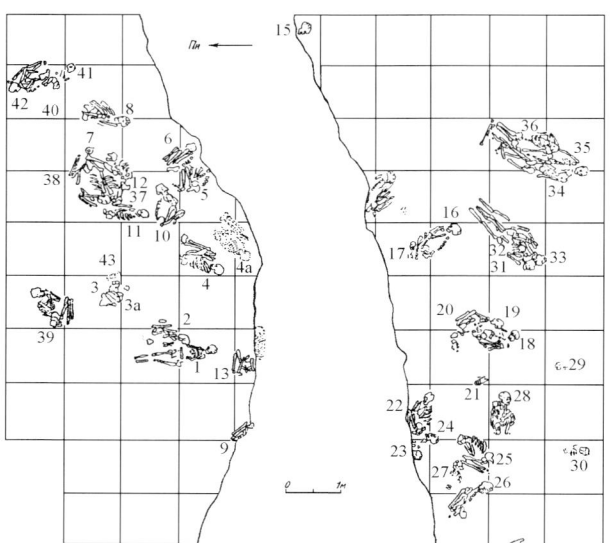

Figure 78.2 Vasilyevka III (Redrawn from Telegin 1982).

extended inhumation representing Neolithic burial practices. As such, a number of the earlier 'Mesolithic' cemeteries, with supposedly later interments, such as Vasilyevka III (Figure 78.2), were used to define the development from earlier Holocene hunter-gatherers through to later Neolithic pastoralists in this region. The combination of the appearance of pottery and the shift from crouched to extended inhumation burial was used to designate the appearance of fully 'Neolithic' culture groups. However, at sites such as Vasilyevka II and Marievka, where the lithic industries retained a Mesolithic character, but burial was in the extended position, a proto-Neolithic designation was applied (Telegin 1987). In general then, the sequence of burial rituals was interpreted as developing from crouched inhumations in the Mesolithic through to Neolithic extended burials, a shift which provided one of the key defining characteristics of the 'so-called' Neolithic period.

Absolute Dating

The preliminary radiocarbon dating of these cemeteries indicated that the crouched and extended inhumations were in fact wholly a Mesolithic, and even an Epipalaeolithic phenomenon in origin (Jacobs 1993). Radiocarbon dating of extended and crouched inhumations at the cemetery of Vasilyevka III indicated that these burials all dated to the period c. 10,000–9000 cal BC (ibid 1993). Similarily, the dates obtained on the earliest 'Neolithic' cemeteries in Telegin's (1987) sequence indicated that these were in fact of later Mesolithic date at 7000–6000 cal BC at sites such as Vasilyevka II and Marievka (Jacobs 1993; Lillie 1998a; Telegin et al. 2000). In addition, some of the burials in the cemetery of Osipovka, all of which were in the extended position, occur at 6500 BC and subsequently at 5500 BC in a cemetery that was traditionally placed at 4300 cal BC in the Neolithic chronology

Sample	Laboratory number	^{14}C age	
		Date BP	cal. RangeBC (2σ)
Vasilyevka III			
Skeleton 3	OxA-3807	10,060±105	10,212-9047
Skeleton 28	OxA-3808	9980±100	10,048-9035
Skeleton 16	OxA-3809	10,080±100	10,230-9050
Vasilyevka II			
Skeleton 20	OxA-3804	7920±85	7050-6450
Skeleton 19	OxA-3805	7620±80	6600-6220
Skeleton 15	OxA-3806	8020±90	7300-6600
Marievka			
Skeleton 10	Ki-6779	7550±80	6510-6220
Skeleton 10	Ki-6781	7585±80	6600-6230
Skeleton 14	Ki-6780	7600±100	6640-6230
Skeleton 10	OXA-6200	7620±160	6989-6060
Skeleton 14	OXA-6269	7630±110	6615-6189
Skeleton 4	Ki-6782	7680±90	6700-6260
Skeleton 4	OXA-6199	7955±50	7036-6604
Vasilyevka V			
Skeleton 29	Ki-6776	6220±60	5400-4850
Skeleton 29	OxA-6198	6280±70	5369-5059
Skeleton 26	Ki-6775	6325±65	5480-5070
Skeleton 8	Ki-6777	6430±50	5480-5310
Skeleton 8	OxA-6171	6470±60	5479-5273
Skeleton 23	Ki-6771	6530±70	5620-5360
Skeleton 10	Ki-6772	6620±80	5710-5380
Skeleton 80	Ki-6773	6675±65	5710-5480
Skeleton 20	OxA-6268	6710±90	5711-5440
Skeleton 10	OxA-6172	6805±60	5738-5531
Osipovka			
Skeleton 53	Ki-519	5940±100	5100-4550
Skeleton 53	Ki-517	6075±125	5300-4700
Skeleton 20	OxA-6168	7675±70	6604-6376
Dereivka I			
Skeleton 11	Ki-3135	4820±40	3700-3510
Skeleton 41, 42, 43	Ki-2177	5190±90	4250-3780
Skeleton 109	OxA-5031	6110±120	5274-4730
Skeleton 11	Ki-6728	6145±55	5280-4850
Skeleton 49	OxA-6160	6165±55	5245-4940
Skeleton 33	OxA-6162	6175±60	5256-4940
Skeleton 42	OxA-6159	6200±60	5263-4950
Skeleton 84	OxA-6161	7270±110	6361-5879
Yasinovatka			
Skeleton 63,64	Ki-2810	5100±40	3980-3790
Skeleton 65	Ki-3580	5890±55	4910-4600
Skeleton 36	Ki-1171	5800±70	4810-4470
Skeleton 15	Ki-3160	5730±40	4690-4460
Skeleton 35	Ki-3162	5810±60	4810-4510
Skeleton 39	Ki-6790	5860±75	4910-4520
Skeleton 18	Ki-3032	5900±90	4980-4530

Figure 78.3 Radiocarbon determinations from the Dnieper Rapids cemeteries of Epipalaeolithic through to Later Neolithic age (after Jacobs 1993 [Vasilyevka III and II], Lillie 1996, 1998a. Telegin et al. 2000), (continued over next page).

Sample	Laboratory number	¹⁴C age	
		Date BP	cal. RangeBC (2σ)
Yasinovatka			
Skeleton 34	Ki-6786	6195±80	5320-4850
Skeleton 41	Ki-6785	6240±95	5500-4850
Skeleton 47, 65	Ki-3033	6240±100	5430-4930
Skeleton 90	Ki-6786	6245±70	5370-4990
Skeleton 18	OxA-6167	6255±65	5313-5053
Skeleton 36	OxA-5057	6260±180	5564-4783
Skeleton 21	Ki-6789	6295±70	5390-5050
Skeleton 45	Ki-6791	6305±80	5480-5050
Skeleton 19	Ki-6788	6310±85	5480-5050
Skeleton 64	OxA-5030	6330±90	5437-5064
Skeleton 17	OxA-6166	6360±75	5437-5090
Skeleton 45	OxA-6164	6360±60	5432-5148
Skeleton 19	OxA-6165	6370±60	5434-5221
Skeleton 5	OxA-6163	6465±60	5476-5271
Nikolskoye			
Skeleton 79a	Ki-3410	5200±30	4216-3976
Skeleton 115	Ki-3284	5200±30	4216-3976
Pit 3	Ki-3158	5230±40	4220-3960
Skeleton 105	Ki-5159	5340±50	4330-4000
Skeleton 125	Ki-3283	5460±40	4450-4220
Skeleton 1	Ki-3575	5560±30	4460-4350
Pit 3	Ki-3125	5560±30	4460-4340
Skeleton 137	OxA-5052	6145±70	5252-4861
Skeleton 125	Ki-6603	6160±70	5300-4850
Skeleton 94	OxA-6155	6225±75	5286-49447
Skeleton 125	OxA-5029	6300±80	5428-5060

Figure 78.3 Continued from previous page.

(Table 1) (cf. Telegin 1987; Telegin and Potekhina 1987). The radiocarbon determinations used in this discussion are in certain cases supplemented by recently published dates from the Kiev conventional radiocarbon facility (Figure 78.3) (cf. Telegin et al. 2000).

On the basis of the new radiocarbon evidence it is apparent that the key shifts in burial ritual occur between the Epipalaeolithic and later Mesolithic periods, as opposed to being at the Neolithic transition, and that extended burials were dominating the burial ritual by the period 7000–6000 BC. As such, this particular characteristic can no longer be used to define the shift from the Mesolithic to Neolithic periods.

Interestingly, this late Mesolithic chronological position for Vasilyevka II and Marievka now indicates that the population migrations suggested by Potekhina (1998, Telegin and Potekhina 1987), as having occurred in the earlier Neolithic, are in effect also a late Mesolithic phenomenon. Therefore, on the basis of the revised chronology, Potekhina's later Mesolithic 'robust individuals' termed northern Europoid-type, are interacting with more gracile Mediterranean-types at a date that significantly precedes the 'traditional' Mesolithic-Neolithic transition. Further support for these initial changes in the anthropological composition of the Dnieper populations is perhaps provided by the identification of 'unique' artefact types such as the bone arm rings from Vasilyevka II which are now dated to the period 7000–6000 BC (Figure 78.4).

The fact that extended inhumation remains the dominant burial mode throughout the Neolithic period, occurring until after 4800 BC at the cemetery of Yasinovatka, and after 4000 BC at Nikolskoye (Figure 78.3), reinforces the suggestion that the later Mesolithic population changes are significant in the historical trajectory of these populations, continuing across the period 7000–3500 BC.

The above observations relating to the hypothesised population shifts remain to fully evaluated against their

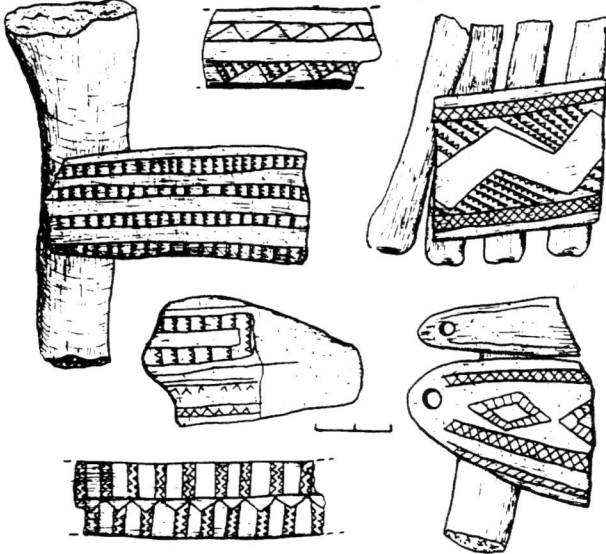

Figure 78.4 Field drawing of inscribed bone bracelets found in the Vasilyevka II cemetery (from Telegin and Potekhina 1987:12). The geometric designs are the only known 'art' form from the Mesolithic in this part of Ukraine. (Scale in cms).

specific socio-political impacts on these societies, but the new radiocarbon seriation has served to clarify certain aspects of the artefactual inventory. Along with shedding light on the 'unique' bone arm bands at Vasilyevka II, the dating of the cemetery of Vasilyevka V, which spans the traditional chronological division of the Mesolithic and Neolithic periods, has shown that there is in fact a discernible shift in the lithic inventories at about 5500 BC. According to Telegin (1987), Telegin and Potekhina (1987) the excavation of the cemetery of Vasilyevka V indicated that two chronologically distinct stages of interment were in evidence. These have been dated to 5700–5450 BC and 5450–5000 BC respectively by Lillie (1998a) (Figure 78.3). The significance of the new dating is that it highlights the shift from Mesolithic, microlithic forms (Figure 78.4:1–17) through to more robust lithic forms as traditionally associated with the subsequent Neolithic period (Figure 78.5:18–20). To date this remains the most securely dated shift in the lithic inventories that we have been able to identify in these cemetery sequences.

When we consider the above evidence it is worth remembering that despite the apparent influx of population in the later Mesolithic a range of artefacts and associated burial goods characterise these populations across the entire span of the Epipalaeolithic, Mesolithic and Neolithic periods.

Artefactual Inventories

In particular the use of red ochre, fish- and deer tooth pendants and numerous flat annular beads (at various times) are ubiquitous aspects of the burial inventory across the entire chronological span being considered. We clearly have considerable evidence for some degree of cultural continuity. This occurs from what is an Epipalaeolithic date at Vasilyevka III, where extended inhumations and ochre are in evidence, right through to the end of the Neolithic period where both extended inhumation, deer and fish-tooth pendants and ochre remain ubiquitous. In the Neolithic period after *c.* 5000 BC artefacts such as beads and boar tusk plates are added to the repertoire, but there is no suggestion that any significant socio-political changes occur at this time. In fact, other than a varying emphasis on the exploitation of fish in the resource procurement spectrum (considered below), the Dnieper populations remain essentially fisher-hunter-gatherer, and predominantly Mesolithic in character until well after *c.* 4800 cal BC.

Unfortunately, despite the addition of over 60 radiocarbon determinations to the absolute dating of the cemetery sequences of the Dnieper Rapids region (Figure 78.3), there still exist some problems in attributing an absolute age to the integration of ceramics to the cultural reperoire. This problem is exaggerated by the fact that at sites such as Yasinovatka, pottery sherds are found 'associated' with the second (b) stage of interment which is dated to after 4900 BC, but there is no secure way to tie the associated ceramics into the absolute chronology. Similarly, the cemetery that is fundamental to Telegin's (1987) ceramic typology for the Dnieper cemeteries, Nikolskoye, has numerous, discrete burial pits, the lower levels of which appear to date to *c.* 5400-4900 BC (Lillie 1998b). To date, none of the ceramics at Nikolskoye can be securely attributed to this early stage of cemetery use.

The upper phase of interment in this cemetery appears to date to after *c.* 4500 BC onwards up to *c.* 3700 BC. In this stage, while the pottery is clearly in association with the interments, no securely dated contextual data exists. This situation persists due to the fact that there is continued re–use of the burial pits throughout the Neolithic period at Nikolskoye, a phenomenon that obscures any evidence for discrete associations due to re-working of the burial contexts.

As such, despite an extensive dating program on the Dnieper Rapids cemeteries, it remains difficult to precisely attribute an age to much of the associated ceramic inventory throughout the earlier Neolithic period. Given that the appearance of pottery is considered to be one of the key defining characteristics of Neolithisation for Ukraine, it is clear that more robust excavation strategies need to be developed in order to further define the chronological boundaries. This approach needs to be employed if we are to understand the mechanisms relating to the integration and dissemination of ceramic technology in this region. At present we have some fundamental insights, but as is often the case, we appear to be creating as many questions as answers, and remain within what is

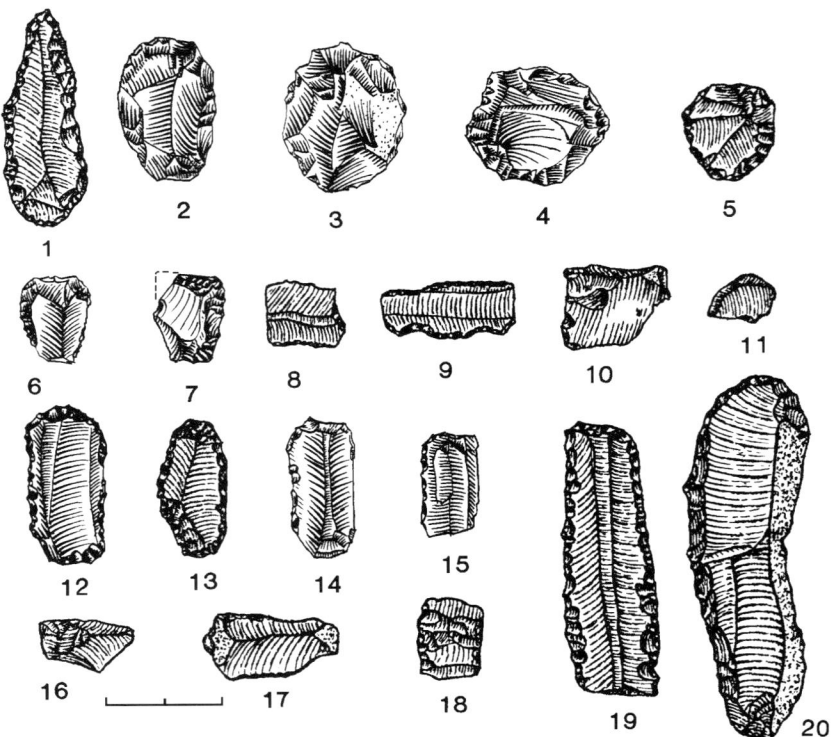

Figure 78.5 Lithics from the cemetery of Vasilyevka V (Scale in cm) (after Telegin and Potekhina 1987:40). Flints 1–17 were found in association with burial 10 and are attributed to the primary phase of interment. Flint 18 is also attributed to this earlier stage of burial. Flints 19 and 20 were associated with burial 29 (flint 19) and a group grave comprising burials 13–16 and 19–20 (flint 20). These artefacts are considered by Telegin to be typologically later than the microlithic artefacts.

effectively a typological periodisation for the ceramics, despite the prevailing radiocarbon chronology.

Obviously, a secure chronology is one of the primary research concerns when studying these cemeteries, and the above discussion advocates further study. However, in addition to refining this chronology, the existence of a large skeletal dataset that spans the Mesolithic to Neolithic periods means that we have the opportunity, via palaeopathology and stable isotope studies, to gain some additional insights into the nature of the subsistence trajectories of these populations across some 6000 years or so of cultural evolution.

Palaeopathology and stable isotopes

The initial study of pathology across these periods has shown that only very low levels of dietary stressors are in evidence (Lillie 1998b). The ubiquitous presence of dental calculus alongside an absence of dental caries suggests that these populations consumed diets that were composed of large quantities of dietary proteins (Lillie 1997). Statistical analysis of the frequencies of calculus deposition appear to support the notion that during the earliest Mesolithic period males may have consumed greater quantities of dietary proteins than females. If this observation is valid however, there is nothing in the expression of dental pathologies such as enamel hypoplasias (reductions in tooth crown thickness due to non-specific sub-adult stress) to suggest that females experienced sub-optimal health during this period (Lillie 1998b).

In contrast, the study of the expression of calculus on the Neolithic populations of the region appears to suggest that more equal levels of dietary proteins were being consumed (ibid. 1998b). In order to further verify these observations stable isotope analyses were carried out on a number of individuals from the later Mesolithic through to Neolithic periods from seven of the cemeteries considered (Lillie and Richards 2000). The evidence obtained clearly supports the notion that protein-dominated diets were being consumed, with fish-based proteins significant across both periods (Figure 78.5). However, there is clear evidence to suggest that other dietary proteins were integral to the diet, with significant quantities of both plant (Osipovka and Yasinovatka) and animal proteins (Dereivka and Vasilyevka V) being consumed (Lillie and Richards 2000:267–8). In addition, recent research has confirmed that certain individuals from the cemetery of Yasinovatka consumed a diet of C3 plants and the herbivores that consumed them (Potekhina 2000). The significant aspects of these studies are that the consumption of fish proteins appears to be a consistent element, and that certain individuals were clearly obtaining their dietary proteins from animal and plant proteins (Lillie and Richards 2000).

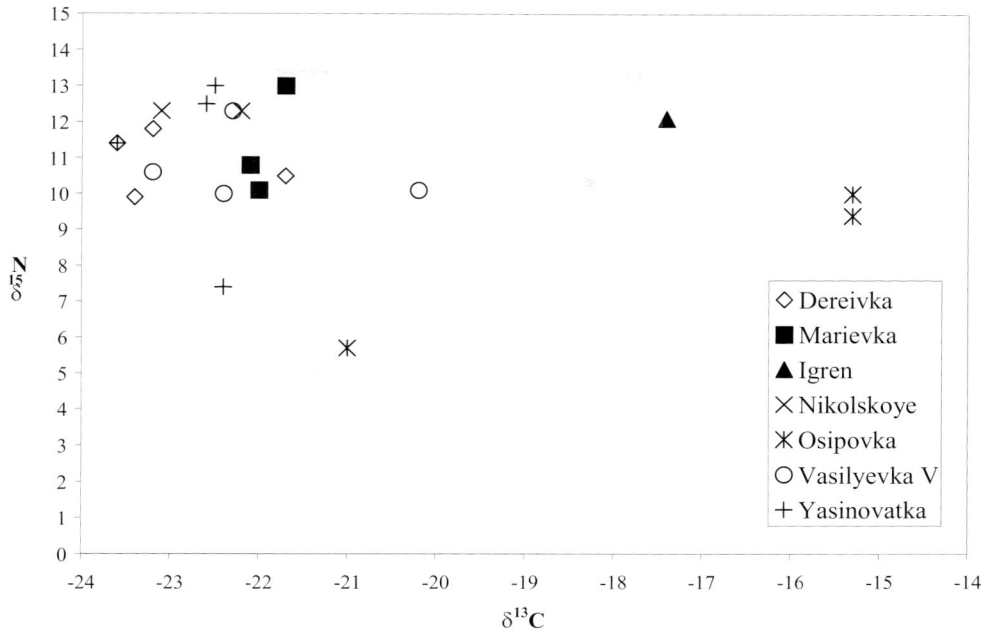

Figure 78.6 Human collagen $\delta^{13}C$ and $\delta^{15}N$ values from the Dnieper Rapids cemeteries.

These preliminary results highlight a picture of dietary protein consumption that is wholly in accord with ethnographic studies of hunter-gatherer societies (cf. Balakin and Nuzhinyi 1995). The observation that fish-based proteins continue into the Neolithic may well highlight intensive food-procurement regimes that reinforce the fisher-hunter-gatherer subsistence base. This would provide a mechanism that avoided the stimulus of a shift towards domesticated species that may have been increasing due to contacts with adjacent farming cultures at c. 5500–4800 cal. BC (Lillie 1998b).

In addition, it is worth noting that until recently, prior to the construction of the hydro-electric dams across the Dnieper, it was quite easy for young children to stand at the food of the rapids along the Dnieper and quite literally knock the fish onto the bank as they traversed the Rapids (Dimitri Telegin, *pers comm* 1992). This activity would have ensured that children were integrated into resource procurement strategies from a very early age and also account for their treatment in the burial ritual, treatment that fully mirrored that afforded to adults in these societies.

Discussion

The evidence from the cemeteries of the Dnieper region supports the notion that some increases in population, possibly from a north eastern origin, are occurring from about 7000–6000 BC – i.e., the later Mesolithic period (cf. Telegin and Potekhina 1987; Potekhina 1998). Despite these hypothesised migrations, a number of the defining characteristics of the Dnieper populations: including extended burials, ochre and fish and deer tooth pendants are in evidence throughout the duration of the Epipalaeolithic, Mesolithic and Neolithic periods between c. 10,000–3500 BC.

It appears that there is some support for the traditional notion of a shift from microlithic to more massive lithic types in the mid sixth millennium BC (c. 5500 cal BC) at the site of Vasilyevka V. However, the significance of this shift in the artefactual inventory, in terms of socio-political directions, remains to be established. Similarly, despite the fact that the later stages of the Dnieper-Donets culture overlap with stage B of Tripolye, and that imported Tripolye pottery has been recovered from the stage-b phases of interment at Nikolskoye, the precise nature of the socio-economic significance of such interactions remains obscure.

The cemeteries of Mariupol-type are a long-term phenomenon, that encompass numerous phases of societal development spanning 6500 years. Unfortunately, despite having obtained in excess of 60 radiocarbon determinations, the complex nature of the burial rituals has served to obscure many of the aspects of socio-economic development that one would hope to highlight in such a study.

Despite these limitations, we can say with some certainty that considerable continuity characterises these populations across the period studied. Not only do numerous aspects of the burial ritual remain constant, across the 6500 years of time being considered, i.e. extended burial, ochre and fish and deer tooth pendants, but a more complete picture of the diet of these populations has been forthcoming.

On the basis of the combined palaeopathological and stable isotopic studies, it appears that the populations exploited fisher-hunter-gatherer subsistence regimes across the Mesolithic and Neolithic periods. The precise degree to which each element of the resource spectrum was exploited remains to be established, but there is strong evidence to support the continued exploitation of riverine resources into the earlier Neolithic. This may well reflect a continuation of the foraging economy which serves to mitigate against any significant shifts in the socio-economic base of the Dnieper fisher-hunter-gatherer groups as contact with adjacent farming groups increases. If this is a realistic assumption, then as a strategy this appears to have worked. At present there is no suggestion of any shifts in the economic system before the final Neolithic, despite the appearance of ceramics at sites such as Yasinovatka and Nikolskoye and Dereivka I.

In summary, continuity with some degree of flexibility is attested across the Mesolithic to Neolithic periods in the Dnieper Rapids region of Ukraine. No 'Mesolithic-Neolithic' transition appears to have occurred in economic terms, and in fact a number of the shifts that are apparent occur in what would traditionally be considered to be a later Mesolithic context.

In order to generate more meaningful conclusions relating to the Neolithic period, we now need to further refine the dating of the more complex burial monuments such as Nikolskoye and the settlement site of Dereivka. Furthermore, our understand of how these particular monuments relate to the expansion of the so-called Dereivka culture groups of nomadic pastoralists, who until recently were thought to have developed horse riding, is in need of additional study. The current research has produced considerable insights into the Mesolithic and earlier Neolithic periods of cultural development in the Dnieper Rapids region. However there are also many more questions that need to be considered in greater detail if we are to attempt to identify the shift towards food producing as opposed to food extracting resource procurement strategies in this region.

Acknowledgements

Colleagues in St.Petersburg and Kiev allowed me access to the Ukrainian skeletal series in 1992 and 1994. In Kiev Prof. Dmitri Telegin and Inna Potekhina not only looked after me but imparted much of their knowledge of the Ukrainian material culture and chronology. Their help proved fundamental to my understanding of this region, and these particular chronological periods. In St.Petersburg Prof. Gokhman and Alexander Kozintsev allowed me unimpeded access to the collections and Prof. Vladimir Timofeev, Lena and Ksenia cared for me and educated me in the ways of Russia culture. Similarily, Inna and family in Kiev gave me their knowledge of Ukrainian traditions in a way that ensured that my research visits proved rewarding on numerous levels. The stable isotopes considered above were analysed and interpreted by Mike Richards at ORAU.

References:

Balakin, S. and Nuzhinyi, D. 1995. The Origins of Graveyards: The Influence of Landscape Elements on Social and Ideological Changes in Prehistoric Communities. *Préhistoire Européenne* 7, 191–202.

Bonsall, C., Lennon, R., McSweeney, K., Stewart, C., Harkness, D., Boroneant, V., Bartosiewicz, L., Payton, R. and Chapman, J. 1997. Mesolithic and Early Neolithic in the Iron Gates: a palaeodietary perspective. *Journal of European Archaeology* 5, No. 1, 50–92.

Jacobs, K. 1993. Human Postcranial Variation in the Ukrainian Mesolithic-Neolithic. *Current Anthropology* 34, 417–30.

Lillie, M.C. 1996. Mesolithic and Neolithic Populations of Ukraine: Indications of Diet from Dental Pathology. *Current Anthropology* 37, 135–142.

—— 1997. Women and Children in Prehistory: Resource Sharing and Social Stratification at the Mesolithic-Neolithic Transition in Ukraine. In: Moore, J. and Scott, E. (eds.) *Invisible People and Processes: Writing Gender and Childhood into European Archaeology,* 213–228. London.

—— 1998a. The Mesolithic-Neolithic transition in Ukraine: new radiocarbon determinations for the cemeteries of the Dnieper Rapids region. *Antiquity* 72, 184–188.

—— 1998b. The Dnieper Rapids Region of Ukraine: A Consideration of chronology, Dental Pathology and Diet at the Mesolithic-Neolithic Transition. Sheffield University: Unpublished PhD Thesis. Sheffield.

Lillie, M.C. and Richards, M. 2000. Stable Isotope Analysis and Dental Evidence of Diet at the Mesolithic-Neolithic Transition in Ukraine. *Journal of Archaeological Science* 27, 965–972.

Potekhina, I.D. 1998. Ancient north Europeans in the Mesolithic-Neolithic transition of southeast Europe. In: Zvelebil, M., Domanska, L. and Dennell, R. (eds.) *Harvesting the Sea, Farming the Forest: the emergence of Neolithic societies in the Baltic region,* 65–69. Sheffield.

—— 2000. North-Pontic Populations in the Mesolithic-Neolithic: Anthropological structure, Diet reconstructions. *Final Programme and Abstracts* of the 6th Annual Meeting of the European Association of Archaeologists, 148. Lisboa.

Telegin, D.Y. 1982. *Mesolitichni pamyatki Ukraine (9–6 tisyacholitta do n.e.).* [Mesolithic Populations of Ukraine (9–6 millennia)], 236–243. Kiev.

—— 1987. Neolithic cultures of the Ukraine and adjacent areas and their chronology. *Journal of World Prehistory* 1, No. 3, 307–331.

Telegin, D.Y. and Potekhina, I.D. 1987. *Neolithic cemeteries and populations in the Dnieper Basin.* B.A.R. Int. Ser., 383. Oxford.

Telegin, D.Y., Potekhina, I.D., Kovaliukh, M.M. and Lillie, M.C. 2000. The chronology of the Mariupol-Type Cemeteries of Ukraine re-visited: implications for the age and chronological periodisation of Mesolithic to Copper Age Cultures. *Radiocarbon and Archaeology* 1, No. 1, 59–74.

79. New Investigations on Submarine Stone Age Settlements in the Wismar Bay Area

Harald Lübke

Since 1998 investigations on submarine Stone Age settlements have taken place in the Wismar Bay area. Several new sites were discovered with different preservation of cultural remains. The most important site so far is "Timmendorf-Nordmole", a coastal settlement of the Late Ertebølle Culture. Numerous implements of flint, bone, antler, ceramic and wood were found in a well-preserved state. The subsistence was based mainly of marine resources. This is well-documented by wooden prongs and bone points of fishing spears, wooden sticks as probable remains of fish weirs, antler harpoons, paddles, fragments of a log boat and a large number of fish bones – especially eel and cod –, sea mammals and birds. In contrary red deer, roe deer, and wild boar are represented by only a few bones. Decorated rim sherds, core axes with specialised cutting edges, truncated blades with basal shaft retouch and transverse arrowheads indicate that the site belongs to the younger Ertebølle culture. Accelerator radiocarbon dates of charred food-waste on ceramics, animal bones and wood indicate that the site was in use during the period from 4400 to 4100 cal BC. In view of new results of excavations in Ostholstein we are now able to prove that at the German Baltic coast the Funnel Beaker Culture did not replace the Ertebølle Culture earlier than 4100 calBC.

Introduction

The present knowledge of the adoption of the Neolithic way of live along the Baltic coast in Germany is fundamentally based on the research of settlements in northeastern Holstein. In the 1970s extensive excavations took place at Grube-Rosenhof and Siggeneben-Süd, Kr. Ostholstein. From the late 1980s until the beginning of the 1990s sites situated in the Trave valley between Bad Segeberg and Bad Oldesloe were excavated. The latest research was done at Wangels, Kr. Ostholstein. All those excavations helped to gain considerable knowledge of the Final Mesolithic Ertebølle- and the Early Neolithic Funnel Beaker Culture (cp. Hartz 1997/98:19 p; Hartz et al. 2000:130 pp; Lübke 2000b:18 p). In the 1980s the first site of the Ertebølle-Culture along the Polish coast was found near Dabki (Ilkiewicz 1997:50 pp).

Compared to its neighbouring areas Mecklenburg-Vorpommern lacks systematical research on Stone Age settlements along its coast. During the past forty years only two sites of this period were excavated and documented, Ralswiek-Augustenhof and Lietzow-Buddelin on the Island of Rügen. In addition, artifacts were found in dredging sites along the Strelasund, but insufficient documentation limits stratigraphic interpretation. According to zooarchaeological and palynological analysis, settlements in Vorpommern of the Lietzow Group, which belonged to the Ertebølle Culture, were not influenced by agricultural elements. Although, from a geographic perspective, they lived close to the Neolithic cultures at the Oder valley and probably had contacts with them. One of the more recent sites was the dredging site Parow Fpl. 4, where pottery of the Funnel Beaker Culture was found. The 14C AMS analysis of food particles, found sticking to pottery, proved the succession of the Funnel Beaker Culture over the Lietzow Group between 4100 to 4000 BC (cp. Lübke et al. 2000:440 p; Mertens and Schirren 2000:451).

According to those results, agricultural elements did not influence Vorpommern in Final Mesolithic times. The same is true for the south of Scandinavia. But there are proofs for the beginning of crop farming and keeping of cattle along Holstein's eastern coast (Kalis and Meurers-Balke 1998:1 pp; Hartz et al. 2000:134 pp), although the people, akin to their neighbours farther north and east, mainly subsisted upon hunting and fishing. It was not before 4100 to 4000 calBC that subsistence based on agricultural production superseded the hunter-gatherer economy. The Early Neolithic Funnel Beaker Culture succeeded the Final Mesolithic Ertebølle Culture. This development was highly influenced by the expansive older Michelberg Culture in the West and the late Lengyel Culture in the East. The interrelation is proven by inventories of the oldest Funnel Beaker Culture, found south of the river Elbe (cp. Lüning 1998:283; Richter 1999:33 pp; Hartz et al. 2000:132 pp) and of the Late

Lengyel Culture in north-central Poland (Grygiel and Bogucki 1997:161 pp; Bogucki 2000:208).

It was only along the coast of northern Germany that those economical changes took place during the 5th millennium BC. Schleswig-Holstein's interior was dominated by groups of the Funnel Beaker Culture with a hunter-gatherer economy until the middle of the 4th millennium BC. Not before the beginning of the second phase of the Nordic Early Neolithic (FN II) did cattle raising and farming economies spread in that area (Hoika 1993:12 pp; Lübke 2000a:245).

Submarine Stone Age Sites in the Wismar Bay Area

The expansion of the Neolithic way of life along the southern Baltic coast is characterised by a unique subsistence pattern. To prepare an ecological and economical profile of this pattern, further excavations on Final Mesolithic and Early Neolithic sites would be useful. However, rapid sea level rise during the Litorina transgression complicates new scientific researches. On the western coast of Mecklenburg only stray finds have been documented up to now. Late- and Final Mesolithic sites are expected to be in about ten meters depth of water or even deeper. In addition, likely settlement areas are situated at former river mouths, sand bars in front of lagoons or at the mouth of bays. Those sites might be destroyed by wave erosion caused by progressive transgression and they might also be covered with younger sediments. All these factors make the location of expressive sites very difficult.

The preservation of submerged sites depends on several determinants. Coastal areas that were not affected by the intensive, dynamic processes along the coast during the Litorina transgression or sites saved by offshore sand bars are likely well preserved. An example is Wismar Bay, which is cut into the hilly ground moraine of northwest Mecklenburg. In the northwest sector shallows separate the Wismar Bay from the Mecklenburg Bay (Figure 79.1). Taking into account the topography and the low water level in Final Mesolithic and Early Neolithic times (Klug 1980:237 pp; Schuhmacher 1991:137 pp) Wismar Bay must have been a fjord like bay with single basins and smaller islands at that time.

Danish research (Sørensen 1983:111 pp; Fischer 1995:374) has shown that such fjord like bays were a preferred area of settlement for Final Mesolithic hunter gatherer and fisher societies. The lack of Mesolithic finds in the Wismar Bay area seem to result from insufficient

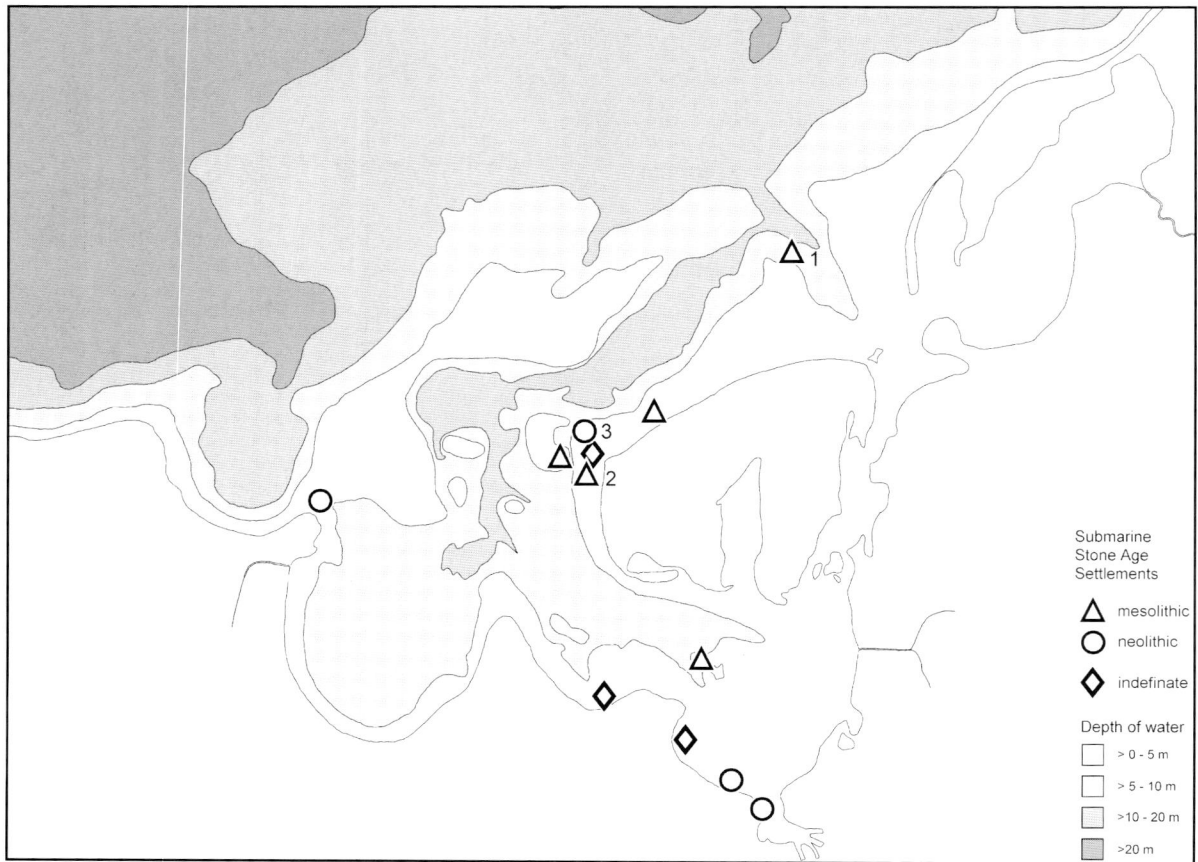

Figure 79.1 The location of submarine stone age sites in the Wismar Bay (1 Jäckelberg-Nord; 2 Timmendorf-Nordmole, 3 Timmendorf-Tonnenhaken). No scale. H. Lübke del.

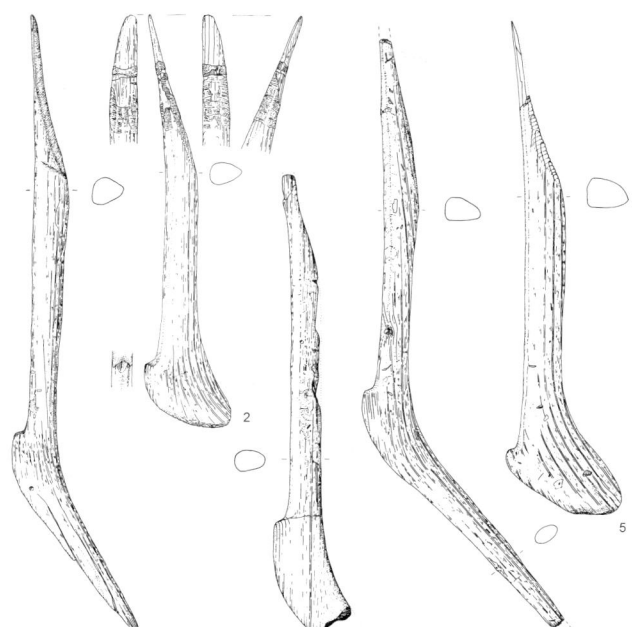

Figure 79.2 Timmendorf-Nordmole (Poel 12, Ostsee II). Wooden implements. 1–5: leister prongs. Scale 1:4. J. Freigang del.

Figure 79.3 Timmendorf-Nordmole (Poel 12, Ostsee II). Wooden implements. 1–2: semi-finished leister prongs, 3: paddle, 4: tool shaft (?), 5: leister shaft and 6: bow. Scale 1:8. J. Freigang del.

research. By a series of underwater surveys, started in 1998, archaeologists hoped to gain more insight into the situation of the bay during the Late and Final Mesolithic. The surveys were conducted together with the Department of Marine Geology of the "Institut für Ostseeforschung" (IOW). "The Landesverband für Unterwasserarchäologie Mecklenburg Vorpommern e. V." (LUMV), an association for sports divers and professional divers, also supported the project. A number of new sites with varying conditions of preservation were discovered (Figure 79.2).

Jäckelberg-Nord

The oldest site up to now is Poel 16 ("Jäckelberg-Nord") which is situated around 1,5 NM north of Poel (Figure 79.2). It was discovered during a survey under the leadership of the IOW with the research vessel "Prof. Albrecht Penck" in October 1999. A peat sediment outcrop was located in 7 m deep water, on the northern edge of the shallow "Jäckelberg" (Figure 79.3). Remains of a stone-age settlement were discovered in the surroundings. According to today's knowledge, parts of the former refuse zone situated off the shore in shallow water are still preserved. Due to its depth of –7 m below mean sea level, Jäckelberg-Nord seemed to be older than the other settlement sites in Wismar Bay. According to the first 14C dates, this site dates back to 5400–5000 calBC (Figures 79.8–79.9). It can thus be assigned to the early Ertebølle period, which began in northern Germany around 5400 BC. Formal analysis of recovered finds confirms these dates (Lübke 2000b:20 p).

Timmendorf-Nordmole

The most important site (Poel 12, Ostsee II – "Timmendorf-Nordmole") discovered up to now presents excellent conditions for the preservation of artifacts and is located off the west coast of the island of Poel. The large Final Mesolithic site is situated about 200 m from the small village of Timmendorf in water 2.5–3.5 m deep (Figure 79.1). Cultural layers in varying states of preservation were located. The area has a length of more than 250 m and is up to 100 m wide. To be able to work effectively a grid with an extension of 210 x 80 m had to be established on the site. Iron measuring posts were put in every ten meters. Afterwards the conditions of the cultural layers in different parts of the settlement were analysed by sounding-trenches. A water dredge with suction head was used to expose the layers. The dredged material was collected in nets at the end of the dredging pipe. Onshore small artifacts and remains of animals and plants were sorted out. Each square meter was drawn and photographed, in addition sections of every trench were documented (Lübke 2000b:22).

The survey showed that large parts of the former settlement surface were destroyed by erosion, as an abraded marl layer appeared directly below a 20 cm thick surface layer consisting of gravel with numerous eroded

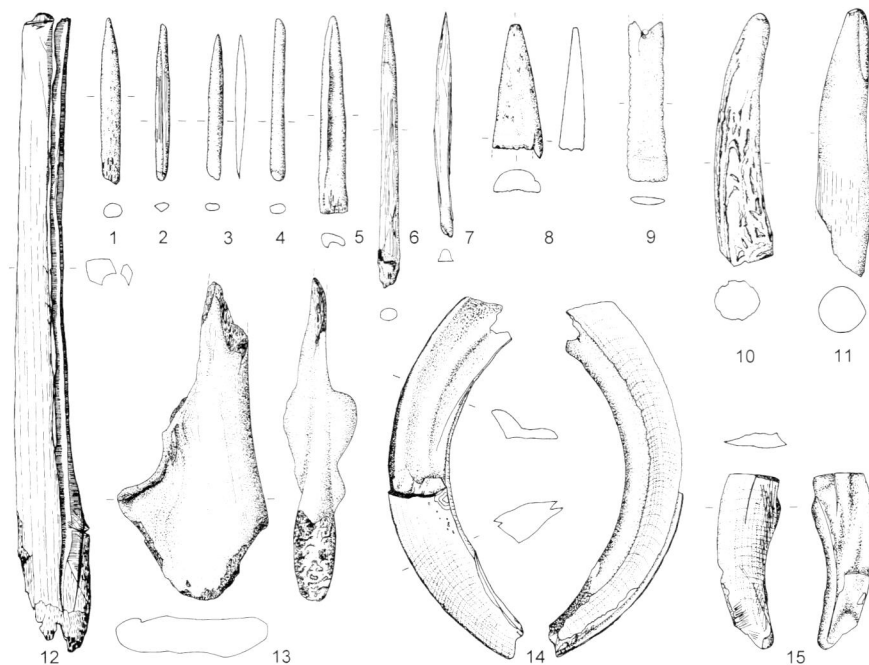

Figure 79.4 Timmendorf-Nordmole (Poel 12, Ostsee II). Bone and antler implements. 1: harpoon head of red deer antler, 2–7: small bone points, 8: red deer antler pendant, 9: red deer long bone with cutting grooves and 10–11: wild boar tusk knifes. Scale 1:3. J. Freigang del.

stone artifacts. Only entrenched settlement features are preserved in this area, as indicated by a 2 m x 3.5 pit – until now not excavated. In deeper water the former border of the settlement and the organogenic shore zone with artifacts such as worked stones, antler, bone, pottery and wood is preserved. In some areas the well-preserved occupation layer could be traced directly below the thin sand layer on the sea bottom. These layers contained unpatinated flint artifacts, large pottery fragments, bone or antler tools as well as wooden implements

The finds

The wooden artifacts found on this site are especially remarkable. The recovered boat remains are up to 2.50 m long fragments of a dugout and further small pieces of lime wood, which could not be assigned to the same boat. This is the first time that fragments of one or even more dugouts, dating back to the Final Mesolithic were found in Northern Germany. In nearby Denmark comparable features were found more frequently in the shore zone of Final Mesolithic settlement sites (Andersen 1987:87 pp, 1991:1 pp; Christensen 1990:119 pp, 1997:282 pp).

Besides indefinable fragments, the majority of the wooden implements found were side prongs of fishing leisters. All together 79 of them were recovered, of which 68 came from an excavated trench, which covers an area of not more than 12 square metres. Most of the prongs are complete apart from smaller damage to the ends. They vary in size and form (Figure 79.2:1–5). The intact ones are from 176 mm to 340 mm long. The pointed upper part can be either slim and wide or broad and short. Some leister prongs show distinct signs of degeneration or have moulds of cord, which are caused by the binding (Figure 79.2:5). Of exceptional note is one prong with a winding of lime-bast on the shaft end (Figure 79.2:2). It is also informative to study the unfinished examples, because they illustrate all production states of these implements. Besides simple bough prongs, cut from trees, and carved semifinished products, almost finished forms also exist (Figure 79.3:1–2).

Another interesting find is a wooden stick, with a carefully carved run around notch on one end (Figure 79.3:5). The other end, which was sticking out of the water was unfortunately destroyed by Teredo navalis. This damage makes it impossible to determinate the sticks' former function. Presumably it is the shaft of a fishing leister. The fragment of an elm bow (Figure 79.3:6) is comparable to similar finds from Denmark (Andersen 1994–95:46). Furthermore a paddle fragment with an oval blade has to be mentioned (Figure 79.3:3). This form doesn't correspond to the known paddle shapes of the Ertebølle Culture. Up to now only long, lean, lancet-like or short paddles with blades formed as a blazon or heart (Andersen 1987:101 pp; Hartz and Lübke 2000:377 pp) were found. The function of another implement (Figure 79.3:4) with moulds of a cord on one end is uncertain. It could be a shaft or a boomerang. Numerous sticks, sharpened on both sides, were probably parts of fishing fences.

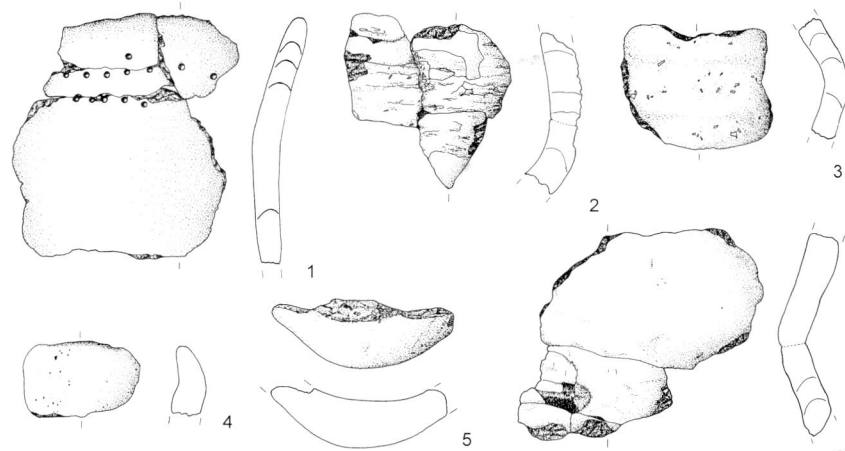

Figure 79.5 Timmendorf-Nordmole (Poel 12, Ostsee II). Pottery. 1: decorated rimsherd, 2–3, 6: body sherds, 4: rimsherd of a lamp and 5: pointed base. Scale 1:3. J. Freigang del.

Hitherto only a few bone and antler remains were recovered. No axes made of antlers were found up to now. Most frequent are small bone points (Figure 79.4:1–7), which were used as inserts for leisters or as parts of composite fishhooks. In addition, waste products were discovered. A long bone of a red deer shows traces of human work, in that a chip is almost completely torn off (Figure 79.4:12). Furthermore, joint ends were cut off by run around notches. Other finds are an elbow dagger (Figure 79.4:13), a harpoon fragment type A (Fig. 4:8; cp. Andersen 1995:59 p), fragments of antler strikers (Figure 79.4:10–11) and two preparations for knifes made of wild boar tusk (Figure 79.4:14–15). A long, rectangular, ornamented pendant, made of a small flat piece of antler, with a bore through its narrow side, was also discovered (Figure 79.4:9).

The pottery consists predominantly of thick-walled potsherds belonging to vessels with pointed bottoms and S-like profiles. Besides some body pieces (Figure 79.5:2–3,6), a not very pronounced pointed pot base (Figure 79.5:5) and a rim potsherd (Figure 79.5:1) are especially remarkable. The latter is decorated with simple stamps. Corresponding pottery has been recovered on the Ertebølle sites Ringkloster and Norsminde in Jutland (Andersen 1994–95:40 pp) as well as in Löddesborg, Sweden (Jennbert 1984:43 pp). A few potsherds were probably parts of clay lamps (Figure 79.5:4).

As expected stone implements and their preparation waste form the largest group of artifacts. Except from a few rock implements the majority of the stone material are flint artifacts. A fragment of a club head with a double conic bore is notable (Figure 79.6:23). Besides numerous flakes and blades some elementary flake cores and a few blade cores were recovered. The amount of irregular blades, prepared in plain hard hammer blade technique is almost 50 percent, much higher than at Jäckelberg-Nord. Still the majority of the blade implements were slim pieces manufactured in the soft hammer blade technique. Among those are truncated blades with a straight or concave retouch, which sometimes have a supplementary developed, proximal shaft retouch (Figure 79.6:10–14). Scrapers, burins and tools with edge retouch were found as well (Figure 79.6:15–16). Among the recovered flake implements, scrapers and various borers are to be mentioned (Figure 79.6:9). The most frequently found artifacts are flake axes. At present more than 100 axes were found. There is a high diversity of axe types (Figure 79.6:17–22). Besides the typical flat-flaked axes, implements with pointed base or flat, adze-like axes were recovered. One of those axes has a specialised cutting edge (Figure 79.6:20), usually common with core axes. Core axes are very rare on this site, but appear in irregular forms. Transverse arrowheads, usually very typical on Stone Age sites, were only sporadically discovered. The 15 projectiles found are trapezoids and have slightly concave or straight retouched edges (Figure 79.6:1–8).

Economy

Numerous charcoal pieces as well as bones of small mammals and fish and floral remains were collected from the dredged material. The excellent state of preservation allows supplementary, scientific studies. According to the preliminary results of the zooarchaeological material (Figure 79.7) seals and sea birds were hunted besides land mammals such as red deer and wild boar. Except for dogs the existence of other domesticated animals could not be proven. The large amount of fish remains is remarkable. On no other site along the German Baltic coast are similar numbers of fish bones registered. The most frequently represented fish is eel, followed by cod and other species. Comparable faunal components were documented at the Danish sites Bjørnholm and Ertebølle (Enghoff 1995:69 p). Taking into account the analysed artifactual material, the people there primarily subsisted on marine resources. Hunting played a secondary role.

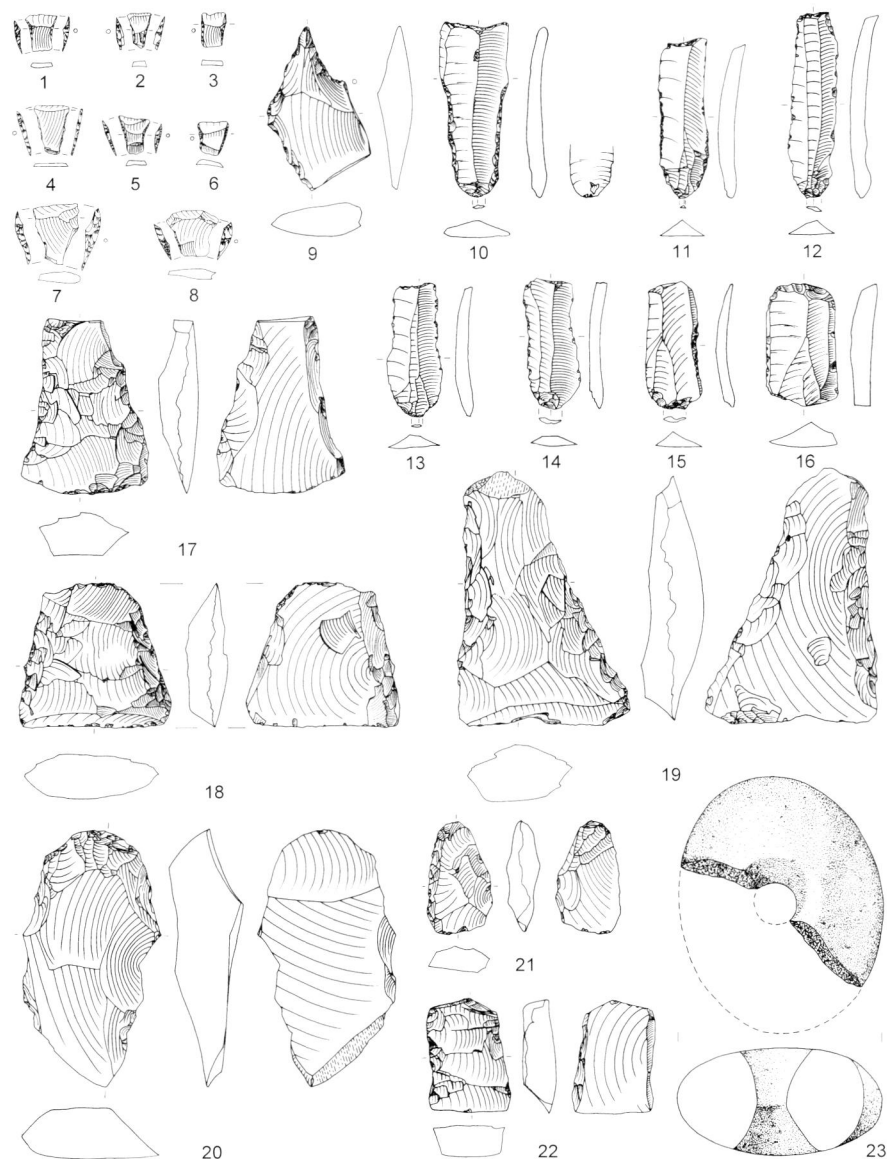

Figure 79.6 Timmendorf-Nordmole (Poel 12, Ostsee II). Stone implements. 1–8: transeversed arrowheads, 9. Borer, 10–14: truncated blades, 15: blade with edge retouch, 16: scraper, 17–22: flake axes and 23: club head. Scale 1:3. J. Freigang del.

When comparing Timmendorf-Nordmole to other Final Mesolithic sites in Ostholstein, this subsistence strategy is the significant difference (Hartz 1997/98:39; Heinrich 1997/98:43 pp; Hartz *et al.* 2000:138 p).

The Dating of Timmendorf-Nordmole and the Beginning of the Neolithic in Northern Germany

Immediately after the discovery of the first archaeological finds, Timmendorf-Nordmole was assigned to the Ertebølle Culture. This assumption was justified by further analysis. The large amount of flake axes dominating the flint implements, the balanced number of blades, manufactured in the soft- and the hard hammer blade technique, as well as the characteristic truncated blades with strong proximal shaft retouch and the axes with specialised cutting edges indicate a younger phase of this culture. Even the coarse, thick walled pottery with simple dot decoration is known from other Ertebølle sites and thus supports this interpretation (Andersen 1994–95:40 pp; Jennbert 1984:43 pp).

At present sixteen AMS dating results of different artifact groups helped to establish dates for Timmendorf-Nordmole (Figures 79.8–79.9). Eight samples were taken from food particle residues attached to pottery, three from animal bones and five samples were taken from wooden implements. With the exception of a clay lamp (KIA - 9500), the dates are remarkable homogeneous. The site dates back to a very late phase of the Ertebølle period from 4500 to 4100 BC. The dates give proof of the

Mammals [Σ ≈ 50]		Birds [Σ ≈ 100]		Fishes [Σ ≈ 800]	
Red Deer *Cervus elaphus*	+ +	Ducks *Anatinae*	+ + +	Eel *Anguilla anguilla*	+ + + +
Roe Deer *Capreolus capreolus*	+ +	Geese, Swans *Anserinae*	+	Cod *Gadus morhua*	+ + +
Wild Boar *Sus scrofa*	+	other	+	Herring *Clupea harengus*	+ +
				Flatfish *Pleuronectidae*	+ +
Seals *Phocidae*	+ +			Three-spined Stickleback *Gasterosteus acul.*	+ +
				Perch *Perca fluviatilis*	+
Dog *Canis lupus f. familaris*	+ +			Cyprinids *Cyprinidae*	+
				Salmon/Trout *Salmo* sp.	+

Figure 79.7 Timmendorf-Nordmole (Poel 12, Ostsee II). List of identified faunal remains (+ + + +: very frequent; + + +: frequent; + +: occasional; +: rare); small mammals (mouses, etc.) and amphibia (tortoise, frogs, etc.) not included. Analyses by D. Heinrich, CAU Kiel.

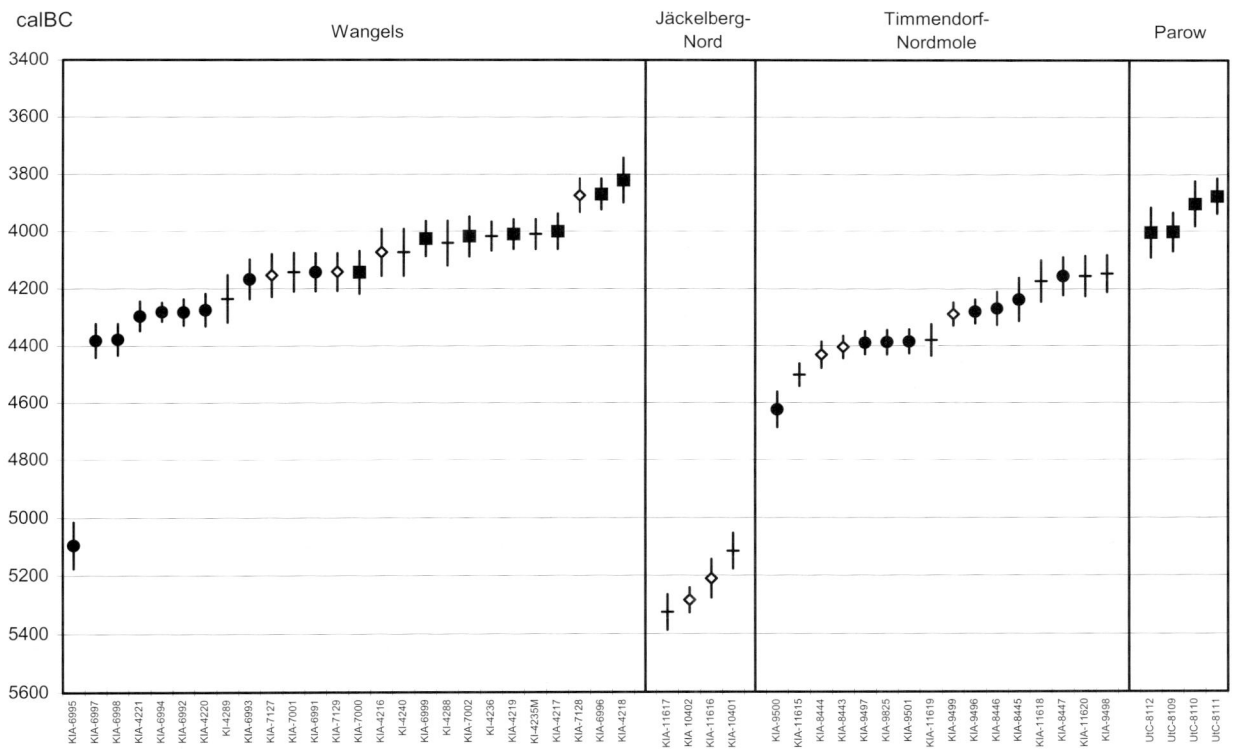

Figure 79.8 Radiocarbon dates (calibrated age ± 1 stdv. B.C.) of Wangels 505, Kr. Ostholstein (Hartz 1997/98; Hartz et al. 2000); Jäckelberg-Nord (Poel 16, Ostsee II); Timmendorf-Nordmole (Poel 12, Ostsee II) and Parow 4, Lkr. Nordvorpommern (Lübke et al. 2001). Circle: Ertebølle-Ceramic; Square: Funnel-Beaker-Ceramic; Cross: Hazelnut, Wooden Implement; Rhombus: Animal Bone.

existence of a younger phase of the Final Mesolithic Ertebølle Culture on the northern Baltic German coast dating from 4500 – 4100 BC. They are in contradiction to the theory of Schwabedissen (1979:203 pp; 1994:373 pp) and Hoika (1994:89), who after the excavation of Grube-Rosenhof LA 58, Kr. Ostholstein, concluded that the Early Neolithic Funnel Beaker Culture appeared in northern Germany in 4400/4300 BC. The stratigraphic problems of the settlement site Grube-Rosenhof, which was used for more than a thousand years, and the insecure chronological

Sample-No.	Age BP	Age calBC	δC13	Artefakt
Timmendorf-Nordmole				
KIA-8443	5604±29	4404±40	-13,8	animal bone, seal
KIA-8444	5621±29	4431±47	-11,0	animal bone, dog
KIA-8445	5362±39	4237±75	-24,3	charred food crust, body sherd
KIA-8446	5380±30	4268±58	-27,3	charred food crust, body herd
KIA-8447	5335±29	4156±65	-26,7	charred food crust, body sherd
KIA-9496	5420±42	4279±42	-23,5	charred food crust, pointed base
KIA-9497	5560±40	4389±41	-23,8	charred food crust, body sherd
KIA-9498	5323±35	4147±64	-31,7	leister prong
KIA-9499	5456±37	4287±41	-22,8	animal bone, red deer
KIA-9500	5791±39	4624±63	-19,8	charred food crust, lamp rimsherd
KIA-9501	5536±32	4384±43	-27,0	charred food crust, body sherd
KIA-9825	5543±43	4387±44	-24,5	charred food crust, decorated rimsherd
KIA-11615	5692±35	4502±40	-24,5	wooden implement
KIA-11618	5343±34	4173±71	-26,2	leister prong
KIA-11619	5505±37	4379±56	-27,6	leister prong
KIA-11620	5327±39	4156±69	-28,2	dug out fragment
Jäckelberg-Nord				
KIA-10401	6.201±41	5115±62	-27,1	wooden post
KIA-10402	6325±35	5283±42	-20,0	animal bone, wild boar
KIA-11616	6253±39	5210±67	-22,6	animal bone, red deer
KIA-11617	6353±46	5326±61	-27,5	wooden post

Figure 79.9 List of Radiocarbon dates of Timmendorf-Nordmole (Poel 12, Ostsee II) and Jäckelberg-Nord (Poel 16, Ostsee II). Calibration after B. Weninger, Cologne (calibrated age ± 1 stdv. B.C.).

classification of the Rosenhof group has been discussed before (Hartz 1999:168 pp; Lübke 2000a:21 pp).

This criticism was confirmed by the results of the excavation of the site Wangels LA 505, Kr. Ostholstein (Hartz 1997/98:19 pp). Here artifacts of the Final Mesolithic Ertebølle and the Early Neolithic Funnel Beaker Culture were recovered in a basal stratum in the shore zone of a Stone Age settlement site. A stratigraphic differentiation of the material was not possible, but the AMS dates of food remains, characteristic potsherds and other artifact groups, helped to verify the existence of more than one phase of use at this site (Figure 79.8). The first phase dates back to 4400 BC, the youngest phase of the Ertebølle Culture, characterised by thick walled, pointed bottom vessels, oval clay lamps, shaft retouched truncated blades, slim blade scrapers, toothed blades, specialised core axes, rock axes and T-axes. From around 4100 BC these are replaced by thin-walled funnel rimmed vessels, open mouthed bowls, bottles, eyelet amphorae and clay disks, all of which are typical for the early Funnel Beaker Culture. Similar artifacts from the site Grube-Rosenhof were also described by Schwabedissen for the Rosenhof Group, which implies that here too, they belonged to a settlement phase dating to 4100 BC and younger. The existence of such a phase at Grube-Rosenhof has already been proven by 14C dates from domesticated animal bones (Hartz *et al.* 2000:136 pp).

The preliminary results of the excavations at Timmendorf-Nordmole are further proof that a younger phase of the Final Mesolithic Ertebølle Culture exists along the German coast until 4100 BC. They also confirm that the Funnel Beaker Culture did not begin before 4100 BC in this region. This is opposed to the situation at Wangels, because at Timmendorf-Nordmole no Early Neolithic settlement phase has yet been established. The material recovered up to now belongs exclusively to the younger Ertebølle Culture and corresponds to the older Final Mesolithic phase in Wangels (Figure 79.8). Future research at Timmendorf-Nordmole will allow a further definition of this younger phase of the Ertebølle Culture in the surroundings of the Mecklenburg Bay. It also has to be established whether, and to what extent, cultural contacts to the southern Epi-Bandceramic Cultures existed and whether animals were domesticated.

Timmendorf-Tonnenhaken

As yet evidence for an Early Neolithic phase in Wismar Bay is lacking. Thus the problem of the origin of the Funnel Beaker Culture and the question of the Neolithic transition connected to it cannot be discussed here. But it has to be mentioned that another submarine settlement site (Poel 15, Ostsee II – "Timmendorf-Tonnenhaken") was discovered about 1000 m to the north of Timmendorf-Nordmole (Figure 79.1). An open peat layer in water 2 m deep contained a Stone Age occupation layer with well preserved potsherds, in addition to stone-, bone-, and antler implements, characteristic of the Funnel Beaker Culture (Lübke 2000b:29). Further research has yet to show whether Tonnenhaken is the succeeding Neolithic settlement to Timmendorf-Nordmole. A survey of this site is planed for 2001. The excellent preservation conditions should provide a strong basis for insight into the economical structure and ecological preconditions of the settlement site.

Conclusions

These researches on submerged Stone Age settlement sites in Wismar Bay deliver an important contribution to the settlement history and history of coastal development in the Baltic coast of Germany. They give new dates for sea level curves and confirm recent research results in Schleswig Holstein which gave a new date for the beginning of the Funnel Beaker Culture, and thus also for the Neolithic transition in Germany. In addition they suggested a possible subdivision of the Ertebølle Culture in this region into several phases, as Timmendorf-Nordmole represents the youngest, and Jäckelberg-Nord the oldest phase of this culture. Further research will give more detailed insight into the material culture and economical structure of these sites. Also further sites have to be located in order to cover the middle phase of the Ertebølle Culture. This would help scholars gain an overview of the development of this culture in Mecklenburg Bay. Another goal will be research on Early Neolithic sites to learn about the emergence of the Funnel Beaker Culture and the Neolithic transition in northern Germany. The excellent conditions of preservation for organic material on submerged Stone Age sites allow for detailed culture ecology studies of the ecological presumptions and economical changes at this time period.

Translated by Katrin Fiedler, Rostock; with additional remarks by James A. R. McClean, Tallahassee.

References

Andersen, S.H. 1987. Mesolithic dug-outs and paddles from Tybrind Vig, Denmark. *Acta Archaeologica* 57, 87–106.
—— 1991. New Finds of Mesolithic Logboats in Denmark. In: Westerdahl, C. (ed.) *Crossroads in Ancient Shipbuilding. Proceedings of the Sixth International Symposium on Boat and Ship Archaeology, Roskilde 1991*. Oxbow Monographs 40, 1–10. Oxford.
—— 1994–95. Ertebølle trappers and wild boar hunters in eastern Jutland. A survey. *Journal Danish Archaeology* 12, 13–59.
—— 1995. Coastal adaptation and marine exploration in Late Mesolithic Danmark – with special emphasis on the Limfjord region. In: Fischer, A. (ed.) *Man and Sea in the Mesolithic. Coastal settlement above and below present sea level. Proceedings of the International Symposium, Kalundborg 1993*. Oxbow Monographs 53, 41–66. Oxford.
Christensen, C. 1990. Stone Age Dug-Out Boats in Denmark: Occurence, Age, Form and Reconstruction. In: Robinson, D.E. (ed.) *Experimentation and Reconstruction in Environmental Archaeology*, 119–141. Oxford.

—— 1997. Boats and navigation in the Stone Age. In: Pedersen, L., Fischer, A. and Aaby, B.(eds.) *The Storebælt Publications. The Danish Storebælt since the Ice Age – man, sea and forest*, 282–289. Copenhagen.
Enghoff, I.B. 1995. Fishing in Denmark during Mesolithic Period. In: Fischer, A. (ed.) *Man and Sea in the Mesolithic. Coastal settlement above and below present sea level. Proceedings of the International Symposium, Kalundborg 1993*. Oxbow Monograph 53, 67–74. Oxford.
Fischer, A. 1995. An entrance to the Mesolithic world below the ocean. Status of ten year's work on the Danish sea floor. In: Fischer, A. (ed.) *Man and Sea in the Mesolithic. Coastal settlement above and below present sea level. Proceedings of the International Symposium, Kalundborg 1993*. Oxbow Monographs 53, 371–384. Oxford.
Hartz, S. 1997/98. Frühbäuerliche Küstenbesiedlung im westlichen Teil der Oldenburger-Graben-Niederung. Ein Vorbericht. *Offa* 54/55, 19–41.
—— 1999. *Die Steinartefakte des endmesolithischen Fundplatzes Grube-Rosenhof LA 58 (Ostholstein). Studien an Flintinventaren zur Zeit der Neolithisierung in Schleswig-Holstein und Südskandinavien*. Untersuchungen und Materialien zur Steinzeit in Schleswig-Holstein 2. Schleswig – Neumünster.
Hartz, S. and Lübke, H. 2001. Stone Age Paddles from Northern Germany. Basic implements of waterborne subsistence and trade. *Schutz des Kulturerbes unter Wasser. Veränderungen europäischer Lebenskultur durch Fluß- und Seehandel. Beiträge zum Internationalen Kongreß für Unterwasserarchäologie (IKUWA '99) 18.–21. Februar in Sassnitz auf Rügen*. Beiträge zur Ur- und Frühgeschichte Mecklenburg-Vorpommerns 35, 377–387. Lübstorf.
Hartz S., Heinrich, D. and Lübke, H. 2000. Frühe Bauern an der Küste. Neue 14C-Daten und Aspekte zum Neolithisierungsprozess im norddeutschen Ostseeküstengebiet. *Prähistorische Zeitschrift* 75, Nr. 2, 129–152.
—— 2001. The neolithisation of northernmost Germany. In: Fischer, A. and Kristiansen, K.(eds.) *The Neolithisation of Denmark. 150 year's debate*. Sheffield (in press).
Heinrich, D. 1997/98: D. Heinrich, Die Tierknochen eines frühneolithischen Wohnplatzes – Fundstelle Wangels LA 505. Ein Vorbericht. *Offa* 54/55, 43–48.
Hoika, J. 1993. Grenzfragen oder: James Watt und die Neolithisierung. *Archäologische Informationen* 16, 6–19.
—— 1994. Zur Gliederung der frühneolithischen Trichterbecherkultur in Holstein. In: Hoika, J. and Meurers-Balke, J. (eds.) *Beiträge zur frühneolithischen Trichterbecherkultur im westlichen Ostseegebiet. 1. Intern. Trichterbechersymposium Schleswig 4. bis 7. März 1985*. Untersuchungen und Materialien zur Steinzeit Schleswig-Holstein 1, 85–132. Schleswig – Neumünster.
Ilkiewicz, J. 1997. From Studies on Ertebølle Type Cultures in the Koszalinian Coastal Area (Dabki 9, Koszalin-Dzierzecino 7). In: Krol, D. (ed.) *The Built Environment of Coast Areas during the Stone Age*. The Baltic Sea-Coast Landscapes Seminar Session No. 1, 50–65. Gdansk.
Jennbert, K. 1984. *Den productiva gåvan. Tradition och innovation i Sydskandinavien för omkring 5300 år sedan*. Acta Archaeologica Lundensia Ser. 4°. No. 16. Lund.
Kalis, A.J. and Meurers-Balke, J. 1998. Die "Landnam"-Modelle von Iversen und Troels-Smith zur Neolithisierung des westlichen Ostseegebietes – ein Versuch ihrer Aktualisierung. *Prähistorische Zeitschrift* 73, Nr. 1, 1–24.
Klug, H. 1980. Der Anstieg des Ostseespiegels im deutschen Küstenraum seit dem Mittelatlantikum. *Eiszeitalter und Gegenwart* 30, 237–252.
Lübke, H. 2000a. *Die steinzeitlichen Fundplätze Bebensee LA 26 und LA 76, Kreis Segeberg. I. Die Steinartefakte. Technologisch-ergologische Studien zum Nordischen Frühneo-

lithikum. Untersuchungen und Materialien zur Steinzeit in Schleswig-Holstein 3. Schleswig – Neumünster.

—— 2000b. Jäckelberg-Nord und Timmendorf-Nordmole. Erste Untersuchungsergebnisse zu submarinen Siedlungsplätzen der endmesolithischen Ertebølle-Kultur in der Wismar-Bucht, Mecklenburg-Vorpommern. *NAU – Nachrichtenblatt Arbeitskreis Unterwasserarchäologie* 7, 17–35

Lübke, H., Schacht, S. and Terberger, T. 2001. Final Mesolithic coastal settlements on the Island of Rügen and in Northern Vorpommern. *Schutz des Kulturerbes unter Wasser. Veränderungen europäischer Lebenskultur durch Fluß- und Seehandel. Beiträge zum Internationalen Kongreß für Unterwasserarchäologie (IKUWA '99) 18.–21. Februar in Sassnitz auf Rügen.* Beiträge zur Ur- und Frühgeschichte Mecklenburg-Vorpommerns 35, 439–449. Lübstorf.

Lüning, J. 1998. Betrachtungen über die Michelsberger Kultur. In: Biel, J., Schlichtherle, H., Strobel, M. and Zeeb, A. (eds.) *Die Michelsberger Kultur und ihre Randgebiete – Probleme der Entstehung, Chronologie und des Siedlungswesens. Kolloquium Hemmenhofen 1997, (Festschrift J. Lüning).* Materialhefte zur Archäologie in Baden-Württemberg 43, 277–289. Stuttgart.

Mertens, E.M. and Schirren, C.M. 2001. Bandkeramik und Stichbandkeramik an der Küste Vorpommerns. *Schutz des Kulturerbes unter Wasser. Veränderungen europäischer Lebenskultur durch Fluß- und Seehandel. Beiträge zum Internationalen Kongreß für Unterwasserarchäologie (IKUWA '99) 18–21. Februar in Sassnitz auf Rügen.* Beiträge zur Ur- und Frühgeschichte Mecklenburg-Vorpommerns 35, 451–456. Lübstorf.

Richter, P.B. 1999. *Das neolithische Erdwerk Walmstorf, Ldkr. Uelzen. Studien zur Besiedlungsgeschichte der Trichterbecherkultur im südlichen Ilmenautal.* Diss. Univ. Hamburg.

Schuhmacher, W. 1991. Das Strandwallsystem des Rustwerder (Insel Poel) und seine Aussagen für die Isostasie und Eustasie im südlichen Ostseeraum. *Meyniana. Veröffentlichungen aus dem Geologischen Institut der Universität Kiel* 43, 137–150.

Schwabedissen, H. 1979. Der Beginn des Neolithikums im nordwestlichen Deutschland. In: Schirnig, H. (ed.) *Großsteingräber in Niedersachsen.* Veröffentlichungen urgeschichtlicher Sammlungen Landesmuseum Hannover 24, 203–222. Hildesheim.

—— 1994. Die Ellerbek-Kultur in Schleswig-Holstein und das Vordringen des Neolithikums über die Elbe nach Norden. In: Hoika, J. and Meurers-Balke, J. (eds.) *Beiträge zur frühneolithischen Trichterbecherkultur im westlichen Ostseegebiet. 1. Intern. Trichterbechersymposium Schleswig 4. bis 7. März 1985.* Untersuchungen und Materialien zur Steinzeit Schleswig-Holstein 1, 361–401. Schleswig – Neumünster.

Sørensen S.A. 1983. Stenalderfund ved Roskilde Fjord. *Fortidsminder og Bygningsbevaring. Antikvariske Studier* 6, 111–119.

Miscellany

Miscellany

80. A short note on the Mesolithic Fauna from Zamostje 2 (Russia)

Louis Chaix

Faunal remains in a Late Mesolithic layer from Zamostje 2 (Russia) are briefly presented. Game animals are dominated by elk and beaver, but they are many other species of fur bearing animals. The presence of reindeer indicates cooler conditions than today. Animals were exploited for fur, meat and marrow, but also for tool making. Some bone carvings show the predominant importance of the elk. The site seems to have been occupied during the summer and autumn but also during the winter.

The site of Zamostje 2 is an important peat bog dwelling which, since 1989, has been excavated by V. Lozovski (Lozovski and Ramseyer 1995; Lozovski 1997; Lozovski and Ramseyer 1997).

Zamostje 2 is located on the left bank of the Dubna River, a tributary of the Volga, about 110 kilometres north of Moscow. During prehistoric times Zamostje was situated on the shore of a large lake and the stratigraphy shows a succession of various layers linked with water level fluctuations.

During the Bølling, between 7950 and 7850 BP, the lake was surrounded by large forests made up of pine and birch with various aquatic plants along the shores (Lozovski 1996:32).

So far 200 m^2 have been excavated along the present course of the Dubna. The stratigraphy reveals many occupation layers, from the Late Mesolithic up to the Late Neolithic ca. 3000 BP.

The preservation of organic remains is exceptional, with a lot of wood and bone artefacts, e.g. bows, arrowheads, tools, bow nets and sculptures (Lozovski 1997:33).

In this short paper I wish to present some preliminary results from layer 8, which belongs to the Late Mesolithic. Two dates are available from this layer, 7380±60 BP (GIN-6201) and 7450±100 BP (GIN-6565).

Animal bones are well preserved, they are of a nice dark brown colour due to their long stay in the peat. They are often broken and their nicely preserved surface reveals various anthropic marks (Chaix 1996).

The faunal spectrum, from un-sieved and sieved material, is presented in figure 80.1.

There is an important difference between the un-sieved

SPECIES	N	% tot.	% mam.
Elk (*Alces alces* (L.)	548	10.72	34.97
Reindeer (*Rangifer tarandus* (L.)	14	0.27	0.89
Wild boar (*Sus scrofa* L.)	7	0.14	0.45
Bear (*Ursus arctos* L.)	36	0.70	2.30
Fox (*Vulpes vulpes* (L.)	8	0.16	0.51
Badger (*Meles meles* (L.)	23	0.45	1.47
Otter (*Lutra lutra* (L.)	9	0.18	0.57
Pine marten (*Martes martes* (L.)	96	1.88	6.13
Beaver (*Castor fiber* L.)	825	16.14	52.65
Hedegehog (*Erinaceus europaeus* L.)	1	0.02	0.06
Total mammals	**1567**		
Birds (*Aves*)	311	6.09	
Fishes (*Pisces*)	3203	62.68	
Dog (*Canis familiaris* L.)	29	0.57	
Total	**5110**		

Figure 80.1 Zamostje 2 : faunal spectrum from the layer 8 (Late Mesolithic)

SPECIES	UNSIEVED		SIEVED	
	NR	%	NR	%
Elk	470	24.0	470	9.5
Reindeer	14	0.7	14	0.3
Wild boar	7	0.4	7	0.1
Bear	32	1.6	32	0.6
Fox	8	0.4	8	0.2
Badger	23	1.2	23	0.5
Otter	9	0.5	9	0.2
Pine marten	96	4.9	96	1.9
Beaver	780	39.9	780	15.7
Hedgehog	1	0.1	1	0.0
Birds	297	15.2	297	6.0
Fishes	190	9.7	3203	64.5
Dog	28	1.4	28	0.6
Total	1955		4968	

Figure 80.2 Zamostje 2 : comparison between unsieved and sieved samples from layer 8

	Elk	Elk	Beaver	Beaver	Marder	Marder
Head	138	29.4	171	21.9	25	26.0
Rachis	97	20.6	260	33.3	6	6.3
Pelvis	5	1.1	28	3.6	4	4.2
Forelimb	48	10.2	136	17.4	30	31.3
Hindlimb	31	6.6	157	20.1	31	32.3
Autopodium	229	48.7	73	9.4		0.0
	548		825		96	

Figure 80.3 Distribution of the skeletal elements for the three main species

and sieved samples concerning the amount of fish bones recovered. From the sieved material they make up 64.5 % of the total, against 9.7 % for the unsieved sample (Figure 80.2). All these figures will change when a more detailed study of the fragments is completed.

The mammal remains in level 8 revel a clear dominance of two species, elk and beaver, representing together 87.6 % of the mammalian fauna. It is evident that these two taxa are not comparable as meat resources, one elk representing a minimum of 15 beavers in terms of weight.

The other species are very poorly represented, but still, the faunal spectrum reveals a good diversity, illustrating a type of "broad spectrum" economy.

The elk bones indicate individuals with a strong built, all the measurements are in the upper part of the range of variation for that species. This is particularly clear when these samples are compared with a modern sample from Western Europe (Chaix and Desse 1981).

The hunters seem to have concentrated on adult animals, the majority were between 10 to 11 years of age while a smaller proportion were between 4 to 5 years of age. Young individuals are rare.

The remains of both male and female elk are present but the males seem to be more common. This preference might best be explained by the need to use antlers for tools and other objects, as attested by the numerous elk antler artefacts that have been discovered on the site (Lozovski 1996; David 1999:616).

All the skeletal elements of the elk are present, indicating that the whole carcass was brought back to the site (Figure 80.3).

Elks were intensively butchered and a lot of cut marks can be observed on the different bones. Evidence of skinning is rare while signs of disarticulation and defleshing are frequent. The sagittal cuts on the first and second phalanxes are the result of deep marrow extraction. The beavers in this sample, represented by numerous bones, belong to a minimum of 80 individuals. From a morphological point of view the beavers at Zamostje 2 were smaller than those from Mesolithic and Neolithic Western Europe (Boessneck et al. 1963; Stampfli 1976; Becker and Johansson 1981). Significant differences are present on many of the bones, particularly in the length of the lower cheek-tooth row and the femur. The osteometry of beavers is not well known as yet and it is possible that the individuals from Zamostje belong to a different subspecies from that which is present in the region today (Freye 1978).

The stages of maturity of the specimens show a predominance of subadults with a few older animals.

Beavers were eaten. This is attested by traces of skinning, disjointing and defleshing.

Some elements, such as the mandibles, were used as tools. The mandibles were processed in a particular fashion, the ascending rami were fractured and the lower incisors used as chisels. Most of the mandibles display a characteristic gloss, testifying to their frequent use. In some cases the posterior end was perforated, this probably represents suspension holes. Similar pieces are well known from various Mesolithic and Neolithic sites in Western and Eastern Europe (Schibler 1981; Zhilin 1997a).

All the skeletal elements of the beaver are present, indicating a local exploitation (Figure 80.3).

Some remains of reindeer were found. They testify to a more southern distribution of this animal during prehistoric times. In fact, nowadays, this cervid is found in the area of Volgoda, 400 kilometres north of Zamostje (Danilov and Markovsky 1983:33). Its presence at Zamostje 2 probably indicates lower mean temperatures in this area during the Bølling.

Fur bearing animals like the brown bear, badger and pine marten are present and numerous marks on their bones are the result of skinning and consumption (Trolle-Lassen 1987). The exploitation of the pine marten was probably made locally (Figure 80.3).

The presence of the hedgehog, oddly enough, is attested by only one half of a mandible. In all other European Mesolithic and Neolithic contexts the mandible is always over represented in comparison with the other

Figure 80.4 Elk's head carved from an elk's rib

hedgehog bones. The significance of this over representation is as yet unknown, but in many cases these mandibles show a typical gloss on the horizontal branch (Vigne 1988:33)

Among the mammals, it is interesting to note the presence of the domestic dog (*Canis familiaris* L.). A minimum of two individuals were found in layer 8. The remains belong to strongly built individuals. Skulls exhibit marked muscular attachments with a clear stop. Crowding of the premolars indicates a shortened snout. Their height was estimated to have been between 52 and 56 cm, placing these animals within the limits of the variation noted for Mesolithic dogs from the East Sea area (Benecke 1993).

These dogs were eaten, as indicated by butchering marks on the humerus and femur, similar to those found in the Danish Mesolithic material (Degerbøl 1962:334).

Birds are well represented with many complete bones. This study is not yet complete but the presence of waterfowl, such as the great crested grebe (*Podiceps cristatus*) and the mallard (*Anas platy-rhynchos*) is attested. Some birds of prey, like the white tailed eagle (*Haliaetus albicilla*) are also present. Their bones show traces of scraping and facetting, but the interpretation of the latter is unclear.

Fishing was practised at Zamostje 2 as indicated by the numerous fish bones, but also by wooden fish traps. A lot of hooks and decorated scaling knives made of elk bone were also discovered (Lozovski and Ramseyer 1995:37; Lozovski 1997:52).

A preliminary examination shows that the fish remains are dominated by small pike (*Esox lucius*) and small Cyprinids.

The great quantity of fish scales found is a good indication that the fish catch was prepared locally.

Some elements reveal the season of occupation of the Zamostje 2 site. If we consider the age of the hunted elks, we can observe the presence of two individuals that were between 12 and 15 months old. This indicates that they were hunted during the summer. Two other elks were 20 and 22 months old. They were killed during the winter.

The presence of various species of aquatic birds and birds of prey seems to show that the site was occupied during the summer and autumn.

With the present state of the research it is difficult to give an exact interpretation concerning the seasonal occupation of the Zamostje 2 site. There are indications of both summer and winter activities. Whether or not the site was continuously occupied throughout the year is still in doubt. The study of the annuli from the fish vertebrae may give more precise information with which to solve this problem.

A number of sculptures and carvings made from antler and bone were recovered from the Zamostje 2 site. In layer 8 a nice sculptured head of an elk was found, carved on a rib from this species (Figure 80.4). In other layers carvings of elk heads or birds were discovered, testifying to the artistic sense of the Mesolithic hunters (Lozovski 1995:423).

In conclusion, the fauna from level 8 at Zamostje 2 has yielded interesting information on the life of the Mesolithic hunters in this area. The exploitation of elk and beaver seems to be common in this part of Europe, as observed on many other sites from both Scandinavia (Andersen *et al.* 1990), Russia (Zhilin 1997b) and from the Baltic countries (Lougas 1995).

The presence of both fur bearing animals and fish attests to the wide diversity of food utilised by the occupants.

The richness and variety of the faunal spectrum indicates that during the Bølling there existed a suitable environment for a year long occupation.

References

Andersen, S.H., Bietti, A., Bonsall, C., Broadbent, N.D., Clark, G.A., Gramsch, B., Jacobi, R.M., Larsson, L., Morrison, A., Newell, R.R., Rozoy, J.G., Straus, L.G. and Woodman, P.C. 1990. Making cultural ecology relevant to Mesolithic research: I.A data base of 413 Mesolithic fauna assemblages. In: Vermeersch, P.M. and Van Peer, P. (eds.) *Contributions to the Mesolithic in Europe*, 23–51. Leuwen.

Becker, C. and Johansson, F. 1981. Die neolithischen Ufersiedlungen von Twann. Band 11: *Tierknochenfunde*. Bern.

Benecke, N. 1993. Zur Kenntnis der mesolithischen Hunden des südlichen Ostseegebietes. *Zeitschrift für Archäologie* 27, 39–65.

Boessneck, J., Jéquier, J.P. and Stampfli, H.R. 1963. Seeberg Burgäschisee-Süd. Die Tierreste. *Acta Bernensia II*, 3.

Chaix, L. 1996. *The fauna of Zamostje*. Guides archéologiques du "Malgré-Tout, 85–95. Treignes.

Chaix, L. and Desse, J. 1981. Contribution à la connaissance de l'élan (*Alces alces* L.) postglaciaire du Jura et du Plateau Suisse. Corpus de mesures. *Quartär* 31/32, 139–190.

Danilov, P.I. and Markovsky, V.A. 1983. Forest reindeer (*Rangifer tarandus fennicus* Lönnb.) in Karelia. *Acta Zoologica Fennica* 175, 33–34.

David, E. 1999. *L'industrie en matières dures animales du Mésolithique ancien et moyen en Europe du Nord. Contribution de l'analyse technologique à la définition du Maglemosien*. Thèse de doctorat, Université de Paris X- Nanterre, 2 vol. Nanterre.

Degerbøl, M. 1962. Der Hund, das älteste Haustier Dänemarks. *Zeitschrift für Tierzüchtung und Züchtungsbiologie* 76, 334–341.

Freye, H.A. 1978. *Castor fiber* Linnaeus, 1758 – Europäischer Biber. In: Niethammer, J. and Krapp, F. (eds.) *Handbuch der Säugetiere Europas*, Band 1, Rodentia 1 (Sciuridae, Castoridae, Gliridae, Muridae), 184–200. Wiesbaden.

Lougas, L. 1995. Analyses of animal remains from the excavations at the Lammasmägi Site, Kunda, Northeastern Estonia. *PACT* 51, 273–291.

Lozovski, V.M. 1995. L'industrie en os du Mésolithique récent en Russie centrale. In: Thévenin, A. (ed.) *L'Europe des derniers chasseurs. Epipaléolithique et Mésolithique*. Actes du 5e Colloque International UISPP, Commission XII, 417–424. Grenoble.

—— 1996. *Zamostje 2. The last prehistoric hunters-fishers of the Russian plain*. Guides archéologiques du "Malgré-Tout", 12–84. Treignes.

—— 1997. Mesolithic and Early Neolithic art of the Volga-Oka region (according to the materials of Zamostje 2 site). Proceedings of the International Symposium "*The Stone Age of the European Plains: objects of organic material and settlement structure as reflections of human culture*", 33–51. Sergiev-Posad.

Lozovski, V.M. and Ramseyer, D. 1995. Le site préhistorique de Zamostje. *Archeologia* 311, 34–41.

Lozovski, V.M. and Ramseyer, D. 1997. Wooden items from the site Zamostje 2.). Proceedings of the International Symposium "*The Stone Age of the European Plains: objects of organic material and settlement structure as reflections of human culture*", 66–73. Sergiev-Posad.

Schibler, J. 1981. Die neolithischen Ufersiedlungen von Twann. Band 17: *Typologische Untersuchungen der cortaillodzeitlichen Knochenartefakte*. Staatlicher Lehrmittelverlag, Bern.

Stampfli, H.R. 1976. *Osteo-archaeologische Untersuchung des Tierknochenmaterials des spätneolithischen Ufersiedlung Auvernier – La Saunerie*. Solothurn.

Trolle-Lassen, T. 1987. Human exploitation of fur animals in Mesolithic Denmark – a case study. *Archaeozoologia*, 1 (2), 85–102.

Vigne, J.D. 1988. De la paléobiogéographie à l'anthropozoologie. *Anthropozoologica* 8, 32–52.

Zhilin, M.G. 1997a. Artifacts made of animals' teeth and jaws in the Mesolithic of Eastern Europe. *Proceedings of the 3rd EAA Meeting*. Ravenna.

—— 1997b. The Mesolithic and Early neolithic settlements of the western part of Dubna river valley.). In: Proceedings of the International Symposium "*The Stone Age of the European Plains: objects of organic material and settlement structure as reflections of human culture*", 164–196. Sergiev-Posad.

81. The contribution of the Technological Study of Bone and Antler Industry for the definition of the Early Maglemose Culture

Eva David

While for many prehistorians the Maglemose culture covers a very large area with, as far as the bone and antler industry is concerned, four characteristic types of tools (Childe 1931), my technological study of almost 3000 bone and antler artefacts from Early and Middle Mesolithic settlements of Northern Europe allows me to propose a more precise definition.

Early Maglemose (M1 and M2) bone and antler industry can now be defined by a considerable production (more than 50% of the industry) of straight and barbed points made by the original "D" and "F" methods on big cervid metapodials and flat bones (ribs and shoulders) associated with shafted heavy tools, which is strictly limited to Zealand island (Denmark) sites. While it offers a mixed assemblage, the interesting late level from Hohen Viecheln (Germany) perhaps indicates a southern geographical limit for the Early Maglemose territory at the end of the Boreal chronozone.

These initial results underline that a technological study of bone and antler material is relevant and while it combined many analyses (typology, statistics, debitage, manufacturing processes and validation by experiments), it provides new insights into the definition of Mesolithic groups. Thus, this study of the Zealand bone and antler industry reveals no difference between Maglemose stage 1 and 2 (as defined by Becker 1953 and Brinch Petersen 1973). Neither Late Maglemosian nor the East Baltic bone and antler collections have yet been reexamined.

Backgound

After the publication of the Mullerup monograph by G. F.-L. Sarauw, in 1903, Abbé Breuil used the term "Maglemose" to distinguish Nordic harpoons from the Magdalenian ones (Breuil 1926:309). Placed in the Mesolithic period by E. Westerby (Westerby 1927:14 pp), the Maglemose was then chronologically defined and divided into five stages by C.J. Becker, mainly using the flint tools from Holmegård IV and Sværdborg I sites (Becker 1953:183), to which E. Brinch Petersen added one further and earlier stage (Brinch Petersen 1973:103).

It was T. Mathiassen who drew up a list over 90 types of bone and antler tools for the whole Danish Mesolithic (Mathiassen 1948:62 pp). B. Bille Henriksen demonstrated an homogeneity of bone and antler tool types between the stages (Bille Henriksen 1980:126 p) and, thus excluded, like G. Sarauw, local Maglemosian groups of Mullerup and Sværdborg (Kozlowski and Kozlowski 1977:224). If the Maglemose cultural group *sensu lato* seems to be restricted to Danish assemblages and Danish archaeologists, it is recognised by severals prehistorians as belonging to a much larger geographical distribution (Schwantes 1928; Schwabedissen 1944). Thus, J. Brøndsted (1960), S.K. Kozlowski (1973), L. Larsson (1978) and T. Galinski (1989) included Scanian sites like Agerød I:H-C in the Maglemose "civilisation". This idea had already been discussed by V.G. Childe, whose "Forest culture" was defined by macrolithic flint tools associated with a specific bone and antler industry (Figure 81.1) : "chisel" (a) ; "adze from metapodial bone of urus" (b) ; "shaft-hole adze" (c) and "adze in a perforated antler haft" (d), (Childe 1931:327). It was in fact J.G.D. Clark (1936:86 pp) who introduced the term Maglemose

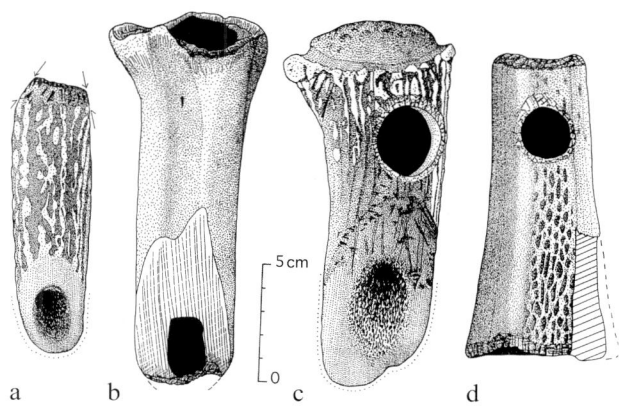

Figure 81.1 Heavy tools from Mullerup I (Sarauw's island, Denmark) – drawings: Eva David. a- blade-axe (cervids tine); b- adze (aurochs metatarsus); c- hammer-axe (red deer antler); d- sleeve (red deer antler).

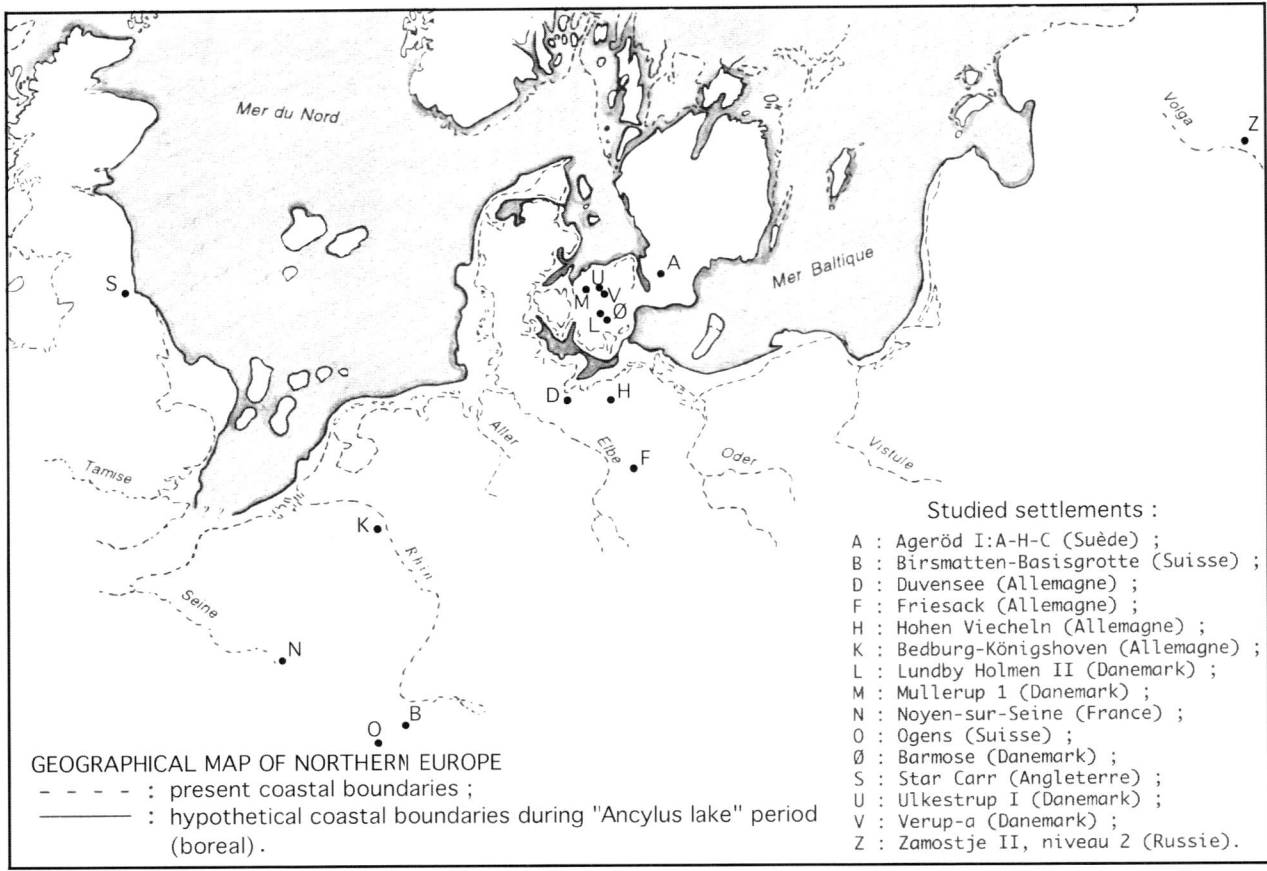

Figure 81.2 Map of Northern Europe during the Boreal chronozone (after Childe 1931:330 and Coles 1998:68): Location of the reexamined Early and Middle Mesolithic bone and antler collections.

"culture" to designate all assemblages belonging to the "Ancylus lake" period distributed from England to Finland. Furthermore, in France, a decorated antler sleeve dredged from the river Oise was also seen as a Maglemosian type (Blanchet and Lambot 1977:76).

Methodology

The bone and antler industry attributed to the Maglemose culture has never been precisely defined. For this reason, I reexamined all the main archaeological collections (Figure 81.2) in order to identify the composition of the assemblages and then isolate elements which could confirm the geographical distribution of the Maglemose cultural group. In face of the numerous sites available, I decided to study collections related to the Early and Middle Mesolithic by pollen analyses (end of Preboreal until end of Boreal) and to the Early Maglemose (stages 0 to 2) which covers the second half of the 10th to the transition of the 9th and 8th millennia. I chose Mullerup I as my reference site because of the overall quality of its data and also because it was the first site to produce a Maglemose industry (David 1999a:28). It includes 221 tools and 309 waste products suitable for elaborating a solid typology and enabling many reconstructions of *chaines opératoires* per anatomical blank on elk, red deer, aurochs and roe deer (David 1999b). The collections from contemporary settlements with similar animals, plants and environment have been added : Ulkestrup Lyng I (M.2) and then those from earlier Maglemose stages ; Barmose (M.0) ; Verup-a and Lundby Holmen II (M.1), all in Denmark. The analyses of morphological, typological, technical and anatomical aspects, in addition to my experimental work, have been undertaken in an interactive way in order to highlight the specific nature of each assemblage. The same study was then made on settlements located in neighbouring regions and the results compared with the Danish material : Hohen Viecheln a, b, c; Friesack I, II, III; Duvensee 1, 2 (all in Germany); Ageröd I:H-C BL, UT, VL (Sweden). Finally, comparisons were made even further afield in order to evaluate the dependance between the desired tools and the technical possibilities within a similar chronological period : Noyen-sur-Seine 1, 2 (France); Ogens; Birsmatten–Basisgrotte 3, 4, 5 (both in Zwitserland – David 2000a); Zamostje II–1991, 2 (Russia – David 1998). Described as a "proto-Maglemosian" industry (Clark *et al.* 1954: 180 pp), the collection from Star Carr (England) has also been taken into account, together with the Bedburg-Königshoven finds (Germany). All this material represents almost 3000 bone and antler artefacts from 15 settlements and 24 archaeological levels.

Three unexpected Methods of Manufacture

In archaeology, technology is "the study of all the procedures employed to produce a tool or a weapon" (Tixier *et al.* 1980:7). It leads to the notion of *systèmes techniques* as a means of studying human behaviour through archaeological data. Every *système technique* involves a project and its realisation. The project implies a *concept opératoire* (of an intellectual nature) which materialises in the form of *chaînes opératoires* (Pelegrin *et al.* 1988) according to a *méthode* or a "reasoned linking together of several actions [in *séquences*] carried out according to one or more *techniques*" (Tixier *et al.* 1992:99). For bone technology, while bones and antlers already have a specific morphology and histology (organic structure), one can suppose that only a few basic methods were used by hunters gatherers faced with similar faunal resources and "hunting economy" (Bridault 1993). In the light of my study, it appears that during Early Mesolithic times all potential techniques were probably known throughout Northern Europe and this may well have been the case since the end of the Upper Paleolithic (David 1998:44). Whereas I expected to find techniques linked in exactly the same sequences for production of a similar piece of equipment (mainly bone throwing spears, arrowheads and antler heavy tool, mostly on cervids species), I discovered that it was the choice and the way the techniques were linked that make the difference for a same anatomical blank. According to my experiments, choices are not related to time-saving (David 1999a). Even if we will never know why choices were made, the Mesolithic methods (debitage, manufacturing and sharpening), as revealed by bone technology, can specify the cultural definition of a group but do not characterise a chronological stage, at least within the Mesolithic.

Since the beginning of my research all the theoretical *chaînes opératoires* suggested (David 1999b) have been validated by experimental work undertaken with flint knappers (David *et al.* 1996, 1997, 1999). A Maglemosian flint tool-kit was reproduced. The techniques which considered relevant were those which delivered similar traces to those observed in the archaeological record. The tools which produced same traces on bones but which have broken very easily have not been taken into account following observations of the archaeological material. The fracture patterns have been checked for flint as well as for bones and antlers. The reconstruction of bone and antler *chaînes opératoires* requires sound knowledge of faunal exploitation (skinning, dismembering, filleting, marrow fracturing) and of taphonomic processes (trampling, gnawing), (Noe-Nygaard 1987, 1989). That is why I have also reexamined the faunal remains for each collection.

At Mullerup and on the other Danish settlements, seven methods of manufacturing bone and antler tools have been recognised (David 1999a). If, in general, the techniques used are in response to the bone or antler mechanical structure, three original methods occurred independently of the raw material:

METHODS	TECHNIQUES
"D" (Danish method)	wedge-splinter dotted perforation groove wedge-splitter
"F" (flat bone method)	groove bilateral scraping bilateral groove wedge-splitter
"C" method	unifacial scraping sawing

"D" Method: production of straight and barbed points on big ungulates metapodials

Our experiments show that it is possible to divide the debitage and manufacturing part of the *chaîne opératoire* of the "D" method into 12 *sequences* (Figure 81.3), 9 of which concern debitage. I will describe our experiments for each sequence separately.

The archaeological worked metapodials show many traces of percussion, in the form of flake negatives (Figure 81.4 A). These were described by U. Møhl (1984) who thought that they could belong to a butchering process. This interpretation seems unlikely to me because the cervids carpus and tarsus (in general firmly joined to metapodials) do not present any percussion traces in the Danish assemblages. Marrow fractures can also be ruled out because the patterns and their localisation are different (David 1999a:636 pp). Furthermore, when the manufacturing traces are superficial, the flake negatives are occasionally visible on the tang of barbed points (*ibid*: contact plate n°80). I believe that direct percussion was not suitable for removing flakes since it is too difficult to strike around a small surface so precisely. After many unsuccessful attemps (David and Johansen 1996), we tried indirect percussion with an unhafted flake axe and with a bone chisel as a punch (David *et al.* 1999). The flake scars resulting from this technique are similar to the ones on the archaeological artefacts. The articular surface of the metapodial is seen as a striking platform on which the bone or flint wedge is placed with a 90° angle and hit with a heavy hammer (about 1 kilo). Flakes are struck off all around the bone and they are not completely detached from it because they remain connected to the bone distally by a thin layer of periosteum (the thin skin covering bones). The tools we used were several flake-axes (unretouched flakes could also have been used) and a bone chisel (David 2000b:Fig.1). The most important point is that the working edge of the tool maintained a 45° angle to avoid damage during percussion. Both flint

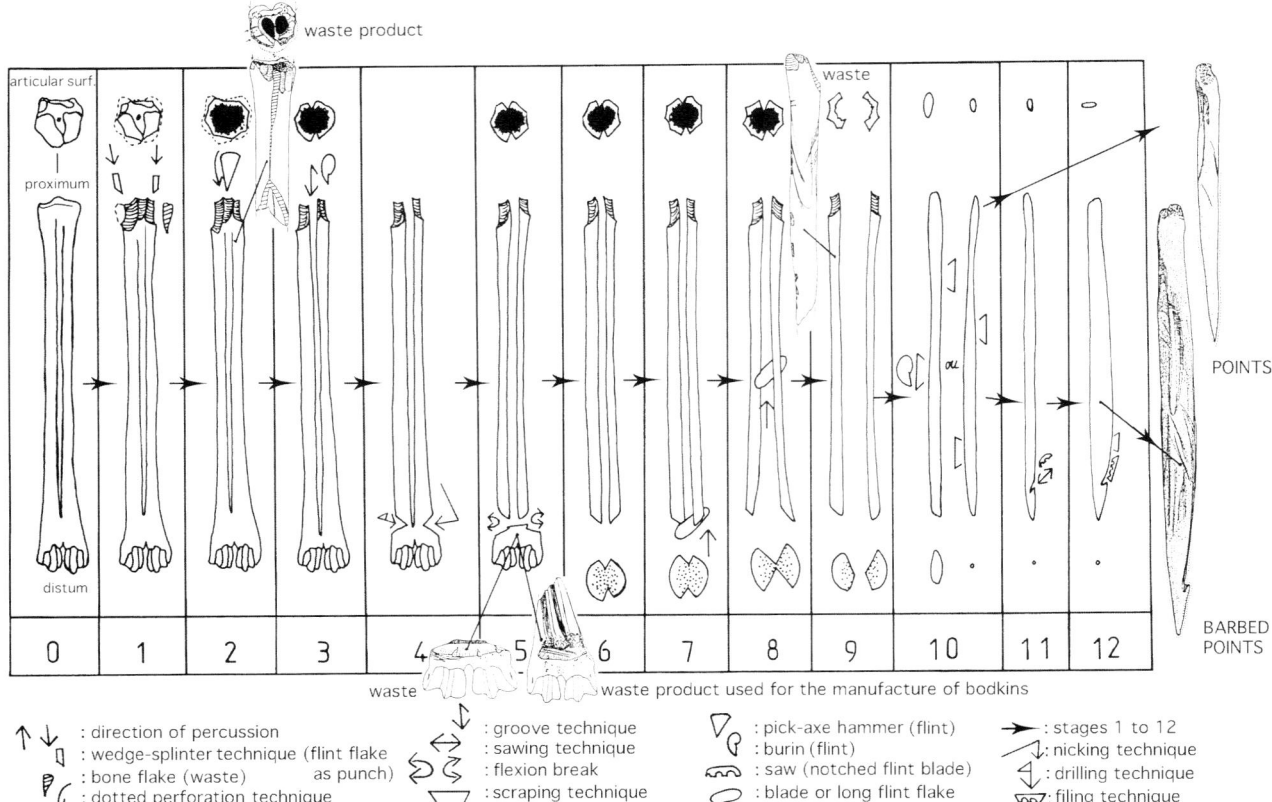

Figure 81.3 "D" Method points validated by experiments (David and Johansen, 1996): linking of the chaîne opératoire to produce Maglemosian straight and barbed points on big ungulates metapodials (mainly cervids) – Schema: Eva David.

and bone wedges, used with indirect percussion, interestingly produced the same patterns on the bone. This technique takes a few minutes. As bone chisels are not very frequent in the Danish assemblages, flint tools were probably used, but an exhaustive study on flint has yet to be undertaken.

Having described this *wedge-splinter technique* (Figure 81.3, sequ. 1), I will now discuss the *dotted perforation technique* which always occurs with the former (sequ. 2). On the archaeological examples (Figure 81.4 B), many small deep triangular percussion marks occur in diffuse manner around the foramen nutricius (the natural perforation in the centre of the metapodial articular surface). After repeated experiments, we concluded that the Maglemosian flint pick-axe (*spidsøkse* in Danish) used by direct percussion on the articular surface, not to flake but to pick, was the right tool. It takes a few minutes to enlarge sufficiently the foramen. Picking with this kind of tool cannot be done very precisely, which explains why the archaeological waste products included many traces of this work just outside the target area. The perforation in the bone was enlarged and deepened until the marrow became visible (David 2000b:Fig.2) and could be removed by shaking.

The goal of sequences 1 and 2 is to get a regularly formed product following preconceived ideas about the shape of the manufactured points. The *wedge-splinter*

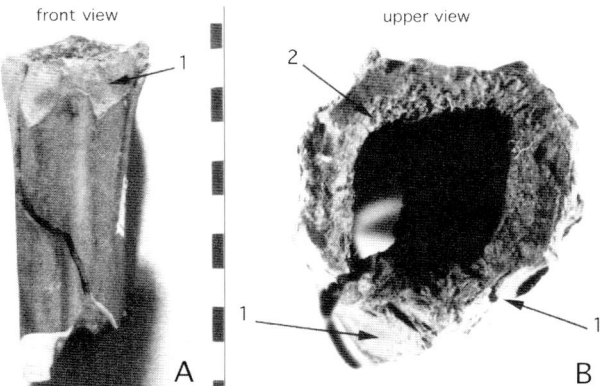

Figure 81.4 A - Mullerup I (Denmark), archaeological waste product showing many removals (flake negatives) on the upper and external anatomical part produced by the wedge-splinter technique, *Cervus elaphus metatarsus. Photo: Eva David. B - Mullerup I (Denmark), archaeological waste product showing many small deep triangular percussion marks on the articular surface produced by the* dotted perforation technique, *Cervus elaphus metatarsus. Photo: Eva David.*

technique (sequence 1) reduces the thickness of the cortical part of the metapodial proximal end and the *dotted perforation technique* (sequence 2) takes off platform and the inner part of the articular surface. So right from the

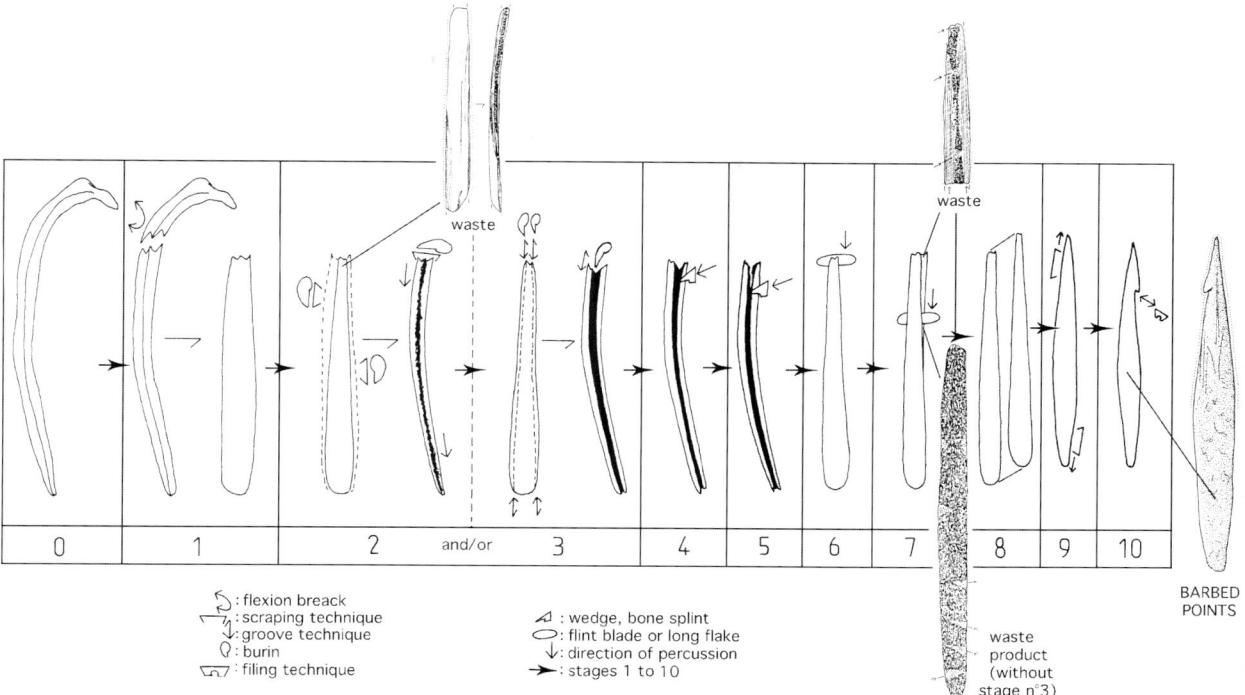

Figure 81.5 "F" method validated by experiments (David and Johansen 1997): linking of the chaîne opératoire *to produce Maglemosian barbed bone points on big ungulates flat bones (ribs and shoulders) – Schema: Eva David.*

first debitage sequences, these two techniques preform the future tang of the straight and barbed points while preserving the maximum length of the metapodial bone.

The next techniques are more well known. The *groove technique* prepares the bone for division. We used the tip of a thick burin to begin the work and then a thinner one to deepen each groove (Figure 81.3, sequ. 3). This sequence is the most time-consuming and is even more so if the bone has to be divided into 4 up to 6 splinters. After being cut off on one anatomical face with a saw (notched flint blade, *sawing technique*) or with a hafted axe by direct percussion (*nicking technique*) or with a hafted drill on a bow (*drilling technique*), the distal end of the bone is knocked off by *flexion breakage on anvil* (sequ. 4 and 5). Then, the edge of a thin flint long flake or blade is placed at the end of the grooves, which were sawed if necessary (sequ. 6) and the blade struck with a soft hammer. The blade splits the bone into blanks (*wedge-splitter technique*) from the end to the proximal part just by sheer strength of arm (sequ. 7 to 9; David 2000b:Fig. 3). Each blank could be now manufactured following three sequences. The tip and tang are created by scraping with the working edge of the same burins (*scraping technique*) in order to obtain points (sequ. 10). To produce barbed points, each barb is made by two obliquely converging saw-cuts on one of the edges (*sawing technique*) and is deepened by filing with the saw, so the barb can be sharpened (*filing technique*). A homogeneous shape is obtained by a last longitudinal scraping under each barb because the filing technique leaves a roughened surface (sequ. 11, 12). Although filing traces are missing under the archaeological barbs, the scraping technique alone cannot reach right under the barb because the working edge of the burin is always too thick. It could be that burin spalls were used instead but an exhaustive study on flint has yet to be undertaken. All points produced with the "D" method show a *high degree of manufacture* {or an "objet of 'class 4' which go through, in all its part, a complete morphological transformation compared to the original anatomical blank" (Stordeur 1978:23)} which prevents a clear view of the original links in the manufacturing chaîne opératoire. The entire *chaîne opératoire* of the "D" method to produce a point or a barbed point on a cervid metapodial takes about 4 hours.

"F" Method: production of barbed points on big ungulates flat bones (ribs and shoulders)

The *chaîne opératoire* of the "F" method shows 10 sequences (Figure 81.5), 8 of which concern debitage. The goal of this method is to separate the two cortical parts which enclosed the spongy core into two long blanks. Thus, after removing the head of a rib by *flexion breakage on anvil* (sequ. 1), both edges are very deeply scraped with the working edge of a thick burin in order to expose the spongy core (sequ. 2). This *scraping* sequence preforms the general shape of the blanks (Figure 81.6 A). Shoulders are less frequently used than ribs and their blanks are taken off by *opposite groove technique* under the scapular crest. Next, a groove is made on both sides of the blank in the spongy core with the tip of a thin burin, and this begins the division of the cortical parts,

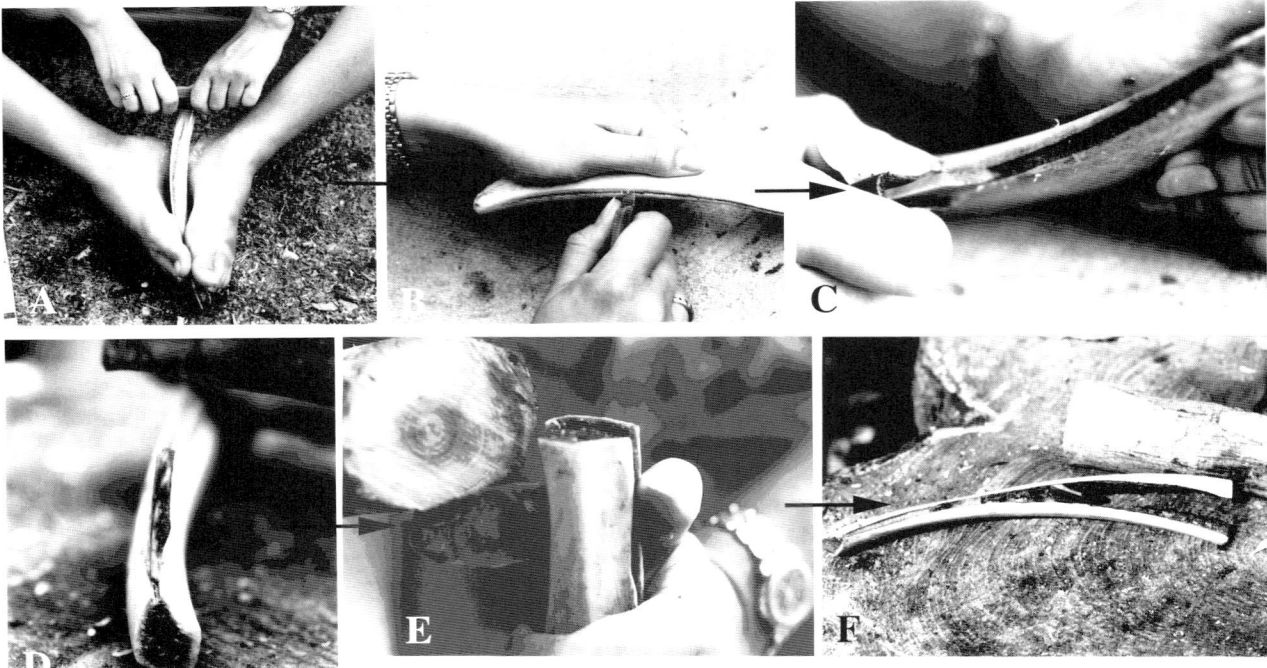

Figure 81.6 Experimental reconstruction of the "F" method linking stages: sequence 2 (A), 3 (B and C), 4 (D), 6 (E) and sequence 7 (F). Photos: Lykke Johansen.

while at the same time the interior of both cortical parts is scraped (Figure 81.5, sequ. 3; Figure 81.6 B, C). So the *groove technique* reduces manufacturing time. The last sequences including the manufacturing are the same as in the "D" method. But as flat bones have more elasticity, the *wedge-splitter technique* is prepared by inserting a small piece of bone by percussion with a soft hammer (Figure 81.6 D), which "presplits" the spongy core before insertion of the blade (Figure 81.6 E–F). This preparation leaves specific long triangular traces inside the spongy core which are very well preserved on the archaeological artefacts (Figure 81.5, waste products). Small pieces of bone used as wedges have not be found but this may be related to the discard, after sieving, of bone chips or flakes, even on today's excavations. The entire *chaîne opératoire* of the "F" method to produce a barbed point on a cervid metapodial takes about 2 hours.

"C" METHOD: production of adzes on aurochs metapodial bones

The *chaîne opératoire* of the "C" method shows 5 *sequences* for which the debitage cannot be separated from the manufacturing sequences (Figure 81.7). The hafted part of the bone is made by the *dotted perforation technique* (sequ. 1). The angle of the working part of the adze is obtained by a very time-consuming scraping sequence (sequ. 2). The distal part of the bone is removed by sawing the reverse side and by *flexion breakage on anvil* (sequ. 3, 4). This helps to obtain a straight working edge which is then completed by scraping (sequ. 5). Our experimental reconstruction taught us that the scraping needs a long and careful attention and that the edge cannot be produced by direct percussion (David *et al.* 1999). The entire *chaîne opératoire* of the "C" method to produce an adze on an aurochs metapodial takes about 4 hours.

Discussion

Even if the Mullerup I, Ulkestrup I, Lundby Holmen II and Verup-a bone and antler industries differ in percentages of shafted points or representation of types, it is clear that the types of shafted points and common tools, as well as the methods and the anatomical blanks, are similar (Figure 81.8). Early Maglemose (M.1, M.2) bone and antler industry can now be defined by a considerable production (more than 50% of the industry) of straight and barbed points made by the original "D" and "F" methods on big cervid metapodials and flat bones (ribs and shoulders) associated with shafted heavy tools. Also, all points are deeply scraped corresponding to a *high degree of manufacture* and in the category of barbed points, those made on flat bones are always much more numerous (70%). The common tools (20%) are well represented by heavy tools used for direct percussion on soft materials (wood, hide…). The adzes on aurochs bone produced by the original "C" method and the engraved adzes, together with the punches for organic materials (David 2002), are specific to the Maglemosian assemblages which are strictly limited to Zealand. As far as

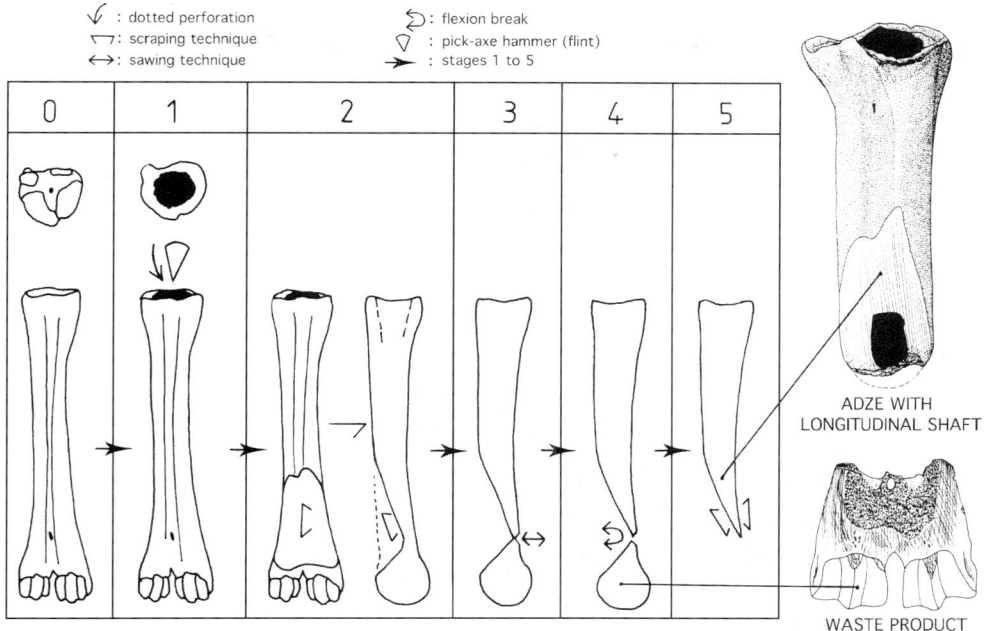

Figure 81.7 "C" method validated by experiments (David and Johansen, 1997): linking of the chaîne opératoire *to produce a Maglemosian adze on an aurochs metapodial – Schema: Eva David.*

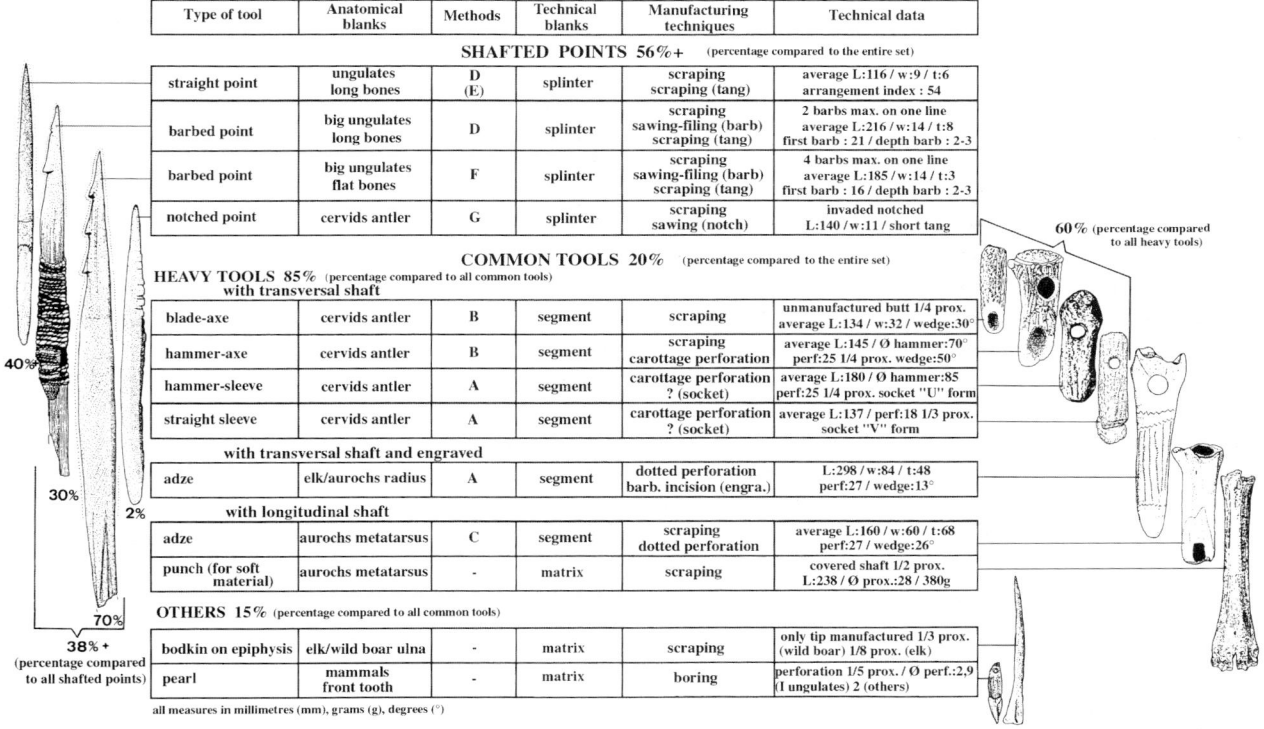

Figure 81.8 General chart of typological, anatomical and technical characteristics of the Maglemosian bone and antler industry common to the Danish settlements of Mullerup I, Ulkestrup Lyng I, Lundby-Holmen II and Verup-a (L: length; w: width; t: thickness; Ø: diameter).

bone and antler artefacts are concerned, this study of the Zealand bone and antler industry reveals no difference between Maglemose stage 1 and 2 (as defined by Becker 1953; Brinch Petersen 1973).

These initial results underline that a technological study of bone and antler material is relevant. It is only a combined analysis of several aspects (typology, debitage, manufacturing and experimental work) for each assem-

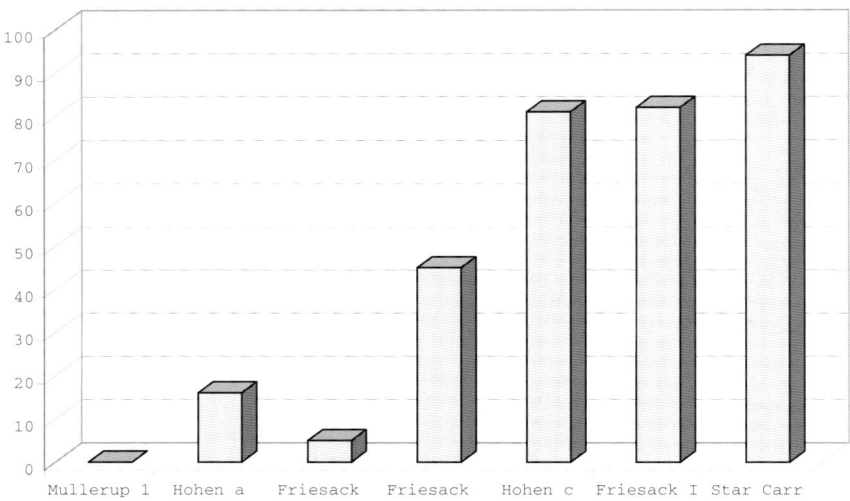

Figure 81.9 Percentage frequency of the common bone and antler industry (bone notched points, antler barbed points, large bone chisels, mattocks, small lissoirs and worked red deer stag frontlets) of studied Early and Middle Mesolithic settlements (David monograph in press).

blage that can provide new insights into the definition of Mesolithic groups. Thus, the blade-axe, hammer-axe, hammer-sleeve and straight sleeve are no longer sufficient to define the Maglemose cultural group *lato sensu,* since they are a common component of many Early and Middle Mesolithic sites. In fact, from the Preboreal to the Late Boreal, it is possible to distinguish at least one "technocomplex" (as defined by Clarke 1968:357) in Northern Europe, so far represented by the Star Carr, Bedburg-Königshoven, Hohen Viecheln-c, Duvensee and all Friesack assemblages which present common tools (Figure 81.9), even if each assemblage can be distinguished by a specific style of shafted point (David 1999a:343 p). Despite my observation of a transformation in hunting equipment, characterised by a strong increase in big cervids barbed and straight points, as well as antler heavy tools, relative to both notched points and roe deer points which emerges between the Friesack II and III chronological stages (at the end of the Early Boreal), it is not possible to demonstrate that the Maglemose cultural group derives from this technocomplex, nor is it possible to term this technocomplex "Maglemosian *lato sensu*". The interesting late level from Hohen Viecheln (Germany) offers a mixed assemblage that could perhaps indicate a southern geographical limit for the Early Maglemose territory at the end of the Boreal chronozone, or possibly a contact zone between Maglemose and this Northeuropean technocomplex. Definitely, the Agerod I:A-H-C bone and antler industries (BL, UT and VL levels) which are made using other methods do not belong to the Maglemosian cultural group (David monograph in press). Future bone and antler studies on the earliest Danish Maglemose cultural group (M.0) and the contemporaneous settlements in the East Baltic regions will hopefully provide a definitive response to all these questions. Further work is also required on the lithic technology of the assemblages described here.

Acknowledgements

This study was supported by a generous grant from the Fyssen Foundation, for which I am extremely grateful. My English was improved by Michael Ilett.

References

Becker, C.J. 1953. Die Maglemosekultur in Dänemark, neue Funde und Ergebnisse. In: Vogt, E. (ed.) *Congrès international des Sciences préhistoriques et protohistoriques – Actes de la IIIème session* – 1950, 180–183. Zürich.

Bille Henriksen, B. 1980. *Lundby-Holmen, Pladser of Maglemose type 1, Sydjælland.* København.

Blanchet, J.-C. and Lambot, B. 1977. Les dragages de l'Oise (première partie). *Cahiers Archéologiques de Picardie,* 61–87.

Breuil, A. 1926. Un harpon maglemosien trouvé à Béthune en 1849. *L'Anthropologie* 36, 309–312.

Bridault, A. 1993. *Les économies de chasse épipaléolithiques et mésolithiques du nord et de l'est de la France.* Thèse de Doctorat, Perlès, C. (dir.), Paris X – Nanterre University. Paris.

Brinch Petersen, E. 1973. A Survey of the Late Paleolithic and the Mesolithic of Denmark. In: Kozlowski, S.K. (ed.) *The Mesolithic in Europe,* 77–127. Warsaw.

Brøndsted, J. 1960. *Steinzeit in Dänemark.* Band 1. Neumünster.

Childe, G.V. 1931. The Forest Cultures of Northern Europe. *Journal of the Royal Anthropological Institution* 61, 325–348.

Clark, J.G.D. 1936, 1970. *The Mesolithic Settlement of Northern Europe: a Study of the Food Gathering Peoples of Northern Europe during the Early Post-Glacial Period.* London.

Clark, J.G.D., Godwin, H., Fraser, F.C., King, J.E., Moore, J.W. and Walker, D. 1954. *Excavations at Star Carr, an Early Mesolithic Site at Seamer near Scarborough, Yorkshire.* Cambridge.

Clarke, D.L. 1968. *Analytical Archaeology.* London.

Coles, B.J. 1998. Doggerland: a Speculative Survey. *Proceedings of the Prehistoric Society* 64, 45–81.

David, E. 1998. Étude technologique de l'industrie en matière dures animales du site mésolithique de Zamostje 2 – fouille 1991 – (Russie). *Archéo-Situla* 26 (1996), 5–62.

―― 1999a. L'industrie en matières dures animales du Mésolithique ancien et moyen en Europe du Nord. Contribution de l'analyse technologique à la définition du Maglemosien. Thèse de doctorat, Julien, M. (dir.), Paris X – Nanterre University (France). Paris.

―― 1999b. Approche technologique des industries en matières dures animales du Mésolithique danois d'après le matériel des gisements maglemosiens de Mullerup 1 (Sarauw's island – 1900) et Ulkestrup Lyng II (1946). In: Thévenin, A. (ed.) *L'Europe des derniers chasseurs, Actes du 5ème Colloque International Épipaléolithique et Mésolithique UISPP Commission XII* – 1995, 167–178. Grenoble.

―― 2000a. L'industrie en matières dures animales des sites mésolithiques de la Baume d'Ogens et de Birsmatten-Basisgrotte (Suisse): résultats de l'étude technologique et comparaisons. In: Crotti, P. (ed.) *Table ronde épipaléolithique et mésolithique. Cahiers d'Archéologie romande* 81, 79–101. Lausanne.

―― 2000b. L'industrie en matières dures animales du "technocomplexes occidental": techniques et définition préliminaire. *Les derniers chasseurs-cueilleurs de l'Europe occidentale (13000 – 5500 av. J.-C.), Actes du colloque international de Besançon, octobre 1998. Collection Annales Littéraires* 699, 143–150. Besançon.

―― 2002. Percuteur de matières tendres sur métapodiens d'aurochs. *Fiches typologiques de l'industrie de l'os préhistorique* cahier X (Os à impressions et éraillures). Société préhistorique française, 133–136.

―― monography in press. *L'industrie en matières dures animales du Mésolithique ancien et moyen en Europe du Nord. Contribution de l'analyse technologique à la définition du Maglemosien.* Librairie archéologique Monique Mergoil Collection Préhistoires.

David, E. and Johansen, L. 1996. *Maglemosian barbed Points made of Metapodials: Reconstructing the chaîne opératoire by Experiments.* Lejre Experimental Center (Denmark) Report No. HAF 26/96. Lejre.

David, E. and Johansen, L. 1997. *Pointes barbelées maglemosiennes sur côte de ruminants: reconstitution et validation de la chaîne opératoire par l'expérimentation.* Lejre Experimental Center (Denmark) Report No. HAF 7/97. Lejre.

David, E., Biard, M. and Sørensen, A.S. 1999. *Maglemosian adzes made on bovids metapodials. Reconstitution and validation of the chaîne opératoire by experiments.* Lejre Experimental Center (Denmark) Report No. HAF 24/99. Lejre.

Galinski, T. 1989. Le Mésolithique de l'Europe. In: Archeologia (ed.) *Le temps de la Préhistoire*, 332–334. Paris.

Kozlowski, S.K. 1973. Introduction to the History of Europe in Early Holocene. In: Kozlowski, S.K. (ed.) *The Mesolithic in Europe*, 331–366. Warsaw.

Kozlowski, J.K. and Kozlowski, S.K. 1977. Pointes, sagaies et harpons du Paléolithique et du Mésolithique en Europe du Centre-Est. *Colloques internationaux du C.N.R.S. 568 – Méthodologie appliquée à l'industrie de l'os préhistorique*, 205–227. Sénanque.

Larsson, L. 1978. Mesolithic Antler and Bone Artefacts from Central Scania. *Meddelander från Lunds Universitets Historiska Museum* 1977–78, 28–67.

Mathiassen, T. 1948. *Danske Oldsager I.* Kobenhavn.

Møhl, U. 1984. Dyreknogler fra Nogle af Borealtidens senere Bopladser i den Sjaellandske Aamosen. *Aarbøger for Nordisk Oldkyndighed og Historie* 1984, 47–60.

Noe-Nygaard, N. 1987. Taphonomy in Archaeology with Special Emphasis on Man as a Biasing Factor. *Journal of Danish Archaeology* 6, 7–52.

―― 1989. Man-Made Trace Fossils on Bones. *Human Evolution* 4, No. 6, 461–491.

Pelegrin, J., Karlin, C. and Bodu, P. 1988. "Chaînes opératoires": un outil pour les préhistoriens. In: Tixier, J. (dir.) *Technologie Préhistorique. Notes et Monographies Techniques* 25, 55–62. Paris.

Sarauw, G.F.L., Jessen, K. and Winge, H. 1903. En Stenalders Boplads, Maglemose ved Mullerup, études sur le premier âge de la pierre du nord de l'Europe. *Aarbøger for Nordisk Oldkyndighed og Historie* 1904, 157–315.

Schwabedissen, H. 1944. *Die Mittlere Steinzeit in Westlichen Norddeutschland.* Neumünster.

Schwantes, G. 1928. Nordisches Paläolithikum und Mesolithikum. *Mitteilungen aus dem Museum für Völkerkunde in Hamburg* 12, 159–252.

Stordeur, D. 1978. Proposition de classement des objets en os selon le degré de transformation imposé à la matière première. *Bulletin de la Société Préhistorique Française* 75 (1), 20–23.

Tixier, J., Inizan, M.L. and Roche, H. 1980. *Préhistoire de la pierre taillée 1 and 2.* Valbonne.

―― 1992. *Technology of knapped Stone.* Meudon.

Westerby, E. 1927. *Stations préhistoriques près de Klampenborg, études sur la période mésolithique.* Copenhague.

Miscellany

82. The Renardières aux Pins, Charente, France. A pre-boreal cave in west central France

Véronique Dujardin and Bruno Boulestin

The Cave of the Renardières is located in the limestone plateau of La Rochefoucauld, to the North of the Aquitaine basin. There are several levels, ranging from the Middle Paleolithic to the Bronze Age. We will present sequence II. We started the excavation and the study in 1997. There are several units in this sequence, separated from each other by a heavy rock fall from the roof of the cave. The lithic series is important and surprising, we found no microliths, in spite of careful sieving, instead we found large tools (up to 10 cm) which included scrapers on cortical flakes and one knife with a notch on its base. This sort of knife is known on 90% of surface sites between the Loire and the Charente rivers and they are well dated: to the Pre-boreal at the Mesolithic necropolis of La Vergne (Charente-Maritime) and from the cave of Rouffignac (Dordogne) to around 9300–9000 BP or 8400–7950 cal BC 2-sigma.

The site

The site of the Renardières is located within the municipality of Les Pins, about 20 kilometers to the north-east of Angoulême (Charente, France, Figure 82.1). It was discovered by prospecting about a dozen years ago. A test pit was opened in 1995, followed by a rescue excavation of the funerary levels dating from the Bronze Age which were being threatened by animal burrows. This excavation also evaluated the stratigraphy of the site and thus of previous occupations. Since 1998 these excavations have been conducted in accord with the framework of a larger research project.

The site is located on the slope of a plateau, on the north side of a small dry valley which cuts through reef-limestone belonging to the Middle Oxfordian period. It consists of a large porch roof covering a rock shelter or wide cave, whose only access today is through a natural chimney opening through the vault. The excavation of the remains that filled the chimney made it possible to highlight several Paleolithic occupations belonging to the Magdalenian, Badegoulian and Gravettian periods. Some evidence of older human presence during the Aurignacian, the Castelperronian and the Mid-Paleolithic is evident from the lithic material found in the animal burrows. Above the principal cavity, contained within the layers beneath the porch roof which were first excavated, a second cavity was discovered, but its vault was now almost entirely collapsed.

In this shelter a significant collection of funerary material, dating from the early Bronze Age (mentioned above) was also discovered. In addition, there were clearly identifiable levels from the early Azilian and late Mesolithic periods. It is this later period which we are concerned with here.

The Mesolithic of Les Renardières

A limited area of Mesolithic level has just been excavated. The lithic series is important because, surprisingly, we found no microliths in spite of careful sieving. What we did discover were large tools (up to 10 cm) which included scrapers on cortical flakes and one knife blade with a notch on its base. We tried to do a radiocarbon dating on the bone from this layer, but the lack of collagen in the bone prevented this. A larger area of this layer will be excavated next year.

The knives with notch(es) on the base

About half of the knife blades have a ratio length/width of between 2 and 3 while the other half have a ratio of between 3 and 4 (Figure 82.4). Only one of these knives, from Bel Air at Villars-les-Bois, is a real blade, with a ratio of 4.08 (Figure 82.5). Most of them are made with a hard hammer technique from local flint.

All of them present an oblique truncation on the distal part. This truncation is generally rectilinear, sometimes convex, in some rare instances sligtly concave. The retouches are direct, very rarely inverse.

On the base there are one or two notches which are made by abrupt or semi-abrupt retouches.

The large majority of these artefacts (77%) have two notches, one on each side. In 16% of these cases they

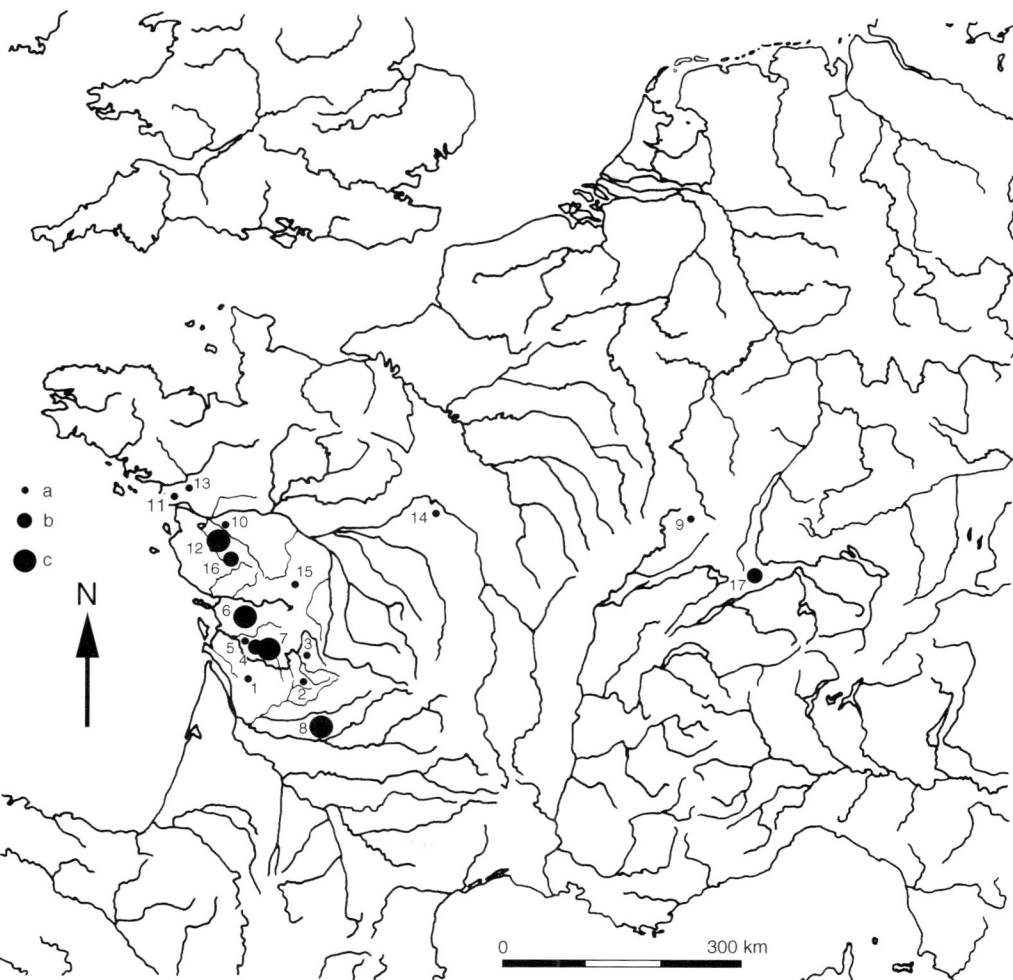

Figure 82.1 Location of the sites where knives with notch(es) on the base have been found. a)1 knife; b) 2 to 5 knives and c) 6 knives or more
From Charente, France: 1) Bouteville, Le Bois de Douvesse; 2) Combiers, Rozet and 3) Les Pins, Les Renardières. From Charente-Maritime, France: 4). Brizambourg, Chez Jouneau and La Sablière; 5) Grandjean, Piphrez; 6) La Vergne, La Grande Pièce; 7) Villars-Les-Bois, Fontbelle and Bel Air. From Dordogne, France: 8) Rouffignac, Le Cro du Cluzeau. From Jura, France: 9) Ruffey-Sur-Seille, À Daupharde. From Loire-Atlantique, France:10) Géneston, Les Garennes; 11) Guérande, Clis B12) Montbert, La Majoire A, B, C and D; 13) Sainte-Reine-de-Bretagne, L'Organais. From Loiret, France: 14) Autry-Le-Châtel, Le Moulin du Saule. From Deux-Sèvres, France: 15) Vasles, La Prouterie. From Vendée, France: 16) Boulogne, Les Vergères. From Switzerland: 17) Birsmatten, Nenzlingen.

have a notch on one side and retouche on the other, while 7% have just one notch.

The mesial part may be natural, without retouches, or the distal retouches can continue up to the notch. The cutting edge of the tool may carry retouches caused by use.

The presence of the notch(es), which would make the fixing of a handle easier, together with the edge ware, would seem to substantiate the interpretation put forward by G. Gouraud (1980) and C. Barrière (1973) that these tools were used as knives, but we cannot completely exclude the possibility that they are arrowheads.

The knives of Rouffignac are squatter, the distal retouches or oblique truncation is less carefully applied and the notches not as carefully made. Barrière (1973) and other authors, P. Bazin and J.-P. Halley (Bazin et al. 1995), for example, have called similar tools, that is to say examples with truncation but no notch, for "Rouffignac Knives".

The lithic material associated with these types of tools, e.g. at Charente and Charente-Maritime, rarely contain microliths. At Les Renardières (Les Pins) there are no microliths. From the necropolis at La Grande Pièce at La Vergne they were found together with just one microlith point with a transverse base. At Bois Douvesse (Bouteville) they were found together with isosceles triangles. They have been found with microliths on a number of surface sites but it is impossible to know for certain if this material is contemporary with the notched knife blades.

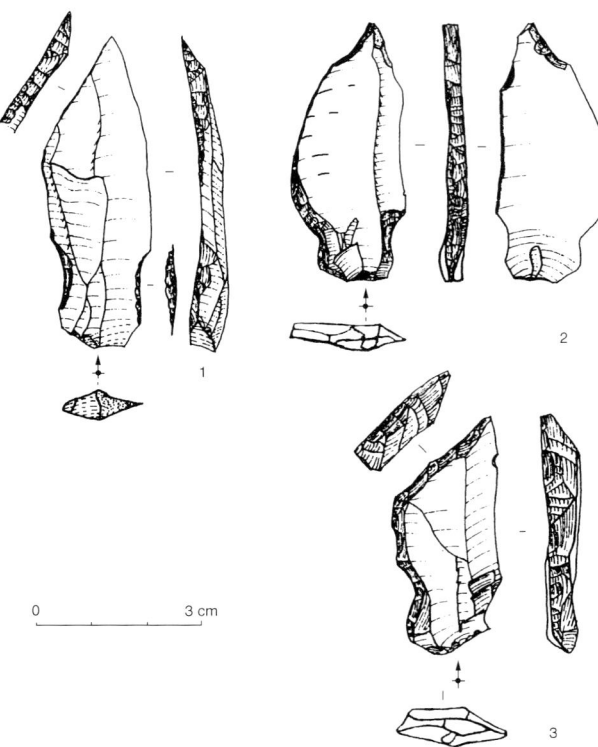

Figure 82.2 Lithic material from the Pre-boreal of Charente 1) Bouteville, Le Bois de Douvesse; 2) Combiers, Rozet and 3) Les Pins, Les Renardières.

1) The knife from Bouteville is the largest and most typical of the series. It consists of a blade with cortical butt, on a black local flint of very good quality, like most of the lithic pieces of the site. The distal truncation is rectilinear, very neat and forms an angle of 141° with the edge of the blade. The mesial part is not reworked. The two notches are carefully arranged by an abrupt direct retouch.
Length 58 mm, width 19 mm, thickness 6 mm, weight 5,97 g.
2) The Combiers knife consists of a short blade on grey flint with white inclusions. The butt is smooth and has a very marked bulb of percussion. An old fracture affects the distal end. The truncation is slightly convex and continues in the arc of a circle on the level of the left notch. The two notches are well released by an abrupt retouch. The cutting edge of the blade is affected by a continuous inverse retouch.
Length 48 mm, width 20 mm, thickness 5 mm, weight 4,60 g.
3) The knife from Les Pins is worked on a short but relatively thick blade of local, rather strongly patinated flint. It is the least regular of the series. The distal truncation is rectilinear, oblique and forms an angle of 132° with the edge of the piece. A first series of direct retouches affects all the thickness of the knife, the markings are supplemented by direct abrupt, scalier retouches. The mesial part, between the truncation and the notch, was redone with a semi-abrupt to abrupt direct retouch which forms the back of the knife. Only one notch is present in the prolongation of the back. On the side opposite the notch, two small lamellate removals can perhaps be interpreted as a preparation for a second notch which was never achieved.
Length 45mm, width 19 mm, thickness 7 mm, weight 5,54 g.
(Drawing by Véronique Dujardin)

Datings

The majority of the known pieces have been found either through surface survey, through excavation in disturbed levels or on sites which have not yet been dated. Only three sites have been reliably C-14 dated: layers 5b and 4c at Rouffignac, level R3 at À Daupharde, Ruffey-sur-Seille (Jura) and three burial pits in the necropolis of La Vergne at Charente-Maritime (Figure 82.6). These dates are supported by the study of the lithic material associated with these knife blades and by the occurence of fauna remains.

At La Vergne, the three dates are concentrated to the Pre-boreal, between 9300 and 9000 BP or 8400–7980 cal BC 2-sigma. These dates, together with a date from layer 5b at Rouffignac, coincide.

The site of À Daupharde at Ruffey-sur-Seille (the Jura) delivered a significant series of radiocarbon datings, from 10,000 BP to the Bronze Age. A notched knife blade was found in level R3, which was dated with 5 radiocarbon samples to 9300–8600 BP or 8300–7500 cal BC 2-sigma (Séara 2000).

Gouraud thought that the site of the Pierre-Saint-Louis to Geay (Charente-Maritime), excavated by Johannes Musch and later by Pascal Foucher, could have had a Pre-boreal component in its central sector that might have contained knives with notches (Gouraud 1996). The two oldest dates from this site would not seem to support this assumption. One date, from structure 15 of sector III, using charcoal gave a value of 8764±93 BP or 8021–7543 cal BC 2-sigma (Lyon-117-OXA). The other, from structure 6 of sector III, dated to 8700±100 BP or 7964–7506 cal BC 2-sigma (Lyon-116-OXA). This means that they postdate the sites which contained knives (and no knife was found during the excavation of this site).

Geographical distribution

More than 92% of the known notched knives originate from the Mid-West of France, with a clear prevalence along the seaboard between the Loire and Charente (Figure 82.1). The three examples from Charente, very recently discovered, would seem to indicate that the distribution of these tools might possibly extend south of the river Charente. The Combiers knife is from the valley of the Nizonne and therefore indicates the extension of the distribution area towards the Dordogne, thus establishing a link with the knives of Rouffignac which are slightly different but contemporary with them.

The four examples from the French Jura (Ruffey-sur-Seille; À Daupharde) and Switzerland (Birsmatten) may indicate the presence of another group, but one which has no direct link with the group of the Mid-West.

Conclusion

The recent discovery of knifes with notches, found in the department of Charente, in the basin of the Nizonne, a

The Renardières aux Pins. Charente, France. A pre-boreal cave in west central France

No. on map	Dpt	Municipality	Locality	Number of knives			References
				Type 1	Type 2	Type 3	
1	16	Bouteville	Bois de Douvesse	1	0	0	Burnez 1993, Dujardin 1999
2	16	Combiers	Rozet	1	0	0	Hutchinson 1999, Dujardin 1999
3	16	Pins (Les)	Les Renardières	0	0	1	Boulestin 1998, Dujardin 1999
4	17	Brizambourg	Chez Jouneau	3	2	0	Foucher & San Juan 1994
4	17	Brizambourg	La Sablière	1	0	0	Blanchet 1999
5	17	Grandjean	Piphrez - Chez Guérin	1	0	0	Favre 1997
6	17	Vergne (La)	La grande Pièce	11	0	0	Duday et al 1995, Gouraud 2000
7	17	Villars-les-Bois	Fontbelle	1	0	0	Favre 1997
7	17	Villars-les-Bois	Bel-Air	8	0	0	Favre 1997, Blanchet 1999, Blanchet 2000a
9	39	Ruffey-sur-Seille	À Daupharde	0	0	1	Séara & Ganard 1996, Séara 2000, Gouraud & Thévenin in press
10	44	Géneston	Les Garennes	2	0	0	Gouraud 1980
11	44	Guérande	Clis B	1	0	0	Gallais 1984
12	44	Montbert	La Majoire A	0	1	0	Gouraud 1980
12	44	Montbert	La Majoire B	2	1	0	Gouraud 1980
12	44	Montbert	La Majoire C	1	0	0	Gouraud 1980
12	44	Montbert	La Majoire D	0	1	2	Gouraud 1980
13	44	Sainte-Reine-de-Bretagne	L'Organais	0	1	0	Gallais et al. 1985, Gouraud & Thévenin in press
14	45	Autry-le-Châtel	Le Moulin du Saule	2	3	0	Bazin et al. 1995
15	79	Vasles	La Prouterie	1	0	0	Blanchet 2000b
16	85	Boulogne	Les Vergères	4	0	1	Prosp. C. Dugast, Gouraud.& Thévenin in press
17	Swiss	Birsmatten	Nenzlingen	3	0	0	Rozoy 1978 pl. 45
		Total		43	9	4	
		Percentage		76.8	16.1	7.1	

Figure 82.3 List of the sites that contain knives with notch(es) on their base. Type 1) two opposed notches; Type 2) one notch with opposing retouches, and Type 3) only 1 notch.
To this list, we must add the 19 knives of The Cro du Cluzeau, level 5b, at Rouffignac (Dordogne, France), which have less marked notches. For the knives of Bel-Air at Villars-les-Bois, we must add two knives with (oblique) truncation, broken at the notch. For Autry-le-Châtel, we just kept back the published knives with well-marked notches associated to a rectilinear or lightly curved distal truncation (Bazin et al. 1995: fig. 15 n° 1 and 3 [type 1] as well as fig. 15 n° 2, 6 and fig. 17 n° 1 [type 2]).

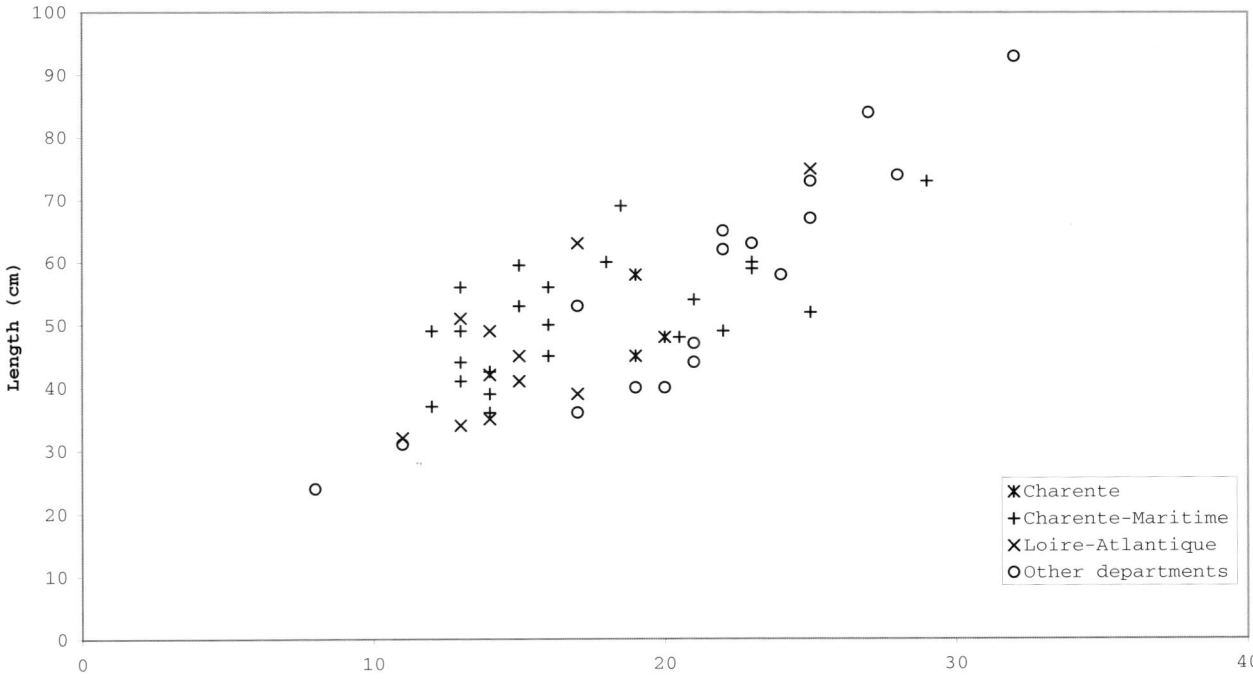

Figure 82.4 Measurement of the knives.

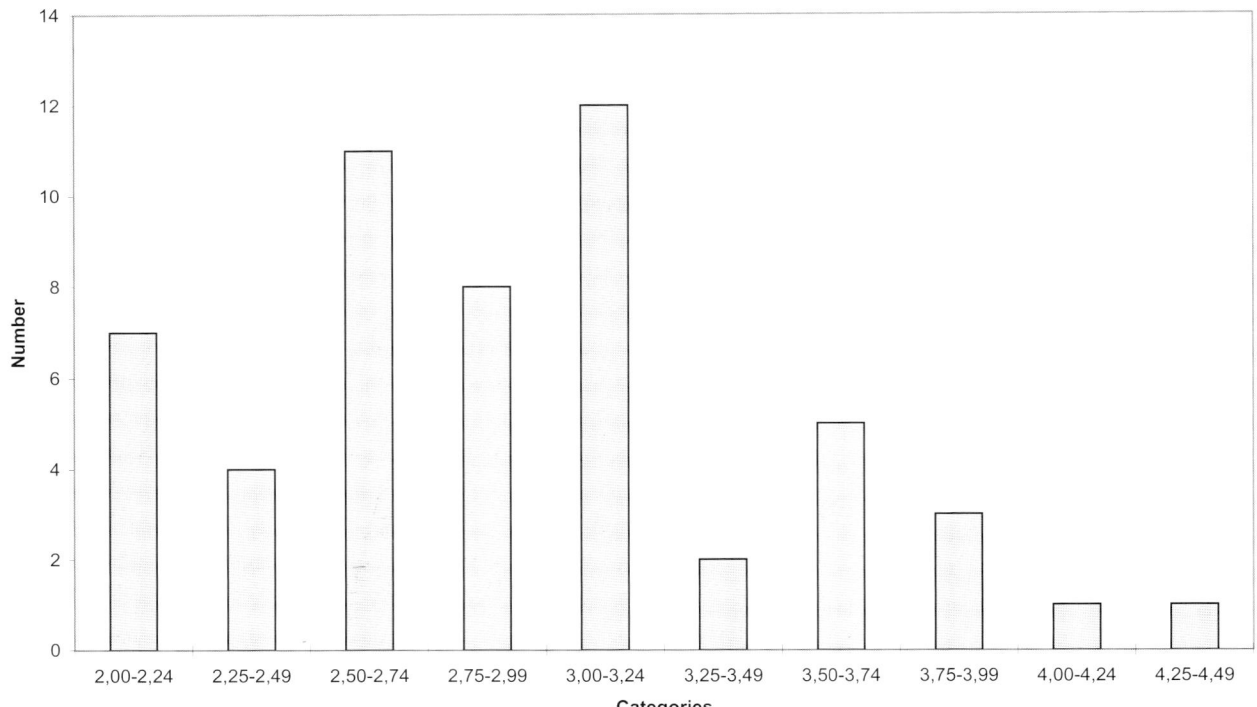

Figure 82.5 Ratio lenght/width.

Dpt	Municipality	Locality	Level	Material	BP Date	cal BC 2-sigma	Reference
17	La Vergne	La Grande Pièce	structure 3	bone	9075±65	8309-7992	OxA 6698 Lyon 368
17	La Vergne	La Grande Pièce	structure 7	bone	9070±70	8313-7981	OxA 6699 Lyon 369
17	La Vergne	La Grande Pièce	structure 10	bone	9215±65	8377-8090	OxA 6700 Lyon 370
24	Rouffignac	Le Cro du Cluzeau	Level 5b	charcoal	9150±90	8400-8012	GrN 5514
24	Rouffignac	Le Cro du Cluzeau	Level 4c	charcoal	8995±105	8326-7737	GrN 2880
39	Ruffey-sur-Seille	A Daupharde	Level R3	hazel nut	9210±70	8378-8087	Lyon 215 (OxA)
39	Ruffey-sur-Seille	A Daupharde	Level R3	hazel nut	9055± 65	8221-7977	Lyon 411 (AA23363)
39	Ruffey-sur-Seille	A Daupharde	Level R3	hazel nut	8980±80	8117-7791	Lyon 241 (OxA)
39	Ruffey-sur-Seille	A Daupharde	Level R3	hazel nut	8710±110	7956-7539	Ly 7353
39	Ruffey-sur-Seille	A Daupharde	Level R3	charcoal	8855±65	8013-7705	Lyon 410 (AA23362)

Figure 82.6 Radiocarbon datings.

tributary of the Dronne and Dordogne, is of a type that is dated to the early Mesolithic of the Pre-boreal. Up until now, this type of tool was primarily and almost exclusively known only from the Atlantic coast of Mid-West France. This discovery has led us to favorably reconsider the hypothesis that there may be a link between these knives and the knives from Rouffignac, which are slightly different but contemporary. The three examples from Charente are very similar to the typical notched knives, and they indicate the presence of an early Mesolithic group of hunter-gatherers akin to those who inhabited the entire area between the Loire and the Charente rivers.

Acknowledgments

We would like to thank Kate Douglas and Carole Hutchinson for correcting our English.

References

Barrière, C. 1973. Rouffignac – L'Archéologie (1ᵉ partie). *Travaux de l'Institut d'Art Préhistorique de la Faculté des Lettres et Sciences Humaines de Toulouse* XV, 1–160.

Bazin, P., Halley, J.-P. and Thévenin, A. 1995. Les stations mésolithiques d'Autry-le-Châtel (Loiret). In: Thévenin, A. (ed.) *Épipaléolithique et Mésolithique entre Seine et Rhin. Table Ronde d'Ancerville 1989*. Annales littéraires de l'université de Besançon, série Archéologie 41, Besançon, 191–212.

Blanchet, F. 1999. *Bel-Air à Villars-les-Bois (Charente-Maritime) : pièces inédites, rapport*, Service Régional de l'Archéologie de Poitou-Charentes, Poitiers.

—— 2000a. *Bel-Air à Villars-les-Bois (Charente-Maritime): deux nouvelles pièces inédites, rapport*, Service Régional de l'Archéologie de Poitou-Charentes, Poitiers.

—— 2000b. *La Prouterie à Vasles (Deux-Sèvres): une nouvelle pièce inédite, rapport*, Service Régional de l'Archéologie de Poitou-Charentes, Poitiers.

Boulestin, B. 1998. *Les Renardières (Les Pins, Charente), niveaux mésolithiques, néolithiques et protohistoriques. Rapport de fouille programmée*, 1998, Service Régional de l'Archéologie de Poitou-Charentes, Poitiers.

Burnez, C. 1993. *Bois de Douvesse à Bouteville (Charente). Rapport de sondage*, Service Régional de l'Archéologie de Poitou-Charentes, Poitiers.

Duday, H., Courtaud, P., Dujardin, V., Martin, H. and Robin, K. 1995. *La Vergne, La Grande Pièce (Charente-Maritime). Complément au DFS de sauvetage urgent*, Service Régional de l'Archéologie de Poitou-Charentes, Poitiers.

Dujardin, V. 1999. Découvertes récentes de couteaux à encoches basilaires en Charente. *Bulletins et Mémoires de la Société Archéologique et Historique de la Charente*, Angoulême, 1999-4, 229–236.

Favre, M. 1997. *Fin Würm, début Holocène sur le littoral charentais. Rapport de prospection thématique*, Service Régional de l'Archéologie de Poitou-Charentes, Poitiers.

Foucher, P. and San Juan, C. 1994. *Fin Würm, début Holocène sur le littoral charentais. Rapport de prospection thématique*, Service Régional de l'Archéologie de Poitou-Charentes, Poitiers.

Gallais, J.-Y. 1984. Stations à microlithes de Clis à Guérande. *Études préhistoriques et protohistoriques des Pays-de-la-Loire* 7, 23–48.

Gallais, J.-Y., Damblon, F., Richard, J., Thiébault, S. and Visset, L. 1985. Le site à microlithes de l'Organais à Sainte-Reine-de-Bretagne (Loire-Atlantique). *Revue Archéologique de l'Ouest* 2, 23–45.

Gouraud, G. 1980. Les couteaux à encoches basilaires des gisements à microlithes en Basse-Loire. *Bulletin de la Société Préhistorique Française* 77 (9), 277–279.

—— 1996. *Le microlithisme de la Pierre Saint-Louis à Geay (Charente-Maritime) dans le cadre du Mésolithique régional*. Mémoire de D.E.A., université de Toulouse Le Mirail et École pratique des Hautes Études en Sciences Sociales, Toulouse.

Gouraud, G. and Thévenin, A. in press. Les couteaux à encoches basilaires. *Table-ronde de Rennes 1996, Supplément à la Revue Archéologique de l'Ouest*.

Hutchinson, C. 1999. *L'abbaye de Rozet à Combiers (Charente). Rapport de fouilles programmées*, Service Régional de l'Archéologie de Poitou-Charentes, Poitiers.

Rozoy, J.-G. 1978. *Les derniers chasseurs*. L'Épipaléolithique en France et en Belgique. Mémoire de la Société archéologie champenoise, Charleville-Mézières.

Séara, F. and Ganard, V. 1996. *Les gisements de Choisey "Aux Campins" et de Ruffey-sur-Seille "À Daupharde" (Jura). Document final de synthèse de fouilles préventives*, Service Régional de l'Archéologie de Franche-Comté, Besançon.

Séara, F. 2000. Les cadres chronologique et culturel des occupations mésolithiques de Ruffey-sur-Seille "À Daupharde" et gisements de Choisey "Aux Campins" (Jura). *Les derniers chasseurs-cueilleurs d'Europe occidentale, actes du Colloque international de Besançon, octobre 1998*. Annales Littéraires 699, série "Environnement, société et archéologie" 1, Besançon, 125–132.

Miscellany

83. Mesolithic settlement during the Preboreal period in Finland

Timo Jussila and Heikki Matiskainen

This overview presents new archaeological finds from Central Finland and the Karelia area in Finland and Russia, at elevations that suggest Preboreal period dates. Extensive excavations at the Ristola site at Lahti, South Finland between 1996–1999, which is dated to the close of the Preboreal period prior to the culmination of Lake Ancylus, have revealed a flint assemblage comparable to the East Baltic Pulli assemblage and those of the Butovo Culture on the Upper Volga This research prompted a search for new evidence of Preboreal settlements in other parts of Finland. The early postglacial history of the large lakes of central Finland are interpreted with the help of three distance diagams. Following the shoreline displacement chronology for the Ancylus stage, previously unknown sites were found in 1999. The oldest of these are situated on Preboreal shorelines. A number of dewlling sites were discovered in Karelia near the Russian border. These sites were located at elevations above the Ancylus transgression culmination point. Flint finds similar to the Lahti Ristola assemblage were found. Some sites were surveyed in the neighbourhood of the Antrea net find on the Karelian Isthmus, Russia.

Brief introduction

Ville Luho suggested in the 1950's that the early Postglacial settlement in Finland should be extended back to the Preboreal period (Luho 1956:146 pp). Luho was also the first to make a systematic study of Finland's Mesolithic dwelling sites and he launched the concept of the "Askola Culture". Working in the parish of Askola along the catchment of the Porvoonjoki River, Luho investigated a number of sites, dating six of them to the shore elevations of the Preboreal Yoldia Sea stage. At the time no Preboreal sites were known from Russia or the Baltic countries and Luho's analogies were based on similarities with the Komsa Culture of Northern Norway. The stratigraphic shoreline displacement chronology lacked fixed points dated by quaternary geology and the incipient Preboreal Mesolithic chronology crumbled when the history of the Baltic became known in greater detail through radiocarbon datings. The oldest sites were now dated to the Boreal period, contemporary with the regressive stage of the Ancylus Lake (Matiskainen 1989:31 p).

In later years Luho's research was alienated by the processualists in Finland (Knutsson 1998:78). The latter ultimately became dogma in a model of economic subsistence according to which the early Postglacial settlement of Finland did not begin until the Boreal period as a result of the utilisation of elk as game (Siiriäinen 1981:25 p). This theory predominated until the late 1990's, by which time the conceptions of quaternary geology regarding the dating, duration and related ecology of climatic and vegetation history and the stages the Baltic have appreciably changed.

Why then was there no Preboreal settlement in Finland, although its existence was indicated by Mesolithic radiocarbon dates from neighbouring countries? One suggested explanation was that the Baltic formed a natural barrier "delaying" the migration of small human populations into the regions north of the Gulf of Finland (Matiskainen 1989:67 p). On the other hand, it was suggested in the mid 1990's that due to its high culmination point – whose age in terms of forest history is slightly older than the boundary of the Preboreal and the Boreal in South Finland – the transgressive Ancylus Lake would have destroyed possible Preboreal sites (Matiskainen 1996:257).

The problem was solved by a dwelling at Ristola in Lahti, South Finland, initially investigated in the late 1960's. Dated to the Corded Ware period, the site included finds of flint artefacts comparable to the material from the Estonian site of Pulli, which had been covered by the transgressive sediments of the Ancylus Lake (Edgren 1984:22). Excavations were continued at Ristola in 1996–1999, with the discovery of more finds of Preboreal flints and of features similar to those found in the Baltic regions and the Butovo Culture in Central Russia (see Takala in this volume).

Shore displacement and Preboreal dwelling sites in Central Finland

Owing to metachronic land upheaval, the Ancylus Lake was continuously regressive in the Baltic basin northwest of the Närke discharge threshold (>5 mm/yr land upheaval isobase). The large lakes of Central Finland were initially isolated from the Ancylus Lake with discharge channels in the northwest. The only distinct and uniformly dated shore level is formed by the chronozone of the IV/V climatic zone, the *Betula – Betula/Pinus* pollen boundary (p.a.z.) (Saarnisto 1971). As this boundary also demarcates the Preboreal and Boreal periods, Stone Age sites at elevations higher than this shore level limit are in theory of Preboreal date. The boundary formed a uniform shore level ca. 8200 cal BC.

The shore level can be described with a distance diagram placed at right angles to the isobases of the land uplift, with morphological and stratigraphic shore observations of different dates marked on it. A uniform dated level – here the IV/V chronozone boundary – forms an ancient shore which is tilted in relation to the NW-SE distance. Other shore levels consisting of dated ancient shorelines can be used as levels in comparison, like the highest shore level of the lakes prior to the formation of the new discharge channels in the south (the Kymijoki and Vuoksi rivers). These, however, are not of importance for the present study.

Recent archaeological surveys in Central Finland have revealed several dwelling sites, with elevations near the shore level of the IV/V zone boundary or considerably higher than this boundary. The most important consideration for successful results was that dwelling sites at Ancylus elevations were explicitly sought after during the surveys. No actual excavations have yet been carried out at these sites and the finds from trial investigations consist of quartz artefacts, quartz debitage and burnt bone.

Assuming that these sites were originally on the shore of the continually regressive Ancylus Lake, some of them can be dated to the Preboreal period. The influence of the saline Yoldia Sea cannot be discerned at all in Central Finland; only to the southeast of the Salpausselkä zone has a weak saline Yoldia influence been observed in diatom flora. The present study presents three distance diagrams from the northern parts of the present Lake Päijänne water system in Central Finland (Figure 83.1). The segments of lines given in the map are the course of the distance diagram in a generalised perpendicular relation to the isobases of land uplift in the area. The study is based on Timo Jussila's (2000:13 pp) recent publication.

The distance diagram in figure 83.2 is drawn through the Lake Saarijärvi system, which belongs to the Päijänne water system, and shows dwelling sites in connection with it. The highest shoreline (1) is the highest uniform shore level, whose age, estimated from tilting, is ca. 8700 cal BC in relation to the IV/V zone boundary (2). The IV/V zone age is based on the mean date of 8200 cal BC obtained from 17 Finnish dates for the B/PB p.a.z. boundary. This date must be regarded as the boundary of the Preboreal and Boreal periods. There is a group of sites observed to be above this dated Baltic shore level. The distance diagram in figure 83.3 is from the Lake Kivijärvi area and the two sites marked are in the vicinity of the shore level of the IV/V zone boundary (2).

The third diagram (Figure 83.4) is from the Laukaa area, north of the city of Jyväskylä. The three sites shown are quartz bearing dwelling sites discovered by the archaeologist Timo Sepänmaa from the Museum of Central Finland in Jyväskylä. Placed in relation to the distance diagram we observe their elevations to be considerably higher than the IV/V zone shore level. They are dated to ca. 8500 cal BC and correspond in age to the Ristola site in Lahti.

The authors feel that shore level analysis applied from quaternary geology is excellently suited for estimating the age of Early Mesolithic sites in the northern parts of the Finnish lake district. The method has been applied not only the Lake Päijänne system but also in the upper reaches of Lake Saimaa, although the number of discovered sites there is small due to a lack of archaeological surveys.

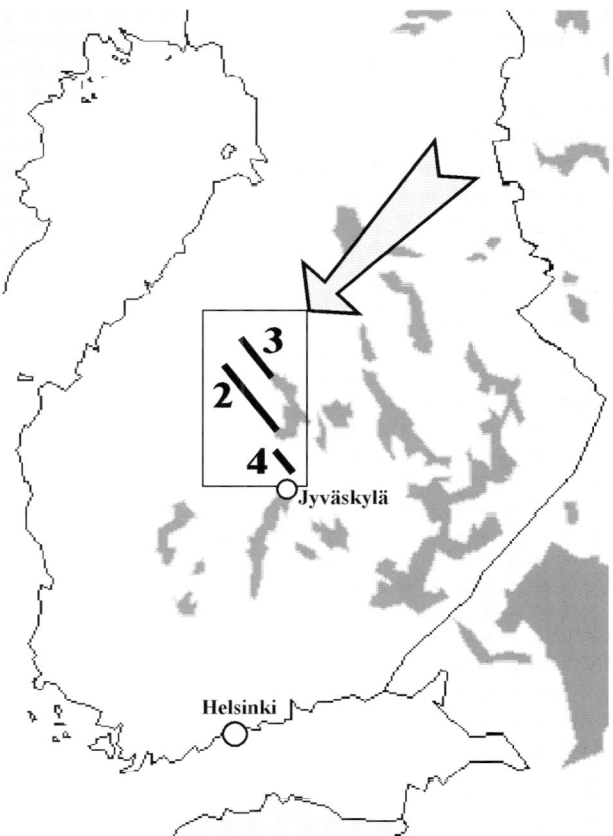

Figure 83.1 Location of presented shoreline distance diagrams of figures 83.2–83.4.

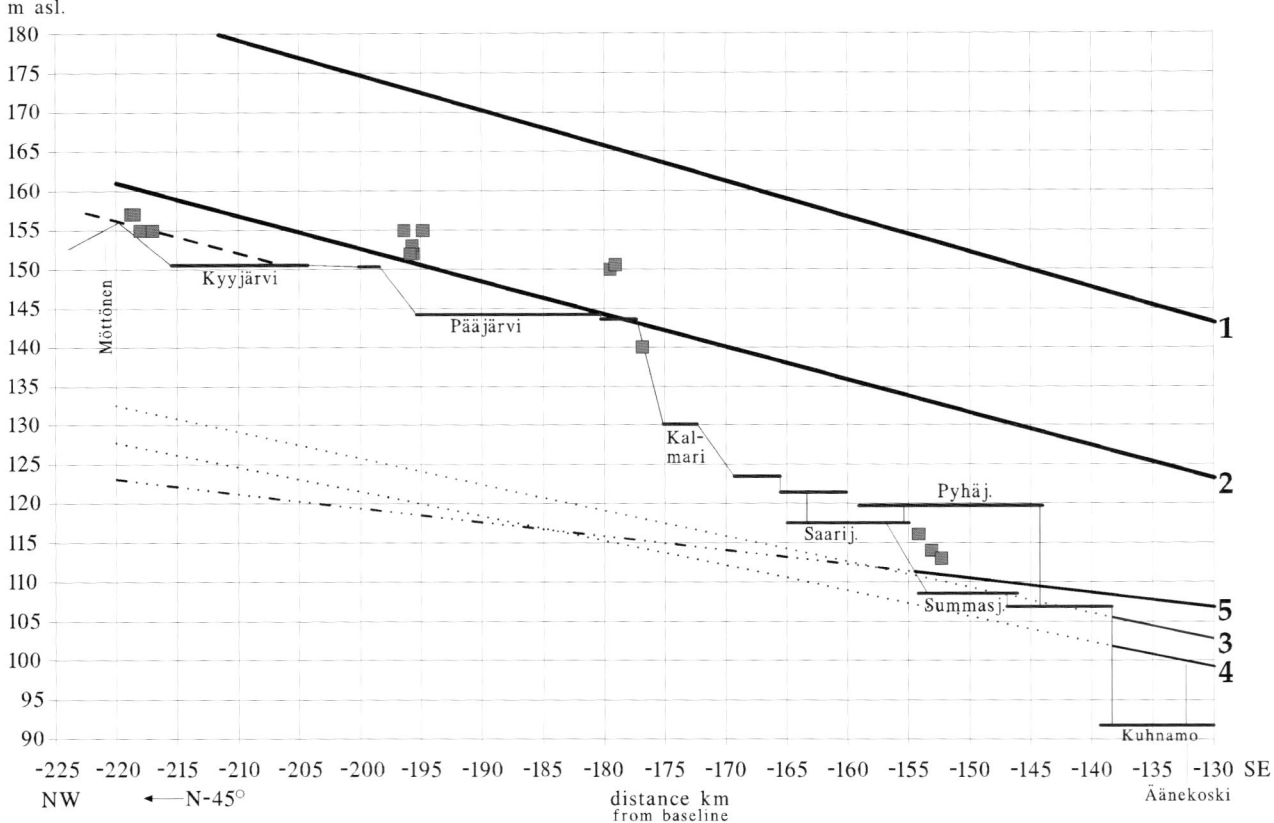

Figure 83.2 1) Ancylus ca. 8700 cal BC, 2) Ancylus IV/V ca. 8200 cal BC, 3) Ancylus V/VI ca. 6600 cal BC, 4) Isolation of Lake Keitele-Päijänne ca. 6700 cal BC, 5) Päijänne transgression maximum 5000 cal BC. — Present lake, n Dwelling site.

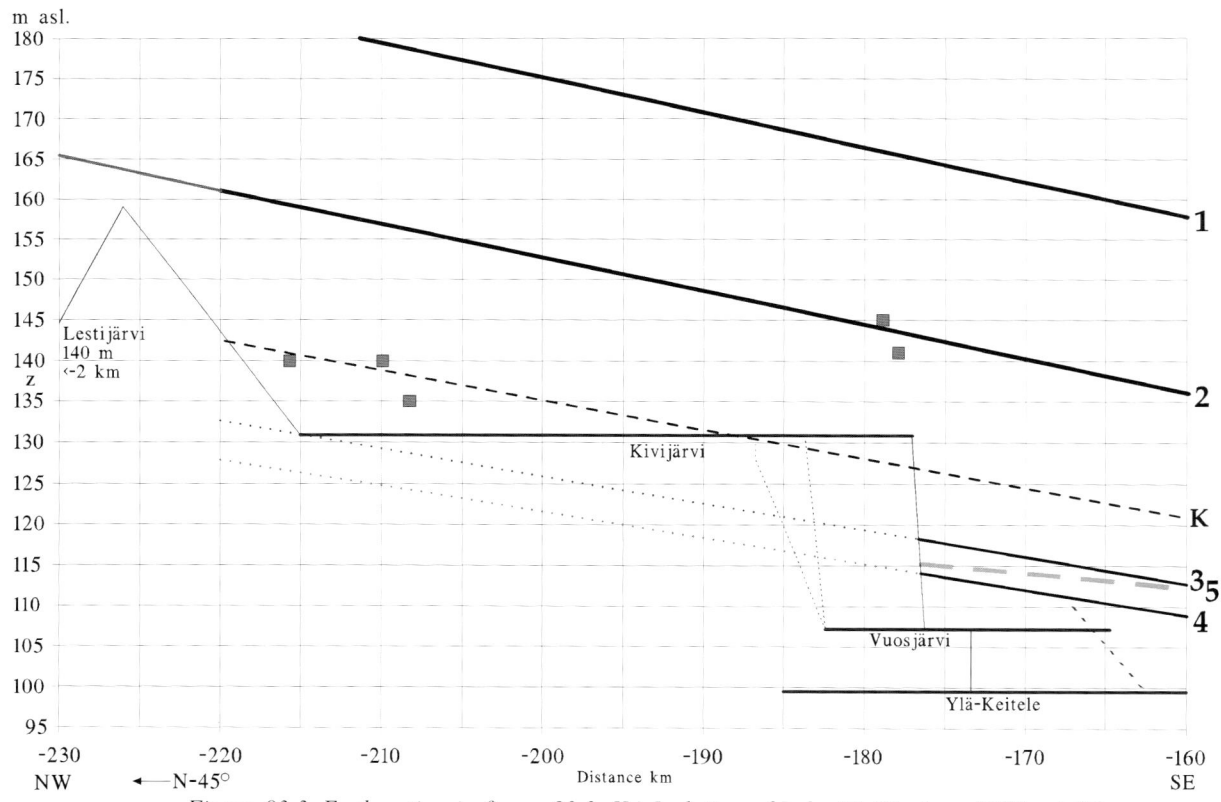

Figure 83.3 Explanation in figure 83.2. K) Isolation of Lake Kivijärvi ca. 7300 cal BC

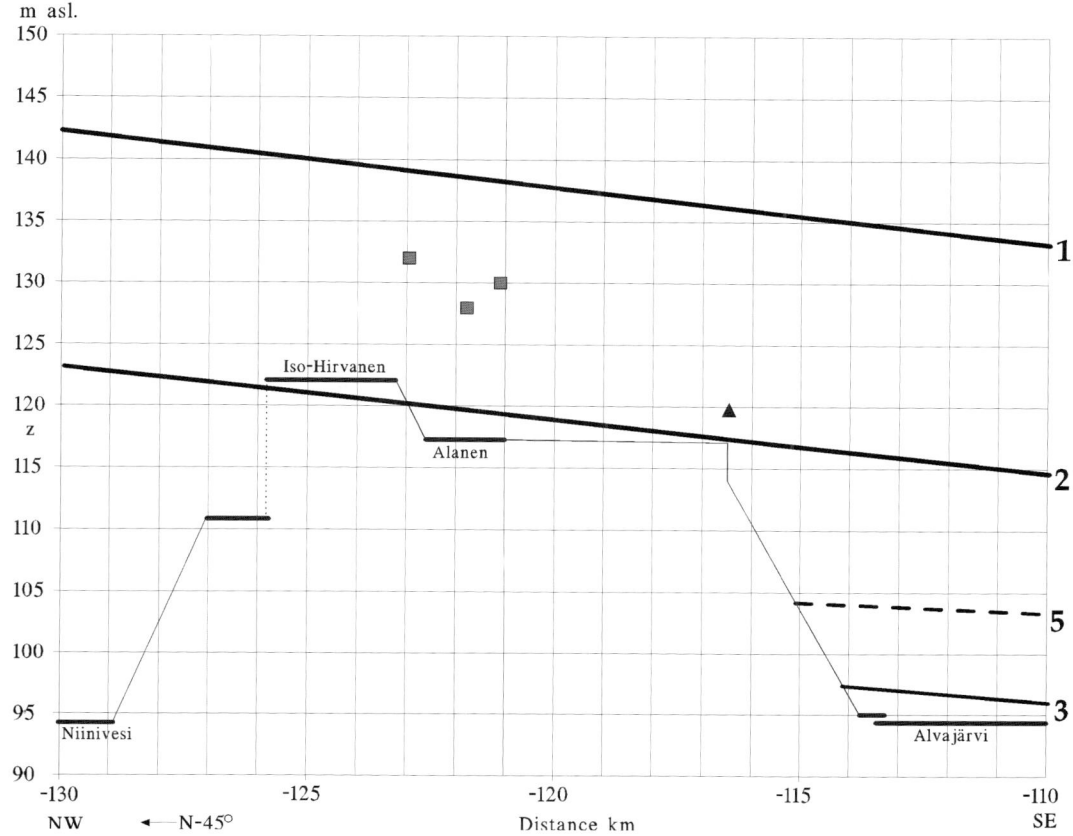

Figure 83.4 Explanation in figure 83.2.

Preboreal sites in Southeast Finland

Timo Jussila discovered a number of quartz bearing dwelling sites during the field survey and inventory work carried out in the summer of 1999 near the Russian border in Southeast Finland. The elevation of these sites in relation to the quaternary geological history of the Baltic suggested that these settlements date from the time of the Ancylus Lake (Figure 83.5). In the Finnish Stone Age material, apart from the classic Comb Ware contexts, flint was only known from the Mesolithic find at Ristola in Lahti. Now, flint artefacts together with flakes and debitage, have been found on four surveyed sites. Finland's Pre-Cambrian bedrock does not contain flint and erratic deposits of flint worn by the glaciations have not been found. Because of this, all flint found on prehistoric sites have, without exception, been interpreted as imported material. A total of 16 sites were discovered in this survey.

Unlike Central Finland, the history of the Ancylus Lake in Southeast Finland was transgressive. In the northern parts of the Gulf of Finland east of the first Salpausselkä zone the transgression has been observed in limnic strata and over the years it has also been possible to date it. By projecting elevation observations it is possible to follow the highest Ancylus boundary as far as the Karelian isthmus.

The shoreline displacement curve (A) in figure 83.6

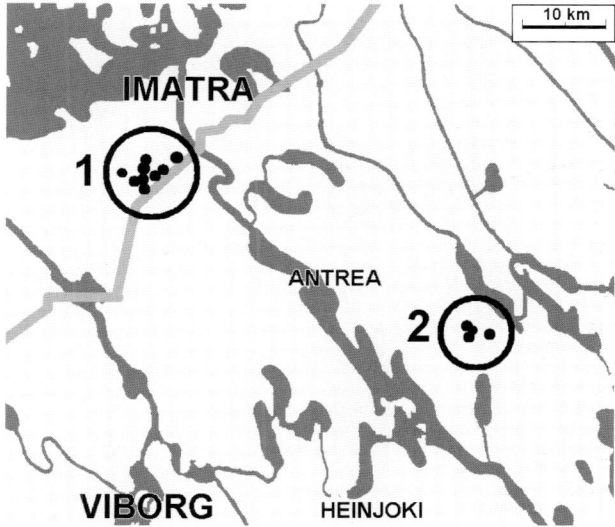

Figure 83.5 SW-Finland and northern part of Karelian Isthmus. 1. Imatra-Joutseno Kuurmanpohja, 2. Antrea net find site and Antrea dwelling sites.

presents an area near the Finnish-Russian border with the above sites placed on it. The starting point here is that sites above the maximum transgression culmination elevation of the Ancylus Lake were originally on the shores of the regressive Yoldia Sea. Curve A is based on

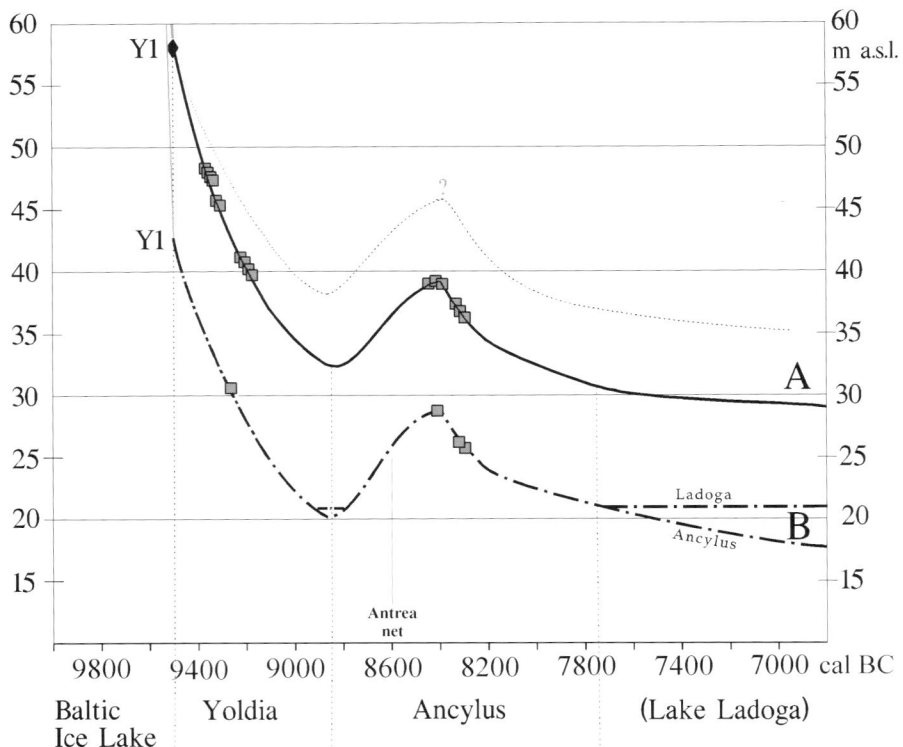

Figure 83.6 Shoreline displacement curves and dwelling sites at the Imatra-Joutseno Kuurmanpohja (A) and at the Antrea net find (B). (Modified from Saarnisto and al. 1996: Fig 2.)

Figure 83.7 Flint assemblage of the Preboreal Joutseno Saarenoja 2 site.

quaternary geological observations that were made in the 1930's, with revisions calculated according to later studies on the Postglacial period.

Curves A and B present the currently accepted conception of the history of the Baltic in Southeast Finland and on the Karelian Isthmus. Until only very recently this area was of secondary importance for research and shore displacement chronology and its dates are based on

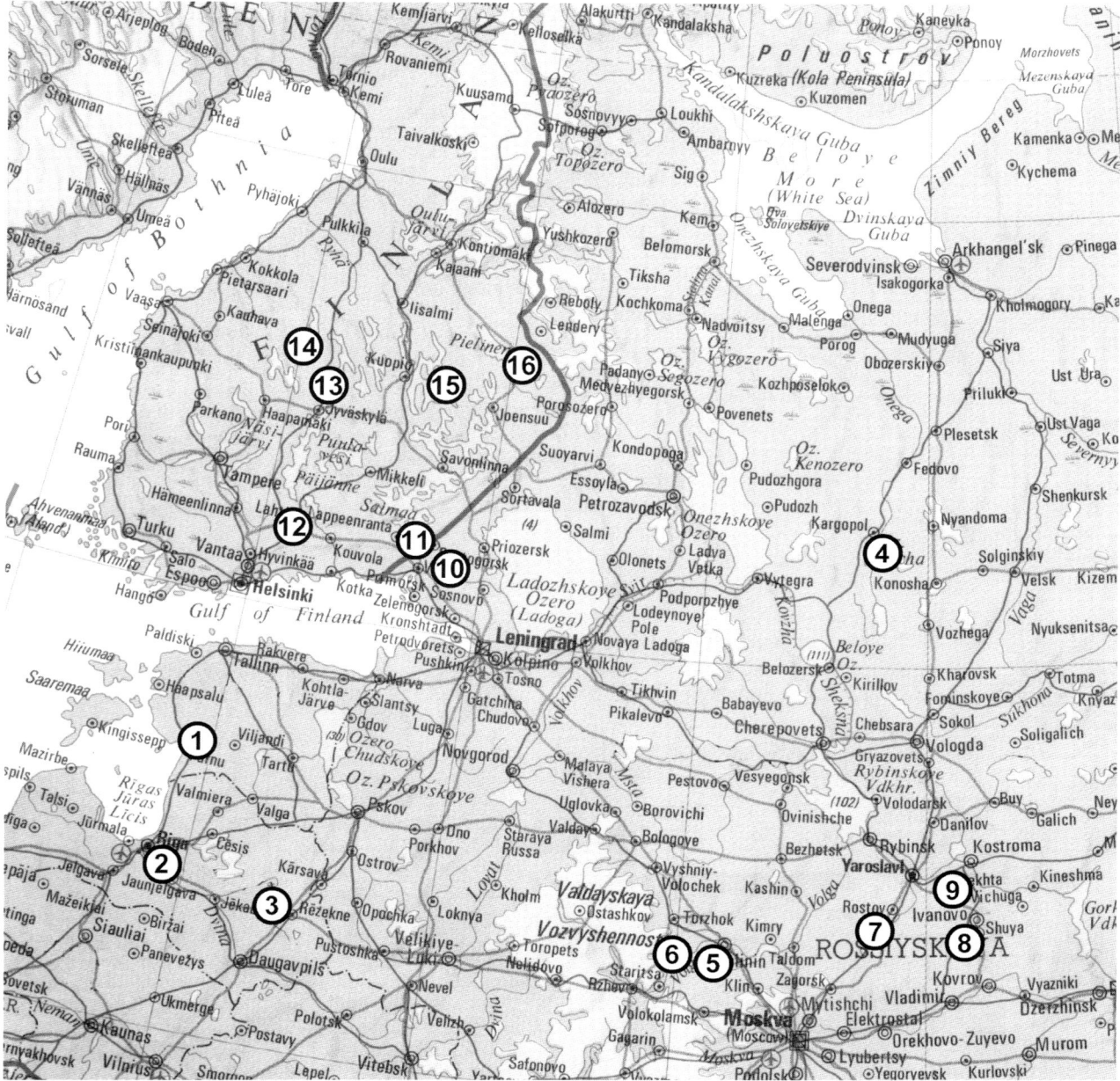

Figure 83.8 Preboreal Mesolithic sites in North Eastern Europe. 1) Pulli, 2) Laukskola, 3) Sulyagals, 4) Veretye, 5) Ozerki, 6) Butovo, 7) Ivanovskoje, 8) Saktysh 14, 9) Stanovoje, 10) Antrea sites, 11) Imatra-Joutseno Kuurmanpohja sites, 12) Ristola, 13) Laukaa, 14) Pylkönmäki-Karstula sites, 15) Tuusniemi, 16) Lieksa sites

radiocarbon dates from points further west and the projections of elevations in accordance with land upheaval. Recent stratigraphic studies have given indications that the Ancylus maximum may have extended to a higher level than previously presented. This level is shown with a dashed line in the diagram.

In the autumn of 2000 Jussila carried out a small trial excavation at the Saarenoja 2 site at Kuurnanpohja in Joutseno. This site is at an elevation of ca. 48 metres a.s.l. approximately 8 metres above the highest Ancylus shoreline. As flakes of flint were found when the site was surveyed, it was assumed to belong to the oldest succession of settlement of the Preboreal in the same way as the Ristola site in Lahti. (One of the objectives of fieldwork was to apply flotation methods to the soil of the occupation layer to obtain macrofossils suitable for AMS dating. At the time of writing the results are still forthcoming).

In addition to quartz, the site revealed an interesting flint assemblage that is significant for Finnish conditions (see Figure 83.7). A backed microblade from the site is similar to a specimen from Ristola in Lahti and is characteristic of the Butovo Culture in Russia. An interesting detail is also a tip fragment of a Shigir bone arrowhead found in connection with fragments of burnt bone.

The Antrea net

In the autumn of 2000 the archaeologists Timo Jussila and Tapani Rosted from Finland and Aivar Kriiska from Estonia carried out a brief expedition to the Riihimäki City Museum in the former Finnish parish of Antrea, present day Kamennogorsk on the Karelian Isthmus in Russia. The purpose of the expedition was to survey for sites of corresponding age in the vicinity of the famous Antrea net find site. The Antrea find is dated to the turn of the Preboreal and Boreal periods.

Conditions and available time, however, were not very favourable for the discovery of hitherto unknown sites, but nevertheless a few sites were found. The most precise maps of the area are from before the Second World War. Used together with a GPS receiver these maps provided relatively good assessments of site elevations. In accordance with research carried out at Heinjoki in Viipuri, the Ancylus Lake culmination, slightly earlier than the Antrea net, is at ca. 28 metres above sea level (Figure 83.6, curve B), (Saarnisto et al. 1999). Four dwelling sites were discovered in a former glacial delta approximately 5–8 kilometres northwest of the net site at the level of 25–30 metres (Figure 83.6).

These results are encouraging, which together with the finds from Imatra in Finland, would suggest that the Karelian Isthmus may yet reveal indications of Preboreal settlements older than the date given to the Antrea net.

Summary

Mesolithic studies in Finland have made considerable progress during the past few years. New research is currently under way and the coming years will either define more closely or revise the present results and views, which are tentative and in some respects superficial.

The Ristola site in Lahti predates the Ancylus Lake culmination, as does the flint bearing sites recently discovered in Southeast Finland. In Central Finland, the sites discovered in Laukaa are also chronologically comparable to the above, and accordingly human settlement would have extended considerably earlier than previously assumed to the northwest into the deglaciated areas.

Figure 83.8 shows the sites dated to the Preboreal Mesolithic in the northern regions of Eastern Europe. The oldest sites of the so called Butovo Culture are from 9500 cal BC (see Zhilin and Matiskainen in this volume). The extent of this cultural phase, to the southern parts of Finland, and its connections with the Pulli technocomplex were prime factors in the Postglacial colonisation of Finland.

Refrerences

Edgren, T. 1984. Kivikausi. *Suomen historia 1*. Helsinki.

Jussila, T. 2000. Pioneerit Keski-Suomessa ja Savossa. Rannansiirtymisajoitusmenetelmien perusteita ja vertailua. *Suomen arkeologinen seura. Muinaistutkija* 2000, No. 2, 13–28.

Luho, V. 1956. Die Askola-Kultur. Die frühmesolithische Zeit in Finnland. *Suomen muinaistoyhdistyksen aikakauskirja* 57. Helsinki.

Knutsson, K. 1998. Convention and Lithic Analysis. In: Holm, L. and Knutsson, K. (eds.) *Proceedings from the Third Flint Alternative Conference at Uppsala, Sweden, October 18–20. 1996*. Dept. of Archaeology and Ancient History, Uppsala University. Occasional Papers 16, 71–93. Uppsala.

Matiskainen, H. 1989. The Palaeolenvironment of Askola, Southern Finland. Mesolithic Settlement and Subsistence 10000–6000 b.p. *Iskos* 6, 1–97.

—— 1996. Discrepancies in Deglaciation Chronology and the Appearance of Man in Finland. In: Larsson, L. (ed.) *The Earliest Settlement in Scandinavia*. Acta Archaeologica Lundensia Series in 8 No 24, 251–262. Lund.

Saarnisto, M. 1971. The Upper Limit of the Flandrian Transgression of Lake Päijänne. *Commentationes Physico-Matematicae* 41, No 2, 149–170.

Saarnisto, M. and Grönlund, T. 1996. Shoreline displacement of Lake Ladoga – new data from Kilpolansaari. In: Simola, H. (ed.) *The First International Lake Ladoga Symposium: proceedings of the First International Lake Ladoga Symposium: ecological problems of Lake Ladoga, St. Petersburg, Russia, 22–26 November 1993*. Hydrobiologia 322, 205–215.

Saarnisto, M., Grönlund, T. and Ikonen, L. 1999. The Yoldia Sea – Lake Ladoga Connexion. Biostratigraphical Evidence from the Karelian Isthmus. In: Huurre, M. (ed.) *Dig it all*, 117–129. Jyväskylä.

Siiriäinen, A. 1981. Problems of the East Fennoscandian Mesolithic. *Finskt Museum* 1977, 5–31.

Miscellany

84. Butchering of Wild Boar (*Sus scrofa*) in the Mesolithic

Ola Magnell

The butchering of wild boar during the Mesolithic in South Scandinavia has been studied through the analysis of cut marks on osteological remains from the sites Ageröd I:HC, Ringsjöholm, Tågerup and Bökeberg III in Scania, Sweden. The study reveals relatively high frequencies of cut marks from dismembering and filleting. The distribution of cut marks indicates a uniformity in the dismembering of wild boar, but it also reveals that two different techniques were used in the skinning of the mandible. A low frequency of dismembering marks on the bones from the lower extremities indicates a less intensive utilisation of the wild boar at Ageröd I:HC. The analysis reveals differences in both the frequency of dismembering marks and the number of black burned bones between sites from Scania, Sweden and Zealand, Denmark. The different age structures of the bones from wild boar recovered from the sites in Scania and Zealand indicate a differentiated processing of juvenile and adult wild boar during the Mesolithic in South Scandinavia.

Introduction

Large quantities of osteological remains have been recovered from the excavations of Mesolithic sites in South Scandinavia during the last century. Bone assemblages contain information on various activities and aspects of Mesolithic society due to the fact that bones undergo a long drawn out process which starts with the hunt and is followed by the transportation of the carcass to the settlement, different stages of butchery, marrow fracturing and cooking and ends with the profane or ritual disposal of the bones. Apart from worked antlers, bones and teeth, osteological remains have rarely been used as sources of information concerning functional behaviour and cultural identity during the Mesolithic in South Scandinavia. An exception to the rule are the works by Nanna Noe-Nygaard (1977, 1995) and Tine Trolle-Lassen (1990). Osteological remains have otherwise mainly been used as ecological indicators through the studies of fauna or to determine economic resource exploitation and the season of occupation (Møhl 1970; Aaris-Sørensen 1976; Lepiksaar 1978; Møhl 1978; Lepiksaar 1982, Lepiksaar 1983; Jonsson 1988).

The large amount of studies on bone surface modification in zooarchaeology over the last thirty years have discussed the possibilities and the problems in the identification and the interpretation of different kinds of marks on bones. For research history, methodological and theoretical discussions about analysis of bone modifications I refer to the works by R. Lee Lyman (1987) and John W. Fisher Jr. (1996) which give a great survey of the subject. Cultural differences in butchery among the Native American tribes on the Plains in North America, between the Masai, Kalenjin and Akamba in Kenya and the Saami in Scandinavia have been noted in ethnographical sources (Manker 1936:40; Lyman 1987:287 p). Lewis Binford states that variation in butchery practices also could be explained by variations in human adaptations to different natural settings (Binford 1978:47). In his studies of the Nunamiut, differences in the butchery of the caribou (*Rangifer tarandus*) was shown, depending on whether the carcasses are stiff or flexible in the joints and further, in the marrow fracturing of bones on hunting stands and on residential campsites (Binford 1981:109 pp). The studies of the marrow fracturing patterns of bones from sites in South Scandinavia and Star Carr, England by Nanna Noe-Nygaard followed by others have shown that different fracturing techniques were used during the Mesolithic (Noe-Nygaard 1977; Trolle-Lassen 1990:24 pp; Lövgren 1998).

This study is an effort to investigate the possibilities of tracing patterns in the butchering of wild boar (*Sus scrofa*) by analysis of bones from different Mesolithic sites in South Scandinavia. Are eventual differences in the butchering of wild boar reflected in bone modifications on osteological remains from different sites? If so, could these differences be explained as cultural expressions or functional adaptations to various natural settings? The reason for studying bones from wild boar is that this species is well represented in osteological remains from Mesolithic sites in South Scandinavia (Jonsson 1988:57; Noe-Nygaard 1995:76 pp; Rowley-Conwy 1999:88). This analysis is also an effort to further study the processing of wild boar during the Mesolithic in South Scandinavia, since most previous analyses of bone modifications only have dealt with or have been focused on the red deer (*Cervus elaphus*) (Noe-Nygaard 1977, 1995; Trolle-Lassen 1990; Magnell 1995; Lövgren 1998).

Material

The material in this study has been chosen to fulfil different criteria. One of the most important factors in analysis of butchering patterns are well preserved osteological remains with bone surfaces relatively little altered by weathering and other processes. If this criteria is not fulfilled it will be impossible to give a representative identification and quantification of the bone modifications. It is also vital to have relatively large quantities of bones to make it possible to observe patterns in the butchering of different anatomical regions.

There are several variables which affect the butchering technique such as prey animals, number of killed animals, environment, technology, cooking, food preservation and ethnicity (Lyman 1987:253). This study focuses on detecting variation in the butchering techniques due to cultural factors such as tradition or preparation and consumption. The material in this study has been chosen to exclude at least some of the other natural variables. While only bones from wild boar are studied, any variations due to taxonomic differences in the butchery could be excluded. On the sites in this study, a similar kind of cutting tools, blades and flakes of flint have been used (Althin 1954:224 pp; Ericsson and Lindblad 1995: 28; Sjöström 1998:8; Knarrström 2000:44 pp). This also excludes any technological explanations of variations in the butchery.

Bones from wild boar excavated at the four sites Ageröd I:HC (upper and white layer), Ringsjöholm, Tågerup (Kongemose layers) and Bökeberg III from Scania, southern Sweden, have been analysed in this study (Figure 84.1). The osteological remains from these sites are well preserved with the majority of bones in weathering category 2, as described by Noe-Nygaard (1995: 69). Relatively large quantities of bones from wild boar have also been recovered from these sites and traces of different taphonomic processes on the bones such as trampling and gnawing by carnivores (probably dogs) are equivalent in the bone assemblages (Figure 84.2).

Method

Reconstruction of the butchering process is based on the analysis of bone surface modifications, mainly cut marks. By comparing the location of cut marks to the anatomy of animals it is often possible to identify marks from skinning, filleting or dismembering (Binford 1981:106 pp). Experimental butchering studies are also useful to test interpretations of functions behind the location of cut marks and to set up reference collections over the

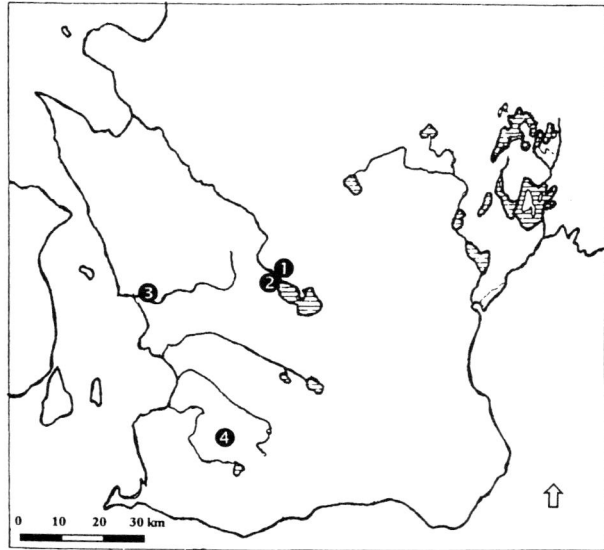

Figure 84.1 Map showing Scania, southern Sweden and the location of the sites in this study. 1. Ageröd I:HC, 2. Ringsjöholm, 3. Tågerup, 4. Bökeberg III.

morphology of cut marks from stone tools. Butchering experiments of skulls and lower extremities from wild boar have been carried out to test the interpretations of cut marks. My experience from experimental butchering of two roe deer (*Capreolus capreolus*), an animal with anatomical similarities to the wild boar, has also been useful in this study (Eriksson *et al.* 2000).

Trampling and carnivore gnawing are taphonomic processes, which sometimes leave marks on bones very similar to cut marks by stone tools (Binford 1981:46; Behrensmayer *et al.* 1986; Fiorillo 1989). Due to this, it is necessary to in detail study each mark found on a bone. By examining the shape and the morphology of the mark under microscope it is often possible to identify the causing agent (Binford 1981:169; Shipman and Rose 1983:81; Olsen and Shipman 1988:549 pp; Noe-Nygaard 1995:187). A cut mark is defined as an elongated striation with a v-formed cross-section with flat sides (Figure 84.3) (Fisher 1995:12; Noe-Nygaard 1995:180 p; Blumenschine *et al.* 1996:496).

Tooth scratches have, compared to cut marks, a u-formed cross-section and a high breadth:depth ratio (Blumenschine *et al.* 1996:496). Another differential characteristic is that flint tools cut into the protrusions of the bone and skip small depressions while the teeth of gnawing carnivores follow the curvature of the bones also across uneven surfaces (Fisher 1996:39). Striations on bones from trampling or other kinds of sedimentary abrasion, are usually shallow compared to cut marks and show a high, random variation in width and orientation. Cut marks have a more regular shape and usually are found in distinct clusters, orientated in one direction (Olsen and Shipman 1988:550 p).

All cut marks in this study have been analysed with an

	Ageröd I:HC	Ringsjöholm	Tågerup	Bökeberg III
Archaeological dating	Late Maglemose-Early Kongemose	Late Maglemose-Early Kongemose	Kongemose	Late Kongemose-Early Ertebølle
^{14}C dating, uncalibrated BP	7910–7220	7910–7150	8095–6770	6650–6400 6150–5800
Site character	Settlement in site complex	Base camp?	Base camp in site complex	Hunting camp
Minimal period of occupation	Autumn* (October-December)	Summer-winter (July-March)	Summer-autumn (June-November)	Late summer-winter (August-March)
Frequency of wild boar of mammal remains (NISP)	25%	29%	31%	12%
NISP / MNI from wild boar	667/24	632/14	490/15	206/9
NISP in this study (teeth and weathered bones excluded)	537	310	283	163
Frequency of bones with tooth marks from carnivores	11%	2%	9%	9%

*Figure 84.2 Description of sites and osteological remains used in the analysis. NISP= number of identified specimens (Payne 1975). MNI= minimal number of individuals (Casteel and Grayson 1977). The figure is based on following literature; Ageröd I:HC (Larsson 1978), Ringsjöholm (Sjöström 1997; Jansson et al. 1998), Tågerup (Karsten and Knarrström 1999:202 pp; Eriksson and Magnell 2001a), Bökeberg III (Regnell et al. 1996; Eriksson and Magnell 2001b). *Revision of previous interpretations by the author based on ageing of juveniles (unpublished data).*

Figure 84.3 Cut mark on a femur fragment of wild boar from the Ringsjöholm site. Left, 7x magnification, and right, 40x magnification. Photo by Ola Magnell.

optical stereomicroscope (7–40x) to detect and examine the morphology of the cut marks. The locations of the cut marks on the bones have been documented by drawings. Also other kinds of modifications such as tooth marks, trampling and conchoidal flake scars have been documented. Presented figures of butchering patterns are syntheses of cut marks from several bones. Quantifications of cut marks are only based on bone fragments with an intact surface, since weathering may have eliminated the bone modifications on less preserved fragments (White 1992:118). The calculation of frequency of cut marks from filleting and dismembering is in a similar way only based on bone fragments where the different types of marks are expected to be found. For instance, filleting marks are not normally found on carpal or tarsal bones and dismembering marks do not occur on long bone diaphyses. The reason for excluding certain bone fragments from the quantification is to consider that differences of bone element representation in the compared assemblages could result in distorted frequencies of filleting and dismembering marks. The quantification of dismembering is based on the number of bone fragments with cut marks compared to the total amount of bone fragments from a specific joint. All bones from each joint have been included in the quantification, i.e. the elbow consists of the distal humeri, the proximal radii and ulna; the wrist of the distal radii and ulna, the carpals and the proximal metacarpals.

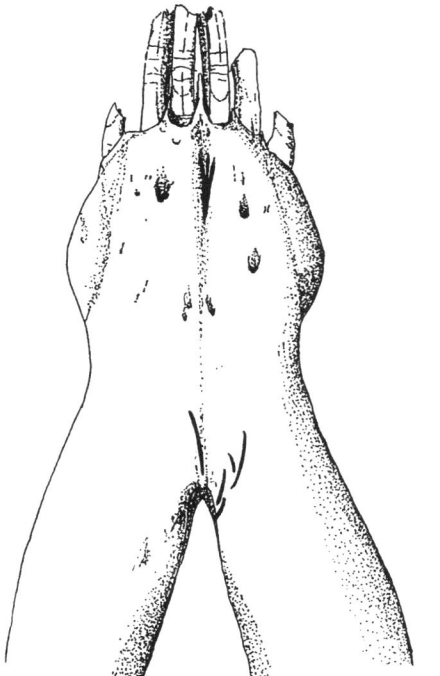
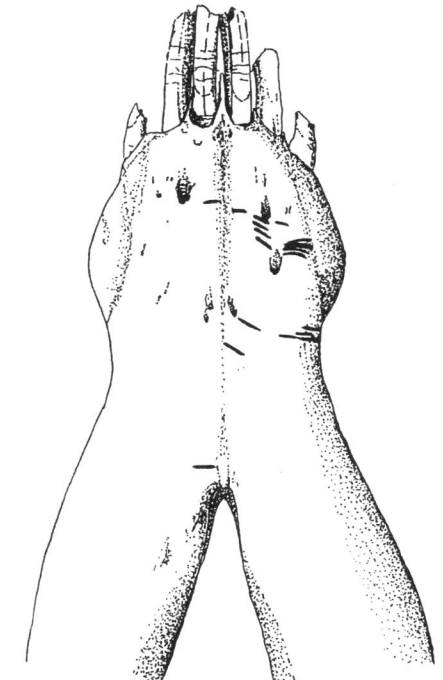

Figure 84.4a Skinning marks with an oral-aboral direction on mandibles of wild boar from Ageröd I:HC and Tågerup. Drawing by Patrik Magnell. Scale 1:2.

Figure 84.4b Transversal cut marks from skinning on the symphysis of the mandibles of wild boar from Ageröd I:HC and Ringsjöholm. Note the concentration of cut marks to the left half of the mandible, which probably is the result of right-handed butchers pulling the skin with their left hand while cutting with their right hand. Drawing by Patrik Magnell. Scale 1:2.

Skinning

Cut marks from skinning are only found in the region of the skeleton which has thin layers of tissue between the bone and the skin. Thus, skinning marks are located to the cranium and the lower extremities (Binford 1981:106 p; Noe-Nygaard 1995:182 p). Cut marks from the skinning of wild boar have been identified on seven mandibles from these four sites and on a fifth metacarpal from Ageröd I:HC. The skinning marks on the mandibles are found in the area of the symphysis. From this part of the mandible 29% of the fragments have cut marks. The orientation of cut marks on the symphysis seems to indicate two different techniques in skinning. Cut marks with an oral-aboral orientation on the symphysis (Figure 84.4a) most likely originate from the making of a ventral cut along the carcass from the tip of the lower jaw to the anus during the skinning. Transversal skinning marks on the mandible indicate that the skin has been forced in a aboral/nuchal-oral/nasal direction over the cranium (Figure 84.4b), probably while the carcass was hanging in a vertical position. Skinning experiments by the author on heads from wild boar confirm variations in the orientation of cut marks depending on whether the skin was forced over the cranium from the back of the skull or cut from the ventral side laying on its forehead.

The presence of cut marks from both skinning techniques on mandibles from one site, Ageröd I:HC, indicate a functional explanation rather than cultural to the use of two different skinning techniques. Oral-aboral oriented cut marks on mandibles may represent animals, which have been butchered at the kill site and skinned lying on their backs on the ground. Mandibles of wild boar with transverse cuts may represent carcasses, which have been skinned, hanging in their Achilles' tendon, transported in one piece to the settlement or to a place suitable for butchering. Cut marks have been observed on the dorsal part of the *processus calcanei* on a calcaneus from Ringsjöholm, which may originate from the hanging of a wild boar in its Achilles' tendon. Cut marks with a similar location are described in studies of the butchering among the Nunamiut. The cut marks have been caused while making a cut through the tissue between the tibia and the calcaneus to insert a rope to hang carcasses in their Achilles' tendon (Binford 1981:119 p).

Dismembering

Cut marks from the dismembering have been observed on 7–16% of the bone fragments from joints of wild boar from the four sites. It is considered difficult to interpret frequency of cut marks (Fisher 1996:55). On bones from an ethnoarchaeological context, the frequency of cut marks often vary between 16–28%. These figures are assumed to be rather high because metal tools are used in these cultures and the use of metal tools in butchering is

Butchering of Wild Boar (Sus scrofa) in the Mesolithic

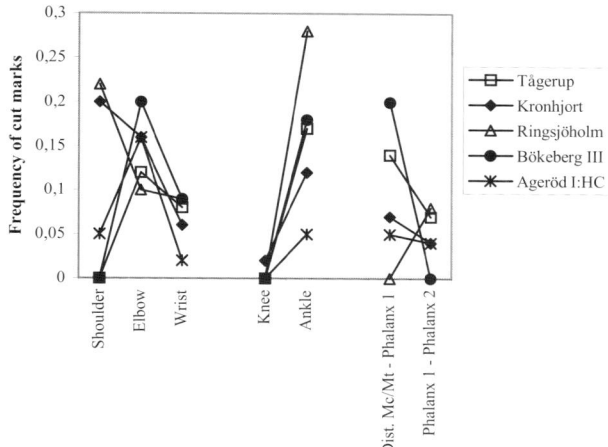

Figure 84.5 Frequency of cut marks from dismembering of the limbs of wild boar on four Mesolithic sites from Scania, Sweden. For quantification see Methods.

supposed to generate more cut marks than the use of stone tools (Lyman 1987:267). When interpreting quantification's of cut marks, it is important to consider different facts. First, butchering does not always leave cut marks on the bones, since soft tissue such as periosteum may protect the tools from getting in contact with the bone (Lyman 1987:261; Fisher 1996:17). Thus, bones without cut marks could have been dismembered even if there are no marks on the bones. Second, dismembering does not usually leave cut marks on all of the bones in a joint. For example, if a wrist is dismembered between the distal radii and the proximal carpals, no cut marks will be caused on the distal carpals or the proximal metacarpals.

The relatively frequent occurrence of cut marks from the dismembering on bones from almost all joints of the wild boar, indicates an intensive processing of the carcasses at these four sites. The cut marks reveal a "butchering scheme" where the following anatomical regions are dismembered; the mandible from the skull, the head from the trunk by the atlas, the neck by the fifth or sixth cervical vertebrate, the ribs from the trunk, the vertebral column joined with sacrum from the pelvis and all of the joints in the extremities, also between the phalanges. The dismembering of the wild boar represents, most likely, both disarticulation of carcasses on kill sites to enable transport to the settlement and further processing before cooking and marrow fracturing.

The quantification of dismembering marks varies a lot between different anatomical regions of the wild boar (Figure 84.5). Most of the variation in the frequency of dismembering marks probably reflect how easily different joints are dismembered without cutting in bone. In enclosed and tight fitted joints like the elbow, cut marks are more common than in the more open joints as the knee (Figure 84.5). No distinct chop marks associated to dismembering, except one on a proximal tibia from Ageröd I:HC, have been observed on the bones. This means that cutting tools rather than axes and adzes have been used during the butchering of wild boar on these sites.

There seems to be no difference in the butchering techniques used on the four sites. The locations of the cut marks indicate a rather systematic dismembering. Cut marks on the atlas show that the skull of wild boar in all cases was cut ventrally from the trunk. On the elbow most of the cut marks are found on the medial (54%) and the cranial/dorsal (25%) parts of the bones (Figure 84.6). The location of the butchering marks probably represents that the elbow regularly was dismembered from the medial and the cranial/dorsal side of the forelimbs. The concentration of cut marks to the dorsal (51%) and the medial (34%) side of the ankle indicates the dismembering pattern of this joint. The systematic dismembering is explained by the anatomy of the animal and the use of the same efficient and functional butchery technique with similar kinds of flint tools on these four sites.

The frequency of dismembering marks is significantly different between the four sites ($\chi^2_3=29,77$, $\alpha=0,05$) Ageröd I:HC differs from the other sites by having a lower frequency of dismembering marks (Figure 84.7). How could this less intensive disarticulation be explained? In Figure 84.5, it is evident that it is the dismembering of the wrist, the ankle and the phalanxes, which is low at Ageröd I:HC. It seems as though the lower extremities of the wild boar were less intensively dismembered at this site. This could be an indication of more favourable dietary conditions at Ageröd I:HC than at the other sites, resulting in a lower level of utilisation of the wild boar and a more frequent disposal of the lower extremities unprocessed.

The marrow fracturing of the limb bones also confirms this interpretation. At these four sites, all the long bones of wild boar have systematically been fractured for the utilisation of the marrow as is the common case with other large mammals on Mesolithic sites in South Scandinavia (Noe-Nygaard 1977; Trolle-Lassen 1990:24 p; Lövgren 1998). Ageröd I:HC is the only one of the four sites where unbroken metacarpals and metatarsals have been recovered. Proximal phalanges are also less frequently broken at Ageröd I:HC than at the other sites. Totally 91% of the metapodials III/IV and 33% of the proximal phalanges III/IV at Ageröd I:HC have been marrow fractured. Out of the proximal phalanges III/IV, 83% from Ringsjöholm and all from Tågerup and Bökeberg III have been broken for marrow. The presence of conchoidal flake scars and percussion striations from impacts of hammer stones indicates that the primary fracturing of the bones is caused by humans. The equal frequency of tooth marks from carnivores on the bones from the sites excludes differences in bone fragmentation due to the gnawing of dogs (Figure 84.2).

The relatively high frequency of dismembering marks on bones from these four sites from Scania differ from the butchering of wild boar on the sites Præstelyng and Kongemose from Zealand, Denmark. Dismembering

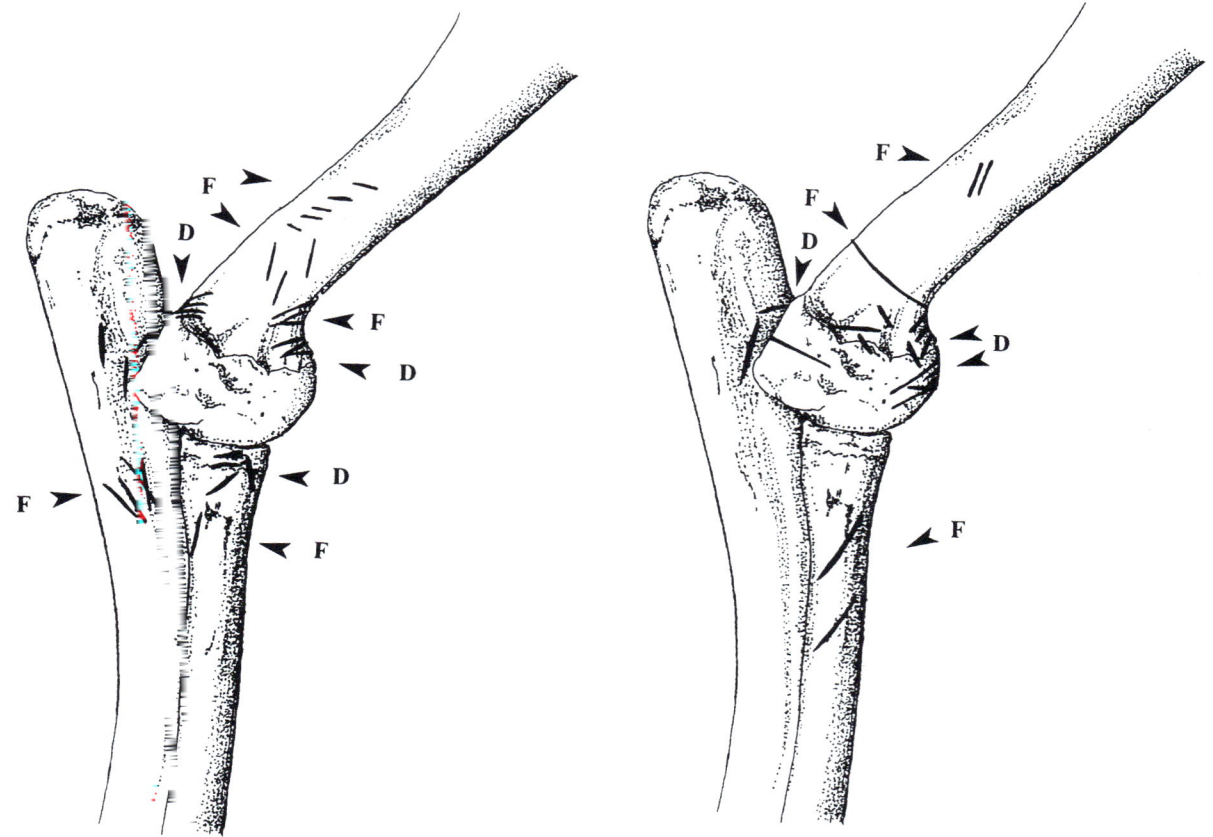

Figure 84.6 Butchering marks on bones of the medial elbow of wild boar from Ageröd I:HC (left) and Tågerup (right). D= dismembering marks, F= filleting marks. Drawings by Patrik Magnell. Scale 1:2.

	Total frequency of cut marks	Frequency of filleting marks	Frequency of dismembering marks
Ageröd I:HC	10% (n=55)	10% (n=35)	7% (n=28)
Ringsjöholm	22% (n=65)	18% (n=33)	16% (n=35)
Tågerup	15% (n=43)	10% (n=15)	15% (n=32)
Bökeberg III	14% (n=23)	12% (n=11)	12% (n=11)

Figure 84.7 Frequencies of cut marks on bones of wild boar from four Mesolithic sites in Scania, Sweden.

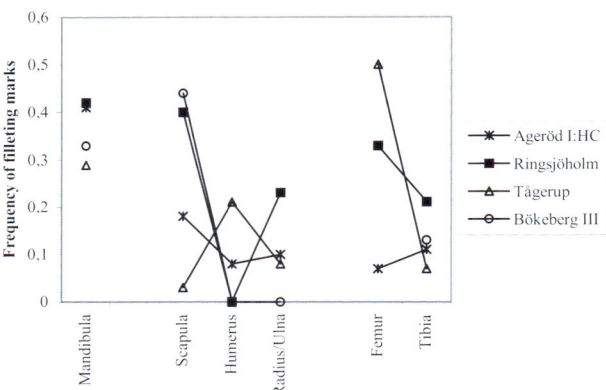

Figure 84.8 Frequency of cut marks from filleting of meat on bones of wild boar from four Mesolithic sites in Scania, Sweden.

marks on bones from wild boar are very few on these two Danish sites. A high percentage of black burned bones have been interpreted as if the wild boar had been roasted whole, which also explains the low frequency of cut marks (Noe-Nygaard 1995 222). Could this be an indication of different regional traditions in the processing of wild boar in Zealand and Scania during the Mesolithic? It could however have an alternative explanation. Most of the wild boar bones from the two Danish sites derive from juveniles, while the bones from the four sites in Scania mainly are from adult individuals. The differences in processing of wild boar could be the result of a tradition during the Mesolithic in South Scandinavia of roasting piglets over fire and filleting meat from the bones of the adult individuals before cooking. Age structure and number of bones with black burned areas on osteological remains of wild boar from sites from Scania support this interpretation. No black burned bones have been identified from Ringsjöholm and Bökeberg III and only one from Ageröd I:HC, while 12 or 4% of the bones of wild boar from Tågerup have traces of slight burning. Bones and teeth of juvenile wild boar are also more frequently represented in

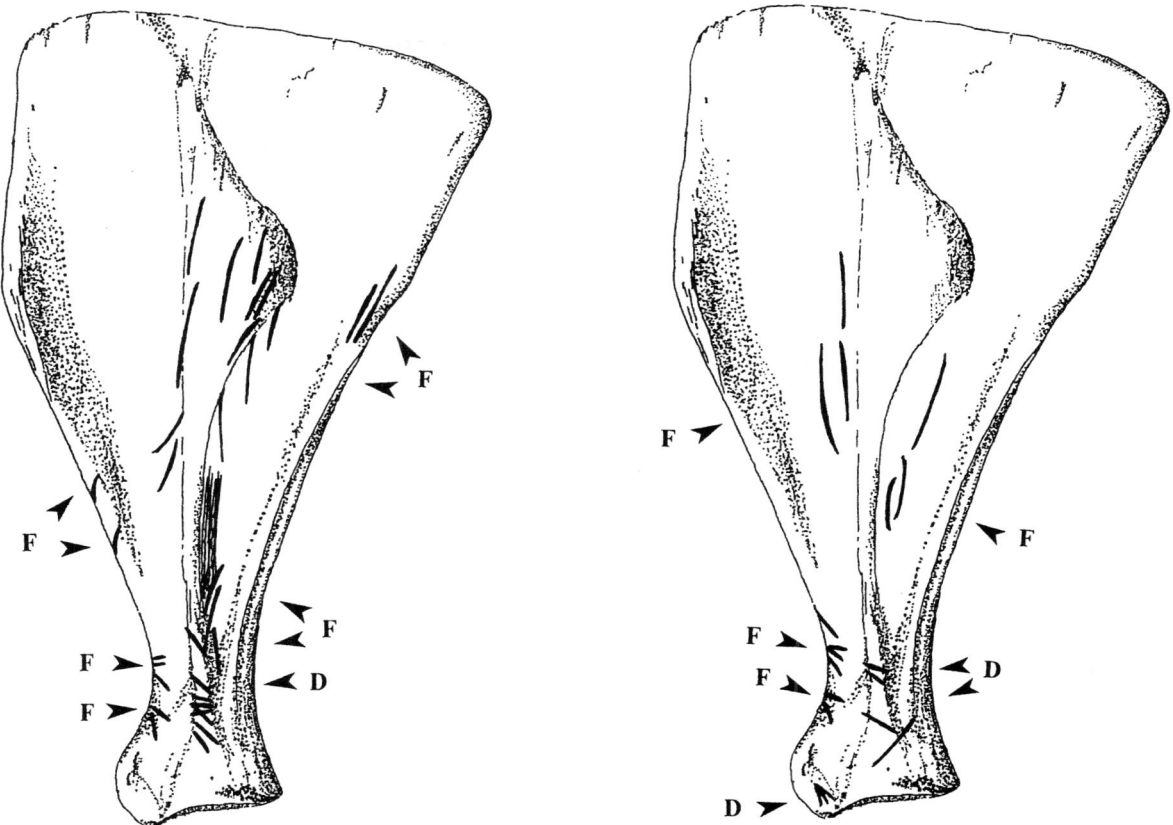

Figure 84.9 Filleting marks on scapulae of wild boar from Ageröd I:HC (left) and Ringsjöholm (right). D= dismembering marks, F= filleting marks. Drawings by Patrik Magnell. Scale 1:2.

the osteological remains from Tågerup, compared to the other three sites (Jansson *et al.* 1998:48 p; Eriksson and Magnell 2001a; Eriksson and Magnell 2001b).

Filleting

Cut marks from the filleting of meat also occur rather frequently on the bones from wild boar from these four sites (Figure 84.7). Meat was probably filleted to minimise the volume to make the cooking more effective and probably also to clean the bones before marrow fracturing. Meat may also have been stripped from the bones in preparation for storage, such as drying and smoking.

Filleting marks have been identified on bone fragments from the mandible, the axial skeleton (cervical and thoracic vertebrae, ribs and pelvis), as well as on the limb bones. The mandible and the scapula are the elements where cut marks from filleting are most commonly found (Figure 84.8). The filleting marks on the mandible are concentrated to the lateral and medial part of *angulus mandibulae* and originate from cutting loose the lateral jaw muscles (*musculus masseter*) respectively the tongue along with the medial jaw muscles. Cut marks from filleting on the scapula are found on both the lateral and the medial surfaces concentrated to the *spina scapulae* and the *margo cranialis/caudalis* (Figure 84.9).

Cut marks from filleting are more frequently found on scapulae from Ringsjöholm and Bökeberg III than on the same element from the other two sites (Figure 84.8). One explanation to this could be that the shoulder at these sites more often was stripped from the scapula during the preparation for storage by smoking and drying. It is interesting to notice that the high frequency of filleting marks, possible associated with the preservation of meat, coincides with the sites with evidence of winter occupation (Figure 84.2). Preservation of meat by drying is favoured in temperatures below 15°C since the microbiological activity is reduced at lower temperatures (Noe-Nygaard 1995:241). A high frequency of longitudinal cut marks on scapulae is typical for sites where meat is dried by the Nunamiut (Binford 1981:98).

The filleting marks on the long bones of the limb appear scattered on the diaphyses and no specific pattern in the orientation and the location of the cut marks has been identified. Also, there is no specific trend in the frequency of the filleting marks on the long bones (Figure 84.8). The large variation of the frequency of filleting marks on the femur is probably due to random factors. The reason to this is that bone fragments from the femur of wild boar are poorly represented in the studied materials, as the case is with several other Mesolithic sites in South Scandinavia. The low presentation of femurs has been interpreted to be the result of transport of the upper hindlimbs from the sites (Noe-Nygaard 1995:222; Rowley-Conwy 1999:94 p).

Conclusions

Butchering marks reveal an intense utilisation of the wild boar during the Mesolithic in South Scandinavia. The location of the cut marks on the bones seems to follow specific patterns, which are indicating a developed tradition in the butchery and the processing of wild boar. The dismembering of the wild boar has been accomplished in a systematic manner and a relatively high frequency of cut marks from filleting indicates that meat usually was stripped from the bones in the preparation for consumption or preservation processes.

Even if no distinct regional or site specific butchering patterns have been identified, variations in the processing of wild boar are evident. Cut marks on mandibles indicate that the wild boar either was skinned lying on the ground or hanging in a vertical position. At Ageröd I:HC, a less intensive utilisation of the wild boar has resulted in a more frequent disposal of the lower extremities unprocessed. The frequency of filleting marks is high on scapulae from the sites Ringsjöholm and Bökeberg III, which may indicate a more intensive stripping of meat during the preparation for storage at settlements occupied during the winter. The low frequency of cut marks from the dismembering and the large amount of black burned bones from juvenile wild boars on two Danish sites compared to the frequent dismembered bones of adult individuals on the sites from Scania, indicates variations in the processing of the wild boar. Piglets have probably more often been roasted over fire, while the meat from the adult wild boar has been filleted before cooking during the Mesolithic in South Scandinavia.

This study reveals that by analysing bone modifications, it is possible to study variations in the butchery during the prehistoric past. To which extent butchery patterns are reflections of the anatomy of the studied animal, and how to interpret the cultural aspect of the location, the orientation and the frequency of cut marks, is still problematic. The similarities of the butchering of wild boar at the four sites may be reflections of a butchery tradition at settlements dated to the Kongemose Culture in the region of western/central Scania as well as the result of a general and functional butchering representing a similar carcass exploitation at these sites. By further studies of butchering marks on osteological remains from Mesolithic sites in South Scandinavia it will probably be possible to confirm or reject the interpretations in this paper. A development of the methodology in studies of bone modifications, standardisation of analysis and further studies will make it possible to "decode" more of the marks found on bones after butchery and processing of the wild boar and other animals during the Mesolithic.

Acknowledgements

Thanks to Elisabeth Iregren for comments on the manuscript. Patrik Magnell deserve thanks for the drawings. I am also grateful to Ylva Olsson for being helpful during my visits to the collections of LUHM (the Historical Museum of the University of Lund) and to Per-Ola Andersson, Sjunkaröds viltslakteri, for providing me with skulls and other parts of the wild boar for experimental butchering.

References

Aaris-Sørensen, K. 1976. Zoological Investigation of the Bone Material from Sværdborg I – 1943. In: Henriksen, B. *Sværdborg I, Excavations 1943–44. A Settlement of the Maglemose Culture*, 137–148. København.

Althin, C-A. 1954. *The Chronology of the Stone Age Settlement of Scania, Sweden. I.* Acta Archaeologica Lundensia. Series in 4. No. 12. Lund.

Behrensmeyer, A.K., Gordon, K.D. and Yanagi, G.T. 1986. Trampling as a Cause of Bone Surface Damage and Pseudo-Cutmarks. *Nature* 319, 768–771.

Binford, L.S. 1978. *Nunamiut Ethnoarchaeology.* New York.

—— 1981. *Bones, Ancient Men and Modern Myths.* New York.

Blumenschine, R.J., Marean, C.W. and Capaldo, D.C. 1996. Blind Tests of Interanalyst Correspondence Accuracy in the Identification of Cut Marks, Percussion Marks and Carnivore Tooth Marks on Bone Surfaces. *Journal of Archaeological Science* 23, 493–507.

Casteel, R.W. and Grayson, D.K. 1977. Terminological Problems in Quantitative Faunal Analysis. *World Archaeology* 9, 235–242.

Ericsson, C. and Lindblad, J. 1995. *I vått och torrt på Bökeberg III. En studie baserad på artefakter från en mesolitisk inlandsboplats i Skåne.* Seminar paper in Archaeology. Institute of Archaeology, University of Lund. Lund.

Eriksson, M., Hanlon, C., Hårdhe, A., Lövgren, A-K. and Magnell, O. 2000. *Styckning och tillvaratagande av rådjur (Capreolus capreolus) med mesolitiska tekniker. Analyser av slaktspår, märgklyvning och slitspår på flintredskap.* Experiment vid Historisk-arkæologisk Forsøgscenter Lejre 12–16 juli 1999. HAF 18/99. Unpublished.

Eriksson, M. and Magnell, O. 2001a. Det djuriska Tågerup. Nya rön kring Kongemose- och Ertebøllekulturens jakt och fiske. In: Karsten, P. and Knarrström, B (eds.) *Tågerup. Specialstudier.* Skånska spår. Arkeologi längs västkustbanan. Riksantikvarieämbetet avdelningen för arkeologiska undersökningar, 156–237. Lund.

—— 2001b. Jakt och slakt. In: Karsten, P. (ed.) *Dansarna från Bökeberg. Om jakt, ritualer och inlandsbosättning vid jägarstenålderns slut.* Riksantikvarieämbetet avdelningen för arkeologiska undersökningar. Skrifter 37, 49–77. Lund.

Fisher, J.W.Jr. 1995. Bone Surface Modifications. *Journal of Archaeological Method and Theory* 2, 7–68.

Fiorillo, A.R. 1989. An Experimental Study of Trampling: Implications for the Fossil Record. In: Bonnichsen, R. and Sorg, M.H. (eds.) *Bone Modification*, 61–71. Orono.

Janson, P., Knöös, S., Larsson, F., Lövgren, A-K., Mårtensson, J. and Rommedahl, H. 1998. *Osteologisk analys av den mesolitiska lokalen Ringsjöholm.* Seminar paper in Historical Osteology. Institute of Archaeology, University of Lund. Lund.

Jonsson, L. 1988. The Vertebrate Faunal Remains from the Late Atlantic Settlement Skateholm in Scania, South Sweden. In: Larsson, L. (ed.). *The Skateholm Project I: Man and Environment*, 56–88. Lund.

Karsten, P. and Knarrström, B. 1999. Tvåtusen år av mesolitisk bosättning i sydvästra Skåne (Sydsverige). In: Burenhult, G. *Arkeologi i Norden,* 202–205. Stockholm.

Knarrström, B. 2000. *Flinta i sydvästra Skåne. En diakron studie av råmaterial, produktion och funktion med fokus på boplatsteknologi och metalltida flintutnyttjande.* Acta Archaeologica Lundensia. Series in 4. No. 12. Lund.

Larsson, L. 1978. *Ageröd I:B – I:D. A Study of Early Atlantic Settlement in Scania.* Acta Archaeologica Lundensia. Series in 4. No. 12. Lund.

Lepiksaar, J. 1978. Bone Remains from the Mesolithic Ageröd I:D and Ageröd I:B – I:D. In: Larsson, L. *Ageröd I:B – I:D. A Study of Early Atlantic Settlement in Scania.* Acta Archaeologica Lundensia. Series in 4. No. 12., 234–244. Lund.

—— 1982. Djurrester från den tidigatlantiska boplatsen vid Segebro nära Malmö i Skåne (Sydsverige). In: Larsson, L. *En tidigatlantisk boplats vid Sege Ås mynning.* Malmöfynd 4, 105–128. Malmö.

—— 1983. Animal Remains from the Mesolithic Bog Site at Ageröd V in Central Scania. In: Larsson, L. *Ageröd V, an Atlantic Bog Site in Central Scania.* Acta Archaeologica Lundensia. Series in 8. No. 12, 59–68. Lund.

Lyman, L. 1987. Archaeofaunas and Butchery Studies: A Taphonomic Perspective. *Advances in Archaeological Method and Theory* 10, 249–337.

Lövgren, A-K. 1998. Märgklyvning. In: Janson, P., Knöös, S., Larsson, F., Lövgren, A-K., Mårtensson, J. and Rommedahl, H. 1998. *Osteologisk analys av den mesolitiska lokalen Ringsjöholm.* Seminar paper in Historical Osteology. Institute of Archaeology, University of Lund, 95–125. Lund.

Magnell, O. 1996. *Mesolitisk slakt. En analys av slaktspår på det osteologiska materialet av kronhjort, älg och rådjur från den sydskandinaviska och senmesolitiska inlandsboplatsen Bökeberg III.* Seminar paper in Historical Osteology. Institute of Archaeology, University of Lund. Lund.

Manker, E. 1936. Renslaktens teknik. Anteckningar från Vittangi skogslappby. *Norrbotten,* 1936, 39–52.

Møhl, U. 1970. Oversigt over dyreknoglerne fra Ølby Lyng –En østsjællandsk kystboplads med Ertebøllekultur. *Aarbøger for nordisk Oldkyndighed og historia* 1970, 43–77.

—— 1978. Aggersund-Bopladsen Zoologiskt belyst. Svanejakt som årsag til bosættelse? *KUML* 1978, 57–75.

Noe-Nygaard, N. 1977. Butchering and Marrow Fracturing as a Taphonomic Factor in Archaeological Deposits. *Palebiology* 3, 217–237.

—— 1995. *Ecological, Sedimentary and Geochemical Evolution of the Late-glacial to Postglacial Åmose Lacustrine Basin, Denmark.* Fossils and Strata 37. Oslo.

Payne, S. 1975. Partial Recovery and Sample Bias. In: Clason, A.T. (ed.). *Archaeozoological Studies,* 7–17. Amsterdam.

Olsen, S.L. and Shipman, P. 1988. Surface Modification on Bone; Trampling Versus Butchery. *Journal of Archaeological Science* 15, 535–553.

Regnell, M., Gaillard, M., Bartholin, T.S. and Karsten, P. 1995. Reconstruction of Environment and History of Plant Use During the Late Mesolithic (Ertebölle Culture) at the Inland Settlement of Bökeberg III, Southern Sweden. *Vegetation, History and Archaeobotany* 4, 67–91.

Rowley-Conwy, P.A. 1999. Meat, Furs and Skins: Mesolithic Animal Bones from Ringkloster, A Seasonal Hunting Camp in Jutland. *Journal of Danish Archaeology* 12 1994–95, 87–98.

Shipman, P. and Rose, J. 1983. Early Hominid Hunting, Butchering and Carcass-Processing Behaviours: Approaches to the Fossil Record. *Journal of Anthropological Archaeology* 2, 57–98.

Sjöström, A. 1997. Ringsjöholm – A Boreal-Early Atlantic Settlement in Central Scania, Sweden. *Lund Archaeological Review* 3, 5–20.

Trolle-Lassen, T. 1990. Butchering of Red Deer. A case study from the Late Mesolithic Settlement of Tybrind Vig, Denmark. *Journal of Danish Archaeology* 9, 7–37.

White, T.D. 1992. *Prehistoric Cannibalism at Mancos 5MTUMR-2346.* Princetown.

Miscellany

85. Another life of bones: the use of Pleistocene faunal remains in the Post-Pleistocene sites of arctic Siberia

Vladimir V. Pitulko

Finds of non-archaeological Pleistocene bone and ivory are common in Siberia, and the tradition of using them as raw materials for tool manufacture which began in the remote past continued long after mammoths and other mega fauna went extinct. Archaeological finds of such materials are uncommon, but a few are known from the Late Paleolithic Dyuktai culture. The Zhokhov site, dated to 8000 BP, has also produced numerous artifacts made from mammoth bones and ivory, but no evidence that its occupants were actually hunting these animals.

The methods of treatment of fresh and fossil ivory are similar, suggesting persistence of this technology from at least 15,000 BP (e.g., Dyuktai culture) to the Late Neolithic (e.g., The Burulgino site located in the lower Indigirka River valley (Fedoseyeva 1980)).

Introduction

In northeast Asia, finds of mammoth tusks and bones, as well as remains of other large Pleistocene animals, are common. Humans from the remote past to the present have utilised these materials, particularly tusks. However, such finds are still rare. The oldest among them are the objects from the Dyuktai cave and Berelekh, while the collection from the Zhokhov site is the largest and most diverse.

In northeast Asia use of these materials in tool manufacture is testified to by a series of isolated finds which, taken together, cover a long period of time. As a rule these are tusk flakes without any secondary treatment (Mochanov 1977:Table 25:3–7; 26:4,–5). It is difficult to say how these things were used since no use wear analyses have yet been published. Many of the artifacts come from the Berelekh site (Mochanov 1977:81). In several instances such flakes were transformed into tools. The latter are recognised as dart heads (Mochanov 1977:Table 5:9, Dyuktai Cave, layer VIII, 15,000 BP) or spear heads (Mochanov 1977:Table 24:38, Berelekh site, 13,000 BP). At the Berelekh site there was also found a perfect spear head made of mammoth tusk. This is a pointed rod 640 mm long, round in cross-section, with a diameter of 25 mm (Vereshchagin and Mochanov 1972:

Fig. 4). The use of bones (mammoth ribs and femora) was reported from three sites (Ust-Mil' II, Ikhine II and Berelekh). In most cases the bones used in tool manufacture were remains of the animals actually hunted by the site inhabitants (which accords well with absolute dates). A probable exception is Berelekh, where people apparently used remains of the animals whose carcasses had accumulated in a natural trap formed by a mort lake (Vereshchagin 1971:93).

The Zhokhov Site collection

To date, the most varied collection of such tools comes from the site on Zhokhov Island (76° north latitude), one of the northernmost islands of the New Siberian archipelago (Pitulko 1991, 1993; Pitulko and Kasparov 1996). Being the only evidence of human penetration into the high latitude regions as early as 8000 years ago, the site represents a very important phenomenon in Arctic prehistory. It is also one of the most important Holocene Stone Age sites investigated in recent decades because a great number of organic artifacts are preserved there in exceptionally good state due to permafrost conditions. Artifacts of fossil mammoth ivory take a special place in the inventory of the site.

The collection includes fragments of composite slotted tools and massive pick-like artifacts, as well as a knife and a side scraper made on ivory flakes. The functions of the latter two tools have been determined by use wear analysis. Unfortunately, the finds from Berelekh (Figures 85.4–85.5) that are very similar to those from Zhokhov in their morphology have never been subjected to such study, so functional comparisons between these assemblages are not possible at present.

One of the specific features of the Zhokhov site inventory is a near total absence of any tools other than composite tools with insets, as well as adzes and chisels. Use wear analysis distinguishes two tools that partly fill this gap. Both served for hide working (Girya and Pitulko 1993:33). These tools were made on large massive flakes of fossil mammoth tusk struck off by a mighty blow

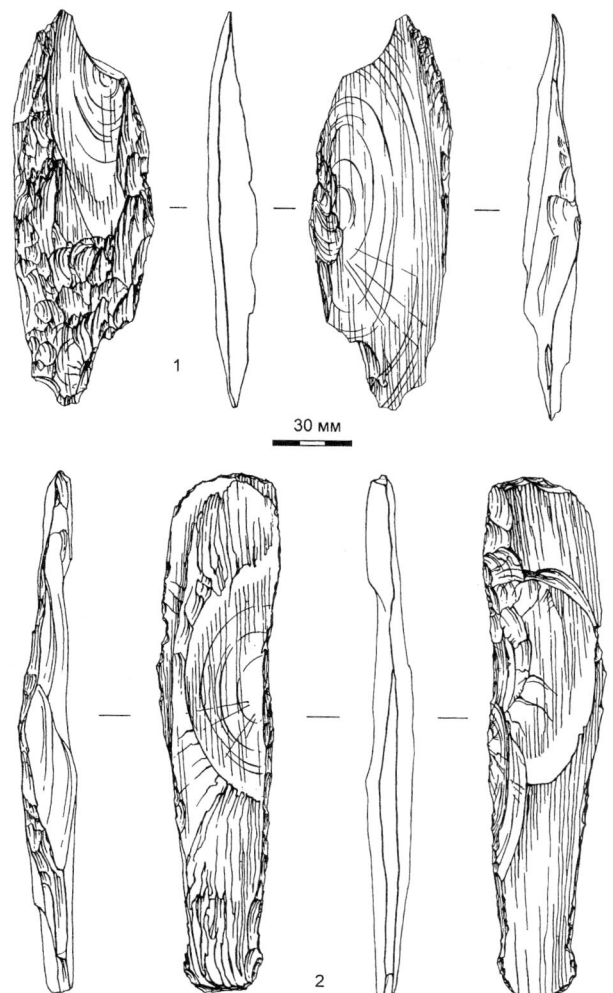

Figure 85.1 Inventory of the Zhokhov site. Tools on flakes of fossil mammoth tusks. 1 – side scraper for hides; 2 – skinning knife.

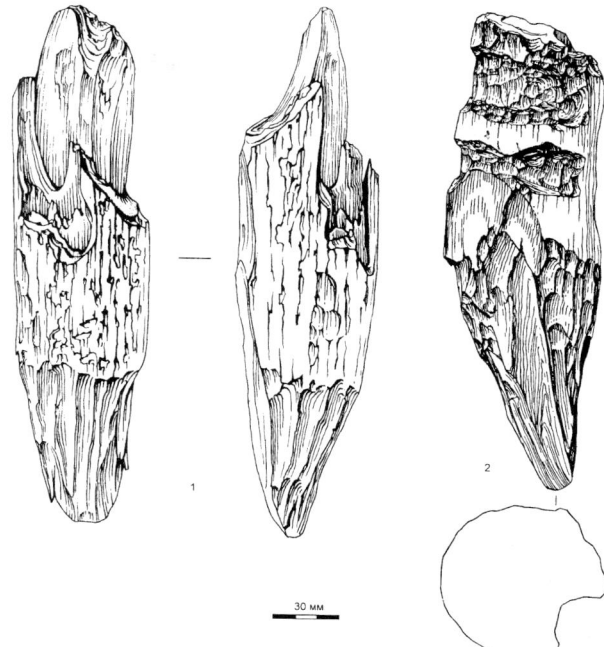

Figure 85.2 Inventory of the Zhokhov site. Pick-like tools of mammoth tusk (1, 2).

oriented along the long axis of the tusk (Figure 85.1). One of the tools has been defined as a skinning knife (Figure 85.1:2). It has secondary treatment forming the handle part of the tool. The use wear traces can be seen over the whole perimeter of the working edge as well as on the lateral surfaces of the knife. They are represented by (1) some rounding (blunting) of the working edge, (2) linear traces oriented along the edge, and (3) light polish covering the micro-relief of the tusk surface.

The second tool (Figure 85.1:1) has been defined as a side scraper for hides. This is a big flake without any signs of secondary retouch. Its dorsal surface bears numerous stepped scars. It is possible that the flake resulted from reshaping of some other tool. The use wear traces are represented by (1) some rounding (blunting) of the working edge, (2) linear traces oriented at right angles to the edge, and (3) polish of the edge and the adjacent areas of the surface. Besides the described use-wear traces, both tools also bear clear traces left by natural agents, but the latter are easily told from the former.

The cultural layer of the site yielded also diverse bone, ivory, and antler flakes testifying to the wide use of these materials and, probably, to standardisation of manufacturing methods.

Pick-like tools made of reindeer antler and mammoth ivory also occupy an important place in the site inventory. This group contains 28 intact and broken objects, including 2 objects transferred to the Institute for the History of Material Culture in St. Petersburg by the members of the Zhokhov polar expedition in the 1970s. Judging by their quantitative ratio, both kinds of raw material were used equally: 13 tools are made of ivory and 15 of antler. It is interesting that the ancient inhabitants of the island gathered and used also shed deer antlers, as is evidenced by the presence in the collection of the peculiar basal parts of the latter. Some of them were used as percussive tools (Pitulko and Kasparov 1996).

Pick-like tools made of fossil mammoth tusks are represented by 13 items. Judging by the available fragments, different pieces of tusks were used. The biggest fragment representing the working part of a tool is 268 mm long. The length of most tools is 200–220 mm, and the diameter reaches 88 mm. The working part is most often sharpened to make it conical and is off-center from the long axis of the tool (Figure 85.2:2), but in one instance the profile of the working edge is wedge-shaped (Figure 85.2:1). The upper end of all these tools (except the latter) is prepared for lashing (Figures 85.2:2; 85.3:4). These tools, as well as antler picks mentioned above, were resharpened, and because of this the intact objects appear to be of strange proportions (Figure 85.3:4), and the working part comprises half to two thirds of their length.

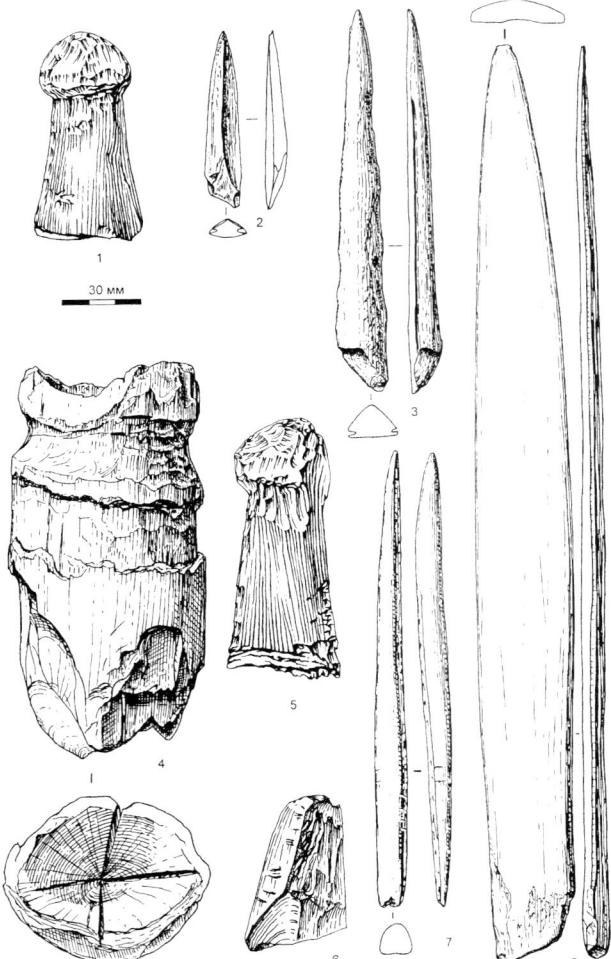

Figure 85.3 Inventory of the Zhokhov site. Tools of undetermined function ("handles" – 1, 5); fragments of double-edged slotted points (3, 4), unfinished double-edged slotted tool in the final stage of manufacture (8), spear head (7); pick-like tool (4), fragment of worked tusk (6). 1–4, 6 – fossil mammoth tusk, 5, 7, 8 – bone (most probably fossil Pleistocene bone well preserved due to permafrost conditions and used alongside with ivory).

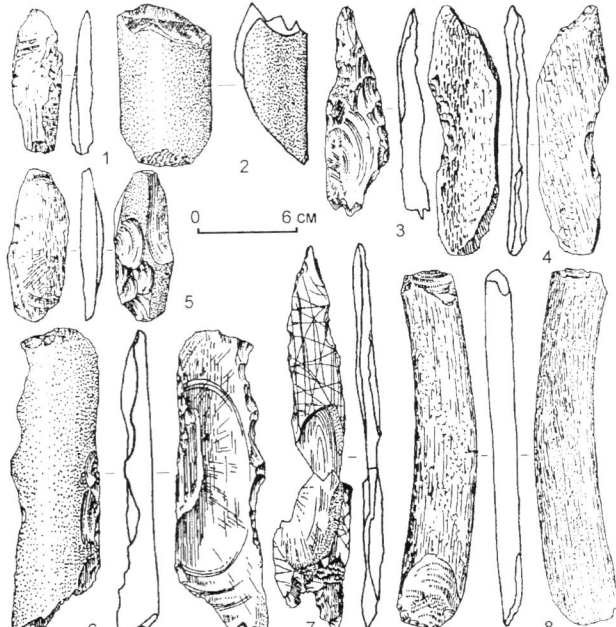

Figure 85.4 Bone artifacts from Berelekh, including ivory flakes (3, 6, 7) or, perhaps, tools on such flakes (after Yu. A. Mochanov 1977).

Unfortunately, the surfaces of most tools are destroyed or heavily damaged, what makes the determination of their functions difficult. However, some of them bear specific linear traces indicative of the contact with soil. This applies to both groups. At the same time, it cannot be ruled out that despite their morphological similarity these tools were used for different purposes. For instance, some antler "picks" could well have served as weapons (bear spears?). A different function can also be proposed for an ivory tool with wedge-shaped working edge (Figure 85.3:1) that appears never to have been utilised. In my view, it could well have served in a capacity of a heavy splitting tool of the adze type, necessary for wood processing. In connection with this it should be noted that many of the ubiquitous wood fragments at the site bear traces of artificial splitting.

Among the Zhokhov artifacts made of organic materials there are some objects with unclear function. Of special interest in this discussion are two of them. These objects are identical in size, design, and the character of damage to one another, but one is made of ivory (Figure 85.3:1), and the other from a massive bone of some very large (Pleistocene?) animal (Figure 85.3:5). They appear as unilaterally flattened handles with a cone-like bulge at the end. Their length is 77 and 103 mm, and the maximum width is 35 and 40 mm respectively.

The group of hunting weapons (composite and non-composite tools, their blanks and unfinished pieces) also includes artifacts made of fossil mammoth tusks and massive bones of large animals. Ivory points are very rare; 2 fragments represent them only. The method of their manufacture was evidently close to that reconstructed by A.K. Filippov (1978), though perhaps less elaborate. Final shaping of the tools was carried out with the use of abrasive rock slabs of different coarseness that are abundant at the site.

Both points are double-edged, massive, and trihedral in cross-section (Figure 85.3:2–3). Judging by the proportions of the fragments, the size of the tools was about 240–280 mm. The depth of the grooves is 3–5 mm, the width 1.5–2 mm. The grooves were incised with the use of a thin straight bladelet and occupied two thirds of the length of the edges. The points have symmetrical elongated-taper outlines. The base lacks any additional working. The collection includes also a large unfinished spearhead (Figure 85.3:8) made of the wall of a long bone of some big animal. Proceeding from its proportions and

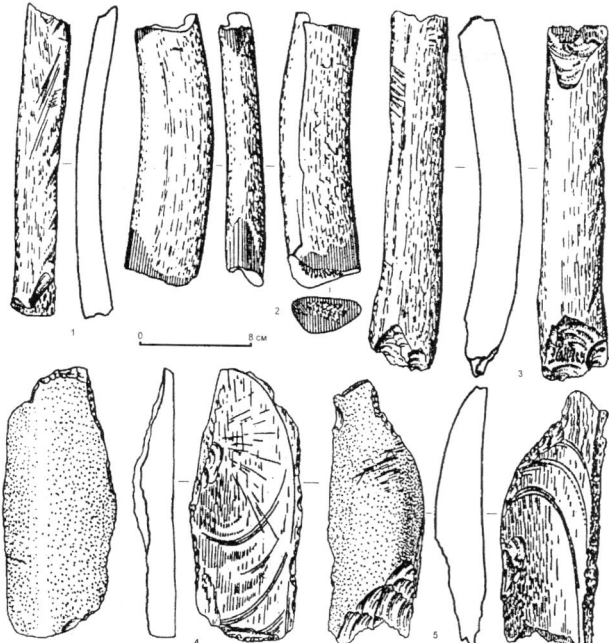

Figure 85.5 Bone artifacts from Berelekh, including ivory flakes (4, 5) or, perhaps, tools on such flakes (after Yu. A. Mochanov 1977).

the massiveness of the bone (even after working its thickness reaches 6–7 mm, while the spongeous substance can be seen on a small area of the base only) it appears probable that the tool is made of a mammoth bone.

Another intact specimen also is made of a massive bone and its surface, as well as that of the previous tool, is carefully worked (Figure 85.3:7). Here too the massiveness of the bone suggests that it belonged to a large Pleistocene animal. The cross-section of the point varies from round at the tip to unilaterally convex at the base, while the base itself is flattened (Figure 85.3:7). On the surface of the tool one can see four small transverse incisions.

Finally, in addition to the Berelekh and Zhokhov finds it is possible to mention a spearhead and axes of mammoth tusk coming from the Late Neolithic (i.e., Ymiyahtakh) layers of the Burulgino site (Fedoseeva 1980:128, Fig. 85, 86) dated to 2950±100 BP (LE – 1002), and "a spearhead of mammoth tusk with flint bladelets fixed along its edge" from another Ymiyahtakh site called Tatianino ozero reported on by Okladnikov (1955:123).

Conclusions

Comparative analysis of the ivory artifacts from the Late Pleistocene sites of northeast Asia and from the Zhokhov site enables us to make the following conclusions:

1. The dorsal surface of the blanks is most often natural, the flakes are short and wide, of oval proportions. Most of them were struck off from unprepared pieces of ivory by a strong lateral blow. As distinct from Old Crow in the Yukon Territory of North America (Morlan and Bonnichsen 1979), there are no known ivory or bone objects in northeast Asia that could be considered cores;

2. the technique of pressure flaking was also sometimes employed (e.g., on a dart head from the Dyuktai cave);

3. the production of big tools (spear heads, picks, mattocks) also involved such methods as planing and cutting. In the case of more delicate objects such as those used in hunting, the final stage of manufacture also involved polishing;

4. the processing methods applied to the "fresh" tusks (those obtained from the hunt) and to the fossilised are similar, suggesting continuity in a tradition of manufacture from the Late Paleolithic to the Late Neolithic.

References

Bonnichsen, R. 1979. Pleistocene bone technology in the Beringian Refugium. *Archaeological Survey of Canada* 89. Ottawa.

Fedoseeva, S.A. 1980. *The Ymyaktakh Culture of North-East Asia.* Novosibirsk.

Filippov, A.K. 1978. Technology of Manufacturing of Bone Points in the Upper Paleolithic Times. *Soviet Archaeology* 2, 23–32.

Girya, Y.Y. and Pitulko, V.V. 1993. Worked Mammoth Bones from the Late Pleistocene and Early Holocene Sites of NE Asia and Siberian High Arctic: sources of raw material and ways of treatment. *Historical Experience of the Developing of the Eastern Regions of Russia.* Abstracts of the conference. Part 1, 33–36. Vladivostok.

Mochanov, Y.A. 1977. *The Oldest Stages of the Human Habitation in North-East Asia.* Novosibirsk.

Morlan, R. and Bonnichsen, R. 1979. Initial Human Habitation in the Old Crow Valley, Yukon. In: Vasilyevsky, R.S. (ed.) *Ancient Cultures of Siberia and of the Pacific,* 48–57. Novosibirsk.

Okladnikov, A.P. 1955. *History of the Yakut ASSR.* Vol. 1. Moscow.

Pitulko, V.V. 1991. On the Fringes of the Stone Age Ecumene. *Priroda* 8, 56–59.

—— 1993. An Early Holocene Site in the Siberian High Arctic. *Arctic Anthropology* 30, No. 1, 13–21.

Pitulko, V.V. and Kasparov, A.K. 1996. Ancient Arctic Hunters: Material Culture and Survival Strategy. *Arctic Anthropology* 33, No. 1, 1–38.

Vereschagin, N.K. 1971. Fauna Remains from the Dwelling Pits of the Baranov Cape. In: Okladnikov, A.P and Beregovaya, N.A. *Old settlements of the Baranov Cape,* 149–156. Novosibirsk.

Vereschagin, N.K. and Mochanov, Y.A. 1972. The Northernmost Traces of the Upper Paleolithic Habitation (the Berelekh Site in the Downstream Area of the Indighirka River). *Soviet Archaeology* 3, 332–336.

Miscellany

86. Recent excavations at the Pre-boreal site of Lahti, Ristola in southern Finland

Hannu Takala

The earliest post glacial settlement of Finland is dated to the Ancylus culmination, to the turn of the Pre-boreal and Boreal periods. The settlement of Lahti, Ristola belongs to this period. The site was excavated in 1970–1971 and 1995–1999. The flint assemblage of Ristola is unique for the Finnish Mesolithic. Nearly 300 objects were found in the recent excavations.

Introduction

The Pre-boreal Mesolithic site of Lahti, Ristola is situated 5 kilometers south of the city of Lahti in southern Finland. The site lies on the Porvoonjoki River which is connected to the Baltic Sea (Figure 86.1). In the 1980's Heikki Matiskainen studied the dating of Ristola through shoreline displacement and dated the Mesolithic phase of the Ristola site to ca. 9250 uncal. BP (Matiskainen 1989:71).

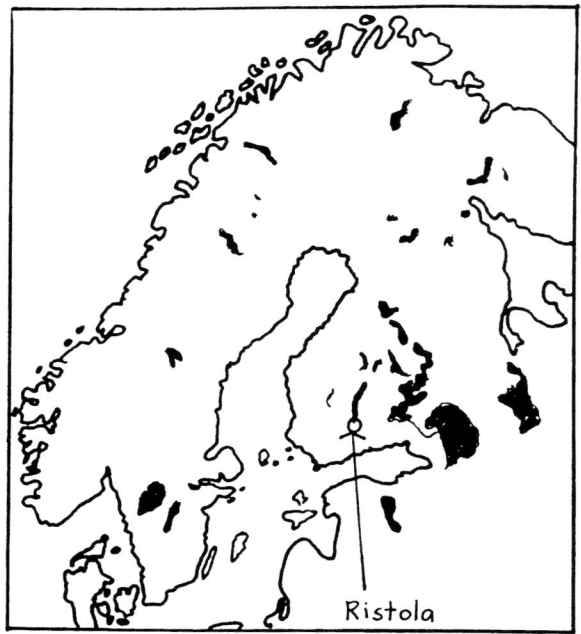

Figure 86.1 Location of Ristola in southern Finland.

In this paper I shall present some preliminary results from the fieldwork. Research on this site is still in progress by the author.

History of research

The first artefacts from the Ristola region were found in the 1960's. Altogether over one hundred quartz scrapers, quartz cores and quartz flakes were collected from three different locations near each other along the river bank. All finds came from a ploughed field as a result of fieldwalking. These finds resulted in two rescue excavations, one in 1970 and the other in 1971, both which were directed by Marianne Schauman from the Finnish National Board of Antiquities. These excavations recorded material from the Mesolithic and Battle Axe Culture. Among the quartz material is a small flint assemblage (Schauman 1972:16 p). The flint artefacts (30 pieces) are of good quality and include flakes, scrapers, inserts and fragments of arrowheads. After the excavation the flint assemblages from Ristola and from the Pulli site in Estonia were studied and compared. This study showed that Ristola may belong to the same age of the Ancylus culmination as Pulli (Edgren 1982:22). According to Matiskainen the flint assemblage from Ristola is similiar to the so called Late Swiderian and this, so far, would make Ristola the northernmost occurrence of the East Baltic Swiderian (Matiskainen 1996:257 p).

Recent excavations at Ristola

Recent excavations started in 1995 and ended in 1999. Earlier finds and the results concerning the dating of Ristola were the main reasons for this new campaign. The author of this paper was the director of these excavations.

During the recent excavations 866 m² were excavated, over 33 000 finds collected and 4 km² prospected by test pitting and phosphate analysis. Additional fieldwalking and test pitting covered another 15 kilometers of the river

Figure 86.2 Excavated areas at Ristola. (Takala 1999, appendix 5).

south of Ristola during which over 40 new sites were found. Excavations at Ristola in 1995 started with testpits in an area with potential occupation layers in and around the site of the old rescue excavations. One clear and large concentration was found. During 1996–1999 several trenches were excavated in that concentration. New test pits were also dug in order to find the limits of the occupation. The Mesolithic concentration at Ristola is clear, but later occupations, especially from the Battle Axe Culture, have produced mixing in some of the layers. The recent study showed that the younger layers lie between 74 and 81 meters above the sea level on sandy terraces. The Mesolithic concentrations are found between 71 and 76 meters on terraces consisting of clayish soils. Cultural layers at Ristola are minimal. But fireplaces and areas with occupation layers have been found. The field has been ploughed and only the lowermost finds are intact. Unfortunately this recent disturbance together with younger occupations has resulted in the mixing of some of the finds. It is important to separate the finds from each period and understand the scale of the disturbance. This study is now under way.

Group	Number of finds
Flakes	168
Blades	77
Burins	14
Scrapers	7
Combined tools	5
Knives	5
Inserts	3
Arrowheads	3
Points	1
Borers	1
Chisels	1
Core axes	1
Total	286

Figure 86.3 Flint finds from the excavations 1995–1999.

Finds

Most of the finds were made from local quartz. The flint artefacts are important because all flint found on Finnish sites is imported. Flint will give information about contacts and migration at the Ristola site. Quartz is also interesting because preliminary research has found examples of objects where flint technology has been used

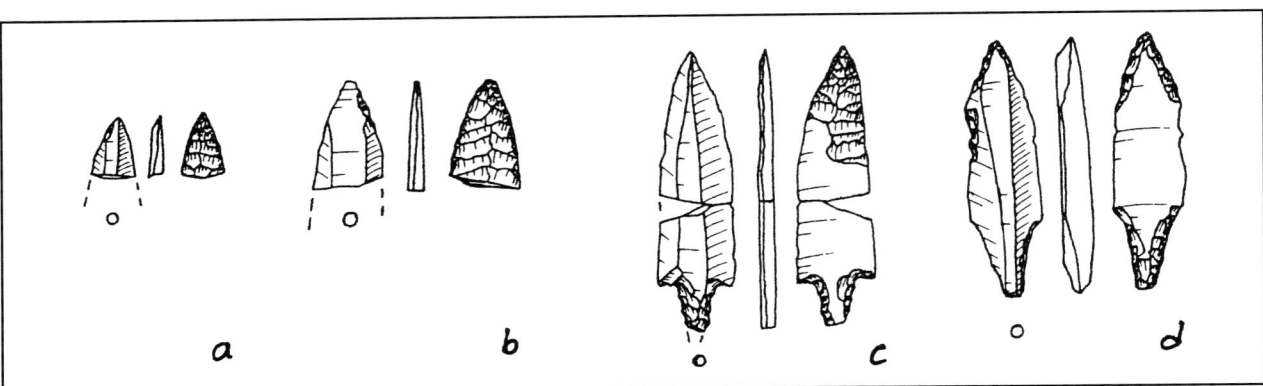

Figure 86.4 Arrowheads. The tanged flintpoint c) also has dorsal retouch on the tang: a) b) and c) flint, d) sandstone. Scale 1:1.

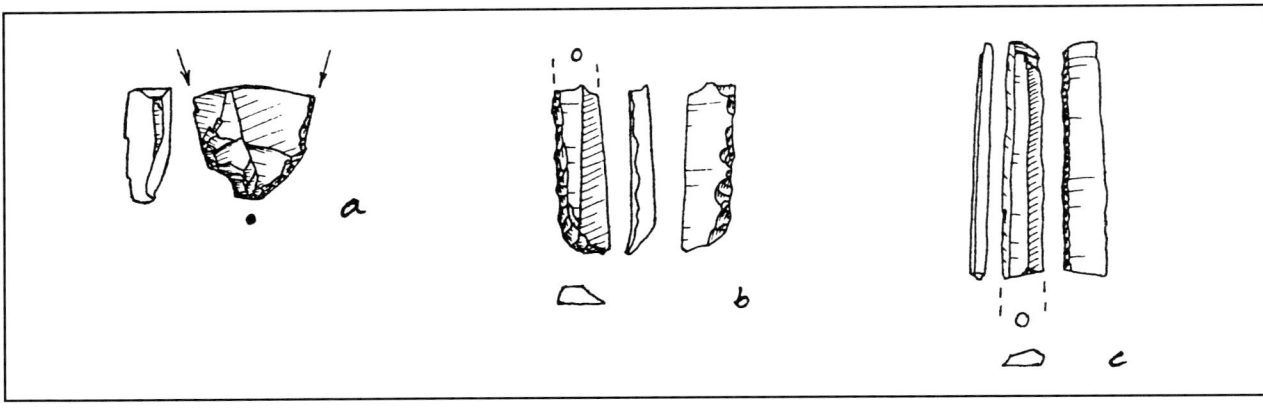

Figure 86.5 a) burin, b) and c) inserts. Scale 1:1.

on quartz. Also, some quartz artefacts can be used for dating, according to the Finnish quartz chronology. The flint assemblage of the recent excavations contains 286 finds. In figure 86.3, the finds are divided into classes. Flakes dominate the assemblage. This presentation of finds is based on a preliminary study of the assemblage and I will present only a small example of finds, a full and detailed presentation of all the flint objects will be published later. Two of the arrowheads are broken but the third is a tanged point with a small fragment missing. All three flint arrowheads (Figure 86.4 a–c) have flat ventral retouch and are similar to the finds from the Pulli assemblage. In addition to flint arrowheads there are two made of siliceous sandstone. One is complete with a tang and ventral retouch on both the tang and point. It also has a weak dorsal retouch on the point (Figure 86.4d). The other one is broken with dorsal retouch on the point and ventral retouch on the left lateral side.

Burins are made of Carboniferous and Cretaceous flint. Nine of the burins were made on blades and five on flakes. There are also three burins made from broken knives and one double burin, also made from a broken knife (Figure 86.5a).

Three inserts were found. Two of them are made on small regular blades (Figure 86.5 b–c). They both have ventral retouch on one lateral side, one also has steep dorsal retouch on the side and base.

Conclusions

Five years of extensive fieldwork at Ristola are over. Now, the main interest is the finds, of both flint and quartz, and the stratigraphy of the site which can be regarded as a multi period settlement. Geological surveys in the summer of 2001 will give us more information as to the dating of the site. Shore displacement curves will be partly renewed. Finds from Ristola will be analysed more carefully, especially the flint assemblage which will be compared to several other assemblages from the East Baltic and Upper Volga. When the study is completed we shall have new information on the Finnish Mesolithic and its cultural contacts.

References

Edgren, T. 1984. Kivikausi. *Suomen historia* 1. Helsinki.
Matiskainen, H. 1989. The paleoenvironment of Askola, southern Finland. Mesolithic settlement and subsistence 10 000–6 000 b.p. Suomen Muinaismuistoyhdistys. *Iskos* 8. Helsinki.
——— 1996. Discrepancies in Deglaciation Chronology and the Appearance of Man in Finland. *Acta Archaeologica Lundensia*, no 24, 251–262.
Schauman, M. 1972. *Kertomus kaivauksesta, jonka hum.kand. Marianne Schauman suoritti Lahden kaupungissa Renkomäen kylässä 1.6.–31.8.1971*. (Excavation report).
Takala, H. 1999. *Kertomus Lahden Renkomäen Ristolan arkeologisista kaivauksista*. (Excavation report).

Miscellany

87. Early Mesolithic communication networks in the East European forest zone

Mickle Zhilin

Excavations of early Mesolithic sites on Upper Volga yielded a number of artifacts, made of imported Cretaceous flint. Among them Butovo site, dated to 9310 BP, uncal. and to Preboreal by pollen. Nearest outcrops of such flint are in Lithuenia and western Belarus about 1000 km from these sites. The same flint was widely used in Pulli site in Estonia, dated to the same period. Similar artifacts, made of this flint were also found in Lahti Ristola in Southern Finland. Some artifacts, made of typical Upper Volga Carboniferous flint were found in Pulli. Nearest outcrops of this flint are about 500 km from Pulli. Besides very strong technological and morphological similarity this indicates emergence and functioning of communication network, covering large areas of East European forest zone in Preboreal and early Boreal. Analysis of early Mesolithic bone industry from the Baltic to Urals also confirms this.

Introduction

The territory of the most part of the East European forest zone is characterised by plain relief, similar soil and hydrological conditions, which determined formation of palaeoecological situation, similar in many aspects from the north-eastern Poland to the Middle Volga. Pollen analyses (Spiridonova and Aleshiskaya 1996:65 pp) showed, that formation of the taiga forest zone started in the very beginning of Preboreal and ended about 9600 years BP uncal. Absence of natural obstacles and well developed river net with easy passes from one basin to another (for example, from the West Dvina to the Volga basin) made favorable conditions for migrations and contacts of ancient population of this vast territory.

In terminal Pleistocene, during the Younger Dryas, periglacial landscapes at the territory of the future forest zone were occupied by the reindeer hunters of two traditions – Swiderian and Lyngby-Ahrensburgian (Rimantene 1971, 1996:15 pp; Koltsov 1978:41 pp; Zaliznyak 1989:76 pp; Zhilin 1996:273 pp). Contacts of Swiderian and Ahrensburgian population are reflected in lithic inventories of sites, combining both traditions. The latter are dated evidently, to the Younger Dryas. Among them are Salaspils Laukskola in Latvia (Zagorska 1996:266 pp), Mergejeris 3 in Lithuania (Rimantene 1996:37) and similar. In the beginning of the Holocene, most probably in the early Preboreal several cultures with traces of Swiderian tradition were formed in the forest zone of Eastern Europe, among them Neman and Kunda in the Eastern Baltic, Veretye to the east from the Onega Lake and Butovo on the Upper Volga and Volga-Oka interflew. The Lyngby-Ahrensburgian tradition, which was the basis of the Ienevo culture on the Upper Volga, is not met in the Mesolithic of the Eastern Baltic.

Kunda culture (Indreko 1948; Koltsov 1978:120 pp; Jaanits 1980:389 pp; Zagorska 1980:73 pp) was spread, mainly, at territories of Latvia and Estonia. The early stage of Kunda culture is represented by Pulli site, dated by C14 to 9675±115 BP uncal. (Ta-176) – charcoal from the bottom of cultural layer; 9600±120 BP uncal. (Ta-245) – unworked wood from the bottom of cultural layer; 9600±120 BP uncal. (Hel-2206A) – peat from cultural layer, insoluble fraction (Junger and Sonninen 1996); 9300±75 BP uncal. (Ta-175) – organic sediments just above cultural layer; 9290±120 BP uncal. (Hel-2206B) – humic fraction of Hel-2206A; 9285±120 BP uncal. (TA-284) – organic sediments just above cultural layer; 9350±60 BP uncal. (Ta-949) – charcoal from a hearth, encircled by stones. The last date determines the occupation time of the site most accurately. Pollen analysis indicates Preboreal age of the site. Lower layer of Zveinieki 2 (Zagorska, 1980: 73pp) and the site Sulagals in Latvia (Lose, 1988:14 pp) are also dated to the Preboreal, most probably to its second half or last quarter. Sites of Kunda culture, dated to the first half of the Preboreal are not known yet, which makes the problem of its origin disputable. Formation of early Kunda culture on the basis of the late Swiderian (Koltsov 1978:132 pp; Zagorska 1980:79 p) seems most probable.

Some sites and stray finds, similar to materials of the early stage of Kunda culture are known from Lithuania (Ostrauskas 1996:192 pp; Rimantene 1996:87 pp). In the north-eastern Poland flint artifacts of early Kunda and

Komornica cultures were found in the same layer at the peat bog site Miluki (Brzozowski and Siemaszko 1996: 229 pp). This layer is dated by C14 to 9280±50 BP uncal. (Gd-7595) and the overlaying layer – 9125±90 (Ua-13086) and 9160±50 BP uncal. (Gd-7594). In southern Finland flint artifacts, resembling finds from Pulli were found at Lahti Ristola site, dated about 9250 BP uncal. (Matiskainen 1996:257 p).

Little is known about Veretye culture in the Preboreal, though C14 dates of a burial in Peschanitsa – 9890±120 BP uncal. (GIN-4858) and burials N 9 – 9730±110 BP uncal. (GIN-4856), N3 – 9520±130 BP uncal. (GIN-4442) and N1 – 9430±150 BP uncal. (GIN-4447) of the cemetery Popovo (Oshibkina 1994) suggest that it existed at that time. Grave furniture is very poor, but strong similarities of early Boreal sites of Veretye, Kunda and Butovo cultures make possible to suppose, that the former was developing during the Preboreal in the same way as two others.

The early stage of Butovo culture is known much better. The earliest site, Stanovoye 4, lower layer (Zhilin 1998b:154, 2001:34 p) is related by pollen to the end of the Younger Dryas. C14 dates obtained from samples of silt and gyttja: 10300±70 (GIN-110112 II), 10060±120 BP (GIN-10127-I), 10040±40 BP (GIN-1027-II), 9970±50 BP (GIN-10126-I), 9940±40 BP (GIN-10125-II), 9850±60 BP (GIN-8379-I) and 9760±150 BP (GIN-8379-II) all uncal. belong to the lake transgressions, when the site was submerged. The next stage is represented by the lower layer of Ivanovskoje 7 (Zhilin 2001:33 p), dated by pollen to the second quarter of Preboreal and by 14-C to 9650±110 BP (GIN-9520) – worked bone, 9640±60 BP (GIN-9516) – wood, gnawed by beaver, both uncal. Gyttja layer, overlaying the cultural layer is dated to 9690±120 BP (GIN-9367), 9500±100 BP (GIN-9385) and 9500±110 BP (GIN-9517), all uncal., indicating that the site was submerged about 9600–9500 BP. A fireplace with finds of the early Butovo culture, including a tanged arrowhead and 3 backed insets in Belivo 4a (Kravtsov 1999:90) is dated to 9550±100 BP uncal. (GIN-3893). Butovo site (Zhilin 1996:278) is dated by pollen to the end of the Preboreal optimum, and has C14 date from charcoal in a hearth in the center of flint concentration – 9310±110 BP uncal. (GIN-5441). The III cultural layer of Stanovoye 4, trench 3 (Zhilin 2001:34 p) is dated by pollen to the last quarter of the Preboreal and has C14 dates: 9280±240 BP (GIN-10122 I), 9090±400 BP (GIN-10124 I) – gyttja with cultural remains, and 9220±60 BP (GIN-8375) – wooden stake, sharpened with stone adze, all uncal. These and similar sites yielded rich collections of lithic, bone and antler artifacts of the early stage of Butovo culture.

The territory between Eastern Baltic and Upper Volga is very poorly studied, there are no sites, which could be reliably dated to the early Mesolithic.

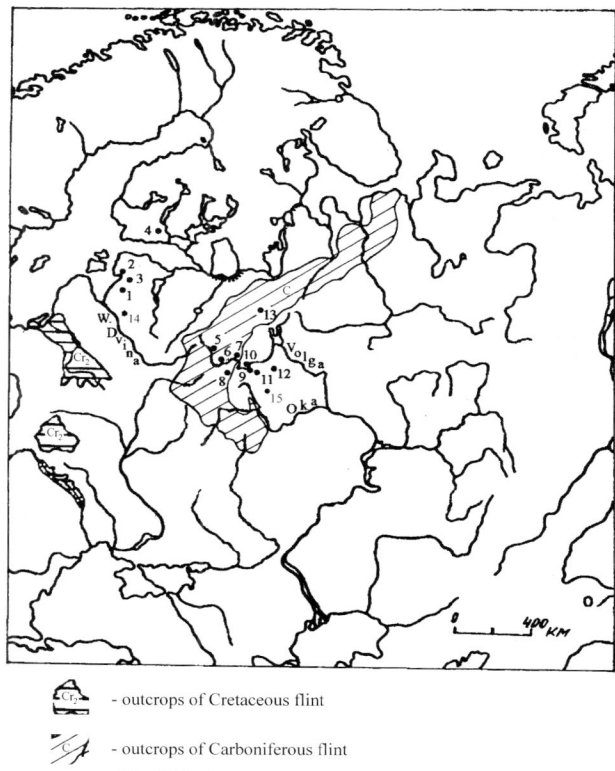

Figure 87.1 Nearest deposits and distribution of artifacts, made of dark gray Cretaseous flint and Carboniferous flint. 1: Zveinieki 2; 2: Pulli; 3: Lepakose; 4: Lahti Ristola; 5: Sukontsevo 3; 6: Butovo; 7: Zaborovje 2; 8: Ozerki 5; 9: Prislon 1; 10: Pekunovo; 11: Okajomovo 5; 12: Ivanovskoje 7; 13: Kurevaniha 5; 14: Sulyagals; 15: Belivo 4a.

Flint imports

Distribution of artifacts, made of imported flint is of special interest for the present paper. Territories of Latvia, Estonia and Southern Finland have no outcrops of flint, good for production of large regular blades – the main blank of the early Kunda culture. Nearest outcrops of such raw material – dark gray, semi-transparent, fine grained Cretaceous flint – are in Lithuania and western Belorussia at a distance of about 300 km from Zveinieki 2, 400 km from Pulli and Lepakoze and 600 km from Lahti Ristola, in the latter case across the sea gulf (Figure 87.1). Most part of lithic artifacts of the earliest site – Pulli – is made from this imported flint (Jaanits 1980:389 pp). Its role is smaller in the lower layer of Zveinieki 2 (Zagorska 1980:73 pp). In Lepakose, which is considered younger than these two, only several tools are made from this imported flint (Jaanits 1980: 389pp). The role of this flint is high in Lahti Ristola (Matiskainen 1996:257), which is later than Pulli, but earlier than Lepakose. In all cases this flint was used, first of all, for production of regular blades, used as blanks for knives, arrowheads and insets (Figure 87.2). In Pulli, Zveinieki 2 and Lahti Ristola finished tools accompanied by blades and flakes were

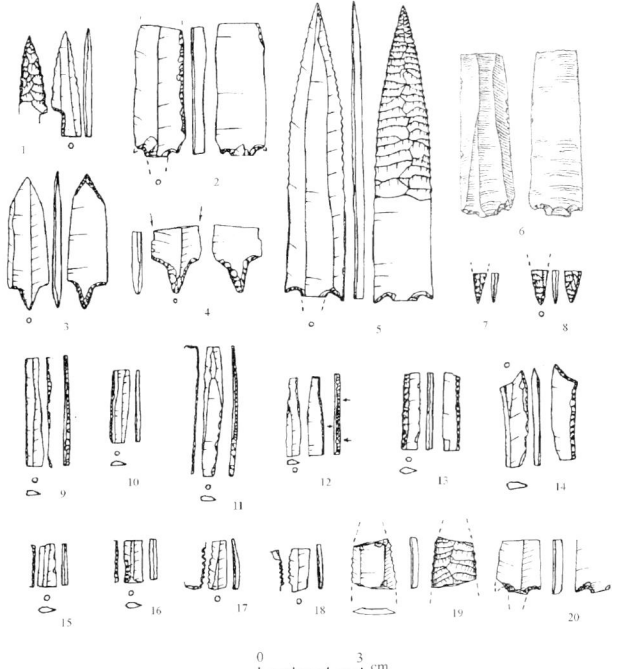

Figure 87.2 Artifacts from early Mesolithic sites of Eastern Baltic region (dark gray Cretaseous flint). 1–5, 7–18: Pulli (after Jaanits, 1980); 6: Zveinieki 2 (After Zagorska, 1980); 19–20: Lahti Ristola (after Matiskainen, 1996).

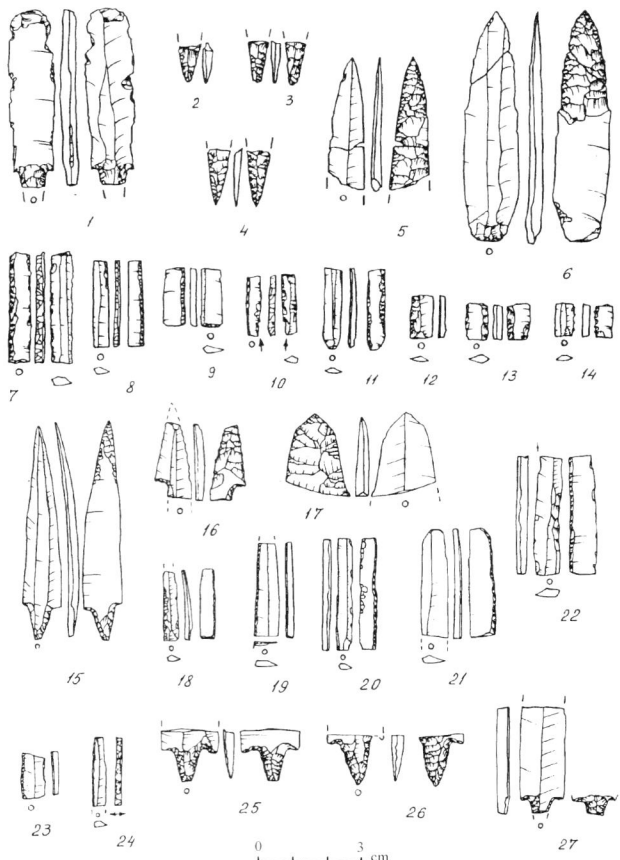

Figure 87.3 Artifacts from early Mesolithic sites of Upper Volga (6,7,13,16,17,25,26: dark gray Cretaseous flint). 1–14: Butovo; 15–22: Prislon 1; 23–27: Zaborovje 2. (After Zhilin, 2000).

found. Prepared cores and blades were brought to the former three sites from distant workshops and played substantial role in their raw material supply. Blade production and the manufacture of tools from this flint were significant for their inhabitants. In Lepakose, on the contrary, this flint played no significant role, and most probably two arrowheads, insert and a retouched blade were brought there as finished artifacts.

Several early Mesolithic sites on the Upper Volga yielded artifacts, made of this kind of Cretaceous flint, nearest outcrops of which are about 600–1000 km from these sites. 10 regular blades, 1 insert and an unfinished arrowhead of the Pulli type (Figure 87.3: 6, 13), made from gray Cretaceous flint of the same variant, as in Pulli, were found at Butovo site (Figure 87.1:6). The other insert from the same flint concentration (Figure 87.3:7) was made of the spotty gray flint. The last variant of flint is also well represented in the inventory of Pulli site, and like dark gray Cretaceous flint is not met in natural deposits on the Upper Volga. An unfinished arrowhead (Figure 87.3:6) was broken into 2 pieces in process of flat ventral retouching, and both pieces were found at a distance about 1,5 m from each other in the same concentration of flint artifacts. It clearly indicates a local attempt to make an arrowhead from imported blade. Two basal fragments of tanged arrowheads of Pulli type (Figure 87.3:25, 26) made of dark gray flint come from the site Zaborovje 2 (Figure 87.1:7). Asymmetric one-winged arrowhead (Figure 87.3:16) and a fragment of a point of a Pulli type arrowhead (possibly unfinished – Figure 87.3:17) also made of the same flint were found at Prislon 1 site (Figure 87.1:9). Basal parts of two tanged arrowheads and several fragments of regular blades, made of this flint come from Pekunovo site (Figure 87.1:10), situated just opposite Prislon 1. An arrowhead of the Pulli type, made of the same flint, was found at Kurevaniha 5 site (Figure 87.1:13), to the north from the Upper Volga. A fragment of a Pulli type arrowhead, made of spotty gray Cretaceous flint was found at Sukontsevo 3 site (Figure 87.1:5). A backed microblade with obliquely truncated end, made of dark gray Cretaceous flint was found in Belivo 4a (Figure 87.1:15).

Several features are easily seen in all Upper Volga finds, described above. First, the number of artifacts, made of imported Cretaceous flint, is very small at each site. They compose 0,6% of all flint artifacts in Butovo; 0,02% in Zaborovje 2; 0,2% in Prislon; less than 0,1% in Pekunovo. Second, only finished tools and regular blades were brought to Upper Volga. Neither flakes, nor nodules or cores were found. Third, almost all finished tools are arrowheads of Pulli types or inserts of composite weapons.

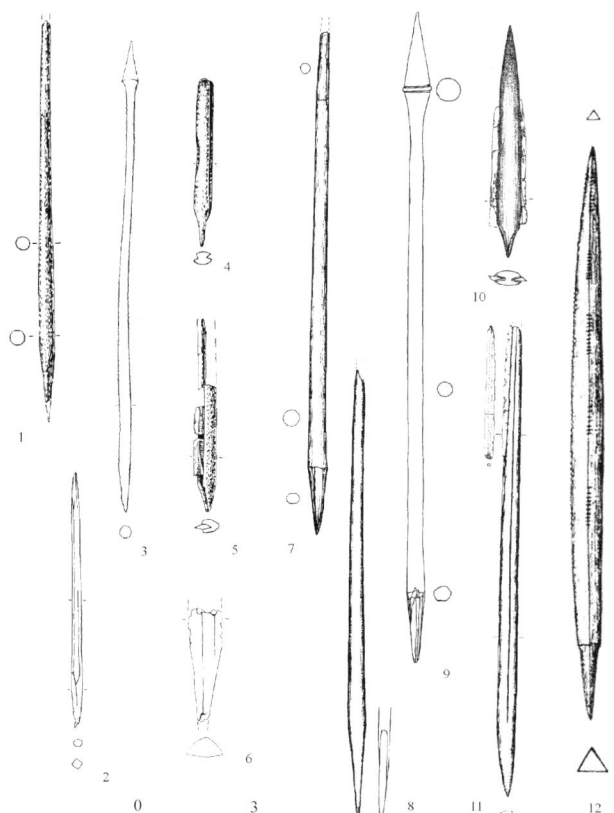

Figure 87.4 Bone arrowheads from early Mesolithic sites of Eastern Baltic and Upper Volga.
1, 4, 5 – Zveinieki 2, lower layer (after Zagorska 1980); 2, 3, 6 – Pulli (after Jaanits 1980);
7, 10 – Ivanovskoje 7, layer 4; 8, 9 – Stanovoje 4, trench 3, layer 3; 11 – Stanovoje 4, layer 4; 12 – Ivanovskoje 3, bottom layer (after Zhilin 2001).

All this means, that imported Cretaceous flint played no significant role as raw material on the Upper Volga. It is easily understandable if we take into consideration, that the Upper Volga region is rich in Carboniferous flint, some varieties of which are as good, as Cretaceous flint. There was no need to import flint raw material.

On the other hand, some regular blades in Pulli are made of typical rose-violet Carboniferous flint, outcrops of which are abundant on the Upper Volga and in Valday regions, the nearest are about 450–500 km from Pulli. In this case it also played no significant role as raw material, and was brought to Pulli in the same pattern, as Cretaceous flint to Upper Volga. More than half of inventory of the other Preboreal site, Sulyagals in Latvia is made of imported yellow and brown Carboniferous flint (Loze 1988:16). Nearest ouncrops of the latter are in the upper branches of the West Dvina (Daugava) river about 400 km from the site. Carboniferous flint was widely used at Lahti Ristola, but its origin is obscure. In both cases it played important role in raw material supply, accompanied in Sulyagals by local gray flint, and by imported Cretaceous flint and local quartz in Lahti Ristola.

Technical and morphological peculiarities of artifacts

If we compare the technology of the manufacture and the morphology of artifacts, made of imported gray Cretaceous flint, found on the Upper Volga (Figure 87.3) with artifacts of the same classes from the Eastern Baltic and Southern Finland (Figure 87.2), we see great similarity, in some cases full identity. Backed microblades are very similar almost everywhere, but the composition of the microlithic group, including also backed microblades with blunted distal or/and proximal ends; with sides, sharpened by slanting or flat retouch; with bifacial retouch of one side; with denticulate sides, is specific for Preboreal sites of Kunda and Butovo cultures. Large slender arrowheads, made of regular blades, with short well pronounced tang, formed by flat ventral and slanting dorsal retouch, and with a point, formed by flat ventral retouch, covering large areas of an arrowhead (Figure 87.2:5) are specific for early Kunda culture. As mentioned above, they are also known from Lithuania, North-Eastern Poland and Southern Finland. In each case the authors wrote about the spread of Kunda culture over their territories. On the Upper Volga such arrowheads are met at late Preboreal sites (Butovo and similar), some made from imported Cretaceous flint (Figure 87.3:17, 25, 26) and in one case an attempt to make such arrowhead from imported blade of such flint was observed in Butovo (Figure 87.3:6). Similar artifacts, but made from local flint are more numerous (Figure 87.3:1–5, 15, 27). Of special interest is a one-winged arrowhead from Prislon 1 (Figure 87.3:16) made from dark gray Cretaceous flint. It is identical to one from Pulli and the second from Lepakose not only typologically, but also stylistically (the same flat ventral retouch with a sharp pressure flaker, which makes lateral edges denticulate). Arrowheads of this very specific type were not met anywhere else, at least, not published. At the same time composition of arrowheads, as well, as of many other tools of early Butovo culture is far from being identical with early Kunda culture. The same could be said about Miluki and Lithuanian sites with early Kunda elements. One tanged arrowhead of Pulli type was met at Popovo site in Eastern Onega lake region (Oshibkina 1999:328, Fig. 3, 14). The dating of this arrowhead is not certain, but it may indicate contacts of Veretje culture during its early stage with early Kunda and Butovo cultures.

Very similar picture is observed, if we compare bone implements from Preboreal sites of Kunda and Butovo cultures (Zhilin 2001). Main types of arrowheads are the same (Figure 87.4): needle-shaped; long slender with biconical head; narrow flat with slots for insets – unretouched regular microblades – along one or both sides. Of special interest are long narrow arrowheads with triangular cross-section, called "the Lubana type". They are specific for Kunda culture and are widespread in the Eastern Baltic during the Preboreal and Boreal (Zagorska,

1974:25 pp). One point of this type was found in the bottom layer of Ivanovskoje 3 (Figure 87.4:12) together with some other implements of the early period of Butovo culture. Fragment of one more such arrowhead was met in Stanovoye 4, trench 3, layer 3. Like flint arrowheads of Pulli style made of dark gray Cretaceous flint, most probably, they were brought (or made?) here as a result of contacts of population of these cultures. One more point of this type was found in Veretje 1 (Oshibkina, 1997), indicating contacts of the population of Kunda and Veretje cultures in early Boreal.

Discussion

Distribution of imported flint over vast territories of the East European forest zone indicates large scale contacts of early Mesolithic populations. Two patterns can be singled out.

1. Import of raw material, when imported flint played significant or even leading role in tool production (Pulli; Zveinieki 2, lower layer; Lahti Ristola; Sulyagals). The first two sites show imports of Cretaceous flint from the south-west and may indicate supply of raw material, which became traditional at least at the territory of Latvia since terminal Paleolithic. Most part of inventory of late Swiderian culture site Salaspils Laukskola is made from the same flint (Zagorska, 1974, 1996:270). At Lahti Ristola both Cretaceous and Carboniferous types of imported flint were used. Pulli and Lahti Ristola may indicate pioneering settlement of the territories of Estonia and Southern Finland by population, which was not familiar with local resources and had to carry necessary amount of flint over long distances. The same process is even better illustrated by Sulyagals, which population carried Carboniferous flint over 500 km, while good Cretaceous flint was available much nearer. If it is so, we observe the very beginning of the early Mesolithic communication network formation, when population density in recently formed East European forest zone was very low.

2. All described Upper Volga sites, Lepakose in Estonia and several regular blades made of Carboniferous flint from Pulli represent the second pattern. Imported flint played no significant role as raw material, and scarce finished tools and regular blades were transported over long distance. Two explanations can be taken into consideration. A) Artifacts, made of exotic flint, reached the sites, where they were found, as a result of exchange. Such model could be best of all illustrated by Pulli: exchange of Cretaceous flint, exotic on the Upper Volga, into Carboniferous flint, exotic at the Eastern Baltic. But in both cases unretouched blades prevail, and in Butovo an attempt to make an arrowhead from imported blade was undertaken. The tip was broken, but the rest of the blade was good for making a new arrowhead (Figure 87.3:6). Still, it was abandoned. It indicates, that at least inhabitants of Butovo did not value imported flint too high. B) Rare finished tools and regular blades were not really "imported", but carried by people, who made and used them. This possibility is supported by the fact, that these tools (arrowheads and insets) are parts of weapons – things, that prehistoric hunters always carry, when they undertake any long distance trip. Small supply of blanks for making any other tools is usually also included in hunter's toolkit. Good knowledge of local resources and friendly population along the way and in the place of destination made unnecessary carrying large amounts of lithic raw material. The populations of Kunda and Butovo cultures, belonging to the same cultural unity, were, most probably, related and friendly. Numerous arrowheads of the Pulli type, made from the local flint on the Upper Volga, indicate adoption of Kunda technological traditions by the population of Butovo culture. This indicates that cultural links between them were stable, and communication network was functioning on a firm basis over large territory. We can expect, that a number of early Mesolithic sites with artifacts, made of imported both Cretaceous and Carboniferous flint will be discovered at now poorly investigated regions between the Baltic and the Upper Volga. Studies of bone and antler artifacts indicate that territories to the north from Upper Volga, such as the eastern Onega Lake region, were also included into it.

It seems reasonable, that emergence of such communication network in the early Mesolithic of the East European forest zone can be explained by large territories, settled by the population with similar cultural traditions in the first half of the Preboreal. Population density was very low, and danger of isolation was very high. The main aim of this network was, most probably, creation of stable system of exogamy links, supplemented by common rituals, hunting etc.

As a result of these contacts a large cultural unity was formed in the forest zone of the Eastern Europe, most probably, during Preboreal optimum, about 9500–9300 BP uncal. It could be named the Kunda-Butovo cultural unity. Western border of this unity is indicated by finds of the Pulli type flint arrowheads and bone points characteristic for Kunda culture in Lithuania and northeastern Poland. Its northern border was running through southern Finland, Karelia and the Eastern Onega lake region, while the eastern border is less clearly seen. Some influence of this unity is traced in Mesolithic bone industry of the Urals region. The Oka formed the southern border of this unity.

In the second half of the Mesolithic it also existed, as indicated by very scarce finds of the artifacts, made from gray Cretaceous flint at late mesolithic sites of the Upper Volga: an insert and knife, made from a blade from Okajomovo 5, dated by C14 to 7910±80 BP (GIN-6191) and 7730±40 BP (GIN 6192), both uncal., and to the late Boreal by pollen; a knife, made from a blade from Ivanovskoje 7, layer 2a, dated to 7530±150 BP (GIN-9361 I), 7520±60 BP (GIN-9361 II), 7490±120 BP (Le-

1260), 7375±170 BP (Le-1261), 7320±190 BP (GIN - 9369), all uncal. And to the early Atlantic by pollen; a burin on broken blade from Ozerki 5 dated to 7410±90 BP (GIN-6659), 7310±120 BP (GIN-7218), 7190±180 BP (GIN-6660), 7120±50 BP (GIN-7217), all uncal and to the early Atlantic by pollen. Flint arrowheads were not produced in the Eastern Baltic during late Mesolithic, but bone arrowheads of this time are very similar to ones from Upper Volga late Mesolithic sites.

References

Brzozowski, J. and Siemaszko, J. 1996. Dolnomezolityczne Obozowsko Kultury Kundajskiej w Milukach, Stanowisko 4, w Swiete Datowan Dendrochronologicznych i Radioweglowych. *Zeszyty Naukowe Politechniki Slaskiej. Seria: Matematyka.Fizyka* z. 80. Geochronometria 14. Nr. Kol. 1331, 229–238.

Indreko, R. 1948. *Die mittlere Steinzeit in Estland.* Stockholm.

Jaanits, K. 1980. Die mesolithischen Siedlungplatze mit Feursteininventar in Estland. *Veroffentlichungen des Museums fur Ur- und Fruhgtschichte. Potsdam.* Band 14/15/1980, 389–399.

Junger, H. and Sonninen, E. 1996. Radiocarbon dates IV. *Radiocarbon Dating Laboratory. University of Helsinki.* Report 4. Helsinki.

Koltsov, L.V. 1978. *Finalniy paleolit i mezolit Yuzhnoi i Yugo-Vostochnoi Pribaltiki.* Moscow.

Kravtsov, A.E. 1999. Nekotoryje resultaty izuchenija ienevskoi kultury v Volgo-Okskom basseine. In: Egorov, V.L. (ed.) *Istoricheskiy muzei – encyklopedija otechestvennoi istorii i kultury. Trudy GIM 103,* 79–108. Moscow.

Lose, I.A. 1988. *Poselenija kamennogo veka Lubanskoi nizini. Mezolit, ranniy i sredniy neolit.* Riga.

Matiskainen, H. 1996. Discrepancies in Deglaciation Chronology and the Appearence of Man in Finland. In: Larsson, L. (ed.) *The Earliest Settlement of Scandinavia.* Acta Archaeologica Lundensia, 8°, No. 24, 251–262. Lund.

Oshibkina, S.V. 1994. Mesoliticheskije pogrebenija Vostochnogo Prionezhja. *Arheologicheskije vesti,* N3. St. Peterburg.

—— 1999. Tanged point industries in the North-West of Russia. In: Kozlowski, S.K., Gurba, J. and Zaliznyak, L.L. (eds.) *Tanged points cultures in Europe,* 325–332. Lublin.

Ostrauskas, T. 1996. Vakaru Lietuvos Mesolitas. *Lietuvos Archeologija* 14, 192–212. Vilnius.

Rimantene, R.K. 1971. *Paleolit i mezolit Litvi.* Vilnius.

—— 1996. *Akmens Amzius Lietuvoje.* Vilnius.

Spiridonova, E.A. and Aleshinskaya, A.S. 1996. Osobennosti formirovanija i struktury rastitelnogo pokrova Volgo-Okskogo mezhdurechja v epohu mezolita. In: Cherhyh, I.N. (ed.). *Tverskoi arheologicheskiy sbornik ,* 2, 65–70. Tver.

Zagorska, I. 1974. Videja Akmens Laikmeta Zivku Skepi Latvija. *Arheologija un etnografija* XI., 25–38. Riga.

—— 1980. Das Fruhmesolithicum in Lettland. In: *Veroffentlichungen des Museums fur Ur- und Fruhgeschichte.* Potsdam. Band 14/15, 73–82.

—— 1996. Late Palaeolithic Finds in the Daugava River Valley. In: Larsson, L. (ed.) *The Earliest Settlement of Scandinavia.* Acta Archaeologica Lundensia 8°, No. 24, 263–272. Lund.

Zaliznyk, L.L. 1989. *Ohotniki na severnogo olenya Ukrainskogo Polesja epohi finalnogo paleolita.* Kiev.

Zhilin, M. 1996. The Western Part of Russia in the Late Palaeolithic – Early Mesolithic. In: Larsson, L. (ed.) *The Earliest Settlement of Scandinavia.* Acta Archaeologica Lundensia 8°, No. 24, 273–284. Lund.

—— 1998a. Adaptacija mezoliticheskih kultur Verhnego Povolzhja k kamennomu sirju. In: Cherhyh, I.N. (ed.). *Tverskoi arheologicheskiy sbornik.* 3, 25–30. Tver.

—— 1998b. Technology of the manufacture of Mesolithic bone arrowheads on the Upper Volga. *European Journal of Achaeology* 2, 149–175.

—— 1999. Hronologija i periodozacija butovskoi mezoliticheskoi kulturi. In: Egorov, V.L. (ed.) *Istoricheskiy muzei: Encyklopediya otechestva..* Trudy GIM: 103, 109–126. Moscow,.

—— 2000. O svyazyah naselenija Pribaltiki i Verhnego Povolzhja v rannem mezolite. In: Cherhyh, I.N. (ed.). *Tverskoi arheologicheskiy sbornik.* 3. 72–79. Tver.

—— 2001. *Kostyanaya industrija mezolita lesnoi zony Vostochnoi Evropy.* Moscow.

Miscellany

88. Deep in Russia, deep in the bog. Excavations at the Mesolithic sites Stanovoje 4 and Sakhtysh 14, Upper Volga region

Mickle G. Zhilin and Heikki Matiskainen

In 2000 the project "Stone Age Wet Sites in Finland and Russia" was started by the authors as a part of a scientific exchange project between the Finnish and Russian Academies of Sciences. Two stratified peat bog sites were excavated on the Upper Volga. Stanovoje 4 has three Mesolithic and one early Neolithic cultural layer. The lower Mesolithic layer is dated by C14 to just before 10300±70 BP uncal. It is the earliest site of the Butovo culture. The middle Mesolithic layer belongs to the Ienevo culture and is dated to 9620±60 BP. A typical asymmetric trapeze was found there. The upper Mesolithic layer belongs to Butovo culture, it is dated to 9220±60 – 8850±90 BP in cut 3 and to 8700±70 – 8540±60 BP in cut 2. Various stone, bone and antler artefacts were found in the Mesolithic layers of Stanovoje 4. Sahtysh 14 was discovered in 1999. It has four Mesolithic cultural layers, the two uppermost are connected with buried soils. C14 samples are being processed. Excavations at Sahtysh 14 will be continued in 2001 and, during following years.

Introduction

Until recent time the Mesolithic of Eastern Europe was almost entirely represented by sites situated on mineral soils where only stone artefacts were preserved. Most of them had no reliable stratigraphy, C14 and pollen data were scarce and insufficient. At the same time several known peat bog sites showed great informative potential.

As a result of extensive surveys, carried out by the Upper Volga expedition during last two decades about 20 Mesolithic peat bog sites were discovered in Central Russia. Twelve of them were excavated in 1989 –2000 by M. Zhilin (1998a:149 pp, 1999:295 pp). These sites are situated in large peat bogs, which developed in former glacial lakes and lake systems, linked with the Upper Volga through the tributaries along its right bank or connected with the river Klyazma, the left tributary of the Oka. (Figure 88.1). There are indications, that similar sites also exist in basins of the tributaries along the left bank of the Upper Volga and in the Oka basin to the south of Klyazma, but these regions are poorly surveyed.

In 2000 the project *Stone Age Wet Sites in Finland and Russia* was started by the authors as a part of bilateral scientific exchange project between the Finnish and Russian Academies of Sciences. Two stratified peat bog sites were excavated on the Upper Volga.

Stanovoje 4

The site is situated at the Podozerskoye peat bog (Komsomolsk district, Ivanovo region – Figure 88.1:15) between Ivanovo and Yaroslavl, 50 km south-east of the latter. The river Lahost, a tributary on the right bank of the river Kotorosl, which is a tributary on the right bank of the Upper Volga, starts from this bog. The site occupies a gentle slope on a promontory in the bog which is a glacial lake terrace at the outlet of the river from a peat bog

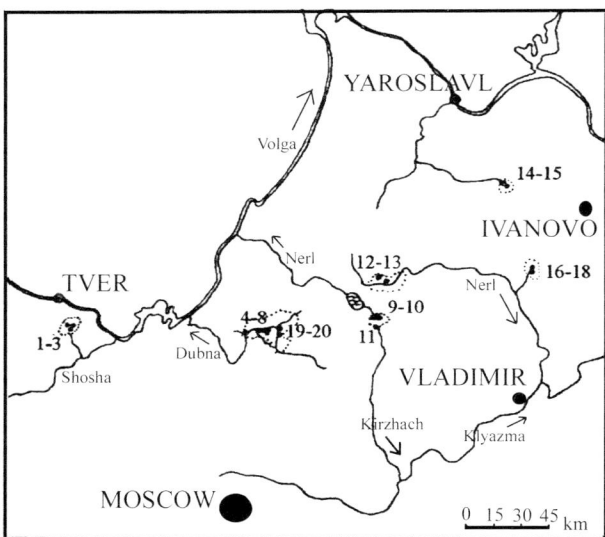

Figure 88.1 Main Mesolithic peat bog sites on the Upper Volga. 1–3: Ozerki 5, 16, 17; 4: Nushpoli 11; 5–8: Okajomovo 4, 5, 18, 29; 9–10: Berendeevo 3, 9; 11: Chernetskoje 8; 12–13: Ivanovskoje 3, 7; 14–15: Stanovoje 1, 4; 16–18: Sahtysh 2a, 9, 14; 19–20: Zamostje 2, 5.

(ancient lake gulf) and a boggy area just below it. The site was discovered in 1992 and 355 square meters were excavated between 1992–2000. A Mesolithic cultural layer belonging to the middle stage of the Butovo culture was discovered in cut 1which is situated at the top of promontory. Sixteen square meters were excavated. It is dated by pollen to the second half of the Boreal. The flint inventory includes various scrapers, burins, insets, cores for microblades, a post-Swiderian tanged point and other tools (Figure 88.2). Fragments of bone arrowheads, harpoon, awls, knives and an ornamented antler punch (Figure 88.2:25) were also found there.

A more complicated stratigraphy was observed in the peat bog in cuts 2 and 3. A total of 139 square meters were excavated in cut 2 between 1992–1999. The stratigraphy of this cut is the following (Figure 88.3a): 1 – modern soil, 5 cm thick; 2 – ground, removed from the artificial bed of the Lahost river during drainage works, 30–160 cm; 3a – brown pea, 10–20 cm; 3b – grey clay with peat, 10–20 cm; 3c – brown peat, 30–40 cm; 4 – dark brown peat or gyttja with thin streaks of sand, 40–50 cm; 4/5 – a streak of yellow sand, 1–5 cm; 5 – black peat with loam, 5–20 cm; 6 – a streak of grey clay in the western part of the cut, up to 10 cm; 7 – gravel with boulders, washed moraine. Besides these, some other layers and streaks were observed at the central part of excavated area between layers 6 and 7. 8 – brown gyttja, gently changing into grey silt, up to 10 cm thick; 9 – grey sand with silt lenses, up to 30 cm. In some areas these layers were represented by separate streaks and lenses, indicating more complex lake sediments near the shore. Two Neolithic and two Mesolithic cultural layers were investigated in cut 2. The first (I) is embedded in the lower half of layer 4. It produced several finds from the middle Neolithic Lyalovo culture. The second (II) is deposited at the very bottom of layer 4, on the surface of a streak of yellow sand (Figure 88.3a). In it were found some flint flakes and blades, lithic and bone artefacts and ceramic fragments of the earliest stage of the early Neolithic Upper Volga culture. Pollen data place this layer in the first half of the Atlantic. Radiocarbon dates of peat with cultural remains are: 7380±170 BP (GIN-10108 I), 7080±40 BP (GIN-10106 II), 6950±50 BP (GIN-10108 II), 6650±160 BP (GIN-10106 II) all uncal. A worked wooden plank 1,5 m long was dated to 7030±100 BP. (GIN-8378), which is the time of the early Neolithic occupation of the site.

The upper Mesolithic layer (III) is embedded in situ in layer 5. The streak of sand (layer 4/5) contains a secondary deposition of bones and artefacts from layer 5which were washed from the slopes of the promontory and transported by the river downstream during floods. Finds from cultural layer III belong to the later part of the middle stage of the Butovo culture.

A lot of animal, fish and bird bones, stone tools and waste, accompanied by bone and antler artefacts were found in layer III. Osteological remains consist of various

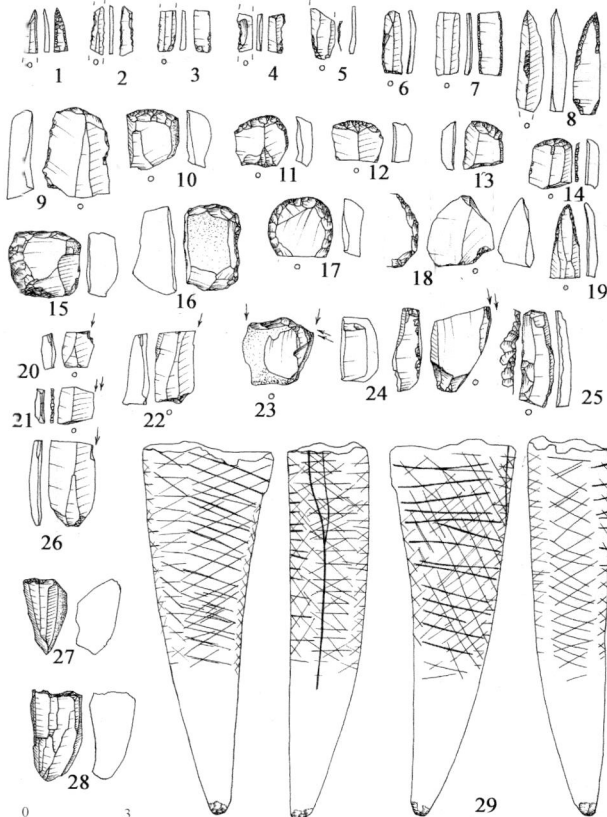

Figure 88.2 Stanovoje 4, cut 1. 1–25 - stone artefacts, 26 - antler punch.

mammals typical for the taiga forest. Elk and beaver bones are most abundant. Pike dominates among fish bones, and various waterfowl dominate in bird remains. Low quality local chert was mainly used in tool production, rare wide regular blades are made of imported Carboniferous Upper Volga flint. Slate was widely used for making polished wood cutting tools. Quartz, quartzite, sandstone and crystalline rocks of local origin were used in small amounts. Blade and microblade technology and production was well developed, but the role of flakes was also high. Finished tools include various scrapers, burins, knives, retouched and unretouched insets, points, a fragment of a willow leaf shaped arrowhead, core and polished axes and adzes, combined tools, hammerstones, polishing slabs and net sinkers. Of special interest are two slate pebbles with engraved geometric designs (Figure 88.5:7).

Bone and antler tools are numerous and impressive, among them various arrowheads (Figure 88.4) some needle shaped; others needle shaped with a biconical bases; some with biconical heads and long stems; narrow flat arrowheads with slots along one or both sides and asymmetric two-winged arrowheads with slots for inserts. Fragments of harpoons or barbed points and spearheads were found, accompanied by massive lance heads made of elk tubular bones and daggers with slots for insets along one or both sides (Figure 88.5). It is worth noting that

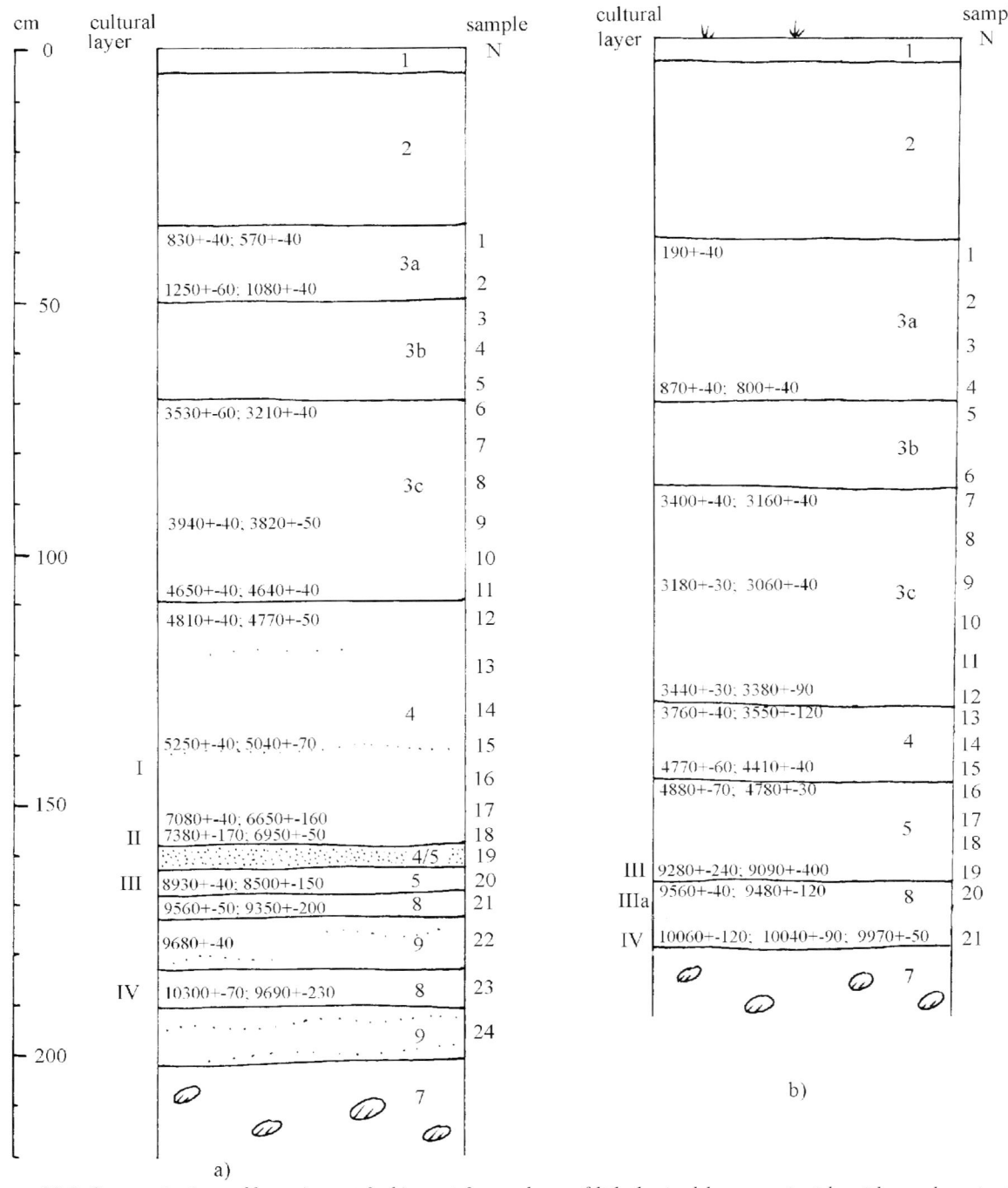

Figure 88.3 Stanovoje 4, profiles: a) - cut 2; b) - cut 3, numbers of lithological layers coincide with numbers in the text.

some slotted artefacts had regular unretouched microblades preserved in their original position in the slots, fixed by dark grey glue. Microscopic analyses showed, that this glue was made of coniferous pitch mixed with bee wax and charcoal dust. Many items were ornamented with engraved geometric designs. Fishing tools include intact hooks and sinkers (Figure 88.5:2, 3, 5). Domestic tools of bone and antler include various knives, scrapers (Figure 88.5:1), awls, needle and needle case and chisels-knives-scrapers made of beaver mandibles (Zhilin 1998b:

26 pp) as well as antler axes, adzes and sleeves for their mounting, bone chisels and gouges, digging tools, punches and pressure flakers. Personal ornaments are represented by various animal teeth pendants with grooves and flat rectangular perforated pendants, made of split ribs. Some of the broad knives made from the shoulder blades of elk are richly ornamented.

Pollen analysis dates this layer to the second quarter of the Boreal (about 8800–8600 BP). C14 dates of peat with cultural remains are: 8930±40 BP (GIN-10109 II),

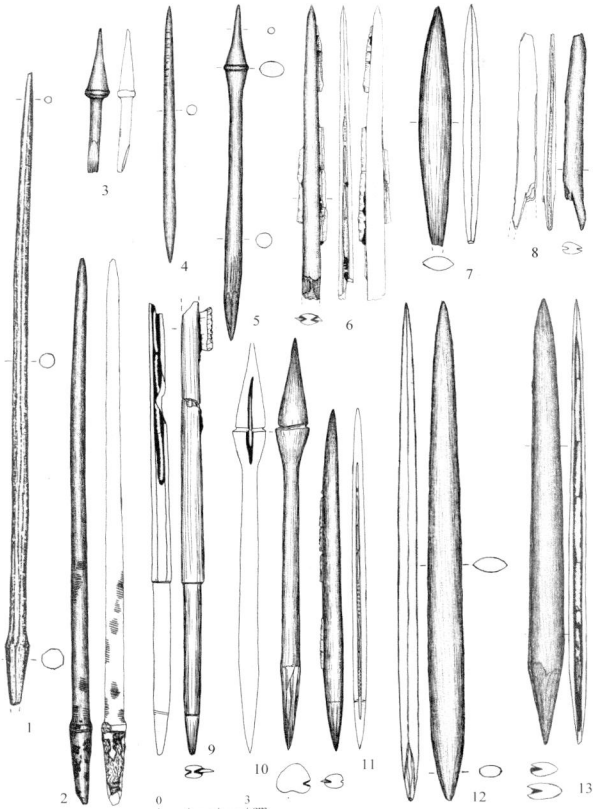

Figure 88.4 Stanovoje 4, cut 2, cultural layer III, bone arrowheads.

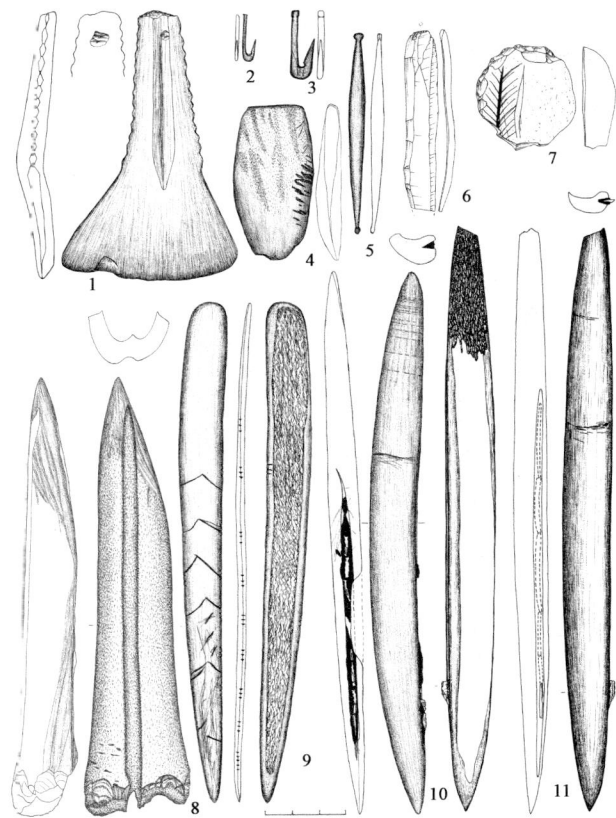

Figure 88.5 Stanovoje 4, cut 2, cultural layer III, bone artefacts (1 - antler).

8640±60 BP (GIN-10110 II), 8540±80 BP (GIN-10109 I), 8500±150 BP (GIN-10110 I). Three wooden stakes from this layer, sharpened with a stone adze, were C14 dated to 8700±70 BP (GIN-8854), 8670±50 BP (GIN-8856) and 8540±60 BP (GIN-8853), which define the occupation period.

The lower Mesolithic layer (IV) was found in cut 2 in a layer embedded in the very bottom of gray silt (layer 8b) and in a layer of gray sand with silt (layer 9) under the latter. A few elk, beaver, pike and bird bones were found there, accompanied by several chert and flint flakes and blades, a double platform core, a burin on broad blade (Figure 88.6:23), fragments of bone artefacts, an antler point (Figure 88.9:4) and a wedge. A sample of silt from the bottom of layer 8b was C dated to 10300±70 BP (GIN-10112 II) and 9690±230 BP (GIN-10112 I). A sample of unworked birch wood from a streak of sand with gyttja just above this layer was C14 dated to 9680±40 BP (GIN-10128).

The stratigraphy of cut 3 is in general similar to cut 2, though there are some variations (Figure 88.3b). 1 – modern soil, 5 cm; 2 – ground removed from artificial river bed during drainage works, 30–300 cm; 3a – brown peat, 20–30 cm; 3b – grey clay with peat, 20 cm; 3c – brown peat, 40 cm; 4 – dark brown gyttja with streaks of sand, in the western part of the cut it changes into pale grey turbulent sand with peat and represents a buried embankment of ancient Lahost river, 40–80 cm; 5 – black peat or gyttja, with some admixture of turbulent sand in upper part, up to 20 cm thick; 6 – a streak of grey clay only in the western part of the trench, up to 5 cm thick; 7 – gravel with boulders, washed moraine. In the central and eastern parts of trench 3 some more layers were observed between layers 5 and 7. Layer 8 – dense brown to greenish-brown gyttja, up to 15 cm thick; 9 – grey sandy loam, up to 10 cm thick. The ancient riverbed of the Lahost was found in the central part of the cut, while traces of the habitation site was located mainly at its western part.

Layer 4 contained a lot of Mesolithic and early Neolithic finds in secondary deposition, especially in the western part of the cut. They had been washed from slopes of the ancient promontory, moved downstream by the river and deposited in the embankment and in the riverbed during floods. Pollen analysis showed that this happened during the late Atlantic and in the Subboreal. The upper part of layer 5 in the central part of trench 3 was also redeposited, while in other parts, where its thickness was smaller, was found in situ. C14 dates of peat samples confirm the pollen data (Figure 88.3b).

Three Mesolithic cultural layers were preserved in situ in cut 3. The upper (III) layer which belongs to the earlier

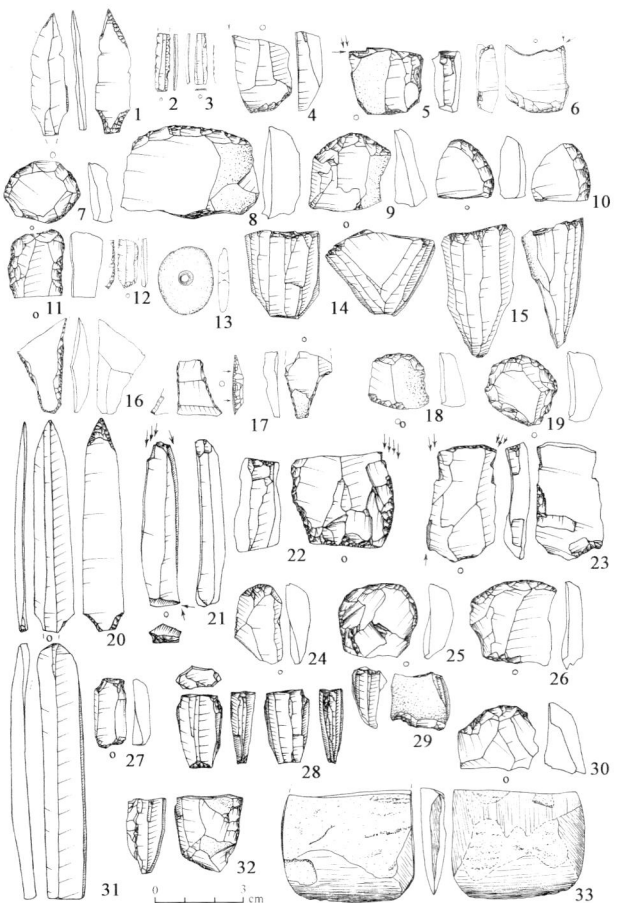

Figure 88.6 Stanovoje 4, stone artefacts: 1–15 - cut 3, cultural layer III; 16–19 - cut 3, cultural layer 3a; 23 - cut 2, cultural layer IV; 20–22, 24–33 - cut 3, cultural layer IV.

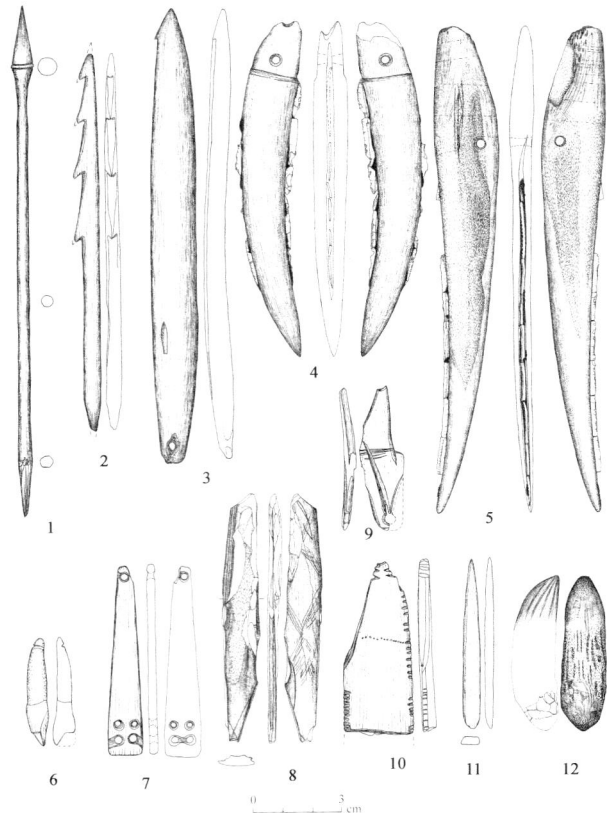

Figure 88.7 Stanovoje 4, cut 3, cultural layer III, bone artefacts.

part of the middle period of the Butovo culture was found in the lower undisturbed level of layer 5 in the central part of the cut while in other areas whole layer 5 was preserved. Numerous wooden stakes from this layer were driven into under laying layers including the ancient riverbed. Most probably, they are remains of fish weirs. Fragments of wooden fishing equipment were also found there. Numerous bones belong to various taiga forest mammals, among which elk and beaver dominate. Pike remains are most numerous among fish bones, birds are represented mainly by waterfowl. The lithic inventory (Figure 88.6:1–15) is much similar to finds from cultural layer III in cut 2, but the number of artefacts and waste is greater. Some finds like tanged post-Swiderian arrowheads, perforated slate pebbles, grooved polishers and a fragment of a perforated mace head deserve special attention. Among the other tools, various scrapers are most numerous, but there are also burins made from broken blades and flakes, knives, perforators, concave scrapers, retouched and unretouched insets, symmetrical and oblique points, core and polished axes, adzes and chisels (Figure 88.8:2–4), combined tools, hammerstones, polishing slabs and net sinkers.

Various bone and antler artefacts were found (Figure 88.7), among them numerous arrowheads: both needle shaped or with biconical heads or bases; others with leaf-shaped heads; narrow flat arrowheads, most with slots for inserts along one or both sides, asymmetric two-winged arrowheads with slots for insets, and others with barbs near the tip or along one side. Barbed points with sparse or dense fine teeth are scarce. Harpoon fragments are also scarce. Slotted spearheads and massive lance heads were found. Straight or slightly curved daggers with microblades, mounted in one or two slots with the help of glue were also recovered. Fragments of fishing hooks indicate their wide use. Numerous bone and antler tools were used for various domestic activities: knives, scrapers, perforated plates for dragging sinew; awls, needle cases, chisels-knives-scrapers made of beaver mandibles; antler axe and adze blades and sleeves for their mounting, narrow bone chisels, punches and a pressure flaker. One adze sleeve was found with a chert core adze still preserved in its groove (Figure 88.8:1a,b). The butt end of a broken antler adze was preserved in the groove of another. An axe sleeve had a fragment of a wooden handle in its shafting hole (Figure 88.8:5). Many items are decorated with engraved geometric designs. Personal ornaments include various teeth pendants and flat rectangular perforated pendants.

This layer is dated to late Preboreal by pollen. C14

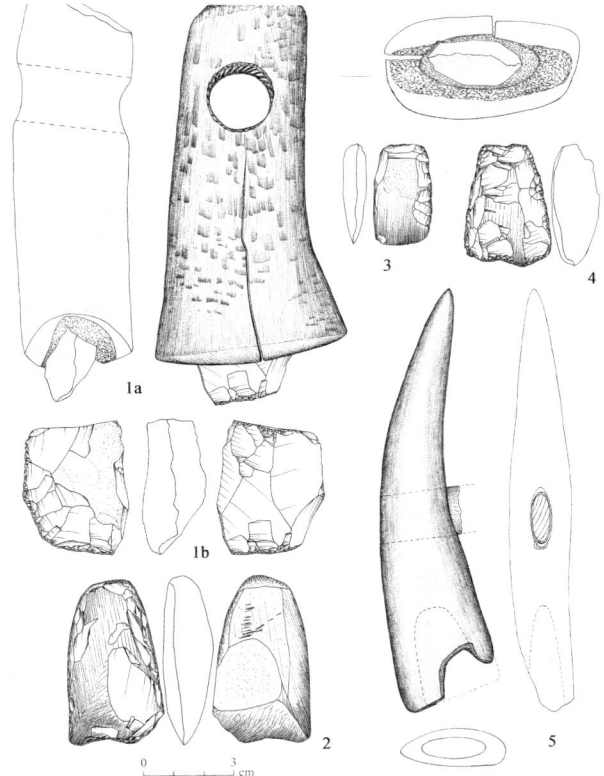

Figure 88.8 Stanovoje 4, cut 3, cultural layer 3. 1a - a sleeve with a chert adze blade in situ, 1b - the blade from the sleeve; 2 - slate adze blade; 3, 4 - chert axe and adze blades; 5 - axe sleeve.

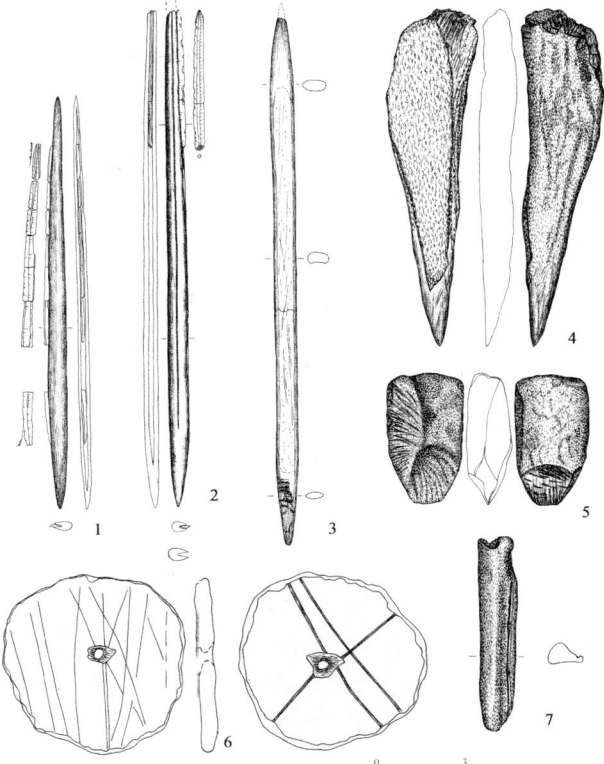

Figure 88.9 Stanovoje 4, cultural layer IV, bone and antler artefacts: 4 - cut 2, the rest - cut 3.

dates taken from the peat samples fall between 9280±240 BP (GIN-10122 I), 9090±400 BP (GIN-10124), 8610±40 BP (GIN-10122 II). The last date probably reflects some later admixture to the sample, while the first two are in good accordance with pollen data. A wooden stake, sharpened with a stone adze is dated to 9220±60 BP (GIN-8375), and which determines the habitation period of the site more accurately. An elk bone from this layer in the western part of the cut was dated to 8850±90 BP (GIN-11093), marking the terminal point of habitation in this area.

The middle (IIIa) cultural layer is separated from the previous by a streak of grey clay in the western part of the trench. It was found on the surface of layer 8 and in its upper 2–3 cm. In the central part of cut 3 the upper 3–5 cm of layer 8 are sterile, and cultural layer IIIa was found just below it (Figure 88.3b). Layer IIIa produced few finds, among them elk and beaver bones, chert flakes, a flint knife made from a blade, scrapers, one high asymmetric trapeze and oblique one-edged arrowheads of the Ienevo culture (Figure 88.6:16–19). Bone artefacts include a massive coarse arrowhead with an irregular sub-biconical head, a gouge, a fragment of a knife and a tubular bone with a deep groove. A fragment of a creel (basket-like fishtrap), carefully woven out of longitudinally split willow branches was found together with a large stone sinker beside it. Pollen analysis places this layer in the first half of the Preboreal, just before its optimum. The top of layer 8, overlaying the cultural layer III is C14 dated to 9560±40 BP (GIN-10125 II) and 9480±120 BP (GIN-10125 I). A wooden stake, sharpened with a stone axe or adze from this layer, found in cut 3 was C14 dated to 9620±60 BP (GIN-8377). Two more similar stakes, found in a horizontal position in cut 2 below cultural layer III in the upper part of layer 8 were C14 dated to 9620±50 BP (GIN-8374) and 9590±40 BP (GIN-8376). This occupation was very short and its chronological limits are well defined.

The finds from the lower (IV) cultural layer were deposited on the gravel and in the bottom 3 cm of layer 8 in the central part of cut 3. Cultural layer IV was separated by the middle sterile part of layer 8 from cultural layer IIIa (Figure 88.3b). In the western part of the cut finds from layer IV were found on the surface of the washed moraine under layer 8, which is thinner here. In the eastern part, where layer 8 is absent, the IV cultural layer is embedded in layer 9. This layer is the earliest scientifically dated site of the Butovo culture. Bones of taiga forest mammals were found, among which elk and beaver dominate. The presence of domestic dog and muskrat is worth noting, as well as the absence of reindeer bones.

Local chert was used for tool production at the site, while larger regular blades and blade tools were made from imported high quality Carboniferous Upper Volga

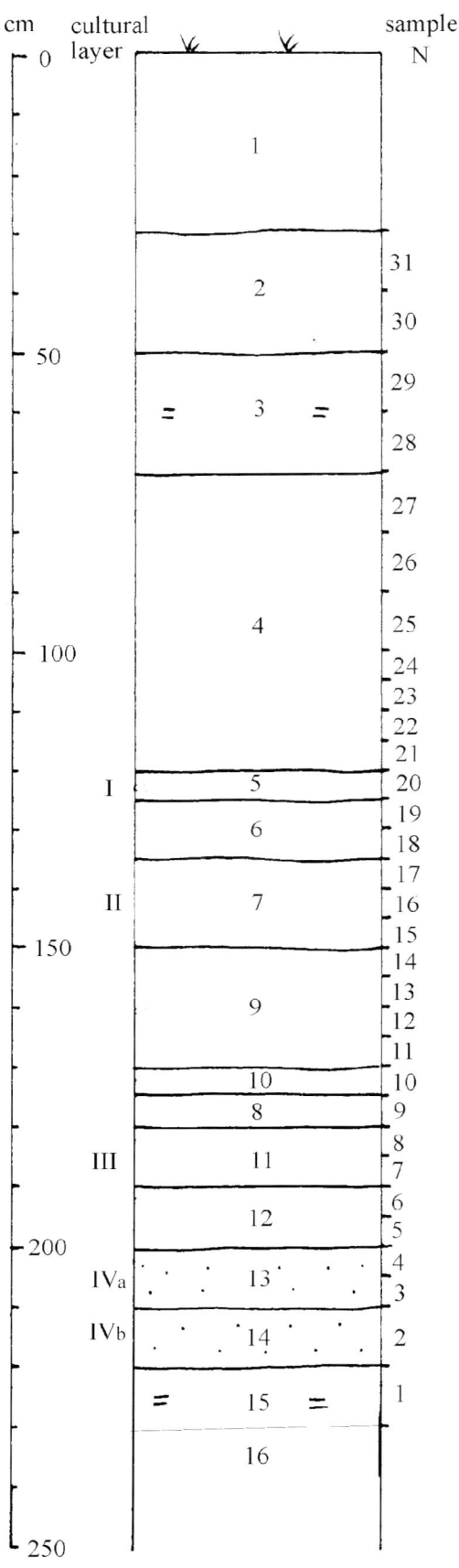

Figure 88.10 Sakhtysh 14, profile, numbers of lithological layers coincide with numbers in the text.

flint. Slate was also used for wood cutting tools. Blades were knocked from sub-prismatic double-platform cores using a soft hammer or punch technique. Smaller regular blades and microblades were obtained from small prismatic, conical and handle cores using a pressure technique. The tool kit (Figure 88.6:20–23) includes end scrapers, side and round scrapers, burins with retouched platform and made from broken blades, a tanged post-Swiderian arrowhead, a hammerstone, preforms of core axes or adzes. A fragment of a slate axe blade, bifacially polished was found in this layer. Bone and antler artefacts (Figure 88.9) include long narrow arrowheads, most with slots for inserts along one or both sides, a fragment of large lance head, an antler dagger with grooves for insets along both sides, a broad knife made from the shoulder blade of an elk, an awl, a hide polisher, a small antler axe and adze blades and two adze sleeves (one with a fragment of a wooden shaft in a shafthole), preforms and cut bones.

Pollen data place the bottom of layer 8, which was deposited during the lake transgression, which flooded the site, to the end of the Younger Dryas. C14 dates of layer 8 are 10060±120 BP (GIN-10127 I), 10040±90 BP (GIN-10027), 9970±50 BP (GIN-10026 I), 9940±50 BP (GIN-10026 II), 9850±60 BP (GIN-8379) all uncal.

This data makes it possible to reconstruct the history of this settlement. It was first occupied in the end of the Younger Dryas slightly before 10300±60 BP uncal by the population of the Butovo culture. The formation of the forest zone of Eastern Europe has just started, sparse birch forests occupied river valleys and lake depressions, while some glacial landscape elements were still present at the watersheds. The faunal complex was typical for the taiga forest where elk and beaver dominated and were the main hunted animals, reindeer was either absent, or not hunted. The site was occupied during regressive stage of the paleolake. As a result of the following transgression the place was abandoned, and a layer of gyttja was deposited. In the second quarter of the Preboreal, about 9600 BP during the next short regression the site was occupied again for a very short period, this time by a population of the Ienevo culture. A birch-pine forest of the northern taiga type played a leading role in the landscape, elk and beaver were the only animals hunted. The next transgression of the lake put this settlement to the end, and a thin streak of clay or gyttja was deposited over its cultural layer. In the last quarter of the Preboreal, about 9220 BP the site was occupied for the third time, again by a population of the Butovo culture. This habitation lasted until the early Boreal, and about 8850 BP the area in cut 3 was abandoned and people moved to a dryer place as revealed in cut 2. Here the settlement functioned until the middle Boreal, and was abandoned about 8500 BP A taiga type forest dominated the landscape and various forest animals were hunted, elk and beaver being the most important. Inland hunting was supplemented by fishing, fowling and food gathering. In the second half of the Boreal the settlement moved to a higher place in cut 1. During the terminal Mesolithic the place was not occupied. It was settled next by a people from the initial phase of the early Neolithic Upper Volga culture in the early Atlantic, about 7000 BP Later it was visited for a short time in the middle Neolithic by a population from the Lyalovo culture, and finally a Bronze Age settlement with textile ceramic emerged at the top of the promontory.

Sahtysh 14

The site is situated at the Sahtysh peat bog (Teikovo district, Ivanovo region) 40 km south-west of Ivanovo (Figure 88.1:18), near the outlet of the river Koika, a tributary on the left bank of the river Nerl, which is a tributary on the left bank of the Klyazma river. The site occupies a place in a peat bog at the foot of a very gentle slope of a promontory, which is part of a terrace which was formed by the late glacial lake. The site was discovered in 1999. Sixty-five square meters were excavated in 1999–2000.

The stratigraphy of the site is the following (Figure 88.10). 1 – modern soil, 30 cm; 2 – brown peat, 20 cm, 3 – dark peat with grey loam, 20 cm, 4 – brown peat, 50 cm; 5 – black peat (buried soil 1), 5–7 cm; 6 – brown peat, 10 cm; 7 – black peat (buried soil 2), 10–15 cm; 8 – brown peat, 5–15 cm; 9 – pale brown peat, found under layer 7 only in the northern part of the trench, which extends further into the peat bog, up to 20 cm thick; 10 – black peat (buried soil 3), also found only in the northern part of the trench, under layer 9 – up to 6 cm thick; 11 – pale yellowish gyttja, is represented in the central and northern parts of the trench under layer 8, up to 15 cm thick; 12 – dark brown peat, in the southern part, nearest to mineral shore, with admixture of sand, 8–15 cm; 13 – grey sand with peat, 6–18 cm; 14 – bluish-grey sand, present in the central and northern parts of the trench, up to 10 cm; 15 – bluish-grey clay, also found in the central and northern parts of the trench, up to 10 cm thick; 16 – gravel with boulders, washed moraine.

Four Mesolithic cultural layers were investigated at the site. The first is connected with the upper buried soil (layer 5), but the excavations only cover a peripheral part of the settlement. Several mammalian and bird bones, a core and several flakes were found. The second cultural layer is embedded in the second buried soil (layer 7). A lot of mammalian, bird and fish bones, accompanied by lithic and bone artefacts were found. Local chert, flint, slate, quartz and crystalline rocks were used to make tools. Blades, microblades and flakes served as blanks for tools, among which various scrapers are the most numerous. Burins, knives, insets, perforators, core and polished wood cutting tools, hammerstones and combined tools were found. Bone and antler tools include needle shaped and long narrow slotted arrowheads; a massive needle shaped spearhead; side scrapers made of elk tubular bones; wide knives; chisels-knives-scrapers made of beaver mandibles; an antler adze and mammalian teeth pendants.

Cultural layer III is embedded in layer 8 in the southern part of the trench, and in the lower part of layer 8 and the upper part of layer 11 in the central and northern areas of the trench. It is separated from cultural layer II in the central and northern parts of the trench by sterile layers 9, 10 and upper part of layer 8. This layer produced numerous bones of forest mammals, birds and fish, chert and flint flakes and blades. Artefacts, made of stone, bone and antler include a quartz core, scrapers, needle shaped arrowheads; a fragment of a flat dagger, a fragment of a slotted dagger, broad knives made of elk scapula, a; fragment of a knife scraper, chisels-knives-scrapers made of beaver mandibles, an antler adze; an antler punch and mammalian teeth pendants.

The next cultural layer (IVa) is embedded in dark brown peat (layer 12), separated from cultural layer IIIa by a streak of gyttja in the central and northern parts of the trench. Besides the remains of forest fauna, finds include wooden stakes, sharpened with a stone adze, chert and flint flakes, blades, a core, scrapers, a slate pressure flaker, an engraved pebble, needle shaped arrowheads, bone knives, scrapers, beaver mandible tools bear and elk tooth pendants.

The bottom cultural layer (IVb) is embedded in a layer of grey sand with peat (layer 13), which was found lying on the bottom deposits of the lake in the central and northern parts of the trench and on a layer of washed moraine in the southern part of the trench. It produced mammalian, fish and bird bones, chert and flint flakes and blades, scrapers, a burin, bone needle shaped arrowhead, an intact fishing hook, a fragment of a broad knife; an awl, a hollow edged gouge, an antler adze and an elk tooth pendant. Pollen data place the lower (IV) cultural layer in the late Preboreal, and other layers in the first half of the Boreal.

Investigation of the Sahtysh 14 site has just started, C14 samples are being processed, the cultural affiliation of most of the layers is not clear yet. Good stratigraphy and preservation of organic materials make this site very promising for future large scale excavations and complex research.

Conclusions

Excavations at Stanovoje 4 showed, that since the very beginning of the Mesolithic the Upper Volga population was practising a complex economy of forest hunting, fishing and gathering. Elk and beaver were most important hunted mammals. Reindeer is not identified in refuse fauna in the lowest layer; its role was minimal in layer III.

The site was occupied several times by a population of different archaeological cultures. This indicates very low population density and high mobility during the Preboreal (cf. Zhilin in this volume). Territorial borders were not established, and contacts between people belonging to different cultures were quite rare.

References

Zhilin, M.G. 1998a. Technology of the Manufacture of Mesolithic Bone Arrowheads on the Upper Volga. *European Journal of Archaeology* 1998, No. 2, 149–175.

—— 1998b. Artefacts, Made of Animals' Teeth and Jaws in the Mesolithic of Eastern Europe. *Proceedings of the Third Annual Meeting of the European Association of Archaeologists*. 1997. Ravenna, 26–31.

—— 1999. New Mesolithic peat sites on the upper Volga. In: Kozlowsk, S., Gurba, I. and Zaliznyak, L. (eds.) *Tanged Points cultures in Europé*, 295–310. Lublin.